Index of English Literary Manuscripts

Volume I *1450–1625*

Volume II *1625–1700*

Volume III *1700–1800*

Volume IV *1800–1900*

Volume V *Indexes of titles, first lines, names, repositories*

Index of English Literary Manuscripts

Volume I

1450–1625

Part 2 *Douglas–Wyatt*

Compiled by Peter Beal

Mansell, London
R. R. Bowker Company, New York
1980

ISBN 0 7201 0898 5 Complete set of five volumes
0 7201 0807 1 Volume I, both parts
0 7201 0808 X Volume I, Part 1
0 7201 0809 8 Volume I, Part 2
Mansell Publishing, 3 Bloomsbury Place, London WC1A 2QA
First published 1980

British Library Cataloguing in Publication Data
Index of English literary manuscripts
Vol.I: 1450-1625.
1. English literature—Manuscripts—Indexes
I. Croft, Peter John II. Hofmann, Theodore
III. Horden, John IV. Beal, Peter
016.82'08 Z6611.LZ
ISBN 0-7201-0807-1
ISBN 0-7201-0808-X (Vol.I Part 1)
ISBN 0-7201-0809-8 (Vol.I Part 2)

Published in North and South America, West Indies and Greenland by R.R. Bowker Company, 1180 Avenue of the Americas, New York, N.Y. 10036

ISBN 0 8352 1216 5 Complete set of five volumes
0 8352 1217 3 Volume I, both parts
0 8352 1218 1 Volume I, Part 1
0 8352 1220 3 Volume I, Part 2
Library of Congress Catalog Card Number 79-88658

Printed in the United Kingdom by J. W. Arrowsmith Ltd., Bristol, and bound by Mansell (Bookbinders) Ltd., Witham, Essex

Contents

List of Facsimiles

Glossary of Terms

Definitions are given below of a number of terms used frequently in Volume I.

autograph written in the hand of the author concerned

commonplace book a compilation arranged as a collection of 'commonplaces' (i.e. notable pieces of wit or wisdom, useful extracts, quotations, anecdotes, or items of information, deemed worth remembering), usually under headings for easy reference or as an aid to study [cp 'miscellany']

compiled by initiated, arranged, or produced by a given person or persons (but not necessarily written in their hand(s) throughout)

composite volume a volume consisting of various physically and textually independent units bound together

copy transcript, not in the hand of the author (unless specifically described as 'autograph copy') [cp 'exemplum']

correction alteration made to rectify a mechanical error of copying [cp 'revision']

draft a text which represents a stage in the composition of the work, or which contains revisions (as distinct from a transcript of an already completed work)

exemplum a printed volume, an individual example of an edition [cp 'copy']

imperfect part of the text is missing because the manuscript is physically damaged or defective [cp 'incomplete' and 'unfinished']

incomplete part of the text is missing because the scribe did not in this instance copy the whole work [cp 'imperfect' and 'unfinished']

miscellany a manuscript consisting of works, or extracts from works, by various authors, usually compiled for pleasure rather than as an aid to study [cp 'commonplace book']

reproduced reproduced as a photographic, engraved, or lithographic facsimile

revision alteration constituting a textual innovation introduced by the author [cp 'correction']

unfinished the work was not completed by the author [cp 'imperfect' and 'incomplete']

Abbreviations

The following is a list of abbreviations used throughout Volume I.

AEB. *Analytical & Enumerative Bibliography* (Bibliographical Society of Northern Illinois)
AL. *American Literature*
AN&Q. *American Notes and Queries*
BC. *The Book Collector*
Bentley. Gerald Eades Bentley, *The Jacobean and Caroline Stage*, 7 vols (Oxford, 1941-68)
BLJ. *British Library Journal*
BLR. *Bodleian Library Record*
BMQ. *British Museum Quarterly*
BNYPL. *Bulletin of the New York Public Library*
BQR. *Bodleian Quarterly Record*
CD. *Comparative Drama*
Chambers, *Elizabethan Stage*. E.K. Chambers, *The Elizabethan Stage*, 4 vols (Oxford, 1923)
CL. *Comparative Literature*
CM. *Cornhill Magazine*
Croft, *Autograph Poetry*. P.J. Croft, *Autograph Poetry in the English Language*, 2 vols (London, 1973)
Cutts, *Musique de la troupe de Shakespeare*. John P. Cutts, *La musique de scène de la troupe de Shakespeare* (Paris, 1959)
De Ricci. Seymour de Ricci (assisted by W.J. Wilson), *Census of Medieval and Renaissance Manuscripts in the United States and Canada*, 3 vols (New York, 1935-40)
De Ricci, *Supplement*. *Supplement to the Census of Medieval and Renaissance Manuscripts in the United States and Canada*, originated by C.U. Fage, continued and edited by W.H. Bond (New York, 1962)
DNB. *The Dictionary of National Biography*, ed. Sir Leslie Stephen and Sir Sidney Lee (The Compact Edition, 2 vols, London 1975)
Doughtie, *Lyrics from English Airs*. *Lyrics from English Airs 1596-1622*, ed. Edward Doughtie (Cambridge, Massachusetts, 1970)
DUJ. *Durham University Journal*
E & S. *Essays & Studies*
EA. *Études Anglaises*
EC. *Essays in Criticism*
EEDS. Early English Drama Series
EETS. Early English Text Society
EHR. *English Historical Review*
ELH. *English Literary History*
ELN. *English Language Notes*
ELR. *English Literary Renaissance*
EM. *English Miscellany*
ES. *Englische Studien*
Facsimiles of Royal, Historical, and Literary Autographs in the British Museum. *Facsimiles of Royal, Historical, Literary and other Autographs in the Department of Manuscripts, British Museum*, ed. George F. Warner, Series I-V (London, 1899)
Flower & Munby, *English Poetical Autographs*. Desmond Flower and A.N.L. Munby, *English Poetical Autographs* (London, 1938)
Greg, *Dramatic Documents*. W.W. Greg, *Dramatic Documents from the Elizabethan Playhouses*, 2 vols (Oxford, 1931)
Greg, *English Literary Autographs*. W.W. Greg, et al., *English Literary Autographs, 1550-1650*, 3 vols, (Oxford 1925-32)
Grosart, *The Dr Farmer MS*. Alexander B. Grosart, *The Dr. Farmer Chetham MS. being a Commonplace-Book in the Chetham Library Manchester*, 2 vols, Chetham Society 89-90 (Manchester, 1873)
HLB. *Harvard Library Bulletin*
HLQ. *Huntington Library Quarterly*
HMC. *Historical Manuscripts Commision*
Hughey, *Arundel Harington MS*. Ruth Hughey, *The Arundel Harington Manuscript of Tudor Poetry*, 2 vols (Columbus, Ohio, 1960)
ILN. *Illustrated London News*
JEGP. *Journal of English and Germanic Philology*
M & L. *Music & Letters*
MD. *Musica Disciplina*
MLN. *Modern Language Notes*
MLR. *Modern Language Review*
MM. *The Mariner's Mirror* (Journal of the Society for Nautical Research)
MP. *Modern Philology*
N & Q. *Notes & Queries*
NCBEL, I. *The New Cambridge Bibliography of English Literature*, ed. George Watson, Volume I: 600-1660 (Cambridge, 1974)
NLWJ. *National Library of Wales Journal*
PBSA. *Papers of the Bibliographical Society of America*
Petti, *English Literary Hands*. Anthony G. Petti,

English Literary Hands from Chaucer to Dryden (London, 1977)

PMLA. *Publications of the Modern Languages Association*

PQ. *Philological Quarterly*

PULC. *Princeton University Library Chronicle*

RD. *Renaissance Drama*

RECTR. *Restoration & Eighteenth-Century Theatre Research*

RES. *Review of English Studies*

RN. *Renaissance News*

RORD. *Research Opportunities in Renaissance Drama*

RQ. *Renaissance Quarterly*

SB. *Studies in Bibliography*

SEL. *Studies in English Literature 1500-1900*

SHR. *Scottish Historical Review*

SP. *Studies in Philology*

SQ. *Shakespeare Quarterly*

SR. *Studies in the Renaissance*

SS. *Shakespeare Survey*

SSL. *Studies in Scottish Literature*

SSt. *Shakespeare Studies*

STS. Scottish Text Society

TLS. *Times Literary Supplement*

TN. *Theatre Notebook*

TQ. *Texas Quarterly*

WMQ. *William and Mary Quarterly*

YES. *The Yearbook of English Studies*

YULG. *Yale University Library Gazette*

Volume I
Part 2

Gavin Douglas
Bishop of Dunkeld

1474?-1522

ABBREVIATIONS

Bawcutt *The Shorter Poems of Gavin Douglas*, ed. Priscilla J. Bawcutt, STS 4th Ser. 3 (Edinburgh & London, 1967).

Coldwell *Virgil's Aeneid translated into Scottish Verse by Gavin Douglas, Bishop of Dunkeld*, ed. David F. C. Coldwell, 4 vols, STS 3rd Ser. 30, 25, 27-8 (Edinburgh & London, 1951-6).

For abbreviations used throughout Volume I, see p.xi.

INTRODUCTION

There are eight known examples of Douglas's autograph, all letters written within the last few years of his life. They are as follows:

(1) To Lord Dacre, 21 January 1514/15 (British Library, Cotton MS Caligula B. I, f. 29r-v); autograph throughout.

(2) To Adam Williamsone, 21 January 1514/15, and enclosing a letter of 18 January 1514/15 (British Library, Cotton MS Caligula B. II, ff. 373-4v); autograph throughout.

(3) Joint letter from Douglas and Robert, Bishop of Ross, to Cardinal Wolsey, 27 June 1517 (British Library, Cotton MS Caligula B. VI, f. 203); in the hand of an amanuensis and signed by Ross and Douglas.

(4) To Cardinal Wolsey, 24 December 1521 (Public Record Office, SP.49/1/127); autograph throughout.

(5) To Cardinal Wolsey, 31 December 1521 (Public Record Office, SP.49/1/128); in the hand of an amanuensis and signed by Douglas.

(6) To Cardinal Wolsey, 1 January 1521/2 (British Library, Cotton MS Caligula B. VI, f. 246r-v); in the hand of an amanuensis and signed by Douglas.

(7) To Cardinal Wolsey, 6 January 1521/2 (British Library, Cotton MS Caligula B. VI, f. 506); autograph throughout. See FACSIMILE XI.

(8) To Cardinal Wolsey, 31 January 1521/2 (Public Record Office, SP.49/1/130); in the hand of an amanuensis and signed by Douglas.

Brief synopses of these letters appear in the Calendars of State Papers, Foreign and Domestic, Henry VIII, Vol. II, part 1 (1864), Nos. 43, 44; Vol. II, part 2 (1864), No. 3407; Vol. III, part 2 (1867), Nos. 1897, 1917, 1930, 1939, and 2007. In addition, a memorial written by Douglas in 1521 against the Duke of Albany is preserved in a scribal copy in the British Library (Cotton MS Caligula B. III, ff. 311-13); the text is summarised in the Calendars cited, Vol. III, part 2 (1867), No. 1898.

Of Douglas's major work, the *Eneados*, five complete MS texts are preserved (DoG 3-7), as well as some MS fragments and extracts (DoG 8-9). The most clearly authoritative of the extant MSS is a transcript of a copy made by Douglas's secretary, Matthew Geddes (DoG 3).

Two other poems which have been generally attributed to Douglas, *Conscience* and *King Hart*, are to be found in the Maitland Folio MS (DoG 1-2).

PB.

ARRANGEMENT

Verse DoG 1-9.

FACSIMILE XI — Gavin Douglas: Letter to Cardinal Wolsey, 6 January 1521/2 (inscribed at the top in a later hand). British Library, Cotton MS Caligula B. VI, volume 2, folio 506 recto. Reproduced by permission of the British Library.

Gawin Douglas Bishop of Dunkeld to Wolsey
6 Jan. 1522

424

Pleis zo^r grace / ze said zisterday sik byssynes at I micht no schaw zo^r grace quhat I thocht twychyng ye cumyng of this Scottis preist Sir Johne Duncanson quhilk zisterday presentit wrytingis to the kingis hienes & zo^r grace for ane salue gard / he is cumyn furth of Scotland wt gret dylligens apon xij days / he is ane famyliar wt ye Duk of Albany & special seruand of a lang tyme to ye archbisschop of Glasgw / he hes brocht wt hym wrytingis & directiones fra thaim baith to be send in France Flanders & Rome as I knaw by his wordis / Alsa thar is cumyn wt hym an Italian callit Evangelista the seruand of a lumbard in Scotland to abyd hym at Sudhampton quhill he pas in Flanders / Gif zo^r grace fynd hym & his directiones I trast ze suld knaw mony thingis tharby And gif zo^r hie prudens think expedient at salue gardis be grantit at ye instance & subscriptioun of ye said duk I report me to zo^r gret wysdom or zit that ye said bisschop of Glasgwis materis & promotion for Sanctandrois suld prosper / considering he is ye mast special man in materis & all ways his partakar wt ye said duk / I dreid alsa this Duncanson is directit in my grevans & to do me hurt / & beseik zo^r grace to gard ye rassar him remeid tharfor / & gif it mycht stand wt zo^r pleiss that he had na passage for ye tyme forthwart onto ye tyme zo^r grace knaw mair fully his directiones / And gif zo^r hie prudens pleisis so do / I wald pray knaw this sam by my desyr / because he knawis him familiar wt me / quharby peraventur I sall knaw sumthing mair of his mynd / albeit I knaw ellis the fynes of the man is rycht mair doubill in our realm / Do as plesis zo^r grace quham God preserf / At London this Epiphanie day wt ye hand of

zo^r humil seruito^r &
chaplain of Dunkeld

511

vide fol. 214, 225.

Gavin Douglas

VERSE

DoG 1 *Conscience* ('Quhen halie kirk first flurist in youthheid').

Copy, untitled, in a folio MS volume of Scottish poetry compiled by Sir Richard Maitland of Lethington (1496-1586); c. 1570-85.

First pub. (from this MS) in *The Poetical Works of Gavin Douglas, Bishop of Dunkeld*, ed. John Small (Edinburgh, 1874), I, 121-2; printed from this MS in Bawcutt, pp. 135-7, and in *The Maitland Folio Manuscript*, ed. W.A. Craigie, STS NS 7 (Edinburgh & London, 1919), 217-18.

Magdalene College, Cambridge, Pepys Library, MS 2553, pp. 192-3.

DoG 2 *King Hart* ('King Hart, in to his cumlie castell strang').

Copy, untitled, in a folio MS volume of Scottish poetry compiled by Sir Richard Maitland of Lethington (1496-1586); c. 1570-85.

First pub. (from this MS) in *Ancient Scotish Poems, never before in print*, ed. John Pinkerton (London, 1786), I, 3-43; printed from this MS in Bawcutt, pp. 139-70, and in *The Maitland Folio Manuscript*, ed. W.A. Craigie, STS NS 7 (Edinburgh & London, 1919), 254-85 (with a facsimile of p. 288 of the MS facing p. 256).

Magdalene College, Cambridge, Pepys Library, MS 2553, pp. 226-56.

DoG 3 *Virgil's Aeneid* ('Lawd, honour, praysyngis, thankis infynyte').

Copy in a scribal hand of a complete transcript made by Douglas's secretary, Matthew Geddes; c. 1515?

First pub. as *The xiii Bukes of Eneados of the famose Poete Virgill*, London, 1553; ed. David F.C. Coldwell, 4 vols, STS 3rd Ser. 30, 25, 27, 28 (Edinburgh & London, 1951-6). Printed from this MS in Coldwell, and described I, 96-7 (where it is mistakenly stated that this copy is in Geddes's hand and that the marginal commentary in the first part of the poem is in Douglas's autograph).

Trinity College, Cambridge, MS O. 3. 12 (James 1184).

DoG 4 -----

Copy of the complete translation, made by John Elphynstoun; owned in 1527 by one William Hay; c. 1515-20.

This MS collated in Coldwell and described I, 97-8.

Edinburgh University Library, MS Dk. 7. 49, ff. 2-367v.

DoG 5 -----

Copy of the complete translation, once owned by William Ruthven, fourth Baron Ruthven and first Earl of Gowrie (1541?-84); [before 1581].

This MS collated in Coldwell and described I, 98.

Edinburgh University Library, MS Dc. 1. 43.

DoG 6 -----

Copy of the complete translation, made by John Mudy with the help of Thomas Bellenden; finished '1545 2o february'.

This MS collated in Coldwell and described I, 98-9.

Lambeth Palace, MS 117.

DoG 7 -----

Copy of the complete translation, made by Henry Aytoun; finished 20 November 1547.

This MS collated in Coldwell and described I, 99-100.

Owned by the Marquess of Bath, Longleat House, MS 252A.

DoG 8 -----

Fragment of a copy, consisting of three folios containing Book I, Chapter II, lines 13-68; Chapter III, lines 1-19, 76-100; Chapter IV, lines 1-35; Chapter VIII, lines 7-70; 1st half 16th century.

This MS recorded in Coldwell, I, 100-1.

Edinburgh University Library, MS La. II. 655.

DoG 9 -----

Copy of the Prologue of Book IV, the Prologue of Book IX (lines 1-18), and the Prologue of Book X, transcribed from the edition of 1553 and corrected from another source, in a volume of Scottish poetry compiled by George Bannatyne; c. 1568.

Printed from this MS in *The Bannatyne Manuscript* ed. J. Barclay Murdoch, Hunterian Club (Glasgow, 1896), IV, 844-53; II, 122-3, 21-7; and in *The Bannatyne Manuscript*, ed. W. Tod Ritchie, STS 3rd Ser. 5, 22, 23, 26 (1928-33), IV, 108-16; II, 113, 20-6; recorded in Coldwell, I, 101.

National Library of Scotland, Adv. MS 1. 1. 6, Vol. II, ff. 291-4v (pp. 637-44); Vol. I, ff. 45r-v, 9-11 (pp. 149-50, 77-82).

Michael Drayton

1563-1631

ABBREVIATIONS

Hebel *The Works of Michael Drayton*, ed. J. William Hebel, Kathleen Tillotson, and Bernard H. Newdigate, 5 vols (Oxford, 1931-41; reprinted, with a new bibliography in Vol. V by B. Juel-Jensen, 1961).

For abbreviations used throughout Volume I, see p.xi.

INTRODUCTION

None of Drayton's poems is known to survive in his autograph and there are only a few extant specimens of his handwriting. A single autograph letter, sent to William Drummond of Hawthornden on 22 November 1620, is preserved in the National Library of Scotland (MS 9931, f. 21). The text is printed, with a reduced facsimile, in Bent Juel-Jensen, 'Michael Drayton and William Drummond of Hawthornden: A Lost Autograph Letter Rediscovered', *The Library*, 5th Ser. 21 (1966), 328-30. For a full-size reproduction of this letter see FACSIMILE XII. A printed exemplum of *The Muses Elizium* (London, 1630) with Drayton's autograph inscription to Sir Richard Brawne is in the Bent Juel-Jensen Drayton collection, now in the Bodleian; a facsimile of the inscription appears in Hebel, V (1961), 266. A printed exemplum of *The Battaile of Agincourt* (London, 1627) with Drayton's autograph inscription to Sir Henry Willoughby is in the Victoria and Albert Museum (Dyce Collection, Cat. No. 3199); facsimiles of the inscription appear in Greg, *English Literary Autographs*, plate VIII(c), and in Bernard H. Newdigate, *Michael Drayton and his Circle* (Oxford, 1961), facing p. 207. A signed autograph receipt of Drayton's for 21 January 1598/9 is in Philip Henslowe's Diary, now at Dulwich College (MS VII, f.31); it is reproduced in Greg, plate VIII(a), in Newdigate, *op. cit.*, facing p. 106, in Petti, *English Literary Hands*, No. 42, and in *The Henslowe Papers*, ed. R. A. Foakes (London, 1977). Another signature, on a slip probably cut from Henslowe's Diary, was formerly pasted in a printed exemplum of *Mortimeriados* (London, 1596) in the Bodleian (Malone 469) and is reproduced in Greg, plate VIII(b), but it has since been removed from the volume and is now unlocated. Two other signatures are pasted in a printed exemplum of Drayton's *Poems* (London, 1605) in the Bodleian (Douce DD 136), though it seems unlikely that the second is genuine; they are both reproduced in W. W. Greg, 'Fragments from Henslowe's Diary', *Collections: Volume IV*, Malone Society (Oxford, 1956), 27-32 (facing p. 32), and in Foakes, *op. cit.* A signature of Drayton's which has not yet been reproduced appears as that of witness to an indenture of 3 December 1613, signed by Sir Henry Goodyer, now in the Birmingham Reference Library (No. 336009); this document is discussed in I. A. Shapiro, 'Drayton at Polesworth', *N & Q*, *194 (12* November 1949), 496. A hitherto unrecorded signature appears as that of witness to an indenture of 31 May 1609, now in the William Salt Library, Stafford (M 593/2); this document, which is also signed by Drayton's patron, Sir Walter Aston, concerns the sale to Aston of the manor of Coulton, Staffordshire, by members of the Gresley family, and its subsequent lease to certain of their servants. Drayton's name is cited (but without his signature) in two other legal documents. He was a witness to the Will of the elder Sir Henry Goodyer (Public Record Office, PROB 10/158 (proved May 1595)), and he was one of the parties in a licence of alienation, of 1 November 1628, concerning land at Polesworth, Warton, and elsewhere (Birmingham Reference Library, No. 597244).

The canon accepted in the *Index* is based on Hebel. The only addition is the lyric *'If the deep sighs of an afflicted breast'* (DrM 38-9), which is attributed to Drayton by several editors. The MSS recorded are chiefly copies of poems in early miscellanies and songbooks. One MS is of some interest because it belonged to Herbert Aston, the son of Drayton's patron (DrM 33). Unless otherwise stated, the MSS recorded have not been noted by editors.

A number of printed exempla of works by Drayton contain minor MS corrections, some probably made by the printer; these are collated in Hebel and have not been given entries. Some other additional items comprise miscellaneous extracts and 18th-century copies. Drayton's longest poem, *Poly-Olbion*, is quoted in John Shrimpton's MS *History of St Albans* (c. 1640), now in the Bodleian (MS Gough Herts. 3, f. 79), and in *An Essay towards the Recovery of the Four Great Roman Ways* by Roger Gale (1672-1744), also in the Bodleian (MS Rawl. D. 400, ff. 14v, 20v). A poem which borrows extracts from poems by Drayton is to be found in a miscellany once owned by Margaret Bellasys (c. 1630), now in the British Library (Add. MS 10309, f. 32B): see Hebel, V, 140, note 2. An 18th-century copy of *To His Coy Love* appears in a miscellany compiled by one Stephen Barrett, now in the Osborn Collection at Yale (c 193, p. 36), and copies of the fourth and sixth sonnets of *Idea* ('Bright starre of Beauty, on whose eye-lids sit' and 'How many paltry, foolish, painted things') (Hebel, II, 312-13) appear in a miscellany of c. 1776-1804 now in the Bodleian (MS Eng. misc. e. 241, f. 126).

PB.

ARRANGEMENT

Verse	DrM 1-69.
Prose	DrM 70.

See also Addenda to Part 2, p. 627

FACSIMILE XII — Michael Drayton: Letter to William Drummond, 22 November 1620; inscribed by Drummond at the foot of the page with the date of receipt. National Library of Scotland, MS 9931, folio 21 recto. Reproduced by permission of the Trustees of the National Library of Scotland.

Noble Mr Drummond: I am oft thinking whether this long silence proceede from you or me; whether I knowe not: but I would have you take it uppon you, & excuse me; and then I would have you laye it uppon me & excuse yor self: but if you will, (if you think it a fault as I doe) lett us devyde it; & both of us amend it. in this long being in the Contrye this Sommer from whence I had no means to send my letter, shall partly speake for me: for beleeve me worthy Will I am most thy a faythfullest frend: whom I love I love forewards: which I hope you shall find. when I writ this letter: o^r Iovall frend Sr. William Alexander was at Court at Newmarkett: but his lady promised me to send this letter safe to you: lett me heare how you doe, so soone as you can and knowe this I am & will ever:

London this 22
of November
in 1618:

Yo^r faythfull frend

M: Drayton

Michael Drayton

VERSE

--- *The Battaile of Agincourt.*

See INTRODUCTION.

--- *'Bright starre of Beauty, on whose eye-lids sit'.*

See INTRODUCTION.

DrM 1 *A Catalogue of the Heroicall Loves* ('The World's faire Rose, and Henries frosty fire').

Copy of a parodied version, followed by a couplet on 'The Admired S^{r}. Philip Sidneye' (beginning 'Divine Sr Philip, I avouch thy writt'), in a miscellany compiled by John Ramsey (b. 1578) of Peterhouse, Cambridge; early 17th century.

First pub. (the original version) without title in *Englands Heroicall Epistles* (London, 1599); Hebel, II, 308. This parody unpublished.

Bodleian, MS Douce 280, f. 124v.

DrM 2 *'Cleere Ankor, on whose Silver-sanded shore'.*

Copy in a verse miscellany compiled by an Oxford man and once owned by one William Bloys; c. 1630s.

First pub. as Amour 13 in *Ideas Mirrour* (London, 1594); Hebel, I, 104; II, 337 (sonnet 53 of *Idea*). This MS recorded in Hebel, V, 16.

Bodleian, MS Rawl. poet. 142, f. 19v.

DrM 3 -----

Copy in a verse miscellany compiled by Arthur Capell; mid-17th century.

This MS recorded in Hebel, V, 16.

British Library, Harley MS 3511, f. 36.

DrM 4 *The Cryer* ('Good Folke, for Gold or Hyre').

Copy, here beginning 'Dear frinds either for loue or hier', in a verse miscellany compiled by Nicholas Burghe (d. 1670); c. 1638.

First pub. among *Odes with Other Lyrick Poesies* in *Poems* (London, 1619); Hebel, II, 371.

Bodleian, MS Ashmole 38, p. 121.

DrM 5 -----

Second copy, also beginning 'Dear frinds eyther for loue or hyer', deleted, in Nicholas Burghe's miscellany; c. 1638.

Bodleian, MS Ashmole 38, p. 122.

DrM 6 -----

Copy, untitled, in a MS volume of poems chiefly by Thomas Carew (the 'Wyburd MS'); c. 1640s.

Bodleian, MS Don. b. 9, f. 18r-v.

DrM 7 -----

Copy, untitled, in a verse miscellany; c. 1640.

Bodleian, MS Eng. poet. c. 53, f. 1v.

DrM 8 -----

Copy in a composite volume of verse collected by Peter Le Neve (1661-1729); 17th century.

Bodleian, MS Eng. poet. d. 152, f. 107v.

DrM 9 -----

Copy, headed 'The complaint of one in his louer absence', in a verse miscellany compiled by an Oxford man and once owned by one Henry Lawson; c. 1630s.

Bodleian, MS Eng. poet. e. 14, f. 20.

DrM 10 -----

Copy, headed 'An Oyes, for a lost Harte', here beginning 'Good ffolks for loue, or else for hire', and ascribed to 'Ben: Johnson', in a verse miscellany probably compiled by a member of Christ Church, Oxford; c. 1630s-40s.

Bodleian, MS Eng. poet. e. 97, p. 163.

DrM 11 -----

Copy in a MS volume of poems chiefly by John Donne compiled by Henry Champernowne (1600-56) of Dartington, Devon; c. 1623.

Bodleian, MS Eng. poet. f. 9, p. 8.

DrM 12 -----

Copy, probably transcribed from *Poems* (London, 1619), in a small MS volume of poems by Drayton once owned by one John Saye or Sayer; mid-17th century.

Bodleian, MS Juel-Jensen Drayton f. 1, fol. 7r-v.

DrM 13 -----

Copy in a verse miscellany compiled by an Oxford man, possibly a member of St John's College; c. 1634-43.

Bodleian, MS Malone 21, f. 66.

The Cryer

DrM 14 -----

Copy, untitled, in a verse miscellany; c. 1630s.

Bodleian, MS Malone 23, p. 8.

DrM 15 -----

Copy, untitled, in a musical setting (set as an Oxford Act song) by Henry Bowman, in a MS songbook (2nd treble part) compiled by Edward Lowe (c.1610-82); c. 1650s.

Bowman's setting first pub. in his *Songs for 1 2 & 3 Voyces* ([no place], 1677).

Bodleian, MS Mus. d. 238, pp. 184-6.

DrM 16 -----

Copy in a musical setting by Henry Bowman; c. 1670-80.

Bodleian, MS Mus. Sch. C. 145, f. 2-8.

DrM 17 -----

Copy, headed 'Cupids inquisition', in a miscellany once owned by Sir Thomas Meres (1634-1715) of Kirton, Lincolnshire; c. 1640s.

This MS recorded in Hebel, V, 147.

British Library, Egerton MS 2725, f. 170 rev.

DrM 18 -----

Copy in a verse miscellany compiled by Arthur Capell; mid-17th century.

This MS recorded in Hebel, V, 147.

British Library, Harley MS 3511, f. 28r-v.

DrM 19 -----

Copy in a verse miscellany; c. 1637.

This MS recorded in Hebel, V, 147.

British Library, Stowe MS 962, f. 132v.

DrM 20 -----

Copy in a miscellany; 1620s.

Cambridge University Library, MS Add. 7196, f. [5 rev.].

DrM 21 -----

Copy in a musical setting by Henry Bowman, in a MS music part book compiled by Thomas Smith (1614-1701) of The Queen's College, Oxford, later Bishop of Carlisle; c. 1637.

Printed from this MS in James Walter Brown, 'Some Elizabethan Lyrics', *CM*, 51 (September 1921), 285-96 (p. 292).

Carlisle Cathedral, Dean & Chapter of Carlisle MSS, Box B1, Bassus, pp. 84-5.

DrM 22 -----

Copy in a musical setting by Henry Bowman, in a MS songbook (1st treble part) compiled by Edward Lowe; c. 1650s.

Edinburgh University Library, MS Dc. 1. 69, ff. 100v-2.

DrM 23 -----

Copy in a verse miscellany; c. 1630.

Folger, MS V. a. 103, Part I, f. 34.

DrM 24 -----

Copy, untitled, in a miscellany compiled by Matthew Day of Windsor; c. 1633-4.

Folger, MS V. a. 160, pp. 3-4 (2nd series).

DrM 25 -----

Copy, headed 'On a man vppon himselfe that made this beeinge in loue', in a verse miscellany compiled by an Oxford man and once owned by one Stephen Welden; mid-17th century.

Folger, MS V. a. 162, ff. 80v-1.

DrM 26 -----

Copy, headed 'A heart lost', in a miscellany later owned by one Joseph Hall; c. 1630s-50.

Folger, MS V. a. 339, ff. 233v-4.

DrM 27 -----

Copy, untitled, in a miscellany compiled by or for Sir Henry Cholmley, brother of Sir Hugh Cholmley (1600-57); c. 1624-41.

Harvard, MS Eng 703, ff. 27v-8.

DrM 28 -----

Copy, headed 'On a heart', in a verse miscellany; c. 1643-50s.

University of Newcastle upon Tyne, MS Bell/White 25, ff. 27-8.

The Cryer

DrM 29 -----

Copy in a verse miscellany; c. 1630.

University of Nottingham, Portland MS Pw V 37, p. 71.

DrM 30 -----

Copy in a verse miscellany; c. 1635.

Rosenbach Foundation, MS 240/7, p. 24.

DrM 31 -----

Copy, headed 'A louers inquest after his heart' and here beginning 'Some good folke for loue, or hire', in a miscellany compiled by or for Sir Thomas Finch, Viscount Maidstone and Earl of Winchelsea; c. 1634.

Rosenbach Foundation, MS 243/4, p. 24.

DrM 32 -----

Copy in a miscellany; c. 1635.

Owned by Edwin Wolf 2nd, Philadelphia, MS, p. 98.

DrM 33 -----

Copy in a verse miscellany compiled by Herbert Aston, son of Sir Walter Aston (1584-1639) of Tixall, Staffordshire; c. 1634.

Yale, Osborn Collection, b 4, f. 54v.

DrM 34 -----

Copy in a MS volume of poems chiefly by John Donne; c. 1622-33.

Yale, Osborn Collection, b 148, p. 23.

DrM 35 -----

Copy in a verse miscellany compiled by Tobias Alston (1620-c.1639) of Sayham Hall, near Sudbury, Suffolk; c. 1639.

Yale, Osborn Collection, b 197, pp. 37-8.

DrM 36 -----

Copy in a miscellany; late 17th century.

Yale, Osborn Collection, b 213, p. 10.

DrM 36.5 See Addenda, p. 627

--- *Englands Heroicall Epistles.*

See DrM 1, 43-4, 49.

DrM 37 *The Heart* ('If thus we needs must goe').

Copy, probably transcribed from *Poems* (London, 1619), in a small MS volume of poems by Drayton once owned by one John Saye or Sayer; mid-17th century.

First pub. among *Odes with Other Lyrick Poesies* in *Poems* (London, 1619); Hebel, II, 355-6.

Bodleian, MS Juel-Jensen Drayton f. 1, fol. 7.

--- *'How many paltry, foolish, painted things'.*

See INTRODUCTION.

--- *Idea.*

See DrM 43-4, 47, 49, and INTRODUCTION.

DrM 38 *'If the deep sighs of an afflicted breast'.*

Copy in a musical setting by John Ward, in a MS songbook compiled by Thomas Hamond (d. 1662) of Suffolk; 1633.

First pub. in John Ward, *First Set of English Madrigals* (London, 1613), xxiii-xxiv; first attributed to Drayton in Thomas Oliphant, *La Musa Madrigalesca* (London, 1837), p. 286; *English Madrigal Verse 1588-1632*, ed. E.H. Fellowes et al., 3rd edition (Oxford, 1967), pp. 270-1.

Bodleian, MS Mus. f. 20-4: f. 20, fol. 79v.

DrM 39 -----

Copy in a musical setting by John Ward in a MS songbook; early 17th century.

This MS collated in John P. Cutts, 'Early Seventeenth-Century Lyrics at St. Michael's College', *M & L*, 37 (1956), 221-33 (p. 232).

St Michael's College, Tenbury Wells, MS 1019, f. 3.

DrM 40 *The Legend of Pierce Gaveston* ('From gloomie shaddowes of eternall Night').

Copy of the last thirty stanzas, probably transcribed from *Poems* (London, 1619), in a small MS volume of poems by Drayton once owned by one John Saye or Sayer; imperfect, lacking the first part of the poem; mid-17th century.

First pub. (1740-line version) London, [1593-4]; Hebel, I, 157-207; 702-line version among *Legends* in *Poems* (London, 1619); Hebel, II, 431-50.

Bodleian, MS Juel-Jensen Drayton f. 1, fols. 3-5v.

Legends

--- *Legends*.

See DrM 40, 70.

DrM 41 *Mr. M.D. To the Author* ('Such was old Orpheus cunning').

Copy in a musical setting in a MS songbook compiled by Thomas Hamond (d. 1662) of Suffolk; c. 1630s-56.

First pub. in Thomas Morley, *First Booke of Balletts to Five Voyces* (London, 1595); Hebel, I, 493.

Bodleian, MS Mus. f. 11-15: f. 11, fol. 50v.

--- *The Muses Elizium*.

See INTRODUCTION.

DrM 42 *'Nature, and Arte are overmatcht by thee'*.

Copy written in Thomas Palmer's MS book of emblems *The Sprite of Trees and Herbes* (1598-9), owned in 1663 by one Margaret Nevill; early 17th century.

First pub. (from this MS) in Percy Simpson, 'Thomas Palmer', *N & Q*, 8th Ser. 8 (28 September 1895), 243-4; printed from this MS in Hebel, I, 497.

British Library, Add. MS 18040, f. 9.

DrM 43 *'Nothing but No and I, and I and No'*.

Copy in a verse miscellany; c. 1630s-40s.

First pub. as sonnet 8 in *Idea* in *Englands Heroicall Epistles* (London, 1599); Hebel, II, 313 (sonnet 5).

Edinburgh University Library, MS La. III. 436, p. 126.

DrM 44 -----

Copy in a verse miscellany compiled by an Oxford man and once owned by one Stephen Welden; mid-17th century.

Folger, MS V. a. 162, f. 26.

DrM 45 *The Owle* ('What time the Sunne by his all-quickning Power').

Copy, complete with dedication to Sir Walter Aston (beginning 'For the shrill Trumpet, and sterne Tragick sounds'), transcribed from the edition of 1604, in a verse miscellany compiled between 6 April and 17 November 1604.

First pub. London, 1604; Hebel, II, 477-514. This MS (formerly in the Phillipps collection) recorded in Hebel, V (1961), 283; a photocopy is in the Bodleian, Juel-Jensen Drayton Collection.

Folger, MS V. b. 210, p. 19 seq.

--- *Peirs Gaveston* ('From gloomy shaddowe of eternall night').

See DrM 40.

DrM 46 *Poly-Olbion*.

Extracts in a miscellany compiled by William Drummond of Hawthornden; c. 1613-20s.

First pub. London, 1612; 1622; Hebel, IV.

National Library of Scotland, MS 2060 (Hawthornden Vol. VIII), ff. 268-75.

--- -----

See also INTRODUCTION.

DrM 47 *'Since to obtaine thee, nothing me will sted'*.

Copy, headed 'Drayton his remedie for Loue', in a verse miscellany; c. 1635.

First pub. as sonnet 15 of *Idea* in *Poems* (London, 1619); Hebel, II, 318 (sonnet 15).

Rosenbach Foundation, MS 240/7, p. 66.

DrM 48 *A Skeltoniad* ('The Muse should be sprightly').

Copy, probably transcribed from *Poems* (London, 1619), in a small MS volume of poems by Drayton once owned by one John Saye or Sayer; mid-17th century.

First pub. in *Poemes Lyrick and pastorall* (London, [1606]); among *Odes with Other Lyrick Poesies* in *Poems* (London, 1619); Hebel, II, 370.

Bodleian, MS Juel-Jensen Drayton f. 1, fol. 8.

DrM 49 *'Some misbeleeving, and prophane in Love'*.

Copy in a verse miscellany; c. 1630s-40s.

First pub. as *Amour* 12 in a version beginning 'Some Atheist or vile Infidel in love' in *Ideas Mirrour* (London, 1594); a version beginning 'Some misbeleeving, and prophane in Love' first pub. as sonnet 35 of *Idea* in *Englands Heroicall Epistles* (London, 1599); Hebel, I, 103; II, 328 (sonnet 35).

Edinburgh University Library, MS La. III. 436, p. 119.

DrM 50 *These verses weare made by Michaell Drayton Esquier Poett Laureatt the night before hee dyed* ('Soe well I love thee, as without thee I').

These verses weare made by Michaell Drayton...the night before hee dyed

Copy in a verse miscellany compiled by Nicholas Burghe (d. 1670); c. 1638.

First pub. (from this MS) in Oliver Elton, *Michael Drayton* (London, 1905), p. 210; printed from this MS in Hebel, I, 507.

Bodleian, MS Ashmole 38, pp. 77-8.

DrM 51 *To His Coy Love, A Canzonet* ('I pray thee leave, love me no more').

Copy, headed 'A Sonnet', in a verse miscellany compiled by an Oxford man, possibly a member of Wadham College, and later used by William Fulman (1632-88); c. late 1630s.

First pub. among *Odes with Other Lyrick Poesies* in *Poems* (London, 1619); Hebel, II, 372.

Bodleian, MS CCC. 328, f. 76.

DrM 52 -----

Copy in a musical setting in a MS songbook; c. 1640s.

Printed from this MS in John P. Cutts, 'A Bodleian Song-Book: Don. C. 57', *M & L*, 34 (1953), 192-211 (p. 205).

Bodleian, MS Don. c. 57, f. 49v.

DrM 53 -----

Copy, headed 'Cant 22', in a verse miscellany compiled by the Yorkshire antiquary John Hopkinson (1610-80); c. 1647.

Bodleian, MS Don. d. 58, f. 28.

DrM 54 -----

Copy, headed 'Sonett', in a verse miscellany once owned by one Peter Daniell; c. 1630s-40s.

Bodleian, MS Eng. poet. c. 50, f. 35.

DrM 55 -----

Copy, untitled, in a verse miscellany compiled by Robert Codrington (1602-65); c. 1638.

Bodleian, MS Eng. poet. f. 27, p. 36.

DrM 56 -----

Copy, probably transcribed from *Poems* (London, 1619), in a small MS volume of poems by Drayton once owned by one John Saye or Sayer; mid-17th century.

Bodleian, MS Juel-Jensen Drayton f. 1, fol. 7v.

DrM 57 -----

Copy of lines 1-4, 12-15, in a miscellany once owned by Margaret Bellasys, probably the daughter of Thomas, first Lord Fauconberg (1577-1653); c. 1630.

This MS recorded in Hebel, V, 147.

British Library, Add. MS 10309, f. 221.

DrM 58 -----

Copy in a composite volume of verse belonging to the Skipwith family of Cotes, Leicestershire; early-mid-17th century.

British Library, Add. MS 25707, f. 95v.

DrM 59 -----

Copy, headed 'On Tantalized by his M[ris]', in a miscellany compiled by Sir John Perceval, Bart. (1629-65), probably while at Magdalene College, Cambridge; constituting Volume CXCII of the Egmont Papers; c. 1646-9.

British Library, Add. MS 47111, f. 11.

DrM 60 -----

Copy in a verse miscellany compiled by Arthur Capell; mid-17th century.

This MS recorded in Hebel, V, 147.

British Library, Harley MS 3511, f. 28v.

DrM 61 -----

Copy in a miscellany; 1620s.

Cambridge University Library, MS Add. 7196, ff. [17v-18 rev.].

DrM 62 -----

Copy in a musical setting, in a MS music part book compiled by Thomas Smith (1614-1701) of The Queen's College, Oxford, later Bishop of Carlisle; c. 1637.

Carlisle Cathedral, Dean & Chapter of Carlisle MSS, Box B1, Bassus, p. 85.

DrM 63 -----

Copy, untitled, in a musical setting in a MS songbook owned and probably compiled by Elizabeth Davenant (sister of Sir William Davenant) of Oxford; c. 1624-30s.

Christ Church, Oxford, MS Mus. 87, ff. 12v-13.

To His Coy Love

DrM 64 -----

Copy, headed 'A Sonett', in a verse miscellany compiled by William Jordan, schoolmaster of Denbigh or Caernarvon; c. 1674-84.

Folger, MS V. a. 276, Part II, f. 18.

DrM 65 -----

Copy, untitled, in a miscellany (p. 2) probably compiled by one or two members of the Calverley family; c. 1623-30s.

Christie's, 13 June 1979 (Arthur A. Houghton, Jr. sale), Lot 135, sold to Maggs; thence to Huntington.

--- -----

See also INTRODUCTION.

DrM 66 *To his Rivall* ('Her lov'd I most').

Copy, probably transcribed from *Poems* (London, 1619), in a small MS volume of poems by Drayton once owned by one John Saye or Sayer; mid-17th century.

First pub. among *Odes with Other Lyrick Poesies* in *Poems* (London, 1619); Hebel, II, 368-9.

Bodleian, MS Juel-Jensen Drayton f. 1, fol. 7v.

DrM 67 *To His Valentine* ('Muse, bid the Morne awake').

Copy in a verse miscellany compiled by Arthur Capell; mid-17th century.

First pub. among *Odes with Other Lyrick Poesies* in *Poems* (London, 1619); Hebel, II, 352-4. This MS recorded in Hebel, V, 146.

British Library, Harley MS 3511, ff. 63v-5.

DrM 68 *To the Cambro-Britans, and their Harpe, his Ballad of Agincourt* ('Faire stood the Wind for France').

A printed exemplum of *Poems* (London, 1619) with annotations in the hand of Richard Butcher (1587-1664), including an extra stanza added to the *Ballad of Agincourt*; c. 1620.

First pub. among *Odes with Other Lyrick Poesies* in *Poems* (London, 1619); Hebel, II, 375-8. This item recorded and the extra stanza printed in Hebel, V (1961), 291; facsimile in Hebel, III (1961), facing p. 9.

Bodleian, Juel-Jensen Drayton d. 6.

DrM 69 *'Upon a Banke with Roses set about'.*

Copy in a musical setting in a MS songbook compiled by Thomas Hamond (d. 1662) of Suffolk; 1633.

First pub. in *Englands Helicon* (London, 1600); musical setting of first stanza pub. in John Ward, *First Set of English Madrigals* (London, 1613), No. xviii; Hebel, II, 525 (lines 105-28 of *The Second Eclogue* of *Pastorals*).

Bodleian, MS Mus. f. 20-4: f. 20, fol. 11v.

PROSE

DrM 70 *To the Reader* ('The word LEGEND...').

Abbreviated version of the Preface to *Legends*, untitled, probably transcribed from *Poems* (London, 1619), in a small MS volume of poems by Drayton once owned by one John Saye or Sayer; mid-17th century.

First pub. in *Poems* (London, 1619); Hebel, II, 382.

Bodleian, MS Juel-Jensen Drayton f. 1, fol. 6.

William Drummond of Hawthornden

1585-1649

ABBREVIATIONS

Fogle French Rowe Fogle, *A Critical Study of William Drummond of Hawthornden* (New York, 1952).

Kastner *The Poetical Works of William Drummond of Hawthornden*, ed. L. E. Kastner, 2 vols, STS NS 3, 4 (Edinburgh & London, 1913).

Laing (1831) David Laing, 'A Brief Account of the Hawthornden Manuscripts in the possession of the Society of Antiquaries of Scotland; with Extracts, containing several unpublished Letters and Poems of William Drummond of Hawthornden', *Transactions of the Society of Antiquaries of Scotland*, 4 (1831), 57-116.

Laing (1833) David Laing, 'Extracts from the Hawthornden Manuscripts, in the possession of the Society of Antiquaries of Scotland', *Transactions of the Society of Antiquaries of Scotland*, 4 (1833), 225-40.

MacDonald (1976) William Drummond, *Poems and Prose*, ed. Robert H. MacDonald (Edinburgh & London, 1976).

MacDonald, *Library of Drummond* Robert H. MacDonald, *The Library of Drummond of Hawthornden* (Edinburgh, 1971).

MacDonald, *SSL*, 7 (1969) Robert H. MacDonald, 'Amendments to L. E. Kastner's Edition of Drummond's Poems', *Studies in Scottish Literature*, 7 (1969), 102-22.

Paganelli Eloisa Paganelli, 'Lettere e Note Inedite di William Drummond of Hawthornden', *English Miscellany*, 19 (1968), 295-333.

Poems (1656) *Poems, by that most famous wit, William Drummond of Hawthornden*, [ed. Edward Phillips] (London, 1656).

Works *The Works of William Drummond of Hawthornden* (Edinburgh, 1711).

For abbreviations used throughout Volume I, see p.xi.

INTRODUCTION

A large collection of Drummond's original papers are preserved, bound in ten volumes in the National Library of Scotland (MSS 2053-62: Hawthornden Vols. I-X); a few other papers are bound with those of his uncle William Fowler (MSS 2063-7: Hawthornden Vols. XI-XV). They represent the most substantial body of working papers of any British poet of the period. The MSS were arranged and bound by the antiquary David Laing (1793-1878) and are described in Laing (1831).

The surviving and identifiable drafts of poems which were published during Drummond's lifetime are recorded in the *Index* in the first section (DrW 1-35). All titles and first lines are taken from Kastner.

The far more numerous drafts of poems which Drummond did not consider worth publishing, and which may be called his 'Posthumous Poems' (DrW 36-302), present serious editorial problems. Some of these poems were printed from Drummond's papers in Phillips's edition of the *Poems* (1656); a few more appeared in the collected *Works* (1711); many more were printed in Laing (1831) and (1833); and others were printed in Kastner (1913). Although this last edition seemed to establish the canon of Drummond's posthumous poems, Kastner did not take account of certain poems among Drummond's papers; moreover, he was inclined to take Drummond's autograph copies as proof of his authorship, whereas Drummond was a habitual copyist of other men's verse. Some of the poems also exist in more than one draft and Kastner failed to make it clear from which he was printing and whether the others contain variant readings. A few poems omitted by Kastner were printed in Fogle (1952), pp. 75, 187-209; some more amendments to Kastner's canon were made in MacDonald, *SSL*, 7 (1969), and two additional poems were printed in MacDonald (1976). No doubt there is room for further amendments.

For practical purposes the *Index* has accepted the canon established in Kastner, Fogle, and MacDonald (1976), except for certain omissions noted below and the addition of three hitherto unpublished verse items which are preserved in other sources besides the Hawthornden volumes. The exact location of two recorded poetical drafts (DrW 138, 196) has not been confirmed. A detailed examination of Drummond's voluminous and sometimes barely legible working papers would possibly bring to light more poems.

The three additional pieces (DrW 68, 74, 94-5) include a Latin poem addressed to Michael Drayton (DrW 94-5) and an item which is not so much a poem as a list of lines and phrases jotted down for future use (DrW 74); this interesting witness to Drummond's methods of composition is reproduced in FACSIMILE XIII.

Two of the poems omitted from the canon may be safely attributed to Sir Robert Ayton (1570-1638) and are included in *The English and Latin Poems of Sir Robert Ayton*, ed. Charles B. Gullans, STS 4th Ser. 1 (Edinburgh & London, 1963), pp. 164-5. They are the verses *'Faire cruel Siluia since thow scornes my teares'* (Kastner, II, 269) and *'Wer these thine eies or lightnings from aboue'*, which is headed in Drummond's transcript 'De Porcheres, on the eies of Madame la Marquise de Monceaux, vret this sonnet' (Kastner, II, 270). The poems appear in the National Library of Scotland, MS 2060 (Hawthornden Vol. VIII), ff. 231, 230. Three other MS copies of the first poem and four other copies of the second are recorded in Gullans (pp. 280-2). A third rejected poem is an elegy on Thomas Sackville (1536-1608). Drummond's version, headed *On a noble man who died at a counsel table* and beginning 'Vntymlie Death that neither wouldst conferre', is included in the *Index* as a very doubtful item (DrW 177), but it should be noted that there are many other copies of a version usually beginning 'Immodest death, that wouldst not once conferre', which have not been given entries: for example, Bodleian (MSS Ashmole 781, p. 136; CCC. 328, f. 97; Don. d. 58, f. 18; Douce f. 5, fol. 11; Eng. poet. e. 14, f. 95v rev; Eng. poet. e. 97, p. 94); British Library (Cotton MS App. L, f. 169); Folger (MSS V. a. 97, p. 153; V. a. 103, Part I, f. 37; V. a. 262, p. 156; V. a. 345, p. 33); Huntington (HM 116, p. 25); Leicestershire Record Office (DG 7/Lit. 2, p. 270); University of Nottingham (Portland MS Pw V 37, p. 37); and Rosenbach Foundation (MSS 1083/16, p. 114; 1083/17, p. 29).

A fourth poem omitted is the satire *For the Kinge* ('From such a face quois excellence'), which is often headed 'The [Five] Senses' (it is a parody on Patrico's blessing of the King's senses in Jonson's *Gypsies Metamorphosed*: see BEN JONSON, JnB 654-70). Kastner printed the poem among his 'Poems of Doubtful Authenticity' (II, 296-9), but its sentiments are alien to those of Drummond and it can be safely rejected from the canon: see C. F. Main, 'Ben Jonson and an Unknown Poet on the King's Senses', *MLN*, 74 (1959), 389-93, and MacDonald, *SSL*, 7 (1969), 118. The poem is of some interest in its own right, however, and was certainly very popular. The following copies are to be found:

Bodleian (MSS Eng. poet. c. 50, f. 25; Eng. poet. e. 37, p. 72; Malone 23, p. 28; Rawl. poet. 26, f. 72; Rawl. poet. 117, ff. 23v-4v; Rawl. poet. 160, f. 14v; Tanner 465, f. 97); Bradford Central Library (Hopkinson MSS, Vol. 34, pp. 65-6); British Library (Add. MS 23229, ff. 99-100; Add. MS 25303, ff. 133-4; Egerton MS 923, f. 30; Harley MS 367, f. 153r-v; Stowe MS 962, ff. 144v-6); Marquess of Bute (4° Vol. Petitions to James I, &c, No. 9, recorded in *HMC*, 3rd Report (1872), Appendix, p. 204: possession confirmed by letter 9 April 1976); Chetham's Library, Manchester (Mun. A 3. 47, ff.1-2); Downing College, Cambridge (Bowtell Collection, MS 'Wickstede Thesaurus', Part II, ff. 106v-7v); Durham Cathedral (Hunter MS 27, ff. 94v-5); Edinburgh University Library (MS H.-P. Coll. 401, f. 51r-v); Folger (MSS V. a. 275, p. 175; V. a. 276, f. 40v; V. a. 339, f. 256; V. a. 345, pp. 59-61; X. d. 235); Harvard (MS Eng 686, ff. 59v-60); Hatfield House (Cecil Papers 206/100r-v, owned by the Marquess of Salisbury, printed in *HMC* 9, Salisbury (Cecil) MSS, XXII (1971), pp. 252-3); Huntington (HM 198, Part I, pp. 30-2); Leicestershire Record Office (DG. 7/Lit. 2, ff. 333v-4v); National Library of Scotland (Adv. MS 19. 3. 8, ff. 47-8v); National Library of Wales (NLW. MS 12443A, Part ii, pp. 125-30); University of Nottingham (Portland MS Pw V 37, pp. 198-200); Pierpont Morgan Library (MA 1057, pp. 80-1); Rosenbach Foundation (MSS 239/27, p. 58 bis; 1083/16, pp. 84-7); St John's College, Cambridge (MS S. 32 (James 423), ff. 31-2); Somerset Record Office (DD/SF C/2635, Box 1); University of Texas at Austin (Ms File/(Herrick, R.)/Works B, pp. 325-7: facsimile in *TQ* 16, No. 4 (Supplement) (Winter 1973), pp. 136-41); Westminster Abbey (MS 41, ff. 21-2); Yale, Osborn Collection (b 54, p. 877).

Also excluded from the entries are some later copies of Drummond's poems. The Epitaph 'Fame, Register of Tyme' and *Armelins Epitaph* ('Neare to this Eglantine') appear in F. Cumming's collection of epitaphs (c. 1784-1800) in the Bodleian (MS Top. gen. e. 32, ff. 72v-3v); the Sonnet 'Sleepe, Silence Child, sweet Father of soft Rest' appears in John Phillips's miscellany (1776-1804) in the Bodleian (MS Eng. misc. e. 241, f. 118); and the Sonnet 'I know that all beneath the Moone decayes' (Kastner, I, 4) appears in Thomas Binns's miscellany (1799) in the Osborn Collection at Yale (c 142, p. 401). A 19th-century transcript of Drummond's published poems is in the National Library of Scotland (MS 2068).

The canon of Drummond's prose presents fewer problems. Although only *A Cypresse Grove* (DrW 306) was published during his lifetime, and although the Hawthornden MSS include Drummond's copies of works by others (e.g. the speeches on Charles I's visit to Edinburgh in Vol. IX, ff. 162-72), it is possible to distinguish the corrected drafts of his own compositions. Of these the most important is his *History of the Five Jameses*, published in 1655, the various drafts of which form Hawthornden Vols I-V (DrW 314-15). Most of his other tracts and essays were printed in *Works* (1711); his account of his own family (DrW 311-13) was printed by one of his descendants in 1831; a few brief essays were printed in Paganelli (1968), and a very few others remain unpublished. For a study of the themes of the main essays see Thomas I. Rae, 'The political attitudes of William Drummond of Hawthornden', *The Scottish Tradition: Essays in Honour of Ronald Gordon Cant*, ed. G. W. S. Barrow (Edinburgh, 1974), 132-46. The original MS of what is perhaps the most interesting of the prose works, Drummond's *Conversations with Ben Jonson*, is no longer among the Hawthornden MSS: it was last seen in the late 17th-early 18th century when Sir Robert Sibbald made a copy of it (DrW 303).

In addition to these works the Hawthornden MSS contain numerous unrecorded fragments, jottings, memoranda, and historical notes (see especially Vol. IX, ff. 26v-7, 59, 92-4, 121, 129, 131v, 141, 146, 152, 155-8, 161). One other volume of historical material of this kind can be found elsewhere, in Edinburgh University Library

MS La. III. 365: see DrW 74). The Hawthornden MSS also contain a fairly large number of draft letters. Thirty-one letters were printed from Vol. IX in Laing (1831), pp. 83-98; a further twenty-eight letters (including the *Dedication to Craigmiller*: DrW 307) were printed from Vol. IX in Paganelli (1968); and a letter to Dr Arthur Johnston 'on the True Nature of Poetry' was printed in MacDonald (1976), pp. 191-2. Two letters are reproduced in part in Greg, *English Literary Autographs*, plate LI(a-c). In other locations, a letter of 7 June 1621 to Sir Robert Kerr, concerning MSS of Daniel and Donne, is among the muniments of the Marquess of Lothian, recorded in *HMC*, 1st Report (1870), Appendix, p. 116, and now on deposit in the Scottish Record Office (GD40/13, f. 26); it is printed in *Correspondence of Sir Robert Kerr, First Earl of Ancram, and his Son William, Third Earl of Lothian*, ed. David Laing, 2 vols (Edinburgh, 1875), I, 24-5. A letter of 1623 is among the Crawford muniments in the John Rylands University Library of Manchester (MS 14/6). A letter of 15 October 1639 to Alexander Lord Kildrummie, discussing translations, was among the muniments of Lord Elphinstone recorded in *HMC*, 9th Report, Part II (1884), Appendix, p. 199; these muniments are now in the Scottish Record Office but they have not yet been catalogued and the letter has not been identified. A signature of Drummond's written in 1637 can also be found in Edinburgh University Library (MS Da. 2. 1, p. 9), and a document bearing his signature in 1640 is at Colorado College.

Two volumes among the Hawthornden MSS which appear to have been Drummond's own miscellanies (as distinct from separate papers bound together by Laing) are recorded in the *Index* in a 'Miscellaneous' section (DrW 352-3), along with a notebook of his now at the University of Dundee (DrW 354).

Five printed books which are known to contain Drummond's substantial autograph annotations have been given entries (DrW 347-51). For an almost complete catalogue of the books in Drummond's library see MacDonald, *Library of Hawthornden* (1971). MacDonald discusses Drummond's marginalia on pp. 33-6 and includes several facsimile examples, as well as printing most of Drummond's own lists of books. Some other books from Drummond's library (at Hawthornden Castle) were sold at Sotheby's, 24 October 1977, Lots 20-2. One other curious item which may be connected with Drummond or his family is a nonce collection of printed works by his friend Sir William Alexander (1567?-1640) formerly in the library of the Duke of Sutherland at Dunrobin Castle and now in the Brotherton Collection at the University of Leeds. Besides containing MS verses in English and Latin dated 1635-6, the volume contains a series of notes, partly in shorthand, signed 'J. Drumond. 1622'.

Some leaves of biographical and critical notes on Drummond written at the end of the 18th century can be found in the University of London (MS 280).

PB.

ARRANGEMENT

Verse: (1) Poems published in Drummond's lifetime	DrW 1-35
(2) Posthumous poems	DrW 36-302
Prose	DrW 303-46
Marginalia in printed books and manuscripts	DrW 347-51
Miscellaneous	DrW 352-4.

FACSIMILE XIII — William Drummond: Poetical jottings beginning 'aboue the circle/circuit of our thoughts' (DrW 74). Edinburgh University Library, MS La. III. 365, folio [22 verso]. Reproduced by permission of Edinburgh University Library.

~~circuit~~

above the circle of our thoughts:

& to nestle, [illegible]

God lisps to Babes,

His more sublime. Summons. clouds,

their clouded life pales fast

his full meridian, and doth not decline

To seed of Grace, whose age doth smack at last

my lifes Summer neare its set.

Globes wth sparkes

Perfumes / consumes /

whose vaste embrace enspheres the earth.

the nastye smell. the Shoals of fish.

where men live a never troubled life, where souls nor [illegible]

Nor irkesome Winter spends his fruitlesse powers.

Zephyre still resumes hath circled mee

a constant breath yt all the fields perfumes.

marble eyes. Glanced on beauties blaze.

To shake the Sanctuaryes of power. i. in time.

These too mighty dayes / to over-see

change / i. bodyes journeyes / abroad

Laughs / extasye. raptures / i. strained in prose.

over ground.

Men cannot prize the pearles they doe not know.

Mole-eyed issue, the shooting orbes

to misticke / [illegible] yon / i. yonder

[illegible] but a figure to show

Those butterflyes [illegible]

Their Painted Wings: [illegible] drinkers [illegible]

The Paper Workes / i. bookes

William Drummond

VERSE

(1) POEMS PUBLISHED IN DRUMMOND'S LIFETIME

*DrW 1 *An Almanacke* ('This strange Ecclipse one sayes').

Autograph draft, with revisions, headed 'on the ecclips of the sune in may anno 1612'; c. 1612.

First pub. in *Poems* ([Edinburgh?, 1614?]); Kastner, II, 151. This MS not mentioned in Kastner.

National Library of Scotland, MS 2062 (Hawthornden Vol. X), f. 174.

*DrW 2 *The Canon* ('When first the Canon from her gaping Throte').

Autograph draft.

First pub. in *Poems* ([Edinburgh?, 1614?]); Kastner, I, 107. This MS not mentioned in Kastner.

National Library of Scotland, MS 2062 (Hawthornden Vol. X), f. 165v.

*DrW 3 *Epitaph* ('Stay Passenger, see where enclosed lyes').

Autograph copy, deleted.

First pub. in *Teares on the Death of Meliades* (Edinburgh, 1613); Kastner, I, 83. This MS not mentioned in Kastner.

National Library of Scotland, MS 2062 (Hawthornden Vol. X), f. 167.

*DrW 4 *Epitaph* ('The Bawd of Iustice, he who Lawes controll'd').

Autograph draft, with revisions.

First pub. in *Poems* ([Edinburgh?, 1614?]); Kastner, II, 152. This MS not mentioned in Kastner.

National Library of Scotland, MS 2062 (Hawthornden Vol. X), f. 186.

*DrW 5 *Floras Flowre* ('Venus doth loue the Rose').

Autograph copy.

First pub. in *Poems* ([Edinburgh?, 1614?]); Kastner, I, 124. This MS not mentioned in Kastner.

National Library of Scotland, MS 2062 (Hawthornden Vol. X), f. 174.

*DrW 6 *For Dorvs* ('Why Nais stand yee nice').

Autograph copy.

First pub. in *Poems* ([Edinburgh?, 1614?]); Kastner, II, 155. Printed from this MS (?) in Kastner, II, 369.

National Library of Scotland, MS 2062 (Hawthornden Vol. X), f. 170.

*DrW 7 *'Great God, whom wee with humble Thoughts adore'*.

Autograph draft of an early version of lines 53-68, here beginning 'O, love and pitie, Vnknown to thes times'.

First pub. among *Vrania, or Spirituall Poems* in *Poems* ([Edinburgh?, 1614?]); Kastner, I, 92-4. This MS recorded in Fogle, p. 201.

National Library of Scotland, MS 2062 (Hawthornden Vol. X), f. 66.

*DrW 8 *Narcissvs* ('Flouds cannot quench my Flames, ah! in this Well').

Autograph dract, on a leaf bound in Drummond's miscellany 'Democritie, a labyrinth of delight'.

First pub. in *Poems* ([Edinburgh?, 1614?]); Kastner, I, 109. This MS not mentioned in Kastner.

National Library of Scotland, MSS 2060 (Hawthornden Vol. VIII), f. 130v.

*DrW 9 -----

Autograph draft, with revisions.

This MS not mentioned in Kastner.

National Library of Scotland, MS 2062 (Hawthornden Vol. X), f. 169v.

*DrW 10 *Of Dametas* ('Dametas dream'd he saw his Wife at Sport').

Autograph copy.

First pub. in *Poems* ([Edinburgh?, 1614?]); Kastner, I, 106. This MS noc mentioned in Kastner.

National Library of Scotland, MS 2062 (Hawthornden Vol. X), f. 158.

*DrW 11 -----

Autograph draft.

This MS not mentioned in Kastner.

National Library of Scotland, MS 2062 (Hawthornden Vol. X), f. 166.

*DrW 12 *'Of Iet'*.

Autograph copy, deleted.

First pub. in *Teares on the Death of Meliades* (Edinburgh, 1613); Kastner, I, 84. This MS not mentioned in Kastner.

National Library of Scotland, MS 2062 (Hawthornden Vol. X), f. 172.

*DrW 13 *Of Phillis* ('In Peticote of Greene').

Autograph copy.

First pub. in *Poems* ([Edinburgh?, 1614?]); Kastner, I, 106. This MS not mentioned in Kastner.

National Library of Scotland, MS 2062 (Hawthornden Vol. X), f. 170.

*DrW 14 *Phoebe* ('If for to be alone and all the Night to wander').

Autograph draft.

First pub. in *Poems* ([Edinburgh?, 1614?]); Kastner, II, 157. This MS not mentioned in Kastner.

National Library of Scotland, MS 2062 (Hawthornden Vol. X), f. 165.

DrW 15 *Polemo-Middinia inter Vitarvam et Nebernam* ('Nymphae quae colitis highissima monta Fifaea').

Copy, ascribed to Gulielmo Drummondo and transcribed from the 1691 Oxford edition, in a composite volume of miscellaneous tracts; 13 leaves; c. 1700.

First pub. [Edinburgh?, 1645?]; Kastner, II, 321-6, in 'Poems of Doubtful Authenticity'; of doubtful authorship: see MacDonald, *SSL*, 7 (1969), 120. This MS not recorded in Kastner.

Durham Cathedral, Hunter MS 76, item 2.

DrW 16 -----

Copy in a verse miscellany; 17th century.

This MS not recorded in Kastner.

Edinburgh University Library, MS La. II. 69, ff. 43-6.

DrW 17 -----

Copy in a verse miscellany of Scottish provenance; [1657-8].

This MS not recorded in Kastner.

National Library of Scotland, Adv. MS 19. 3. 4, ff. 70v-3v.

DrW 18 -----

Copy, ascribed to Gulielmo Drummond de Hauthornden, made by Robert Veitch, a skipper in Leith; 12 pages; among the muniments of the Earl of Haddington; 1731.

This MS not recorded in Kastner.

Scottish Record Office, RH13/46.

*DrW 19 *The Pourtrait of Mars and Venvs* ('Faire Paphos wanton Queene').

Autograph draft, with revisions.

First pub. in *Poems* ([Edinburgh?, 1614?]); Kastner, I, 101. This MS not mentioned in Kastner.

National Library of Scotland, MS 2062 (Hawthornden Vol. X), f. 171.

DrW 20 *The Praise of a Solitarie Life* ('Thrice happie hee, who by some shadie Groue').

Copy, headed 'Another Poem in praise of Solitude or Retirement, by S. Will. Drumond of Hauthornden; a little altered', in a miscellany compiled by Robert Fleming; c. 1670-85.

First pub. in *Flowres of Sion* ([Edinburgh?], 1623); Kastner, II, 30. This MS not recorded in Kastner.

Bodleian, MS Rawl. poet. 213, f. 58.

*DrW 21 *The Shadow of the Ivdgement* ('Aboue those boundlesse Bounds where Starrs do moue').

Autograph draft of lines 67-406, 427-58, beginning 'To those black Sprightes which thou dost keepe in chaines'.

First pub. in *Flowres of Sion* ([Edinburgh?], 1623); Kastner, II, 50-63. This MS not mentioned in Kastner.

National Library of Scotland, MS 2062 (Hawthornden Vol. X), ff. 120-36.

*DrW 22 *Son.* ('If crost with all Mis-haps bee my poore Life').

Autograph draft, with revisions.

First pub. in *Poems* ([Edinburgh?, 1614?]); Kastner, I, 30. This MS not mentioned in Kastner.

National Library of Scotland, MS 2062 (Hawthornden Vol. X), f. 156.

DrW 23 *Son.* ('My Lute, bee as thou wast when thou didst grow').

Copy in a 19th-century hand, written in a

miscellany originally compiled c. 1644 by one William Han.

First pub. in *Poems* ([Edinburgh?, 1614?]); Kastner, I, 60. This MS not recorded in Kastner.

Yale, Osborn Collection, b 150, p. 218.

*DrW 24 *Son.* ('My Teares may well Numidian Lions tame').

Autograph draft.

First pub. in *Poems* ([Edinburgh?, 1614?]); Kastner, I, 24. Facsimile and transcript of this MS in Croft, *Autograph Poetry*, I, 29; not mentioned in Kastner.

National Library of Scotland, MS 2062 (Hawthornden Vol. X), f. 7.

*DrW 25 -----

Autograph draft, with revisions.

This MS not mentioned in Kastner.

National Library of Scotland, MS 2062 (Hawthornden Vol. X), f. 162v.

DrW 26 *Son.* ('Sleepe, Silence Child, sweet Father of soft Rest').

Copy in a 19th-century hand, written in a miscellany originally compiled c. 1644 by one William Han.

First pub. in *Poems* ([Edinburgh?, 1614?]); Kastner, I, 7. This MS not recorded in Kastner.

Yale, Osborn Collection, b 150, p. 218.

*DrW 27 *Son.* ('You restlesse Seas, appease your roaring Waues').

Autograph copy, with corrections.

First pub. in *Poems* ([Edinburgh?, 1614?]); Kastner, I, 28. This MS collated in Kastner, I, 190.

National Library of Scotland, MS 2062 (Hawthornden Vol. X), f. 4.

*DrW 28 *The Statue of Medvsa* ('Of Medvsa strange').

Autograph draft, with revisions, headed 'Medusaes Image'.

First pub. in *Poems* ([Edinburgh?, 1614?]); Kastner, I, 99. This MS not mentioned in Kastner.

National Library of Scotland, MS 2062 (Hawthornden Vol. X), f. 171v.

*DrW 29 *To S.W.A.* ('Though I haue twice beene at the Doores of Death').

Autograph draft, with revisions, headed 'Damon to Alexis'.

First pub. in *A Cypresse Grove* ([Edinburgh?], 1612); Kastner, II, 106. Printed from this MS in Kastner, II, 355-6; facsimile in Laing (1831), facing p. 57.

National Library of Scotland, MS 2062 (Hawthornden Vol. X), f. 10.

*DrW 30 -----

Autograph, bound with a printed exemplum of Drummond's *Poems* (1656); c. 1630.

This MS not recorded in Kastner.

Folger, D 2200.

DrW 31 -----

Copy in a small MS collection of poems by Sir William Alexander; early 17th century.

This MS not recorded in Kastner.

Chetham's Library, Manchester, Halliwell-Phillipps No. 26, p. 4.

*DrW 32 *To S^r^. W.A.* ('Like Sophocles (the hearers in a trance)').

Autograph copy of a version beginning 'Whidder braue sprit like Sophocles thou pranse'.

First pub. in Sir William Alexander, *Doomes-Day* (Edinburgh, 1614); Kastner, II, 161. Printed from this MS in Kastner, II, 371.

National Library of Scotland, MS 2061 (Hawthornden Vol. IX), f. 59.

DrW 33 *The Trojane Horse* ('A Horse I am, whom Bit').

Autograph draft, with revisions.

First pub. in *Poems* ([Edinburgh?, 1614?]); Kastner, I, 99. This MS not mentioned in Kastner.

National Library of Scotland, MS 2062 (Hawthornden Vol. X), f. 171v.

--- *Vrania.*

See DrW 7, 34.

*DrW 34 *'What haplesse Hap had I now to bee borne'.*

Autograph copy.

'What haplesse Hap had I now to bee borne'

First pub. among *Vrania, or Spirituall Poems* in *Poems* ([Edinburgh?, 1614?]); Kastner, I, 90. This MS not mentioned in Kastner.

National Library of Scotland, MS 2062 (Hawthornden Vol. X), f. 36.

*DrW 35 *A Wish* ('To forge to mightie Ioue').

Autograph draft.

First pub. in *Poems* ([Edinburgh?, 1614?]); Kastner, I, 120. This MS not mentioned in Kastner.

National Library of Scotland, MS 2062 (Hawthornden Vol. X), f. 169v.

(2) POSTHUMOUS POEMS

*DrW 36 *'A foolish change made vretchet Chremes dead'.*

Autograph draft.

First pub. in Kastner (1913), II, 286.

National Library of Scotland, MS 2062 (Hawthornden Vol. X), f. 158v.

*DrW 37 -----

Autograph copy.

National Library of Scotland, MS 2062 (Hawthornden Vol. X), f. 165v.

*DrW 38 *'A lady in her prime to whom was giuen'.*

Autograph copy, in Drummond's miscellany 'Democritie, a labyrinth of delight'; c. 1620s.

First pub. in Kastner (1913), II, 284; of doubtful authorship: see MacDonald, *SSL*, 7 (1969), 116.

National Library of Scotland, MS 2060 (Hawthornden Vol. VIII), f. 126.

*DrW 39 *'Against the king, sir, now why would yee fight?'.*

Autograph draft of lines 13-26, beginning 'Giue me a thousand couenants, I'll subscriue'.

First pub. in *Works* (1711); Kastner, II, 206.

National Library of Scotland, MS 2062 (Hawthornden Vol. X), f. 177B.

*DrW 40 *'Ah! eyes, deare eyes, how could the Heuens consent'.*

Autograph draft, headed 'A Lady Weeping'.

First pub. in Kastner (1913), II, 271.

National Library of Scotland, MS 2062 (Hawthornden Vol. X), f. 3.

*DrW 41 -----

Autograph draft.

National Library of Scotland, MS 2062 (Hawthornden Vol. X), f. 67.

*DrW 42 -----

Autograph third draft.

National Library of Scotland, MS 2062 (Hawthornden Vol. X), f. 67.

*DrW 43 *'Alexis, Flora, Damon, Cloris, Myris'.*

Autograph draft of one of two poems headed 'Pastorells from Maria Bonardo frattegiano'.

First pub. in Fogle (1952), p. 199.

National Library of Scotland, MS 2062 (Hawthornden Vol. X), f. 55.

*DrW 44 *All Changeth* ('The angrye winds not ay').

Autograph draft.

First pub. in *Poems* (1656); Kastner, II, 185.

National Library of Scotland, MS 2062 (Hawthornden Vol. X), f. 31.

*DrW 45 *'All good hath left this age, all trackes of shame'.*

Autograph copy.

First pub. in *Poems* (1656); Kastner, II, 174.

National Library of Scotland, MS 2062 (Hawthornden Vol. X), f. 36.

*DrW 46 *Amarillis to her dog Perlin* ('Faire Perlin doe not barke').

Autograph copy.

First pub. in Kastner (1913), II, 281.

National Library of Scotland, MS 2062 (Hawthornden Vol. X), f. 53.

*DrW 47 *Amphion of marble* ('This Amphion, Phidias frame').

Autograph copy.

Amphion of marble

First pub. in Laing (1831); Kastner, II, 236.

National Library of Scotland, MS 2062 (Hawthornden Vol. X), f. 170.

*DrW 48 *'Are these the Shores, is this the happye sand'.*

Autograph draft of a poem in a series headed 'De Materia Prima'.

First pub. in Fogle (1952), p. 189.

National Library of Scotland, MS 2062 (Hawthornden Vol. X), f. 44.

*DrW 49 *A Ball of Snow* ('With whitest hand, white snow').

Autograph draft.

First pub. in Fogle (1952), p. 193.

National Library of Scotland, MS 2062 (Hawthornden Vol. X), f. 54.

*DrW 50 *'Be reasons good Jhon him a christian proueth'.*

Autograph draft.

First pub. in Kastner (1913), II, 287.

National Library of Scotland, MS 2062 (Hawthornden Vol. X), f. 159.

*DrW 51 *The Beare of loue* ('In woodes and desart Boundes').

Autograph draft, with revisions.

First pub. in *Poems* (1656); Kastner, II, 178.

National Library of Scotland, MS 2062 (Hawthornden Vol. X), f. 8.

*DrW 52 -----

Autograph copy.

National Library of Scotland, MS 2062 (Hawthornden Vol. X), f. 40.

*DrW 53 -----

Autograph copy, deleted.

National Library of Scotland, MS 2062 (Hawthornden Vol. X), f. 144v.

*DrW 54 *Beauties Frailtye* ('Looke how the maying Rose').

Autograph draft, with revisions, headed 'Jodel in Dido'.

First pub. in *Poems* (1656); Kastner, II, 175.

National Library of Scotland, MS 2062 (Hawthornden Vol. X), f. 3.

*DrW 55 -----

Autograph copy, untitled.

National Library of Scotland, MS 2062 (Hawthornden Vol. X), f. 38.

*DrW 56 -----

Autograph draft.

National Library of Scotland, MS 2062 (Hawthornden Vol. X), f. 152.

*DrW 57 -----

Autograph draft, with revisions.

National Library of Scotland, MS 2062 (Hawthornden Vol. X), f. 152.

*DrW 58 *'Behold (O Scots!) the reueryes of your King'.*

Autograph draft, deleted, with a second autograph version beginning 'Britannes, admire the extravagancyes of our King'.

First pub. in Laing (1831); Kastner, II, 243.

National Library of Scotland, MS 2062 (Hawthornden Vol. X), f. 185.

*DrW 59 *Bembo in his Rime. 2 Son.*

Copy by Drummond of a sonnet by Cardinal Bembo, with three different autograph translations by Drummond; the first beginning 'As the yong faune, vhen vinters gone avay' and headed 'In the same sort of Rime'; the second beginning 'As the yong stag, vhen vinter hids his face' and headed 'In rime more frie'; the third beginning 'As the yong hart, when sunne with goldin beames' and headed 'Paraphrasticalie translated'.

First pub. in Laing (1833); Kastner, II, 233-4.

National Library of Scotland, MS 2062 (Hawthornden Vol. X), ff. 161-2.

*DrW 60 *'Bishopes are like the turnores, most men say'.*

Autograph draft, with revisions.

First pub. in Laing (1831); Kastner, II, 243.

National Library of Scotland, MS 2062 (Hawthornden Vol. X), f. 178.

*DrW 61 -----

Autograph draft.

National Library of Scotland, MS 2062 (Hawthornden Vol. X), f. 214.

*DrW 62 *The Boares head* ('Amidst a pleasant greene').

Autograph draft, with revisions.

First pub. in *Poems* (1656); Kastner, II, 177.

National Library of Scotland, MS 2062 (Hawthornden Vol. X), f. 39.

*DrW 63 -----

Autograph copy, untitled.

National Library of Scotland, MS 2062 (Hawthornden Vol. X), f. 49v.

*DrW 64 -----

Autograph copy.

National Library of Scotland, MS 2062 (Hawthornden Vol. X), f. 50.

*DrW 65 *'Bold Scotes, at Bannochburne yee killd your king'*.

Autograph draft.

First pub. in *Works* (1711); Kastner, II, 207.

National Library of Scotland, MS 2062 (Hawthornden Vol. X), f. 179.

*DrW 66 -----

Autograph copy, with revisions.

National Library of Scotland, MS 2062 (Hawthornden Vol. X), f. 180.

*DrW 67 -----

Autograph copy.

National Library of Scotland, MS 2062 (Hawthornden Vol. X), f. 201.

DrW 68 *Carmina lugubria in mortem illustrissimi regis Jacobi* ('Occidit ille decus summorum nobile regum').

Copy of a Latin elegy of three 12-line stanzas ascribed to 'Drummond Scotum', in a bound collection of papers of Sir Julius Caesar (1558-1636); c. 1625.

Believed to be unpublished.

British Library, Add. MS 34324, f. 322.

*DrW 69 *A Character of the Anti-Couenanter, or Malignant* ('Would yee know these royall knaues').

Autograph draft of lines 1-18, 73-106.

First pub. in *Works* (1711); Kastner, II, 218-21.

National Library of Scotland, MS 2062 (Hawthornden Vol. X), ff. 189B, 190.

*DrW 70 -----

Autograph draft of part of the poem, with revisions.

National Library of Scotland, MS 2062 (Hawthornden Vol. X), f. 191.

*DrW 71 *Charles the IX of France* ('Vhy, vomets Charles so much blood from his brest?').

Autograph copy.

First pub. in Kastner (1913), II, 287.

National Library of Scotland, MS 2062 (Hawthornden Vol. X), f. 173.

*DrW 72 *Chloris enamoured* ('Amintas, now at last').

Autograph copy.

First pub. in Laing (1831); Kastner, II, 237.

National Library of Scotland, MS 2062 (Hawthornden Vol. X), f. 35.

*DrW 73 *'Chremes did hing him selff vpon a tree'*.

Autograph draft.

First pub. in Kastner (1913), II, 287.

National Library of Scotland, MS 2062 (Hawthornden Vol. X), f. 166.

*DrW 74 *'Circūit aboue the circle of our thoughts'*.

Autograph poetical jottings, the first line reading 'aboue the circūit / circle of our thoughts', on a single leaf bound in a volume of transcripts made by Drummond of letters from Queen Elizabeth to James VI.

Hitherto unpublished. See FACSIMILE XIII.

Edinburgh University Library, MS La. III. 365, f. [22v].

*DrW 75 *The country Maid* ('A country Maid amazon-like did ryde').

Autograph draft, with revisions.

First pub. in *Works* (1711); Kastner, II, 210.

National Library of Scotland, MS 2062 (Hawthornden Vol. X), f. 198.

The country Maid

*DrW 76 -----

Autograph draft of lines 1-6.

National Library of Scotland, MS 2062 (Hawthornden Vol. X), f. 199.

*DrW 77 *The creed* ('How is the Creed thus stollen from vs away?').

Autograph draft; c. 1619.

First pub. in Laing (1831); Kastner, II, 244.

National Library of Scotland, MS 2061 (Hawthornden Vol. IX), f. 140.

*DrW 78 -----

Autograph copy; c. 1619.

National Library of Scotland, MS 2062 (Hawthornden Vol. X), f. 184.

*DrW 79 -----

Autograph copy; c. 1619.

National Library of Scotland, MS 2062 (Hawthornden Vol. X), f. 189.

*DrW 80 *D.A. Johnstones Eden-Bourgh* ('Install'd on Hills, her Head neare starrye bowres').

Autograph draft, with revisions.

First pub. in Laing (1831); Kastner, II, 227.

National Library of Scotland, MS 2062 (Hawthornden Vol. X), f. 76v.

*DrW 81 -----

Autograph copy.

National Library of Scotland, MS 2062 (Hawthornden Vol. X), f. 77.

*DrW 82 -----

Autograph copy, with two copies of Johnston's original Latin verses, headed 'The same inglished'.

National Library of Scotland, MS 2062 (Hawthornden Vol. X), ff. 77-8.

*DrW 83 *D.O.M.S.* ('Justice, Truth, Peace, and Hospitalitie').

Autograph draft, untitled.

First pub. in Laing (1831); Kastner, II, 250.

National Library of Scotland, MS 2062 (Hawthornden Vol. X), f. 86.

*DrW 84 *D.O.M.S.* ('So falles by Northern blast a Virgine rose').

Autograph draft.

First pub. in Laing (1831); Kastner, II, 254.

National Library of Scotland, MS 2062 (Hawthornden Vol. X), f. 87.

*DrW 85 *Daphnè* ('Now Daphnès armes did grow').

Autograph draft, with revisions.

First pub. in *Poems* (1656); Kastner, II, 178.

National Library of Scotland, MS 2062 (Hawthornden Vol. X), f. 8.

*DrW 86 -----

Autograph copy.

National Library of Scotland, MS 2062 (Hawthornden Vol. X), f. 40.

*DrW 87 -----

Autograph copy, deleted.

National Library of Scotland, MS 2062 (Hawthornden Vol. X), f. 144v.

--- *De Porcheres, on the eies of Madame la Marquise de Monceaux, vret this sonnet* ('Wer these thine eies, or lightnings from aboue').

[Kastner, II, 270].

See INTRODUCTION.

*DrW 88 *'Deare Steed that Choisen art now to sustaine'*.

Autograph draft of a poem in a series headed 'De Materia Prima'.

First pub. in Fogle (1952), p. 190.

National Library of Scotland, MS 2062 (Hawthornden Vol. X), f. 46.

*DrW 89 *Discontented Phillis* ('Blacke are my thoughts as is my Husbands haire').

Autograph draft, with revisions.

First pub. in Kastner (1913), II, 288.

National Library of Scotland, MS 2062 (Hawthornden Vol. X), f. 26.

*DrW 90 -----

Autograph copy.

National Library of Scotland, MS 2062 (Hawthornden Vol. X), f. 197.

Discontented Phillis

*DrW 91 -----

Autograph draft, with revisions.

National Library of Scotland, MS 2062 (Hawthornden Vol. X), f. 199.

*DrW 92 *'Doth then the world goe thus, doth all thus moue?'*.

Autograph copy.

First pub. in *Poems* (1656); Kastner, II, 174.

National Library of Scotland, MS 2062 (Hawthornden Vol. X), f. 37.

DrW 93 *Drummonds Lines one the Bischopes: 14 Appryll 1638* ('Doe all pens slumber still, darr not one tray').

Copy of verses here ascribed to Drummond, in a MS volume of pasquinades compiled by Sir James Balfour, Lyon King of Arms (1600-57); [1637-47].

First pub. in the 'Third Book' of James Maidment's *Book of Scotish Pasquils* (Edinburgh, 1827); Kastner, II, 293, in 'Poems of Doubtful Authenticity'; probably by Drummond: see MacDonald, *SSL*, 7 (1969), 117.

National Library of Scotland, Adv. MS 19. 3. 8, ff. 14-15v.

*DrW 94 *'Dum tua melliflui specto pigmenta Libelli'*.

Autograph copy of an eight-line Latin poem addressed to Michael Drayton.

Unpublished.

National Library of Scotland, MS 2062 (Hawthornden Vol. X), f. 84.

*DrW 95 -----

Autograph copy on a single leaf.

Edinburgh University Library, MS La. II. 320.

*DrW 96 *Eclogue* ('Damon and Moeris by a christal spring').

Autograph draft.

First pub. in Kastner (1913), II, 257-62.

National Library of Scotland, MS 2062 (Hawthornden Vol. X), ff. 108-14v.

*DrW 97 *Eclogue* ('Vhile dayes bright coachman makes our schadows schort').

Autograph draft.

First pub. in Kastner (1913), II, 263-7.

National Library of Scotland, MS 2062 (Hawthornden Vol. X), ff. 115-19.

*DrW 98 *Encomiastike verses before a book entitled Follies* ('At ease I red your Worke, and am right sorrye').

Autograph draft, with revisions.

First pub. in Laing (1831); Kastner, II, 248.

National Library of Scotland, MS 2062 (Hawthornden Vol. X), ff. 195-6.

*DrW 99 *Epitaph* ('Fame, Register of Tyme').

Autograph draft.

First pub. in *Poems* (1656); Kastner, II, 198.

National Library of Scotland, MS 2062 (Hawthornden Vol. X), f. 2.

*DrW 100 *Epitaph* ('Heer lyes a cooke who went to buye ylles').

Autograph copy in Drummond's miscellany 'Democritie, a labyrinth of delight'; c. 1620s.

First pub. in Kastner (1913), II, 284; of doubtful authorship: see MacDonald, *SSL*, 7 (1969), 116.

National Library of Scotland, MS 2060 (Hawthornden Vol. VIII), f. 31v.

*DrW 101 *Epitaph* ('Heere lyes a Doctor who with droges and pelfe').

Autograph copy in Drummond's miscellany 'Democritie, a labyrinth of delight'; c. 1620s.

First pub. in Kastner (1913), II, 284; of doubtful authorship: see MacDonald, *SSL*, 7 (1969), 116.

National Library of Scotland, MS 2060 (Hawthornden Vol. VIII), f. 31v.

*DrW 102 -----

Second autograph copy in Drummond's miscellany 'Democritie, a labyrinth of delight'; c. 1620s.

National Library of Scotland, MS 2060 (Hawthornden Vol. VIII), f. 117v.

*DrW 103 *Epitaph* ('Heere Rixus lies, a Nouice in the lawes').

Autograph copy.

Epitaph ('Heere Rixus lies')

First pub. in *Works* (1711); Kastner, II, 211.

National Library of Scotland, MS 2062 (Hawthornden Vol. X), f. 197.

*DrW 104 *Epitaph* ('Heer S—— lyes, most bitter gall').

Autograph draft, with revisions.

First pub. in *Poems* (1656); Kastner, II, 184.

National Library of Scotland, MS 2062 (Hawthornden Vol. X), f. 186.

*DrW 105 *Epitaph* ('If Monumentes were lasting wee would raise').

Autograph draft.

First pub. in Laing (1831); Kastner, II, 251.

National Library of Scotland, MS 2062 (Hawthornden Vol. X), f. 104.

*DrW 106 *Epitaph* ('Sancher whom this earth scarce could containe').

Autograph copy; c. 1619.

First pub. in Laing (1831); Kastner, II, 245.

National Library of Scotland, MS 2062 (Hawthornden Vol. X), f. 220.

*DrW 107 *Epitaph* ('Truth hatred breedes').

Autograph copy.

First pub. in Kastner (1913), II, 288.

National Library of Scotland, MS 2062 (Hawthornden Vol. X), f. 174.

*DrW 108 -----

Autograph draft, with revisions.

National Library of Scotland, MS 2062 (Hawthornden Vol. X), f. 186.

*DrW 109 *Epitaph of a Judge* ('Peace, Passenger, heere sleepeth vnder ground').

Autograph draft, with revisions.

First pub. in Laing (1831); Kastner, II, 243.

National Library of Scotland, MS 2062 (Hawthornden Vol. X), f. 172.

*DrW 110 *Epitaphe on a Cooke* ('Heere lyes a sowre and angry cooke').

Autograph copy in Drummond's miscellany 'Democritie, a labyrinth of delight'; c. 1620s.

First pub. in Kastner (1913), II, 285; of doubtful authorship: see MacDonald, *SSL*, 7 (1969), 117.

National Library of Scotland, MS 2060 (Hawthornden Vol. VIII), f. 77v.

*DrW 111 -----

Autograph copy.

National Library of Scotland, MS 2062 (Hawthornden Vol. X), f. 103B.

*DrW 112 *Essay out of the Italien* ('Melpomene in Athenes neuer song').

Autograph draft.

First pub. in Kastner (1913), II, 273.

National Library of Scotland, MS 2062 (Hawthornden Vol. X), f. 164v.

*DrW 113 *'Faire art thou if thy lockes of curling gold'.*

Autograph draft of a poem in a series headed 'De Materia Prima'.

First pub. in Fogle (1952), p. 187.

National Library of Scotland, MS 2062 (Hawthornden Vol. X), f. 41.

--- *'Faire cruel Siluia since thow scornes my teares'.*

[Kastner, II, 269].

See INTRODUCTION.

*DrW 114 *'First in the orient raign'd th'assyrian kings'.*

Autograph copy in Drummond's miscellany 'Democritie, a labyrinth of delight'; c. 1620s.

First pub. in Laing (1831); Kastner, II, 229; of doubtful authorship: see MacDonald, *SSL*, 7 (1969), 114-15.

National Library of Scotland, MS 2060 (Hawthornden Vol. VIII), f. 292v.

DrW 115 -----

Copy inscribed by Sir James Murray of Tibbermure or by someone in his household at the end of a 14th century MS of John Lydgate's *Destruction of Troy*; c. 1612.

Cambridge University Library, MS Kk. 5. 30, (II), f. 78v.

*DrW 116 *'Flyting no reason hath, for at this tyme'.*

Autograph draft.

'Flyting no reason hath, for at this tyme'

First pub. in Laing (1831); Kastner, II, 245.

National Library of Scotland, MS 2062 (Hawthornden Vol. X), f. 154.

*DrW 117 *For a Ladyes Summonds of Nonentree* ('Kite.| Summond not mee to enter, there's no doubt').

Autograph draft.

First pub. in MacDonald (1976), pp. 141-3.

National Library of Scotland, MS 2062 (Hawthornden Vol. X), ff. 193-5.

--- *For the Kinge* ('From such a face quhois excellence').

See INTRODUCTION.

*DrW 118 *Fragment* ('A faire, a sueet, a pleasant heunlie creature').

Autograph copy, with revisions.

First pub. in Kastner (1913), II, 276.

National Library of Scotland, MS 2062 (Hawthornden Vol. X), f. 64.

*DrW 119 *Fragment* ('It Autumne vas, and cheereful chantecleare').

Autograph draft.

First pub. in Laing (1831); Kastner, II, 241.

National Library of Scotland, MS 2062 (Hawthornden Vol. X), f. 63.

*DrW 120 *Fragment* ('Like vnto her nothing can be namd').

Autograph copy.

First pub. in Kastner (1913), II, 275.

National Library of Scotland, MS 2062 (Hawthornden Vol. X), ff. 64-5.

*DrW 121 *Fragment* ('Now Phoebus vhept his horse vith al his might').

Autograph copy.

First pub. in Laing (1831); Kastner, II, 241.

National Library of Scotland, MS 2062 (Hawthornden Vol. X), f. 63.

*DrW 122 *Fragment of a greater work* ('As vhen a sheaphard boy from fearful hight').

Autograph draft.

First pub. in Fogle (1952), p. 202.

National Library of Scotland, MS 2062 (Hawthornden Vol. X), f. 66v.

*DrW 123 *Galateas Sonnets* ('Joas in vaine thou brings thy rimes and songs').

Autograph draft of five sonnets, with revisions.

First pub. in *Poems* (1656); Kastner, II, 179-83.

National Library of Scotland, MS 2062 (Hawthornden Vol. X), ff. 22-4.

*DrW 124 -----

Autograph draft of the second, third, fourth and fifth sonnets.

National Library of Scotland, MS 2062 (Hawthornden Vol. X), ff. 162, 168r-v.

*DrW 125 *'Gods iudgments seldome vse to cease, vnlease'.*

Autograph draft, on a leaf bound in Drummond's miscellany 'Democritie, a labyrinth of delight'.

First pub. in *Works* (1711); Kastner, II, 211.

National Library of Scotland, MS 2060 (Hawthornden Vol. VIII), f. 199v.

*DrW 126 -----

Autograph copy.

National Library of Scotland, MS 2062 (Hawthornden Vol. X), f. 184.

*DrW 127 -----

Autograph copy.

National Library of Scotland, MS 2062 (Hawthornden Vol. X), f. 189.

*DrW 128 *'Great lyes they preach who tell the church cannot err'.*

Autograph draft.

First pub. in *Works* (1711); Kastner, II, 208.

National Library of Scotland, MS 2062 (Hawthornden Vol. X), f. 182.

*DrW 129 *'Great Queene whom to the liberall Heauens propine'.*

Autograph copy in Drummond's miscellany

'Great Queene whom to the liberall Heauens propine'

'Democritie, a labyrinth of delight'; c. 1620s.

First pub. in Kastner (1913), II, 269; of doubtful authorship: see MacDonald, *SSL*, 7 (1969), 114-15.

National Library of Scotland, MS 2060 (Hawthornden Vol. VIII), f. 293.

*DrW 130 *'Happie to be, trulye is in some schoole--'*.

Autograph copy; c. 1639.

First pub. in Laing (1831); Kastner, II, 242.

National Library of Scotland, MS 2062 (Hawthornden Vol. X), f. 177A.

*DrW 131 *'Hear lyeth Jean that some tyme vas a maid'*.

Autograph draft.

First pub. in Kastner (1913), II, 286.

National Library of Scotland, MS 2062 (Hawthornden Vol. X), f. 158.

*DrW 132 -----

Autograph copy.

National Library of Scotland, MS 2062 (Hawthornden Vol. X), f. 165v.

*DrW 133 *'Heere beneath | Wee allwayes sayle towards the port of death'*.

Autograph draft of a poem with accompanying philosophical observations.

First pub. in Fogle (1952), pp. 208-9.

National Library of Scotland, MS 2062 (Hawthornden Vol. X), ff. 105A-B.

*DrW 134 *'Heere couered lies vith earth, vithout a tombe'*.

Autograph copy.

First pub. in Laing (1831); Kastner, II, 244.

National Library of Scotland, MS 2062 (Hawthornden Vol. X), f. 171v.

*DrW 135 *'Heere lye the Bones of a gentle horse'*.

Autograph draft of the complete poem, after a false start (lines 1-2 on f. 223).

First pub. in Kastner (1913), II, 289.

National Library of Scotland, MS 2062 (Hawthornden Vol. X), ff. 223-4.

*DrW 136 *His Flames are Quenched* ('Phillis the knots are broke').

Autograph draft.

First pub. in Fogle (1952), p. 192.

National Library of Scotland, MS 2062 (Hawthornden Vol. X), f. 54.

*DrW 137 *'I feare to me such fortune be assigned'*.

Autograph copy in Drummond's miscellany 'Democritie, a labyrinth of delight'; c. 1620s.

First pub. in Laing (1831); Kastner, II, 230; of doubtful authorship: see MacDonald, *SSL*, 7 (1969), 114-15.

National Library of Scotland, MS 2060 (Hawthornden Vol. VIII), f. 292v.

*DrW 138 *'I write but Inke is teares'*.

Autograph draft.

First pub. in Fogle (1952), p. 193.

National Library of Scotland, MS 2062 (Hawthornden Vol. X) [? unconfirmed].

*DrW 139 *'Idas to schune sunnes beames'*.

Autograph copy.

First pub. in Kastner (1913), II, 283.

National Library of Scotland, MS 2062 (Hawthornden Vol. X), f. 174.

*DrW 140 *'If it be trew that Echo doth remaine'*.

Autograph draft, with revisions.

First pub. in Kastner (1913), II, 283.

National Library of Scotland, MS 2062 (Hawthornden Vol. X), f. 172.

*DrW 141 *'If of the dead save good nought should be said'*.

Autograph draft; c. 1640s.

First pub. in MacDonald (1976), p. 143.

National Library of Scotland, MS 2062 (Hawthornden Vol. X), f. 91.

*DrW 142 *'Ilas of the Nymfes'*.

Autograph draft of a poem in a series headed 'Madrigals di Mauritio Moro'; incomplete.

'Ilas of the Nymfes'

First pub. in Fogle, p. 192.

National Library of Scotland, MS 2062 (Hawthornden Vol. X), f. 53.

*DrW 143 *An image to the pilgrime* ('To worship mee, why come ye, Fooles, abroad?').

Autograph draft.

First pub. in Laing (1831); Kastner, II, 246.

National Library of Scotland, MS 2062 (Hawthornden Vol. X), f. 158v.

*DrW 144 -----

Autograph copy.

National Library of Scotland, MS 2062 (Hawthornden Vol. X), f. 165v.

*DrW 145 *'In ashe her lies the wanton God of loue'.*

Autograph copy.

First pub. in Kastner (1913), II, 280.

National Library of Scotland, MS 2062 (Hawthornden Vol. X), f. 41.

*DrW 146 *'In parlament one voted for the king'.*

Autograph copy.

First pub. in *Works* (1711); Kastner, II, 207.

National Library of Scotland, MS 2062 (Hawthornden Vol. X), f. 181.

*DrW 147 -----

Autograph copy.

National Library of Scotland, MS 2062 (Hawthornden Vol. X), f. 202.

*DrW 148 *In S^r. P. d. R.* ('Great Paragon, of Poets richest Pearle').

Autograph copy in Drummond's miscellany 'Ephemeris'; c. 1606-14.

First pub. in Kastner (1913), II, 268; of doubtful authorship: see MacDonald, *SSL*, 7 (1969), 113-14.

National Library of Scotland, MS 2059 (Hawthornden Vol. VII), f. 23v.

*DrW 149 *'Into the sea al cornards Thomas vist'.*

Autograph draft.

First pub. in Kastner (1913), II, 287.

National Library of Scotland, MS 2062 (Hawthornden Vol. X), f. 166.

*DrW 150 *'Jeane cal not your husband hart vhen ye him kis'.*

Autograph draft.

First pub. in Kastner (1913), II, 286.

National Library of Scotland, MS 2062 (Hawthornden Vol. X), f. 158.

*DrW 151 -----

Autograph copy.

National Library of Scotland, MS 2062 (Hawthornden Vol. X), f. 165v.

*DrW 152 *'Killd by ingratitude heere blest within doth rest'.*

Autograph copy in Drummond's miscellany 'Democritie, a labyrinth of delight'; c. 1620s.

First pub. in Kastner (1913), II, 284; of doubtful authorship: see MacDonald, *SSL*, 7 (1969), 116.

National Library of Scotland, MS 2060 (Hawthornden Vol. VIII), f. 126.

*DrW 153 *A Locke desired* ('I neuer long'd for gold').

Autograph draft.

First pub. in Laing (1831); Kastner, II, 239.

National Library of Scotland, MS 2062 (Hawthornden Vol. X), f. 9.

*DrW 154 -----

Autograph copy, deleted.

National Library of Scotland, MS 2062 (Hawthornden Vol. X), f. 28.

*DrW 155 *'Loue once thy lawes'.*

Autograph copy in Drummond's miscellany 'Democritie, a labyrinth of delight'; c. 1620s.

First pub. in Kastner (1913), II, 279; of doubtful authorship: see MacDonald *SSL*, 7 (1969), 116-17.

National Library of Scotland, MS 2060 (Hawthornden Vol. VIII), f. 63v.

*DrW 156 *'Momus, with venom'd tooth, why wouldst thou teare'.*

Autograph draft.

'Momus, with venom'd tooth, why wouldst thou teare'

First pub. in Laing (1831); Kastner, II, 246.

National Library of Scotland, MS 2062 (Hawthornden Vol. X), f. 213.

*DrW 157 *'Mops gaue his fath to Anne and Helen, yet doth ow'.*

Autograph draft.

First pub. in Kastner (1913), II, 285.

National Library of Scotland, MS 2062 (Hawthornden Vol. X), f. 158.

*DrW 158 *'Most royall sir, heere I doe you beseech'.*

Autograph draft.

First pub. in *Works* (1711); Kastner, II, 209.

National Library of Scotland, MS 2062 (Hawthornden Vol. X), f. 216.

*DrW 159 *Neroes image* ('A cunning hand it was').

Autograph draft, with revisions.

First pub. in Laing (1831); Kastner, II, 235.

National Library of Scotland, MS 2062 (Hawthornden Vol. X), f. 170v.

*DrW 160 *A New Precisian* ('Why should this nice world blame').

Autograph draft.

First pub. in Fogle (1952), p. 205.

National Library of Scotland, MS 2062 (Hawthornden Vol. X), f. 25.

*DrW 161 *Non vltra* ('When Idmon saw the eyne').

Autograph draft.

First pub. in Laing (1831); Kastner, II, 240.

National Library of Scotland, MS 2062 (Hawthornden Vol. X), f. 25.

*DrW 162 *'Nor Amaranthes nor Roses doe bequeath'.*

Three autograph versions; the first untitled; the second headed 'Guazzo hath this Epitaph on a Drunckard' and beginning 'Nor Roses to my tomb, nor Lillies giue'; the third headed 'Out of the Italian' and beginning 'Nor roses to my tombe nor lilies giue'.

First pub. in *Poems* (1656); Kastner, II, 184, 379.

National Library of Scotland, MS 2062 (Hawthornden Vol. X), f. 185.

*DrW 163 *'Now let these Hills sweet aire sigh forth'.*

Autograph draft of a poem in a series headed 'De Materia Prima'.

First pub. in Fogle (1952), p. 187.

National Library of Scotland, MS 2062 (Hawthornden Vol. X), f. 42.

*DrW 164 *'O leave (Ulisses) in their cave the Winds'.*

Autograph draft of a poem headed 'Of Dido' in a series headed 'Madrigals di Mauritio Moro'.

First pub. in Fogle (1952), p. 192.

National Library of Scotland, MS 2062 (Hawthornden Vol. X), f. 52.

*DrW 165 *'O most perfidious face'.*

Autograph draft.

First pub. in Kastner (1913), II, 283.

National Library of Scotland, MS 2062 (Hawthornden Vol. X), f. 241v.

*DrW 166 *'O Tymes, o Heauen that still in motion art'.*

Autograph draft.

First pub. in Laing (1831); Kastner, II, 228. Facsimile of this MS in Kastner, I, frontispiece.

National Library of Scotland, MS 2062 (Hawthornden Vol. X), f. 21.

*DrW 167 *Of a Be* ('Ingenious was that Bee').

Autograph copy.

First pub. in Laing (1831); Kastner, II, 236.

National Library of Scotland, MS 2062 (Hawthornden Vol. X), f. 9.

*DrW 168 -----

Autograph copy, deleted.

National Library of Scotland, MS 2062 (Hawthornden Vol. X), f. 28.

*DrW 169 *Of a Kisse* ('Lips, double port of loue').

Autograph draft.

First pub. in Laing (1831); Kastner, II, 239.

National Library of Scotland, MS 2062 (Hawthornden Vol. X), f. 29.

*DrW 170 *'Of all these Rebelles raisd against the king'*.

Autograph copy.

First pub. in *Works* (1711); Kastner, II, 223.

National Library of Scotland, MS 2062 (Hawthornden Vol. X), f. 177Av.

*DrW 171 *Of Anthea* ('When Hylas saw the eyne').

Autograph draft, with revisions.

First pub. in Kastner (1913), II, 279.

National Library of Scotland, MS 2062 (Hawthornden Vol. X), f. 33.

*DrW 172 *Of Chloris* ('Forth from greene Thetis Bowers').

Autograph draft, with revisions.

First pub. in Laing (1831); Kastner, II, 236.

National Library of Scotland, MS 2062 (Hawthornden Vol. X), f. 10.

*DrW 173 *The oister* ('With open shells in seas, on heauenly due').

Autograph copy, deleted.

First pub. in *Poems* (1656); Kastner, II, 185.

National Library of Scotland, MS 2062 (Hawthornden Vol. X), f. 12.

*DrW 174 *On a Book* ('Litel but blissed Booke').

Autograph draft, heavily deleted.

First pub. in Fogle (1952), p. 205.

National Library of Scotland, MS 2062 (Hawthornden Vol. X), f. 29.

*DrW 175 *On a glasse sent to his best beloued* ('Oft ye me aske vhome my sweet faire can be?').

Autograph draft.

First pub. in Laing (1831); Kastner, II, 247.

National Library of Scotland, MS 2062 (Hawthornden Vol. X), f. 167.

*DrW 176 *On a lamp* ('Faithfull and loued light').

Autograph copy.

First pub. in Kastner (1913), II, 280.

National Library of Scotland, MS 2062 (Hawthornden Vol. X), f. 51.

*DrW 177 *On a noble man who died at a counsel table* ('Vntymlie Death that neither wouldst conferre').

Autograph copy in Drummond's miscellany 'Democritie, a labyrinth of delight'; c. 1620s.

First pub. in Kastner (1913), II, 285; of doubtful authorship: see MacDonald, *SSL*, 7 (1969), 116. For other copies, see INTRODUCTION.

National Library of Scotland, MS 2060 (Hawthornden Vol. VIII), f. 31.

*DrW 178 *On Marye Kings pest* ('Turne, citezenes, to God; repent, repent').

Autograph copy; c. 1645.

First pub. in Laing (1831); Kastner, II, 244.

National Library of Scotland, MS 2062 (Hawthornden Vol. X), f. 184.

*DrW 179 -----

Autograph copy; c. 1645.

National Library of Scotland, MS 2062 (Hawthornden Vol. X), f. 189.

*DrW 180 *On Pime* ('When Pime last night descended into Hell').

Autograph draft.

First pub. in *Works* (1711); Kastner, II, 208.

National Library of Scotland, MS 2062 (Hawthornden Vol. X), f. 91.

*DrW 181 *On Pomponatius* ('Trade softlie, passenger, vpon this stone').

Autograph copy.

First pub. in Laing (1831); Kastner, II, 245.

National Library of Scotland, MS 2062 (Hawthornden Vol. X), f. 197.

*DrW 182 *'On some greene meade if shee her virgine side'*.

Autograph draft.

First pub. in Fogle (1952), p. 189.

National Library of Scotland, MS 2062 (Hawthornden Vol. X), f. 46.

*DrW 183 *On the Death of a Margarite* ('In shelles and gold pearles are not keept alone').

Autograph draft, with revisions, deleted.

On the Death of a Margarite

First pub. in *Poems* (1656); Kastner, II, 184.

National Library of Scotland, MS 2062 (Hawthornden Vol. X), f. 26.

*DrW 184 -----

Autograph copy.

National Library of Scotland, MS 2062 (Hawthornden Vol. X), f. 31.

*DrW 185 *On the image of Lucrece* ('Wise Hand, which wiselie wroght').

Autograph copy.

First pub. in Laing (1831); Kastner, II, 235.

National Library of Scotland, MS 2062 (Hawthornden Vol. X), f. 170v.

*DrW 186 -----

Autograph draft, deleted.

National Library of Scotland, MS 2062 (Hawthornden Vol. X), f. 171.

*DrW 187 *On the isle of Rhe* ('Charles, would yee quaile your foes, haue better lucke').

Autograph draft; c. 1627.

First pub. in Laing (1831); Kastner, II, 245.

National Library of Scotland, MS 2062 (Hawthornden Vol. X), f. 185.

*DrW 188 -----

Autograph copy; c. 1627.

National Library of Scotland, MS 2062 (Hawthornden Vol. X), f. 188.

*DrW 189 -----

Autograph copy; c. 1627.

National Library of Scotland, MS 2062 (Hawthornden Vol. X), f. 220.

*DrW 190 *On the lut of Margarite* ('The harmonie vherto the heauens doe dance').

Autograph draft.

First pub. in Kastner (1913), II, 282.

National Library of Scotland, MS 2062 (Hawthornden Vol. X), f. 165v.

*DrW 191 -----

Second autograph draft.

National Library of Scotland, MS 2062 (Hawthornden Vol. X), f. 165v.

*DrW 192 *On the poems of* ----- ('Thocht poets skil her vant, thinke it no crime').

Autograph draft.

First pub. in Kastner (1913), II, 286.

National Library of Scotland, MS 2062 (Hawthornden Vol. X), f. 165.

*DrW 193 *'Or the vinged boy my thochts to the made thral'*.

Autograph draft.

First pub. in Kastner (1913), II, 272.

National Library of Scotland, MS 2062 (Hawthornden Vol. X), f. 162v.

*DrW 194 *'Our faults thy wrath deserued haue, alas!'*.

Autograph draft, deleted.

First pub. in Kastner (1913), II, 272.

National Library of Scotland, MS 2062 (Hawthornden Vol. X), f.151.

*DrW 195 *Out of the Passerat* ('Vho cuckhold is & tries it not').

Autograph copy.

First pub. in Kastner (1913), II, 287.

National Library of Scotland, MS 2062 (Hawthornden Vol. X), f. 172.

*DrW 196 *Par.* ('Old dotard (Pasquill) thou mistaketh it').

Autograph draft.

First pub. in Laing (1831); Kastner, II, 243.

National Library of Scotland, MS 2062 (Hawthornden Vol. X) [? unconfirmed].

*DrW 197 *'Paule vent to Toune to saue him selfe from horning'*.

Autograph draft.

First pub. in Kastner (1913), II, 286.

National Library of Scotland, MS 2062 (Hawthornden Vol. X), f. 165.

'Paule vent to Toune to saue him selfe from horning'

*DrW 198 -----

Autograph copy.

National Library of Scotland, MS 2062 (Hawthornden Vol. X), f. 165v.

*DrW 199 *Persuasive dissuading* ('Show mee not lockes of Gold').

Autograph copy.

First pub. in Laing (1831); Kastner, II, 240.

National Library of Scotland, MS 2062 (Hawthornden Vol. X), f. 32.

*DrW 200 -----

Autograph copy.

National Library of Scotland, MS 2062 (Hawthornden Vol. X), f. 33.

*DrW 201 *'Phebus wher'ere thou stayst in Cynthe or Dele'.*

Autograph draft of a poem in a series headed 'De Materia Prima'.

First pub. in Fogle (1952), p. 189.

National Library of Scotland, MS 2062 (Hawthornden Vol. X), f. 45.

*DrW 202 *'Phillis when first amongst us thou camst downe'.*

Autograph draft of a poem in a series headed 'De Materia Prima'.

First pub. in Fogle (1952), p. 188.

National Library of Scotland, MS 2062 (Hawthornden Vol. X), f. 43.

--- *Polemo-Middinia inter Vitarvam et Nebernam* ('Nymphae quae colitis highissima monta Fifaea').

See DrW 15-18.

*DrW 203 *'Prometheus am I'.*

Autograph copy in Drummond's miscellany 'Democritie, a labyrinth of delight'; c. 1620s.

First pub. in Laing (1831); Kastner, II, 240; of doubtful authorship: see MacDonald, *SSL*, 7 (1969), 116.

National Library of Scotland, MS 2060 (Hawthornden Vol. VIII), f. 300.

*DrW 204 *A prouerbe* ('God neuer had a Church but there, Men say').

Autograph copy.

First pub. in Laing (1831); Kastner, II, 245.

National Library of Scotland, MS 2062 (Hawthornden Vol. X), f. 193.

*DrW 205 -----

Autograph copy.

National Library of Scotland, MS 2062 (Hawthornden Vol. X), f. 220.

*DrW 206 *A prouerbe* ('To singe as was of old, is but a scorne').

Autograph draft; c. 1639.

First pub. in Laing (1831); Kastner, II, 244.

National Library of Scotland, MS 2062 (Hawthornden Vol. X), f. 214.

*DrW 207 *'Rames ay runne backward when they would aduance'.*

Autograph draft.

First pub. in Laing (1831); Kastner, II, 246.

National Library of Scotland, MS 2062 (Hawthornden Vol. X), f. 183.

*DrW 208 *Regrat* ('In this Worlds raging sea').

Autograph copy, with revisions.

First pub. in Laing (1831); Kastner, II, 237.

National Library of Scotland, MS 2062 (Hawthornden Vol. X), f. 35.

*DrW 209 *A Replye* ('Swadl'd is the Babye, and almost two yeeres').

Autograph draft, here beginning 'The Babyes swadled & almost two yeers'.

First pub. in *Works* (1711); Kastner, II, 207.

National Library of Scotland, MS 2062 (Hawthornden Vol. X), f. 179.

*DrW 210 -----

Autograph copy.

National Library of Scotland, MS 2062 (Hawthornden Vol. X), f. 180.

*DrW 211 -----

Autograph copy.

National Library of Scotland, MS 2062 (Hawthornden Vol. X), f. 201.

*DrW 212 *A Replye* ('Who do in good delight').

Autograph draft, deleted.

First pub. in *Poems* (1656); Kastner, II, 175.

National Library of Scotland, MS 2062 (Hawthornden Vol. X), f. 15.

*DrW 213 -----

Autograph copy.

National Library of Scotland, MS 2062 (Hawthornden Vol. X), f. 37.

*DrW 214 *A Replye* ('Who loue enjoyes, and placed hath his Minde').

Autograph draft.

First pub. in *Poems* (1656); Kastner, II, 188.

National Library of Scotland, MS 2062 (Hawthornden Vol. X), f. 73.

*DrW 215 -----

Autograph copy.

National Library of Scotland, MS 2062 (Hawthornden Vol. X), f. 75.

*DrW 216 *'Rise to my soule, bright Sunne of Grace, o rise!'*.

Autograph draft, with revisions, deleted.

First pub. in Laing (1831); Kastner, II, 229.

National Library of Scotland, MS 2062 (Hawthornden Vol. X), f. 13.

*DrW 217 *'S. Andrew, why does thou giue up thy Schooles'*.

Autograph copy on a leaf bound in Drummond's miscellany 'Democritie, a labyrinth of delight'.

First pub. in Laing (1831); Kastner, II, 243.

National Library of Scotland, MS 2060 (Hawthornden Vol. VIII), f. 199v.

*DrW 218 *Saint Peter, after the denying his master* ('Like to the solitarie pelican').

Autograph draft, with revisions.

First pub. in *Works* (1711); Kastner, II, 214.

National Library of Scotland, MS 2062 (Hawthornden Vol. X), f. 15v.

*DrW 219 *'Samarias Motheres when to Death they steru'd'*.

Autograph copy.

First pub. in Kastner (1913), II, 288.

National Library of Scotland, MS 2062 (Hawthornden Vol. X), f. 177B.

*DrW 220 *Sextain* ('With elegies, sad songs, and murning layes').

Autograph copy.

First pub. in Laing (1831); Kastner, II, 247.

National Library of Scotland, MS 2062 (Hawthornden Vol. X), f. 158v.

*DrW 221 *A sigh* ('Sigh, stollen from her sweet brest').

Autograph draft.

First pub. in Laing (1831); Kastner, II, 238.

National Library of Scotland, MS 2062 (Hawthornden Vol. X), f. 2.

*DrW 222 *Silenus to King Midas* ('The greatest Gift that from their loftie Thrones').

Autograph copy, untitled, in Drummond's miscellany 'Ephemeris'; c. 1606-14.

First pub. in *Poems* (1656); Kastner, II, 186; of doubtful authorship: see MacDonald, *SSL*, 7 (1969), 113-14.

National Library of Scotland, MS 2059 (Hawthornden Vol. VII), f. 23v.

*DrW 223 -----

Autograph copy.

National Library of Scotland, MS 2062 (Hawthornden Vol. X), f. 2.

*DrW 224 -----

Autograph copy.

National Library of Scotland, MS 2062 (Hawthornden Vol. X), f. 137v.

*DrW 225 *'Sith God ordaines and Natures lawes require'*.

Autograph draft.

First pub. in Fogle (1952), p. 209.

National Library of Scotland, MS 2062 (Hawthornden Vol. X), f. 79.

*DrW 226 *'Some men desire spouses that come of noble Houses'.*

Autograph copy.

First pub. in Thomas Weelkes, *Ayeres of Phantastique Spirites* (1608); printed from this MS in Fogle (1952), p. 208; of uncertain authorship: see [J.P. Cutts], 'William Drummond of Hawthornden', *N & Q*, 202 (April 1957), 148-50.

National Library of Scotland, MS 2062 (Hawthornden Vol. X), f. 70.

*DrW 227 *Song of Passerat* ('Shephard loueth thow me vell?').

Autograph draft.

First pub. in *Works* (1711); Kastner, II, 221-2.

National Library of Scotland, MS 2062 (Hawthornden Vol. X), f. 176r-v.

*DrW 228 *Sonnet before a poëme of Irene* ('Mourne not (faire Grece) the ruine of thy kings').

Autograph copy, with two lines added in pencil.

First pub. in Laing (1831); Kastner, II, 230.

National Library of Scotland, MS 2062 (Hawthornden Vol. X), f. 202.

*DrW 229 -----

Autograph copy.

National Library of Scotland, MS 2062 (Hawthornden Vol. X), f. 203.

*DrW 230 *Sonnet qu'un poet Italien fit pour vn bracelet de cheveux qui lui auoit estè donnè par sa maistresse.*

Copy by Drummond of a sonnet by Antonio Tebaldeo, with three different autograph translations by Drummond; the first headed 'In the same sort of rime' and beginning 'O haire, sueet haire, part of the tresse of gold'; the second headed 'In frier sort of rime' and beginning 'O haire, faire haire, some of the goldin threeds'; the third headed 'Paraphrasticalie translated' and beginning 'Haire, suet haire, tuitchet by Midas hand'.

First pub. in Laing (1833); Kastner, II, 231-2.

National Library of Scotland, MS 2062 (Hawthornden Vol. X), f. 160r-v.

*DrW 231 *The Statue of Alcides* ('Flora vpon a tyme').

Autograph draft.

First pub. in *Works* (1711); Kastner, II, 208.

National Library of Scotland, MS 2062 (Hawthornden Vol. X), f. 220v.

*DrW 232 -----

Autograph draft, with revisions.

National Library of Scotland, MS 2062 (Hawthornden Vol. X), f. 220v.

*DrW 233 -----

Autograph draft, with revisions.

National Library of Scotland, MS 2062 (Hawthornden Vol. X), f. 221.

*DrW 234 -----

Autograph draft, with revisions.

National Library of Scotland, MS 2062 (Hawthornden Vol. X), f. 222.

*DrW 235 *Stollen pleasure* ('My sweet did sweetlie sleep').

Autograph draft.

First pub. in Laing (1831); Kastner, II, 238.

National Library of Scotland, MS 2062 (Hawthornden Vol. X), f. 137v.

*DrW 236 -----

Autograph second draft.

National Library of Scotland, MS 2062 (Hawthornden Vol. X), f. 137v.

*DrW 237 *'Strange is his end, his death most rare and od'.*

Autograph copy in Drummond's miscellany 'Democritie, a labyrinth of delight'; c. 1620s.

First pub. in Kastner (1913), II, 284; of doubtful authorship: see MacDonald, *SSL*, 7 (1969), 116.

National Library of Scotland, MS 2060 (Hawthornden Vol. VIII), f. 79.

*DrW 238 -----

Autograph copy in Drummond's miscellany 'Democritie, a labyrinth of delight'; c. 1620s.

National Library of Scotland, MS 2060 (Hawthornden Vol. VIII), f. 126.

Sur les oeuures poetiques de Guillaume Alexandre

*DrW 239 *Sur les oeuures poetiques de Guillaume Alexandre, Sieur De Menstre* ('Menstre, Mignon de Pinde, astre des escossois').

Autograph draft.

First pub. in Kastner (1913), II, 278.

National Library of Scotland, MS 2062 (Hawthornden Vol. X), f. 163v.

*DrW 240 *'Sweet are the thoughts that harbour full content'.*

Autograph draft.

First pub. in Fogle (1952), p. 207; discussed in [J.P. Cutts], 'William Drummond of Hawthornden', *N & Q*, 202 (April 1957), 148-50.

National Library of Scotland, MS 2062 (Hawthornden Vol. X), f. 70.

*DrW 241 *'That burning lampe so gloriouslie that lustres'.*

Autograph draft, headed 'fragment'.

First pub. in Fogle (1952), p. 201.

National Library of Scotland, MS 2062 (Hawthornden Vol. X), f. 65.

*DrW 242 *'That which preserueth cherries, peares and plumes'.*

Autograph copy in Drummond's miscellany 'Democritie, a labyrinth of delight'; c. 1620s.

First pub. in Kastner (1913), II, 284; of doubtful authorship: see MacDonald, *SSL*, 7 (1969), 116.

National Library of Scotland, MS 2060 (Hawthornden Vol. VIII), f. 38.

*DrW 243 *'The boyling sighs, and hote flaming fire'.*

Autograph draft.

First pub. in Fogle (1952), p. 191.

National Library of Scotland, MS 2062 (Hawthornden Vol. X), f. 48.

--- *'The daughter of a king, of princelye parts'.*

[Kastner, II, 200].

See DrW 279.

*DrW 244 *'The dolorous accents, the most ruthfull plaints.*

Autograph draft, headed 'Eclogue Damon'.

First pub. in Fogle (1952), pp. 193-8.

National Library of Scotland, MS 2062 (Hawthornden Vol. X), ff. 57-62, 211.

*DrW 245 *'The feilds vith flours var Pant in divers heu'.*

Autograph poetical fragment.

First pub. in Fogle (1952), p. 200.

National Library of Scotland, MS 2062 (Hawthornden Vol. X), f. 63.

*DrW 246 *'The Gods haue heard my vowes'.*

Autograph copy.

First pub. in Kastner (1913), II, 282.

National Library of Scotland, MS 2062 (Hawthornden Vol. X), f. 71.

*DrW 247 *'The King a Negative Voice most justly hath'.*

Autograph copy.

First pub. in *Works* (1711); Kastner, II, 207.

National Library of Scotland, MS 2062 (Hawthornden Vol. X), f. 181.

*DrW 248 *'The king good subiectes can not saue: then tell'.*

Autograph copy; c. 1639.

First pub. in Laing (1831); Kastner, II, 242.

National Library of Scotland, MS 2062 (Hawthornden Vol. X), f. 177A.

*DrW 249 *'The king nor Bond nor oath had him to follow'.*

Autograph copy.

First pub. in *Works* (1711); Kastner, II, 207.

National Library of Scotland, MS 2062 (Hawthornden Vol. X), f. 180.

*DrW 250 *'The Nightingale, the organ of delight'.*

Autograph copy.

First pub. in Thomas Weelkes, *Ayeres of Phantastique Spirites* (1608); printed from this MS in Fogle (1952), p. 208; of uncertain authorship: see [J.P. Cutts], 'William Drummond of Hawthornden', *N & Q*, 202 (April 1957), 148-50.

National Library of Scotland, MS 2062 (Hawthornden Vol. X), f. 70.

*DrW 251 *'The parlament lordes haue sitten twice fiue weekes'.*

Autograph copy.

First pub. in Laing (1831); Kastner, II, 242.

National Library of Scotland, MS 2062 (Hawthornden Vol. X), f. 181.

'The parlament lordes haue sitten twice fiue weekes'

*DrW 252 -----

Autograph draft.

National Library of Scotland, MS 2062 (Hawthornden Vol. X), f. 215v.

*DrW 253 *'The parlament the first of June will sit'.*

Autograph copy.

First pub. in Laing (1831); Kastner, II, 243.

National Library of Scotland, MS 2062 (Hawthornden Vol. X), f. 181.

*DrW 254 *'The scottish kirke the English church doe name'.*

Autograph draft, with revisions; c. 1639.

First pub. in *Works* (1711); Kastner, II, 205.

National Library of Scotland, MS 2062 (Hawthornden Vol. X), f. 177A.

*DrW 255 *'The time that rests in feast, in dance, in pleasure'.*

Autograph copy.

First pub. in Fogle (1952), pp. 205-7.

National Library of Scotland, MS 2062 (Hawthornden Vol. X), f. 209.

*DrW 256 *'The woefull Marie midst a blubbred band'.*

Autograph draft, with revisions.

First pub. in *Works* (1711); Kastner, II, 215.

National Library of Scotland, MS 2062 (Hawthornden Vol. X), ff. 16-19.

*DrW 257 *'There where the pleasant Eske'.*

Autograph draft of one of two poems headed 'Pastorells from Maria Bonardo frattegiano'.

First pub. in Fogle (1952), p. 199.

National Library of Scotland, MS 2062 (Hawthornden Vol. X), f. 55.

*DrW 258 *'This Monument vnder'.*

Autograph draft, with revisions.

First pub. in Kastner (1913), II, 281.

National Library of Scotland, MS 2062 (Hawthornden Vol. X), f. 54v.

*DrW 259 *'Thocht louers lie borne by the streame of yuth'.*

Autograph draft.

First pub. in Kastner (1913), II, 286.

National Library of Scotland, MS 2062 (Hawthornden Vol. X), f. 159.

*DrW 260 *To a swallow, building neare the statue of Medea* ('Fond Prognèe, chattering wretch').

Autograph copy.

First pub. in *Poems* (1656); Kastner, II, 186.

National Library of Scotland, MS 2062 (Hawthornden Vol. X), f. 38.

*DrW 261 -----

Autograph copy.

National Library of Scotland, MS 2062 (Hawthornden Vol. X), f. 51.

*DrW 262 *To an Owle* ('Ascalaphus tell mee').

Autograph draft, with revisions.

First pub. in *Poems* (1656); Kastner, II, 177.

National Library of Scotland, MS 2062 (Hawthornden Vol. X), f. 39.

*DrW 263 *To Anne, the french Queen, new come from Spaine, and applyable to Marye of England, meeting the King at Douer* ('At length heere shee is: wee haue got those bright eyes').

Autograph copy of a French poem and an English translation in Drummond's miscellany 'Democritie, a labyrinth of delight'; c. 1620s.

First pub. in Kastner (1913), II, 274; of doubtful authorship: see MacDonald, *SSL*, 7 (1969), 115.

National Library of Scotland, MS 2060 (Hawthornden Vol. VIII), f. 171.

*DrW 264 *'To build a tombe Jhone doth him daylie paine'.*

Autograph draft.

First pub. in Kastner (1913), II, 285.

National Library of Scotland, MS 2062 (Hawthornden Vol. X), f. 158.

*DrW 265 -----

Autograph copy.

National Library of Scotland, MS 2062 (Hawthornden Vol. X), f. 165v.

*DrW 266 *To his amorous Thoughts* ('Sweet wanton thought which art of Beautye borne').

Autograph copy, deleted.

First pub. in *Poems* (1656); Kastner, II, 186.

National Library of Scotland, MS 2062 (Hawthornden Vol. X), f. 11.

DrW 267 *To my Ladye Mary Wroath* ('For beautye onlye, armd with outward grace').

Fair copy in an italic hand.

First pub. in Kastner (1913), II, 271.

National Library of Scotland, MS 2062 (Hawthornden Vol. X), f. 83.

*DrW 268 *To my ladye Mary Wroath* ('Who can (great lady) but adore thy name').

Autograph copy.

First pub. in Kastner (1913), II, 277.

National Library of Scotland, MS 2062 (Hawthornden Vol. X), ff. 80-1.

DrW 269 -----

Fair copy in an italic hand.

National Library of Scotland, MS 2062 (Hawthornden Vol. X), ff. 82-3.

*DrW 270 *To the Author* ('Whiles dark, unknowne, neglectd your Glorie').

Autograph, inscribed on a flyleaf of Drummond's printed exemplum of William Alexander, *Monarchicke Tragedies* (London, 1607) (see DrW 347).

First pub. in Fogle (1952), p. 75.

National Library of Scotland, MS 1692, f. iii.

*DrW 271 *To the honorable Author, Sir John Skene* ('All lawes but cob-webes are, but none such right').

Autograph draft.

First pub. in Laing (1831); Kastner, II, 228.

National Library of Scotland, MS 2062 (Hawthornden Vol. X), f. 5.

*DrW 272 -----

Autograph copy.

National Library of Scotland, MS 2062 (Hawthornden Vol. X), f. 6.

*DrW 273 *To the Memorie of ...* ('As nought for splendour can with sunne compare').

Autograph draft.

First pub. in Laing (1831); Kastner, II, 252.

National Library of Scotland, MS 2062 (Hawthornden Vol. X), f. 90.

*DrW 274 *To the Memorie of his much louing and beloued Master, M.F.R.* ('No Wonder now if Mistes beclowde our Day').

Autograph draft, with revisions.

First pub. in Laing (1831); Kastner, II, 249.

National Library of Scotland, MS 2062 (Hawthornden Vol. X), f. 88.

*DrW 275 -----

Autograph draft, with revisions.

National Library of Scotland, MS 2062 (Hawthornden Vol. X), f. 89.

*DrW 276 *To the Memorie of the excellent ladye Isabell, Countesse of Lawderdale* ('Fond wight, who dreamest of Greatnesse, Glorie, State').

Autograph draft, untitled.

First pub. in *Poems* (1656); Kastner, II, 194.

National Library of Scotland, MS 2062 (Hawthornden Vol. X), f. 101r-v.

*DrW 277 -----

Autograph copy.

National Library of Scotland, MS 2062 (Hawthornden Vol. X), f. 102.

*DrW 278 -----

Autograph copy.

National Library of Scotland, MS 2062 (Hawthornden Vol. X), ff. 103B-4.

*DrW 279 *To the Memorie of the vertuous Gentlewoman Rachell Lindsay* ('The Daughter of a king, of princelye partes').

Autograph draft.

First pub. in Laing (1831); Kastner, II, 251.

National Library of Scotland, MS 2062 (Hawthornden Vol. X), f. 85.

*DrW 280 *To the Memorie of the worthye ladye, the ladye Craigmillare* ('This Marble needes no teares, let these be powr'd').

Autograph draft.

First pub. in Laing (1831); Kastner, II, 253.

National Library of Scotland, MS 2062 (Hawthornden Vol. X), f. 94.

*DrW 281 -----

Autograph draft, with revisions.

National Library of Scotland, MS 2062 (Hawthornden Vol. X), f. 94A.

*DrW 282 -----

Autograph copy.

National Library of Scotland, MS 2062 (Hawthornden Vol. X), f. 95.

*DrW 283 -----

Autograph copy

National Library of Scotland, MS 2062 (Hawthornden Vol. X), f. 96.

*DrW 284 *To the Memory of John, Earl of Lauderdale* ('Of those rare worthyes which adorn'd our North').

Autograph copy of three epitaphs; [1645].

First pub. in *Poems* (1656); Kastner, II, 192-3.

National Library of Scotland, MS 2062 (Hawthornden Vol. X), ff. 97-9.

*DrW 285 *'Tom moneyless his agnus dei hath sold'.*

Autograph draft.

First pub. in Kastner (1913), II, 285.

National Library of Scotland, MS 2062 (Hawthornden Vol. X), f. 158.

*DrW 286 *Translation of the death of a sparrow, out of Passerat* ('Ah! if yee aske (my friendes) why this salt shower').

Autograph draft.

First pub. in *Works* (1711); Kastner, II, 212-13.

National Library of Scotland, MS 2062 (Hawthornden Vol. X), f. 175.

*DrW 287 -----

Autograph draft.

National Library of Scotland, MS 2062 (Hawthornden Vol. X), f. 175v.

*DrW 288 *'Two Bittes of Noses may make on tall nose'.*

Autograph copy.

First pub. in Kastner (1913), II, 288.

National Library of Scotland, MS 2062 (Hawthornden Vol. X), f. 184.

*DrW 289 *Venus armed* ('As to trye new alarmes').

Autograph draft, with revisions.

First pub. in *Poems* (1656); Kastner, II, 176.

National Library of Scotland, MS 2062 (Hawthornden Vol. X), f. 38.

*DrW 290 *'Why byeth old Chremes land so near his death?'.*

Autograph draft.

First pub. in Kastner (1913), II, 287.

National Library of Scotland, MS 2062 (Hawthornden Vol. X), f. 159.

*DrW 291 -----

Autograph draft.

National Library of Scotland, MS 2062 (Hawthornden Vol. X), f. 166.

*DrW 292 *Vindiciae against the Comones for B.C.* ('Some are that thinke it no way can agree').

Autograph draft, with revisions.

First pub. in Kastner (1913), II, 289.

National Library of Scotland, MS 2062 (Hawthornden Vol. X), f. 204.

*DrW 293 *'What course of life should wretched Mortalles take?'.*

Autograph copy, with an alteration in a later hand.

First pub. in *Poems* (1656); Kastner, II, 173.

National Library of Scotland, MS 2062 (Hawthornden Vol. X), f. 20.

'What groning ghost is this that goes'

*DrW 294 *'What groning ghost is this that goes'.*

Autograph draft, here beginning 'What ghostlie grones be those that goes'.

First pub. in Fogle (1952), p. 203.

National Library of Scotland, MS 2062 (Hawthornden Vol. X), f. 207.

*DrW 295 *'What pen is there so bold'.*

Autograph draft of a poem in a series headed 'De Materia Prima'.

First pub. in Fogle (1952), p. 190.

National Library of Scotland, MS 2062 (Hawthornden Vol. X), f. 47.

*DrW 296 *'When Charles was yong, to walke straight and vpright'.*

Autograph draft, with revisions.

First pub. in Laing (1831); Kastner, II, 242.

National Library of Scotland, MS 2062 (Hawthornden Vol. X), f. 178.

*DrW 297 *'When discord in a Towne the Toxan ringes'.*

Autograph copy.

First pub. in Laing (1831); Kastner, II, 244.

National Library of Scotland, MS 2062 (Hawthornden Vol. X), f. 188.

*DrW 298 *'While yee raise you to heauen shrill Swan'.*

Autograph draft.

First pub. in Fogle (1952), p. 202.

National Library of Scotland, MS 2062 (Hawthornden Vol. X), f. 56.

--- *'Why byeth old Chremes land so near his death?'.*

See DrW 290-1.

*DrW 299 *'Ye veep as if your husbands death yow griuit'.*

Autograph draft.

First pub. in Kastner (1913), II, 286.

National Library of Scotland, MS 2062 (Hawthornden Vol. X), f. 158.

*DrW 300 -----

Autograph copy.

National Library of Scotland, MS 2062 (Hawthornden Vol. X), f. 165v.

*DrW 301 *'Zanzummines they obeye the king doe sweare'.*

Autograph copy.

First pub. in Laing (1831); Kastner, II, 243.

National Library of Scotland, MS 2062 (Hawthornden Vol. X), f. 178.

*DrW 302 *'Zoilus eies in glasse did see them selues looke euen'.*

Autograph draft.

First pub. in Kastner (1913), II, 286.

National Library of Scotland, MS 2062 (Hawthornden Vol. X), f. 165.

PROSE

DrW 303 *Ben Jonson's Conversations with William Drummond.*

Copy, headed 'Informations be Ben Johnston to W.D. when he came to Scotland upon foot 1619', transcribed from Drummond's autograph by the antiquary Sir Robert Sibbald (1641-1722) in his MS collection 'Adversaria'; late 17th-early 18th century.

First pub. (in an abridged form) in *Works* (1711). Printed from this MS in Laing (1833), pp. 241-70, and in *Ben Jonson*, ed. C.H. Herford and Percy and Evelyn Simpson, I (Oxford, 1925), 132-51. Of Drummond's original MS only the cover remains, in MS 2061 (Hawthornden Vol. IX), f. 140.

National Library of Scotland, Adv. MS 33. 3. 19, ff. 25v-31.

*DrW 304 -----

Copy made by Drummond of Ben Jonson's 'epitaph' and of two anecdotes told to Drummond by Jonson, which correspond to passages in the Conversations with Jonson, in Drummond's miscellany 'Democritie, a labyrinth of delight'; c. 1619-20s.

These MS passages printed in Laing (1831), pp. 78-9.

National Library of Scotland, MS 2060 (Hawthornden Vol. VIII), ff. 3-4.

--- -----

See also DrW 351.

*DrW 305 *Bibliotheca Edinburgena Lectori.*

Two autograph drafts.

First pub. in *Works* (1711), p. 222.

National Library of Scotland, MS 2061 (Hawthornden Vol. IX), ff. 174-3, 175-8.

*DrW 306 *A Cypresse Grove.*

Autograph draft, with revisions, of a portion of the essay, here beginning 'If on the Great Theater of this Earth...' and ending '...in the midst of multitudes rather garded than regarded', in Drummond's miscellany 'Democritie, a labyrinth of delight'; c. 1620s.

First pub. appended to *Flowres of Sion* ([Edinburgh], 1623]; Kastner, II, 65-104 (11. 115-274).

National Library of Scotland, MS 2060 (Hawthornden Vol. VIII), ff. 204-8.

*DrW 307 *A dedication of some poems to Craigmiller.*

Autograph, the title added in a later hand.

First pub. (from this MS) in Paganelli (1968), pp. 327-8.

National Library of Scotland, MS 2061 (Hawthornden Vol. IX), f. 131.

*DrW 308 *Discourse in commendation of kinglie government.*

Autograph draft; 1626.

Believed to be unpublished.

National Library of Scotland, MS 2061 (Hawthornden Vol. IX), ff. 159-60.

*DrW 309 *For the geneologie of the house of Drummond.*

Autograph draft.

Believed to be unpublished.

National Library of Scotland, MS 2061 (Hawthornden Vol. IX), ff. 144v-5.

*DrW 310 *The Hermitage.*

Autograph draft.

Believed to be unpublished.

National Library of Scotland, MS 2061 (Hawthornden Vol. IX), f. 151.

--- *The History of Scotland.*

See DrW 314-16.

DrW 311 *History of the Family of Perth.*

Copy in a volume of antiquarian transcripts made by Robert Mylne (1643?-1747); late 17th-early 18th century.

First pub. in William Drummond, *The Genealogy of the House of Drummond* (Edinburgh, 1831), Appendix I, pp. 241-56.

National Library of Scotland, Adv. MS 34. 6. 9, ff. 264-79v.

DrW 312 -----

Abridgement made by Robert Mylne, in one of his bound antiquarian collections; late 17th-early 18th century.

National Library of Scotland, Adv. MS 34. 6. 12, pp. 410-23.

DrW 313 -----

Abridgement in a volume of antiquarian papers compiled by Robert Mylne, engraver, son of the antiquary Robert Mylne; with a note saying this account 'I had from Mr Alexr Nisbet Herauld his transcript who had it from the principal (wch he borrowed from the present S^r^ W^m^. Drũmond of Hawthornden his son the 7. Aũg. 1701) copie writen with Mr Williams own hand'; early 18th century.

National Library of Scotland, Adv. MS 23. 3. 24, ff. 78-80.

*DrW 314 *The History of the Five Jameses, Kings of Scotland.*

Autograph rough drafts bound in three volumes; Vol. I (James I-II) dated 1633; Vol. II (James III) dated 1642-3; Vol. III (James IV-V) dated 1623, 1639 and 1644.

First pub. as *The History of Scotland* (London, 1655); *Works* (1711), pp. 1-116. These drafts discussed in Thomas I. Rae, 'The historical writing of Drummond of Hawthornden', *SHR*, 54, 1 (April 1975), 22-62.

National Library of Scotland, MSS 2053-5 (Hawthornden Vols. I-III).

*DrW 315 -----

Fair copy or later drafts bound in two volumes (Vol. IV: James I-III; Vol. V: James IV-V), mainly in the hand of an amanuensis, with Drummond's autograph revisions and additions; James IV entirely in Drummond's autograph; entitled 'The Historie of the Lives and Raignes of five Kinges of Scotland'; c. 1644-9.

These MSS discussed in Rae; a speech in MS. 2057, ff. 202-8, printed in MacDonald (1976), pp. 174-8.

National Library of Scotland, MSS 2056-7 (Hawthornden Vols. IV-V).

DrW 316 -----

Copy; late 17th-early 18th century.

National Library of Scotland, Adv. MS 35. 5. 4.

In praise of letters

*DrW 317 *In praise of letters.*

Autograph draft of a brief essay.

First pub. (from this MS) in Paganelli (1968), pp. 332-3.

National Library of Scotland, MS 2061 (Hawthornden Vol. IX), f. 147.

*DrW 318 *In praise of the allegorie in poesie.*

Autograph draft of a brief essay.

First pub. (from this MS) in Paganelli (1968), pp. 331-2.

National Library of Scotland, MS 2061 (Hawthornden Vol. IX), f. 143.

*DrW 319 *Irene.*

Autograph first draft, with revisions, inscribed at the end 'This copie of Irene is uerie imperfite and not to be made use of'; 1638.

First pub. in *Works* (1711), pp. 163-73.

National Library of Scotland, MS 2058 (Hawthornden Vol. VI), ff. 42-87.

*DrW 320 -----

Autograph second draft, with revisions; 1638.

National Library of Scotland, MS 2058 (Hawthornden Vol. VI), ff. 89-133.

*DrW 321 -----

Autograph third draft, with revisions; lacking the title and incomplete; [1638].

National Library of Scotland, MS 2058 (Hawthornden Vol. VI), ff. 136-47.

*DrW 322 -----

Autograph fourth draft, the final version; 1638.

Extracts from this MS printed in MacDonald (1976), pp. 179-99.

National Library of Scotland, MS 2058 (Hawthornden Vol. VI), ff. 149-86.

DrW 323 -----

Copy in a MS volume of Drummond's prose tracts; 17th century.

National Library of Scotland, Adv. MS 13. 2. 5, ff. 1-38v.

DrW 324 -----

Copy in a composite volume of historical papers once owned by the antiquary Robert Mylne (1643?-1747); 17th century.

National Library of Scotland, Adv. MS 31. 2. 1, ff. 213-69.

DrW 325 -----

Copy in a MS volume of Drummond's prose tracts; 17th century.

National Library of Scotland, Adv. MS 32. 4. 9, ff. 1-22.

*DrW 326 *The Load-Star.*

Autograph draft, with one section deleted.

First pub. in *Works* (1711), pp. 183-4.

National Library of Scotland, MS 2058 (Hawthornden Vol. VI), ff. 242-8.

DrW 327 -----

Copy in a MS volume of Drummond's prose tracts; 17th century.

National Library of Scotland, Adv. MS 13. 2. 5, ff. 41-5v.

DrW 328 -----

Copy in a MS volume of Drummond's prose tracts; 17th century.

National Library of Scotland, Adv. MS 32. 4. 9, ff. 23-6v.

*DrW 329 *The Magical Mirror.*

Autograph first draft, with revisions; incomplete; [1639].

First pub. in *Works* (1711), pp. 174-6.

National Library of Scotland, MS 2058 (Hawthornden Vol. VI), ff. 227-32v.

*DrW 330 -----

Autograph second draft, with revisions; incomplete; [1639].

National Library of Scotland, MS 2058 (Hawthornden Vol. VI), ff. 233-9v.

*DrW 331 -----

Autograph draft, the final version; imperfect,

lacking the final page; 1639.

National Library of Scotland, MS 2058 (Hawthornden Vol. VI), ff. 211-26.

DrW 332 -----

Copy in a MS volume of Drummond's prose tracts; 17th century.

National Library of Scotland, Adv. MS 13. 2. 5, ff. 48v-55v.

DrW 333 -----

Copy in a MS volume of Drummond's prose tracts; 17th century.

National Library of Scotland, Adv. MS 32. 4. 9, ff. 27-32v.

*DrW 334 *New-Scotland.*

Autograph draft.

Believed to be unpublished.

National Library of Scotland, MS 2061 (Hawthornden Vol. IX), ff. 148-9.

*DrW 335 [*Note on Painters and Poets*].

A brief autograph note.

First pub. (from this MS) in Paganelli (1968), pp. 330-1.

National Library of Scotland, MS 2061 (Hawthornden Vol. IX), f. 77.

*DrW 336 *Of change of religion.*

Autograph.

Believed to be unpublished.

National Library of Scotland, MS 2061 (Hawthornden Vol. IX), ff. 136v-7.

*DrW 337 *Of Impresas.*

Autograph.

First pub. in *Works* (1711), pp. 228-31.

National Library of Scotland, MS 2061 (Hawthornden Vol. IX), f. 128.

*DrW 338 [*Of the Country of Amauria*].

Autograph drafts, untitled.

Believed to be unpublished.

National Library of Scotland, MS 2066 (Hawthornden Vol. XIV), ff. 70v, 71v.

*DrW 339 *Queries of State.*

Autograph first draft.

First pub. in *Works* (1711), pp. 177-8.

National Library of Scotland, MS 2058 (Hawthornden Vol. VI), ff. 190-5v.

*DrW 340 -----

Autograph second draft.

National Library of Scotland, MS 2058 (Hawthornden Vol. VI), ff. 197-202.

*DrW 341 -----

Autograph draft, the final version.

National Library of Scotland, MS 2058 (Hawthornden Vol. VI), ff. 205-9.

DrW 342 -----

Copy in a MS volume of Drummond's prose tracts; 17th century.

National Library of Scotland, Adv. MS 13. 2. 5, ff. 58-61.

DrW 343 -----

Copy in a MS volume of Drummond's prose tracts; 17th century.

National Library of Scotland, Adv. MS 32. 4. 9, ff. 33-5v.

DrW 344 *Remoras for the National League between Scotland and England, 1642.*

Copy in a MS volume of Drummond's prose tracts; 17th century.

First pub. in *Works* (1711), pp. 188-9.

National Library of Scotland, Adv. MS 13. 2. 5, ff. 62v-6.

DrW 345 -----

Copy in a MS volume of Drummond's prose tracts; 17th century.

National Library of Scotland, Adv. MS 32. 4. 9, ff. 36-9.

*DrW 346 *Skiamachia*

Autograph draft; 1643.

First pub. in *Works* (1711), pp. 190-205.

National Library of Scotland, MS 2058 (Hawthornden Vol. VI), ff. 260-318.

MARGINALIA IN PRINTED BOOKS AND MANUSCRIPTS [and see also INTRODUCTION]

*DrW 347 Alexander, William. *The Monarchicke Tragedies* (London, 1607).

Extensive autograph annotations and an autograph sonnet to Sir William Alexander (see DrW 270).

MacDonald, *Library of Drummond*, No. 698 (and see p. 34); see also INTRODUCTION.

National Library of Scotland, MS 1692.

*DrW 348 Boethius. *De consolatione philosophiae* (Lyons, 1486).

Autograph annotations on the invention of printing.

MacDonald, *Library of Drummond*, No. 425.

British Library, Department of Printed Books, I. B. 41526 a & b.

*DrW 349 Estienne, Robert. *Les mots francois selon lordre des lettres* (Paris, 1544).

Autograph annotations; c. 1607.

MacDonald, *Library of Drummond*, No. 1037 (and facsimile of one page on p. 133).

Edinburgh University Library, De. 4. 15.

*DrW 350 Fairfax, Edward. *Godfrey of Bulloigne* (London, 1600).

Extensive autograph annotations.

MacDonald, *Library of Drummond*, No. 931 (discussed pp. 34-6).

Owned by Lord Home of the Hirsel [possession confirmed by letter 15 September 1975].

*DrW 351 Jonson, Ben. *Workes* (London, 1616).

Autograph annotations, a number of which repeat information given in Drummond's Conversations with Jonson (see DrW 303-4); c. 1616.

MacDonald, *Library of Drummond*, No. 850, with a facsimile of p. 782 on p. 36. These annotations discussed in J.R. Barker, 'A Pendant to Drummond of Hawthornden's *Conversations*', *RES*, NS 16 (1965), 284-8.

University of Dundee, Brechin Diocesan Library, Br Q822.34.

MISCELLANEOUS

*DrW 352 [*Miscellany*].

Autograph miscellany entitled 'Ephemeris', containing lists of books, extracts from other authors, &c; 403 leaves, folio; c. 1606-14.

Drummond's lists of books read by him 1606-14 (ff. 359-67) printed in Laing (1831), pp. 73-7, and in MacDonald, *Library of Drummond*, pp. 228-31. Other lists of 1611 and earlier (ff. 3, 370-97) incorporated in MacDonald's catalogue, with facsimiles of ff. 3 & 370 between pp. 144 & 145. Individual poems and works in this MS are given separate entries in the *Index*.

National Library of Scotland, MS 2059 (Hawthornden Vol. VII).

*DrW 353 -----

Autograph miscellany, containing extracts from other authors, &c; beginning with a collection of anecdotes, pasquils, &c, entitled 'Democritie, a labyrinth of delight'; 300 leaves, folio; c. 1618-20s.

Some extracts from this MS printed in Laing (1831), pp. 78-82. Drummond's 'Catalogue of Comedies' (ff. 122-3) printed in MacDonald, *Library of Drummond*, pp. 231-2. Individual poems and works in this MS are given separate entries in the *Index*.

National Library of Scotland, MS 2060 (Hawthornden Vol. VIII).

*DrW 354 -----

A MS volume entitled 'Memorialls', chiefly in Drummond's autograph with a few notes by his son William; consisting of genealogical notes relating to the Drummonds of Carnock and a diary recording family births, deaths, marriages, accidents and illnesses between 1606 and 1647, with additions by William the son for the period 1649-1700; 87 pages plus 301 blank pages.

This MS discussed in MacDonald, *Library of Drummond*, pp. 11-12. The initial 'Memorialls' printed in MacDonald (1976), pp. 193-5.

University of Dundee, Brechin Diocesan Library, BrMS/Vol. 5.

--- -----

See also DrW 74 and INTRODUCTION.

William Dunbar

1460?-1513?

ABBREVIATIONS

Bennett *Devotional Pieces in Verse and Prose,* ed. J. A. W. Bennett, STS 3rd Ser. 23 (Edinburgh & London, 1955).

Craigie *The Maitland Folio Manuscript,* ed. W. A. Craigie, 2 vols, STS NS 7, 20 (Edinburgh & London, 1919-27).

Craigie, *Asloan MS* *The Asloan Manuscript,* ed. W. A. Craigie, 2 vols, STS NS 14, 16 (Edinburgh & London, 1923-5).

Mackenzie *The Poems of William Dunbar,* ed. W. Mackay Mackenzie (London, 1932; reprinted 1966).

Murdoch *The Bannatyne Manuscript,* ed. J. Barclay Murdoch, 4 vols Hunterian Club (Glasgow, 1896; reprinted New York, 1966).

Ritchie *The Bannatyne Manuscript,* ed. W. Tod Ritchie, 4 vols, STS 3rd Ser. 5, 22, 23, 26 (Edinburgh & London, 1928-33).

Small *The Poems of William Dunbar,* ed. John Small (with introduction and notes by A. J. G. Mackay and Walter Gregor), 3 vols, STS 2.4, 16, 21.29 (Edinburgh & London, 1883-93).

Stevenson *Pieces from the Makculloch and the Gray MSS. together with the Chepman and Myllar Prints,* ed. George Stevenson, STS 65 (Edinburgh & London, 1918).

For abbreviations used throughout Volume I, see p.xi.

INTRODUCTION

The main MS sources of Dunbar's poems have long been known to scholars. They are as follows:

(1) The BANNATYNE MS (National Library of Scotland, Adv. MS. 1.1.6). An anthology of Scottish poetry compiled by George Bannatyne; dated 1568 but probably written during the course of some years. Contains fifty-one poems at present attributed to Dunbar. Complete text printed in Murdoch and Ritchie. Complete facsimile, introduced by Denton Fox, published by the Scolar Press, 1979. The MS is now bound in two volumes with three sets of foliation and pagination, the most recent of which (foliating each volume separately) is not cited by editors and has been ignored in the *Index*.

(2) The MAITLAND FOLIO MS (Magdalene College, Cambridge, Pepys Library, MS 2553). An anthology of Scottish poetry compiled by Sir Richard Maitland of Lethington (1496-1586), written by several amanuenses, c. 1570-85. Contains sixty-three poems at present attributed to Dunbar. Complete text printed in Craigie. This MS is not to be confused with another anthology, the 'Maitland Quarto MS', which is also in the Pepys Library. A MS transcript of both the Folio and Quarto MSS made by John Pinkerton (1758-1826) for his edition of *Ancient Scotish Poems,* 2 vols (London, 1786), is preserved at the University of Newcastle upon Tyne (MS Bell/White 18) (this transcript is not hereafter cited in the *Index*).

(3) The REIDPETH MS (Cambridge University Library, MS Ll. 5. 10.). A partial transcript of the Maitland Folio MS (including parts of the MS no longer preserved) made by John Reidpeth in 1622-3. Contains fifty poems at present attributed to Dunbar. Variant readings are recorded in Craigie.

(4) The ASLOAN MS. (National Library of Scotland, [MS Acc. 4233]). A miscellany of verse and prose compiled by John Asloan, c. 1515. Contains six poems at present attributed to Dunbar. Complete text printed in Craigie, *Asloan MS*.

A few other MSS in which particular poems appear are recorded in the *Index* (DuW 55, 75, 130, 151-2, 159, 181-4, 189). There are no surviving autographs of Dunbar.

The only other early textual source is 'the Chepman and Myllar Prints'. This is a collection of printed tracts, the only extant but imperfect exemplum of which is preserved in the National Library of Scotland. The first nine of the tracts, which include seven poems at present attributed to Dunbar, were printed in Edinburgh in or about the year 1508 by Walter Chepman and Androw Myllar. The collection was reprinted in Stevenson (1918) and reproduced in facsimile in *The Chepman and Myllar Prints,* ed. William Beattie (Edinburgh Bibliographical Society, 1950). Otherwise, so far as is known, Dunbar's poems were not printed until the 18th century, when Scottish anthologists like Allan Ramsay, Lord Hailes, and John Pinkerton published selections from the MS sources (details are not included in the *Index*).

No collected edition of Dunbar's poems has appeared since Mackenzie (1932), although they are currently being re-edited by Professor James Kinsley of the University of Nottingham. Mackenzie's edition should be used in conjunction with the STS edition by John Small. The canon accepted in the *Index* is based on Mackenzie, and titles and first lines are cited from that work. It should be noted that when Mackenzie 'printed from' any of the main MSS he was, in fact, using the editions of these texts noted above.

A few additional transcripts of poems by Dunbar made in 1793 and afterwards by Joseph Ritson, George Chalmers, and David Laing can be found in Edinburgh University Library (MS La. III. 476).

PB.

ARRANGEMENT

Verse DuW 1-196.

William Dunbar

VERSE

DuW 1 *Advice to Spend anis Awin Gude* ('Man, sen thy lyfe is ay in weir').

Copy, untitled, in the Bannatyne MS; c. 1568.

Printed from this MS in Mackenzie, No. 72, pp. 147-8; Murdoch, III, 383-4; Ritchie, III, 11-13.

National Library of Scotland, Adv. MS 1. 1. 6, Vol. I, f. 136r-v (pp. 331-2).

DuW 2 -----

Copy, untitled, in the Maitland Folio MS; c. 1570-85.

Printed from this MS in Craigie, I, 253-4; collated in Mackenzie, p. 223.

Magdalene College, Cambridge, Pepys Library, MS 2553, pp. 225-6.

DuW 3 *Aganis the Solistaris in Court* ('Be divers wyis and operatiounes').

Copy in the Maitland Folio MS; c. 1570-85.

Printed from this MS in Mackenzie, No. 29, pp. 55-6; Craigie, I, 7.

Magdalene College, Cambridge, Pepys Library, MS 2553, p. 8.

DuW 4 -----

Second copy in the Maitland Folio MS; c. 1570-85.

Printed from this MS in Craigie, I, 377-8; collated in Mackenzie, p. 209.

Magdalene College, Cambridge, Pepys Library, MS 2553, p. 316.

DuW 5 -----

Copy in the Reidpeth MS; 1622-3.

This MS collated in Craigie, II, 37.

Cambridge University Library, MS Ll. 5. 10, f. 10.

DuW 6 *All Erdly Joy Returnis in Pane* ('Off lentren in the first mornyng').

Copy, untitled, in the Bannatyne MS; c. 1568.

Printed from this MS in Mackenzie, No. 71, pp. 145-6; Murdoch, II, 131-2; Ritchie, II, 121-2.

National Library of Scotland, Adv. MS 1. 1. 6, Vol. I, f. 48v (p. 156).

DuW 7 -----

Copy, untitled, in the Maitland Folio MS; c. 1570-85.

Printed from this MS in Craigie, I, 382-3; collated in Mackenzie, p. 223.

Magdalene College, Cambridge, Pepys Library, MS 2553, pp. 319-20.

DuW 8 *The Amendis to the Telyouris and Sowtaris for the Turnament Maid on Thame* ('Betuix twell houris and ellevin').

Copy in the Bannatyne MS; c. 1568.

Printed from this MS in Mackenzie, No. 59, pp. 126-7; Murdoch, II, 319-21; Ritchie, II, 298-300.

National Library of Scotland, Adv. MS 1. 1. 6, ff. 112v-13 (pp. 284-5).

DuW 9 -----

Copy, subscribed 'quhone he drank to ye Dekynnis ffor amendis to ye bodeis of thair craftis', in the Maitland Folio MS; c. 1570-85.

Printed from this MS in Craigie, I, 378-9; collated in Mackenzie, p. 220.

Magdalene College, Cambridge, Pepys Library, MS 2553, p. 317.

DuW 10 *Ane His Awin Ennemy* ('He that hes gold and grit riches').

Copy, untitled, in the Bannatyne MS; c. 1568.

Printed from this MS in Mackenzie, No. 2, pp. 2-3; Murdoch, II, 329-30; Ritchie, II, 308-9.

National Library of Scotland, Adv. MS 1. 1. 6, Vol. I, ff. 115v-16 (pp. 290-1).

DuW 11 -----

Copy, untitled, in the Maitland Folio MS; c. 1570-85.

Printed from this MS in Craigie, I, 239-40.

Magdalene College, Cambridge, Pepys Library, MS 2553, pp. 212-13.

DuW 12 *The Ballad of Kynd Kittok* ('My gudame wes a gay wif, bot scho wes ryght gend').

Copy, untitled, in the Bannatyne MS; c. 1568.

The Ballad of Kynd Kittok

First pub. in the Chepman and Myllar Prints (Edinburgh, 1508); Mackenzie, No. 85, pp. 169-70. Printed from this MS in Murdoch, III, 382-3; Ritchie, III, 10-11; collated in Mackenzie, pp. 227-8.

National Library of Scotland, Adv. MS 1. 1. 6, Vol. I, ff. 135v-6 (pp. 330-1).

DuW 13 *Ane Ballat of Our Lady* ('Hale, sterne superne! Hale, in eterne').

Copy in the Asloan MS; c. 1515.

Printed from this MS in Mackenzie, No. 82, pp. 160-2; Craigie, *The Asloan MS*, II, 275-8.

National Library of Scotland, [MS Acc. 4233], ff. 303-4v.

DuW 14 *Best to be Blyth* ('Full oft I mus and hes in thocht').

Copy, untitled, in the Bannatyne MS; c. 1568.

Printed from this MS in Mackenzie, No. 69, pp. 143-4; Murdoch, II, 281-2; Ritchie, II, 260-1.

National Library of Scotland, Adv. MS 1. 1. 6, Vol. I, f. 98v (p. 258).

DuW 15 -----

Copy of lines 1-9, deleted and untitled, in the Bannatyne MS; c. 1568.

Printed from this MS in Murdoch, II, 329; Ritchie, II, 308.

National Library of Scotland, Adv. MS 1. 1. 6, Vol. I, f. 115v (p. 290).

DuW 16 -----

Copy, untitled, in the Maitland Folio MS; c. 1570-85.

Printed from this MS in Craigie, I, 410-11; collated in Mackenzie, p. 222.

Magdalene College, Cambridge, Pepys Library, MS 2553, p. 337.

DuW 17 -----

Copy, untitled, in the Reidpeth MS; 1622-3.

This MS collated in Craigie, II, 126.

Cambridge University Library, MS Ll. 5. 10, f. 43r-v.

DuW 18 *Bewty and the Presoneir* ('Sen that I am a presoneir').

Copy, untitled, in the Bannatyne MS; c. 1568.

Printed from this MS in Mackenzie, No. 54, pp. 104-7; Murdoch, III, 607-10; Ritchie, III, 249-52.

National Library of Scotland, Adv. MS 1. 1. 6, Vol. II, ff. 214-15 (pp. 487-9).

DuW 19 -----

Copy of lines 1-16, untitled, in the Reidpeth MS; 1622-3.

Printed from this MS in Craigie, II, 58; collated in Mackenzie, p. 218.

Cambridge University Library, MS Ll. 5. 10, f. 8.

DuW 20 *The Birth of Antichrist* ('Lucina schynnyng in silence of the nicht').

Copy, untitled, in the Bannatyne MS; c. 1568.

Printed from this MS in Mackenzie, No. 39, pp. 70-1; Murdoch, III, 375-7; Ritchie, III, 4-5.

National Library of Scotland, Adv. MS 1. 1. 6, Vol. I, ff. 133-4 (pp. 325-7).

DuW 21 -----

Copy, untitled, in the Maitland Folio MS; c. 1570-85.

Printed from this MS in Craigie, I, 405-7; collated in Mackenzie, p. 213.

Magdalene College, Cambridge, Pepys Library, MS 2553, pp. 334-5.

DuW 22 -----

Copy, untitled, in the Reidpeth MS; 1622-3.

This MS collated in Craigie, II, 126.

Cambridge University Library, MS Ll. 5. 10, ff. 42v-3.

DuW 23 *Complaint to the King* ('Complane I wald, wist I quhome till').

Copy, untitled, in the Maitland Folio MS; c. 1570-85.

Printed from this MS in Mackenzie, No. 19, pp. 39-41; Craigie, I, 17-19.

Magdalene College, Cambridge, Pepys Library, MS 2553, pp. 16-18.

DuW 24 -----

Copy, untitled, in the Reidpeth MS; 1622-3.

This MS collated in Craigie, II, 39; Mackenzie, p. 206.

Complaint to the King

Cambridge University Library, MS Ll. 5. 10, ff. 13v-14.

DuW 25 *Complaint to the King Aganis Mure* ('Schir, I complane off injuris').

Copy, untitled, in the Maitland Folio MS; c. 1570-85.

Printed from this MS in Mackenzie, No. 5, p. 5; Craigie, I, 10.

Magdalene College, Cambridge, Pepys Library, MS 2553, pp. 10-11.

DuW 26 -----

Copy, untitled, in the Reidpeth MS; 1622-3.

This MS collated in Craigie, II, 37.

Cambridge University Library, MS Ll. 5. 10, f. 11.

DuW 27 *The Dance of the Sevin Deidly Synnis* ('Off Februar the fyistene nycht').

Copy in the Bannatyne MS; c. 1568.

Printed from this MS in Mackenzie, No. 57, pp. 120-3; Murdoch, II, 312-15; Ritchie, II, 291-4.

National Library of Scotland, Adv. MS 1. 1. 6, Vol. I, ff. 110-11 (pp. 279-81).

DuW 28 -----

Copy, untitled, in the Maitland Folio MS; imperfect; c. 1570-85.

Printed from this MS in Craigie, I, 12-16 (with a facsimile of p. 14); recorded in Mackenzie, pp. 219-20.

Magdalene College, Cambridge, Pepys Library, MS 2553, pp. 12-16.

DuW 29 -----

Copy of lines 1-12, 109-20, untitled and prefixed to *The Sowtar and Tailyouris War* (see DuW 154), in the Maitland Folio MS; c. 1570-85.

Printed from this MS in Craigie, I, 183.

Magdalene College, Cambridge, Pepys Library, MS 2553, pp. 161-2.

DuW 30 -----

Copy, untitled, in the Reidpeth MS; 1622-3.

This MS collated in Craigie, II, 38-9.

Cambridge University Library, MS Ll. 5. 10, ff. 11v-13.

DuW 31 *The Devillis Inquest* ('This nycht in my sleip I wes agast').

Copy of a 17-stanza version, untitled, in the Bannatyne MS; c. 1568.

Edited from this MS in Mackenzie, No. 42, pp. 76-9 (see pp. 238-9); Murdoch, III, 372-5; Ritchie, III, 1-4.

National Library of Scotland, Adv. MS 1. 1. 6, Vol. I, ff. 132v-3 (pp. 324-5).

DuW 32 -----

Copy of a 13-stanza version, untitled and beginning 'Dremand me thocht that I did heir', in the Maitland Folio MS; c. 1570-85.

Edited from this MS in Mackenzie (see pp. 238-9); Craigie, I, 62-4.

Magdalene College, Cambridge, Pepys Library, MS 2553, pp. 55-7.

DuW 33 -----

Copy of a 13-stanza version, untitled and beginning 'Dremand me thocht that I did heir', in the Reidpeth MS; 1622-3.

This MS collated in Craigie, II, 64-5.

Cambridge University Library, MS Ll. 5. 10, ff. 18v-19.

DuW 34 *The Dream* ('This hinder nycht, halff sleiping as I lay').

Copy, untitled, in the Reidpeth MS; 1622-3.

Printed from this MS in Mackenzie, No. 60, pp. 127-30; Craigie, II, 46-50.

Cambridge University Library, MS Ll. 5. 10, ff. 3v-5.

DuW 35 *The Dregy of Dunbar* ('We that ar heir in hevins glory').

Copy in the Bannatyne MS; c. 1568.

Printed from this MS in Mackenzie, No. 30, pp. 56-9; Murdoch, II, 292-6; Ritchie, II, 271-5.

National Library of Scotland, Adv. MS 1. 1. 6, Vol. I, ff. 102-3v (pp. 265-8).

DuW 36 -----

Copy, subscribed 'Dumbaris dirige to ye king', in the Maitland Folio MS; c. 1570-85.

Printed from this MS in Craigie, I, 337-41; collated in Mackenzie, pp. 209-10.

Magdalene College, Cambridge, Pepys Library, MS 2553, pp. 290-2.

The Dregy of Dunbar

DuW 37 -----

Copy, subscribed 'Dumbaris dirige to ye king', in the Reidpeth MS; 1622-3.

This MS collated in Craigie, II, 116.

Cambridge University Library, MS Ll. 5. 10, ff. 55v-6v.

DuW 38 *Dunbar at Oxinfurde* ('To speik of science, craft, or sapience').

Copy in the Maitland Folio MS; c. 1570-85.

Printed from this MS in Mackenzie, No. 53, p. 104; Craigie, I, 9.

Magdalene College, Cambridge, Pepys Library, MS 2553, pp. 9-10.

DuW 39 -----

Second copy in the Maitland Folio MS; c. 1570-85.

Printed from this MS in Mackenzie; Craigie, I, 379-80.

Magdalene College, Cambridge, Pepys Library, MS 2553, pp. 317-18.

DuW 40 -----

Copy in the Reidpeth MS; 1622-3.

This MS collated in Craigie, II, 37.

Cambridge University Library, MS Ll. 5. 10, f. 10v.

DuW 41 *Elegy on the Death of Bernard Stewart, Lord of Aubigny* ('Illuster Lodovick, of France most Cristin king').

Copy, untitled, in the Reidpeth MS; 1622-3.

Printed from this MS in Mackenzie, No. 62, pp. 133-4; Craigie, II, 54-5.

Cambridge University Library, MS Ll. 5. 10, ff. 6v-7.

DuW 42 *Epetaphe for Donald Owre* ('In vice most vicius he excellis').

Copy in the Bannatyne MS; c. 1568.

Printed from this MS in Mackenzie, No. 36, pp. 65-6; Ritchie, I, 87-8 (with a facsimile of p. 53).

National Library of Scotland, Adv. MS 1. 1. 6, Vol. I, pp. 53-4.

DuW 43 -----

Copy, untitled, in the Maitland Folio MS; c. 1570-85.

Printed from this MS in Craigie, I, 11-12.

Magdalene College, Cambridge, Pepys Library, MS 2553, pp. 11-12.

DuW 44 -----

Copy, untitled, in the Reidpeth MS; 1622-3.

This MS collated in Craigie, II, 38.

Cambridge University Library, MS Ll. 5. 10, f. 11r-v.

DuW 45 *The Fenyeit Freir of Tungland* ('As yung Awrora, with cristall haile').

Copy in the Bannatyne MS; c. 1568.

Printed from this MS in Mackenzie, No. 38, pp. 67-70; Murdoch, II, 333-7; Ritchie, II, 311-15.

National Library of Scotland, Adv. MS 1. 1. 6, Vol. I, ff. 117-18v (pp. 293-6).

DuW 46 -----

Copy of lines 1-69 in the Asloan MS; c. 1515.

Printed from this MS in Craigie, *The Asloan MS*, II, 92-4; collated in Mackenzie, p. 212.

National Library of Scotland, [MS Acc. 4233], ff. 211v-12v.

DuW 47 *The Flyting of Dunbar and Kennedie* ('Schir Johine the Ros, ane thing thair is compild').

Copy of lines 1-315 in the Bannatyne MS; c. 1568.

First pub. in the Chepman and Myllar Prints (Edinburgh, 1508); Mackenzie, No. 6, pp. 5-20. Printed from this MS in Murdoch, III, 420-37; Ritchie, III, 44-62; lines 1-315 printed from this MS in Mackenzie.

National Library of Scotland, Adv. MS 1. 1. 6, Vol. I, ff. 147-54 (pp. 353-61).

DuW 48 -----

Copy, untitled, in the Maitland Folio MS; imperfect; c. 1570-85.

Printed from this MS in Craigie, I, 71-88; collated in Mackenzie, pp. 198-201.

Magdalene College, Cambridge, Pepys Library, MS 2533, pp. 53-4, 59-63, 69-70, 77-80.

The Flyting of Dunbar and Kennedie

DuW 49 -----

Copy, untitled, in the Reidpeth MS; 1622-3.

This MS collated in Craigie, II, 69-70.

Cambridge University Library, MS Ll. 5. 10, ff. 58-65.

DuW 50 *The Freiris of Berwick* ('At Tweidis mowth thair standis a nobill toun').

Copy in the Bannatyne MS; c. 1568.

Of doubtful authorship. Printed from this MS in Mackenzie, No. 93, pp. 182-95; Murdoch, IV, 1004-20; Ritchie, IV, 261-77.

National Library of Scotland, Adv. MS 1. 1. 6, Vol. II, ff. 348v-54v (pp. 746-58).

DuW 51 -----

Copy in the Maitland Folio MS; c. 1570-85.

Printed from this MS in Craigie, I, 133-48; collated in Mackenzie, pp. 231-4.

Magdalene College, Cambridge, Pepys Library, MS 2553, pp. 113-29.

DuW 52 *A General Satyre* ('Doverrit with dreme, devysing in my slummer').

Copy, untitled, in the Bannatyne MS; c. 1568.

Of doubtful authorship. Printed from this MS in Mackenzie, No. 77, pp. 151-3; Murdoch, II, 162-5; Ritchie, II, 147-50.

National Library of Scotland, Adv. MS 1. 1. 6, Vol. I, ff. 60-1 (pp. 181-3).

DuW 53 -----

Copy, untitled, in the Bannatyne MS; c. 1568.

Printed from this MS in Ritchie, I, 79-82.

National Library of Scotland, Adv. MS 1. 1. 6, Vol. I, pp. 47-8.

DuW 54 -----

Copy, untitled, in the Maitland Folio MS; c. 1570-85.

Printed from this MS in Craigie, I, 211-13; collated in Mackenzie, pp. 224-6.

Magdalene College, Cambridge, Pepys Library, MS 2553, pp. 187-9.

DuW 55 *'Gladethe thoue Queyne of Scottis regioun'.*

Copy written on a blank page between two deeds dated 25 October 1505 and 28 March 1506 in a Minute Book of Sasines in Aberdeen, 1501-4, Vol. II.

Printed from this MS in Mackenzie, No. 90, pp. 179-80. A transcript made for David Laing by R. Stephens (1835) is in Edinburgh University Library, MS La. III. 476.

Corporation Charter Room, Aberdeen.

DuW 56 *The Goldyn Targe* ('Ryght as the stern of day begouth to schyne').

Copy in the Bannatyne MS; c. 1568.

First pub. in the Chepman and Myllar Prints (Edinburgh, 1508); Mackenzie, No. 56, pp. 112-19. Printed from this MS in Murdoch, IV, 995-1003; Ritchie, IV, 252-61; recorded in Mackenzie, pp. 218-19. Facsimile of f. 345 in Small, I, at the end.

National Library of Scotland, Adv. MS 1. 1. 6, Vol. II, ff. 345-8v (pp. 739-46).

DuW 57 -----

Copy in the Maitland Folio MS; imperfect; c. 1570-85.

Printed from this MS in Craigie, I, 89-97; recorded in Mackenzie, pp. 218-19.

Magdalene College, Cambridge, Pepys Library, MS 2553, pp. 64-6, 73-6, 81.

DuW 58 *Gude Counsale* ('Be ye ane luvar, think ye nocht ye suld').

Copy, untitled, in the Bannatyne MS; c. 1568.

Printed from this MS in Mackenzie, No. 68, pp. 142-3; Murdoch, III, 602-3; Ritchie, III, 244-5.

National Library of Scotland, Adv. MS 1. 1. 6, Vol. II, f. 212v (p. 484).

DuW 59 *How Dumbar wes Desyrd to be Ane Freir* ('This nycht, befoir the dawing cleir').

Copy in the Bannatyne MS; c. 1568.

Printed from this MS in Mackenzie, No. 4, pp. 3-4; Murdoch, II, 327-8; Ritchie, II, 306-7.

National Library of Scotland, Adv. MS 1. 1. 6, Vol. I, f. 115r-v (pp. 289-90).

DuW 60 -----

Copy of lines 1-20, 26-50, in the Maitland Folio MS; c. 1570-85.

Printed from this MS in Craigie, I, 404-5; collated in Mackenzie, p. 197.

Magdalene College, Cambridge, Pepys Library, MS 2553, pp. 333-4.

DuW 61 -----

Copy of lines 1-20, 26-50, untitled, in the Reidpeth MS; 1622-3.

This MS collated in Craigie, II, 126.

Cambridge University Library, MS Ll. 5. 10, f. 42r-v.

DuW 62 *How Sall I Governe Me?* ('How sould I rewill me or in quhat wys').

Copy, untitled, in the Bannatyne MS; c. 1568.

Mackenzie, No. 9, pp. 24-6. Printed from this MS in Murdoch, II, 178-80; Ritchie, II, 162-3; collated in Mackenzie, p. 203.

National Library of Scotland, Adv. MS 1. 1. 6, Vol. I, ff. 65v-6v (pp. 192-4).

DuW 63 -----

Copy, untitled, in the Maitland Folio MS; c. 1570-85.

Printed from this MS in Mackenzie; Craigie, I, 388-9.

Magdalene College, Cambridge, Pepys Library, MS 2553, pp. 323-4.

DuW 64 -----

Copy, untitled, in the Reidpeth MS; 1622-3.

This MS collated in Craigie, II, 123.

Cambridge University Library, MS Ll. 5. 10, f. 38r-v.

DuW 65 *In Prais of Wemen* ('Now of wemen this I say for me').

Copy, untitled, in the Bannatyne MS; c. 1568.

Printed from this MS in Mackenzie, No. 45, pp. 83-4; Murdoch, IV, 809-10; Ritchie, IV, 75-6.

National Library of Scotland, Adv. MS 1. 1. 6, Vol. II, f. 278v (p. 612).

DuW 66 -----

Copy, here beginning 'Off women now this I say for me', in the Maitland Folio MS; c. 1570-85.

Printed from this MS in Craigie, I, 345; collated in Mackenzie, p. 215.

Magdalene College, Cambridge, Pepys Library, MS 2553, pp. 294-5.

DuW 67 *'In secreit place this hyndir nycht'*.

Copy in the Bannatyne MS; c. 1568.

Mackenzie, No. 28, pp. 53-5. Printed from this MS in Murdoch, II, 296-8; Ritchie, II, 275-7; collated in Mackenzie, pp. 208-9.

National Library of Scotland, Adv. MS 1. 1. 6, Vol. I, ff. 103v-4 (pp. 268-9).

DuW 68 -----

Copy, untitled, in the Maitland Folio MS; c. 1570-85.

Printed from this MS in Mackenzie; Craigie, I, 368-70.

Magdalene College, Cambridge, Pepys Library, MS 2553, pp. 308, 311.

DuW 69 -----

Copy, untitled, in the Reidpeth MS; 1622-3.

This MS collated in Craigie, II, 121.

Cambridge University Library, MS Ll. 5. 10, ff. 34v-5.

DuW 70 *Inconstancy of Luve* ('Quha will behald of luve the chance').

Copy, untitled, in the Bannatyne MS; c. 1568.

Printed from this MS in Mackenzie, No. 51, pp. 100-1; Murdoch, IV, 816; Ritchie, IV, 81-2.

National Library of Scotland, Adv. MS 1. 1. 6, Vol. II, f. 281 (p. 617).

DuW 71 *Lament for the Makaris* ('I that in heill wes and gladnes').

Copy, untitled, in the Bannatyne MS; c. 1568.

First pub. in the Chepman and Myllar Prints (Edinburgh, 1508); Mackenzie, No. 7, pp. 20-3. Printed from this MS in Murdoch, II, 308-11; Ritchie, II, 287-91; collated in Mackenzie, pp. 202-3.

National Library of Scotland, Adv. MS 1. 1. 6, Vol. I, ff. 109-10 (pp. 277-9).

DuW 72 -----

Copy, untitled, in the Maitland Folio MS; c. 1570-85.

Lament for the Makaris

Printed from this MS in Craigie, I, 214-17; collated in Mackenzie, pp. 202-3.

Magdalene College, Cambridge, Pepys Library, MS 2553, pp. 189-92.

DuW 73 *The Manere of the Crying of ane Playe* ('Harry, harry, hobbillschowe!').

Copy, headed 'Ane littill Interlud of the Droichis Part of the [Play]', in the Bannatyne MS; c. 1568.

Mackenzie, No. 86, pp. 170-4. Printed from this MS in Murdoch, II, 337-41; Ritchie, II, 315-20; collated in Mackenzie, pp. 228-30.

National Library of Scotland, Adv. MS 1. 1. 6, Vol. I, ff. 118v-20 (pp. 296-9).

DuW 74 -----

Copy of lines 1-165 in the Asloan MS; c. 1515.

Printed from this MS in Mackenzie; Craigie, *The Asloan MS*, III, 149-54.

National Library of Scotland, [MS Acc. 4233], ff. 240-2v.

DuW 75 *The Maner of Passing to Confessioun* ('O synfull man, thir ar the fourty dayis').

Copy in a Scottish miscellany of devotional verse and prose; c. 1530s.

Printed from this MS in Mackenzie, No. 84, pp. 167-9; Bennett, pp. 257-9.

British Library, Arundel MS 285, ff. 161-2v.

DuW 76 *Meditatioun in Wyntir* ('In to thir dirk and drublie dayis').

Copy, untitled, in the Maitland Folio MS; c. 1570-85.

Printed from this MS in Mackenzie, No. 10, pp. 26-7; Craigie, I, 380-2.

Magdalene College, Cambridge, Pepys Library, MS 2553, pp. 318-19.

DuW 77 -----

Copy of lines 23-50, untitled and here beginning 'And lat fortoune wirk furthe hir rage', in the Maitland Folio MS; c. 1570-85.

Printed from this MS in Craigie, I, 1-2; recorded in Mackenzie, p. 203.

Magdalene College, Cambridge, Pepys Library, MS 2553, p. 3.

DuW 78 -----

Copy of lines 1-22, untitled, in the Reidpeth MS; 1622-3.

Printed from this MS in Craigie, II, 34-5; recorded in Mackenzie, p. 203.

Cambridge University Library, MS Ll. 5. 10, f. 1.

DuW 79 *The Merle and the Nychtingaill* ('In May as that Aurora did upspring').

Copy, untitled, in the Bannatyne MS; c. 1568.

Printed from this MS in Mackenzie, No. 63, pp. 134-7; Murdoch, IV, 822-6; Ritchie, IV, 87-91.

National Library of Scotland, Adv. MS 1. 1. 6, Vol. II, ff. 283-4v (pp. 621-4).

DuW 80 -----

Copy of lines 1-16, 33-120, untitled, in the Maitland Folio MS; c. 1570-85.

Printed from this MS in Craigie, I, 188-91; collated in Mackenzie, pp. 221-2.

Magdalene College, Cambridge, Pepys Library, MS 2553, pp. 165-8.

DuW 81 *A New Year's Gift to the King* ('My Prince, in God gif the guid grace').

Copy, untitled, in the Reidpeth MS; 1622-3.

Printed from this MS in Mackenzie, No. 26, p. 51; Craigie, II, 44-5.

Cambridge University Library, MS Ll. 5. 10, ff. 2v-3.

DuW 82 *No Tressour Availis without Glaidnes* ('Be mirry, man! and tak nocht far in mynd').

Copy, headed 'Hermes the Philosopher', in the Bannatyne MS; c. 1568.

Printed from this MS in Mackenzie, No. 73, pp. 148-9; Murdoch, II, 279-80; Ritchie, II, 259-60.

National Library of Scotland, Adv. MS 1. 1. 6, Vol. I, ff. 97v-8v (pp. 256-8).

DuW 83 -----

Copy, untitled, in the Maitland Folio MS; c. 1570-85.

Printed from this MS in Craigie, I, 249-50; collated in Mackenzie, pp. 223-4.

Magdalene College, Cambridge, Pepys Library, MS 2553, pp. 221-2.

DuW 84 *None May Assure in this Warld* ('Quhom to sall I compleine my wo').

Copy, untitled, in the Bannatyne MS; c. 1568.

Mackenzie, No. 21, pp. 44-6. Printed from this MS in Murdoch, II, 234-6; Ritchie, II, 215-17 (with a facsimile of f. 84v); collated in Mackenzie, p. 207.

National Library of Scotland, Adv. MS 1. 1. 6, Vol. I, ff. 84-5 (pp. 229-31).

DuW 85 -----

Copy, untitled, in the Maitland Folio MS; c. 1570-85.

Printed from this MS in Mackenzie; Craigie, I, 401-3.

Magdalene College, Cambridge, Pepys Library, MS 2553, pp. 331-3.

DuW 86 -----

Copy, untitled, in the Reidpeth MS; 1622-3.

This MS collated in Craigie, II, 125-6.

Cambridge University Library, MS Ll. 5. 10, ff. 40v-2.

DuW 87 *Of a Dance in the Quenis Chalmer* ('Sir Jhon Sinclair begowthe to dance').

Copy in the Maitland Folio MS; c. 1570-85.

Printed from this MS in Mackenzie, No. 32, pp. 60-1; Craigie, I, 415-16.

Magdalene College, Cambridge, Pepys Library, MS 2553, pp. 340-1.

DuW 88 -----

Copy in the Reidpeth MS; 1622-3.

This MS collated in Craigie, II, 128.

Cambridge University Library, MS Ll. 5. 10, f. 45r-v.

DuW 89 *Of Ane Blak-Moir* ('Lang heff I maed of ladyes quhytt').

Copy in the Maitland Folio MS; c. 1570-85.

Printed from this MS in Mackenzie, No. 37, pp. 66-7; Craigie, I, 416-17.

Magdalene College, Cambridge, Pepys Library, MS 2553, pp. 341-2.

DuW 90 -----

Copy in the Reidpeth MS; 1622-3.

This MS collated in Craigie, II, 128.

Cambridge University Library, MS Ll. 5. 10, ff. 45v-6.

DuW 91 *Of Content* ('Quho thinkis that he hes sufficence').

Copy, untitled, in the Maitland Folio MS; c. 1570-85.

Printed from this MS in Mackenzie, No. 70, pp. 144-5; Craigie, I, 366-7.

Magdalene College, Cambridge, Pepys Library, MS 2553, p. 307.

DuW 92 -----

Copy, untitled, in the Reidpeth MS; 1622-3.

Printed from this MS in Craigie, II, 50-1; collated in Mackenzie, p. 223.

Cambridge University Library, MS Ll. 5. 10, f. 5r-v.

DuW 93 *Of Covetyce* ('Fredome, honour, and nobilnes').

Copy, untitled, in the Bannatyne MS; c. 1568.

Printed from this MS in Mackenzie, No. 67, pp. 141-2; Murdoch, II, 175-6; Ritchie, II, 159-60.

National Library of Scotland, Adv. MS 1. 1. 6, Vol. I, ff. 64v-5 (pp. 190-1).

DuW 94 -----

Copy, untitled, in the Maitland Folio MS; imperfect; c. 1570-85.

Printed from this MS in Craigie, I, 5-6; collated in Mackenzie, p. 222.

Magdalene College, Cambridge, Pepys Library, MS 2553, pp. 6-7.

DuW 95 -----

Copy, untitled, in the Reidpeth MS; 1622-3.

This MS collated in Craigie, II, 36.

Cambridge University Library, MS Ll. 5. 10, f. 9r-v.

DuW 96 *Of Deming* ('Musing allone this hinder nicht').

Copy, untitled, in the Bannatyne MS; c. 1568.

Of doubtful authorship. Printed from this MS in Mackenzie, No. 8, pp. 23-4; Murdoch, II, 171-3; Ritchie, II, 156-7.

National Library of Scotland, Adv. MS 1. 1. 6, Vol. I, ff. 63v-4 (pp. 188-9).

Of Deming

DuW 97 -----

Copy, untitled and lacking lines 26-30, in the Maitland Folio MS; c. 1570-85.

Printed from this MS in Craigie, I, 191-3; collated in Mackenzie, p. 203.

Magdalene College, Cambridge, Pepys Library, MS 2553, pp. 168-70.

DuW 98 -----

Copy, untitled, in the Maitland Folio MS; c. 1570-85.

Printed from this MS in Craigie, I, 372-4; collated in Mackenzie, p. 203.

Magdalene College, Cambridge, Pepys Library, MS 2553, pp. 313-14.

DuW 99 *Of Discretioun in Asking* ('Off very asking followis nocht').

Copy, untitled, in the Bannatyne MS; c. 1568.

Printed from this MS in Mackenzie, No. 14, pp. 31-3; Murdoch, II, 165-7; Ritchie, II, 150-2.

National Library of Scotland, Adv. MS 1. 1. 6, Vol. I, f. 61r-v (pp. 183-4).

DuW 100 -----

Copy, untitled, in the Bannatyne MS; c. 1568.

Printed from this MS in Ritchie, I, 76-7.

National Library of Scotland, Adv. MS 1. 1. 6, Vol. I, pp. 45-6.

DuW 101 -----

Copy, untitled, in the Maitland Folio MS; c. 1570-85.

Printed from this MS in Craigie, I, 289-90; recorded in Mackenzie, p. 204.

Magdalene College, Cambridge, Pepys Library, MS 2553, pp. 259-60.

DuW 102 -----

Copy, untitled, in the Reidpeth MS; 1622-3.

This MS collated in Craigie, II, 110.

Cambridge University Library, MS Ll. 5. 10, ff. 21r-v.

DuW 103 *Of Discretioun in Geving* ('To Speik of gift or almous deidis').

Copy in the Bannatyne MS; c. 1568.

Printed from this MS in Mackenzie, No. 15, pp. 33-4; Murdoch, II, 167-9; Ritchie, II, 152-4.

National Library of Scotland, Adv. MS 1. 1. 6, Vol. I, ff. 61v-2v (pp. 184-6).

DuW 104 -----

Copy in the Bannatyne MS; imperfect at the end; c. 1568.

Printed from this MS in Ritchie, I, 77-8.

National Library of Scotland, Adv. MS 1. 1. 6, Vol. I, p. 46.

DuW 105 -----

Copy, immediately following on from *Of Discretioun in Asking* (see DuW 101), in the Maitland Folio MS; c. 1570-85.

Printed from this MS in Craigie, I, 290-2; collated in Mackenzie, pp. 204-5.

Magdalene College, Cambridge, Pepys Library, MS 2553, pp. 260-1.

DuW 106 -----

Copy, immediately following on from *Of Discretioun in Asking* (see DuW 102), in the Reidpeth MS; 1622-3.

This MS collated in Craigie, II, 110.

Cambridge University Library, MS Ll. 5. 10, ff. 21v-2v.

DuW 107 *Of Discretioun in Taking* ('Eftir Geving I speik of taking').

Copy in the Bannatyne MS; c. 1568.

Printed from this MS in Mackenzie, No. 16, pp. 35-6; Murdoch, II, 170-1; Ritchie, II, 154-5.

National Library of Scotland, Adv. MS 1. 1. 6, Vol. I, ff. 62v-3 (pp. 186-7).

DuW 108 -----

Copy, immediately following on from *Of Discretioun in Geving* (see DuW 105), in the Maitland Folio MS; c. 1570-85.

Printed from this MS in Craigie, I, 292-4; collated in Mackenzie, p. 205.

Magdalene College, Cambridge, Pepys Library, MS 2553, pp. 261-2.

DuW 109 -----

Copy, immediately following on from *Of*

Discretioun in Geving (see DuW 106), in the Reidpeth MS; 1622-3.

This MS collated in Craigie, II, 110.

Cambridge University Library, MS Ll. 5. 10, ff. 22v-3.

DuW 110 *Of Folkis Evill to Pleis* ('Four Maner of folkis ar evill to pleis').

Copy, untitled, in the Bannatyne MS; c. 1568.

Mackenzie, No. 23, pp. 48-9. Printed from this MS in Murdoch, II, 180-1; Ritchie, II, 163-4; recorded in Mackenzie, p. 208.

National Library of Scotland, Adv. MS 1. 1. 6, Vol. I. f. 66v (p. 194).

DuW 111 -----

Copy in the Bannatyne MS; imperfect at the beginning; c. 1568.

Printed from this MS in Ritchie, I, 78-9.

National Library of Scotland, Adv. MS 1. 1. 6, Vol. I, p. 47.

DuW 112 -----

Copy, untitled, in the Reidpeth MS; 1622-3.

Printed from this MS in Mackenzie; Craigie, II, 45-6.

Cambridge University Library, MS Ll. 5. 10, f. 3r-v.

DuW 113 *Of James Dog, Kepar of the Quenis Wardrop* ('The wardraipper of Venus boure').

Copy in the Maitland Folio MS; c. 1570-85.

Printed from this MS in Mackenzie, No. 33, pp. 61-2; Craigie, I, 413.

Magdalene College, Cambridge, Pepys Library, MS 2553, p. 339.

DuW 114 -----

Copy in the Reidpeth MS; 1622-3.

This MS collated in Craigie, II, 127.

Cambridge University Library, MS Ll. 5. 10, f. 44r-v.

DuW 115 *Of Luve Erdly and Divine* ('Now culit is Dame Venus brand').

Copy, untitled, in the Bannatyne MS; c. 1568.

Printed from this MS in Mackenzie, No. 52, pp. 101-4; Murdoch, IV, 826-9; Ritchie, IV, 91-4.

National Library of Scotland, Adv. MS 1. 1. 6, Vol. II, ff. 284v-5v (pp. 624-6).

DuW 116 *Of Lyfe* ('Quhat is this lyfe bot ane straucht way to deid').

Copy, untitled, in the Maitland Folio MS; c. 1570-85.

Printed from this MS in Mackenzie, No. 76, p. 151; Craigie, I, 350.

Magdalene College, Cambridge, Pepys Library, MS 2553, p. 310.

DuW 117 *Of Manis Mortalitie* ('Memento, homo, quod cinis es!').

Copy, untitled, in the Bannatyne MS; c. 1568.

Printed from this MS in Mackenzie, No. 74, pp. 149-50; Murdoch, II, 127-9; Ritchie, II, 117-19.

National Library of Scotland, Adv. MS 1. 1. 6, Vol. I, f. 47r-v (pp. 153-4).

DuW 118 -----

Copy, untitled, in the Maitland Folio MS; c. 1570-85.

Printed from this MS in Craigie, I, 218-19; collated in Mackenzie, p. 224.

Magdalene College, Cambridge, Pepys Library, MS 2553, pp. 193-4.

DuW 119 *Of Sir Thomas Norny* ('Now lythis off ane gentill knycht').

Copy, untitled, in the Maitland Folio MS; imperfect; c. 1570-85.

Printed from this MS in Mackenzie, No. 35, pp. 63-4; Craigie, I, 2-4.

Magdalene College, Cambridge, Pepys Library, MS 2553, pp. 3-5.

DuW 120 -----

Copy, untitled, in the Reidpeth MS; 1622-3.

This MS collated in Craigie, II, 35-6.

Cambridge University Library, MS Ll. 5. 10, f. 8r-v.

DuW 121 *Of the Changes of Lyfe* ('I seik about this warld unstabille').

Copy, untitled, in the Maitland Folio MS;

Of the Changes of Lyfe

slightly imperfect; c. 1570-85.

Printed from this MS in Mackenzie, No. 66, pp. 140-1; Craigie, I, 4.

Magdalene College, Cambridge, Pepys Library, MS 2553, pp. 5-6.

DuW 122 -----

Second copy, untitled, in the Maitland Folio MS; c. 1570-85.

Printed from this MS in Craigie, I, 376; recorded in Mackenzie, p. 222.

Magdalene College, Cambridge, Pepys Library, MS 2553, p. 315.

DuW 123 -----

Copy, untitled, in the Reidpeth MS; 1622-3.

This MS collated in Craigie, II, 36; recorded in Mackenzie, p. 222.

Cambridge University Library, MS Ll. 5. 10, ff. 8v-9.

DuW 124 *Of the Ladys Solistaris at Court* ('Thir ladyis fair, That makis repair').

Copy, untitled, in the Bannatyne MS; c. 1568.

Printed from this MS in Mackenzie, No. 48, pp. 97-8; Murdoch, IV, 762-3; Ritchie, IV, 30-1.

National Library of Scotland, Adv. MS 1. 1. 6, Vol. II, f. 261r-v (p. 577).

DuW 125 -----

Copy, untitled, in the Maitland Folio MS; c. 1570-85.

Printed from this MS in Craigie, I, 390-1; text corrected from this MS in Mackenzie (p. 217).

Magdalene College, Cambridge, Pepys Library, MS 2553, pp. 324-5.

DuW 126 -----

Copy, untitled, in the Reidpeth MS; 1622-3.

This MS collated in Craigie, II, 123.

Cambridge University Library, MS Ll. 5. 10, ff. 38v-9.

DuW 127 *Of the Nativitie of Christ* ('Rorate celi desuper!').

Copy, untitled, in the Bannatyne MS; c. 1568.

Printed from this MS in Mackenzie, No. 79, pp. 154-5; Murdoch, II, 69-70; Ritchie, II, 65-6.

National Library of Scotland, Adv. MS 1. 1. 6, Vol. I, f. 27r-v (pp. 113-14).

DuW 128 *Of the Passioun of Christ* ('Amang thir freiris, within ane cloister').

Copy, untitled, in the Maitland Folio MS; c. 1570-85.

Printed from this MS in Mackenzie, No. 80, pp. 155-9; Craigie, I, 229-34.

Magdalene College, Cambridge, Pepys Library, MS 2553, pp. 203-7.

DuW 129 -----

Copy of lines 1-32, 41-96, headed 'ye passioun of Ihesu', in the Asloan MS; c. 1515.

Printed from this MS in Craigie, *The Asloan MS*, II, 242-5; recorded in Mackenzie, p. 226.

National Library of Scotland, [MS Acc. 4233], ff. 290v-2.

DuW 130 -----

Copy in a Scottish miscellany of devotional verse and prose; c. 1530s.

Printed from this MS in Bennett, pp. 266-9.

British Library, Arundel MS 285, ff. 168r-v, 171, 169, 170.

DuW 131 *Of the Said James, Quhen he had plesett him* ('O Gracious Princes, guid and fair').

Copy in the Maitland Folio MS; c. 1570-85.

Printed from this MS in Mackenzie, No. 34, pp. 62-3; Craigie, I, 414.

Magdalene College, Cambridge, Pepys Library, MS 2553, pp. 339-40.

DuW 132 -----

Copy in the Reidpeth MS; 1622-3.

This MS collated in Craigie, II, 127-8.

Cambridge University Library, MS Ll. 5. 10, f. 44v-5.

DuW 133 *Of the Warldis Instabilitie* ('This waverand warldis wretchidnes').

Copy, untitled, in the Maitland Folio MS;

Of the Warldis Instabilitie

c. 1570-85.

Printed from this MS in Mackenzie, No. 13, pp. 28-31; Craigie, I, 202-5.

Magdalene College, Cambridge, Pepys Library, MS 2553, pp. 178-81.

DuW 134 -----

Copy, untitled, in the Reidpeth MS; 1622-3.

This MS collated in Craigie, II, 101.

Cambridge University Library, MS Ll. 5. 10, ff. 27-8v.

DuW 135 *Of the Warldis Vanitie* ('O wreche, be war! this warld will wend the fro').

Copy, untitled, in the Maitland Folio MS; c. 1570-85.

Printed from this MS in Mackenzie, No. 75, pp. 150-1; Craigie, I, 221.

Magdalene College, Cambridge, Pepys Library, MS 2553, pp. 195-6.

DuW 136 *On His Heid-ake* ('My heid did yak yester nicht').

Copy, untitled, in the Reidpeth MS; 1622-3.

Printed from this MS in Mackenzie, No. 3, p. 3.

Cambridge University Library, MS Ll. 5. 10, f. 6.

DuW 137 *On the Resurrection of Christ* ('Done is a battel on the dragon blak').

Copy, untitled, in the Bannatyne MS; c. 1568.

Printed from this MS in Mackenzie, No. 81, pp. 159-60; Murdoch, II, 94-6; Ritchie, II, 88-9.

National Library of Scotland, Adv. MS 1. 1. 6, Vol. I, f. 35 (p. 129).

DuW 138 *Ane Orisoun* ('Salviour, suppois my sensualitie').

Copy, untitled, in the Maitland Folio MS; c. 1570-85.

Printed from this MS in Mackenzie, No. 78, p. 154; Craigie, I, 393.

Magdalene College, Cambridge, Pepys Library, MS 2553, p. 326.

DuW 139 -----

Copy, untitled, in the Reidpeth MS; 1622-3.

This MS collated in Craigie, II, 102.

Cambridge University Library, MS Ll. 5. 10, f. 40.

DuW 140 *The Petition of the Gray Horse, Auld Dunbar* ('Now Lufferis cummis with larges lowd').

Copy of lines 23-53, untitled and here beginning 'Schir lat It neuer In toume be tald', in the Maitland Folio MS; c. 1570-85.

Edited partly from this MS in Mackenzie, No. 22, pp. 46-8; printed in Craigie, I, 19-20.

Magdalene College, Cambridge, Pepys Library, MS 2553, p. 18.

DuW 141 -----

Copy, untitled, in the Reidpeth MS; 1622-3.

Edited partly from this MS in Mackenzie; collated in Craigie, II, 39-41.

Cambridge University Library, MS Ll. 5. 10, ff. 1r-v, 14r-v.

DuW 142 *Quhen the Governour Past in France* ('Thow that in hevin, for our salvatioun').

Copy in the Maitland Folio MS; c. 1570-85.

Printed from this MS in Mackenzie, No. 65, pp. 139-40; Craigie, I, 210-11.

Magdalene College, Cambridge, Pepys Library, MS 2553, pp. 186-7.

DuW 143 -----

Copy in the Reidpeth MS; 1622-3.

This MS recorded in Mackenzie, p. 222.

Cambridge University Library, MS Ll. 5. 10, ff. 28v-9.

DuW 144 *Quhone he List to Feyne* ('My hartis tresure, and swete assured so').

Copy in the Maitland Folio MS; c. 1570-85.

Printed from this MS in Mackenzie, No. 50, pp. 99-100; Craigie, I, 386-7.

Magdalene College, Cambridge, Pepys Library, MS 2553, pp. 322-3.

DuW 145 *Quhone Mony Benefices Vakit* ('Schir, at this feist of benefice').

Copy in the Maitland Folio MS; c. 1570-85.

Mackenzie, No. 11, pp. 27-8. Printed from this MS in Craigie, I, 6-7; recorded in Mackenzie, p. 203.

Magdalene College, Cambridge, Pepys Library, MS 2553, pp. 7-8.

Quhone Mony Benefices Vakit

DuW 146 -----

Copy in the Maitland Folio MS; c. 1570-85.

Printed from this MS in Mackenzie; Craigie, I, 376-7.

Magdalene College, Cambridge, Pepys Library, MS 2553, p. 316.

DuW 147 -----

Copy in the Reidpeth MS; 1622-3.

This MS collated in Craigie, II, 36.

Cambridge University Library, MS Ll. 5. 10, ff. 9v-10.

DuW 148 *Remonstrance to the King* ('Schir, ye have mony servitouris').

Copy, untitled, in the Maitland Folio MS; c. 1570-85.

Printed from this MS in Mackenzie, No. 17, pp. 36-8; Craigie, I, 222-4.

Magdalene College, Cambridge, Pepys Library, MS 2553, pp. 196-8.

DuW 149 *Rewl of Anis Self* ('To dwell in court, my freind, gife that thow list').

Copy, untitled, in the Bannatyne MS; c. 1568.

Printed from this MS in Mackenzie, No. 41, pp. 75-6; Murdoch, II, 184-6; Ritchie, II, 167-9.

National Library of Scotland, Adv. MS 1. 1. 6, Vol. I, ff. 68-9 (pp. 197-9).

DuW 150 *Ros Mary: Ane Ballat of Our Lady* ('Ros Mary, most of vertewe virginale').

Copy in the Asloan MS; c. 1515.

Edited partly from this MS in Mackenzie, No. 87, pp. 175-7; printed in Craigie, *The Asloan MS*, II, 271-2.

National Library of Scotland, [MS Acc. 4233], f. 301r-v.

DuW 151 -----

Copy made by a certain 'Johannes', possibly John Purde, in a MS book of lecture notes on logic written in Louvain in 1477 by Magnus Makculloch, clerk to Archbishop William Schevez (d. 1497); late 15th-early 16th century.

Printed from this MS in Stevenson, pp. 24-5; recorded in Mackenzie, p. 230.

Edinburgh University Library, MS Borl. 205, f. 183v.

DuW 152 -----

Copy of an eight-stanza version, in a MS book of religious poems chiefly composed and probably transcribed by the priest William Forrest; c. 1581.

Printed from this MS in Henry Noble MacCracken, 'New Stanzas by Dunbar', *MLN*, 24 (1909), 110-11; edited partly from this MS in Mackenzie.

British Library, Harley MS 1703, ff. 79v-80.

DuW 153 *The Sowtar and Tailyouris War* ('Nixt that a turnament wes tryid').

Copy, headed 'The Turnament', in the Bannatyne MS; c. 1568.

Printed from this MS in Mackenzie, No. 58, pp. 123-6; Murdoch, II, 316-19; Ritchie, II, 295-8.

National Library of Scotland, Adv. MS 1. 1. 6, Vol. I, ff. 111-12v (pp. 281-4).

DuW 154 -----

Copy, here beginning 'Syn till ane turnament fast thai hyit', prefixed by lines 1-12, 109-20 of *The Dance of the Sevin Deidly Synnis* (see DuW 29) and untitled, in the Maitland Folio MS; c. 1570-85.

Printed from this MS in Craigie, I, 183-7; recorded in Mackenzie, p. 220.

Magdalene College, Cambridge, Pepys Library, MS 2553, pp. 162-5.

DuW 155 -----

Copy, headed 'The Iustis betuix ye talyeour & ye sowtar', in the Asloan MS; c. 1515.

Printed from this MS in Craigie, *The Asloan MS*, II, 89-92; collated in Mackenzie, p. 220.

National Library of Scotland, [MS Acc. 4233], ff. 210-11v.

DuW 156 *The Tabill of Confession* ('To The, O mercifull Salviour, Jesus').

Copy in the Bannatyne MS; c. 1568.

Printed from this MS in Mackenzie, No. 83, pp. 163-7; Murdoch, II, 43-8; Ritchie, II, 42-7.

National Library of Scotland, Adv. MS 1. 1. 6, Vol. I, ff. 17v-19v (pp. 94-8).

DuW 157 -----

Copy in the Bannatyne MS; c. 1568.

Printed from this MS in Ritchie, I, 13-18;

recorded in Mackenzie, p. 227.

National Library of Scotland, Adv. MS 1. 1. 6, Vol. I, pp. 9-11.

DuW 158 -----

Copy, subscribed 'ane confessioun generale', in the Maitland Folio MS; c. 1570-85.

Printed from this MS in Craigie, I, 224-9; recorded in Mackenzie, p. 227.

Magdalene College, Cambridge, Pepys Library, MS 2553, pp. 199-203.

DuW 159 -----

Copy in a Scottish miscellany of devotional verse and prose; c. 1530s.

Printed from this MS in Bennett, pp. 1-6; partly printed from this MS in Mackenzie.

British Library, Arundel MS 285, ff. 1-4v.

DuW 160 *The Testament of Mr. Andro Kennedy* ('I, Maister Andro Kennedy').

Copy in the Bannatyne MS; c. 1568.

First pub. in the Chepman and Myllar Prints (Edinburgh, 1508); Mackenzie, No. 40, pp. 71-4. Printed from this MS in Murdoch, III, 438-41; Ritchie, III, 62-6; text corrected from this MS in Mackenzie (p. 213).

National Library of Scotland, Adv. MS 1. 1. 6, Vol. I, ff. 154-5v (pp. 367-70).

DuW 161 -----

Copy, untitled, in the Maitland Folio MS; c. 1570-85.

Printed from this MS in Craigie, I, 155-9; recorded in Mackenzie, p. 213.

Magdalene College, Cambridge, Pepys Library, MS 2553, pp. 135-8.

DuW 162 -----

Copy, untitled, in the Reidpeth MS; 1622-3.

Cambridge University Library, MS Ll. 5. 10, ff. 24v-6.

DuW 163 *The Thrissil and the Rois* ('Quhen Merche wes with variand windis past').

Copy in the Bannatyne MS; c. 1568.

Printed from this MS in Mackenzie, No. 55, pp. 107-12; Murdoch, IV, 988-94; Ritchie, IV, 246-52.

National Library of Scotland, Adv. MS 1. 1. 6, Vol. II, ff. 342v-5 (pp. 734-9).

DuW 164 *To a Ladye* ('Sweit rois of vertew and of gentilnes').

Copy, untitled, in the Maitland Folio MS; c. 1570-85.

Printed from this MS in Mackenzie, No. 49, p. 99; Craigie, I, 383-4.

Magdalene College, Cambridge, Pepys Library, MS 2553, p. 320.

DuW 165 *To Aberdein* ('Blyth Aberdeane, thow beriall of all tounis').

Copy, untitled, in the Reidpeth MS; 1622-3.

Printed from this MS in Mackenzie, No. 64, pp. 137-9; Craigie, II, 55-8.

Cambridge University Library, MS Ll. 5. 10, f. 7r-v.

DuW 166 *To the Gouvernour in France* ('We lordis hes chosin a chiftane mervellus').

Copy, untitled, in the Bannatyne MS; c. 1568.

Printed from this MS in Mackenzie, No. 92, pp. 181-2; Murdoch, II, 215-16; Ritchie, II, 197-9.

National Library of Scotland, Adv. MS 1. 1. 6, Vol. I, ff. 78v-9 (pp. 218-19).

DuW 167 *To the King* ('Off benefice, Schir, at everie feist').

Copy, untitled, in the Maitland Folio MS; c. 1570-85.

Mackenzie, No. 12, p. 28. Printed from this MS in Craigie, I, 8-9; text corrected from this MS in Mackenzie.

Magdalene College, Cambridge, Pepys Library, MS 2553, pp. 8-9.

DuW 168 -----

Copy, untitled, in the Maitland Folio MS; c. 1570-85.

Printed from this MS in Mackenzie; Craigie, I, 385-6.

Magdalene College, Cambridge, Pepys Library, MS 2553, pp. 321-2.

To the King

DuW 169 -----

Copy, untitled, in the Reidpeth MS; 1622-3.

This MS collated in Craigie, II, 37.

Cambridge University Library, MS Ll. 5. 10, f. 10r-v.

DuW 170 *To the King* ('Sanct Salvatour! send silver sorrow').

Copy in the Bannatyne MS; c. 1568.

Printed from this MS in Mackenzie, No. 1, pp. 1-2; Murdoch, II, 322-4; Ritchie, II, 301-2.

National Library of Scotland, Adv. MS 1. 1. 6, Vol. I, ff. 113v-14 (pp. 286-7).

DuW 171 *To the King* ('Schir, yit remembir as of befoir').

Copy, untitled, in the Bannatyne MS; c. 1568.

Mackenzie, No. 20, pp. 41-3. Printed from this MS in Murdoch, II, 271-4; Ritchie, II, 251-4; collated in Mackenzie, pp. 206-7.

National Library of Scotland, Adv. MS 1. 1. 6, Vol. I, ff. 94v-5v (pp. 250-2).

DuW 172 -----

Copy, untitled, in the Maitland Folio MS; c. 1570-85.

Printed from this MS in Mackenzie; Craigie, I, 346-8.

Magdalene College, Cambridge, Pepys Library, MS 2553, pp. 295-6, 309.

DuW 173 -----

Copy of lines 76-83, untitled and beginning 'How suld I leif and I not landit', in the Reidpeth MS; 1622-3.

Cambridge University Library, MS Ll. 5. 10, f. 34.

DuW 174 *To the King That He war Johne Thomosunis Man* ('Schir, for your Grace bayth nicht and day').

Copy, untitled, in the Maitland Folio MS; c. 1570-85.

Printed from this MS in Mackenzie, No. 18, pp. 38-9; Craigie, I, 220-1.

Magdalene College, Cambridge, Pepys Library, MS 2553, pp. 194-5.

DuW 175 *To the Lordis of the Kingis Chalker* ('My Lordis of Chalker, pleis yow to heir').

Copy, untitled, in the Reidpeth MS; 1622-3.

Printed from this MS in Mackenzie, No. 25, pp. 50-1; Craigie, II, 53-4.

Cambridge University Library, MS Ll. 5. 10, f. 6r-v.

DuW 176 *To the Merchantis of Edinburgh* ('Quhy will ye, merchantis of renoun').

Copy, untitled, in the Reidpeth MS; 1622-3.

Printed from this MS in Mackenzie, No. 44, pp. 81-3; Craigie, II, 41-4.

Cambridge University Library, MS Ll. 5. 10, ff. 1v-2v.

DuW 177 *To the Princess Margaret* ('Now fayre, fayrest off every fayre').

Copy in a musical setting in a MS volume of madrigals and musical pieces; early 16th century.

Printed from this MS in Mackenzie, No. 89, pp. 178-9. Facsimile in Small, I, at the end.

British Library, Royal MS App. 58, f. 15v.

DuW 178 *To the Quene* ('Madam, your men said thai wald ryd').

Copy, untitled, in the Maitland Folio MS; c. 1570-85.

Printed from this MS in Mackenzie, No. 31, pp. 59-60; Craigie, I, 417-18.

Magdalene College, Cambridge, Pepys Library, MS 2553, p. 342.

DuW 179 -----

Copy, untitled, in the Reidpeth MS; 1622-3.

This MS collated in Craigie, II, 129; Mackenzie, p. 210.

Cambridge University Library, MS Ll. 5. 10, f. 46r-v.

DuW 180 *To the Queen Dowager* ('O lusty flour of yowth, benying and bricht').

Copy, untitled, in the Bannatyne MS; c. 1568.

Printed from this MS in Mackenzie, No. 91, pp. 180-1; Murdoch, III, 689-91; Ritchie, III, 323-4.

National Library of Scotland, Adv. MS 1. 1. 6, Vol. II, f. 238v (p. 532).

DuW 181 *To the City of London* ('London, thou art of townes A per se').

Copy, headed 'ye treatise of London made at Mr. Shaa table when he was mayre', in a

To the City of London

miscellany compiled by Richard Hill of London; c. 1520.

Mackenzie, No. 88, pp. 177-8. Printed from this MS in *Songs, Carols, and other Miscellaneous Poems*, ed. Roman Dyboski, EETS ES 101 (London, 1907-8), pp. 100-2; text corrected from this MS in Mackenzie (pp. 230-1).

Balliol College, Oxford, MS 354, ff. 199v-200.

DuW 182 -----

Copy in a MS 'chronicle of England, containing the remarkable passages of what happened; together with the mayors and sheriffs of London, from A° 1215 to A° 1509'; early 16th century.

Printed from this MS in Mackenzie.

British Library, Cotton MS Vitellius A. XVI, ff. 200-1.

DuW 183 -----

Copy, headed 'An honour to London', in a miscellany; 16th century.

Printed from this MS in T. Wright and James Orchard Halliwell[-Phillipps], *Reliquiae Antiquae* (London, 1841), I, 205-7; recorded in Mackenzie, pp. 230-1.

British Library, Lansdowne MS 762, f. 7v.

DuW 184 -----

Copy, headed 'A balad mayde at London when my Lorde Prince Arthur was wed, by a Skotte hauyng muche money of dyuerse lordes for hys Indytyng', formerly bound in a printed exemplum of William Caxton's *Cordiale* (1479); c. 1501-9.

Printed from this MS in Curt F. Bühler, 'London Thow Art The Flowre Of Cytes All', *RES*, 13 (1937), 1-9.

Pierpont Morgan Library, MA 717.

DuW 185 *The Tretis of the Tua Mariit Wemen and the Wedo* ('Apon the Midsummer evin, mirriest of nichtis').

Copy in the Maitland Folio MS; c. 1570-85.

First pub. in the Chepman and Myllar Prints (Edinburgh, 1508); Mackenzie, No. 47, pp. 85-97. Printed from this MS in Mackenzie (lines 1-103); Craigie, I, 98-115.

Magdalene College, Cambridge, Pepys Library, MS 2553, pp. 81-96.

DuW 186 *The Twa Cummeris* ('Rycht airlie on Ask Weddinsday').

Copy, untitled, in the Bannatyne MS; c. 1568.

Printed from this MS in Mackenzie, No. 46, p. 84; Murdoch, III, 386-7; Ritchie, III, 14-15.

National Library of Scotland, Adv. MS 1. 1. 6, Vol. I, f. 137 (p. 333).

DuW 187 -----

Copy, untitled and here beginning 'Airlie on als wodnisday', in the Maitland Folio MS; c. 1570-85.

Printed from this MS in Craigie, I, 64-5; recorded in Mackenzie, p. 215.

Magdalene College, Cambridge, Pepys Library, MS 2553, pp. 57-8.

DuW 188 -----

Copy, untitled, in the Reidpeth MS; 1622-3.

This MS collated in Craigie, II, 65.

Cambridge University Library, MS Ll. 5. 10, f. 19v.

DuW 189 -----

Copy, written on a blank page in a Minute Book of Sasines in Aberdeen, 1501-4, Vol. II; c. 1501-4.

This MS recorded in Mackenzie, p. 215. A transcript made for David Laing by R. Stephens (1835) is in Edinburgh University Library, MS La. III. 476.

Corporation Charter Room, Aberdeen.

DuW 190 *Tydingis fra the Sessioun* ('Ane murlandis man of uplandis mak').

Copy, untitled, in the Bannatyne MS; c. 1568.

Printed from this MS in Mackenzie, No. 43, pp. 79-80; Murdoch, II, 160-2; Ritchie, II, 145-7.

National Library of Scotland, Adv. MS 1. 1. 6, Vol. I, f. 59r-v (pp. 179-80).

DuW 191 -----

Copy, untitled, in the Maitland Folio MS; c. 1570-85.

Printed from this MS in Craigie, I, 374-5; recorded in Mackenzie, p. 214.

Magdalene College, Cambridge, Pepys Library, MS 2553, pp. 314-15.

DuW 192 -----

Copy, untitled, in the Reidpeth MS; 1622-3.

Tydingis fra the Sessioun

This MS collated in Craigie, II, 121-2.

Cambridge University Library, MS Ll. 5. 10, ff. 37-8.

DuW 193 *Welcome to the Lord Treasurer* ('I thocht lang quhill sum lord come hame').

Copy, untitled, in the Reidpeth MS; 1622-3.

Printed from this MS in Mackenzie, No. 24, pp. 49-50; Craigie, II, 51-2.

Cambridge University Library, MS Ll. 5. 10, ff. 5v-6.

DuW 194 *The Wowing of the King quhen he was in Dumfermeling* ('This hindir nycht in Dumfermeling').

Copy in the Bannatyne MS; c. 1568.

Printed from this MS in Mackenzie, No. 27, pp. 51-3; Murdoch, II, 330-3; Ritchie, II, 309-11.

National Library of Scotland, Adv. MS 1. 1. 6, Vol. I, f. 116r-v (pp. 291-2).

DuW 195 -----

Copy, untitled, in the Maitland Folio MS; c. 1570-85.

Printed from this MS in Craigie, I, 407-9; text corrected from this MS in Mackenzie (p. 208).

Magdalene College, Cambridge, Pepys Library, MS 2553, pp. 335-7.

DuW 196 -----

Copy of lines 1-14, untitled, in the Reidpeth MS; 1622-3.

This MS collated in Craigie, II, 126.

Cambridge University Library, MS Ll. 5. 10, f. 58.

Sir Thomas Elyot

1489/90?-1546

For abbreviations used throughout Volume I, see p.xi.

None of Sir Thomas Elyot's known works is preserved in manuscript. However, ten original letters, addressed chiefly to Thomas Cromwell, and written between 1528 and 1536, are in the Public Record Office (SP. 1/72/36-7; 1/75/81; 1/76/149; 1/104/248; 1/235/242; 3/10/96) and in the British Library (Cotton MSS Cleopatra E. IV, f. 260; Cleopatra E. VI, f. 254; Titus B. I, ff. 376-7; and Vitellius B. XXI, ff. 58-9). Another autograph letter to Cromwell, originally, it seems, accompanying a presentation exemplum of Elyot's *Of the Knowledeg whiche Maketh a Wise Man* (London, 1533), is likewise in the British Library (Harley MS 6989, f. 33). In addition, Elyot inscribed a Latin dedicatory epistle to Cromwell in a presentation exemplum of *The Dictionary of Syr Thomas Elyot* (London, 1538), now in the British Library (Department of Printed Books, C. 28, m. 2). These items, together with Elyot's Will, now in the Public Record Office (PROB 11/31, f. 110), and other documents relating to his life, are cited in Stanford E. Lehmberg, *Sir Thomas Elyot: Tudor Humanist* (Austin, Texas, 1960); they are printed in full in K. J. Wilson, 'The Letters of Sir Thomas Elyot', *SP*, 73, No. 5 (December 1976). Elyot's letter to Cromwell, 8 December 1532 (Titus B. I, f. 377), is reproduced in Lehmberg, facing p. 32, and his letter to Cromwell, autumn 1536 (Cleopatra E. IV, f. 260), is reproduced in Wilson, p. viii.

A Latin translation of part of Elyot's *Image of Governance* (1541) is preserved in the British Library (Royal MS 12 A. IV). It belongs to a series of Latin exercises written c. 1553 by the twelve or thirteen year old Lady Mary Fitzalan (d. 1557), assisted by John Radcliffe, (son of Robert Radcliffe, first Earl of Sussex), as a new year's gift for her father, the twelfth Earl of Arundel.

PB.

Edward Fairfax

d. 1635

ABBREVIATIONS

Atterbury Correspondence *The Epistolary Correspondence . . . of the Right Reverend Francis Atterbury, D.D., Lord Bishop of Rochester*, ed. John Nichols, 5 vols (London, 1783-90).

For abbreviations used throughout Volume I, see p.xi.

INTRODUCTION

Edward Fairfax's reputation as a poet rests on *Godfrey of Bulloigne or the Recoverie of Jerusalem* (London, 1600), his much-admired translation of Tasso's *Gerusalemme Liberata*. His other poetical works, perhaps of comparable quality, are either lost or preserved only in fragments. A text of Fairfax's twelve pastoral Eclogues has not been seen since 1789. The poet's own MS — one annotated by his son William in 1636 — was in the possession of his great-nephew Brian Fairfax (1633-1711) in 1705 (see Brian Fairfax's letters to Bishop Atterbury, 12 and 24 March 1704/5, in *Atterbury Correspondence*, III, 255-69). Mrs Elizabeth Cooper evidently saw this MS and printed from it the Fourth Eclogue ('Whilst on the rough and heath-strewed wilderness') in *The Muses Library* (London, 1737). Richard Gough saw the MS and quoted from it the two opening lines of the Fifth Eclogue ('Upon Verbeia's willow-wattled brim') in his edition of Camden's *Britannia* (London, 1789), III, 50. The MS then disappeared from view. No other copy of all twelve Eclogues is known to have existed apart from one transcribed for the Duke of Richmond and Lennox which perished in the great fire at Whitehall in January 1618/19 (see *Atterbury Correspondence*, III, 258-9). A MS copy of most of the Eighth Eclogue (FaE 2) and a MS copy of one other unnumbered Eclogue (FaE 1) are the only other texts known.

In his edition of *The Fairfax Correspondence* (2 vols, London, 1848) — in his not entirely reliable account of the Fairfax papers formerly preserved at Leeds Castle, Kent, and sold in 1822 — George W. Johnson claims that among them was 'an autograph epitaph by Edward Fairfax on the late monarch': the *Epitaph upon King James* beginning 'All that have eyes now wake and weep' (I, 2-3). Even if the copy was made by Edward Fairfax, however, this is no proof of his authorship. In fact, the poem was written by George Morley, later Bishop of Winchester (1597-1684). Of some forty-two MS copies of this epitaph known to the Compiler, nine (including Morley's own miscellany in Westminster Abbey (MS 41, f. 48v)) ascribe the poem to Morley; one (Rosenbach Foundation, MS 1083/15, f. 89r-v) ascribes it (mistakenly) to 'd[r] Corbet', and the rest are anonymous.

Of Fairfax's prose works, his most notable piece — his account of the effects of 'witchcraft' on his family in Fuyston, Yorkshire, in 1621 — is preserved in his autograph (FaE 5). It is, however, slightly imperfect, but a few complete copies are preserved (FaE 6-9) and probably more were once in circulation, including Ebenezer Sibly's (see FaE 8) and a copy owned before 1784 by 'Mr. [Isaac?] Reed of Staple-Inn' (*Atterbury Correspondence*, III, 263).

According to Roger Dodsworth, in his MS *Sancti et Scriptores Ebor* (1631), Fairfax's unprinted works included a 'History of Edward the Black Prince' (*Atterbury Correspondence*, III, 262-3); this work too is unlocated. So is a series of letters on theological matters which, according to Brian Fairfax, who owned them in 1705, passed between Edward Fairfax and John Dorrell or Darrell, a Catholic priest imprisoned in York Castle. These letters, said Brian Fairfax, 'deserve to be published' (*Atterbury Correspondence*, III, 260).

Fairfax's lost works — and 'the many valuable manuscripts' which, according to Brian Fairfax, he 'has left in the library of Lord Fairfax at Denton, both in verse and prose' (*Atterbury Correspondence*, III, 257-8) — eluded the enquiries of a researcher as recently as 1954 (see Charles G. Bell, 'Edward Fairfax — Base Son and Lost Eclogues', *N & Q*, 199 (April 1954), 143-5), although a very few letters and documents relating to his life have been found (see Bell, 'Edward Fairfax, a Natural Son', *MLN*, 62 (1947), 24-7, and T. M. Gang, 'The Quarrel between Edward Fairfax and his Brother', *N & Q*, 214 (January 1969), 28-33). It is, however, by no means certain that the lost works have all been destroyed. The papers of the Fairfax family have been widely dispersed, but many survive in record offices and other repositories, chiefly in Yorkshire, and in institutions such as the Bodleian, the British Library, and Harvard. A recent account of the papers which might provide the impetus for a fresh search is W. J. Connor, 'The Fairfax Archives: A Study in Dispersal', *Archives*, XI, No. 50 (Autumn 1973), 76-85.

PB.

ARRANGEMENT

Verse	FaE 1-4
Prose	FaE 5-9
Miscellaneous	FaE 10.

Edward Fairfax

VERSE

FaE 1 *Eclogue. Hermes and Lycaon* ('The sweaty sithe-man with his razor keen').

Copy, headed 'An Egloge maide by my vncle M[r] Ed: Fairfax in a Dialoge betwixt two sheapards', in a verse miscellany entitled *The Imployment of my Solitude* compiled by Thomas, third Lord Fairfax (1612-71); c. 1660-70.

First pub. (from this MS) in *Miscellanies of the Philobiblon Society*, 12 (London, 1868-9), No. 4, ed. Clements R. Markham; ed. William Grainge in Edward Fairfax, *Daemonologia* (Harrogate, 1882; reprinted London, 1971), pp. 181-9.

Bodleian, MS Fairfax 40, pp. 647-56.

FaE 2 *Eclogue the Eighth. Ida and Opilio* ('Bright may this riseing beame on Ida shine!').

Copy in a composite volume of verse written by or relating to members of the Fairfax family; imperfect at the end; early 17th century.

First pub. (from this MS) in W.W. Greg, 'Fairfax Eighth Eclogue', *MLQ*, 4 (1901), 85-91, and additional notes in 6 (1903), 73-4; reprinted in Greg, *Collected Papers* (Oxford, 1966), 29-43.

British Library, Add. MS 11743, ff. 5-6v.

--- *Eclogues*.

See INTRODUCTION.

--- *Epitaph upon King James* ('All that have eyes now wake and weep').

See INTRODUCTION.

FaE 3 *Godfrey of Bulloigne*.

Copy of Canto I, lines 14-21, the description of Gabriel descending from Heaven, beginning 'On silver wings he tooke a shining paire', in a composite volume of verse written by or relating to members of the Fairfax family; early 17th century.

First pub. London, 1600; ed. R. Weiss (Carbondale, 1962). This MS recorded in Charles C. Bell, 'A History of Fairfax Criticism', *PMLA*, 62.1 (1947), 644-56 (p. 645).

British Library, Add. MS 11743, f. 26.

FaE 4 -----

Extracts in a verse miscellany compiled by Bishop White Kennett (1660-1728); late 17th-early 18th century.

British Library, Lansdowne MS 928, ff. 1-20v.

PROSE

*FaE 5 *A Discourse of Witchcraft*.

Autograph, with corrections or revisions in the introduction; imperfect, lacking the first part of the introduction; 32 leaves; [1621-3].

First pub. (from this MS) in *Miscellanies of the Philobiblon Society*, 5 (London, 1858-9), No. 3, ed. R. Monckton Milnes; ed. William Grainge as *Daemonologia* (Harrogate, 1882; reprinted London, 1971). Facsimile of part of f. 12 in Greg, *English Literary Autographs*, plate XLVI(c).

British Library, Add. MS 32495.

FaE 6 -----

Copy of the complete work in a miscellany compiled by Miles Gale, rector of Keighley, Yorkshire (d. 1721); early 18th century.

This MS recorded but not collated by editors. Following the text are ink drawings by Gale of members of the Fairfax family and of witches and their familiars, etc. (ff. 43-79).

British Library, Add. MS 32496, ff. 3v-42v.

FaE 7 -----

Copy of the complete work in a composite volume of Fairfax papers and state tracts; 91 pages; mid-late 17th century.

Formerly among the Ingilby papers at Ripley Castle, Yorkshire, this MS recorded in *HMC*, 6th Report (1877), Appendix, p. 362.

National Maritime Museum, AND/25, item 1.

FaE 8 -----

Copy of a transcript of the complete work, 'With many Curious Plates', made 'from an Old Manuscript by Ebenezer Sibly. M.D. 1793'; 55 pages; watermark 1825.

University of Texas at Austin, Ms File/(Fairfax, E)/Works B.

EDWARD FAIRFAX

A Discourse of Witchcraft

FaE 9 -----

Copy, with drawings, from the Fairfax papers; 332 pages; 17th century.

This MS formerly Phillipps MS 10666.

Sotheby's, 8 June 1898, Lot 430, sold to Hodgkin; unlocated.

--- -----

See also INTRODUCTION.

MISCELLANEOUS

*FaE 10 *Armada, Roccolta di Pasquinate Diverse.*

A MS volume of various Italian poems and other pieces, 'said to be the autograph of Edward Fairfax', entitled 'Armada, Raccolta di Pasquinate Diverse in Diverse Lingue Scritte'; once in the library of James I and afterwards among the Fairfax papers; 4°; c. 1610.

Sotheby's, 8 June 1898 (Phillipps sale of Fairfax MSS), Lot 390, sold to Ellis; unlocated.

Giles Fletcher the Younger

1588?-1623

ABBREVIATIONS

Boas *The Poetical Works of Giles Fletcher and Phineas Fletcher,* ed. Frederick S. Boas, 2 vols (Cambridge, 1908-9).

For abbreviations used throughout Volume I, see p.xi.

INTRODUCTION

The small corpus of extant poetical works by Giles Fletcher the Younger is almost entirely printed in Boas (I, 1-90, 265-73). Only one of the poems in that edition is preserved in MS (FIG 1), though there also exists in MS a poem by Fletcher not known to Boas: Fletcher's contribution to the gratulatory anthology presented by Cambridge University to Frederick V, the Elector Palatine (FIG 2).

Boas notes (I, ix-x) that a MS entitled *Aegidii Fletcheri Versio Poetica Lamentationum Jeremiae* was formerly preserved in the library of King's College, Cambridge, but cannot now be located. It was described by William Cole (1714-82) as 'a small MS. given to it [the library] Febr. 2. 1654-5 by S. Th. Socius' [i.e. Samuel Thomson] and containing a 19-verse dedication to Dr 'Whytgyfte'. Cole assumed that the MS was the work of Giles Fletcher the Younger, but there is reason for attributing it to Giles Fletcher the Elder (1549?-1611), who (unlike his son) was a member of King's College and was in residence at the same time as John Whitgift, the future Archbishop of Canterbury (1530?-1604).

One other poem, found in MS sources, has some connection with Giles Fletcher. He contributed to the *Epicedium Cantabrigiense* (1612) an eight-line Latin elegy on Prince Henry, *Carmen Sepulchrale* ('Miraris quî Saxa loqui didicere, Viator?') (Boas, I, 270). An English version, beginning 'Reader, wonder thinke it none', achieved considerable popularity and occurs in very many 17th-century miscellanies, but there is no evidence that Fletcher was its author. The English version, which has been doubtfully attributed to Ben Jonson, is discussed in William Dinsmore Briggs, 'Studies in Ben Jonson. III', *Anglia,* 39 (1916), 16-44 (pp. 32-41), and in *Ben Jonson,* ed. C. H. Herford and Percy and Evelyn Simpson, 11 vols (Oxford, 1925-52), VIII, 432-3. It may be noted that in two sources (Folger, MS V. a. 103, Part I, f. 3, and University of Nottingham, Portland MS Pw V 37, p. 4), both written by the same scribe, the poem is ascribed to 'M[r] C. W.'

Research for the *Index* has brought to light two examples of Giles Fletcher's autograph. A signed letter of 21 May 1611, sent to his benefactor Sir Nathaniel Bacon of Stiffkey, Norfolk, is in the Norfolk Record Office (Bradfer-Lawrence VII b (1)), and Fletcher's subscription for the degree of B.D. on 3 July 1619 is preserved in the Cambridge University Archives (*Subscriptiones I,* p. 66): for reproductions of both, see FACSIMILE XIV.

PB.

ARRANGEMENT

Verse FIG 1-2.

FACSIMILE XIV — Giles Fletcher the Younger: (a) Letter to Sir Nathaniel Bacon, 21 May 1611. Norfolk Record Office, Bradfer-Lawrence VII b (1). Reproduced by permission of the Norfolk Record Office. (b) Subscription for the degree of B.D., 3 July 1619. Cambridge University Archives, Subscription I, page 66. Reproduced by permission of the University Archives, Cambridge University Library.

Right worshipfull Sr

Yr desire was (as I heard) to knowe as soon as might bee, of yr Nephewe Mr Townshends arrivall: that so (if I misguesse not) yu might sende him a man rather speedily then hastily, to wayte, not so much upon his comming as himselfe. I was bould therfore upon this first occasion to signifie so much unto yu, & to desire so much favour of yr worship (if it please yu, & yu bee so well pleased) to write unto him (as nowe at his first comming wth yr good & right fatherly perswasions to forwarde both his present desire of study, & my future paynes: because I knowe yr worships authoritie wth him plurimum et potest, et debet. wch I doe not as doubting of yr worships great care, & love of him, or his owne care of himselfe, & love of his book, both wch I am glad to see & hear, but out of (it may bee) an over earnest desire of an unexperienced Tutor, to have him bee, whilest hee is here (as most here bee not) a constant Student. Pardon good Sr my much bouldness at this time, if I have presumed to write, & to write thus unto yu, & I will promise yr worship here after rather to be faulty in silence, then in this boulder kinde of writing. So wth my most respected duety to yr good worship, I humbly take my leave.

May 21. 1611

Yr worships in all good service [illegible],

Giles Fletcher

STP R. 1619 66

Julij 2 I Rich: Palmer doe willinglie and ex animo subscribe to these articles sett downe in the begin-ning of this booke and to all things conteined ~~ther~~ in them. BD

Rich: Palmer (C.C.)

Julij 3° I Giles Fletcher doe willinglie & ex animo subscribe to these Articles sett downe in the beginning of this booke & to all things conteyned in them. – BD

Giles Fletcher (Trin)

Julij 5° I John Euerarde do willingly & ex animo subscribe to these Articles sette downe in the begin-ning of this booke & to all thinges contayned in them. BD

Jo: Euerarde (Cla)

Giles Fletcher the Younger

VERSE

--- *Carmen sepulchrale* ('Miraris quî Saxa loqui didicere, Viator?').

See INTRODUCTION.

FlG 1 *A Description of Encolpius* ('It was at evening, & in Aprill mild').

Copy, headed 'Nisus amore pio pueri &c.' and endorsed in another hand ''tis Encolpus in Petronius. I had it of Mr. Blois', in a verse miscellany compiled by Archbishop William Sancroft (1617-93); mid-late 17th century.

First pub. (from this MS) in *Miscellanies of the Fuller Worthies Library*, ed. A.B. Grosart, III (1872), 510-12; printed from this MS in Boas, I, 89-90.

Bodleian, MS Tanner 465, f. 42r-v.

--- *Aegidii Fletcheri versio poetica lamentationum Ieremiae.*

See INTRODUCTION.

FlG 2 *'Surgens coerulco lotus ab aquore'.*

Copy of Fletcher's Latin poem in honour of Frederick V, Elector Palatine, in one of the two MS volumes of gratulatory verse presented to Frederick by the University of Cambridge on 6 March 1612/13.

Unpublished. This MS recorded in Leicester Bradner, 'New Poems by George Herbert: The Cambridge Latin Gratulatory Anthology of 1613', *RN*, 15 (1962), 208-11.

Vatican Library, MS Palat. lat. 1736, f. 13.

John Fletcher

1579-1625

ABBREVIATIONS

Dyce *The Works of Beaumont and Fletcher*, ed. Alexander Dyce, 11 vols (London, 1843-6).

For abbreviations used throughout Volume I, see p.xi.

INTRODUCTION

There is a single known MS containing John Fletcher's handwriting: his verse epistle to the Countess of Huntingdon (FlJ 8), first published in 1929. The MS was then regarded as entirely autograph but is now considered to be a scribal copy with a few autograph additions.

With one exception, the remaining meagre canon of Fletcher's poems accepted in the *Index* is based on Dyce (I, liii-liv; III, 453-6; XI, 517-18). A work added to Dyce's version of the canon is the song *'Hither we come into this world of woe'* (FlJ 1-6). The ascription of this song to 'J. Fletcher' in Henry Lawes's *Second Book of Ayres and Dialogues* (1655) probably refers to John Fletcher, and is accepted as such in the Oxford *English Madrigal Verse*. A possible but less likely alternative author would be the religious poet Joseph Fletcher (1582?-1637).

Unless otherwise stated, the MSS recorded in the *Index* have not been previously noted by editors. For Fletcher's dramatic works see above, DRAMATIC WORKS IN THE BEAUMONT AND FLETCHER CANON

PB.

ARRANGEMENT

Verse FlJ 1-15.

John Fletcher

VERSE

F1J 1 *'Hither we come into this world of woe'.*

Copy in a musical setting by Henry Lawes in a MS songbook; c. 1640s.

First pub. (anon) in Walter Porter, *Madrigales and Ayres* (London, 1632); ascribed to J. Fletcher in Henry Lawes, *Second Book of Ayres and Dialogues* (London, 1655); *English Madrigal Verse*, ed. E.H. Fellowes, et al., 3rd edition (Oxford, 1967), p. 644. See also INTRODUCTION.

Bodleian, MS Don. c. 57, f. 32.

F1J 2 -----

Copy in a musical setting by John Wilson, in Wilson's corrected MS volume of his own songs; possibly in Wilson's autograph or else in the hand of someone similarly associated with Edward Lowe (c. 1610-82); c. 1656.

This MS collated in John P. Cutts, 'Seventeenth Century Lyrics', *MD*, 10 (1956), 142-209 (p. 156).

Bodleian, MS Mus. b. 1, f. 16.

F1J 3 -----

Copy in a musical setting by Henry Lawes in a MS songbook compiled by one 'T.C.'; c. 1656-9.

British Library, Add. MS 11608, f. 9.

F1J 4 -----

Copy in a musical setting by Henry Lawes, in Lawes's autograph songbook; mid-17th century.

British Library, Add. MS 53723, f. 67.

F1J 5 -----

Copy in a musical setting in a MS songbook; mid-17th century.

British Library, Egerton MS 2013, f. 15.

F1J 6 -----

Copy, headed 'An Epitaph on a Child' in a verse miscellany; c. 1630.

Rosenbach Foundation, MS 239/23, p. 183.

F1J 7 *A Sonnet* ('Come, sorrow, come! bring all thy cries').

Copy of an epicede ascribed to 'I.F.' in a verse miscellany compiled by one Thomas Crosse; c. 1630s.

First pub. (from this MS) in Dyce (1843), I, liii-liv.

British Library, Harley MS 6057, f. 34.

*F1J 8 *To the most Excelent and best Lady the Countess of Huntington* ('There ys not any Sculler of o[r] Tyme').

Verse epistle sent to the Countess of Huntingdon, in the hand of an amanuensis with Fletcher's autograph address, signature and a one-word insertion; c. 1619-20.

First pub. (from this MS, with a facsimile) in Samuel A. Tannenbaum, 'A Hitherto Unpublished John Fletcher Autograph', *JEGP*, 28 (1929), 35-40; discussed (with another facsimile) in Greg, *English Literary Autographs*, plate XCIII; in Tannenbaum, 'The John Fletcher Holograph', *PQ*, 13 (1934), 401-4; in Greg, 'John Fletcher's Autograph', *PQ*, 14 (1935), 373; in Tannenbaum, 'The John Fletcher Holograph', *PQ*, 15 (1936), 221; in Petti, *English Literary Hands*, No. 52. Tannenbaum, unlike Greg and Petti, believed the MS to be entirely autograph.

Huntington, HA 13333.

F1J 9 *Upon An Honest Man's Fortune* ('You that can look through heaven, and tell the stars').

Copy, untitled, in a verse miscellany owned by one Peter Daniell; c. 1630s-40s.

First pub. appended to *The Honest Man's Fortune* in *Comedies and Tragedies* (London, 1647); Dyce, III, 453-6.

Bodleian, MS Eng. poet. c. 50, ff. 78v-80.

F1J 10 -----

Copy, untitled, in a verse miscellany; c. 1630s.

Bodleian, MS Rawl. poet. 160, ff. 45-6.

F1J 11 -----

Copy, indexed as 'verses by Jack: Flecher', in a composite volume of verse belonging to the Skipwith family of Cotes, Leicestershire; early-mid-17th century.

British Library, Add. MS 25707, ff. 66-7.

F1J 12 -----

Copy, untitled, in a verse miscellany owned in 1640 by Anthony St John (1618-73) and Ann St John of Bletsoe, Bedfordshire; c. 1630s.

Harvard, fMS Eng 626, ff. 10v-12.

Upon An Honest Man's Fortune

FlJ 13 -----

Copy, headed 'Against astrolagers' and ascribed to 'John Fletcher', in a verse miscellany owned by Edward Denny, Charles Cokes, Edward Randolpe, and Thomas Cassy; c. 1630s.

Huntington, HM 198, Part I, pp. 1-2.

FlJ 14 -----

Copy, untitled, in a verse miscellany; c. 1630.

Rosenbach Foundation, MS 239/23, pp. 85-90.

FlJ 15 -----

Copy in a verse miscellany compiled by Tobias Alston (1620-c.1639) of Sayham Hall, near Sudbury, Suffolk; c. 1639.

Yale, Osborn Collection, b 197, pp. 123-5.

DRAMATIC WORKS

See BEAUMONT AND FLETCHER

Phineas Fletcher

1582-1650

ABBREVIATIONS

Boas *The Poetical Works of Giles Fletcher and Phineas Fletcher*, ed. Frederick S. Boas, 2 vols (Cambridge, 1908-9).

Seaton *Venus & Anchises (Brittain's Ida) and other Poems by Phineas Fletcher*, ed. Ethel Seaton (London, 1926).

For abbreviations used throughout Volume I, see p.xi.

INTRODUCTION

Three important literary autographs of Phineas Fletcher survive, all copies of his Latin poem *Locustae, vel pietas Jesuitica* (FlP 4-6). In addition, various printed exempla of *The Purple Island...together with Piscatorie Eclogs and other Poetical Miscellanies* (Cambridge, 1633) are known to contain Fletcher's autograph inscriptions. They include volumes at King's College, Cambridge (Keynes C. 3. 11), and in the Pierpont Morgan Library; another (the 'Sykes-Britwell copy') which in 1940 was in the possession of Maggs Brothers (see *The Carl H. Pforzheimer Library: English Literature 1475-1700* (New York, 1940), I, 360), and yet another which was owned before 1909 by Mr F.T. Sabin (the inscription in this volume is reproduced in Boas, II, frontispiece). The inscription in the King's College volume reads 'Esse suj voluit Monumentū Pignus Amoris'; the inscriptions in the other recorded volumes are similar. An exemplum in the British Library (Department of Printed Books, C. 34. g. 33) has bound in at the beginning a leaf, evidently extracted from some other book, bearing the inscription 'Ex dono Phineae ffletcheri authoris' and, in a different hand, two lines in Latin subscribed 'Phinees ffletcher', but none of this writing is in Fletcher's hand (see Boas, I, xii; II, vii). All these printed volumes have, or originally had, bindings stamped with the arms of Edward Benlowes (1603?-76), the dedicatee of the work. The King's College volume also has Fletcher's autograph annotations on two pages in the text of *The Purple Island*: a marginal note on page 147 and a textual correction on page 177. An exemplum of the same edition in the Widener Library at Harvard has a ten-line marginal note on page 59 of the *Poetical Miscellanies*, but it is not in Fletcher's hand.

One other important MS containing Fletcher's autograph survives. It is the register of baptisms, burials, and marriages of All Saints Church, Hilgay, Norfolk, in which Fletcher made entries while he was Rector from 1621 to 1650. This register is the evidence for establishing the authenticity of the other autographs cited. It is at present still preserved at Hilgay but will shortly be transferred to the Norfolk Record Office. Part of one leaf is reproduced in Boas (I, frontispiece).

Evidence of another autograph of Fletcher's, which survived at least until the 18th century, is provided by one 'W. Thomson' of The Queen's College, Oxford, who annotated a volume of Fletcher's printed works, now in the British Library (Department of Printed Books, 239. i. 23). On page 3 of the *Piscatorie Eclogs* Thomson notes, 'I have a Vol: of Latin Poems in 4to in the Authors own MS: dedicated [? to the Archbishop of Canterbury]'. Nothing more of this MS volume is known.

Among other sources, there survive contemporary transcripts of Fletcher's academic play *Sicelides* (FlP 18-19), and important copies of early versions of *Venus and Anchises (Brittain's Ida)* and other poems are found in a MS at Sion College, London (FlP 2, 8-11, 13, 16). This last MS is edited and described in Seaton; it was not known to Boas and it adds to his version of the canon one more poem, an *Epithalamium* (FlP 2). Other texts recorded in the entries below (chiefly copies in a journal of 1657 compiled by one Thomas Grocer) probably derive from printed sources; they have not been noted by editors.

PB.

ARRANGEMENT

Verse	FlP 1-17
Dramatic works	FlP 18-20.

Phineas Fletcher

VERSE

FlP 1 *Against a rich man despising povertie* ('If well thou view'st us with no squinted eye').

Copy in a journal compiled by one Thomas Grocer; 1657.

First pub. in *The Purple Island* (Cambridge, 1633); Boas, II, 236-7.

Huntington, HM 93, p. 151.

--- *Brittain's Ida.*

See FlP 16-17.

FlP 2 *Epithalamium* ('Harke gentle sheppeardes that on Norwiche plaines').

Copy in a composite volume of mathematical, theological, and other MSS; c. 1616-28.

First pub. (from this MS) in Seaton (1926), pp. 21-9, with a facsimile of f. 243 facing p. 21.

Sion College, MS ARC L 40.2/L 40, ff. 243-7.

FlP 3 *An Hymen at the Marriage of my most deare Cousins M^r. W. and M.R.* ('Chamus, that with thy yellow-sanded stream').

Copy, untitled, beginning at stanza 12 ('Oh happy pair, where nothing wants to either'), in a journal compiled by one Thomas Grocer; 1657.

First pub. in *The Purple Island* (Cambridge, 1633); Boas, II, 223-5.

Huntington, HM 93, p. 149.

*FlP 4 *Locustae, vel pietas Jesuitica* ('Panditur Inferni limen, patet intima Ditis').

Autograph, with a dedicatory epistle to James Montagu, Bishop of Bath and Wells; [1611].

First pub. Cambridge, 1627; Boas, I, 97-123. This MS discussed in Boas, I, x-xvi, and collated I, 279-87; facsimiles of the dedication in Boas, I, following p. 96, and in Greg, *English Literary Autographs*, plate L(d).

British Library, Sloane MS 444.

*FlP 5 -----

Autograph, with a dedicatory epistle to Prince Henry, bound with a theological treatise; [1611-12].

This MS formerly owned by A.B. Grosart and by Bertram Dobell; discussed in Boas, I, x-xvi, and collated I, 279-87; facsimile of the third leaf in Boas I, following p. 96.

British Library, Egerton MS 2875, ff. 153-79.

*FlP 6 -----

Autograph, with a dedicatory epistle to Prince Charles and a preliminary epistle to the Prince's tutor, Thomas Murray; c. 1612-21.

This MS discussed in Boas, I, x-xvi, and collated I, 279-87; facsimile of part of the epistle to Murray in Boas, I, following p. 96.

British Library, Harley MS 3196.

FlP 7 *On womens lightnesse* ('Who sowes the sand? or ploughs the easie shore?').

Copy in a journal compiled by one Thomas Grocer; 1657.

First pub. in *The Purple Island* (Cambridge, 1633); Boas, II, 239.

Huntington, HM 93, p. 156.

FlP 8 *Piscatorie Eclogues. II* ('Myrtil, why idle sit we on the shore?').

Copy of stanzas 5-25, headed 'Ecloga. Thomalin. Thirsill' and here beginning 'Thirsil what wicked Chaunce or luckeles starre', in a composite volume of mathematical, theological, and other MSS; c. 1616-28.

First pub. in *The Purple Island* (Cambridge, 1633); Boas, II, 180-6. Printed from this MS in Seaton, pp. 55-64.

Sion College, MS ARC L 40.2/L 40, ff. 260-3.

FlP 9 ----- *IV* ('Chromis my joy, why drop thy rainie eyes?').

Copy, headed 'Ecloga. Thelgon. Chronis', in a composite volume of mathematical, theological, and other MSS; c. 1616-28.

Boas, II, 192-8. Printed from this MS in Seaton, pp. 33-41.

Sion College, MS ARC L 40.2/L 40, ff. 251-4v.

FlP 10 ----- *V* ('The well known fisher-boy, that late his name').

Copy, headed 'Ecloga. Algon. Daphnis. Nicaea', in a composite volume of mathematical, theological, and other MSS; c. 1616-28.

Boas, II, 199-204. Printed from this MS in Seaton, pp. 65-76.

Sion College, MS ARC L 40.2/L 40, ff. 264-7.

Piscatorie Eclogues. VI

FlP 11 ----- *VI* ('A fisher-boy that never knew his peer').

Copy, headed 'Ecloga. Thomalin. Thirsill' and here beginning 'A gentle boye whoe never knew his peere', in a composite volume of mathematical, theological and other MSS; c. 1616-28.

Boas, II, 205-12. Printed from this MS in Seaton, pp. 42-54.

Sion College, MS ARC L 40.2/L 40, ff. 255-9.

FlP 12 *The Purple Island, or The Isle of Man* ('The warmer Sun the golden Bull outran').

Extracts, beginning at Canto I, stanza 36 ('Vain men, too fondly wise, who plough the seas'), and at Canto XII, stanza 75 ('There sweet delights, which know nor end, nor measure'), in a journal compiled by one Thomas Grocer; 1657.

First pub. Cambridge, 1633; Boas, II, 1-171.

Huntington, HM 93, pp. 162,5.

--- -----

See also INTRODUCTION.

FlP 13 *To M^r. Jo. Tomkins* ('Thomalin my lief, thy musick strains to heare').

Copy, headed 'Non invisa Cano', in a composite volume of mathematical, theological, and other MSS; c. 1616-28.

First pub. in *The Purple Island* (Cambridge, 1633); Boas, II, 233-5. Printed from this MS in Seaton, pp. 30-2.

Sion College, MS ARC L 40.2/L 40, ff. 249-50.

FlP 14 *A translation of Boëthius, book 2 verse 7* ('Who onely honour seeks with prone affection').

Copy, headed 'Equality', in a journal compiled by one Thomas Grocer; 1657.

First pub. in *The Purple Island* (Cambridge, 1633); Boas, II, 245.

Huntington, HM 93, p. 158.

FlP 15 *Upon the B. of Exon. Doct. Hall his Meditations* ('Most wretched soul, that here carowsing pleasure').

Copy, untitled, in a journal compiled by one Thomas Grocer; 1657.

First pub. in *The Purple Island* (Cambridge, 1633); Boas, II, 246.

Huntington, HM 93, p. 159.

FlP 16 *Venus and Anchises: Brittain's Ida* ('In Ida Vale (who knowes not Ida Vale?)').

Copy of a version with two new introductory stanzas beginning 'Thirsil (poore ladd) whose Muse yet scarcely fledge', in a composite volume of mathematical, theological, and other MSS; c. 1616-28.

First pub. as *Brittain's Ida*, ascribed to Edmund Spenser, [London], 1628; Boas, II, 343-63; *Elizabethan Minor Epics*, ed. Elizabeth Story Donno (London, 1963), pp. 305-24, emending the printed text from this MS. Printed from this MS in Seaton, pp. 1-20, with a facsimile of f. 235 as the frontispiece.

Sion College, MS ARC L 40.2/L 40, ff. 235-42.

FlP 17 -----

Extract, untitled and beginning at Canto II, stanza 7 ('Fond men, whose wretched care the life soone ending'), in a miscellany later owned by one Joseph Hall; c. 1630s-50.

Folger, MS V. a. 339, f. 182.

DRAMATIC WORKS

FlP 18 *Sicelides, A Piscatory.*

Copy, with corrections possibly in another hand; early 17th century.

Performed at King's College, Cambridge, 13 March 1614/15; first pub. London, 1631; Boas I, 187-264. This MS discussed in Boas, I, xvi-xix, and collated I, 288-309.

British Library, Add. MS 4453.

FlP 19 -----

Copy; early 17th century.

This MS discussed in Boas, I, xvi-xix, and collated I, 288-309.

Bodleian, MS Rawl. poet. 214, ff. 1-86.

FlP 20 -----

Copy of the *Epilogus*, headed 'A Comedy' and beginning 'As in a Feast, so in a Comedy', in a miscellany; mid-17th century.

Boas, I, 264.

Yale, Osborn Collection, b 205, f. 42.

John Florio

1553?-1626

ABBREVIATIONS

Yates Frances A. Yates, *John Florio* (Cambridge, 1934).

For abbreviations used throughout Volume I, see p.xi.

INTRODUCTION

Florio claims a place in British literary history chiefly through his translation of Montaigne's *Essays* (London, 1603). No MS of this work is known, although extracts can be found in some 17th-century miscellanies (e.g. MSS Ogden 7/7 and 7/10 at University College London), and some printed exempla contain annotations by early readers (e.g. Ben Jonson's volume, now in the British Library (Department of Printed Books, C. 28. m. 8)). Two other works of Florio, however, both in his native Italian, are preserved in his autograph (Flo 1-2).

In addition, there is a printed exemplum of his book *A Worlde of Wordes* (London, 1598) which contains an autograph presentation sonnet *To the right Honorable S^r. Thomas Egerton, knight Lord keeper of the greate seale of England* (beginning 'Cato in yeares learn't Greeke, for Romanes weare'). The poem is signed 'Il Candido', which was the soubriquet used by Florio's friend Matthew Gwinne, so evidently the poem was originally composed by Gwinne and only copied out by Florio. (For some discussion on this matter see correspondence by Bent Juel-Jensen and John Kerr in *TLS*, 23 December 1965, p. 1204, and 20 January 1966, p. 43). The volume was sold at Sotheby's, 8 November 1965, Lot 122, to Blackwell, and a facsimile of the sonnet appears in the sale catalogue. The volume was subsequently offered for sale by Zeitlin and Ver Brugge, catalogue No. 246 (Autumn 1978), item 132. It may be added that lines 1-10 of the sonnet were first published in James Wardrop, *The Script of Humanism* (Oxford, 1963), p. 49.

There have also survived four autograph letters of Florio. One, probably sent to Sir Robert Cotton and dated 11 March 1600, is in the British Library (Cotton MS Julius C. III, f. 174); it is reproduced in part in Greg, *English Literary Autographs*, plate LXXVIII(d). Another letter, written in Italian to Sir Francis Windebank on 9 December 1619, is in the Public Record Office (SP. 14/3, f. 68). Two more letters were both written to Lord Cranfield, one on 11 November 1621, the other in 1623; they are among the Cranfield Papers (Nos. 2323 and 985) in the Kent Archives Office. All these letters are printed in Yates, pp. 218-19, 293-4, 296-7, and 299-300.

A printed exemplum of *Florio his First Fruites* (London, 1578) containing particularly interesting MS annotations by Gabriel Harvey (1545?-1630) is to be found at Harvard: see Clifford Chalmers Huffman, 'Gabriel Harvey on John Florio and John Eliot', *N & Q*, 220 (July 1975), 300-2.

PB.

ARRANGEMENT

Verse and prose FloJ 1-3.

John Florio

VERSE AND PROSE

*FloJ 1 *Giardino di recreatione.*

Autograph, including (f. 12v) a poem in the hand of Matthew Gwinne (1558?-1627); 145 leaves; with a dedication to Sir Edward Dyer dated 12 November 1582.

First pub. in *Second Fruits* (London, 1591). This MS recorded in Yates, pp. 45, 345. See also SAMUEL DANIEL, DaS 18.

British Library, Add. MS 15214.

*FloJ 2 James I, *Basilicon Doron.*

Autograph translation into Italian of the 1603 edition of King James's treatise; 68 leaves; c. 1603.

Unpublished. This MS recorded in Yates, pp. 248, 345.

British Library, Royal MS 14 A. V.

--- Montaigne's *Essays.*

See INTRODUCTION.

FloJ 3 *Second Fruits.*

Copy of 59 verse proverbs taken from Chapter VI, headed 'Wise Politique Italian Admonicōns & Counsells', written on a single folded vellum leaf; c. 1595.

First pub. London, 1591.

Owned by Peter Beal, Leeds.

--- *To the right Honorable S^{r}. Thomas Egerton, knight Lord keeper of the greate seale of England* ('Cato in yeares learn't Greeke, for Romanes weare').

See INTRODUCTION.

John Ford

1586?-1639?

ABBREVIATIONS

Bang *John Fordes Dramatische Werke*, ed. Willy Bang, *Materialien zur Kunde des älteren Englischen Dramas*, Ser. I, Vol. 23 (Louvain, 1908; reprinted by Kraus Reprint Ltd, 1967).

De Vocht *John Ford's Dramatic Works*, ed. Henry De Vocht, *Materials for the Study of the Old English Drama*, Ser. II, Vol. 1 (Louvain, 1927; reprinted by Kraus Reprint Ltd, 1967).

Dyce *The Works of John Ford*, ed. William Gifford and revised by Alexander Dyce, 3 vols (London, 1869; 1895 edition reprinted New York, 1965).

For abbreviations used throughout Volume I, see p.xi.

INTRODUCTION

No MSS of Ford's most famous plays, *The Broken Heart* and *'Tis Pity she's a Whore*, are known, and of his other plays only a few early MS copies of particular songs are recorded. On the other hand, presentation copies of the poem *Fame's Memorial* (FoJ 2) and the religious prose piece *A Line of Life* (FoJ 3) are preserved. Their formal appearance suggests that they are both scribal copies rather than autographs, but there appears to be no independent example of Ford's handwriting with which to compare them.

Apart from the Poem *A Contract of Love and Truth*, which is ascribed to 'J. Foord' and has been tentatively added to the canon (see FoJ 1), the *Index* accepts the canon established in Dyce. Unless otherwise stated, the MSS recorded have not been previously noted by editors. For references to other works which have been at some time attributed to Ford, see Bentley, III, 433-64.

Bentley records (III, 464) a prompt book of *'Tis Pity she's a Whore* which was offered for sale in A. S. W. Rosenbach's catalogue of English plays to 1700 (1940), item 204. This item, now in the Robert H. Taylor Collection at Princeton, is an exemplum of the edition of 1633 marked up probably for a performance after 1660. A Restoration prompt book of *The Lover's Melancholy* (an exemplum of the edition of 1629 with extensive MS excisions) is preserved in the Folger (STC 11163/copy 3) and is discussed in Clifford Leech, 'A Projected Restoration Performance of Ford's "The Lover's Melancholy"?', *MLR*, 56 (1961), 378-81. Another exemplum of the edition of 1629, now in the Harvard Theatre Collection, was revised and prepared as a prompt book by Charles Macklin (1699-1797) for performances at Drury Lane on 28 April, 5 and 20 May 1748: see Robert R. Findlay, 'Macklin's 1748 Adaptation of Ford's *The Lover's Melancholy*', *RECTR*, 8 (1969), 13-22. A MS adaptation of *Perkin Warbeck* in the Bodleian (MS Rawl. poet. 122) was probably prepared (by several hands) for a performance at Goodman's Fields Theatre on 19 December 1745: see Donald K. Anderson, Jr, 'The Date and Handwriting of a Manuscript Copy of Ford's "Perkin Warbeck"', *N & Q*, 208 (September 1963), 340-1, and Margaret Crum, 'A Manuscript of Ford's "Perkin Warbeck": An additional Note', *N & Q*, 210 (March 1965), 104-5.

One other additional item is a copy of lines 1-4 of the song 'Pleasures, beauty, youth attend ye' from *The Lady's Trial*, a copy in an 18th-century Scottish miscellany in the Bodleian (MS Rawl. poet. 196, f. 1v).

PB.

ARRANGEMENT

Verse	FoJ 1-2
Prose	FoJ 3
Dramatic works	FoJ 4-14.

John Ford

VERSE

FoJ 1 *A Contract of Love and Truth* ('Soe gold is priz'd, and being chastly pure').

Copy of a poem ascribed to 'J. Foord' in a miscellany once owned by Sir Thomas Meres (1634-1715) of Kirton, Lincolnshire; c. 1640s.

First pub. (from this MS) in Bertram Lloyd, 'An Unprinted Poem by John Ford (?)', *RES*, 1 (1925), 217-19.

British Library, Egerton MS 2725, ff. 134v-5.

FoJ 2 *Fame's Memorial* ('Swift Time, the speedy pursuivant of heaven').

Fair copy, complete with dedication and the anagram from Camden, written for presentation to Lady Penelope Rich; bound in a volume of Ford's printed plays; [1606].

First pub. London, 1606; Dyce, III, 277-327. This MS discussed and unpublished stanzas printed in Bertram Lloyd, 'An Inedited MS. of Ford's *Fames Memoriall*', *RES*, 1 (1925), 93-5.

Bodleian, Malone 238.

PROSE

FoJ 3 *A Line of Life.*

Fair copy, with a dedicatory preface, written for presentation to Lord Haye, Viscount Doncaster (later Earl of Carlisle); bound in a volume of religious tracts; c. 1618.

First pub. [London], 1620; Dyce, III, 381-419. This MS recorded in M. Joan Sargeaunt, 'Writings Ascribed to John Ford by Joseph Hunter in *Chorus Vatum*', *RES*, 10 (1934), 165-76 (pp. 174-5), and in George F. Reinecke, 'John Ford's "Missing" Ralegh Passage', *ELN*, 6 (1968-9), 252-4.

British Library, Lansdowne MS 350, ff. 143-83.

DRAMATIC WORKS

FoJ 4 *The Lady's Trial*, II, iv. Song: 'Pleasures, beauty, youth attend ye'.

Copy in a musical setting by William Lawes, in Lawes's autograph songbook; c. 1638-45.

First pub. London, 1639; Dyce, III, 1-99 (pp. 40-1); De Vocht, pp. 329-408 (p. 363, lines 1011-26). This MS recorded in John P. Cutts, 'British Museum Additional MS. 31432: William Lawes' writing for the Theatre and the Court', *The Library*, 5th Ser. 7 (1952), 225-34 (p. 231).

British Library, Add. MS 31432, f. 19.

FoJ 5 ----- -----

Copy in a musical setting in a MS songbook ('Earl Ferrers' MS'); c. 1640.

This MS collated in John P. Cutts, 'Drexel Manuscript 4041', *MD*, 18 (1964), 151-202 (pp. 182-3).

New York Public Library, Music Division, Drexel MS 4041, No. 68, f. 48.

FoJ 6 ----- -----

Copy in a musical setting in a MS songbook owned (in 1659) and partly compiled by the composer John Gamble; c. 1630s-50s.

Facsimile of this MS in John H. Long, *Shakespeare's Use of Music* (Gainesville, Florida, 1961), p. 146.

New York Public Library, Music Division, Drexel MS 4257, No. 178.

--- ----- -----

See also INTRODUCTION.

FoJ 7 ----- IV, ii. Song: 'What, ho! we come to be merry'.

Copy in a musical setting by William Lawes, in Lawes's autograph songbook; c. 1638-45.

Dyce, III, 70. Printed from this MS in Cutts, *The Library*, 5th Ser. 7 (1952), 230.

British Library, Add. MS 31432, f. 18v.

FoJ 8 *The Lover's Melancholy*, III, ii. Song: 'They that will learn to drink a health in hell'.

Copy of Cuculus's song, headed 'On dispraise of Tabacco' and here beginning 'He that will learn to drink a health in hell', in a verse miscellany; c. 1640.

First pub. London, 1629; Dyce, I, 1-106 (p. 66); Bang, pp. 1-86 (p. 67, lines 1629-33).

Bodleian, MS Rawl. poet. 153, f. 21v.

FoJ 9 ----- -----

Copy, headed 'Tobacco' and here beginning 'He that would learn to drink a health in hell'; c. 1660.

Rosenbach Foundation, MS 239/18, p. 49.

The Lover's Melancholy, III, ii. Song

FoJ 10 ----- -----

Copy, headed 'An Epigram of Tobackoe' and here beginning 'Hee that will learne to drink a helth in hell', in a miscellany compiled by or for Sir Thomas Finch, Viscount Maidstone and Earl of Winchelsea; c. 1634.

Rosenbach Foundation, MS 243/4, p. 7.

FoJ 11 ----- -----

Copy, beginning 'He y[t] would learne to pledge a health in hell', in a verse miscellany probably compiled by a member of an Inn of Court; c. 1630.

Rosenbach Foundation, MS 1083/15, f. 71.

FoJ 12 ----- V, i. Song: 'Fly hence, shadows, that do keep'.

Copy of the Boy's song in a musical setting by John Wilson, in Wilson's corrected MS volume of his own songs; possibly in Wilson's autograph or else in the hand of someone similarly associated with Edward Lowe (c.1610-82); c. 1656.

Dyce, I, 95; Bang, p. 77 (lines 2437-46). This MS collated in John P. Cutts, 'Seventeenth Century Lyrics', *MD*, 10 (1956), 142-209 (p. 181).

Bodleian, MS Mus. b. 1, f. 99.

FoJ 13 ----- -----

Copy in a musical setting by John Wilson, in a MS songbook (2nd treble part) compiled by Edward Lowe; c. 1650s.

Bodleian, MS Mus. d. 238, p. 124.

FoJ 14 ----- -----

Copy in a musical setting by John Wilson, in a MS songbook (1st treble part) compiled by Edward Lowe; c. 1650s.

Edinburgh University Library, MS Dc. 1. 69, f. 71v.

--- *Perkin Warbeck*.

See INTRODUCTION.

John Foxe

1516-87

ABBREVIATIONS

Mozley J. F. Mozley, *John Foxe and his Book* (London, 1940).

Smith, *ELR*, 1 (1971) John Hazel Smith, 'John Foxe on Astrology', *English Literary Renaissance*, 1 (1971), 210-25.

For abbreviations used throughout Volume I, see p.xi.

INTRODUCTION

A large collection of Foxe's papers is preserved in the British Library (Harley MSS 416-26, 590, 783, and Lansdowne MSS 335, 353, 388-9, 819, 1045). It contains various materials relating to his work as a martyrologist and includes a number of drafts of original writings. The contents of the MSS in this collection are to some extent analysed in the published catalogues of the Harley and Lansdowne MSS.

There is no complete bibliography of Foxe's published and unpublished writings. Some of Foxe's works are cited in 19th-century editions of *Actes and Monuments*; a list of his 'minor works' is supplied in Mozley, pp. 243-5; and a list of works ascribed to Foxe, including lost or unidentified items which might still be among his papers, appears in John Bale, *Scriptorum illustrium Maioris Brytanniae catalogus* (Basle, 1557), pp. 733-4. Entries are given in the *Index* to MSS of identified works by Foxe which have been published or discussed in print; apart from a single unpublished item (FxJ 12), the remaining heterogeneous material is briefly summarised in the MISCELLANEOUS section (FxJ 21-5).

Other theological or historical MSS which were owned or used by Foxe can be found in the Bodleian (MS Auct. F. 5. 26) and at Trinity College, Cambridge (MSS B. 2. 7 (James 50); B. 2. 35 (James 78); and B. 3. 34, 35 (James 113-14)). His annotated printed exemplum of Jan Hus et al., *Historia et monumenta, prima pars* (Nuremberg, 1558), which also contains notes by Lancelot Andrewes (see AndL), is at Pembroke College, Cambridge (4.11.22-3). The detached title leaf of a printed exemplum of Paulus Constantinus Phrygio, *Chronicum regum* (1534), bearing the signature 'Joh. Foxii' — probably Foxe's, though the leaf was once owned by the forger J. P. Collier — is in the Folger (MS X. d. 459 (6)).

Foxe's letter to Sir William Cecil (6 July 1568) requesting special permission to have *Actes and Monuments* printed by more than four printers is in Lansdowne MS 10 (ff. 211-12v). Other letters of Foxe, apart from those in the main collection of his papers, can be found in the following repositories:

> University of Basle (Ki.-Ar. 18a, 181: a letter to Boniface Amerbach, 25 November 1556, originally accompanying a presentation exemplum of *Locorum communium tituli* (Basle, '1557') and printed in *Original Letters relative to the English Reformation, Second portion*, ed. Hastings Robinson, Parker Society 28 (Cambridge, 1847), p. 767); Bodleian (MSS Rawl. C. 936, ff. 6-11; Rawl. D. 825, f. 47); British Library (Add. MSS 19400, f. 97; 34727, f. 2); Corpus Christi College, Cambridge (MS 114, No. 198, p. 537); Lambeth Palace (MS 2019, ff. 1-2: a joint letter to Archbishop Parker and others, 20 March 1564/5, to which Foxe was one of the signatories); Magdalen College, Oxford (the letter accompanying the printed exemplum of *Actes and Monuments* (1563) which Foxe presented to his old college, reproduced in Josiah Pratt's edition, I (1870), facing p. 42); Staatsarchiv, Zurich (E II 375, 580-4: six letters of 1559, printed in translation in *The Zurich Letters*, ed. Hastings Robinson, Parker Society 7 (Cambridge, 1842), pp. 22, 25-6, 35-8, 41-3); and Zentralbibliothek, Zurich (Ms. F 62, f. 411: to Heinrich Bullinger, 21 January '1559').

Several of Foxe's letters in the main MS collection are printed in Pratt's edition of *Actes and Monuments*, in the appendices of Vol. I, and part of the letter in Harley MS 416, f. 157, is reproduced in Greg, *English Literary Autographs*, plate LXV(c). Some later transcripts of letters by Foxe are in the Bodleian (Rawlinson K (Hearne) 45, f. 4v); Bradford Central Library (Hopkinson MSS, Vol. 19, f. 37r-v); Cambridge University Library (MS Mm. 1. 42, pp. 55, 82); Lambeth Palace (MS 2010, f. 117); and The Queen's College, Oxford (MS 284, f. 41).

Printed exempla of Foxe's *Pandectae locorum communium*, a huge commonplace book (published in 1572 and 1585) consisting of a preface, an index, and titles at the top of blank leaves, can be found in the British Library (Add. MS 6038, with extensive notes by Sir Julius Caesar, which he finished 12 December 1629; Harley MS 783, with MS entries possibly by Samuel Foxe?; Lansdowne MS 679, with MS entries by Samuel Foxe and his son Thomas Foxe); and in Cambridge University Library (MS Mm. 3. 7, with anonymous entries).

Foxe's *Actes and Monuments* — popularly known as *The Book of Martyrs* — was one of the most popular books of the 16th and 17th centuries and was frequently quoted in commonplace books and miscellanies. Among the many MSS of this kind which contain extracts and which have not received entries in the *Index* are the following:

University of Birmingham (MSS 13/i/19: a MS book of sayings of 16th-century English martyrs, taken from Foxe?); Bodleian (MSS Ashmole 1139, f. 106r-v; Gough London 8, f. 13v seq.; Rawl. D. 400, ff. 99-100); British Library (Add. MSS 21070, f. 37 seq.: 39830: Harley MS 785, ff. 76-9v; Sloane MS 922, pp. 3-34); Cambridge University Library (MS Gg. 4. 13, pp. 157-205); Durham Cathedral (Hunter MS 112); Huntington (EL 6162; also the Hastings Collection, in a MS tract by Thomas Cartwright?, printed in *HMC* 78, Hastings MSS, I (1928), 442-6); Inner Temple Library (Petyt MSS 511, Vols. 11, 17; 512, Vol. 1; 553, Vols. 5, 8, 25; 538, Vols. 7, 13, 17); Lambeth Palace (MS 113, ff. 107v, 175v-6); Northamptonshire Record Office (F.H. 4218); University College London (MS Ogden 7/24); and in a folio volume relating to Chester among the Wilbraham MSS recorded in *HMC*, 4th Report (1874), Appendix, p. 416 (unlocated: not found among Chester City and County archives).

The exemplum of the first edition of *Actes and Monuments* (1563) which the printer, John Day, presented to King's College, Cambridge, is still preserved there (pressmark M. 33. 59) but now lacks the title leaf.

PB.

ARRANGEMENT

See also Addenda to Part 2, p. 627

FACSIMILE XV — John Foxe: Draft of an untitled preface (inscribed at the top in a later hand) (FxJ 12). British Library, Harley MS 416, folio 145 recto. Reproduced by permission of the British Library.

Fox's Preface to a Booke

Although the studious mynd of this godly brother writer therof, and the worthynes of the work, hauyng in yt matter enough to commende yt self, hath no neede of any furtherance of other commendation, especially beyng assigned and sufficiently authorised by the approbation of the right Reverend in God the L. Archbisshop now of Yorke, then bisshop of London, yet notwithstandyng beyng so requested both by the author and the printer also therof to adioyne somewhat by waye of preface, I thought yt not amisse to satisfie [illegible]

and so much the more, for that perceavyng the contents of this treatise collected as principall flowres out of the best learned writers, I thinke the same not so very frutefull only, but especially for the staying of them which want comfort and consolation, nothyng doubtyng but by readyng therof, thou shalt better understand, gentle reader, thy self neyther any labour lost, nor tyme misspent, bestowed and employed in the readyng and tastyng therof.

John Foxe

PROSE

FxJ 1 *Actes and Monuments.*

Copy of an abbreviated version, transcribed from a printed edition; imperfect, lacking the beginning and end; c. 1650.

First pub. (complete) London, 1563; ed. Josiah Pratt, 8 vols (London, 1870, 1853-68).

University of Chicago, MS f-115.

--- -----

See also FxJ 3, *Miscellaneous Papers* (FxJ 21-5), and INTRODUCTION.

*FxJ 2 *An omnis mundi inferioris gubernatio ab influentiis dependent coelestibus.*

Autograph treatise on astrology written while Foxe was a fellow of Magdalen College, Oxford; one in a series of 'Letters & Writings of J. Fox in y[e] University' bound in a composite volume of MSS (see FxJ 22); [1544-5].

First pub. (from this MS, with a translation) in Smith, *ELR*, 1 (1971), 210-25.

British Library, Lansdowne MS 388, ff. 62-5.

--- *Book of Martyrs.*

See FxJ 1.

*FxJ 3 *Commentarii rerum in ecclesia gestarum.*

Autograph Latin account of John Wicliffe and his followers, first printed in *Commentarii rerum* (Strasbourg, 1554), later translated into English and incorporated in *Actes and Monuments*; together with Foxe's original dedication (to Duke Christopher of Würtemberg); [1554].

British Library, Lansdowne MS 335.

*FxJ 4 *De contemnendis opibus.*

Autograph inspirational piece written while Foxe was a fellow of Magdalen College, Oxford; one in a series of 'Letters & Writings of J. Fox in ye University' bound in a composite volume of MSS (see FxJ 22); [1544-5].

Unpublished; recorded in Smith, *ELR*, 1 (1971), 211.

British Library, Lansdowne MS 388, ff. 92v-100.

*FxJ 5 *De re eucharistica.*

Autograph; one in a series of 'Letters & Writings of J. Fox in y[e] University' bound in a composite volume of MSS (see FxJ 22); [1544-5].

Unpublished; recorded in John Bale, *Scriptorum illustrium* (Basle, 1557), p. 733. This MS recorded in Mozley, p. 245.

British Library, Lansdowne MS 388, ff. 175-82.

*FxJ 6 *De regno clauium disputatio adversus perturbatas conscientias.*

Autograph inspirational piece written while Foxe was a fellow of Magdalen College, Oxford; one in a series of 'Letters & Writings of J. Fox in y[e] University' bound in a composite volume of MSS (see FxJ 22); [1544-5].

Unpublished; recorded in Smith, *ELR*, 1 (1971), 211.

British Library, Lansdowne MS 388, ff. 105-10v.

*FxJ 7 *De tota sacramenti eucharistiae causa.*

Autograph translation into Latin of Thomas Cranmer's *Answer unto a Crafty and Sophistical Cavillation*; [1556-7].

Unpublished; discussed in Mozley, p. 56.

British Library, Harley MS 418.

*FxJ 8 [*Digest of Erasmus's Querimonia pacis*].

Autograph, written while Foxe was a fellow of Magdalen College, Oxford; one in a series of 'Letters & Writings of J. Fox in y[e] University' bound in a composite volume of MSS (see FxJ 22); [1544-5].

Unpublished; recorded in Smith, *ELR*, 1 (1971), 211.

British Library, Lansdowne MS 388, ff. 66-71.

*FxJ 9 *Expostulatio Jesu Christi cum humano genere.*

Autograph, in a composite volume of Foxe's papers; c. 1550.

Publication not traced; recorded in John Bale, *Scriptorum illustrium* (Basle, 1557), p. 733, as 'Expostulationem Christicum homine'. This MS recorded in Mozley, p. 243.

British Library, Harley MS 423, ff. 129-47.

--- *Pandectae locorum communium.*

See INTRODUCTION.

*FxJ 10 *Papa confutatus.*

Autograph, in a composite volume of theological tracts; imperfect; [1580].

First pub. London, 1580.

British Library, Lansdowne MS 353, ff. 225-384.

*FxJ 11 *Praefationis operibus D. Johann Chrysostomi praemittendae.*

Autograph Latin preface to an edition of the works of St Chrysostom, in a composite volume of Foxe's papers; [1557].

First pub. in *Opera D. Ioannis Chrysostomi*, Vol. I (Basle, 1557).

British Library, Harley MS 416, ff. 148-9.

*FxJ 12 [*Preface*].

Autograph untitled preface, beginning 'Although ye arduous mynd of thys godly brother cōpiler herof...', inscribed in a later hand 'Fox's Preface to a Book', in a composite volume of Foxe's papers.

Publication not traced. See FACSIMILE XV.

British Library, Harley MS 416, f. 145.

*FxJ 13 *Reformatio legum ecclesiasticarum.*

Copy of canon laws, formerly belonging to Archbishop Thomas Cranmer, with Foxe's autograph annotations; used for Foxe's edition of the *Reformatio*; [1571].

First pub. London, 1571. This MS discussed in Mozley, p. 80.

British Library, Harley MS 426.

--- *Rerum in ecclesia gestarum commentarii.*

See FxJ 3.

FxJ 14 *A Sermon of Christ Crucified.*

Notes of Foxe's sermon on 24 March 1569/70, headed 'Mr foxe at paules crosse in good frydaye the xxiiii of februari anno 1570' and inscribed 'getherde bi the pson of S agnes and corrected by master fox', in a composite volume of Foxe's papers; [1570].

First pub. London, 1570.

British Library, Harley MS 425, ff. 131-3v.

FxJ 15 *Syllogisticon, hoc est argumenta... de re et materia sacramenti eucharistici &c.*

Copy, entitled 'Syllogisticon. hoc est: Argvmenta sev Probationes & Resolutiones... De re materia Sacramenti Eucharistici. Cum Epistola ad Papistas hortatoria'; mid-16th century.

First pub. London, [1560-4?].

Christ Church, Oxford, MS 140.

*FxJ 16 *Tables of Grammar.*

Autograph page of Latin grammar with an English explanation, probably used in the compilation of Foxe's *Tables of Grammar*, in a composite volume of papers relating to Foxe and his descendants (see FxJ 24); c. 1551-2.

First pub. 1552 (no exemplum extant). This MS recorded in Mozley, p. 35. Foxe's autograph letter to Sir William Cecil asking for a licence to print this work is in the British Library, Add. MS 34727, f. 2.

British Library, Lansdowne MS 819, f. 90.

*FxJ 17 [*Tract on Rhetoric and Dialectics*].

Autograph, written while Foxe was a fellow of Magdalen College, Oxford; one in a series of 'Letters & Writings of J. Fox in ye University' bound in a composite volume of MSS (see FxJ 22); [1544-5].

Unpublished; recorded in Smith, *ELR*, 1 (1971), 211.

British Library, Lansdowne MS 388, ff. 71v-7v.

DRAMATIC WORKS

*FxJ 18 *Christus triumphans.*

Autograph draft, with extensive revisions, in a composite volume of MSS; c. 1556.

First pub. Basle, 1556; edited (with a translation) by John Hazel Smith in *Two Latin Comedies by John Foxe the Martyrologist* (Ithaca & London, 1973), pp. 199-371. This MS collated in Smith, with a facsimile of f. 132 on p. 201.

British Library, Lansdowne MS 1045, ff. 132-55.

FxJ 19 -----

Exemplum of the edition of 1556 containing MS annotations, possibly used as a prompt book for a production (at Oxford or Cambridge?); c. 1562?

This item collated in Smith, p. 376 seq.

Harvard, *53-1371.

*FxJ 20 *Titus et Gesippus.*

Autograph draft, with extensive revisions, written while Foxe was a fellow of Magdalen College, Oxford; one in a series of 'Letters & Writings of J. Fox in ye University' bound in a composite volume of MSS (see FxJ 22); [1544-5].

First pub. (from this MS, with a translation) in

Titus et Gesippus

Two Latin Comedies by John Foxe the Martyrologist, ed. John Hazel Smith (Ithaca & London, 1973), pp. 50-197, with a facsimile of f. 121 on p. 53.

British Library, Lansdowne MS 388, ff. 121-46, 112-16.

MISCELLANEOUS

*FxJ 21 [*Miscellaneous Papers*].

A large collection of Foxe's papers bound in ten volumes, consisting of numerous letters, notes, transcripts and theological tracts, some autograph, some in other hands, many relating to his work as a martyrologist; once owned by John Strype (1643-1737); 16th century.

These MSS analysed in *A Catalogue of the Harleian Manuscripts in the British Museum* (London, 1808), I, 236-50, 359. For individual works see FxJ 9, 11, 12, 14.

British Library, Harley MSS 416-17, 419-25, 590.

*FxJ 22 -----

A composite volume of papers formerly owned by John Strype, including a life of Foxe by his son Samuel Foxe (ff. 2-52), Foxe's autograph drafts of letters and other writings composed while he was a fellow of Magdalen College, Oxford [1544-5] (ff. 53v-148), Foxe's autograph extracts from a book by John Purvey on the Eucharist (ff. 166-75), and letters and exercises by Samuel Foxe (ff. 184-250); 16th and 17th centuries.

This MS analysed in *A Catalogue of the Lansdowne Manuscripts in the British Museum*, Part II (London, 1819), pp. 112-13. For individual works see FxJ 2, 4-6, 8, 17, 20.

British Library, Lansdowne MS 388.

*FxJ 23 -----

A bound collection of Foxe's papers, consisting of documents and transcripts used in the writing of *Actes and Monuments*, most of them being printed in that work; 16th century.

British Library, Lansdowne MS 389.

*FxJ 24 -----

A composite volume of papers collected by John Strype, consisting chiefly of documents relating to Foxe and his descendants, particularly concerning property, from 1584 to 1654, including (f. 95) a list of books and manuscripts belonging to Foxe.

See also FxJ 16.

British Library, Lansdowne MS 819.

FxJ 25 -----

Two composite volumes of historical tracts and documents including 18 items owned and used by Foxe; these items are included in a list of 23 'Manuscripts out of John Fox his study' in a late 16th century hand in Vol. 46, f. 29; chiefly 16th century.

The list of MSS is printed in J. Conway Davies, *Catalogue of Manuscripts in the Library of the Honourable Society of the Inner Temple* (London, 1972), I, 43-4; the volumes are analysed in this catalogue, Vol. II, 847-83.

Inner Temple Library, Petyt MS 538, Vols. 46, 47.

--- -----

See also INTRODUCTION.

George Gascoigne

1542?-77

ABBREVIATIONS

Cunliffe *The Complete Works of George Gascoigne*, ed. John W. Cunliffe, 2 vols (Cambridge, 1907-10).

Prouty George Gascoigne, *A Hundreth Sundrie Flowres*, ed. C. T. Prouty, University of Missouri Studies, 17 (Columbia, 1942).

For abbreviations used throughout Volume I, see p.xi.

INTRODUCTION

None of the works attributed wholly or in part to Gascoigne in Cunliffe is known to survive in the author's hand. Of scribal MSS, the most important are the copies that Gascoigne presented to Queen Elizabeth of *Hemetes the Hermit* (GaG 4) and *The Grief of Joye* (GaG 3), the former signed and with some drawings probably in his hand. Beside these two MSS, an early copy of *Jocasta* is preserved (GaG 6), and there is an early copy of the anonymous English version of *Hemetes* (GaG 5). The only other MSS of Gascoigne's works are verse extracts in miscellanies; they have not been previously recorded by editors.

For an argument that two poems in a miscellany compiled by Edward Pudsey (1573-1613) may perhaps be attributed to Gascoigne on stylistic evidence, see Juliet Mary Gowan, *An Edition of Edward Pudsey's Commonplace Book (c. 1600-1615)* (unpublished M. Phil., University of London, 1967). These poems are verses beginning 'Pleasure on whome senses as seruants wayt' (Bodleian, MS Eng. poet. d. 3, f. 1v) and 'Dy dy desire and bid delight adew' (*ibid.*, f. 2). They have not been given entries in the *Index*.

Two letters sent by Gascoigne to Lord Burghley are in the Public Record Office: one, of 15 September 1576, in SP.70/139, the other, of 7 October 1576, in SP.70/140. These letters are reproduced in Greg, *English Literary Autographs*, plate XXXVII. Another possibly autograph letter, now unlocated, was sent to Sir Nicholas Bacon on 1 January 1576/7. This letter, formerly among Lord Townshend's papers recorded in *HMC*, 11th Report, Appendix IV (1887), p. 3, is printed in B. M. Ward, 'George Gascoigne and his Circle', *RES*, 2 (1926), 32-41. Ward notes that it includes a six-line verse (beginning 'Before the sturdye colte will byde the bytt') and a drawing of a man on horseback which supports the probability that the drawings in *Hemetes* (GaG 4) were executed by the poet himself.

Various other documents relating to Gascoigne's life are cited by Ward and by C. T. Prouty in his biography, *George Gascoigne: Elizabethan Courtier, Soldier, and Poet* (New York, 1942). Prouty reproduces as his frontispiece the title page of a printed exemplum of Petrarch, *Il Petrarcha con la spositione di M. Giovanni Andrea* (1553?) bearing Gascoigne's signature, a volume owned in 1942 by Mr Leon Mandel of Chicago. The signature of a George Gascoigne, probably the poet, is also found in a MS political discourse originally presented to Henry VIII, now in the British Library (Royal MS 12 A. LXIII, f. 48).

A printed exemplum of *The Whole woorkes of George Gascoigne* (London, 1587) in the British Library (Department of Printed Books, C. 34. f. 8) has three leaves at the end containing MS copies of additional poems by Gascoigne transcribed from printed sources; the hand is probably that of an 18th-century scholar. A copy of *Gascoignes Lullabie* (beginning 'Sing lullabie, as women do') (Prouty, p. 150) in the Folger (MS V. a. 339, f. 181) is a forgery by J. P. Collier: see Giles E. Dawson, 'John Payne Collier's Great Forgery', *SB*, 24 (1971), 1-26 (pp. 10-11).

PB.

ARRANGEMENT

Verse	GaG 1-3
Prose	GaG 4-5
Dramatic works	GaG 6.

George Gascoigne

VERSE

GaG 1 *The arraignment of a Lover* ('At Beautyes barre as I dyd stande').

Copy, untitled, here beginning 'At beautyse bar where I dyd stand', in a verse miscellany owned in 1642 by one Gabriell Penne; mid-late 16th century.

First pub. in *A Hundreth sundrie Flowres* (London, [1573]); Cunliffe, I, 38-9; Prouty, pp. 144-5.

Bodleian, MS Ashmole 48, ff. 139-8v.

--- *'Before the sturdye colte will byde the bytt'.*

See INTRODUCTION.

--- *Gascoignes araignement.*

See GaG 1.

GaG 2 *Gascoignes good morrow* ('You that have spent the silent night').

Copy in a miscellany compiled by Robert Dobbes, Vicar of Runcorn, Cheshire; c. 1601-7.

First pub. in *A Hundreth sundrie Flowres* (London, [1573]); Cunliffe, I, 55-7; Prouty, pp. 161-3.

British Library, Add. MS 30076, f. 3v.

GaG 3 *The Grief of Joye* ('The griefe of joye, in worthie wise to write').

Copy, written as a New Year's gift for Queen Elizabeth, complete with dedication, preface, &c.; the references to the Queen in gilt; presented to the Queen on 1 January 1576/7.

First pub. (from this MS) in *The Complete Poems of George Gascoigne*, ed. W.C. Hazlitt (London, 1869-70), II, 253-302; Cunliffe, II, 511-57. Facsimile of the dedication (f. 3) in Alfred Fairbank and Bruce Dickins, *The Italic Hand in Tudor Cambridge*, Cambridge Bibliographical Society Monograph No. 5 (London, 1962), plate 20.

British Library, Royal MS 18 A. LXI.

PROSE

*GaG 4 *The Tale of Hemetes the Heremyte.*

Copy, the anonymous English text accompanied by Gascoigne's translations into Latin, Italian, and French; written as a New Year's Gift for Queen Elizabeth, with a dedicatory letter signed by Gascoigne (f. 6v), pen and ink drawings of Gascoigne presenting his book to the Queen, and other emblems, the drawings apparently all in Gascoigne's hand; presented to the Queen c. 1 January 1575/6.

First pub. (English and Latin) in Synesius, Bishop of Cyrene, *A Paradoxe* ([London], 1579). Printed from this MS, with the drawings, in Cunliffe, II, 473-510. Facsimile of the dedicatory epistle in Greg, *English Literary Autographs*, plate XXXVII(d). In the dedicatory epistle Gascoigne specifically disclaims authorship of the English version, which originally formed part of the royal entertainment at Woodstock in 1575.

British Library, Royal MS 18 A. XLVIII.

GaG 5 -----

Copy of the English version in a volume of entertainments presented by Sir Henry Lee (1530-1610) and others before Queen Elizabeth; once owned by Lee; imperfect; c. 1575.

British Library, Add. MS 41499, ff. 4-5v.

DRAMATIC WORKS

GaG 6 *Jocasta.*

Copy, entitled 'Jocasta: a tragedie written in Greke by Euripedes translated and digested into Acte by George Gascoign and ffraunces Kynwelmershe of Grays ynne, 1566'; once owned by Roger North, second Baron North (1530-1600); late 16th century.

First pub. in *A Hundreth sundrie Flowres* (London, [1573]); Cunliffe, I, 244-324. This MS collated in Cunliffe.

British Library, Add. MS 34063.

--- *The Tale of Hemetes the Heremyte.*

See GaG 4-5.

Robert Greene

1558-92

ABBREVIATIONS

Grosart *The Life and Complete Works in Prose and Verse of Robert Greene*, ed. Alexander B. Grosart, 15 vols, The Huth Library (privately printed, 1881-6; reprinted New York, 1964).

For abbreviations used throughout Volume I, see p.xi.

INTRODUCTION

No example of Greene's autograph is known. As the frontispiece to the first volume of his edition of Greene (1881) Grosart reproduced a MS Latin prayer taken from St Augustine's *Meditations* and signed 'Robert Grene', a MS which he said was 'believed to be' Greene's autograph. The MS was then owned by 'a private collector in London' and is now unlocated. In fact, all circumstances militate against this manuscript's having any connection with Robert Greene the writer and dramatist. Not only is the spelling of the name different (without the medial double e), but there is also the inherent improbability of Greene's making excerpts from St Augustine, besides which the writing may well belong to the early-17th century. In any case, the MS might be a transcript of a transcript made by one 'Robert Grene' (and the name is hardly uncommon). Grosart's facsimile is reproduced (reduced) in A. D. Wraight and Virginia F. Stern, *In Search of Christopher Marlowe* (London, 1965), p. 185.

Three notable items are recorded in the entries below. The most important is what is probably Edward Alleyn's part in *Orlando Furioso* (GrR 9). A printed exemplum of *A Looking Glasse for London and England* (GrR 8) is of some interest since it is one of the earliest surviving printed plays marked up as a contemporary prompt book. There also survives a playhouse MS copy of a sequel to Greene's *Friar Bacon* (GrR 7) which can probably be likewise attributed to that author.

In addition there are just a few known extracts from Greene's prose works in miscellanies (GrR 1-6), items which have not been noted by editors. Extracts from his *Pandosto: The Triumph of Time* (1588) also appear in John Evans's miscellany *Hesperides, or the Muses' Garden* (c. 1655), for details of which see WILLIAM SHAKESPEARE, INTRODUCTION.

PB.

ARRANGEMENT

Prose	GrR 1-6
Dramatic works	GrR 7-9.

Robert Greene

PROSE

GrR 1 *Arbasto: The Anatomie of Fortune.*

Extracts in a MS book of extracts from prose romances; c. 1600.

First pub. London, 1584; Grosart, III, 171-253.

Folger, MS V. b. 83, ff. 8-11.

GrR 2 *Ciceronis Amor. Tullies Loue.*

Extracts in a MS book of extracts from prose romances; c. 1600.

First pub. London, 1589; Grosart, VII, 95-216.

Folger, MS V. b. 83, ff. 5-8.

GrR 3 *Greenes Farewell to Folly.*

Extracts in a MS book of extracts from prose romances; c. 1600.

First pub. London, 1591; Grosart, IX, 223-348.

Folger, MS V. b. 83, ff. 41-7.

GrR 4 *Menaphon.*

Extracts in a miscellany possibly compiled by one William Parkyn (fl. 1588); late 16th century.

First pub. London, 1589; Grosart, VI, 1-146.

Folger, MS V. a. 307.

GrR 5 *Orpharion.*

Extracts in a MS book of extracts from prose romances; c. 1600.

First known publication London, 1599; Grosart, XII, 1-94.

Folger, MS V. b. 83, ff. 49-54.

--- *Pandosto: The Triumph of Time.*

See INTRODUCTION.

GrR 6 *Planetomachia.*

Extracts in a MS book of extracts from prose romances; c. 1600.

First pub. London, 1585; Grosart, V, 1-135.

Folger, MS V. b. 83, ff. 36-41.

DRAMATIC WORKS

GrR 7 *John of Bordeaux or The Second Part of Friar Bacon.*

Copy of a sequel to Greene's *Friar Bacon* probably also by Greene, with insertions in another hand and revisions by at least three more hands associated with the playhouse including the playwright Henry Chettle; untitled; c. 1590-4.

First pub. (from this MS) Oxford, 1936, ed. W.L. Renwick and W.W. Greg, Malone Society, with eight pages of facsimiles. This MS discussed in Harry R. Hoppe, 'John of Bordeaux: A Bad Quarto that never reached print', *Studies in Honor of A.H.R. Fairchild* (Columbia, 1946), 121-32; Greene's authorship supported in Waldo F. McNeir, 'Robert Greene and *John of Bordeaux*', *PMLA*, 64. i (1949), 781-801.

Owned by the Duke of Northumberland, Alnwick Castle, MS 507.

GrR 8 *A Looking Glasse for London and England.*

Exemplum of the fourth edition [1603-7] with numerous MS annotations, used as a prompt book by a London theatrical company; imperfect; early 17th century.

First pub. London, 1594; Grosart, XIV, 1-113; ed. W.W. Greg, Malone Society (Oxford, 1932). This item (formerly owned by F. Locker) recorded in Grosart, XIV, 2; described, with facsimile pages, in Charles Read Baskervill, 'A Prompt Copy of *A Looking Glass for London and England*', *MP*, 30 (1932-3), 29-51; see also Berta Sturman, 'A Date and a Printer for *A Looking Glasse for London and England*, Q4', *SB*, 21 (1968), 248-53.

University of Chicago, PR 2297.L8 160 - Rare bk.

GrR 9 *Orlando Furioso.*

The part of Orlando in the hand of a playhouse scribe, with additions probably made by the actor Edward Alleyn (1566-1626), probably used for a performance by Lord Strange's company in February 1591/2; imperfect; [1591-2].

First pub. London, 1594; Grosart, XIII, 111-98; ed. W.W. Greg and R.B. McKerrow, Malone Society (Oxford, 1907). This MS collated in Grosart; printed, with facsimile pages, in *Two Elizabethan Stage Abridgements: The Battle of Alcazar and Orlando Furioso*, ed. W.W. Greg, Malone Society (Oxford, 1922), and in Greg, *Dramatic Documents*, I, 176-87, & Vol. II; complete facsimile in *The Henslowe Papers*, ed. R.A. Foakes (London, 1977), II, in endpocket.

Dulwich College, Alleyn Papers, Vol. I, No. 138, ff. 261-71.

Fulke Greville
Lord Brooke
1554-1628

ABBREVIATIONS

Bullough *Poems and Dramas of Fulke Greville*, ed. Geoffrey Bullough, 2 vols (Edinburgh & London, [1939]).

Grosart *The Works in Verse and Prose Complete of the Right Honourable Fulke Greville*, ed. Alexander B. Grosart, 4 vols, Fuller Worthies Library (privately printed, 1870).

Wilkes, *Remains* Fulke Greville, *The Remains*, ed. G. A. Wilkes (Oxford, 1965).

For abbreviations used throughout Volume I, see p.xi.

INTRODUCTION

The six bound volumes of Fulke Greville's literary MSS formerly at Warwick Castle and now in the British Library (Add. MSS 54566-71) have been described as the most substantial existing authorised MS text of any distinguished Elizabethan or Jacobean poet. The Warwick MSS, which are all fair copies made by scribes, some containing the author's autograph corrections and revisions, were first collated in Grosart (1870), and have since been used by other editors, notably Bullough (1939) and Professor G. A. Wilkes of the University of Sydney, who is currently re-editing Greville's complete poetry and plays. The six volumes are generally cited by the letters A-F (see Bullough, I, 27-9), and Bullough designated the scribal hands by the letters a-d (I, 32), although scribes a and b have since been recognised as one and the same and it is possible that this hand is also that of scribe d. The MSS are described in some detail in W. Hilton Kelliher, 'The Warwick Manuscripts of Fulke Greville', *BMQ*, 34 (1969-70), 107-21.

Apart from the Warwick MSS, the most notable MS texts of Greville's works are additional copies of his play *Mustapha* (GrF 29-31), certain variant readings for that play recorded by his editor Sir Kenelm Digby (GrF 32), and early copies of his *Life of Sidney* (GrF 24-6). There are also a few early copies of particular poems and a draft letter by Sir John Coke (1563-1644) (GrF 6) which gives us some idea of what Greville's lost Latin epitaph on Sidney was like. One poem, which begins 'A tale I once did heare a true man tell' and which did not appear either in Greville's *Certaine Learned and Elegant Workes* (London, 1633) or in his *Remains* (London, 1670), can be added to the canon on the basis of ascription to 'Mr Grevell' and to 'Sr F. G.' in miscellanies owned by Sir John Harington and Sir Robert Cecil respectively (GrF 8-9); as regards the dating of these copies it should be noted that Greville was not knighted till 1603 (his father was knighted in 1565). Six other poems are attributed to Greville in Grosart (II, 131-47) but without any evidence except for the poem 'Away with these selfe-louing-Lads' (II, 137-9) which he failed to notice is Sonnet lii of *Caelica* (GrF 4). An 18th-century copy of John Dowland's setting of that sonnet in the British Library (Add. MS 29291, f. 12) has not been given an entry. The MSS recorded in the *Index* have not been previously noted by editors unless otherwise stated.

Greville's known prose works are all printed in Grosart, Vol. IV. Greville's *Letter to an Honourable Lady* (GrF 15) and the so-called *Letter to Grevill Varney on his Travels* (GrF 16-23) are included in the entries since they are basically essays in epistolary form. The latter, however, is not an orginal composition of Greville's but is one version of a 'formula' letter perhaps originated by Sir Thomas Bodley (1545-1613) and also used by Bacon or the Earl of Essex (see GrF 16). Grosart mentions an unspecified copy of 'Greville's' letter in the 'British Museum' (IV, 301), but this may be a mistake; it is possible, though, that other volumes of state letters are to be found containing copies of the letter besides those recorded in the *Index*.

A prose work entitled *The Five Yeares of King James* which was published under Greville's name in 1643 was rejected from the canon in Grosart (I, xiii-xiv), and also in an article by him in *N & Q*, 4th Ser. 2 (21 November 1868), 489-90. MS copies of the work include one owned by the Duke of Northumberland at Alnwick Castle (MS 528 (Safe No. 1)), two in Cambridge University Library (MSS Dd. 3. 86, (4), and Ee. 4. 14, ff. 1-60v), and one at The Queen's College, Oxford (MS 32, ff. 48-101).

A large number of original letters of Greville and other documents containing his handwriting are preserved in the British Library, the Public Record Office, the Bodleian, Warwick Castle, the Warwickshire Record Office (CR 136 B/190), Hatfield House, Melbourne Hall, the Folger, the Robert H. Taylor Collection at Princeton, the Osborn Collection at Yale, and in other repositories. A useful list of MS materials used by one biographer appears in Ronald A. Rebholz, *The Life of Fulke Greville, First Lord Brooke* (Oxford, 1971), pp. 353-5. A few relevant documents are also cited in Grosart. Facsimiles of letters in Greville's hand appear in Greg, *English Literary Autographs*, plate XLIII (his example b, however, is the hand of Greville's father: see iii. 1932. addenda); in the Sotheby sale catalogue for 4 July 1955, Lot 790 (one of six letters to Richard Bagot, now in the Robert H. Taylor Collection); and (a letter in which Greville admits to the illegibility of his hand) in FACSIMILE XVI. Facsimile examples of letters in the hand of one of his scribes appear in *BMQ*, 34 (1969-70), plate XXVI; a letter of 10 March 1599/1600 in the hand of a scribe and signed by Greville is reproduced in Sir Henry James, *Facsimiles of National Manuscripts from William the Conqueror to Queen Anne*, 4 vols (Southampton, 1865-8), III, plate XCIII; and two documents signed by him in 1573 and 1616, now in the Hyde Collection, Somerville, New Jersey, are reproduced in the printed catalogue of the R.B. Adam Library (1929), III, facing p. 221 and after p. 11. For a printed exemplum of Bandello's works with the schoolboy scribblings of both Greville and Sidney, see SIR PHILIP SIDNEY, INTRODUCTION. Features of Greville's handwriting are discussed in Bullough, I, 29-30, and in Croft, *Autograph Poetry*, I, 15.

PB.

ARRANGEMENT

Verse	GrF 1-14
Prose	GrF 15-26
Dramatic works	GrF 27-46.

See also Addenda to Part 2, p. 627

FACSIMILE XVI — Fulke Greville: Letter to Sir Robert Cecil, 25 September 1607. Hatfield House, Cecil Papers 122/87. Reduced by approx. 10 per cent. Reproduced by courtesy of The Marquess of Salisbury.

Right honorable & my very good lord, I had
busines of myne, ther hathe falen out som questio
since it pleasd your lordship to make reference of
it to Sr ffrauncis Baron. The perticulers I
shame to desier you, I am other mans hand
more lejible of. I must acknowledge the hole to
your lordes favor and accordingly hath proceded
In my offers, in the Equallest sence, that either
my father, or I, could gather out of yor lordships
words or letters. In the rest, my most humble
desire is, that your honor would vouchsafe, to
sygnefy your fynall pleasure to Sr ffrauncis, that
I whose fortune can be of no use to you, may cease
to be further troublesome. & so most humbly
craving pardon, I commit your honor to god, from
Warwicks parke this 25 of Octeber

your lordships humble frend
& servant

since the next day after I
came hither, I have never bene
well, ther and your lordships
own [illegible] to the [illegible]
of I [illegible] & following the
busines, I hope will excuse
my not waiting upon you
myself

ffulke Grevyll

Fulke Greville

VERSE

*GrF 1 *Caelica.*

Copy of the original sequence of 109 'sonnets' made by one of Greville's amanuenses (Bullough's 'scribe a'), with Greville's autograph revisions, some of the revisions copied again fairly by a second amanuensis ('scribe d'); constituting 'Warwick MSS, Vol. E'; c. 1619.

The entire sonnet sequence first pub. in *Certaine Learned and Elegant Workes* (London, 1633); Bullough, I, 73-153. This MS collated in Bullough. Facsimiles of sonnets lxxvi and lxxviii in Bullough, I, facing pp. 32 and 112; sonnet lxxvii in *BMQ*, 34 (1969-70), plate XXIV; sonnet xciii in Croft, *Autograph Poetry*, I, 15; sonnets lxxvii and lxxviii, with texts and discussion, in Norman K. Farmer, Jr., 'Holograph Revisions in Two Poems by Fulke Greville', *ELR*, 4 (1974), 98-110.

British Library, Add. MS 54570.

GrF 2 ----- *Sonnet v* ('Who trusts for trust, or hopes of loue for loue').

Copy of the incipit of an early version, here 'Who euer thinks or hopes', in a musical setting by John Dowland, in a MS virginal book compiled by one 'R: Cr.' (? Richard Creighton); c. 1635-8.

This sonnet first pub. in John Dowland, *First Booke of Songes or Ayres* (London, 1597); Bullough, I, 75.

Bibliothèque Nationale, Paris, Département de la Musique, MS Conservatoire Rés. 1186, f. 6v.

GrF 3 ----- -----

Copy of an early version, beginning 'Whoever thinks or hopes of love for love', in a musical setting by John Dowland, in a MS songbook compiled by Thomas Hamond (d. 1662) of Suffolk; c. 1630.

Bodleian, MS Mus. f. 7-10: f. 7, fol. 2v.

GrF 4 ----- *Sonnet lii* ('Away with these self-louing lads').

Copy, after a false start (on f. 146v), in a verse miscellany compiled by John Harington of Stepney (1520?-82) and his son Sir John Harington of Kelston (1560-1612); late 16th century.

This sonnet first pub. in John Dowland, *First Booke of Songes or Ayres* (London, 1597); Bullough, I, 104. Printed from this MS in Hughey, *Arundel Harington MS*, I, No. 198, pp. 242-3; collated in Bullough.

Owned by the Duke of Norfolk, Arundel Castle, MSS (Special Press), 'Harrington MS. Temp. Eliz.', f. 147.

GrF 4.3, 4.5, 4.8 See Addenda, p. 627.

--- ----- -----

See also INTRODUCTION.

GrF 5 ----- *Sonnet lxxxiv* ('Farewell sweet Boy, complaine not of my truth').

Copy in a miscellany later owned by one Joseph Hall; c. 1630s-50.

This sonnet first pub. in Martin Peerson, *Mottects* (London, 1630); Bullough, I, 134-5.

Folger, MS V. a. 339, f. 43.

GrF 6 [*Epitaph on Sir Philip Sidney*].

Sir John Coke's autograph draft of his letter to Greville in which he quotes from and comments on Greville's lost Latin verse epitaph on Sidney; endorsed by one of Coke's sons 'To S[r] F G. Sent by my father Sept. 16 1615'.

This MS printed in Norman Farmer, Jr., 'Fulke Greville and Sir John Coke: An Exchange of Letters on a History Lecture and Certain Latin Verses on Sir Philip Sidney', *HLQ*, 33 (1969-70), 217-36; see also Joan Rees, 'Fulke Greville's Epitaph on Sidney', *RES*, NS 19 (1968), 47-51.

Owned by the Marquess of Lothian, Melbourne Hall, Cowper (Coke) MSS, packet 15.

GrF 7 *An Inquisition upon Fame and Honour* ('What are Mens liues, but labyrinths of error').

Copy made by one of Greville's amanuenses (Bullough's 'scribe d'), in a MS volume of Greville's works ('Warwick MSS, Vol. B'); c. 1625.

First pub. in *Certaine Learned and Elegant Workes* (London, 1633); Bullough, I, 192-213. This MS collated in Bullough; facsimile of stanza 75 in Bullough, II, facing p. 48.

British Library, Add. MS 54567, ff. 52-66.

GrF 8 *A tale put in verse by M[r] Grevell* ('A tale I once did heare a true man tell').

Copy, headed 'A tale put in verse by M[r] Grevell The ptyes that weare Authores of y[e] true reporte weare M[r] of the Rolles y[t] nowe is and his ladye | to S[r]. M. A.', in a verse miscellany compiled by John Harington of Stepney (1520?-82) and his son Sir John Harington of Kelston (1560-1612); late 16th century.

First pub. (from this MS) in Hughey, *Arundel Harington MS* (1960), I, No. 69, pp. 113-15.

A tale put in verse by Mr Grevell

Owned by the Duke of Norfolk, Arundel Castle, MSS (Special Press), 'Harrington MS. Temp. Eliz.', ff. 35-6.

GrF 9 -----

Copy, untitled, subscribed 'finis Sr F.G.', in a volume of state letters compiled (chiefly by Simon Willis) for Robert Cecil, Earl of Salisbury (1563?-1612); [1603-12].

Owned by the Marquess of Salisbury, Hatfield House, Cecil Papers 286, ff. [23-4].

*GrF 10 *A Treatie of Humane Learning* ('The Mind of Man is this worlds true dimension').

Copy made by one of Greville's amanuenses (Bullough's 'scribe c'), with Greville's autograph corrections or revisions, in a MS volume of his works ('Warwick MSS, Vol. B'); c. 1625.

First pub. in *Certaine Learned and Elegant Workes* (London, 1633); Bullough, I, 154-91. This MS collated in Bullough. Facsimiles of stanza 25 in *BMQ*, 34 (1969-70), plate XXVII; stanzas 61-2 in Bullough, II, facing p. 16.

British Library, Add. MS 54567, ff. 5-30.

GrF 11 *A Treatie of Warres* ('Peace is the haruest of Mans rich creation').

Copy made by one of Greville's amanuenses (Bullough's 'scribe d'), in a MS volume of Greville's works ('Warwick MSS, Vol. B'); c. 1625.

First pub. in *Certaine Learned and Elegant Workes* (London, 1633); Bullough, I, 214-30. This MS collated in Bullough.

British Library, Add. MS 54567, ff. 68-79.

*GrF 12 *A Treatise of Monarchy* ('There was a tyme before the tymes of story').

Copy made by one of Greville's amanuenses (Bullough's 'scribe b'), with corrections in another hand and some corrections in Greville's autograph; untitled; constituting 'Warwick MSS, Vol. A'; c. 1619.

First pub. in *The Remains of Sir Fulk Grevill* (London, 1670). Printed from this MS in Wilkes, *Remains*, pp. 35-202. Facsimiles of stanzas 169-70 in *BMQ*, 34 (1969-70), plate XXV; stanzas 588-90 in Bullough, I, facing p. 160.

British Library, Add. MS 54566.

GrF 13 -----

Copy in the hand of Richard Graves, allegedly transcribed from a MS bequeathed by Greville to his chaplain, Graves's brother; incomplete; 34 pages; mid-17th century.

Harvard, MS Eng 36.

GrF 14 *A Treatise of Religion* ('What makes these manie lawes, these reynes of Power').

Copy made by one of Greville's amanuenses (Bullough's 'scribe d'), in a MS volume of Greville's works ('Warwick MSS, Vol. B'); c. 1625.

First pub. in *The Remains of Sir Fulk Grevill* (London, 1670). Printed from this MS in Wilkes, *Remains*, pp. 203-31.

British Library, Add. MS 54567, ff. 32-50v.

PROSE

GrF 15 *A Letter to an Honourable Lady*.

Copy made by one of Greville's amanuenses (Bullough's 'scribe b'); untitled; constituting 'Warwick MSS, Vol. F'; c. 1619.

First pub. in *Certaine Learned and Elegant Workes* (London, 1633); Grosart, IV, 233-99. Facsimile of part of Chapter III of this MS in Bullough, I, facing p. 224.

British Library, Add. MS 54571.

GrF 16 *Letter to Grevill Varney on his Travels*.

Copy in a volume of letters and state papers owned in the 17th century by William Goswell, James Bedford and Gerard Langbaine; 1st half 17th century.

First pub. in *Certaine Learned and Elegant Workes* (London, 1633); Grosart, IV, 301-6. This essay perhaps originally written by Thomas Bodley and also used by Francis Bacon and/or the Earl of Essex (see FRANCIS BACON, INTRODUCTION); possibly sent by Greville to John Harris rather than Greville Varney: see Norman K. Farmer, Jr., 'Fulke Greville's Letter to a Cousin in France and the Problem of Authorship in Cases of Formula Writing', *RQ*, 22 (1969), 140-7. This MS collated in Grosart and discussed in Farmer, p. 141.

Bodleian, MS University College 152, pp. 13-17.

GrF 16.5 See Addenda, p. 627.

GrF 17 -----

Copy, headed 'Sir Ffulke Grevill to a couzin of his residing in Ffrance', in a volume of letters and state papers; 1st half 17th century.

This MS described in Farmer, pp. 140-1.

Owned by the Marquess of Bute, D 18, item 26.

GrF 18 -----

Copy, headed 'A Letter written by Sr Ffulke Greuill to his cousin Grevill Varney then residing in France...', in a miscellany compiled by a Cambridge man; early 17th century.

Cambridge University Library, MS Add. 7958, ff. 18v-19v.

GrF 19 -----

Copy, headed 'A letter written by S[r] ffulke Grevill to his cousin Grevill Varney...', among the papers of the Gell family formerly of Hopton Hall, Derbyshire; early 17th century.

This MS recorded in *HMC*, 9th Report, Part II (1884), Appendix, p. 386.

Derbyshire Record Office, D 258/56/35, ff. [1v-2v].

GrF 20 -----

Copy, headed 'S[r] Fulk Grevill to a Cosen of his residing in France wherein hee setteth downe what obseruacōns hee thinkes fitt for him to make vse of in his Trauailes', in a volume of state letters and speeches among the papers of the Fuller family of Brightling Park and possibly once owned by Ambrose Trayton of Lewes, Esquire of the Body to James I and Charles I; c. 1620s.

East Sussex Record Office, RAF/F/13/1, ff. 44-5.

GrF 21 -----

Copy, headed 'Sir fulke Grevill to his Kinsman in France', in a volume of state papers and tracts; early-mid-17th century.

This MS recorded in Farmer, p. 141.

Inner Temple Library, Petyt MS 538, Vol. 36, ff. 82-3.

GrF 22 -----

Copy in a volume of essays on travel; early 17th century.

This MS recorded in *BC*, 15 (Summer 1966), p. 156.

Owned by Bent E. Juel-Jensen, Oxford.

GrF 22.5 See Addenda, p. 627.

GrF 23 -----

Copy made by or for Francis Bacon, in a collection of Bacon's letters constituting Volume VIII of the collections of Edmund Gibson, Bishop of London (1669-1748); apparently a letter sent by the Earl of Essex to the Earl of Rutland; imperfect, now lacking signature and address; [1596].

Printed from this MS in *The Works of Francis Bacon*, ed. James Spedding et al. (London, (1857-74), IX, 16-18; see INTRODUCTION and FRANCIS BACON, INTRODUCTION.

Lambeth Palace, MS 936, f. 218.

GrF 23.5 See Addenda, p. 627.

--- -----

See also INTRODUCTION.

GrF 24 *Life of Sir Philip Sidney.*

Copy of an early version; 1st half 17th century.

First pub. London, 1652; Grosart, IV, 1-224; ed. Nowell Smith (Oxford, 1907); now being re-edited for the Clarendon Press by John Gouws. This MS recorded in *BC*, 15 (Summer 1966), p. 156.

Owned by Bent E. Juel-Jensen, Oxford.

GrF 25 -----

Copy of an early version; 1st half 17th century.

This MS described in S. Blaine Ewing, 'A New Manuscript of Greville's "Life of Sidney"', *MLR*, 49 (1954), 424-7.

Shrewsbury Library, MS 295.

GrF 26 -----

Copy bound in two volumes, each volume in a different hand; entitled 'A Dedication to S[r]. Phillip Sidney'; 1st half 17th century.

This MS collated in Grosart and in Smith.

Trinity College, Cambridge, MSS R. 7. 32, 33 (James 774).

DRAMATIC WORKS

GrF 27 *Alaham.*

Copy made by one of Greville's amanuenses (Bullough's 'scribe d'), with pencil markings possibly made by Greville; untitled; constituting 'Warwick MSS, Vol. C'; c. 1625.

First pub. in *Certaine Learned and Elegant Workes* (London, 1633); Bullough, II, 138-213. This MS collated in Bullough; facsimile of p. 108 (part of Act III) in Bullough, II, facing p. 192.

British Library, Add. MS 54568.

GrF 28 *Mustapha.*

Copy of the later version made by one of Greville's amanuenses (Bullough's 'scribe d'), with pencil markings possibly made by Greville; constituting 'Warwick MSS, Vol. D'; c. 1625.

An early version first pub. London, 1609; later version first pub. in *Certaine Learned and Elegant Workes* (London, 1633); Bullough, II, 63-137. This MS collated in Bullough. Facsimiles of part of Chor. 2 in Bullough, II, facing p. 96; III, i, 9-14 in *BMQ*, 34 (1969-70), plate XXVII(b).

British Library, Add. MS 54569.

GrF 29 -----

Copy of an early version; untitled; 28 leaves plus blanks; c. 1609.

This MS collated in Bullough (his 'C text').

Cambridge University Library, MS Ff. 2. 35.

GrF 30 -----

Copy of an early version, the chorus at the end in another hand; imperfect at the end; c. 1609.

Formerly Phillipps MS 9060; this MS briefly discussed in Ronald A. Rebholz, *Life of Fulke Greville* (Oxford, 1971), 101-2.

Folger, MS V. b. 223.

GrF 31 -----

Copy of an early version in two hands, with alterations on f. 19 in another hand; lacking a title leaf; 25 leaves; c. 1609.

This MS sold at Parke-Bernet Galleries, 13 November 1968, Lot 86.

Princeton, Robert H. Taylor Collection.

GrF 32 -----

Printed exemplum of *Certaine Learned and Elegant Workes* (London, 1633) with MS notes on pp. 158-9 at the end of *Mustapha* in the hand of the editor, Sir Kenelm Digby (1603-65), recording an original reading for the *Chorus Quintvs* and noting that the *Chorus Sacerdotvm* 'is misplaced', &c; c. 1633.

This item discussed in W. Hilton Kelliher, 'The Warwick Manuscripts of Fulke Greville', *BMQ*, 34 (1969-70), 107-21 (pp. 117-18, 121).

Bibliothèque Nationale, Paris.

GrF 33 -----

Copy of the *Chorus Sacerdotvm* at the end, headed 'A Chorus of Turkish Priests in Mustapha, by Lord Brooks' and here beginning 'O wearisome condition of humanity!', in a verse miscellany compiled by George Clarke (1660-1736); late 17th-early 18th century.

Bullough, II, 136-7.

Worcester College, Oxford, MSS 6. 13, p. 237.

GrF 34 -----

Copy of the first ten lines of Achmat's soliloquy (II, i, 1-10), headed 'Sir ffulke Greuille of ambition' and here beginning 'Who standing in the shade of humble valleyes', in a miscellany; early 17th century.

Bullough, II, 79-80.

University of Leeds, Brotherton Collection, MS Lt. 25, f. 6v.

GrF 35 ----- IV, iv, 116-17: 'Mischiefe is like the Cockatrices eyes'.

Copy of the couplet, here beginning 'Treason is like a Basiliscus eye', in a composite volume of verse collected by Elias Ashmole (1617-92); mid-17th century.

Bullough, II, 118.

Bodleian, MS Ashmole 36/37, f. 145.

GrF 36 ----- -----

Copy, headed 'On Treason' and here beginning 'Treason is like ye Basiliscus eye', in a verse miscellany compiled by an Oxford man; mid-17th century.

Bodleian, MS CCC. 176, f. 8v.

GrF 37 ----- -----

Copy, here beginning 'Treason is like the Basiliscus eye', in a verse miscellany compiled by an Oxford man and once owned by one Henry Lawson; c. 1630s.

Bodleian, MS Eng. poet. e. 14, f. 89v.

GrF 38 ----- -----

Copy, here beginning 'Treason is like ye Basiliscus Eye', in a verse miscellany compiled by a member of Christ Church, Oxford; c. 1630s-40s.

Bodleian, MS Eng. poet. e. 97, p. 114.

GrF 39 ----- -----

Copy, here beginning 'Treason is like a Basiliscus eye', in a verse miscellany probably compiled by a member of New College, Oxford; c. 1620s-30s.

Bodleian, MS Malone 19, p. 40.

GrF 40 ----- -----

Copy, headed 'Mr Clapham from Mr Foucke Greuill' and here beginning 'Treason is like a Cocatrices eies', in a miscellany compiled by Sir Stephen Powle, Clerk of the Crown; 29 November 1606.

Printed from this MS in G.A. Wilkes, 'The Sequence of the Writings of Fulke Greville, Lord Brooke', *SP*, 56 (1959), 489-503 (p. 491).

Bodleian, MS Tanner 169, f. 43.

GrF 41 ----- -----

Copy, headed 'On Treason' and here beginning 'Treason is like the basiliscus eye', in a verse miscellany compiled by an Oxford man and once owned by one Stephen Welden; mid-17th century.

Folger, MS V. a. 162, f. 35v.

GrF 42 ----- -----

Copy, here beginning 'Treason is like a Basiliscus eye', in a verse miscellany compiled by one or two Oxford men, possibly connected with New College and afterwards with the Inns of Court; 1630s.

Harvard, MS Eng 686, f. 10.

GrF 43 ----- -----

Copy, headed 'On treason' and here beginning 'Treason is like a Basiliscus eye', in a miscellany; c. 1630s.

John Rylands University Library of Manchester, Rylands English MS 410, f. 22v.

GrF 44 ----- -----

Copy, headed 'On Treason' and here beginning 'Treason is like a Basiliske his eye', in a verse miscellany; c. 1634.

Rosenbach Foundation, MS 239/27, p. 52.

GrF 45 ----- -----

Copy, headed 'On Treason' and here beginning 'Treason is like a Basiliscus eye', in a verse miscellany compiled by one Robert Bishop; c. 1630.

Rosenbach Foundation, MS 1083/16, p. 146.

GrF 46 ----- -----

Copy, headed 'Another' [on Treason] and here beginning 'Treason is like the basiliske his eye', in a verse miscellany; c. 1640.

Yale, Osborn Collection, b 62, p. 96.

Joseph Hall
Bishop of Exeter and Norwich

1574-1656

ABBREVIATIONS

Davenport *The Collected Poems of Joseph Hall*, ed. Arnold Davenport (Liverpool, 1949).

Wynter *The Works of the Right Reverend Joseph Hall, D.D.*, ed. Philip Wynter, 10 vols (Oxford, 1863; reprinted New York, 1969).

For abbreviations used throughout Volume I, see p.xi.

INTRODUCTION

For a writer who was as prolific and as controversial as Joseph Hall, there are remarkably few surviving MSS of his works. The only autograph to receive an entry is the draft of *Certain Irrefragable Propositions* which he sent to Archbishop William Laud (HlJ 12 and see FACSIMILE XVII), a document which, with Laud's alterations, was the basis for Hall's *Episcopacy by Divine Right* (1640). A few of his miscellaneous poems are preserved in early copies, but, apart from one extract (HlJ 8), there is no MS of his important satire *Virgidemiae*. A few scattered copies of certain prose works are to be found, including his popular contribution to 17th-century 'character' literature (HlJ 14-16) and an unpublished English translation by Moses Wall of his *Henochismus* (HlJ 53). His most frequently copied piece was his plea for moderation addressed to the House of Commons in 1628 (HlJ 17-30), of which, no doubt, other copies are to be found besides those recorded. The MSS of Hall's works recorded below have not been previously noted by editors unless otherwise stated.

The only notable MS collection of works by Hall, one which accounts for twenty-two entries, is a MS in my own possession. It is a folio volume of 137 leaves (29.5 x 18.5 cm), closely written in a single neat scribal hand, with some of the titles ornamented, and now in an 18th-century binding (the spine lettered 'BISHOP HALL'S WORKS'). The MS contains works published between 1605 and 1623, but the repeated references in titles to 'Josep: Hall now B^p^. of Exon.' indicate a date of transcription after 23 December 1627 and before 15 November 1641, when Hall became Bishop of Norwich. It was possibly copied out before 1633, since it contains his paraphrase on *The Song of Songs* following the text of the Geneva Bible (HlJ 57), a work which he revised following the text of the Authorised Version and incorporated in *An Explication ... of all the Hard Texts in the Old and New Testament* (1633). It is not immediately apparent whether the collection was made from printed or from MS sources, or indeed whether it was made for private use or whether it was some kind of authorised 'file' or library copy made for a member of Hall's circle, for another ecclesiastical body, or for an intended publisher. The very last page of the MS (f. 137v) contains a series of eight untitled religious aphorisms (beginning 'The law before o^r^ sauiour Christs time, was like the rod in Moses hand turned into a serpent ...'), which were obviously added by a scribe to fill up the volume; though not given an entry, they too may derive from Hall's works or papers.

The one other recorded MS which contains several works of Hall is that compiled by one Nehemiah Wellington (or 'Nehemia Wallington' as he wrote his name), now in the British Library (Sloane MS 922). On ff. 34-51v of a miscellany apparently kept between 1635 and 1652 he copied out 'Some Epiesels or Letters of Ios Hall D of Diuinitie and Deane of Worchester in 1620', noting at the end 'Their be many more excellent letters in D Halls Booke which I let passe for preuitis sake'. Wellington probably took his text from the 1620 edition of Hall's collected works.

The canon of VERSE accepted here is based on Davenport, with the addition of two poems (HlJ 3, 4-5) which are ascribed to Hall in MS sources. Of the first edition of *The Kings Prophecie: or Weeping Ioy* (London, 1603) Davenport records (p. lxxv) only two surviving exempla, both containing MS corrections probably made in the printing house. One (an imperfect exemplum) is in the British Library (Department of Printed Books, C. 39. b. 54); the other was formerly in the Loveday Library at Williamscote House, Banbury, but was sold to Maggs Brothers in 1971. Another additional item mentioned in Davenport (p. 270) is a Latin version by William Dillingham of Hall's commendatory verses *To William Bedell* (see HlJ 7) in the British Library (Sloane MS 1815, f. 57). A transcript of Hall's English version made c. 1798 by Edmond Malone (1741-1812) is in the Bodleian (MS Malone 8, p. 3).

Entries are not given to verses written about Hall, although these are of some biographical interest since they represent contemporary reactions to certain of his ecclesiastical and administrative policies. A poem variously titled *The Curate of Doctor Hall* or *Dr Hall's Curate's petition to the Kinge* (beginning 'I serve under Dr Hall') is to be found in a number of miscellanies, including those in the Bodleian (MSS Ashmole 781, p. 118; Rawl. poet. 26, f. 2v (subscribed 'Mannynge')), in Bradford Central Library (Hopkinson MSS, Vol. 34,

p. 90), in the British Library (Egerton MS 2560, f. 79), at Downing College, Cambridge (Bowtell Collection, MS 'Wickstede Thesaurus', Part II, f. 78), and in Durham Cathedral (Hunter MS 27, f. 92v). A poem *Vpon the Dedication of Hall's Workes* (beginning 'Joseph foreseeing these hard times of dearth') is to be found in a miscellany compiled by Thomas Manne (1582?-1641), now in the British Library (Add. MS 58215, p. 107), and in one compiled by Peter Calfe (1610-67), also in the British Library (Harley MS 6917, f. 96). A Latin epigram on Hall is in the MS volume of Latin poems on various authors written by Thomas Porter in 1614 and dedicated to Sir John Heveningham; this MS is owned by the Earl of Leicester at Holkham Hall, Norfolk (MS 436). For a poem on Hall written by Phineas Fletcher, see FlP 15.

An interesting argument in favour of an addition to the Hall canon, under the category of 'Dramatic Works', is advanced in Frank Livingstone Huntley, *Bishop Joseph Hall, 1574-1656: A Biographical and Critical Study* (Cambridge, 1978), p. 30 seq. There is reason to believe that Hall was the 'major author' of the second part of *The Returne from Parnassus*, the third in a trilogy of Cambridge student plays acted in 1598-1601. This play was twice printed in Cambridge in 1606 and a contemporary MS copy, once owned by James Orchard Halliwell-Phillipps, is preserved in the Folger (MS V. a. 355). It is possible that Hall also 'had a hand in' the first two plays of the trilogy, *The Pilgrimage to Parnassus* and the first part of *The Returne from Parnassus*. The text of these two plays is preserved in a contemporary MS copy, once owned by Thomas Hearne, now in the Bodleian (MS Rawl. D. 398, ff. 200-20), and published in facsimile in the Old English Drama Students' Facsimile series, 1912. The two plays were first printed by W. D. Macray in 1886. The whole trilogy is re-edited from the MS and printed sources by J. B. Leishman in *The Three Parnassus Plays (1598-1601)* (London, 1949). Hall's participation in these entertainments would help to explain some of the references in John Marston's satires against him, and they may even be the 'lost pastorals' which Hall is supposed to have written (see Huntley, p. 40).

Hall's PROSE writings, like those of most ecclesiastical writers, do not fall into clearly defined 'literary' and 'non-literary' categories. For present purposes the canon is based on Wynter (1863), excluding the final section in that edition, Hall's 'Miscellaneous Letters and Papers' (X, 499-544). That is to say, entries are given to the MSS of tracts, sermons, and epistles published during, or in two cases (HlJ 17-30, 55) just after Hall's lifetime.

Hall's miscellaneous papers, which were only published by later editors or which remain unpublished, can be summarised as follows. Thirteen of his letters, written between 1619 and 1639, were printed in Wynter (X, 505-20) from the originals in the Public Record Office (SP. 14/108/72; 14/110/71; 14/155/70; 14/164/14; 16/58/50; 16/118/35.I; 16/159/35; 16/166/40; 16/166/71; 16/193/69; 16/401/53; 16/430/50; 16/430/51). Part of the first of these letters is reproduced in Petti, *English Literary Hands*, No. 51. Six letters to Laud written in 1639-40 (though the date of one is misprinted in Wynter as '1629'), including important discussions on *Episcopacy by Divine Right* (see Wynter, IX, 142-281), were printed in Wynter (X, 533-44) from early published texts, but the original letters are in the Public Record Office (SP. 16/429/40; 16/431/2; 16/431/65; 16/432/63; 16/436/45; 16/442/35). Laud's reply of 11 November 1639 (not printed in Wynter), containing his comments on Hall's book as read in MS, is SP. 16/432/38. Four more of Hall's letters, written between 1619 and 1646[/7?], were printed in Wynter (X, 503-5, 507, 520) from the originals in the Bodleian (MSS Tanner 74, ff. 113-14, 159-60, 214-15; Tanner 59/2, f. 689), and one letter of 1651 was printed (X, 525-7) from a copy of the lost original made by William Fulman (1632-88), now also in the Bodleian (MS CCC. 306, ff. 67-8). Wynter printed a further ten letters (X, 499-503, 514-15, 521-5, 527-32) from early printed texts. One of them (X, 524-5), written to Thomas Fuller on 30 August 1651, is also preserved in a copy made by the Yorkshire antiquary John Hopkinson (1610-80), now in Bradford Central Library (Hopkinson MSS, Vol. 19, ff. 97v-8v).

Since Wynter's time a number of additional items have come to light. Hall's letter [? February 1628/9] to Thomas Turner, Laud's chaplain and licenser, giving him the authority to omit certain passages in *The Reconciler* (London, 1629; Wynter, VIII, 719-57), is in the Public Record Office (SP. 16/136/81). A letter to Laud, of 31 December 1634, is SP. 16/278/97, and a letter sent to the Council by Hall and Sir Nicholas Martyn on 17 January 1639/40 is SP. 16/442/27. The Public Record Office also has a petition sent by Hall, 12 June 1636, to the King (SP. 16/326/7), a document written by Hall and others in January 1637/8 supporting a petition sent to the Council by Western clothiers (SP. 16/380/88), and Hall's explanation on 18 August 1640 of the clauses 'stuck at' in the oath appointed by the recent Synod (SP. 16/464/30). The British Library has a letter sent to Sir Edward Nicholas, 10 December [1641] (Egerton MS 2533, f. 256); one sent to a certain Mrs Goring, 15 August [1608-27] (Harley MS 3783, f. 10), and one to William (later Archbishop) Sancroft, 19 February [c. 1648-56] (Harley MS 3783, f. 101). The last two letters are reproduced in part in Greg, *English Literary Autographs*, plate LXXIX. Five letters written between 1629 and 1634 to the Lord Mayor of Exeter are now in the Devon Record Office, Exeter (L. 325, 326, 352, 353, 363). Also preserved in this office are a joint letter to the Corporation of Exeter, 19 July 1630, to which Hall was a signatory (L. 337), and a scribal copy of Hall's endorsement of a letter by his predecessor in the bishopric of Exeter, Valentine Cary (L. 276). Some of these documents are cited in *HMC* 73, Records of the City of Exeter (1916), pp. 26, 47-8, 142-4. Exeter Cathedral still retains some official documents bearing Hall's signature or notes (Dean & Chapter of Exeter 3601), including the second part of his Bishop's register; in this repository are also preserved some notes on Hall's family and descendants written c. 1730 (Dean & Chapter of Exeter 3499/2961). Certain of these items are recorded in *HMC* 55, Various Collections IV (1907), pp. 14, 95. A signed decree of Hall's regulating Plymouth burial fees in 1637 is in the Devon Record Office, Plymouth (W 374).

Several original letters or documents are preserved in other repositories. A letter of 2 May 1636 to Sir John Coke (1563-1644), recorded in *HMC*, 12th Report, Appendix II (1888), p. 116, is owned by the Marquess of Lothian at

Melbourne Hall, Derbyshire. A letter written after 1625 to Sir John Eliot (1592-1632) is in Volume 10 of Eliot's correspondence owned by the present Lord Eliot at Port Eliot, Cornwall; the collection is recorded in *HMC*, 1st Report (1870), Appendix, pp. 43-4. An interesting letter concerning a deposition against Hall for extortion of fees, sent by Hall on 21 September [1628] to Sir Henry Spelman (1564?-1641), was formerly in the Alfred Morrison collection and is now in the Pforzheimer Library (MS 142); it is printed in *The Carl H. Pforzheimer Library; English Literature 1475-1700* (New York, 1940), III, 1263-4. A signed licence to preach which Hall granted on 31 May 1639 to one Thomas Brancker is in the Osborn Collection at Yale. The earliest known signatures of Hall are those under the dates 2 October 1595, 17 October 1598, and 8 April 1600 in the earliest of the College Order Books for the library at Emmanuel College, Cambridge (COL 14 1, pp. 11, 12, 13). The last document bearing his hand is his Will, dated 21 July 1654 and emended 7 September 1656, now in the Public Record Office (PROB 10/837 (proved 18 September 1656)); a registered copy is PROB 11/258, ff. 161-3, and another is in the Norfolk Record Office (1656, 263/251).

A particularly interesting original letter (now unfortunately damaged) is preserved in the Bodleian (MS Lincoln College 146, ff. 9-10). It was sent on 14 August 1645 to Edmund Lynolde, Pastor of Heling, near Grimsby, Lincolnshire, and is bound up in Lynolde's own MS compilation (consisting of 47 leaves) entitled 'Meditations Vnmused And Vowes Vnvoted In An Epistle written to Doctor Joseph Hall late Bishop of Exceter wherein he is argued for a great wrong done to A Man of His Owne Profession in y[e] late High Commission Court about an vniust and illegall sentence there passed'. Hall's letter contains his defence against Lynolde's accusations, a revealing comment on Laud, who had been executed in the previous January, and notable comments on his own plight (having had his 'whole estate...seized by the Parliament...and...hauing not so much as a comptency allowed mee, as yet, for the necessary sustentaō̄n of my family').

Some other unpublished letters of Hall are preserved in contemporary transcripts. A Latin epistle 'De colloquio Lipsiaco' (on the doctrine of Justus Lipsius), dated 'Febr: 25 1632', is copied in a miscellany belonging to John Dury, now in the British Library (Sloane MS 402, ff. 180-2), and again in another MS volume associated with Dury, now at Trinity College, Dublin (MS 293, ff. 106-7v). A copy of an undated four-page epistle (?1639) headed 'The Bishop of Exceter his Apology vpon a Report that went of him to bee a fauourer of Puritans Written to a frind of his liuing at the Kings Court', and beginning 'But can it bee thus? What? That a Divine of my Diocesse should so defile his owne nest ...', is preserved in the Somerset Record Office, among the papers of the Phelips family of Montacute House (DD/PH 221/40). Three letters from Hall to Sir Thomas Bodley's librarian, Thomas James (1572-1629), two of them written in 1619 and one written while Hall was still at Emmanuel College, Cambridge, are preserved in copies made by James himself, in Bodleian MS Ballard 44, ff. 146 rev, 177, 179. There was also at one time a 17th-century transcript of correspondence of Marco Antonio de Dominis (1560-1624), the Archbishop of Spalato who became a martyr of the Inquisition; the MS included a letter of his to Hall and Hall's *Responsum*, possibly the correspondence which was published in de Dominis, *De pace religionis* (Vesuntione Sequanorum, 1666): see Wynter, X, 208-14. This MS, once part of the Libri collection, was sold at Sotheby's, 19 June 1893, Lot 254, and the sale catalogue notes that a 'similar MS' was sold at Sotheby's on 30 March 1859.

In view of the huge correspondence which Hall must have conducted, with correspondents both in Britain and on the Continent, it is possible that more letters of his are to be found. It is unlikely, however, that many of his papers concerning official diocesan business would have survived his virtual ejection from the bishopric of Norwich in 1641 and the parliamentary sequestration of the property of malignants in 1643. Neither is there any trace of the books and MSS mentioned in Hall's Will. Most of his library he bequeathed to his son, Samuel, who also received his 'paper bookes', except for those containing 'the notes of my sermons', which he divided between his other sons, Robert and George. He also specified 'the papers in my litle black Trunke, contayning Letters of intercourse w[t] forraine Diuines, and some sermons and tractates', directing that these should 'not be medled w[th], or disposed, w[t]out the ioynt consent of my said three sonnes, whom I thank God I haue liued to see learned, iudicious and paynfull diuines'.

Hall's works were often cited in 17th-century miscellanies and commonplace books. Extracts from Hall's works can be found, for instance, in the Bodleian (MS Rawl. D. 1500, ff. 34-5 rev., from *Quo Vadis?*); the British Library (Add. MS 52585, ff. 7-18v, 20r-v, and passim; Harley MS 980, ff. 39v-40, from *The Honour of the Married Clergy Maintained*); Chetham's Library, Manchester (Mun. A 6. 33, passim); the Dorset Record Office (D51/5, pp. 1-9, including extracts from *Occasional Meditations*); Durham Cathedral ('Arguments agt Anabaptists out of Hall' in Hunter MS 132); the Norfolk Record Office (MS 11349, p. 58); and the Plume Library, Maldon (Plume MS 31). It is also not uncommon to find printed exempla of Hall's works containing MS annotations by early readers. For instance, a bound collection of printed works by Hall (*Epistles, Characters of Virtues and Vices*, and *Pharisaism and Christianity*) in the Bodleian (8° Rawl. 597) has numerous marginal annotations; so has an exemplum of *Quo Vadis?* (London, 1617) in the Huntington (RB 61290).

PB.

ARRANGEMENT

Verse	HlJ 1-8
Prose	HlJ 9-60.

See also Addenda to Part 2, p. 627

FACSIMILE XVII — Joseph Hall: First page of *Certain Irrefragable Propositons* sent to Archbishop Laud (received 29 December 1639), with Laud's inscription at the top and some alterations in his hand (HlJ 12). Public Record Office, SP 16/436/45.I, recto. Reduced by approx. 5 per cent.

Concerninge Church-governement & ye Estate of Episcopacye.

45 I

1 God had never any Church upon earth that was ruled by a Parity.

The first Church of God wch was reduced to a publick polity, amonge ye Jewes, was by his owne appointment reall governed by a setled imparity of High Priest, Priests, Levites

3 The Evangelicall Church was founded by our Saviour in a knowne imparity; for though the Apostles were equall among themselves, yet they were ~~in a degree~~ above the 70. and all other disciples and were specially indued wth power from on high.

4 The same God and Saviour after his ascension did set severall rankes and orders of the holy ministery; first Apostles, secondly Prophets, thirdly teachers &c: all wch acknowledged the eminence

Cor. 12 28 and authority of the Apostles.

5 The Apostles after the ascension of our Saviour by the direccon of Gods spirit, did exercise that power and superiority of spirituall iurisdiccon over the rest of the Church wch was given them by Christ; and stood upon their maiority above all other ministers of the Gospell.

6 The same Apostles did not carry that power up to heaven wth them, and leave the Church unfurnished wth the due helpes of her further propagation & governement; but by vertue of this power, and by the same direccon of Gods spirit ordayned in severall parts spirituall guides and governors of Gods people to ayd and succeed them

7 These spirituall persons so by them ordayned were at the first promiscuously called ~~[illegible]~~ Bishops, and presbyters; and managed the Church affayres, by common advise, but still under the governement of the Apostles, their Ordayners, & Overseers.

8 But when the Apostles found that quarrells and emulations grew in the Church, even while many of them were livinge, through the parity of presbyters, and side takings of the people; The same Apostles by the appointment and direction of the same Spirit, raysed in each city, where the Church was more frequent, one amongst the presbyters, to a more eminent authority then the rest to succeed them in their ordinary power of ordination and censure; and encharged them peculiarly wth the care of Church governement; such were Timothy, & Titus, and those wch were styled the Angells of the seven Asian Churches

7 These selected persons were then, and ever since distinguished from the rest by the name of Episcopi, Bishops.

Joseph Hall

VERSE

HlJ 1 *Cearten veerses written by Doctor Hall upon the kings coming into Scotland* ('Doe not repyine fayre sun to see these eyne').

Copy of a series of three poems, transcribed from HlJ 2, in a MS heraldic book relating to Scotland; c. 1627.

First pub. (from this MS) in Arnold Davenport, 'Three Uncollected Poems by Joseph Hall', *N & Q*, 182 (31 January 1942), 58-9; printed from this MS in Davenport (1949), p. 150.

British Library, Harley MS 1423, f. 102.

HlJ 2 -----

Copy of the three poems, untitled and ascribed to 'Dr Hall', on two leaves bound in a volume of Scottish genealogical collections compiled by William Camden (see CmW 160); c. 1627.

National Library of Scotland, Adv. MS 33. 2. 36, ff. 76-7.

HlJ 3 *An Epitaph on Gustavus Adolphus King of Sweden* ('He sleeps within this Tombe').

Copy of a Latin epitaph 'by an Italian Friar' (beginning 'Dormit Mistè in hoc Tumulo') followed by a 23-line English version, headed 'Sequitur Anglice' and endorsed 'Translated by Jo: Hall &c: In: 1634. - It is wrote in the Hand of that Time, & probably translated by Joseph Hall, who was Bp. of Exeter in 1627', all in the hand of William Cole (1714-82), Volume XXXI of his miscellaneous collections; 18th century.

Believed to be unpublished.

British Library, Add. MS 5832, f. 216.

--- *The Kings Prophecie: or Weeping Ioy* ('What Stoick could his steely brest containe').

See INTRODUCTION.

HlJ 4 *'On the Altar Royall Melvin frownes to fynde'.*

Copy of a twelve-line poem, preceded by a two-line Latin motto and headed 'Josephus Hall in Melv.', in a volume of theological and state tracts; mid-17th century.

Believed to be unpublished.

Cambridge University Library, MS Gg. 1. 29, f. 15v.

HlJ 5 -----

Copy, here beginning 'On ye Altar Royall, Melvjn frowns to find' and ascribed to 'Hall', in a verse miscellany compiled by a Cambridge man; c. 1648-60.

Bodleian, MS Rawl. poet. 246, f. 16.

HlJ 6 *To Camden* ('One fayre Par-royall hath our Iland bred').

Copy, untitled and ascribed to 'Ios Hall. Imman.', in a notebook compiled by Brian Twyne (1579?-1644); early 17th century.

First pub. (from this MS) in Helen E. Sandison, 'Three Spenser Allusions', *MLN*, 44 (1929), 159-62; printed from this MS in Davenport, p. 105.

Bodleian, MS Wood D. 32, f. 260.

HlJ 7 *To William Bedell* ('Willy, thy Rhythms so sweetly run and rise').

Copy of Hall's commendatory verses, headed 'In Autorem', prefixed to a copy of Bedell's poem *A Protestant Memorial*, in a composite volume of verse; 17th century.

First pub. in William Bedell, *A Protestant Memorial: or, The Shepherd's Tale of the Pouder-Plott* (London, 1713); Davenport, p. 123. This MS recorded in Wynter, IX, 707.

Bodleian, MS Rawl. poet. 154, f. 12.

--- -----

See also INTRODUCTION.

HlJ 8 *Virgidemiae.*

Copy of Book IV, Satire 3, lines 1-27, here beginning 'What botes it (Pontice, tho thou couldst discours', in the hand of one Thomas Dutton, in a MS book of heraldry and other matter owned in 1658 by one Robert Wever; c. 1603-34.

Books IV-VI first pub. as *Virgidemiarvm. The three last Bookes* (London, 1598); Davenport, pp. 44-99 (59-60).

British Library, Add. MS 26705, f. 130.

PROSE

HlJ 9 *The Art of Divine Meditation.*

Copy, complete with the appended *A Meditation of Death, According to the Former Rules*, in a MS volume of Hall's works; imperfect, lacking one leaf between ff. 125 and 126 containing the end of Chapter XXIV and the beginning of Chapter XXV; [1627-41].

First pub. London, 1606; Wynter, VI, 46-88.

Owned by Peter Beal, Leeds, Hall MS, ff. 117v-33v.

HlJ 10 *The Best Bargain: A Sermon Preached to the Court at Theobald's on Sunday, September 21, 1623.*

Copy in a MS volume of Hall's works; [1627-41].

First pub. London, 1623; Wynter, V, 174-85.

Owned by Peter Beal, Leeds, Hall MS, ff. 41-5.

HlJ 11 *A Brief Sum of the Principles of Religion.*

Copy, entitled 'A breife Summe of the Principles of Religion by waye of Catechisme' and ascribed to 'M[r] Doctor Josuah Hall', in a volume of tracts; c. 1623.

First pub. (?) in *A Recollection of such Treatises as haue beene heretofore seuerally published* (London, 1615); Wynter, VIII, 219-21.

British Library, Harley MS 969, ff. 3-4v.

*HlJ 12 *Certain Irrefragable Propositions, worthy of Serious Consideration.*

Autograph draft of Hall's 'short and full propositions' concerning church government and episcopacy enclosed with his autograph letter on the subject to Archbishop Laud (received 29 December 1639); bearing Laud's additions and alterations and his endorsement 'These phaps may be thought fitt for a subscriptiō of others'; a single leaf.

First pub. London, '1639' [i.e. 1640]; Wynter, IX, 138-41. See **FACSIMILE XVII.** The accompanying letter to Laud is printed in Wynter, X, 541-2.

Public Record Office, SP. 16/436/45.I.

HlJ 13 -----

Copy of the complete work, including the dedicatory letter to the King; [end of 1639-early 1640].

Public Record Office, SP. 16/433/55 and 55.I-IV.

HlJ 14 *Characters of Virtues and Vices.*

Copy in a MS volume of Hall's works; [1627-41].

First pub. London, 1608; Wynter, VI, 89-125; ed. Rudolf Kirk, together with *Heaven vpon Earth* (New Brunswick, N.J., 1948).

Owned by Peter Beal, Leeds, Hall MS, ff. 10v-21v.

HlJ 15 -----

Copy in a miscellany compiled by one Thomas Parsons; c. 1635.

Huntington, HM 1338, ff. 7-13v.

HlJ 16 -----

Copy of nineteen 'Characterisms of Vice' in a miscellany once owned by Margaret Bellasys, probably the daughter of Thomas, first Lord Fauconberg (1577-1653); c. 1630.

British Library, Add. MS 10309, ff. 1-39.

--- -----

See also INTRODUCTION.

--- *Episcopacy by Divine Right.*

See INTRODUCTION.

HlF 17 *Episcopal Admonition, Sent in a Letter to the House of Commons, April 28, 1628.*

Copy in a volume chiefly of speeches and proceedings in the House of Commons, March-June 1628; 17th century.

First pub. in *Cabala* (London, 1663), p. 113; Wynter, VIII, 272.

Bodleian, MS Rawl. C. 687, ff. 41v-2.

HlJ 18 -----

Copy in a volume of speeches and proceedings in the House of Commons; 17th century.

Bodleian, MS Rawl. C. 807, pp. 283-5.

HlJ 19 -----

Copy in a volume of state papers; 17th century.

Bodleian, MS Tanner 82, f. 311r-v.

HlJ 20 -----

Copy in a volume of state papers; 17th century.

British Library, Add. MS 44848, f. 230v.

HlJ 21 -----

Copy in a volume of speeches and proceedings in the House of Commons, 1627-8; 17th century.

British Library, Harley MS 2217, f. 31.

HlJ 22 -----

Copy in a volume chiefly of speeches and proceedings in the House of Commons, 1627-8; 17th century.

British Library, Harley MS 2305, ff. 207v-8.

Episcopal Admonition, Sent in a Letter to the House of Commons, April 28, 1628

H1J 23 -----

Copy on a single leaf in a composite volume of state papers; c. 1628.

British Library, Stowe MS 180, f. 57.

H1J 24 -----

Copy in a volume of state letters and speeches; mid-17th century.

Cambridge University Library, MS Gg. 4. 13, p. 103.

H1J 25 -----

Copy in a volume of state tracts and papers; 17th century.

Formerly among the Carew MSS at Crowcombe Court, Somerset, this MS recorded in *HMC*, 4th Report (1874), Appendix, p. 373.

Harvard, MS Eng 1266.2 (22), f. 140.

H1J 26 -----

Copy in a volume of proceedings in Parliament in 1628; 17th century.

House of Lords Record Office, Historical Collections, No. 50, p. 251.

H1J 27 -----

Copy in a volume of state tracts and papers; 17th century.

Inner Temple Library, Petyt MS 538, Vol. 18, f. 414.

H1J 27.5 See Addenda, p. 627.

H1J 28 -----

Copy in a volume of historical collections compiled by Henry Wharton (1664-94); 17th century.

Lambeth Palace, MS 595, p. 94.

H1J 28.5 See Addenda, p. 628.

H1J 29 -----

Copy on a single leaf in an unbound collection of state papers; imperfect; c. 1628.

St John's College, Cambridge, MS K. 56 (James 542), No. 21.

H1J 29.5, 29.8 See Addenda, p. 628.

H1J 30 -----

Copy on f. 47v in a volume of state letters; 17th century.

Formerly among the MSS of Lord Braye at Stanford Hall, Rugby, this MS recorded in *HMC* 15, 10th Report, Appendix VI (1887), p. 116.

Unlocated.

H1J 31 *Epistles. Decade I, Epistle 1. To Jacob Wadsworth; lately revolted, in Spain.*

Copy in a MS volume of Hall's works; [1627-41].

First pub. in *Epistles*, Vol. I (London, 1608); Wynter, VI, 128-31.

Owned by Peter Beal, Leeds, Hall MS, ff. 107v-8v.

H1J 32 *Epistles. Decade I, Epistle 2. To My Lord and Patron, The Lord Denny. Of the contempt of the World.*

Copy in a MS volume of Hall's works; [1627-41].

First pub. in *Epistles*, Vol. I (London, 1608); Wynter, VI, 131-3.

Owned by Peter Beal, Leeds, Hall MS, ff. 133v-4v.

H1J 33 *Epistles. Decade I, Epistle 10. Written to Mr. J.B. and Dedicated to My Father, Mr. J. Hall. Against the fear of death.*

Copy in a MS volume of Hall's works; [1627-41].

First pub. in *Epistles*, Vol. I (London, 1608); Wynter, VI, 156-8.

Owned by Peter Beal, Leeds, Hall MS, ff. 134v-5.

H1J 34 -----

Copy in a miscellany compiled by one Nehemiah Wellington; c. 1650.

British Library, Sloane MS 922, ff. 50-1v.

H1J 35 *Epistles. Decade II, Epistle 1. To Sir Robert Darcy. The estate of a true but weak Christian.*

Copy in a MS volume of Hall's works; [1627-41].

First pub. in *Epistles*, Vol. I (London, 1608); Wynter, VI, 158-9.

Owned by Peter Beal, Leeds, Hall MS, f. 135r-v.

H1J 36 -----

Copy in a miscellany compiled by one Nehemiah Wellington; c. 1650.

British Library, Sloane MS 922, ff. 34-5v.

H1J 37 *Epistles. Decade II, Epistle 2. To Sir Edmund Bacon. Of the benefit of retiredness and secresy.*

Copy in a miscellany compiled by one Nehemiah Wellington; c. 1650.

First pub. in *Epistles*, Vol. I (London, 1608); Wynter, VI, 160-2.

British Library, Sloane MS 922, ff. 40-1v.

H1J 38 *Epistles. Decade II, Epistle 4. To my Sister Mrs. B. Brinsly. Of the sorrow not to be repented of.*

Copy in a miscellany compiled by one Nehemiah Wellington; c. 1650.

First pub. in *Epistles*, Vol. I (London, 1608); Wynter, VI, 169-71.

British Library, Sloane MS 922, ff. 38-9v.

H1J 39 *Epistles. Decade II, Epistle 8. To my Father-in-Law, Mr. George Wenyffe. Exciting to Christian cheerfulness.*

Copy in a miscellany compiled by one Nehemiah Wellington; c. 1650.

First pub. in *Epistles*, Vol. I (London, 1608); Wynter, VI, 178-89.

British Library, Sloane MS 922, ff. 41v-2v.

H1J 40 *Epistles. Decade II, Epistle 9. To Mr. W.R. Dedicated to Mr. Thomas Burlz. Consolations of immoderate grief for the death of friends.*

Copy in a miscellany compiled by Nehemiah Wellington; c. 1650.

First pub. in *Epistles*, Vol. I (London, 1608); Wynter, VI, 180-3.

British Library, Sloane MS 922, ff. 48-50.

H1J 41 *Epistles. Decade II, Epistle 10. To Mr. I.A. Merchant. Against sorrow for worldly losses.*

Copy in a miscellany compiled by one Nehemiah Wellington; c. 1650.

First pub. in *Epistles*, Vol. I (London, 1608); Wynter, VI, 183-4.

British Library, Sloane MS 922, f. 45r-v,

J1J 42 *Epistles. Decade III, Epistle 3. To Mr. Samuel Burton. A discourse of the trial and choice of the true religion.*

Copy in a MS volume of Hall's works; [1627-41].

First pub. in *Epistles*, Vol. II (London, 1608); Wynter, VI, 191-8.

Owned by Peter Beal, Leeds, Hall MS, ff. 22-4v.

H1J 43 *Epistles. Decade III, Epistle 8. To Mr. Rob. Hay. A discourse of the continual exercise of a Christian; how he may keep his heart from hardness and his ways from error.*

Copy in a MS volume of Hall's works; [1627-41].

First pub. in *Epistles*, Vol. II (London, 1608); Wynter, VI, 208-10.

Owned by Peter Beal, Leeds, Hall MS, ff. 135v-6v.

H1J 44 -----

Copy in a miscellany compiled by one Nehemiah Wellington; c. 1650.

British Library, Sloane MS 922, f. 43r-v.

H1J 45 *Epistles. Decade IV, Epistle 6. A discourse of the signs and proofs of a true faith.*

Copy in a miscellany compiled by one Nehemiah Wellington; c. 1650.

First pub. in *Epistles*, Vol. II (London, 1608); Wynter, VI, 231-4.

British Library, Sloane MS 922, f. 44r-v.

H1J 46 *Epistles. Decade IV, Epistle 7. To Mr. Ed. Alleyne. A direction how to conceive of God in our devotions and meditations.*

Copy in a MS volume of Hall's works; [1627-41].

First pub. in *Epistles*, Vol. II (London, 1608); Wynter, VI, 234-6.

Owned by Peter Beal, Leeds, Hall MS, ff. 136v-7.

H1J 47 *Epistles. Decade V, Epistle 5. To Sir Richard Lea, since deceased. Discoursing of the comfortable remedies of all afflictions.*

Copy in a miscellany compiled by one Nehemiah Wellington; c. 1650.

First pub. in *Epistles*, Vol. III (London, 1611); Wynter, VI, 260-3.

British Library, Sloane MS 922, ff. 46-7v.

H1J 48 *Epistles. Decade VI, Epistle 2. To Mr. T.S. Dedicated to Sir Fulke Grevill. Discoursing how we may use the world without danger.*

Copy in a MS volume of Hall's works; [1627-41].

First pub. in *Epistles*, Vol. III, Part 2 (London, 1610); Wynter, VI, 283-5.

Owned by Peter Beal, Leeds, Hall MS, ff. 108v-9.

H1J 49 *Epistles. Decade VI, Epistle 3. To Sir George Fleetwood. Of the remedies of sin, and motives to avoid it.*

Epistles. Decade VI, Epistle 3. To Sir George Fleetwood

Copy in a miscellany compiled by one Nehemiah Wellington; c. 1650.

First pub. in *Epistles*, Vol. III, Part 2 (London, 1610); Wynter, VI, 285-8.

British Library, Sloane MS 922, ff. 36-7v.

--- *Epistles.*

See also INTRODUCTION.

--- *An Explication by way of Paraphrase of all the Hard Texts in the Old and New Testament.*

See H1J 57.

H1J 50 *The Free Prisoner, or The Comfort of Restraint, written some while since in the Tower.*

Copy, headed 'Bishop Hall upon his emprisonm^{t}. Tower 1641' and subscribed 'To my much respected & obliged freind Mr A.B. these', in a volume of transcripts of historical documents made by the Yorkshire antiquary John Hopkinson (1610-80); 1660.

First pub. in *Three Tractates* (London, 1646); Wynter, VI, 539-50.

Bradford Central Library, Hopkinson MSS, Vol. 18, ff. 138-45v.

H1J 51 *The Great Impostor: Laid open in a Sermon at Gray's Inn, February 2, 1623.*

Copy in a MS volume of Hall's works; [1627-41].

First pub. London, 1623; Wynter, V, 158-73.

Owned by Peter Beal, Leeds, Hall MS, ff. 35-40v.

H1J 52 *Heaven upon Earth.*

Copy in a MS volume of Hall's works; [1627-41].

First pub. London, 1606; Wynter, VI, 1-45; ed. Rudolf Kirk, together with *Characters of Virtues and Vices* (New Brunswick, N.J., 1948).

Owned by Peter Beal, Leeds, Hall MS, ff. 76-91v.

H1J 53 *Henochismus.*

MS English translation made by one Moses Wall, written for presentation to Elizabeth St John and with a dedicatory epistle to her (ff. 5-8); 1639.

Original Latin version first pub. London, 1635; Wynter, X, 188-207. Wall's translation unpublished.

Harvard, MS Eng 740.

H1J 54 *Holy Observations.*

Copy in a MS volume of Hall's works; [1627-41].

First pub. London, 1607; Wynter, VII, 522-43.

Owned by Peter Beal, Leeds, Hall MS, ff. 92-9v.

--- *The Honour of the Married Clergy Maintained.*

See INTRODUCTION.

H1J 55 *A Letter for the Observation of the Feast of Christ's Nativity.*

Copy, headed 'Joseph Hall on the observance of Christmasse day', in a composite volume of ecclesiastical and historical tracts; early-mid-17th century.

First pub. as *A letter concerning Christmasse* (London, 1659); Wynter, IX, 128-37.

Gonville and Caius College, Cambridge, MS 291/274, pp. 325-9.

--- *A Meditation of Death.*

See H1J 9.

H1J 56 *Meditations and Vows; Divine and Moral. Three Centuries.*

Copy in a MS volume of Hall's works; [1627-41].

First pub. London, 1605; Wynter, VII, 439-521.

Owned by Peter Beal, Leeds, Hall MS, ff. 45v-75v.

--- *Occasional Meditations.*

See INTRODUCTION.

H1J 57 *An Open and Plain Paraphrase upon the Song of Songs.*

Copy in a MS volume of Hall's works; [1627-41].

First pub. in *Salomon's Divine Arts* (London, 1609); later incorporated in *An Explication by way of Paraphrase of all the Hard Texts in the Old and New Testament* (London, 1633); printed in Wynter, III, 290-316, as part of the latter work. See INTRODUCTION.

Owned by Peter Beal, Leeds, Hall MS, ff. 1-10.

H1J 58 *The Passion Sermon. Preached at Paul's Cross on Good-Friday, April 14, 1609.*

Copy in a MS volume of Hall's works; [1627-41].

First pub. London, 1609; Wynter, V, 24-54.

Owned by Peter Beal, Leeds, Hall MS, ff. 24v-34v.

HlJ 59 *Pharisaism and Christianity: Compared and set forth in a Sermon at Paul's Cross, May 1, 1608.*

Copy in a MS volume of Hall's works; [1627-41].

First pub. London, 1608; Wynter, V, 1-23.

Owned by Peter Beal, Leeds, Hall MS, ff. 109v-17v.

--- -----

See also INTRODUCTION.

--- *Quo Vadis? A Just Censure of Travel.*

See INTRODUCTION.

--- *The Reconciler.*

See INTRODUCTION.

HlJ 60 *A Serious Dissuasive from Popery. To W.D. Revolted, &c.*

Copy in a MS volume of Hall's works; [1627-41].

First pub. with *The Peace of Rome* (London, 1609); Wynter, VIII, 352-73.

Owned by Peter Beal, Leeds, Hall MS, ff. 100-7.

DRAMATIC WORKS

See INTRODUCTION.

Sir John Harington

1560-1612

ABBREVIATIONS

1615 *Epigrams Both Pleasant and Serious, Written by that All-worthy Knight, Sir Iohn Harrington* (London, 1615).

1618 *The most elegant and witty epigrams of Sir Iohn Harrington, digested into foure Bookes* (London, 1618).

Hughey Ruth Hughey, *The Arundel Harington Manuscript of Tudor Poetry*, 2 vols (Columbus, Ohio, 1960).

McClure *The Letters and Epigrams of Sir John Harington together with The Prayse of Private Life*, ed. Norman Egbert McClure (Philadelphia, 1930; reprinted New York, 1970).

Nugae Antiquae *Nugae Antiquae*, ed. Henry Harington, 2 vols (London & Bath, 1769-75); 2nd edition, 3 vols (London & Bath, 1779; reprinted 1792); 3rd edition revised by Thomas Park, 2 vols (London, 1804; reprinted New York, [1970s]).

For abbreviations used throughout Volume I, see p.xi.

INTRODUCTION

Sir John Harington of Kelston, Somerset, was an industrious literary figure who was responsible for the production of a considerable number of MSS, both of his own and of other authors' works. Of his own compositions there survive autograph, or partly autograph, MSS of his *Orlando Furioso* (HrJ 7-10, including the printer's copy); of his collected *Epigrams* (HrJ 20-2) and of particular epigrams (HrJ 84, 296, 300, 302); of his translation of Virgil's *Aeneid, Book VI* (HrJ 18); of certain of his *Metrical Paraphrases of the Psalms* (HrJ 2-3); of his *Metamorphosis of Ajax* (HrJ 317, the printer's copy); of his *Supplie or Addicion to the Catalogue of Bishops* (HrJ 328-9); and of his epistolary *Short View of the State of Ireland* (HrJ 326). Three of these MSS (HrJ 18, 21, 328) were written for presentation to Prince Henry. At least five printed exempla of *The Metamorphosis of Ajax* contain Harington's autograph sidenotes and footnotes (HrJ 318-22). Among other notable MSS, there survive scribal copies, evidently produced at Harington's direction, of *The Englishman's Doctor* (HrJ 1), of his *Tract on the Succession to the Crown* (HrJ 333), of his discourse on Elias (HrJ 315), and of his *Treatise on Playe* (HrJ 336), and there is a scribal draft of an unfinished epistolary discourse addressed to Joseph Hall (HrJ 316). It is quite possible that certain other MSS recorded in the entries below were produced by Harington's scribes.

One MS, a formal scribal copy of an anonymous translation of Virgil's *Aeneid, Book IV* sold at auction in 1978 (HrJ 17), was identified as Harington's on stylistic grounds and because of the newly-discovered autograph translation of *Book VI* (HrJ 18). Against the certainty of the attribution to Harington of *Book IV* is the fact that the MS is unascribed and in an unknown hand. Unlike *Book VI*, it has no accompanying Latin text, no elaborate glosses, commentary, or appendices, and no preliminary epistle to explain why the translation was made. Neither is there any known reference to Harington's ever having concerned himself with *Book IV*, whereas his attention to *Book VI* is established from a reference in his *View of the State of Ireland* (1605) to having written for Prince Henry 'a comment on the sixt booke of Vergill'. On the other hand, the style of the translation of *Book IV* is so characteristic of Harington that it is difficult to believe that it could have been written by anyone else. It is written in six-line rhyming stanzas, perhaps an experimental variation of the *ottava rima* of his *Book VI* and of his *Orlando Furioso*; the MS was very probably owned by William, Lord Compton, with whom Harington was well acquainted (see McClure, pp. 141-2); and while the hand cannot be positively identified as one of the Harington 'household' hands, it is stylistically and generically similar to them. In the dedicatory epistle to King James prefixed to *Book VI* Harington explains that this work, as presented to James, represents a revision of an earlier translation written 'for my sonns better vnderstandinge', one 'done fyrst for the benefyt of myne own chylde, and now commented on and amplyfyed for the vse of the Peerles Prince'. Although Harington adds that he found it 'so hard and so harsh for owr Englysh verse that I never durst meddle with any more of yt', it is possible that he had earlier translated other parts of the *Aeneid* but that, for various reasons, *Book VI* was suitable for special revised treatment in 1604.

Besides these texts, at least seven MS miscellanies owned by Harington survive (HrJ 337-44), several containing pieces by other authors in his hand, as well as certain of his own works. It is, however, no easy matter to distinguish Harington's autograph from the writing of his scribes, who were clearly encouraged to model their penmanship on his own and, indeed, to make the transitions from one hand to another as imperceptible as possible. This is especially true of one of the most important of the Harington MSS, the Arundel miscellany (HrJ 337). Here is frequent evidence of a characteristic practice of Harington, which was to begin transcribing a poem, then after a line or a few lines (sometimes in the middle of a line) resign the rest of the task to a scribe, possibly making his own corrections afterwards. The common, if understandable, failure of scholars to distinguish Harington's autograph correctly has led in the past to frequent inaccuracies of description.

Four of the Harington miscellanies (HrJ 340-3), as well as MSS of four of his prose works (HrJ 315, 317, 329, 336), belong to the single most important collection of MSS relating to him: the Harington Papers, which were acquired by the British Library in 1947 (Add. MSS 46366-73B, 46374-6B, 46377-8B, 46379-82C, 46383-4). Of these twenty-four volumes (some not yet bound), which comprise papers of the Harington family from the 16th to the 19th century, the first eight (including one of Harington's copies of Sidney's *Psalms*: see SiP 76) belonged to him, and certain other documents of his are combined with later papers in the ninth and nineteenth volumes. Some of the papers have been considerably rearranged since the 1920s, when McClure examined them, and they also contain important material to which he makes no reference. Certain of the miscellanies recorded in the entries were previously owned and, in particular instances, perhaps chiefly compiled by Sir John's father, John Harington of Stepney (1520?-82), whose literary interests and activities were considerable in their own right: see Ruth Hughey, *John Harington of Stepney: Tudor Gentleman* (Columbus, Ohio, 1971). Another of the miscellanies (HrJ 342) is of special interest since it is a notebook relating to the Earl of Essex's expedition to Ireland, a campaign in which Harington took part. His cousin, Robert Markham, advised him to keep an 'accounte' or 'journal' as a matter of precaution (see McClure, p. 19). Probably a similar but more detailed notebook (now unlocated) was the 'Journale' which, according to his own report, he was obliged to show Queen Elizabeth on his return from Ireland and which he later sent to Markham (McClure, pp. 121-2). These notebooks, and the authorship of the main report on Essex's expedition contained in the extant MS, are discussed in R. H. Miller, 'Sir John Harington's Irish Journals', *SB*, 32 (1979), 179-86.

A number of other MSS and works of Harington are known to have existed, though now unlocated. References in two of his draft letters (McClure, pp. 142-4) indicate that in or after 1609 Harington presented a MS of his *Metrical Paraphrases of the Psalms* to James I. An earlier and more elaborate gift to the King was his New Year's gift in 1602/3 of a set of verses accompanying a highly ornate and perfumed lantern made of four metals, the silver reflector plate engraved with a series of religious pictures. The verses (the original presentation MS of which may have survived as late as the 19th century) are preserved in transcripts (HrJ 20-1, 26), one containing illustrations of the lantern and its designs. Scribal copies made for Harington of three letters sent to him from the Scottish Court partly in response to this gift are among the Harington Papers (Add. MS 46381, ff. 138v, 141v, 145v). At about the same time Harington also sent James an autograph copy of his collected *Epigrams*, a copy 'sent by Cap. Hunter' and described in the special dedicatory epigram as 'a present heer of skribled pages. . .A work in which my pen yt self engages' (McClure No. 347, p. 287). Perhaps it was this MS which Harington had particularly in mind when he referred in the dedicatory epistle of his *Aeneid, Book VI* to 'some other of my toys w[ch] yowr Ma[tie] was pleasd to look on. . .written of to lyght matters'. He probably also sent more MSS to Prince Henry besides those which are known. For instance, he sent him 'by my servant such matters as your Highness did covet to see, in regard to Bishop Gardener of Winchester, which I shall sometime more largely treat of' (McClure, p. 127). Fortunately the larger treatise which Harington promised, his *Supplie or Addicion to the Catalogue of Bishops*, is preserved in the copy later presented to the Prince (HrJ 328). At an earlier period, Harington must certainly have presented copies of some of his epigrams to Queen Elizabeth, employing contrived stratagems to bring them to her notice, such as on the occasion when he left a copy of his epigram 'in praise of her reading' (HrJ 56-60) 'behinde her cushion at my departinge from her presence' (*Nugae Antiquae* (1804), I, 172). For another notable deployment of a 'Booke', for the entertainment of the Queen's ladies, see HrJ 302. Not long before Elizabeth's death he tried to cheer her with some more verses, but by then she was understandably 'paste [her] relishe for such matters' (McClure, p. 97).

Among Harington's 'lost' works, a diary for 1594-1603, entitled *Breefe Notes and Remembraunces*, survived at least until the early 19th century; extracts are printed in *Nugae Antiquae* (1804), I, 165-82. In the notes after Book XXIII of *Orlando Furioso* (1591) Harington mentions having written 'a litle dialogue of mariage' in his 'young dayes'. In the notes after Book XLIV he refers to Foxe's account of the 'troubles' of the future Queen Elizabeth in the reign of Queen Mary, an account which Harington, Thomas Arundell (1560-1639), and Sir Edward Hoby (1560-1617) were obliged to translate at Eton. 'This litle booke', he says, 'was given to her Majestie'. In the notes after Book XVII he claims that 'the felicitie of our realme of England' and 'the gracious and myld government of our Soveraigne' are subjects requiring 'an entire treatise. . .and therefore I reserve it wholly for an other worke of mine owne, if God give me abilitie to performe it'. It is not clear whether Harington did 'performe it' or whether his politic desire to praise the reign of Elizabeth manifested itself sufficiently in his known works. Elsewhere it is evident that more ink must have been spilt in the controversy with Joseph Hall concerning the marriage of clergy and the voluntary separation of married partners. Hall's 'apologeticall discourse' on the subject, published in his *Epistles* (1608), Decade II, Epistle 3, must have prompted a reply from Harington, to which Hall made a counter-reply in his letter to Harington published in *Epistles* (1611), Decade V, Epistle 9, a work which in turn provoked Harington's unfinished discourse (HrJ 316).

A more substantial work by Harington is mentioned in the anonymous pamphlet (? by one Young) *Ulysses upon Ajax* (London, 1596), sig. D3[v]. After heartily condemning Harington's *Metamorphosis of Ajax*, his *Orlando Furioso*, and his 'obscene' Epigrams, the writer turns for more favourable comment to 'his succinct collection of historie: his compendious & apt obseruatiōs in the Emperors līues', for 'thus much touching his succinct obseruations out of the Emperors liues...I like that [work] best which, is lōgest'. Perhaps the writer's last remark should not be taken literally. It seems unlikely that Harington would ever have produced anything longer than *Orlando Furioso*, but his work on the Emperors may well have been longer than *The Metamorphosis of Ajax*, which is the main target of *Ulysses upon Ajax*. There are many references in *Orlando Furioso* and Harington's other works indicating his familiarity with the lives of the Emperors. In the notes after Book XXXV, for instance, he says, 'Of Augustus Caesars faultes both Suetonius and Plutarke have written at large, and I am loth to renew the memorie of them except I did also [i.e. unless I were also to] recite his many vertues which made large recompence for his few vices'. Possibly the work was planned as a collection of imperial biographies rather like the *Scriptores historiae Augustae*, which is cited in *The Metamorphosis of Ajax* (ed. Elizabeth Donno, p. 107). A complete text of *Observations on the Emperors' Lives* is unknown, but a historical essay which may well constitute a chapter in that work has now been discovered in a MS among the Cecil Papers at Hatfield House (HrJ 325). The MS, entitled 'The Fall of Nero and beginning of Galba', is written in a scribal hand possessing immediately recognisable characteristics of the Harington 'household' hands, together with neat italic sidenotes very similar to the autograph marginalia found in many of Harington's MSS. The prose style reads somewhat like a translation from Latin, but the text does not correspond with any of the standard ancient accounts of Nero (Suetonius, Tacitus, Plutarch, Dio Cassius, and others); it would seem, therefore, to be an original account, the style of which is partly influenced by its Latin historical sources. The discovery of this piece raises the possibility of identifying other portions of the work. For instance, in a neatly written miscellany among the Ormsby-Gore papers in the National Library of Wales (Brogyntyn (1938 deposit) MS 13 (=Brogyntyn MS 29), pp. 217-29) is a formal account of the Emperor Tiberius, beginning 'Augustus of famous memorie having concluded the Last Act of his Life and Empire, the Citie was partly possest wth a Lamentacōn for the great losse of a gracious Soveraigne...'. The piece is anonymous and the mid-17th-century hand is not one that can be associated with Harington, but both subject and style immediately invite comparison with the Hatfield text.

The extent of Harington's literary activities and the corresponding dissemination of his MSS, as well as printed works, are well attested. In the dedicatory epistle of his *Aeneid, Book VI*, for instance, he says that he would like to have all his earlier works burnt 'in one fyer, save that so many of them are so flown abroad in England and Scotland, as not my reclamacion, nay hardly yor Maties proclamacion myght call them in'. It is indeed possible that more of his MSS are to be found. The extant libraries of his known associates present obvious possibilities. For instance, a large part of the collections in York Minster almost certainly belonged to Archbishop Tobie Matthew (1546-1628) and certain MS tracts to be found among them have striking similarities, in binding, appearance, and style of handwriting, to the MS *Tract on the Succession to the Crown* (HrJ 333) which Harington evidently presented to Matthew. On the other hand, MSS which have been associated with Harington in the past on slight evidence provide examples of the need for caution in matters of attribution. In his catalogue *English Poetry to 1700* (1941), A.S.W. Rosenbach claimed that his item 186, a miscellany now at the Rosenbach Foundation (MS 1083/15), was perhaps compiled by Harington since one of the hands had certain similarities with his, as indeed it does. Another miscellany, now in the Bodleian (MS Rawl. poet. 31), was inaccurately described by one of its owners as a collection of 'Sir John Harringtons Poems Written in the Reign of Queen Elizabeth'. However, since this MS contains a number of poems addressed to his cousin, Lucy, Countess of Bedford, it is possible that the owner made his assumption on the basis of some positive connection it had with one branch of the Harington family. Similar associations were responsible for McClure's attributing to Harington the discourse *The Prayse of Private Life*, although it seems more likely to be the work of his friend Samuel Daniel (see DaS 45-6). A MS text of one of Harington's epigrams (HrJ 82) is part of a volume (now in the East Sussex Record Office) which may also conceivably have had some association with the Harington family. It is a large volume of state letters and poems, including Donne's obsequy on the Countess of Bedford's brother, Sir John Harington, second Baron Harington of Exton (1592-1614), and a private letter of consolation written to their mother by one John Grange.

Harington must, of course, have possessed a library. His works provide abundant evidence of his wide reading and of the probable nature of his library. Lists of some of his (and perhaps his son's) books — including tracts by Hall, Donne, and Lancelot Andrewes, plays by Shakespeare and others, and such items as 'Two paper bookes to translate Latin into englishe & englishe into latin' and 'One Booke for Examples of The Educacōn of youthe' — appear in one of his miscellanies (HrJ 338). His library must have been dispersed, to other branches of the Harington family and perhaps elsewhere, before the total demolition of his house at Kelston in the 18th century (see Ian Grimble, *The Harington Family* (London, 1957), pp. 236-7). Apart from his annotated exemplum of Godwin's *Catalogue of Bishops* (see HrJ 328), the only printed volumes belonging to him known at present are exempla of his own works. The annotated exempla of *The Metamorphosis of Ajax* (HrJ 318-22) have already been mentioned, though no doubt he would have presented many others to friends and relatives, including one to Sir Robert Cecil (see McClure, pp. 93-4). Of the various exempla of *Orlando Furioso* which he must have presented, one, inscribed to Sir Thomas Coningsby, was item 392 in Rosenbach's catalogue of *English Poetry to 1700* (1941), and another, apparently presented to Lord Burghley, is in the British Library (Department of Printed Books, C. 57. h. 1) (see Howard M. Nixon, 'A London Binding for Lord Burghley, 1591', *BC*, 26 (Spring 1977), 84-5). For the volume presented to his mother-in-law, see HrJ 22. Volumes from Harington's personal library might perhaps be expected to contain, if not his signature, his device (representing his family name) of a hare, with a ring in its mouth, on a barrel (or tun).

Of Harington's correspondence, sixty-two letters are

printed from various sources in McClure. The texts of seventeen letters are printed from *Nugae Antiquae*; texts of four of these letters (McClure, pp. 68-80) are found in Harington's Irish notebook (HrJ 342) and two others (McClure, pp. 132-4, 96-8) are preserved in later transcripts among the Harington Papers (Add. MSS 46382A, ff. 1-2v; 46382B, ff. 12v-13), but the originals of the remaining eleven letters have not been seen by editors since the early 19th century. Of the forty-five letters not in *Nugae Antiquae*, the texts of six are printed in McClure from other published sources, four are printed from later transcripts among the Harington Papers (Add. MS 46382B, ff. 3v-4v), one from a transcript in the Bodleian (MS Tanner 169, f. 62), and one from a transcript in the Inner Temple Library (see HrJ 25). McClure prints the remaining thirty-three letters from the originals (that is, either the actual letters sent or autograph drafts which Harington retained). These are to be found at Hatfield House (nineteen letters among the Cecil Papers, owned by the Marquess of Salisbury), in the British Library (Add. MS 12049, pp. e, 194; Add. MS 27632, ff. 31r-v, 37, 42r-v, 45; Lansdowne MSS 13, No. 38, and 82, No. 88), in the Public Record Office (SP.12/102/325; SP.14/49/33), at Gonville and Caius College, Cambridge (MS 606/513, p, 61), and in Cambridge University Library (see HrJ 22). Harington's letter to Lady Russell in Lansdowne MS 82 (McClure, pp. 65-6) is reproduced in part in Greg, *English Literary Autographs*, plate XLV(a). The letter to Prince Henry accompanying an autograph copy of the *Epigrams*, a letter which McClure printed (p. 126) from Harington's draft in Add. MS 12049 (page e), can be found in the copy actually presented to the Prince (HrJ 21). In addition to the sixty-two letters printed in full by McClure there are some letters of Harington sent to Gilbert Talbot, Earl of Shrewsbury, now in the College of Arms, letters which McClure was only allowed to cite briefly. Two of them (Talbot Papers, Vol. M, ff. 61, 285) were printed by McClure (pp. 94-5, 112) from the texts printed in Edmund Lodge, *Illustrations of British History, Biography, and Manners* (1838) and in *Nugae Antiquae*. Unpublished letters are in the Talbot Papers, Vol. M, ff. 84, 204, and 210, and on f. 249 is a scribal summary of a law suit involving Harington (June 1604). McClure established that the Talbot letters were written by Sir John Harington and not by his cousin, the second Baron Harington of Exton (to whom they are still assigned in catalogues of the Talbot Papers). A draft letter of Harington overlooked by McClure (besides the address to Hall: HrJ 316) is in the British Library (Add. MS 27632, f. 46): see the review in *TLS* (4 September 1930), p. 697. Also in existence is an unpublished letter from Harington to Lady Arabella Stuart, now owned by the Duke of Norfolk, Arundel Castle ('Autograph Letters 1585 to 1617', No. 169), and a revealing autograph letter to Sir Robert Cecil, 12 June 1600, referring to Harington's writings in Ireland, is in the Public Record Office (SP. 63/207, part iii/105); the latter is noted in R.H. Miller's article in *SB*, 32 (1979). Other letters of 'Sir John Harington' found in various repositories (e.g. in the British Library (Add. MS 34727, f. 8, a Latin epistle to Prince Henry), in the Berkshire Record Office (among the Trumbull MSS), and in the Österreichische Nationalbibliothek, Vienna (Cod. 9737[rst])) prove to be written by his cousin or other members of his family. One further document of Harington's, a signed conveyance of land, dated 30 September 1588 and containing his pedigree, was sold at Sotheby's, 12 December 1977, Lot 87, to J.F. Fleming.

Of all Harington's literary works, those which may have had the widest manuscript circulation among his contemporaries are his Epigrams (which were written under his pseudonym, 'Misacmos', meaning 'a hater of filthiness'). Copies of individual epigrams, or groups of them, evidently circulated at Court, within the Inns of Court, and elsewhere, and they were frequently recopied in 17th-century miscellanies. The texts found in miscellanies usually represent early versions. Harington made numerous revisions when preparing fair copies of large numbers of epigrams from his 'scatterd papers', and it was revised versions which were posthumously published (from unspecified copy-texts) in 1615 and 1618. Some eighty or more epigrams found in his own MS collections (a number of these epigrams also occuring in miscellanies) were not published until the 20th century, but even then McClure's edition is not complete (see HrJ 213). A few other epigrams are found ascribed to Harington in MS sources, probably without authority, although the instances of patently false ascription are rare. A 26-line poem *Against D[r]. Prickett* ('Prickett, ye phisicke doct[r], loues a whore') is subscribed 'S[r]. J: Harrington' in an Oxford miscellany of the 1630s now in the New York Public Library, Arents Collection (Cat. No. S288, pp. 111-12). A couplet *On a Lawyer* ('God works wonders now and then'), found in innumerable miscellanies, is occasionally ascribed to Harington, or appears among other epigrams of his. It was printed under the heading 'An Epitaph by a man of his Father' as the eighth of nine 'Epigrammes by Sir I. H. and others' appended to I[ohn] C[lapham], *Alcilia, Philoparthens Louing Folly* (London, 1613). This circumstance might account for its connection with Harington, but he is not known to have written any epitaphs, either serious or satirical. The couplet also features in the Jonson apocrypha: see *Ben Jonson*, ed. C.H. Herford and Percy and Evelyn Simpson, VIII (Oxford, 1947), 444, and C.F. Main, 'Two Items in the Jonson Apocrypha', *N & Q*, 199 (June 1954), 243-5. Another epitaph associated with Harington is one on his mother, Isabella Markham, beginning 'A body chast, a vertuous mind, a temperat toung, an humble hart'. He quotes this in his notes after Book XXIX of *Orlando Furioso* as an epitaph written by 'a better pen then mine', but by someone 'well acquainted with her conditions'. At least one of his contemporaries believed that Harington composed this epitaph himself. On an end-paper in a printed exemplum of Nicolo Contarini, *De perfectione rerum* (Lyons, 1587), a volume once in Archbishop Sancroft's library and now at Emmanuel College, Cambridge (S. 14. 3. 37.), there is written a slightly variant version subscribed 'hir son, I am. J. H. vpō his Mother...'. This text is followed by a parody, headed 'Art tho[u] hir son whi than in the ' We shall the Dams true Image see', the last line containing an allusion to *The Metamorphosis of Ajax*.

It is likely that other texts of Harington's known epigrams are to be found in miscellanies in addition to those recorded in the entries below. For instance, in one of the notebooks of Sir Richard Dyott, M.P. (1590-1659), now in the Staffordshire Record Office (D. 661/11/1/7, p. 84), one of Harington's epigrams is paraphrased, perhaps from memory: 'Sir Jo: Harrington in his epigrammes brings in a country fellow who had taken advise of a lawyer and when his deeds 3 weekes had bin perused told the lawyer he had no mony to give him...'. Dyott presumably refers to the epigram *Of taking a Hare* (McClure No. 331, p. 278). Extracts from *Orlando Furioso* probably also occur in miscellanies. One couplet is quoted, for instance, in a miscellany belonging to the printer Christopher Wase (1627-90), a MS now in the Bodleian (MS Rawl. poet. 117, f. 275 rev.). McClure did not search texts of Harington's poems in miscellanies; indeed, unless otherwise stated, the MSS noted in the *Index* are unrecorded by editors.

As a footnote to Harington's translation of the *Regimen sanitatis Salernitanum* (see HrJ 1) it may be added that another English translation of the work is to be found in MSS. This begins 'All Salerne Schoole thus write to Englands King' and was made by the 'Translator Generall in his Age', Philemon Holland (1552-1637). A MS text of this version is found, for instance, in a medical miscellany in the British Library (Sloane MS 738, ff. 114-26). A twenty-three page MS of what appears to be the same version, described in a sale catalogue as probably the (anonymous) author's autograph and dated as c. 1650, was sold at Sotheby's, 6 February 1973, Lot 270, to Maggs. Holland's translation was first published in 1617, but a new edition appeared in 1649.

PB.

ARRANGEMENT

See also Addenda to Part 2, p. 628

FACSIMILE XVIII — Sir John Harington: Two pages of *Virgil's Aeneid, Book VI*, [1604] (HrJ 18). Berkshire Record Office, Trumbull Add. MS. 23, unnumbered opening containing stanzas 2, 3 and 4 in English on the left-hand page and the original Latin surrounded by Harington's English commentary on the right-hand page. Reproduced from the manuscripts of The Marquess of Downshire in the Berkshire Record Office by permission of the County Archivist.

2

But good Æneas marcheth to the towre
that joyn on great appollos sacred cave
to sage [a]Sybilla and her secret bowre
wheare Phebus spryte doth make her strawngly rave
forshewing her th'events of future howres
at [b]Trybias grove and Temple gilted brave.
by [c]Dedalus with art and cost most sumptuous
then when he made that vyage most presumptuous.

3.

This dedalus as elder folke have told
the wrathe of myghty Mynos did eschew
by flying to the Northern clymat cold
I sayd by flying for with wings he flew
[o]To Calcis cast. ~~aloft in skyes~~, an hyghe attempt and bold
and here arryving furst he thought yt dew
to consecrat to phebus sundry things
but cheefly these his artificiall wings

4

And here this stately temple he did make
to vew the front of which Æneas stayd
[e]Androgeus death was graven, and for his sake
how all the Greeks that bloody tribute payd
Male Children seavn eche yeere by lot they take
One tother syde lay Gnossyan land displayd
wheare Queen Pasyphae with stupendious frame
Conceavd a Monster Mynotawr by name.

a Sibilla was a generall name of certayne cunning women or pro
phitesses of theise wear ten but one of speciall fame whose wrytings wear
kept in Rome. and she prophesyed of Chryst as in the book of Sent
Augustin yt appeers in Civitate wch I have farder occasyon to quote here
after.

At pius Æneas arces, quibus altus Apollo
Præsidet, horrendæque procul secreta Sybillæ
Antrum immane petit: magnã cui mentẽ, animumq;
Delius inspirat vates, aperitq; futura.
Jam subeunt Triviæ lucos atq; aurea tecta.
Dædalus, vt fama est, fugiens Minoia regna,
Præpetibus pennis ausus se credere cœlo,
Insuetum per iter gelidas enauit ad Arctos,
Chalcidicaq; leuis tandem super astitit arce.
Redditus his primum terris, tibi Phœbe sacrauit
Remigium alarum, posuitq; immania templa.
In foribus, lethum Androgeo: tum pendere pœnas
Cecropidæ iussi, miserũm septena quotannis
Corpora gnatorum stat ductis sortibus vrna.
Contra elata mari respondet Gnosia tellus:
Hic crudelis amor tauri, suppostaque furto
Pasiphaë, mistumq; genus, prolesq; biformis
Minotaurus inest, Veneris monumenta nefandæ.

b. Trivias grove was a wood by the lake of Avernus, Tryvia ys one of the names of diana.

c Dedalus, an excellent goldsmith and archytect

d. Calcis a town of Euboea made by the athenians, and so named of the store of brasse and copper im ployed therein. theise as I sayd buylt Cumea as the inhabitants of Atenry in Irland built the fyne town of Galoway, in the pro vince of Connort.

e. Androgeus sonne of the Just king Mynos. who was a passing actyve yong man, and slayne by the Athenians of envy, and therfore they payd that trybute.

f. Gnossius a chefe cytty of Creet king Minos seat.

g. Pasiphae wyfe of king Minos who loving one Taurus in dishonorable sort gave occasyon of that absurd
fiction that she was put into a wodden cow to take the bull, ~~but~~ and so bare a
monster. but the truth was that in dedalus house she was got with chyld by
this Taurus and had twinns of wch one was lyke the kyng, and the other
lyke this Taurus and therce came the name of Minotaurus.

Sir John Harington

VERSE

(1) TRANSLATIONS

HrJ 1 *The Englishman's Doctor, or The School of Salerne* ('The Salerne Schoole doth by these lines impart').

Copy, with corrections, of Harington's translation of the late 11th-early 12th-century poem *Regimen sanitatis Salernitanum* (by Joannes de Mediolano?); untitled; early 17th century.

First pub. London, 1607; ed. Francis R. Packard and Fielding H. Garrison as *The School of Salernum* (London, 1922); ed. anonymously as *The School of Salernum* (Salerno, 1953). A version of lines 1-8 quoted in *The Metamorphosis of Ajax* (see HrJ 317-22.8). Formerly Phillipps MS 9132 and Bibliotheca Osleriana No. 7623, this MS recorded but not collated by editors; described by H.F.B. Brett-Smith in *BQR*, 5 (1926-9), 307. Facsimiles of p. 1 in 1922 edition, facing p. 75, and in 1953 edition, p. 12. The variants in this MS from the early printed text are listed by Edmond Malone (1741-1812) in his exemplum of the edition of 1624 in the Bodleian, Mal. 507.

Bodleian, MS Eng. poet. e. 32.

--- *The Hermaphrodite.*

See HrJ 71.

*HrJ 2 *Metrical Paraphrases of the Psalms* ('Right happie hee that neither walked hath').

Copy of Harington's translation of the Seven Penitential Psalms (Nos. 6, 32, 38, 51, 102, 130, 143), partly autograph, partly in the hand of an amanuensis with autograph revisions; forming part of a Harington miscellany (see HrJ 344); c. 1609.

Harington's complete Psalter unpublished. Psalms 38, 102, and 130 printed from this MS in Karl E. Schmutzler, 'Harington's Metrical Paraphrases of the Seven Penitential Psalms: Three Manuscript Versions', *PBSA*, 53 (1959), 240-51. Facsimile of part of f. 104 (Psalm 6) in Petti, *English Literary Hands*, No. 31 (where it is mistakenly described as entirely autograph, but see P.J. Croft's review in *TLS* (24 February 1978), p. 241).

British Library, Egerton MS 2711, ff. 104-7.

*HrJ 3 -----

Autograph draft, with revisions, of Harington's translation of Psalms 1, 3, and 4, in a Harington miscellany (see HrJ 338); c. 1609.

British Library, Add. MS 27632, f. 33.

HrJ 4 -----

Copy of Harington's translation of Psalms 42 and 50 in the same hand as the scribal hand in HrJ 2, in Harington's notebook relating to Ireland in 1599-1600 (see HrJ 342); c. 1609.

British Library, Add. MS 46369, ff. 18v-19v.

HrJ 5 -----

Copy of Harington's complete Psalter, entitled 'King Davids Psalmes', inscribed in a later hand on a flyleaf 'The Psalmes putt into verse by Sr John Harrington'; owned in 1701 by Algernon Capell, Earl of Essex; 93 leaves; early 17th century.

Psalms 24, 112, and 137 printed from this MS in *Nugae Antiquae* (1804), II, 403-6; discussed in Schmutzler.

Bodleian, MS Douce 361.

HrJ 6 -----

Copy of Harington's complete Psalter, entitled 'King Davids Psalmes', once owned by 'James Harington' (? Sir James Harington of Merton, Oxfordshire); 231 pages; imperfect; early 17th century.

This MS discussed in Schmutzler.

Ohio State University, English Department Library, [no ref. number].

--- -----

See also INTRODUCTION.

--- *Of a faire woman; translated out of Casaneus his Catalogus gloriae mundi.*

See HrJ 100-1.

*HrJ 7 *Orlando Furioso* ('Of Dames, of Knights, of armes, of loves delight').

Fair copy of Books I-XXIV, almost entirely in the hand of an amanuensis, with the first stanza, italic headings and sidenotes, and some corrections and additions in Harington's autograph; prepared as a trial lay-out of the text before the full printing; with inserted engravings, some coloured, from both Italian and English printed editions; c. 1590.

First pub. London, 1591; ed. Robert McNulty (Oxford, 1972). This MS collated in McNulty; discussed, with facsimile examples, in Kathleen M. Lea, 'Harington's *Folly*', *Elizabethan and Jacobean Studies Presented to F.P. Wilson* (Oxford, 1959), 42-58, and in Philip Gaskell, *From Writer to Reader* (Oxford, 1978), p. 11 seq. NB. this MS is not entirely autograph.

Bodleian, MS Rawl. poet. 125.

Orlando Furioso

*HrJ 8 -----

Fair copy of Books XIV to the 'Briefe and Summarie Allegorie' after Book XLVI, largely autograph, with some extensive passages towards the end in the hand of an amanuensis; the printer's copy for the first edition; imperfect; c. 1590-1.

This MS collated in McNulty; discussed, with facsimile pages, in W.W. Greg, 'An Elizabethan Printer and his Copy', *The Library*, 4th Ser. 4 (1923-4), 102-18, reprinted in Greg, *Collected Papers* (Oxford, 1966), pp. 95-109; Greg, *English Literary Autographs*, plate XLV(b); Percy Simpson, *Proof-Reading in the Sixteenth, Seventeenth and Eighteenth Centuries* (London, 1935), pp. 71-5; Kathleen M. Lea, *op. cit.*; Croft, *Autograph Poetry*, I, 20; Gaskell, *op. cit.*, p. 11 seq. NB. this MS is not entirely autograph.

British Library, Add. MS 18920.

*HrJ 9 -----

Copy, probably autograph, of Harington's English translation of a four-line Latin verse by Sir Walter Mildmay (here beginning 'fflye Sinne for sharp Revendge doth follow sinne') which is cited in the notes to Book XXII of *Orlando Furioso*; in the Arundel Harington MS (see HrJ 337); late 16th century.

McNulty, p. 249. Printed from this MS in Hughey, I, No. 92, p. 143.

Owned by the Duke of Norfolk, Arundel Castle, MSS (Special Press), 'Harrington MS. Temp. Eliz.', f. 59v.

*HrJ 10 -----

Copy of various lines of verse, possibly early translations of parts of *Orlando Furioso* made by Harington or by his father John Harington of Stepney (namely Book XXXI, stanza 2, lines 7-8; Book XLIV, stanza 33, lines 7-8; Book XXXI, stanza 1, line 1 seq.; Book V, stanza 54, lines 5-6; Book XLVI, stanza 91, lines 7-8), with some revisions in Sir John's autograph, in the Arundel Harington MS (see HrJ 337); mid-late 16th century.

These lines printed from this MS in Hughey, I, No. 35, p. 100; No. 38, p. 100; No. 44, p. 101; No. 50, p. 102; No. 54, p. 102, and discussed in II, pp. 44-8, 50-1.

Owned by the Duke of Norfolk, Arundel Castle, MSS (Special Press), 'Harrington MS. Temp. Eliz.', ff. 28-9.

HrJ 11 -----

Copy of Book XIX, stanza 1, here beginning 'None can deame right who faythfull frends do rest', in a Harington miscellany (see HrJ 339); late 16th century.

British Library, Add. MS 36529, f. 44.

HrJ 12 -----

Extensive extracts, in a volume also containing letters (1623-5) of Richard Newall, merchant; 1645.

Bodleian, MS Malone 2, ff. 14-129.

HrJ 13 -----

Copy of Harington's English translation of a Latin verse by Sir Walter Mildmay cited in the notes to Book XXII of *Orlando Furioso* (see HrJ 9), in a miscellany compiled by one Katherine Austen; [1664-8].

This MS recorded in Hughey, II, 123.

British Library, Add. MS 4454, f. 61v.

HrJ 14 -----

Copy of Book IX, stanzas 24-5 (beginning 'For first he is of limbs and bodie strong'), and Book XI, stanzas 19-24, in a scribal hand, in a volume of antiquarian collections of William Camden (see CmW 149); late 16th-early 17th century.

British Library, Cotton MS Julius F. XI, f. 307.

HrJ 15 -----

Extracts in a miscellany compiled by William Drummond of Hawthornden; c. 1609.

National Library of Scotland, MS 2059 (Hawthornden Vol. VII), ff. 226-7v.

--- -----

See also HrJ 22, 243, and INTRODUCTION.

HrJ 16 ----- *A Preface or Rather, A Briefe Apologie cf Poetrie and of the Author and Translator of this Poem.*

Copy of 'Sir John Harrington his apologie of poetrie', subscribed 'The preface or rather a briefe apologie of poetrie, the apologie of S^{r}: John Harrington worke of translation called Orlando: furioso finis.', in a miscellany compiled by one Jacob Blenkinsop; 16 pages; c. 1639.

York Minster, MX XVI. L. 15, [no page numbers].

--- *Ouids confession translated into English for Generall Norreys. 1593.*

See HrJ 296.

--- *The School of Salerne, or The English Doctor.*

See HrJ 1.

HrJ 17 *Virgil's Aeneid. Book IV* ('Now Cupids quickning shafts had moved desire').

Copy of a verse translation in 170 six-line stanzas (ending with a two-line envoy) probably by Harington; 35 pages of text; from the papers of the Marquess of Northampton at Castle Ashby and probably once owned by William Compton, first Earl of Northampton (d. 1630); early 17th century.

Unpublished. This MS sold at Christie's, 5 July 1978, Lot 47; facsimile of one page in the sale catalogue. See INTRODUCTION.

British Library, Add. MS 60283.

*HrJ 18 *Virgil's Aeneid. Book VI* ('While thus with tears hee spake, his Navy glydes').

Autograph fair copy of a verse translation in 134 eight-line stanzas, with accompanying original Latin text, made for the instruction of Prince Henry; complete with a dedicatory epistle to James I, explanatory notes and glosses, and a series of seven appendices: namely (1) 'Of Enchauntements, and prophecies'; (2) 'Of funerals'; (3) 'Of hel and the state of the ded'; (4) 'Of Paradise and the state of the godly'; (5) 'Of the sowl of man and the original thereof'; (6) 'Of the Citty and Empyre of Room'; (7) 'Of reeding poetry'; 156 pages; among the papers of the Trumbull family of Easthampstead Park and owned by the Marquess of Downshire; [1604].

Unpublished. See FACSIMILE XVIII and INTRODUCTION.

Berkshire Record Office, Trumbull Add. MS 23.

HrJ 19 -----

Copy of the commentary, 'Taken out of a MS of his late Majesty [? Charles I] Composed by Sr John Harrington K^t^', entitled 'To φως φισεως or the light of Nature in Heathens, being breife notes upon the sixth booke of Virgils Aeneads'; the work dated 19 June 1604; c. 1650?

Owned by Marcus Selden Goldman, Urbana, Illinois.

(2) EPIGRAMS

(i) COLLECTIONS OF EPIGRAMS

*HrJ 20 *Epigrams.*

Copy of 409 Epigrams (including one by Surrey: see SuH 41), plus a few additional scraps of verse, in the hand of an amanuensis, with a few autograph revisions and additions; also (p. c) Latin and English verses by Francis Harington; (pp. e, 194) two of Harington's letters [printed in McClure, pp. 126, 95-6]; (pp. 195-201) Latin 'exercyses' (with translations) by his son, John; (pp. 203-5) more Latin and English verses; (pp. 207-15) the English and Latin verses for Harington's 'new yeeres guifte' to King James in 1602/3 [printed in *Nugae Antiquae* (1804), I, 325-31, and see HrJ 21, 26]; (pp. 216-17) Harington's welcome to King James and to Queen Anne [McClure Nos. 425-6]; (pp. 217-18) his verses 'Musa jocosa meos solari assueta dolores' [*Nugae Antiquae* (1804), I, 332-3; the Latin version of McClure No. 427]; (pp. 219-50) an index to the volume; and (p. 251) a Latin epigram on tobacco, with a translation; 251 numbered pages; imperfect, lacking pp. 11-12; [1603-12].

Seven Epigrams first pub. in *Epigrammes by Sir J.H. and others* appended to J[ohn] C[lapham], *Alcilia, Philoparthens Louing Folly* (London, 1613); 116 Epigrams pub. London, 1615; 346 Epigrams pub. London, 1618; 428 Epigrams printed in McClure (1930), pp. 145-322; and see also HrJ 27-314.5. This MS collated in McClure, which prints from it McClure Nos. 347-428 (pp. 287-322) (but see HrJ 213). Extracts also printed from this MS by 'EU. HOOD' (i.e. Joseph Haslewood) in *Gentleman's Magazine*, 97. ii (1827), pp. 119-21, 128, 392. Facsimiles of p. 27 in Greg, *English Literary Autographs*, plate XLV(d), and of pp. 132-3 in McClure, facing p. 298. NB. this MS is not entirely autograph, neither are the pages autograph in the cited facsimiles.

British Library, Add. MS 12049.

*HrJ 21 -----

Autograph fair copy of 408 Epigrams (including one by Surrey: see SuH 42), with revisions; also (pp. 257-63) a watercolour drawing of the lantern, with accompanying English and Latin verses, which Harington gave to King James as a New Year's gift in 1602/3; (p. 264) Harington's welcome to King James and to Queen Anne; and (pp. 265-6) his verses 'Musa jocosa meos solari assueta dolores'; with a dedicatory epistle to Prince Henry, dated (and probably presented to him shortly after) 19 June 1605.

This MS recorded, and those epigrams which also occur in the Arundel Harington MS are collated, in Hughey. See also HrJ 20, 26, and 213.

Folger, MS V. a. 249.

*HrJ 22 -----

Autograph fair copy of about 52 Epigrams, bound with a printed exemplum of *Orlando Furioso* (London, 1591), presented to Harington's mother-in-law, Lady Jane Rogers; with a dedicatory epistle to her dated 19 December 1600.

This MS collated in McClure, and the epistle printed pp. 86-7. Facsimile pages in Greg, *English Literary Autographs*, plate XLV(c), and in Flower & Munby, *English Poetical Autographs*, p. 4.

Cambridge University Library, MS Adv. b. 81.

Epigrams

HrJ 23 -----

Fair copy of 65 Epigrams in a composite volume of verse belonging to the Skipwith family of Cotes, Leicestershire; early 17th century.

British Library, Add. MS 25707, ff. 120-32v.

HrJ 24 -----

Fair copy of 18 Epigrams (McClure Nos. 261, 5, 67, 308, 262, 326, 338, 121, 122 (same as 329), 142, 356, 337, 366, 246, 270, 263, 248, 421), plus a Latin version of No. 421 (beginning 'Stirpis Haringtoniae Soboles pulcherrima Sara'); inscribed in a later hand 'A Booke of verses made by S^{r}: John Harrington knight who dwelt at Bathe'; early 17th century.

Harvard, MS Eng 121.

HrJ 25 -----

Copy of ten Epigrams (McClure Nos. 188, 271, 31, 302, 337, 67, 90, 267, 338, and 329), together with (f. 303v) a copy of Harington's letter of 19 December 1600 to Lucy, Countess of Bedford, in which he presents these epigrams to her; this MS probably a copy deriving from the MS he sent to her; in a verse miscellany bound in a composite volume of state papers; early 17th century.

This MS recorded in McClure, p. 390, and the letter printed p. 87; also discussed in Frances Berkeley Young, '*The Triumphe of Death* translated out of Italian by the Countesse of Pembrooke', *PMLA*, 27 (1912), 47-75.

Inner Temple Library, Petyt MS 538, Vol. 43, ff. 289-90v.

HrJ 26 -----

Transcript of Harington's Latin and English verses written in 1602 to accompany his new year's gift of a lantern to King James (see HrJ 20-1), made by John Leyden (1775-1811) 'from the original in the University Library, Edinburgh'; 4 leaves; 26 March 1802.

Printed from this transcript in *Nugae Antiquae* (1804), I, 325-35. What Leyden calls 'the original' is no longer in Edinburgh University Library and is unlocated.

National Library of Scotland, Adv. MS 19. 3. 2.

(ii) INDIVIDUAL EPIGRAMS
[in addition to those in HrJ 20-6]

--- *Against D^{r}. Prickett* ('Prickett, ye phisicke doct^{r}, Loues a whore').

See INTRODUCTION.

HrJ 27 *Against Swearing* ('In elder times an ancient custome was').

Copy, headed 'Of Othes' and subscribed 'Authore Ben: Jonsonio', in a miscellany compiled by Leweston Fitzjames of the Middle Temple; c. 1595.

First pub. in Henry Fitzsimon, S.J., *The Justification and Exposition of the Divine Sacrifice of the Masse* (Douai, 1611); *1615*; *1618*, Book IV, No. 9; McClure No. 263, p. 256.

Bodleian, MS Add. B. 97, f. 39.

HrJ 28 -----

Copy in a composite volume of verse collected by Elias Ashmole (1617-92); mid-17th century.

Bodleian, MS Ashmole 36/37, f. 117v.

HrJ 29 -----

Second copy in a composite volume of verse collected by Elias Ashmole; mid-17th century.

Bodleian, MS Ashmole 36/37, f. 126.

HrJ 30 -----

Copy in a verse miscellany partly compiled by Elias Ashmole; c. 1630s-40s.

Bodleian, MS Ashmole 47, f. 47.

HrJ 31 -----

Copy in a miscellany compiled by one John Stansby; c. 1669.

Bodleian, MS Ashmole 1463, p. 2.

HrJ 32 -----

Copy in a verse miscellany; c. 1630s.

Bodleian, MS Douce f. 5, fol. 34.

HrJ 33 -----

Copy in a verse miscellany probably compiled by a member of New College, Oxford; c. 1620s-30s.

Bodleian, MS Malone 19, p. 51.

HrJ 34 -----

Copy, untitled, in a verse miscellany; c. 1620-33.

Bodleian, MS Rawl. poet. 31, f. 3r-v.

Against Swearing

HrJ 35 -----

Copy in a miscellany once owned by Margaret Bellasys, probably the daughter of Thomas, first Lord Fauconberg (1577-1653); c. 1630.

British Library, Add. MS 10309, f. 62v.

HrJ 36 -----

Copy, headed 'Juramenta antiqua', in a verse miscellany probably compiled by a Cambridge man; c. 1630s.

British Library, Add. MS 15227, f. 5v.

HrJ 37 -----

Copy in a verse miscellany probably compiled by a Cambridge man; mid-17th century.

British Library, Add. MS 22603, f. 32v.

HrJ 38 -----

Copy, headed 'Against Dr Patton who preached against swearing by the crosse and masse made by a Papist', in a verse miscellany once owned by Francis Norreys (? Sir Francis Norris (1609-69)) and Henry Balle; mid-17th century.

British Library, Egerton MS 2421, f. 19.

HrJ 39 -----

Copy in a verse miscellany; c. 1620-33.

British Library, Harley MS 4064, f. 233.

HrJ 40 -----

Copy in a verse miscellany probably compiled by Francis Baskerville of Malmesbury, Wiltshire, and owned in 1663 by William Wallrond; c. 1633.

British Library, Sloane MS 1446, f. 41v.

HrJ 41 -----

Copy in a miscellany probably compiled by a Cambridge man; c. 1627.

British Library, Sloane MS 1489, f. 10.

HrJ 42 -----

Copy in a verse miscellany probably compiled by a member of an Inn of Court; mid-17th century.

Folger, MS V. a. 262, p. 83.

HrJ 43 -----

Copy, headed 'The degrees of Swearing', in a verse miscellany compiled by one or two Oxford men, possibly connected with New College and afterwards with the Inns of Court; 1630s.

Harvard, MS Eng 686, f. 17v.

HrJ 44 -----

Copy, untitled, in a MS volume of poems chiefly by John Donne once owned by one Meriall Tracy; c. 1620-33.

Huntington, HM 198, Part II, f. 45v.

HrJ 45 -----

Copy, untitled, in a miscellany; early 17th century.

University of Leeds, Brotherton Collection, MS Lt. 25, f. 9.

HrJ 46 -----

Copy, here beginning 'In older times an auncient custome was', in a verse miscellany owned and probably compiled by Hugh Barrow (b. 1617/18), of Brasenose College, Oxford; c. 1638.

New York Public Library, Arents Collection, Cat. No. S288, p. 81.

HrJ 47 -----

Copy in a verse miscellany compiled by one Robert Bishop; c. 1630.

Rosenbach Foundation, MS 1083/16, p. 119.

HrJ 48 -----

Copy, untitled, in a verse miscellany; c. 1620.

Victoria and Albert Museum, Dyce Collection, Cat. No. 44 (Pressmark 25. F. 39), f. 79v.

HrJ 49 -----

Copy in a verse miscellany; c. 1640.

Yale, Osborn Collection, b 62, p. 22.

HrJ 50 -----

Copy in a miscellany; mid-17th century.

Yale, Osborn Collection, b 200, pp. 23-4.

Against Swearing

HrJ 51 -----

Copy in a miscellany; mid-17th century.

Yale, Osborn Collection, b 205, f. 47.

HrJ 52 *The Author, of his own fortune* ('Take fortune as it falles, as one aduiseth').

Copy in a verse miscellany compiled by the Yorkshire antiquary John Hopkinson (1610-80); mid-17th century.

First pub. in *1618*, Book I, No. 29; McClure No. 30, p. 160.

Bradford Central Library, Hopkinson MSS, Vol. 34, p. 81.

HrJ 53 -----

Copy, headed 'Of Fortune', in a verse miscellany once owned by Elizabeth Herrick (1684-1745) and William Herrick (1689-1773); c. 1630.

Leicestershire Record Office, DG. 9/2796, p. 33.

HrJ 54 *The Author to his wife* ('Mall, once in pleasant company by chance').

Copy written in a verse miscellany probably compiled by a member of an Inn of Court; c. 1630.

First pub. in *1615*; *1618*, Book IV, No. 45; McClure No. 299, pp. 268-9. See also HrJ 55.

Rosenbach Foundation, MS 1083/15, ff. 86v-7.

HrJ 55 -----

Copy, 'Taken out of Burton's Abstract upon Malincholy', in a verse miscellany; late 17th-early 18th century.

This epigram is quoted in Robert Burton, *Anatomy of Melancholy* (Oxford, 1621), Part 2, Sect. 2, Memb. 6, subs. 4.

Yale, Osborn Collection, fb 142, pp. 32-3.

HrJ 56 *The Author to Queene Elizabeth, in praise of her reading* ('For euer deare, for euer dreaded Prince').

Copy, headed 'To y[e] Prince', in a verse miscellany partly compiled by Elias Ashmole (1617-92); c. 1630s-40s.

First pub. in *1615*; *1618*, Book IV, No. 13; McClure No. 267, p. 258. This epigram is also quoted in *Breefe Notes and Remembraunces* (*Nugae Antiquae* (1804), I, 172): see INTRODUCTION.

Bodleian, MS Ashmole 47, f. 21.

HrJ 57 -----

Copy, headed 'Sir John Harrington to Quee: Elizabeth' and here beginning 'Dreade, Soveraigne, and ever loueinge Prince', in a verse miscellany; c. 1620-33.

Bodleian, MS Rawl. poet. 31, f. 3.

HrJ 58 -----

Copy, headed 'Ad. reg: Elizab:', in a verse miscellany probably compiled by a Cambridge man; c. 1630s.

British Library, Add. MS 15227, f. 6.

HrJ 59 -----

Copy, headed 'S[r] John Harrington to Queene Elizabeth' and here beginning 'Dread Soveraigne and ever loving Prince', in a verse miscellany; c. 1620-33.

British Library, Harley MS 4064, f. 233.

HrJ 60 -----

Copy, headed 'S[r] John Harrington to Quee. Eliza.' and here beginning 'Dread Soueraigne & ever Loving Prince', in a miscellany probably compiled by someone connected with the Inns of Court; c. 1620s.

Printed from this MS in Grosart, *The Dr Farmer MS* (1873), I, 83.

Chetham's Library, Manchester, Mun. A 4. 15, p. 75.

HrJ 60.5 See Addenda, p. 628.

--- *The authors farewell to his Muse written at Eaton 1603 the 14th of April* ('Musa jocosa meos solari assueta dolores').

[The Latin version of McClure No. 427, printed in *Nugae Antiquae* (1804), I, 332-3, appears in the British Library, Add. MS 12049, pp. 217-18 (see HrJ 20) and in the Folger, MS. V. a. 249, pp. 265-6 (see HrJ 21); also in *A Short View of the State of Ireland* (HrJ 326-7).]

HrJ 61 *A comparison of a Booke, with Cheese* ('Old Haywood writes, & proues in some degrees').

Copy, here beginning 'Heiwood affirms & proves in some degrees', in a miscellany probably compiled by a Cambridge man; c. 1627.

First pub. in *1615*; *1618*, Book IV, No. 72; McClure No. 326, pp. 276-7.

British Library, Sloane MS 1489, f. 10v.

HrJ 62 -----

Copy, headed 'Vt caseus liber' and here

beginning 'Heywood affirmes & prooues in some degrees', in a verse miscellany compiled by an Oxford man and once owned by one Stephen Welden; mid-17th century.

Folger, MS V. a. 162, f. 34.

HrJ 63 *A dish of dainties for the Diuell* ('A godly Father, sitting on a draught').

Copy of an early version, untitled, in the Arundel Harington MS (see HrJ 337); late 16th century.

First pub. in *The Metamorphosis of Ajax* (London, 1596); *1618*, Book I, No. 48; McClure No. 49, p. 166. Printed from this MS in Hughey, I, No. 197, p. 242. See also HrJ 317-24.

Owned by the Duke of Norfolk, Arundel Castle, MSS (Special Press) 'Harrington MS. Temp. Eliz.', f. 146v.

HrJ 64 *A good answere of a Gentlewoman to a Lawyer* ('A vertuous Dame, that saw a Lawyer rome').

Copy, headed 'A gentlewomans answeare to a Lawyer', in a verse miscellany compiled by the Yorkshire antiquary John Hopkinson (1610-80); mid-17th century.

First pub. in *1618*, Book III, No. 39; McClure No. 240, pp. 248-9.

Bradford Central Library, Hopkinson MSS, Vol. 34, p. 76.

HrJ 65 -----

Copy, untitled, in a verse miscellany probably compiled by a Cambridge man; c. 1630s.

British Library, Add. MS 15227, f. 90v.

HrJ 66 -----

Copy, headed 'Of a Lawyers absence', in a MS volume of epigrams once owned by one Richard Wharfe; c. 1631.

British Library, Harley MS 1836, ff. 15v-16.

HrJ 67 -----

Copy in a verse miscellany compiled by an Oxford man and once owned by one Stephen Welden; imperfect; mid-17th century.

Folger, MS V. a. 162, f. 1v.

HrJ 68 -----

Copy, headed 'A lady to a Lawyer', in a verse miscellany; c. 1640.

Folger, MS V. a. 319, f. 51.

HrJ 69 -----

Copy, headed 'A Lady to a Lawyer', in a verse miscellany; mid-17th century.

Folger, MS V. a. 322, p. 47.

HrJ 70 -----

Copy, untitled, in a verse miscellany; c. 1620.

Victoria and Albert Museum, Dyce Collection, Cat. No. 44 (Pressmark 25. F. 39), f. 65v.

HrJ 70.5 See Addenda, p. 628.

HrJ 71 *The Hermaphrodite* ('When first my mother bore me in her wombe').

Copy, headed 'The Hermophrodite translated', in a verse miscellany; c. 1634.

A version (a translation of a Latin poem by Pulix) first pub. in Timothy Kendall, *Flowers of Epigrammes* (London, 1577); *1615*; *1618*, Book III, No. 37; McClure No. 238, pp. 246-7.

Rosenbach Foundation, MS 239/27, p. 170.

HrJ 72 *How England may be reformed* ('Men say that England late is bankrout grown').

Copy, untitled and here beginning 'England men say of late is Banquerout growen', in a miscellany; c. 1621-31.

Not pub. before the 19th century (?); quoted at the end of the *Tract on the Succession to the Crown* (see HrJ 333-5); McClure No. 375, p. 301. This MS recorded in McClure, p. 425.

Bodleian, MS Ashmole 781, p. 134.

HrJ 73 -----

Copy, untitled and here beginning 'England men say of late is banquerout growne', in a verse miscellany later owned by William Fulman (1632-88); c. 1630.

Bodleian, MS CCC. 327, f. 24.

HrJ 74 -----

Copy, untitled and here beginning 'Englande (men say) of late is bankerupte growne', in a verse miscellany owned in 1619 and possibly compiled by Simon Sloper (b. 1596/7) of Magdalen Hall, Oxford; c. 1620s.

Bodleian, MS Eng. poet. f. 10, fol. 97.

HrJ 75 -----

Copy, untitled and here beginning 'England men say of late is bankerupt growne', in a verse miscellany; c. 1630s.

Bodleian, MS Malone 23, p. 121.

How England may be reformed

HrJ 76 -----

Copy, untitled and here beginning 'England men say of late is bankroute growne', in a miscellany compiled by an Oxford man; early 17th century.

Bodleian, MS Rawl. poet. 212, f. 87v.

HrJ 77 -----

Copy, headed 'S[r] Jo. Harrington On K. James his Coming in' and here beginning 'England (Men say) of late is banckrupt grown', in a MS book of jests compiled by Archbishop William Sancroft (1617-93); mid-late 17th century.

Bodleian, MS Sancroft 53, p. 47.

HrJ 78 -----

Second copy, untitled and here beginning 'England, Men say, of late is Bankrupt grown', in Archbishop Sancroft's book of jests; mid-late 17th century.

Bodleian, MS Sancroft 53, p. 57.

HrJ 79 -----

Copy, here beginning 'England (men say) of late is bankrupt growne', in a miscellany once owned by Margaret Bellasys, probably the daughter of Thomas, first Lord Fauconberg (1577-1653); c. 1630.

British Library, Add. MS 10309, f. 120.

HrJ 80 -----

Copy, untitled and here beginning 'England, men say of late, is bankrupte growne', in a miscellany compiled by someone connected with the Court; c. 1605.

Printed from this MS in J.O. Halliwell, *Poetical Miscellanies from a Manuscript Collection of the time of James I*, Percy Society (London, 1845), p. 37.

British Library, Add. MS 22601, f. 60v.

HrJ 81 -----

Copy, untitled and here beginning 'England men say of late is bankrout growen', in a verse miscellany among the papers of the Gell family, formerly of Hopton Hall, perhaps owned by Sir John Gell (1593-1671); c. 1620s-30s.

Derbyshire Record Office, D258/60/26a, ff. [38v-9].

HrJ 82 -----

Copy, untitled and here beginning 'England, men say of late is banquerot growne', in a group of poems in the middle of a MS volume of state letters; among the papers of the Fuller family of Brightling Hall and possibly once owned by Ambrose Trayton of Lewes, Esquire of the Body to James I and Charles I; c. 1614-20s.

East Sussex Record Office, RAF/F/13/1, [no page number].

HrJ 83 -----

Copy, headed 'Upon England' and here beginning 'England men say of late is Bankrupt growne', in a verse miscellany; c. 1630.

University of Nottingham, Portland MS Pw V 37, p. 174.

*HrJ 84 *In defence of Lent* ('Our belly-gods dispraise the Lenton fast').

Copy, lines 1-4 in Harington's autograph, the rest probably autograph, untitled, in the Arundel Harington MS (see HrJ 337); late 16th century.

First pub. in *1618*, Book II, No. 90; McClure No. 186, pp. 222-3. Printed from this MS in Hughey, I, No. 91, p. 142.

Owned by the Duke of Norfolk, Arundel Castle, MSS (Special Press), 'Harrington MS. Temp. Eliz.', f. 59v.

HrJ 85 *In prayse of the Countesse of Darby, married to the Lord Keeper* ('This noble Countesse liued many yeeres').

Copy, headed 'The praise of the Countess of Derby married to the Lord Chancellour', in a verse miscellany compiled by the Yorkshire antiquary John Hopkinson (1610-80); mid-17th century.

First pub. in *1618*, Book III, No. 47; McClure No. 248, p. 251.

Bradford Central Library, Hopkinson MSS, Vol. 34, p. 80.

HrJ 86 -----

Copy, headed 'The sam Author vppon y[e] countes of Darby the wiff of ffernando', written at the end of a MS copy of *Leicester's Commonwealth*; c. 1620s.

Emmanuel College, Cambridge, MS 1. 3. 28 (James 80), f. 58.

HrJ 87 *In Romam* ('Hate, and debate, Rome through the world hath spread').

Copy, headed 'Roma, Amor', in a verse miscellany probably compiled by a Cambridge man; c. 1630s.

First pub. in *1618*, Book IV, No. 92; McClure No. 346, p. 286.

British Library, Add. MS 15227, f. 76v.

HrJ 88 -----

Copy, headed 'Of Rome', in a verse miscellany; c. 1643-50s.

University of Newcastle upon Tyne, MS Bell/White 25, f. 42v.

HrJ 89 -----

Copy, headed 'An Epigram of Rome', in a miscellany compiled by or for Sir Thomas Finch, Viscount Maidstone and Earl of Winchelsea; c. 1634.

Rosenbach Foundation, MS 243/4, p. 3.

HrJ 90 -----

Copy, subscribed 'Colb. Claney. 30th. Augt. 62', in a miscellany; c. 1662.

Yale, Osborn Collection, b 52/1, p. 120.

HrJ 91 *Of a certaine Man* ('There was (not certain when) a certaine preacher').

Copy, headed 'On Quidam Homo' and here beginning 'There was not certaine, when a Certaine Teacher', in a verse miscellany probably compiled by a Cambridge man; c. 1630s.

First pub. in *1615*; *1618*, Book IV, No. 23; McClure No. 277, p. 262. The MS text followed by 'The Answ: to it by the Lady cheeke' (here beginning 'That noe man yet could in the Bible find').

British Library, Add. MS 15227, f. 16.

HrJ 92 -----

Copy, headed 'Vpon the death of mr Pate of Brasennose Colledge Oxford', in a verse miscellany owned in 1623 and probably compiled by one Richard Jackson; c. 1620s-30s.

Edinburgh University Library, MS H.-P. Coll. 401, f. 100v.

HrJ 93 -----

Copy in a miscellany; c. 1630.

Folger, MS V. a. 345, p. 171.

HrJ 94 -----

Copy, untitled and here beginning 'A time not certaine when a certaine preacher', in a MS volume of poems chiefly by John Donne once owned by one Meriall Tracy; c. 1620-33.

Huntington, HM 198, Part II, ff. 38v-9.

HrJ 95 -----

Copy, headed 'Erat quidam Homo. Or An invective against Women' and here beginning 'It is not certaine when, a certaine Preacher', in a verse miscellany; c. 1630.

The text followed by 'Erat quaedam Mulier. Or The Womans Reply' (here beginning 'That no man yet could in the scripture find').

University of Nottingham, Portland MS Pw V 37, p. 172.

HrJ 96 -----

Copy, headed 'A Certaine Woman' and here beginning 'It was not certaine when a certaine Preacher', in a verse miscellany compiled by one Robert Bishop; c. 1630.

The text followed by 'The reply' (here beginning 'That noe man yet could in the Bible find').

Rosenbach Foundation, MS 1083/16, p. 16.

HrJ 96.5 See Addenda, p. 628.

HrJ 97 -----

Copy, untitled and here beginning 'It is of certaine that a ceraine preacher', in a verse miscellany once owned by Sir Henry Spelman (1564?-1641); c. 1630s.

The text followed by an answer (here beginning 'That no man yett could in the Scriptures find').

South African Library, Cape Town, MS Grey 7 a 29, pp. 157-8.

HrJ 98 -----

Copy, untitled and here beginning 'It was not certaine when a cteine teacher', in a miscellany compiled by a Cambridge man; c. 1630s.

Trinity College, Dublin, MS 690, f. 150v.

HrJ 98.5, 98.8 See Addenda, p. 628.

HrJ 99 *Of a faire Shrew* ('Faire, rich, and yong? how rare is her perfection').

Copy, headed 'Upon a shrewd mrs', in a verse miscellany compiled by the Yorkshire antiquary John Hopkinson (1610-80); mid-17th century.

First pub. in *1615*; *1618*, Book IV, No. 37; McClure No. 291, p. 266.

Bradford Central Library, Hopkinson MSS, Vol. 34, p. 8.

HrJ 100 *Of a faire woman; translated out of Casaneus his Catalogus gloriae mundi* ('These thirty things that Hellens fame did raise').

Copy, headed in another hand 'Calmeydas verses translated by Iohn Harington', in the Arundel

Of a faire woman; translated out of Casaneus

Harington MS (see HrJ 337); late 16th century.

First pub. in *1618*, Book I, No. 15; McClure No. 16, p. 154. Printed from this MS in Hughey, I, No. 226, p. 257. The text followed by a copy of the original Latin verses by Barthélemy de Chasseneux (lines 1-10 in Harington's autograph).

Owned by the Duke of Norfolk, Arundel Castle, MSS (Special Press), 'Harrington MS. Temp. Eliz.', ff. 156v-7.

HrJ 101 -----

Copy in a verse miscellany compiled by the Yorkshire antiquary John Hopkinson (1610-80); mid-17th century.

Bradford Central Library, Hopkinson MSS, Vol. 34, p. 75.

HrJ 102 *Of a Lady that giues the cheek* ('Is't for a grace, or is't for some disleeke').

Copy, headed 'To his M^rs^', in a verse miscellany compiled by an Oxford man; mid-17th century.

First pub. in *1615*; *1618*, Book III, No. 3; McClure No. 201, p. 230.

Bodleian, MS CCC. 176, f. 29v.

HrJ 103 -----

Copy, headed 'On a gentelwoman tha pained her face' and here beginning 'If for a grace or if for some mislike', in a verse miscellany compiled by an Oxford man and once owned by one Henry Lawson; c. 1630s.

Bodleian, MS Eng. poet. e. 14, f. 81v.

HrJ 104 -----

Copy, untitled, in a verse miscellany; c. 1620-33.

Bodleian, MS Rawl. poet. 31, f. 4.

HrJ 105 -----

Copy, headed 'To a proud Lady', in a miscellany compiled by William Eliot (a nephew of Sir Simonds D'Ewes), bound in a composite volume; c. 1640-55.

Bodleian, MS Rawl. poet. 116, f. 53.

HrJ 106 -----

Copy, headed 'Coynesse', in a verse miscellany compiled by the Yorkshire antiquary John Hopkinson (1610-80); late 17th century.

Bradford Central Library, Hopkinson MSS, Vol. 17, f. [9v].

HrJ 107 -----

Copy, headed 'Upon a gentlewoman painted', in a verse miscellany compiled by John Hopkinson; mid-17th century.

Bradford Central Library, Hopkinson MSS, Vol. 34, p. 33.

HrJ 108 -----

Copy, headed 'On a gent'woman who painted her face', in a musical setting in a MS songbook compiled by one Giles Earle; c. 1615-26.

This MS collated in John P. Cutts, 'Sir John Harington's Epigrammatic Lyric', *N & Q*, 205 (February 1960), 60-1.

British Library, Add. MS 24665, f. 49r-v.

HrJ 109 -----

Copy in a musical setting in a MS songbook once owned by one Richard Elliotts and possibly by the composer Adrian Batten (d. 1637); c. 1630.

Printed from this MS in Cutts, *N & Q* (1960), 60-1.

British Library, Add. MS 29481, f. 12.

HrJ 110 -----

Copy, headed 'On a gentlewoman who painted her face', in a verse miscellany compiled by Daniel Leare (a distant cousin of William Strode) probably while at Christ Church, Oxford; c. 1631-3.

British Library, Add. MS 30982, f. 23.

HrJ 111 -----

Copy, headed 'Of a Painted Lady', in a miscellany probably compiled by someone connected with the Inns of Court; c. 1620s.

Printed from this MS in Grosart, *The Dr Farmer MS* (1873), I, 82.

Chetham's Library, Manchester, Mun. A 4. 15, p. 75.

HrJ 112 -----

Copy, headed 'To a Scornefull Ladye', in a miscellany compiled by one Richard Archard; c. 1650-7.

Folger, MS V. a. 124, f. 41v.

HrJ 113 -----

Copy in a verse miscellany probably compiled

by a member of an Inn of Court; mid-17th century.

Folger, MS V. a. 262, p. 102.

HrJ 114 -----

Copy, headed 'Of a gentlewoman that painted her face', in a verse miscellany compiled by one or two Oxford men, possibly connected with New College and afterwards with the Inns of Court; 1630s.

Harvard, MS Eng 686, f. 54.

HrJ 115 -----

Copy, headed 'Of Kissing' and here beginning 'Its for a grace or else for some dislike', in a miscellany compiled by an Oxford man, possibly a member of Brasenose College; c. late 1630s.

Huntington, HM 116, p. 53.

HrJ 116 -----

Copy in a musical setting in a MS songbook once owned by a certain Anne Twice; c. 1620.

This MS collated in Cutts, *N & Q* (1960), 60-1.

New York Public Library, Music Division, Drexel MS 4175, No. xx.

HrJ 117 -----

Copy, headed 'A woman giving her cheek to be Kissed', in a verse miscellany; c. 1643-50s.

University of Newcastle upon Tyne, MS Bell/White 25, f. 44v.

HrJ 118 -----

Copy, untitled, in a verse miscellany; c. 1638-45.

Rosenbach Foundation, MS 239/22, f. 7v.

HrJ 119 -----

Copy, headed 'On a painted Lady', in a verse miscellany; c. 1634.

Rosenbach Foundation, MS 239/27, p. 202.

HrJ 120 -----

Copy, headed 'A painted creature Kist', in a verse miscellany compiled by one Robert Bishop; c. 1630.

Rosenbach Foundation, MS 1083/16, p. 59.

HrJ 121 -----

Copy, untitled and here beginning 'Yst for a fauor, or for some dislike', in a MS volume of poems chiefly by John Donne, among the family papers of the Earl of Dalhousie; c. 1620-5.

Scottish Record Office, GD45/26/95/1, f. 18.

HrJ 122 -----

Copy, untitled and here beginning 'Yst for a fauour, or for some dislike', probably transcribed from HrJ 121, in a MS volume of poems chiefly by Donne, among the family papers of the Earl of Dalhousie and once owned by Andrew Ramsey; c. 1622-9.

Scottish Record Office, GD45/26/95/2, f. 13.

HrJ 122.5 See Addenda, p. 628.

HrJ 123 -----

Copy, headed 'On a Gentlewoman paynted', in a miscellany; c. 1635.

Owned by Edwin Wolf 2nd, Philadelphia, MS, p. 88.

HrJ 124 -----

Copy, headed 'Another' and here beginning 'I'st for a fauo[r] or for some dislike', in a fragment of a verse miscellany bound with a MS translation of the *Song of Solomon* transcribed in 1622 by one Robert Eliot; c. 1630s.

Worcester College, Oxford, MSS. 4. 29, f. [14].

HrJ 125 *Of a Lady that left open her Cabbinett* ('A vertuose Lady sitting in a muse').

Copy in a verse miscellany partly compiled by Elias Ashmole (1617-92); c. 1630s-40s.

First pub. in 'Epigrammes' appended to J[ohn] C[lapham], *Alcilia, Philoparthens Louing Folly* (London, 1613); McClure No. 404, p. 312.

Bodleian, MS Ashmole 47, f. 53v.

HrJ 126 -----

Copy, headed 'A Lady musinge', with two additional lines, in a verse miscellany compiled by an Oxford man, possibly a member of Wadham College, and later used by William Fulman (1632-88); c. late 1630s.

Bodleian, MS CCC. 328, f. 44.

HrJ 127 -----

Copy, untitled and here beginning 'A Gentle Lady sitting in a muse', transcribed by Peter Le Neve (1661-1729) 'from a MS. written 1612', in a composite volume of verse collected by

Of a Lady that left open her Cabbinett

Le Neve; late 17th century.

Bodleian, MS Eng. poet. d. 152, f. 96.

HrJ 128 -----

Copy, with four additional lines, in a verse miscellany compiled by an Oxford man and once owned by one Henry Lawson; c. 1630s.

Bodleian, MS Eng. poet. e. 14, f. 81v.

HrJ 129 -----

Copy, headed 'S[r]. John Keys to his Lady' and here beginning 'A gallant lady sitting in a muse', in a verse miscellany owned in 1619 and possibly compiled by Simon Sloper (b. 1596/7) of Magdalen Hall, Oxford; c. 1620s.

Bodleian, MS Eng. poet. f. 10, fol. 89.

HrJ 130 -----

Copy in a miscellany compiled by Edward Natley, fellow of Queens' College, Cambridge; c. 1635-44.

Bodleian, MS Eng. poet. f. 25, fol. 15v.

HrJ 131 -----

Copy, headed 'On a Lady which sate museing', in a verse miscellany compiled by Robert Codrington (1602-65); c. 1638.

Bodleian, MS Eng. poet. f. 27, p. 50.

HrJ 132 -----

Copy in a verse miscellany probably compiled by a member of New College, Oxford; c. 1620s-30s.

Bodleian, MS Malone 19, p. 75.

HrJ 133 -----

Copy, untitled, in a miscellany compiled by William Eliot (a nephew of Sir Simonds D'Ewes), bound in a composite volume; c. 1640-55.

Bodleian, MS Rawl. poet. 116, f. 53.

HrJ 134 -----

Copy, untitled, in a verse miscellany apparently compiled by an Oxford man and once owned by one William Bloys; c. 1630s-40s.

Bodleian, MS Rawl. poet. 142, f. 40.

HrJ 135 -----

Copy, here beginning 'A beauteous lady sitting in a muse', in a composite volume of verse and prose; early 17th century.

Bodleian, MS Rawl. poet. 172, f. 2.

HrJ 136 -----

Copy, headed 'Upon a vertuous Ladye falling asleepe', in a verse miscellany compiled by the Yorkshire antiquary John Hopkinson (1610-80); mid-17th century.

Bradford Central Library, Hopkinson MSS, Vol. 34, p. 9.

HrJ 137 -----

Copy, headed 'S[r] John Harrington on his wife', in a verse miscellany probably compiled by a Cambridge man; c. 1630s.

British Library, Add. MS 15227, f. 6.

HrJ 138 -----

Copy, headed 'A Ladyes answer to her husband', in a verse miscellany; c. 1630s.

British Library, Add. MS 22118, f. 34v.

HrJ 139 -----

Copy, headed 'Upon a Lady', in a verse miscellany once owned by one W. Allen; c. early 1630s.

British Library, Egerton MS 923, f. 52.

HrJ 140 -----

Copy, headed 'On a lady and her Knight', in a verse miscellany once owned by Francis Norreys (? Sir Francis Norris (1609-69)) and Henry Balle; mid-17th century.

British Library, Egerton MS 2421, f. 15.

HrJ 141 -----

Copy, headed 'Epigramata', in a portion of a verse miscellany compiled for writing practice by Feargod Barbon of Daventry, Northamptonshire (? a relation of the Anabaptist politician Praisegod Barbon (1596?-1679)), bound in a composite volume of verse; early-mid-17th century.

British Library, Harley MS 7332, f. 46.

HrJ 142 -----

Copy, headed 'On a Lady', in a verse miscellany once owned by the physician Nathaniel Highmore (1613-85); c. 1630s.

British Library, Sloane MS 542, f. 12.

Of a Lady that left open her Cabbinett

HrJ 143 -----

Copy, untitled, in a verse miscellany bound with a collection of printed amatory poems and pamphlets; early 17th century.

Printed from this MS in *Love-Poems and Humourous Ones*, ed. Frederick J. Furnivall, Ballad Society (Hertford, 1874; reprinted New York, 1977), p. 21.

British Library, Department of Printed Books, C. 39. a. 37, f. 13.

HrJ 144 -----

Copy, untitled, in a verse miscellany; c. 1630s-40s.

Edinburgh University Library, MS La. III. 436, p. 58.

HrJ 145 -----

Copy, headed 'On a Museing lady', in a miscellany compiled by one Richard Archard; c. 1650-7.

Folger, MS V. a. 124, f. 5.

HrJ 146 -----

Copy, untitled and here beginning 'A gallant lady sitting in a muse', in a verse miscellany probably compiled by a member of an Inn of Court; mid-17th century.

Folger, MS V. a. 262, p. 80.

HrJ 147 -----

Copy, headed 'On ye lady J: S. musinge', in a verse miscellany compiled by William Jordan, schoolmaster of Denbigh or Caernarvon; c. 1674-84.

Folger, MS V. a. 276, Part II, f. 50v.

HrJ 148 -----

Copy, headed 'On a musing Lady', in a verse miscellany; c. 1640.

Folger, MS V. a. 319, f. 9v.

HrJ 149 -----

Copy, with four additional lines and the marginal note 'A couplet or two fastened to S^r Io: Harrington his epigrā, to doe his Townes knight yeomans seruice?', in a miscellany later owned by one Joseph Hall; c. 1630s-50.

Folger, MS V. a. 339, f. 275.

HrJ 150 -----

Copy, headed 'Of a Lady musing', with four additional lines, in a miscellany; c. 1630.

Folger, MS V. a. 345, pp. 29-30.

HrJ 151 -----

Copy, untitled, in a verse miscellany compiled by one or two Oxford men, possibly connected with New College and afterwards with the Inns of Court; 1630s.

Harvard, MS Eng 686, f. 34v.

HrJ 152 -----

Copy in the hand of William Parkhurst (fl. 1604-67), untitled, in a composite volume of MSS collected by Parkhurst; among the papers of the Finch family of Burley-on-the-Hill, Rutland; 1600s-41.

Leicestershire Record Office, DG. 7/Lit. 2, f. 351v.

HrJ 153 -----

Copy, headed 'On a lady', among poems on a single folio leaf in a collection of unbound literary papers assembled by Adam Ottley (1685-1752), Registrar of the diocese of St David's; c. 1630s.

National Library of Wales, Ottley (unnumbered bundle of literary papers).

HrJ 154 -----

Copy, headed 'Upon a Vertuous Lady', in a verse miscellany; c. 1643-50s.

University of Newcastle upon Tyne, MS Bell/White 25, f. 45r-v.

HrJ 155 -----

Copy, headed 'Vpon a Ladie', with four additional lines, in a miscellany; c. 1660.

Rosenbach Foundation, MS 239/18, p. 45.

HrJ 156 -----

Copy, untitled, in a verse miscellany; c. 1634.

Rosenbach Foundation, MS 239/27, p. 159.

HrJ 157 -----

Copy, headed 'A Knight to his Lady beeing in a

muse', in a miscellany compiled by or for Sir Thomas Finch, Viscount Maidstone and Earl of Winchelsea; c. 1634.

Rosenbach Foundation, MS 243/4, p. 17.

HrJ 158 -----

Copy, headed 'A Lady', in a verse miscellany compiled by one Robert Bishop; c. 1630.

Rosenbach Foundation, MS 1083/16, p. 19.

HrJ 159 -----

Copy, untitled, in a verse miscellany; c. 1620.

Victoria and Albert Museum, Dyce Collection, Cat. No. 44 (Pressmark 25. F. 39), f. 82.

HrJ 159.5 See Addenda, p. 628.

HrJ 160 -----

Copy, headed 'Vir ad Dominam', in a miscellany; mid-17th century.

Yale, Osborn Collection, b 205, f. 46v.

HrJ 161 *Of a Lady that sought remedy at the Bathe* ('A Lady that none name, nor blame none hath').

Copy in a miscellany; c. 1630.

First pub. in *1618*, Book III, No. 8; McClure No. 206, pp. 232-3.

Folger, MS V. a. 345, p. 51.

HrJ 162 *Of a Preacher that sings Placebo* ('A smooth-tong'd Preacher that did much affect').

Copy, headed 'On a Preacher', in a miscellany compiled by one Thomas Watson; c. 1680s.

First pub. in *1618*, Book II, No. 56; McClure No. 152, p. 207.

Merton College, Oxford, MS D. 1. 2, f. 13.

HrJ 163 *Of a Precise Cobler, and an ignorant Curat* ('A Cobler, and a Curat, once disputed').

Copy, headed 'On a curate and a Cobbler', in a verse miscellany probably compiled by a member of New College, Oxford; c. 1620s-30s.

First pub. in *1618*, Book I, No. 66; McClure No. 67, p. 173.

Bodleian, MS Malone 19, p. 55.

HrJ 164 -----

Copy, headed 'On a Curate and a Cobler', in a verse miscellany probably compiled by a Cambridge man; c. 1630s.

British Library, Add. MS 15227, f. 6v.

HrJ 164.5 See Addenda, p. 628.

HrJ 165 -----

Copy in a verse miscellany compiled by John Cruso (1618-81) of Gonville and Caius College, Cambridge; c. 1630s.

St John's College, Cambridge, MS U. 26 (James 548), p. 44.

HrJ 166 *Of a Precise Lawyer* ('A Lawyer call'd vnto the Barre but lately').

Copy in a verse miscellany compiled by the Yorkshire antiquary John Hopkinson (1610-80); mid-17th century.

First pub. in *1618*, Book I, No. 82; McClure No. 83, pp. 179-80.

Bradford Central Library, Hopkinson MSS, Vol. 34, p. 129.

HrJ 167 *Of a Precise Tayler* ('A Taylor, thought a man of vpright dealling').

Copy in a verse miscellany compiled by Nicholas Burghe (d. 1670); c. 1638.

First pub. in *1618*, Book I, No. 20; McClure No. 21, pp. 156-7.

Bodleian, MS Ashmole 38, p. 85.

HrJ 168 -----

Copy in a composite volume of verse and prose owned c. 1669 by one John Cooke of Bury St Edmunds, Suffolk; c. 1620s-30s.

Bodleian, MS Rawl. poet. 26, f. 3v.

HrJ 169 -----

Copy, headed 'A Translation', in a verse miscellany; c. 1620-33.

Bodleian, MS Rawl. poet. 31, ff. 4-5.

HrJ 170 -----

Copy in a composite volume of verse and prose; early 17th century.

Bodleian, MS Rawl. poet. 172, f. 12.

HrJ 171 -----

Copy in a miscellany compiled by an Oxford man; early 17th century.

Bodleian, MS Rawl. poet. 212, f. 101.

HrJ 172 -----

Copy, headed 'Upon a precise Taylor', in a verse miscellany compiled by the Yorkshire

Of a Precise Tayler

antiquary John Hopkinson (1610-80); mid-17th century.

Bradford Central Library, Hopkinson MSS, Vol. 34, p. 92.

HrJ 173 -----

Copy, headed 'The Taylors reformation', in a verse miscellany probably compiled by a Cambridge man; c. 1630s.

British Library, Add. MS 15227, f. 14.

HrJ 174 -----

Copy, headed 'A reformed Taylor', in a verse miscellany probably compiled by a Cambridge man; mid-17th century.

British Library, Add. MS 22603, ff. 52v-3.

HrJ 175 -----

Copy in a verse miscellany; c. 1620-33.

British Library, Harley MS 4064, f. 233v.

HrJ 176 -----

Copy, untitled, in a MS volume of poems chiefly by John Donne; c. 1620s.

British Library, Lansdowne MS 740, f. 128v.

HrJ 177 -----

Copy, headed 'A Reformed Taylour', in a verse miscellany owned by Edward Denny, Charles Cokes, Edward Randolpe, and Thomas Cassy; c. 1630s.

Huntington, HM 198, Part I, pp. 27-8.

HrJ 178 -----

Copy, headed 'A storie of a Taylor by S^r. John Harrington', in a verse miscellany possibly once owned by Sir John Reresby (d. 1646); among the papers of the Savile family, formerly of Methley Hall, near Pontefract; c. 1630s.

Leeds Archives Department, MX 237, f. 18v.

HrJ 179 -----

Copy in the hand of William Parkhurst (fl. 1604-67), untitled, in a composite volume of MSS collected by Parkhurst; among the papers of the Finch family of Burley-on-the-Hill, Rutland; 1600s-41.

Leicestershire Record Office, DG. 7/Lit. 2, f. 322.

HrJ 180 -----

Copy in a verse miscellany; c. 1634.

Rosenbach Foundation, MS 239/27, pp. 170-1.

HrJ 181 -----

Copy in a verse miscellany compiled by one Robert Bishop; c. 1630.

Rosenbach Foundation, MS 1083/16, pp. 186-7.

HrJ 182 -----

Copy, headed 'Vppon a Puritan Taylor', in a verse miscellany compiled by John Cruso (1618-81) of Gonville and Caius College, Cambridge; c. 1630s.

St John's College, Cambridge, MS U. 26 (James 548), pp. 22-3.

HrJ 183 -----

Copy, untitled, in a MS volume of poems chiefly by John Donne, among the family papers of the Earl of Dalhousie; c. 1620-5.

Scottish Record Office, GD45/26/95/1, f. 57.

HrJ 183.5 See Addenda, p. 628.

HrJ 184 -----

Copy in a verse miscellany; c. 1640.

Yale, Osborn Collection, b 62, pp. 94-5.

HrJ 185 -----

Copy in a verse miscellany compiled by Tobias Alston (1620-c.1639) of Sayham Hall, near Sudbury, Suffolk; c. 1639.

Yale, Osborn Collection, b 197, p. 99.

HrJ 186 -----

Copy in a miscellany; mid-17th century.

Yale, Osborn Collection, b 205, ff. 47v-8.

HrJ 187 *Of a pregnant pure sister* ('I learned a tale more fitt to be forgotten').

Copy of a ten-line version, headed 'On a maid gott wth child' and here beginning 'A godlie maid wth one of her societie', in a verse miscellany compiled by the Yorkshire antiquary John Hopkinson (1610-80); c. 1647.

First pub. (13-line version) in *The Epigrams of Sir John Harington*, ed. N.E. McClure (Philadelphia, 1926), but see HrJ 197; McClure (1930), No. 413, p. 315.

Bodleian, MS Don. d. 58, f. 35.

Of a pregnant pure sister

HrJ 188 -----

Copy of a ten-line version, headed 'On a precise mayd wth childe' and here beginning 'A godly mayd by one of her societie', in a verse miscellany compiled by an Oxford man and once owned by one Henry Lawson; c. 1630s.

Bodleian, MS Eng. poet. e. 14, f. 89v.

HrJ 189 -----

Copy of a ten-line version, headed 'On a holy sister got with childe by a holy brother' and here beginning 'A sister once by one of her society', in a verse miscellany compiled by Robert Codrington (1602-65); c. 1638.

Bodleian, MS Eng. poet. f. 27, p. 167.

HrJ 190 -----

Copy of a ten-line version, untitled and here beginning 'A Puritan, with one of her society', in a composite volume of verse and prose owned c. 1669 by one John Cooke of Bury St Edmunds, Suffolk; c. 1620s-30s.

Bodleian, MS Rawl. poet. 26, f. 8v.

HrJ 191 -----

Copy of a ten-line version, headed 'The Godlye mayde' and here beginning 'A godlye Mayde wth one of her societye', in a verse miscellany; c. 1620-33.

Bodleian, MS Rawl. poet. 31, f. 3v.

HrJ 192 -----

Copy of a variant 16-line version, headed 'A saintlike sister' and here beginning 'A saintlike sister late turnd votarie', in a composite volume of verse and prose; early 17th century.

Bodleian, MS Rawl. poet. 172, f. 12.

HrJ 193 -----

Copy of a ten-line version, headed 'Parturiens Puritana' and here beginning 'A godly sister, by one of her Society', in a verse miscellany probably compiled by a Cambridge man; c. 1630s.

Edited partly from this MS in John Wardroper, *Love and Drollery* (London, 1969), p. 174.

British Library, Add. MS 15227, f. 14v.

HrJ 194 -----

Copy of a ten-line version, headed 'On a Puritan maide' and here beginning 'A Puritan maide by one of hir societie', in a miscellany compiled by Anthony Scattergood (1611-87) of Trinity College, Cambridge; c. 1632-40.

British Library, Add. MS 44963, f. 36v.

HrJ 195 -----

Copy of a variant 14-line version, headed 'On a Puritaine' and here beginning 'A s^t^ like sister late turnd votary', in a verse miscellany once owned by one W. Allen; c. 1630s.

British Library, Egerton MS 923, p. 71.

HrJ 196 -----

Copy of a ten-line version, untitled and here beginning 'A godlye maide wth one of her societye', in a verse miscellany; c. 1630.

British Library, Egerton MS 2230, f. 13v.

HrJ 197 -----

Copy of a ten-line version, untitled and here beginning 'A puritane, with one of hir societie', in a verse miscellany bound with a collection of printed amatory poems and pamphlets; early 17th century.

Printed from this MS in *Love-Poems and Humourous Ones*, ed. Frederick J. Furnivall, Ballad Society (Hertford, 1874; reprinted New York, 1977), p. 22.

British Library, Department of Printed Books, C. 39. a. 37, f. 13v.

HrJ 198 -----

Copy of a ten-line version, headed 'Upon A Holy Sister' and here beginning 'A Godly sister by one of her society', in a verse miscellany; mid-17th century.

Folger, MS V. a. 262, p. 147.

HrJ 199 -----

Copy of a ten-line version, untitled and here beginning 'A [ ] sister wth one of her society', partly deleted, in a miscellany; c. 1630.

Folger, MS V. a. 345, p. 47.

HrJ 200 -----

Copy of a ten-line version, headed 'On a maiden conceived by a scholler' and here beginning 'A godly maiden wth one of her societie', in a verse miscellany compiled by one or two Oxford men, possibly connected with New College and afterwards with the Inns of Court; 1630s.

Harvard, MS Eng 686, f. 54v.

Of a pregnant pure sister

HrJ 201 -----

Copy of a ten-line version, headed 'On a Mayd got wth child' and here beginning 'A godly Mayd with one of her society', in a miscellany compiled by an Oxford man, possibly a member of Brasenose College; c. late 1630s.

Huntington, HM 116, p. 49.

HrJ 202 -----

Copy of a ten-line version, headed 'Upon a Puritan mayde' and here beginning 'A puritan mayde by one of her society', in a verse miscellany; c. 1643-50s.

University of Newcastle upon Tyne, MS Bell/White 25, ff. 40v-1.

HrJ 203 -----

Copy of a ten-line version headed 'A Puritan maide' and here beginning 'A Puritan maide by one of her society', in a miscellany; c. 1660.

Rosenbach Foundation, MS 239/18, p. 46.

HrJ 204 -----

Copy of a ten-line version, untitled and here beginning 'A godly maide by one of her society', in a verse miscellany; c. 1638-45.

Rosenbach Foundation, MS 239/22, f. 8.

HrJ 205 -----

Copy of a ten-line version, headed 'On a Puritan' and here beginning 'A holy made, by one of her society', in a verse miscellany; c. 1634.

Rosenbach Foundation, MS 239/27, p. 206.

HrJ 206 -----

Copy of a ten-line version, untitled and here beginning 'A holy maide by one of her society', in a verse miscellany partly compiled by one Robert Berkeley; c. 1640.

Rosenbach Foundation, MS 240/2, p. 147.

HrJ 207 -----

Copy of a ten-line version, headed 'On A Purytan Maide' and here beginning 'A vertuous maide (with one of her society)', in a miscellany compiled by or for Sir Thomas Finch, Viscount Maidstone and Earl of Winchelsea; c. 1634.

Rosenbach Foundation, MS 243/4, p. 15.

HrJ 208 -----

Copy of a ten-line version, untitled and here beginning 'A Godly maide with one of her society', in a verse miscellany compiled by one Robert Bishop; c. 1630.

Rosenbach Foundation, MS 1083/16, p. 29.

HrJ 208.5 See Addenda, p. 628.

HrJ 209 -----

Copy of a ten-line version, headed 'On a puritan maide' and here beginning 'A holy maid with one of her society', in a verse miscellany; c. 1640.

Yale, Osborn Collection, b 62, p. 41.

HrJ 209.5, 209.8 See Addenda, p. 629.

HrJ 210 *Of a sawcy Cator* ('A Cator had of late some wild-fowle bought').

Copy, headed 'Of a Cater', in a verse miscellany probably compiled by a member of an Inn of Court; mid-17th century.

First pub. in *1615*; *1618*, Book IV, No. 22; McClure No. 276, p. 261.

Folger, MS V. a. 262, p. 103.

HrJ 211 -----

Copy in a miscellany; c. 1630.

Folger, MS V. a. 345, p. 171.

HrJ 212 -----

Copy in a verse miscellany compiled by one Robert Bishop; c. 1630.

Rosenbach Foundation, MS 1083/16, p. 176.

HrJ 213 *Of a word in welch mistaken in English* ('An English lad long Woode a lasse of wales').

Copy, headed 'Nil refert loqui dũ vbi liceat' and here ascribed to 'JD', in a MS volume of poems chiefly by John Donne compiled by Henry Champernowne (1600-56) of Dartington, Devon; c. 1623.

Believed to be unpublished; this epigram occurs in Harington's collections in the British Library, Add. MS 12049, pp. 157-8 (see HrJ 20), and in the Folger, MS V. a. 249, pp. 210-11 (see HrJ 21), but omitted in McClure.

Bodleian, MS Eng. poet. f. 9, p. 18.

HrJ 214 -----

Copy, headed 'An Epigram', in a verse miscellany; c. 1630s.

Bodleian, MS Rawl. poet. 160, f. 158v.

HrJ 215 -----

Copy, headed 'Epigr', in a portion of a verse

miscellany compiled for writing practice by Feargod Barbon of Daventry, Northamptonshire (? a relation of the Anabaptist politician Praisegod Barbon (1596?-1679)), bound in a composite volume of verse; early-mid-17th century.

British Library, Harley MS 7332, f. 45.

HrJ 216 -----

Copy, headed 'of mistaking of a word', deleted, in a verse miscellany compiled by a Cambridge man; c. 1630.

A 19th-century transcript of this MS is in the Bodleian, MS Firth d. 7, f. 162.

Cambridge University Library, MS Add. 4138, f. 49r-v.

HrJ 217 -----

Copy, untitled, in a verse miscellany owned by Edward Denny, Charles Cokes, Edward Randolpe, and Thomas Cassy; c. 1630s.

Huntington, HM 198, Part I, p. 165.

HrJ 218 -----

Copy, headed 'Nil refert loqui dum vbi liceat', in a MS volume of poems chiefly by John Donne; c. 1622-33.

Yale, Osborn Collection, b 148, p. 3.

HrJ 219 -----

Copy, headed 'An Epigram', in a verse miscellany compiled by Tobias Alston (1620-c.1639) of Sayham Hall, near Sudbury, Suffolk; c. 1639.

Yale, Osborn Collection, b 197, p. 111.

HrJ 220 *Of bagge and baggage* ('A man appointed, vpon losse of life').

Copy in a verse miscellany compiled by one Robert Bishop; c. 1630.

First pub. in *1615*; *1618*, Book IV, No. 42; McClure No. 296, p. 267.

Rosenbach Foundation, MS 1083/16, p. 33.

HrJ 221 *Of Blessing without a crosse* ('A Priest that earst was riding on the way').

Copy, headed 'Of Blessing w^th^out the Crosse', in a verse miscellany compiled by the Yorkshire antiquary John Hopkinson (1610-80); mid-17th century.

First pub. in *1618*, Book I, No. 17; McClure No. 18, p. 155.

Bradford Central Library, Hopkinson MSS, Vol. 34, p. 81.

HrJ 222 -----

Copy, headed 'Sacerdotis benedictis' and here beginning 'A certaine preist once riding on the way', in a verse miscellany probably compiled by a Cambridge man; c. 1630s.

British Library, Add. MS 15227, f. 6.

HrJ 223 -----

Copy, headed 'On A Vicar' and here beginning 'An honest Viccar riding by the way', in a verse miscellany compiled by an Oxford man, possibly a member of Christ Church; c. late 1630s.

Folger, MS V. a. 97, p. 54.

HrJ 224 -----

Copy, here beginning 'An honest Vicar ridinge by the way', in a verse miscellany compiled by an Oxford man and once owned by one Stephen Welden; mid-17th century.

Folger, MS V. a. 162, f. 34.

HrJ 225 -----

Copy, headed 'A Vicar and a blind man' and here beginning 'An honest vicar riding on the way', in a verse miscellany possibly once owned by Sir John Reresby (d. 1646); among the papers of the Savile family, formerly of Methley Hall, near pontefract; c. 1630s.

Leeds Archives Department, MX 237, f. 73v.

HrJ 226 -----

Copy, headed 'Of Blessinge' and here beginning 'A Preist in hast was riding on ye waye', in a verse miscellany once owned by Elizabeth Herrick (1684-1745) and William Herrick (1689-1773); c. 1630.

Leicestershire Record Office, DG. 9/2796, p. 34.

HrJ 227 -----

Copy, here beginning 'A certayne priest once riding on ye way', in a verse miscellany; c. 1620.

Victoria and Albert Museum, Dyce Collection, Cat. No. 44 (Pressmark 25. F. 39), f. 79v.

HrJ 228 -----

Copy, here beginning 'A certaine preist once riding on the way', in a verse miscellany; c. 1640.

Yale, Osborn Collection, b 62, p. 114.

HrJ 229 *Of certain puritan wenches* ('Six of the weakest sex and purest sect').

Copy, headed 'The conference of 6 Puritanicall wenches', in a verse miscellany; c. 1630s.

First pub. (anonymously) in *Rump: or An Exact Collection of the Choycest Poems and Songs* (London, 1662), II, 158-9; McClure No. 356, p. 292.

Bodleian, MS Douce f. 5, fol. 19v.

HrJ 230 -----

Copy, headed 'The conference of 6 Puritanicall wenches', in a composite volume of verse and prose owned c. 1669 by one John Cooke of Bury St Edmunds, Suffolk; c. 1620s-30s.

Bodleian, MS Rawl. poet. 26, f. 6.

HrJ 231 -----

Copy, headed 'Verses on Puritan women', in a miscellany once owned by Margaret Bellasys, probably the daughter of Thomas, first Lord Fauconberg (1577-1653); c. 1630.

British Library, Add. MS 10309, f. 148.

HrJ 232 -----

Copy, headed 'verses on a proposal to substitute another name for preaching', in a volume of state papers compiled by Sir Peter Manwood (d. 1625) of Hackington, Kent; c. 1618-25.

British Library, Add. MS 38139, f. 58.

HrJ 233 -----

Copy, headed 'Upon six holy Sisters that mett at a Conuenticle to alter the Popish word of Preaching', in a verse miscellany; late 17th century.

British Library, Harley MS 6913, f. 55r-v.

HrJ 234 -----

Copy, headed 'The conference of 6 puritanicall wenches', partly deleted, in a miscellany; c. 1630.

Folger, MS V. a. 345, p. 43.

HrJ 235 -----

Copy, headed 'The conference of 6 Puritan wenches', in a verse miscellany; c. 1634.

Rosenbach Foundation, MS 239/27, p. 165.

HrJ 236 -----

Copy, untitled and here beginning 'Sixe of the weakest sort & purest sect', in a verse miscellany probably compiled by a member of an Inn of Court; c. 1598-1600s.

Rosenbach Foundation, MS 1083/15, f. 52.

HrJ 237 -----

Copy, headed 'Six Puritane wenches', in a verse miscellany compiled by one Robert Bishop; c. 1630.

Rosenbach Foundation, MS 1083/16, p. 17.

HrJ 237.5 See Addenda, p. 629.

HrJ 238 -----

Copy, untitled, in a verse miscellany compiled by John Cruso (1618-81) of Gonville and Caius College, Cambridge; c. 1630s.

St John's College, Cambridge, MS U. 26 (James 548), p. 91.

HrJ 239 -----

Copy, untitled, in a verse miscellany appended to a MS volume of poems by John Donne; c. 1630s.

Trinity College, Dublin, MS 877, ff. 203v-4.

HrJ 240 *Of cursing Cuckolds* ('A Lord that talked late in way of scorne').

Copy, untitled and here beginning 'A great man speaking one day in scorne', in a miscellany; early 17th century.

First pub. in *1615*; *1618*, Book IV, No. 26; McClure No. 280, p. 263.

University of Leeds, Brotherton Collection, MS Lt. 25, f. 7v.

HrJ 241 *Of Fortune* ('Fortune, men say, doth giue too much to many').

Copy of an early version, untitled and here beginning '[blynde *added in another hand*] ffortune gevs tomoche to manye', in the Arundel Harington MS (see HrJ 337); mid-late 16th century.

First pub. in *1615*; *1618*, Book IV, No. 56; McClure No. 310, p. 272. Printed from this MS in Hughey, I, No. 56, p. 103.

Owned by the Duke of Norfolk, Arundel Castle, MSS (Special Press), 'Harrington MS. Temp. Eliz.', f. 29.

Of Fortune

HrJ 242 -----

Copy, untitled, in a miscellany probably compiled by a Cambridge man; c. 1627.

British Library, Sloane MS 1489, f. 10.

HrJ 243 *Of Galla's goodly Periwigge* ('You see the goodly hayre that Galla weares').

Copy of a four-line version, untitled and here beginning 'The goodly heare Gella doth weare', in a verse miscellany probably compiled by a member of an Inn of Court; c. 1598-1600s.

First pub. in *Orlando Furioso* (London, 1591), in notes at the end of Book XXXII; *1618*, Book II, No. 66; McClure No. 162, p. 211.

Rosenbach Foundation, MS 1083/15, f. 29v.

HrJ 244 *Of Garlick to my Lady Rogers* ('If Leekes you like, and doe the smell disleeke').

Copy, untitled, in a miscellany later owned by one Joseph Hall; c. 1630s-50.

First pub. in *The Metamorphosis of Ajax* (London, 1596); *1618*, Book I, No. 47; McClure No. 48, p. 166. See also HrJ 317-24.

Folger, MS V. a. 339, f. 274.

HrJ 245 *Of inclosing a Common* ('A Lord, that purpos'd for his more auaile').

Copy, headed 'Vpon a Lord who would haue inclosed a Common', in a verse miscellany; c. 1634.

First pub. in *1615*; *1618*, Book IV, No. 68; McClure No. 322, p. 275.

Rosenbach Foundation, MS 239/27, p. 51.

HrJ 246 -----

Copy, headed 'On A Lord who would haue inclosed a Commons', in a verse miscellany compiled by one Robert Bishop; c. 1630.

Rosenbach Foundation, MS 1083/16, p. 177.

HrJ 247 *Of Lynus borrowing* ('Lynus came late to me, sixe crownes to borrow').

Copy in a miscellany; imperfect, lacking the beginning; early 17th century.

First pub. in *1615*; *1618*, Book IV, No. 16; McClure No. 270, p. 259.

University of Leeds, Brotherton Collection, MS Lt. 25, f. 10.

HrJ 248 *Of one that vow'd to dis-inherit his sonne, and giue his goods to the poore* ('A citizen that dwelt neere Temple-barre').

Copy in a verse miscellany once owned by Elizabeth Herrick (1684-1745) and William Herrick (1689-1773); c. 1630.

First pub. in *1618*, Book I, No. 65; McClure No. 66, pp. 172-3.

Leicestershire Record Office, DG. 9/2796, p. 35.

HrJ 249 *Of Plaine dealing* ('My writings oft displease you: what's the matter?').

Copy, headed 'Of plaine dealings' and here beginning 'My writings still displease thee, what the matter?', in a verse miscellany once owned by Elizabeth Herrick (1684-1745) and William Herrick (1689-1773); c. 1630.

First pub. in *1618*, Book I, No. 59; McClure No. 60, p. 170. This epigram is also quoted in the *Tract on the Succession to the Crown* (see HrJ 333-5).

Leicestershire Record Office, DG. 9/2796, p. 34.

HrJ 250 *Of sixe sorts of Fasters* ('Sixe sorts of folkes I find vse fasting dayes').

Copy in a verse miscellany compiled by one Robert Bishop; c. 1630.

First pub. in *1615*; *1618*, Book IV, No. 30; McClure No. 284, p. 264.

Rosenbach Foundation, MS 1083/16, pp. 178-9.

HrJ 251 *Of swearing first betweene the wife and the Husband* ('Cis, by that Candle, in my sleepe, I thought').

Copy in a verse miscellany compiled by the Yorkshire antiquary John Hopkinson (1610-80); mid-17th century.

First pub. in *1618*, Book II, No. 80; McClure No. 176, p. 218.

Bradford Central Library, Hopkinson MSS, Vol. 34, p. 76.

--- *Of taking a Hare* ('Vnto a Lawyer rich, a Client poore').

[McClure No. 331, p. 278].

See INTRODUCTION.

HrJ 252 *Of the Bishopricke of Landaffe* ('A learned Prelate late dispos'd to laffe').

Copy in a verse miscellany compiled by a Cambridge man; c. 1630.

Of the Bishopricke of Landaffe

First pub. in *1618*, Book II, No. 2; McClure No. 98, p. 187.

Cambridge University Library, MS Add. 4138, f. 49v.

HrJ 253 *Of the commodities that men haue by their Marriage* ('A fine yong Clerke, of kinne to Fryer Frappert').

Copy, headed 'Ludicrū of marriage' and here beginning 'A fine younge Preist of kin to ffryar ffrapp', in a miscellany compiled by Leweston Fitzjames of the Middle Temple; c. 1595.

First pub. in *1618*, Book II, No. 70; McClure No. 166, pp. 213-14.

Bodleian, MS Add. B. 97, f. 38v.

HrJ 254 -----

Copy, untitled and here beginning 'A ffine yong priest of kin to ffrier ffrapper', in a MS volume of poems chiefly by John Donne; c. 1620s.

British Library, Lansdowne MS 740, f. 128.

HrJ 255 -----

Copy, here beginning 'A fine yong Priest of kin to frier ffrapper', in a MS volume of poems chiefly by John Donne, among the family papers of the Earl of Dalhousie; c. 1620-5.

Scottish Record Office, GD45/26/95/1, f. 56v.

HrJ 256 *Of Treason* ('Treason doth neuer prosper, what's the reason?').

Copy in a verse miscellany once owned by Elizabeth Lane and John Finch; c. 1630s.

First pub. in *1615*; *1618*, Book IV, No. 5; McClure No. 259, p. 255. This epigram also quoted in a letter to Prince Henry, 1609 (McClure, p. 136).

Aberdeen University Library, MS 29, p. 57.

HrJ 257 -----

Copy in a composite volume of verse collected by Elias Ashmole (1617-92); mid-17th century.

First pub. in *1615*; *1618*, Book IV, No. 5; McClure No. 259, p. 255.

Bodleian, MS Ashmole 36/37, f. 145.

HrJ 258 -----

Second copy in a composite volume of verse collected by Elias Ashmole; mid-17th century.

Bodleian, MS Ashmole 36/37, f. 159v.

HrJ 259 -----

Copy in a verse miscellany; c. 1630s.

Bodleian, MS Douce f. 5, fol. 31.

HrJ 260 -----

Copy in a verse miscellany probably compiled by a member of New College, Oxford; c. 1620s-30s.

Bodleian, MS Malone 19, p. 40.

HrJ 261 -----

Copy of a version beginning 'Some say treason is unlawful; what's the reason?', in a MS songbook compiled by Thomas Hamond (d. 1662) of Suffolk; 1633.

Bodleian, MS Mus. f. 20-4: f. 24, fol. 108v.

HrJ 262 -----

Copy in a miscellany; late 17th century.

Bodleian, MS Top. Oxon. e. 280, p. 707.

HrJ 263 -----

Copy in a verse miscellany compiled by Daniel Leare (a distant cousin of William Strode) probably while at Christ Church, Oxford; c. 1631-3.

British Library, Add. MS 30982, f. 39.

HrJ 264 -----

Copy in a verse miscellany once owned by Francis Norreys (? Sir Francis Norris (1609-69)) and Henry Balle; mid-17th century.

British Library, Egerton MS 2421, f. 46v.

HrJ 265 -----

Copy in the hand of Sir William Dugdale (1605-86), untitled, in one of his volumes of antiquarian collections; mid-late 17th century.

British Library, Harley MS 6193, f. iii.

HrJ 266 -----

Copy in a verse miscellany probably compiled by one 'I.A.' of Christ Church, Oxford, and later owned by Robert Killigrew; c. early 1630s.

British Library, Sloane MS 1792, f. 22v.

Of Treason

HrJ 267 -----

Copy in a verse miscellany compiled by an Oxford man and once owned by one Stephen Welden; mid-17th century.

Folger, MS V. a. 162, f. 35v.

HrJ 268 -----

Copy in a verse miscellany compiled by one or two Oxford men, possibly connected with New College and afterwards with the Inns of Court; 1630s.

Harvard, MS Eng 686, f. 10.

HrJ 268.5 See Addenda, p. 629.

HrJ 269 -----

Copy in a verse miscellany compiled by one Robert Bishop; c. 1630.

Rosenbach Foundation, MS 1083/16, p. 146.

HrJ 270 -----

Copy, here beginning 'Treason nere prospers, true, but what's the reason', in a notebook probably compiled by Sir Richard Dyott (1590-1659), MP for Stafford and Lichfield; early-mid-17th century.

Staffordshire Record Office, D. 661/11/1/7, p. 20.

HrJ 271 -----

Copy in a verse miscellany; c. 1640.

Yale, Osborn Collection, b 62, p. 96.

HrJ 272 *Of two Welsh Gentlemen* ('I heard among some other pretty Tales').

Copy of a 12-line version, headed 'An Epigram of Sr John Harrington' and here beginning 'Two Squires of Wales came ridinge to a Towne', in a composite volume of verse and dramatic works compiled by members of the Salusbury family of Llewenni, Denbighshire; early 17th century.

First pub. (the short version) in *1615*; the longer version in *1618*, Book I, No. 62; McClure No. 63, p. 171. The MS text followed by a 20-line 'replie', beginning 'Once out of England ridde a companie' and subscribed 'Ignoto'.

National Library of Wales, NLW. MS 5390D, p. 163.

HrJ 273 *Of Women learned in the tongues* ('You wisht me to a wife, faire, rich and young').

Copy, headed 'A refusall of a Learned wife', in a verse miscellany partly compiled by Elias Ashmole (1617-92); c. 1630s-40s.

First pub. in *1615*; *1618*, Book IV, No. 7; McClure No. 261, pp. 255-6.

Bodleian, MS Ashmole 47, f. 48.

HrJ 274 -----

Copy, headed 'A learned wife', in a verse miscellany compiled by an Oxford man, possibly a member of Wadham College, and later used by William Fulman (1632-88); c. late 1630s.

Bodleian, MS CCC. 328, f. 47v.

HrJ 275 -----

Copy, untitled, in a verse miscellany compiled by an Oxford man and once owned by one Henry Lawson; c. 1630s.

Bodleian, MS Eng. poet. e. 14, f. 87.

HrJ 276 -----

Copy, headed 'A refusall of a learned wife' and here beginning 'You wish me to a wife that's faire & young', in a verse miscellany compiled by Robert Codrington (1602-65); c. 1638.

Bodleian, MS Eng. poet. f. 27, p. 133.

HrJ 277 -----

Copy, headed 'Upon Comending a wife to a gent.' and here beginning 'I wish you to a wife thats faire & younge', in a verse miscellany compiled by the Yorkshire antiquary John Hopkinson (1610-80); mid-17th century.

Bradford Central Library, Hopkinson MSS, Vol. 34, p. 83.

HrJ 278 -----

Copy, headed 'A refusall of a learned wife' and here beginning 'You wish me to a wife thats faire & younge', in a verse miscellany compiled by Daniel Leare (a distant cousin of William Strode) probably while at Christ Church, Oxford; c. 1631-3.

British Library, Add. MS 30982, f. 20v.

HrJ 279 -----

Copy, headed 'In amorosom. Epi. 7:' and here beginning 'A wife you wisht me (Sir) rich, faire and young', in a MS volume of epigrams once owned by one Richard Wharfe; c. 1631.

Printed from this MS in *The Complete Poems of Sir John Davies*, ed. Alexander B. Grosart (London, 1876), II, 48-9.

British Library, Harley MS 1836, f. 16v.

Of Women learned in the tongues

HrJ 280 -----

Copy in a verse miscellany compiled by an Oxford man and once owned by one Stephen Welden; mid-17th century.

Folger, MS V. a. 162, f. 32v.

HrJ 281 -----

Copy, headed 'Upon one that would not marry a learned wife' and here beginning 'You wisht mee to a wife that's fayre and young', in a verse miscellany probably compiled by a member of an Inn of Court; mid-17th century.

Folger, MS V. a. 262, p. 69.

HrJ 282 -----

Copy, untitled and here beginning 'Youle wishe mee to a wife that is rich faire & yonge', in a verse miscellany compiled by one or two Oxford men, possibly connected with New College and afterwards with the Inns of Court; 1630s.

Harvard, MS Eng 686, f. 85.

HrJ 283 -----

Copy, headed 'Of a learned wife', in a miscellany compiled by an Oxford man, possibly a member of Brasenose College; c. late 1630s.

Huntington, HM 116, p. 13.

HrJ 284 -----

Copy, headed 'A refusall of a learned wife' and here beginning 'You wish mee to a wife that's faire & young', in a verse miscellany compiled by one Edward Hyde, possibly the future first Earl of Clarendon (1609-74); c. 1630s.

Owned by Sir Geoffrey Keynes, *Bibliotheca Bibliographici* No. 1863, f. 8v.

HrJ 285 -----

Copy, untitled and here beginning 'S^r I do wish to you a wife, rich, faire & yong', in a miscellany; early 17th century.

University of Leeds, Brotherton Collection, MS Lt. 25, f. 7v.

HrJ 286 -----

Copy, headed 'On a Learned wife' and here beginning 'One proferd mee a wife, rich, faire & yonge', in a verse miscellany; c. 1634.

Rosenbach Foundation, MS 239/27, p. 187.

HrJ 287 -----

Copy, headed 'Learned Wife', in a verse miscellany compiled by one Robert Bishop; c. 1630.

Rosenbach Foundation, MS 1083/16, p. 20.

HrJ 288 -----

Copy, untitled, in a MS volume of poems chiefly by John Donne, among the family papers of the Earl of Dalhousie; c. 1620-5.

Scottish Record Office, GD45/26/95/1, f. 57.

HrJ 289 -----

Copy, untitled, in a miscellany compiled by a Cambridge man; c. 1630s.

Trinity College, Dublin, MS 690, f. 140v.

HrJ 289.5 See Addenda, p. 629.

HrJ 290 *Of writing with double pointing* ('Dames are indude with vertues excellent?').

Copy of a version beginning 'Wemen or noble vertuos excellent', in a verse miscellany compiled by Nicholas Burghe (d. 1670); c. 1638.

First pub. in *1618*, Book I, Nos. 33 and 35; McClure Nos. 34 and 36, pp. 161-2.

Bodleian, MS Ashmole 38, p. 84.

HrJ 291 -----

Copy in a verse miscellany; early 17th century.

Bodleian, MS Rawl. poet. 172, f. 9v.

HrJ 292 -----

Copy, headed 'Another' [i.e. verse employing a double sense], with a prose preamble concerning King Edward at Berkeley Castle, in a miscellany; c. 1630.

Folger, MS V. a. 345, pp. 13-14.

HrJ 293 -----

Copy, headed 'Of Women in a double sense', in a miscellany compiled by one Thomas Watson; c. 1680s.

Merton College, Oxford, MS D. 1. 2, f. 12v.

HrJ 294 -----

Copy of a four-line version beginning 'Weomen are godely wyse & excellent', in a verse miscellany probably compiled by a member of an Inn of Court; c. 1598-1600s.

Rosenbach Foundation, MS 1083/15, f. 39.

Of writing with double pointing

HrJ 295 -----

Copy, untitled, in a miscellany compiled by Sir Francis Fane (c.1612-80); c. 1672.

Shakespeare Birthplace Trust Record Office, ER 93/2, f. 192v.

*HrJ 296 *Ouids confession translated into English for Generall Norreys. 1593* ('To liue in Lust I make not my profession').

An early version, lines 1-6 in Harington's autograph, the rest in the hand of an amanuensis with autograph revisions, headed by Harington 'Ovids Confession. Non ego mendosos ausim defendere mores', in the Arundel Harington MS (see HrJ 337); late 16th century.

First pub. in *1618*, Book II, No. 85; McClure No. 181, pp. 219-21. Printed from this MS in Hughey, I, No. 222, pp. 253-4.

Owned by the Duke of Norfolk, Arundel Castle, MSS (Special Press), 'Harrington MS. Temp. Eliz.', f. 153r-v.

HrJ 297 *A pretty questions of Lazarus soule well answered* ('Once on occasion two good friends of mine').

Copy in a verse miscellany compiled by the Yorkshire antiquary John Hopkinson (1610-80); mid-17th century.

First pub. in *1615*; *1618*, Book II, No. 46; McClure No. 142, pp. 203-4.

Bradford Central Library, Hopkinson MSS, Vol. 34, p. 76.

HrJ 298 *A Tale of a Bayliffe distraining for rent. To my Ladie Rogers* ('I heard a pleasant tale at Cammington').

Copy in a verse miscellany compiled by the Yorkshire antiquary John Hopkinson (1610-80); mid-17th century.

First pub. in *1618*, Book I, No. 91; McClure No. 93, pp. 183-5.

Bradford Central Library, Hopkinson MSS, Vol. 34, pp. 77-8.

HrJ 299 -----

Copy of a shortened version beginning 'I hard the Tale once of an arrant Baily', in a verse miscellany compiled by one Robert Bishop; c. 1630.

Rosenbach Foundation, MS 1083/16, pp. 187-8.

--- *To her Daughter, vpon the same point, reading the same verse with another point* ('Dames are indude with vertues excellent?').

[McClure No. 36].

See HrJ 290-5.

HrJ 299.5 See Addenda, p. 629.

*HrJ 300 *To Master Cooke, the Queenes Atturney, that was incited to call Misacmos into the Starre-chamber, but refused it* ('Those that of dainty fare make deare prouision').

Autograph, untitled and here beginning 'They that of dainty food make deer provision'; imperfect, with part of lines 5-6, 7-8, and a title added in an 18th-century hand; written on an end-paper in a printed exemplum of *The Metamorphosis of Ajax* (London, 1596) (see HrJ 321); c. 1596.

First pub. in *1618*, Book I, No. 45; McClure No. 46, p. 165.

University of Texas at Austin, Wh/H224/596n.

HrJ 301 *To Mr. Bastard, the minister that writes the pleasant Epigrams* ('Had yow been known to me ear yow wear maryd').

Copy, headed 'In Thom: Bastard Theolog:' and here beginning 'Bastard had I knowne ere thou hadst bene married', in a verse miscellany compiled by one Robert Bishop; c. 1630.

First pub. in *The Epigrams of Sir John Harington*, ed. N.E. McClure (Philadelphia, 1926); McClure (1930), No. 358, p. 293.

Rosenbach Foundation, MS 1083/16, p. 245.

*HrJ 302 *To the ladies of the Queenes Priuy-Chamber, at the making of their perfumed priuy at Richmond, The Booke hanged in chaines saith thus:* ('Faire Dames, if any tooke in scorne, and spite').

Autograph, headed 'An Epigram of the booke hanging in cheyns. to ye Ladyes' and here beginning 'Fayr dames yf any tooke in skorn or spyte', written on the back of the title leaf of a printed exemplum of *The Metamorphosis of Ajax* (London, 1596) (see HrJ 321); c. 1596.

First pub. in *1618*, Book I, No. 44; McClure No. 45, p. 165.

University of Texas at Austin, Wh/H224/596n.

HrJ 303 *A Tragicall Epigram* ('When doome of Peeres & Iudges fore-appointed').

Copy, headed 'On ye beheading of Mary Q. of Scots' and here beginning 'When doome of death by Judgem^t^ foreappointed', in a verse miscellany compiled by an Oxford man and once owned by one Henry Lawson; c. 1630s.

A Tragicall Epigram

First pub. in *1615*; *1618*, Book IV, No. 82; McClure No. 336, pp. 280-1. This epigram is also quoted in the *Tract on the Succession to the Crown* (see HrJ 333-5).

Bodleian, MS Eng. poet. e. 14, f. 100.

HrJ 304 -----

Copy, untitled and here beginning 'When doome of death by Judgment foreappointed', in a miscellany compiled by an Oxford man; early 17th century.

Bodleian, MS Rawl. poet. 212, f. 87v.

HrJ 305 -----

Copy, here beginning 'When doome of Death by Judgem^{t} fore-appointed', in a miscellany once owned by Margaret Bellasys, probably the daughter of Thomas, first Lord Fauconberg (1577-1653); c. 1630.

British Library, Add. MS 10309, f. 148v.

HrJ 306 -----

Copy, untitled and here beginning 'When doome of death by iudgm^{ts} force appointed', in a miscellany compiled by someone connected with the Court; c. 1605.

Printed from this MS in J.O. Halliwell, *Poetical Miscellanies from a Manuscript Collection of the time of James I*, Percy Society (London, 1845), p. 38.

British Library, Add. MS 22601, ff. 60v-1.

HrJ 307 -----

Copy, here beginning 'When Doome of Death by Judgem^{t} foreappoynted' and subscribed 'Sr John Harrington vpon the Death of the Queen of Scotts', written at the end of a MS volume of tracts on Mary Queen of Scots; early 17th century.

Durham Cathedral, Hunter MS 51, [no page number].

HrJ 308 -----

Copy, headed 'Sr John Harringtons Epigram vppon the deathe of his magesties Mother Mary quen of Scotland', written at the end of a MS copy of *Leicester's Commonwealth*; c. 1620s.

Emmanuel College, Cambridge, MS I. 3. 28 (James 80), f. 56.

HrJ 309 -----

Copy, headed 'On the beheading of Mary Queene of Scotts' and here beginning 'When doome of death by judgment foreappointed', in a verse miscellany; c. 1630.

Folger, MS V. a. 103, Part I, f. 2v.

HrJ 310 -----

Copy, headed 'An elegie on ye queene of Scots' and here beginning 'When doome of death by iudgment foreappointed', in a verse miscellany; c. 1640.

Folger, MS V. a. 319, f. 21.

HrJ 311 -----

Copy, headed 'An elegye on ye Queene of Scotts' and here beginning 'When doome of death by iudgment foreappointed', in a verse miscellany; mid-17th century.

Folger, MS V. a. 322, p. 35.

HrJ 312 -----

Copy, headed 'On ye Q. of Scots Execution' and here beginning 'When doom of death by iudgment soe appointed', in a miscellany; c. 1630.

Folger, MS V. a. 345, p. 103.

HrJ 313 -----

Copy, headed 'On the beheading of Mary Queene of Scots' and here beginning 'When doome of death by judgment foreappointed', in a verse miscellany; c. 1630.

University of Nottingham, Portland MS Pw V 37, p. 2.

HrJ 313.5 See Addenda, p. 629.

HrJ 314 -----

Copy, untitled and here beginning 'when peeres and judges had by doome appointed', in a miscellany owned and partly compiled by Robert Herrick; c. 1612-23.

Facsimile and transcript of this MS in Norman K. Farmer, Jr., 'Poems from a Seventeenth-Century Manuscript with the Hand of Robert Herrick', *TQ*, 16, No. 4 (supplement) (Winter 1973), (pp. 20-1), and see also P.J. Croft, 'Errata in "Poems from a Seventeenth-Century Manuscript"', *TQ*, 19, No. 1 (Spring 1976), 160-73 (p. 162).

University of Texas at Austin, Ms File/(Herrick, R)/Works B, p. 63.

HrJ 314.5 See Addenda, p. 629.

PROSE

[and see also HrJ 338-44 and INTRODUCTION]

--- *A Briefe Apologie of Poetrie.*

See HrJ 16.

Breefe Notes and Remembraunces

--- *Breefe Notes and Remembraunces.*

See INTRODUCTION.

--- *Breife Notes upon the Sixth Booke of Virgils Aeneads.*

See HrJ 18-19.

--- *A Briefe View of the State of the Church of England.*

See HrJ 328-32.

HrJ 315 *A Discourse shewing that Elyas must personally come before the Day of Judgment.*

Copy in the hand of an amanuensis, in Volume VI of the Harington Papers; c. 1597?

First pub. (from this MS) in *Nugae Antiquae* (1775), pp. 39-56; *Nugae Antiquae* (1804), II, 281-304. This MS briefly described in Ruth Hughey, 'The Harington Manuscript at Arundel Castle and Related Documents', *The Library*, 4th Ser. 15 (1934-5), 388-444 (p. 402).

British Library, Add. MS 46371, ff. 31-45v.

--- *The Fall of Nero and beginning of Galba.*

See HrJ 325.

HrJ 316 *Letter to the Rev. Joseph Hall, on the Marriage of the Clergy.*

Unfinished draft in the hands of amanuenses of an epistle to Joseph Hall, probably intended for publication, in a Harington miscellany (see HrJ 338); [1611-12].

First pub. (from this MS) in M.H.M. MacKinnon, 'Sir John Harington and Bishop Hall', *PQ*, 37 (1958), 80-6. NB. this MS is not autograph.

British Library, Add. MS 27632, ff. 35-40.

*HrJ 317 *The Metamorphosis of Ajax.*

MS, largely autograph (but some pages in the hand of an amanuensis); the printer's copy for the first edition; imperfect; constituting Volume III of the Harington Papers; [1596].

First pub. London, 1596; ed. Elizabeth Story Donno (New York, 1962). This MS collated in Donno; described in Ruth Hughey, 'The Harington Manuscript at Arundel Castle and Related Documents', *The Library*, 4th Ser. 15 (1934-5), 388-444 (pp. 403-4).

British Library, Add. MS 46368.

*HrJ 318 -----

Exemplum of one of the editions of 1596 with Harington's autograph marginal annotations; once owned by John, Lord Lumley (1534?-1609).

This item (the 'Lumley-Folger' copy) collated in Donno; facsimile of title page in Donno, frontispiece.

Folger, STC 12779; STC 12772.3/copy 1; STC 12774.2/copy 1.

*HrJ 319 -----

Exemplum of one of the editions of 1596 with Harington's autograph marginal annotations; imperfect, the missing first part ('A New Discourse') supplied from an exemplum of the third edition.

This item (the 'Nares-Folger' copy) collated in Donno.

Folger, STC 12781.2; STC 12772.3/copy 2; STC 12774.2/ copy 2.

*HrJ 320 -----

Exemplum of one of the editions of 1596 with Harington's autograph marginal annotations; imperfect.

This item collated in Donno.

University of Sheffield, *827.32.

*HrJ 321 -----

Exemplum of one of the editions of 1596 with Harington's autograph marginal annotations; also containing various annotations in 18th- and 19th-century hands, including an 18th-century transcript on the flyleaf facing the title page of a dedication by Harington to his uncle, Thomas Markham, dated 3 August 1596 (see HrJ 322).

This item (the 'Markham-Wrenn' copy) collated in Donno. See also HrJ 300, 302.

University of Texas at Austin, Wh/H224/596n.

*HrJ 322 -----

Exemplum of one of the editions of 1596 with Harington's autograph marginal annotations, two autograph epigrams, and his autograph dedication to his uncle, Thomas Markham, dated 3 August 1596 (on the back of the title page); also containing five pages of notes in the hand of Isaac Reed (1742-1807).

This item described in William Beloe, *Anecdotes of Literature and Scarce Books*, 2 vols (London, 1814), II, 372-84; also recorded in *Proceedings and Papers of the Oxford Bibliographical Society*, 2 (1927-30), 212. See also HrJ 321, 323-4.

Privately owned in U.S.A.

The Metamorphosis of Ajax

HrJ 323 -----

Exemplum of one of the editions of 1596 containing transcripts in an early 19th-century hand of Harington's autograph dedication to Thomas Markham and marginal annotations in HrJ 322; the inside cover bearing a note in another hand stating (incorrectly) 'Note. written by Walter Scott April 18 1815', together with the bookplate of the Carleton House Library (i.e. of the Prince Regent, afterwards George IV).

Royal Library, Windsor, III. 34. E.

HrJ 324 -----

Exemplum of one of the editions of 1596 containing transcripts of Harington's autograph dedication to Thomas Markham and marginal annotations in HrJ 322; the MS notes here in the hands of Richard Farmer (1735-97), James Bindley (1737-1818), and Sir Francis Freeling (1764-1836).

This item sold at Sotheby's, 29 January 1873, Lot 748.

University of Texas at Austin, Wh/H224/596nb.

HrJ 325 [*Observations on the Emperors' Lives*].

Copy of a historical narrative, headed 'The Fall of Nero and beginning of Galba' and beginning 'Galerius, Trachalus, and Silius Italicus being Consuls: Caius Julius Vindex, Lieutenant of Gallia Lugdunensis, perceyuing that priuate conspiracies...', in the hand of an amanuensis, with a few marginal annotations in an italic hand; probably part of Harington's lost 'succinct collection of historie: his compendious & apt obseruatiōs in the Emperors liues'; among the papers of Sir Robert Cecil; c. 1580s-90s.

Unpublished. See INTRODUCTION.

Owned by the Marquess of Salisbury, Hatfield House, Cecil Papers 139/194-203v.

--- *The Prayse of Private Life.*

See SAMUEL DANIEL, DaS 45-6.

*HrJ 326 *A Short View of the State of Ireland.*

Autograph copy, with revisions, of Harington's letter to Charles Blount, Earl of Devonshire, and Sir Robert Cecil, Viscount Cranborne, applying for the Chancellorship of Ireland; 1605.

First pub. (from this MS) Oxford, 1879, ed. W.D. Macray. Facsimile of f. 13 (which includes the epigram 'Musa Jocosa, meos solari assueta dolores') in Kathleen M. Lea, 'Harington's *Folly*', *Elizabethan and Jacobean Studies Presented to F.P. Wilson* (Oxford, 1959), pp. 42-58 (facing p. 48). The original autograph letter which accompanied the copy of this memorial (now unlocated) sent by Harington to Sir Robert Cecil on 20 April 1605 is owned by the Marquess of Salisbury, Hatfield House, Cecil Papers 110/97, and is printed in McClure, p. 118.

Bodleian, MS Rawl. B. 162, ff. 1-13.

HrJ 327 -----

Copy in a composite volume of state tracts once owned by Sir Richard Grosvenor (1585-1645); c. 1634.

Formerly owned by the Duke of Westminster, Eaton Hall, Cheshire, this MS recorded in *HMC*, 3rd Report (1872), Appendix, p. 212. A microfilm is in the British Library (RP 170).

Harvard, MS Eng 1266 (20), v. 2, ff. 282-94v.

*HrJ 328 *A Supplie or Addicion to the Catalogue of Bishops, to ye Yeare 1608.*

Autograph fair copy, appended (ff. 314-407) to a printed exemplum of Bishop Francis Godwin, *A Catalogue of the Bishops of England* (London, 1601), presented to Prince Henry; the printed volume (ff. 1-279) containing Harington's extensive autograph annotations, with an index (ff. 230-301v) in the hand of an amanuensis, and 'A table Alphabeticall annexed to the Booke of the Catalogue of Bishops' (ff. 302-13) also in Harington's autograph; 18 February 1607/8.

First pub. as *A Briefe View of the State of the Church of England*, ed. John Chetwind (London, 1653). Printed from this MS in *Nugae Antiquae* (London, 1804), II, 1-278; discussed in R.H. Miller, 'Sir John Harington's *A Supplie or Addicion to the Catalogue of Bishops, to the Yeare 1608*: Composition and Text', *SB*, 30 (1977), 145-61. See also INTRODUCTION.

British Library, Royal MS 17 B. XXII.

*HrJ 329 -----

Copy of an early version in the hand of an amanuensis, with some italic headings in Harington's autograph; untitled; imperfect; constituting Volume V of the Harington Papers; [1607-8].

This MS discussed in Miller. NB. the MS is not entirely autograph.

British Library, Add. MS 46370.

HrJ 330 -----

Copy in two hands; ff. 169-248v in an early 17th-century hand; ff. 134-68v in a mid-17th-century hand, evidently replacing a lost portion of the original copy; bound in a composite volume of historical MSS.

A Supplie or Addicion to the Catalogue of Bishops

This MS discussed and some previously unpublished portions of the text printed from it in Miller.

British Library, Harley MS 1220, ff. 134-248v.

HrJ 331 -----

Copy, once owned by the publisher Moses Pitt (fl. 1654-96); mid-late 17th century.

This MS discussed in Miller.

British Library, Sloane MS 1675.

HrJ 332 -----

Copy of about four-fifths of the work; imperfect, breaking off in the section on Dr Edwin Sandys; in a composite volume of historical papers once owned by one John Saunders; early-mid-17th century.

Trinity College, Dublin, MS 806, ff. 142-75v.

HrJ 333 *A Tract on the Succession to the Crown.*

Fair copy in the hand of an amanuensis of Harington, given to Tobie (later Archbishop) Matthew (1546-1628), with Matthew's autograph annotations; untitled; [1602].

First pub. (from this MS) London, 1880, ed. Clements R. Markham, Roxburghe Club; reprinted New York, 1969.

York Minster, MS XVI. L. 6.

HrJ 334 -----

Extracts from the introduction, concerning 'the 3 sorts of religions in Engla[nd]e', in the hand of a member of, or someone associated with, the Harington family, inscribed 'Some notes for remembrance out of Sir Jo. Harringtons booke on the behalfe of the K. of Sc. succession', among the papers of Sir Robert Cecil; early 17th century.

This MS recorded in McClure, p. 29 (n).

Owned by the Marquess of Salisbury, Hatfield House, Cecil Papers 139/108-9v.

HrJ 335 -----

Copy of the last chapter, headed 'The eight chapiter; of quyeting the contrauersies of Religion', with 'Out of S[r] John Haringtons boke' added above in a different ink; in a MS volume of theological tracts; 35 pages; dated 10 December 1602; early 17th century.

York Minster, MS XVI. K. 18, [no page numbers].

HrJ 336 *A Treatise on Playe.*

Copy in the hand of an amanuensis, headed 'Of Play', in Volume VI of the Harington Papers; c. 1597.

First pub. (from this MS) in *Nugae Antiquae*, (1775), pp. 3-38; *Nugae Antiquae* (1804), I, 186-232. This MS briefly described in Ruth Hughey, 'The Harington Manuscript at Arundel Castle and Related Documents', *The Library*, 4th Ser. 15 (1934-5), 388-444 (p. 402).

British Library, Add. MS 46371, ff. 1-30.

MISCELLANEOUS

*HrJ 337 [*Miscellany*].

A large verse miscellany begun by John Harington of Stepney (1520?-82) and continued by his son, Sir John Harington of Kelston; in several hands, including a considerable amount in Sir John's autograph; imperfect, once consisting of 228 leaves of which 145 remain; mid-late 16th century.

This MS described, and the text printed, with facsimile examples of ff. 53, 66v, in Hughey; also discussed in Ruth Hughey, 'The Harington Manuscript at Arundel Castle and Related Documents', *The Library*, 4th Ser. 15 (1934-5), 388-444. A number of poems in this MS are recorded elsewhere in the *Index* under their individual titles. A transcript made c. 1810 for George F. Nott is in the British Library, Add. MS 28635. See also INTRODUCTION.

Owned by the Duke of Norfolk, Arundel Castle, MSS (Special Press), 'Harrington MS. Temp. Eliz.'.

*HrJ 338 -----

A volume of papers collected by Harington, in several hands, a large part in the hand of one amanuensis; consisting of miscellaneous tracts, notes, drafts of letters, and memoranda; including Harington's translation of three Psalms (see HrJ 3), his Letter to Joseph Hall (see HrJ 316), lists of books and plays owned by Harington (ff. 11v, 30, 43r-v, 47); two copies of an anonymous tract entitled 'The Order of a Christian Common wealth' (ff. 54-60v, 116v-21); and anonymous tracts entitled 'Of the Trinitie' (ff. 61-8v), 'A question of the Trynytye, Dialogue wyse' (ff. 72-93), 'Whether usurye be Lawfull among Christians' (ff. 94v-103), 'Of the Sabbothe' (ff. 105-9v), 'A Dialogue betwene Neshama, the Sowle, Nephes, the Bodye, and Orthodoxus' (ff. 110-15v), and 'Whether it be dampnation for a man to kill hymself' (ff. 122-5v); Harington's autograph occurring chiefly on ff. 30-2 (a book list of 1609, notes, and letters), 33 (Psalms),

34 (notes), and 41-6 (notes and letters, including 'Names of Comedies'); the signature of Francis Harington of Compton, dated 7 February 1609, appearing on f. 41; 135 leaves; late 16th century-1612.

Most (but not all) of the draft letters in this MS printed in McClure.

British Library, Add. MS 27632.

*HrJ 339 -----

A miscellany almost entirely compiled for John Harington of Stepney (1520?-82) but also used by Sir John Harington; in several hands; consisting of poems by Surrey and Wyatt (see HENRY HOWARD, EARL OF SURREY, and SIR THOMAS WYATT), poems by John Harington the Elder, translations of Ovid by Sir Thomas Chaloner (d. 1565) and of Virgil by Thomas Phaer (d. 1560), an extract from Harington's *Orlando Furioso* (see HrJ 11), a Latin poem by Edmund Campion (d. 1581), a deathbed speech of 'Mr. Diringe' (? Edward Dering, d. 1576), various anonymous pieces, and Harington's autograph copy of an anonymous six-line verse beginning 'Now hope, now feare, now ioye, now wofull cace' (f. 46v); the signature of Ellina Harington appearing on ff. 29v and 82 and the signature of Francis Harington appearing on f. 29v; 82 leaves; mid-late 16th century.

Formerly Phillipps MS 9474. Some pieces in this MS (notably works by John Harington the Elder) printed in the various editions of *Nugae Antiquae* and in Ruth Hughey, *John Harington of Stepney: Tudor Gentleman* (Columbus, Ohio, 1971).

British Library, Add. MS 36529.

HrJ 340 -----

A MS volume owned by Sir John Harington (also probably by his father), consisting of historical tracts and state papers chiefly relating to Queen Elizabeth and Mary Queen of Scots, including Sir Thomas Smith's 'Dialogue concerning the Queen's Marriage' and Sidney's 'Letter to the Queen' (see SiP 191); written chiefly in a single scribal hand, with additions in one or more other hands; constituting Volume I of the Harington Papers; 'Prose N^{o} I' stamped on the spine; 126 leaves; late 16th century.

This MS briefly discussed by Hughey in *The Library*, 4th Ser. 15 (1934-5), 399-400 et passim, and in McClure, p. 11 (n).

British Library, Add. MS 46366.

HrJ 341 -----

A MS volume owned by Sir John Harington (also probably by his father), consisting of letters chiefly by Sir John Cheke (1514-57), with some by Sir Christopher Hatton and others, and extracts from Seneca's Epistles, written mainly in three scribal hands, with some additional matter probably in later hands, including a Dialogue of Plato; constituting Volume II of the Harington Papers; 'Prose N° II' stamped on the spine; imperfect, now comprising 140 leaves (some original leaves probably extracted by the printers of *Nugae Antiquae*); late 16th century.

Portions printed in the various editions of *Nugae Antiquae*; this MS briefly discussed by Hughey in *The Library*, 15 (1934-5), 399-401 et passim.

British Library, Add. MS 46367.

*HrJ 342 -----

A notebook, chiefly in the hands of amanuenses, partly autograph, entitled on the cover 'Sr John Harringtons own MSS relating to the war in Ireland 1599'; containing copies of state letters and documents relating to Ireland in 1597-1600 and reports of events at that time; including (ff. 7-18) 'A Journal of my lords Jorney, beginning the 9. of May. 1599' (f. 7r-v and sidenotes throughout in Harington's autograph), (f. 20) a copy of letters of Captain MacDermon to the Constable of Boyle, 15 August 1599 (in Harington's autograph), (ff. 21-3) a 'Report of my Jorney into the North to Justice Cary. In Ierland' (in Harington's autograph), (ff. 41-3v) 'The chiefe causes of the wante of reformation of Irelande', and (ff. 45-51v) copies of three of Harington's letters of August 1599 and February 1599/1600; also (ff. 18v-19v) copies of Harington's translation of two Psalms, probably written in later (see HrJ 4); constituting Volume IV of the Harington Papers; 62 leaves; c. 1599-1600 (and additions c. 1609).

Some texts in this MS (notably the 'Report...to Justice Cary' and Harington's letters) printed in the various editions of *Nugae Antiquae*; the three letters reprinted from this publication in McClure, pp. 68-76, 79-80. The 'Journal of my lords Jorney' is different from the 'Report concerning...Essex's Journeys' attributed (probably incorrectly) to Harington in *Nugae Antiquae* (1804), I, 268-93: see Timothy G.A. Nelson, 'Sir John Harington -- A Mistaken Attribution', *N & Q*, 214 (December 1969), 457. See also INTRODUCTION.

British Library, Add. MS 46369.

*HrJ 343 -----

A volume of transcripts of documents relating to lands formerly belonging to Sir James Harington of Brierley from the time of their forfeiture in 1485 until the grant of their reversion to John Harington of Stepney in 1570, compiled by Sir John Harington of Kelston apparently for Sir Henry Hobart and inscribed 'The booke of Haryngtons Lands for Sr Henry Hubbert [his] Maties attorney general'; chiefly in the hands of amanuenses, with Harington's autograph annotations and with some pages or substantial additions in his autograph (notably ff. 25, 26v, 33, 35v-6, 37v-8); 44 leaves;

[*Miscellany*]

constituting Volume VIII of the Harington Papers; c. 1606-12.

Two documents probably relating to this volume, the first (a pedigree of the Harington family from the 13th to the 16th century) in Harington's autograph, are in Volume IX of the Harington Papers (Add. MS 46373B, ff. 1-2v).

British Library, Add. MS 46373A.

*HrJ 344 -----

A MS volume originally owned by Sir Thomas Wyatt and containing (ff. 3-101) copies of his poems (see SIR THOMAS WYATT); later owned by Sir John Harington, who entered his translation of the Psalms on ff. 104-7 (see HrJ 2); then used by various members of the Harington family, chiefly in the 1630s-50s, as a rough notebook; imperfect, now comprising 120 leaves; 16th-17th century.

This MS discussed by editors of Wyatt: see SIR THOMAS WYATT, INTRODUCTION.

British Library, Egerton MS 2711.

Stephen Hawes

fl. 1503-11

ABBREVIATIONS

Gluck & Morgan *The Minor Poems of Stephen Hawes*, ed. Florence W. Gluck and Alice B. Morgan, EETS 271 (London, 1974).

For abbreviations used throughout Volume I, see p.xi.

INTRODUCTION

There are no known examples of Hawes' autograph. Extracts from three of his works appear in two 16th-century miscellanies. There survives also a MS of an elegy on Henry VII which used to be attributed to John Skelton but which has been more recently assigned to Hawes on stylistic grounds (see HaS 3).

PB.

ARRANGEMENT

Verse HaS 1-4.

Stephen Hawes

VERSE

HaS 1 *The Comfort of Lovers* ('The gentyll poetes vnder cloudy fygures').

Copy of anonymous love poems made up of lines transcribed from an early printed edition of *The Comfort of Lovers*, in a verse miscellany; c. 1537.

First pub. [London, 1515?]; Gluck & Morgan, pp. 93-122. This MS printed in Frederick Morgan Padelford, 'The Songs in Manuscript Rawlinson C. 813', *Anglia*, 31 (1908), 309-97; recorded in Gluck & Morgan, pp. xx-xxii.

Bodleian, MS Rawl. C. 813, f. 14v seq. (poems No. 13, lines 148-54, and No. 16).

HaS 2 *The Conversion of Swearers* ('The fruytfull sentence & the noble werkes').

Copy of lines 234-89 (beginning 'Wo worthe your hartes so planted in pryde'), written in a 15th-century MS book of verse questions and answers; early 16th century.

First pub. London, 1509; Gluck & Morgan, pp. 73-84. This MS recorded in Gluck & Morgan, p. xx.

British Library, Harley MS 4294, f. 80.

HaS 3 *An Elegy on the Death of Henry VII* ('O wauering Worlde all Wrapped in Wretchidnes').

Copy of a poem possibly by Hawes in a monastic letter book; c. 1509.

First pub. [c. 1509]; ed. Alexander Dyce in *Poetical Works of John Skelton* (London, 1843), II, 399-400; printed from this MS and attributed to Hawes in G.V. Scammell and H.L. Rogers, 'An Elegy on Henry VII', *RES*, NS 8 (1957), 167-70.

Durham Cathedral, Prior's Kitchen, Durham Dean and Chapter Muniments, Registrum Parvum IV, ff. 176v-7.

HaS 4 *The Pastime of Pleasure* ('Oh my lady dear both regard and see').

Copy of anonymous love poems made up of lines transcribed from an early printed edition of *The Pastime of Pleasure*, in a verse miscellany; c. 1537.

First pub. London, [1509]; ed. William Edward Mead, EETS 173 (London, 1928). This MS printed in F.M. Padelford, 'The Songs in Manuscript Rawlinson C. 813', *Anglia*, 31 (1908), 309-97; recorded in Mead, p. xxxviii.

Bodleian, MS Rawl. C. 813, f. 14v seq. (poems No. 13, 14, 15, 47, 48, and possibly 1 and 51).

Robert Henryson

1425?-1506?

ABBREVIATIONS

Craigie *The Maitland Folio Manuscript*, ed. W. A. Craigie, 2 vols, STS NS 7, 20 (Edinburgh & London, 1919-27).

Craigie, *Asloan MS* *The Asloan Manuscript*, ed. W. A. Craigie, 2 vols, STS NS 14, 16 (Edinburgh & London, 1923-5).

Gregory Smith *The Poems of Robert Henryson*, ed. G. Gregory Smith, 3 vols, STS 55, 58, 64 (Edinburgh & London, 1906-14).

Murdoch *The Bannatyne Manuscript*, ed. J. Barclay Murdoch, 4 vols, Hunterian Club (Glasgow, 1896; reprinted New York, 1966).

Ritchie *The Bannatyne Manuscript*, ed. W. Tod Ritchie, 4 vols, STS 3rd Ser. 5, 22, 23, 26 (Edinburgh & London, 1928-33).

Stevenson *Pieces from the Makculloch and the Gray MSS. together with the Chepman and Myllar Prints*, ed. George Stevenson, STS 65 (Edinburgh & London, 1918).

Wood *The Poems and Fables of Robert Henryson*, ed. H. Harvey Wood (Edinburgh, 1933; 2nd edition 1958).

For abbreviations used throughout Volume I, see p.xi.

INTRODUCTION

The main MS sources of Henryson's poems are the same as those of Dunbar's poems: namely, the Bannatyne MS, the Maitland Folio MS, and the Asloan MS (for details see WILLIAM DUNBAR, INTRODUCTION). Three poems also appear in the Makculloch MS (HnR 12, 18, 24), one poem appears in the Gray MS (HnR 7), and independent transcripts of *The Morall Fabillis of Esope* (HnR 10) and *The Testament of Cresseid* (HnR 29-30) are preserved.

The last two poems, Henryson's most important works, were first published in the 16th century. Three other poems (HnR 14, 16, 35) appeared in the Chepman and Myllar Prints in 1508 (see again the Introduction to Dunbar). The remaining pieces were not printed until the 18th or 19th centuries, when they were edited from the MS sources.

The standard collected edition of Henryson (from which titles and first lines are cited in the *Index*) remains Wood. It is indebted to the STS edition by G. Gregory Smith.

PB.

ARRANGEMENT

Verse HnR 1-35.

Robert Henryson

VERSE

HnR 1 *The Abbay Walk* ('Allone as I went up and doun').

Copy, untitled, in the Bannatyne MS; c. 1568.

Wood, pp. 195-6. Printed from this MS in Ritchie, I, 50-2; collated in Wood.

National Library of Scotland, Adv. MS 1. 1. 6, Vol. I, pp. 30-2.

HnR 2 -----

Copy, untitled, in the Bannatyne MS; c. 1568.

Printed from this MS in Wood; Murdoch, II, 125-7; Ritchie, II, 116-17.

National Library of Scotland, Adv. MS 1. 1. 6, Vol. I, ff. 46v-7 (pp. 152-3).

HnR 3 -----

Copy, untitled, in the Maitland Folio MS; c. 1570-85.

Printed from this MS in Craigie, I, 351-2; collated in Wood.

Magdalene College, Cambridge, Pepys Library, MS 2553, pp. 296-7.

HnR 4 -----

Copy, headed 'Ane Sonnet' and subscribed 'Finis, quod Riddell', written in a small MS volume by one Alexander Riddell at Bowland in 1636.

This MS recorded in *The Poems and Fables of Robert Henryson*, ed. David Laing (Edinburgh, 1865), pp. 240-1.

In 1865 'in the library of Mr [George] Chalmers of Aldbar'; unlocated.

HnR 5 *Aganis Haisty Credence of Titlaris* ('Ffals titlaris now growis up full rank').

Copy, untitled, in the Bannatyne MS; c. 1568.

Printed from this MS in Wood, pp. 215-16; Murdoch, II, 182-4; Ritchie, II, 165-7.

National Library of Scotland, Adv. MS 1. 1. 6, Vol. I, ff. 67v-8 (pp. 196-7).

HnR 6 -----

Copy, untitled, in the Maitland Folio MS; c. 1570-85.

Printed from this MS in Craigie, I, 348-50; collated in Wood.

Magdalene College, Cambridge, Pepys Library, MS 2553, pp. 309-10.

HnR 7 *The Annunciation* ('Forcy as deith Is likand lufe').

Copy in a miscellany compiled by James Gray, priest of the diocese of Dunblane and secretary to William Schevez (d. 1497) and James Stewart (d. 1504), successive Archbishops of St Andrews; end 15th-early 16th century.

Printed from this MS in Wood, pp. 199-201; Stevenson, pp. 43-5.

National Library of Scotland, Adv. MS 34. 7. 3, ff. 70-1v.

HnR 8 *The Bludy Serk* ('This hindir yeir I hard be tald').

Copy, the title added in a later hand, in the Bannatyne MS; c. 1568.

Printed from this MS in Wood, pp. 173-6; Murdoch, IV, 942-6; Ritchie, IV, 202-5.

National Library of Scotland, Adv. MS 1. 1. 6, Vol. II, ff. 325-6v (pp. 699-702).

HnR 9 *The Garment of Gud Ladeis* ('Wald my gud lady lufe me best').

Copy in the Bannatyne MS; c. 1568.

Printed from this MS in Wood, pp. 169-70; Murdoch, III, 611-12; Ritchie, III, 252-4.

National Library of Scotland, Adv. MS 1. 1. 6, Vol. II, f. 215r-v (pp. 489-90).

HnR 10 *The Morall Fabillis of Esope the Phrygian* ('Thocht feinyeit fabils of ald poetre').

Copy, with two coloured illustrations; 75 leaves; 1571.

First pub. Edinburgh, 1570; Wood, pp. 1-102. This MS collated in Wood. Facsimiles of various pages in Wood, facing pp. xiv, 5, and in Gregory Smith, II, facing pp. x, 7, 121. A transcript of the MS made by John Dougald (1821) is in the National Library of Scotland, Adv. MS 19. 3. 5.

British Library, Harley MS 3865.

HnR 11 -----

Copy of ten fables in the Bannatyne MS; c. 1568.

Printed from this MS in Murdoch, IV, 855-66, 898-922, 946-88; Ritchie, IV, 116-28, 158-82, 206-45, with a facsimile of f. 301v facing p. 123; collated in Wood.

The Morall Fabillis of Esope the Phrygian

National Library of Scotland, Adv. MS 1. 1. 6, Vol. II, ff. 298-302, 310v-17v, 326v-42v (pp. 645-53, 670-84, 702-34).

HnR 12 ----- *The Prolog and The Taill of the Cok, and the Jasp.*

Copy, untitled, made by a certain 'Johannes', possibly John Purde, on the fly-leaves of a MS book of lecture notes on logic written in Louvain in 1477 by Magnus Makculloch, clerk to Archbishop William Schevez (d. 1497); late 15th-early 16th century.

Printed from this MS in Stevenson, pp. 3-8; collated in Wood.

Edinburgh University Library, MS Borl. 205, ff. ii^{v}-iii.

HnR 13 ----- *The Taill of the Uponlandis Mous, and the Burges Mous.*

Copy in the Asloan MS; c. 1515.

Printed from this MS in Craigie, *Asloan MS*, II, 141-9 (with a facsimile of f. 236); collated in Wood.

National Library of Scotland, [MS Acc. 4233], ff. 236-9v.

HnR 14 *Orpheus and Eurydice* ('The nobilnes and grit magnificens').

Copy of a 633-line version in the Bannatyne MS; c. 1568.

First pub. in the Chepman and Myllar Prints (Edinburgh, 1508). Printed from this MS in Wood, pp. 129-48; Murdoch, IV, 922-42; Ritchie, IV, 182-201.

National Library of Scotland, Adv. MS 1. 1. 6, Vol. II, ff. 317v-25 (pp. 684-99).

HnR 15 -----

Copy of a 578-line version in the Asloan MS; c. 1515.

Printed from this MS in Craigie, *Asloan MS*, II, 155-74; collated in Wood.

National Library of Scotland, [MS Acc. 4233], ff. 247-56v.

HnR 16 *The Prais of Aige* ('Wythin a garth, under a rede rosere').

Copy, untitled, in the Bannatyne MS; c. 1568.

First pub. in the Chepman and Myllar Prints (Edinburgh, 1508); Wood, pp. 185-6. Printed from this MS in Ritchie, I, 73-4; collated in Wood.

National Library of Scotland, Adv. MS 1. 1. 6, Vol. I, p. 44.

HnR 17 -----

Copy, untitled, in the Bannatyne MS; c. 1568.

Printed from this MS in Murdoch, II, 155-6; Ritchie, II, 141-2; collated in Wood.

National Library of Scotland, Adv. MS 1. 1. 6, Vol. I, f. 57r-v (pp. 173-4).

HnR 18 -----

Copy, untitled, made by a certain 'Johannes' possibly John Purde, in a MS book of lecture notes on logic written in Louvain in 1477 by Magnus Makculloch, clerk to Archbishop William Schevez (d. 1497); late 15th-early 16th century.

Printed from this MS in Stevenson, pp. 15-16; collated in Wood.

Edinburgh University Library, MS Borl. 205, f. 87.

HnR 19 *Ane Prayer for the Pest* ('O eterne god, of power infinyt').

Copy in the Bannatyne MS; c. 1568.

Wood, pp. 163-5. Printed from this MS in Ritchie, I, 33-6; collated in Wood.

National Library of Scotland, Adv. MS 1. 1. 6, Vol. I, pp. 20-2.

HnR 20 -----

Copy in the Bannatyne MS; c. 1568.

Printed from this MS in Wood; Murdoch, II, 61-4; Ritchie, II, 58-60.

National Library of Scotland, Adv. MS 1. 1. 6, Vol. I, ff. 24-5v (pp. 107-10).

HnR 21 *The Ressoning betuix Aige and Yowth* ('Quhen fair flora, the godes of the flowris').

Copy in the Bannatyne MS; c. 1568.

Wood, pp. 179-80. Printed from this MS in Ritchie, I, 68-71; collated in Wood.

National Library of Scotland, Adv. MS 1. 1. 6, Vol. I, pp. 42-3.

HnR 22 -----

Copy in the Bannatyne MS; c. 1568.

Printed from this MS in Wood; Murdoch, II, 149-52; Ritchie, II, 137-9.

National Library of Scotland, Adv. MS 1. 1. 6, Vol. I, ff. 55-6 (pp. 169-71).

HnR 23 -----

Copy, untitled, in the Maitland Folio MS; c. 1570-85.

Printed from this MS in Craigie, I, 200-2; collated in Wood.

Magdalene College, Cambridge, Pepys Library, MS 2553, pp. 176-8.

HnR 24 -----

Copy made by a certain 'Johannes', possibly John Purde, in a MS book of lecture notes on logic written in Louvain in 1477 by Magnus Makculloch, clerk to Archbishop William Schevez (d. 1497); late 15th-early 16th century.

Printed from this MS in Stevenson, pp. 22-3; collated in Wood.

Edinburgh University Library, MS Borl. 205, f. 181v.

HnR 25 *The Ressoning betuix Deth and Man* ('O mortall man, behold, tak tent to me').

Copy in the Bannatyne MS; c. 1568.

Wood, pp. 211-12. Printed from this MS in Ritchie, I, 71-3; collated in Wood.

National Library of Scotland, Adv. MS 1. 1. 6, Vol. I, pp. 43-4.

HnR 26 -----

Copy in the Bannatyne MS; c. 1568.

Printed from this MS in Wood; Murdoch, II, 153-5; Ritchie, II, 139-41.

National Library of Scotland, Adv. MS 1. 1. 6, Vol. I, ff. 56-7 (pp. 171-3).

HnR 27 *Robene and Makyne* ('Robene sat on gud grene hill').

Copy, untitled, in the Bannatyne MS; c. 1568.

Printed from this MS in Wood, pp. 151-4; Murdoch, IV, 1050-4; Ritchie, IV, 308-12.

National Library of Scotland, Adv. MS 1. 1. 6, Vol. II, ff. 365-6v (pp. 779-82).

HnR 28 *Sum Practysis of Medecyne* ('Guk, guk, gud day, ser, gaip quhill ye get it').

Copy in the Bannatyne MS; c. 1568.

Printed from this MS in Wood, pp. 157-60; Murdoch, III, 401-4; Ritchie, III, 28-31.

National Library of Scotland, Adv. MS 1. 1. 6, Vol. I, ff. 141v-2v (pp. 342-4).

HnR 29 *The Testament of Cresseid* ('Ane doolie sessoun to ane cairfull dyte').

Copy, bound with a MS copy of Chaucer's *Troilus and Criseide*; 16th century.

First pub. in *Workes of Geoffrey Chaucer*, ed. William Thynne (London, 1532); Wood, pp. 105-26. This MS collated in Wood.

St John's College, Cambridge, MS L. 1. (James 235), ff. 121v-8v.

HnR 30 -----

Copy transcribed for Sir Francis Kinaston (1587-1642) from an early printed edition but with editorial emendations; together with Kinaston's Latin version of the poem; 1639-40.

Printed from this MS in Gregory Smith, I, xcvii-clxii; collated in Wood.

Bodleian, MS Add. C. 287, pp. 475-509.

HnR 31 -----

Copy of the first three stanzas written on the last leaf of a MS copy of Gavin Douglas's *Aeneid* once owned by William Ruthven, fourth Baron Ruthven and first Earl of Gowrie (1541?-84); 16th century.

This MS recorded in *Virgil's Aeneid translated into Scottish Verse by Gavin Douglas, Bishop of Dunkeld*, ed. David F.C. Coldwell, 4 vols, STS (Edinburgh & London, 1951-6), I, 98; not recorded in Wood.

Edinburgh University Library, MS Dc. 1. 43, f. 301v.

HnR 32 *The Thre Deid Pollis* ('O sinfull man, in to this mortall se').

Copy, here ascribed to Patrick Johnstoun, in the Bannatyne MS; c. 1568.

Printed from this MS in Wood, pp. 205-7; Murdoch, II, 157-9; Ritchie, II, 142-4.

National Library of Scotland, Adv. MS 1. 1. 6, Vol. I, ff. 57v-8v (pp. 174-8).

HnR 33 -----

Copy, untitled, in the Maitland Folio MS; c. 1570-85.

Printed from this MS in Craigie, I, 394-5; collated in Wood.

The Thre Deid Pollis

Magdalene College, Cambridge, Pepys Library, MS 2553, pp. 327-8.

HnR 34 -----

Copy of the incipit, here 'O mortill man', in a musical setting, in a MS songbook compiled by Sir William Mure of Rowallan; c. 1600s-20.

This MS recorded in Wood, p. xxx.

Edinburgh University Library, MS La. III. 488, f. 24v.

HnR 35 *The Want of Wyse Men* ('Me ferlyis of this grete confusioun').

Copy, here beginning 'Me mervellis of this grit Confusioun', in the Bannatyne MS; c. 1568.

First pub. in the Chepman and Myllar Prints (Edinburgh, 1508); Wood, pp. 189-91. Printed from this MS in Murdoch, II, 213-15; Ritchie, II, 195-7; collated in Wood.

National Library of Scotland, Adv. MS 1. 1. 6, Vol. I, f. 78r-v (pp. 217-18).

Edward, Lord Herbert of Cherbury

1582?-1648

ABBREVIATIONS

Occasional Verses (1665) *Occasional Verses of Edward Lord Herbert, Baron of Cherbury and Castle-Island*, [ed. Sir Henry Herbert] (London, 1665).

Rossi Mario M. Rossi, *La vita, le opere, i tempi di Edoardo Herbert di Chirbury*, 3 vols (Florence, 1947).

Smith *The Poems English and Latin of Edward, Lord Herbert of Cherbury*, ed. G. C. Moore Smith (Oxford, 1923; reprinted 1968).

For abbreviations used throughout Volume I, see p.xi.

INTRODUCTION

Herbert of Cherbury's papers have survived in considerable number, as have the archives of the Herbert family in general. Most of the main collection, formerly preserved at Powis Castle, Welshpool, is now in the National Library of Wales. A few of the Powis MSS are in the Public Record Office, and certain items have been sold elsewhere (e.g. HrE 143, now at Harvard).

There is no collected edition of Herbert's works and a number of his papers remain unpublished. The most extensive account of his work ever undertaken is Rossi's. A useful (though not absolutely accurate) checklist of his published works can also be found in J. M. Shuttleworth, 'Edward, Lord Herbert of Cherbury (1583-1648): A Preliminary, Annotated Checklist of Works by and about him', *NLWJ*, 20 (1977), 151-68.

Most of Herbert's poems were first published posthumously by his brother, Sir Henry Herbert, in *Occasional Verses* (1665). This text is the basis of Moore Smith's edition (1923). Smith collates fully one particularly important MS of Herbert's poems, now in the British Library (Add. MS 37157). This MS appears to have been Herbert's own 'official' collection of his poems, and is now bound up in a composite volume of Herbert family papers. It is a fair copy made by an amanuensis, who often left spaces for letters or words he evidently could not decipher in his copy-texts; Herbert then went through the MS filling in the spaces and making a number of minor autograph corrections and revisions. The MS is dated by Herbert at the end (f. 25) '1630', although some of it must have been written a little later (see Smith, pp. xxv-xxvi). Smith also collates a few copies of particular poems in early miscellanies — notably Bodleian, MS Rawl. poet. 31. Some of Herbert's poems were evidently in circulation in the Inns of Court and other circles long before the edition of 1665 materialised, and a number of additional copies not known to Smith are recorded below. Smith was also unaware of a few autographs of certain poems among the Powis MSS (HrE 8, 30, 32, 35-6).

Rossi (III, 393-8) has argued for the addition to the canon of several poems and verse fragments to be found in a packet of 'Poems: notes and draft[s]' among the Powis MSS now in the National Library of Wales ((1959 deposit), Series II, '(Envelope) Taken from Bundle 26'). The poems in this packet (a series of loose or detached leaves) are chiefly in Herbert's autograph and include, as Rossi notes (III, 398-400), his copies of verses by others. In fact, it is likely that all the poems in this packet are other men's compositions, and none should be accepted as Herbert's without further evidence of authorship. The doubtful or spurious poems which Rossi attributes to Herbert are as follows:

> *'Iris Caeruleo Fluore cingens'* (14 lines, anon.); *'My Lord, I suit my garments to my minde'* (4 lines, probably the conclusion of a poem, anon.); *On ye Death of S^r. Th. Pelham*, beginning 'Merely for Death to grieve, and mourne' (by William Strode: see Volume II of the *Index*); *An opposite to Melancholy*, beginning 'Returne my Joyes, and hither bring' (also by Strode: see Volume II of the *Index*); *'The being yours can make even Vices good'* (17 lines, probably the conclusion of a poem, anon.); *'Tis not enough for one that is a wife'* (36 lines, anon.); *To Dianas earthly Deputesse of my Worthy Sister Mrs Jane Carye*, beginning 'When daies cleare light his compast course hath runne' (23 lines, incomplete?, anon.).

A poem which can certainly be rejected from the canon is *Echo to a Rock* (beginning 'Thou heaven-threat'ning Rock, gentler then she'), printed in *Occasional Verses* (1665) and consequently in Smith (pp. 46-7). This poem was written by Henry Reynolds (c.1563/4-1635) and is clearly ascribed to him in the Stoughton MS (p. 73) owned by Rosemary Williams: see Mary Hobbs, 'Drayton's "Most Dearely-Loved Friend Henery Reynolds Esq."', *RES*, NS 24 (1973), 414-28 (p. 426). It was mistaken in 1665 for one of Herbert's poems since he obviously had a copy among his papers, for he wrote a sequel to it, *Echo in a Church*, of which three autograph drafts survive (HrE 8, and see FACSIMILE XIX).

The PROSE section (HrE 92-143) includes all those works expressly attributed to Herbert in Rossi's bibliography (III, 538-42). One of them, the English *Religio Laici*, has been previously known from two drafts (HrE 136-7), but what appears to be a more complete text, with two unpublished appendices, exists (HrE 138). Titles are supplied in the entries for those works without a heading (HrE 92-3, 128, 139-43). The present reference for each of the relevant Powis MSS is cited in this section as accurately as possible (some have been rearranged, as well as relocated, since Mario Rossi examined them). In view of the general disorder of the various drafts, many of which are not easily recognisable, there is an obvious need for the whole Powis collection to be catalogued in detail.

It may be noted that one work sometimes attributed to Sir Timothy Baldwin (1620-96)— the Latin version of *The Expedition to the Isle of Rhé* — is proved to be Herbert's by the existence of his autographs (HrE 117-18) and also by his own testimony. In a letter of 9 February 1638/9 to Secretary Windebank, now in the Public Record Office (SP.16/412/77), Herbert specifically refers to his expenses in 'writing the Expedition to the Isle of Ré in Latin and in Englishe'. On the other hand, a prose work which can be safely rejected from the canon is *A Dialogue between a Tutor and his Pupil*, a treatise published as Herbert's by Horace Walpole in 1768. Walpole's attribution has been supported by a mistaken belief that one of the five known MSS is in the hand of one of Herbert's amanuenses (see R. I. Aaron in *Mind*, 54 (1945), 355-6) and by the fact that another of the MSS was owned by a later member of the Herbert family. Rossi rejected the work in 1947 (III, 530-3) because of its inconsistency with Herbert's philosophy, and he did so again, on conclusive evidence, in 'Herbert of Cherbury's *Religio Laici*: A Bibliographical Note', *Edinburgh Bibliographical Society Transactions*, 4, Part 2 (1962), 45-52. The MS of the dialogue in the National Library of Wales (NLW. MS 5296E) is part of a heavily revised draft evidently in the hand of the anonymous author: it has no connection with Herbert. Neither have the other MSS, all later copies, in the Bodleian (MS Ballard 54; MS Rawl. C. 95, once owned by 'Anglesey'), and in the British Library (Add. MS 29770; and Add. MS 4366, an 18th-century copy owned by Henry Herbert, ninth Earl of Pembroke).

The only prose work of Herbert's which seems to be represented in miscellanies is *The Life and Reign of King Henry VIII*, published in 1649. Since extracts in miscellanies were evidently taken from the printed edition, however, they have not been included in the entries. The work is quoted or précised, for instance, in MSS in the Bodleian (MS Rawl. C. 848, pp. 143-95), in a MS owned by Lord Egremont at Petworth House (HMC MS 128, pp. 109-40), in the Inner Temple Library (Miscellaneous MSS 17 and 38; Petyt MSS 535, Vol. 6, ff. 267-70, and 536, Vol. 10, ff. 245-8), and at University College London (MS Ogden 7/10). On the other hand, several transcripts of the work made for Herbert himself survive, and also his collection of historical documents used in its composition (see HrE 121-5). In the letter of 9 February 1638/9 cited earlier Herbert refers to these, noting his expenses in 'keeping Schollers and Clerkes, for coppyinge Records, and making Transcripts of the History of king H.VIII'. Similar copies of historical documents used by Herbert when writing *The Expedition to the Isle of Rhé* are preserved among the Powis MSS (1959 deposit), Series II, Bundle XII, Nos. 3-6.

The MISCELLANEOUS section includes Herbert's lute-book (HrE 144). Many other miscellaneous items are among the Powis MSS. Some papers on state affairs which were owned though probably not composed by Herbert (such as *A short Narration of occurrences in . . . Scotland* and *Questions touching upon Obedience to Magistrate in eminency*, both now in the '(Envelope) Taken from Bundle 26') are printed in Rossi (III, 492-504). A Herbert MS of some peripheral interest which has received attention is the household book (1601) of his mother, Magdalene Herbert, still in the possession of the Earl of Powis at Powis Castle; it is discussed, with a facsimile example, in Amy Charles, 'Mrs. Herbert's Kitchin Booke', *ELR*, 4 (1974), 164-73. Among miscellaneous items elsewhere, an account apparently by Herbert of negotiations concerning the English liturgy at St Germain-en-Leye is in the National Library of Wales (NLW. MS 550B). Herbert's Will is preserved in the Public Record Office (PROB 10/697, proved October 1648).

The Powis MSS also contain a large amount of Herbert's correspondence. Some of his letters are printed in Rossi (III, 400-5, 408-9, 443-72, 487-8, 521-6), and some in *Herbert Correspondence*, ed. W. J. Smith (Cardiff, 1963), pp. 71-2, 79-80, 86-8, 97-9, 104-5, 107, 110-12, 117-18, 121-3, 125-30, 132. Thirteen volumes of Herbert family papers, containing the bulk of Lord Herbert's correspondence and diplomatic papers, are now in the Public Record Office (PRO. 30/53). Those volumes containing Herbert's correspondence from 1615 to 1639, together with miscellaneous family papers between 1586 and 1735 (PRO. 30/53/10-11), are described in *HMC*, 10th Report, Appendix IV (1885), pp. 378-99, and printed in part in *Old Herbert Papers at Powis Castle and in the British Museum*, ed. Morris Charles Jones, Montgomeryshire Collections Vol. 20 (London, 1886). This last publication also includes the text of Herbert's book of despatches for 1619, now in the British Library (Add. MS 7082). There are numerous other letters and despatches of Herbert in the Public Record Office, the British Library, and elsewhere. Four letters to Robert Harley are among the Portland papers now on deposit in the British Library (Loan MS 29/202, f. 165 seq.). One of Herbert's letters in the British Library, written to Sir Dudley Carleton, 25 June 1617, is reproduced in Sir Henry James, *Facsimiles of National Manuscripts from William the Conqueror to Queen Anne*, 4 vols (Southampton, 1865-8), IV, plate XXI. A letter of 23 August 1644, apparently sent to Prince Rupert, and similarly in the British Library (Add. MS 18981, f. 229), is reproduced in part in Greg, *English Literary Autographs*, plate XLIX(c). Four letters sent to Sir George More are printed in *The Losely Manuscripts*, ed. Alfred John Kempe (London, 1836), pp. 347-59; the originals are still at Loseley Park (Vol. 2014, Nos. 98, 100-2), in the possession of Brigadier F. G. More-Molyneux-Longbourne. Two letters to Gerard Voss bound in a presentation exemplum of Walpole's edition of Herbert's *Autobiography* are discussed in R. W. Chapman, 'Lord Herbert of Cherbury and the Bodleian', *BQR*, 7 (1932-4), 174-5; the letters were in the library of the Cowper family at Panshanger, Hertfordshire — a library which was dispersed in 1953 before the house was demolished — but they are printed in *Gerardi Joan. Vossii et clarorum virorum ad eum epistolae* (London, 1690).

Some correspondence of Herbert and his son Richard, now among the Ellesmere MSS in the Huntington, is printed and discussed in James H. Hanford, 'Lord Herbert of Cherbury and his Son', *HLQ*, 5 (1942), 317-32. Three letters of 1643 owned in the early 19th century by Rebecca Warner and now unlocated are printed in her book *Epistolary Curiosities* (Bath, 1818), pp. 30-2. A Latin letter of 19/29 October 1625 to Hugo Grotius was once owned by Alfred Morrison (1821-97) and is recorded in the printed catalogue of his autograph collection, Vol. II (1885), p. 286. The same catalogue reproduces Herbert's signature on a receipt of 4 February 1646. Some letters of Herbert are also among the Trumbull MSS (Alphabetical Series, Vol. XXVI) in the Berkshire Record Office.

The *Index* does not include a section on Herbert's Marginalia in Printed Books and Manuscripts. Most of Herbert's Greek and Latin books (about 931 volumes, including many with his autograph annotations) were given to Jesus College, Oxford; a complete catalogue can be found in C. J. Fordyce and T. M. Knox, 'The Library of Jesus College, Oxford', Appendix, *Proceedings and Papers of the Oxford Bibliographical Society*, 5, Part 2 (1937), 71-115. About 230 of his other books, formerly at Powis Castle, have been dispersed in various sales (notably Sotheby's, 16 January 1956, and 20 March 1967, and see Maggs Brothers catalogue No. 837 (1956) and Dawson catalogues Nos. 208, 216, and 217). Herbert's own catalogue of his library, written chiefly by an amanuensis (c. 1636-7), is in the National Library of Wales (NLW. MS 5298E).

PB.

ARRANGEMENT

Verse:	(1) Poems by Herbert	HrE 1-76
	(2) Poems of uncertain authorship	HrE 77-91
Prose		HrE 92-143
Miscellaneous		HrE 144.

See also Addenda to Part 2, p. 629

FACSIMILE XIX — Edward, Lord Herbert of Cherbury: Draft, *Echo in a Church*, [1625] (HrE 8). Public Record Office, PRO 30/53/9/10, folio 1 recto. Reproduced by permission of the Earl of Powis.

1

Eccho Heav'n

When shall my troubled soule at large
it selfe discharge

Or wounded conscience comfort find. O when. Eccho. Even
Eccho Heav'n

Whence comes the voice I heare,

Who is it that of thy words repeats the first and last, E. the first and last

I now should growe agast

Did I not hope that it thou o Lord

Who doest thee grace afford

Wilt thou then heare my words when I do call. E. all

And wilt thou supply grant, when I do cry. E. I.

Then though I fall

Thy grace will my defaults supply

What shall I do yet if oft I thy grace attempt & tempt

But since no man from frailtys exempt

What should I do ... to be of ... the same & pray

But who will teach the way

... who will raise my soule from ill

quench bad desires, reforme my will. I will.

I must confess at least but wilt not yet thy favor show

that mortall may face to face I may thee know. E. no

I pray thee

Thee then yet to my prayers incline

Tell art thou God or but a voice divine. E. divine

I can not reade, but growe with crying now so faint

I must desire thee to acquaint

Whether thou be the Lord or but a voice

Or tell before I wholy weary am

From heaven ... came

Or tell before I wholy weary am E. I am

Edward, Lord Herbert of Cherbury

VERSE

(1) POEMS BY HERBERT

HrE 1 *Another Sonnet to Black it self* ('Thou Black, wherein all colours are compos'd'.

Copy in Herbert's MS collection of his own poems; c. 1630-1.

First pub. in *Occasional Verses* (1665); Smith, p. 39. This MS collated in Smith, p. 130.

British Library, Add. MS 37157, f. 18.

HrE 2 *The Brown Beauty* ('While the two contraries of Black and White').

Copy in Herbert's MS collection of his own poems; c. 1630-1.

First pub. in *Occasional Verses* (1665); Smith, p. 60. This MS collated in Smith, p. 133.

British Library, Add. MS 37157, f. 11r-v.

--- *De Vita coelesti, ex iisdem principiis conjectura* ('Toto lustratus Genio, mihi gratulor ipsi').

[Smith, pp. 103-6].

A version of this poem appears in Herbert's *Autobiography*: see HrE 94-5.

--- *De vita humana philosophica disquisitio* ('Prima fuit quondam genitali femine Vita').

[Smith, pp. 99-102].

A short version of this poem appears in Herbert's *Autobiography*: see HrE 94-5.

HrE 3 *A Description* ('I sing her worth and praises hy').

Copy, headed 'Idea: Off S^r: Edw: Harbert', in a verse miscellany; c. 1620-33.

First pub. in *Occasional Verses* (1665); Smith, pp. 2-5. This MS collated in Smith, p. 125.

Bodleian, MS Rawl. poet. 31, ff. 14-15v.

HrE 4 -----

Copy, untitled, in a MS volume of poems chiefly by John Donne once owned by one Meriall Tracy; c. 1620-33.

Huntington, HM 198, Part II, ff. 6-7.

HrE 5 *Ditty* ('If you refuse me once, and think again').

Copy in Herbert's MS collection of his own poems; c. 1630-1.

Stanzas 1-3 first pub. (prefixed to verses by Sir Robert Ayton) in *The Last Remains of Sr John Suckling* (London, 1659); first pub. complete in *Occasional Verses* (1666); Smith, pp. 31-2. This MS collated in Smith, pp. 128-9.

British Library, Add. MS 37157, ff. 2v-3.

HrE 6 -----

Copy, transcribed from *The Last Remains of Sr John Suckling* (1659), in a miscellany; late 17th century.

This MS recorded in *The Works of Sir John Suckling: The Non-Dramatic Works*, ed. Thomas Clayton (Oxford, 1971), p. 98.

Yale, Osborn Collection, b 213, pp. 106-7.

HrE 7 *Ditty* ('Why dost thou hate return instead of love?').

Copy of the first stanza in Herbert's MS collection of his own poems; c. 1630-1.

First pub. in *Occasional Verses* (1665); Smith, pp. 56-7. This MS collated in Smith, p. 132.

British Library, Add. MS 37157, f. 17.

*HrE 8 *Echo in a Church* ('Where shall my troubled soul, at large').

Three successive autograph drafts, with revisions, in a collection of Herbert's papers formerly preserved at Powis Castle; [1625].

First pub. in *Occasional Verses* (1665); Smith, pp. 47-8. These MSS discussed in Rossi, III, 389-91. See FACSIMILE XIX.

Public Record Office, PRO.30/53/9/10, ff. 1, 2, 25v.

HrE 9 -----

Copy, untitled, in Herbert's MS collection of his own poems; c. 1630-1.

This MS collated in Smith, p. 131, with a facsimile after p. xxiv.

British Library, Add. MS 37157, f. 25.

HrE 10 -----

Copy, headed 'The Ecchoe', in a verse miscellany owned by one Peter Daniell; c. 1630s-40s.

Bodleian, MS Eng. poet. c. 50, f. 55.

Echo in a Church

HrE 11 -----

Copy in a musical setting by Henry Lawes, in Lawes's autograph songbook; mid-17th century.

Facsimile of f. 83 of this MS in Pamela J. Willetts, *The Henry Lawes Manuscript* (London, 1969), plate I.

British Library, Add. MS 53723, ff. 82v-3.

--- *Echo to a Rock* ('Thou heaven-threat'ning Rock, gentler then she').

[Smith, pp. 46-7].

See INTRODUCTION.

*HrE 12 *Elegy for Doctor Dunn* ('What though the vulgar and received praise').

Copy, with seven autograph corrections and revisions, in Herbert's MS collection of his own poems; c. 1631.

First pub. in *Occasional Verses* (1665); Smith, pp. 57-9. This MS collated in Smith, p. 132.

British Library, Add. MS 37157, ff. 19-20v.

HrE 13 *Elegy for the Prince* ('Must he be ever dead? Cannot we add').

Copy in a composite volume of verse and prose owned c. 1669 by one John Cooke of Bury St Edmunds, Suffolk; c. 1620s-30s.

First pub. among 'Sundry Funeral Elegies' appended to Joshua Sylvester, *Lachrymae Lachrymarum*, 3rd edition (London, 1613); *Occasional Verses* (1665); Smith, pp. 22-4. This MS collated in Smith, pp. 127-8.

Bodleian, MS Rawl. poet. 26, f. 91.

HrE 14 -----

Copy, headed 'SCH his Eligie', transcribed from HrE 15, in a verse miscellany possibly compiled by a member of an Inn of Court; c. 1630s.

This MS collated in Smith, pp. 127-8.

British Library, Add. MS 21433, ff. 169-70v.

HrE 15 -----

Copy, headed 'S^{r} Ed. H. his Elegy on Prince Harry', in a miscellany possibly compiled by a member of an Inn of Court; c. 1620s-30s.

This MS collated in Smith, pp. 127-8.

British Library, Add. MS 25303, ff. 81v-2v.

HrE 16 -----

Copy, headed 'One Prince Henery an Elegy by S^{r} Ed: Her:', in a verse miscellany possibly compiled by a member of an Inn of Court; c. 1620s.

This MS collated in Smith, pp. 127-8.

British Library, Harley MS 3910, ff. 119v-20v.

HrE 17 -----

Copy, subscribed 'Sr Edwarde Harbort one the Prince', in a MS volume of poems chiefly by John Donne, bound in a composite volume of MSS; c. 1620-33.

This MS collated in Smith, pp. 127-8.

Cambridge University Library, MS Ee. 4. 14, ff. 70v-1.

HrE 18 -----

Copy in the hand of Sir Robert Phelips (1586?-1638), endorsed 'S^{r}. E^{d} Herbert of the prin[ce]', among the papers of the Phelips family of Montacute House, Somerset; early 17th century.

Somerset Record Office, DD/PH221/51.

HrE 19 -----

Copy in a miscellany entitled *A Collection of Witt and Learning*; c. 1677-81.

Yale, Osborn Collection, b 54, p. 882.

*HrE 20 *Elegy over a Tomb* ('Must I then see, alas! eternal night').

Copy, with three autograph corrections or revisions, in Herbert's MS collection of his own poems; c. 1630-1.

First pub. in *Occasional Verses* (1665); Smith, pp. 32-4. This MS collated in Smith, p. 129.

British Library, Add. MS 37157, ff. 3v-4.

HrE 21 *Epitaph. Caecil. Boulstr.* ('Methinks Death like one laughing lyes').

Copy, headed 'On Mrs. Bulstreed', in a MS volume of poems chiefly by John Donne compiled by Henry Champernowne (1600-56) of Dartington, Devon; c. 1623.

First pub. in *Occasional Verses* (1665); Smith, pp. 20-1. This MS collated in Smith, p. 127.

Bodleian, MS Eng. poet. f. 9, p. 207.

Epitaph. Caecil. Boulstr.

HrE 22 -----

Copy, headed 'Another Sir Edw: Harbert', in a verse miscellany; c. 1620-33.

This MS collated in Smith, p. 127.

Bodleian, MS Rawl. poet. 31, ff. 36v-7.

HrE 23 -----

Copy, headed 'Another', in a verse miscellany; c. 1620-33.

This MS collated in Smith, p. 127.

British Library, Harley MS 4064, ff. 261v-2.

HrE 24 -----

Copy of lines 11-21, untitled, here beginning 'This mightie warrier was deceived yet', in a MS volume of poems chiefly by John Donne once owned by one Meriall Tracy; c. 1620-33.

Huntington, HM 198, Part II, f. 8.

HrE 25 -----

Copy of lines 1-2, untitled, in a MS volume of poems chiefly by John Donne; c. 1622-33.

Yale, Osborn Collection, b 148, p. 150.

HrE 26 *Epitaph of a stinking Poet* ('Here stinks a Poet, I confess').

Copy, headed 'An Epitaph on one who had a stinking breath' and here beginning 'Here lyes one stinks I must confesse', in a miscellany compiled by an Oxford man, possibly a member of Brasenose College; c. late 1630s.

First pub. in *Occasional Verses* (1665); Smith, p. 29.

Huntington, HM 116, p. 166.

HrE 27 -----

Copy, headed 'On a stinking breath' and here beginning 'Haere lies one stinks I must confesse', in a verse miscellany compiled by one Robert Bishop; c. 1630.

Rosenbach Foundation, MS 1083/16, p. 105.

*HrE 28 *Epitaph on Sir Edward Saquevile's Child, who dyed in his Birth* ('Reader, here lies a Child that never cry'd').

Copy, headed 'On my L. of Dorsets first sonne', with Herbert's autograph addition 'who dyed in his birth', in Herbert's MS collection of his own poems; c. 1630-1.

First pub. in *Occasional Verses* (1665); Smith, p. 30. This MS collated in Smith, p. 128.

British Library, Add. MS 37157, f. 1v.

HrE 29 *Epitaph on Sir Philip Sidney lying in St. Paul's without a Monument* ('Within this Church Sir Philip Sidney lies').

Copy, untitled, in a verse miscellany compiled by John Cruso (1618-81) of Gonville and Caius College, Cambridge; c. 1630s.

First pub. in *Wits Recreations* (London, 1640); *Occasional Verses* (1665); Smith, p. 53. This MS collated in Smith, p. 132.

St John's College, Cambridge, MS U. 26 (James 548), p. 127.

*HrE 30 *Euryale maerens* ('Depressae valles piceis irriguae fontibus').

Four autograph drafts, early versions of parts of the poem, among Herbert's papers formerly preserved at Powis Castle; [1632].

First pub. in *Occasional Verses* (1665); Smith, p. 93. These MSS discussed in Rossi, III, 391.

National Library of Wales, Powis MSS (1959 deposit), Series II, Bundle XIX, No. 6.

*HrE 31 *The first Meeting* ('As sometimes with a sable Cloud').

Copy, with four autograph corrections and revisions, in Herbert's MS collection of his own poems; c. 1630-1.

First pub. in *Occasional Verses* (1665); Smith, pp. 39-42. This MS collated in Smith, p. 130.

British Library, Add. MS 37157, ff. 7v-8v.

*HrE 32 *For a Dyal* ('Discurrens dubiae placidus compendia vitae').

Autograph, with one alteration, written on the back end-paper of Herbert's printed exemplum of Antonio de Herrera, *Tercera parte de la historia general del mundo* (Madrid, 1612); 12 September 1622.

First pub. in *Occasional Verses* (1665); Smith, p. 89. Facsimile of this MS in Sotheby's sale catalogue, 20 March 1967.

Sotheby's, 20 March 1967 (Powis Castle Sale), Lot 176; Dawson's catalogue No. 208, item 108, sold to Deighton Bell; unlocated.

*HrE 33 *The Green-Sickness Beauty* ('From thy pale look, while angry Love doth seem').

Copy of a seven-stanza version, with an autograph correction, in Herbert's MS collection of his own poems; c. 1630-1.

First pub. in *Occasional Verses* (1665); Smith, pp. 68-9. This MS collated and the last two stanzas printed in Smith, pp. 134-5.

British Library, Add. MS 37157, ff. 11v-12.

*HrE 34 *The Green-Sickness Beauty* ('Though the pale white within your cheeks compos'd').

Copy, with an autograph alteration, in Herbert's MS collection of his own poems; c. 1630-1.

First pub. in *Le Prince d'Amour* (London, 1660); *Occasional Verses* (1665); Smith, pp. 67-8. This MS collated in Smith, p. 134.

British Library, Add. MS 37157, ff. 12v-13.

*HrE 35 *Haered. ac nepot. suis praecepta & consilia* ('Si tibi chara Dei sunt Jussa, & Jussa Parentis').

Autograph, with revisions, of an early 110-line version, among Herbert's papers formerly preserved at Powis Castle; 1642.

First pub. subjoined to *De causis errorum* (London, 1645); Smith, pp. 106-18. This MS discussed in Rossi, III, 391-2.

National Library of Wales, Powis MSS (1959 deposit), Series II, Bundle XIX, No. 1.

*HrE 36 *The Idea, Made of Alnwick in his Expedition to Scotland with the Army, 1639* ('All Beauties vulgar eyes on earth do see').

Autograph of an early, 84-line version, now contained in an opening glass frame in a navy blue box, among Herbert's papers formerly preserved at Powis Castle.

First pub. in *Occasional Verses* (1665); Smith, pp. 75-9. This MS discussed in Frank J. Warnke, 'Two Previously Unnoted MSS. of Poems by Lord Herbert of Cherbury', *N & Q*, 199 (April 1954), 141-2.

National Library of Wales, Powis MSS (1965 deposit).

--- *Imilce pleads that her son may not be sacrificed* ('What is this with blood to stain').

[Smith, p. 99].

A translation of Silius Italicus's lines, attributed by Smith to Herbert, appears in *A Dialogue between a Tutor and his Pupil* (see INTRODUCTION).

--- *'Iris caeruleo fluore cingens'*.

See INTRODUCTION.

HrE 37 *Kissing* ('Come hither Womankind, and all their worth').

Copy of a version headed 'More diuersity of kissing' and beginning at line 5 (here 'The sweetly melting kisse that doth consume'), in a verse miscellany compiled by one Robert Bishop; c. 1630.

First pub. in *Occasional Verses* (1665); Smith, pp. 30-1.

Rosenbach Foundation, MS 1083/16, pp. 279-80.

--- *'...My Lord, I suit my garments to my minde'*.

See INTRODUCTION.

*HrE 38 *An Ode upon a Question moved, Whether Love should continue for ever?* ('Having interr'd her Infant-birth').

Copy of a 38-stanza version, with several autograph corrections and revisions, in Herbert's MS collection of his own poems; c. 1630-1.

First pub. in *Occasional Verses* (1665); Smith, pp. 61-6. This MS collated and the last three stanzas printed in Smith, pp. 133-4; facsimile of f. 13v in Smith, after p. xxiv.

British Library, Add. MS 37157, ff. 13v-16v.

--- *On y[e] Death of S[r]. Th. Pelham* ('Merely for Death to grieve, and mourne').

See INTRODUCTION.

--- *An opposite to Melancholy* ('Returne my Joyes, and hither bring').

See INTRODUCTION.

HrE 39 *Sonnet* ('Innumerable Beauties, thou white haire').

Copy in Herbert's MS collection of his own poems; c. 1630-1.

First pub. (from this MS) in Smith (1923), p. 97.

British Library, Add. MS 37157, f. 17.

*HrE 40 *Sonnet* ('You well compacted Groves, whose light & shade').

Copy, with an autograph revision, headed 'Sonnet', with Herbert's autograph addition 'at Merlou 1620 in France', in Herbert's MS collection of his own poems; c. 1630-1.

First pub. in *Occasional Verses* (1665); Smith, p. 54. This MS collated in Smith, p. 132.

British Library, Add. MS 37157, f. 10v.

HrE 41 *Sonnet of Black Beauty* ('Black beauty, which above that common light').

Copy in Herbert's MS collection of his own poems; c. 1630-1.

First pub. in *Occasional Verses* (1665); Smith, p. 38. Printed from this MS in Norman Ault, *Seventeenth Century Lyrics*, 2nd edition (New York, 1950), p. 3; collated in Smith, p. 130.

British Library, Add. MS 37157, f. 7.

*HrE 42 *'Tears, flow no more, or if you needs must flow'.*

Copy, with an autograph revision, headed by Herbert 'Ditty', in Herbert's MS collection of his own poems; c. 1630-1.

First pub. in *Occasional Verses* (1665); Smith, p. 26. This MS collated in Smith, p. 128.

British Library, Add. MS 37157, f. 2.

HrE 43 -----

Copy in a verse miscellany appended to a MS volume of poems by John Donne; c. 1630s.

Formerly MS G. 2. 21, p. 357; this MS collated in Smith, p. 128.

Trinity College, Dublin, MS 877, f. 191v.

HrE 44 -----

Copy in a MS volume of poems chiefly by Henry King belonging to the Stoughton family of Warwick; c. 1636.

Owned by Rosemary Williams, London, Stoughton MS, pp. 95-6.

--- *'...The being yours can make even Vices good'.*

See INTRODUCTION.

HrE 45 *The Thought* ('If you do love, as well as I').

Copy in Herbert's MS collection of his own poems; c. 1630-1.

First pub. in *Occasional Verses* (1665); Smith, pp. 43-4. This MS collated in Smith, p. 131.

British Library, Add. MS 37157, f. 9r-v.

HrE 46 -----

Copy in a musical setting by John Wilson in Wilson's corrected MS volume of his own songs; possibly in Wilson's autograph or else in the hand of someone similarly associated with Edward Lowe (c.1610-82); c. 1656.

This MS collated in John P. Cutts, 'Seventeenth Century Lyrics', *MD*, 10 (1956), 142-209 (p. 168).

Bodleian, MS Mus. b. 1, ff. 51-3.

HrE 47 -----

Copy in a composite volume of verse belonging to the Skipwith family of Cotes, Leicestershire; early-mid-17th century.

This MS collated in Smith, p. 131.

British Library, Add. MS 25707, f. 156r-v.

HrE 48 -----

Copy in a verse miscellany compiled by Peter Calfe (1610-67) and his son Peter (d. 1693); c. 1642-50.

This MS collated in Smith, p. 131.

British Library, Harley MS 6918, ff. 20v-1.

HrE 49 -----

Copy in a verse miscellany owned in 1640 by Anthony St John (1618-73) and Ann St John, of Bletsoe, Bedfordshire; c. 1630s.

Harvard, fMS Eng 626, ff. 18v-19.

HrE 50 -----

Copy in a verse miscellany; c. 1630.

Rosenbach Foundation, MS 239/23, pp. 47-8.

HrE 51 -----

Copy, here ascribed to 'Ro: Herrick', in a verse miscellany once owned by Sir Henry Spelman (1564?-1641); c. 1630s.

South African Library, Cape Town, MS Grey 7 a 29, pp. 134-5.

--- *'Tis not enough for one that is a wife'.*

See INTRODUCTION.

HrE 52 *To a Lady who did sing excellently* ('When our rude & unfashion'd words, that long').

Copy in Herbert's MS collection of his own poems; c. 1630-1.

First pub. in *Occasional Verses* (1665); Smith, pp. 44-5. This MS collated in Smith, p. 131.

British Library, Add. MS 37157, f. 1r-v.

--- *To Dianas earthly Deputesse of my Worthy Sister Mrs Jane Carye* ('When daies cleare light his compast course hath runne').

See INTRODUCTION.

HrE 53 *To her Body* ('Regardful Presence! whose fix'd Majesty').

Copy in a verse miscellany; c. 1620-33.

First pub. in *Occasional Verses* (1665); Smith, pp. 5-6. This MS collated in Smith, p. 126.

Bodleian, MS Rawl. poet. 31, ff. 15v-16.

*HrE 54 *To her Eyes* ('Black eyes if you seem dark').

Copy, with three autograph corrections, in Herbert's MS collection of his own poems; c. 1630-1.

First pub. in *Occasional Verses* (1665); Smith, pp. 35-6. This MS collated in Smith, p. 129.

British Library, Add. MS 37157, f. 5r-v.

HrE 55 *To her Face* ('Fatal Aspect! that hast an Influence').

Copy in a verse miscellany; c. 1620-33.

First pub. in *Occasional Verses* (1665); Smith, p. 5. This MS collated in Smith, p. 125.

Bodleian, MS Rawl. poet. 31, f. 15v.

HrE 56 -----

Copy in a MS volume of poems chiefly by John Donne once owned by one Meriall Tracy; c. 1620-33.

Huntington, HM 198, Part II, f. 7r-v.

*HrE 57 *To her Hair* ('Black beamy hairs, which so seem to arise').

Copy, with eight autograph corrections and revisions, in Herbert's MS collection of his own poems; c. 1630-1.

First pub. in *Occasional Verses* (1665); Smith, pp. 37-8. This MS collated in Smith, p. 130.

British Library, Add. MS 37157, f. 6r-v.

HrE 58 *To her Mind* ('Exalted Mind! whose Character doth bear').

Copy, here beginning 'Exalted minde, that guid'st thee beautious spheare', in a verse miscellany; c. 1620-33.

First pub. in *Occasional Verses* (1665); Smith, p. 6. This MS collated in Smith, p. 126.

Bodleian, MS Rawl. poet. 31, f. 16.

HrE 59 -----

Copy in a MS volume of poems chiefly by John Donne once owned by one Meriall Tracy; c. 1620-33.

Huntington, HM 198, Part II, f. 7v.

HrE 60 *To his Friend Ben. Johnson, of his Horace made English* (''Twas not enough, Ben Johnson, to be thought').

Copy in a MS volume of poems by Ben Jonson transcribed by one 'S.H.' (born 1665) from *Horace: his Art of Poetry* (London, 1640); c. 1680.

First pub. in Ben Jonson, *Horace: his Art of Poetry* (London, 1640); *Occasional Verses* (1665); Smith, pp. 19-20.

Edinburgh University Library, MS Dc. 7. 94, f. 19v.

*HrE 61 *To his Mistress for her true Picture* ('Death, my lifes Mistress, and the soveraign Queen').

Copy, with at least twelve autograph corrections and revisions, headed 'To my M^tris &c.', in Herbert's MS collection of his own poems; c. 1630-1.

First pub. in *Occasional Verses* (1665); Smith, pp. 48-53. This MS collated in Smith, pp. 131-2.

British Library, Add. MS 37157, ff. 21v-4.

*HrE 62 *To Mrs. Diana Cecyll* ('Diana Cecyll, that rare beauty thou dost show').

Copy, with two autograph revisions, in Herbert's MS collection of his own poems; c. 1630-1.

First pub. in *Occasional Verses* (1665); Smith, pp. 34-5. This MS collated in Smith, p. 129.

British Library, Add. MS 37157, ff. 4v-5.

HrE 63 -----

Copy in a composite volume of verse collected by Elias Ashmole (1617-92); mid-17th century.

This MS collated in Smith, p. 129.

Bodleian, MS Ashmole 36/37, f. 305.

HrE 64 -----

Copy in a verse miscellany compiled by one 'H.S.', a Cambridge man; c. 1640s-50s.

This MS collated in Smith, p. 129.

Bodleian, MS Rawl. poet. 147, p. 75.

To Mrs. Diana Cecyll

HrE 65 -----

Copy, omitting the first two words, transcribed from HrE 66, in a verse miscellany possibly compiled by a member of an Inn of Court; c. 1620s-30s.

This MS collated in Smith, p. 129.

British Library, Add. MS 21433, ff. 96v-7.

HrE 66 -----

Copy, omitting the first two words, in a miscellany possibly compiled by a member of an Inn of Court; c. 1620s-30s.

This MS collated in Smith, p. 129.

British Library, Add. MS 25303, f. 92v.

HrE 67 -----

Copy, omitting the first two words, in a miscellany once owned by Sir Thomas Meres (1634-1715) of Kirton, Lincolnshire; c. 1640s.

This MS collated in Smith, p. 129.

British Library, Egerton MS 2725, f. 65.

HrE 68 -----

Copy, untitled, in a verse miscellany possibly compiled by a member of an Inn of Court; c. 1620s.

This MS collated in Smith, p. 129.

British Library, Harley MS 3910, ff. 59v-60.

HrE 69 -----

Copy, untitled, in a verse miscellany; c. 1640.

Folger, MS V. a. 319, f. 27r-v.

HrE 70 -----

Copy, untitled, in a verse miscellany; mid-17th century.

Folger, MS V. a. 322, p. 52.

HrE 71 -----

Copy, untitled and omitting the first two words, in a miscellany compiled by or for Sir Henry Cholmley, brother of Sir Hugh Cholmley (1600-57); c. 1624-41.

Harvard, MS Eng 703, f. 19.

HrE 72 -----

Copy, untitled and omitting the first two words, in a verse miscellany owned by Edward Denny, Charles Cokes, Edward Randolpe, and Thomas Cassy; c. 1630s.

Huntington, HM 198, Part I, p. 166.

HrE 73 -----

Copy in a verse miscellany appended to a MS volume of poems by John Donne; c. 1630s.

Formerly MS G. 2. 21, p. 307, this MS collated in Smith, p. 129.

Trinity College, Dublin, MS 877, f. 166r-v.

HrE 74 *To one Blacke, and not very Hansome, who expected coṁendation* ('What though your eyes bee starres, your haire, bee night').

Copy in Herbert's MS collection of his own poems; c. 1630-1.

First pub. (from this MS) in Smith (1923), pp. 97-8.

British Library, Add. MS 37157, ff. 17v-18.

*HrE 75 *To the C. of D.* ('Since in your face, as in a beauteous sphere').

Copy, with an autograph correction, in Herbert's MS collection of his own poems; c. 1630-1.

First pub. in *Occasional Verses* (1665); Smith, p. 55. This MS collated in Smith, p. 132.

British Library, Add. MS 37157, f. 21.

HrE 76 -----

Copy, untitled and deleted, in Herbert's MS collection of his own poems; c. 1630-1.

British Library, Add. MS 37157, f. 10.

(2) POEMS OF UNCERTAIN AUTHORSHIP

HrE 77 *Inconstancy* ('Inconstancy's the greatest of synns').

Copy, untitled and ascribed to 'Sir Edw: Harbert', in a verse miscellany; c. 1620-33.

First pub. (from this MS) in Smith (1923), p. 119.

Bodleian, MS Rawl. poet. 31, f. 36.

Inconstancy

HrE 78 -----

Copy, untitled, in a verse miscellany; c. 1620-33.

Printed from this MS in Frank J. Warnke, 'Two Previously Unnoted MSS. of Poems by Lord Herbert of Cherbury', *N & Q*, 199 (April 1954), 141-2.

British Library, Harley MS 4064, f. 259v.

HrE 78.5 See Addenda, p. 629.

HrE 79 *Ode: Of our Sense of Sinne* ('Vengeance will sit above our faults; but till').

Copy, untitled and here ascribed to 'JD', in a MS volume of poems chiefly by John Donne compiled by Henry Champernowne (1600-56) of Dartington, Devon; c. 1623.

First pub. in John Donne, *Poems* (London, 1635); *The Poems of John Donne*, ed. Herbert J.C. Grierson (Oxford, 1912), I, 350; Smith, pp. 119-20. This MS collated in Grierson and in Smith, p. 139.

Bodleian, MS Eng. poet. f. 9, pp. 81-2.

HrE 80 -----

Copy, ascribed to 'S[r] Edw. Herbert', in a verse miscellany; c. 1620-33.

This MS collated in Grierson and in Smith, p. 139.

Bodleian, MS Rawl. poet. 31, f. 13v.

HrE 81 -----

Copy in a verse miscellany; c. 1620-33.

This MS collated in Grierson and in Smith, p. 139.

British Library, Harley MS 4064, f. 241v.

HrE 82 -----

Copy, untitled, in a verse miscellany; c. 1637.

This MS collated in Smith, p. 139.

British Library, Stowe MS 962, f. 209.

HrE 83 -----

Copy, untitled, in a MS volume of Donne's poems (the 'Carnaby MS'); c. 1620-33.

This MS collated in Grierson and in Smith, p. 139.

Harvard, fMS Eng 966.1, f. 41r-v.

HrE 84 -----

Copy, untitled, in a MS volume of works by Donne (the 'Dobell MS'); c. 1623-33.

Harvard, fMS Eng 966.4, f. 211v.

HrE 85 -----

Copy in a MS volume of Donne's poems completed on 12 October 1632 and corrected after 1633 by two other hands (the 'O'Flahertie MS').

This MS collated in Grierson and in Smith, p. 139.

Harvard, MS Eng 966.5, f. 28v.

HrE 86 -----

Copy, untitled, in a MS volume of Donne's poems (the 'Stephens MS'); 1620.

This MS collated in Grierson and in Smith, p. 139.

Harvard, MS Eng 966.6, f. 130v.

HrE 87 -----

Copy, untitled, in a MS volume of poems chiefly by Donne; c. 1620s.

Harvard, MS Eng 966.7, f. 22v.

HrE 88 -----

Copy, untitled, in a MS volume of Donne's poems once owned by John Egerton, first Earl of Bridgewater (1579-1649); c. 1622-33.

This MS collated in Grierson and in Smith, p. 139.

Huntington, EL 6893, f. 32.

HrE 89 -----

Copy, untitled and here ascribed to 'J[ohn] D[onne]', in a volume of poems chiefly by Donne once owned by one Meriall Tracy; c. 1620-33.

Huntington, HM 198, Part II, ff. 11v-12.

HrE 90 -----

Copy, here ascribed to 'J[ohn]. D[onne]', written on the back of the title leaf of a printed exemplum of Donne's *Deaths Duell* (London, 1633); mid-17th century.

Princeton, Robert H. Taylor Collection.

Ode: Of our Sense of Sinne

HrE 91 -----

Copy, untitled, in a MS volume of poems chiefly by Donne; c. 1622-33.

Yale, Osborn Collection, b 148, pp. 93-4.

--- *To a Lady that desired I would love her* ('Now you have freely given me leave to love').

[Smith, pp. 122-3].

See VOLUME II: THOMAS CAREW.

PROSE

*HrE 92 [*Address to the King on the Present Estate of the Kingdom and Foreign Affairs*].

Autograph fair copy, with alterations, of a memorial beginning 'My most gratious Soveraine. It is observd amonge Statesmen that wise Princes have ever receivd their Counsailors advises in forraine affaires...', among Herbert's papers formerly preserved at Powis Castle; 3 leaves; 10 April 1635.

First pub. (from this MS) in a condensed form in W.J. Smith, *Herbert Correspondence* (Cardiff, 1963), pp. 86-8; discussed in Rossi, II, 475-85, and III, 542.

National Library of Wales, Powis MSS (1959 deposit), Series II, Bundle XII, No. 10.

*HrE 93 [*Advice to the King during the War with Spain*].

Autograph draft, with revisions, of a memorial to the King, in a collection of Herbert's papers formerly preserved at Powis Castle; 1624.

Unpublished; discussed in Rossi, II, 407-16, and III, 542.

Public Record Office, PRO.30/53/9/10, ff. 3-20.

*HrE 94 *Autobiography.*

Draft in the hand of an amanuensis, with revisions entered in another hand, one or two possibly in Herbert's autograph; imperfect, consisting of pp. 13-28, 33-72, 85-100, 105-20, 137-44; in a blue binding lettered 'Life of Lord Herbert of Cherbury', among Herbert's papers formerly preserved at Powis Castle; c. 1643.

First pub. Strawberry Hill, 1764, ed. Horace Walpole; edited from this MS in *The Life of Edward, First Lord Herbert of Cherbury written by himself*, ed. J.M. Shuttleworth (London, 1976). This MS discussed (as 'AuE') in Shuttleworth, pp. xviii-xx, with a facsimile of p. 58 facing p. 4; discussed (as 'Draft A') in R.I. Aaron, 'The "Autobiography" of Edward, First Lord Herbert of Cherbury: The Original Manuscript Material', *MLR*, 36 (1941), 184-94, with a facsimile of p. 59 facing p. 161; and (as MS 'E') in Rossi, III, 508-20. N.B. the revisions are not all autograph.

National Library of Wales, Powis MSS (1965 deposit).

HrE 95 -----

Copy of the complete work, transcribed from a lost intermediate MS ('AuX'), with alterations in three other hands; the MS used for Horace Walpole's edition; in a brown binding lettered 'The Life of Edward Lord Herbert of Cherbury written by Himself', among the Herbert family papers formerly preserved at Powis Castle; late 17th-early 18th century.

Text corrected from this MS in Shuttleworth and discussed (as 'AuW') pp. xx-xxi; discussed (as 'Draft B') in Aaron, and (as MS 'W') in Rossi, III, 508-20. See also HrE 95.5

National Library of Wales, Powis MSS (1965 deposit).

HrE 95.5 See Addenda, p. 629.

--- -----

See also HrE 136-8.

*HrE 96 *De causis errorum.*

Single autograph leaf, part of the first draft, among Herbert's papers formerly preserved at Powis castle.

First pub. London, 1645; facsimile of this edition introduced by Günter Gawlick (Stuttgart, 1966). This MS recorded in Rossi, III, 490-1.

National Library of Wales, Powis MSS (1959 deposit), Series II, Bundle XIX, No. 6 (III).

*HrE 97 -----

Part of the autograph first draft, on 26 leaves irregularly numbered from 104 to 128 (?), among Herbert's papers formerly preserved at Powis Castle.

This MS recorded in Rossi, III, 490-1.

National Library of Wales, Powis MSS (1959 deposit), Series II, (Envelope) Taken from Bundle 26.

*HrE 98 -----

Single autograph leaf, headed 'Rectum Judex sui et obliqui', part of the second draft, among Herbert's papers formerly preserved at Powis Castle.

De causis errorum

This MS recorded in Rossi, III, 490-1.

National Library of Wales, Powis MSS (1959 deposit), Series II, Bundle XIX, No. 6 (I).

*HrE 99 -----

Autograph second draft of part of the work, on 46 pages, among Herbert's papers formerly preserved at Powis Castle.

This MS recorded in Rossi, III, 490-1.

National Library of Wales, Powis MSS (1959 deposit), Series II, Bundle XIX, No. 6 (IV).

*HrE 100 -----

Autograph third draft of part of the work, on 41 pages, among Herbert's papers formerly preserved at Powis Castle.

This MS recorded in Rossi, III, 490-1.

National Library of Wales, Powis MSS (1959 deposit), Series II, Bundle XIX, No. 5a.

*HrE 101 -----

Autograph third draft of part of the work, on 35 leaves, the pages numbered 41-67, among Herbert's papers formerly preserved at Powis Castle.

This MS recorded in Rossi, III, 490-1.

National Library of Wales, Powis MSS (1959 deposit), Series II, Bundle XIX, No. 7.

HrE 102 -----

Copy of part of the work, on 34 pages, inscribed by the third Baron Herbert of Cherbury 'De Causis Errorum (Manuscripts of my Grand Father given me by M[r] Edw: Griffith of Satten June 29. 1680 wherof I have...taken a catalogue', among Herbert family papers formerly preserved at Powis Castle.

This MS recorded in Rossi, III, 490-1.

National Library of Wales, Powis MSS (1959 deposit), Series II, Bundle XIX, No. 6 (II).

HrE 103 -----

Copy of part of the work, on pages numbered 42-59, among Herbert's papers formerly preserved at Powis Castle.

This MS recorded in Rossi, III, 490-1.

National Library of Wales, Powis MSS (1959 deposit), Series II, Bundle XIX, No. 5c.

HrE 104 -----

Fair copy of the complete work, on 143 numbered pages, among Herbert's papers formerly preserved at Powis Castle; 1640.

This MS recorded in Rossi, III, 490-1.

National Library of Wales, Powis MSS (1959 deposit), Series II, Bundle XIX, No. 6 (V).

*HrE 105 *De religione Gentilium.*

Autograph draft of the table of contents and part of Chapter I, among Herbert's papers formerly preserved at Powis Castle; c. 1642-4.

First pub. Amsterdam, 1663. This MS recorded in Rossi, III, 506.

National Library of Wales, Powis MSS (1959 deposit), Series II, Bundle XX, No. 1.

*HrE 106 -----

Draft of Chapters II-X, chiefly autograph, partly in the hand of an amanuensis, on 126 pages, among Herbert's papers formerly preserved at Powis Castle; c. 1642-4.

This MS recorded in Rossi, III, 506.

National Library of Wales, Powis MSS (1959 deposit), Series II, Bundle XIX, No. 5b.

*HrE 107 -----

Autograph draft of 'Pars secunda' and 'Pars tertia', among Herbert's papers formerly preserved at Powis Castle; c. 1642-4.

This MS recorded in Rossi, III, 506.

National Library of Wales, Powis MS (1959 deposit), Series II, Bundle XX, No. 2.

*HrE 108 -----

Two leaves of autograph alterations to the original draft, among Herbert's papers formerly preserved at Powis Castle; c. 1642-4.

This MS recorded in Rossi, III, 506.

National Library of Wales, Powis MSS (1959 deposit), Series II, (Envelope) Taken from Bundle 26.

HrE 109 -----

Copy of the complete work, among Herbert's papers formerly preserved at Powis Castle; c. 1642-4.

This MS recorded in Rossi, III, 507.

National Library of Wales, Powis MSS (1959 deposit), Series II, Bundle XX, No. 3.

--- *De religione laici.*

See HrE 130-5.

*HrE 110 *De veritate.*

Autograph early draft; untitled; dated 20 July 1619.

First pub. Paris, 1624; translated by Meyrick H. Carré (Bristol, 1937); facsimile of the 1645 London edition introduced by Günter Gawlick (Stuttgart, 1966). This MS discussed in Rossi, III, 412-16, and in Gawlick, pp. xi-xii; for an account of its history see H.F.J. Vaughan, 'Lord Herbert of Chirbury's MSS.', *Transactions of the Shropshire Archaeological Society*, 1st Ser. 3 (1880), 353-77.

British Library, Add. MS 7081.

*HrE 111 -----

Copy, with autograph revisions; imperfect; the dedication dated 15 December 1622; [1622-3].

This MS discussed in Rossi, III, 416-17, and in Gawlick, pp. xii-xiii. Facsimile of two pages in Greg, *English Literary Autographs*, plate XLIX (a-b).

British Library, Sloane MS 3957.

*HrE 112 -----

Autograph draft, heavily revised, bound in two volumes; dated Paris, 20/30 June 1623.

These MSS discussed in Rossi, III, 417, and in Gawlick, p. xiii.

St John's College, Cambridge, MSS I. 5, 6 (James 306, 307).

*HrE 113 *A designe for a perpetuall intertainment of about 15,000 Foote and 3000 Horse for his Maties service.*

Autograph draft, in a collection of Herbert's papers formerly preserved at Powis Castle; 14 February 1625.

First pub. (from this MS) in Rossi, III, 484-6.

Public Record Office, PRO.30/53/9/10, ff. 21-2v.

--- *A Dialogue between a Tutor and his Pupil.*

See INTRODUCTION.

--- *Expeditio in Ream Insulam.*

See HrE 114-20.

*HrE 114 *The Expedition to the Isle of Rhé.*

Autograph fair copy of the complete English version, with the dedicatory epistle to the King but without the preface; the MS presented by Herbert to Charles I, with some alterations and underlinings in an unidentified hand; in a green binding lettered 'Edward Lord Herbert of Cherbury's Commentaries of the Duke of Buckingham's Expedition to the Isle of Ré in France in 1627', among Herbert family papers formerly preserved at Powis Castle; c. 1630.

Latin version (*Expeditio in Ream Insulam*) first pub. London, 1656, ed. Timothy Baldwin; English version first pub. London, 1860, ed. Lord Powis, Philobiblon Society. This MS recorded in Rossi, III, 486-7.

National Library of Wales, Powis MSS (1965 deposit).

HrE 115 -----

Copy of Chapters III-VIII of the English version, among Herbert's papers formerly preserved at Powis Castle; c. 1630.

This MS recorded in Rossi, III, 486.

National Library of Wales, Powis MSS (1959 deposit), Series II, Bundle XVIII, No. 7c.

*HrE 116 -----

Autograph draft of the beginning of Chapter I of the English version, headed 'To the Corte'; two leaves; among Herbert's papers formerly preserved at Powis Castle; c. 1630.

This MS recorded in Rossi, III, 487.

National Library of Wales, Powis MSS (1959 deposit), Series II, Bundle XII, No. 9.

*HrE 117 -----

Autograph draft of the complete Latin version, among Herbert's papers formerly preserved at Powis Castle; 1630.

This MS recorded in Rossi, III, 487.

National Library of Wales, Powis MSS (1959 deposit), Series II, Bundle XVIII, No. 7b.

*HrE 118 -----

Autograph copy of the complete Latin version, with revisions, bound in yellow vellum, among Herbert's papers formerly preserved at Powis Castle; the dedicatory epistle to the King dated 1 August 1631.

Formerly P. II. XVIII. 7a; this MS recorded in Rossi, III, 487.

National Library of Wales, Powis MSS (1965 deposit).

The Expedition to the Isle of Rhê

HrE 119 -----

Copy of the complete Latin version, with a dedicatory epistle to the King dated 10 August 1630 and a preface 'Ad Lectorem'; c. 1630.

Bodleian, MS e. Mus. 95.

*HrE 120 -----

Autograph draft of the dedicatory epistle to Charles I, in Latin, among Herbert's papers formerly preserved at Powis Castle; dated Montgomery, 10 August 1630.

This MS recorded in Rossi, III, 487.

National Library of Wales, Powis MSS (1959 deposit), Series II, Bundle XVIII, No. 7d.

--- -----

See also INTRODUCTION.

*HrE 121 *The Life and Reign of King Henry VIII.*

Draft of the complete work, partly autograph, chiefly in the hand of an amanuensis with Herbert's revisions, and with some corrections and the dedicatory epistle in the hand of Thomas Master of New College, Oxford; bound in three volumes (MSS 71-3) together with some of Herbert's historical notes; with a fourth volume (MS 74) comprising a collection of relevant historical documents transcribed for Herbert by Thomas Master; 1634-8.

First pub. London, 1649; London, 1880 (with *Autobiography*). These MSS described in Rossi, III, 488-90. See also INTRODUCTION.

Bodleian, MSS Jesus College 71-4.

*HrE 122 -----

Copy in the hand of an amanuensis, with autograph revisions; c. 1638.

This MS described in Rossi, III, 490.

Bodleian, MS Ashmole 1143.

*HrE 123 -----

Copy, prefixed at p. iii by an autograph letter to John Rouse, Bodley's Librarian; given to the Bodleian by Herbert via Thomas Master; 1638.

This MS (s.c. 3074) recorded in Rossi, III, 490.

Bodleian, MS Bodl. 910.

*HrE 124 -----

Autograph rough draft of part of the work, on four leaves, among Herbert's papers formerly preserved at Powis Castle; c. 1634-8.

This MS recorded in Rossi, III, 490.

National Library of Wales, Powis MSS (1959 deposit), Series II, Bundle XVIII, No. 5b.

HrE 125 -----

Copy of part of the work, on 21 leaves of writing, among Herbert's papers formerly preserved at Powis Castle; c. 1634-8.

This MS recorded in Rossi, III, 490.

National Library of Wales, Powis MSS (1959 deposit), Series II, Bundle XVIII, No. 5a.

--- -----

See also INTRODUCTION.

--- *The Life of Edward, First Lord Herbert of Cherbury written by himself.*

See HrE 94-94.5.

*HrE 126 *The new Philosophy of Beauty.*

Autograph draft of the beginning of an unfinished work on aesthetics, among Herbert's papers formerly preserved at Powis Castle.

First pub. (from this MS) in Rossi (1947), III, 442-3.

National Library of Wales, Powis MSS (1959 deposit), Series II, (Envelope) Taken from Bundle 26.

HrE 127 *Of Knowledge and the Power cognitive in general.*

Copy of an English redaction in twelve chapters of part of an early version of Thomas Hobbes's *De corpore* (Chapters VII, VIII, XI, XII), possibly in the hand of Francis Herbert; with the sub-headings '1° De principiis cognitionis| 2° De principiis actionis'; 4 leaves; unfinished or perhaps imperfect; c. 1637-40?

First pub. (from this MS) in Mario M. Rossi, 'L'evoluzione del pensiero di Hobbes alla luce di un nuovo manuscritto', *Civilità Moderna*, 13 (1941), 125-50, 217-46, 366-402; reprinted in Rossi, *Alle fonti del deismo e del materialismo moderno* (Florence, 1942), pp. 104-19. Edited from this MS in Thomas Hobbes, *Critique du De Mundo de Thomas White*, ed. Jean Jacquot and Harold Whitmore Jones (Paris, 1973), Appendix II, pp. 448-60; also discussed in R.I. Aaron,

Of Knowledge and the Power cognitive in general

'A Possible Early Draft of Hobbes' *De Corpore*', *Mind*, 54 (1945), 342-56, and in Arrigo Pacchi, *Convenzione e ipotesi nella formazione della filosofia naturale di Thomas Hobbes* (Florence, 1965), pp. 15-18, 42 seq.

National Library of Wales, NLW. MS 5297E.

HrE 128 [*On the King's Supremacy in the Church*].

Copy, inscribed by someone on 14 May 1635 'shewed to his Grace the Arch Bpp of Canterbury by the Kings Command'; [1635].

First pub. (from this MS) in Herbert, *De religione laici*, ed. Harold R. Hutcheson (New Haven, 1944), pp. 183-6; discussed in Rossi, II, 485-95, and III, 542.

Public Record Office, SP.16/288/88.

HrE 129 -----

Copy in a volume of transcripts of state papers made by John Brydall; 1677.

Text corrected from this MS in Hutcheson; recorded in Rossi, II, 493, and III, 542.

The Queen's College, Oxford, MS 157, pp. 158-78.

--- *Quid laicus*.

See HrE 130-5.

*HrE 130 *Religio laici* [*in Latin*].

Autograph first draft, incomplete, on four pages, among Herbert's papers formerly preserved at Powis Castle; c. 1643-4.

First pub. as *De religione laici*, with *De causis errorum* &c (London, 1645); facsimile of this edition introduced by Günter Gawlick (Stuttgart, 1966); edited and translated by Harold R. Hutcheson (New Haven, 1944). This MS described in Rossi, III, 504.

National Library of Wales, Powis MSS (1959 deposit), Series II, Bundle XIX, (no number).

*HrE 131 -----

Series of leaves belonging to the second autograph draft, among Herbert's papers formerly preserved at Powis Castle; c. 1643-4.

This MS described in Rossi, III, 504.

National Library of Wales, Powis MSS (1959 deposit), Series II, Bundle XIX, (no number).

*HrE 132 -----

Autograph fair copy of the complete work, among Herbert's papers formerly preserved at Powis Castle; c. 1643-5.

This MS described in Rossi, III, 504-5.

National Library of Wales, Powis MSS (1959 deposit), Series II, Bundle XIX, No. 6 ('43').

*HrE 133 -----

Autograph draft, the title deleted, on 14 leaves, among Herbert's papers formerly preserved at Powis Castle.

This MS recorded in Rossi, III, 505.

National Library of Wales, Powis MSS (1959 deposit), Series II, (Envelope) Taken from Bundle 26.

*HrE 134 -----

Autograph early draft of the *Quid laicus*, entitled 'Resp. J.G. petentis Quid Laicus de relligione optima statuerit', on seven leaves of writing, among Herbert's papers formerly preserved at Powis Castle; c. 1643-4.

This MS recorded in Rossi, III, 505.

National Library of Wales, Powis MSS (1959 deposit), Series II, Bundle XIX, No. 3.

HrE 135 -----

Fair copy of the complete work, entitled 'Appendix Libr. De Veritate', comprising (ff. 1-8) 'Religio laici' and (ff. 8v-10v) 'Quid laicus', in the hand of an amanuensis, among Herbert's papers formerly preserved at Powis Castle; c. 1643-5.

This MS described in Rossi, III, 505.

National Library of Wales, Powis MSS (1965 deposit).

HrE 136 *Religio Laici* [*in English*].

Copy of an independent English work entitled 'Religio Laici' and beginning 'Having [formerly] spoken of all Learning fitt to bee obtaynd in youth I shall say something of Religion...', in the hand of an amanuensis, with revisions entered in another hand; 9 leaves; c. 1642-4.

First pub. (from this MS) in Herbert G. Wright, 'An Unpublished Manuscript by Lord Herbert of Cherbury Entitled "Religio Laici"', *MLR*, 28 (1933), 295-307. This MS discussed in Rossi, III, 505; in R.I. Aaron, 'A Possible Early Draft of Hobbes' *De Corpore*', *Mind*, 54 (1945), 342-56 (pp. 354-5); in Gawlick, pp. xlvii-xlviii; and in Rossi, 'Herbert of Cherbury's *Religio Laici*: A Bibliographical Note', *Edinburgh Bibliographical Society Transactions*, 5, Part 2 (1962), 45-52 (where it is argued that the piece may belong to the *Autobiography*, but see HrE 138). N.B. the revisions are not autograph.

National Library of Wales, NLW. MS 5295E.

Religio Laici [in English]

*HrE 137 -----

Copy of a version of the English 'Religio Laici', with autograph revisions; 18 leaves (written on one side); c. 1642-5.

This MS discussed in S.E. Sprott, 'The Osler Manuscript of Herbert's *Religio Laici*', *The Library*, 5th Ser. 11 (1956), 120-2; but see also Rossi, *Edinburgh Bibliographical Society Transactions* (1962), 45-6 (n).

McGill University, Montreal, Osler Library, Cat. No. 4589.

HrE 138 -----

Copy of a version of the English 'Religio Laici', entitled 'Religio Laici offered to the consideration of all men (whether Dependants, or Independants) for the setling of some ffundamentall grounds of Religion' (pp. 1-40), followed by 'An Appendix to the Preists touching Religio Laici' (beginning 'If, notwithstanding the Preists of whatsoever Religious order, in whatsoever Country...') (pp. 41-59) and 'The common notions touching Religion' (beginning 'Being about to speake of Revelation, wee thinke fitt to premise certaine praecognita thereof...') (pp. 60-4); inscribed on the first page in another hand 'Lord Harbert'; 12°; mid-17th century.

Leconfield MS 129, this MS recorded in *HMC*, 6th Report (1877), pp. 312-13. The appendices are unpublished.

Owned by Lord Egremont, Petworth House, HMC MS 129.

HrE 139 [*Reply to D. Molin*].

Copy, among Herbert's papers formerly preserved at Powis Castle; September 1633.

Unpublished; discussed in Rossi, I, 474-5, 589 seq.; II, 524-5, and III, 542.

National Library of Wales, Powis MSS (1959 deposit), Series II, Bundle XXIX, No. 5g.

*HrE 140 -----

Autograph notes for the first five pages of Herbert's reply, among Herbert's papers formerly preserved at Powis Castle; September 1633.

This MS recorded in Rossi, III, 542 (n).

National Library of Wales, Powis MSS (1959 deposit), Series II, Bundle XIX, No. 5a.

*HrE 141 [*Reply to P. Mersenne*].

Autograph draft of Herbert's reply to Mersenne's objections to *De veritate*, among Herbert's papers formerly preserved at Powis Castle; [1638?].

Unpublished; discussed in Rossi, I, 481; II, 529-39, and III, 542.

National Library of Wales, Powis MS (1959 deposit), Series II, (Envelope) Taken from Bundle 26.

*HrE 142 [*Translation of Bacon's Elogium Elizabethae*].

Part of an autograph draft of Herbert's translation of Francis Bacon's *In felicem memoriam Elizabethae, Angliae Reginae*, beginning 'Indeed about the 10th of her Raigne, some tumults were attempted in the North', on four folio leaves, among Herbert's papers formerly preserved at Powis Castle; imperfect.

Unpublished; recorded in Rossi, III, 542. See also FRANCIS BACON, BcF 298-300.

National Library of Wales, Powis MSS (1959 deposit), Series II, (Envelope) Taken from Bundle 26.

*HrE 143 [*Translation of Descartes' Discours de la méthode*].

Autograph draft of Herbert's translation of Chapter IV and part of Chapter V of Descartes' *Discours*, beginning 'I know not whether I may entertaine you with my first Meditations...'; 6 leaves; formerly among Herbert's papers at Powis Castle; [1645?].

Unpublished; discussed in Rossi, II, 537-8, and III, 542. This MS sold at Sotheby's, 16 January 1956, Lot 216. A microfilm is in the British Library (M/471).

Harvard, MS Eng 995.

--- [*Translation of Hobbes's De principiis*].

See HrE 127.

MARGINALIA IN PRINTED BOOKS AND MANUSCRIPTS

See INTRODUCTION

MISCELLANEOUS

*HrE 144 [*Lute-Book*].

Herbert's MS lute-book, mainly autograph, partly in the hand of an amanuensis; inscribed by Herbert 'The Lutebooke of Edward Lord Herbert, of Cherbury and Castle Island, containing diverse selected Lessons of excellent Authors in severall Countreys. Wherein also are some few of my owne Composition'; formerly among Herbert's papers preserved at Powis Castle; c. 1624-40.

This MS described in Thurston Dart, 'Lord Herbert of Cherbury's Lute-Book', *M & L*, 38 (1957), 136-48, and in Rossi, III, 405-7.

Fitzwilliam Museum, Cambridge, MU 3 - 1956.

George Herbert

1593-1633

ABBREVIATIONS

Amy Charles Amy M. Charles, *A Life of George Herbert* (Ithaca & London, 1977).

Grosart *The Complete Works in Verse and Prose of George Herbert*, ed. Alexander B. Grosart, 3 vols (London, 1874).

Hutchinson *The Works of George Herbert*, ed. F. E. Hutchinson (Oxford, 1941; reprinted 1967).

Palmer *The English Works of George Herbert*, ed. George Herbert Palmer, 3 vols (London, 1905).

For abbreviations used throughout Volume I, see p.xi.

INTRODUCTION

There are two important MSS of Herbert's poems.

(1) The DR WILLIAMS MS (Dr Williams's Library, MS Jones B. 62). This MS is of special interest since it is the only MS of his poems known to have been handled by Herbert himself. Like the Tanner MS, it evidently came into the possession of Nicholas Ferrar (1593-1637), who was in effect Herbert's literary executor (the MS is known to have belonged to the Mapletoft family, with whom Ferrar was connected by the marriage of his niece); however, it is certainly not the 'little Book' which, according to Herbert's biographer, Izaak Walton (1670), Herbert gave on his death-bed to Edmund Duncon to convey to Ferrar for printing. It is a volume of 106 leaves (plus blanks) containing copies of early versions of 78 English poems in all, including several not subsequently published in *The Temple*. All are in the neat and conventional hand of a scribe, but the MS bears the author's distinctive autograph corrections and revisions throughout. The MS cannot be dated precisely, nor is it clear whether it was written and corrected at a particular time or over a period. It must have been written long enough before Herbert's death for him to have been able to make the further revisions to his poems which are represented in the Tanner MS. It may (as is argued in Amy Charles, p. 80 seq.) belong to his Cambridge years (1609-24). The volume concludes with a series of Latin poems, composed no earlier than 1623, and written entirely in Herbert's autograph. The first editor to make use of this MS was Grosart in 1874. It is fully collated in Hutchinson's edition, which also prints from it those poems not in the Tanner MS. A complete facsimile, introduced by Amy M. Charles, is published as *The Williams Manuscript of George Herbert's Poems* (Scholars' Facsimiles & Reprints, Delmar, New York, 1977). It should be noted that the view tentatively put forward by Amy Charles in her Life of Herbert (pp. 79-80, 214-16) that the Dr Williams MS may be in Herbert's autograph throughout is quite untenable.

(2) The TANNER MS (Bodleian, MS Tanner 307). This MS comprises 152 leaves and is a transcript of those poems (167 in all) which were subsequently published as *The Temple* (Cambridge, 1633). It was produced very shortly after Herbert's death for the Cambridge University licensers and was presumably copied from Herbert's final and definitive MS of his poems. It is likely that it was produced by a member of the Little Gidding community under the direct supervision of Nicholas Ferrar. The hand cannot be identified with certainty; that of one (or even both) of Ferrar's nieces, Anna and Mary Collett, has been suggested (see Amy Charles, pp. 182-4). The MS was later owned by Archbishop William Sancroft (1617-93) and by Bishop Thomas Tanner (1674-1735). A complete facsimile is published as *The Bodleian Manuscript of George Herbert's Poems* (Scholars' Facsimiles & Reprints, Delmar, New York, 1977). The Tanner MS was chosen as copy-text for Hutchinson's edition; however, its exact authority remains a matter of dispute: see Hutchinson, pp. l-lii, lxxii-lxxiv; J. Max Patrick, 'Critical Problems in Editing George Herbert's *The Temple*', *The Editor as Critic and the Critic as Editor* (Los Angeles, 1973), pp. 1-40; and Amy Charles, p. 182 seq. Against the view that this MS could be the actual MS from which the first edition of *The Temple* was set up are its total lack of printers' marks or of signs of rough handling, its considerable number of mechanical errors of transcription (despite its meticulous calligraphic appearance), and its numerous differences from the text of the 1633 edition. There seems no good reason to doubt that the first edition was set up directly from Herbert's definitive MS and that the Tanner MS was prepared only for the specific purpose of obtaining a license. The edition was produced with considerable speed (by October 1633), suggesting that preparations for it did not wait upon the formalities of licensing or the return of a 'printers' MS'. This would help to explain why it should be the licensers' MS which survived while Herbert's own MS, like nearly all printers' MSS of the 17th century, has not.

Besides the Dr Williams MS, a very small number of autographs are known. They are listed in Amy Charles (pp. 211-12). The most notable examples are letters.

Herbert's letter of 26 December 1618 to Sir Robert Harley is now among the Portland MSS deposited in the British Library (Loan MS 29/202, ff. 171-2v); the text is printed in Hutchinson, pp. 367-9, and see FACSIMILE XX. Contrary to the assumption made by Amy Charles (whose discussion of Herbert's handwriting (pp. 210-16) is somewhat confused and inaccurate), and as is quite common in letters of the period, the superscribed address is not in the hand of the letter-writer himself. A second letter, an undated Latin epistle to Bishop Lancelot Andrewes, probably written in the autumn of 1619, is in the British Library (Sloane MS 118, ff. 34-5); it is printed in Hutchinson, pp. 471-3, and reproduced in part in Greg, *English Literary Autographs*, plate XLIX(d-e). A third letter, now among the Ferrar Papers at Magdalene College, Cambridge, is a memorandum written in October 1631 for one or more members of the Little Gidding community on 'Reasons for Arth. Woodenoths Liuing wth S[r] Jhon Dau̅ers'; it is printed in Hutchinson, pp. 380-1, and was first discussed in Bernard Blackstone, 'A Paper by George Herbert', *TLS* (15 August 1936), p. 664. The first page is reproduced in *The Ferrar Papers*, ed. B. Blackstone (Cambridge, 1938), facing p. 269. The texts of three other letters of Herbert are printed in Hutchinson (pp. 378-9, 470-1) from scribal copies preserved in Cambridge University Library (MS Mm. 1. 46, ff. 410-11) and in Dr Williams's Library (MS Jones B. 57), and the texts of fifteen more letters are printed in Hutchinson (pp. 363-7, 369-77, 379, and also 304-5) from published texts. Hutchinson also prints (pp. 456-69) sixteen official letters in Latin written by Herbert during his period as Praelector and Public Orator at Cambridge (1618-28). These letters were copied by a scribe into the official orator's book, *Epistolae Academiae, Tom. II*, preserved in the Cambridge University Archives (*Lett. 2*). Herbert's personal attention to these copies is witnessed by his autograph annotations: for instance, a note at the top of p. *537/280 and a three-line signed inscription, dated '19 Jan. 1619' [i.e. 1619/20], on p. *532.

Certain other academic and ecclesiastical documents bear his signature or inscriptions. The Admission Books at Trinity College, Cambridge, contain his signatures on 3 October 1614 (as a minor fellow), on 15 March 1615/16 (as a major fellow), and on 2 October 1617 (as a sublector fourth class). On 26 February 1628/9 he signed his Marriage License Bond, now preserved in the Salisbury Diocesan Record Office. At his Institution to Bemerton Rectory (26 April 1630) and at his Ordination (19 September 1630) he made appropriate entries in the Bishop's first Subscription Book (ff. 95v, 99), preserved in the same office; these subscriptions are printed in Amy Charles, pp. 147, 153, and are reproduced in Palmer, III, facing pp. 6 and 64. Herbert also signed an official transcript of Bemerton parish register for 1631, which is similarly preserved in the Salisbury Diocesan Record Office; the original parish register is preserved in the Wiltshire Record Office (WRO 930/1) but bears no trace of Herbert's hand. Elsewhere Herbert signed (as witness) the Will of his neice Dorothy Vaughan (proved 19 October 1632), now in the Public Record Office (PROB 1/35). His own Will (proved 12 March 1632/3) is signed by him but the text is in the hand of his curate, Nathaniel Bostocke; it is likewise preserved in the Public Record Office (PROB 1/36) and the text is printed in Hutchinson, pp. 382-3.

In addition to the poems in the Dr Williams MS and the Tanner MS, the entries below include a number of copies of particular poems in miscellanies dating before 1701. Hutchinson ignored such copies as having no independent authority (see Hutchinson, p. lvi). The entries specifically state which texts he did not record to distinguish them from the rest, which were known to him. A few other transcripts not given entries are to be found. An anonymous 236-page MS adaptation of most of *The Temple*, written in 1681-2 and based on a printed text, is now at Harvard (Her 2.5*); this MS was recorded in Grosart, I, 25, 30. Thirty-one poems were transcribed in 1671 from the sixth edition of *The Temple* (Cambridge, 1641) in a verse miscellany compiled by the Stirling schoolmaster Andrew Symson (1639-1712); it is now in Edinburgh University Library (MS La. III. 432, ff. 21-53v). Twenty-two poems were copied from a printed source in an 18th-century verse miscellany now in the Bodleian (MS Rawl. poet. 90, ff. 134v-46). Various extracts from a printed source were copied c. 1700 in a miscellany compiled by Dame Sarah Cowper (1644-1720), now in the Hertfordshire Record Office (D/EP F44, pp. 348-56). Another 18th-century miscellany in the Bodleian (MS Rawl. D. 1275) includes a copy of *The Church-porch* (f. 26), and a similar miscellany in the Osborn Collection at Yale (c 139) includes copies of *Dialogue*, *The Call*, and *Discipline* (pp. 126, 137-8). Also to be found in the Bodleian (MS Rawl. D. 199) is a MS treatise by George Ryley, *Mr. Herbert's Temple and Church Militant explained and improved by a discourse upon each poem critical and practical*, dated 'March y[e] 24, 1714/5'; this is mentioned in Hutchinson (p. lvi).

Two more items of some interest are Latin verse translations of poems by Herbert made in 1634 by James Leeke (1605-54), Fellow of Peterhouse, Cambridge: one a translation of *Good Friday*, the other a translation of *The Church Militant*. These translations are preserved in Durham Cathedral (Hunter MS 27, ff. 190-202, 203r-v). They are discussed and printed in part in P. G. Stanwood, 'Poetry Manuscripts of the Seventeenth Century in the Durham Cathedral Library', *DUJ*, 62 (1969-70), 81-90 (pp. 88-90).

Some other MSS of Herbert's works which have been reported at various times since his death remain unlocated. A printed exemplum of Bacon's *Certaine Psalmes* with Herbert's Latin poem to Bacon inscribed on a flyleaf was last recorded in 1870 (see HrG 310), but there is only the unreliable testimony of Alexander Grosart to suggest that the poem was in Herbert's autograph. The 'small quarto volume of MS. Latin poetry' from which J. Fry printed in 1816 the English poem to Bacon (see HrG 299) is likewise unlocated; nor can the MS copy from which William Pickering printed his text of *Inventa Bellica* in 1836 be identified, unless perchance it is either HrG 322 or HrG 323, the former interestingly ascribed to the playwright and translator Thomas May (1595-1650). At the time of his edition of 1941 Hutchinson had similarly failed to discover the whereabouts of a Little Gidding story book containing a copy of *Outlandish Proverbs*, one recorded by John Jones (1700-70), and the whereabouts of four of Herbert's letters which were published in 1818 by Rebecca Warner: see F. E. Hutchinson, 'Missing Herbert Manuscripts', *TLS* (15 July 1939), p. 421.

Herbert's personal papers were bequeathed to his widow, who, according to Izaak Walton, intended to make them public; however, 'they and Highnam House were burnt together by the late rebels' in the Civil War. According to John Aubrey (*Brief Lives*, ed. Andrew Clark (Oxford, 1898), I, 309-10), those papers included a 'folio in Latin' which, because the parson of Highnam 'could not read' it, was 'condemned' by Herbert's widow 'to the uses of good houswifry'. Although perhaps an indication of the fate of many 17th-century MSS, Aubrey's account is viewed with scepticism by Amy Charles (p. 180), who thinks it likely that any MSS of consequence (like the 'little Book' given to Edmund Duncon) were sent by Herbert to Nicholas Ferrar and that it was only family papers and letters which were retained by his widow until destroyed in the Civil War.

The canon accepted in the *Index* is based on Hutchinson, with the addition of three Latin poems (HrG 314, 326-7) discovered in more recent years.

PB.

ARRANGEMENT

Verse:	(1) English poems by Herbert	HrG 1-290
	(2) English poems of uncertain authorship	HrG 291-301
	(3) Latin poems by Herbert	HrG 302-27
Prose		HrG 328-30.

See also Addenda to Part 2, p. 629

FACSIMILE XX — George Herbert: First page of a letter to Sir Robert Harley, 26 December 1618. British Library, Loan MS 29/202, folio 171 recto. Reproduced by permission of the owner.

Sr

This letter runs to you with much eagernes. for I am enioined to write to you by Sr John Davess. to which mine owne obligations were occasion inough. & therfore I am not over much beholding to those busnesses wch iustly excuse him from writing at this time, because my recompence of your favours consist in this only. Now his desire is to acquaint you with those passages of newes wch this time affords; for though it is likely that the time after the holydays will bee fruitfuller of novelties, yet his love expects them not but first certifies you that there are come agents hither from the low-Cuntries to treat of divers matters, as of certaine iniuries wch they are thought to have offerd to our Merchants at the Indies, wherin they have satisfied the king reasonably. but yet he will heare of no other affairs, untill they have satisfied him also concerning the fishing wch the Hollanders use in our coasts. wch the King would so appropriate to himselfe, as that either his subiects only should practise it. or at least that the Hollanders should pay him tribute out of their fishing. now to the answering of this demaund of the kinge those Agents pretend they have no comission, & therfore deferr it untill they have farther from the States. My Lord of Buckingham was observed on Christmas day to bee so devout as to come to the Chappell an howre before prayers began, of wch is doubted whether it have some farther meaning. Sr Charls Howard & his Lady are at much difference. & shee being at London sent for him (as shee sayes) to make peace with him. wch he refusing to doe hath given her occasion to protest shee will never speake with him againe. & to threaten him that if he will not give his [illegible] her estate

George Herbert

VERSE

(1) ENGLISH POEMS BY HERBERT

HrG 1 *Aaron* ('Holinesse on the head').

Copy in the Tanner MS; [1633].

First pub. in *The Temple* (1633); Hutchinson, p. 174.

Bodleian, MS Tanner 307, f. 128r-v.

*HrG 2 *Affliction (I)* ('When first thou didst entice to thee my heart').

Copy, with an autograph correction, in the Dr Williams MS; c. 1620s.

First pub. in *The Temple* (1633); Hutchinson, pp. 46-8.

Dr Williams's Library, MS Jones B. 62, ff. 48v-50.

HrG 3 -----

Copy in the Tanner MS; [1633].

Bodleian, MS Tanner 307, ff. 29-30v.

HrG 4 *Affliction (II)* ('Kill me not ev'ry day').

Copy in the Tanner MS; [1633].

First pub. in *The Temple* (1633); Hutchinson, p. 62.

Bodleian, MS Tanner 307, f. 41v.

HrG 5 *Affliction (III)* ('My heart did heave, and there came forth, O God!').

Copy in the Tanner MS; [1633].

First pub. in *The Temple* (1633); Hutchinson, p. 73.

Bodleian, MS Tanner 307, f. 50r-v.

HrG 6 *Affliction (IV)* ('Broken in pieces all asunder').

Copy, headed 'Tentation', in the Dr Williams MS; c. 1620s.

First pub. in *The Temple* (1633); Hutchinson, pp. 89-90.

Dr Williams's Library, MS Jones B. 62, ff. 58v-9.

HrG 7 -----

Copy in the Tanner MS; [1633].

Bodleian, MS Tanner 307, f. 62r-v.

HrG 8 *Affliction (V)* ('My God, I read this day').

Copy in the Dr Williams MS; c. 1620s.

First pub. in *The Temple* (1633); Hutchinson, p. 97.

Dr Williams's Library, MS Jones B. 62, ff. 65v-6.

HrG 9 -----

Copy in the Tanner MS; [1633].

Bodleian, MS Tanner 307, f. 67r-v.

HrG 10 *The Agonie* ('Philosophers have measur'd mountains').

Copy in the Tanner MS; [1633].

First pub. in *The Temple* (1633); Hutchinson, p. 37.

Bodleian, MS Tanner 307, f. 23.

*HrG 11 *The Altar* ('A broken Altar, Lord, thy servant reares').

Copy, with an autograph revision, in the Dr Williams MS; c. 1620s.

First pub. in *The Temple* (1633); Hutchinson, p. 26.

Dr Williams's Library, MS Jones B. 62, f. 15v.

HrG 12 -----

Copy in the Tanner MS; [1633].

Bodleian, MS Tanner 307, f. 15v.

HrG 13 -----

Copy in a verse miscellany compiled by an Oxford man and once owned by one Stephen Welden; mid-17th century.

This MS not recorded in Hutchinson.

Folger, MS V. a. 162, f. 12v.

Ana-$^{MARY}_{ARMY}$}*gram*

HrG 14 *Ana-*$^{MARY}_{ARMY}$}*gram* ('How well her name an Army doth present').

Copy in the Tanner MS; [1633].

First pub. in *The Temple* (1633); Hutchinson, p. 77.

Bodleian, MS Tanner 307, f. 44v.

HrG 15 -----

Copy in a verse miscellany; late 17th century.

This MS not recorded in Hutchinson.

Yale, Osborn Collection, b 137, p. 201.

HrG 16 *The Answer* ('My comforts drop and melt away like snow').

Copy in the Tanner MS; [1633].

First pub. in *The Temple* (1633); Hutchinson, p. 169.

Bodleian, MS Tanner 307, f. 124r-v.

HrG 17 *Antiphon (I)* ('Let all the world in ev'ry corner sing').

Copy in the Tanner MS; [1633].

First pub. in *The Temple* (1633); Hutchinson, p. 53.

Bodleian, MS Tanner 307, f. 34v.

HrG 18 *Antiphon (II)* ('Praised be the God of love').

Copy, headed 'Ode', in the Dr Williams MS; c. 1620s.

First pub. in *The Temple* (1633); Hutchinson, pp. 92-3.

Dr Williams's Library, MS Jones B. 62, f. 65.

HrG 19 -----

Copy in the Tanner MS; [1633].

Bodleian, MS Tanner 307, f. 64r-v.

HrG 20 *Artillerie* ('As I one ev'ning sat before my cell').

Copy in the Tanner MS; [1633].

First pub. in *The Temple* (1633); Hutchinson, p. 139.

Bodleian, MS Tanner 307, ff. 100v-1v.

HrG 21 *Assurance* ('O spitefull bitter thought!').

Copy in the Tanner MS; [1633].

First pub. in *The Temple* (1633); Hutchinson, pp. 155-6.

Bodleian, MS Tanner 307, ff. 113v-14v.

HrG 22 *Avarice* ('Money, thou bane of blisse, & sourse of wo').

Copy in the Tanner MS; [1633].

First pub. in *The Temple* (1633); Hutchinson, p. 77.

Bodleian, MS Tanner 307, f. 53.

HrG 23 -----

Copy in a composite volume of tracts and papers; late 17th century.

This MS not recorded in Hutchinson.

Bodleian, MS Rawl. D. 924, f. 341.

HrG 24 -----

Copy, transcribed from the edition of 1678, in a medical miscellany; late 17th century.

This MS not recorded in Hutchinson.

British Library, Sloane MS 3796, f. 17v.

HrG 25 *The Bag* ('Away despair! my gracious Lord doth heare').

Copy in the Tanner MS; [1633].

First pub. in *The Temple* (1633); Hutchinson, pp. 151-2.

Bodleian, MS Tanner 307, ff. 110-11.

HrG 26 -----

Copy, transcribed from George Swinnock's *Christian-Man's Calling* (1668) and inscribed 'wrot by my grandmother Moye', in a miscellany of religious verse and prose; [1668-78].

This MS not recorded in Hutchinson.

Bodleian, MS Rawl. C. 580, p. 314.

HrG 27 *The Banquet* ('Welcome sweet and sacred cheer').

Copy in the Tanner MS; [1633].

First pub. in *The Temple* (1633); Hutchinson, pp. 181-2.

Bodleian, MS Tanner 307, ff. 133v-4v.

Bitter-sweet

HrG 28 *Bitter-sweet* ('Ah my deare angrie Lord').

Copy in the Tanner MS; [1633].

First pub. in *The Temple* (1633); Hutchinson, p. 171.

Bodleian, MS Tanner 307, f. 126.

HrG 29 -----

Copy in a miscellany compiled by Robert Fleming; c. 1670-85.

This MS not recorded in Hutchinson.

Bodleian, MS Rawl. poet. 213, f. 57v.

HrG 29.5 See Addenda, p. 629.

HrG 30 *The British Church* ('I joy, deare Mother, when I view').

Copy in the Tanner MS; [1633].

First pub. in *The Temple* (1633); Hutchinson, pp. 109-10.

Bodleian, MS Tanner 307, ff. 76v-7v.

HrG 31 *The Bunch of Grapes* ('Joy, I did lock thee up: but some bad man').

Copy in the Tanner MS; [1633].

First pub. in *The Temple* (1633); Hutchinson, p. 128.

Bodleian, MS Tanner 307, ff. 91v-2v.

HrG 32 *Businesse* ('Canst be idle? canst thou play').

Copy in the Tanner MS; [1633].

First pub. in *The Temple* (1633); Hutchinson, pp. 113-14.

Bodleian, MS Tanner 307, ff. 79v-80v.

HrG 33 *The Call* ('Come, my Way, my Truth, my Life').

Copy in the Tanner MS; [1633].

First pub. in *The Temple* (1633); Hutchinson, p. 156.

Bodleian, MS Tanner 307, f. 114v.

HrG 34 -----

Copy of lines 1-4, 9-12, inscribed with extracts from other works inside the back cover of a MS book of sermons written by Stephen Machin; late 17th century.

This MS not recorded in Hutchinson.

Yale, Osborn Collection, b 245.

--- -----

See also INTRODUCTION.

HrG 33 *Charms and Knots* ('Who reade a chapter when they rise').

Copy in the Dr Williams MS; c. 1620s.

First pub. in *The Temple* (1633); Hutchinson, pp. 96-7.

Dr Williams's Library, MS Jones B. 62, ff. 66v-7.

HrG 36 -----

Copy in the Tanner MS; [1633].

Bodleian, MS Tanner 307, ff. 66v-7.

HrG 37 -----

Copy in a volume of state letters and speeches; mid-17th century.

This MS not recorded in Hutchinson.

Cambridge University Library, MS Gg. 4. 13, p. 236 rev.

HrG 38 -----

Copy in a verse miscellany; late 17th century.

This MS not recorded in Hutchinson.

Yale, Osborn Collection, b 137, p. 84.

HrG 39 *Christmas* ('All after pleasures as I rid one day').

Copy of lines 1-14, headed 'Christmas-Day', in the Dr Williams MS; c. 1620s.

First pub. in *The Temple* (1633); Hutchinson, pp. 80-1.

Dr Williams's Library, MS Jones B. 62, f. 45.

HrG 40 -----

Copy in the Tanner MS; [1633].

Bodleian, MS Tanner 307, ff. 55v-6.

HrG 41 -----

Copy of lines 15-34, untitled and beginning 'The shepherds sing; and shall I silent be?', in a musical setting by John Jenkins (1592-1678), in three MS music part books; early-mid-17th century.

Christmas

This MS discussed in Vincent Duckles, 'John Jenkins's Settings of Lyrics by George Herbert', *MQ*, 48 (1962), 461-75; not recorded in Hutchinson.

Christ Church, Oxford, MSS Mus. 736-7, ff. 24v-5; 738, ff. 25v-6.

HrG 42 *The Church-floore* ('Mark you the floore? that square & speckled stone').

Copy in the Tanner MS; [1633].

First pub. in *The Temple* (1633); Hutchinson, pp. 66-7.

Bodleian, MS Tanner 307, f. 45r-v.

HrG 43 *Church-lock and key* ('I know it is my sinne, which locks thine eares').

Copy, headed 'Prayer', in the Dr Williams MS; c. 1620s.

First pub. in *The Temple* (1633); Hutchinson, p. 66.

Dr Williams's Library, MS Jones B. 62, f. 35.

HrG 44 -----

Copy in the Tanner MS; [1633].

Bodleian, MS Tanner 307, ff. 44v-5.

*HrG 45 *The Church Militant* ('Almightie Lord, who from thy glorious throne').

Copy, with autograph revisions, in the Dr Williams MS; c. 1620s.

First pub. in *The Temple* (1633); Hutchinson, pp. 190-8.

Dr Williams's Library, MS Jones B. 62, ff. 82v-9.

HrG 46 -----

Copy in the Tanner MS; [1633].

Bodleian, MS Tanner 307, ff. 141-7.

--- -----

See also INTRODUCTION.

HrG 47 *Church-monuments* ('While that my soul repairs to her devotion').

Copy in the Dr Williams MS; c. 1620s.

First pub. in *The Temple* (1633); Hutchinson, pp. 64-5.

Dr Williams's Library, MS Jones B. 62, ff. 45v-6.

HrG 48 -----

Copy in the Tanner MS; [1633].

Bodleian, MS Tanner 307, ff. 43v-4.

HrG 49 *Church-musick* ('Sweetest of sweets, I thank you: when displeasure').

Copy in the Dr Williams MS; c. 1620s.

First pub. in *The Temple* (1633); Hutchinson, pp. 65-6.

Dr Williams's Library, MS Jones B. 62, f. 32.

HrG 50 -----

Copy in the Tanner MS; [1633].

Bodleian, MS Tanner 307, f. 44r-v.

*HrG 51 *The Church-porch* ('Thou, whose sweet youth and early hopes inhance').

Copy, with autograph revisions, in the Dr Williams MS; c. 1620s.

First pub. in *The Temple* (1633); Hutchinson, pp. 6-24.

Dr Williams's Library, MS Jones B. 62, ff. 1-13v.

HrG 52 -----

Copy in the Tanner MS; [1633].

Bodleian, MS Tanner 307, ff. 2-14v.

HrG 53 -----

Copy in a miscellany probably compiled by members of the Cartwright family of Aynho, Northamptonshire; mid-17th century.

This MS not recorded in Hutchinson.

Bodleian, MS Don. e. 6, f. 16v.

HrG 54 -----

Copy of stanzas 58 (beginning 'Slight not the smallest losse, whether it be') and 53, transcribed from the edition of 1678, in a medical commonplace book; late 17th century.

This MS not recorded in Hutchinson.

British Library, Sloane MS 3796, f. 17v.

HrG 55 -----

Copy of various stanzas, beginning with stanza 2 ('Beware of lust: it doth pollute and foul'), among 'Choice Verses written out of the Sacred Poems, of Mr George Herbert' in a verse miscellany probably compiled by Robert Clarke of Wadham College, Oxford; c. 1663.

This MS not recorded in Hutchinson.

Duke University, MS 12-14-71, pp. 2-4.

HrG 56 -----

Copy in a verse miscellany; late 17th century.

This MS not recorded in Hutchinson.

Yale, Osborn Collection, b 137, pp. 76-84.

--- -----

See also INTRODUCTION.

HrG 57 *Church-rents and schismes* ('Brave rose, (alas!) where art thou? in the chair').

Copy in the Tanner MS; [1633].

First pub. in *The Temple* (1633); Hutchinson, p. 140.

Bodleian, MS Tanner 307, ff. 101v-2.

HrG 58 *Clasping of hands* ('Lord, thou art mine, and I am thine').

Copy in the Tanner MS; [1633].

First pub. in *The Temple* (1633); Hutchinson, p. 157.

Bodleian, MS Tanner 307, f. 115.

HrG 59 *The Collar* ('I struck the board, and cry'd, No more').

Copy in the Tanner MS; [1633].

First pub. in *The Temple* (1633); Hutchinson, pp. 153-4.

Bodleian, MS Tanner 307, ff. 11v-12v.

HrG 60 *Coloss. 3. 3. Our life is hid with Christ in God* ('My words & thoughts do both expresse this notion').

Copy in the Dr Williams MS; c. 1620s.

First pub. in *The Temple* (1633); Hutchinson, pp. 84-5.

Dr Williams's Library, MS Jones B. 62, f. 60.

HrG 61 -----

Copy in the Tanner MS; [1633].

Bodleian, MS Tanner 307, f. 58v.

HrG 62 *Complaining* ('Do not beguile my heart').

Copy in the Tanner MS; [1633].

First pub. in *The Temple* (1633); Hutchinson, pp. 143-4.

Bodleian, MS Tanner 307, f. 104r-v.

HrG 63 *Confession* ('O what a cunning guest').

Copy in the Tanner MS; [1633].

First pub. in *The Temple* (1633); Hutchinson, p. 126.

Bodleian, MS Tanner 307, f. 90r-v.

HrG 64 *Conscience* ('Peace pratler, do not lowre').

Copy in the Tanner MS; [1633].

First pub. in *The Temple* (1633); Hutchinson, pp. 105-6.

Bodleian, MS Tanner 307, ff. 73v-4v.

HrG 65 *Constancie* ('Who is the honest man?').

Copy in the Tanner MS; [1633].

First pub. in *The Temple* (1633); Hutchinson, pp. 72-3.

Bodleian, MS Tanner 307, ff. 49-50.

HrG 66 -----

Copy in the hand of Francis Knollys, in his MS translation of the Psalms; 1660.

This MS not recorded in Hutchinson.

Bodleian, MS Rawl. poet. 60, p. 1.

*HrG 67 *Content* ('Peace mutt'ring thoughts, and do not grudge to keep').

Copy, with an autograph revision, in the Dr Williams MS; c. 1620s.

First pub. in *The Temple* (1633); Hutchinson, pp. 68-9.

Dr Williams's Library, MS Jones B. 62, ff. 47-8.

HrG 68 -----

Copy in the Tanner MS; [1633].

Bodleian, MS Tanner 307, ff. 46-7.

HrG 69 -----

Copy in a musical setting by John Wilson, in Wilson's corrected MS volume of his own songs;

Content

possibly in Wilson's autograph or else in the hand of someone similarly associated with Edward Lowe (c.1610-82); c. 1656.

Printed from this MS in Norman Ault, *A Treasury of Unfamiliar Lyrics* (London, 1938); pp. 240-1; music edited in André Souris, *Poèmes de Donne Herbert et Crashaw mis en musique par leur contemporains* (Paris, 1961), pp. 20-3; not recorded in Hutchinson.

Bodleian, MS Mus. b. 1, ff. 50v-1.

HrG 70 -----

Copy, headed 'Against Vaineglorie', in a verse miscellany appended to a MS volume of poems by John Donne; c. 1630s.

This MS not recorded in Hutchinson.

Trinity College, Dublin, MS 877, ff. 164v-5v.

HrG 71 *The Crosse* ('What is this strange and uncouth thing?').

Copy in the Tanner MS; [1633].

First pub. in *The Temple* (1633); Hutchinson, pp. 164-5.

Bodleian, MS Tanner 307, ff. 120v-1v.

HrG 72 -----

Copy of lines 19-24, here beginning 'Alas things sort not to my will', inscribed with extracts from other works inside the back cover of a MS book of sermons written by Stephen Machin; late 17th century.

This MS not recorded in Hutchinson.

Yale, Osborn Collection, b 245.

HrG 73 *The Dawning* ('Awake sad heart, whom sorrow ever drowns').

Copy in the Tanner MS; [1633].

First pub. in *The Temple* (1633); Hutchinson, p. 112.

Bodleian, MS Tanner 307, ff. 78v-9.

HrG 74 -----

Copies, untitled, in a musical setting by John Jenkins (1592-1678), in three MS music part books; early-mid-17th century.

This MS discussed in Vincent Duckles, 'John Jenkins's Settings of Lyrics by George Herbert', *MQ*, 48 (1962), 461-75; not recorded in Hutchinson.

Christ Church, Oxford, MSS Mus. 736-7, ff. 25v-6; 738, ff. 26v-7.

HrG 75 *Death* ('Death, thou wast once an uncouth hideous thing').

Copy in the Dr Williams MS; c. 1620s.

First pub. in *The Temple* (1633); Hutchinson, pp. 185-6.

Dr Williams's Library, MS Jones B. 62, ff. 76v-7.

HrG 76 -----

Copy in the Tanner MS; [1633].

Bodleian, MS Tanner 307, f. 137r-v.

HrG 77 *Decay* ('Sweet were the dayes, when thou didst lodge with Lot').

Copy in the Tanner MS; [1633].

First pub. in *The Temple* (1633); Hutchinson, p. 99.

Bodleian, MS Tanner 307, f. 69.

HrG 78 *The Dedication* ('Lord, my first fruits present themselves to thee').

Copy in the Dr Williams MS; c. 1620s.

First pub. in *The Temple* (1633); Hutchinson, p. 5. Facsimile of this MS in Palmer, II, 108.

Dr Williams's Library, MS Jones B. 62, [before f. 1].

HrG 79 -----

Copy in the Tanner MS; [1633].

Bodleian, MS Tanner 307, f. 1.

*HrG 80 *Deniall* ('When my devotions could not pierce').

Copy, with an autograph revision, in the Dr Williams MS; c. 1620s.

First pub. in *The Temple* (1633); Hutchinson, pp. 79-80.

Dr Williams's Library, MS Jones B. 62, ff. 53v-4.

HrG 81 -----

Copy in the Tanner MS; [1633].

Bodleian, MS Tanner 307, f. 55r-v.

HrG 82 *Dialogue* ('Sweetest Saviour, if my soul').

Copy in the Tanner MS; [1633].

First pub. in *The Temple* (1633); Hutchinson, pp. 114-15.

Bodleian, MS Tanner 307, ff. 80v-1.

--- -----

See also INTRODUCTION.

HrG 83 *A Dialogue-Antheme* ('Alas, poore Death, where is thy glorie?').

Copy in the Tanner MS; [1633].

First pub. in *The Temple* (1633); Hutchinson, p. 169.

Bodleian, MS Tanner 307, ff. 124v-5.

HrG 84 *The Discharge* ('Busie enquiring heart, what wouldst thou know?').

Copy in the Tanner MS; [1633].

First pub. in *The Temple* (1633); Hutchinson, pp. 144-5.

Bodleian, MS Tanner 307, ff. 105-6.

HrG 85 *Discipline* ('Throw away thy rod').

Copy in the Tanner MS; [1633].

First pub. in *The Temple* (1633); Hutchinson, pp. 178-9.

Bodleian, MS Tanner 307, ff. 131v-2.

--- -----

See also INTRODUCTION.

HrG 86 *Divinitie* ('As men, for fear the starres should sleep and nod').

Copy in the Tanner MS; [1633].

First pub. in *The Temple* (1633); Hutchinson, pp. 134-5.

Bodleian, MS Tanner 307, f. 97r-v.

HrG 87 *Dooms-day* ('Come away').

Copy in the Dr Williams MS; c. 1620s.

First pub. in *The Temple* (1633); Hutchinson, pp. 186-7.

Dr Williams's Library, MS Jones B. 62, ff. 77v-8.

HrG 88 -----

Copy in the Tanner MS; [1633].

Bodleian, MS Tanner 307, ff. 137v-8v.

HrG 89 *Dotage* ('False glozing pleasures, casks of happinesse').

Copy in the Tanner MS; [1633].

First pub. in *The Temple* (1633); Hutchinson, p. 167.

Bodleian, MS Tanner 307, f. 123.

HrG 90 *Dulnesse* ('Why do I languish thus, drooping and dull').

Copy in the Tanner MS; [1633].

First pub. in *The Temple* (1633); Hutchinson, pp. 115-16.

Bodleian, MS Tanner 307, ff. 81v-2.

*HrG 91 *Easter* ('Rise heart; thy Lord is risen. Sing his praise').

Copy, with an autograph revision; with lines 19-30 (here beginning 'I had prepared many a flowre') as a separate poem entitled 'Easter'; in the Dr Williams MS; c. 1620s.

First pub. in *The Temple* (1633); Hutchinson, pp. 41-2.

Dr Williams's Library, MS Jones B, 62, ff. 26v-7.

HrG 92 -----

Copy in the Tanner MS; [1633].

Bodleian, MS Tanner 307, ff. 25v-6.

*HrG 93 *Easter-wings* ('Lord, who createdst man in wealth and store').

Copy, with autograph revisions, in the Dr Williams MS; c. 1620s.

First pub. in *The Temple* (1633); Hutchinson, p. 43. Facsimile of this MS in Petti, *English Literary Hands*, No. 57.

Dr Williams's Library, MS Jones B. 62, ff. 27v-8.

HrG 94 -----

Copy in the Tanner MS; [1633].

Bodleian, MS Tanner 307, ff. 26v-7.

*HrG 95 *The Elixir* ('Teach me, my God and King').

Copy of an early version beginning 'Lord teach mee to referr', with extensive autograph revisions; originally entitled 'Perfection', the title 'The Elixir' added by Herbert; in the Dr Williams MS; c. 1620s.

First pub. in *The Temple* (1633); Hutchinson, pp. 184-5. Facsimiles of this MS in Palmer, I, after p. 120; Flower & Munby, *English Poetical Autographs*, p. 10; Croft, *Autograph Poetry*, I, 34.

Dr Williams's Library, MS Jones B. 62, ff. 74v-5.

HrG 96 -----

Copy in the Tanner MS; [1633].

Bodleian, MS Tanner 307, f. 136r-v.

HrG 97 *Employment (I)* ('If as a flowre doth spread and die').

Copy in the Dr Williams MS; c. 1620s.

First pub. in *The Temple* (1633); Hutchinson, p. 57.

Dr Williams's Library, MS Jones B. 62, ff. 35v-6.

HrG 98 -----

Copy in the Tanner MS; [1633].

Bodleian, MS Tanner 307, ff. 37v-8.

*HrG 99 *Employment (II)* ('He that is weary, let him sit').

Copy, the title added by Herbert, in the Dr Williams MS; c. 1620s.

First pub. in *The Temple* (1633); Hutchinson, pp. 78-9.

Dr Williams's Library, MS Jones B. 62, ff. 55v-6.

HrG 100 -----

Copy in the Tanner MS; [1633].

Bodleian, MS Tanner 307, f. 54r-v.

*HrG 101 *L'Envoy* ('King of Glorie, King of Peace').

Copy, with an autograph revision and the title added by Herbert, in the Dr Williams MS; c. 1620s.

First pub. in *The Temple* (1633); Hutchinson, p. 199.

Dr Williams's Library, MS Jones B. 62, f. 89v.

HrG 102 -----

Copy in the Tanner MS; [1633].

Bodleian, MS Tanner 307, f. 147r-v.

HrG 103 *Ephes. 4. 30. Grieve not the Holy Spirit, &c.* ('And art thou grieved, sweet and sacred Dove').

Copy in the Tanner MS; [1633].

First pub. in *The Temple* (1633); Hutchinson, pp. 135-6.

Bodleian, MS Tanner 307, ff. 97v-8v.

HrG 104 -----

Copies of lines 1-18, untitled, in a musical setting by John Jenkins (1592-1678), in three MS music part books; early-mid-17th century.

This MS discussed in Vincent Duckles, 'John Jenkins's Settings of Lyrics by George Herbert', *MQ*, 48 (1962), 461-75; not recorded in Hutchinson.

Christ Church, Oxford, MSS Mus. 736-7, ff. 31v-2; 738, ff. 32v-3.

HrG 105 -----

Copies of lines 19-36, untitled and beginning 'Oh take thy lute, and tune it to a strain', treated as a separate song, in a musical setting by John Jenkins (different from that in HrG 104), in three MS music part books; early-mid-17th century.

This MS discussed in Duckles; not recorded in Hutchinson.

Christ Church, Oxford, MSS Mus. 736-7, f. 31; 738, f. 32.

HrG 106 *Even-song* ('Blest be the God of love').

Copy in the Tanner MS; [1633].

First pub. in *The Temple* (1633); Hutchinson, pp. 63-4.

Bodleian, MS Tanner 307, ff. 42v-3v.

HrG 107 *Euen-song* ('The Day is spent, & hath his will on mee').

Copy in the Dr Williams MS; c. 1620s.

First pub. (from this MS) in Grosart (1874); printed from this MS in Hutchinson, p. 203.

Dr Williams's Library, MS Jones B. 62, f. 44r-v.

*HrG 108 *Faith* ('Lord, how couldst thou so much appease').

Copy, with autograph revisions, in the Dr Williams MS; c. 1620s.

First pub. in *The Temple* (1633); Hutchinson, pp. 49-51.

Dr Williams's Library, MS Jones B. 62, ff. 60v-1v.

HrG 109 -----

Copy in the Tanner MS; [1633].

Bodleian, MS Tanner 307, ff. 32-3.

HrG 110 *The Familie* ('What doth this noise of thoughts within my heart').

Copy in the Tanner MS; [1633].

First pub. in *The Temple* (1633); Hutchinson, pp. 136-7.

Bodleian, MS Tanner 307, ff. 98v-9.

HrG 111 *The Flower* ('How fresh, O Lord, how sweet and clean').

Copy in the Tanner MS; [1633].

First pub. in *The Temple* (1633); Hutchinson, pp. 165-7.

Bodleian, MS Tanner 307, ff. 121v-2v.

HrG 112 *The Foil* ('If we could see below').

Copy in the Tanner MS; [1633].

First pub. in *The Temple* (1633); Hutchinson, pp. 175-6.

Bodleian, MS Tanner 307, f. 129v.

HrG 113 *The Forerunners* ('The harbingers are come. See, see their mark').

Copy in the Tanner MS; [1633].

First pub. in *The Temple* (1633); Hutchinson, pp. 176-7.

Bodleian, MS Tanner 307, ff. 129v-30v.

*HrG 114 *Fraltie* ('Lord, in my silence how do I despise').

Copy, with an autograph revision, in the Dr Williams MS; c. 1620s.

First pub. in *The Temple* (1633); Hutchinson, pp. 71-2.

Dr Williams's Library, MS Jones B. 62, f. 46r-v.

HrG 115 -----

Copy in the Tanner MS; [1633].

Bodleian, MS Tanner 307, ff. 48v-9.

HrG 116 *Giddinesse* ('Oh, what a thing is man! how farre from power').

Copy in the Tanner MS; [1633].

First pub. in *The Temple* (1633); Hutchinson, p. 127.

Bodleian, MS Tanner 307, f. 91r-v.

HrG 117 *The Glance* ('When first thy sweet and gracious eye').

Copy in the Tanner MS; [1633].

First pub. in *The Temple* (1633); Hutchinson, pp. 171-2.

Bodleian, MS Tanner 307, f. 126r-v.

HrG 118 *The Glimpse* ('Whither away delight?').

Copy in the Tanner MS; [1633].

First pub. in *The Temple* (1633); Hutchinson, pp. 154-5.

Bodleian, MS Tanner 307, ff. 112v-13.

HrG 119 *Good Friday* ('O my chief good').

Copy, with lines 21-32 (here beginning 'Since nothing Lord can bee so good') as a separate poem entitled 'The Passion', in the Dr Williams MS; c. 1620s.

First pub. in *The Temple* (1633); Hutchinson, pp. 38-9.

Dr Williams's Library, MS Jones B. 62, ff. 25v, 24v.

HrG 120 -----

Copy in the Tanner MS; [1633].

Bodleian, MS Tanner 307, f. 24r-v.

--- -----

See also INTRODUCTION.

*HrG 121 *Grace* ('My stock lies dead, and no increase').

Copy, with autograph revisions, in the Dr Williams MS; c. 1620s.

First pub. in *The Temple* (1633); Hutchinson, pp. 60-1.

Dr Williams's Library, MS Jones B. 62, ff. 42v-3.

HrG 122 -----

Copy in the Tanner MS; [1633].

Bodleian, MS Tanner 307, f. 40r-v.

HrG 123 *Gratefulnesse* ('Thou that hast giv'n so much to me').

Copy in the Tanner MS; [1633].

First pub. in *The Temple* (1633); Hutchinson, pp. 123-4.

Bodleian, MS Tanner 307, f. 88r-v.

HrG 124 *Grief* ('O who will give me tears? Come all ye springs').

Copy in the Tanner MS; [1633].

First pub. in *The Temple* (1633); Hutchinson, p. 164.

Bodleian, MS Tanner 307, f. 120r-v.

HrG 125 *H. Baptisme (I)* ('As he that sees a dark and shadie grove').

Copy of an early version beginning 'When backward on my sins I turne mine eyes' in the Dr Williams MS; c. 1620s.

First pub. in *The Temple* (1613); Hutchinson, pp. 43-4.

Dr Williams's Library, MS Jones B. 62, f. 28v.

HrG 126 -----

Copy in the Tanner MS; [1633].

Bodleian, MS Tanner 307, f. 27v.

HrG 127 *H. Baptisme (II)* ('Since, Lord, to thee').

Copy in the Dr Williams MS; c. 1620s.

First pub. in *The Temple* (1633); Hutchinson, p. 44.

Dr Williams's Library, MS Jones B. 62, f. 29.

HrG 128 -----

Copy in the Tanner MS; [1633].

Bodleian, MS Tanner 307, f. 28.

HrG 129 *The H. Communion* ('Not in rich furniture, or fine aray').

Copy of lines 25-40, headed 'Prayer' and beginning 'Give me my captive soul, or take', in the Dr Williams MS; c. 1620s.

First pub. in *The Temple* (1633); Hutchinson, pp. 52-3.

Dr Williams's Library, MS Jones B. 62, f. 34v.

HrG 130 -----

Copy in the Tanner MS; [1633].

Bodleian, MS Tanner 307, ff. 33v-4v.

HrG 131 -----

Copy of lines 25-40 in a journal compiled by one Thomas Grocer; 1657.

This MS not recorded in Hutchinson.

Huntington, HM 93, p. 36.

HrG 132 *The H. Communion* ('O gratious Lord, how shall I know').

Copy in the Dr Williams MS; c. 1620s.

First pub. (from this MS) in Grosart (1874); printed from this MS in Hutchinson, pp. 200-1.

Dr Williams's Library, MS Jones B. 62, ff. 30v-1v.

HrG 133 *The H. Scriptures. I* ('Oh Book! infinite sweetnesse! let my heart').

Copy in the Dr Williams MS; c. 1620s.

First pub. in *The Temple* (1633); Hutchinson, p. 58.

Dr Williams's Library, MS Jones B. 62, f. 37v.

HrG 134 -----

Copy in the Tanner MS; [1633].

Bodleian, MS Tanner 307, f. 38v.

HrG 135 *The H. Scriptures. II* ('Oh that I knew how all thy lights combine').

Copy in the Dr Williams MS; c. 1620s.

First pub. in *The Temple* (1633); Hutchinson, p. 58.

Dr Williams's Library, MS Jones B. 62, f. 38.

HrG 136 -----

Copy in the Tanner MS; [1633].

Bodleian, MS Tanner 307, f. 39.

HrG 137 *Heaven* ('O who will show me those delights on high?').

Copy in the Dr Williams MS; c. 1620s.

First pub. in *The Temple* (1633); Hutchinson, p. 188.

Dr Williams's Library, MS Jones B. 62, f. 79.

HrG 138 -----

Copy in the Tanner MS; [1633].

Bodleian, MS Tanner 307, f. 139.

HrG 139 *The Holdfast* ('I threatned to observe the strict decree').

Copy in the Tanner MS; [1633].

First pub. in *The Temple* (1633); Hutchinson, p. 143.

Bodleian, MS Tanner 307, f. 104.

HrG 140 *Home* ('Come Lord, my head doth burn, my heart is sick').

Copy in the Tanner MS; [1633].

First pub. in *The Temple* (1633); Hutchinson, pp. 107-9.

Bodleian, MS Tanner 307, ff. 75-6v.

HrG 141 -----

Copy in a miscellany compiled by one Robert Fleming; c. 1670-85.

This MS not recorded in Hutchinson.

Bodleian, MS Rawl. poet. 213, f. 57v.

HrG 142 -----

Copy among 'Choice Verses written out of the Sacred Poems, of Mr George Herbert' in a verse miscellany probably compiled by Robert Clarke of Wadham College, Oxford; c. 1663.

This MS not recorded in Hutchinson.

Duke University, MS 12-14-71, pp. 23-4.

HrG 143 *Hope* ('I gave to Hope a watch of mine: but he').

Copy in the Tanner MS; [1633].

First pub. in *The Temple* (1633); Hutchinson, p. 121.

Bodleian, MS Tanner 307, f. 86v.

HrG 144 *Humilitie* ('I saw the Vertues sitting hand in hand').

Copy in the Dr Williams MS; c. 1620s.

First pub. in *The Temple* (1633); Hutchinson, pp. 70-1.

Dr Williams's Library, MS Jones B. 62, ff. 50v-1.

HrG 145 -----

Copy in the Tanner MS; [1633].

Bodleian, MS Tanner 307, ff. 47v-8.

HrG 146 *The Invitation* ('Come ye hither All, whose taste').

Copy in the Tanner MS; [1633].

First pub. in *The Temple* (1633); Hutchinson, pp. 179-80.

Bodleian, MS Tanner 307, ff. 132v-3.

HrG 147 *Jesu* ('Jesu is in my heart, his sacred name').

Copy in the Tanner MS; [1633].

First pub. in *The Temple* (1633); Hutchinson, p. 112.

Bodleian, MS Tanner 307, f. 79.

HrG 148 -----

Copy in a miscellany compiled by Sir John Gibson (1606-65) of Welburn, near Kirkby Moorside, Yorkshire, a Royalist prisoner in Durham Castle c. 1653-60; [1655-60].

This MS not recorded in Hutchinson.

British Library, Add. MS 37719, f. 272.

HrG 149 -----

Copy in a miscellany of hymns &c. compiled by one Mary Webber; c. 1694.

This MS not recorded in Hutchinson.

Yale, Osborn Collection, b 202, p. 97.

HrG 150 *The Jews* ('Poore nation, whose sweet sap and juice').

Copy in the Tanner MS; [1633].

First pub. in *The Temple* (1633); Hutchinson, p. 152.

Bodleian, MS Tanner 307, f. 111r-v.

*HrG 151 *Jordan (I)* ('Who sayes that fictions onely and false hair').

Copy, with an autograph revision, in the Dr Williams MS; c. 1620s.

First pub. in *The Temple* (1633); Hutchinson, pp. 56-7.

Dr Williams's Library, MS Jones B. 62, f. 53.

HrG 152 -----

Copy in the Tanner MS; [1633].

Bodleian, MS Tanner 307, f. 37r-v.

HrG 153 *Jordan (II)* ('When first my lines of heav'nly joyes made mention').

Copy in the Dr Williams MS; c. 1620s.

First pub. in *The Temple* (1633); Hutchinson, pp. 102-3.

Dr Williams's Library, MS Jones B. 62, f. 74.

HrG 154 -----

Copy in the Tanner MS; [1633].

Bodleian, MS Tanner 307, f. 71v.

HrG 155 *Josephs coat* ('Wounded I sing, tormented I indite').

Copy in the Tanner MS; [1633].

First pub. in *The Temple* (1633); Hutchinson, p. 159.

Bodleian, MS Tanner 307, f. 116v.

HrG 156 *Judgement* ('Almightie Judge, how shall poore wretches brook').

Copy in the Dr Williams MS; c. 1620s.

First pub. in *The Temple* (1633); Hutchinson, pp. 187-8.

Dr Williams's Library, MS Jones B. 62, f. 78v.

HrG 157 -----

Copy in the Tanner MS; [1633].

Bodleian, MS Tanner 307, f. 138v.

HrG 158 *Justice (I)* ('I cannot skill of these thy wayes').

Copy in the Tanner MS; [1633].

First pub. in *The Temple* (1633); Hutchinson, pp. 95-6.

Bodleian, MS Tanner 307, f. 66v.

HrG 159 *Justice (II)* ('O dreadfull Justice, what a fright and terrour').

Copy in the Tanner MS; [1633].

First pub. in *The Temple* (1633); Hutchinson, p. 141.

Bodleian, MS Tanner 307, f. 102r-v.

HrG 160 *The Knoll* ('The Bell doth tolle').

Copy in the Dr Williams MS; c. 1620s.

First pub. (from this MS) in Grosart (1874); printed from this MS in Hutchinson, p. 204.

Dr Williams's Library, MS Jones B. 62, f. 75v.

--- *L'Envoy* ('King of Glorie, King of Peace').

See HrG 101-2.

*HrG 161 *Lent* ('Welcome deare feast of Lent: who loves not thee').

Copy, with an autograph revision, in the Dr Williams MS; c. 1620s.

First pub. in *The Temple* (1633); Hutchinson, pp. 86-7.

Dr Williams's Library, MS Jones B. 62, ff. 62-3.

HrG 162 -----

Copy in the Tanner MS; [1633].

Bodleian, MS Tanner 307, ff. 59v-60v.

HrG 163 *Life* ('I made a posie, while the day ran by').

Copy in the Tanner MS; [1633].

First pub. in *The Temple* (1633); Hutchinson, p. 94.

Bodleian, MS Tanner 307, f. 65v.

HrG 164 *Longing* ('With sick and famisht eyes').

Copy in the Tanner MS; [1633].

First pub. in *The Temple* (1633); Hutchinson, pp. 148-50.

Bodleian, MS Tanner 307, ff. 108-10.

Love

HrG 165 *Love* ('Thou art too hard for me in Love').

Copy in the Dr Williams MS; c. 1620s.

First pub. (from this MS) in Grosart (1874); printed from this MS in Hutchinson, pp. 201-2.

Dr Williams's Library, MS Jones B. 62, ff. 38v-9.

HrG 166 *Love I* ('Immortall Love, authour of this great frame').

Copy in the Dr Williams MS; c. 1620s.

First pub. in *The Temple* (1633); Hutchinson, p. 54.

Dr Williams's Library, MS Jones B. 62, f. 29v.

HrG 167 -----

Copy in the Tanner MS; [1633].

Bodleian, MS Tanner 307, f. 35.

HrG 168 *Love II* ('Immortall Heat, O let thy greater flame').

Copy in the Dr Williams MS; c. 1620s.

First pub. in *The Temple* (1633); Hutchinson, p. 54.

Dr Williams's Library, MS Jones B. 62, f. 30.

HrG 169 -----

Copy in the Tanner MS; [1633].

Bodleian, MS Tanner 307, f. 35v.

HrG 170 *Love III* ('Love bade me welcome: yet my soul drew back').

Copy in the Dr Williams MS; c. 1620s.

First pub. in *The Temple* (1633); Hutchinson, pp. 188-9. Facsimile of this MS in Palmer, I, 84.

Dr Williams's Library, MS Jones B. 62, f. 79v.

HrG 171 -----

Copy in the Tanner MS; [1633].

Bodleian, MS Tanner 307, f. 139v.

HrG 172 -----

Copy, headed 'Herberts poem, p. 183. called Loue', written by Oliver Heywood (1629-1702) at the end of his MS tract *Safe custody or A Discourse of a Christians committing his soul into the hands of god*; c. 1700.

This MS not recorded in Hutchinson.

University of Leeds, MS 13, p. 53.

HrG 173 *Love-joy* ('As on a window late I cast mine eye').

Copy in the Tanner MS; [1633].

First pub. in *The Temple* (1633); Hutchinson, p. 116.

Bodleian, MS Tanner 307, f. 82.

HrG 174 *Love unknown* ('Deare Friend, sit down, the tale is long and sad').

Copy in the Tanner MS; [1633].

First pub. in *The Temple* (1633); Hutchinson, pp. 129-31.

Bodleian, MS Tanner 307, ff. 92v-4.

*HrG 175 *Man* ('My God, I heard this day').

Copy, with autograph corrections and the title added by Herbert, in the Dr Williams MS; c. 1620s.

First pub. in *The Temple* (1633); Hutchinson, pp. 90-2.

Dr Williams's Library, MS Jones B. 62, ff. 63v-4v.

HrG 176 -----

Copy in the Tanner MS; [1633].

Bodleian, MS Tanner 307, ff. 63-4.

HrG 177 *Mans medley* ('Heark, how the birds do sing').

Copy in the Tanner MS; [1633].

First pub. in *The Temple* (1633); Hutchinson, pp. 131-2.

Bodleian, MS Tanner 307, ff. 94-5.

HrG 178 *Marie Magdalene* ('When blessed Marie wip'd her Saviours feet').

Copy in the Tanner MS; [1633].

First pub. in *The Temple* (1633); Hutchinson, p. 173.

Bodleian, MS Tanner 307, f. 127v.

HrG 179 *Mattens* ('I cannot ope mine eyes').

Copy in the Dr Williams MS; c. 1620s.

Mattens

First pub. in *The Temple* (1633); Hutchinson, pp. 62-3.

Dr Williams's Library, MS Jones B. 62, f. 43r-v.

HrG 180 -----

Copy in the Tanner MS; [1633].

Bodleian, MS Tanner 307, f. 42.

HrG 181 *The Method* ('Poore heart, lament').

Copy in the Tanner MS; [1633].

First pub. in *The Temple* (1633); Hutchinson, pp. 133-4.

Bodleian, MS Tanner 307, f. 96r-v.

HrG 182 *Miserie* ('Lord, let the Angels praise thy name').

Copy in the Dr Williams MS; c. 1620s.

First pub. in *The Temple* (1633); Hutchinson, pp. 100-2.

Dr Williams's Library, MS Jones B. 62, ff. 69v-71v.

HrG 183 -----

Copy in the Tanner MS; [1633].

Bodleian, MS Tanner 307, ff. 69v-71.

HrG 184 *Mortification* ('How soon doth man decay!').

Copy in the Dr Williams MS; c. 1620s.

First pub. in *The Temple* (1633); Hutchinson, pp. 98-9.

Dr Williams's Library, MS Jones B. 62, ff. 68v-9.

HrG 185 -----

Copy in the Tanner MS; [1633].

Bodleian, MS Tanner 307, f. 68r-v.

*HrG 186 *Nature* ('Full of rebellion, I would die').

Copy, with an autograph revision, in the Dr Williams MS; c. 1620s.

First pub. in *The Temple* (1633); Hutchinson, p. 45.

Dr Williams's Library, MS Jones B. 62, f. 42.

HrG 187 -----

Copy in the Tanner MS; [1633].

Bodleian, MS Tanner 307, f. 28v.

HrG 188 *Obedience* ('My God, if writings may').

Copy in the Dr Williams MS; c. 1620s.

First pub. in *The Temple* (1633); Hutchinson, pp. 104-5.

Dr Williams's Library, MS Jones B. 62, ff. 72v-3v.

HrG 189 -----

Copy in the Tanner MS; [1633].

Bodleian, MS Tanner 307, ff. 72v-3v.

HrG 190 *The Odour. 2. Cor. 2. 15.* ('How sweetly doth My Master sound! My Master!').

Copy in the Tanner MS; [1633].

First pub. in *The Temple* (1633); Hutchinson, pp. 174-5.

Bodleian, MS Tanner 307, ff. 128v-9.

HrG 191 -----

Copy in a verse miscellany probably compiled by Robert Clarke of Wadham College, Oxford; c. 1663.

This MS not recorded in Hutchinson.

Duke University, MS 12-14-71, pp. 150-1.

HrG 192 *An Offering* ('Come, bring thy gift. If blessings were as slow').

Copy in the Tanner MS; [1633].

First pub. in *The Temple* (1633); Hutchinson, pp. 147-8.

Bodleian, MS Tanner 307, ff. 107-8.

HrG 193 -----

Copy of lines 25-42, beginning 'Since my sadnesse', among 'Choice Verses written out of the Sacred Poems, of M[r] George Herbert' in a verse miscellany probably compiled by Robert Clarke of Wadham College, Oxford; c. 1663.

This MS not recorded in Hutchinson.

Duke University, MS 12-14-71, p. 24.

HrG 194 *Paradise* ('I blesse thee, Lord, because I Grow').

Copy in the Tanner MS; [1633].

First pub. in *The Temple* (1633); Hutchinson, pp. 132-3.

Bodleian, MS Tanner 307, ff. 95v-6.

HrG 195 *A Parodie* ('Souls joy, when thou art gone').

Copy in the Tanner MS; [1633].

First pub. in *The Temple* (1633); Hutchinson, pp. 183-4.

Bodleian, MS Tanner 307, ff. 135-6.

HrG 196 -----

Copy, headed 'Songe', in a MS volume of John Donne's poems probably prepared for an intended edition, owned in 1680 by Narcissus Luttrell; c. 1632.

This MS not recorded in Hutchinson.

Owned by Sir Geoffrey Keynes, *Bibliotheca Bibliographici* No. 1861, ff. 124v-5.

HrG 197 *Peace* ('Sweet Peace, where dost thou dwell? I humbly crave').

Copy in the Tanner MS; [1633].

First pub. in *The Temple* (1633); Hutchinson, pp. 124-5.

Bodleian, MS Tanner 307, ff. 89-90.

*HrG 198 *The Pearl. Matth. 13. 45.* ('I know the wayes of Learning; both the head').

Copy, with autograph revisions, in the Dr Williams MS; c. 1620s.

First pub. in *The Temple* (1633); Hutchinson, pp. 88-9.

Dr Williams's Library, MS Jones B. 62, ff. 57v-8.

HrG 199 -----

Copy in the Tanner MS; [1633].

Bodleian, MS Tanner 307, ff. 61-2.

HrG 200 *Perseverance* ('My God, the poore expressions of my Love').

Copy in the Dr Williams MS; c. 1620s.

First pub. (from this MS) in Grosart (1874); printed from this MS in Hutchinson, pp. 204-5.

Dr Williams's Library, MS Jones B. 62, f. 76.

HrG 201 *The Pilgrimage* ('I travell'd on, seeing the hill, where lay').

Copy in the Tanner MS; [1633].

First pub. in *The Temple* (1633); Hutchinson, pp. 141-2.

Bodleian, MS Tanner 307, f. 103r-v.

HrG 202 *The Posie* ('Let wits contest').

Copy in the Tanner MS; [1633].

First pub. in *The Temple* (1633); Hutchinson, pp. 182-3.

Bodleian, MS Tanner 307, f. 135.

HrG 203 -----

Copy in a volume of state letters and speeches; mid-17th century.

This MS not recorded in Hutchinson.

Cambridge University Library, MS Gg. 4. 13, p. 236 rev.

HrG 204 *Praise (I)* ('To write a verse or two is all the praise').

Copy in the Dr Williams MS; c. 1620s.

First pub. in *The Temple* (1663); Hutchinson, p. 61.

Dr Williams's Library, MS Jones B. 62, f. 41v.

HrG 205 -----

Copy in the Tanner MS; [1633].

Bodleian, MS Tanner 307, f. 41r-v.

HrG 206 *Praise (II)* ('King of Glorie, King of Peace').

Copy in the Tanner MS; [1633].

First pub. in *The Temple* (1633); Hutchinson, p. 146.

Bodleian, MS Tanner 307, ff. 106-7.

HrG 207 *Praise (III)* ('Lord, I will mean and speak thy praise').

Copy in the Tanner MS; [1633].

First pub. in *The Temple* (1633); Hutchinson, pp. 157-9.

Bodleian, MS Tanner 307, ff. 115v-16v.

HrG 208 *Prayer (I)* ('Prayer the Churches banquet, Angels age').

Copy in the Dr Williams MS; c. 1620s.

First pub. in *The Temple* (1633); Hutchinson, p. 51.

Dr Williams's Library, MS Jones B. 62, f. 34.

HrG 209 -----

Copy in the Tanner MS; [1633].

Bodleian, MS Tanner 307, f. 33.

HrG 210 -----

Copy, headed 'Verses out of Herbert, oratour to ye vniusitie of Cambridge Touching prayer', in a volume of state letters and speeches; mid-17th century.

This MS not recorded in Hutchinson.

Cambridge University Library, MS Gg. 4. 13, p. 236 rev.

HrG 211 *Prayer (II)* ('Of what an easie quick accesse').

Copy in the Dr Williams MS; c. 1620s.

First pub. in *The Temple* (1633); Hutchinson, p. 103.

Dr Williams's Library, MS Jones B. 62, ff. 71v-2.

HrG 212 -----

Copy in the Tanner MS; [1633].

Bodleian, MS Tanner 307, f. 72r-v.

HrG 213 *The Priesthood* ('Blest Order, which in power dost so excell').

Copy in the Tanner MS; [1633].

First pub. in *The Temple* (1633); Hutchinson, pp. 160-1.

Bodleian, MS Tanner 307, ff. 117v-18v.

HrG 214 -----

Copy in a composite volume of tracts and papers; late 17th century.

This MS not recorded in Hutchinson.

Bodleian, MS Rawl. D. 924, ff. 339-40.

HrG 215 *Providence* ('O sacred Providence, who from end to end').

Copy in the Tanner MS; [1633].

First pub. in *The Temple* (1633); Hutchinson, pp. 116-21.

Bodleian, MS Tanner 307, ff. 82v-6v.

HrG 216 -----

Copy of part of the poem, beginning at line 61 ('Each creature hath a wisdome for his good'), among 'Choice Verses written out of the Sacred Poems, of Mr George Herbert' in a verse miscellany probably compiled by Robert Clarke of Wadham College, Oxford; c. 1663.

This MS not recorded in Hutchinson.

Duke University, MS 12-14-71, p. 4.

HrG 217 *The Pulley* ('When God at first made man').

Copy in the Tanner MS; [1633].

First pub. in *The Temple* (1633); Hutchinson, pp. 159-60.

Bodleian, MS Tanner 307, f. 117r-v.

HrG 218 *The Quidditie* ('My God, a verse is not a crown').

Copy, headed 'Poetry', in the Dr Williams MS; c. 1620s.

First pub. in *The Temple* (1633); Hutchinson, pp. 69-70.

Dr Williams's Library, MS Jones B. 62, f. 48.

HrG 219 -----

Copy in the Tanner MS; [1633].

Bodleian, MS Tanner 307, f. 47r-v.

HrG 220 *The Quip* ('The merrie world did on a day').

Copy in the Tanner MS; [1633].

First pub. in *The Temple* (1633); Hutchinson, pp. 110-11.

Bodleian, MS Tanner 307, ff. 77v-8.

*HrG 221 *Redemption* ('Having been tenant long to a rich Lord').

Copy, with autograph revisions, in the Dr Williams MS; c. 1620s.

Redemption

First pub. in *The Temple* (1633); Hutchinson, p. 40.

Dr Williams's Library, MS Jones B. 62, f. 25.

HrG 222 -----

Copy in the Tanner MS; [1633].

Bodleian, MS Tanner 307, ff. 24v-5.

*HrG 223 *Repentance* ('Lord, I confesse my sinne is great').

Copy, with an autograph revision, in the Dr Williams MS; c. 1620s.

First pub. in *The Temple* (1633); Hutchinson, pp. 48-9.

Dr Williams's Library, MS Jones B. 62, ff. 40v-1.

HrG 224 -----

Copy in the Tanner MS; [1633].

Bodleian, MS Tanner 307, f. 31r-v.

HrG 225 *The Reprisall* ('I have consider'd it, and finde').

Copy, headed 'The Second Thanks-giving', in the Dr Williams MS; c. 1620s.

First pub. in *The Temple* (1633); Hutchinson, pp. 36-7.

Dr Williams's Library, MS Jones B. 62, f. 24.

HrG 226 -----

Copy in the Tanner MS; [1633].

Bodleian, MS Tanner 307, f. 22v.

HrG 227 *The Rose* ('Presse me not to take more pleasure').

Copy in the Tanner MS; [1633].

First pub. in *The Temple* (1633); Hutchinson, pp. 177-8.

Bodleian, MS Tanner 307, ff. 130v-1v.

HrG 228 -----

Copy of a version of the second stanza, here beginning 'Sure there is no pleasure here', inscribed with extracts from other works inside the back cover of a MS book of sermons written by Stephen Machin; late 17th century.

This MS not recorded in Hutchinson.

Yale, Osborn Collection, b 245.

*HrG 229 *The Sacrifice* ('Oh all ye, who passe by, whose eyes and minde').

Copy, with autograph revisions, in the Dr Williams MS; c. 1620s.

First pub. in *The Temple* (1633); Hutchinson, pp. 26-34.

Dr Williams's Library, MS Jones B. 62, ff. 16-22.

HrG 230 -----

Copy in the Tanner MS; [1633].

Bodleian, MS Tanner 307, ff. 16-21.

HrG 231 *The Search* ('Whither, O, whither art thou fled').

Copy in the Tanner MS; [1633].

First pub. in *The Temple* (1633); Hutchinson, pp. 162-3.

Bodleian, MS Tanner 307, ff. 118v-20.

HrG 232 *Self-condemnation* ('Thou who condemnest Jewish hate').

Copy in the Tanner MS; [1633].

First pub. in *The Temple* (1633); Hutchinson, pp. 170-1.

Bodleian, MS Tanner 307, f. 125r-v.

HrG 233 *Sepulchre* ('O blessed bodie! Whither art thou thrown?').

Copy in the Tanner MS; [1633].

First pub. in *The Temple* (1633); Hutchinson, pp. 40-1.

Bodleian, MS Tanner 307, f. 25r-v.

HrG 234 -----

Copy in a journal compiled by one Thomas Grocer; 1657.

This MS not recorded in Hutchinson.

Huntington, HM 93, p. 35.

HrG 235 *Sighs and Grones* ('O do not use me').

Copy in the Tanner MS; [1633].

First pub. in *The Temple* (1633); Hutchinson, p. 83.

Bodleian, MS Tanner 307, ff. 57-8.

HrG 236 *Sinne (I)* ('Lord, with what care hast thou begirt us round!').

Copy in the Dr Williams MS; c. 1620s.

First pub. in *The Temple* (1633); Hutchinson, pp. 45-6.

Dr Williams's Library, MS Jones B. 62, f. 66.

HrG 237 -----

Copy in the Tanner MS; [1633].

Bodleian, MS Tanner 307, f. 29.

HrG 238 *Sinne (II)* ('O that I could a sinne once see!').

Copy in the Dr Williams MS; c. 1620s.

First pub. in *The Temple* (1633); Hutchinson, p. 63.

Dr Williams's Library, MS Jones B. 62, f. 39.

HrG 239 -----

Copy in the Tanner MS; [1633].

Bodleian, MS Tanner 307, f. 42v.

HrG 240 *The Sinner* ('Lord, how I am all ague, when I seek').

Copy in the Dr Williams MS; c. 1620s.

First pub. in *The Temple* (1633); Hutchinson, p. 38.

Dr Williams's Library, MS Jones B. 62, f. 26.

HrG 241 -----

Copy in the Tanner MS; [1633].

Bodleian, MS Tanner 307, f. 23v.

HrG 242 *Sinnes round* ('Sorrie I am, my God, sorrie I am').

Copy in the Tanner MS; [1633].

First pub. in *The Temple* (1633); Hutchinson, p. 122.

Bodleian, MS Tanner 307, ff. 86v-7.

HrG 243 *Sion* ('Lord, with what glorie wast thou serv'd of old').

Copy in the Tanner MS; [1633].

First pub. in *The Temple* (1633); Hutchinson, pp. 106-7.

Bodleian, MS Tanner 307, ff. 74v-5.

HrG 244 *The Size* ('Content thee, greedie heart').

Copy in the Tanner MS; [1633].

First pub. in *The Temple* (1633); Hutchinson, pp. 137-8.

Bodleian, MS Tanner 307, ff. 99v-100v.

HrG 245 *The Sonne* ('Let forrain nations of their language boast').

Copy in the Tanner MS; [1633].

First pub. in *The Temple* (1633); Hutchinson, pp. 167-8.

Bodleian, MS Tanner 307, f. 123v.

HrG 246 *The Starre* ('Bright spark, shot from a brighter place').

Copy in the Tanner MS; [1633].

First pub. in *The Temple* (1633); Hutchinson, p. 74.

Bodleian, MS Tanner 307, ff. 50v-1.

HrG 247 -----

Copies of lines 1-16, untitled, in a musical setting by John Jenkins (1592-1678), in three MS music part books; early-mid-17th century.

This MS discussed in Vincent Duckles, 'John Jenkins's Settings of Lyrics by George Herbert', *MQ*, 48 (1962), 461-75; not recorded in Hutchinson.

Christ Church, Oxford, MSS Mus. 736-7, f. 33; 738, f. 34.

HrG 248 -----

Copies of lines 17-32, untitled and beginning 'Then with our trinitie of light', treated as a separate song, in a musical setting by John Jenkins (different from that in HrG 247), in three MS music part books; early-mid-17th century.

This MS discussed in Duckles; not recorded in Hutchinson.

Christ Church, Oxford, MSS Mus. 736-7, f. 32v; 738, f. 33v.

HrG 249 *The Storm* ('If as the windes and waters here below').

Copy in the Tanner MS; [1633].

First pub. in *The Temple* (1633); Hutchinson, p. 132.

Bodleian, MS Tanner 307, f. 95r-v.

HrG 250 *Submission* ('But that thou art my wisdome, Lord').

Copy in the Tanner MS; [1633].

First pub. in *The Temple* (1633); Hutchinson, p. 95.

Bodleian, MS Tanner 307, f. 66.

HrG 251 -----

Copy of lines 1-4, 13-16, inscribed with extracts from other works inside the back cover of a MS book of sermons written by Stephen Machin; late 17th century.

This MS not recorded in Hutchinson.

Yale, Osborn Collection, b 245.

*HrG 252 *Sunday* ('O day most calm, most bright').

Copy, with an autograph revision, in the Dr Williams MS; c. 1620s.

First pub. in *The Temple* (1633); Hutchinson, pp. 75-7.

Dr Williams's Library, MS Jones B. 62, ff. 51-2v.

HrG 253 -----

Copy in the Tanner MS; [1633].

Bodleian, MS Tanner 307, ff. 51v-2v.

HrG 254 *Superliminare* ('Thou, whom the former precepts have').

Copy, the first quatrain headed 'Perirranterium', in the Dr Williams MS; c. 1620s.

First pub. in *The Temple* (1633); Hutchinson, p. 25.

Dr Williams's Library, MS Jones B. 62, ff. 14v-15.

HrG 255 -----

Copy in the Tanner MS; [1633].

Bodleian, MS Tanner 307, f. 15.

HrG 256 *The Temper (I)* ('How should I praise thee, Lord! how should my rymes').

Copy, headed 'The Christian Temper', in the Dr Williams MS; c. 1620s.

First pub. in *The Temple* (1633); Hutchinson, p. 55.

Dr Williams's Library, MS Jones B. 62, ff. 32v-3.

HrG 257 -----

Copy in the Tanner MS; [1633].

Bodleian, MS Tanner 307, f. 36r-v.

HrG 258 *The Temper (II)* ('It cannot be. Where is that mightie joy').

Copy, headed 'The Christian Temper', in the Dr Williams MS; c. 1620s.

First pub. in *The Temple* (1633); Hutchinson, p. 56.

Dr Williams's Library, MS Jones B. 62, f. 33v.

HrG 259 -----

Copy in the Tanner MS; [1633].

Bodleian, MS Tanner 307, ff. 36v-7.

*HrG 260 *The Thanksgiving* ('Oh King of grief! a title strange, yet true').

Copy, with an autograph revision, in the Dr Williams MS; c. 1620s.

First pub. in *The Temple* (1633); Hutchinson, pp. 35-6.

Dr Williams's Library, MS Jones B. 62, ff. 22v-3v.

HrG 261 -----

Copy in the Tanner MS; [1633].

Bodleian, MS Tanner 307, ff. 21v-2v.

HrG 262 *Time* ('Meeting with Time, Slack thing, said I').

Copy in the Tanner MS; [1633].

First pub. in *The Temple* (1633); Hutchinson, pp. 122-3.

Bodleian, MS Tanner 307, ff. 87-8.

*HrG 263 *To all Angels and Saints* ('Oh glorious spirits, who after all your bands').

Copy, with an autograph revision, in the Dr Williams MS; c. 1620s.

First pub. in *The Temple* (1633); Hutchinson, pp. 77-8.

Dr Williams's Library, MS Jones B. 62, ff. 56v-7.

HrG 264 -----

Copy in the Tanner MS; [1633].

Bodleian, MS Tanner 307, ff. 53-4.

To all Angels and Saints

HrG 265 -----

Copy in the hand of Thomas Traherne, in his MS book of Meditations and Devotions on the festivals of the Church; c. 1660-74.

This MS not recorded in Hutchinson.

Bodleian, MS Eng. th. e. 51, f. 112v.

*HrG 266 *Trinitie Sunday* ('Lord, who hast form'd me out of mud').

Copy, with an autograph revision, in the Dr Williams MS; c. 1620s.

First pub. in *The Temple* (1633); Hutchinson, p. 68.

Dr Williams's Library, MS Jones B. 62, f. 39v.

HrG 267 -----

Copy in the Tanner MS; [1633].

Bodleian, MS Tanner 307, f. 46.

HrG 268 *Trinity Sunday* ('He that is one').

Copy in the Dr Williams MS; c. 1620s.

First pub. (from this MS) in Grosart (1874); printed from this MS in Hutchinson, pp. 202-3.

Dr Williams's Library, MS Jones B. 62, f. 40.

HrG 269 *A true Hymne* ('My joy, my life, my crown!').

Copy in the Tanner MS; [1633].

First pub. in *The Temple* (1633); Hutchinson, p. 168.

Bodleian, MS Tanner 307, ff. 123v-4.

HrG 270 -----

Copy in the hand of Francis Knollys, in his MS translation of the Psalms; 1660.

This MS not recorded in Hutchinson.

Bodleian, MS Rawl. poet. 60, p. 3.

HrG 271 *The 23d Psalme* ('The God of love my shepherd is').

Copy in the Tanner MS; [1633].

First pub. in *The Temple* (1633); Hutchinson, pp. 172-3.

Bodleian, MS Tanner 307, ff. 126v-7.

HrG 272 -----

Copy in a verse miscellany compiled by Archbishop William Sancroft (1617-93); mid-late 17th century.

This MS not recorded in Hutchinson.

Bodleian, MS Tanner 466, f. 18r-v.

HrG 273 -----

Copy in a musical setting by Henry Lawes, in Lawes's autograph songbook; mid-17th century.

This MS not recorded in Hutchinson.

British Library, Add. MS 53723, f. 78v.

HrG 274 -----

Copy, signed 'W.F.', on a loose leaf; 17th century.

This MS not recorded in Hutchinson.

Yale, Osborn Collection, P.B. VI/41.

HrG 275 *Ungratefulnesse* ('Lord, with what bountie and rare clemencie').

Copy in the Dr Williams MS; c. 1620s.

First pub. in *The Temple* (1633); Hutchinson, p. 82.

Dr Williams's Library, MS Jones B. 62, ff. 54v-5.

HrG 276 -----

Copy in the Tanner MS; [1633].

Bodleian, MS Tanner 307, ff. 56v-7.

HrG 277 *Unkindnesse* ('Lord, make me coy and tender to offend').

Copy in the Dr Williams MS; c. 1620s.

First pub. in *The Temple* (1633); Hutchinson, pp. 93-4.

Dr Williams's Library, MS Jones B. 62, ff. 67v-8.

HrG 278 -----

Copy in the Tanner MS; [1633].

Bodleian, MS Tanner 307, ff. 64v-5.

HrG 279 *Vanitie (I)* ('The fleet Astronomer can bore').

Copy in the Tanner MS; [1633].

First pub. in *The Temple* (1633); Hutchinson, pp. 85-6.

Bodleian, MS Tanner 307, f. 59r-v.

HrG 280 *Vanitie (II)* ('Poore silly soul, whose hope and head lies low').

Copy in the Tanner MS; [1633].

First pub. in *The Temple* (1633); Hutchinson, p. 111.

Bodleian, MS Tanner 307, f. 78r-v.

HrG 281 *Vertue* ('Sweet day, so cool, so calm, so bright').

Copy in the Tanner MS; [1633].

First pub. in *The Temple* (1633); Hutchinson, pp. 87-8.

Bodleian, MS Tanner 307, ff. 60v-1.

HrG 281.5 See Addenda, p. 630.

HrG 282 -----

Copy among 'Choice Verses written out of the Sacred Poems, of M[r] George Herbert' in a verse miscellany probably compiled by Robert Clarke of Wadham College, Oxford; c. 1663.

This MS not recorded in Hutchinson.

Duke University, MS 12-14-71, p. 23.

HrG 283 *The Water-course* ('Thou who dost dwell and linger here below').

Copy in the Tanner MS; [1633].

First pub. in *The Temple* (1633); Hutchinson, p. 170.

Bodleian, MS Tanner 307, f. 125.

HrG 284 *Whitsunday* ('Listen sweet Dove unto my song').

Copy of an early version beginning 'Come blessed doue charm'd wth my song' in the Dr Williams MS; c. 1620s.

First pub. in *The Temple* (1633); Hutchinson, pp. 59-60.

Dr Williams's Library, MS Jones B. 62, ff. 36v-7.

HrG 285 -----

Copy in the Tanner MS; [1633].

Bodleian, MS Tanner 307, ff. 39v-40.

HrG 286 *The Windows* ('Lord, how can man preach thy eternall word?').

Copy in the Tanner MS; [1633].

First pub. in *The Temple* (1633); Hutchinson, pp. 67-8.

Bodleian, MS Tanner 307, f. 45v.

HrG 287 *The World* ('Love built a stately house; where Fortune came').

Copy in the Dr Williams MS; c. 1620s.

First pub. in *The Temple* (1633); Hutchinson, p. 84.

Dr Williams's Library, MS Jones B. 62, ff. 59v-60.

HrG 288 -----

Copy in the Tanner MS; [1633].

Bodleian, MS Tanner 307, f. 58r-v.

HrG 289 *A Wreath* ('A wreathed garland of deserved praise').

Copy in the Dr Williams MS; c. 1620s.

First pub. in *The Temple* (1633); Hutchinson, p. 185.

Dr Williams's Library, MS Jones B. 62, f. 56.

HrG 290 -----

Copy in the Tanner MS; [1633].

Bodleian, MS Tanner 307, ff. 136v-7.

(2) ENGLISH POEMS OF UNCERTAIN AUTHORSHIP

--- *L'Envoy* ('Shine on, Maiestick soule, abide').

See HrG 294-8.

HrG 291 *A Paradox. That the Sicke are in better State then the Whole* ('You whoe admire yourselues because').

Copy in a verse miscellany compiled by one 'H.S.', a Cambridge man; 1640s-50s.

First pub. (from this MS) in *Works of George Herbert*, ed. William Pickering, II (London, 1835); Hutchinson, pp. 209-11. This MS collated in Hutchinson.

Bodleian, MS Rawl. poet. 147, p. 78.

A Paradox. That the Sicke are in better State then the Whole

HrG 292 -----

Copy in a miscellany possibly compiled by a member of an Inn of Court; c. 1620s-30s.

Printed from this MS in Hutchinson.

British Library, Add. MS 25303, ff. 98v-9.

HrG 293 -----

Copy, ascribed to George Herbert, in a verse miscellany possibly compiled by a member of an Inn of Court; c. 1620s.

This MS collated in Hutchinson.

British Library, Harley MS 3910, ff. 53v-4.

HrG 294 *To the Queene of Bohemia* ('Bright soule, of whome if any countrey knowne').

Copy, complete with 'L'Envoy' (beginning 'Shine on, Maiestick soule, abide'), in a verse miscellany owned by one Peter Daniell; c. 1630s-40s.

First pub. in *Inedited Poetical Miscellanies 1584-1700*, ed. W.C. Hazlitt ([London], 1870), pp. [186-92]; Hutchinson, pp. 211-13. Herbert's authorship supported in Kenneth Alan Hovey, 'George Herbert's Authorship of "To the Queene of Bohemia"', *RQ*, 30 (1977), 43-50, and in Ted-Larry Pebworth, 'George Herbert's Poems to the Queen of Bohemia: A Rediscovered Text and a New Edition', *ELR* (forthcoming). This MS collated in Pebworth.

Bodleian, MS Eng. poet. c. 50, f. 60r-v.

HrG 295 -----

Copy, complete with 'L'Envoy', ascribed to 'G: H:', transcribed from HrG 298, in a transcript of two 17th-century verse miscellanies; 19th century.

This MS recorded in Pebworth.

Bodleian, MS Firth d. 7, ff. 173-7.

HrG 296 -----

Copy, complete with 'L'Envoy', ascribed to 'G. H.', in a verse miscellany; c. 1630s.

This MS collated in Pebworth.

Bodleian, MS Rawl. poet. 160, f. 84r-v.

HrG 297 -----

Copy, complete with 'L'Envoy', ascribed to 'G. H.', in a verse miscellany possibly compiled by a member of an Inn of Court; c. 1620s.

Printed from this MS in Hutchinson; collated in Pebworth.

British Library, Harley MS 3910, ff. 121-2.

HrG 298 -----

Copy, complete with 'L'Envoy', ascribed to 'G: H:', in a verse miscellany compiled by a Cambridge man; c. 1630.

Formerly owned by F.W. Cosens; printed from this MS in Hazlitt and in Pebworth.

Cambridge University Library, MS Add. 4138, ff. 52v-3v.

HrG 299 *To the Right Hon. the L. Chancellor (Bacon)* ('My Lord. A diamond to mee you sent').

Copy in a composite volume of verse and prose owned c. 1669 by one John Cooke of Bury St Edmunds, Suffolk; c. 1620s-30s.

First pub. 'from a small quarto volume of MS. Latin poetry' in J. Fry, *Bibliographical Memoranda* (Bristol, 1816); Hutchinson, p. 209. This MS not recorded in Hutchinson.

Bodleian, MS Rawl. poet. 26, f. 48.

HrG 300 -----

Copy in a verse miscellany compiled by a Cambridge man; c. 1648-60.

This MS collated in Hutchinson.

Bodleian, MS Rawl. poet. 246, f. 46v.

HrG 301 -----

Copy in a verse miscellany; mid-17th century.

Printed from this MS in Hutchinson.

British Library, Add. MS 22602, f. 32.

(3) LATIN POEMS BY HERBERT

HrG 302 *Ad Autorem Instaurationis Magnae* ('Per strages licet autorum veterúmque ruinam').

Copy, headed 'Ad Eundem', in a verse miscellany compiled by a Cambridge man; c. 1648-60.

First pub. in James Duport, *Ecclesiastes Solomonis* (Cambridge, 1662); Hutchinson, p. 435. This MS collated in Hutchinson.

Bodleian, MS Rawl. poet. 246, f. 46.

HrG 302.5 See Addenda, p. 630.

Aethiopissa ambit Cestum Diuersi Coloris Virum

HrG 303 *Aethiopissa ambit Cestum Diuersi Coloris Virum* ('Qvid mihi si facies nigra est? hoc, Ceste, colore').

Copy in a verse miscellany compiled by a Cambridge man; c. 1648-60.

First pub. in James Duport, *Ecclesiastes Solomonis* (Cambridge, 1662); Hutchinson, p. 437. This MS collated in Hutchinson.

Bodleian, MS Rawl. poet. 246, ff. 46v-7.

HrG 304 -----

Copy in a verse miscellany; mid-17th century.

This MS collated in Hutchinson.

British Library, Add. MS 22602, f. 32.

HrG 304.5 See Addenda, p. 630.

HrG 305 *Comparatio inter Munus Summi Cancellariatus et Librum* ('Mvnere dum nobis prodes, Librôque futuris').

Copy in a verse miscellany compiled by a Cambridge man; c. 1648-60.

First pub. in James Duport, *Ecclesiastes Solomonis* (Cambridge, 1662); Hutchinson, p. 435. This MS collated in Hutchinson.

Bodleian, MS Rawl. poet. 246, f. 46v.

HrG 306 *Dum petit Infantem* ('Dvm petit Infantem Princeps, Grantâmque Iacobus').

Copy made by Joseph Mede in a letter to Sir Martin Stutevile, in a bound collection of Mede's letters; 15 March 1622/3.

First pub. in *True Copies Of all the Latine Orations, made on the 25. and 27. of Februarie 1622* (London, 1623); Hutchinson, pp. 437-8. This MS collated in Hutchinson. A transcript of this letter made by Thomas Baker (1656-1740) is in Harley MS 7041.

British Library, Harley MS 389, ff. 298, 300.

HrG 307 -----

Copy of lines 1-4, here beginning 'Dum petit Hispanam Princeps, Grantamq Jacobus', in a volume of theological and state tracts; mid-17th century.

This MS collated in Hutchinson.

Cambridge University Library, MS Gg. 1. 29, f. 21 rev.

HrG 308 -----

Copy pasted on the flyleaf of a printed exemplum of Izaak Walton, *The Life of Mr. George Herbert* (London, 1670); 17th century.

This MS collated in Hutchinson.

Harvard, *EC.H4157.W670w2.

HrG 309 -----

Copy, among the papers of the Clifton family of Clifton Hall, Nottinghamshire; 17th century.

This MS not recorded in Hutchinson. It is accompanied by a transcript and a translation into English made by Rosslyn Bruce, 18 June 1905.

University of Nottingham, Clifton MS Cl LM 59.

HrG 310 *In Honorem Illustr. D.D. Verulamij, S*[ti] *Albani, Mag. Sigilli Custodis post editam ab eo Instaurationem Magnam* ('Qvis iste tandem? non enim vultu ambulat').

Copy, alleged by Grosart to be autograph, inscribed on the flyleaf of a printed exemplum of Francis Bacon, *Certaine Psalmes* (London, 1625); c. 1625?

First pub. in Emanuele Tesauro, *Caesares*, 2nd edition (Oxford, 1637); Hutchinson, pp. 436-7. This item recorded in *Miscellanies of The Fuller Worthies Library*, ed. A.B. Grosart, I (London, 1870).

Owned in 1870 by one Mrs Seaman of Tunbridge Wells, Kent; unlocated.

HrG 311 -----

Copy in a verse miscellany compiled by a Cambridge man; c. 1648-60.

This MS collated in Hutchinson.

Bodleian, MS Rawl. poet. 246, f. 46r-v.

HrG 312 -----

Copy in a composite volume perhaps partly compiled by a member of an Inn of Court; c. 1640s.

This MS not recorded in Hutchinson.

British Library, Harley MS 4931, f. 16.

HrG 313 -----

Copy, here ascribed to 'Gulielmus Herbert', on a leaf pasted in a volume of autograph drafts of Bacon (see BcF 287, 294); mid-17th century.

This MS collated in Hutchinson.

Owned by the Duke of Devonshire, Chatsworth House, MS Hardwick 72A, f. 1.

HrG 314 *In nobilissimi Cornitis Palatini Ad Rhenum, et illustrissa: Domina Elizabethe Nuptiae Epithal.* ('En Aurora vocat, lectus genialis in aula est').

Copy of a sixteen-line epithalamium on the marriage of Frederick, the Elector Palatine, to Princess Elizabeth, in the MS volume of gratulatory verse presented to the Elector Palatine by the University of Cambridge on 6 March 1612/13.

First pub. (from this MS) in Leicester Bradner, 'New Poems by George Herbert: The Cambridge Latin Gratulatory Anthology of 1613', *RN*, 15 (1962), 208-11; translated in Kenneth Alan Hovey, 'George Herbert's Authorship of "To the Queene of Bohemia"', *RN*, 30 (1977), 43-50 (p. 45).

Vatican Library, MS Palat. lat. 1736, f. 36.

*HrG 315 *Lucus* ('Svm, quis nescit, Imago Dei, sed sexea certè').

Autograph of 35 Latin poems in the Dr Williams MS; c. 1620s.

First pub. (from this MS) in Grosart (1874) (but see HrG 317 and 321); printed from this MS in Hutchinson, pp. 410-21. Facsimiles of poems xxv, xxvi and xxvii in Petti, *English Literary Hands*, No. 58; poems xxx and xxi in John J. Daniell, *The Life of George Herbert* (London, 1902), facing p. 317.

Dr Williams's Library, MS Jones B. 62, ff. 107v-19.

HrG 316 ----- *X. Papae titulus Nec Deus Nec Homo* ('Qvisnam Antichristus cessemus quaerere; Papa').

Copy, headed 'In adulatorium Papae titulam "Nec deus est nec homo"', among the papers of the Clifton family of Clifton Hall, Nottinghamshire; 17th century.

This MS not recorded in Hutchinson. It is accompanied by a transcript and a translation into English made by Rosslyn Bruce, 18 June 1905.

University of Nottingham, Clifton MS Cl LM 59.

HrG 317 ----- *XXV. Roma. Anagr.* ('Roma, tuum nomen quam non pertransijt Oram').

Copy in Volume II of a bound MS antiquarian collection once owned by Ralph Thoresby (1658-1725); late 17th-early 18th century.

This poem first pub. in James Duport, *Ecclesiastes Solomonis* (Cambridge, 1662). This MS collated in Hutchinson, p. 416.

British Library, Add. MS 4275, f. 273.

HrG 318 ----- -----

Copy in a miscellany bound in a composite volume of MSS; mid-17th century.

The text followed by an English version beginning 'Rome, Thou that cal'st thyselfe a queene a whore'. This MS not recorded in Hutchinson.

British Library, Harley MS 1221, f. 102r-v.

HrG 319 ----- -----

Copy, dated 1618, in a miscellany bound in a composite volume of MSS; mid-17th century.

The text followed on f. 16 by an English version (see HrG 318). This MS not recorded in Hutchinson.

British Library, Harley MS 6038, f. 15v.

HrG 320 ----- -----

Copy in a miscellany; c. 1630.

This MS not recorded in Hutchinson.

Folger, MS V. a. 345, p. 156.

HrG 321 ----- *XXXII. Triumphus Mortis* ('O mea suspicienda manus, ventèrque perennis!').

Copy of a version headed 'Inuenta Bellica' and beginning 'O mortis longaeua fames, venterque perennis', in a small MS volume of Latin poems; early-mid-17th century.

This poem first pub. (from a MS in Pickering's possession) in *The Works of George Herbert*, ed. William Pickering, I (London, 1836). Printed from this MS in G.M. Story, 'George Herbert's *Inventa Bellica*: A New Manuscript', *MP*, 59 (1962), 270-2; not recorded in Hutchinson.

Chetham's Library, Manchester, Mun. A 3. 48, ff. 1-2.

HrG 322 ----- -----

Copy of a version headed 'Inventa Bellica', here ascribed to 'T: May', and beginning 'O martis longava fames! vanterq perennis', in a verse miscellany compiled by an Oxford man; c. 1630s.

This MS not recorded by editors.

Folger, MS V. a. 170, pp. 206-10.

HrG 323 ----- -----

Copy of a version headed 'Inventa Bellica' and beginning 'O mortis longaeua fames, verterque perennis', in a verse miscellany; c. 1638-45.

Lucus XXXII. Triumphus Mortis

This MS not recorded by editors.

Rosenbach Foundation, MS 239/22, ff. 53v-5.

HrG 324 *Memoriae Matris Sacrum. II* ('Corneliae sanctae, graues Semproniae').

Copy of lines 1-51 in a verse miscellany compiled by a Cambridge man; c. 1640s.

First pub. in *A Sermon of Commemoration of the Lady Dãuers. By John Donne. Together with other Commemorations of Her* (London, 1627); Hutchinson, pp. 422-31 (pp. 422-4). This MS recorded in Hutchinson.

Bodleian, MS Rawl. poet. 62, f. 7r-v.

*HrG 325 *Passio Discerpta* ('Cvm lacrymas oculôsque duos tot vulnera vincant').

Autograph of 21 Latin poems in the Dr Williams MS; c. 1620s.

First pub. (from this MS) in Grosart (1874); printed from this MS in Hutchinson, pp. 404-9. Facsimiles of f. 103 in Palmer, I, 168; f. 106 in Hutchinson, frontispiece.

Dr Williams's Library, MS Jones B. 62, ff. 102-7.

HrG 326 *'Peregrinis Almam Matrem Invisentibus'.*

Copy of a poem ascribed to 'G. Herbert Orator' written on a flyleaf in a printed exemplum of the *Workes* of James I (London, 1616 [1620 issue]); c. 1620s.

First pub. (from this MS) in J. Gibbs, 'An Unknown Poem of George Herbert', *TLS* (30 December 1949), p. 857, where it is mistakenly described as autograph. Facsimile in *The Houghton Library 1942-1967* (Cambridge, Mass., 1967), p. 53.

Harvard, *fEC.H4157.Zz620j.

HrG 327 *'Sume Palatini versus de numine Phoebi'.*

Copy of an untitled eight-line poem on the visit of Frederick, the Elector Palatine, to the University of Cambridge, in the MS volume of gratulatory verse presented to Frederick by the University on 6 March 1612/13.

First pub. (from this MS) in Leicester Bradner, 'New Poems by George Herbert: The Cambridge Latin Gratulatory Anthology of 1613', *RN*, 15 (1962), 208-11; translated in Kenneth Alan Hovey, 'George Herbert's Authorship of "To the Queene of Bohemia"', *RQ*, 30 (1977), 43-50 (pp. 44-5).

Vatican Library, MS Palat. lat. 1736, f. 13v.

PROSE

HrG 328 *Oratio in Discessum Regis ab Academiã Cantabrigiae habita 12º die Martij 1622.*

Copy; [1622-3].

First pub. (from this MS) in Hutchinson (1941), pp. 443-4.

Public Record Office, SP.14/139/90.

HrG 329 *Outlandish Proverbs.*

Copy of 204 proverbs, headed 'In the Name of God, IHS. Amen. Proverbs', on preliminary leaves in one of the MS story books of the Little Gidding community; c. 1630s.

First pub. London, 1640; Hutchinson, pp. 321-55. Formerly owned by Lady Langman, this MS collated in Hutchinson and described p. 571.

Clare College, Cambridge.

HrG 330 -----

Copy of 72 proverbs made by George Herbert's brother, Sir Henry Herbert (1595-1673), headed 'Outlandishe Prouerbs selected out of seuerall Languages & entered here the vi. August 1637. At Ribsford. H.H.', in a bound volume of Herbert family papers.

This MS collated in Hutchinson and discussed p. 572.

National Library of Wales, NLW. MS 5301E, ff. 1-7.

--- -----

See also INTRODUCTION.

--- *Reasons for Arth. Woodenoths Liuing wth Sr Jhon Daũers.*

See INTRODUCTION.

John Heywood

1497?-1580?

ABBREVIATIONS

Halliwell *The Moral Play of Wit and Science and Early Poetical Miscellanies from an Unpublished Manuscript*, ed. James Orchard Halliwell [later Halliwell-Phillipps], Shakespeare Society (London, 1848).

Milligan John Heywood, *Works and Miscellaneous Short Poems*, ed. Burton A. Milligan (Urbana, 1956).

For abbreviations used throughout Volume I, see p.xi.

INTRODUCTION

Only a very few autographs of John Heywood survive. The most important are two letters written in his old age to Lord Burghley. One, of 18 April 1575, is in the Public Record Office (SP.12/24/17); the other, which he states is written in his seventy-ninth year (1576?), is among the MSS of the Marquess of Salisbury at Hatfield House (Cecil Papers 8/44). These letters are printed in A. W. Reed, *Early Tudor Drama* (London, 1926), pp. 35-7, 237-8, with a facsimile of part of the first letter facing p. 124. The same plate includes a reproduction of Heywood's signature on a lease of 20 February 1538/9 among the Conventual Leases (Essex 46) in the Public Record Office. Reed believed that these examples showed that the extant MS of Heywood's play *Wytty and Wytless* (HyT 20) was also in his autograph, but in fact a close comparison shows this not to be so: the hand in the latter has peculiar characteristics not shared by Heywood and it also spells his name differently from the undoubted examples of his signature. One other signature of his appears as witness to the Will of Margaret Cox (John Redford's sister) made on 30 September 1556 and preserved in St Paul's Cathedral (Vol. A, f. 117): see Arthur Brown, 'Two Notes on John Redford', *MLR*, 43 (1948), 508-10. Another document of biographical interest, a contemporary copy of the grant to Heywood of Haydon Manor in 1521, can be found in the British Library (Add. MS 24844, ff. 38v-9); it is printed in Robert W. Bolwell, *The Life and Works of John Heywood* (New York, 1921), p. 159.

A few of Heywood's poems and epigrams appear in 16th or 17th-century MS copies, but since his epigrams were readily available in several printed editions they were not a popular choice for miscellanies. The copies recorded in the *Index* have not been noted by editors unless otherwise stated. The most important of the miscellaneous MSS recorded is British Library Add. MS 15233, a mid-16th-century volume of works by Heywood, John Redford (c. 1486-1547), and others, possibly owned in the late 16th century by one Edward Heyborn. The MS was evidently produced by someone close to the Redford-Heywood circle and includes a number of poems ascribed to Heywood which were not published in his lifetime. The MS was first printed in Halliwell (1848).

Heywood's non-dramatic works have been edited in Milligan (1956); various other works have been edited by John S. Farmer in *The Dramatic Writings of John Heywood* (London, 1905; reprinted 1966) and in *The Spider and the Fly* (London, 1908; reprinted 1966). For additions to Farmer's version of the canon, see *NCBEL*, I, col. 1413.

An item not given an entry in the *Index* is a couplet ascribed to 'Hewodd' in a miscellany of the 1590s compiled by John Lilliat, now in the Bodleian (MS Rawl. poet. 148, f. 3). The couplet, which does not appear to be among Heywood's published epigrams, is headed 'of ffeasters' and begins 'One fat feeder, an other feedeth in fine feast'. Two other MS items which have been similarly excluded from the entries are late 18th-century transcripts of early printed ballads by Heywood: *A Brief Ballet touching the Traitorous Taking of Scarborough Castle* ('Oh, valiant invaders! gallantly gay') and *A Ballad specifying partly the Manner, partly the Matter, in the ... Marriage between ... the King's and Queen's Highness* ('The eagle bird hath spread his wings'). These transcripts are in the Mitchell Library, Glasgow (308897), and are recorded in G. Neilson, 'A Bundle of Ballads', *E & S*, 7 (1921), 108-42 (pp. 118-19). Two of Heywood's poems can also be found in a miscellany in the Folger (MS V. a. 339, ff. 109, 118v): *A Song in praise of a Ladie* ('Giue place. yea ladies, and be gone') and '*What hart can thynk or toong expres*'. The copies are, however, forgeries by J. P. Collier: see Giles E. Dawson. 'John Payne Collier's Great Forgery', *SB*, 24 (1971), 1-26 (p. 4).

Heywood's ballads and songs are listed in the *Index* according to their original titles or, if untitled, their first lines, and not according to the titles supplied in Halliwell or Milligan.

PB.

ARRANGEMENT

Verse: (1) Proverbs and epigrams	HyJ 1-4
(2) Songs and ballads	HyJ 5-19
Dramatic works	HyJ 20.

John Heywood

VERSE

(1) PROVERBS AND EPIGRAMS

HyJ 1 *A dialogue conteynyng the number of thē effectuall prouerbes in the Englishe tounge.*

Extracts from the 1576 edition of Heywood's *Woorkes*, bound with an exemplum of that edition; c. 1576-1600.

First pub. London, 1546; Milligan, pp. 17-101; ed. Rudolph E. Habenicht (Berkeley & Los Angeles, 1963).

Folger, STC 13287.

HyJ 2 *Epigrams.*

Copy of 34 epigrams (*First Hundred*, Nos. 20, 21, 35, 53, 59, 62, 68, 72, 79, 83; *Three Hundred*, Nos. 59, 169; *Fifth Hundred*, Nos. 12, 21, 33, 36, 44, 49, 57, 60, 62, 68, 72, 74, 87, 99, 108, 114, 186, 192, 212, 226, 236 and 272), not in sequence, in a verse miscellany probably compiled by a member of an Inn of Court; c. 1598-1600s.

First pub. London, 1550-60; first collected in *Woorkes* (London, 1562); Milligan, pp. 103-224.

Rosenbach Foundation, MS 1083/15, ff. 14v, 20v-2, 28, 50v-1.

HyJ 3 -----

Copy of eight epigrams (*First Hundred*, Nos. 11, 25, 38, 39, 42; *Fifth Hundred*, No. 2; *Sixth Hundred*, Nos. 96, 100); also a deleted copy of a ninth epigram (*Sixth Hundred*, No. 98), written in the middle of a copy of Sir David Lindsay's *Satyre of the Thrie Estaitis*, in a MS volume of Scottish poetry compiled by George Bannatyne; c. 1568.

A sixt hundred of Epigrammes first pub. in *Woorkes* (London, 1562); Milligan, pp. 225-48. Printed from this MS in *The Bannatyne Manuscript*, ed. J. Barclay Murdoch, Hunterian Club (Glasgow, 1896), III, 450-2, 456-7; IV, 1079; *The Bannatyne Manuscript*, ed. W. Tod Ritchie, III, STS NS 23 (Edinburgh & London, 1928), 74-6, 79-81, 130.

National Library of Scotland, Adv. MS 1. 1. 6, Vol. I, ff. 159r-v, 161r-v, 177 (pp. 377-8, 381-2, 413).

HyJ 4 -----

Copy of one epigram (*First Hundred*, No. 79) in a verse miscellany compiled by one Robert Bishop; c. 1630.

Rosenbach Foundation, MS 1083/16, p. 61.

(2) SONGS AND BALLADS

HyJ 5 *'All a grene wyllow is my garland'.*

Copy in a MS volume of works by John Redford and others; c. 1530s-40s.

First pub. (from this MS) in Halliwell (1848), pp. 86-8; printed from this MS in Milligan, pp. 257-9.

British Library, Add. MS 15233, f. 48r-v.

--- *A ballad against slander and detraction.*

See HyJ 8.

HyJ 6 *'Be merye, frendes, take ye no thowghte'.*

Copy in a MS volume of works by John Redford and others; c. 1530s-40s.

First pub. (from this MS) in Halliwell (1848), pp. 104-6; printed from this MS in Milligan, pp. 259-61.

British Library, Add. MS 15233, ff. 58-9.

HyJ 7 *A discription of a most noble Ladye* ('Geue place, ye ladyes, all bee gone').

Copy in a MS volume of religious poems chiefly composed and probably transcribed by the priest William Forrest; 1581.

First pub. (?) in *The Proverbs, Epigrams and Miscellanies of John Heywood*, ed. John S. Farmer (London, 1906). Printed from this MS in Milligan, pp. 250-2. See also HyJ 15-16.

British Library, Harley MS 1703, ff. 108-9.

HyJ 8 *'Gar call hym downe'.*

Copy in a MS volume of works by John Redford and others; c. 1530s-40s.

First pub. as a broadside entitled *A ballad against sklander and detraccion* (London, [1562]). Printed from this MS in Milligan, pp. 263-7.

British Library, Add. MS 15233, ff. 62v-3v.

HyJ 9 *'I desyre no number of manye thynges for store'.*

Copy in a MS volume of works by John Redford and others; c. 1530s-40s.

First pub. (from this MS) in Halliwell (1848), pp. 61-2; printed from this MS in Milligan, p. 254.

British Library, Add. MS 15233, f. 33v.

'Yf loue for loue of long tyme had'

HyJ 10 *'Yf loue for loue of long tyme had'.*

Copy, plus the first stanza mistakenly copied in *'Be merye, frendes'* (see HyJ 6) and deleted, in a MS volume of works by John Redford and others; 1530s-40s.

First pub. (from this MS) in Halliwell (1848), pp. 106-7; printed from this MS in Milligan, p. 261.

British Library, Add. MS 15233, f. 59r-v.

HyJ 11 *'Long haue I bene a singyng man'.*

Copy, here ascribed to Heywood, in a miscellany once owned by John Anstis and Henry Savile; mid-16th century.

First pub. (from this MS) in John Payne Collier, *The History of English Dramatic Poetry to the Time of Shakespeare: and Annals of the Stage to the Restoration* (London, 1831), I, pp. 70, 72; Milligan, pp. 275-7; possibly written by John Redford. This MS collated in Milligan.

British Library, Cotton MS Vespasian A. XXV, f. 141v.

HyJ 12 -----

Copy, here ascribed to John Redford, in a MS volume of works by Redford and others; c. 1530s-40s.

Printed from this MS in Milligan.

British Library, Add. MS 15233, f. 45r-v.

HyJ 13 *'Man, for thyne yll lyfe formerly'.*

Copy in a MS volume of works by John Redford and others; c. 1530s-40s.

First pub. (from this MS) in Halliwell (1848), pp. 77-8; printed from this MS in Milligan, pp. 255-6.

British Library, Add. MS 15233, f. 43r-v.

HyJ 14 *'Man, yf thow mynd heuen to obtayne'.*

Copy in a MS volume of works by John Redford and others; c. 1530s-40s.

First pub. (from this MS) in Halliwell (1848), pp. 118-19; printed from this MS in Milligan, pp. 268-9.

British Library, Add. MS 15233, f. 64r-v.

HyJ 15 *A song in praise of a Ladie* ('Giue place, yea ladies, and be gone').

Copy in a verse miscellany; c. 1616.

First pub. in *Songes and Sonettes*, ed. Richard Tottel (London, 1557). Printed from this MS in Milligan, pp. 252-4. See also HyJ 7.

British Library, Add. MS 15225, f. 16v.

HyJ 16 -----

Copy, headed 'In praise of a gentlewomā', in a miscellany compiled by one 'Jo. Tempest'; mid-17th century.

University of Leeds, Brotherton Collection, MS Lt. q. 9, f. 65.

--- -----

See also INTRODUCTION.

HyJ 17 *'What hart can thynk or toong expres'.*

Copy in a MS volume of works by John Redford and others; c. 1530s-40s.

First pub. (from this MS) in Halliwell (1848), pp. 79-80; printed from this MS in Milligan, pp. 256-7.

British Library, Add. MS 15233, f. 44r-v.

HyJ 18 -----

Copy in a musical setting, among songs added to a MS ecclesiastical tract, constituting Volume XLIV of the collections of Sir Joseph Banks (1743-1820); early 17th century.

British Library, Add. MS 4900, ff. 58v-9.

--- -----

See also INTRODUCTION.

HyJ 19 *'Ye be wellcum, ye be wellcum'.*

Copy in a MS volume of works by John Redford and others; c. 1530s-40s.

First pub. (from this MS) in Halliwell (1848), pp. 111-13; printed from this MS in Milligan, pp. 261-3.

British Library, Add. MS 15233, ff. 61v-2.

DRAMATIC WORKS

HyJ 20 *Wytty and Wytless.*

Copy, subscribed 'John Heywod', in a composite volume of MSS partly compiled by John Stow (1525?-1605); imperfect and lacking title; mid-16th century.

Thomas Heywood

1574?-1641

ABBREVIATIONS

Dramatic Works *The Dramatic Works of Thomas Heywood,* [ed. R. H. Shepherd], 6 vols (1874; reprinted New York, 1964).

For abbreviations used throughout Volume I, see p.xi.

INTRODUCTION

Both on internal and external evidence the MS plays known as *The Captives* (HyT 4) and *The Escapes of Jupiter* (HyT 6) can be assigned to Heywood and are clearly in the author's hand. The same hand has been tentatively identified with 'Hand B' in the celebrated *Booke of Sir Thomas Moore* (HyT 12). The only other known autographs of Heywood are three signatures on his deposition in a law-suit between Baskerville and Worth, 3 October 1623, now in the Public Record Office (Chancery Depositions, 500 (9, 103)); they are reproduced in Greg, *English Literary Autographs,* plate XCVIII(f-h).

Scribal copies are preserved of two other plays probably by Heywood: *Dick of Devonshire* (HyT 5), and the more recently discovered *Tom a Lincoln* (HyT 13). After receiving considerable publicity in the national press in 1973, the latter was refused an export license when sold at Sotheby's and it remains the property of the Marquess of Lothian. Two other notable MSS are copies of what is apparently Heywood's unpublished verse translation of Ovid (HyT 2-3), the first of which was submitted to the licenser in 1623 and may have belonged to Heywood himself.

Heywood's dramatic canon is discussed in Bentley, IV, 553-86, and V, 1318-20, and most of his plays are printed in *Dramatic Works* (1874). Some of his non-dramatic works have not been reprinted since the 17th century. For the canon, see Arthur Melville Clark, 'A Bibliography of Thomas Heywood', *Proceedings and Papers of the Oxford Bibliographical Society,* 1 (1922-6), 97-153, and *NCBEL,* I, cols. 1682-6. For the possibility that the play *The Seven Champions of Christendom* may have been written by Heywood, see Paul Merchant, 'Thomas Heywood's Hand in *The Seven Champions of Christendom*', *The Library,* 5th Ser. 33 (1978), 226-30. That article includes a facsimile of a MS list of Heywood's plays inscribed by Ferdinando Marsham in a printed exemplum of *The Iron Age* (1632) now at Yale.

A poem on the death of Queen Elizabeth, probably by Thomas Dekker, is ascribed to Heywood in one MS source (see DkT 3), evidently because it was reprinted in his *Life and Death of Queene Elizabeth* (1639). Another poem on Queen Elizabeth, beginning 'Chast Virgin, Royal Queen, Belov'd and fear'd', is ascribed to 'M[r] Thomas Haywood' in a miscellany in the Rosenbach Foundation (MS 239/16, p. 100), but is not included in the entries. Extracts from two of Heywood's plays, *If You Know not Me, You Know No Bodie; or, The Troubles of Queene Elizabeth* (1605) and *The Rape of Lucrece* (1609), also appear in John Evans's miscellany *Hesperides, or the Muses' Garden;* for details of this see WILLIAM SHAKESPEARE, INTRODUCTION.

PB.

ARRANGEMENT

Verse	HyT 1-3
Dramatic works	HyT 4-13.

Thomas Heywood

VERSE

HyT 1 *Of Lucrece* ('If to thy bed the adulterer welcome came').

Copy in a verse miscellany compiled by an Oxford man and once owned by one Stephen Welden; mid-17th century.

First pub. in *Pleasant Dialogves and Dramma's* (London, 1637), p. 268.

Folger, MS V. a. 162, f. 10.

HyT 2 *Ovid's De Arte Amandi or, The Art of Love* ('If there be any in this multitude').

Fair copy with corrections, probably in the hand of an amanuensis; licensed by George Cottington 8 June 1623.

Believed to be unpublished; see W.W. Greg, *Licensers for the Press &c. to 1640*, Oxford Bibliographical Society, NS 10 (Oxford, 1962), pp. 25-6. This is not the translation of Ovid which Arthur Melville Clark attributed to Heywood in 'Thomas Heywood's *Art of Love* Lost and Found', *The Library*, 4th Ser. 3 (1922-3), 210-22, and in 'A Bibliography of Thomas Heywood', *Proceedings & Papers of the Oxford Bibliographical Society*, 1 (1922-6), 97-153 (pp. 113-14).

Bodleian, MS Rawl. poet. 198.

HyT 3 -----

Copy, with corrections; imperfect at the beginning (here beginning 'More eares of ripe corne growes not in the feildes'); in a MS volume of amatory poems; early 17th century.

Bodleian, MS Rawl. poet. 216, ff. 2-91.

DRAMATIC WORKS

--- *Calisto or The Escapes of Jupiter.*

See HyT 6.

*HyT 4 *The Captives, or The Lost Recovered.*

Autograph. untitled, prepared for use as a prompt book by another hand, in a composite volume of MS plays; [1624].

First pub. (from this MS) in *A Collection of Old English Plays*, ed. A.H. Bullen, IV (London, 1885), 99-217; ed. Arthur Brown, Malone Society (Oxford, 1953). This MS discussed in Greg, *Dramatic Documents*, I, 284-8, and in Bentley, IV, 560-2. Facsimile pages in Malone Society edition; Greg, *Dramatic Documents*, II, plate 7; Greg, *English Literary Autographs*, plate XXII(a); Petti, *English Literary Hands*, No. 55.

British Library, Egerton MS 1994, ff. 52-73.

HyT 5 *Dick of Devonshire.*

Copy of a play probably written or revised by Heywood, in the hand of a playhouse scribe, in a composite volume of MS plays; this MS in the same hand as *Blurt Master Constable* (MiT 6) and the verse miscellany, Add. MS 33998; [1626?].

First pub. (from this MS) in *A Collection of Old English Plays*, ed. A.H. Bullen, II (London, 1883), 1-99; ed. James G. and Mary R. McManaway, Malone Society (Oxford, 1955). This MS discussed in Greg, *Dramatic Documents*, I, 329-32; in Bentley, V, 1318-20; and in James G. McManaway, 'Latin Title-Page Mottoes as a Clue to Dramatic Authorship', *The Library*, 4th Ser. 26 (1945-6), 28-36, reprinted in McManaway, *Studies in Shakespeare, Bibliography and Theater* (New York, 1969), 55-66. Facsimile pages in Malone Society edition and McManaway article.

British Library, Egerton MS 1994, ff. 30-51.

*HyT 6 *The Escapes of Jupiter.*

Autograph, the first act entitled 'Calisto'; the play entitled at the end in another hand 'The Escapes of Iupiter'; in a composite volume of MS plays; c. 1625?

This play is made up of scenes from *The Golden Age* (London, 1611; *Dramatic Works*, III, 1-79) and *The Silver Age* (London, 1613; *Dramatic Works*, III, 81-164). Not published as a separate play but discussed in W.W. Greg, 'The Escapes of Jupiter', *Palaestra*, 148 (1925), reprinted in Greg, *Collected Papers* (Oxford, 1966), pp. 156-83; also discussed in Greg, *Dramatic Documents*, I, 318-21; in Bentley, III, 567; and in Henry D. Janzen, 'A Note on the Authorship of *The Escapes of Jupiter*', *ELN*, 10 (1972-3), 270-3.

British Library, Egerton MS 1994, ff. 74-95.

--- *The Golden Age* and *The Silver Age.*

See HyT 6.

HyT 7 *How a Man may chuse a Good Wife from a Bad.*

Extracts in a miscellany compiled by Edward Pudsey (1573-1613); 1600s.

First pub. London, 1602.

Bodleian, MS Eng. poet. d. 3, f. 86.

If You Know not Me, You Know no bodie

--- *If You Know not Me, You Know no bodie; or, The Troubles of Queene Elizabeth.*

See INTRODUCTION.

HyT 8 *The Iron Age (Part I).*

Exemplum of the edition of 1632 containing an original proofsheet (sigs. $F1^v$, $F3^v$) with a printer's MS corrections.

First pub. London, 1632; *Dramatic Works*, III, 257-345. This item discussed, with a facsimile, in Arthur Brown, 'A Proof-Sheet in Thomas Heywood's *The Iron Age*', *The Library*, 5th Ser. 10 (1955), 275-8.

Boston Public Library, G. 3972. 13.

HyT 9 *The Rape of Lucrece.*

Exemplum of the edition of 1609 with the text of the missing leaf sig. H1 supplied in MS; 17th century?

First pub. London, 1608; *Dramatic Works*, V, 161-257; ed. Allan Holaday (Urbana, 1950).

Victoria and Albert Museum, Dyce Collection, Cat. No. 4719 (Pressmark 26 Box 18/5).

--- -----

See also INTRODUCTION.

--- ----- Song: 'Now what is love I will thee tell'.

[*Dramatic Works*, V, 180; Holaday, lines 568-79].

See SIR WALTER RALEGH, RaW 434-7.

HyT 10 ----- Song: 'The Gentry to the Kings head'.

Copy of a 16-line version of the tavern song in a musical setting by John Wilson in a MS songbook compiled by John Playford (1623-86?); c. 1660s.

Dramatic Works, V, 190; Holaday, lines 1148-71. Printed from this MS in John P. Cutts, 'Thomas Heywood's "The Gentry to the King's Head" in "The Rape of Lucrece" and John Wilson's setting', *N & Q*, 206 (October 1961), 384-7.

Bibliothèque Nationale, Paris, Département de la Musique, MS Conservatoire Rés. 2489, pp. 294-5 [f. 23r-v].

HyT 11 ----- *The Cries of Rome:* 'Thus go the cries in Romes faire towne'.

Copy of one of the two songs 'which were added' to Heywood's play 'by the stranger that lately acted Valerius his part', in a scrapbook of MS verse bought by Joseph Haslewood (1769-1833) from an old Catholic family named Hawkins seated at Boughton, near Canterbury, Kent; 19th century.

Dramatic Works, V, 254-6. This MS formerly Phillipps MS 8923.

Huntington, HM 183, f. 24.

--- -----

See also INTRODUCTION.

*HyT 12 *Sir Thomas More.*

MS, entitled 'The Booke of Sir Thomas Moore', of a play originally by Anthony Munday and chiefly in his autograph, with additions in five other hands, one of which (contributing a short scene on f. 7 and generally known as 'Hand B') has been identified as possibly Heywood's autograph; c. mid-1590s.

First pub. (from this MS) London, 1844, ed. Alexander Dyce, Shakespeare Society; ed. W.W. Greg, Malone Society (Oxford, 1911). For facsimiles and discussions see WILLIAM SHAKESPEARE (ShW 88). The identification of 'Hand B' with Heywood's autograph is disputed in J.M. Nosworthy, 'Hand B in *Sir Thomas More*', *The Library*, 5th Ser. 11 (1956), 47-50.

British Library, Harley MS 7368.

HyT 13 *Tom a Lincoln.*

Copy, partly in the hand of Morgan Evans of Lantwit Major, Glamorgan, partly in two other hands, in a miscellany compiled by Evans; probably transcribed at Gray's Inn from a theatrical playbook; imperfect and lacking a title; among the papers of Sir John Coke (1563-1644); c. 1611-15.

Unpublished. This MS described in Sotheby's sale catalogue, 20 November 1973. See INTRODUCTION.

Owned by the Marquess of Lothian, Melbourne Hall.

Richard Hooker

1554-1600

ABBREVIATIONS

Elrington *The Whole Works of the Most Rev. James Ussher*, Vols. 1-14 ed. Charles Richard Elrington; Vols. 15-17 ed. James H. Todd (Dublin, 1847-64).

Keble *The Works of Mr. Richard Hooker*, ed. John Keble [first pub. 1836], 7th edition revised by R. W. Church and F. Paget, 3 vols (Oxford, 1888).

For abbreviations used throughout Volume I, see p.xi.

INTRODUCTION

Hooker's complete works are currently being edited for *The Folger Library Edition of the Works of Richard Hooker*, general editor W. Speed Hill. The edition is expected to appear in six volumes as follows:

Volume I: *Of the Laws of Ecclesiastical Polity*, Preface and Books I-IV. Text, edited by Georges Edelen (Cambridge, Mass., & London, 1977).
Volume II: *Of the Laws of Ecclesiastical Polity*, Book V. Text, edited by W. Speed Hill (Cambridge, Mass., & London, 1977).
Volume III: *Of the Laws of Ecclesiastical Polity*, Books VI-VIII. Text, edited by P. G. Stanwood (scheduled for publication in 1979/80).
Volume IV: *Hooker's 'Laws': Attack and Response*. Text and commentary by John Booty (scheduled for publication in 1981).
Volume V: *Tractates and Sermons*. Text edited by Laetitia Yeandle; commentary by Egil Grislis (scheduled for publication in 1982).
Volume VI: *Commentary on the 'Laws', Index*, by William P. Haugaard, Lee W. Gibbs, John Booty, Arthur S. McGrade, and W. Speed Hill (scheduled for publication in 1984).

Two companion volumes by W. Speed Hill have also been published:

(i) *Richard Hooker: A Descriptive Bibliography of the Early Editions: 1593-1724* (Cleveland, 1970).
(ii) *Studies in Richard Hooker: Essays preliminary to an Edition of his Works*, ed. W. Speed Hill (Cleveland, 1972).

Until this edition appears the standard edition of Hooker's works remains Keble (1888). The Folger edition will add to the canon established in Keble three sermons (HkR 24, 26, 27) which have been hitherto incorporated in the works of Archbishop James Ussher (1581-1656).

Several examples of Hooker's autograph have survived. Perhaps the most important are, firstly, the printer's copy of Book V of the *Polity* containing Hooker's autograph additions (HkR 10) and, secondly, twenty-seven pages of autograph notes for the *Polity* (HkR 8). An autograph draft of part of the *Sermon on Pride* (HkR 6) and a scribal copy of the *Sermon of the Certainty and Perpetuity of Faith in the Elect* containing autograph additions (HkR 23) are extant; so also is Hooker's annotated printed exemplum of the anonymous *Christian Letter*, a pamphlet attacking his doctrine (HkR 53).

In view of the mystery surrounding the fate of most of Hooker's MSS and the delay in the posthumous publication of his works, a number of early scribal MSS are of special significance in establishing the text, particularly of Books VI-VIII of the *Polity*: see, for instance, W. Speed Hill, 'Hooker's *Polity*: The Problem of the "Three Last Books"', *HLQ*, 34 (1970-1), 317-36. The number of known copies of the problematical Book VIII now stands at eight (HkR 14-21); the number of copies of the even more problematical Book VI (apart from the Cranmer-Sandys notes on the original version: HkR 11) stands at two (HkR 12-13). Despite its traditional, if anomalous place in the *Polity*, the Folger editors have decided to treat the bulk of 'Book VI' as a separate Tractate of Penance.

The single most important collection of MSS of Hooker's works is at Trinity College, Dublin. This collection belonged to Archbishop Ussher and probably came to him via Bishop Lancelot Andrewes. It is described in P. G. Stanwood, 'The Richard Hooker Manuscripts', *Long Room* (Spring-Summer 1975), 7-10. One other notable collection which contains relevant MSS is the so-called Fairhurst Papers at Lambeth Palace. These papers are ecclesiastical documents belonging to the official archives of the Church of England; they were removed for safe keeping by John Selden during the Civil War and were re-acquired by Lambeth Palace at a sale at Sotheby's in 1963. The collection is described by Geoffrey Bill in 'Lambeth Palace Library', *The Library*, 5th Ser. 21 (1966), 192-206 (pp. 201-3), and in the *Catalogue of Manuscripts in Lambeth Palace Library: MSS 1907-2340* (Oxford, 1976), pp. 29-66.

In addition to the MSS of Hooker's theological tracts, the *Index* includes documents relating to the major controversy in which he was engaged: that is, his doctrinal dispute with Walter Travers (1548?-1635) in 1585-86 (HkR 28-52). Travers's *Supplication to the Council* and various reports of his doctrinal objections to Hooker are included, as well as Hooker's *Answer to Travers* and Hooker's accounts of his own preaching. Travers's letter to Lord Burghley of 28 March 1586 and his arguments for being reinstated as minister in the Temple following the success of Hooker's defence are preserved in official copies annotated by Archbishop John Whitgift (1530?-1604) in the British Library (Lansdowne MS 50, ff. 169, 178r-v). The whole debate is treated in S. J. Knox, *Walter Travers: Paragon of Elizabethan Puritanism* (London, 1962), pp. 70-88.

Hooker's *Polity* was frequently quoted, sometimes extensively, in 17th and 18th-century miscellanies and commonplace books; these quotations invariably derive from printed editions, however, and have not received entries in the *Index*. Among those MSS which contain extracts from Hooker are the following:

Bodleian (MS Eng. misc. c. 144, pp. 152-63; MS Rawl. D. 1275, f. 30); British Library (Harley MS 980, ff. 38-40v; Lansdowne MS 924, between ff. 1 & 25; Lansdowne MS 932, ff. 64-73; Sloane MS 3828, ff. 92-5); Chetham's Library, Manchester (Mun. A 6. 33 & 34); Folger (MS V. b. 154); Inner Temple Library (Petyt MS 512, Vols. S & U); Public Record Office (SP. 12/246/112, ff. 317-20: a copy of Book V, Chapter LXXVI); and University College London (MS Ogden 7/17, ff. [3-18v]: a copy of parts of the Preface and Book I).

Printed exempla of the *Polity* are often found containing marginal annotations by early readers, but, again, these items are not included in the *Index*. There are volumes of this kind, for instance, in the British Library (Department of Printed Books). William Fulman's annotated exemplum of Books VI and VIII at Corpus Christi College, Oxford, is mentioned in Keble (1888), I, xxxiii.

A copy has recently been discovered (in Folger, MS V. b. 314) of the Latin translation of the *Polity*, Books I-V, which John Earle made for continental use during the Interregnum: see W. Speed Hill's letter in *TLS* (31 January 1975), p. 112, and Volume II of the *Index*: JOHN EARLE. This work was thought to have been lost since Earle's original MS was destroyed by his servants after his death: see David Novarr, *The Making of Walton's Lives* (Ithaca, New York, 1958), pp. 207-8 (n).

A few other documents of interest may be mentioned. Two letters from Hooker to John Rainolds are preserved in transcripts made by William Fulman (1632-88) at Corpus Christi College, Oxford (MS 303, ff. 208, 210); the texts are printed in Keble (1888), I, 109-14. 'The Inventarie of the goodes and chattells' (including the library) left by Hooker at his death — a document dated 26 November 1600 — is preserved in the Kent Archives Office (PRC 11/1); it is printed in Rosemary Keen, 'Inventory of Richard Hooker, 1601', *Archaeologia Cantiana* (Kent Archaeological Society), 70 (1956), 231-6. Hooker's Will is preserved in the same record office (PRC 32/38/291). Reports of the proceedings in the case of Hooker versus Sandys — documents of major importance in establishing what happened to Hooker's *Polity* after his death — are in the Public Record Office (C. 24/390/100 and C. 24/394/73); these and other documents relating to the legacies of Hooker's daughters are printed in C. J. Sisson, *The Judicious Marriage of Mr Hooker and the Birth of The Laws of Ecclesiastical Polity* (Cambridge, 1940), pp. 127-73. An anonymous 'examinacion of M[r] Hooker's doctrine' written about the 1650s is in the Northamptonshire Record Office, among the papers of the Isham family of Lamport Hall (I.L. 3382). An anonymous 18th-century analysis of the *Polity*, Books I-IV, is in the British Library (Stowe MS 110). Certain other MS works which are found ascribed to 'Mr Hooker' appear to be writings by another 'Hooker' (? Thomas Hooker). For instance, in the British Library there is a MS 'Treatise of the Will of Man written by Mr Hooker, sometime Preacher of God's Word at Chelmsford in Essex' (Harley MS 6828, ff. 65-82), and in York Minster a collection of MS transcripts of anti-episcopal tracts surreptitously printed in the 1630s (MS XVI. L. II) includes 'A Briefe discourse touchinge kneeling in the Act of receiuinge the Lords Supper: Written by M[r]. Hooker'.

Apart from the annotated *Christian Letter* (HkR 53) no printed books owned or annotated by Hooker have been identified. The late Elsie Smith, in 'Hooker at Salisbury', *TLS* (30 March 1962), p. 223, intimated that a number of theological books in the library of Salisbury Cathedral were 'heavily annotated' by Hooker, but, although Hooker certainly had access to this library, no annotations in his autograph are to be found.

PB.

ARRANGEMENT

Prose:	(1) Prose works by Hooker	HkR 1-27
	(2) Documents relating to the Hooker-Travers controversy	HkR 28-52
Marginalia in printed books and manuscripts		HkR 53.

FACSIMILE XXI — Richard Hooker: Page of notes for *Of the Laws of Ecclesiastical Polity*, c.1597-8 (HkR 8). Trinity College, Dublin. MS 364, folio 75 recto. Reduced by approx. 5 per cent. Last three lines of page omitted. Reproduced by permission of The Board of Trinity College, Dublin.

75

An [illegible] upon [illegible] of [illegible] [illegible] about [illegible] [illegible]

[illegible] and [illegible] [illegible]

1 ~~Of the definition of the church [illegible] [illegible] with in a Christian kingdome~~

2 What the power of Dominion is.

3 By what right, [after what fashion, in what manner] and with what conveniency christian kings may have dominion.

[illegible] kings of [illegible] [illegible]

8 Of the power ~~of the kings of England~~ in making ecclesiasticall governors.

7 Of their power in the judgment of causes ecclesiasticall.

9 Of their exemption from the judgment of others.

6 Of their power in ~~[illegible]~~ making ecclesiasticall lawes.

4 Of their title of Headship.

5 Of their prerogative to ~~call generall~~ [call generall] councils about the affaires of the church.

1

The state of a christian kingdome is as the state of Israel gods own people which people was not part of the the common wealth and part of the the church of god, but the self same people whole and intire in both.

2

Power of dominion is a supremacie above them to whome the personall exercise of jurisdiction belongeth. supremacy is in regard of all other persons conteined as parts within that politique bodie over which they have supremacy, and not in regard of the lawe it self. Rex non debet esse sub homine sed sub Deo et lege. ~~[illegible]~~ For the kings supremacy as it excludeth forein persons writers have writte. But little hitherto hath been particularly and of purpose set down in defence of the said supremacy as it respecteth persons at home.

3

It is a common errour which ~~[illegible]~~ Stapleton's worke in saying that ~~the Englishe protestant~~ which is not puritan holdeth the power of dominion to belong ad ius regale principis christiani et potestatem principaliter et necessario planeque essentialiter. Stapl. de doctr. princip. l. 5. ca. 17. That which doth so belong unto kings, all kings have it equally in them. whereas in power of dominion all kings have not an equall latitude. The reason is because the originall subject of power is that whole intire body or societie whereof the king is made a principall member by receiving principalitie of power [illegible] it. And [illegible] with what largenes or restraint a politique societie ~~[illegible]~~ doth make to it self a king and impart supreme power unto him will impart or sharpe [at the first] the same it is in the voluntary choise and discretion of the said societie ~~[illegible]~~ ~~the king of kings [illegible] [illegible] [illegible] [illegible] [illegible]~~ The whole bodie of the church the subject originall wherinto as into a cisterne from god as a fountain by christ as a conduit ~~all~~ power of dominion is derived. ~~[illegible]~~ Touching which point in haue all their consents [illegible] in the church of Rome it self who stand for the authority of councils generall above popes. Of the power of a church nationall subject unto a christian king. A nation being free and independent may without repugnancy to any law either of god or nature graunt supremacy of power in religion to his king and ~~[illegible]~~ consequently a nation imbracing christianity the like power to a christian king. [Unto] which [illegible] be against it. What may be objected against ~~[illegible]~~ a christian kings dominion ecclesiasticall.

The [illegible] of [illegible] [illegible] [illegible] [illegible] that [illegible] [illegible] [illegible] [illegible] for [illegible] [illegible] [illegible] [illegible] [illegible] will [illegible] [illegible] [illegible] [illegible] [illegible] [illegible] the body of the clergy [illegible] synod.

Ambros. ep. 32. [illegible] l. 4. c. 11. [illegible] 4.

Quid honorificentius quam ut Imperator ecclesiae filius esse dicatur? Imperator enim bonus intra ecclesiam non supra ecclesiam est.

Non negatur principi, Magistratui, vel communitati potestas { Perversa docentes corporali poena puniendi. / Leges pro ecclesiae pace ferendi. / Dogmata { Probata [illegible] / Defendendi / Contra violatores vindicandi. } } Stapl. l. 5. c. 17.

How much the adversaries of kingly power doe graunt it may doe, and what consequents may be drawen out of their graunts.

Whether a societie having given supreme power over it self unto any and finding afterwards inconvenience therin may resume the same. [illegible] no. But which supremacie of power doth return unto it than [illegible] may it help it self. How many waies the said power may return as it came by [illegible] unto the body from whence it came.

[illegible] in loc. com. ~~[illegible]~~ [illegible] [illegible] Ec. [illegible] [illegible] [illegible] in pro[l]egom.

4 7

Look the statute which prohibiteth that the Dean and chapter in cathedrall churches should sollicit the k. for leave to elect their prelate, and that [illegible] a Bishop[rick] should not continue void for above six months. Docet ~~[illegible]~~ Musculus in corrupto Ecclesiae statu non esse causam cur Minister christianus pro Magistratu vel principe ad praedicandum Evangelium vocatus de vocatione sua haesitet. ‖ Adversus istos temere dubitantes [illegible] non posse authoritatem principem saecularem aut alium quemque magistratum vel etiam communitatem politicam non posse auctoritatem dare. Staplet. l. 5. c. 17. [illegible] [illegible] non [illegible] contendimus sed de potestate regia [illegible] in ecclesiasticis [illegible] [illegible] conferendi.

[illegible] co. de Magist. civ. [illegible] eod. loc.

[illegible] in prolegomen.

[illegible] [illegible]. doctr. princ. l. 5. ca. 17.

5 8

Melancthon pertinere vult emendationem Ecclesiarum ad Magistratus officium praesertim cessantibus Episcopis et adversantibus Evangelio. Quod aliqui (inquit) dicunt magistratum prophanum non esse judicem controversiarum de dogmatibus, vera et explicata responsio est Ecclesiam esse judicem et sequi normam Evangelii in judicando. Cum autem magistratus pius sit [illegible] membrum Ecclesiae judicet et ipse cum aliis piis et eruditis iuxta normam quam dixi. Omnibus enim Ecclesiae membris dictum est, Attendite vobis a falsis prophetis. ‖ Sicut quilibet privatus privatam ita princeps publicam habet de doctrina religionis judicandi potestatem. The same which Joshua spake concerning him self and his houshold belongeth unto every king as concerning him self and his people, I and mine will serve the Lord.

Isti Laicocephali quorum facile princeps Brentius videri potest volunt principes christianos etiam de ipsa doctrina cognoscere et judicare, posse ac debere non solum falsos prophetas punire sed etiam [illegible] ac pronunciare qui sint falsi Prophetae [illegible] [illegible] [illegible] hac [illegible] habere eos potestatem instituendi ministros et deponendi non solum in [illegible] [illegible] qui non [illegible] [illegible] [illegible] [illegible] habuerunt sed etiam semper in quovis ecclesiae statu.

Richard Hooker

PROSE

(1) PROSE WORKS BY HOOKER

--- *Answer to Walter Travers's Supplication to the Council.*

[Keble, III, 570-96].

See HkR 36-9.

HkR 1 *A Discovery of the Causes of the Continuance of these Contentions concerning Church Government.*

Copy in the hand of a scribe who worked for Archbishop Ussher and who also wrote HkR 2, 6 and 12, with corrections and annotations in Ussher's hand; used as the printer's copy in 1641; bound in a volume of Ussher's papers; c. 1641.

First pub. in *Certain briefe Treatises, written by diverse learned men, concerning the ancient and modern Government of the Church* (Oxford, 1641); Keble, III, 460-5. This MS and its authenticity discussed in Keble, I, xlviii-xlix.

Trinity College, Dublin, MS 774, f. 56r-v.

HkR 2 *Fragments of an Answer to the Letter of certain English Protestants.*

Copy of untitled fragments of a treatise on Grace, the Sacraments and Predestination partly or wholly intended as a reply to the *Christian Letter* (pub. 1599), in the hand of a scribe who worked for Archbishop Ussher and who also wrote HkR 1, 6 and 12, in a MS volume of works chiefly by Hooker once owned by Ussher; c. 1630s-40s.

First pub. (from this MS) in Keble (1836); Keble (1888), II, 537-97.

Trinity College, Dublin, MS 121, ff. 52-67.

HkR 3 *A Learned Discourse of Justification, Works, and How the Foundation of Faith is Overthrown.*

Copy, with a few annotations in another hand, once owned by Archbishop Ussher; 22 leaves; late 16th-early 17th century.

First pub. Oxford, 1612; Keble, III, 483-547. This MS collated in Keble (see I, liii).

Trinity College, Dublin, MS 118.

HkR 4 -----

Copy in a composite volume of MS tracts and papers; late 16th-early 17th century.

This MS not recorded in Keble.

British Library, Harley MS 4888, ff. 92-117.

HkR 5 -----

Copy; inscribed 'Mr. Hooker' by the second Earl of Bridgewater (1622-86); late 16th-early 17th century.

This MS not recorded in Keble.

Huntington, EL 8178E.

*HkR 6 *A Learned Sermon of the Nature of Pride.*

Autograph draft of the first portion as published in 1612 (ff. 33-42v); c. 1586; together with a fair copy of an additional portion in the hand of a scribe who worked for Archbishop Ussher and who also wrote HkR 1, 2 and 12 (ff. 43-50v); late 1630s-early '40s; bound in a MS volume of works chiefly by Hooker once owned by Ussher.

First portion pub. Oxford, 1612; additional portion first pub. (from this MS) in Keble (1836); Keble (1888), III, 597-642. This MS described in Laetitia Yeandle and P.G. Stanwood, 'An Autograph Manuscript by Richard Hooker', *Manuscripta*, 18 (1974), 38-41.

Trinity College, Dublin, MS 121, ff. 33-50v.

HkR 7 -----

A few notes taken from the first part of the sermon (that published in 1612) in the hand of Archbishop Ussher, in a bound volume of Ussher's papers; c. 1640s.

This MS not recorded in Keble.

Trinity College, Dublin, MS 774, f. 60.

*HkR 8 *Of the Laws of Ecclesiastical Polity.*

Autograph notes for the *Polity*, principally on Book VIII but also on Books V, VI and VII; 16 leaves with 27 pages in Hooker's writing; bound in a composite volume of legal and ecclesiastical tracts; c. 1597-8.

Book VII first pub. in John Gauden's edition of the 'complete' *Polity*, London, 1662; for publication of other books see individual Books below. This MS not recorded in Keble; described, with a facsimile of f. 71, in P.G. Stanwood, 'The Richard Hooker Manuscripts', *Long Room* (Spring-Summer 1975), 7-10. See also FACSIMILE XXI

Trinity College, Dublin, MS 364, ff. 69-84v.

HkR 9 -----

Notes made by Archbishop Ussher from Hooker's autograph notes (HkR 8), in a bound volume of Ussher's papers; c. 1640s.

This MS not recorded in Keble.

Trinity College, Dublin, MS 774, ff. 68v-71.

Of the Laws of Ecclesiastical Polity

--- -----

See also INTRODUCTION.

*HkR 10 ----- *Book V.*

Fair copy in the hand of Benjamin Pullen with Hooker's autograph marginal notes and corrections; bearing the signature and licence of Archbishop Whitgift and used as the printer's copy in 1597.

First pub. London, 1597; Keble, II, 1-533. Edited from this MS in Folger edition, II (1977); described in Keble (1888), II, v-xvii, and in Percy Simpson, *Proof-Reading in the Sixteenth, Seventeenth and Eighteenth Centuries* (London, 1935), pp. 76-9. Various facsimile examples in Folger edition; Keble, II, v; Greg, *English Literary Autographs*, plate LXXVIII; Simpson, facing p. 78.

Bodleian, MS Add. C. 165.

HkR 11 ----- *Book VI.*

Notes made by George Cranmer and Edwin Sandys on the original version of Book VI; a MS sent to Hooker; inscribed in an unidentified hand 'Mr. S. and Mr. Cr. Notes upon the 6 and 7 bookes' and by William Fulman (1632-88) 'Written with their own hands and given me by my friend M. Isaac Walton 1673. W.F.'; c. 1594-6.

These notes first pub. (from this MS) in Keble (1836); Keble (1888), III, 108-39. Facsimile examples of this MS in Keble, I, after p. cxxii.

Bodleian, MS CCC. 295.

HkR 12 ----- -----

Copy in the hand of a scribe who worked for Archbishop Ussher and who also wrote HkR 1, 2 and 6, with corrections in Ussher's hand, in a MS volume of works chiefly by Hooker once owned by Ussher; late 1630s-early '40s.

First pub. (with Book VIII) London, 1648; Keble, III, 1-107. The bulk of the so-called 'Book VI' is to be removed from the *Polity* in the Folger edition of Hooker and be included in Vol. V of the edition as a 'Tractate of Penance'. This MS collated in Keble (see I, xxxiv).

Trinity College, Dublin, MS 121, ff. 1-32.

HkR 13 ----- -----

Copy of a text deriving from HkR 12 in a composite volume of MS tracts and papers; 1st half 17th century.

This MS not recorded in Keble.

British Library, Harley MS 3787, ff. 1-32.

HkR 14 ----- *Book VIII.*

Copy, with annotations by Archbishop Ussher; 167 leaves; 1st half 17th century.

First pub. in an incomplete form (with 'Book VI'), London, 1648; some additions pub. in Nicholas Bernard, *Clavi Trabales* (London, 1661), and in John Gauden's 'complete' edition of the *Polity* (London, 1662); Keble, III, 326-455 (and pp. 456-60 for a passage found in MSS but not in the first edition, possibly part of a Sermon on Civil Disobedience); ed. Raymond Aaron Houk, *Hooker's Ecclesiastical Polity Book VIII* (New York, 1931). Printed from this MS in Keble (see I, xlv-xlvi) and in Houk.

Trinity College, Dublin, MS 120.

HkR 15 ----- -----

Copy of Chapters 6 and 8, headed 'Of the autoritye of making lawes', in a volume of miscellaneous theological papers; 1st half 17th century.

This MS collated in Houk.

Bodleian, MS Rawl. D. 843, ff. 20-4.

HkR 16 ----- -----

Copy, transcribed from HkR 19, in a composite volume of MS tracts and papers; 1st half 17th century.

This MS not in the same hand as the MS of Book VI bound with it (HkR 13); not recorded in Keble or in Houk.

British Library, Harley MS 3787, ff. 33-80v.

HkR 17 ----- -----

Copy; 1st half 17th century.

This MS collated in Houk.

British Library, Sloane MS 2750, ff. 1-50.

HkR 18 ----- -----

Copy in a composite volume of ecclesiastical and historical tracts; 1st half 17th century.

This MS collated in Keble (see I, xlv) and in Houk.

Gonville and Caius College, Cambridge, MS 291/274, pp. 241-73.

HkR 19 ----- -----

Copy in a composite volume of historical MSS

among the collections of Archbishop Thomas Tenison (1636?-1715); c. 1625.

This MS collated in Keble (see I, xlv) and in Houk.

Lambeth Palace, MS 711, ff. 9-42.

HkR 20 ----- -----

Copy of part of Book VIII in a composite volume of MSS relating to the Church of England (among the Fairhurst Papers); 1st half 17th century.

This MS not recorded in Keble or in Houk.

Lambeth Palace, MS 2014, ff. 1-46.

HkR 21 ----- -----

Copy, with corrections by Dr Thomas Barlow, Bishop of Lincoln (1607-91), in a composite volume of theological tracts; mid-17th century.

This MS collated in Keble (see I, xliv-xlv) and in Houk.

The Queen's College, Oxford, MS 292, pp. 1-79.

HkR 22 *A Remedy against Sorrow and Fear: Delivered in a Funeral Sermon.*

A few brief references to the sermon in the hand of Archbishop Ussher, in a bound volume of Ussher's papers; c. 1640s.

First pub. Oxford, 1612; Keble, III, 643-53. This MS not recorded in Keble.

Trinity College, Dublin, MS 774, f. 60.

*HkR 23 *A Sermon of the Certainty and Perpetuity of Faith in the Elect.*

Copy made by two amanuenses, with Hooker's autograph corrections and additions to the portion copied by the first amanuensis (ff. 54-9v), in a composite volume of theological and historical documents; c. 1584-5.

First pub. [Oxford], 1612; Keble, III, 469-81. This MS not recorded in Keble.

Bodleian, MS CCC. 288, ff. 54-62v.

HkR 24 *Sermon on Hebrews ii. 14, 15.*

Copy of a sermon beginning 'God gave his people, the Jewes, a law, which law is set down in the 25th of Leviticus...', in the hand of Archbishop Ussher, in a bound volume of Ussher's papers; mid-17th century.

First pub. (from this MS) in Elrington, XVII (1864), xxvii-xxxviii; discussed and attributed to Hooker in Laetitia Yeandle and P.G. Stanwood, 'Three Manuscript Sermon Fragments by Richard Hooker', *Manuscripta*, 21, No. 1 (March 1977), 33-7.

Trinity College, Dublin, MS 774, ff. 57-9.

--- *Sermon on Justification.*

See HkR 3-5.

HkR 25 *A Sermon (on Matthew vii. 7, 8) found among the papers of Bishop Andrews.*

Copy, with corrections in another hand, headed 'Ric. Hooker Math. 7. 7' and endorsed 'Sermon m[r] Hooker', in a composite volume of theological and historical documents; 17th century.

First pub. in Izaac Walton, *Life of Dr. Sanderson* (London, 1678); Keble, III, 700-9. This MS not recorded in Keble.

Bodleian, MS CCC. 288, ff. 223v-8.

HkR 26 *Sermon on Matthew xxvii. 46.*

Copy of a sermon beginning 'There is a dereliction of probation and reprobation, of utter refuseal, and a dereliction of triall onely', in the hand of Archbishop Ussher, in a bound volume of Ussher's papers; mid-17th century.

First pub. (from this MS) in Elrington, XVII (1864), xxiv-xxvi; discussed and attributed to Hooker in Laetitia Yeandle and P.G. Stanwood, 'Three Manuscript Sermon Fragments by Richard Hooker', *Manuscripta*, 21, No. 1 (March 1977), 33-7.

Trinity College, Dublin, MS 774, ff. 56v-7.

HkR 27 *Sermon on Proverbs iii. 9, 10.*

Copy of part of a sermon beginning 'Unto the precept of honouring the Lord with our riches...', in the hand of Archbishop Ussher, in a bound volume of Ussher's papers; incomplete; mid-17th century.

First pub. (from this MS) in Elrington, XVII (1864), xxxix-xli; discussed and attributed to Hooker in Laetitia Yeandle and P.G. Stanwood, 'Three Manuscript Sermon Fragments by Richard Hooker', *Manuscripta*, 21, No. 1 (March 1977), 33-7.

Trinity College, Dublin, MS 774, f. 59v.

--- *Supposed Fragment of a Sermon on Civil Obedience, hitherto printed as part of the Eighth Book.*

[Keble, III, 456-60].

See HkR 14-21.

A Tractate of Penance.

--- *A Tractate of Penance.*

See HkR 12-13.

(2) DOCUMENTS RELATING TO THE HOOKER-TRAVERS CONTROVERSY

HkR 28 *Walter Travers's Supplication to the Council.*

Copy in the hand of Dr Robert Clay (d. 1628), in a volume of state papers; c. 1603-20.

First pub. Oxford, 1612; Keble, III, 548-9. This MS collated in Keble (see I, liii).

Bodleian, MS e. Mus. 55, ff. 83-6v.

HkR 29 -----

Copy in a composite volume of MS tracts and papers; late 16th-early 17th century.

This MS not recorded in Keble.

British Library, Harley MS 4888, ff. 66-73.

HkR 30 -----

Copy; 10 leaves; late 16th century.

This MS not recorded in Keble.

Folger, MS X. d. 74.

HkR 31 -----

Copy among the papers of the Earls Fitzwilliam of Milton, Northamptonshire; late 16th century.

This MS not recorded in Keble; see also HkR 42.

Northamptonshire Record Office, F (M) P. 139.

HkR 32 -----

Copy in a composite volume of ecclesiastical tracts; late 16th century.

This MS not recorded in Keble.

Dr Williams's Library, MS Morrice A, Part I, ff. 109-16.

HkR 33 -----

Copy transcribed from HkR 32 by an amanuensis working for Roger Morrice (1628-1701/2), in a composite volume of ecclesiastical tracts; late 17th century.

This MS not recorded in Keble.

Dr Williams's Library, MS Morrice A, Part II, ff. 244v-51v (pp. 64-78).

HkR 34 -----

Second copy transcribed from HkR 32 by an amanuensis working for Roger Morrice, in a composite volume of ecclesiastical tracts; late 17th century.

This MS not recorded in Keble.

Dr Williams's Library, MS Morrice C, ff. 805-13.

HkR 35 -----

Copy in a folio volume with three other theological tracts (one by John Rainolds, 1593); late 16th century.

Formerly owned by W. Bromley-Davenport of Baginton Hall, Warwickshire, this MS recorded in *HMC*, 2nd Report (1871), Appendix, p. 78; not recorded in Keble.

Unlocated: it is not among Bromley-Davenport MSS in the John Rylands University Library of Manchester, the Warwickshire Record Office, the Chester City Record Office, or those owned by Sir Walter Bromley-Davenport of Capesthorne Hall (confirmed by letter 7 November 1977), and it was not included in the sale at Sotheby's, 8-9 May 1903; it may have perished in a fire at Baginton in 1884.

HkR 36 *Hooker's Answer to Walter Travers's Supplication to the Council.*

Copy; late 16th-early 17th century.

First pub. (with Travers's *Supplication*) Oxford, 1612; Keble, III, 570-96. This MS collated in Keble (see I, liii).

Trinity College, Dublin, MS 119, ff. 1-18.

HkR 37 -----

Copy in the hand of Dr Robert Clay (d. 1628), in a volume of state papers; c. 1603-20.

This MS collated in Keble.

Bodleian, MS e. Mus. 55, ff. 87-92.

HkR 38 -----

Copy in a composite volume of MSS collected by the classical scholar Meric Casaubon (1599-1671); late 16th-early 17th century.

This MS not recorded in Keble.

British Library, Burney MS 362, ff. 96-114v.

HkR 39 -----

Copy in a composite volume of MS tracts and papers; late 16th-early 17th century.

Hooker's Answer to Walter Travers's Supplication

This MS not recorded in Keble.

British Library, Harley MS 4888, ff. 74v-85.

HkR 40 *A shorte note of vnsounde pointes of Doctrine at divers times deliuered by Mr: Hooker in his publicke sermons.*

Copy in a volume of state and ecclesiastical papers; late 16th century.

These statements printed in Keble I, 59-60. This MS not recorded in Keble.

British Library, Lansdowne MS 96, f. 50r-v.

HkR 41 -----

Copy in a composite volume of papers once owned by Archbishop William Laud (1573-1645); early 17th century.

This MS not recorded in Keble.

Lambeth Palace, MS 943, pp. 63-4.

HkR 42 -----

Copy, together with a copy of Travers's *Supplication* (HkR 31), among the papers of the Earls Fitzwilliam of Milton, Northamptonshire; late 16th century.

This MS not recorded in Keble.

Northamptonshire Record Office, F (M) P. 139.

--- -----

See also HkR 43-4.

HkR 43 *Doctrin preached by mr Hooker in the Temple the fyrst of Marche 1585.*

MS in a composite volume of historical documents chiefly relating to transactions between England and Scotland; late 16th century.

This MS is a different version of the statements printed in Keble, I, 59-60 (see HkR 40-2); recorded in Keble's footnotes.

British Library, Harley MS 291, ff. 184v-5.

HkR 44 *Propositions taught and maynteined by mr Hooker the same breefly confuted by L.T. <Lawrence Tomson> in a privat letter the 20th of marche 1585.*

Copy in a composite volume of historical documents chiefly relating to transactions between England and Scotland; late 16th century.

This MS is a different version of the statements printed in Keble, I, 59-60 (see HkR 40-2); recorded in Keble's footnotes; (see also HkR 50).

British Library, Harley MS 291, ff. 183-4.

HkR 45 *Notes of mr Hookers Sermon.*

Copy of Hooker's account of what he preached in his Temple sermons on Habakkuk, endorsed apparently by Archbishop Whitgift (on f. 177v) '28 Mart. 1586. Inter Hooker et Travers', in a volume of tracts and state papers.

This MS conforms to the text printed in Keble, I, 60-4; (see also HkR 49).

British Library, Lansdowne MS 50, ff. 174-6v.

HkR 46 -----

Copy, with an endorsement by Archbishop Whitgift, in a composite volume of papers on church government (among the Fairhurst Papers); late 16th century.

This MS is a version of the account printed in Keble, I, 60-4.

Lambeth Palace, MS 2006, ff. 9-13v.

HkR 47 [*Hooker's vindication of his preaching in the Temple*].

Copy of an untitled passage by Hooker defending his doctrine and identifying some of his references in the *Sermon on Justification* (see HkR 3-5), beginning 'I have bene greuouslye vsed {openly / secretly} and for boulstringe of Heresye...', in a composite volume of papers on church government (among the Fairhurst Papers); late 16th century.

This MS unpublished.

Lambeth Palace, MS 2006, ff. 13v-15v.

HkR 48 [*Answer to Hooker's Account*].

Copy of a series of untitled paragraphs, beginning 'Our fathers are no presidense for us to follow in error', apparently written in answer to Hooker's account of his preaching in the Temple (HkR 45-6), in a volume of tracts and state papers; [1586].

This MS believed to be unpublished.

British Library, Lansdowne MS 50, ff. 171-3.

HkR 49 [*Statement on the Hooker-Travers Controversy*].

Copy of a statement of doctrinal differences between Hooker and Travers, in a composite volume of papers on church government (among the Fairhurst Papers); late 16th century.

This MS believed to be unpublished; one paragraph corresponds with the footnote in Keble, I, 61 (see HkR 45-6).

Lambeth Palace, MS 2006, ff. 6-8v.

HkR 50 [*Lawrence Tomson's Letter on the Hooker-Travers Controversy*].

A letter written from Laleham by Lawrence Tomson to 'Mrs Crane' discussing Hooker's propositions concerning the salvation of Papists, in a composite volume of ecclesiastical tracts; 26 February 1585/6.

This MS believed to be unpublished; recorded in *The Seconde Parte of a Register*, ed. Albert Peel (Cambridge, 1915), II, p. 48, No. 197. A late 17th century copy of this letter is in MS Morrice C, pp. 640-1; (see also HkR 44).

Dr Williams's Library, MS Morrice A, Part I, f. 35.

HkR 51 [*Christopher Tayler's Letter on the Hooker-Travers Controversy*].

A letter from Christopher Tayler 'To the godlie and his louinge brother in Christe Mr Houldesworth preacher of gods holie woord at Newcastle' in which he records and comments on Hooker's opinions in his Temple sermons; 6 April 1586.

This MS believed to be unpublished.

Public Record Office, SP. 12/188/5.

HkR 52 *Sr Hew Herberts treatise against Hooker*.

A MS treatise discussing at length the Hooker-Travers controversy, in a composite volume of ecclesiastical tracts; c. 1588?

This MS believed to be unpublished; recorded in *The Seconde Parte of a Register*, ed. Albert Peel (Cambridge, 1915), II, p. 48, No. 198.

Dr Williams's Library, MS Morrice A, Part I, ff. 178-83.

MARGINALIA IN PRINTED BOOKS AND MANUSCRIPTS

*HkR 53 *A Christian Letter of certaine English Protestants* [Middelburg, 1599].

Interleaved exemplum of an anonymous printed pamphlet containing Hooker's extensive autograph annotations towards a self-vindication; [1599].

Independent early 17th-century transcripts of Hooker's annotations are to be found in two other interleaved exempla of this pamphlet: (i) Corpus Christi College, Oxford, MS 215A (Thomas Norgrove's transcript); (ii) Trinity College, Dublin, MS 119, ff. 20-70v (anonymous). All three texts collated in Keble (see I, xviii-xxv), and the annotations cited in footnotes, with facsimile examples of Hooker's autograph notes on pp. 20, 22, 24 of the pamphlet in I, after p. cxxii. The annotations discussed in Vincent Mahon, 'The "Christian Letter": Some Puritan Objections to Hooker's Work; and Hooker's "Undressed" Comments', *RES*, NS 25 (1974), 305-12.

Corpus Christi College, Oxford, MS 215B.

Ben Jonson

1572-1637

ABBREVIATIONS

Herford & Simpson *Ben Jonson*, ed. C. H. Herford and Percy and Evelyn Simpson, 11 vols (Oxford, 1925-52).

John Benson's 4to edition (1640) *Ben: Ionson's Execration against Vulcan. With divers epigrams by the same Author ... Printed by J. O. for John Benson* (London, 1640).

John Benson's 12mo edition (1640) *Q. Horatius Flaccus: His Art of Poetry. Englished by Ben: Jonson. With other Workes of the Author ... Printed by J. Okes, for John Benson* (London, 1640).

Sabol, *400 Songs & Dances* *Four Hundred Songs and Dances from the Stuart Masque*, ed. Andrew J. Sabol (Providence, Rhode Island, 1978).

For abbreviations used throughout Volume I, see p.xi.

INTRODUCTION

There are many MS texts of Jonson's works, including a number of autographs. The complete autograph copy of his *Masque of Queens* presented to Prince Henry survives (JnB 685), and so does an autograph of the opening speech of an entertainment presented before King James and King Christian of Denmark (JnB 580). Altogether twelve poems are preserved in his own hand: five presentation poems to various patrons or influential friends (JnB 386, 504-5, 512, 529), three satires on Inigo Jones (JnB 248, 474, 488), a translation of Martial given to his friend Edward Alleyn (JnB 319), an epitaph included in a letter to another friend, George Garrard (JnB 102), and two poems written out for presentation to William Drummond of Hawthornden (JnB 270, 352). The leaf containing the last two items was not seen by editors since 1711 until research for the *Index* brought it to light in 1978 (see FACSIMILE XXII).

Besides the letter of 1609 to George Garrard (see JnB 102), three of Jonson's autograph letters are preserved: (1) to Sir Robert Cecil, [1605] (owned by the Marquess of Salisbury, Hatfield House, Cecil Papers 114/58); printed in Herford & Simpson, I, 194-6; (2) to Sir Robert Cecil, 8 November 1605 (Public Record Office, SP. 14/16/30); printed in Herford & Simpson, I, 202; reproduced in Greg, *English Literary Autographs*, plate XXIII(a-b), and in Ann Morton, *Men of Letters*, Public Record Office Museum Pamphlets No. 6 (London, 1974), plate III; (3) to Sir Robert Cotton, [c. 1635] (British Library, Cotton MS Julius C. III, f. 222); printed in Herford & Simpson, I, 215; reproduced in Greg, *English Literary Autographs*, plate XXIII(c). What could be described as another autograph letter is a Latin epistle to Richard Briggs, 10 August 1623, written by Jonson in a printed exemplum of Martial, *Epigrammaton libri*, ed. Thomas Farnaby (London, 1615), now in the Folger; it is printed in Herford & Simpson, I, 215-16. The texts of some additional letters are printed in Herford & Simpson (I, 193-214) from published sources and from certain scribal transcripts in the Folger (MS V. a. 321 (the Dobell-White MS: see GEORGE CHAPMAN, INTRODUCTION)) and in the British Library (Harley MS 4955 (the Newcastle MS)).

A further series of autograph items is Jonson's inscriptions in his own printed works. There are at least five surviving exempla of Jonson's *Workes* (1616) with presentation inscriptions. One, inscribed 'To his most worthy, & learned Freind M^r: John Wilson', is in the Pierpont Morgan Library; another, inscribed 'To his most learned and honor'd Freind Mr Edward Heyward', is in the Huntington (HEH 62101, vol. 1); a third, inscribed to his 'Amicissimo ... Francis Yong', is in the Yale Elizabethan Club; a fourth, inscribed to his 'worthy, and deseruing Brother M^r. Alexander Glouer', is recorded in Herford & Simpson (VIII, 666) as being in 1947 in the possession of Mr Frank Capra; and a fifth, inscribed 'To my most learn'd and honor'd friend M^r. Tho. Farnabie', was sold at Christie's, 14 June 1979 (Arthur A. Houghton, Jr. sale), Lot 275, to Fleming. Another exemplum of Jonson's *Workes*, sold at Sotheby's, 24 October 1977, Lot 29, to A. Scott, has inlaid in an accompanying volume of the 1640 edition a leaf containing a lengthy autograph inscription to Jonson's 'worthy Friend M^r. John Achmoty, for the hospitable favors I receivd of him in Scotland', dated 3 July 1619 (a facsimile appears in the Sotheby hard-cover sale catalogue). Since the inscription refers to 'this small present', however, and the leaf is a small quarto in size, it clearly belongs not to the 1616 Folio but probably to a quarto of one of Jonson's individual works. Several other quartos bear his presentation inscriptions. The inscribed exemplum of *The Masques of Blackness and of Beauty* (1608) which he presented to Queen Anne (see Herford & Simpson, VIII, 663) is in the British Library (Department of Printed Books, C. 34. d. 4); so too is the exemplum of *The Masque of Queens* (1609) with his autograph dedication to Queen Anne (C. 28. g. 5). This dedication is printed in Herford & Simpson, VII, 279, and reproduced in Greg, *English Literary Autographs*, plate XXIV(a). An exemplum of *Sejanus his Fall* (1605) inscribed to Francis Crane (see

Herford & Simpson, VIII, 665) is in the Huntington (RB 60659); another exemplum of the same edition, inscribed to Sir Robert Townshend and with contemporary textual emendations (see Herford & Simpson, IV, 331; VIII, 665), is in the British Library (Department of Printed Books, Ashley 3464). An exemplum of *Volpone* (1607) inscribed to John Florio (see Herford & Simpson, VIII, 665) is in the British Library (Department of Printed Books, C. 12. e. 17); the inscription is reproduced in Herford & Simpson, I, 56, and also in the Scolar Press facsimile of this exemplum (Menston, 1968). A single leaf, possibly detached from an exemplum of one of Johnson's own works, and with the autograph inscription, 'To the most noble M^{r}. William St. Maure. Ben: Jonsons guift. A testimony of obseruance', is reproduced in the printed catalogue of the R. B. Adam Library (London & New York, 1929), III, after p. 142, and is now in the Hyde Collection, Somerville, New Jersey.

Many printed books (and a few MSS) once owned by Jonson bear his signature, motto, inscriptions, or marginal annotations. A checklist of books and MSS from Jonson's library is printed in Herford & Simpson, I, 250-71, and XI, 593-603; a more comprehensive catalogue is printed in David McPherson, 'Ben Jonson's Library and Marginalia: An Annotated Catalogue', *SP*, 71, No. 5 (December 1974). In view of the availability and extensiveness of this catalogue, which includes facsimile examples of Jonson's signature and marginalia, Jonson's marginalia in printed books and MSS are not included in the *Index*. McPherson's catalogue can be amended in the following instances. Three of his items (Nos. 111, 195, 200: i.e. *Malleus maleficarum* (Lyons, 1615), Otto van Veen, *Amorum emblemata* (Antwerp, 1608), and Marcus Vitruvius Pollio, *De architectura* (Venice, 1567)) are now at University College London (Ogden A 291-3). His item No. 156 (Fernando de Rojas, *The Spanish Bawd* (London, 1631)) is now in the Robert H. Taylor Collection at Princeton, and the title page, with Jonson's signature, is reproduced in *PULC*, 38 (1977), 139. What appears to be his item No. 69 (Fulke Greville, *Certaine Learned and Elegant Workes* (London, 1633)) is now at Shrewsbury School. McPherson's 'doubtful' item No. 6 (the Gollancz exemplum of Tacitus, *Annales* and *Description of Germàine* (London, 1598), with annotations relating to Sejanus) is also at University College London (Ogden A 302), and it can be confirmed that the annotations are definitely not in Jonson's hand, nor is there any mark of his ownership. Neither are the annotations by Jonson in two other volumes which, though not mentioned by McPherson, have been mistakenly catalogued or cited by others as belonging to Jonson: one, an exemplum of Cicero, *Opera omnia* (Basle, 1534) in the University of London Library (Bb [Cicero] fol. Strongroom), with annotations relating to Catiline (II, 287-92); the other, an exemplum of George Chapman, *Twelve Bookes of Homers Iliades* (London, [1609?]) at Trinity College, Cambridge (VI. 9. 58), with annotations discussed in H. C. Fay, 'Critical Marks in a Copy of Chapman's *Twelve Bookes of Homers Iliades*', *The Library*, 5th Ser. 8 (1953), 117-21. One or two authentic items may be added to McPherson's catalogue. In one of James Orchard Halliwell-Phillipps's collections in the Folger (MS Z. e. 7, p. 23) is a detached half title leaf of *Iani Gruteri ad Martialem notae* with Jonson's signature. In an autograph collection of Thomas Rawlinson (1681-1725) in the Bodleian (MS Rawl. D. 1387, ff. 46-8) are three similar items: one, the title leaf of [Thomas Cooper], *An Admonition to the People of England* (London, 1589) with Jonson's signature; secondly, the title leaf of *Flores epigrammatum ex optimis quisbusque authoribus excerpti per Leodegarium tomus primus* (Paris, 1560) with Jonson's signature and motto ('tanquā Explorator'); and thirdly, a slip with Jonson's motto and signature of ownership cut from an unidentified volume. One other possible addition — though it cannot be confirmed — is a printed exemplum of Joachimus Camerarius, *Commentarii utriusque linguae* (Basle, 1551) which was sold at Sotheby's, 18 December 1908, Lot 308. According to the sale catalogue, the volume had copious MS marginal notes possibly in Jonson's hand (and which the book collector James Crossley of Manchester claimed were Jonson's), and the title page bore the monogram 'B.I.'

One or two additional examples of Jonson's hand may be mentioned. Jonson seems to have been one of the earliest English poets to leave 'autographs' in the modern sense, that is, inscriptions consciously written out as mementos of himself and which his contemporaries evidently requested or valued as such: witness particularly his presentation leaf to Drummond (FACSIMILE XXII). There are at least two recorded inscriptions of his in contemporary autograph albums (a form of compilation which became fashionable on the Continent in the 16th century). One was written c.1599-1611 in the *Liber amicorum* of Captain Francis Segar, now in the Huntington (HM 743, f. 84); the inscription is printed in Herford & Simpson, VIII, 664-5. The other was written on 1 January 1619/20 in the *Album academicum et apodemicum* of Joachim Morsius (1593-1643). This album was formerly in the Municipal Library of Lübeck, West Germany, but cannot now be located and was almost certainly destroyed in World War II; however, Jonson's inscription was reproduced in Heinrich Schneider, *Joachim Morsius und sein Kreis* (Lübeck, 1929), p. 25, and is printed in Herford & Simpson, VIII, 664. Another kind of inscription, Jonson's epitaph on Robert Jermyn of Rushbrooke (1623), was carved on a monument in St Margaret's, Lothbury, but this church was largely destroyed in the Fire of London (1666). Early copies of the inscription are written in a miscellany in the Bodleian (MS Rawl. poet. 142, f. 48) and in a printed exemplum of Camden, *Annales* (London, 1615) in the Folger (STC 4496/copy 1); the text is printed in Herford & Simpson, VIII. 661. For a copy made by Jonson of Wotton's poem *The Character of a Happy Life*, see WoH 2.

Apart from the main autograph items, the most important MSS of Jonson's works are contemporary scribal copies of the complete text of various masques and entertainments. Eleven such copies are known (JnB 563, 574-576.5, 611-12, 676, 680, 683, 691), and there also survives (not previously recorded by editors) a French version of the *Entertainment of the King and Queen at Theobalds* in 1607 which was evidently made for the use of the distinguished French spectators (JnB 577). Although all the texts represented in these copies are presumably close to the author's own MSS, only one is known for certain to have been handled by Jonson himself: the copy of *The Masque of Blackness* which he signed and presented to Queen Anne (JnB 683). What would have been a scribal copy of comparable authority of another entertainment, the *Panegyre on the King's Opening of Parliament*, which Jonson presented to King James, is no longer to be found among the Royal MSS except for the detached title leaf (JnB 690). Four of the copies of entertainments (JnB 574, 611, 676, 680) belong to a single MS volume, known as the Newcastle MS. This volume, now in the British Library (Harley MS 4955), is the single most important MS collection of Jonson's works. It is a formal anthology compiled by two scribes during the 1620s and 1630s evidently for the Cavendish family, perhaps principally for Sir William Cavendish, first Earl of Newcastle (1592-1676), who was one of Jonson's patrons. It consists chiefly of works by Jonson and Donne. Besides containing copies of four entertainments and of some letters of Jonson, the MS includes extracts from three other masques (JnB 564, 606, 735) and copies of 29 of Jonson's poems (recorded in the entries below).

The number of surviving MS copies of Jonson's masques reflects the value which Court circles, and Jonson himself, evidently attached to these productions. A complementary survival of MSS is that of the original costume and scenic designs for masques, including Jonson's, made by Inigo Jones, preserved among the collections of the Duke of Devonshire at Chatsworth House; they are extensively catalogued, with numerous illustrations, in Stephen Orgel and Roy Strong, *Inigo Jones: The Theatre of the Stuart Court*, 2 vols (Sotheby Parke Bernet, University of California Press, 1973). No special conditions favoured the survival of MSS of Jonson's plays written for the public stage, however. The plays are represented in the *Index* only by various extracts (probably derived from printed texts) in miscellanies, and by some early copies of the songs. The latter are of some interest because a number of the songs introduced in Jonson's plays (and masques) clearly circulated in MS as independent pieces, sometimes being revised before publication; moreover, certain MS copies preserve contemporary musical settings. Various other musical pieces preserved in MSS may belong to particular dances in Jonson's masques: see Sabol, *400 Songs & Dances*, passim.

Some additional extracts from the dramatic works may be noted. By far the most extensive collection of quotations from Jonson to be found anywhere is in John Evans's miscellany *Hesperides, or the Muses' Garden* (c. 1655); for details of this compilation, see WILLIAM SHAKESPEARE, INTRODUCTION. The surviving indexes of the miscellany include the titles of 45 of Jonson's plays and masques, as well as of ten other works (or groups of works) by him. Elsewhere, a transcript of a speech from *Catiline* (I, i, 61 seq.) made by Thomas Hearne (1678-1735) can be found in the Bodleian (MS Rawl. D. 260, f. 26). The Witches' chants in *The Masque of Queens* (lines 155-204) appear in a later musical setting by R. J. S. Stevens (1757-1837) in the British Library (Add. MS 31815, ff. 55-64). The song beginning 'If I freely may discouer' from *The Poetaster* (II, ii, 163 seq.) was the basis for a 38-line poem by John Grainge beginning 'To the world I'll now discover', the text of which is printed in John Wardroper, *Love and Drollery* (London, 1969), pp. 102-3. The poem is preserved in miscellanies in the British Library (Add. MS 25707, f. 104; Sloane MS 1446, f. 68v); in the Folger (MS V. a. 322, pp. 197-8); and at the Rosenbach Foundation (MS 239/23, pp. 171-3).

There are numerous copies of Jonson's poems in miscellanies and other MS sources. Those texts often represent early versions which circulated in MS before being revised for publication. Jonson established his definitive text of the *Epigrammes* and *The Forrest* in the First Folio of his *Workes* (1616), which he personally supervised, but he never completed a second collected edition. The Second Folio of his *Workes*, including *The Vnder-wood*, was edited after his death by Sir Kenelm Digby (1603-65) and by the printer Thomas Walkley and was published in 1640-1 (the title page is dated 1640). Digby and Walkley allegedly worked from Jonson's 'true & perfect Copies'; this was as opposed to John Benson's 'pirated' 4to and 12mo editions of Jonson's poems, which were printed in 1640 from 'false & imperfect Copies' (see Herford & Simpson, IX, 98). Nonetheless, certain of the texts (e.g. Nos. xx and lxxxiv of *The Vnder-wood*) were evidently imperfect and at least three poems by other authors (Nos. xxxix, lxxx, and lxxxi) were included by mistake. MS copies of poems in *The Vnder-wood* are arguably of textual importance in providing useful checks against the readings of the Second Folio. The early versions of the poems which they sometimes preserve are those which were, in fact, most widely known to Jonson's own contemporaries.

Among the more notable of the miscellaneous MS sources are copies of certain poems owned by Sir Kenelm Digby himself; however, they clearly had no connection with the MSS Jonson bequeathed to him and which, after being sold to Walkley for printing, suffered the usual fate of printers' MSS and have disappeared without trace. What was described by a later owner, Henry Bright, as 'a small packet of old discoloured papers' containing 19 poems by various authors (six in Digby's autograph) included three poems by Jonson (JnB 193, 226, 307), two relating to Digby's wife, Venetia Stanley. This collection cannot now be traced, though the texts were fortunately printed by Bright in 1877. Another unlocated miscellany reported to have contained poems by Jonson, a 12mo MS volume of poems by Jonson, Strode, Corbett, et al compiled by Jeremie Baines (fl. 1639-51) of Hampshire, was formerly owned by Rev. T. M. Webb of Hardwick Vicarage, Herefordshire, and was last recorded in *HMC*, 7th Report, Part I (1879), Appendix, p. 691.

There are a few other miscellaneous copies of poems by Jonson which are not given entries. Copies of the *Epitaph on Elizabeth, L.H.* appear in a volume of Thomas Percy's (c.1749) in the Bodleian (MS Eng. misc. e. 219, f. 6v), in a verse miscellany of 1747 in the Osborn Collection at Yale (fc 60, p. 119), and in a miscellany of Gabriel Lepipre's (c.1744-53) also in the Osborn Collection (c 360/1, p. 185). A short version of Jonson's extempore *Grace ... before King James*, here ascribed to 'King Charles 2ds Fool' and beginning 'The King God bless; the Queen no less', appears in an early 18th-century miscellany in the Brotherton Collection at the University of Leeds (MS Lt. 13, f. 42v). An early 18th-century verse miscellany at the University of Chicago contains a copy of

A Nymphs Passion (MS 554, p. 9). Thomas Hearne's transcript of *Horace his Art of Poetry* (lines 1-314) is in the Bodleian (MS Rawl. D. 261, pp. 104-15). E. T. W. Horne's copy of the song 'Drinke to me, onely, with thine eyes' in Henry Harrington's musical setting is in the British Library (Add. MS 29386, f. 12v). John Genest's copy of *To the worthy Author M. Iohn Fletcher* is written in an exemplum of Jonson's *Workes* (1640) in the Folger (STC 14753/copy 1).

One of Jonson's poems, *The Houre-glasse* (JnB 270-307), survives in slightly variant forms, but entries are not given to what appears to be a quite independent and anonymous translation of the original Latin poem by Girolamo Amaltei. This other version, beginning 'This dust y[t] quite runs out to runne againe', is printed in Herford & Simpson (XI, 53) from a MS in the British Library (Add. MS 30982, f. 57). There are also MS copies in Aberdeen University Library (MS 29, p. 178) and in the British Library (Sloane MS 1446, f. 26v).

The canon of Jonson's verse accepted in the *Index* is based entirely on Herford & Simpson and excludes what is regarded in that edition as the Jonson apocrypha (VIII, 424-52) as well as other verses which can be found ascribed to Jonson in MS sources. (At Harvard, for instance (Autograph file), is a late 17th-century copy of a poem which is alleged to have been copied from his autograph: the poem *Written by Ben: Jonson under Sir Ben: Rudyards Picture*, beginning 'Could we (as here this figure) see his Mind'). As with Donne, Jonson's popularity seems to have led to his name being uncritically linked with a variety of contemporary verses, though not only with poems written in his style but also with assorted trivial jokes and pieces of doggerel. He was likewise the subject of many 17th-century anecdotes, usually concerning witty things he is supposed to have said on various occasions; some of these are cited in Herford & Simpson, in J. F. Bradley and J. Q. Adams, *The Jonson Allusion-Book* (New Haven, 1922), and in Hilton Kelliher, 'Anecdotes of Jonson and Cleveland', *N & Q*, 217 (May 1972), 172-3. The frequency and earliness with which some of these references occur suggest that at least certain of them have their basis in fact. For instance, the verse on Noye the Attorney ('When the world was drown'd') is cited in Herford & Simpson (VIII, 447) from a copy in a notebook of Thomas Plume (1630-1704), but an earlier version, claiming that Jonson composed the verse in a tavern in Chancery Lane, is to be found in a notebook of Sir Richard Dyott, M.P. (1590-1659), now in the Staffordshire Record Office (D. 661/11/1/7, p. 54); Dyott's source is cited as 'M[r] James Povey'. The one invaluable record of Jonson's views and conversation is, of course, William Drummond's account: see DrW 303-4. Drummond's report is also the only evidence of a number of presumably genuine works which Jonson had written (for instance, 'a discourse of Poesie both against Campion & Daniel') and of certain works which, in 1618, he intended to write (such as 'ane Epick Poeme jntitled Heroologia of the Worthies of his Country'), but of which no texts are known. Some other 'lost' works can be inferred from references in certain of Jonson's poems: see William Dinsmore Briggs, 'Studies in Ben Jonson. IV', *Anglia*, 39 (1916), 209-52 (p. 219 seq.).

Some of Jonson's printed works bear interesting annotations by 17th-century readers, but they are not included in the entries below. For the annotations in one privately owned exemplum of the *Workes* (1616), see James A. Riddell, 'Seventeenth-Century Identifications of Jonson's Sources in the Classics', *RQ*, 28 (1975), 204-18. For annotations made by Charles Stanhope, second Lord Stanhope (1595-1675), in an exemplum of the *Workes* (1640) now in the Osborn Collection at Yale, see James M. Osborn, 'Ben Jonson and the Eccentric Lord Stanhope', *TLS* (4 January 1957), p. 16. For William Drummond's annotated exemplum of the *Workes* (1616), see DrW 351.

A considerable number of the MSS recorded in the *Index* have been collated in Herford & Simpson, but unless so stated the MSS here recorded have not been previously noted by editors.

PB.

ARRANGEMENT

See also Addenda to Part 2, p. 630

FACSIMILE XXII — Ben Jonson: *The Houre-glasse* and *My Picture left in Scotland*, 19 January 1618/19 (JnB 270 and 352). Scottish Record Office, GD18/4312. Reduced by approx. 15 per cent and processed to eliminate the heavy waterstaining on the original leaf. Reproduced by permission of Sir John Clerk of Penicuik, Bt., C.B.E., V.R.D.

To the honoring respect
borne
to the Freindship contracted wth
the right vertuous and learned
Mr William Drummond.

And the perpetuating the same by all offices of Loue
hereafter.

I Beniamin Jonson.
whome he hath honord wth the leaue to be calld his,
haue, wth mine owne hand, to satisfie his request
written this imperfect song.

On a Louers dust, made sand for an Howreglasse.

Do but consider this small dust here running in the glasse
by atomes moud;
Could you beleeue that this the body euer was
of one that lou'd?
And, in his mistress' flame, playing like the flye,
Turnd to cinders by her eye!
Yes: and in death, as life, unblest,
To haue it exprest
Euen ashes of louers find no rest.

Yet. that Loue when it is at full, may admit heaping,
Receiue another; and this a picture of my selfe.

I doubt that Loue is rather deafe, then blind.
For else it could not be
That shee,
Whom I adore so much, should so slight mee,
And cast my suite behind.
I'm sure my language to her is as sweete,
And all my closes meete
In numbers of as subtile feete,
As makes the yongest hee
That sits in shadow of Apollos tree.
O but my conscious feares,
That flye my thoughts betweene,
Prompt mee, that shee hath seene
My hundreds of gray haires,
Told sixe, and fortie yeares,
Read so much wast as she cannot embrace
My mountaine belly, and my rockye face,
And all these, through her eyes have stopt her eares.

Ben: Jonson

Januar 19
1619.

Ben Jonson

VERSE

[and, for songs from dramatic works, see also JnB 556-739]

JnB 1 *'And must I sing? what subiect shall I chuse?'.*

Copy in a verse miscellany owned in 1623 and probably compiled by one Richard Jackson; c. 1620s-30s.

First pub. in *Diuerse Poetical Essaies* appended to Robert Chester, *Loues Martyr* (London, 1601); *The Forrest* (x) in *Workes* (London, 1616); Herford & Simpson, VIII, 107-8.

Edinburgh University Library, MS H.-P. Coll. 401, f. 73v.

--- -----

See also JnB 423-4.

JnB 2 *Another. In defence of their Inconstancie. A Song* ('Hang up those dull, and envious fooles').

Copy, headed 'A Song Apologetique: In defence of womens inconstancy', in a miscellany; c. 1660.

First pub. in *The Vnder-wood* (vi) in *Workes* (London, 1640); Herford & Simpson, VIII, 146.

Rosenbach Foundation, MS 239/18, pp. 3-4.

JnB 3 -----

Copy in a miscellany owned and probably compiled by one John Hale; late 17th century.

Yale, Osborn Collection, b 104, pp. 116-17.

JnB 4 *An Answer to Alexander Gill* ('Shall the prosperity of a Pardon still').

Copy, headed 'Another answeare' and here beginning 'Doth the prosperitie of a pardon still', in a verse miscellany; c. 1630s.

First pub. in *Wit and Drollery* (London, 1656); Herford & Simpson, VIII, 410-11. This MS evidently the Dobell MS collated in Herford & Simpson.

Folger, MS V. a. 245, f. 70v.

JnB 4.5 See Addenda, p. 630.

JnB 5 -----

Copy, headed 'An Answer' and here beginning 'Doth the prosperity of a pardon still', in a MS volume; c. 1632-42.

Printed from his transcript of this MS in John Payne Collier, 'Ben Jonson and Alexander Gill', *The Athenaeum*, No. 1957 (29 April 1865), pp. 587-8; collated from this publication in Herford & Simpson.

Formerly owned by Richard Heber (1773-1833); unlocated.

JnB 6 -----

Copy, headed 'To Alexander Gill' and here beginning 'Doth the prosperity of a pardon still', in a verse miscellany; 17th century.

Printed from this MS in John Payne Collier, *An Old Man's Diary* (London, 1871-2), part ii, p. 13; collated from this publication in Herford & Simpson.

Formerly owned by John Payne Collier (1789-1883); unlocated.

JnB 7 -----

Copy, headed 'Ben Johnson against Gill', in a heraldic miscellany (f. 75) compiled by John Cooper, a scribe of Sir Christopher Hatton's; c. 1632-43.

This MS formerly Phillipps MS 13185.

Sotheby's, 29 October 1975, Lot 78 (unsold); unlocated.

JnB 8 *A Celebration of Charis in ten Lyrick Peeces. 4. Her Triumph* ('See the Chariot at hand here of Love').

Copy, headed 'In Dominam amatoriam' and here beginning 'See now ye chariot at hand heere of Loue', in a verse miscellany probably compiled by a Cambridge man; c. 1630s.

First pub. (all ten poems) in *The Vnder-wood* (ii) in *Workes* (London, 1640); Herford & Simpson, VIII, 131-42 (pp. 134-5). Lines 11-30 of poem 4 (beginning 'Doe but looke on her eyes, they do light') first pub. in *The Devil is an Ass*, II, vi, 94-113 (London, 1631). This MS collated in Herford & Simpson.

British Library, Add. MS 15227, f. 89.

JnB 9 ----- -----

Copy in a musical setting by Robert Johnson in a MS music book owned (in 1659) and partly compiled by the composer John Gamble; c. 1630s-50s.

This MS recorded in Cutts, *Musique de la troupe de Shakespeare*, pp. 150-1.

New York Public Library, Music Division, Drexel MS 4257, No. 2.

JnB 10 ----- -----

Copy in a verse miscellany compiled by Tobias

Alston (1620-c.1639) of Sayham Hall near Sudbury, Suffolk; c. 1639.

Yale, Osborn Collection, b 197, pp. 186-7.

JnB 11 ----- -----

Copy of lines 11-30 in a verse miscellany compiled by one Thomas Crosse; c. 1630s.

This MS collated in Herford & Simpson.

British Library, Harley MS 6057, f. 4v.

JnB 12 ----- -----

Copy of lines 21-30 (beginning 'Have you seene but a bright Lillie grow'), headed 'A song' and here beginning 'Haue you seene ye white Lilly grow', in a verse miscellany once owned by Elizabeth Lane and John Finch; c. 1630s.

Aberdeen University Library, MS 29, p. 176.

JnB 13 ----- -----

Copy of lines 21-30, here beginning 'Haue you^u seene the white lillye grow', with two additional stanzas, in a verse miscellany compiled by the Yorkshire antiquary John Hopkinson (1610-80); c. 1647.

Bodleian, MS Don. d. 58, f. 26v.

JnB 14 ----- -----

Copy of lines 21-30 in a miscellany compiled by Edward Natley, fellow of Queens' College, Cambridge; c. 1635-44.

Bodleian, MS Eng. poet. f. 25, fol. 64v.

JnB 15 ----- -----

Copy of lines 21-30 in a miscellany compiled by William Eliot (a nephew of Sir Simonds D'Ewes), bound in a composite volume of MSS; c. 1640-55.

This MS collated in Herford & Simpson.

Bodleian, MS Rawl. poet. 116, f. 50v.

JnB 16 ----- -----

Copy of lines 21-30 in a verse miscellany; c. 1620s-30s.

Bodleian, MS Rawl. poet. 199, p. 74.

JnB 17 ----- -----

Copy of lines 21-30, here beginning 'Haue you^u seene but a Whyte Lillie grow', in a musical setting by Robert Johnson, in a MS songbook owned in 1630 by one Hugh Floyd; c. 1614-30.

Printed from this MS in Cutts, *Musique de la troupe de Shakespeare*, pp. 54-5; recorded in Herford & Simpson, XI, 609. Facsimile in F.H. Potter, *Reliquary of English Song* (London, 1915), facing p. x.

British Library, Add. MS 15117, f. 17v.

JnB 18 ----- -----

Copy of lines 21-30, headed 'Another' and here beginning 'Have you seen ye white lilie growe', in a verse miscellany once owned by one John Philips; c. 1630s.

British Library, Add. MS 19268, f. 14.

JnB 19 ----- -----

Copy of lines 21-30 in a musical setting by Robert Johnson, in a MS songbook once owned by one Richard Elliotts and possibly by the composer Adrian Batten (d. 1637); c. 1630.

This MS collated in Cutts, *Musique de la troupe de Shakespeare*, pp. 150-3.

British Library, Add. MS 29481, f. 10r-v.

JnB 20 ----- -----

Copy of lines 21-30 in a verse miscellany probably compiled by one 'I.A.' of Christ Church, Oxford, and later owned by Robert Killigrew; c. early 1630s.

British Library, Sloane MS 1792, f. 92.

JnB 21 ----- -----

Copy of lines 21-30, here beginning 'Haue you seene the white lilly growe', with an additional verse beginning 'Haue you seene the faire christall rocke', in a verse miscellany bound with a collection of printed amatory poems and pamphlets; early 17th century.

Printed from this MS in *Love-Poems and Humourous Ones*, ed. Frederick J. Furnivall, Ballad Society (Hertford, 1874; reprinted New York, 1977), pp. 16-17.

British Library, Department of Printed Books, C. 39, a. 37, ff. 9v-10.

JnB 22 ----- -----

Copy of lines 21-8, headed 'A song' and here beginning 'Did you ever see ye white lilly grow', in a verse miscellany once owned by William Godolphin and Henry Savile; late 17th century.

Cambridge University Library, MS Dd. 6. 43, f. 25v.

JnB 23 ----- -----

Copy of lines 21-30, here beginning 'Have you seene the white lilly grow', in a musical setting by Robert Johnson, in a MS songbook owned and probably compiled by Elizabeth Davenant (sister of Sir William Davenant) of Oxford; c. 1624-30s.

This MS collated in Cutts, *Musique de la troupe de Shakespeare*, pp. 150-1; recorded in Herford & Simpson, XI, 609.

Christ Church, Oxford, MS Mus. 87, ff. 4v-5.

JnB 24 ----- -----

Copy of lines 21-30, headed 'A Lover to his Mistrisse' and here beginning 'Haue you seene the whyte lillye grow', in a verse miscellany; c. 1630.

Folger, MS V. a. 103, Part I, f. 31v.

JnB 25 ----- -----

Copy of lines 21-30, headed 'A Sonnet' and here beginning 'Have you seene the white Lilly grow', in a verse miscellany compiled by an Oxford man; c. 1630s.

This MS probably the Dobell MS collated in Herford & Simpson.

Folger, MS V. a. 170, pp. 30-1.

JnB 26 ----- -----

Copy of lines 21-30 in a musical setting by Robert Johnson in a MS songbook once owned by a certain Anne Twice; c. 1620.

Printed from this MS in Cutts, *Musique de la troupe de Shakespeare*, p. 56.

New York Public Library, Music Division, Drexel MS 4175, No. xlix.

JnB 27 ----- -----

Copy of lines 21-30, headed 'A Lover on his Mistresse' and here beginning 'Have you seene the white Lilly grow', in a verse miscellany; c. 1630.

University of Nottingham, Portland MS Pw V 37, p. 64.

JnB 28 ----- -----

Copy of lines 21-30, headed 'A Songe' and here beginning 'Haue you seene the white Lillye Growe', in a verse miscellany; c. 1635.

Rosenbach Foundation, MS 240/7, p. 90.

JnB 29 ----- -----

Copy of lines 21-30, headed 'On My Lady Lucy Percy' and here beginning 'Haue you seene the bright-Lilly growe', in a miscellany compiled by or for Sir Thomas Finch, Viscount Maidstone and Earl of Winchelsea; c. 1634.

Rosenbach Foundation, MS 243/4, p. 9.

JnB 30 ----- -----

Copy of lines 21-30, here beginning 'Heave you not seen bot a bright lillie grow', in a musical setting by Robert Johnson, written in one of the MS part books of the 'St Andrews Psalter'; early 17th century.

This MS collated in Cutts, *Musique de la troupe de Shakespeare*, pp. 150-1.

Trinity College, Dublin, MS 412, f. 31v.

JnB 31 ----- -----

Copy of lines 21-30, here beginning 'Have y^{u} seene the white lilly grow', in a verse miscellany connected with Christ Church, Oxford, owned and perhaps partly compiled by George Morley, later Bishop of Winchester (1598-1684); 1620s-30s.

Westminster Abbey, MS 41, f. 88v.

JnB 32 ----- -----

Copy of lines 21-30, headed 'A song' and here beginning 'Have you seene the white lilly grew', in a miscellany; mid-17th century.

Yale, Osborn Collection, b 205, f. 73.

JnB 33 ----- -----

Copy of lines 21-30, here beginning 'Have you seen ye white lilly grow', in a miscellany; late 17th century.

Yale, Osborn Collection, b 213, p. 65b.

JnB 34 ----- -----

Copy of lines 21-30, here beginning 'Haue you seene ye white lilly grow', with two additional stanzas, in a miscellany (p. 3) probably compiled by one or two members of the Calverley family; c. 1623-30s.

Formerly Phillipps MS 9624 and owned before 1947 by N.M. Broadbent; printed from this MS in Herford & Simpson, VIII, 135-6. Facsimile in Christie's sale catalogue, 13 June 1979, plate 20.

Christie's, 13 June 1979 (Arthur A. Houghton, Jr. sale), Lot 135, sold to Maggs; thence to Huntington.

A Celebration of Charis in ten Lyrick Peeces. 4. Her Triumpn

JnB 35 ----- -----

Copy of line 21 in a musical setting by Robert Johnson, written in the bass MS part book of the 'St Andrews Psalter'; early 17th century.

This MS recorded in Cutts, *Musique de la troupe de Shakespeare*, pp. 150-3.

Edinburgh University Library, MS La. III. 483, Bassus, p. 201.

JnB 36 ----- *7. Begging another, on colour of mending the former* ('For Loves-sake, kisse me once againe').

Copy, headed 'On Begging A kiss of his M[ris]', in a verse miscellany compiled by Nicholas Burghe (d. 1670); c. 1638.

Herford & Simpson, VIII, 139. This MS collated in Herford & Simpson.

Bodleian, MS Ashmole 38, p. 84.

JnB 37 ----- -----

Copy of a version of lines 1-6, untitled, in a miscellany once owned by Margaret Bellasys, probably the daughter of Thomas, first Lord Fauconberg (1577-1653); c. 1630.

British Library, Add. MS 10309, f. 57v.

JnB 38 ----- -----

Copy, untitled, in a composite volume of verse belonging to the Skipwith family of Cotes, Leicestershire; early-mid-17th century.

This MS collated in Herford & Simpson.

British Library, Add. MS 25707, f. 63.

JnB 39 ----- -----

Copy, untitled, in a verse miscellany owned in 1691 by one Thomas White; c. 1640.

Folger, MS V. a. 96, ff. 51v-2.

JnB 40 ----- -----

Copy, headed 'To his M[rs]', in a miscellany compiled by one Richard Archard; c. 1650-7.

Folger, MS V. a. 124, f. 43v.

JnB 41 ----- -----

Copy, untitled, in a verse miscellany; mid-17th century.

Folger, MS V. a. 322, p. 128.

JnB 42 ----- -----

Copy, untitled, in a verse miscellany owned in 1640 by Anthony St John (1618-73) and Ann St John, of Bletsoe, Bedfordshire; c. 1630s.

Harvard, fMS Eng 626, f. 78v.

JnB 43 ----- -----

Copy, untitled, in a verse miscellany; c. 1630.

Rosenbach Foundation, MS 239/23, pp. 35-6.

JnB 44 ----- -----

Copy in a miscellany partly compiled by one Robert Berkeley; c. 1640s.

Rosenbach Foundation, MS 240/2, pp. 81-2.

JnB 44.5 See Addenda, p. 630.

JnB 45 ----- *9. Her man described by her own Dictamen* ('Of your Trouble, Ben, to ease me').

Copy, headed 'The Man', in the Newcastle MS; c. 1620s-30s.

Herford & Simpson, VIII, 140-2. This MS collated in Herford & Simpson.

British Library, Harley MS 4955, ff. 34v-5.

JnB 46 ----- *10. Another Ladyes exception present at the hearing* ('For his Mind, I doe not care').

Copy, headed 'A Lady's Choyce', in a composite volume of verse collected by Peter Le Neve (1661-1729), his brother Oliver, and Thomas Martin (1697-1771) of Palgrave; 17th century.

Herford & Simpson, VIII, 142. This MS collated in Herford & Simpson.

British Library, Add. MS 27406, f. 110.

JnB 47 *Charles Cauendish to his posteritie* ('Sonnes, seeke not me amonge these polish'd stones').

Copy in the Newcastle MS; c. 1620s-30s.

First pub. (from this MS) in *The Works of Ben Jonson*, ed. William Gifford, 9 vols (London, 1816). Printed from this MS in Herford & Simpson, VIII, 387-8, and collated with the monument at Bolsover.

British Library, Harley MS 4955, f. 54v.

JnB 48 *The Dreame* ('Or Scorne, or pittie on me take').

Copy in a musical setting by John Wilson, in Wilson's corrected MS volume of his own songs; possibly in Wilson's autograph or else in the hand of someone similarly associated with Edward Lowe (c.1610-82); c. 1656.

First pub. in *The Vnder-wood* (xi) in *Workes* (London, 1640); Herford & Simpson, VIII, 150-1. This MS collated (no variants) in John P. Cutts, 'Seventeenth Century Lyrics', *MD*, 10 (1956), 142-209 (p. 167).

Bodleian, MS Mus. b. 1, f. 48v.

JnB 49 -----

Copy, untitled, in a verse miscellany owned in 1691 by one Thomas White; c. 1640.

Folger, MS V. a. 96, ff. 38v-9.

JnB 50 -----

Copy, untitled, in a verse miscellany owned in 1640 by Anthony St John (1618-73) and Ann St John, of Bletsoe, Bedfordshire; c. 1630s.

Harvard, fMS Eng 626, ff. 66v-7.

JnB 51 -----

Copy, untitled, in a miscellany compiled by or for Sir Henry Cholmley, brother of Sir Hugh Cholmley (1600-57); c. 1624-41.

Harvard, MS Eng 703, f. 34v.

JnB 52 -----

Copy, untitled, in a miscellany; c. 1630.

Huntington, HM 172, f. 25r-v.

JnB 53 -----

Copy, headed 'On a Virgin fallen in loue in her sleepe not knowing with whome', in a verse miscellany possibly once owned by Sir John Reresby (d. 1646); among the papers of the Savile family, formerly of Methley Hall, near Pontefract; c. 1630s.

Leeds Archives Department, MX 237, f. 54v.

JnB 54 -----

Copy in the hand of William Parkhurst (fl. 1604-67) in a composite volume of MSS collected by him; among the papers of the Finch family of Burley-on-the-Hill, Rutland; 1600s-41.

Leicestershire Record Office, DG. 7/Lit. 2, f. 260v.

JnB 55 -----

Copy, written at the back of a MS volume of poems by Donne once owned by one E. Puckering; c. 1620s-30s.

Trinity College, Cambridge, MS R. 3. 12 (James 592), p. 242.

JnB 56 *An Elegie On the Lady Jane Pawlet, Marchion: of Winton* ('What gentle Ghost, besprent with April deaw').

Copy in a transcript by one 'S.H.' (born 1665) of John Benson's 12mo edition of Jonson's poems (1640); c. 1680.

First pub. in John Benson's 4to edition (1640) and in *The Vnder-wood* (lxxxiii) in *Workes* (London, 1640); Herford & Simpson, VIII, 268-72. This MS recorded in Herford & Simpson.

Edinburgh University Library, MS Dc. 7. 94, ff. 7v-9v.

JnB 57 -----

Copy in a miscellany of religious verse compiled by Constance, daughter of Sir Walter Aston (1584-1639) of Tixall, Staffordshire; c. 1630-50.

Huntington, HM 904, ff. 137-9.

JnB 58 -----

Copy in a verse miscellany appended to a MS volume of poems by Donne; c. 1630s.

This MS collated in Herford & Simpson.

Trinity College, Dublin, MS 877, ff. 176-7v.

JnB 59 *An Epigram on the Princes birth* ('And art thou borne, brave Babe? Blest be thy birth').

Copy in the Newcastle MS; c. 1630s.

First pub. in John Benson's 4to edition of Jonson's poems (1640) and in *The Vnder-wood* (lxv) in *Workes* (London, 1640); Herford & Simpson, VIII, 237-8. This MS collated in Herford & Simpson.

British Library, Harley MS 4955, f. 193.

JnB 60 -----

Copy, lacking the first two lines, in a verse miscellany compiled by an Oxford man and once owned by one Henry Lawson; c. 1630s.

Bodleian, MS Eng. poet. e. 14, f. 48.

JnB 61 -----

Copy in a composite volume of verse and prose owned c. 1669 by one John Cooke of Bury St Edmunds, Suffolk; c. 1620s-30s.

This MS collated in Herford & Simpson.

Bodleian, MS Rawl. poet. 26, f. 10v.

JnB 62 -----

Copy in a verse miscellany belonging to the Paulet family and owned in 1659 by one Egigius Frampton; mid-17th century.

This MS collated in Herford & Simpson.

Bodleian, MS Rawl. poet. 84, f. 61.

An Epigram on the Princes birth

JnB 63 -----

Copy in a verse miscellany compiled by one 'H.S.', a Cambridge man; c. 1640s-50s.

This MS collated in Herford & Simpson.

Bodleian, MS Rawl. poet. 147, p. 232 rev.

JnB 64 -----

Copy in a verse miscellany; c. 1630s.

This MS collated in Herford & Simpson.

Bodleian, MS Rawl. poet. 160, f. 12v.

JnB 65 -----

Copy in a verse miscellany probably compiled by a member of New College, Oxford; c. 1630s.

This MS collated in Herford & Simpson.

Bodleian, MS Rawl. poet. 206, p. 57.

JnB 66 -----

Copy in a verse miscellany once owned by one John Philips; c. 1630s.

British Library, Add. MS 19268, f. 18v.

JnB 67 -----

Copy in a verse miscellany compiled by Thomas Manne (1582?-1641) of Christ Church, Oxford; c. 1630s.

British Library, Add. MS 58215, p. 123.

JnB 68 -----

Copy in a verse miscellany once owned by Francis Norreys (? Sir Francis Norris (1609-69)) and Henry Balle; mid-17th century.

This MS collated in Herford & Simpson.

British Library, Egerton MS 2421, f. 16v.

JnB 69 -----

Copy in a miscellany once owned by Sir Thomas Meres (1634-1715) of Kirton, Lincolnshire; c. 1640s.

This MS collated in Herford & Simpson.

British Library, Egerton MS 2725, f. 35.

JnB 70 -----

Copy, headed 'Another', in a verse miscellany compiled by a Cambridge man; c. 1660s.

Cambridge University Library, MS Add. 79, f. 46.

JnB 71 -----

Copy in a transcript by one 'S.H.' (born 1665) of John Benson's 12mo edition of Jonson's poems (1640); c. 1680.

Edinburgh University Library, MS Dc. 7. 94, ff. 6v-7.

JnB 72 -----

Copy in a verse miscellany; c. 1634.

Rosenbach Foundation, MS 239/27, p. 225.

JnB 73 -----

Copy in a verse miscellany appended to a MS volume of poems by Donne; c. 1630s.

This MS collated in Herford & Simpson.

Trinity College, Dublin, MS 877, ff. 169v-70.

JnB 74 *An Epigram To my Mvse, the Lady Digby, on her Husband, Sir Kenelme Digby* ('Tho', happy Muse, thou know my Digby well').

Copy in a verse miscellany compiled by one Thomas Crosse; c. 1630s.

First pub. in John Benson's 4to edition of Jonson's poems (1640) and in *The Vnder-wood* (lxxviii) in *Workes* (London, 1640); Herford & Simpson, VIII, 262-3. This MS collated in Herford & Simpson.

British Library, Harley MS 6057, f. 20.

JnB 75 -----

Copy in a transcript by one 'S.H.' (born 1665) of John Benson's 12mo edition of Jonson's poems (1640); c. 1680.

This MS recorded in Herford & Simpson.

Edinburgh University Library, MS Dc. 7. 94, f. 14r-v.

JnB 76 -----

Copy in a verse miscellany compiled by William Jordan, schoolmaster of Denbigh or Caernarvon; c. 1674-84.

Folger, MS V. a. 276, Part II, f. 43r-v.

JnB 77 -----

Copy in a verse miscellany; mid-17th century.

Folger, MS V. a. 322, pp. 7-8.

JnB 78 *An Epigram. To our great and good K. Charles On his Anniversary Day* ('How happy were the Subject, if he knew').

Copy, headed 'To the great and Gratious King Charles. On the Vniuersary day of his Raigne. 1629', in the Newcastle MS; c. 1630s.

First pub. in *The Vnder-wood* (lxiv) in *Workes* (London, 1640); Herford & Simpson, VIII, 236-7. This MS collated in Herford & Simpson.

British Library, Harley MS 4955, f. 192v.

JnB 79 *An Epigram to the Queene, then lying in* ('Haile Mary, full of grace, it once was said').

Copy in the Newcastle MS; c. 1630s.

First pub. in John Benson's 4to edition of Jonson's poems (1640) and in *The Vnder-wood* (lxvi) in *Workes* (London, 1640); Herford & Simpson, VIII, 238. This MS collated in Herford & Simpson.

British Library, Harley MS 4955, f. 193.

JnB 80 -----

Copy in a transcript by one 'S.H.' (born 1665) of John Benson's 12mo edition of Jonson's poems (1640); c. 1680.

Edinburgh University Library, MS Dc. 7. 94, f. 6v.

JnB 81 -----

Copy in a verse miscellany appended to a MS volume of poems by Donne; c. 1630s.

This MS collated in Herford & Simpson.

Trinity College, Dublin, MS 877, f. 170.

JnB 82 *An Epigram. To William Earle of Newcastle* ('They talke of Fencing, and the use of Armes').

Copy in the Newcastle MS; c. 1620s-30s.

First pub. in John Benson's 4to edition of Jonson's poems (1640) and in *The Vnder-wood* (lix) in *Workes* (London, 1640); Herford & Simpson, VIII, 232-3. This MS collated in Herford & Simpson.

British Library, Harley MS 4955, f. 39.

JnB 83 -----

Copy in a verse miscellany compiled by one Thomas Crosse; c. 1630s.

This MS collated in Herford & Simpson.

British Library, Harley MS 6057, f. 20v.

JnB 84 -----

Copy in a transcript by one 'S.H.' (born 1665) of John Benson's 12mo edition of Jonson's poems (1640); c. 1680.

This MS recorded in Herford & Simpson.

Edinburgh University Library, MS Dc. 7. 94, ff. 13v-14.

JnB 85 *An Epigram. To William, Earle of Newcastle* ('When first, my Lord, I saw you backe your horse').

Copy, headed 'To the Right Honorable William viscount Mansfield: On his Horsemanship, and Stable', in the Newcastle MS; c. 1620s-30s.

First pub. in John Benson's 4to edition of Jonson's poems (1640) and in *The Vnder-wood* (liii) in *Workes* (London, 1640); Herford & Simpson, VIII, 288. This MS collated in Herford & Simpson.

British Library, Harley MS 4955, f. 40.

JnB 86 -----

Copy in a transcript by one 'S.H.' (born 1665) of John Benson's 12mo edition of Jonson's poems (1640); c. 1680.

This MS recorded in Herford & Simpson.

Edinburgh University Library, MS Dc. 7. 94, f. 13r-v.

JnB 87 -----

Copy in a verse miscellany compiled by William Jordan, schoolmaster of Denbigh or Caernarvon; c. 1674-84.

Folger, MS V. a. 276, Part II, f. 42v.

JnB 88 -----

Copy in a verse miscellany; mid-17th century.

Folger, MS V. a. 322, p. 4.

JnB 89 *An Epistle to a Friend* ('Censure, not sharplye then, but mee advise').

Copy, untitled, in a MS volume of poems chiefly by Donne compiled by Henry Champernowne (1600-56) of Dartington, Devon; c. 1623.

Lines 12-26 (beginning 'Little knowe they that professe Amitye') first pub. as lines 19-33 of 'An Epistle to a friend' in *The Vnder-wood* (xxxvii) in *Workes* (London, 1640); lines 1-11 first pub. in William Dinsmore Briggs, 'Studies in Ben Jonson. IV', *Anglia*, 39 (1916), 209-51 (pp. 230-1); Herford & Simpson, VIII, 421-2. This MS collated in Herford & Simpson.

Bodleian, MS Eng. poet. f. 9, pp. 12-13.

An Epistle to a Friend

JnB 90 -----

Copy, untitled, in a verse miscellany; c. 1620-33.

Printed from this MS in Briggs (lines 1-11) and in Herford & Simpson.

Bodleian, MS Rawl. poet. 31, ff. 23v-4.

JnB 91 -----

Copy, untitled, in a MS volume of poems chiefly by Donne; c. 1622-33.

Yale, Osborn Collection, b 148, p. 5.

JnB 92 *An Epistle to a Friend, to perswade him to the Warres* ('Wake friend, from forth thy Lethargie: the Drum').

Copy, headed 'To a Freind', in the Newcastle MS; c. 1620s-30s.

First pub. in *The Vnder-wood* (xv) in *Workes* (London, 1640); Herford & Simpson, VIII, 162-8. This MS collated in Herford & Simpson.

British Library, Harley MS 4955, ff. 31-4.

JnB 93 *Epistle To Elizabeth Covntesse of Rvtland* ('Whil'st that, for which, all vertue now is sold').

Copy, headed 'To the Countesse Off Rutland: An Elegie', in a verse miscellany; c. 1620-33.

First pub. in *The Forrest* (xii) in *Workes* (London, 1616); Herford & Simpson, VIII, 113-16. This MS collated in Herford & Simpson.

Bodleian, MS Rawl. poet. 31, ff. 18v-20v.

JnB 94 -----

Copy, headed 'To the Countesse of Rutland An Elegie', in a verse miscellany; c. 1620-33.

This MS collated in Herford & Simpson.

British Library, Harley MS 4064, ff. 243v-5v.

JnB 95 -----

Copy of lines 65-7, 35-6, untitled and here beginning 'You, and that other starre, that purest light', in a verse miscellany; mid-17th century.

Folger, MS V. a. 219, f. 34v (Nos. 18, 19).

JnB 96 -----

Copy of lines 2-4, here beginning 'Allmighty gold' and subscribed 'fforrest to Eliz. Coun: of Rutland', followed by lines 41-7, 72, 89-90, in a fragment of a miscellany; early 17th century (after 1616).

Worcester College, Oxford, (inserted loose in MSS 6. 13), f. [6v].

JnB 97 *Epistle. To Katherine, Lady Avbigny* (''Tis growne almost a danger to speake true').

Copy of lines 1-6, 26-32, 43-52, 121-4, 71-80, untitled, in a verse miscellany; mid-17th century.

First pub. in *The Forrest* (xiii) in *Workes* (London, 1616); Herford & Simpson, VIII, 116-20.

Folger, MS V. a. 219, ff. 33v-4 (Nos. 8-12).

JnB 98 -----

Copy of lines 49-50, here beginning 'Great title, birth, but virtue most' and subscribed 'fforrest to Kath: La. Aubigny', followed by lines 68-70, 85-6, in a fragment of a miscellany; early 17th century (after 1616).

Worcester College, Oxford, (inserted loose in MSS 6. 13), f. [7].

JnB 99 *An Epistle to Master Iohn Selden* ('I know to whom I write. Here, I am sure').

Copy in a heraldic miscellany; late 17th century.

First pub. in John Selden, *Titles of Honor* (London, 1614); *The Vnder-wood* (xiv) in *Workes* (London, 1640); Herford & Simpson, VIII, 158-61. This MS collated in Herford & Simpson.

Bodleian, MS Rawl. B. 20, f. 42v.

JnB 100 *Epistle. To my Lady Covell* ('You won not Verses, Madam, you won mee').

Copy, untitled, in the Newcastle MS; c. 1620s-30s.

First pub. in *The Vnder-wood* (lvi) in *Workes* (London, 1640); Herford & Simpson, VIII, 230-1. This MS collated in Herford & Simpson.

British Library, Harley MS 4955, f. 42v.

JnB 101 *An Epistle to Sir Edward Sacvile, now Earle of Dorset* ('If, Sackvile, all that have the power to doe').

Copy, headed 'A Poeme by the way of thankfull acknowledgment sent and dedicated to S[r] Edward Sackvile', in a verse miscellany; c. 1630.

An Epistle to Sir Edward Sacvile, now Earle of Dorset

First pub. in *The Vnder-wood* (xiii) in *Workes* (London, 1640); Herford & Simpson, VIII, 153-8.

University of Nottingham, Portland MS Pw V 37, pp. 232-6,

*JnB 102 *Epitaph* [*on Cecilia Bulstrode*] ('Stay, view this stone: And, if thou beest not such').

Autograph fair copy, in a letter to George Garrard; [1609].

First pub. in John A. Harper, 'Ben Jonson and Mrs. Bulstrode', *N & Q*, 3rd Ser. 4 (5 September 1863), 198-9. Printed from this MS (when it was among the Bromley-Davenport MSS at Baginton Hall, Warwickshire) in *HMC*, 2nd Report (1871), Appendix, p. 79, and also in Herford & Simpson, VIII, 371-2. Facsimiles in *The Houghton Library 1942-1967* (Cambridge, Mass., 1967), p. 83; Croft, *Autograph Poetry*, I, 27.

Harvard, Lowell autograph.

JnB 103 -----

Copy, headed 'Vppon A Virgine wch liued and died att Courte', in a verse miscellany compiled by Nicholas Burghe (d. 1670); c. 1638.

This MS collated in Herford & Simpson.

Bodleian, MS Ashmole 38, p. 187.

JnB 104 -----

Copy in a verse miscellany; c. 1620-33.

This MS collated in Herford & Simpson.

Bodleian, MS Rawl. poet. 31, f. 36r-v.

JnB 105 -----

Copy, untitled, in a miscellany compiled by William Eliot (a nephew of Sir Simonds D'Ewes), bound in a composite volume of MSS; c. 1640-55.

This MS collated in Herford & Simpson.

Bodleian, MS Rawl. poet. 116, f. 55v.

JnB 106 -----

Copy, headed 'On the death of Mistris Boulstead', in a verse miscellany; c. 1630s.

This MS collated in Herford & Simpson.

Bodleian, MS Rawl. poet. 160, f. 25v.

JnB 107 -----

Copy in the hand of a playhouse scribe in a verse miscellany probably compiled for the lawyer Chaloner Chute and belonging to his family in Hampshire; this MS in the same hand as *Dick of Devonshire* (HyT 5) and *Blurt Master Constable* (MiT 6); c. 1630s.

This MS recorded but not collated in Herford & Simpson.

British Library, Add. MS 33998, f. 33r-v.

JnB 108 -----

Copy, untitled, in a verse miscellany; c. 1630.

British Library, Egerton MS 2230, f. 35v.

JnB 109 -----

Copy in a verse miscellany; c. 1620-33.

This MS collated in Herford & Simpson.

British Library, Harley MS 4064, f. 261v.

JnB 110 -----

Copy, headed 'on the death of Mrs. Boulstred', in a verse miscellany compiled by one Thomas Crosse; c. 1630s.

This MS collated in Herford & Simpson.

British Library, Harley MS 6057, f. 33v.

JnB 111 -----

Copy in a verse miscellany; c. 1637.

British Library, Stowe MS 962, f. 90v.

JnB 112 -----

Copy in a miscellany probably compiled by someone connected with an Inn of Court; c. 1620s.

Formerly MS 8012; printed from this MS in Harper (1863) and in Grosart, *The Dr Farmer MS* (1873), II, 190; collated in Herford & Simpson.

Chetham's Library, Manchester, Mun. A 4. 15, p. 162.

JnB 113 -----

Copy in a miscellany; c. 1630.

Edinburgh University Library, MS La. III. 493, f. 94.

JnB 114 -----

Copy, untitled, in a verse miscellany owned in 1691 by one Thomas White; c. 1640.

Folger, MS V. a. 96, f. 76.

Epitaph [*on Cecilia Bulstrode*]

JnB 115 -----

Copy, headed 'Upon the same Mrs Boulstred', in a MS volume of poems by Donne (the 'O'Flahertie MS') completed on 12 October 1632.

This MS collated in Herford & Simpson.

Harvard, MS Eng 966.5, f. 87.

JnB 116 -----

Copy, headed 'On the death of M^ris Boulstred', in a MS volume of poems by Donne once owned by John Egerton, first Earl of Bridgewater (1579-1649); c. 1622-33.

This MS collated in Herford & Simpson.

Huntington, EL 6893, f. 26r-v.

JnB 117 -----

Copy in a MS volume of poems chiefly by Donne once owned by one Meriall Tracy; c. 1620-33.

Huntington, HM 198, Part II, f. 113v.

JnB 118 -----

Copy, headed 'Vpon the same', in a MS volume of poems by Donne owned in 1680 by Narcissus Luttrell; c. 1632.

Owned by Sir Geoffrey Keynes, *Bibliotheca Bibliographici* No. 1861, f. 49v.

JnB 119 -----

Copy in a miscellany compiled by William Drummond of Hawthornden; c. 1620s.

National Library of Scotland, MS 2060 (Hawthornden Vol. VIII), f. 164.

JnB 120 -----

Copy in a verse miscellany used by members of the Holgate family of Saffron Walden, Essex; c. 1630s.

Pierpont Morgan Library, MA 1057, p. 94.

JnB 121 -----

Copy, headed 'On the death of Mrs Boulstred', in a verse miscellany compiled by one Robert Bishop; c. 1630.

Rosenbach Foundation, MS 1083/16, p. 274.

JnB 122 *Epitaph on Elizabeth, L.H.* ('Would'st thou heare, what man can say').

Copy, headed 'An Epitaph on a gentelwoman whose name was Elizabeth', in a verse miscellany compiled by Nicholas Burghe (d. 1670); c. 1638.

First pub. in *Epigrammes* (cxxiiii) in *Workes* (London, 1616); Herford & Simpson, VIII, 79. This MS collated in Herford & Simpson.

Bodleian, MS Ashmole 38, p. 168.

JnB 123 -----

Copy in a miscellany probably compiled by members of the Cartwright family of Aynho, Northamptonshire; mid-17th century.

Bodleian, MS Don. e. 6, f. 24.

JnB 124 -----

Copy, headed 'An Epitaph on Queene Elizabeth', in a verse miscellany compiled by an Oxford man; c. 1640.

This MS collated in Herford & Simpson.

Bodleian, MS Rawl. D. 1092, f. 267v.

JnB 125 -----

Copy of lines 3-6, beginning 'Vnderneath this stone doth lye', in a miscellany compiled partly by the Oxford printer Christopher Wase (1627-90); mid-17th century.

This MS collated in Herford & Simpson.

Bodleian, MS Rawl. poet. 117, f. 269 rev.

JnB 126 -----

Copy of lines 3-6, here beginning 'Here vnderneath this stone doth ly', in a verse miscellany; c. 1640.

Bodleian, MS Rawl. poet. 153, f. 20.

JnB 127 -----

Copy, headed 'An other' [epitaph on Mrs Bulstrode] and here beginning 'Wilt thou heare w^t. man can saye', in a verse miscellany; c. 1630s.

This MS collated in Herford & Simpson.

Bodleian, MS Rawl. poet. 160, f. 25v.

JnB 128 -----

Copy of lines 1-8, headed 'On a Gentlewom: Tomb' and here beginning 'Wilt thou heare what wee can say', in a verse miscellany probably compiled by a Cambridge man; c. 1630s.

Epitaph on Elizabeth, L.H.

This MS collated in Herford & Simpson.

British Library, Add. MS 15227, f. 97v.

JnB 129 -----

Copy, headed 'on M[rs]. Boulstred', in a verse miscellany compiled by one Thomas Crosse; c. 1630s.

This MS collated in Herford & Simpson.

British Library, Harley MS 6057, f. 30.

JnB 130 -----

Copy of lines 3-12, here beginning 'Underneath this stone there lies', in a MS volume of poems by William Browne of Tavistock possibly compiled by a member of an Inn of Court; c. 1637-50.

Printed from this MS in *The Poems of William Browne of Tavistock*, ed. Gordon Goodwin (London, 1894), II, 295.

British Library, Lansdowne MS 777, f. 60.

JnB 131 -----

Copy in a verse miscellany; c. 1637.

British Library, Stowe MS 962, f. 81v.

JnB 132 -----

Copy, untitled, in a verse miscellany possibly once owned by Sir John Reresby (d. 1646); among the papers of the Savile family, formerly of Methley Hall, near Pontefract; c. 1630s.

Leeds Archives Department, MX 237, f. 92v.

JnB 133 -----

Copy, headed 'An Epitaph', in a verse miscellany; c. 1634.

Rosenbach Foundation, MS 239/27, p. 357.

JnB 134 -----

Copy, headed 'Epitaph: on El: F:' and here beginning 'Wilt thou heare what man can say?', in a verse miscellany compiled by one Robert Bishop; c. 1630.

Rosenbach Foundation, MS 1083/16, p. 275.

JnB 135 -----

Copy in a verse miscellany owned and possibly compiled by John Pike of Cambridge; c. 1636-40s.

This MS collated in Herford & Simpson.

St John's College, Cambridge, MS S. 32 (James 423), f. 8v.

JnB 136 -----

Copy of lines 1-8, headed 'On the death of a most fayre and vertuous Lady' and here ascribed to 'S[r] Edw: Hastings', in a verse miscellany appended to a MS volume of poems by Donne; c. 1630s.

This MS collated in Herford & Simpson.

Trinity College, Dublin, MS 877, f. 257.

JnB 136.5 See Addenda, p. 630

--- -----

See also INTRODUCTION.

JnB 137 *Epitaph on Katherine, Lady Ogle* ('T'is a Record in heauen, You, that were').

Copy, with a faintly pencilled rough sketch of a design for a memorial tablet, in the Newcastle MS; c. 1629-30s.

First pub. (from this MS) in *The Works of Ben Jonson*, ed. William Gifford, 9 vols (London, 1816); printed from this MS in Herford & Simpson, VIII, 399-400.

British Library, Harley MS 4955, f. 55.

JnB 138 *An Epitaph on Master Vincent Corbet* ('I have my Pietie too, which could').

Copy of lines 1-36 in a verse miscellany probably compiled by one 'I.A.' of Christ Church, Oxford, and later owned by Robert Killigrew; c. early 1630s.

First pub. in *The Vnder-wood* (xii) in *Workes* (London, 1640); Herford & Simpson, VIII, 151-2. This MS collated in Herford & Simpson.

British Library, Sloane MS 1792, ff. 61-2.

JnB 139 -----

Copy, headed 'Vpon D[r]. C: father: B: J:' and here beginning 'I hope my piety too, which could', in a verse miscellany compiled by an Oxford man; c. 1630s.

This MS probably the Dobell MS collated in Herford & Simpson.

Folger, MS V. a. 170, pp. 224-6.

JnB 140 -----

Copy in a verse miscellany probably compiled by a member of an Inn of Court; mid-17th century.

Folger, MS V. a. 262, p. 42.

An Epitaph on Master Vincent Corbet

JnB 141 -----

Copy, untitled, in a verse miscellany used by members of the Holgate family of Saffron Walden, Essex; c. 1630s.

Pierpont Morgan Library, MA 1057, p. 10.

JnB 142 -----

Copy beginning at line 7 ('Deare Vincent Corbet, who so long') in a miscellany; c. 1660.

Rosenbach Foundation, MS 239/18, p. 4.

JnB 143 *Epitaph on S<alomon> P<avy> a Child of Q. El<izabeths> Chappel* ('Weepe with me all you that read').

Copy, headed 'Vppon Sal: Pauye a boy of 13 years of age and on of the Companye of the Reuells to Queene Elizabeth', in a verse miscellany compiled by Nicholas Burghe (d. 1670); c. 1638.

First pub. in *Epigrammes* (cxx) in *Workes* (London, 1616); Herford & Simpson, VIII, 77. This MS collated in Herford & Simpson.

Bodleian, MS Ashmole 38, p. 171.

JnB 144 -----

Copy, headed 'Epitaphium', in a miscellany; early 17th century.

Formerly among the Isham MSS at Lamport Hall, this MS recorded in *HMC*, 3rd Report (1872), Appendix, p. 252; printed from this MS in *The Complete Poems of Richard Barnfield*, ed. Alexander B. Grosart (London, 1876), pp. 217-18.

Folger, MS V. a. 161, pp. 20-1.

JnB 145 *Epithalamion; or, A Song: Celebrating the Nvptials of Hierome Weston with Frances Stuart* ('Though thou hast past thy Summer standing, stay').

Copy in the Newcastle MS; c. 1630s.

First pub. in *The Vnder-wood* (lxxv) in *Workes* (London, 1640); Herford & Simpson, VIII, 252-8. This MS collated in Herford & Simpson.

British Library, Harley MS 4955, ff. 176v-9v.

JnB 146 *Epode* ('Not to know vice at all, and keepe true state').

Copy, headed 'Epos', in a composite volume of verse and dramatic works compiled by members of the Salusbury family of Llewenni, Denbighshire; early-mid-17th century.

First pub. in *Diuerse Poeticall Essaies* appended to Robert Chester, *Loues Martyr* (London, 1601); *The Forrest* (xi) in *Workes* (London, 1616); Herford & Simpson, VIII, 109-13. This MS collated in Herford & Simpson.

National Library of Wales, NLW. MS 5390D, pp. 504-2 rev.

JnB 147 -----

Copy of lines 1-4, 55-62, 65-74, 91-103, 115-16, untitled, in a verse miscellany; mid-17th century.

Folger, MS V. a. 219, f. 34r-v (Nos. 13-17).

JnB 148 -----

Copy, headed 'Epos'; mid-17th century.

Formerly owned by G. Thorn-Drury, this MS collated in Herford & Simpson.

Folger, MS X. d. 246.

JnB 149 -----

Copy of lines 37-51, here beginning 'The thing, they here call loue, is blind Desire' and subscribed 'Ben: Jo: fforrest. Epod. 11.', followed by lines 72-4, 76-82, 87-90, 113-16, 17-18, in a fragment of a miscellany; early 17th century (after 1616).

Worcester College, Oxford, (inserted loose in MSS 6. 13), f. [6r-v].

JnB 150 -----

Copy of the final couplet, here beginning 'And to yor sence obiect this sentence euer', in a miscellany compiled partly by the Oxford printer Christopher Wase (1627-90); mid-17th century.

Bodleian, MS Rawl. poet. 117, f. 276v rev.

JnB 151 *Eupheme; or, The Faire Fame Left to Posteritie Of that truly noble Lady, the Lady Venetia Digby. 3. The Picture of the Body* ('Sitting, and ready to be drawne').

Copy in the Newcastle MS; c. 1620s-30s.

First pub. (Nos. 3 and 4) in John Benson's 4to edition of Jonson's poems (1640) and (all poems) in *The Vnder-wood* (lxxxiv) in *Workes* (London, 1640); Herford & Simpson, VIII, 272-89 (pp. 275-7). This MS collated in Herford & Simpson.

British Library, Harley MS 4955, f. 35v.

JnB 152 ----- -----

Copy in a verse miscellany once owned by Elizabeth Lane and John Finch; c. 1630s.

Aberdeen University Library, MS 29, pp. 82-3.

Eupheme. 3. The Picture of the Body

JnB 153 -----

Copy, here ascribed to 'Geo: Ghapman', in a verse miscellany compiled by Nicholas Burghe (d. 1670); c. 1638.

This MS collated in Herford & Simpson.

Bodleian, MS Ashmole 38, pp. 5-6.

JnB 154 -----

Copy, headed 'A Gentlewoman sitting in a chaire to have her picture drawne', in a verse miscellany compiled by an Oxford man; mid-17th century.

Bodleian, MS CCC. 176, f. 17.

JnB 155 -----

Copy in a verse miscellany once owned by one Peter Daniell; c. 1630s-40s.

Bodleian, MS Eng. poet. c. 50, f. 111r-v.

JnB 156 ----- -----

Copy, headed 'A Sonnett', in a verse miscellany; c. 1640.

This MS collated in Herford & Simpson.

Bodleian, MS Firth e. 4, p. 73.

JnB 157 ----- -----

Copy, headed 'Vpon Venetia Stanley her picture', in a composite volume of verse and prose owned c. 1669 by one John Cooke of Bury St Edmunds, Suffolk; c. 1620s-30s.

This MS collated in Herford & Simpson.

Bodleian, MS Rawl. poet. 26, f. 16.

JnB 158 ----- -----

Copy of lines 13-28, headed 'On M[rs] Venetia Stanlye to ye paynter' and here beginning 'Draw first a cloud all saue her neck', in a verse miscellany probably compiled by an Oxford man and once owned by one William Bloys; c. 1630s.

This MS collated in Herford & Simpson.

Bodleian, MS Rawl. poet. 142, f. 16v.

JnB 159 ----- -----

Copy, headed 'Ben Ionson To the Painter', in a verse miscellany; c. 1630s.

This MS collated in Herford & Simpson.

Bodleian, MS Rawl. poet. 160, ff. 110v-11.

JnB 160 ----- -----

Copy, headed 'The same Ben: Jhonsons description of m[rs] Venetia Stanly, since wife of S[r]. kel: Digby', in a MS volume of poems chiefly by and probably in the hand of one 'Alphonso Mervall' (i.e. James Cobbes?); c. 1629.

This MS collated in Herford & Simpson.

Bodleian, MS Rawl. poet. 166, pp. 85-6.

JnB 161 ----- -----

Copy in a verse miscellany compiled by the Yorkshire antiquary John Hopkinson (1610-80); mid-17th century.

Bradford Central Library, Hopkinson MSS, Vol. 34, p. 130.

JnB 162 ----- -----

Copy, headed 'On a Gentlewoman Sittinge to hav hir Picktur Drawne', in a verse miscellany partly compiled by Brian Fairfax (1633-1711); late 17th century.

This MS collated in Herford & Simpson.

British Library, Add. MS 22582, f. 2r-v.

JnB 163 ----- -----

Copy in a miscellany possibly compiled by a member of an Inn of Court; c. 1620s-30s.

This MS collated in Herford & Simpson.

British Library, Add. MS 25303, f. 75v.

JnB 164 ----- -----

Copy, untitled, in a composite volume of verse belonging to the Skipwith family of Cotes, Leicestershire; early-mid-17th century.

This MS collated in Herford & Simpson.

British Library, Add. MS 25707, ff. 152v-3.

JnB 165 ----- -----

Copy in a MS volume of elegies on Venetia Digby; c. 1633.

This MS (erroneously cited as 'Add 17') collated in Herford & Simpson.

British Library, Add. MS 30259, ff. 1-2.

JnB 166 ----- -----

Copy, headed 'The Body. Vpon m[ris]. Ven: S:', in a verse miscellany compiled by Thomas Manne (1582?-1641) of Christ Church, Oxford; c. 1630s.

British Library, Add. MS 58215, pp. 87-8.

Eupheme. 3. The Picture of the Body

JnB 167 ----- -----

Copy, headed '[On Mrs Venetia Stanly *deleted*] The body', in a verse miscellany compiled by Arthur Capell; mid-17th century.

This MS collated in Herford & Simpson.

British Library, Harley MS 3511, ff. 49v-50.

JnB 168 ----- -----

Copy, headed 'Of his M^{rs} sitting to be drawne', in a verse miscellany probably compiled by Francis Baskerville of Malmesbury, Wiltshire, and owned in 1663 by William Wallrond; c. 1633.

This MS collated in Herford & Simpson.

British Library, Sloane MS 1446, f. 91r-v.

JnB 169 ----- -----

Copy in a verse miscellany probably compiled by one 'I.A.' of Christ Church, Oxford, and later owned by Robert Killigrew; c. early 1630s.

This MS collated in Herford & Simpson.

British Library, Sloane MS 1792, f. 56r-v.

JnB 170 ----- -----

Copy in a verse miscellany; c. 1637.

British Library, Stowe MS 962, f. 146v-7.

JnB 171 ----- -----

Copy, headed 'His Mistresse Drawne', in a transcript by one 'S.H.' (born 1665) of John Benson's 12mo edition of Jonson's poems (1640); c. 1680.

This MS recorded in Herford & Simpson.

Edinburgh University Library, MS Dc. 7. 94, ff. 14v-15.

JnB 172 ----- -----

Copy in a verse miscellany; c. 1630s-40s.

Edinburgh University Library, MS La. III. 436, pp. 8-9.

JnB 173 ----- -----

Copy in a verse miscellany owned in 1691 by one Thomas White; c. 1640.

Folger, MS V. a. 96, ff. 41-2.

JnB 174 ----- -----

Copy, headed 'On the Lady Digby', in a miscellany compiled by Richard Boyle, Viscount Dungarvon, later Earl of Burlington (1612-98); c. 1630s.

Folger, MS V. a. 125, Part I, f. 26.

JnB 175 ----- -----

Copy in a verse miscellany compiled by an Oxford man; c. 1630s.

This MS probably 'Dobell MS II' collated in Herford & Simpson.

Folger, MS V. a. 170, pp. 159-60.

JnB 176 ----- -----

Copy, headed 'Vpon Mrs Venetia Stanley. The body', in a verse miscellany; mid-17th century.

Folger, MS V. a. 322, pp. 8-9.

JnB 177 ----- -----

Copy in a verse miscellany owned in 1640 by Anthony St John (1618-73) and Ann St John, of Bletsoe, Bedfordshire; c. 1630s.

Harvard, fMS Eng 626, ff. 67v-8.

JnB 178 ----- -----

Copy, headed 'By Ben Johnson upon Mrs Venetia Stanley', in a miscellany compiled by or for Sir Henry Cholmley, brother of Sir Hugh Cholmley (1600-57); c. 1624-41.

Harvard, MS Eng 703, ff. 59r-v.

JnB 179 ----- -----

Copy in a miscellany; c. 1630.

Huntington, HM 172, ff. 26v-7.

JnB 180 ----- -----

Copy in a verse miscellany owned by Edward Denny, Charles Cokes, Edward Randolpe, and Thomas Cassy; c. 1630s.

Huntington, HM 198, Part I, pp. 54-5.

JnB 181 ----- -----

Copy, headed 'Of his m^{rs} sitting to have her picture drawne. Body', in a verse miscellany possibly once owned by Sir John Reresby

(d. 1646); among the papers of the Savile family, formerly of Methley Hall, near Pontefract; c. 1630s.

Leeds Archives Department, MX 237, f. 45.

JnB 182 ----- -----

Copy, untitled, in a verse miscellany once owned by Elizabeth Herrick (1684-1745) and William Herrick (1689-1773); c. 1630.

Leicestershire Record Office, DG. 9/2796, pp. 38-40.

JnB 183 ----- -----

Copy, here ascribed to 'Daniell. poett:', written at the end of a MS copy of Sir Francis Hubert's *Edward II*; mid-17th century.

Printed from this MS in Sir John Simeon, 'Inedited Poems of Daniel', *Miscellanies of the Philobiblon Society*, 2 (London, 1855-6), No. 13 (pp. 8-9).

University of London Library, MS 304, [no page numbers].

JnB 184 ----- -----

Copy in a miscellany; c. 1660.

Rosenbach Foundation, MS 239/18, p. 3.

JnB 185 ----- -----

Copy in a verse miscellany; c. 1630.

Rosenbach Foundation, MS 239/23, pp. 80-2.

JnB 186 ----- -----

Copy, headed 'A Picture', in a miscellany compiled by or for Sir Thomas Finch, Viscount Maidstone and Earl of Winchelsea; c. 1634.

Rosenbach Foundation, MS 243/4, pp. 124-5.

JnB 187 ----- -----

Copy in a verse miscellany once owned by Sir Henry Spelman (1564?-1641); c. 1630s.

South African Library, Cape Town, MS Grey 7 a 29, pp. 128-9.

JnB 188 ----- -----

Copy, untitled, in a verse miscellany appended to a MS volume of poems by Donne; c. 1630s.

This MS collated in Herford & Simpson.

Trinity College, Dublin, MS 877, ff. 197v-8.

JnB 189 ----- -----

Second copy, untitled, in a verse miscellany appended to a MS volume of poems by Donne; c. 1630s.

This MS collated in Herford & Simpson.

Trinity College, Dublin, MS 877, ff. 228v-9.

JnB 190 ----- -----

Copy in a verse miscellany connected with Christ Church, Oxford, owned and perhaps partly compiled by George Morley, later Bishop of Winchester (1598-1684); 1620s-30s.

Westminster Abbey, MS 41, f. 34r-v.

JnB 191 ----- -----

Copy in a miscellany; c. 1635.

Owned by Edwin Wolf 2nd, Philadelphia, MS, p. 91.

JnB 192 ----- -----

Copy in a miscellany; mid-17th century.

Yale, Osborn Collection, b 205, ff. 87-8.

JnB 192.5 See Addenda, p. 630.

JnB 193 ----- -----

Copy in a MS collection of poems once owned by Sir Kenelm Digby (1603-65); 17th century.

Printed from this MS in *Poems from Sir Kenelm Digby's Papers, in the possession of Henry A. Bright*, Roxburghe Club (London, 1877), pp. 21-2; collated from this publication in Herford & Simpson.

Unlocated.

JnB 194 ----- *4. The Mind* ('Painter, yo'are come, but may be gone').

Copy in the Newcastle MS; c. 1620s-30s.

Herford & Simpson, VIII, 277-81. This MS collated in Herford & Simpson.

British Library, Harley MS 4955, ff. 36-7.

JnB 195 ----- -----

Copy in a verse miscellany once owned by Elizabeth Lane and John Finch; c. 1630s.

Aberdeen University Library, MS 29, pp. 83-5.

JnB 196 ----- -----

Copy in a verse miscellany compiled by Nicholas Burghe (d. 1670); c. 1638.

This MS collated in Herford & Simpson.

Bodleian, MS Ashmole 38, p. 5.

JnB 197 ----- -----

Copy in a verse miscellany once owned by one Peter Daniell; c. 1630s-40s.

Bodleian, MS Eng. poet. c. 50, ff. 111v-12v.

JnB 198 ----- -----

Copy in a verse miscellany; c. 1630s.

This MS collated in Herford & Simpson.

Bodleian, MS Rawl. poet. 160, ff. 111-12.

JnB 199 ----- -----

Copy in a MS volume of poems chiefly by and probably in the hand of one 'Alphonso Mervall' (i.e. James Cobbes?); c. 1629.

This MS collated in Herford & Simpson.

Bodleian, MS Rawl. poet. 166, pp. 86-9.

JnB 200 ----- -----

Copy in a verse miscellany compiled by the Yorkshire antiquary John Hopkinson (1610-80); mid-17th century.

Bradford Central Library, Hopkinson MSS, Vol. 34, pp. 130-2.

JnB 201 ----- -----

Copy in a miscellany possibly compiled by a member of an Inn of Court; c. 1620s-30s.

This MS collated in Herford & Simpson.

British Library, Add. MS 25303, ff. 76-7.

JnB 202 ----- -----

Copy in a composite volume of verse belonging to the Skipwith family of Cotes, Leicestershire; early-mid-17th century.

This MS collated in Herford & Simpson.

British Library, Add. MS 25707, ff. 153-4.

JnB 203 ----- -----

Copy in a MS volume of elegies on Venetia Digby; c. 1633.

This MS (erroneously cited as 'Add 17') collated in Herford & Simpson.

British Library, Add. MS 30259, ff. 2-4v.

JnB 204 ----- -----

Copy in a verse miscellany compiled by Thomas Manne (1582?-1641) of Christ Church, Oxford; c. 1630s.

British Library, Add. MS 58215, pp. 89-92.

JnB 205 ----- -----

Copy in a verse miscellany compiled by Arthur Capell; mid-17th century.

This MS collated in Herford & Simpson.

British Library, Harley MS 3511, ff. 50-1v.

JnB 206 ----- -----

Copy in a verse miscellany compiled by one Thomas Crosse; c. 1630s.

This MS collated in Herford & Simpson.

British Library, Harley MS 6057, f. 21v.

JnB 207 ----- -----

Copy in a verse miscellany probably compiled by Francis Baskerville of Malmesbury, Wiltshire, and owned in 1663 by William Wallrond; c. 1633.

This MS collated in Herford & Simpson.

British Library, Sloane MS 1446, ff. 89v-90.

JnB 208 ----- -----

Copy in a verse miscellany probably compiled by one 'I.A.' of Christ Church, Oxford, and later owned by Robert Killigrew; c. early 1630s.

This MS collated in Herford & Simpson.

British Library, Sloane MS 1792, ff. 56v-8.

JnB 209 ----- -----

Copy in a verse miscellany; c. 1637.

British Library, Stowe MS 962, ff. 177v-9.

JnB 210 ----- -----

Copy in a transcript by one 'S.H.' (born 1665) of John Benson's 12mo edition of Jonson's poems (1640); c. 1680.

This MS recorded in Herford & Simpson.

Edinburgh University Library, MS Dc. 7. 94, ff. 15-16.

Eupheme. 4. The Mind

JnB 211 ----- -----

Copy in a verse miscellany; c. 1630s-40s.

Edinburgh University Library, MS La. III. 436, pp. 9-11.

JnB 212 ----- -----

Copy in a verse miscellany owned in 1691 by one Thomas White; c. 1640.

Folger, MS V. a. 96, ff. 42-4.

JnB 213 ----- -----

Copy in a verse miscellany compiled by an Oxford man; c. 1630s.

This MS probably 'Dobell MS II' collated in Herford & Simpson.

Folger, MS V. a. 170, pp. 160-3.

JnB 214 ----- -----

Copy in a verse miscellany; mid-17th century.

Folger, MS V. a. 322, pp. 9-11.

JnB 215 ----- -----

Copy in a verse miscellany owned in 1640 by Anthony St John (1618-73) and Ann St John, of Bletsoe, Bedfordshire; c. 1630s.

Harvard, fMS Eng 626, ff. 68v-9v.

JnB 216 ----- -----

Copy of a ten-line version, untitled, in a miscellany compiled by or for Sir Henry Cholmley, brother of Sir Hugh Cholmley (1600-57); c. 1624-41.

Harvard, MS Eng 703, f. 59v.

JnB 217 ----- -----

Copy in a miscellany; c. 1630.

Huntington, HM 172, ff. 27-8v.

JnB 218 ----- -----

Copy in a verse miscellany owned by Edward Denny, Charles Cokes, Edward Randolpe, and Thomas Cassy; c. 1630s.

Huntington, HM 198, Part I, pp. 55-6.

JnB 219 ----- -----

Copy in a verse miscellany possibly once owned by Sir John Reresby (d. 1646); among the papers of the Savile family, formerly of Methley Hall, near Pontefract; c. 1630s.

Leeds Archives Department, MX 237, f. 45v.

JnB 220 ----- -----

Copy in a verse miscellany once owned by Elizabeth Herrick (1684-1745) and William Herrick (1689-1773); c. 1630.

Leicestershire Record Office, DG. 9/2796, pp. 38-40.

JnB 221 ----- -----

Copy, written at the end of a MS copy of Sir Francis Hubert's *Edward II* (see JnB 183); mid-17th century.

Printed from this MS in Sir John Simeon, 'Inedited Poems of Daniel', *Miscellanies of the Philobiblon Society*, 2 (London, 1855-6), No. 13 (pp. 9-12).

University of London Library, MS 304, [no page numbers].

JnB 222 ----- -----

Copy in a verse miscellany; c. 1630.

Rosenbach Foundation, MS 239/23, pp. 82-5.

JnB 223 ----- -----

Copy, ascribed in a different ink to 'Rob: Herrick', in a verse miscellany once owned by Sir Henry Spelman (1564?-1641); c. 1630s.

South African Library, Cape Town, MS Grey 7 a 29, pp. 129-30.

JnB 224 ----- -----

Copy in a verse miscellany connected with Christ Church, Oxford, owned and perhaps partly compiled by George Morley, later Bishop of Winchester (1598-1684); 1620s-30s.

Westminster Abbey, MS 41, ff. 34v-5v.

JnB 225 ----- -----

Copy in a miscellany; c. 1635.

Owned by Edwin Wolf 2nd, Philadelphia, MS, p. 92.

Eupheme. 4. The Mind

JnB 226 ----- -----

Copy in a MS collection of poems once owned by Sir Kenelm Digby (1603-65); 17th century.

Printed from this MS in *Poems from Sir Kenelm Digby's Papers, in the possession of Henry A. Bright*, Roxburghe Club (London, 1877), pp. 23-5; collated from this publication in Herford & Simpson.

Unlocated.

JnB 227 ----- *8. To Kenelme, Iohn, George* ('Boast not these Titles of your Ancestors').

Copy, complete with prose introduction, in a MS 'Discourse of the Pedigree of Percy's and Stanley's' once owned by Sir Kenelm Digby (1603-65); early-mid-17th century.

Herford & Simpson, VIII, 281-2.

National Library of Wales, Peniarth MS 444C, p. 17.

JnB 228 ----- *9. Elegie on my Muse* (''Twere time that I dy'd too, now shee is dead').

Copy in a MS volume of elegies on Venetia Digby; c. 1633.

Herford & Simpson, VIII, 283-9. This MS (erroneously cited as 'Add 17') collated in Herford & Simpson.

British Library, Add. MS 30259, ff. 4-10v.

JnB 229 ----- -----

Copy in a miscellany; c. 1630s.

This MS collated in Herford & Simpson.

Bodleian, MS Eng. poet. e. 37, pp. 80-6.

JnB 230 *An Execration upon Vulcan* ('Any why to me this, thou lame Lord of fire').

Copy in the Newcastle MS; c. 1620s-30s.

First pub. in John Benson's 4to edition of Jonson's poems (1640) and in *The Vnder-wood* (xliii) in *Workes* (London, 1640); Herford & Simpson, VIII, 202-12. This MS collated in Herford & Simpson.

British Library, Harley MS 4955, ff. 43-6.

JnB 231 -----

Copy, headed 'Ben Johnson upon the burning of his bookes', in a verse miscellany compiled by an Oxford man and once owned by one Henry Lawson; c. 1630s.

This MS collated in Herford & Simpson.

Bodleian, MS Eng. poet. e. 14, ff. 22v-4.

JnB 232 -----

Copy of lines 1-10, deleted, in a verse miscellany owned by one Henry Lawson; c. 1630s.

Bodleian, MS Eng. poet. e. 14, f. 78.

JnB 233 -----

Copy in a verse miscellany probably compiled by a member of Christ Church, Oxford; c. 1630s-40s.

Bodleian, MS Eng. poet. e. 97, pp. 71-6.

JnB 234 -----

Copy of lines 191-216, headed 'Ben: Johnson against Vulcan' and beginning 'Pox on your flameship, Vulcan; if it be', in a verse miscellany compiled by the Yorkshire antiquary John Hopkinson (1610-80); late 17th century.

Bradford Central Library, Hopkinson MSS, Vol. 17, ff. [13v-14].

JnB 235 -----

Copy, transcribed from JnB 236, in a verse miscellany possibly compiled by a member of an Inn of Court; c. 1630s.

This MS collated in Herford & Simpson.

British Library, Add. MS 21433, ff. 97-102v.

JnB 236 -----

Copy in a miscellany possibly compiled by a member of an Inn of Court; c. 1620s-30s.

This MS collated in Herford & Simpson.

British Library, Add. MS 25303, ff. 94-8.

JnB 237 -----

Copy in a verse miscellany possibly compiled by a member of an Inn of Court; c. 1620s.

This MS collated in Herford & Simpson.

British Library, Harley MS 3910, ff. 61v-4v.

JnB 238 -----

Copy, headed 'Ben: Jonson upon the burning of his study and bookes', in a verse miscellany possibly compiled by one 'I.A.' of Christ Church, Oxford, and later owned by Robert Killigrew; c. early 1630s.

This MS collated in Herford & Simpson.

British Library, Sloane MS 1792, ff. 101-4v.

An Execration upon Vulcan

JnB 239 -----

Copy in a verse miscellany; c. 1637.

British Library, Stowe MS 962, f. 238-42.

JnB 240 -----

Copy in a transcript by one 'S.H.' (born 1665) of John Benson's 12mo edition of Jonson's poems (1640); c. 1680.

Edinburgh University Library, MS Dc. 7. 94, ff. 2-5.

JnB 241 -----

Copy, headed 'Ben Johnson against Vulcane', in a verse miscellany compiled by an Oxford man, possibly a member of Christ Church; c. late 1630s.

Folger, MS V. a. 97, pp. 156-61.

JnB 242 -----

Copy, headed 'Johnsons: Inuectiue against Vulcan', in a verse miscellany compiled by William Jordan, schoolmaster of Denbigh or Caernarvon; c. 1674-84.

Folger, MS V. a. 276, Part II, ff. 43v-4.

JnB 243 -----

Copy, written on both sides of a single folio leaf in a disbound collection of MS poems probably once belonging to the Newdegate family of Arbury Hall, Nuneaton, Warwickshire; early-mid-17th century.

This MS sold at Hodgson's, 21 November 1958, Lot 572.

University of Leeds, Brotherton Collection, MS Lt. q. 11, No. 51.

JnB 244 -----

Copy, headed 'Ben Johnsons Verses on the burning of his Studye', in a verse miscellany; c. 1638-45.

Rosenbach Foundation, MS 239/22, ff. 39-42v.

JnB 245 -----

Copy in a verse miscellany; c. 1634.

Rosenbach Foundation, MS 239/27, pp. 17-24.

JnB 246 -----

Copy in two hands, untitled, in a verse miscellany connected with Christ Church, Oxford, owned and perhaps partly compiled by George Morley, later Bishop of Winchester (1598-1684); 1620s-30s.

Westminster Abbey, MS 41, ff. 63-5v.

JnB 247 -----

Copy, headed 'An Execration against Vulcan for burninge his Papers', and 'Vulcans Cursse' inscribed on a separate page; on unbound leaves among the papers of the Middletons, a Yorkshire recusant family; early-mid-17th century.

Yorkshire Archaeological Society, Leeds, MD 59/22, [no item number].

*JnB 248 *An Expostulac̄on wth Inigo Iones* ('Mr Suruey^r^, you y^t^ first begann').

Autograph; [1631].

First pub. in *The Works of Ben Jonson*, 7 vols, ed. Peter Whalley (London, 1756). Printed from this MS in Herford & Simpson, VIII, 402-6.

Huntington, EL 8729, ff. 42-3v.

JnB 249 -----

Copy in the Newcastle MS; c. 1630s.

This MS collated in Herford & Simpson.

British Library, Harley MS 4955, ff. 174v-5v.

JnB 250 -----

Copy, transcribed from a MS source, in a note-book compiled by the engraver and antiquary George Vertue (1684-1756); [1713-54].

This MS collated in Herford & Simpson.

British Library, Add. MS 23070, ff. 29-30v.

JnB 251 -----

Copy in a verse miscellany owned in 1691 by one Thomas White; c. 1640.

Folger, MS V. a. 96, ff. 90v-3v.

JnB 252 -----

Copy in a verse miscellany; mid-17th century.

Folger, MS V. a. 322, pp. 11-14.

JnB 253 -----

Copy; c. 1631.

This MS the Dobell MS collated in Herford & Simpson.

Folger, MZ X. d. 245 (a-b).

An Expostulacōn wth Inigo Iones

JnB 254 -----

Transcript of an early MS, on unbound leaves among the MSS of the Duke of Portland, of Welbeck Abbey, Nottinghamshire; late 18th-early 19th century.

University of Nottingham, Portland MS Pw 2V 154.

JnB 255 -----

Copy in a verse miscellany appended to a MS volume of poems by Donne; c. 1630s.

This MS collated in Herford & Simpson.

Trinity College, Dublin, MS 877, ff. 178-80.

JnB 256 *A Fragment of Petronius Arbiter* ('Doing, a filthy pleasure is, and short').

Copy in a verse miscellany compiled by Nicholas Burghe (d. 1670); c. 1638.

First pub. in *The Vnder-wood* (lxxxviii) in *Workes* London, 1640); Herford & Simpson, VIII, 294. This MS collated in Herford & Simpson.

Bodleian, MS Ashmole 38, p. 62.

JnB 257 *A Grace by Ben: Johnson. extempore. before King James* ('Our King and Queen the Lord-God blesse').

Copy of a short version beginning 'Our Royall king & Queene, God Bless', in a verse miscellany compiled by Nicholas Burghe (d. 1670); c. 1638.

First pub. (?) in John Aubrey, *Brief Lives*, ed. Andrew Clark (Oxford, 1898), II, 14; Herford & Simpson, VIII, 418-19. This MS collated in Herford & Simpson.

Bodleian, MS Ashmole 38, p. 117.

JnB 258 -----

Copy made by John Aubrey (1626-97) in the third volume of his autograph *Brief Lives*; 1681.

Printed from this MS in Clark and in Herford & Simpson.

Bodleian, MS Aubrey 8, f. 55.

JnB 259 -----

Copy of a version headed 'A Grace said before the King by a Jester' and beginning 'The King, the Queene, the Prince god blesse', in a verse miscellany compiled by a member of New College, Oxford; c. 1620s-30s.

Printed from this MS in Herford & Simpson, VIII, 419 (n).

Bodleian, MS Malone 19, p. 138.

JnB 260 -----

Copy of a version perhaps spoken at Lady Bedford's table, headed 'A forme of a Grace' and beginning 'The Kinge, ye Queene, the Prince god blesse', in a composite volume of verse and prose owned c. 1669 by John Cooke of Bury St Edmunds, Suffolk; c. 1620s-30s.

Bodleian, MS Rawl. poet. 26, f. 1v.

JnB 261 -----

Copy of a version beginning 'God blesse ye king, ye queene, god blesse', in a verse miscellany; c. 1630s.

This MS collated in Herford & Simpson.

Bodleian, MS Rawl. poet. 160, f. 175v.

JnB 262 -----

Copy of a version headed 'A grace said before ye king by his Jester' and beginning 'The Kinge and eke ye Queene God blesse', in a verse miscellany compiled by an Oxford man and once owned by one Stephen Welden; mid-17th century.

Folger, MS V. a. 162, f. 58.

JnB 263 -----

Copy of an eight-line version headed 'A grace said before the King by a Jester' and beginning 'The King, the Queen the Prince God bless', in a verse miscellany compiled by one or two Oxford men, possibly connected with New College and afterwards with the Inns of Court; 1630s.

Harvard, MS Eng 686, f. 38v.

JnB 264 -----

Copy of a version headed 'An Extemporary Grace by Ben. Iohnson before the kings' and beginning 'God blesse the King the Quene noe lesse', in a verse miscellany compiled by one Robert Bishop; c. 1630.

Rosenbach Foundation, MS 1083/16, pp. 181-2.

--- -----

See also INTRODUCTION.

JnB 265 *<Horace. Epode 2.> The praises of a Countrie life* ('Happie is he, that from all Businesse cleere').

Copy in the Newcastle MS; c. 1620s-30s.

First pub. in *The Vnder-wood* (lxxxv) in *Workes* (London, 1640); Herford & Simpson, VIII, 289-91.

British Library, Harley MS 4955, ff. 37v-8v.

<Horace. Epode 2.> The praises of a Countrie life

JnB 266 -----

Copy in a verse miscellany; c. 1620-33.

This MS collated in Herford & Simpson.

Bodleian, MS Rawl. poet. 31, ff. 28-9v.

JnB 267 -----

Copy in a verse miscellany; c. 1620-33.

This MS collated in Herford & Simpson.

British Library, Harley MS 4064, ff. 250-1v.

JnB 268 *Horace his Art of Poetry* ('If to a Womans head a Painter would').

Extracts in a miscellany probably compiled by members of the Cartwright family of Aynho, Northamptonshire; mid-17th century.

First pub. in John Benson's 12mo edition of Jonson's poems (1640) and in *Workes* (London, 1640); Herford & Simpson, VIII, 297-355.

Bodleian, MS Don. e. 6, f. 18v.

JnB 269 -----

Copy of lines 229-36, headed 'In a Translation of Hor: The Young Gentlemans Life' and beginning 'Th' unbearded Youth, his Guardian once being gone', written by one Katherine Butler at the back of Knightley Chetwode's MS volume of sermons by Donne which she used as a commonplace book; 1696.

St Paul's Cathedral, MS 52. D. 14.

--- -----

See also INTRODUCTION.

*JnB 270 *The Houre-glasse* ('Doe but consider this small dust').

Autograph fair copy (together with JnB 352) on a single leaf presented to William Drummond of Hawthornden, now among the papers of the Clerk family of Penicuik; headed 'To the honoring respect | borne | to the Freindship contracted w^{t}h | the right vertuous, and learned | M^{r}. William Drummond: | And the perpetuating the same by all offices of Loue | herafter, | I Beniamin Jonson, | Whome he hath honord w^{t}h the leaue to be calld his, | haue, w^{t}h mine owne hand, to satisfie his request, | written this imperfect song, | On a Louers dust, made sand for an Howerglasse'; signed at the bottom and dated January 19th 1619 [i.e. 1618/19].

First pub. in John Benson's 4to edition of Jonson's poems (1640) and in *The Vnder-wood* (viii) in *Workes* (London, 1640); Herford & Simpson, VIII, 148-9. Printed from this MS in *The Works of William Drummond* (Edinburgh, 1711), p. 155 (see Herford & Simpson, I, 177-8), and cited in Drummond's *Conversations with Jonson* (see Herford & Simpson, I, 150, and DrW 303). See FACSIMILE XXII. The MS accompanied by an 18th-century transcript on a single leaf endorsed 'Copy of Ben Johnsone's verses of which I have the oreginal in the Charter house'.

Scottish Record Office, GD18/4312.

JnB 271 -----

Copy in a composite volume of verse collected by Elias Ashmole (1617-92); mid-17th century.

This MS collated in Herford & Simpson. The text accompanied by the original Latin version by Girolamo Amaltei.

Bodleian, MS Ashmole 36/37, f. 257.

JnB 272 -----

Copy, headed 'One y^{t} sent an hour glasse to his M^{rs}', in a verse miscellany compiled by an Oxford man; mid-17th century.

Bodleian, MS CCC. 176, f. 8.

JnB 273 -----

Copy, untitled, in a verse miscellany once owned by one Peter Daniell; c. 1630s-40s.

Bodleian, MS Eng. poet. c. 50, f. 113.

JnB 274 -----

Copy, here beginning 'See this small dust here running in the glass', in a miscellany compiled by Edward Natley, fellow of Queens' College, Cambridge; c. 1635-44.

Bodleian, MS Eng. poet. f. 25, fol. 19v.

JnB 275 -----

Copy, untitled, in a verse miscellany compiled by Robert Codrington (1602-65); c. 1638.

Bodleian, MS Eng. poet. f. 27, p. 66.

JnB 276 -----

Copy, here beginning 'Consider the dust moving in this glass', in a verse miscellany; c. 1640.

This MS collated in Herford & Simpson.

Bodleian, MS Firth e. 4, p. 51.

The Houre-glasse

JnB 277 -----

Copy, headed 'Of the Ashes of a dead Lover put in an hower glasse', in a composite volume of verse and prose; early 17th century.

This MS collated in Herford & Simpson.

Bodleian, MS Rawl. poet. 172, f. 74v.

JnB 278 -----

Copy, headed 'Of the sand running In an hower glasse', in a composite volume of verse; mid-17th century.

This MS collated in Herford & Simpson.

British Library, Add. MS 11811, f. 31.

JnB 279 -----

Copy, headed 'Of Sand in an houreglasse', in a verse miscellany probably compiled by a Cambridge man; c. 1630s.

This MS collated in Herford & Simpson.

British Library, Add. MS 15227, f. 96v.

JnB 280 -----

Copy in a verse miscellany once owned by one John Philips; c. 1630s.

This MS collated in Herford & Simpson.

British Library, Add. MS 19268, f. 4v.

JnB 281 -----

Copy in a verse miscellany probably compiled by a Cambridge man; mid-17th century.

This MS collated in Herford & Simpson.

British Library, Add. MS 22603, f. 49r-v.

JnB 282 -----

Copy in the hand of a playhouse scribe, headed 'On y[e] Sand in an houreglasse', in a verse miscellany possibly compiled for the lawyer Chaloner Chute and belonging to his family in Hampshire; this MS in the same hand as *Dick of Devonshire* (HyT 5) and *Blurt Master Constable* (MiT 6); c. 1630s.

This MS collated in Herford & Simpson.

British Library, Add. MS 33998, f. 14r-v.

JnB 283 -----

Copy, headed 'A lovers ashes put into an houre glasse by his M[ris]', in a miscellany once owned by Sir Thomas Meres (1634-1715) of Kirton, Lincolnshire; c. 1640s.

British Library, Egerton MS 2725, f. 112v.

JnB 284 -----

Copy in a MS volume of poems by Donne; c. 1623-33.

This MS collated in Herford & Simpson.

British Library, Stowe MS 961, f. 69v.

JnB 285 -----

Copy in a verse miscellany; c. 1637.

British Library, Stowe MS 962, f. 144.

JnB 286 -----

Copies in a musical setting by Alfonso Ferrabosco, in two MS music part books compiled by Thomas Smith (1614-1701) of The Queen's College, Oxford, later Bishop of Carlisle; c. 1637.

Printed from this MS in Edward Doughtie, 'Ferrabosco and Jonson's "The Houre-glasse"', *RQ*, 22 (1969), 148-50.

Carlisle Cathedral, Dean & Chapter of Carlisle MSS, Box B1, Altus, p. 8; Bassus, p. 8.

JnB 287 -----

Copy, untitled, in a verse miscellany among the papers of the Gell family, formerly of Hopton Hall, possibly once owned by Sir John Gell (1593-1671); c. 1620s-30s.

Derbyshire Record Office, D258/31/16, p. 9.

JnB 288 -----

Copy, headed 'On a Gentle-Woman working by an Houre-glasse', in a transcript by one 'S.H.' (born 1665) of John Benson's 12mo edition of Jonson's poems (1640); c. 1680.

This MS recorded in Herford & Simpson.

Edinburgh University Library, MS Dc. 7. 94, f. 17v.

JnB 289 -----

Copy in a verse miscellany compiled by an Oxford man and once owned by one Stephen Welden; mid-17th century.

Folger, MS V. a. 162, f. 90.

The Houre-glasse

JnB 290 -----

Copy in a verse miscellany compiled by an Oxford man; c. 1630s.

This MS probably the Dobell MS collated in Herford & Simpson.

Folger, MS V. a. 170, p. 76.

JnB 291 -----

Copy in a verse miscellany; c. 1630s.

Folger, MS V. a. 245, f. 55v.

JnB 292 -----

Copy in a verse miscellany; c. 1630.

Facsimile of this MS in Giles E. Dawson and Laetitia Kennedy-Skipton, *Elizabethan Handwriting 1500-1650* (London, 1968), plate 42.

Folger, MS V. b. 43, f. 9v.

JnB 293 -----

Copy, untitled, in a verse miscellany owned in 1640 by Anthony St John (1618-73) and Ann St John, of Bletsoe, Bedfordshire; c. 1630s.

Harvard, fMS Eng 626, f. 73.

JnB 294 -----

Copy in a MS volume of poems by Donne (the 'O'Flahertie MS') completed on 12 October 1632.

Harvard, MS Eng 966.5, f. 139v.

JnB 295 -----

Copy, untitled, in a MS volume of poems chiefly by Donne; c. 1620s.

Harvard, MS Eng 966.7, f. 32.

JnB 296 -----

Copy in a verse miscellany owned by Edward Denny, Charles Cokes, Edward Randolpe, and Thomas Cassy; c. 1630s.

Huntington, HM 198, Part I, p. 53.

JnB 297 -----

Copy, headed 'On a Gentlewoman working by an houreglasse', in a miscellany compiled by Sir Henry Rainsford (1599-1641) of Clifford Chambers, near Stratford-upon-Avon; c. 1630.

Owned by Sir Geoffrey Keynes, *Bibliotheca Bibliographici* No. 15, [no page numbers].

JnB 298 -----

Copy in a MS volume of poems by Donne owned in 1680 by Narcissus Luttrell; c. 1632.

Owned by Sir Geoffrey Keynes, *Bibliotheca Bibliographici* No. 1861, f. 113.

JnB 299 -----

Copy, untitled and here beginning 'Consider but this dust heere in this glass', in a verse miscellany possibly once owned by Sir John Reresby (d. 1646); among the papers of the Savile family, formerly of Methley Hall, near Pontefract; c. 1630s.

Leeds Archives Department, MX 237, f. 34.

JnB 300 -----

Copy, headed 'On the Sand runninge in an hower glass', in a verse miscellany used by members of the Holgate family of Saffron Walden, Essex; c. 1630s.

Pierpont Morgan Library, MA 1057, p. 132.

JnB 301 -----

Copy, headed 'On the sand running in an Houre glasse', in a verse miscellany compiled by one Robert Bishop; c. 1630.

Rosenbach Foundation, MS 1083/16, p. 291.

JnB 302 -----

Copy, headed 'On a faire Ladie working by an hower glasse', in a verse miscellany owned in 1642 by one Horatio Carey; c. 1638-42.

Rosenbach Foundation, MS 1083/17, p. 15.

JnB 303 -----

Copy in a verse miscellany owned and possibly compiled by John Pike of Cambridge; c. 1636-40s.

This MS collated in Herford & Simpson.

St John's College, Cambridge, MS S. 32 (James 423), f. 7v.

JnB 304 -----

Copy, untitled, in a verse miscellany once owned by Sir Henry Spelman (1564?-1641); c. 1630s.

South African Library, Cape Town, MS Grey 7 a 29, p. 75.

The Houre-glasse

JnB 305 -----

Copy in a verse miscellany compiled by Tobias Alston (1620-c.1639) of Sayham Hall, near Sudbury, Suffolk; c. 1639.

Yale, Osborn Collection, b 197, p. 59.

JnB 306 -----

Copy in a miscellany; mid-17th century.

Yale, Osborn Collection, b 205, f. 73v.

JnB 307 -----

Copy in a MS collection of poems once owned by Sir Kenelm Digby (1603-65); 17th century.

Printed from this MS in *Poems from Sir Kenelm Digby's Papers, in the possession of Henry A. Bright*, Roxburghe Club (London, 1877), p. 31; collated from this publication in Herford & Simpson.

Unlocated.

--- -----

See also INTRODUCTION.

JnB 308 *The humble Petition of poore Ben. To th' best of Monarchs, Masters, Men, King Charles* ('That whereas your royall Father').

Copy, headed 'To the Kings Most Excellent Maiesty The humble Petcōn of your Poet To your Maiestye dooth shew it' and here beginning 'Whereas late your Royal father', in the hand of Elias Ashmole (1617-92) in a composite volume of verse collected by him; mid-late 17th century.

First pub. in *The Vnder-wood* (lxxvi) in *Workes* (London, 1640); Herford & Simpson, VIII, 259-60. This MS collated in Herford & Simpson.

Bodleian, MS Ashmole 36/37, f. 48v.

JnB 309 -----

Copy, headed 'Ben: Johnsons peticion to ye k^s: ma^tie' and here beginning 'Whereas yor late [?] father', in a miscellany of English and Welsh poems compiled by Richard Roberts, Justice of the Peace; c. 1620s.

Bodleian, MS Don. c. 54, f. 3v.

JnB 310 -----

Copy, headed 'Mr Ben: Johnsons Petition to the Kings most Excell^t Matie the humble Petition of yor Poet to your Matie doth shewe it' and here beginning 'Whereas late your Royall Father', in a verse miscellany; c. 1630.

Rosenbach Foundation, MS 239/23, pp. 201-2.

JnB 311 *A Hymne to God the Father* ('Heare mee, O God!').

Copy in a MS volume of the words of anthems used in one of the royal chapels, possibly used by Charles I; c. 1635.

First pub. in *The Vnder-wood* (i.2) in *Workes* (London, 1640); Herford & Simpson, VIII, 129-30. This MS collated in Herford & Simpson.

Bodleian, MS Rawl. poet. 23, p. 158.

JnB 312 -----

Copy, headed 'A Sacred Song', in a musical setting by Alfonso Ferrabosco in a MS songbook; mid-17th century.

This MS collated in Herford & Simpson.

British Library, Egerton MS 2013, f. 57v.

JnB 313 -----

Copy, untitled, in a miscellany compiled by or for Sir Henry Cholmley, brother of Sir Hugh Cholmley (1600-57); c. 1624-41.

Harvard, MS Eng 703, f. 63r-v.

JnB 314 -----

Copy in a musical setting by Alfonso Ferrabosco in a MS volume of songs, madrigals and motets; early 17th century.

This MS collated in John P. Cutts, 'Early Seventeenth-Century Lyrics at St. Michael's College', *M & L*, 37 (1956), 221-33 (pp. 225-6).

St Michael's College, Tenbury Wells, MS 1018, f. 31.

JnB 315 *Inviting a Friend to Svpper* ('To night, graue sir, both my poore house, and I').

Copy in a verse miscellany compiled by Peter Calfe (1610-67); c. 1641.

First pub. in *Epigrammes* (ci) in *Workes* (London, 1616); Herford & Simpson, VIII, 64-5. This MS collated in Herford & Simpson.

British Library, Harley MS 6917, f. 84r-v.

JnB 316 -----

Copy in a verse miscellany compiled by William Jordan, schoolmaster of Denbigh or Caernarvon; c. 1674-84.

Folger, MS V. a. 276, Part II, ff. 20v-1v.

--- *The iust indignation the Author tooke at the vulgar censure of his Play, by some malicious Spectators begat this following Ode to himselfe* ('Come leaue the lothed stage').

See JnB 367-81.

JnB 317 *A little Shrub growing by* ('Aske not to know this Man. If fame should speake').

Copy, headed 'Another by Ben:', in a miscellany; c. 1660.

First pub. in *The Vnder-wood* (xxi) in *Workes* (London, 1640); Herford & Simpson, VIII, 172.

Rosenbach Foundation, MS 239/18, p. 5.

JnB 318 *Lord Bacon's Birth-day* ('Haile, happie Genius of this antient pile!').

Copy made by John Aubrey (1617-92) in the first part of his autograph *Brief Lives*; 1679/80.

First pub. in *The Vnder-wood* (li) in *Workes* (London, 1640); Herford & Simpson, VIII, 225. This MS collated in Herford & Simpson.

Bodleian, MS Aubrey 6, f. 69.

*JnB 319 *Martial. <Epigram XLVII, Book X.>* ('The Things that make the happier life, are these').

Autograph, among the papers of the actor Edward Alleyn (1566-1626).

First pub. (from this MS) in John Payne Collier, *Memoirs of Edward Alleyn* (London, 1841), p. 54; printed from this MS in Herford & Simpson, VIII, 295. Facsimile in *The Henslowe Papers*, ed. R.A. Foakes (London, 1977), II, 135.

Dulwich College, Alleyn Papers, Vol. I, No. 135, f. 259.

JnB 320 -----

Copy, untitled, in a composite volume of MSS; early 17th century.

This MS collated in Herford & Simpson.

British Library, Harley MS 791, f. 59v.

JnB 321 -----

Copy in a verse miscellany compiled by William Jordan, schoolmaster of Denbigh or Caernarvon; c. 1674-84.

Folger, MS V. a. 276, Part II, f. 42r-v.

JnB 322 *The Musicall strife; In a Pastorall Dialogue* ('Come, with our Voyces, let us warre').

Copy in a musical setting in a MS songbook; c. 1640s.

First pub. in *The Vnder-wood* (iii) in *Workes* (London, 1640); Herford & Simpson, VIII, 143-4. This MS collated in John P. Cutts, 'A Bodleian Song-Book: Don. C. 57', *M & L*, 34 (1953), 192-211 (p. 204).

Bodleian, MS Don. c. 57, f. 48v.

JnB 323 -----

Copy, headed 'Two Ladies invitinge each other to singe', in a verse miscellany; c. 1640.

Bodleian, MS Eng. poet. c. 53, f. 2v.

JnB 324 -----

Copy in a musical setting by John Wilson in Wilson's corrected MS volume of his own songs; possibly in Wilson's autograph or else in the hand of someone similarly associated with Edward Lowe (c.1610-82); c. 1656.

This MS collated in John P. Cutts, 'Seventeenth Century Lyrics', *MD*, 10 (1956), 142-209 (p. 176).

Bodleian, MS Mus. b. 1, f. 81.

JnB 325 -----

Copy in a musical setting by John Wilson, used as an Oxford Act Song; c. 1660-70.

Bodleian, MS Mus. Sch. C. 142.

JnB 326 -----

Copy, headed 'Cantilena', in a verse miscellany probably compiled by a Cambridge man; c. 1630s.

This MS collated in Herford & Simpson.

British Library, Add. MS 15227, f. 88v.

JnB 327 -----

Copy, untitled, in a composite volume of verse belonging to the Skipwith family of Cotes, Leicestershire; early-mid-17th century.

This MS collated in Herford & Simpson.

British Library, Add. MS 25707, ff. 4v-5.

JnB 328 -----

Copy, headed 'Two Ladies ioyning each other to sing', in a verse miscellany compiled by Daniel Leare (a distant cousin of William Strode) probably while at Christ Church, Oxford; c. 1631-3.

This MS collated in Herford & Simpson.

British Library, Add. MS 30982, ff. 37v-8.

The Musicall strife; In a Pastorall Dialogue

JnB 329 -----

Copy, headed 'Sonnett', in a verse miscellany probably compiled by Francis Baskerville of Malmesbury, Wiltshire, and owned in 1663 by William Wallrond; c. 1633.

This MS collated in Herford & Simpson.

British Library, Sloane MS 1446, f. 55.

JnB 330 -----

Copy, headed 'The Operatione of Musicke', in a verse miscellany; c. 1637.

British Library, Stowe MS 962, ff. 207v-8.

JnB 331 -----

Copy, headed 'A Dialogue in Song betweene A Nimph & à Shephard'; 17th century.

This MS collated in Herford & Simpson.

Chetham's Library, Manchester, Halliwell-Phillipps No. 2217.

JnB 332 -----

Copy, untitled, in a verse miscellany; c. 1630.

Formerly MS. 1. 8, this MS recorded in Cutts, *MD*, 10 (1956), 176.

Folger, MS V. b. 43, ff. 28v-9.

JnB 333 -----

Copy, headed 'A Dialogue in Song betweene a Nymph and a Shepheard', in a verse miscellany owned in 1640 by Anthony St John (1618-73) and Ann St John, of Bletsoe, Bedfordshire; c. 1630s.

Harvard, fMS Eng 626, f. 80r-v.

JnB 334 -----

Copy, headed 'To Ladyes enviting each other to sing', in a verse miscellany possibly once owned by Sir John Reresby (d. 1646); among the papers of the Savile family, formerly of Methley Hall, c. 1630s.

Leeds Archives Department, MX 237, f. 23.

JnB 335 -----

Copy, headed 'A Dialogue in Songe Betweene a Nymphe & a Shepheard', in a verse miscellany; c. 1630.

Rosenbach Foundation, MS 239/23, pp. 30-1.

JnB 336 -----

Copy, headed 'Two sheapheards inuiting each other to singe', in a verse miscellany owned in 1642 by one Horatio Carey; c. 1638-42.

Rosenbach Foundation, MS 1083/17, ff. 109v-10.

JnB 337 -----

Copy, headed 'A dialog betweene two Ladies', in a verse miscellany; c. 1630s-40s.

This MS collated in Herford & Simpson.

St John's College, Cambridge, MS S. 23 (James 416), f. 53r-v.

JnB 338 -----

Copy, untitled and here ascribed to 'Corbett', with a stave of music by Nicholas Lanier, in a composite miscellany; c. 1620s.

Trinity College, Cambridge, MS B. 14. 22 (James 307), f. 87.

JnB 339 -----

Copy, untitled, in a verse miscellany appended to a MS volume of poems by Donne; c. 1630s.

This MS collated in Herford & Simpson.

Trinity College, Dublin, MS 877, ff. 187v-8.

JnB 340 -----

Copy, headed 'Sonnet', in a MS volume of poems chiefly by Henry King belonging to the Stoughton family of Warwick; c. 1636.

Owned by Rosemary Williams, London, Stoughton MS, pp. 101-2.

JnB 341 *My Answer. The Poet to the Painter* ('Why? though I seeme of a prodigious wast').

Copy in the Newcastle MS; c. 1620s-30s.

First pub. in John Benson's 4to edition of Jonson's poems (1640) and in *The Vnder-wood* (lii) in *Workes* (London, 1640); Herford & Simpson, VIII, 226-7. This MS collated in Herford & Simpson.

British Library, Harley MS 4955, f. 42.

JnB 342 -----

Copy of lines 7-24, here beginning 'You are not tied by any painters Law', in a verse miscellany once owned by one Peter Daniell; c. 1630s-40s.

Bodleian, MS Eng. poet. c. 50, f. 131v.

My Answer. The Poet to the Painter

JnB 343 -----

Copy of lines 1-15, headed 'B. Johnson, to Burlace the Painter', in a verse miscellany probably compiled by an Oxford man and once owned by one William Bloys; c. 1630s-40s.

This MS collated in Herford & Simpson.

Bodleian, MS Rawl. poet. 142, f. 43v.

JnB 344 -----

Copy, headed 'Ben Ionson to ye Painter', in a verse miscellany compiled by Daniel Leare (a distant cousin of William Strode) probably while at Christ Church, Oxford; c. 1631-3.

This MS collated in Herford & Simpson.

British Library, Add. MS 30982, ff. 58v-9.

JnB 345 -----

Copy, headed 'Ben: Iohnsons Reply', in a verse miscellany compiled by Peter Calfe (1610-67); c. 1641.

This MS collated in Herford & Simpson.

British Library, Harley MS 6917, f. 63.

JnB 346 -----

Copy in a verse miscellany; c. 1640.

This MS collated in Herford & Simpson.

British Library, Harley MS 6931, f. 58r-v.

JnB 347 -----

Copy, headed 'B.I. to the paynter', in a verse miscellany probably compiled by one 'I.A.' of Christ Church, Oxford, and later owned by Robert Killigrew; c. early 1630s.

This MS collated in Herford & Simpson.

British Library, Sloane MS 1792, ff. 119v-20.

JnB 348 -----

Copy in a transcript by one 'S.H.' (born 1665) of John Benson's 12mo edition of Jonson's poems (1640); c. 1680.

This MS recorded in Herford & Simpson.

Edinburgh University Library, MS Dc. 7. 94, ff. 16v-17.

JnB 349 -----

Copy in a verse miscellany compiled by an Oxford man, possibly a member of Christ Church; c. late 1630s.

Folger, MS V. a. 97, p. 127.

JnB 350 -----

Copy in a verse miscellany possibly once owned by Sir John Reresby (d. 1646); among the papers of the Savile family, formerly of Methley Hall, near Pontefract; c. 1630s.

Leeds Archives Department, MX 237, f. 64.

JnB 351 -----

Copy in a miscellany; mid-17th century.

Yale, Osborn Collection, b 200, pp. 247-8.

*JnB 352 *My Picture left in Scotland* ('I now thinke, Love is rather deafe, then blind').

Autograph fair copy (following JnB 270) on a single leaf presented to William Drummond of Hawthornden, now among the papers of the Clerk family of Penicuik; headed 'Yet, that Loue when it is at full, may admit heaping, | Receiue another; and this a picture of my selfe'; signed and dated January 19th 1619 [i.e. 1618/19].

First pub. in John Benson's 4to edition of Jonson's poems (1640) and in *The Vnder-wood* (ix) in *Workes* (London, 1640); Herford & Simpson, VIII, 149-50. Printed from this MS in *The Works of William Drummond* (Edinburgh, 1711), p. 155 (see Herford & Simpson, I, 177-8), and cited in Drummond's *Conversations with Jonson* (see Herford & Simpson, I, 150-1, and DrW 303). See FACSIMILE XXII. The MS accompanied by an 18th-century transcript on a single leaf endorsed 'Copy of Ben Johnsone's verses of which I have the oreginal in the Charter house'.

Scottish Record Office, GD18/4312.

JnB 353 -----

Copy, headed 'Verses on his Picture', in the Newcastle MS; c. 1620s-30s.

This MS collated in Herford & Simpson.

British Library, Harley MS 4955, f. 47v.

JnB 354 -----

Copy, untitled, in a verse miscellany once owned by one Peter Daniell; c. 1630s-40s.

Bodleian, MS Eng. poet. c. 50, f. 118.

My Picture left in Scotland

JnB 355 -----

Copy in a transcript by one 'S.H.' (born 1665) of John Benson's 12mo edition of Jonson's poems (1640); c. 1680.

This MS recorded in Herford & Simpson.

Edinburgh University Library, MS Dc. 7. 94, f. 17r-v.

JnB 356 -----

Copy, untitled, in a verse miscellany owned in 1691 by one Thomas White; c. 1640.

Folger, MS V. a. 96, f. 51r-v.

JnB 357 -----

Copy, untitled, in a verse miscellany; mid-17th century.

Folger, MS V. a. 322, pp. 127-8.

JnB 358 -----

Copy, untitled, in a verse miscellany owned in 1640 by Anthony St John (1618-73) and Ann St John, of Bletsoe, Bedfordshire; c. 1630s.

Harvard, fMS Eng 626, f. 78r-v.

JnB 359 -----

Copy, untitled, in a miscellany; c. 1630.

Huntington, HM 172, f. 32b.

JnB 360 -----

Copy, untitled, in a verse miscellany; c. 1630.

Rosenbach Foundation, MS 239/23, pp. 34-5.

JnB 361 *A New-yeares-Gift sung to King Charles, 1635* ('To day old Janus opens the new yeare').

Copy of lines 56-65 (beginning 'Hee gives all plentie, and encrease') incorporated as lines 14-23 in a copy of Nicholas Lanier's 'A Pastorall Song to the King on Newyeares day: Ano. Dni. 1663[/4?]' (beginning 'Looke shephards looke, old Janus doth vnfold'), in a composite volume of verse collected by Elias Ashmole (1617-92); late 17th century.

First pub. in *The Vnder-wood* (lxxix) in *Workes* (London, 1640); Herford & Simpson, VIII, 263-5. This MS recorded in Herford & Simpson, XI, 605.

Bodleian, MS Ashmole 36/37, f. 166.

JnB 362 *A Nymphs Passion* ('I love, and he loves me again').

Copy in a volume of state papers once owned by Robert Drake and Stephen Foster; c. 1630s.

First pub. in *The Vnder-wood* (vii) in *Workes* (London, 1640); Herford & Simpson, VIII, 147-8. This MS collated in Herford & Simpson.

British Library, Egerton MS 2026, f. 67v.

--- -----

See also INTRODUCTION.

JnB 363 *Ode* ('Yff Men, and tymes were nowe').

Copy, untitled, in a verse miscellany; c. 1620-33.

First pub. in William Dinsmore Briggs, 'Did Jonson Write a Third "Ode to Himself"?', *The Athenaeum* (13 June 1914), p. 828. Printed from this MS in Herford & Simpson, VIII, 419-21.

Bodleian, MS Rawl. poet. 31, ff. 8v-9.

JnB 364 -----

Copy in a verse miscellany; c. 1620-33.

Printed from this MS in Briggs; collated in Herford & Simpson.

British Library, Harley MS 4064, f. 237r-v.

JnB 365 *Ode Enthousiastike* ('Splendor! O more then mortall').

Copy, headed 'To L:C: off: B' and here beginning 'Beautye, more then Mortall', in a verse miscellany; c. 1620-33.

First pub. in *Diuerse Poeticall Essaies* appended to Robert Chester, *Loues Martyr* (London, 1601); Herford & Simpson, VIII, 364-5. This MS collated in Herford & Simpson.

Bodleian, MS Rawl. poet. 31, ff. 20v-1.

JnB 366 *An Ode, or Song, by all the Muses. In celebration of her Majesties birth-day* ('Up publike joy, remember').

Copy, headed 'To the Queen on her Birth-day', in a transcript by one 'S.H.' (born 1665) of John Benson's 12mo edition of Jonson's poems (1640); c. 1680.

First pub. in Benson's 4to edition (1640) and in *The Vnder-wood* (lxvii) in *Workes* (London, 1640); Herford & Simpson, VIII, 239-40.

Edinburgh University Library, MS Dc. 7. 94, ff. 5v-6v.

JnB 367 *Ode to himselfe* ('Come leaue the lothed stage').

Copy in the Newcastle MS; c. 1630s.

First pub., with the heading 'The iust indignation the Author tooke at the vulgar censure of his Play, by some malicious spectators, begat this following Ode to himselfe', in *The New Inn* (London, 1631); Herford & Simpson, VI, 492-4.

British Library, Harley MS 4955, f. 207.

JnB 368 -----

Copy in a verse miscellany compiled by Nicholas Burghe (d. 1670); c. 1638.

Printed from this MS in *The New Inn*, ed. G.B. Tennant (New York, 1908); collated in Herford & Simpson, and in Tom Davis, 'Ben Johnson's Ode to Himself: An Early Version', *PQ*, 51.i (1972), 410-21.

Bodleian, MS Ashmole 38, pp. 80-1.

JnB 369 -----

Copy in a verse miscellany compiled by an Oxford man, possibly a member of Wadham College, and later used by William Fulman (1632-88); c. late 1630s.

This MS recorded in Davis, p. 411.

Bodleian, MS CCC. 328, ff. 45v-6.

JnB 370 -----

Copy in a verse miscellany; c. 1640.

This MS collated in Davis.

Bodleian, MS Firth e. 4, pp. 30-5.

JnB 371 -----

Copy in a verse miscellany compiled by a Cambridge man; c. 1640s.

This MS collated in Davis.

Bodleian, MS Rawl. poet. 62, ff. 38v-40v.

JnB 372 -----

Copy in a MS volume of poems chiefly by and probably in the hand of one 'Alphonso Mervall' (i.e. James Cobbes?); c. 1629.

This MS collated in Davis.

Bodleian, MS Rawl. poet. 166, pp. 83-5.

JnB 373 -----

Copy in a verse miscellany partly compiled (after 1646) by one John Peverell; c. 1630s.

This MS collated in Davis.

Bodleian, MS Rawl. poet. 209, ff. 11-12.

JnB 374 -----

Copy, headed 'Ben: Johnsons discontented Soliloquy upon ye sinister Censure of his play called ye New Inne...', together with a Latin version and Thomas Randolph's verse-for-verse answer, in a verse miscellany compiled by a Cambridge man; c. 1660s.

Cambridge University Library, MS 79, ff. 28v-31.

JnB 375 -----

Copy in a transcript by one 'S.H.' (born 1665) of John Benson's 12mo edition of Jonson's poems (1640); c. 1680.

Edinburgh University Library, MS Dc. 7. 94, ff. 18-19.

JnB 376 -----

Copy on leaves removed from a verse miscellany compiled by an Oxford man, possibly a member of Christ Church; c. late 1630s.

The MS to which these leaves belong is now Folger, MS V. a. 97.

Folger, MS V. a. 152, pp. 77-8.

JnB 377 -----

Copy in a verse miscellany compiled by an Oxford man; c. 1630s.

Folger, MS V. a. 170, pp. 184-7.

JnB 378 -----

Copy, headed 'Mr Ionsons farewell to the stage', together with Thomas Randolph's verse-for-verse answer and Latin versions by William Strode and Randolph, in a verse miscellany; mid-17th century.

Folger, MS V. a. 322, pp. 170-81.

JnB 379 -----

Copy in a verse miscellany owned by Edward Denny, Charles Cokes, Edward Randolpe, and Thomas Cassy; c. 1630s.

Huntington, HM 198, Part I, pp. 114-15.

JnB 379.5 See Addenda, p. 630.

JnB 380 -----

Copy in a verse miscellany once owned by one John Nutting; c. 1630s-40s.

St John's College, Cambridge, MS S. 23 (James 416), ff. 1-2.

JnB 380.5 See Addenda, p. 630.

JnB 381 -----

Printed exemplum of *The New Inn* (London, 1631) with MS annotations made by Joseph Haslewood (1769-1833) collating the text of the 'Ode to himselfe' with a 17th-century MS once in his possession; early 19th century.

This item collated in Herford & Simpson.

Victoria and Albert Museum, Dyce Collection, Cat. No. 5363.

JnB 382 *An Ode. to himselfe* ('Where do'st thou carelesse lie').

Copy, untitled, in a verse miscellany; c. 1620-33.

First pub. in *The Vnder-wood* (xxiii) in *Workes* (London, 1640); Herford & Simpson, VIII, 174-5. This MS collated in Herford & Simpson.

Bodleian, MS Rawl. poet. 31, ff. 7v-8v.

JnB 383 -----

Copy in a verse miscellany once owned by one W. Allen; c. 1630s.

This MS collated in Herford & Simpson.

British Library, Egerton MS 923, f. 19.

JnB 384 -----

Copy in a verse miscellany; c. 1620-33.

This MS collated in Herford & Simpson.

British Library, Harley MS 4064, ff. 236-7.

JnB 385 -----

Copy in a MS volume of poems chiefly by Donne once owned by one Meriall Tracy; c. 1620-33.

Huntington, HM 198, Part II, ff. 5v-6.

*JnB 386 *An Ode to Iames Earle of Desmond* ('Where art thou, Genius? I should use').

Autograph, untitled and here beginning 'Genius where art thow', bound in a verse and heraldic miscellany compiled by William Cynwal of Penmachno for Catherine of Berain, wife of Sir Richard Clough.

First pub. in *The Vnder-wood* (xxv) in *Workes* (London, 1640); Herford & Simpson, VIII, 176-80. This MS collated in Herford & Simpson, with a facsimile of lines 1-23 facing p. 179.

Christ Church, Oxford, MS 184, f. 40r-v.

JnB 387 *Ode. To Sir William Sydney, on his Birth-Day* ('Now that the harth is crown'd with smiling fire').

Copy of lines 39-40, here beginning 'They y^{t} swell' and subscribed 'fforrest to Sr Wil. Sydney', in a fragment of a miscellany; early 17th century (after 1616).

First pub. in *The Forrest* (xiiii) in *Workes* (London, 1616); Herford & Simpson, VIII, 120-1.

Worcester College, Oxford, (inserted loose in MSS 6. 13), f. [7].

JnB 388 *Of Life, and Death* ('The ports of death are sinnes; of life, good deeds').

Copy of lines 5-8, untitled and beginning 'This world deaths region is, the other lifes', in a composite volume of verse collected by Peter Le Neve (1661-1729), his brother Oliver, and Thomas Martin (1697-1771) of Palgrave; 17th century.

First pub. in *Epigrammes* (lxxx) in *Workes* (London, 1616); Herford & Simpson, VIII, 53-4. This MS collated in Herford & Simpson.

Bodleian, Add. MS 27406, f. 74v.

JnB 389 -----

Copy, headed 'Epitaph', in a miscellany compiled by one George Turner; c. 1630s.

Folger, MS V. a. 275, p. 133.

JnB 390 *On Banck the Vsvrer* ('Banck feeles no lamenesse of his knottie gout').

Copy in a verse miscellany partly compiled by Elias Ashmole (1617-92); c. 1630s-40s.

First pub. in *Epigrammes* (xxxi) in *Workes* (London, 1616); Herford & Simpson, VIII, 36. This MS recorded in Herford & Simpson.

Bodleian, MS Ashmole 47, f. 45v.

JnB 391 -----

Copy in a verse miscellany owned and probably compiled by Hugh Barrow (b. 1617/18) of Brasenose College, Oxford; c. 1638.

New York Public Library, Arents Collection, Cat. No. S288, p. 79.

JnB 392 *On English Movnsievr* ('Would you beleeue, when you this Movnsievr see').

Copy in a miscellany probably compiled by members of the Cartwright family of Aynho, Northamptonshire; mid-17th century.

First pub. in *Epigrammes* (lxxxviii) in *Workes* (London, 1616); Herford & Simpson, VIII, 56.

Bodleian, MS Don. e. 6, f. 23.

JnB 393 -----

Copy, beginning at line 7, here 'He is French soe much', in a miscellany compiled by Sir Francis Fane (c.1612-80); imperfect at the beginning and lacking a title; c. 1655-6.

Folger, MS V. a. 180, f. 97.

JnB 394 *On Giles and Ione* ('Who sayes that Giles and Ione at discord be?').

Copy in a verse miscellany partly compiled by Elias Ashmole (1617-92); c. 1630s-40s.

First pub. in *Epigrammes* (xlii) in *Workes* (London, 1616); Herford & Simpson, VIII, 40. This MS collated in Herford & Simpson.

Bodleian, MS Ashmole 47, f. 46r-v.

JnB 395 -----

Copy in a miscellany probably compiled by members of the Cartwright family of Aynho, Northamptonshire; mid-17th century.

Bodleian, MS Don. e. 6, f. 22.

JnB 396 -----

Copy in a miscellany probably compiled by a Cambridge man; c. 1627.

This MS collated in Herford & Simpson.

British Library, Sloane MS 1489. f. 35v.

JnB 397 -----

Copy, untitled, in a miscellany later owned by one Joseph Hall; c. 1630s-50.

Folger, MS V. a. 339, f. 230.

JnB 398 -----

Copy in a miscellany; c. 1630.

Folger, MS V. a. 345, p. 282.

JnB 399 *On Groyne* ('Groyne, come of age, his state sold out of hand').

Copy, untitled, in a miscellany compiled by William Drummond of Hawthornden; c. 1620s.

First pub. in *Epigrammes* (cxvii) in *Workes* (London, 1616); Herford & Simpson, VIII, 75.

National Library of Scotland, MS 2060 (Hawthornden Vol. VIII), f. 238.

JnB 400 -----

Copy in a fragment of a miscellany; early 17th century (after 1616).

Worcester College, Oxford, (inserted loose in MSS 6. 13), f. [5v].

JnB 401 *On Gvt* ('Gvt eates all day, and lechers all the night').

Copy in a verse miscellany; c. 1638-45.

First pub. in *Epigrammes* (cxviii) in *Workes* (London, 1616); Herford & Simpson, VIII, 76.

Rosenbach Foundation, MS 239/22, f. 25.

JnB 402 -----

Copy, untitled, written in a verse miscellany probably compiled originally by a member of an Inn of Court; c. 1630.

Rosenbach Foundation, MS 1083/15, f. 86v.

JnB 403 -----

Copy in a fragment of a miscellany; early 17th century (after 1616).

Worcester College, Oxford, (inserted loose in MSS 6. 13), f. [5v].

JnB 404 *On Margaret Ratcliffe* ('Marble, weepe, for thou dost couer').

Copy in a verse miscellany partly compiled by Elias Ashmole (1617-92); c. 1630s-40s.

First pub. in *Epigrammes* (xl) in *Workes* (London, 1616); Herford & Simpson, VIII, 39. This MS collated in Herford & Simpson.

Bodleian, MS Ashmole 47, ff. 45v-6.

JnB 405 -----

Copy in a verse miscellany owned and probably compiled by Hugh Barrow (b. 1617/18) of Brasenose College, Oxford; c. 1638.

New York Public Library, Arents Collection, Cat. No. S288, p. 79.

JnB 406 *On My First Sonne* ('Farewell, thou child of my right hand, and ioy').

Copy of lines 9-12, headed 'Bens Epitaph on his eldest son dyinge in Infancy' and here beginning 'Rest in soft peace and Ask't, say heare doth lye', in a miscellany compiled by Sir Francis Fane (c. 1612-80); c. 1672.

On My First Sonne

First pub. in *Epigrammes* (xlv) in *Workes* (London, 1616); Herford & Simpson, VIII, 41.

Shakespeare Birthplace Trust Record Office, ER 93/2, f. 157v.

JnB 407 *On Some-Thing, That Walkes Some-Where* ('At court I met it, in clothes braue enough').

Copy in a verse miscellany partly compiled by Elias Ashmole (1617-92); c. 1630s-40s.

First pub. in *Epigrammes* (xi) in *Workes* (London, 1616); Herford & Simpson, VIII, 30. This MS collated in Herford & Simpson.

Bodleian, MS Ashmole 47, f. 45v.

JnB 408 -----

Copy, here beginning 'In Courte I mett it in cloths braue enough', in a MS volume of poems chiefly by Donne once owned by one Meriall Tracy; c. 1620-33.

Huntington, HM 198, Part II, f. 118v.

JnB 409 -----

Copy in a verse miscellany owned and probably compiled by Hugh Barrow (b. 1617/18) of Brasenose College, Oxford; c. 1638.

New York Public Library, Arents Collection, Cat. No. S288, p. 79.

JnB 410 *On the new Motion* ('See you yond' Motion? Not the old Fa-ding').

Copy of lines 19-20, untitled and beginning 'What then so swells each lim?', in a verse miscellany; imperfect; mid-17th century.

First pub. in *Epigrammes* (xcvii) in *Workes* (London, 1616); Herford & Simpson, VIII, 62-3.

Folger, MS V. a. 219, f. 33 (No. 4).

JnB 411 *On the Right Honourable, and vertuous Lord Weston, L. high Treasurer of England, Vpon the Day, Hee was made Earle of Portland, To the Envious* ('Looke up, thou seed of envie, and still bring').

Copy in a verse miscellany compiled by Nicholas Burghe (d. 1670); c. 1638.

First pub. in *The Vnder-wood* (lxxiii) in *Workes* (London, 1640); Herford & Simpson, VIII, 250. This MS collated in Herford & Simpson.

Bodleian, MS Ashmole 38, p. 67.

JnB 412 *On the Vnion* ('When was there contract better driuen by Fate?').

Copy in a verse miscellany partly compiled by Elias Ashmole (1617-92); c. 1630s-40s.

First pub. in *Epigrammes* (v) in *Workes* (London, 1616); Herford & Simpson, VIII, 28. This MS collated in Herford & Simpson.

Bodleian, MS Ashmole 47, f. 45.

JnB 413 -----

Copy, here beginning 'Never was bargaine better driven by fate', in a miscellany of English and Welsh poems compiled by Richard Roberts, Justice of the Peace; c. 1620s.

Bodleian, MS Don. c. 54, f. 3v.

JnB 414 -----

Second copy, also beginning 'Never was bargaine better driven by fate', in a miscellany of English and Welsh poems compiled by Richard Roberts; c. 1620s.

Bodleian, MS Don. c. 54, f. 11.

JnB 415 -----

Copy, here beginning 'Never was marriage better driven by fate', in a miscellany compiled partly by the Oxford printer Christopher Wase (1627-90); mid-17th century.

This MS collated in Herford & Simpson.

Bodleian, MS Rawl. poet. 117, f. 164v rev.

JnB 416 -----

Copy, here beginning 'Was ever cóntract driven by better fate', in a verse miscellany; c. 1630s.

This MS collated in Herford & Simpson.

Bodleian, MS Rawl. poet. 160, f. 34v.

JnB 417 -----

Copy, headed 'In Vnionem Angliae & Scotiae' and here beginning 'Was ever Contract better drawne by fate?', in a verse miscellany probably compiled by a Cambridge man; c. 1630s.

This MS collated in Herford & Simpson.

British Library, Add. MS 15227, f. 8v.

JnB 417.5, 417.8 See Addenda, p. 631

On the Vnion

JnB 418 -----

Copy, headed 'King James his coming to the croune', in a verse miscellany possibly once owned by Sir John Reresby (d. 1646); among the papers of the Savile family, formerly of Methley Hall, near Pontefract; c. 1630s.

Leeds Archives Department, MX 237, f. [82d^{v}].

JnB 419 -----

Copy in the hand of William Parkhurst (fl. 1604-67), here beginning 'Was ever contract better driven by fate', in a composite volume of MSS collected by Parkhurst; among the papers of the Finch family of Burley-on-the-Hill, Rutland; [1616-41].

Leicestershire Record Office, DG. 7/Lit. 2, f. 288A.

JnB 420 -----

Copy in a verse miscellany owned and probably compiled by Hugh Barrow (b. 1617/18) of Brasenose College, Oxford; c. 1638.

New York Public Library, Arents Collection, Cat. No. S288, pp. 78-9.

JnB 421 -----

Copy, here beginning 'Never was Vnion better driven by fate', in a verse miscellany; c. 1630.

University of Nottingham, Portland MS Pw V 37, p. 180.

JnB 422 -----

Copy in a verse miscellany appended to a MS volume of poems by Donne; c. 1630s.

This MS collated in Herford & Simpson.

Trinity College, Dublin, MS 877, f. 243.

JnB 422.5 See Addenda, p. 631.

--- *A Poẽme sent me by Sir William Burlase* ('To paint thy Worth, if rightly I did know it').

See JnB 341-51.

--- *The praises of a Countrie life* ('Happie is he, that from all Businesse cleere').

See JnB 265-7.

JnB 423 *Proludium* ('An elegie? no, muse; yt askes a straine').

Copy; mid-17th century.

This version of 'And must I sing?...' (see JnB 1) first pub. (from this MS, then owned by Thorn-Drury) in G. Thorn-Drury, *A Little Ark* (London, 1921), p. 1; edited partly from this MS in Herford & Simpson, VIII, 108.

Folger, MS X. d. 246.

JnB 424 -----

Copy in a composite volume of MS verse and dramatic works compiled by members of the Salusbury family of Llewenni, Denbighshire; early-mid-17th century.

Edited partly from this MS in Herford & Simpson.

National Library of Wales, NLW. MS 5390D, p. 504 rev.

JnB 425 *A Satyricall Shrub* ('A Womans friendship! God whom I trust in').

Copy of lines 17-24, untitled and here beginning 'Aske not to knowe this woman, she is worse', in a verse miscellany compiled by Nicholas Burghe (d. 1670); c. 1638.

First pub. in *The Vnder-wood* (xx) in *Workes* (London, 1640); Herford & Simpson, VIII, 171-2. Some texts of this poem discussed in Peter Beal, 'Ben Jonson and "Rochester's" *Rodomontade on his Cruel Mistress*', *RES*, NS 29 (1978), 320-4. This MS collated in Herford & Simpson and in Beal.

Bodleian, MS Ashmole 38, p. 155.

JnB 426 -----

Copy of a version of lines 17-24, headed 'Lord Buckhurst Rodomandado upon his Mistris', here beginning 'Seek not to know a woman, for she's worse', and subscribed 'Cōmunicat: á Mrs Sam: Naylour Aug: 14. 1672', in a miscellany compiled by one John Watson.

This version printed in *Westminster-Drollery* (London, 1671), p. 14. Printed from this MS in Brice Harris, *Charles Sackville, Sixth Earl of Dorset* (Urbana, 1940), p. 37; collated in Beal; recorded in Herford & Simpson, XI, 60.

British Library, Add. MS 18220, f. 103.

JnB 427 -----

Copy of lines 17-24, untitled and here beginning 'Aske not to know this woman she is worse', in a miscellany compiled by Richard Boyle, Viscount Dungarvon, later Earl of Burlington (1612-98); c. 1630s.

This MS collated in Beal.

Folger, MS V. a. 125, Part I, f. 54.

A Satyricall Shrub

JnB 428 -----

Copy of lines 17-24, untitled and here beginning 'Aske not to know this woman: shee is worse', in a verse miscellany possibly once owned by Sir John Reresby (d. 1646); among the papers of the Savile family, formerly of Methley Hall, near Pontefract; c. 1630s.

Printed from this MS in Beal.

Leeds Archives Department, MX 237, f. 52v.

JnB 429 -----

Copy of a version of lines 17-24, untitled, here beginning 'Trust not y[t] thing call'd woman, she is worse', and subscribed 'Rochester', in a miscellany compiled by one Thomas Watson; c. 1680s.

Formerly MS P. 3. 1; edited from this MS in *The Complete Poems of John Wilmot, Earl of Rochester*, ed. David M. Vieth (New Haven & London, 1968), p. 159; collated in Beal.

Merton College, Oxford, MS D. 1. 2, f. 144.

JnB 430 -----

Copy of lines 17-24, beginning 'Doe not you aske to know her, she is worse', in a miscellany; c. 1660.

This MS recorded (but not seen) in Beal.

Rosenbach Foundation, MS 239/18, p. 5.

--- Song: 'Cock-Lorell would needes haue the Diuell his guest'.

See JnB 625-53.

--- Song: 'ffrom a Gypsie in the morninge'.

See JnB 654-670.5.

--- Song: 'If I freely may discouer'.

See JnB 693-714.

--- Song: 'Still to be neat, still to be drest'.

See JnB 582-601.

--- Song: 'Though I am young, and cannot tell'.

See JnB 715-28.

JnB 431 *A Song of the Moon* ('To the wonders of the Peake').

Copy, untitled, in the Newcastle MS; c. 1620s-30s.

First pub. (from this MS) in *The Works of Ben Jonson*, ed. William Gifford, 9 vols (London, 1816); printed from this MS in Herford & Simpson, VIII, 416-18.

British Library, Harley MS 4955, f. 53r-v.

JnB 432 *A Song of Welcome to King Charles* ('Fresh as the Day, and new as are the Howers').

Copy, untitled, in the Newcastle MS; c. 1620s-30s.

First pub. (from this MS) in *The Works of Ben Jonson*, ed. William Gifford, 9 vols (London, 1816); printed from this MS in Herford & Simpson, VIII, 416.

British Library, Harley MS 4955, f. 52v.

JnB 433 *Song. That Women are bvt Mens shaddowes* ('Follow a shaddow, it still flies you').

Copy in a verse miscellany compiled by an Oxford man and once owned by one Henry Lawson; c. 1630s.

First pub. in *The Forrest* (vii) in *Workes* (London, 1616); Herford & Simpson, VIII, 104. This MS recorded in Herford & Simpson.

Bodleian, MS Eng. poet. e. 14, f. 75v.

JnB 434 -----

Copy in a miscellany compiled by John Abbott (b. 1653/4) of St John's College, Oxford; c. 1670s.

Bodleian, MS Rawl. D. 954, f. 44.

JnB 435 -----

Copy in a verse miscellany partly compiled (after 1646) by one John Peverell; mid-17th century.

Bodleian, MS Rawl. poet. 209, f. 34.

JnB 436 -----

Copy in a miscellany compiled by Anthony Scattergood (1611-87) of Trinity College, Cambridge; c. 1632-40.

British Library, Add. MS 44963, f. 10.

JnB 437 -----

Copy, headed 'Women', in a verse miscellany compiled by Arthur Capell; mid-17th century.

This MS collated in Herford & Simpson.

British Library, Harley MS 3511, ff. 60v-1.

JnB 438 -----

Copy in a verse miscellany owned in 1623 and probably compiled by one Richard Jackson; c. 1620s-30s.

Edinburgh University Library, MS H.-P. Coll. 401, f. 73.

JnB 439 -----

Copy in a miscellany compiled by William

Drummond of Hawthornden; c. 1620s.

National Library of Scotland, MS 2060 (Hawthornden Vol. VIII), f. 238.

JnB 440 -----

Copy, headed 'A Woman', in a verse miscellany; c. 1643-50s.

University of Newcastle upon Tyne, MS Bell/White 25, f. 42v.

JnB 441 -----

Copy, headed 'Women', in a miscellany; c. 1660.

Rosenbach Foundation, MS 239/18, p. 49.

JnB 442 -----

Copy in a verse miscellany compiled by one Robert Bishop; c. 1630.

Rosenbach Foundation, MS 1083/16, pp. 55-6.

JnB 443 *Song. To Celia* ('Come my Celia let vs proue').

Copy, untitled and here beginning 'Come: sweete (Celia) lett vs prove', in a verse miscellany; c. 1620-33.

First pub. in *Volpone*, III, vii, 166-83 (London, 1607); *The Forrest* (v) in *Workes* (London, 1616); Herford & Simpson, VIII, 102; Doughtie, *Lyrics from English Airs*, p. 294. This MS collated in Herford & Simpson and in Doughtie, pp. 563-4.

Bodleian, MS Rawl. poet. 31, f. 7.

JnB 444 -----

Copy in a composite volume of verse and prose; early 17th century.

This MS collated in Herford & Simpson and in Doughtie, pp. 563-4.

Bodleian, MS Rawl. poet. 172, f. 2.

JnB 445 -----

Copy in a miscellany once owned by Margaret Bellasys, probably the daughter of Thomas, first Lord Fauconberg (1577-1653); c. 1630.

This MS collated in Herford & Simpson and in Doughtie, pp. 563-4.

British Library, Add. MS 10309, f. 117.

JnB 446 -----

Copy in a musical setting by Alfonso Ferrabosco in a MS songbook owned in 1630 by one Hugh Floyd; c. 1614-30.

Printed from this MS in Cutts, *Musique de la troupe de Shakespeare*, pp. 3-5, and in Doughtie, pp. 563-4.

British Library, Add. MS 15117, f. 20v.

JnB 447 -----

Copy in a verse miscellany owned in 1623 and probably compiled by one Richard Jackson; c. 1620s-30s.

Edinburgh University Library, MS H.-P. Coll. 401, f. 73.

JnB 448 -----

Copy, headed 'A Song', in a verse miscellany probably compiled by a member of an Inn of Court; mid-17th century.

This MS collated in Doughtie, pp. 563-4.

Folger, MS V. a. 262, p. 101.

JnB 449 -----

Copy, untitled, in a miscellany later owned by one Joseph Hall; c. 1630s-50.

This MS collated in Doughtie, pp. 563-4.

Folger, MS V. a. 339, f. 191v.

JnB 450 -----

Copy, headed 'Another' and here beginning 'Come sweet M[rs] lett us proue', in a verse miscellany owned in 1642 by one Horatio Carey; c. 1638-42.

This MS collated in Doughtie, pp. 563-4.

Rosenbach Foundation, MS 1083/17, ff. 91v-2.

JnB 451 *Song. To Celia* ('Drinke to me, onely, with thine eyes').

Copy in a verse miscellany compiled by an Oxford man and once owned by one Henry Lawson; c. 1630s.

First pub. in *The Forrest* (ix) in *Workes* (London, 1616); Herford & Simpson, VIII, 106. This MS collated in Herford & Simpson.

Bodleian, MS Eng. poet. e. 14, f. 21.

JnB 452 -----

Copy in a verse miscellany; c. 1640.

This MS collated in Herford & Simpson.

Bodleian, MS Firth e. 4, p. 25.

JnB 453 -----

Copy in a verse miscellany; mid-17th century.

This MS collated in Herford & Simpson.

British Library, Add. MS 22602, f. 2v.

Song. To Celia

JnB 454 -----

Copy, untitled, in a composite volume of verse belonging to the Skipwith family of Cotes, Leicestershire; early-mid-17th century.

This MS collated in Herford & Simpson.

British Library, Add. MS 25707, f. 69v.

JnB 455 -----

Copy in a verse miscellany compiled by Arthur Capell; mid-17th century.

This MS collated in Herford & Simpson.

British Library, Harley MS 3511, f. 61.

JnB 456 -----

Copy, headed 'To his M[rs]', in a verse miscellany probably compiled by Francis Baskerville of Malmesbury, Wiltshire, and owned in 1663 by William Wallrond; c. 1633.

This MS collated in Herford & Simpson.

British Library, Sloane MS 1446, f. 54v.

JnB 457 -----

Copy in a verse miscellany; c. 1637.

British Library, Stowe MS 962, f. 235.

JnB 458 -----

Copy in a verse miscellany owned in 1623 and probably compiled by one Richard Jackson; c. 1620s-30s.

Edinburgh University Library, MS H.-P. Coll. 401, f. 73v.

JnB 459 -----

Copy, headed 'To his Mistress', in a miscellany compiled by Richard Boyle, Viscount Dungarvon, later Earl of Burlington (1612-98); c. 1630s.

Folger, MS V. a. 125, Part I, f. 43.

JnB 460 -----

Copy, headed 'A lover's health', in a verse miscellany probably compiled by a member of an Inn of Court; mid-17th century.

Folger, MS V. a. 262, p. 39.

JnB 461 -----

Copy, untitled, in a miscellany compiled by one George Turner; c. 1630s.

Folger, MS V. a. 275, p. 156.

JnB 462 -----

Copy, headed 'A health to a louer', in a miscellany; c. 1630.

Folger, MS V. a. 345, p. 286.

JnB 463 -----

Copy in a verse miscellany; c. 1630.

Folger, MS V. b. 43, f. 25v.

JnB 464 -----

Copy of an eight-line version in a miscellany compiled by William Drummond of Hawthornden; c. 1620s.

National Library of Scotland, MS 2060 (Hawthornden Vol. VII), f. 238.

JnB 465 -----

Copy, headed 'A health to his M[ris]', in a verse miscellany compiled by one Robert Bishop; c. 1630.

Rosenbach Foundation, MS 1083/16, p. 56.

JnB 466 -----

Copy, headed 'A health to a Louer', in a verse miscellany owned in 1642 by one Horatio Carey; c. 1638-42.

Rosenbach Foundation, MS 1083/17, f. 108.

JnB 467 -----

Copy in a verse miscellany appended to a MS volume of poems by Donne; c. 1630s.

This MS collated in Herford & Simpson.

Trinity College, Dublin, MS 877, f. 272.

JnB 468 -----

Copy, headed 'To his Mistresse' and here beginning 'Drink to mee Caelia with thine Eye', in a MS volume of poems chiefly by Henry King belonging to the Stoughton family of Warwick; c. 1636.

Owned by Rosemary Williams, London, Stoughton MS, p. 100.

JnB 469 *A speech out of Lucane* ('Just and fit actions Ptolemy (he saith)').

Copy in a verse miscellany; c. 1620-33.

First pub. in William Dinsmore Briggs, 'Studies in Ben Jonson. IV', *Anglia*, 39 (1916), 209-51 (pp. 247-8); Herford & Simpson, VIII, 422-3. This MS collated in Herford & Simpson.

Bodleian, MS Rawl. poet. 31, f. 18r-v.

A speech out of Lucane

JnB 470 -----

Copy in a verse miscellany; c. 1620-33.

Printed from this MS in Briggs and in Herford & Simpson.

British Library, Harley MS 4064, f. 243r-v.

JnB 471 *A speach presented vnto king James at a tylting in the behalfe of the two noble Brothers s^r^ Robert & s^r^ Henrye Rich, now Earles of warwick and Hollande* ('Two noble knightes, whom true desire and zeale').

Copy in a verse miscellany compiled by Nicholas Burghe (d. 1670); c. 1638.

First pub. (?) (from this MS) in Herford & Simpson, VIII (1947), 382-3.

Bodleian, MS Ashmole 38, p. 103.

JnB 472 *This was Mr Ben: Johnsons Answer of the suddayne* ('Il may Ben Johnson slander so his feete').

Copy in the Newcastle MS; c. 1620s-30s.

First pub. (from this MS) in William Dinsmore Briggs, 'Studies in Ben Jonson', *Anglia*, 37 (1913), 463-93 (p. 470); printed from this MS in Herford & Simpson, VIII, 418.

British Library, Harley MS 4955, f. 47v.

JnB 473 *To a Friend* ('To put out the word, whore, thou do'st me woo').

Copy in a miscellany probably compiled by members of the Cartwright family of Aynho, Northamptonshire; mid-17th century.

First pub. in *Epigrammes* (lxxxiii) in *Workes* (London, 1616); Herford & Simpson, VIII, 54.

Bodleian, MS Don. e. 6, f. 22v.

*JnB 474 *To a ffreind an Epigram Of him* ('Sr Inigo doth feare it as I heare').

Autograph; [1631].

First pub. in *The Works of Ben Jonson*, ed. Peter Whalley, 7 vols (London, 1756). Printed from this MS in Herford & Simpson, VIII, 407-8.

Huntington, EL 8729, f. 44.

JnB 475 -----

Copy in the Newcastle MS; c. 1630s.

This MS collated in Herford & Simpson.

British Library, Harley MS 4955, f. 176.

JnB 476 -----

Copy, transcribed from a MS source, in a notebook compiled by the engraver and antiquary George Vertue (1684-1756); [1713-54].

This MS collated in Herford & Simpson.

British Library, Add. MS 23070, f. 31.

JnB 477 -----

Copy in a verse miscellany compiled by one Thomas Crosse; c. 1630s.

This MS collated in Herford & Simpson.

British Library, Harley MS 6057, f. 19.

JnB 478 -----

Copy in a verse miscellany owned in 1691 by one Thomas White; c. 1640.

Folger, MS V. a. 96, f. 94r-v.

JnB 479 -----

Copy in a verse miscellany; mid-17th century.

Folger, MS V. a. 322, p. 15.

JnB 480 -----

Copy; c. 1631.

This MS the Dobell MS collated in Herford & Simpson. Facsimile in Giles E. Dawson and Laetitia Kennedy-Skipton, *Elizabethan Handwriting 1500-1650* (London, 1968), plate 43.

Folger, MS X. d. 245(a).

JnB 481 -----

Transcript of an early MS, on unbound leaves among the MSS of the Duke of Portland, of Welbeck Abbey, Nottinghamshire; late 18th-early 19th century.

University of Nottingham, Portland MS Pw 2V 154.

JnB 482 -----

Copy in a verse miscellany appended to a MS volume of poems by Donne; c. 1630s.

This MS collated in Herford & Simpson.

Trinity College, Dublin, MS 877, f. 178.

JnB 483 *To Doctor Empirick* ('When men a dangerous disease did scape').

Copy, untitled, in a verse miscellany later used by William Fulman (1632-88); c. 1630.

To Doctor Empirick

First pub. in *Epigrammes* (xiii) in *Workes* (London, 1616); Herford & Simpson, VIII, 31.

Bodleian, MS CCC. 327, f. 32v.

JnB 484 -----

Copy in a miscellany compiled by Anthony Scattergood (1611-87) of Trinity College, Cambridge; c. 1632-40.

Printed from this MS in *Poetical and Dramatic Works of Thomas Randolph*, ed. W.C. Hazlitt (London, 1875), p. 655.

British Library, Add. MS 44963, f. 9v.

JnB 485 *To Fine Lady Wovld-Bee* ('Fine Madame Wovld-Bee, wherefore should you feare').

Copy in a miscellany probably compiled by members of the Cartwright family of Aynho, Northamptonshire; mid-17th century.

First pub. in *Epigrammes* (lxii) in *Workes* (London, 1616); Herford & Simpson, VIII, 46.

Bodleian, MS Don. e. 6, f. 22v.

JnB 486 -----

Copy of lines 8-12, beginning 'To make amends, yo'are thought a wholesome creature', in a composite volume of verse and prose owned c. 1669 by one John Cooke of Bury St Edmunds, Suffolk; c. 1620s-30s.

This MS collated in Herford & Simpson.

Bodleian, MS Rawl. poet. 26, f. 1v.

JnB 487 *To Foole, or Knave* ('Thy praise, or dispraise is to me alike').

Copy, untitled and here beginning 'ffooles praise or dispraise is to me alike', in a verse miscellany compiled by one Robert Bishop; c. 1630.

First pub. in *Epigrammes* (lxi) in *Workes* (London, 1616); Herford & Simpson, VIII, 46.

Rosenbach Foundation, MS 1083/16, p. 282.

*JnB 488 *To Inigo Marquess Would be A Corollary* ('But cause thou hearst ye mighty k. of Spaine').

Autograph; [1631].

First pub. in *The Works of Ben Jonson*, ed. Peter Whalley, 7 vols (London, 1756). Printed from this MS in Herford & Simpson, VIII, 406-7.

Huntington, EL 8729, ff. 43v-4.

JnB 489 -----

Copy in the Newcastle MS; c. 1630s.

This MS collated in Herford & Simpson.

British Library, Harley MS 4955, f. 176.

JnB 490 -----

Copy, transcribed from a MS source, in a notebook compiled by the engraver and antiquary George Vertue (1684-1756); [1713-54].

This MS collated in Herford & Simpson.

British Library, Add. MS 23070, ff. 30v-1.

JnB 491 -----

Copy in a verse miscellany compiled by one Thomas Crosse; c. 1630s.

This MS collated in Herford & Simpson.

British Library, Harley MS 6057, f. 18v.

JnB 492 -----

Copy in a verse miscellany owned in 1691 by one Thomas White; c. 1640.

Folger, MS V. a. 96, ff. 93v-4.

JnB 493 -----

Copy in a verse miscellany; mid-17th century.

Folger, MS V. a. 322, pp. 14-15.

JnB 494 -----

Copy; c. 1631.

This MS the Dobell MS collated in Herford & Simpson. Facsimile of first page in Giles E. Dawson and Laetitia Kennedy-Skipton, *Elizabethan Handwriting 1500-1650* (London, 1968), plate 43.

Folger, MS X. d. 245(a).

JnB 495 -----

Transcript of an early MS, on unbound leaves among the MSS of the Duke of Portland, of Welbeck Abbey, Nottinghamhsire; late 18th-early 19th century.

University of Nottingham, Portland MS Pw 2V 154.

JnB 496 -----

Copy in a verse miscellany appended to a MS volume of poems by Donne; c. 1630s.

This MS collated in Herford & Simpson.

Trinity College, Dublin, MS 877, f. 180r-v.

JnB 497 *To Iohn Donne* ('Donne, the delight of Phoebvs, and each Muse').

Copy in a verse miscellany partly compiled by Elias Ashmole (1617-92); c. 1630s-40s.

First pub. in *Epigrammes* (xxiii) in *Workes* (London, 1616); Herford & Simpson, VIII, 34. This MS collated in Herford & Simpson.

Bodleian, MS Ashmole 47, f. 45v.

JnB 498 -----

Copy in a verse miscellany owned and probably compiled by Hugh Barrow (b. 1617/18) of Brasenose College, Oxford; c. 1638.

New York Public Library, Arents Collection, Cat. No. S288, p. 80.

JnB 499 *To Lvcy, Countesse of Bedford, with Mr. Donnes Satyres* ('Lvcy, you brightnesse of our spheare, who are').

Copy of lines 13-16, untitled and here beginning 'They, though few | Bee of the best: and 'mongst those, best are you', in a verse miscellany; imperfect; mid-17th century.

First pub. in *Epigrammes* (xciiii) in *Workes* (London, 1616); Herford & Simpson, VIII, 60-1.

Folger, MS V. a. 219, f. 33 (No. 1).

JnB 500 *To Mary Lady Wroth* ('Madame, had all antiquitie beene lost').

Copy in a miscellany probably compiled by members of the Cartwright family of Aynho, Northamptonshire; mid-17th century.

First pub. in *Epigrammes* (cv) in *Workes* (London, 1616); Herford & Simpson, VIII, 67-8.

Bodleian, MS Don. e. 6, f. 23v.

--- *To Mr Ben: Johnson in his Jorney by Mr Crauen* ('When witt, and learninge are so hardly sett').

See JnB 472.

JnB 501 *To my Detractor* ('My verses were commended, thou dar'st say').

Copy in the Newcastle MS; c. 1630s.

First pub. in John Benson's 4to edition of Jonson's poems (1640). Printed from this MS in Herford & Simpson, VIII, 408-9.

British Library, Harley MS 4955, f. 173v.

JnB 502 -----

Copy in a verse miscellany compiled by Nicholas Burghe (d. 1670); c. 1638.

This MS collated in Herford & Simpson.

Bodleian, MS Ashmole 38, p. 82.

JnB 503 -----

Copy in a transcript by one 'S.H.' (born 1665) of John Benson's 12mo edition of Jonson's poems (1640); c. 1680.

Edinburgh University Library, MS Dc. 7. 94, f. 13.

*JnB 504 *To Robert Earle of Salisbvrie* ('What need hast thou of me? or of my Muse?').

Autograph fair copy, headed 'To the most Worthy of his Honors. Robert, Earle of Salisbury. Epigramme', together with JnB 505, on a single leaf; endorsed in a contemporary hand '1606 Mr Johnsons Epigr'.

First pub. in *Epigrammes* (xliii) in *Workes* (London, 1616); Herford & Simpson, VIII, 40-1. This MS collated in Herford & Simpson; facsimile in T. Bolt, 'The Manuscripts at Hatfield House', *The Connoisseur*, 8 (Jan.-April 1904), 32-6 (p. 36).

Owned by the Marquess of Salisbury, Hatfield House, Cecil Papers 144/266.

*JnB 505 *To Robert Earl of Salisbvrie* ('Who can consider thy right courses run').

Autograph fair copy, headed 'Another', together with JnB 504, on a single leaf; endorsed in a contemporary hand '1606 Mr Johnsons Epigr'.

First pub. in *Epigrammes* (lxiii) in *Workes* (London, 1616); Herford & Simpson, VIII, 47. This MS collated in Herford & Simpson; facsimile in *The Connoisseur*, 8 (1904), p. 36.

Owned by the Marquess of Salisbury, Hatfield House, Cecil Papers 144/266.

JnB 506 -----

Copy in a verse miscellany; mid-17th century.

Folger, MS V. a. 219, f. 33 (No. 3).

JnB 507 *To Sicknesse* ('Why, Disease, dost thou molest').

Copy in a verse miscellany; c. 1620-33.

First pub. in *The Forrest* (viii) in *Workes* (London, 1616); Herford & Simpson, VIII, 104-6. This MS collated in Herford & Simpson.

Bodleian, MS Rawl. poet. 31, ff. 12v-13.

JnB 508 -----

Copy in a verse miscellany; c. 1620-33.

This MS collated in Herford & Simpson.

British Library, Harley MS 4064, ff. 240v-1.

JnB 509 -----

Copy in a MS volume of poems chiefly by Donne; c. 1620s.

This MS collated in Herford & Simpson.

British Library, Lansdowne MS 740, f. 127v.

JnB 510 *To Sir Henrie Savile* ('If, my religion safe, I durst embrace').

Copy of lines 25-36, untitled and here beginning 'Although to write bee lesser then to doe', in a verse miscellany; mid-17th century.

First pub. in *Epigrammes* (xcv) in *Workes* (London, 1616); Herford & Simpson, VIII, 61-2.

Folger, MS V. a. 219, f. 33 (No. 2).

JnB 511 -----

Copy in a fragment of a miscellany; early 17th century (after 1616).

Worcester College, Oxford, (inserted loose in MSS 6. 13), ff. [3, 5].

*JnB 512 *To Sir Horace Vere* ('Which of thy names I take, not onely beares').

Autograph fair copy, in a composite volume of verse among the 'Conway Papers' chiefly descended from Sir Edward Conway, Viscount Conway (d. 1631) of Conway Castle.

First pub. in *Epigrammes* (xci) in *Workes* (London, 1616); Herford & Simpson, VIII, 58. This MS collated in Herford & Simpson.

British Library, Add. MS 23229, f. 87.

JnB 513 *To Sir Robert Wroth* ('How blest art thou, canst loue the countrey, Wroth').

Copy in a verse miscellany; c. 1620-33.

First pub. in *The Forrest* (iii) in *Workes* (London, 1616); Herford & Simpson, VIII, 96-100. This MS collated in Herford & Simpson.

Bodleian, MS Rawl. poet. 31, ff. 34-6.

JnB 514 -----

Copy in a verse miscellany; c. 1620-33.

This MS collated in Herford & Simpson.

British Library, Harley MS 4064, ff. 257-9.

JnB 515 -----

Copy of a version of lines 75-6, 79-80, here beginning 'An vniust Lawyer | Changes possessions oftner wth his breath' and subscribed 'Ben: Johns: fforrest. 3. med to Sr Rob: Wroth.', followed by lines 85-90, in a fragment of a miscellany; early 17th century (after 1616).

Worcester College, Oxford, (inserted loose in MSS 6. 13), f. [5v].

JnB 516 *To Sir Thomas Roe* ('Thou hast begun well, Roe, which stand well too').

Copy of lines 3-6, 9-12, untitled and here beginning 'Hee that is round within himselfe, and streight', in a verse miscellany; mid-17th century.

First pub. in *Epigrammes* (xcviii) in *Workes* (London, 1616); Herford & Simpson, VIII, 63.

Folger, MS V. a. 219, f. 33v (No. 5).

JnB 517 -----

Copy in a fragment of a miscellany; early 17th century (after 1616).

Worcester College, Oxford, (inserted loose in MSS 6. 13), f. [5].

JnB 518 *To Svsan Covntesse of Montgomery* ('Were they that nam'd you, prophets? Did they see').

Copy of lines 1-8 in a verse miscellany; mid-17th century.

First pub. in *Epigrammes* (ciiii) in *Workes* (London, 1616); Herford & Simpson, VIII, 67.

Folger, MS V. a. 219, f. 33v (No. 7).

JnB 519 *To the Ghost of Martial* ('Martial, thou gau'st farre nobler Epigrammes').

Copy, headed 'Upon K. James', in a miscellany; c. 1660.

To the Ghost of Martial

First pub. in *Epigrammes* (xxxvi) in *Workes* (London, 1616); Herford & Simpson, VIII, 38.

Rosenbach Foundation, MS 239/18, p. 54.

JnB 520 *To the immortall memorie, and friendship of that noble paire, Sir Lvcivs Cary, and Sir H. Morison* ('Brave Infant of Saguntum, cleare').

Copy, headed 'To Sr Lucius Carey, on the death of his Brother Morison', in the Newcastle MS; c. 1630s.

First pub. in John Benson's 4to edition of Jonson's poems (1640) and in *The Vnder-wood* (lxx) in *Workes* (London, 1640); Herford & Simpson, VIII, 242-7. This MS collated in Herford & Simpson.

British Library, Harley MS 4955, ff. 180-1v.

JnB 521 -----

Copy, headed 'Ode on the death of S^r: Henry Morison to the noble S^r: Lucius Cary', in the hand of Elias Ashmole (1617-92) in a composite volume of verse collected by him; mid-17th century.

This MS collated in Herford & Simpson.

Bodleian, MS Ashmole 36/37, ff. 49-50.

JnB 522 -----

Copy, headed 'Ode Pindarick to ye Noble Sir Lucius Cary', in a transcript by one 'S.H.' (born 1665) of John Benson's 12mo edition of Jonson's poems (1640); c. 1680.

This MS recorded in Herford & Simpson.

Edinburgh University Library, MS Dc. 7. 94, ff. 9v-11v.

JnB 523 -----

Copy in a verse miscellany; mid-17th century.

Folger, MS V. a. 322, pp. 16-19.

JnB 524 -----

Copy, headed 'Ode Pindarique', in a verse miscellany once owned by one John Nutting; c. 1630s-40s.

This MS collated in Herford & Simpson.

St John's College, Cambridge, MS S. 23 (James 416), ff. 23-5v.

JnB 525 *To the King. On his Birth-day. An Epigram Anniversarie* ('This is King Charles his Day. Speake it, thou Towre').

Copy of lines 1-18 in a verse miscellany compiled by Nicholas Burghe (d. 1670); c. 1638.

First pub. in John Benson's 4to edition of Jonson's poems (1640) and in *The Vnder-wood* (lxii) in *Workes* (London, 1640); Herford & Simpson, VIII, 249. This MS collated in Herford & Simpson.

Bodleian, MS Ashmole 38, p. 74.

JnB 526 -----

Copy in a verse miscellany compiled by one Thomas Crosse; c. 1630s.

This MS collated in Herford & Simpson.

British Library, Harley MS 6057, f. 19v.

JnB 527 -----

Copy in a transcript by one 'S.H.' (born 1665) of John Benson's 12mo edition of Jonson's poems (1640); c. 1680.

This MS recorded in Herford & Simpson.

Edinburgh University Library, MS Dc. 7. 94, f. 5r-v.

JnB 528 *To ye memorye of that most honoured Ladie Jane, eldest Daughter, to Cuthbert Lord Ogle: and Countesse of Shrewsbury* ('I could begin with that graue forme, Here lies').

Copy in the Newcastle MS; c. 1620s-30s.

First pub. (from this MS) in *The Works of Ben Jonson*, ed. William Gifford, 9 vols (London, 1816); printed from this MS in Herford & Simpson, VIII, 394.

British Library, Harley MS 4955, f. 54.

*JnB 529 *To the most noble, and aboue his Titles, Robert, Earle of Somerset* ('They are not those, are present wth theyre face').

Autograph, inserted in a printed exemplum of Jonson's *Workes* (London, 1640), with a MS note 'These Verses were made by the aucthor of this booke, and were deliuered to the Earle of Somersett vpon his lo:^pps wedding day; they are written by his owne hand'; [1613].

First pub. (from this MS) in anon., 'Ben Jonson's Verses on the Marriage of the Earl of

Somerset', *N & Q*, 5 (28 February 1852), 193-4; printed from this MS in Herford & Simpson, VIII, 384. Facsimile in Flower & Munby, *English Poetical Autographs*, p. 8.

British Library, Department of Printed Books, C. 28. m. 11.

JnB 530 *To the Parliament* ('There's reason good, that you good lawes should make').

Copy in a composite volume of verse collected by Elias Ashmole (1617-92); mid-17th century.

First pub. in *Epigrammes* (xxiiii) in *Workes* (London, 1616); Herford & Simpson, VIII, 34. This MS collated in Herford & Simpson.

Bodleian, MS Ashmole 36/37, f. 159v.

JnB 531 *To the Right hon[ble] Hierome, L. Weston. An Ode gratulatorie, For his Returne from his Embassie* ('Such pleasure as the teeming Earth').

Copy in a transcript by one 'S.H.' (born 1665) of John Benson's 12mo edition of Jonson's poems (1640); c. 1680.

First pub. in Benson's 4to edition (1640) and in *The Vnder-wood* (lxxiv) in *Workes* (London, 1640); Herford & Simpson, VIII, 250-1. This MS recorded in Herford & Simpson.

Edinburgh University Library, MS Dc. 7. 94, ff. 11v-12.

JnB 532 *To the right Honourable, the Lord Treasurer of England. An Epigram* ('If to my mind, great Lord, I had a state').

Copy in the Newcastle MS; c. 1630s.

First pub. in John Benson's 4to edition of Jonson's poems (1640) and in *The Vnder-wood* (lxxvii) in *Workes* (London, 1640); Herford & Simpson, VIII, 260-1. This MS collated in Herford & Simpson.

British Library, Harley MS 4955, f. 173.

JnB 533 -----

Copy, headed 'Benn Johnsons Newyears gift To my lord Treasurer', in a verse miscellany once owned by one Peter Daniell; c. 1630s-40s.

Bodleian, MS Eng. poet. c. 50, f. 58r-v.

JnB 534 -----

Copy in a transcript by one 'S.H.' (born 1665) of John Benson's 12mo edition of Jonson's poems (1640); c. 1680.

This MS recorded in Herford & Simpson.

Edinburgh University Library, MS Dc. 7. 94, f. 12r-v.

JnB 535 -----

Copy, headed 'Ben Johnsons newyeares guift to the lord treasurer Weston', in a miscellany; c. 1650-70.

Folger, MS E. a. 6, f. 6.

JnB 536 -----

Copy in a verse miscellany; mid-17th century.

Folger, MS V. a. 322, pp. 4-5.

JnB 537 -----

Copy, headed 'A new yeares giuft sent to the Right Honorable', in a verse miscellany possibly once owned by Sir John Reresby (d. 1646); among the papers of the Savile family, formerly of Methley Hall, near Pontefract; c. 1630s.

Leeds Archives Department, MX 237, f. [82f^{v}].

JnB 538 -----

Copy in a verse miscellany once owned by one John Nutting; c. 1630s-40s.

This MS collated in Herford & Simpson.

St John's College, Cambridge, MS S. 23 (James 416), ff. 37v-8.

JnB 539 -----

Copy, headed 'Ben: Iohnsons verses to Sir Richard Weston Lord Trēr Jan: 10 for w[ch] hee gaue him 40[lr]', in a verse miscellany owned and possibly compiled by John Pike of Cambridge; c. 1636-40s.

This MS collated in Herford & Simpson.

St John's College, Cambridge, MS S. 32 (James 423), f. 19.

JnB 540 *To the Right Honourable, the Lord high Treasurer of England. An Epistle Mendicant* ('Poore wretched states, prest by extremities').

Copy, headed 'To my Lord Weston, Lo: Treasurer. A Letter', in the Newcastle MS; c. 1630s.

First pub. in *The Vnder-wood* (lxxi) in *Workes* (London, 1640); Herford & Simpson, VIII, 248. This MS collated in Herford & Simpson.

British Library, Harley MS 4955, f. 174.

JnB 541 -----

Copy in a verse miscellany compiled by William Jordan, schoolmaster of Denbigh or Caernarvon; c. 1674-84.

Folger, MS V. a. 276, Part II, f. 44v.

JnB 542 *To the Same* ('Kisse me, sweet: The warie louer').

Copy, headed 'Of kissing', in a verse miscellany compiled by an Oxford man and once owned by one Henry Lawson; c. 1630s.

Lines 19-22 first pub. in *Volpone*, III, vii, 236-9 (London, 1607); pub. complete in *The Forrest* (vi) in *Workes* (London, 1616); Herford & Simpson, VIII, 103.

Bodleian, MS Eng. poet. e. 14, f. 42.

JnB 543 -----

Copy in a verse miscellany; c. 1640.

This MS collated in Herford & Simpson.

Bodleian, MS Firth e. 4, f. 71.

JnB 544 -----

Copy, untitled, in a verse miscellany; c. 1620-33.

This MS collated in Herford & Simpson.

Bodleian, MS Rawl. poet. 31, f. 7r-v.

JnB 545 -----

Copy in a miscellany once owned by Margaret Bellasys, probably the daughter of Thomas, first Lord Fauconberg (1577-1653); c. 1630.

This MS collated in Herford & Simpson.

British Library, Add. MS 10309, f. 117v.

JnB 546 -----

Copy in a verse miscellany owned in 1623 and probably compiled by one Richard Jackson; c. 1620s-30s.

Edinburgh University Library, MS H.-P. Coll. 401, f. 73.

JnB 547 -----

Copy, headed 'A Louer', in a miscellany; c. 1630.

Folger, MS V. a. 345, pp. 286-7.

JnB 548 -----

Copy in a verse miscellany compiled by one Robert Bishop; c. 1630.

Rosenbach Foundation, MS 1083/16, pp. 53-4.

JnB 549 *To the worthy Author M. Iohn Fletcher* ('The wise, and many-headed Bench, that sits').

Copy, headed 'On Fletcher's faithfull Sheepheardesse', on a loose leaf inserted in a composite volume of MSS collected by Joseph Haslewood (1769-1833); mid-late 17th century.

First pub. in John Fletcher, *The Faithfull Shepheardesse* (London, [1609?]); Herford & Simpson, VIII, 370-1.

Yorkshire Archaeological Society, Leeds, MS 312.

--- -----

See also INTRODUCTION.

JnB 550 *To William Camden* ('Camden, most reuerend head, to whom I owe').

Copy, headed 'His Own Epigram', in a MS volume of biographical extracts; c. 1670.

First pub. in *Epigrammes* (xiiii) in *Workes* (London, 1616); Herford & Simpson, VIII, 31.

Folger, MS V. a. 306, f. 12.

JnB 551 -----

Copy, headed 'Ben: Johnsons Epigram on himself', in a miscellany compiled by Sir Francis Fane (c.1612-80); c. 1672.

Shakespeare Birthplace Trust Record Office, ER 93/2, f. 157v.

JnB 552 *To William Earle of Pembroke* ('I doe but name thee Pembroke, and I find').

Copy in a verse miscellany partly compiled by Elias Ashmole (1617-92); c. 1630s-40s.

First pub. in *Epigrammes* (cii) in *Workes* (London, 1616); Herford & Simpson, VIII, 66. This MS collated in Herford & Simpson.

Bodleian, MS Ashmole 47, f. 44v.

JnB 553 -----

Copy of lines 9-12, untitled and here beginning 'They follow vertue for reward to day', in a verse miscellany; mid-17th century.

Folger, MS V. a. 219, f. 33v (No. 6).

JnB 554 -----

Copy in a verse miscellany owned and probably compiled by Hugh Barrow (b. 1617/18) of Brasenose College, Oxford; c. 1638.

New York Public Library, Arents Collection, Cat. No. S288, p. 78.

'When late (graue Palmer) these thy graffs and flowers'

JnB 555 *'When late (graue Palmer) these thy graffs and flowers'.*

Copy written in Thomas Palmer's MS book of emblems *The Sprite of Trees and Herbes* (1598-9), owned in 1663 by one Margaret Nevill; early 17th century.

First pub. (from this MS) in Percy Simpson, 'Thomas Palmer', *N & Q*, 8th Ser. (28 September 1895), 243-4; printed from this MS in Herford & Simpson, VIII, 361-2.

British Library, Add. MS 18040, f. 10.

PROSE

--- *Ben Jonson's Conversations with William Drummond of Hawthornden.*

See WILLIAM DRUMMOND, DrW 303-4.

MARGINALIA IN PRINTED BOOKS AND MANUSCRIPTS

See INTRODUCTION.

DRAMATIC WORKS
[and see also INTRODUCTION]

JnB 556 *Bartholomew Fair.*

Extracts, with comments on the play, in a miscellany compiled by Abraham Wright (1611-90); c. 1640.

First pub. London, 1631; Herford & Simpson, VI, 1-141. Wright's comments on the play printed in Arthur C. Kirsch, 'A Caroline Commentary on the Drama', *MP*, 66 (1968-9), 256-61 (pp. 256-7).

British Library, Add. MS 22608, ff. 70v-2v.

JnB 557 ----- III, v, 69 seq. Song: 'My masters and friends, and good people draw neere'.

Copy of Nightingale's song in a miscellany; c. 1660.

Rosenbach Foundation, MS 239/18, pp. 74-5.

JnB 558 *The Case is Altered.*

Extracts, headed 'Tis a mad world', in a miscellany compiled by Edward Pudsey (1573-1613); 1600s.

First pub. London, 1609; Herford & Simpson, III, 93-190.

Bodleian, MS Eng. poet. d. 3, f. 80.

JnB 559 *Catiline.*

Copy of various speeches transcribed from a printed source in a miscellany; c. 1672.

First pub. London, 1611; Herford & Simpson, V, 409-550.

British Library, Sloane MS 161, ff. 22-7.

JnB 560 ----- I, i, 73-97: 'It is decree'd. Nor shall thy Fate, o Rome'.

Copy of Catiline's speech in a miscellany; c. 1700.

University of Leeds, Brotherton Collection, MS Lt. 48, f. [42].

JnB 561 ----- -----

Copy in a musical setting by Cesare Morelli, in a MS volume of music compiled by Morelli for the use of Samuel Pepys; c. 1680-93.

This MS discussed in MacDonald Emslie, 'Three Early Settings of Jonson', *N & Q*, 198 (November 1953), 466-9.

Magdalene College, Cambridge, Pepys Library, MS 2591, ff. 41-3v.

JnB 562 ----- -----

Copy in a musical setting (by Samuel Pepys and John Hingston?), in a MS songbook compiled for Pepys by Cesare Morelli; c. 1680-93.

This MS discussed in Emslie.

Magdalene College, Cambridge, Pepys Library, MS 2803, ff. 108v-11v.

--- -----

See also INTRODUCTION.

JnB 563 *Christmas his Masque.*

Copy of an early version without the descriptions of the characters, dresses and properties and entitled 'Christmas his Showe', in a miscellany of verse and dramatic works; c. 1616.

First pub. in *Workes* (London, 1640); Herford & Simpson, VII, 431-47. This MS collated in Herford & Simpson.

Folger, MS J. a. 1, ff. 168-74.

JnB 564 ----- lines 71-8, 93-101, 172-9, 182-245. Song: 'Now God preserve, as you well doe deserve'.

Copy of the song of Christmas in the Newcastle MS; c. 1620s-30s.

This MS collated in Herford & Simpson.

British Library, Harley MS 4955, ff. 46v-7.

Christmas his Masque

JnB 565 ----- -----

Copy, headed 'Ben Iohnsons Maske before the Kinge &c;', in a verse miscellany; c. 1630s.

This MS collated in Herford & Simpson.

Bodleian, MS Rawl. poet. 160, ff. 173-4.

JnB 566 ----- -----

Copy in a verse miscellany owned by Edward Denny, Charles Cokes, Edward Randolpe, and Thomas Cassy; c. 1630s.

Huntington, HM 198, Part I, pp. 60-1.

JnB 566.5 See Addenda, p. 631.

JnB 567 *Cynthia's Revels.*

Extracts in a miscellany compiled by Edward Pudsey (1573-1613); 1600s.

First pub. London, 1601; Herford & Simpson, IV, 1-184.

Bodleian, MS Eng. poet. d. 3, f. 40r-v.

JnB 568 -----

Extracts, including Amorphus's song beginning 'Thou more then most sweet gloue' (IV, iii, 305-16), in a verse miscellany probably compiled by an Oxford man and once owned by one William Bloys; c. 1630s.

Bodleian, MS Rawl. poet. 142, f. 45v.

JnB 569 ----- IV, iii, 242-53. Song: 'O, That ioy so soone should waste!'.

Copy of Hedon's song, headed 'On a Kisse', in a verse miscellany probably compiled by a Cambridge man; c. 1630s.

British Library, Add. MS 15227, f. 82v.

JnB 570 ----- -----

Copy in a musical setting by Henry Lawes, in Lawes's autograph songbook; mid-17th century.

This MS recorded in Herford & Simpson, XI, 606.

British Library, Add. MS 53723, f. 5.

JnB 571 ----- -----

Copy in a musical setting in a MS songbook; early 17th century.

This MS recorded in Andrew J. Sabol, 'A Newly Discovered Contemporary Song Setting for Jonson's "Cynthia's Revels"', *N & Q*, 203 (September 1958), 384-5; printed in Sabol, 'Two Unpublished Stage Songs for the "Aery of Children"', *RN*, 13 (1960), 222-32 (p. 229); facsimile in Mary Chan, '*Cynthia's Revels* and Music for a Choir School: Christ Church Manuscript Mus 439', *SR*, 18 (1971), 134-72 (pp. 138-9).

Christ Church, Oxford, MS Mus. 439, pp. 38-9.

JnB 572 ----- -----

Copy in a verse miscellany; c. 1690-1730.

Folger, MS V. a. 308, f. 5v.

JnB 573 ----- *The Epilogue* ('Gentles be't knowne to you, since I went in').

Copy in a verse miscellany owned in 1623 and probably compiled by one Richard Jackson; c. 1620s-30s.

Edinburgh University Library, MS H.-P. Coll. 401, f. 36.

--- *The Devil is an Ass*, II, vi, 94-103. Song: 'Doe but looke, on her eyes! They doe light', and II, vi, 104-13. Song: 'Haue you seene but a bright Lilly grow'.

See JnB 8-35.

JnB 574 *An Entertainment at the Blackfriars.*

Copy in the Newcastle MS; c. 1620s-30s.

First pub. (from this MS) in *The Monthly Magazine; or British Register*, Part I (February 1816); printed from this MS in Herford & Simpson, VII, 765-86, with a facsimile of f. 48 facing p. 768.

British Library, Harley MS 4955, ff. 48-52v.

JnB 575 *An Entertainment of the King and Queen at Theobalds, 22 May 1607.*

Copy of an early version of lines 1-125 (without the prose description) in a volume of miscellaneous verse and prose transcribed from the papers of Sir Christopher Yelverton (1535?-1612); early 17th century.

First pub. in *Workes* (London, 1616); Herford & Simpson, VII, 151-8. This MS recorded in Herford & Simpson, p. 153.

All Souls College, Oxford, MS 155, ff. 319-21.

JnB 576 -----

Copy of an early version of lines 1-125 (without the prose description) in a volume of papers compiled for, and chiefly relating to, Francis Fane, Earl of Westmoreland (1582/3-1628); c. 1607.

This MS recorded in *HMC*, 10th Report, Appendix IV (1885), p. 6; collated in Herford & Simpson.

British Library, Add. MS 34218, ff. 23v-4.

An Entertainment of the King and Queen at Theobalds, 22 May 1607

JnB 576.5 See Addenda, p. 631.

JnB 577 -----

Copy of the masque in a French version, beginning 'Le genie: Ne vous estonnez pas Seigneurs si ceste place' and ending 'Et les loyaux subiectz s'auancent soubz leurs Roys'; presumably a file copy of a translation made for the use of Charles de Lorraine and his party; endorsed in a contemporary hand 'French verses at Tibbald 24 May 1607'.

This MS recorded in *HMC*, 9 Salisbury (Cecil) MSS, XIX (1965), 138.

Owned by the Marquess of Salisbury, Hatfield House, Cecil Papers 140/110-11v.

JnB 578 -----

Copy of an 89-line version on two of eight leaves removed from a miscellany; early 17th century.

Folger, MS X. d. 475.

JnB 579 ----- lines 130-41. Song: 'O blessed change!'.

Copy of the concluding song in the hand of Robert Kirkham, a secretary of Sir Robert Cecil; endorsed in a contemporary hand '1606 Song'.

This MS collated in Herford & Simpson.

Owned by the Marquess of Salisbury, Hatfield House, Cecil Papers 144/271.

*JnB 580 *The Entertainment of the Two Kings at Theobalds. 24 July 1606.*

Autograph of the opening speech (lines 8-15), here beginning 'Enter, o long'd-for Princes', with corrections in another hand; endorsed in a contemporary hand 'Sp: 1607'.

First pub. in *Workes* (London, 1616); Herford & Simpson, VII, 145-50. Printed from this MS in Herford & Simpson, VII, 147 (where it is incorrectly stated that the corrections are in the hand of Robert Cecil, Earl of Salisbury).

Owned by the Marquess of Salisbury, Hatfield House, Cecil Papers 144/272.

JnB 581 -----

Copy of the opening speech 'by Ewmone by Dice and Irene the 3 houres which do represent Time' (lines 8-15), here beginning 'Enter (o lord), for princes blesse these bowers', in a miscellany compiled by one Gilbert Frevile of Bishop Middleham, County Durham; c. 1630.

British Library, Egerton MS 2877, f. 162v rev.

JnB 582 *Epicoene*, I, i, 92-102. Song: 'Still to be neat, still to be drest'.

Copy of Clerimont's song, headed 'On a spruce Ladye', in a verse miscellany compiled by Nicholas Burghe (d. 1670); c. 1638.

First pub. London, 1616; Herford & Simpson, V, 139-272.

Bodleian, MS Ashmole 38, p. 152.

JnB 583 ----- -----

Copy of the second stanza, headed 'His choice' and here beginning 'Giue mee a forme, giue me a face', in a verse miscellany compiled by the Yorkshire antiquary John Hopkinson (1610-80); c. 1647.

Bodleian, MS Don. d. 58, f. 14.

JnB 584 ----- -----

Copy in a verse miscellany compiled by an Oxford man and once owned by one Henry Lawson; c. 1630s.

Bodleian, MS Eng. poet. e. 14, f. 12.

JnB 585 ----- -----

Copy in a verse miscellany compiled by a member of New College, Oxford; c. 1620s-30s.

Bodleian, MS Malone 19, p. 44.

JnB 586 ----- -----

Copy in a verse miscellany; c. 1620-33.

Bodleian, MS Rawl. poet. 31, f. 9v.

JnB 587 ----- -----

Copy in a verse miscellany; c. 1620s-30s.

Bodleian, MS Rawl. poet. 199, p. 11.

JnB 588 ----- -----

Copy in a miscellany once owned by Margaret Bellasys, probably the daughter of Thomas, first Lord Fauconberg (1577-1653); c. 1630.

British Library, Add. MS 10309, f. 100v.

JnB 589 ----- -----

Copy in a verse miscellany; c. 1630.

British Library, Egerton MS 2230, f. 13.

JnB 590 ----- -----

Copy, headed 'A song', in a miscellany once owned by Sir Thomas Meres (1634-1715) of Kirton, Lincolnshire; c. 1640s.

British Library, Egerton MS 2725, f. 105v.

Epicoene. Song: 'Still to be neat'

JnB 591 ----- -----

Copy, headed 'To a curious Lady', in a miscellany probably compiled by someone connected with an Inn of Court; c. 1620s.

Printed from this MS in Grosart, *The Dr Farmer MS* (1873), I, 113.

Chetham's Library, Manchester, Mun. A 4. 15, p. 102.

JnB 592 ----- -----

Copy in a miscellany compiled by Andrew Symson (1639-1712), schoolmaster of Stirling; c. 1671.

Edinburgh University Library, MS La. III. 432, f. 18v.

JnB 593 ----- -----

Copy in a verse miscellany; c. 1630s-40s.

Edinburgh University Library, MS La. III. 436, p. 7.

JnB 594 ----- -----

Copy in a verse miscellany compiled by an Oxford man and once owned by one Stephen Welden; mid-17th century.

Folger, MS V. a. 162, f. 32v.

JnB 595 ----- -----

Copy in a miscellany; c. 1630s.

John Rylands University Library of Manchester, Rylands English MS 410, f. 17.

JnB 596 ----- -----

Copy, headed 'To a spruse Lady', in a verse miscellany possibly once owned by Sir John Reresby (d. 1646); among the papers of the Savile family, formerly of Methley Hall, near Pontefract; c. 1630s.

Leeds Archives Department, MX 237, f. 53.

JnB 597 ----- -----

Copy in the hand of William Parkhurst (fl. 1604-67) in a composite volume of MSS collected by him; among the papers of the Finch family of Burley-on-the-Hill, Rutland; [1616-41].

Leicestershire Record Office, DG. 7/Lit. 2, f. 288A.

JnB 598 ----- -----

Copy in a musical setting by William Lawes in a MS songbook ('Earl Ferrers' MS'); c. 1640.

Printed from this MS in Murray Lefkowitz, *William Lawes* (London, 1960), pp. 197-8; recorded in Herford & Simpson, XI, 606.

New York Public Library, Music Division, Drexel MS 4041, No. 64, f. 45v.

JnB 599 ----- -----

Copy in a musical setting in a MS music book owned (in 1659) and partly compiled by the composer John Gamble; c. 1630s-50s.

New York Public Library, Music Division, Drexel MS 4257, No. 179.

JnB 600 ----- -----

Copy, headed 'On a Gentlewoman that used to trick upp her selfe over-curiously', in a verse miscellany; c. 1630.

University of Nottingham, Portland MS Pw V 37, p. 187.

JnB 601 ----- -----

Copy in a miscellany; late 17th century.

Yale, Osborn Collection, b 213, p. 7.

JnB 602 *Every Man in his Humour*.

Extracts in a miscellany compiled by Edward Pudsey (1573-1613); 1600s.

First pub. London, 1601; Herford & Simpson, III, 191-403.

Bodleian, MS Eng. poet. d. 3, f. 41.

JnB 603 -----

Extracts in a miscellany compiled by Archbishop William Sancroft (1617-93); late 17th century.

Bodleian, MS Sancroft 29, pp. 68, 127.

JnB 604 -----

Two pages of extracts from Act I, scene i, in a notebook compiled by Thomas Plume (1630-1704); late 17th century.

This MS recorded in Herford & Simpson, I, 186.

Plume Library, Maldon, Plume MS 22, f. [68r-v].

Every Man out of his Humour

JnB 605 *Every Man out of his Humour.*

Extracts in a miscellany compiled by Edward Pudsey (1573-1613); 1600s.

First pub. London, 1600; Herford & Simpson, III, 405-604.

Bodleian, MS Eng. poet. d. 3, f. 39v.

JnB 606 *The Fortunate Isles, and their Union*, lines 586 seq. Song: 'Come, noble Nymphs, and doe not hide'.

Copy, headed 'A Song at Court to inuite the Ladies to Dance', in the Newcastle MS; c. 1630s.

First pub. London, 1625; Herford & Simpson, VII, 701-29 (p. 727).

British Library, Harley MS 4955, f. 192.

JnB 607 ----- -----

Copy in the hand of Elias Ashmole (1617-92), in a composite volume of verse collected by him; mid-17th century.

Bodleian, MS Ashmole 36/37, f. 29.

JnB 608 ----- -----

Copy of the incipit in a musical setting in a MS songbook; c. 1640s.

Printed from this MS in David Fuller, 'The Jonsonian Masque and its Music', *M & L*, 54 (1973), 440-52 (p. 451); edited in Sabol, *400 Songs & Dances*, No. 35.

Bodleian, MS Don. c. 57, f. 53.

JnB 609 ----- -----

Copy, headed 'To ye Ladies of ye Court. An Ode', in a transcript by one 'S.H.' (born 1665) of John Benson's 12mo edition of Jonson's poems (1640); c. 1680.

Edinburgh University Library, MS Dc. 7. 94, ff. 17v-18.

JnB 610 ----- -----

Copy, headed 'Some Ladyes richly adorn'd and refusing to Dance at a Masque, wer woo'd to it after this manner', in a verse miscellany possibly once owned by Sir John Reresby (d. 1646); among the papers of the Savile family, formerly of Methley Hall, near Pontefract; c. 1630s.

Leeds Archives Department, MX 237, f. 62v.

JnB 611 *The Gypsies Metamorphosed.*

Copy of a composite text representing both the version used for the performances at Burley-on-the-Hill and Belvoir in August 1621 and that used for the performance at Windsor c. September 1621, in the Newcastle MS; probably transcribed from Jonson's own MS as used for the 1640 edition of his *Workes*; c. 1620s-30s.

First pub. in John Benson's 12mo edition of Jonson's poems (1640) and in *Workes* (London, 1640); Herford & Simpson, VII, 539-622; ed. George Watson Cole (New York, 1931); ed. W.W. Greg as *Jonson's Masque of Gipsies* (London, 1952). This MS collated in Herford & Simpson and in Greg; facsimiles of ff. 1 and 6 in Greg, plates X-XI.

British Library, Harley MS 4955, ff. 2-30.

JnB 612 -----

Copy of a composite text representing both the version used for the performances at Burley-on-the-Hill and Belvoir in August 1621 and that used for the performance at Windsor c. September 1621; once in the library of the first and second Earls of Bridgewater; c. 1620s.

Edited from this MS in Herford & Simpson and in Greg; the complete MS reproduced, with a transcript, in Cole; facsimile pages in Herford & Simpson, VII, facing pp. 564, 622, and in Greg, plates VI-XI.

Huntington, HM 741.

JnB 613 -----

Copy of the King's, the Prince's, and the Ladies' fortunes, in a hand similar to that of Sir Henry Goodyer (1571-1627) (see JOHN DONNE, INTRODUCTION); inscribed at the end 'The Gypsies Maaske att Burley'; imperfect; c. 1620s.

Herford & Simpson, lines 272-556; Greg, Burley version, lines 248-480. This MS collated in Herford & Simpson and in Greg; facsimile of p. 4 in Greg, plate XII.

Public Record Office, SP.14/122/58.

JnB 614 -----

Copy of the Lord Keeper's, the Lord Steward's, the Lord Treasurer's and the Lord Chamberlain's fortunes, in a composite volume of verse and prose; c. 1620s.

Herford & Simpson, lines 565-84, 631-43, 588-97, 681-97; Greg, Windsor version, lines 392-411, 455-67, 414-23, 373-89.

This MS collated in Greg; recorded in Herford & Simpson, VII, 551.

Bodleian, MS Rawl. poet. 172, f. 78r-v.

The Gypsies Metamorphosed

JnB 615 -----

Copy of the Lord Keeper's, the Lord Steward's, the Lord Treasurer's, and the Lord Chamberlain's fortunes, in a composite volume of MSS partly compiled by Archbishop William Sancroft (1617-93); 1620s.

Herford & Simpson, lines 565-84, 631-9, 588-97, 681-97; Greg, Windsor version, lines 392-411, 455-63, 414-23, 373-89. This MS collated in Greg; recorded in Herford & Simpson, VII, 551.

Bodleian, MS Tanner 306, ff. 252-3.

JnB 616 ----- Lady Purbeck's fortune: 'Helpe me wonder, here's a booke'.

Copy in a verse miscellany owned in 1691 by one Thomas White; c. 1640.

Herford & Simpson, lines 522-43; Greg, Burley version, lines 447-68.

Folger, MS V. a. 96, ff. 37v-8.

JnB 617 ----- -----

Copy, headed 'Looking on a Gentlewoman's Hand to tell her Fortune' and here beginning 'Bless me wonder, here's a booke', in a verse miscellany; c. 1630.

Folger, MS V. b. 43, f. 26.

JnB 618 ----- -----

Copy in a verse miscellany owned in 1640 by Anthony St John (1618-73) and Ann St John, of Bletsoe, Bedfordshire; c. 1630s.

Harvard, fMS Eng 626, ff. 65v-6.

JnB 619 -----

Copy in a verse miscellany; c. 1630.

Rosenbach Foundation, MS 239/23, p. 40.

JnB 620 ----- Song: 'The faery beame vppon you'.

Copy in a miscellany compiled by William Eliot (a nephew of Sir Simonds d'Ewes), bound in a composite volume of MSS; c. 1640-55.

Herford & Simpson, lines 262-71; Greg, Burley version, lines 237-46; Windsor version, lines 231-40.

Bodleian, MS Rawl. poet. 116, f. 50v.

JnB 621 ----- -----

Copy in a verse miscellany appended to a MS volume of poems by Donne; c. 1630s.

Trinity College, Dublin, MS 877, f. 189.

JnB 622 ----- Song: 'To the old, longe life and treasure'.

Copy in a musical setting in a MS music book owned (in 1659) and partly compiled by the composer John Gamble; c. 1630s-50s.

Herford & Simpson, lines 301-11; Greg, Burley version, lines 277-86; Windsor version, lines 271-80. Edited from this MS in Sabol, *400 Songs & Dances*, No. 29.

New York Public Library, Music Division, Drexel MS 4257, No. 177.

JnB 623 ----- -----

Copy in a verse miscellany appended to a MS volume of poems by Donne; c. 1630s.

Trinity College, Dublin, MS 877, f. 188v.

JnB 624 ----- Song: 'Why, this is a sport'.

Copy of the song sung by Patrico and Jackman in a musical setting by Edmund Chilmead (1611-54) in a MS songbook compiled by Edward Lowe (c.1610-82); c. 1654-70s.

Herford & Simpson, lines 706-31; Greg, Windsor version, lines 508-26. Edited from this MS in Sabol, *400 Songs & Dances*, No. 30; collated in Greg; recorded in Herford & Simpson, XI, 607. Facsimiles in Cole, pp. 16-18, and in Greg, plate V.

British Library, Add. MS 29396, ff. 71v-2v.

JnB 625 ----- Song: 'Cock-Lorell would needes haue the Diuell his guest'.

Copy of the ballad, headed 'Ben's Johnsons Cooklorrel', in a composite volume of papers of the Herrick family of Leicestershire; late 17th century.

Herford & Simpson, lines 1061-1125; Greg, Burley version, lines 821-84; Windsor version, lines 876-939.

Bodleian, MS Eng. hist. c. 476, f. 139r-v.

JnB 626 ----- -----

Copy, headed 'Ben Iohnson on the Peake', in a verse miscellany compiled by an Oxford man and once owned by one Henry Lawson; c. 1630s.

This MS recorded in Herford & Simpson, X, 635.

Bodleian, MS Eng. poet. e. 14, f. 16r-v.

The Gypsies Metamorphosed. Song: 'Cock-Lorell'

JnB 627 ----- -----

Copy, headed 'Ben: Johnsons diuells dish before y[e] Kinge', in a verse miscellany owned in 1619 and possibly compiled by Simon Sloper (b. 1596/7) of Magdalen Hall, Oxford; c. 1620s.

This MS recorded in Herford & Simpson, X, 634-5.

Bodleian, MS Eng. poet. f. 10, fols. 100v-1.

JnB 628 ----- -----

Copy, headed 'The devills feast', in a verse miscellany compiled by Robert Codrington (1602-65); c. 1638.

Bodleian, MS Eng. poet. f. 27, pp. 229-32.

JnB 629 ----- -----

Copy, headed 'Ben Johnson on the Peake', in a verse miscellany probably compiled by a member of New College, Oxford; c. 1620s-30s.

This MS recorded in Herford & Simpson, X, 634.

Bodleian, MS Malone 19, pp. 95-8.

JnB 630 ----- -----

Copy, headed 'The Devills Arse a' Peake, alias Satans tayle in y[e] Peake', in a verse miscellany compiled by a Cambridge man; c. 1640s.

This MS recorded in Herford & Simpson, X, 634.

Bodleian, MS Rawl. poet. 62, ff. 32-3.

JnB 631 ----- -----

Copy, headed 'A Song', in a verse miscellany; c. 1630s.

This MS recorded in Herford & Simpson, X, 634.

Bodleian, MS Rawl. poet. 160, f. 175r-v.

JnB 632 ----- -----

Copy of a seven-stanza version in a composite volume of verse and prose; c. 1620s.

This MS recorded in Herford & Simpson, X, 634.

Bodleian, MS Rawl. poet. 172, f. 78v.

JnB 633 ----- -----

Copy, headed 'A feast for the devill, at the divells arse ith' Peake', in a verse miscellany compiled by Archbishop William Sancroft (1617-93); mid-late 17th century.

This MS recorded in Herford & Simpson, X, 634.

Bodleian, MS Tanner 465, f. 85r-v.

JnB 634 ----- -----

Copy in a composite volume of MSS; c. 1620s.

Bodleian, MS Wood F. 34, f. 161.

JnB 635 ----- -----

Copy, with five extra stanzas, in a MS volume of ballads (the 'Percy Folio'); mid-17th century.

Printed from this MS in *Bishop Percy's Folio Manuscript*, ed. John W. Hales, Frederick J. Furnivall, et al., 4 vols (London, 1867-8); additional stanzas printed in Herford & Simpson, X, 633-4.

British Library, Add. MS 27879, f. 91.

JnB 636 ----- -----

Copy in a verse miscellany once owned by one W. Allen; c. 1630s.

This MS recorded in Herford & Simpson, X, 634.

British Library, Egerton MS 923, ff. 22v-3.

JnB 637 ----- -----

Copy in a verse miscellany compiled by Arthur Capell; mid-17th century.

This MS recorded in Herford & Simpson, X, 634.

British Library, Harley MS 3511, ff. 30v-2.

JnB 638 ----- -----

Copy in a verse miscellany; late 17th century.

This MS recorded in Herford & Simpson, X, 634.

British Library, Harley MS 3991, ff. 22-3v.

JnB 639 ----- -----

Copy, headed 'M[r] Johnson to the King', in a verse miscellany probably compiled by one 'I.A.' of Christ Church, Oxford, and later owned by Robert Killigrew; c. early 1630s.

This MS recorded in Herford & Simpson, X, 634.

British Library, Sloane MS 1792, ff. 55-6.

JnB 640 ----- -----

Copy, headed 'Ben Johnson on the Peake', in a verse miscellany compiled by an Oxford man and once owned by one Stephen Welden; mid-17th century.

Folger, MS V. a. 162, f. 51r-v.

The Gypsies Metamorphosed. Song: 'Cock-Lorell'

JnB 641 ----- -----

Copy, headed 'The Deuils Entertaynment at the Deuils arse a peake', in a verse miscellany probably compiled by a member of an Inn of Court; mid-17th century.

Folger, MS V. a. 262, pp. 103-6.

JnB 642 ----- -----

Copy, headed 'Ben. John: The Divells feast', in a verse miscellany; c. 1630.

Folger, MS V. a. 345, pp. 178-9.

JnB 643 ----- -----

Copy in the hand of William Parkhurst (fl. 1604-67) in a composite volume of MSS collected by him; among the papers of the Finch family of Burley-on-the-Hill, Rutland; [1621-41].

Leicestershire Record Office, DG. 7/Lit. 2, ff. 325v-6.

JnB 644 ----- -----

Copy in a verse miscellany of Welsh origin bound with a miscellany owned by one Edward Lewis; c. 1630s.

National Library of Wales, NLW. MS 12443A, Part ii, pp. 78-81.

JnB 645 ----- -----

Copy (words only) in a MS music book owned (in 1659) and partly compiled by the composer John Gamble; c. 1630s-50s.

New York Public Library, Music Division, Drexel MS 4257, No. 92.

JnB 646 ----- -----

Copy in a verse miscellany; c. 1630.

University of Nottingham, Portland MS Pw V 37, pp. 140-1.

JnB 647 ----- -----

Copy in a verse miscellany; c. 1634.

Rosenbach Foundation, MS 239/27, pp. 84-6.

JnB 648 ----- -----

Copy written in a verse miscellany probably compiled originally by a member of an Inn of Court; c. 1630.

Rosenbach Foundation, MS 1083/15, ff. 72v-3v.

JnB 649 ----- -----

Copy, headed 'The reason why it was called the Deuills Arse in the Peake', in a verse miscellany compiled by one Robert Bishop; c. 1630.

Rosenbach Foundation, MS 1083/16, pp. 178-9.

JnB 650 ----- -----

Copy, headed 'Mr Johnson to the King', in a verse miscellany connected with Christ Church, Oxford, owned and perhaps partly compiled by George Morley, later Bishop of Winchester (1598-1684); 1620s-30s.

Westminster Abbey, MS 41, ff. 28v-9v.

JnB 651 ----- -----

Copy, headed 'A Songe by Benn: Johnson', in a verse miscellany; c. 1640.

Yale, Osborn Collection, b 62, pp. 127-31.

JnB 652 ----- -----

Copy, headed 'The diuells Banquett', in a verse miscellany compiled by Tobias Alston (1620-c.1639) of Sayham Hall, near Sudbury, Suffolk; c. 1639.

Yale, Osborn Collection, b 197, pp. 180-1.

JnB 653 ----- -----

Copy, headed 'Ben Johnson on ye Peake', in a miscellany; mid-17th century.

Yale, Osborn Collection, b 200, pp. 360-2.

JnB 654 ----- Song: 'ffrom a Gypsie in the morninge'.

Copy of Patrico's blessing of the King's senses, headed 'To ye king: B: I.', in a verse miscellany once owned by Elizabeth Lane and John Finch; c. 1630s.

Herford & Simpson, lines 1329-89; Greg, Windsor version, lines 1129-89. For a parody of this song, see WILLIAM DRUMMOND, INTRODUCTION.

Aberdeen University Library, MS 29, pp. 80-2.

JnB 655 ----- -----

Copy, headed 'Ben Johnson to King James' and here beginning at the third line ('ffrom ye Goblin and ye Spectar'), in a verse miscellany partly compiled by Elias Ashmole (1617-92); c. 1630s-40s.

Bodleian, MS Ashmole 47, ff. 90-1.

The Gypsies Metamorphosed. Song: 'ffrom a Gypsie'

JnB 656 ----- -----

Copy, headed 'prayer for King James, a Caracter of his humours', in a verse miscellany compiled by John Polwhele of Polwhele and Treworgan, Cornwall; c. 1623-32.

Bodleian, MS Eng. poet. f. 16, fol. 9.

JnB 657 ----- -----

Copy, headed 'In Eusden' [i.e. 'The fiue Senses'], in a verse miscellany compiled by the Yorkshire antiquary John Hopkinson (1610-80); mid-17th century.

Bradford Central Library, Hopkinson MSS, Vol. 34, pp. 67-8.

JnB 658 ----- -----

Copy, headed 'To the King', in a verse miscellany compiled by Daniel Leare (a distant cousin of William Strode), probably while at Christ Church, Oxford; c. 1631-3.

British Library, Add. MS 30982, ff. 155-4v rev.

JnB 659 ----- -----

Copy, headed 'To the King', in a verse miscellany probably compiled by one 'I.A.' of Christ Church, Oxford, and later owned by Robert Killigrew; c. early 1630s.

British Library, Sloane MS 1792, ff. 64-6.

JnB 660 ----- -----

Copy in a miscellany compiled by Richard Boyle, Viscount Dungarvon, later Earl of Burlington (1612-98); c. 1630s.

Folger, MS V. a. 125, Part I, f. 20v.

JnB 661 ----- -----

Copy, headed 'To K: James B: J.', in a verse miscellany compiled by an Oxford man; c. 1630s.

Either this MS or JnB 662 probably the Dobell MS recorded in Greg, p. 10.

Folger, MS V. a. 170, pp. 67-8 (bis).

JnB 662 ----- -----

Copy, headed 'To the King', in a verse miscellany; c. 1630s.

See JnB 661.

Folger, MS V. a. 245, f. 62r-v.

JnB 663 ----- -----

Copy on one page of a single bifolium among the papers of the Clifton family of Clifton Hall, Nottinghamshire; 1620s.

University of Nottingham, Clifton MS Cl LM 43.

JnB 664 ----- -----

Copy, headed 'The five Senses', in a verse miscellany; c. 1630.

University of Nottingham, Portland MS Pw V 37, pp. 197-8.

JnB 665 ----- -----

Copy in a verse miscellany used by members of the Holgate family of Saffron Walden, Essex; c. 1630s.

Pierpont Morgan Library, MA 1057, pp. 82-3.

JnB 666 ----- -----

Copy, headed 'Another to K: James', in a verse miscellany; c. 1634.

Rosenbach Foundation, MS 239/27, pp. 60-2.

JnB 667 ----- -----

Copy in a verse miscellany owned and possibly compiled by John Pike of Cambridge; c. 1636-40s.

St John's College, Cambridge, MS S. 32 (James 423), ff. 27v-8v.

JnB 668 ----- -----

Copy on a single leaf among the papers of the Hay family of Haystoun; c. 1620s.

Scottish Record Office, GD34/996.

JnB 669 ----- -----

Copy, headed 'B. J. 5 senses', in a verse miscellany connected with Christ Church, Oxford, owned and perhaps partly compiled by George Morley, later Bishop of Winchester (1598-1684); 1620s-30s.

Westminster Abbey, MS 41, ff. 27v-8v.

JnB 670 ----- -----

Copy in a miscellany; c. 1635.

Owned by Edwin Wolf 2nd, Philadelphia, MS, p. 47.

JnB 670.5 See Addenda, p. 631.

JnB 671 *The Haddington Masque*, lines 86 seq. Song: 'Beauties, haue yee seene this toy'.

Copy of the Graces' song in a musical setting by Henry Lawes (three-part setting f. 81; solo version f. 80v), in a MS songbook chiefly compiled by one 'T.C.'; c. 1656-9.

First pub. together with *The Masques of Blackness and Beauty* (London, [1608]); Herford & Simpson, VII, 243-63 (p. 252). This MS recorded in Herford & Simpson, XI, 606.

British Library, Add. MS 11608, ff. 80v-1.

JnB 672 ----- -----

Copy in a musical setting by Henry Lawes, in Lawes's autograph songbook; mid-17th century.

This MS recorded in Herford & Simpson, XI, 606; facsimile in Willa McClung Evans, *Henry Lawes* (New York & London, 1941), p. 27.

British Library, Add. MS 53723, f. 36v.

JnB 673 ----- -----

Copy, headed 'Cupid run from Venus', in a verse miscellany owned and probably compiled by Hugh Barrow (b. 1617/18) of Brasenose College, Oxford; c. 1638.

New York Public Library, Arents Collection, Cat. No. S288, p. 26.

JnB 674 ----- -----

Copy in a musical setting by Henry Lawes in a MS music book owned (in 1659) and partly compiled by the composer John Gamble; c. 1630s-50s.

This MS recorded in Herford & Simpson, XI, 606.

New York Public Library, Music Division, Drexel MS 4257, No. 37.

JnB 674.5 See Addenda, p. 631.

JnB 675 ----- lines 415-24. Song: 'Why stayes the Bride-grome to inuade'.

Copy in a musical setting by Alfonso Ferrabosco in a MS songbook; early 17th century.

This MS recorded in David Fuller, 'The Jonsonian Masque and its Music', *M & L*, 54 (1973), 440-52 (p. 446), and in Doughtie, *Lyrics from English Airs*, p. 568.

Christ Church, Oxford, MS Mus. 439, pp. 60-1.

JnB 676 *The King's Entertainment at Welbeck.*

Copy, transcribed from the acting copy (1633), in the Newcastle MS; c. 1633.

First pub. in *Workes* (London, 1640); Herford & Simpson, VII, 789-803. This MS collated in Herford & Simpson, with a facsimile of f. 194 facing p. 790.

British Library, Harley MS 4955, ff. 194-8v.

JnB 677 ----- lines 5-18. Song: 'What softer sounds are these salute the Eare'.

Copy of the opening song in a musical setting by William Lawes, in Lawes's autograph songbook; c. 1638-45.

This MS discussed in John P. Cutts, 'British Museum Additional MS. 31432: William Lawes' writing for the Theatre and the Court', *The Library*, 5th Ser. 7 (1952), 225-34 (p. 231).

British Library, Add. MS 31432, f. 20v.

JnB 678 *The King's Entertainment in passing to his Coronation.*

Extracts, untitled, in a fragment of a miscellany; early 17th century (after 1616).

First pub. London, 1604; Herford & Simpson, VII, 81-109.

Worcester College, Oxford, (inserted loose in MSS 6, 13), ff. [7-8].

JnB 679 *Love Freed from Ignorance and Folly*, lines 338-42. Song: 'O What a fault, nay, what a sinne'.

Copy, with an additional stanza, in a musical setting by Alfonso Ferrabosco in a MS volume of songs, madrigals and motets; early 17th century.

First pub. in *Workes* (London, 1616); Herford & Simpson, VII, 357-71. Printed from this MS in John P. Cutts, 'Early Seventeenth-century Lyrics at St. Michael's College', *M & L*, 37 (1956), 221-33 (p. 227); edited in Sabol, *400 Songs & Dances*, No. 17.

St Michael's College, Tenbury Wells, MS 1018, ff. 36v-7v.

JnB 680 *Love's Welcome at Bolsover.*

Copy, transcribed from the acting copy (1634), in the Newcastle MS; c. 1634.

First pub. in *Workes* (London, 1640); Herford & Simpson, VII, 805-14. This MS collated in Herford & Simpson, with a facsimile of f. 199 facing p. 806.

British Library, Harley MS 4955, ff. 199-202.

JnB 681 *The Masque of Augurs*, lines 411-23. Song: 'Doe not expect to heare of all'.

Copy of Apollo's song in a musical setting by Nicholas Lanier in a MS songbook chiefly compiled by one 'T.C.'; c. 1656-9.

First pub. London, 1622; Herford & Simpson, VII, 623-47. Edited from this MS in Sabol, *400 Songs & Dances*, No. 33; discussed in MacDonald Emslie, 'Three Early Settings of Jonson', *N & Q*, 198 (November 1953), 466-9.

British Library, Add. MS 11608, f. 17v.

The Masque of Beauty

JnB 682 *The Masque of Beauty*, lines 341-63. Songs: 'If all these Cupids now were blind'.

Copy of three consecutive songs in a composite musical setting by Alfonso Ferrabosco in a MS songbook; early 17th century.

First pub. together with *The Masque of Blackness* (London, [1608]); Herford & Simpson, VII, 181-94. This MS recorded in Doughtie, *Lyrics from English Airs*, p. 569.

Christ Church, Oxford, MS Mus. 439, pp. 93-4, 96.

--- -----

For the exemplum inscribed to Queen Anne, see INTRODUCTION.

*JnB 683 *The Masque of Blackness.*

Copy in the hand of an amanuensis, with Jonson's autograph signature at the end; entitled 'The Twelvth nights Reuells'; the copy submitted to Queen Anne for the performance on 6 January 1604/5.

First pub. together with *The Masque of Beauty* (London, [1608]); Herford & Simpson, VII, 161-80. Printed from this MS in Herford & Simpson, VII, 195-201. See also JnB 690.

British Library, Royal MS 17 B. XXXI.

--- -----

For the exemplum inscribed to Queen Anne, see INTRODUCTION.

JnB 684 ----- lines 295-300. Song: 'Come away, come away'.

Copy in a musical setting by Alfonso Ferrabosco in a MS songbook; early 17th century.

This MS recorded in Doughtie, *Lyrics from English Airs*, p. 562.

Christ Church, Oxford, MS Mus. 439, p. 31.

*JnB 685 *The Masque of Queens.*

Autograph fair copy presented to Prince Henry; 1609.

First pub. London, 1609. Printed from this MS in Herford & Simpson, VII, 265-317; the complete MS reproduced, with Inigo Jones's designs, London, 1930, ed. Guy Chapman. Facsimile pages in *Facsimiles of Royal, Historical and Literary Autographs in the British Museum* (1899), plate 94; *Shakespeare's England* (Oxford, 1917), I, facing p. 292; *British Museum Catalogue of Western Manuscripts in the Old Royal and King's Collections* (London, 1921), IV, plate 103; Greg, *English Literary Autographs*, plate XXIV (b-c); Herford & Simpson, VII, facing p. 290, Petti, *English Literary Hands*, No. 46.

British Library, Royal MS 18 A. XLV.

JnB 686 -----

Copy of the 'argument', or summary of the plot, which was submitted to the Court before the performance of the masque, in a verse miscellany; c. 1609.

Printed from this MS in Herford & Simpson, VII, 318-19.

British Library, Harley MS 6947, f. 143.

--- -----

For the exemplum inscribed to Queen Anne, see INTRODUCTION.

JnB 687 ----- lines 743-8. Song: 'When all the Ages of the earth'.

Copy in a musical setting in Alfonso Ferrabosco in a MS songbook; early 17th century.

This MS recorded in Doughtie, *Lyrics from English Airs*, p. 570.

Christ Church, Oxford, MS Mus. 439, p. 95.

--- *Neptune's Triumph for the Return of Albion*, lines 472-82. Song: 'Come, noble Nymphs, and doe not hide'.

See JnB 606-10.

--- *The New Inn.*

See JnB 367-81.

JnB 688 *Oberon, The Fairy Prince*, lines 396-406. Song: 'Nay, nay, You must not stay'.

Copy in a musical setting by Alfonso Ferrabosco in a MS volume of songs, madrigals and motets; early 17th century.

First pub. in *Workes* (London, 1616); Herford & Simpson, VII, 337-56. Printed from this MS in John P. Cutts, 'Le rôle de la musique dans les masques de Ben Jonson', *Les fêtes de la Renaissance*, ed. Jean Jacquot, I (Paris, 1956), 285-303 (p. 300); edited in Sabol, *400 Songs & Dances*, No. 15.

St Michael's College, Tenbury Wells, MS 1018, f. 36.

JnB 689 ----- lines 425-32. Song: 'Gentle knights, Knowe some measure of your nights'.

Copy in a musical setting by Alfonso Ferrabosco in a MS volume of songs, madrigals and motets; early 17th century.

Printed from this MS in Cutts, *op. cit.*, I, 298-9; edited in Sabol, No. 16.

St Michael's College, Tenbury Wells, MS 1018, ff. 37v-8.

JnB 690 *A Panegyre on the King's Opening of Parliament. 19 March 1603/4.*

Title page of a MS copy of the masque sent by Jonson to James I (the rest of the text now missing); erroneously bound up as the dedication to Jonson's MS copy of *The Masque of Blackness* (see JnB 683); 1604.

First pub. together with *B. Jon: His Part of King James his Royall and Magnificent Entertainement through his Honorable Cittie of London* (London, 1604); Herford & Simpson, VII, 111-17. This MS recorded in Herford & Simpson, VII, 69.

British Library, Royal MS 17 B. XXXI.

--- *Part of the Kings Entertainment in Passing to his Coronation.*

See JnB 678.

JnB 691 *Pleasure Reconciled to Virtue.*

Copy in the hand of Ralph Crane, probably made for presentation to a courtier; 12 leaves; [1619].

First pub. in *Workes* (London, 1640). Printed from this MS in Herford & Simpson, VII, 473-91, with facsimiles of ff. 5 and 10 facing pp. 478, 492. For the identification of the hand see F.P. Wilson, 'Ben Jonson and Ralph Crane', *TLS* (8 November 1941), p. 555; further details of Crane in Wilson, 'Ralph Crane, Scrivener to The King's Players', *The Library*, 4th Ser. 7 (1926-7), 194-215.

Owned by the Duke of Devonshire, Chatsworth House.

JnB 692 *The Poetaster.*

Extracts in a miscellany compiled by Edward Pudsey (1573-1613); 1600s.

First pub. London, 1602; Herford & Simpson, IV, 185-325.

Bodleian, MS Eng. poet. d. 3, ff. 41v-2.

JnB 693 ----- II, ii, 163 seq. Song: 'If I freely may discouer'.

Copy in a verse miscellany later used by William Fulman (1632-88); c. 1630.

Bodleian, MS CCC. 327, f. 23.

JnB 694 ----- -----

Copy in a verse miscellany compiled by the Yorkshire antiquary John Hopkinson (1610-80); c. 1647.

Bodleian, MS Don. d. 58, f. 29.

JnB 695 ----- -----

Copy in a verse miscellany compiled by an Oxford man and once owned by one Henry Lawson; c. 1630s.

Bodleian, MS Eng. poet. e. 14, f. 21.

JnB 696 ----- -----

Copy, headed 'How to choose a M^rs', in a verse miscellany compiled by Robert Codrington (1602-65); c. 1638.

Bodleian, MS Eng. poet. f. 27, pp. 96-7.

JnB 697 ----- -----

Copy in a miscellany compiled by a member of St John's College, Oxford; c. 1680-90.

Bodleian, MS Rawl. poet. 65, f. 27.

JnB 698 ----- -----

Second copy in a miscellany compiled by a member of St John's College, Oxford; c. 1680-90.

Bodleian, MS Rawl. poet. 65, f. 35v.

JnB 699 ----- -----

Copy in a miscellany compiled partly by the Oxford printer Christopher Wase (1627-90); mid-17th century.

Bodleian, MS Rawl. poet. 117, f. 32v.

JnB 700 ----- -----

Copy, headed 'A sonnet', in a verse miscellany once owned by one John Philips; c. 1630s.

British Library, Add. MS 19268, f. 8v.

JnB 701 ----- -----

Copy in a musical setting in a MS songbook compiled by one Giles Earle; c. 1615-26.

Printed from this MS in David Fuller, 'Ben Jonson's Plays and their contemporary Music', *M & L*, 58 (1977), 60-75 (p. 65); recorded in Herford & Simpson, XI, 605-6; facsimile in Willa McClung Evans, *Ben Jonson and Elizabethan Music* (Lancaster, Philadelphia, 1929), frontispiece.

British Library, Add. MS 24665, ff. 59v-60.

JnB 702 ----- -----

Copy in a musical setting by Henry Lawes, in Lawes's autograph songbook; mid-17th century.

The Poetaster. Song: 'If I freely may discouer'

This MS recorded in Herford & Simpson, XI, 605-6.

British Library, Add. MS 53723, f. 7.

JnB 703 ----- -----

Copy, headed 'Sonnett', in a MS volume of poems by Donne; c. 1623-33.

British Library, Stowe MS 961, f. 79v.

JnB 704 ----- -----

Copy in a verse miscellany; c. 1637.

British Library, Stowe MS 962, f. 86v.

JnB 705 ----- -----

Copy in a miscellany; c. 1620s-43.

Cambridge University Library, MS Add. 7196, f. [18 rev].

JnB 706 ----- -----

Copy, headed 'Sonnet', in a MS volume of poems by Donne (the 'O'Flahertie MS') completed on 12 October 1632.

Harvard, MS Eng 966.5, f. 154.

JnB 707 ----- -----

Copy, headed 'J.D. Sonnett', in a MS volume of poems chiefly by Donne; c. 1620s.

Harvard, MS Eng 966.7, f. 25v.

JnB 708 ----- -----

Copy in a miscellany compiled by an Oxford man, possibly a member of Brasenose College; c. late 1630s.

Huntington, HM 116, pp. 53-4.

JnB 709 ----- -----

Copy, headed 'Sonnet. quaere, if Donnes', in a MS volume of poems by Donne owned in 1680 by Narcissus Luttrell; c. 1632.

Owned by Sir Geoffrey Keynes, *Bibliotheca Bibliographici* No. 1861, f. 124.

JnB 710 ----- -----

Copy in a musical setting by Henry Lawes in a MS music book owned (in 1659) and partly compiled by the composer John Gamble; c. 1630s-50s.

This MS recorded in Herford & Simpson, XI, 606.

New York Public Library, Music Division, Drexel MS 4257, No. 25.

JnB 711 ----- -----

Copy in a verse miscellany compiled by one Robert Bishop; c. 1630.

Rosenbach Foundation, MS 1083/16, p. 53.

JnB 712 ----- -----

Copy, headed 'A sonnett', in a verse miscellany owned in 1642 by one Horatio Carey; c. 1638-42.

Rosenbach Foundation, MS 1083/17, f. 121r-v.

JnB 713 ----- -----

Copy, headed 'Canzone', in a MS volume of poems by Donne; c. 1620-33.

Yale, Osborn Collection, b 114, pp. 310-11.

JnB 714 ----- -----

Copy in a MS volume of poems chiefly by Donne; c. 1622-33.

Yale, Osborn Collection, b 148, p. 4.

JnB 714.5 See Addenda, p. 631.

--- -----

See also INTRODUCTION.

JnB 715 *The Sad Shepherd*, I, v, 65-80. Song: 'Though I am young, and cannot tell'.

Copy of Karolin's song in a verse miscellany once owned by one Peter Daniell; c. 1630s-40s.

First pub. in *Workes* (London, 1641); Herford & Simpson, VII, 1-49.

Bodleian, MS Eng. poet. c. 50, f. 120v.

JnB 716 ----- -----

Copy in a verse miscellany probably compiled by a member of Christ Church, Oxford; c. 1630s-40s.

Bodleian, MS Eng. poet. e. 97, p. 215.

JnB 717 ----- -----

Copy, headed 'Death & Loue Paraaleld', in a verse miscellany; c. 1625-31.

Bodleian, MS Malone 16, p. 13.

The Sad Shepherd. Song: 'Though I am young'

JnB 718 ----- -----

Copy in a musical setting by John Wilson in Wilson's corrected MS volume of his own songs; possibly in Wilson's autograph or else in the hand of someone similarly associated with Edward Lowe (c. 1610-82); c. 1656.

This MS collated in John P. Cutts, 'Seventeenth Century Lyrics', *MD*, 10 (1956), 142-209 (p. 196).

Bodleian, MS Mus. b. 1, ff. 137v-8.

JnB 719 ----- -----

Copy, headed 'A comparison twixt loue & death', in a composite volume of verse belonging to the Skipwith family of Cotes, Leicestershire; early-mid-17th century.

British Library, Add. MS 25707, f. 67.

JnB 720 ----- -----

Copy, headed 'A Sonnet', in a transcript by one 'S.H.' (born 1665) of John Benson's 12mo edition of Jonson's poems (1640); c. 1680.

Edinburgh University Library, MS Dc. 7. 94, f. 19.

JnB 721 ----- -----

Copy in a verse miscellany owned in 1691 by one Thomas White; c. 1640.

Folger, MS V. a. 96, f. 53r-v.

JnB 722 ----- -----

Copy, headed 'Loue and Death', in a verse miscellany compiled by William Jordan, schoolmaster of Denbigh or Caernarvon; c. 1674-84.

Folger, MS V. a. 276, Part II, f. 21v.

JnB 723 ----- -----

Copy, headed 'Of love and death', in a verse miscellany; c. 1630.

Folger, MS V. b. 43, f. 9.

JnB 724 ----- -----

Copies in a musical setting by Nicholas Lanier, in four MS music part books compiled by John Playford (1623-86?); c. 1660.

This setting first pub. in John Playford, *Select Musical Ayres and Dialogues in Three Books* (London, 1653).

University of Glasgow, MSS R. d. 58-61; i, f. 46; ii, f. 35v; iii, f. 45; iv, f. 32.

JnB 725 ----- -----

Copy, untitled, in a verse miscellany owned in 1640 by Anthony St John (1618-73) and Ann St John, of Bletsoe, Bedfordshire; c. 1630s.

Harvard, fMS Eng 626, f. 79v.

JnB 726 ----- -----

Copy in a miscellany compiled by Sir Henry Rainsford (1599-1641) of Clifford Chambers, near Stratford-upon-Avon; c. 1630.

Owned by Sir Geoffrey Keynes, *Bibliotheca Bibliographici* No. 15, [no page numbers].

JnB 727 ----- -----

Copy in a verse miscellany; c. 1630.

Rosenbach Foundation, MS 239/23, p. 33.

JnB 728 ----- -----

Copy, headed 'Of Loue and Death', in a MS volume of poems chiefly by Henry King belonging to the Stoughton family of Warwick; c. 1636.

Owned by Rosemary Williams, London, Stoughton MS, p. 44.

JnB 729 *Sejanus his Fall.*

Extracts in a miscellany compiled partly by the Oxford printer Christopher Wase (1627-90); mid-17th century.

First pub. London, 1605; Herford & Simpson, IV, 327-486.

Bodleian, MS Rawl. poet. 117, f. 149v rev.

JnB 730 -----

Extracts (11 pages) in a miscellany of proverbs, extracts, &c; mid-17th century.

Folger, MS V. a. 263, [no page numbers].

JnB 731 -----

Extracts in a miscellany; c. 1634-40.

University College London, MS Ogden 7/29, [no page numbers].

JnB 731.5 See Addenda, p. 631.

JnB 732 -----

Copy of part of Macro's speech beginning 'By you, that fooles call gods' (V, 390-9), in a miscellany; c. 1672.

British Library, Sloane MS 161, f. 28.

Sejanus his Fall

JnB 733 -----

Copy of the couplet beginning 'He that will thrive in state, he must neglect' (III, 736-7), in a miscellany probably compiled by members of the Cartwright family of Aynho, Northamptonshire; mid-17th century.

Bodleian, MS Don. e. 6, f. 17v.

--- -----

For the exempla inscribed by Jonson, see INTRODUCTION.

--- *The Silent Woman.*

See JnB 582-601.

JnB 734 *The Staple of News.*

Extracts, with comments on the play, in a miscellany compiled by Abraham Wright (1611-90); c. 1640.

First pub. London, 1631; Herford & Simpson, VI, 271-382. Wright's comments on f. 72v printed in Arthur C. Kirsch, 'A Caroline Commentary on the Drama', *MP*, 66 (1968-9), 256-61 (p. 256).

British Library, Add. MS 22608, ff. 69-70v, 72v.

JnB 735 *The Vision of Delight.*

Copy of the speeches of Phantasy (lines 57-125, beginning 'Bright Night, I obey thee, and am come at thy call'), transcribed probably from a text used at the original performance in 1617, in the Newcastle MS; c. 1620s-30s.

First pub. in *Workes* (London, 1640); Herford & Simpson, VII, 461-71. This MS collated in Herford & Simpson.

British Library, Harley MS 4955, ff. 40v-1.

JnB 736 ----- lines 237-42. Song: 'I was not wearier where I lay'.

Copy of Aurora's song in a musical setting probably by Nicholas Lanier in a MS songbook; mid-17th century.

Printed from this MS in J.P. Cutts, 'Ben Jonson's Masque "The Vision of Delight"', *N & Q*, 201 (February 1956), 64-7, and in MacDonald Emslie, 'Nicholas Lanier's Innovations in English Song', *M & L*, 41 (1960), 13-27 (pp. 23-4); edited in Sabol, *400 Songs & Dances*, No. 26.

British Library, Egerton MS 2013, f. 45v.

JnB 737 *Volpone.*

Extract in a verse miscellany probably compiled by an Oxford man and once owned by one William Bloys; c. 1630s.

First pub. London, 1607; Herford & Simpson, V, 1-137.

Bodleian, MS Rawl. poet. 142, f. 19v.

JnB 738 -----

Exemplum of the edition of 1607 with the text of the missing title page and last leaf supplied in MS; mid-late 17th century.

This item recorded in Herford & Simpson, V, 6, and collated.

Bodleian, Mal. 225 (4).

JnB 739 -----

Exemplum of the edition of 1607 with the text of the missing first two leaves and signature O supplied in MS; early 17th century.

This item recorded in Herford & Simpson, V, 7, and collated.

Owned before 1937 by the Clifton Shakspere Society; unlocated.

--- -----

For the exemplum inscribed to John Florio, see INTRODUCTION.

--- ----- III, vii, 166-83. Song: 'Come my Celia, let vs proue'.

See JnB 443-50.

--- ----- III, vii, 236-9. Song: 'That the curious may not know'.

See JnB 542-8.

MARGINALIA AND INSCRIPTIONS IN PRINTED BOOKS AND MANUSCRIPTS

See INTRCDUCTION.

Thomas Kyd

1558-94

ABBREVIATIONS

Boas *The Works of Thomas Kyd,* ed. Frederick S. Boas (Oxford, 1901).

For abbreviations used throughout Volume I, see p.xi.

INTRODUCTION

Except for two copies of an answer by 'T.K.', possibly Kyd, to well-known verses by Chidiock Tichborne, there are no known MSS of any of Kyd's works. Not even his *Spanish Tragedy* is to be found quoted in miscellanies.

Kyd's autograph is preserved, however, in the form of two letters which he wrote in 1593 denouncing the atheism of Marlowe and defending himself against a similar charge. Both are in the British Library. One letter (Harley MS 6949, ff. 218-19) is addressed to Sir John Puckering. It is reproduced in Boas (frontispiece, and text on pp. cviii-cx); in A. D. Wraight and Virginia F. Stern, *In Search of Christopher Marlowe* (London, 1965), p. 314; in Greg, *English Literary Autographs,* plate XV; and in Petti, *English Literary Hands,* No. 32. The second letter (Harley MS 6848, f. 154) was sent to Puckering or to one of the Lords of the Privy Council. It is reproduced in Wraight and Stern, p. 316, and in Greg, plate XV.

Fragments of an anonymous heretical disputation found among Kyd's papers (though not in his hand) are preserved in Harley MS 6848, ff. 187-9v. The fragments are printed, with a facsimile of one page, in Boas, pp. cx-cxiii; a facsimile of another page appears in Wraight and Stern, p. 239.

PB.

ARRANGEMENT

Verse KdT 1-2.

Thomas Kyd

VERSE

KyT 1 *Hendecasyllabon T.K. in Cygneam Cantionam Chidiochi Tychborne* ('Thy prime of youth is frozen with thy faults').

Copy, headed 'Answer', in a miscellany; early 17th century.

First pub. in *Verses of Prayse and Ioye* (London, 1586); Boas, pp. 340-1. Formerly among the Isham MSS at Lamport Hall, Northamptonshire, this MS recorded in *HMC*, 3rd Report (1872), Appendix, p. 252; printed from this MS in *The Complete Poems of Richard Barnfield*, ed. A.B Grosart (London, 1876), pp. 211-12: see RICHARD BARNFIELD, INTRODUCTION; not recorded in Boas.

Folger, MS V. a. 161, pp. 13-14.

KyT 2 -----

Copy, headed 'The Aunsweare to the same' [i.e. Tichborne's poem] and here beginning 'Thy theyme of youthe, is frozen with the faults', in a volume of state papers; c. 1610.

Not recorded in Boas.

Yale, Osborn Collection, fb 9, f. 30v.

John Leland

1506-52

ABBREVIATIONS

Smith *The Itinerary of John Leland*, ed. Lucy Toulmin Smith, 5 vols (London, 1907-10; reprinted, with a foreword by T. Kendrick, Carbondale, [1964]).

For abbreviations used throughout Volume I, see p.xi.

INTRODUCTION

The topographical and antiquarian writings of the 'King's Antiquary' to Henry VIII, John Leland, present extraordinary problems to the textual editor because of the state of disorder and incompleteness in which he left his major works and because of the proliferation of transcripts (many of original MSS which have subsequently decayed or been lost). Voluminous autographs of the so-called *Collectanea* (LeJ 16) and the *Itinerary* (LeJ 54) are preserved in the Bodleian, and there are a few other autograph portions belonging to these works (LeJ 17, 18, 55-6). To reconstruct anything approaching the complete texts, however, it would be necessary also to consult a variety of transcripts and extracts made by 16th, 17th and 18th-century antiquaries. The most extensive account of the MSS of these works remains that in Smith; page references to Smith are given in the entries below for all MSS mentioned or discussed in that edition.

Leland has left some autographs of other works (LeJ 3, 8, 12, 50, 90, 96-8), including his presentation verses on the coronation of Anne Boleyn (LeJ 8). The scribal copy of *Antiphilarchia* which he must have presented to Henry VIII likewise survives (LeJ 9). At least two more autographs are to be found, which have not received entries. One is a letter to Thomas Cromwell, 25 January 1536/7, now in the Public Record Office (SP. 1/115, p. 63); it is printed in *Letters and Papers Foreign and Domestic of Henry VIII*, Vol. XII, part 1 (1890), No. 230. The other is Leland's signature on an official document of 20 May 1545, also in the Public Record Office (E322/16/191): see *op. cit.*, Vol. XX, part 1 (1905), No. 776. In his account of Leland in the *DNB*, Sidney Lee claims that a printed exemplum of *Sedulii Scoti comment. in epistolas Pauli* (Basle, 1527) in Cambridge University Library has at the beginning an epigram in Leland's hand; however, neither of the two exempla of that edition now in this library (B*. 4. 15(c) and Sel. 3. 74[1]) contains such an epigram.

A list of works ascribed to Leland appears in John Bale, *Scriptorum illustrium Maioris Brytanniae catalogus* (Basle, 1557), pp. 671-2. A number of these works have never been identified, but some of Bale's titles (such as 'Descriptio Angliae') may well refer to transcripts of documents among Leland's miscellaneous collections rather than to original works: see T. C. Skeat, 'Two "Lost" Works by John Leland', *EHR*, 65 (1950), 505-8. The preface to the *Itinerary* — the account of his research which Leland presented to Henry VIII (preserved in his autograph: LeJ 90) — was printed by Bale in 1549 under the title *The Laboriouse Journey and Serche of Johan Leylande for Englandes Antiquitees* and so is listed in the *Index* as an independent work (LeJ 90-5). Two exempla of Bale's edition in the British Library (Department of Printed Books, 291. a. 48 and G. 2931), and possibly others elsewhere, have a missing word near the top of sig. F6^{v} supplied in Bale's autograph: see W. W. Greg, 'Pen-and-Ink Corrections', *RES*, 7 (1931), 337. Two transcripts of Bale's edition are not included in the entries. One, made by Robert Vaughan of Hengwrt (1592?-1667), is now in the National Library of Wales (Peniarth MS 274D, pp. 143-93); the other, made by Thomas Hearne (1678-1735), is now in the Bodleian (MS Rawl. B. 254, ff. 1-17).

There are a few other miscellaneous items of interest. A transcript of *Laudatio pacis* (London, 1546) made by Richard Rawlinson (1690-1755) and owned in 1710 by Thomas Hearne is in the Bodleian (MS Rawl. D. 1208, ff. 11-17). A contemporary transcript of Hearne's entire edition of the *Itinerary* (9 vols, Oxford, 1710-12) is also in the Bodleian (MSS St Edmund Hall 41-9). A 19th-century extract from the same edition is among the archives of Lord Egremont at Petworth House (Archives 2954). In his *Remarks and Collections* (ed. C. E. Doble, II (Oxford, 1886), 227) Hearne notes that an Elizabethan transcript of the *Itinerary* ('being taken from the originals before they took wet, as is suppos'd') was once owned by James Wright (1643-1713) but was consumed in a fire at the Middle Temple in 1678. Various printed exempla of Leland's works contain notable annotations by readers: for instance, exempla of three of his poems and tracts in the British Library (Department of Printed Books, C. 95. c. 15 (1, 3,4)) have annotations by the antiquary William Lambarde (1536-1601). Copies are also to be found of medieval documents which Leland used in his work (e.g. MS Dugdale 11, ff. 1-8, in the Bodleian, and Cotton MSS Cleopatra C. III, f. 220, and Domitian A. VIII, ff. 119-20v, in the British Library), but it would be impossible to determine all his sources of information or exactly which extant documents he is likely to have handled. Indeed, the value of Leland's *Collectanea* lies in the uniqueness of his position as the King's Antiquary at the time of the dissolution of the monasteries, when he was able to examine and transcribe so much material which was subsequently lost or dispersed.

A brief early-18th-century account of Leland was published as *The Life of John Leland (the First English Antiquary) with extensive notes and a bibliography of his works ... printed from a hitherto unpublished work (by the learned Edward Burton)* (London, 1896). Eight pages of Burton's working papers of his account (formerly Phillipps MS 8232) are now in the Bodleian (MS Eng. misc. a. 21).

PB.

ARRANGEMENT

Verse	LeJ 1-8
Prose	LeJ 9-95
Marginalia in printed books and manuscripts	LeJ 96-8.

FACSIMILE XXIII — John Leland: Two pages of *The Itinerary of John Leland*, c. 1540-45 (LeJ 54). Bodleian Library, MS Top. gen. e. 9, folios 18 verso and 19 recto. Reproduced by permission of the Curators of the Bodleian Library.

possessions and as in that gave
hym S. Waleries.

Robert Dilley had a brother caullid
Nigellus, of whom be no verre
famose thinges written
Nigellus had a sunne caullid
Robert that provid a very noble
man
This Robert the 2. had a wife
caullid Edith Forne a woman
of fame and highly estemid with
Henry the Kyng, by whose procuration
Robert weddid hir
This Robert began the priorie of
blake chanons at Oseney by Oxford
emong the isles that Isis ryver
ther makith.
Sum write that this was the occasion of making of it. Edith usid
to walk out of Oxford castelle with
her gentilwomen to solace and that
often tymes. Wher yn a certen
place in a tre as often as she cam
a certen pies usid to gether to it
and ther to chattre, and as it wer
to speke on to her

mater and this [illegible] tyme sore fe-
rid as of a wonder
Wherapon she sent for one Radulph
a chanon of S. Fridiswides a man
of a vertuus life and her confessor
asking hym counsel: to who he answe-
rid after that he had seene
the fascion of the pies chattering
oly at her cumming, that she should buil-
de in church or monasterie in that
place: then she entreatid her husband
to build a priorie and so he did
making Radulph the first prior
of it.
The cumming of Edith to Oseney
and Radulph waiting on her: and
the tre with the chattering pies
be paintid in the walle of tharch
over Edith tumbe in Oseney priorie.
There lyith an image of Edith of stone in thab-
bite of a wowes holding a hart
in her right hond on the north side
of the high altare
Robert Dilley the 2. fonder of
Oseney priorie was buried in thabbay
of Eynesham a 3 mile fro Oxford

John Leland

VERSE

LeJ 1 *Laudatio pacis* ('Martia bella canant alij, gladiosque cruentos').

Exemplum of the edition of 1546 with a few MS corrections; 16th century.

First pub. London, 1546; reprinted in *Joannis Lelandi...collectanea*, ed. Thomas Hearne, 3rd edition (London, 1774), V, 69-78. This item recorded in James Hutton, 'John Leland's *Laudatio pacis*', *SP*, 58 (1961), 616-26.

British Library, Department of Printed Books, 1075. m. 16 (3), pp. 219-33.

--- -----

See also INTRODUCTION.

LeJ 2 [*Poemata*].

Copy of Leland's Latin epigrams transcribed from his autograph by John Stow (1525?-1605); c. 1576.

Many of Leland's Latin epigrams pub. in *Principum, ac illustrium aliquot & eruditorum in Anglia virorum, encomia, trophaea, genethliaca & epithalamia*, ed. Thomas Newton (London, 1589); reprinted in *Joannis Lelandi... collectanea*, ed. Thomas Hearne, 3rd edition (London, 1774), V, 79-167. Twenty-eight poems printed from this MS in Leicester Bradner, 'Some Unpublished Poems by John Leland', *PMLA*, 71.ii (1956), 827-36. Leland's original autograph is now lost.

Bodleian, MS Tanner 464, Vol. IV.

*LeJ 3 -----

Autograph Latin verses, beginning 'Aethelstanus erat nostre pars maxima cure', inscribed in a 10th-century MS of the Four Gospels in Latin.

These verses appear in Stow's transcript (LeJ 2), p. 17.

British Library, Royal MS 1 A. XVIII, f. 2v.

LeJ 4 -----

Copy of a large number of Leland's Latin poems in a miscellany compiled by one John Jones of Gellilvydy; imperfect; c. 1611.

National Library of Wales, Peniarth MS 364B, Part i, pp. [27-86].

LeJ 5 -----

Copy of five of Leland's Latin epigrams in the hand of John Bale, in his MS epitome of Leland's *Commentarii de scriptoribus Britannicis* (see BaJ 23); c. 1552-7.

Trinity College, Cambridge, MS R. 7. 15 (James 753), ff. 3-5.

LeJ 6 -----

Copy of two Latin poems ascribed to 'Lelandus' in an antiquarian miscellany compiled by William Wyrley (1565-c.1613); late 16th-early 17th century.

Formerly Phillipps MS 13152; this MS sold at Sotheby's, 15 June 1971, Lot 1649.

University of Birmingham, MS 7/i/16, f. 106.

LeJ 7 -----

Copy of an epigram on Cambridge University, headed 'Jhoannes Lelandus antiquarius composuit sequens epigramma' and beginning 'Olim granta fuit titulis vrbs inclyta multis', in a MS copy of William Whitlock's *Chronicon Lichefeldensis Ecclesie*; 2nd half 16th century.

Bodleian, MS Ashmole 770, f. 12v.

--- -----

See also LeJ 9-11.

*LeJ 8 [*Verses made at the Coronation of Queen Anne*].

Autograph fair copy of Leland's Latin verses, together with Nicholas Udall's autograph English and Latin verses (see UdN 1), for the coronation procession of Queen Anne Boleyn, 31 May 1533; presumably the copy presented to the Queen; [1533].

First pub. (from this MS) in John Nichols, *The Progresses and Public Processions of Queen Elizabeth*, I (London, 1788), i-xx; printed from this MS in F.J. Furnivall, 'Leland's and Udall's Verses before the Coronation of Anne Boleyn', *Ballads from Manuscripts*, Ballad Society (London, 1870), I, 364-401. Facsimile of one page (Leland's hand in the lower half) in Alfred Fairbank and Berthold Wolpe, *Renaissance Handwriting: An Anthology of Italic Scripts* (London, 1960), plate 23. J.P. Collier's transcript of the MS (c. 1850) is in the Folger, MS N. b. 48.

British Library, Royal MS 18 A. LXIV.

PROSE

LeJ 9 *Antiphilarchia.*

Fair copy, with two preliminary Latin epigrams, in a single scribal hand; the copy presented by Leland to Henry VIII; owned in 1586 by Thomas Knyvet; 187 leaves; 1540s.

Unpublished.

Cambridge University Library, MS Ee. 5. 14.

LeJ 10 -----

Copy transcribed from LeJ 9; once owned by Thomas Baker (1656-1740) who gave it to Thomas Hearne; 13 June 1625.

Bodleian, MS Rawl. C. 186.

LeJ 11 -----

Copy in a volume of papers collected by Thomas Hearne; c. 1717.

Bodleian, MS Rawl. B. 198.

*LeJ 12 *Antiquitates Britanniae.*

Autograph; imperfect and lacking a title; in a composite volume of Leland's works; c. 1535-45.

Unpublished; discussed in T.C. Skeat, 'Two "Lost" Works by John Leland', *EHR*, 65 (1950), 505-8.

British Library, Cotton MS Julius C. VI, ff. 1-89.

LeJ 13 -----

Extracts from Leland's autograph transcribed by John Bale in his *Index Britanniae scriptorum* (see BaJ 22); c. 1549-57.

Printed from this MS in John Bale, *Index Britanniae scriptorum*, ed. R.L. Poole and M. Bateson (Oxford, 1902); recorded in Skeat, p. 506.

Bodleian, MS Selden Supra 64, ff. 7v, 114, 262v-3.

LeJ 14 -----

Extracts from Leland's autograph transcribed by William Camden, in a composite volume of historical MSS (see CmW 148); late 16th-early 17th century.

This MS recorded in Skeat, p. 506.

British Library, Cotton MS Julius F. X, ff. 103, 157v-9, 163-4v.

LeJ 15 *Assertio inclytissimi Arturii regis Britanniae.*

Copy of an anonymous English translation of Leland's work (not Robinson's translation); imperfect; late 16th century.

First pub. London, 1544; ed. William Edward Mead in Christopher Middleton, *The famous Historie of Chinon of England*, EETS, 165 (London, 1925); Richard Robinson's translation pub. London, 1582.

Bodleian, MS Top. gen. e. 46.

*LeJ 16 *Collectanea.*

Autograph, bound in three volumes, a few pages in a scribal hand with autograph corrections and revisions; c. 1545.

First pub. (from this MS) in *J. Lelandi antiquarii de rebus Britannicis collectanea*, ed. Thomas Hearne, 6 vols (Oxford, 1715; 2nd. edition London, 1770; 3rd edition London, 1774). This MS recorded in Smith, I, xx.

Bodleian, MSS Top. gen. c. 1-3.

*LeJ 17 -----

A portion of the *Collectanea*, all in Leland's autograph except a list of religious houses (ff. 28-38) which is in the hand of a scribe with autograph corrections and revisions; owned in 1677 by Sir Henry St George (1625-1715); c. 1536-45.

Formerly Phillipps MS 12111; this MS recorded in Smith, I, xxx, et passim. Facsimile examples of ff. 16v, 17v, in Greg, *English Literary Autographs*, plate CI, and Petti, *English Literary Hands*, No. 21.

British Library, Add. MS 38132.

*LeJ 18 -----

List of books in monastic libraries and extracts from Latin poets and other writers, partly autograph, partly in a scribal hand, in a composite volume of historical MSS; imperfect; c. 1535-43.

This MS recorded in Smith, V, xiv.

British Library, Cotton MS Vitellius C. IX, ff. 233-4v, 240-51v.

LeJ 19 -----

Lists of MSS in Lincolnshire monasteries probably compiled by Leland, in a scribal hand, prepared for and annotated by Henry VIII; headed 'Tabula librorum de Historiis antiquitatum ac diuinitate tractancium in librariis et domibus religiosis'; c. 1536-8.

Printed from this MS in J.R. Liddell, '"Leland's"

Lists of Manuscripts in Lincolnshire Monasteries', *EHR*, 213 (1939), 88-95; discussed, with a facsimile page, in Francis Wormald and C.E. Wright, *The English Library before 1700* (London, 1958), pp. 161-2 and plate 12.

British Library, Royal MS App. 69.

LeJ 20 ----- [*Stow transcript*].

Portions of the *Collectanea* transcribed from Leland's autograph by John Stow (1525?-1605); c. 1576.

This MS recorded in Smith, I, xxiii.

Bodleian, MS Tanner 464, Vol. I.

LeJ 21 ----- -----

Extracts transcribed by John Stow, in a composite volume of antiquarian MSS collected by Francis Thynne, Lancaster Herald (1545?-1608); late 16th century.

This MS recorded in Smith, V, xii.

British Library, Cotton MS Cleopatra C. III, ff. 301-19v.

LeJ 22 ----- -----

Extracts transcribed by John Stow, headed 'Excerpta ex Lelando de libris, quos ille reperit in biblothecis Monasteriorum', in a composite volume of historical MSS; imperfect; 1576.

British Library, Cotton MS Tiberius E. VIII, ff. 237-54v.

LeJ 23 ----- -----

Extracts transcribed from one of John Stow's transcripts, in a volume of antiquarian collections compiled by Robert Glover, Somerset Herald (1544-88); late 16th century.

Bodleian, MS Ashmole 848, ff. 1-6.

LeJ 24 ----- -----

Portions of the *Collectanea* transcribed from one of John Stow's transcripts by Robert Vaughan of Hengwrt (1592?-1667); imperfect; mid-17th century.

National Library of Wales, Peniarth MS 273, Part i, pp. 1-360.

LeJ 25 ----- [*Burton transcript*].

Extracts transcribed from Leland's autograph by William Burton (1575-1645), in Burton's MS volume of Leland's works; [1628-41].

This MS recorded in Smith, I, xxv-xxvii.

Bodleian, MS Gough, Gen. Top. 2, ff. 157-62, 165.

LeJ 26 ----- -----

Extracts transcribed by William Burton, in a MS volume of Leland's works; [1628-41].

This MS recorded in Smith, V, xii.

British Library, Cotton MS Julius C. VI, ff. 233-43.

LeJ 27 ----- [*Dugdale transcript*].

Copy of parts of the *Collectanea* in three volumes; Volume I entirely in the hand of Sir William Dugdale (1605-86); Volumes II and III in the hand of an amanuensis; all three volumes containing Dugdale's autograph indexes, dated July-August 1657; among the papers of the Hatton family, formerly of Holdenby and Kirby Hall, Northamptonshire.

These MSS recorded in *HMC*, 1st Report (1870), Appendix, p. 31.

Northamptonshire Record Office, F.H. 2664, 114, 115.

LeJ 28 ----- -----

Copy of parts of the *Collectanea* in the hand of Sir William Dugdale; c. 1657?

This MS recorded in Smith, V, xiii.

British Library, Harley MS 6193.

LeJ 29 ----- -----

Copy of a portion of the *Collectanea*, transcribed from Leland's autograph (LeJ 17) by Sir William Dugdale, in a small volume of Dugdale's antiquarian collections; 1677.

This MS recorded in Smith, I, xxx; II, 117.

Bodleian, MS Eng. hist. c. 9, ff. 33-41.

LeJ 30 ----- -----

Extracts from Leland's works -- probably the *Collectanea* and perhaps the *Itinerary* -- transcribed from a book of notes (notebook 'M') made by Sir William Dugdale, in a volume of historical collections compiled by the antiquary Roger Dodsworth (1585-1654); c. 1642-51.

Bodleian, MS Dodsw. 105, f. 97.

LeJ 31 ----- [*Other transcripts and extracts*].

Brief extracts transcribed by Elias Ashmole (1617-92) in his MS collection for a History of the Order of the Garter; mid-late 17th century.

Bodleian, MS Ashmole 1115, f. 94r-v.

Collectanea [Other transcripts and extracts]

LeJ 32 ----- -----

Extracts transcribed by Anthony Wood (1632-95), in a MS volume of his papers and those of Thomas Rawlins; 17 June 1660.

Bodleian, MS Ballard 70, ff. 1-15.

LeJ 33 ----- -----

Copy of a portion of the *Collectanea*, transcribed from Leland's autograph (LeJ 17) for the antiquary Robert Plot (1640-96); 1682.

This MS recorded in Smith, I, xxx; II, 117.

Bodleian, MS Bodl. 353.

LeJ 34 ----- -----

Extracts in a composite volume of theological and state tracts; mid-17th century.

Bodleian, MS CCC. 288, ff. 290-2.

LeJ 35 ----- -----

Extracts, transcribed from an antiquarian collection of St Loe Kniveton of Gray's Inn, together with extracts from Francis Thynne's calendars of public records, in a volume of historical collections compiled by the antiquary Roger Dodsworth (1585-1654); c. 1636.

Bodleian, MS Dodsw. 82, ff. 1-10.

LeJ 36 ----- -----

Extracts in a volume of historical collections compiled by the historian Sir James Ware (1594-1666); c. 1644-55.

Bodleian, MS Rawl. B. 479, ff. 30v-3.

LeJ 37 ----- -----

Notes of Leland's list of books in various monastic libraries taken from the *Collectanea*, in a miscellany; late 17th century.

Bodleian, MS Rawl. D. 1493, ff. 196-9v.

LeJ 38 ----- -----

List of the contents of the *Collectanea* in the hand of the antiquary Browne Willis (1682-1760) of Whaddon Hall, near Winslow, Buckinghamshire, in a volume of Willis's antiquarian collections; early 18th century.

Bodleian, MS Willis 5, ff. 106v-14.

LeJ 39 ----- -----

Extract relating to Staffordshire families, transcribed by Sir Henry St George (1625-1715) from a leaf of Leland's autograph which once formed part of LeJ 17 (and is now lost), in a MS volume of genealogical and historical collections; [1703].

This MS recorded in Smith, I, xxi, xxx; printed II, 117 seq.

British Library, Add. MS 5937, ff. 203-5.

LeJ 40 ----- -----

Extracts in a MS volume of Leland's works; late 16th century.

This MS recorded in Smith, V, xii.

British Library, Cotton MS Julius C. VI, passim between ff. 90 and 191.

LeJ 41 ----- -----

List of witnesses from eight or nine old charters, copied 'ex Lelando', probably from the *Collectanea*, in a volume of historical collections; 16th century.

This MS recorded in Smith, V, xiv.

British Library, Cotton MS Vespasian B. XV, f. 40.

LeJ 42 ----- -----

Notes 'ex aliis diversis Collectaneis Johanni Leilandi', in a volume of antiquarian collections compiled by William Camden (see CmW 155); 1573.

This MS recorded in Smith, V, xii.

British Library, Lansdowne MS 229, ff. 88-99.

LeJ 43 ----- -----

Extracts in Volume XXIX of the miscellaneous historical collections of Bishop White Kennett (1660-1728); the first group headed 'ex Collectaneis Johannis Lelandi, MS., 4to, vol. 2' (i.e. transcribed either from a lost volume of the *Collectanea* or partly from a MS of Part II of the *Itinerary*); 17th century.

This MS recorded in Smith, V, xiii-xiv.

British Library, Lansdowne MS 963, ff. 15v-16v, 177-86.

LeJ 44 ----- -----

Extract in a volume of historical collections; 18th century.

This MS recorded in Smith, V, xiv.

British Library, Stowe MS 305, f. 296.

Collectanea [*Other transcripts and extracts*]

LeJ 45 ----- -----

Notes taken from the *Collectanea* by one 'R.K.', in a volume of historical, topographical and antiquarian collections; 18th century.

This MS recorded in Smith, V, xiv.

British Library, Stowe MS 1048, ff. 24, 12v rev.

LeJ 46 ----- -----

Extract in a volume of collections on ecclesiastical history compiled by Henry Wharton (1664-95); late 17th century.

Lambeth Palace, MS 585, p. 120.

LeJ 47 ----- -----

Latin extracts from the Life of St Winifred by Robert, Prior of Shrewsbury, transcribed from Leland's autograph of the *Collectanea*, in a MS volume of extracts from antiquarian collections possibly transcribed for Sir Thomas Mostyn (1651-c.1700); late 17th century.

Formerly Mostyn MS 255, this MS recorded in *HMC*, 4th Report (1874), Appendix, p. 360.

National Library of Wales, NLW. MS 21246D, ff. 47-8v.

LeJ 48 ----- -----

An index of Leland's sources for his *Collectanea*, probably compiled by Thomas Gale (1635?-1702); late 17th century.

Trinity College, Cambridge, MS O. 3. 33 (James 1205).

LeJ 49 ----- -----

Copy (on ff. 1-25) of a portion of the *Collectanea*, transcribed from Leland's autograph (LeJ 17), with annotations in a different ink; followed by various extracts from the *Collectanea* in another hand with an index at the end; 17th century.

See also LeJ 88.

Trinity College, Cambridge, MS O. 10. 25 (James 1477).

--- -----

See also INTRODUCTION.

--- ----- *Antiquitates Britanniae.*

See LeJ 12-14.

*LeJ 50 *Commentarii de scriptoribus Britannicis.*

Autograph, entitled c. 1612 by William Burton (1575-1645) 'De Scriptoribus Illustribus Britanniae'; c. 1545.

First pub. Oxford, 1709, ed. A. Hall, 2 vols. Facsimile of p. 198 of this MS in Theodore Besterman, *The Beginnings of Systematic Bibliography*, 2nd edition (London, 1936), facing p. 20.

Bodleian, MS Top. gen. c. 4.

LeJ 51 -----

Exemplum of the edition of 1709 with annotations in the hand of Thomas Hearne collating the printed text to p. 132 with Leland's autograph; c. 1709-16.

Bodleian, 8° Rawl. 57.

LeJ 52 -----

Extracts transcribed from Leland's autograph, in a volume of historical collections compiled by the historian Sir James Ware (1594-1666); 25 November 1644.

Bodleian, MS Rawl. B. 479, ff. 1-22v.

LeJ 53 -----

Copy in two hands, with additions and indexes by Thomas Gale (1635?-1702); 17th century.

Trinity College, Cambridge, MSS O. 10. 6, 7 (James 1458-9).

--- -----

See also JOHN BALE, BaJ 23.

*LeJ 54 *The Itinerary of John Leland.*

Autograph, bound in eight volumes; imperfect; c. 1540-45.

First pub. (from this MS) Oxford, 1710-12, ed. Thomas Hearne, 9 vols; edited from this MS in Smith. See FACSIMILE XXIII.

Bodleian, MSS Top. gen. e. 8-15.

*LeJ 55 -----

Autograph of several passages belonging to the *Itinerary*, in the third volume of the autograph of the *Collectanea*; c. 1535-43.

This MS recorded in Smith, I, xxx; printed III, 127; IV, 164 seq.

Bodleian, MS Top. gen. c. 3, pp. 96-8, 107, 117-24, 149-52, et passim.

The Itinerary

*LeJ 56 -----

Autograph fragment, consisting of two leaves taken from one of Leland's quarto MS volumes of the *Itinerary*, in a composite volume of historical papers; c. 1535-43.

Printed from this MS in Smith, I, 327-9.

British Library, Cotton MS Vespasian F. IX, ff. 198-9.

LeJ 57 ----- [*Stow transcript*].

Copy of the *Itinerary* in ten parts, transcribed from Leland's autograph by John Stow (1525?-1605); entitled 'Comentaria Angliae John Layland'; c. 1576.

This MS recorded in Smith, I, xxii-xxiv.

Bodleian, MS Tanner 464, Vols. II, III and V.

LeJ 58 ----- -----

Copy, transcribed from John Stow's transcript (LeJ 57) by Robert Vaughan of Hengwrt (1592?-1667); headed 'Comentarii Angliae John Leyland 1542 of late written by Jon Stow An^o Dni 1576'; incomplete; mid-17th century.

This MS recorded in Smith, III, vi (n).

National Library of Wales, Peniarth MS 273, Part i, pp. 361-741.

LeJ 59 ----- -----

Copy of part of the fifth volume of Leland's autograph transcribed from Stow's transcript (LeJ 57) for Robert Vaughan of Hengwrt; headed 'Comentarij Anglia 4. bookes by Jo^n Leyland written by John Stow in Anno. 1576. Collegis in Kent'; imperfect; mid-17th century.

This MS recorded in Smith, III, vi (n).

National Library of Wales, Peniarth MS 273, Part ii.

LeJ 60 ----- [*Burton transcript*].

Copy of five 'parts', transcribed from Leland's autograph by William Burton (1575-1645), in Burton's MS volume of Leland's works; [1628-c.1641].

This MS recorded in Smith, I, xxv.

Bodleian, MS Gough, Gen. Top. 2, ff. 1-156, 224-8, 241-52.

LeJ 61 ----- -----

Copy of five 'parts', transcribed from Leland's autograph for William Burton and presented by him to the Bodleian; c. 1632.

This MS recorded in Smith, I, xxvi.

Bodleian, MS Bodl. 470.

LeJ 62 ----- -----

Copy of five 'parts', transcribed from William Burton's scribal transcript (LeJ 61) in two hands; late 17th-early 18th century.

This MS recorded in Smith, I, xxix.

Bodleian, MS Gough, Gen. Top. 1.

LeJ 63 ----- [*Dugdale transcript*].

Copy of nine 'books' in the hand of Sir William Dugdale (1605-86); ff. 263-323 comprising 'Divers Passages omitted in the Copy in the Oxford Library transcribed out of Stows Copy in the Custody of Mr Robert Vaughan of Henwrt in Merioneth'; with (ff. 260-2v) Dugdale's index, dated 15 July 1657.

This MS recorded in Smith, I, xxviii-xxix.

British Library, Harley MS 6266, ff. 8-323.

LeJ 64 ----- -----

Copy of seven 'parts' transcribed for Sir William Dugdale, with his autograph index, dated 15 July 1657; among the papers of the Hatton family, formerly of Holdenby and Kirby Hall, Northamptonshire.

This MS recorded in *HMC*, 1st Report (1870), Appendix, p. 31.

Northamptonshire Record Office, F.H. 116.

LeJ 65 ----- -----

Copy of seven 'books', transcribed probably for Sir William Dugdale and including (ff. 254-61) his index (dated 15 July 1657); c. 1657?

This MS recorded in Smith, I, xxix.

British Library, Harley MS 1346.

LeJ 66 ----- -----

Copy of seven 'parts', including Dugdale's index; containing a note by Narcissus Luttrell (1657-1732) saying that the MS was copied from one belonging to Robert Harley (? LeJ 65) and that Luttrell had checked it against the original; 2nd half 17th century.

All Souls College, Oxford, MS 99.

LeJ 67 ----- [*Other transcripts and extracts*].

Copy of most of the first three volumes of Leland's autograph, transcribed by Thomas Gale

(1635?-1702); late 17th century.

This MS recorded in Smith, I, xxix.

Trinity College, Cambridge, MS O. 5. 25 (James 1306).

LeJ 68 ----- -----

Copy of most of the first four volumes of Leland's autograph transcribed by Browne Willis (1682-1760) while at Christ Church, Oxford; May 1704.

This MS recorded in Smith, I, xxix-xxx.

Bodleian, MS Top. gen. c. 5.

LeJ 69 ----- -----

Extracts, in a volume of antiquarian collections concerning Lichfield compiled by Elias Ashmole (1617-92); mid-late 17th century.

Bodleian, MS Ashmole 855, pp. 3-9.

LeJ 70 ----- -----

Extracts from seven 'books', followed by an attempt to draw up a regular itinerary of Leland's journeys, in a volume of antiquarian collections compiled by Elias Ashmole; 8 October 1659.

This MS recorded in Smith, I, xxix.

Bodleian, MS Ashmole 861, ff. 354-407.

LeJ 71 ----- -----

Copy of part of the fourth volume of Leland's autograph, in a volume of theological and state tracts; mid-17th century.

Bodleian, MS CCC. 288, ff. 293-351.

LeJ 72 ----- -----

Copy of the pedigree of the Tregoz family taken from Leland's *Itinerary*, in a volume of heraldic and genealogical collections compiled by Sir Richard St George (c.1555-1635); c. 1586-1619.

Bodleian, MS Rawl. B . 103, f. 113.

LeJ 73 ----- -----

Part of a transcript of Leland's autograph made by Thomas Hearne, in one of Hearne's miscellaneous collections; early 18th century.

Bodleian, MS Rawl. D. 732, ff. 187-289.

LeJ 74 ----- -----

Copy of a list of monastic houses in England, 'abstracted chiefly from Leland's Itinerary', with corrections and additions in another hand; c. 1565-1600.

Bodleian, MS Rawl. D. 1075.

LeJ 75 ----- -----

Fragment of a copy of the *Itinerary* in a volume of collections relating to Devon compiled by Jeremiah Milles, Dean of Exeter (1714-84); 18th century.

Bodleian, MS Top. Devon. b. 6, ff. 23-49.

LeJ 76 ----- -----

Extracts transcribed by Dr Richard Furney, archdeacon of Surrey (d. 1753), in a volume of collections relating to Gloucestershire; early 18th century.

Bodleian, MS Top. Glouc. c. 2, f. 226 seq.

LeJ 77 ----- -----

Extracts in a volume of collections relating to Gloucestershire; 1st half 18th century.

Bodleian, MS Top. Glouc. c. 6, f. 4 seq.

LeJ 78 ----- -----

Extracts transcribed from MS sources in the Bodleian, in a volume of collections relating to Salop compiled by William Mytton (1694/5-1746) of Halston and Edward Lloyd of Trenewith; c. 1733.

British Library, Add. MS 30323, ff. 19v-22.

LeJ 79 ----- -----

Extracts from Part II transcribed by Francis Thynne, Lancaster Herald (1545?-1608) (ff. 67v-87v); 17 December 1589; with a few other miscellaneous notes from the *Itinerary* (ff. 179v, 199v-201); in one of Thynne's volumes of antiquarian collections.

This MS recorded in Smith, V, xii.

British Library, Cotton MS Cleopatra C. III, ff. 67v-87v, 179v, 199v-201.

LeJ 80 ----- -----

Copy of Part I, with a few other extracts in another hand, in a MS volume of Leland's works; late 16th-17th century.

This MS recorded in Smith, V, xii.

British Library, Cotton MS Julius C. VI, ff. 192-232, and passim after f. 90.

The Itinerary [*Other transcripts and extracts*]

LeJ 81 ----- -----

Extracts arranged according to the counties of England and Wales; late 16th-early 17th century.

This MS recorded in Smith, V, xii-xiii.

British Library, Harley MS 842.

LeJ 82 ----- -----

Notes from the *Itinerary* in a volume of antiquarian collections compiled by William Camden (see CmW 155); 1573.

This MS recorded in Smith, V, xii.

British Library, Lansdowne MS 229, ff. 83-7v.

LeJ 83 ----- -----

List of the names of counties and towns along Leland's routes and, in another hand, an extract concerning the Priory of Snelleshall, Staunford, &c; in a composite volume of MSS; late 17th-early 18th century.

This MS recorded in Smith, V, xiii.

British Library, Lansdowne MS 825, ff. 19-21, 53-4v.

LeJ 84 ----- -----

Extracts in several hands, in Volume VI of the miscellaneous historical collections of Bishop White Kennett (1660-1728); 17th century.

This MS recorded in Smith, V, xiii.

British Library, Lansdowne MS 940, ff. 122-54.

LeJ 85 ----- -----

Extracts transcribed from Leland's autograph, in a volume of collections on ecclesiastical history compiled by Henry Wharton (1664-95); late 17th century.

Lambeth Palace, MS 585, pp. 115-18.

LeJ 86 -----

Extracts relating to Pontefract, transcribed from the papers of Dr Nathaniel Johnston (1627-1705) of Pontefract, in a volume of antiquarian collections; 18th century.

Formerly among the Bacon Frank papers at Campsall Hall, Yorkshire, this MS recorded in *HMC*, 6th Report (1877), Appendix, p. 448.

Leeds Archives Department, BF. B. 3, pp. 104-26.

LeJ 87 ----- -----

Copy of part of the *Itinerary* relating to Wales, possibly transcribed for Sir Thomas Mostyn (1651-c.1700); late 17th century.

Formerly Mostyn MS 255, this MS recorded in *HMC*, 4th Report (1874), Appendix, p. 360.

National Library of Wales, NLW. MS 21246D, ff. 1-42.

LeJ 88 ----- -----

Extracts in a MS copy of parts of the *Collectanea* (see LeJ 49); 17th century.

Trinity College, Cambridge, MS O. 10. 25 (James 1477), passim.

LeJ 89 ----- -----

Copy of part of the *Itinerary* relating to Kent, in a composite volume of MSS chiefly concerning Kent; 18th century?

Formerly MS XXXI (item 4) among the papers of the Towneley family at Towneley Hall, Burnley, Lancashire; this MS recorded in *HMC*, 4th Report (1874), Appendix, p. 412.

Unlocated.

--- -----

See also LeJ 43, 90-5, and INTRODUCTION.

*LeJ 90 *The Laboryouse Journey and Serche of Johan Leylande for Englandes Antiquitees.*

Autograph, untitled, at the end of the third volume of the *Collectanea* (see LeJ 16); c. 1545.

First pub. London, 1549, ed. John Bale. Printed from this MS in Smith, I, xxxvii-xliii.

Bodleian, MS Top. gen. c. 3, p. 281 seq.

LeJ 91 -----

Copy transcribed from Leland's autograph by William Burton (1575-1645), in Burton's MS volume of Leland's works; 1628.

This MS recorded in Smith, I, xxv.

Bodleian, MS Gough Gen. Top. 2, f. 1 seq.

LeJ 92 -----

Copy transcribed from Leland's autograph for William Burton, at the beginning of a MS copy of the *Itinerary* presented by Burton to the Bodleian (see LeJ 61); c. 1632.

Bodleian, MS Bodl. 470, ff. 1-2.

LeJ 93 -----

Copy, transcribed from LeJ 92, at the beginning of a MS copy of the *Itinerary* (see LeJ 62); late 17th-early 18th century.

This MS recorded in Smith, I, xxix.

Bodleian, MS Gough Gen. Top. 1.

LeJ 94 -----

Copy in the hand of Sir William Dugdale (1605-86), at the beginning of his copy of the *Itinerary* (see LeJ 63); 1657.

British Library, Harley MS 6266, ff. 5-7.

LeJ 95 -----

Copy in a volume of historical collections compiled by William Petyt (1637-1707); 17th century.

Inner Temple Library, Petyt MS 535, Vol. 6, ff. 129-33.

--- -----

See also INTRODUCTION.

--- *Tabula librorum de historiis antiquitatum ac diuinitate tractancium in librariis et domibus religiosis.*

See LeJ 19.

MARGINALIA IN PRINTED BOOKS AND MANUSCRIPTS

--- *The Four Gospels.*

See LeJ 3.

*LeJ 96 Giraldus Cambrensis. *De instructione principium.*

14th-century MS with Leland's autograph annotations.

This probably the MS referred to in John Bale, *Index Britanniae scriptorum*, ed. R. Lane Poole and M. Bateson (Oxford, 1902), p. 425.

British Library, Cotton MS Julius B. XIII, ff. 48-173.

*LeJ 97 Homer's *Iliad*: Latin translation by L. Valla (Cologne, 1522).

Autograph annotations.

British Library, Department of Printed Books, 832. a. 34.

*LeJ 98 *Vitae illustrium virorum.*

A MS volume of lives of saints (entitled by Leland 'Vitae illustrium virorum') owned by Henry VIII, with Leland's autograph note (f. ii^{v}) comparing Plutarch and Sulpicius Severus as biographers; c. 1528-43.

Bodleian, MS Bodl. 354.

Sir David Lindsay

1490?-1555

ABBREVIATIONS

Hamer *The Works of Sir David Lindsay of the Mount 1490-1555*, ed. Douglas Hamer, 4 vols, STS 3rd Ser. 1, 2, 6, 8 (Edinburgh & London, 1930-4).

For abbreviations used throughout Volume I, see p.xi.

INTRODUCTION

The few extant MSS of works by Sir David Lindsay are all collated or described in Hamer. None is in Lindsay's own hand. What appears to be his only surviving autograph is a letter he sent to the Scottish Secretary from Antwerp, 23 August 1531, now in the British Library (Cotton MS Caligula B. I, f. 313). It is printed in Hamer, IV, 255. It is also transcribed, with a facsimile of the signature alone, in *The Poetical Works of Sir David Lyndsay of the Mount*, ed. David Laing, 2 vols (Edinburgh, 1879), I, xxiv-xxvi, and see FACSIMILE XXIV. For information about other early documents relating to Lindsay, see Hamer, IV, 241-77.

PB.

ARRANGEMENT

FACSIMILE XXIV — Sir David Lindsay: Letter to the Secretary of State for Scotland, 23 August 1531. British Library, Cotton MS Caligula B.I, folio 313 recto. Reproduced by permission of the British Library.

My lord I recommend me hartly seruice on to your l. plese your l. to wit yt I com to brussellis ye iij day of Julij
quhar I fand ye empriour and gat presens of his maiestie ye iiij day eftir my cuming and hes gottin gud expeditioun
of ye commissioun and yt I was send for and hes gottin ye auld alliances and confirmationis conforme for ye space
of ane hundreth yeir for ye quhilk confirmatioun I haiff [illegible] to deliuer to ye conservatour and
and [illegible] to bring with me in [illegible] under ye empriouris gret sell and hes deliuerit to his maiestie the kingis
our souerane [illegible] under his [illegible] gret sell for ye said space of ane hundreth yeiris
my lord ye sall understand yt ye empriour [illegible] in ye court lang tyme efter yt I com yair
to quham I deliuerit your l. writtingis quhilk ressauit yame rycht thankfully and schew me gret humanitie
for your l. saik bot he gaiff me na ansuer of your writtingis quhill I was reddy to depart furth of ye
court [illegible] quhilk ye sall ressaiff fra this berar I remanit in ye court viij dayis and [illegible]
[illegible] apon ye [illegible] to ye [illegible] quhen ye [illegible] was heir [illegible] all [illegible] quhen I [illegible] to ye court
yt ye kingis grace our souerane was deid for ye quhilk causit ye quene of hungary send for me and inquirit
diligentlie of yt mater at me and was rycht glaid quhen I schew hir ye verite of ye kingis grace
our souerane prosperitie It was schawin to me yt ye quene maist gart all ye kirkis in brussellis
pray for his grace saull yai nocht [illegible] was send for verite furth of Ingland and war haldin for
effect ay quhill my cuming to ye court
my l. it war to lang to me to writ to your l. ye triumphis yt I haiff sene sen my cuming to ye
court [illegible] yt is to say ye triumphand iustingis ye terribill tornamentis ye fechtyn on fut
in barras ye nammis of lordis and knychtis yt war hurt ye day of ye gret tornament quhairfoir
nochtstandand I haiff writtin at lenth in articlis to schaw ye kingis grace at my hame cuming
[illegible] ye empriour purposis to depart at ye end of yis moneth and passis up in almany for reformatioun
of ye lutherianis ye quene of hungarie remanis heir regent of all yir contreis and was confermit regent
be ye iij estaitis in ye town of brussellis ye v day of Julij and as for vyir nouellis I refer to ye
[illegible] writtin wt my hand at handwarp ye [illegible] day of [illegible] be your seruitour at his power

David lyndsay harrauld
to [illegible]

Sir David Lindsay

VERSE

LiD 1 *The Complaynt of Schir Dauid Lindesay* ('Schir, I beseik thyne Excellence').

Copy made by David Anderson of Aberdeen; bound up with the Elphynstoun MS of Douglas's *Aeneid*; [1563-6].

First pub. [Edinburgh, 1529-30?]; Hamer, I, 39-53. This MS described in Hamer, IV, 8-11.

Edinburgh University Library, MS Dk. 7. 49, Part II, ff. 118v-124.

LiD 2 *The Deploratioun of the Deith of Quene Magdalene* ('O Cruell Deith, to greit is thy puissance').

Copy made by David Anderson of Aberdeen; bound up with the Elphynstoun MS of Douglas's *Aeneid*; [1563-6].

First pub. [Edinburgh, 1537]; Hamer, I, 105-12. This MS described in Hamer, IV, 8-11.

Edinburgh University Library, MS Dk. 7. 49, Part II, ff. 125-7v.

LiD 3 -----

Copy, written in a transcript of Robert Lindesay of Pitscottie, *Historie and Cronicles of Scotland*, Book XXI, chapter xxix; c. 1598.

Formerly Phillipps MS 3107 and owned in 1896 by John Scott, CB, of Halkshill; printed from this MS in *Pitscottie's Chronicles of Scotland*, ed. A.J.G. Mackay, I, STS 42 (Edinburgh & London, 1899), 370-6, and described pp. lxxx-lxxxiv; collated in Hamer, III, 119.

John Rylands University Library of Manchester, MS 84/1/1, ff. 83v-5.

LiD 4 *Ane Descriptioun of Peder Coffeis having na Ragaird till honestie in thair vocatioun* ('It is my purpoiss to discryve').

Copy, ascribed to Lindsay, in a MS volume of Scottish poetry compiled by George Bannatyne; c. 1568.

First pub. (from this MS) in Allan Ramsay, *The Ever Green* (Edinburgh, 1724), II, 219-22; printed from this MS in Hamer, I, 389-92.

National Library of Scotland, Adv. MS 1. 1. 6, Vol. I, f. 162r-v (pp. 383-4).

LiD 5 *Ane Dialog betuix Experience and Ane Courteour of the Miserabyll Estait of the Warls (The Monarche)* ('Into that Park I sawe appeir').

Copy, complete with the Epistle to the Reader and Prologue, probably transcribed, from a printed edition, by William Hay and David Anderson of Aberdeen; bound up with the Elphynstoun MS of Douglas's *Aeneid*; [1563-6].

First pub. [St Andrews *or* Edinburgh, c. 1554]; Hamer, I, 197-386. This MS described in Hamer, IV, 8-11.

Edinburgh University Library, MS Dk. 7. 49, Part II, ff. 1-99.

LiD 6 -----

Copy; begun 2 June 1556.

This MS described in Hamer, IV, 5-8, and partly collated, III, 233 seq.

Lambeth Palace, MS 332.

LiD 7 *The Dreme of Schir Dauid Lyndesay* ('Me thocht ane lady, of portratour perfyte').

Copy, complete with the Epistle and Prologue, made by David Anderson of Aberdeen; bound up with the Elphynstoun MS of Douglas's *Aeneid*; [1563-6].

First pub. [Edinburgh, 1528-30?]; Hamer, I, 3-38. This MS described in Hamer, IV, 8-11.

Edinburgh University Library, MS Dk. 7. 49, Part II, ff. 99v-118v.

LiD 8 *The Historie of Squyer Meldrum* ('Quho that Antique Stories reidis').

Copy transcribed from a printed edition by one James Clark of Glasgow; 1631.

First pub. [Edinburgh, 1579-80?]; Hamer, I, 145-96; ed. James Kinsley (London & Edinburgh, 1959). This MS recorded in Hamer, IV, 12, and in Kinsley, p. 2.

Formerly owned by John Pinkerton (1758-1826), by Richard Heber (1774-1833), and (in 1836) by J. Bohn; unlocated.

LiD 9 *The Testament and Complaynt of the Papyngo* ('Suppose I had Ingyne Angelicall').

Copy made by David Anderson of Aberdeen; bound up with the Elphynstoun MS of Douglas's *Aeneid*; [1563-6].

First pub. [Edinburgh, 1530]; Hamer, I, 55-90. This MS described in Hamer, IV, 8-11.

Edinburgh University Library, MS Dk. 7. 49, Part II, ff. 128-44v.

DRAMATIC WORKS

LiD 10 *Ane Satyre of the Thrie Estaitis.*

Extracts, headed 'The Play, made be Dauid Lynsayis, of the Month, Knicht', comprising seven long passages (called 'Interludes'), in an irregular order, together with the prefatory 'banns', from a version performed on the Castle Hill, Cupar, Fifeshire, on 7 June 1552 (Hamer's 'Version II'), in a MS volume of Scottish poetry compiled by George Bannatyne; c. 1568.

First pub. (in Hamer's 'Version III') Edinburgh, 1602; printed from this MS (in a parallel text with the 1602 edition) in Hamer, Vol. II; ed. James Kinsley (London, 1954). Also printed from this MS in *The Bannatyne Manuscript*, Hunterian Club (Glasgow, 1896), III, 463-597; *The Bannatyne Manuscript*, ed. W. Tod Ritchie, III, STS NS 23 (1928), 87-238. The different versions of the play discussed in Anna J. Mill, 'Representations of Lyndsay's *Satyre of the Thrie Estaitis*', *PMLA*, 47. i (1932), 636-51, with corrigenda in *PMLA*, 48 (1933), 315-16; Raymond A. Houk, 'Versions of Lindsay's *Satire of the Three Estates*', *PMLA*, 55. i (1940), 396-405; John MacQueen, 'Ane Satyre of the Thrie Estaitis', *SSL*, 3 (1965-6), 129-43; Anna Jean Mill, 'The Original Version of Lindsay's *Satyre of the Thrie Estaitis*', *SSL*, 6 (1968-9), 67-75.

National Library of Scotland, Adv. MS 1. 1. 6, Vol. II, ff. 164-210 (pp. 387-479).

LiD 11 -----

Prose summary of the version performed in the Banquetting Hall in the Palace at Linlithgow before James V and Marie de Lorraine on 6 January 1539/40 (Hamer's 'Version I'), written by a Protestant Scotsman and sent by Sir William Eure to Thomas Cromwell with a covering letter dated from Berwick Castle, 26 January [1539/40]; bound in a composite volume of state papers.

Printed from this MS in Hamer, II, 1-6.

British Library, Royal MS 7 C. XVI, ff. 137-8.

LiD 12 -----

A MS of 'Sir Dauid Lindesay A Satyre of the three Estates', owned in 1627 by William Drummond of Hawthornden.

This MS recorded in Drummond's catalogue of his library, *Auctarium Bibliothecae Edinburgenae* (Edinburgh, 1627), p. 22; see Hamer, IV, 12, and Robert H. MacDonald, *The Library of Drummond of Hawthornden* (Edinburgh, 1971), No. 1371.

The main part of Drummond's library was given to Edinburgh University but a number of volumes were dispersed and this MS is unlocated.

Thomas Lodge

1558-1625

ABBREVIATIONS

Gosse *The Complete Works of Thomas Lodge*, [ed. Edmund Gosse], 4 vols, Hunterian Club (Glasgow, 1883; reprinted New York, 1963).

For abbreviations used throughout Volume I, see p.xi.

INTRODUCTION

The only surviving autographs of Thomas Lodge are a few letters. A letter of 17 January 1610/11 to Sir Thomas Edmondes is in the British Library (Stowe MS 171, f. 352) and is reproduced in Greg, *English Literary Autographs*, plate XIX. Nine letters to William Trumbull — eight written between 13 April 1607 and 22 November 1609, and one written 7 October 1613 — are among the Trumbull papers in the Berkshire Record Office. They are printed in *HMC* 75, Downshire, II (1936), pp. 24-5, 91-4, 112-15, 140, 189-90, 249-50, and in Downshire, IV (1940), p. 215, and they are discussed in Joseph W. Houppert, 'Thomas Lodge's Letters to William Trumbull', *RN*, 18 (1965), 117-23. For one of these letters, see FACSIMILE XXV.

Another letter, a medical prescription sent to Sir Stephen Powle on 20 August 1618, is preserved in a transcript made by Powle, now in the Bodleian (MS Tanner 169, ff. 191-2); it is printed in N. Burton Paradise, *Thomas Lodge: The History of an Elizabethan* (New Haven, 1931), pp. 61-2.

The *Index* records a few extracts from Lodge's works in miscellanies and songbooks, and also two apparently contemporary scribal copies of his medical handbook *The Poore Mans Talentt* (LoT 13-14). Except where otherwise stated, these MSS have not been previously noted by editors. One item which has not received an entry is an 18th-century copy of Lodge's *Ode* in Thomas Ford's song-version beginning 'Now I see thy looks were feigned', a copy in a MS songbook of one Philip Hayes, now in the Bodleian (MS Mus. d. 8, f. 14v).

PB.

ARRANGEMENT

Verse	LoT 1-10
Prose	Lot 11-16.

FACSIMILE XXV — Thomas Lodge: Letter to William Trumbull, 13 April 1607. Berkshire Record Office, Trumbull Miscellaneous Correspondence, Volume II, folio 12 recto. Reproduced from the manuscripts of The Marquess of Downshire in the Berkshire Record Office by permission of the County Archivist.

12

My very best Sonne: I have receaved in yor last letters, not only a confirmation of yor pietye and love towards me; but also a manifest demonstration both of the one and the other in yor expedition: wch is of that nature in respect of expectation, that it redoubleth the benefitt. Should I spend all the vowels of Rhetorique in complement, I could not expresse my thankfulnes; yow only may accomplish them by yor kind acceptance and gave them there and they have all, by the vertue of the goodnesse that shineth in yow: The good wch I have receaved thereby is the beginning of a greater sorrow, for thereby we understand of the desperate sicknes (if not death) of my Lady Cooke my wives daughter wch hath so dismayed my poore wife that Senecas verse may be truly said of her. Curae leves loquuntur ingentes stupent.
for so astonished is she at this newes as she is wholie altered from her former contentments. And alas the fortunes of our misfortunes that have ate before us were enough to make us stoope; yet now this last of sorrow that ladeth us backward is ready quite to overturne us: And uppon this only occasion have I beene silent so long. It remaineth now that as ever hitherto so now likewise yow will stand or frend so mery, as to send away the enclosed to Mr Grout wch I had for till wee gett an answer and certaintie of our daughters estate, my wife will be still a woman that is the subiect of physick. I pray yow likewise (if my lord have any stuff to come over out of England this May) advertise me by the next whether I may wright tymely enough to have my books sent over for if I may I will send yow letters by the next post to have them delivered to yor assignee. wth such other things as concerne me: trust me I should be ashamed to presse yow so farr but that I assure my self of yor entire affection towards me and mine. for wch I will recompence wth my prayers if wch I would otherwise performe in actions and offices of kindnes and wish yow now and ever to be commanded by yow, wch have ever without any desert of myne devoted me unto yow by yor humanitie. 13 Aprilis

Yors if his owne, and no otherwise.

Tho: Lodge

What a chorle was my memory that had almost (throw forgetfulnes) made me close up my letters without acknowledgment of those kind salutations you presented me in your last letters. I pray you as in all thinges so sted me in this to redouble my thankes to each one according to their worthines and good will that have remembred me by you, and let both male and female know that altho they outstrip me in fortune, thy shall not nor cannot conquer me in affection wth wch resolution and my wifes humble and harty commendation to all wee once more bid you farwell.

Thomas Lodge

VERSE

LoT 1 *'First shall the heauens want starrie light'.*

Copy, headed 'A Sonet of Constant assurance to his M[rs]', in a verse miscellany; c. 1634-50s.

First pub. in *Rosalynde. Euphues golden legacie* (London, 1590); Gosse, I (*Rosalynde*, p. 38).

University of Newcastle upon Tyne, MS Bell/White 25, f. 60v.

LoT 2 *An Ode* ('Now I find thy lookes were fained').

Copy, here beginning 'Now I see thy looks were feigned', in a musical setting, in a MS songbook compiled by one Giles Earle; c. 1615-26.

First pub. in *The Phoenix Nest* (London, 1593); *Phillis: Honoured with Pastorall Sonnets, Elegies, and amorous delights* (London, 1593); Gosse, II, (p. 58). The song-version beginning 'Now I see thy looks were feigned' first pub. in Thomas Ford, *Musicke of Sundrie Kindes* (London, 1607).

British Library, Add. MS 24665, ff. 56v-7.

LoT 3 -----

Copy, here beginning 'Now I see thy looks were feigned', in a musical setting by John Ford, in a MS music part-book compiled by Thomas Smith (1614-1701), of The Queen's College, Oxford, later Bishop of Carlisle; c. 1637.

This MS collated in John P. Cutts, *Bishop Smith's Part-Song Books in Carlisle Cathedral Library* (American Institute of Musicology, 1972), p. 61.

Carlisle Cathedral, Dean & Chapter of Carlisle MSS, Box B1, Bassus, p. 92.

LoT 4 -----

Copy, here beginning 'Now I see thy Loue is fained', in a verse miscellany; c. 1630s-40s.

Edinburgh University Library, MS La. III. 436, pp. 72-3.

LoT 5 -----

Copy, here beginning 'Now I see thy looks were fained', in a musical setting in a MS music book compiled by one John Squyer; [1697-1701].

Edinburgh University Library, MS La. III. 490, p. 73.

LoT 6 -----

Copy, headed 'A Song' and here beginning 'Now I see thy lookes are fained', in a miscellany; c. 1630.

Folger, MS V. a. 345, pp. 137-8.

LoT 7 -----

Copy, here beginning 'Now I sie thy lookes wer fainzied', in a musical setting, in a MS songbook possibly compiled by one William Stirling with later additions by John Leyden (1775-1811); c. 1639.

Printed from this MS in Nelly Diem, *Beiträge zur Geschichte der Schottischen Musik im XVII. Jahrhundert* (Zürich & Leipzig, 1919), pp. 99-100.

National Library of Scotland, Adv. MS 5. 2. 14, f. 21r-v.

LoT 8 -----

Copy, here beginning 'Now I sie thy lucks ar fained', in a musical setting in a MS songbook owned in 1669 by Robert Ker of Ferniehurst, later fourth Lord Jedburgh; c. 1630.

National Library of Scotland, MS 5448, ff. 9v-10.

LoT 9 -----

Copy, headed 'A songe' and here beginning 'Now I see thy lookes were fained', in a verse miscellany; c. 1634.

Rosenbach Foundation, MS 239/27, pp. 113-14.

--- -----

See also INTRODUCTION.

LoT 10 *Phoebes Sonnet a replie to Montanus passion* ('Downe a downe: | Thus Phillis sung').

Copy in a musical setting by Francis Pilkington in a MS songbook compiled by Thomas Hamond (d. 1662) of Suffolk; c. 1630.

First pub. in *Rosalynde. Euphues golden legacie* (London, 1590); Gosse, I (*Rosalynde*, p. 47). This setting first pub. in Francis Pilkington, *The First Booke of Songs or Ayres* (London, 1605). This MS collated in Doughtie, *Lyrics from English Airs*, p. 539.

Bodleian, MS Mus. f. 7-10: f. 7, fols. 22-21v.

The Divel coniured.

PROSE

LoT 11 *The Divel coniured.*

Extracts in a miscellany compiled by Edward Pudsey (1573-1613); 1600s.

First pub. London, 1596; Gosse, Vol. III.

Bodleian, MS Eng. poet. d. 3, f. 78r-v.

LoT 12 *Euphves Shadow, The Battaile of the Sences.*

Extracts in a MS book of extracts from prose romances; c. 1600.

First pub. London, 1592; Gosse, Vol. II.

Folger, MS V. b. 83, ff. 11-14v.

LoT 13 *The Poore Mans Talentt.*

Copy of Lodge's medical handbook in twelve chapters, with a dedicatory epistle to Lady Anne, Countess of Arundel, and with five pages of additional receipts in two other hands; c. 1623?

First pub. (from this MS) in Gosse, Vol. IV (1883), with a facsimile of the dedicatory epistle. Gosse mistakenly believed the epistle to be autograph.

Folger, MS V. a. 136.

LoT 14 -----

Copy, with the dedicatory epistle, and with four leaves of additional receipts (ff. 32-5) as in LoT 13, in a volume of medical treatises and prescriptions; c. 1623?

The text followed on ff. 36-94 by miscellaneous medical works in the same hand (all unpublished) conceivably also by Lodge.

British Library, Add. MS 34212, ff. 1-35.

LoT 15 *Rosalynde. Euphues Golden Legacie.*

Extracts in a MS book of extracts from prose romances; c. 1600.

First pub. London, 1590; Gosse, Vol. I.

Folger, MS V. b. 83, ff. 3-5.

--- -----

See also LoT 1 and 10.

LoT 16 *The Workes of L.A. Seneca both morrall and naturall.*

Extracts from Lodge's translation on 23 leaves in a miscellany once owned by William Drake (1606-69) of Shardeloes, near Amersham, Buckinghamshire; c. 1659.

First pub. London, 1614. This MS recorded in Stuart Clark, 'Wisdom Literature of the Seventeenth Century: A Guide to the Contents of the "Bacon-Tottel" Commonplace Books. Part II', *Transactions of the Cambridge Bibliographical Society*, 6, Part 6 (1978), 46-73 (p. 59).

DRAMATIC WORKS

--- *A Looking Glasse for London and England.*

See ROBERT GREENE, GrR 8.

John Lyly

1554-1606

ABBREVIATIONS

Bond *The Complete Works of John Lyly*, ed. R. Warwick Bond, 3 vols (Oxford, 1902; reprinted 1967).

For abbreviations used throughout Volume I, see p.xi.

INTRODUCTION

There are eight important autographs of John Lyly, all of them letters. These letters are printed in Bond and also in Albert Feuillerat, *John Lyly* (Cambridge, 1910), pp. 522-64. They may be listed as follows:

(1) To Lord Burghley, July 1582 (British Library, Lansdowne MS 36, ff. 192-3). Bond, I, 28-9. Facsimile in Greg, *English Literary Autographs*, plate XVII.

(2) To Sir Robert Cecil, 17 January 1594/5 (owned by the Marquess of Salisbury, Hatfield House, Cecil Papers 24/99). Bond, I, 390.

(3) To Sir Robert Cecil, 22 December 1597 (Public Record Office, SP. 12/265/61, ff. 128-9). Bond, I, 68-9.

(4) To Sir Robert Cecil, 23 January 1597/8 (owned by the Marquess of Salisbury, Hatfield House, Cecil Papers 59/113). Bond, I, 391.

(5) To Sir Robert Cecil, 9 September 1598 (owned by the Marquess of Salisbury, Hatfield House, Cecil Papers 64/5). Bond, I, 392-3.

(6) To Sir Robert Cecil, 27 February 1600/1 (owned by the Marquess of Salisbury, Hatfield House, Cecil Papers 77/14). Bond, I, 395.

(7) To Sir Robert Cecil, 4 February 1602/3 (owned by the Marquess of Salisbury, Hatfield House, Cecil Papers 91/103). Bond, I, 75. Facsimile in Bond, III, frontispiece.

(8) To Sir Robert Cotton, 30 April 1605 (British Library, Cotton MS Julius C. III, f. 246). Bond, I, 395-6. Facsimile in Greg, *English Literary Autographs*, plate XVIII(a).

A Latin epistle from Lyly to Lord Burghley, 16 May 1574, in the British Library (Lansdowne MS 19, f. 31; printed in Bond, I, 13-14) is apparently in the hand of a scribe.

Two other letters of Lyly are known: his petitions to Queen Elizabeth, probably written in 1598 and 1601 respectively. Although the original letters seem to be no longer preserved among the state papers, a large number of copies were evidently put in circulation and the letters were a popular choice for 17th-century letter-manuals and anthologies of state correspondence. The petitions are printed in Bond (I, 64-5, 70-1) from British Library, Harley MS 1323, ff. 249-50, and he collates two other copies in the British Library (Harley MS 1877, f. 71, and Hargrave MS 225, p. 36). Bond records (I, 377) further copies now in the Bodleian (MSS Ashmole 781, ff. 76-7; Tanner 82, ff. 23v-4v; University College 152, pp. 2-5) and in Cambridge University Library (MS Ee. 5. 23, pp. 434-5). Two copies of the two petitions which Bond records (I, 64, 75n) but did not see are (i) Leconfield MS 61, pp. 23-7 (now owned by Lord Egremont, Petworth House; recorded in *HMC*, 6th Report (1877), Appendix, p. 306); and (ii) a MS volume of tracts owned by the Marquess of Bute (D. 18, ff. 52-3; recorded in *HMC*, 3rd Report (1872), Appendix, p. 204). Other, unrecorded copies of the two petitions are in the Bodleian (MS CCC. 327, ff. 24-5v), Bradford Central Library (Hopkinson MSS, Vol. 44, pp. 16-20), the British Library (Add. MSS 4108, ff. 5-6; 44848, ff. 22-3v), East Sussex Record Office (RAF/F/13/1, f. 36), the Folger (MSS V. a. 239, pp. 42-8; V. b. 234, pp. 32-6), the Huntington (HM 36836, pp. 19-21 (the Michael Lort volume sold at Sotheby's, 24 October 1972, Lot 383)), and the Inner Temple Library (Petyt MS 538, Vol. 36, f. 78). Sir Stephen Powle's copy of the second petition only (Bodleian, MS Tanner 169, f. 69) is printed in Bond, I, 378; there are other, unrecorded copies of this petition alone in Cambridge University Library (MS Add. 4138, f. 51v) and in the Northamptonshire Record Office (F.H. 2617).

Certain other original documents bearing Lyly's signature were discovered by William Urry among the archives at Canterbury Cathedral; they are discussed by him in 'John Lyly and Canterbury', *Thirty-third Annual Report of the Friends of Canterbury Cathedral* (April 1960), 19-25 (p. 24). One is an indenture for the sale of 'The Splayed Eagle' in Canterbury, 10 January [1571], signed by both 'John Lyllye' and his mother, Jane; another is a quitclaim from John to his mother, 3 October [1581], signed in an italic script 'Per me Joannē Liliē' (or 'Liliū'). These two documents are now in the Kent Archives Office (Boteler MSS, 116a and 116e). Two title deeds concerning the same property, both signed in 1581 by Jane Lyly, are items 116b and 116c in the same collection. John Lyly's name is also cited as witness to a receipt for money granted by the ecclesiastical court to one Edward Braine, 20 July

1570, a document preserved at Canterbury Cathedral (Diocesan Register of Licences, I, f. 20).

There are very few extant literary MSS relating to Lyly. Bond prints (III, 434-502) a large number of poems which he tentatively attributes to Lyly on stylistic grounds, many of them preserved in MS sources. Since a number of his attributions (e.g. poems by Sidney) are plainly erroneous, however, and since they are all in any case purely conjectural, these poems are not included in the *Index*.

Bond's attribution to Lyly of various entertainments should also be viewed with scepticism. The *Entertainment at Elvetham* (Bond, I, 431-52) is the work of various writers: see Harry H. Boyle, 'Elizabeth's Entertainment at Elvetham: War Policy in Pageantry', *SP*, 68 (1971), 146-66, and NICHOLAS BRETON, BrN 61-76. For the authorship of the Gardner's and Molecatcher's speeches on the Queen's visit to Theobald's in May 1591 (British Library, Egerton MS 2623, ff. 15-19; printed in Bond, I, 417-19), see W. W. Greg, 'A Collier Mystification', *RES*, 1 (1925), 452-4. For the *Sonet At the Tilt Yard, Nov. 17, 1590* (Bond, I, 411-12), see GEORGE PEELE, PlG 10-21. For the *Entertainment at Harefield* (Bond, I, 491-504), see SIR JOHN DAVIES, DaJ 290-300. For the *Lord of Combrlande's Speeche to ye Queene, upon ye 17 day of November, 1600* (Bond, I 415-16), see SIR JOHN DAVIES, INTRODUCTION.

What Bond entitles *Speeches to Queen Elizabeth at Quarrendon: August, 1592* (I, 453-70) and conjecturally assigns to Lyly on stylistic grounds (I, 526-7) is a collection of speeches probably belonging to devices presented by Sir Henry Lee but not necessarily presented on one occasion, or in August 1592, or at Quarrendon: see Chambers, III, 404-7. These speeches were printed in William Harper, *Masques: Performed before Queen Elizabeth* (Chiswick, 1820), from MS copies in a historical collection made by Henry Ferrers of Baddesley Clinton, Warwickshire. For the fate of Ferrers's MSS see Elizabeth K. Berry, 'Henry Ferrers an early Warwickshire antiquary 1550-1633', *Dugdale Society Occasional Papers*, No. 16 (Oxford, 1965). These 'masques' were probably among the eight volumes of Ferrers's papers which were destroyed in a fire at Birmingham Reference Library in 1879. The same speeches occur, together with other related speeches not known to Bond, in a collection of entertainments connected with Sir Henry Lee and formerly preserved at Lee's home, Ditchley Hall, Oxfordshire; it is now in the British Library (Add. MS 41499A, ff. 2, 12-16). Two of the speeches appear in a collection in the Inner Temple Library (Petyt MS 538, Vol. 43, ff. 298-300v) ascribed to Dr [Richard] Edes (1555-1604), the Queen's chaplain; one of the speeches in this text is collated in *The Phoenix Nest 1593*, ed. Hyder Edward Rollins (Cambridge, Mass., 1931), p. 137 seq. The lost Ferrers collection contained three other short pieces which Bond printed (I, 412-14) from Harper's 1820 volume and attributed to Lyly: *A Cartell for a Challeng, Sir Henry Lee's Challenge before the Shampanie*, and *The Supplication of the Owld Knight*. These pieces too occur in the Lee collection (Add. MS 41499A, ff. 1-2), and there is more reason to associate them with Lee than with Lyly: see Chambers, III, 404-5.

Besides extracts from two plays printed as Lyly's in the 17th century, the *Index* includes only two entertainments. One (LyJ 2) is clearly ascribed to him in the MS source; the other (LyJ 3) is anonymous but has been attributed to Lyly by Leslie Hotson.

PB.

ARRANGEMENT

See also Addenda to Part 2, p. 631

John Lyly

DRAMATIC WORKS

LyJ 1 *Campaspe.*

Extracts in a miscellany compiled by Edward Pudsey (1573-1613); 1600s.

First pub. London, 1584; Bond, II, 313-60.

Bodleian, MS Eng. poet. d. 3, f. 86v.

LyJ 2 *The Entertainment at Chiswick.*

Copy of two speeches by an Angler, headed 'At Sr William Russels howse at Cheswick', the second speech headed 'At her Majesties departure', subscribed 'John: Lilly' and endorsed 'To the Right Worshipfull Roger Wilbraham Esquior Master of Requestes geve these'; on a single leaf among the papers of the Finch and Hatton families; [28-9 July 1602].

First pub. (from this MS) in *Queen Elizabeth's Entertainment at Mitcham*, ed. Leslie Hotson (New Haven, 1953).

Northamptonshire Record Office, F.H. 2414.

LyJ 3 *The Entertainment at Mitcham.*

Copies of parts of an entertainment possibly by Lyly among the papers of Sir Julius Caesar (1558-1636); ff. 253-62v endorsed by Caesar 'The 2. speeches dialogue wise to Q. Elizabeth at my howse at Mitcham 13. Sept. 1598'; f. 233 endorsed in a different hand 'A copy of the supplication deliuered to her Maiesty at D. Caesars howse, 12. Septemb. 1598'; f. 281 endorsed by Caesar 'The dite of the Greak song, before the Queens Maiesty at mine howse at Mitcham'.

First pub. (from these MSS) in *Queen Elizabeth's Entertainment at Mitcham*, ed. Leslie Hotson (New Haven, 1953).

British Library, Add. MS 12497, ff. 233, 253-62v, 281.

LyJ 4 *Loves Metamorphosis.*

Extracts in a miscellany compiled by Edward Pudsey (1573-1613); 1600s.

First pub. London, 1601; Bond, III, 289-332.

Bodleian, MS Eng. poet. d. 3, f. 86v.

Sir Thomas Malory

fl. c.1470

For abbreviations used throughout Volume I, see p.xi.

INTRODUCTION

The single extant MS of Malory's *Morte D'Arthur* was discovered in 1934 among the MSS in the Warden and Fellows' Library, Winchester College (MS 13). Through a public fund the MS was bought by the British Library on 26 March 1976 for £150,000.

The text of the MS differs considerably from that printed by Caxton in 1485. However, recent research by Lotte Hellinga, using modern scientific aids, has revealed that the MS must have passed through Caxton's hands, for it bears unmistakable smudges of printers' ink and the impressions of certain of Caxton's types. Unless he finally turned to one or more other MSS for his text (or for part of his text), it is possible that Caxton's printed text is his own 'edited' version of Malory's work based on the extant MS.

Additional research by Hilton Kelliher into the provenance of the MS, through the name of a former owner, Richard Followell, lends support to its authority by linking it with the Malory family in Northamptonshire.

One other item recorded (MaT 2) is a 16th-century index of Malory's work, not generally known until its appearance at auction in 1978.

PB.

ARRANGEMENT

Prose MaT 1-2.

Sir Thomas Malory

PROSE

MaT 1 *Morte D'Arthur.*

Copy in two scribal hands; used by William Caxton; once owned by one Richard Followell, probably a member of the Fowlwell or Fellwell family of Litchborough, Northamptonshire, tenants to a branch of the Malory family; imperfect, now consisting of part of Chapter VIII until near the end of Chapter CLXXII; 473 leaves, folio; c. 1470-83.

First pub. by William Caxton (London, 1485). Edited from this MS, with three facsimile pages, in *The Works of Sir Thomas Malory*, ed. Eugène Vinaver, 3 vols (Oxford, 1947; 2nd edition revised, 1967); facsimile edition of the MS in *The Winchester Malory: A Facsimile*, introduced by N.R. Ker, EETS SS4 (Oxford University Press, 1976). Discussed extensively in Lotte Hellinga and Hilton Kelliher, 'The Malory Manuscript', *BLJ*, 3 (1977), 91-113.

British Library, Add. MS 59678.

MaT 2 -----

A MS compilation of the principal deeds of King Arthur and the Knights of the Round Table as they appear in Malory's *Morte D'Arthur*, written by one John Grinken; comprising five pages of preface, seven pages of alphabetical list of names (a further page now missing), and 147 entries, with a number of armorial devices; 54 leaves (including 11 blanks); incomplete; slightly imperfect and lacking title; 2nd half 16th century.

This MS formerly Phillipps MS 100.

Christie's, 29 November 1978, Lot 27, sold to Quaritch.

Christopher Marlowe

1564-93

ABBREVIATIONS

Bakeless John Bakeless, *The Tragicall History of Christopher Marlowe*, 2 vols (Cambridge, Mass., 1942).

Bowers *The Complete Works of Christopher Marlowe*, ed. Fredson Bowers, 2 vols (Cambridge, 1973).

Tucker Brooke *The Works of Christopher Marlowe*, ed. C. F. Tucker Brooke (Oxford, 1910).

Wraight & Stern A. D. Wraight and Virginia F. Stern, *In Search of Christopher Marlowe* (London, 1965).

For abbreviations used throughout Volume I, see p.xi.

INTRODUCTION

The only known example of Marlowe's hand is his signature as witness to the Will of Katherine Benchkin in November 1585, a document now preserved in the Kent Archives Office (PRC 16/86). The signature is reproduced in Bakeless, I, facing p. 208; in Wraight & Stern, pp. 229-30; and in Petti, *English Literary Hands*, No. 34. Despite the claims made in Wraight & Stern, a comparison between this signature and the much-discussed MS fragment of *A Massacre at Paris* (MrC 23) renders untenable the view that the latter could be autograph. On the contrary, the fragment is the work of an unskilled scribe. Neither is there any good reason to suppose that it is a forgery, even though once owned by John Payne Collier. Some discernible unevenness in the pen strokes and flow of ink is to be attributed to the scribe's lack of skill.

No other early MSS of the plays are known apart from one or two quotations (including interesting early quotations from *Doctor Faustus* in the hand of Thomas Nashe: MrC 20) and two MS leaves making up an imperfect printed exemplum of *Edward II* (MrC 21). There are early MS copies of just a few of the poems, notably of Marlowe's most famous lyric 'Come live with mee' (MrC 10-19), which exists in several early versions, one text (MrC 18) apparently assigned by its scribe to Thomas Blundeville's *Exercises* (first pub. 1594). The MSS recorded in the *Index* have not been noted by editors unless otherwise stated.

A few additional items may be mentioned. An 18th-century MS copy of *Dido Queen of Carthage*, transcribed for George Steevens (1736-1800) by the actor John Henderson (1747-85) from what was then thought to be a unique exemplum of the 1594 edition, is in the British Library (Add. MS 5142). (A transcript made from Henderson's transcript by Brownlow Waight in 1832 is in the Folger, MS D. a. 10). A late 18th-century transcript of an early edition of *A Massacre at Paris*, with the title page and ff. 3-8 perhaps in the hand of the actor John Philip Kemble (1757-1823), is in the British Library (King's MS 443). Charles Lamb's MS copy of 'Come live with mee' is at Harvard (MS Eng 959).

Numerous documents in public records relating to Marlowe's life are reproduced in Wraight & Stern. They include various academic records, the warrant for his arrest in 1593, the testimonies of Richard Baines and others concerning his atheism, and the coroner's inquest on his death (see also THOMAS KYD, INTRODUCTION). Other records concerning Marlowe and his family are cited in William Urry's forthcoming book, *The Marlowes of Canterbury*.

PB.

ARRANGEMENT

Verse	MrC 1-19
Dramatic works	MrC 20-3.

See also Addenda to Part 2, p. 631

Christopher Marlowe

VERSE

MrC 1 *Hero and Leander* ('On Hellespont guiltie of True-loves blood').

Four lines (Second Sestyad, lines 131-4, here beginning 'Oh none have power but Gods their love to hide') quoted in Henry Oxinden's draft of a letter to Elizabeth Dallison, in a bound collection of Oxinden family correspondence; [1641].

First pub. London, 1598; Bowers, II, 423-515 (p. 448); Tucker Brooke, pp. 485-548 (p. 507). For George Chapman's continuation of the poem see ChG 3-4. Printed from this MS in *The Oxinden Letters 1607-1642*, ed. Dorothy Gardiner (London, 1933), pp. 252-3.

British Library, Add. MS 28000, f. 369.

MrC 2 -----

Copy of eight lines in the Second Sestyad (lines 131-4, 287-90), in a miscellany compiled by Sir Henry Oxinden (1609-70) of Kent; c. 1642-70.

Bowers, II, 448, 452; Tucker Brooke, pp. 507, 511. This MS discussed in Mark Eccles, 'Marlowe in Kentish Tradition', *N & Q*, 169 (20 July 1935), 39-41.

Folger, MS V. b. 110, pp. 48, 58.

MrC 3 *In obitum honoratissimi viri Rogeri Manwood militis, quaestorii Reginalis Capitalis Baronis* ('Noctivagi terror, ganeonis triste flagellum').

Copy inscribed in a printed exemplum of *Hero and Leander* (London, 1629); 17th century.

First pub. (from this MS) in *The Works of William Shakespeare*, ed. John Payne Collier (London, 1844), I, xliv; Bowers, II, 540. This MS discussed in Mark Eccles, 'Marlowe in Kentish Tradition', *N & Q*, 169 (13 July 1935), 20-3, and in Bakeless, I, 116-19. See also NICHOLAS BRETON, INTRODUCTION.

Sotheby's, 15 February 1917, Lot 2521, sold to P.J. Dobell; unlocated.

MrC 4 -----

Copy, subscribed 'C. Marlo. Auth: Hero & Lean.', in a miscellany compiled by Sir Henry Oxinden (1609-70) of Kent; c. 1642-70.

Printed from this MS in Bowers; discussed in Mark Eccles, *N & Q*, 169 (20 July 1935), 39-41.

Folger, MS V. b. 110, flyleaf.

MrC 5 -----

Second copy, subscribed 'These verses above written were made by Christopher Marlo, who was a Shomakers son of Canterbury; it was this Marlo, who made the 2 first bookes of Hero & Leander, witnes M[r] Alderich', in a miscellany compiled by Sir Henry Oxinden; c. 1642-70.

This MS collated in Bowers.

Folger, MS V. b. 110, p. 42.

MrC 6 *Ovid's Elegies. I, v* ('In summers heate, and midtime of the day').

Copy, headed 'Corinne concubitus Aeleg 5. Lib: Amorum', in a verse miscellany compiled by John Hopkinson (1610-80); c. 1647.

Ten of Marlowe's Elegies (including I, v and II, iv) first pub. 'Middleburg' [i.e. London], [c. 1595-6]; Bowers, II, 307-421 (p. 321); Tucker Brooke, pp. 553-627 (pp. 564-5).

Bodleian, MS Don. d. 58, f. 46v.

MrC 7 ----- -----

Copy, headed 'Corinna concubitus Ovid. lib. 1° Amorum Eleg. 5 AEstas erat &c.', in a verse miscellany compiled by one or two Oxford men, possibly connected with New College and afterwards with the Inns of Court; 1630s.

Harvard, MS Eng 686, f. 32.

MrC 8 ----- -----

Copy, untitled and beginning 'In so̅mers heat at midtyme of the day', in a verse miscellany probably compiled by a member of an Inn of Court; c. 1598-1600s.

Rosenbach Foundation, MS 1083/15, f. 22.

MrC 9 ----- *II, iv* ('I meane not to defend the scapes of any').

Copy on a leaf formerly bound in J.P. Collier's extra-illustrated printed exemplum of his *History of English Dramatic Poetry* (London, 1879), II, 487; c. 1600?

Bowers, II, 345-6; Tucker Brooke, pp. 585-6.

Folger, MS X. d. 459 (13).

MrC 9.5, 9.8 See Addenda, p. 631.

MrC 10 *The Passionate Shepherd to his Love* ('Come live with mee, and be my love').

Copy of a four-stanza version in a composite volume of alchemical papers compiled by Dr Simon Forman (1552-1611); c. 1598.

The Passionate Shepherd to his Love

First pub. in a four-stanza version in *The Passionate Pilgrime* (London, 1599); printed in a six-stanza version in *Englands Helicon* (London, 1600); Bowers, II, 536-7; Tucker Brooke, pp. 550-1. For Ralegh's 'Answer' see RaW 189-99. This MS collated in Bowers; facsimile in Bakeless, II, facing p. 184.

Bodleian, MS Ashmole 1486, II, f. 6v.

MrC 11 -----

Copy of a four-stanza version in a verse miscellany compiled by John Lilliat (c.1550-c.1599); c. 1589-99.

This MS collated in Bowers.

Bodleian, MS Rawl. poet. 148, f. 96v.

MrC 12 -----

Copy of a six-stanza version, headed 'The milkemaids song', apparently transcribed from Izaak Walton, *The Compleat Angler* (London, 1653), in a miscellany owned by James Bateman (b. 1633/4) of Christ's College, Cambridge, by Robert Pierrepont (either the son of Col. Francis Pierrepont, M.P. (d. 1659), or the third Earl of Kingston (1650/1-82)) of Holme-Pierrepoint, Nottinghamshire, and by the poet John Oldham (1653-83); c. 1650s-60s.

This MS collated in Bowers.

Folger, MS V. a. 169, Part II, f. 2r-v.

MrC 13 -----

Copy of a seven-stanza version in a miscellany possibly once owned by John Thornborough, Bishop of Limerick (1551-1641); late 16th-early 17th century.

Formerly MS 297.3 and V. b. 75; this MS collated in Bowers and in Tucker Brooke; facsimile in Wraight & Stern, p. 130.

Folger, MS Z. e. 28, f. 100v.

MrC 14 -----

Copy of a four-stanza version, headed 'A Pastoral made by Sr Walter Raleigh' and apparently transcribed from an early MS source; written on a blank leaf in a printed exemplum of Ralegh's *History of the World* (London, 1614); late 18th-early 19th century.

Printed from this MS in Susanne Woods, '"The Passionate Sheepheard" and "The Nimphs Reply": A Study of Transmission', *HLQ*, 34 (1970), 25-33 (pp. 25-6).

Huntington, RB 69107.

MrC 15 -----

Copy of a four-stanza version, untitled, in a composite verse miscellany, including a section owned by one David Williams, used c. 1666-74 by members of the Lloyd family of Llwydiarth; early 17th century.

National Library of Wales, Sotheby MS B2, p. 151.

MrC 16 -----

Copy of a four-stanza version, headed in a later hand 'Poemes written in the Reigne of Queen Elizabeth | A sonnet Madrigal by S^r philipp Sydney', in a collection of state papers; c. 1600-10.

Printed from this MS in Curt F. Bühler, 'Four Elizabethan Poems', *Joseph Quincy Adams Memorial Studies* (Washington, D.C., 1948), 695-706 (p. 696).

Pierpont Morgan Library, R-V. R. of E. (Eliz. 1), No. 48.

MrC 17 -----

Copy of a four-stanza version, untitled and here beginning 'If thou wilt liue and by my loue', in a verse miscellany probably compiled by a member of an Inn of Court; c. 1598-1600s.

Printed from this MS in Samuel A. Tannenbaum, 'Unfamiliar Versions of Some Elizabethan Poems', *PMLA*, 45 (1930), 809-21 (pp. 815-16); collated in Bowers.

Rosenbach Foundation, MS 1083/15, f. 29.

MrC 18 -----

Copy of an eight-stanza version (plus two lines), headed 'Blundwells exercise', in a miscellany of poems and state papers; among the papers of the Troyte-Bullock family, formerly of Zeals House, Mere, and probably deriving from the papers of the Chafyn family of Bulford and Chisenbury or the Reymes family of Waddon, near Dorchester; c. 1620s.

Wiltshire Record Office, 865/500, f. [11v].

MrC 19 -----

Copy in a musical setting, endorsed 'NB. This Tune was found in an old MS. as old as Shakespears Time by Sr J. Hawkins'; 18th century.

Yale, Osborn Collection, Files/Marlowe.

DRAMATIC WORKS

MrC 20 *Doctor Faustus.*

A printed exemplum of John Leland, *Principum Ac illustrium aliquot & eruditorum in Anglia virorum Encomia* (London, 1589), with Thomas Nashe's signature and annotations on the title page (recto and verso) and pp. 130, 132, including the quotations 'Che sara sara deuinynitie adie' (cp. *Faustus*, I, i, 74-5) and 'studie in indian silke' (cp. *Faustus*, I, i, 117-18); c. 1589-1601.

First pub. [London, 1601?] (earliest extant edition London, 1604); Bowers, II, 121-271 (pp. 163-4); Tucker Brooke, pp. 139-229 (pp. 148-9). These annotations printed, with facsimiles, in Paul H. Kocher, 'Some Nashe Marginalia concerning Marlowe', *MLN*, 57 (1942), 45-9.

Folger, STC 15447.

MrC 21 *Edward II.*

Printed exemplum of the edition of 1598 with the text of the missing first two leaves (title page and 70 lines of text) supplied in MS, probably transcribed from the edition of 1594; 1598-early 17th century.

First pub. London, 1594; Bowers, II, 1-119; Tucker Brooke, pp. 307-85. This item has been thought to demonstrate the existence of a 1593 edition: see Bowers, II, 3 seq. Facsimiles in W.W. Greg's edition, Malone Society (Oxford, 1925), and in Bakeless, II, facing p. 24.

Victoria and Albert Museum, Dyce Collection, Cat. No. 6209 (Pressmark 25. D. 40).

MrC 22 -----

Copy of Mortimer's lines beginning 'Base fortune, now I see, that in thy wheele' (V, vi, 59-61), in a miscellany compiled by Sir Henry Oxinden (1609-70) of Kent; c. 1642-70.

Bowers, II, 95; Tucker Brooke, p. 384. This MS discussed in Mark Eccles, 'Marlowe in Kentish Tradition', *N & Q*, 169 (20 July 1935), 39-41.

Folger, MS V. b. 110, p. 58.

MrC 23 *The Massacre at Paris.*

One leaf fragment, consisting of a draft of part of one scene; c. 1590s.

First pub. London, [1594?]; Bowers, I, 353-417; Tucker Brooke, pp. 440-84. This fragment printed in Bowers, I, 390-1, as scene xvii, lines 806-20 (with a facsimile as frontispiece), and in Tucker Brooke as an Appendix, pp. 482-3; first pub. in J.P. Collier's introduction to *The Jew of Malta* in his edition of Dodsley's *Old Plays* (London, 1825), VIII, 244; also printed in *The Massacre at Paris*, ed. W.W. Greg, Malone Society (Oxford, 1928). For discussions of this MS, which has been mistakenly considered an autograph, see particularly J.Q. Adams, '*The Massacre at Paris* Leaf', *The Library*, 4th Ser. 14 (1934), 447-69; J.M. Nosworthy, 'The Marlowe Manuscript', *The Library*, 4th Ser. 26 (1946), 158-71; Wraight & Stern, pp. 224-32 (with facsimiles); Croft, *Autograph Poetry*, I, xiv; R.E. Alton, 'Marlowe Authenticated', *TLS* (26 April 1974), pp. 446-7; Petti, *English Literary Hands*, No. 35 (with a facsimile); P.J. Croft, *TLS* (24 February 1978), p. 241.

Folger, MS J. b. 8.

John Marston

1576-1634

ABBREVIATIONS

Bullen *The Works of John Marston*, ed. A. H. Bullen, 3 vols (London, 1887).

Davenport *The Poems of John Marston*, ed. Arnold Davenport (Liverpool, 1961).

For abbreviations used throughout Volume I, see p.xi.

INTRODUCTION

Two extant MSS of dramatic works by Marston are partly in his autograph (MaJ 3, 6). There also survives a single autograph letter, addressed to Sir Gervase Clifton and now at the University of Nottingham (Clifton MS Cl C 567). It is printed and discussed in W. H. Grattan Flood, 'A John Marston Letter', RES, 4 (1928), 86-7; Robert E. Brettle, 'The "Poet Marston" Letter to Sir Gervase Clifton, 1607', *RES*, 4 (1928), 212-14; Brettle, 'Notes on John Marston', *RES*, NS 13 (1962), 390-3; and Albert H. Tricomi, 'Identifying Sir Gervase Clifton, the Addressee of Marston's Letter, 1607', *N & Q*. 222 (May-June 1977), 202-3. The letter is reproduced in FACSIMILE XXVI.

Another letter, from a certain 'John Marston' to Lord Kimbolton, was formerly among the Duke of Manchester's papers in the Public Record Office but was sold and is now in the possession of Mr R. M. Willcocks (a postal specialist) of 7 Shooters Hill Road, London SE3 (confirmed by letter 6 September 1976). This letter was first recorded in *Shakespeare's Comedies, Histories, Tragedies and Poems*, ed. John Payne Collier (London, 1858), I, 179, and was also printed in *HMC*, 8th Report (1881), Appendix, Part II, p. 58, and in Robert E. Brettle, 'John Marston and the Duke of Buckingham 1627-1628', *N & Q*, 212 (September 1967), 326-30. Albert H. Tricomi has now established beyond doubt, however, that this letter was not written by John Marston the dramatist but was written in 1642 by John Marston, rector of St Mary Magdalen Church, Canterbury. Professor Tricomi's findings, together with facsimiles of the letters of the two John Marstons, are set forth in 'The Provenance of John Marston's letter to Lord Kimbolton', *PBSA*, 72 (1978), 213-19. This article also includes a facsimile of the subscription written by John Marston, the Canterbury cleric, in the Oxford *Liber Subscriptionum Clericorum, 1628-46*, now in the Oxford University Archives (MS Oxf. Dioc. e. 13, p. 82).

A third letter, supposedly from John Marston to Philip Henslowe, was 'discovered' by John Payne Collier at Dulwich College (Alleyn Papers, Vol. I, No. 103, f. 148). This letter is one of Collier's forgeries: see George F. Warner, *Catalogue of the Manuscripts and Muniments of Alleyn's College of God's Gift at Dulwich* (London, 1881), p. 49. A facsimile, which clearly shows it to be a forgery, appears in Clement Mansfield Ingilby, *A Complete View of the Shakspere Controversy* (London, 1861), p. 273. This document is also reproduced and discussed by Professor Tricomi in 'John Marston's Manuscripts', *HLQ* (forthcoming, 1979).

Four other genuine specimens of Marston's handwriting have been discovered by Robert E. Brettle. One is Marston's boyish signature of 4 February 1591/2 in the Oxford University Archives (Subscription Register, 1581-1615, S.P./38, Register Ab, f. 75v). Two more are brief Latin statements and signatures written when he subscribed to the Thirty-nine Articles on his ordination in 1609: one dated 24 September on f. 14, the other dated 24 December on f. 17 of the *Liber Subscriptionum Clericorum, 1605-35*, in the Oxford University Archives. A fourth signature is on his Will of 17 June 1634, now in the Public Record Office (PROB 10/528, proved 9 July 1634); the text is printed in *The Works of John Marston*, ed. James Orchard Halliwell (London, 1856), I, viii-ix. All these documents are discussed by Brettle in 'John Marston, Dramatist at Oxford, 1591(?)-1594, 1609', *RES*, 3 (1927), 398-405; 'John Marston, Dramatist: Some New Facts about his Life', *MLR*, 22 (1927), 7-14; and 'Notes on John Marston', *RES*, NS 13 (1962), 390-3.

In his article on Marston and the Duke of Buckingham, *N & Q*, 212 (September 1967), 326-30, Brettle drew attention to three satirical poems on Buckingham which he thought might have been written by Marston. These poems are (1) *Upon the Dukes Goeing into Fraunce* ('And wilt thou goe, great duke, and leave us heere'), (2) *The Duke Return'd Againe. 1627* ('And art return'd againe with all thy faults'), and (3) the chronogram *Georg IVs DVX BVCkIngaMIae MDCXXVVVIII* ('Thy numerous name with this yeare doth agree'). The chronogram is ascribed to 'John Marston' in Nicholas Burghe's miscellany in the Bodleian (MS Ashmole 38, p. 25). There are anonymous copies in the Bodleian (MS Ashmole 38, p. 19; MS Rawl. poet. 160, f. 198; MS Tanner 475, f. 100), the British Library (Add. MS 10309, f. 39v; Sloane MS 826, f. 181v), Cambridge University Library (MS Gg. 4. 13, pp. 115, 150 (two copies)), Emmanuel College, Cambridge (MS 1. 3. 16 (James 68), [VI, No. 1]), and in a miscellany (p. 88) of Sir John Oglander (1585-1655) owned by the Oglander family on the Isle of Wight. The first two poems have been associated with Marston because an anonymous copy of them in the Huntington (HM 742) was at one time believed to be in Marston's autograph, a circumstance which, together with the single attribution of the third poem, suggested that all three poems were Marston's compositions. In fact the Huntington MS is certainly not in Marston s hand (nor in the hand of John Marston, the Canterbury cleric). It is, however, possible that the two John Marstons have again been confused. There is evidence that the Canterbury cleric was a political dissident who may well have penned the chronogram which is expressly attributed to him; but there is no direct evidence for linking the first two poems with either Marston. This matter is discussed by Professor Tricomi in his article on 'John Marston's Manuscripts' (*HLQ*, 1979). It may be added that in one copy (MS Ashmole 38, pp. 133-5) the second poem is ascribed to 'Mr. [John] Heappe'. Anonymous copies of the first poem can be found in the Bodleian (MSS Douce f. 5, fol. 21v; Eng. poet. c. 50, f. 13v; Malone 23, p. 105; Rawl. poet. 26, f. 80v; Rawl. poet. 160, f. 198), the British Library (Add. MS 10309, f. 42; Sloane MS 826, f. 161; Sloane MS 1792, f. 5), Cambridge University Library (MS Gg. 4. 13, p. 111), Harvard (MS Eng 686, f. 52), Northamptonshire Record Office (I.L. 4333), Rosenbach Foundation (MS 239/27, p. 57 bis), and Yale, Osborn Collection (b 54, p. 881). Anonymous copies of the second poem are in the Berkshire Record Office (Trumbull Add. MS 51), Bodleian (MSS Ashmole 36/37, f. 50v; CCC. 317, f. 150r-v; Douce f. 5, fol. 5v; Eng. poet. c.50, f. 27v; Malone 21, f. 56v; Malone 23, p. 106; Rawl. poet. 26, f. 79; Rawl. poet. 160, f. 198; Tanner 306, f. 264; Tanner 465, ff. 98v-100; Bradford Central Library (Spencer-Stanhope, Calendar No. 2795, Bundle 10, No. 34, ff. [17v-18v]); the British Library (Add. MSS 10309, ff. 42-4v; 19268, f. 31r-v; 22591, f. 315r-v; 27408, ff. 146-7, 148 (two copies); Sloane MS 826, ff. 32-3v, 161v-4 (two copies)); Cambridge University Library (MS Gg. 4. 13, pp. 111-13); Chester City Record Office (CR 63/2/19, ff. 63v-4 (the Davenport of Bramhall MS recorded in *HMC*, 12th Report, Appendix IX (1891), pp. 545-52)); Huntington (HM 198, Part I, pp. 44-6); Leeds Archives Department (TN/F7 (two copies)); Northamptonshire Record Office (I.L. 4287); Yale, Osborn Collection (b 200, p. 50); Yorkshire Archaeological Society, Leeds (MD 59/22, [no item number]); and one sold at Sotheby's, 21 February 1978, Lot 367, to Theodore Hofmann.

One other work has been somewhat bedevilled by Collier and by a tenuous attribution to Marston. That is the Gray's Inn entertainment of February 1617/18 known variously as *The Mountbank's Masque* or as *The First Antimasque of Mountebanks*, printed by Collier and Peter Cunningham in *Inigo Jones ... and Five Court Masques*, The Shakespeare Society (London, 1848), pp. 111-30, and reprinted in Bullen, III, 417-43. Collier's copy-text was a MS now in the Huntington (HM 21), which has on the first page the pencil note 'By J. Marstone' and has a few other pencil annotations in the text. In fact, as Professor Tricomi makes clear in his article on Marston's manuscripts, these notations are obviously in a modern hand, possibly Collier's own hand, and cannot be taken as the slightest evidence of any connection between this entertainment and John Marston. Marston's authorship is also rejected in Bentley, V, 1376-8. The other known contemporary copies of the work are all anonymous: i.e. Bodleian, MS Rawl. D. 1021; British Library, Add. MS 5956, ff. 74-82v; and two hitherto unrecorded versions: one in Gray's Inn Library (MS 29), the other belonging to H. M. FitzRoy Newdegate of Arbury Hall, Nuneaton (MS A 414, ff. 1-12v).

Of Marston's genuine works, none of the poems is known to survive in MS. Apart from the two autograph MSS of dramatic works (MrJ 3, 6), there is a contemporary copy of part of the Derby entertainment (MrJ 7); there are early settings of a song from *The Dutch Courtezan* (MrJ 4-5), and there are a few extracts from printed editions of the plays in miscellanies. Unless otherwise stated, these MSS have not been recorded by editors. Marston's dramatic canon is taken to be that established in Chambers, III, 427-34, including *Jack Drum's Entertainment* which Marston evidently helped to revise but which is not printed in Bullen.

PB.

ARRANGEMENT

Verse	(see INTRODUCTION)
Dramatic works	MrJ 1-10.

FACSIMILE XXVI — John Marston: Letter to Sir Gervase Clifton, [1607]. University of Nottingham, Clifton MS Cl C567. Reproduced by permission of Lieutenant Colonel P.T. Clifton and the University of Nottingham.

Mr lett me intreate you to admitt my most inforced excuse
for not yett sending the booke. First wth my owne hand
I writt one coppye: for all the rest wch I had caused to
be transcribed were given ~~at~~ and stolne from me at my
Lord Spencers. Then wth all speedie care I gave my
coppy unto a Scrivener to write out: who is now sicke
and will instantly have ended it. You shall find it attend
you at yor returne from Sr John Harringtons.
I shall attended my Lady Derby if I could possible
have provided yor booke wch only busines kept me at home.
And so I beseech you Sr as this is most true so lett it be a
most sufficient satisfaction for detaining my promise.
As for yor carefull tendering yor warde, it approves you worthy
yor name and noble auncestors whose virtues the Rumor of
this Contry hath given me at large.
Be you ever the heire of their virtues as of their
possessions and my unworthy Spirit shall ever acknowledge
due honor to such merritt. I have now but one request
to you wch is that our acquaintance may grow to the
deare title of frendshipp wch respects not outward fortune
but inward ~~one~~ desert. wherein I will ever be most industrious
to equall you. And so desiring ever to live in
yor loving remembrance I rest

The harty lover of you & yor virtues

John Marston

John Marston

VERSE

--- *The Duke Return'd Againe. 1627* ('And art returned again with all thy faults').

See INTRODUCTION.

--- *Georg IVs DVX BVCkIngaMIae MDCXVVVIII* ('Thy numerous name with this yeare doth agree').

See INTRODUCTION.

--- *Upon the Dukes Goeing into Fraunce* ('And wilt thou goe, great duke, and leave us heere').

See INTRODUCTION.

DRAMATIC WORKS

MrJ 1 *Antonio and Mellida, The First Part.*

Extracts in a miscellany compiled by Edward Pudsey (1573-1613); 1600s.

First pub. London, 1602; Bullen, I, 1-93; ed. W.W. Greg, Malone Society (Oxford, 1921); ed. G.K. Hunter (London, 1965).

Bodleian, MS Eng. poet. d. 3, f. 41v.

MrJ 2 *Antonio's Revenge.*

Extracts in a miscellany compiled by Edward Pudsey (1573-1613); 1600s.

First pub. London, 1602; ed. W.W. Greg, Malone Society (Oxford, 1921); ed. G.K. Hunter (London, 1966).

Bodleian, MS Eng. poet. d. 3, f. 41v.

*MrJ 3 *The Argument of the Spectacle presented to the Sacred Maiestys of great Brittan, and Denmark as they Passed through London.*

Copy, partly autograph; five leaves; presented to James I on or shortly after 31 July 1606.

First pub. (from this MS) in Bullen (1887), III, 405-11; Davenport, pp. 183-8. This MS discussed in R.E. Brettle, 'Notes on John Marston', *RES*, NS 13 (1962), 390-3 (p. 391). Facsimile of one page in Greg, *English Literary Autographs*, plate XVIII(b-c).

British Library, Royal MS 18 A. XXXI.

MrJ 4 *The Dutch Courtezan*, I, ii, 220-7. Song: 'The dark is my delight'.

Copy of Franceschina's song in a musical setting, in a MS songbook compiled by one Giles Earle; c. 1615-26.

First pub. London, 1605; Bullen, II, 1-103 (p. 19); ed. M.L. Wine (London, 1965), pp. 19-20; ed. Peter Davison (Edinburgh, 1968), p. 29. Printed from this MS in Andrew J. Sabol, 'Two Unpublished Stage Songs for the "Aery of Children"', *RN*, 13 (1960), 222-32 (p. 230); recorded in Wine and in Davison.

British Library, Add. MS 24665, f. 61r-v.

MrJ 5 ----- -----

Copy in a musical setting in a MS songbook once owned by one Robius Downes; early 17th century.

British Library, Egerton MS 2971, ff. 8v-9.

*MrJ 6 *The Entertainment of the Dowager-Countess of Darby.*

Copy, partly autograph, partly in two other hands, headed 'The ho[ble]: Lorde & Lady of Huntingdons Entertainement of theire right Noble Mother Alice: Countesse Dowager of Darby the firste nighte of her honors arrivall att the house of Ashby'; the MS presented to the Dowager Countess of Derby; [1607].

First pub. (from this MS) in *Poems of John Marston*, ed. Alexander B. Grosart (Manchester, 1879); Bullen, III, 383-404 (reprinting Grosart); Davenport, pp. 189-207. This MS discussed in R.E. Brettle, 'Notes on John Marston', *RES*, NS 13 (1962), 390-3 (p. 391). Facsimile pages in Davenport, p. 191; R.B. Haselden, 'Scientific Aids for the Study of Manuscripts', *Transactions of the Bibliographical Society*, Supplement 10 (Oxford, 1935), fig. XIII; Croft, *Autograph Poetry*, I, 28.

Huntington, EL 34. B9.

MrJ 7 -----

Draft of an abbreviated form of the preliminary description of the arrangements at the Park Gates and the whole of Merymna's first speech, in a composite volume of MSS; August 1607.

This MS collated in Davenport.

British Library, Sloane MS 848, f. 9.

MrJ 8 *The Fawn.*

Extracts, transcribed from one of the editions of 1606, in a miscellany compiled by William Drummond of Hawthornden; c. 1609.

First pub. as *Parasitaster, or The Fawn* (London, 1606); Bullen, II, 105-229; ed. Gerald A. Smith (London, 1965).

National Library of Scotland, MS 2059 (Hawthornden Vol. VII), ff. 344-8v.

Jack Drum's Entertainment

MrJ 9 *Jack Drum's Entertainment.*

Extracts in a miscellany compiled by Edward Pudsey (1573-1613); 1600s.

First pub. London, 1601; ed. John S. Farmer, Tudor Facsimile Texts (1912).

Bodleian, MS Eng. poet. d. 3, f. 40v.

--- *The Mountbank's Masque.*

See INTRODUCTION.

MrJ 10 *What You Will.*

Extracts in a miscellany compiled by Edward Pudsey (1573-1613); 1600s.

First pub. London, 1607; Bullen, II, 317-419.

Bodleian, MS Eng. poet. d. 3, ff. 80v, 81.

Philip Massinger

1583-1640

ABBREVIATIONS

Edwards & Gibson *The Plays and Poems of Philip Massinger*, ed. Philip Edwards and Colin Gibson, 5 vols (Oxford, 1976).

For abbreviations used throughout Volume I, see p.xi.

INTRODUCTION

Several of Massinger's autographs have survived. The most important is the complete autograph of his play *Believe as You List* (MsP 14). A printed exemplum of *The Duke of Milan* (1623) contains autograph corrections (MsP 17) and autograph presentation verses to Sir Francis Foljambe (MsP 9). Six other printed exempla of Massinger's plays contain autograph corrections (MsP 15, 18, 20, 32, 34, 37). These six plays were bound together with unannotated exempla of *The Fatal Dowry* (1632) and *The Maid of Honour* (1632), probably for Massinger himself, but the collection was broken up and the plays individually rebound by Edmund Gosse (1849-1928). The collection, known as the 'Harbord volume' since it was sold from the Harbord Library at Gunton, Norfolk, in 1853, is described in the following works: A. H. Cruickshank, *Philip Massinger* (Oxford, 1920), pp. 215-23; W. W. Greg, 'More Massinger Corrections', *The Library*, 4th Ser. 5 (1925), 59-91, reprinted in Greg, *Collected Papers* (Oxford, 1966), pp. 120-48; Cruickshank, 'Massinger Corrections', *The Library*, 4th Ser. 5 (1925), 175-9; J. E. Gray, 'Still More Massinger Corrections', *The Library*, 5th Ser. 5 (1951), 132-9; A. K. McIlwraith, 'The Manuscript Corrections in Massinger's Plays', *The Library*, 5th Ser. 6 (1952), 213-16; and Edwards & Gibson, I, xxxii-xxxiii.

Massinger's signature appears on the presentation MS of his consolatory verses to the Earl of Pembroke and Montgomery (MsP 8). His signature is also found on five documents among the Alleyn Papers at Dulwich College: on three leases of Edward Alleyn (Vol. VII, No. 8, ff. 114, 115, 116), on a letter from Nathan Field to Philip Henslowe (probably July 1613) which has autograph additions by Massinger and Robert Daborne (Vol. I, No. 68, f. 96), and on a bond of 4 July 1615 between Massinger and Daborne on the one part and Henslowe on the other (Vol. I, No. 102, f. 146). The relevant portion of the letter from Field is reproduced in Cruickshank, *Philip Massinger* (Oxford, 1920), facing p. 4, and in Greg, *English Literary Autographs*, plate XIII(b). Both this letter and the bond of 1615 are reproduced in *The Henslowe Papers*, ed. R. A. Foakes (London, 1977), II, Nos. 68, 102. The signature on the bond of 1615 is also reproduced in Irvine E. Gray, 'Philip Massinger: An Archival Problem', *Journal of the Society of Archivists*, 2 (1960-4), 319-21 (fig. b). One other 'signature' — the inscription 'Philip Massinger his booke' on a printed exemplum of Phineas Fletcher, *Sicelides* (Cambridge, 1631) in the Dyce Collection in the Victoria and Albert Museum — is a suspected forgery (see Edwards & Gibson, I, xliv).

Printed exempla of two of Massinger's plays with interesting MS alterations made by unidentified hands have been collated in Edwards & Gibson and are included in the entries (MsP 19, 38). In addition, there is a similarly corrected exemplum of *The Maid of Honour* (MsP 28), and an exemplum of *The Renegado* contains an original proof sheet (MsP 35). Some printed exempla of *The City Madam* (London, 1658 or 1659) also have what is probably a printer's MS emendation of the word 'Boman' to 'Roman' on sig. I1[r] (IV, ii, 113): e.g. volumes in the Bodleian (Malone Q 23 and Malone 185 (4)); the British Library (Department of Printed Books, Ashley 1128); University of Chicago; Worcester College, Oxford (Plays 4.78); and one with the bookplate of Sir Thomas Hanmer formerly owned by Dobell. These volumes are discussed in Edwards & Gibson, IV, 7, and in A. K. McIlwraith, 'Pen-and-ink Corrections in Books of the Seventeenth Century', *RES*, 7 (1931), 204-7.

Other items recorded in the *Index* include the important scribal copy of *The Parliament of Love* (MsP 31), various MS copies of poems by Massinger, and some extracts and songs from the plays in early miscellanies. Items MsP 1 and 7 are of special interest in being hitherto unrecorded verses, which throw light on a theatrical war in which Massinger is known to have been engaged in 1630. The Trumbull MS in which Massinger's Prologue to *The Maid of Honour* appears (MsP 7) also contains an anonymous attack on this prologue headed *To my honored ffriend M[r] Thomas Carew at S[r]: Richard Leightons house in Boswell Court*, and beginning 'Soe the rude Carpenter or Mason may', an attack which provoked in turn Massinger's bitter retaliation, *A Charme for a Libeller* (MsP 1). The MSS recorded in the entries have not been noted in Edwards & Gibson unless specifically stated.

The canon of Massinger's plays accepted in the *Index* is based on Edwards & Gibson. For various other plays in which Massinger probably had a hand see BEAUMONT AND FLETCHER and the discussion of the canon in Bentley, IV, 749-830. There exist many later adaptations and prompt books of the plays (particularly of *A New Way to Pay Old Debts*, which Edmund Kean made popular in the 19th century), but, except for a 17th-century adaptation of *The Renegado* (MsP 36), they have not been given entries. A MS adaptation of the *City Madam* called *The Cure of Pride*, preserved in the Huntington (HM 95), has been sometimes assigned to the late 17th century but may have been written early in the 18th century (see Edwards & Gibson, IV, 12).

PB.

ARRANGEMENT

Verse MsP 1-13
Dramatic works MsP 14-38.
See also Addenda to Part 2, p. 631.

Philip Massinger

VERSE

MsP 1 *A Charme for a Libeller* ('I'me in my Circle & I haue thee here').

Copy of a 150-line satirical poem signed 'Phillip Massinger', written in a MS journal of proceedings in Parliament from January to March 1628/9, owned on 1 May 1629 by one Arthur Langford; among the papers of the Trumbull family of Easthampstead Park; c. 1630.

First pub. (from this MS) in Peter Beal, 'Massinger at Bay', *YES* (forthcoming, 1980).

Berkshire Record Office, Trumbull Add. MS 51, ff. [64v-6v].

MsP 2 *The Copie of a Letter written vpon occasion to the Earle of Pembrooke Lo: Chamberlaine* ('Soe subiect to the worser fame').

Copy in a verse miscellany appended to a MS volume of poems by John Donne; c. 1630s.

First pub. in *Poems consisting of Epistles & Epigrams, Satyrs, Epitaphs and Elegies* <chiefly by John Eliot> (London, 1658). Printed from this MS in Edwards & Gibson, IV, 389-91.

Trinity College, Dublin, MS 877, ff. 274-5v (pp. 554-7).

MsP 3 *A funerall Poem Sacred to the memorie of the trewly noble and most accomplishid gentleman Sr Warham Sentliger Knight lineally descended from &c:* ('Such were his noble Ancesters, and yet').

Copy of a 108-line elegy, subscribed 'Written by his truly devoted servant Philip Massinger', in a miscellany compiled by the minor playwright John Clavell (1601-43); among the papers of the Troyte-Bullock family formerly of Zeals House, Mere; c. 1635.

First pub. (from this MS) in J.H.P. Pafford, 'A New Poem by Philip Massinger', *N & Q*, 223 (December 1978), 503-5.

Wiltshire Record Office, 865/502, ff. [11-12 rev.].

MsP 4 *Londons Lamentable Estate, in any great Visitation* ('O London; Where are now those powerfull Charmes').

Copy, containing a dedication to John Piers dated 23 October 1626, in a MS volume of religious pieces compiled by the scrivener Ralph Crane; c. 1626.

First pub. (from this MS) in H.W. Garrod, *Genius Loci and other Essays* (Oxford, 1950); printed from this MS in Edwards & Gibson, IV, 399-405.

Bodleian, MS Rawl. poet. 61, ff. 71-6.

MsP 5 -----

Copy, headed 'A trewe discription of the lamentable estate of the Cittie of London in the visitation of 1625', in a verse miscellany once owned by one John Nutting; c. 1630s-40s.

This MS collated in Edwards & Gibson.

St John's College, Cambridge, MS S. 23 (James 416), ff. 26-30.

MsP 6 *A Newyeares Guift presented to my Lady and M:^{rs} the then Lady Katherine Stanhop now Countesse of Chesterfeild* ('Before I ow'd to you the name').

Copy in a verse miscellany appended to a MS volume of poems by John Donne; c. 1630s.

First pub. (from this MS) in A.B. Grosart, 'Literary-Finds in Trinity College, Dublin, and Elsewhere', *ES*, 26 (1899), 1-19 (pp. 6-7); printed from this MS in Edwards & Gibson, IV, 393-4.

Trinity College, Dublin, MS 877, ff. 275v-6v (pp. 557-9).

MsP 7 *Prologue to ye Mayde of honour* ('To all y^{t} are come hither, and haue brought').

Copy of a 32-line prologue for a revival of *The Maid of Honour* at the Cockpit early in 1630, written in a MS journal of proceedings in Parliament from January to March 1628/9, owned on 1 May 1629 by one Arthur Langford; among the papers of the Trumbull family of Easthampstead Park; c. 1630.

First pub. (from this MS) in Peter Beal, 'Massinger at Bay', *YES* (forthcoming, 1980).

Berkshire Record Office, Trumbull Add. MS 51, f. [63].

*MsP 8 *Serio, sed Serio. To the right ho:^{ble} my most singular good Lord and Patron Philip Earle of Pembrooke and Montgomerye, Lord Chamberlaine of his Ma:^{ties} Houshould &c. Vppon The deplorable and vntimely death of his late truely noble Sonne Charles Lord Herbert &c.* ('T'was ffate, nott want of dutie did mee wronge').

Copy in the hand of an amanuensis with Massinger's autograph signature; [1636].

First pub. in *The Dramatic Works of Mr. Philip Massinger*, ed. Thomas Coxeter (London, 1759). Printed from this MS in Edwards & Gibson, IV, 418-20.

British Library, Royal MS 18 A. XX.

*MsP 9 *To my Honorable ffreinde S^{r} ffrancis ffoliambe knight and Baronet* ('S^{r}. wth my service I praesent this booke').

Autograph verses written on the flyleaf of a

To my Honorable ffreinde S^r ffrancis ffoliambe

printed exemplum of *The Duke of Milan* (London, 1623) presented to Sir Francis Foljambe (see MsP 17); [1623].

First pub. (from this MS) in *The Plays of Philip Massinger*, ed. William Gifford, 2nd edition (London, 1813); printed from this MS in Edwards & Gibson, IV, 396. Facsimiles in *The Handbook of the Dyce and Forster Collections* (London, 1880); in R. Garnett and E. Gosse, *English Literature*, II (London, 1903); and in Greg, *English Literary Autographs*, plate XIV(a). A transcript made by Dawson Turner (1775-1858) is in the British Library, Add. MS 28655, ff. 194v-5.

Victoria and Albert Museum, Dyce Collection, Cat. No. 6323 (Pressmark 25. A. 106).

MsP 10 *The Virgins Character* ('Such as doe Trophies striue to raise').

Copy in a verse miscellany once owned by one Peter Daniell; c. 1630s-40s.

First pub. in A.K. McIlwraith, '*The Virgins Character:* A New Poem by Philip Massinger', *RES*, 4 (1928), 64-8; Edwards & Gibson, IV, 409-13. This MS collated in Edwards & Gibson.

Bodleian, MS Eng. poet. c. 50, ff. 106v-8v.

MsP 11 -----

Copy in a verse miscellany compiled by Peter Calfe (1610-67) and his son Peter (d. 1693); c. 1642-50.

Printed from this MS in McIlwraith and in Edwards & Gibson.

British Library, Harley MS 6918, ff. 52-4.

MsP 12 -----

Copy in a verse miscellany owned in 1640 by Anthony St John (1618-73) and Ann St John, of Bletsoe, Bedfordshire; c. 1630s.

This MS collated in Edwards & Gibson.

Harvard, fMS Eng 626, ff. 60-2v.

MsP 13 -----

Copy in a verse miscellany; c. 1630.

Rosenbach Foundation, MS 239/23, pp. 24-9.

DRAMATIC WORKS

--- *Beggars' Bush.*

See BEAUMONT and FLETCHER, B&F 1-13.

*MsP 14 *Believe as You List.*

Autograph fair copy, with revisions made by Edward Knight, book-keeper and prompter of the King's Company, and some further corrections in another hand; prepared for use in the theatre; 29 leaves; licensed and slightly emended by Sir Henry Herbert, Master of the Revels, 6 May 1631.

First pub. (from this MS) London, 1849, ed. T.C. Croker and F.W. Fairholt, Percy Society; printed from this MS in Edwards & Gibson, III, 303-90; reproduced in Tudor Facsimile Texts (London, 1907). Facsimile pages in Greg, *English Literary Autographs*, plate XIV(b); Greg, *Dramatic Documents*, Vol. II; A.H. Cruickshank, *Philip Massinger* (Oxford, 1920), after p. 176; Flower & Munby, *English Poetical Autographs*, p. 9; Edwards & Gibson, III, after p. 302; Petti, *English Literary Hands*, No. 56.

British Library, Egerton MS 2828.

--- *The Bloody Brother.*

See BEAUMONT and FLETCHER, B&F 14-26.

*MsP 15 *The Bondman.*

Exemplum of the edition of 1624 with Massinger's numerous autograph corrections (part of the 'Harbord volume'); c. 1624-33.

First pub. London, 1624; Edwards & Gibson, I, 311-95. This item collated in Edwards & Gibson.

Folger, STC 17632/copy 2.

MsP 16 -----

Extracts, headed 'The bond mā by Massengeoure', in a notebook probably compiled by Thomas Frewen (1630-1702) of Brickwall; c. 1648.

East Sussex Record Office, FRE 686, p. 23 seq.

--- *The City Madam.*

See INTRODUCTION.

*MsP 17 *The Duke of Milan.*

Exemplum of the edition of 1623 with Massinger's autograph verse presentation inscription to Sir Francis Foljambe (see MsP 9) and about 50 autograph textual corrections; c. 1623.

First pub. London, 1623; Edwards & Gibson, I, 213-300. This item collated in Edwards & Gibson; discussed, with a facsimile of the first page of the text, in W.W. Greg, 'Massinger's Autograph Corrections in *The Duke of Milan*, 1623', *The Library*, 4th Ser. 4 (1923), 207-11, reprinted in Greg, *Collected Papers* (Oxford, 1966), pp. 110-19.

Victoria and Albert Museum, Dyce Collection, Cat. No. 6323 (Pressmark 25. A. 106).

The Duke of Milan

*MsP 18 -----

Exemplum of the edition of 1623 with a few corrections in Massinger's autograph made chiefly to replace lines cut away by the binder (part of the 'Harbord volume'); c. 1623-33.

This item recorded in Edwards & Gibson, I, 207.

Folger, STC 17634/copy 1.

MsP 19 -----

Exemplum of the edition of 1623 with 33 substantive MS corrections; 17th century.

This item collated in Edwards & Gibson.

Library of Congress, PR2704.D8 1623.

--- *The Elder Brother.*

See BEAUMONT and FLETCHER, B&F 43-5.

*MsP 20 *The Emperor of the East.*

Exemplum of the edition of 1632 with 81 corrections in Massinger's autograph (part of the 'Harbord volume'); c. 1632-3.

First pub. London, 1632; Edwards & Gibson, III, 401-88. This item collated in Edwards & Gibson.

Folger, STC 17636/copy 1.

--- *The False One.*

See BEAUMONT and FLETCHER, B&F 56-7.

MsP 21 *The Fatal Dowry*, IV, ii, 51-8. Song: 'Courtier, if thou needs wilt wiue'.

Copy of a 16-line version of the Citizen's Song of the Courtier in a verse miscellany; c. 1630.

First pub., as by 'P.M. and N[athan] F[ield]', London, 1632; Edwards & Gibson, I, 13-95 (p. 71). Printed from this MS in Cutts, *Musique de la troupe de Shakespeare*, p. 168; discussed in Edwards & Gibson, V, 107.

Folger, MS V. b. 43, f. 25v.

MsP 21.5 See Addenda, p. 631

MsP 22 ----- IV, ii, 71-86. Song: 'Poore Citizen, if thou wilt be'.

Copy of the Courtier's Song of the Citizen in a musical setting in a MS songbook; c. 1640s.

Edwards & Gibson, I, 72. Printed from this MS and discussed in Cutts, *Musique de la troupe de Shakespeare*, pp. 78-80, and in Edwards & Gibson, I, 97-103 (Appendix B); V, 107.

Bodleian, MS Don. c. 57, ff. 96v-7.

MsP 23 ----- -----

Copy in a composite volume of verse; c. 1625-50.

Bodleian, MS Rawl. poet. 152, f. 19.

MsP 24 ----- -----

Copy in a verse miscellany; c. 1690-1730.

Folger, MS V. 1. 308, f. 9.

MsP 25 ----- -----

Copy in a verse miscellany; c. 1630.

This MS collated in Cutts, *Musique de la troupe de Shakespeare*, pp. 167-8.

Folger, MS V. b. 43, f. 26.

MsP 26 ----- -----

Copy in a verse miscellany entitled *The Theatre of Complements erected*, owned in 1682 by Narcissus Luttrell (1657-1732); c. 1670s.

Yale, Osborn Collection, fb 107, pp. 42-3.

MsP 27 *The Great Duke of Florence.*

Extracts in a miscellany perhaps partly compiled by one William How; mid-17th century.

First pub. London, 1636; Edwards & Gibson, III, 101-80.

Folger, MS V. a. 87, ff. 21v-2v.

--- *The Honest Man's Fortune.*

See BEAUMONT and FLETCHER, B&F 58.

--- *Love's Cure.*

See BEAUMONT and FLETCHER, B&F 65-72.

--- *The Lover's Progress.*

See BEAUMONT and FLETCHER, B&F 73-6.

MsP 28 *The Maid of Honour.*

Exemplum of the edition of 1632 (second issue) with the text of the missing leaves sig. I1-3 supplied in MS and with numerous MS corrections throughout; 17th century.

First pub. London, 1632; Edwards & Gibson, I, 117-97.

British Library, Department of Printed Books, C. 142. d. 16.

The Maid of Honour

MsP 29 -----

Extracts in a miscellany perhaps partly compiled by one William How; mid-17th century.

Folger, MS V. a. 87, ff. 24-33.

--- ----- *Prologue.*

See MsP 7.

MsP 30 *A New Way to Pay Old Debts.*

Extracts, with comments on the play, in a miscellany compiled by Abraham Wright (1611-90); c. 1640.

First pub. London, 1633; Edwards & Gibson, II, 293-377. Printed from this MS in Edwards & Gibson, II, 378-9.

British Library, Add. MS 22608, f. 93r-v.

MsP 31 *The Parliament of Love.*

Copy in the hand of a playhouse scribe who also wrote the MS of Dekker's *Welsh Embassador* (DkT 46), made for use in the theatre, with corrections in the fourth and fifth acts in another hand; imperfect; probably the copy submitted to Sir Henry Herbert, Master of the Revels, for licensing in 1624.

First pub. (from this MS) in *The Plays of Philip Massinger*, ed. William Gifford (London, 1805); edited from this MS in Edwards & Gibson, II, 107-76; literal transcript and facsimile pages in Malone Society edition, ed. K.M. Lea and W.W. Greg (Oxford, 1929).

Victoria and Albert Museum, Dyce Collection, Cat. No. 39 (Pressmark 25. F. 33).

*MsP 32 *The Picture.*

Exemplum of the edition of 1630 with nearly 60 corrections in Massinger's autograph in the first two acts (part of the 'Harbord volume'); c. 1630-3.

First pub. London, 1630; Edwards & Gibson, III, 193-287. This item collated in Edwards & Gibson.

Folger, STC 17640.2/copy 1.

MsP 33 ----- III, v, 26-37. Song: 'The blushing rose and purple flower'.

Copy of the 'song of pleasure' in a musical setting, in a MS songbook owned (in 1659) and partly compiled by the composer John Gamble; c. 1630s-50s.

Edwards & Gibson, III, 244. Printed from this MS in Edwards & Gibson, III, 288-92.

New York Public Library, Music Division, Drexel MS 4257, No. 78.

--- *The Queen of Corinth.*

See BEAUMONT and FLETCHER, B&F 158-65.

*MsP 34 *The Renegado.*

Exemplum of the edition of 1630 with Massinger's numerous autograph corrections and revisions (part of the 'Harbord volume'); c. 1630-3.

First pub. London, 1630; Edwards & Gibson, II, 11-96. This item collated in Edwards & Gibson.

Folger, STC 17641/copy 1.

MsP 35 -----

Exemplum of the edition of 1630 with an original proof sheet (the inner forme of sheet F) containing three MS corrections; [1630].

British Library, Department of Printed Books, C. 142. b. 19.

MsP 36 -----

MS of an adaptation, untitled, possibly written for performances by the King's Company in 1662; 2nd half 17th century.

This MS discussed in Edwards & Gibson, II, 8-9; in W.J. Lawrence, 'The Renegado', *TLS* (24 October 1929), p. 846; in J.G. McManaway, 'Philip Massinger and the Restoration Drama', *Studies in Shakespeare, Bibliography and Theater* (New York, 1969), 3-30 (pp. 14-15); and in Bentley, IV, 814.

Bodleian, MS Rawl. poet. 20.

*MsP 37 *The Roman Actor.*

Exemplum of the edition of 1629 with Massinger's numerous autograph corrections (part of the 'Harbord volume'); c. 1629-33.

First pub. London, 1629; Edwards & Gibson, III, 13-93. This item collated in Edwards & Gibson; facsimile of one page in W.W. Greg, *Collected Papers* (Oxford, 1966), facing p. 128.

Folger, STC 17642/copy 3.

MsP 38 -----

Exemplum of the edition of 1629 with MS corrections; 17th century.

This item collated in Edwards & Gibson.

British Library, Department of Printed Books, 162. d. 8.

--- *Sir John van Olden Barnavelt.*

See BEAUMONT and FLETCHER, B&F 167.

--- *The Spanish Curate.*

See BEAUMONT and FLETCHER, B&F 168-70.

--- *The Virgin Martyr.*

See THOMAS DEKKER, INTRODUCTION.

Thomas Middleton

1580-1627

ABBREVIATIONS

Bullen *The Works of Thomas Middleton*, ed. A. H. Bullen, 8 vols (London, 1885-6; reprinted New York, [1960s]).

For abbreviations used throughout Volume I, see p.xi.

INTRODUCTION

An undoubted example of Middleton's autograph is the signature he wrote in the subscription register on matriculating at The Queen's College, Oxford, 7 April 1598, a register now preserved in the Oxford University Archives (Subscription Register, 1581-1615, S.P./38, Register Ab, f. 93). Five of the six extant MSS of *A Game at Chess*, written twenty-six years later (MiT 14-18), contain handwriting consistent with this signature and can be accepted as in part the author's autograph; one of them (MiT 14) is entirely autograph. For one page of this MS, together with Middleton's Oxford subscription, see FACSIMILE XXVII.

The survival of so many MSS of *A Game at Chess*, all earlier than the first edition, can be accounted for by the special topical interest the play had in 1624 and by the ban imposed upon it by the Government. There survive, besides, important scribal copies of *The Mayor of Queenborough* (MiT 22-3), of *The Witch* (MiT 28), and of one of the many entertainments Middleton wrote for the Lord Mayor of London (MiT 20). Printed exempla of three other plays have the text of missing leaves supplied in MS (MiT 6, 12, 13); one (MiT 6) is of particular interest since the hand can be identified with that of a playhouse scribe, a scribe later associated with the lawyer Challoner Chute or his family.

The entries include early MS copies of various songs and extracts from Middleton's plays and of two poems ascribed to him. The authenticity of one of these poems, a verse written by the author to the King in defence of *A Game at Chess* (MiT 1-4), has been the subject of unnecessary scholarly debate. Unless otherwise stated, the MSS recorded have not been previously noted by editors.

A few additional items may be mentioned. Extracts from *The Phoenix* (1607), *The Family of Love* (1608), and *A Mad World, My Masters* (1608) appear in John Evans's miscellany *Hesperides, or the Muses' Garden* (c. 1655), for details of which see WILLIAM SHAKESPEARE, INTRODUCTION. Some printed exempla of *Two New Playes* [i.e. *More Dissemblers besides Women* and *Women Beware Women*] (London, 1657) are to be found with annotations by early owners. These annotations, which seem to be of little textual or theatrical interest apart from one note in an exemplum at Yale which explains how Livia kills Isabella in the second of the two plays, are discussed in J. R. Mulryne, 'Annotations in some Copies of *Two New Playes by Thomas Middleton*, 1657', *The Library*, 5th Ser. 30 (1975), 217-21. There is also some MS music for Middleton's plays. Music for the first dance by the Witches in *The Witch* can be found in the British Library (Add. MSS 10444, ff. 21, 74v; 17786-9, f. 5v; 38539, f. 4) and at Trinity College, Dublin (MS 408); music for the second dance of the Witches is in the British Library (Add. MS 10444, ff. 21v, 75) and at Christ Church, Oxford (MS Mus. 92, f. 15r-v). This music is printed and discussed by John P. Cutts in 'Jacobean Masque and Stage Music', *M & L*, 35 (1954), 185-200, and in *Musique de la troupe de Shakespeare* (1959), pp. 14-16, 125-6.

Individual plays by Middleton have been edited at various times but the only collected edition remains Bullen. The canon, like that of other Jacobean dramatists, is still a subject of scholarly debate: for general assessments see Bentley, IV, 855-911, and David J. Lake, *The Canon of Thomas Middleton's Plays* (Cambridge, 1975).

PB.

ARRANGEMENT

Verse	MiT 1-5
Dramatic works	MiT 6-34.

See also Addenda to Part 2, p. 632

FACSIMILE XXVII — Thomas Middleton: (a) First page of the Induction to *A Game at Chess*, [1624] (MiT 14). Trinity College, Cambridge, MS 0. 2. 66, folio 1 recto. Reproduced by permission of the Master and Fellows of Trinty College, Cambridge. (b) Subscription on matriculating at The Queen's College, Oxford, 7 April 1598. Oxford University Archives, Subscription Register, 1581-1615, S.P./38, Register Ab, folio 93 recto. Reproduced by permission of the Keeper of the Archives, University of Oxford.

The Induction!

Ignatius Loyola appearing, Error
at his foote as asleepe.

Ign. Hah! where? what Angle of the world is this?
that I can neyther see the politick face
nor with my refinde Nostrills taste the footsteps
of any of my disciples, sonnes and heires
as well of my designes as Institution,
I thought they'de spread over the world by this time
coverd the Earths face and made darke the Land
like the Ægiptian Grasshoppers;
here's too much Light appeares shot from the Eyes
of truth and goodnes never yet deflowrde,
sure they were never here, then is their Monarchie
unperfect yet, a iust reward I see
for their Ingratitude so long to mee
their father and their Founder,
tis not 5 yeares since I was sainted by em,
where slept my honor all the time before
could they be so forgetfull to canonize
their prosperous Institutor, when they had sainted mee
they found no roome in all their Kalendar
to place my name that should have remoovde princes

1598.

Mar. 17. George Walter,
Christofer Darlston,
William Vuedale,
Richarde Vuedale,
Queen's Edward Barrett,
Walter Barrett,
John Leneson,
Thomas Mowlton,
Henry Finman,

Apr. 7. Joseph Hall Univ.
Thomas Middleton Queen's
Edward Evans [illegible]
Apr. 28. Henry Gethen
Jesus Thomas Johnes
John [illegible]
George Ball Ball.
John Crowdman Exeter
May 5. Edmund Wiseman

Thomas Middleton

VERSE

MiT 1 *Petition to King James* ('A harmless game raised merely for delight').

Copy, here beginning 'A hormless game: royd only for delight' and preceded by a note on the success and suppression of *A Game at Chess*, inscribed in an exemplum of the first edition of that play; c. 1625?

First pub. (from this MS) in Edward Capell, *The School of Shakespeare*, III (London, [1780]), p. 31; Bullen, I, lxxxiii; *A Game at Chesse*, ed. R.C. Bald (Cambridge, 1929), p. 166. Printed from this MS, with a facsimile, in Samuel A. Tannenbaum, 'A Middleton Forgery', *PQ*, 12 (1933), 33-6. Tannenbaum considered this MS a forgery (perhaps by George Steevens), but see Bernard M. Wagner, '"A Middleton Forgery"', *PQ*, 14 (1935), 287-8. Tannenbaum also prints a facsimile of a similar MS note, but without the verse, inscribed in a printed exemplum of *A Game at Chess* formerly owned by A.S.W. Rosenbach.

Victoria and Albert Museum, Dyce Collection, Cat. No. 6561 (No. 1) (Pressmark 25. D. 42).

MiT 2 -----

Copy, headed 'On the author of the play called ye game at chesse', in a verse miscellany; c. 1630s.

This MS collated in Wagner, *PQ*, 14 (1935), 288.

Bodleian, MS Douce f. 5, fol. 22v.

MiT 3 -----

Copy, headed 'The petition of poet Midleton Autho^r of ye Game at Chess, to king Iames', in a composite volume of verse; c. 1624-40s.

Printed from this MS in Wagner, *PQ*, 14 (1935), 288.

Bodleian, MS Rawl. poet. 152, f. 3.

MiT 4 -----

Copy of an eight-line version, headed 'Verses sent to King James', in a miscellany compiled by Sir Thomas Dawes; c. 1624-8.

Printed from this MS in Geoffrey Bullough, '"The Game at Chesse": How it Struck a Contemporary', *MLR*, 49 (1954), 156-63 (p. 163); reprinted in *A Game at Chess*, ed. J.W. Harper (London, 1966), p. xvii.

British Library, Add. MS 29492, f. 43.

MiT 4.5 See Addenda, p. 632.

MiT 5 *On the death of that great master in his art and quality, painting and playing, R[ichard] Burbage* ('Astronomers and star-gazers this year').

Copy, ascribed to 'Tho: Middleton', in a verse miscellany compiled by one Robert Bishop; c. 1630.

First pub. (from this MS, formerly belonging to Richard Heber (1774-1833)) in John Payne Collier, *New Facts regarding the Life of Shakespeare* (London, 1835), p. 26; Bullen, VII, 413.

Rosenbach Foundation, MS 1083/16, p. 271.

DRAMATIC WORKS

MiT 6 *Blurt, Master-Constable*.

Exemplum of the edition of 1602 with the text of the missing leaves H2 and H3 supplied in MS by a playhouse scribe; probably transcribed from a prompt book; this MS in the same hand as *Dick of Devonshire* (HyT 5) and a verse miscellany in the British Library (Add. MS 33998); c. 1620s-30s.

First pub. London, 1602; Bullen, I, 1-98. This MS discussed, with a facsimile, in James G. McManaway, 'Latin Title-Page Mottoes as a Clue to Dramatic Authorship', *The Library*, 4th Ser. 26 (1945-6), 28-36, reprinted in McManaway, *Studies in Shakespeare, Bibliography, and Theater* (New York, 1969), 55-66.

Folger, STC 17876.

MiT 7 -----

Extracts in a miscellany compiled by Edward Pudsey (1573-1613); 1600s.

This MS discussed in Juliet Gowan, '*Edward Pudsey's Booke* and the Authorship of *Blurt Master Constable*', *RORD*, 8 (1965), 46-8 (where Dekker's authorship of the play is argued).

Bodleian, MS Eng. poet. d. 3, ff. 41v, 42v, 86.

MiT 8 ----- I, ii, 209-16. Song: 'What meat eats the Spaniard?'.

Copies in a musical setting in six MS music part-books; early 17th century.

Bullen, I, 24. Printed from these MSS in Andrew J. Sabol, 'Two Songs with Accompaniment for an Elizabethan Choirboy Play', *SR*, 5 (1958), 149-59.

British Library, Add. MSS 17786-91, No. 28, (i-iv, vi, f. 13v; v, f. 9v).

A Chaste Maid in Cheapside, IV, i, 162-72, 174-9

MiT 9 *A Chaste Maid in Cheapside*, IV, i, 162-72, 174-9. Song: 'Cupid is Venus' only joy'.

Copy of the Welshwoman's song in a musical setting, in a MS songbook once owned by one Richard Elliotts and possibly by the composer Adrian Batten (d. 1637); c. 1630.

First pub. London, 1630; Bullen, V, 1-115 (pp. 80-1); ed. R.B. Parker (London, 1969), (pp. 84-5); this song also occurs in *More Dissemblers besides Women* (I, iv, 89-99). This MS collated in Cutts, *Musique de la troupe de Shakespeare*, pp. 144-6; see also Cutts, 'The Music for *A Chaste Maid in Cheapside*', Appendix II in Parker, pp. 84-5, 128-37.

British Library, Add. MS 29481, f. 6v.

MiT 10 ----- -----

Copy in a musical setting in a MS songbook once owned by a certain Anne Twice; c. 1620.

This MS collated in Cutts, *Musique de la troupe de Shakespeare*, pp. 144-6, and in Parker, pp. 84-5, 128-37.

New York Public Library, Music Division, Drexel MS 4175, No. xxiiii.

MiT 11 ----- -----

Second copy in a musical setting in a MS songbook once owned by a certain Anne Twice; c. 1620.

This MS collated in Cutts, *Musique de la troupe de Shakespeare*, pp. 144-6, and in Parker, pp. 84-5, 128-37.

New York Public Library, Drexel MS 4175, No. lvi.

MiT 12 *A Fair Quarrel*.

Exemplum of the second edition (1622) with the text of the missing last leaf (sig. K4) supplied in MS; 17th century.

First pub., as written by Middleton and William Rowley, London, 1617; Bullen, IV, 153-276; ed. R.V. Holdsworth (London, 1974); ed. George R. Price (London, 1977).

Worcester College, Oxford, Plays 2.1(1).

MiT 13 *The Family of Love*.

Exemplum of the edition of 1608 with the text of the various missing leaves (title page, address to the reader, prologue, parts of A3 and A4, I3 and the epilogue on I4) supplied in MS; 17th century.

First pub. London, 1608; Bullen, III, 1-120.

Worcester College, Oxford, Plays 2.1(2).

--- -----

See also INTRODUCTION.

*MiT 14 *A Game at Chess*.

Autograph; 106 pages; [1624].

First pub. London, [1625]; Bullen, VII, 1-136; edited from this MS by R.C. Bald (Cambridge, 1929) and by J.W. Harper (London, 1966). Facsimile pages in Bald, facing p. 34; Harper, p. 1; Greg, *English Literary Autographs*, plate XCIV(a); Petti, *English Literary Hands*, No. 54. See also FACSIMILE XXVII.

Trinity College, Cambridge, MS O. 2. 66 (James 1170).

*MiT 15 -----

Copy in two scribal hands, with the title page, two sections of the text and two corrections in Middleton's autograph; 108 pages; [1624].

This MS collated in Bald and in Harper; discussed in George R. Price, 'The Huntington MS of *A Game at Chess*', *HLQ*, 17 (1953-4), 83-8; facsimile pages in Bald, facing pp. 27 and 39, and in Greg, *English Literary Autographs*, plate XCIV(c).

Huntington, EL 34. B. 17.

*MiT 16 -----

Copy of an abridged version made by the scrivener Ralph Crane, with Middleton's autograph dedication to William Hammond; 1624.

This MS collated and two scenes printed in Bald; recorded in Harper. Facsimile pages in Bald, facing p. 33; F.P. Wilson, 'Ralph Crane, Scrivener to the King's Players', *The Library*, 4th Ser. 7 (1926-7), 194-215 (plate V); Greg, *English Literary Autographs*, plate XCIV(b).

Bodleian, MS Malone 25.

*MiT 17 -----

Copy in two scribal hands, with the title page in Middleton's autograph; [1624].

This MS described in R.C. Bald, 'A New Manuscript of Middleton's "Game at Chesse"', *MLR*, 25 (1930), 474-8; recorded in Harper. Facsimile of title page in Greg, *English Literary Autographs*, plate XCIV(d-e).

Folger, MS V. a. 342.

*MiT 18 -----

Copy of an early version made by Ralph Crane, with one annotation on p. 32 in Middleton's autograph, and with corrections or revisions in other hands; once owned by Mervyn Archdale (1723-91); 13 August 1624.

This MS described in R.C. Bald, 'An Early Version of Middleton's "Game at Chesse"', *MLR*, 38 (1943), 177-80; recorded in Harper. Facsimile of a page in James G. McManaway, 'The Authorship of Shakespeare', *Studies in Shakespeare, Bibliography, and Theater* (New York, 1969), 175-210 (p. 203).

Folger, MS V. a. 231.

MiT 19 -----

Copy made by Ralph Crane; 102 pages; 1624.

This MS collated in Bald; facsimile of p. 21 in Wilson, *The Library*, 4th Ser. 7 (1926-7), 194-215 (plate IV).

British Library, Lansdowne MS 690.

--- -----

See also MiT 1-4.

--- *Hengist, King of Kent; or The Mayor of Queenborough.*

See MiT 22-3.

MiT 20 *An Invention for the Service of the Right Honourable Edward Barkham, Lord Mayor.*

Copy, with the lacunae badly cropped, in a composite volume of 'Conway Papers', probably descended from Sir Edward Conway, Viscount Conway (d. 1631) of Conway Castle; [1622].

Performed 1622 (see Bentley, IV, 883); first pub. (from this MS) in Bullen, VII (1886), 369-78. The MS accompanied by a modern transcript with the missing lacunae supplied in brackets.

Public Record Office, SP.14/129/53.

MiT 21 *A Mad World, My Masters.*

Extracts transcribed from the edition of 1608 in a miscellany compiled by William Drummond of Hawthornden; c. 1609.

First pub. London, 1608; Bullen, III, 247-359; ed. Standish Henning (London, 1965).

National Library of Scotland, MS 2059 (Hawthornden Vol. VII), ff. 221-2v.

--- -----

See also INTRODUCTION.

MiT 22 *The Mayor of Queenborough.*

Copy, with some corrections in another hand; entitled at the end 'Hengist King off Kent'; c. 1650-70.

First pub. London, 1661; Bullen, II, 1-115. Edited from this MS, with four pages of facsimiles, by R.C. Bald as *Hengist, King of Kent: Or The Mayor of Queenborough* (New York & London, 1938); see also C.J. Sisson's review in *MLR*, 34 (1939), 261-2. This MS formerly part of the 'Lambarde volume' of plays.

Folger, MS J. b. 6.

MiT 23 -----

Copy, entitled at the end 'Hengist King of Kent', among the collections of the Duke of Portland, of Welbeck Abbey, Nottinghamshire; c. 1650-70.

This MS collated in Bald (with two pages of facsimiles), where it is incorrectly stated that this MS and MiT 22 are in the same hand.

University of Nottingham, Portland MS Pw V 20.

--- *More Dissemblers besides Women*, I, iv, 89-95, 98-9. Song: 'Cupid is Venus' only joy'.

See MiT 9-11.

--- *The Nice Valour.*

See BEAUMONT and FLETCHER, B&F 112-53.

--- *The Phoenix.*

See INTRODUCTION.

MiT 24 *The Widow*, III, i, 22-37. Song: 'I keep my horse, I keep my whore'.

Copy of Latrocinio's song, headed 'Thee Highe Lawyers Song in the playe called the Widdowe', in a verse miscellany compiled by Nicholas Burghe (d. 1670); c. 1638.

First pub. London, 1652; Bullen, V, 117-235 (pp. 168-9); ed. Robert T. Levine, Salzburg Studies in English Literature (1975).

Bodleian, MS Ashmole 38, p. 127.

MiT 25 ----- -----

Copy, headed 'On a purse Taker', in a miscellany once owned by Margaret Bellasys, probably the daughter of Thomas, first Lord Fauconberg (1577-1653); c. 1630.

This MS recorded in Bullen, V, 168(n) (misprinted as 'Add. 10319').

British Library, Add. MS 10309, f. 96.

The Widow. Song: 'I keep my horse'

MiT 26 ----- -----

Copy in a musical setting by William Lawes in a MS songbook compiled by Edward Lowe (c.1610-82); [1654-70s].

Printed from this MS and collated in Cutts, *Musique de la troupe de Shakespeare*, pp. 57, 153-4.

British Library, Add. MS 29396, ff. 77v-8.

MiT 27 ----- -----

Copy in a verse miscellany; late 17th century.

British Library, Harley MS 3991, f. 92r-v.

MiT 28 *The Witch.*

Copy made by the scrivener Ralph Crane; c. 1619-27.

First pub. London, 1778; Bullen, V, 351-453. Edited from this MS, with facsimile pages, by W.W. Greg and F.P. Wilson, Malone Society (Oxford, 1950). This MS discussed in Bentley, IV, 903-5, and, with a facsimile of one page, in F.P. Wilson, 'Ralph Crane, Scrivener to the King's Players', *The Library*, 4th Ser. 7 (1926-7), 194-215. A transcript made by George Steevens (1736-1800) for the edition of 1778 is in the Folger, MS D. a. 47.

Bodleian, MS Malone 12.

--- -----

See also INTRODUCTION.

MiT 29 ----- II, i, 128-35. Song: 'In a maiden-time profest'.

Copy of a three-strophe version of Isabella's song in a musical setting by Robert Johnson (as edited by John Wilson), in Wilson's corrected MS volume of his own songs; possibly in Wilson's autograph or else in the hand of someone similarly associated with Edward Lowe (c.1610-82); c. 1656.

Bullen, V, 386; Malone Society edition, p. 25, lines 590-7. This MS collated in Cutts, *Musique de la troupe de Shakespeare*, pp. 7, 122-3.

Bodleian, MS Mus. b. 1, f. 21.

MiT 30 ----- -----

Copy, headed 'Songe', in a verse miscellany compiled by Daniel Leare (a distant cousin of William Strode), probably while at Christ Church, Oxford; c. 1631-3.

British Library, Add. MS 30982, f. 36v.

MiT 31 ----- -----

Copy in a musical setting by Robert Johnson in a MS music book owned (in 1659) and partly compiled by the composer John Gamble; c. 1630s-50s.

This MS collated in Cutts, *Musique de la troupe de Shakespeare*, pp. 7, 122-3.

New York Public Library, Music Division, Drexel MS 4257, No. 32.

MiT 32 ----- III, iii, 39-75. Song: 'Come away, come away, Hecate'.

Copy of the witches' song in a musical setting possibly by Robert Johnson, in a MS music book partly compiled by John Bull (c.1562-1628); early 17th century.

Bullen, V, 416-18; Malone Society edition, pp. 57-9, lines 1331-71. This MS printed and collated in Cutts, *Musique de la troupe de Shakespeare*, pp. 11-13, 123-4.

Fitzwilliam Museum, Cambridge, MS 52. D. 25, ff. 107v-8.

MiT 33 ----- -----

Copy in a musical setting possibly by Robert Johnson, in a MS songbook once owned by a certain Anne Twice; c. 1620.

This MS printed and collated in John P. Cutts, 'The Original Music to Middleton's *The Witch*', *SQ*, 7 (1956), 203-9, and in *Musique de la troupe de Shakespeare*, pp. 8-10, 123-4.

New York Public Library, Music Division, Drexel MS 4175, No. liiii.

--- *Women Beware Women.*

See INTRODUCTION.

MiT 34 *Your Five Gallants.*

Extracts transcribed from the first edition in a miscellany compiled by William Drummond of Hawthornden; c. 1609.

First pub. London, [1608?]; Bullen, III, 121-245.

National Library of Scotland, MS 2059 (Hawthornden Vol. VII), ff. 209v-10v.

Sir Thomas More

1478-1535

ABBREVIATIONS

Bradner & Lynch *The Latin Epigrams of Thomas More*, ed. Leicester Bradner and Charles A. Lynch (Chicago, 1953).

Yale *The Yale Edition of the Complete Works of St Thomas More* [volumes listed below].

For abbreviations used throughout Volume I, see p.xi.

INTRODUCTION

More's works are currently being published in *The Yale Edition of the Complete Works of St Thomas More*, executive editor R. S. Sylvester (deceased, July 1978), as follows:

Volume 1. *English Poems, Life of Pico, Four Last Things*, ed. Richard S. Sylvester and Nicolas Barker (scheduled for publication in 1984).

Volume 2. *The History of King Richard III*, ed. Richard S. Sylvester (New Haven & London, 1963; third printing, 1975).

Volume 3: Part I. *Translations of Lucian*, ed. Craig R. Thompson (New Haven & London, 1974).

Part II. *Latin Poems*, ed Leicester Bradner, Charles A. Lynch, R. P. Oliver, and Clarence H. Miller (scheduled for publication in 1983).

Volume 4. *Utopia*, ed. Edward Surtz, S.J., and J. H. Hexter (New Haven & London, 1965; fourth printing, 1979).

Volume 5: Parts I & II. *Responsio ad Lutherum*, ed. John M. Headley (New Haven & London, 1969).

Volume 6. *Dialogue concerning Heresies*, ed. T. M. C. Lawler, Richard C. Marius, and G. Marc'hadour (scheduled for publication in 1980).

Volume 7. *Letter against Frith, Letter to Bugenhagen*, ed. Elizabeth F. Rogers, Richard C. Marius, and Frank Manley; *Supplication of Souls*, ed. G. Marc'hadour (scheduled for publication in 1983).

Volume 8: Parts I-III. *The Confutation of Tyndale's Answer*, ed. Louis A. Schuster, Richard C. Marius, James P. Lusardi, and Richard J. Schoeck (New Haven & London, 1973).

Volume 9. *Apology*, ed. J. B. Trapp (New Haven & London, 1979).

Volume 10. *Debellation of Salem and Bizance*, ed. Richard J. Schoeck and Ruth McGugan (scheduled for publication in 1982).

Volume 11. *Answer to a Poisoned Book*, ed. Clarence H. Miller (scheduled for publication in 1981).

Volume 12. *A Dialogue of Comfort against Tribulation*, ed. Louis L. Martz and Frank Manley (New Haven & London, 1976).

Volume 13. *Treatise on the Passion, Treatise on the Blessed Body, Instructions and Prayers*, ed. Garry E. Haupt (New Haven & London, 1976).

Volume 14: Parts I & II. *De Tristitia Christi*, ed. Clarence H. Miller (New Haven & London, 1976).

Volume 15. *Correspondence*, ed. H. Schulte Herbrüggen and Elizabeth F. Rogers (scheduled for publication in 1985-6).

Companion volumes:

R. W. Gibson and J. M. Patrick, *St. Thomas More: A Preliminary Bibliography of his Works and of Moreana to the year 1750* (New Haven & London, 1961).

Thomas More's Prayer Book, ed. Louis L. Martz and Richard S. Sylvester (New Haven & London, 1969).

H. Schulte Herbrüggen, *A Checklist of Manuscript Materials relating to St. Thomas More* (in progress).

Selected Works Series (modern spelling):

Selected Letters, ed. Elizabeth F. Rogers (New Haven & London, 1961).

Utopia, ed. Edward Surtz (New Haven & London, 1964; seventeenth printing, 1979).

Richard III and Selections from the English and Latin

Poems, ed. Richard S. Sylvester (New Haven & London, 1976).

A Dialogue of Comfort, ed. Frank Manley (New Haven & London, 1977).

The Tower Works: Devotional Writings, ed. Garry E. Haupt and Clarence H. Miller (scheduled for publication in 1980).

All the main MSS recorded in the *Index* have been or will be collated and described by the Yale editors; the occasional MS extracts from More's works which they may not already have considered are unlikely to have any textual significance. Volumes 1 and 3 (Part II) of the Yale edition will record a number of MS copies of More's English and Latin poems in addition to those recorded in the *Index*, but they invariably derive from printed sources.

The most important surviving autographs of More are the Valencia MS of *De tristitia Christi* (MrT 19), which he wrote in the Tower before his execution, and his annotations in the Yale Prayer Book (MrT 46), probably made at the same time. In addition, there are a number of surviving autograph letters. Most of the *Correspondence* is printed in Elizabeth Rogers's edition (Princeton, 1947), but the Yale edition (Volume 15) will also include more recently discovered letters. Part of More's letter to Cardinal Wolsey, 3 September 1523 (British Library, Harley MS 6989, f. 16) is reproduced in Elizabeth Rogers (1947), facing p. 282; part of another letter to Wolsey, 30 October 1523 (British Library, Cotton MS Galba B. VIII, f. 95) is reproduced in Petti, *English Literary Hands*, No. 17; More's letter to Henry VIII, 5 March 1533/4 (Cotton MS Cleopatra E. VI, f. 177) is reproduced in *Facsimiles of Royal, Historical, and Literary Autographs in the British Museum* (1899), plate 8, and in the Yale edition of *More's Prayer Book* (1969), p. xxviii. For a discussion of More's English and Latin handwriting, with various facsimile examples, see G. Marc'hadour, 'A Godly Meditation', *Moreana*, No. 5 (1965), 53-72.

Apart from the autographs, the most important MSS are the original scribal copy of five *epigrammata* which More presented to Henry VIII on his coronation (MrT 6), and various early transcripts of his theological works. A number of these were probably produced by members of More's own circle during the reign of Queen Mary.

A few additional and miscellaneous items may be mentioned. Extracts from *Utopia* in English appear in a miscellany compiled by Edward Pudsey (1573-1613), now in the Bodleian (MS Eng. poet. d. 3, f. 26), and in a 16th-century MS volume of law readings owned by one Edward Shorland or Shurlande, now in the British Library (Hargrave MS 89, f. 3r-v). A 16th-century MS translation of *Utopia* into Castilian is preserved in the Biblioteca de Palacio, Madrid (Sig. II-1087). Quotations from *The History of King Richard III* appear in a fragmentary early 17th-century miscellany (f. [8r-v]), at Worcester College, Oxford (inserted loose in MSS 6. 13), and in a mid-17th-century miscellany compiled by one Robert Knight, now in the British Library (Add. MS 5482, f. 4). Extracts from *The Life of John Picus, Earl of Mirandula* appear in a 17th-century miscellany in the British Library (Sloane MS 848, f. 12). A prayer beginning 'Helpe me dere father' is ascribed to 'sir Thomas Moore' in Robert Parkyn's miscellany in the Bodleian (MS Lat. th. d. 15, f. 116v) — see A. G. Dickens, 'A New Prayer of Sir Thomas More', *The Church Quarterly Review*, 124 (1937), 224-37 — but it is actually by John Fisher, two of whose autograph drafts of the prayer are in the Public Record Office: see David Rogers, 'St. John Fisher: An Unpublished Prayer to God the Father', *The Month*, NS 7 (1952), 106-11. A two-line epitaph on 'Jo: Calfe', beginning 'O Deus omnipotens vituli miserere Johannis', is ascribed to 'Tho: Morus eques' in an early 17th-century miscellany in Chetham's Library, Manchester (Mun. A 4. 15, p. 138, printed in Grosart, *The Dr Farmer MS*, II, 158), but there seems to be no good reason to connect it with More. Various Latin and English versions of the epitaph can be found in numerous early 17th-century miscellanies, an English version first being published in Richard Johnson, *The Pleasant Conceites of Old Hobson the Merry Londoner* (London, 1607).

Another group of additional MSS is of the various lives of More. Thirteen MSS of William Roper's *Life of More* (which also contains the verse *Lewis the Lost Lover*: see MrT 5) are collated in the edition of that life by Elsie Vaughan Hitchcock, EETS 197 (London, 1935). Eight more MS copies are in the Bodleian (MS CCC. 318, ff. 119-28), in Cambridge University Library (MS Add. 7958, ff. 25-48), in the John Rylands University Library of Manchester (Rylands English MS 875, ff. 9-49), in the University of London Library ([S.L.] V. 21), in the National Library of Scotland (Adv. MS 33. 7. 16), at Yale (MS 367), and in the Osborn Collection at Yale (a 25 and b 10). In her edition of Nicholas Harpsfield's *Life of More*, EETS 186 (London, 1932), Elsie Hitchcock collates eight MSS (the fifth of which, Yelverton MS 72, is now in the British Library (Add. MS 48066)); another MS is at Harvard (MS Eng 749). In their edition of a *Life of More* by one 'Ro: Ba:', EETS 222 (London, 1950), Elsie Hitchcock and P. E. Hallett collate eight MSS, and a ninth is at Harvard (MS Eng 765). There is also a *Life of More* by Cresacre More, which is currently being edited by Michael A. Anderegg of the University of North Dakota. MS copies of this life are in the British Library (Royal MS 17 B. XXVII); at Chatsworth House (Hardwick Vol 52, owned by the Duke of Devonshire); at the English Province of the Society of Jesus, London (MS Gillow 993); in the Inner Temple Library (Petyt MS 538, Vol. 45, ff. 177-264v); in the Gleeson Library at the University of San Francisco; and at Yale (two copies in MSS Vault Shelves/More (uncatalogued) and Vault Shelves/Cavendish). A four-page account of More, possibly based on one of these *Lives*, can also be found in a late 17th-century miscellany, perhaps compiled by a Jesuit, preserved at Georgetown University [no ref. number].

PB.

ARRANGEMENT

Verse:	(1) English verse	MrT 1-5
	(2) Latin verse	MrT 6-14
Prose (including prayers)		MrT 15-45
Miscellaneous		MrT 46-7.

Sir Thomas More

VERSE

(1) ENGLISH VERSE

MrT 1 *Davy the Dicer* ('Longe was I, ladye lucke, your seruynge man').

Copy in a MS volume of More's works probably produced by members of the More circle; c. 1550-7.

First pub. in *Workes* (London, 1557), p. 1433; Yale, Vol. 1.

British Library, Royal MS 17 D. XIV, 453.

MrT 2 *Fortune* ('Mine high estate power and auctoritie').

Copy of More's verses on Fortune (in 37 stanzas), in a miscellany compiled by Richard Hill, citizen of London; c. 1503-36.

First pub. as part of the preface in *The Boke of the fayre Gentylwoman...Lady Fortune* (London, [after February 1536]); pub. as the fourth of *These fowre thinges* in *Workes* (London, 1557), sig. C5^{v}-C8^{v}; Yale, Vol. 1. Printed from this MS in *Songs, Carols, and other Miscellaneous Poems*, ed. Roman Dyboski, EETS, ES 101 (London, 1907-8), 72-80. The texts of this poem are discussed in Hubertus Schulte Herbrüggen, 'Sir Thomas Mores Fortuna-Verse', *Lebende Antike Symposion für Rudolf Sühnel* (Berlin, 1967), 155-72.

Balliol College, Oxford, MS 354, ff. 104-6.

MrT 3 *A Lamentation of the Death of Queen Elizabeth* ('O ye that put your trust and confidence').

Copy in a miscellany compiled by Richard Hill, citizen of London; c. 1503-36.

First pub. as the third of *These fowre thinges* in *Workes* (London, 1557), sig. CIIII-C5; Yale, Vol. 1. Printed from this MS in *Songs, Carols, and other Miscellaneous Poems*, ed. Roman Dyboski, EETS, ES 101 (London, 1907-8), 97-9.

Balliol College, Oxford, MS 354, ff. 175-6.

MrT 4 -----

Copy written in a 15th-century MS of the poems of Thomas Hoccleve; 16th century.

British Library, Sloane MS 1825, f. 88v.

MrT 5 *Lewis the Lost Lover* ('Ey flatteringe fortune, looke thow neuer so faire').

Copy in a MS volume of More's works probably produced by members of the More circle; c. 1550-7.

First pub. in *Workes* (London, 1557), p. 1432; Yale, Vol. 1.

British Library, Royal MS 17 D. XIV, f. 453.

--- -----

This verse also appears in manuscripts of William Roper's *Life of More*: see INTRODUCTION.

--- *A Prayer of Picus Mirandula unto God* ('O holy God of dreadfull maiestee').

See MrT 34.

--- *These Four Things*.

See MrT 2-4.

(2) LATIN VERSE

MrT 6 *Epigrammata. 1-5* ('Si qua dies unquam, si quod fuit Anglia tempus').

Illuminated copy on vellum of five Latin epigrams, with a prose preface, written for the coronation of Henry VIII on 24 June 1509; the MS presented to the King; [1509].

255 *Epigrammata* first pub. Basle, 1518; Yale, Vol. 3, Part II. Printed from this MS in Bradner & Lynch (1953), pp. 15-24.

British Library, Cotton MS Titus D. IV, ff. 1-14.

MrT 7 ----- -----

Copy of the five epigrams and the prose preface in a miscellany; imperfect; early 17th century.

University of Leeds, Brotherton Collection, MS Lt. 25, ff. 1-6.

MrT 8 ----- *38. Aliud* ('Fleres, si scires unum tua tempora mensem').

Copy of the Latin epigram with an English translation beginning 'Knowest thow a moneth should end thy dayes', in a miscellany later owned by one Joseph Hall; c. 1630s-50.

Bradner & Lynch, p. 32.

Folger, MS V. a. 339, f. 22.

MrT 9 ----- *141. Epitaphium Abyngdonii cantoris* ('Attrahat huc oculos, aures attraxerat olim').

Copy in a MS volume of biographical memoranda compiled by Bishop White Kennett (1660-1728); late 17th-early 18th century.

Epigrammata. 141. Epitaphium Abyngdonii cantoris

Bradner & Lynch, p. 68.

British Library, Lansdowne MS 978, f. 152.

MrT 10 ----- *219. In pvellam divaricatis tibiis eqvitantem* ('Ergo, puella, uiri quis te negat esse capacem').

Copy, headed 'Thomae Mori equitis aurati epigramma in mulierem diuaricatis pedibus equitante', in a miscellany compiled by one John Morris; [1604-5].

Bradner & Lynch, p. 95.

British Library, Royal MS 12 B. V, f. 4.

MrT 11 ----- *242. Epitaphivm in sepvlchro Iohannae olim vxoris Mori destinantis idem sepvlchrvm et sibi et Aliciae posteriori vxori* ('Chara Thomae iacet hic Iohanna uxorcula Mori').

Copy of the epitaph More made for his tomb at Chelsea, consisting of a Latin prose epitaph and a Latin epigram, in a MS also containing other works of More (see MrT 24); end 16th-early 17th century.

Epigram first pub. in *Epigrammata* (Basle, 1518); Bradner & Lynch, pp. 104-5. Prose epitaph (with epigram) first pub. in Desiderius Erasmus, *De praeparatione ad mortem* (Basle, 1534); Nicholas Harpsfield, *Life and Death of Sir Thomas More*, ed. Elsie V. Hitchcock, EETS 186 (London, 1932), pp. 278-81; *Opus epistolarum Des. Erasmi Roterodami*, ed. P.S. Allen, X, (Oxford, 1941), pp. 260-1. This MS discussed in Clarence H. Miller, 'A Vatican Manuscript containing Three Brief Works by St. Thomas More', *Moreana*, No. 26 (1970), 41-4.

Vatican Library, MS Barbarinus latinus 2567, ff. 49-50.

--- [*Epitaph on More's Tomb*].

See MrT 11.

MrT 12 *More's Verses Punning on his Name* ('Moraris si sit spes tibi longa morandi').

Copy in a MS volume of More's works probably produced by members of the More circle; c. 1550-7.

First pub. in Nicholas Harpsfield, *Life and Death of Sir Thomas More*, ed. Elsie V. Hitchcock, EETS 186 (London, 1932); Bradner & Lynch, p. 122; Yale, Vol. 3, Part II.

British Library, Royal MS 17 D. XIV, f. 453.

MrT 13 -----

The epigram quoted in one of two brief anecdotes about More in a miscellany; c. 1670.

Worcester College, Oxford, MSS 2. 23, ff. [83v-4].

MrT 14 *Versus in tabulam duplicem.*

Copy of More's verses on pictures of Erasmus and Peter Gilles ('Tabella loquitur', beginning 'Quanti olim fuerant Pollux et Castor amici', and 'Ipse loqvor Morvs', beginning 'Tu quos aspicis, agnitos opinor'), in a copy of More's letter to Gilles, 7 October [1517], in a MS letterbook compiled for Erasmus by his pupils; [1517].

First pub. in Desiderius Erasmus, *Auctarium selectarum aliquot epistolarum* (Basle, 1518); Bradner & Lynch, pp. 120-1; Yale, Vol. 3, Part II. The handwriting of this MS designated 'Hand B' in *Opus epistolarum Des. Erasmi Roterdami*, ed. P.S. Allen, I (Oxford, 1906), p. 605.

Athenaeum Library, Deventer, Holland, I, 91 (101 G 6), f. 207v.

PROSE

(including Prayers)

MrT 15 *Assertio quod omne perjurium sit mortale peccatum.*

Copy of a Latin meditation on the meaning of perjury in a MS volume of More's works probably produced by members of the More circle; c. 1550-7.

Unpublished; to be published in Yale as an appendix to Vol. 6.

British Library, Royal MS 17 D. XIV, ff. 436v- 7v.

MrT 16 -----

Copy in a volume of documents relating to More and John Fisher; mid-16th century.

British Library, Arundel MS 152, f. 313.

MrT 17 -----

Second copy in a volume of documents relating to More and Fisher; mid-16th century.

British Library, Arundel MS 152, f. 320.

MrT 18 *The Confutation of Tyndale's Answer.*

Copy of the 'preface to the crysten reader' in a MS volume of More's works apparently transcribed from *Workes* (1557); mid-16th century.

First pub. 2 vols, London, 1532-3; Yale, Vol. 8, Parts I-III (1973). This MS recorded in Yale, Part III, p. 1420.

Bodleian, MS Ballard 72, ff. 51v-81.

*MrT 19 *De tristitia Christi.*

Autograph draft, with extensive revisions, written while More was a prisoner in the Tower of London (17 April 1534 - 6 July 1535, but before 12 June 1535 when he was denied writing materials); left unfinished; entitled 'De tristitia tedio pauore et oratione Christi ante captionem eius'; together with rough notes and drafts for the same work and for other passages (see MrT 23).

First pub. as *Expositio passionis Domini* in *Thomae Mori...omnia...latina opera* (Louvain, 1565); Mary Basset's English translation, *An exposicion of a parte of the passion of our saviour Iesus Christe*, pub. in *Workes* (London, 1557), pp. 1350-1404. This MS reproduced, with a transcript and translation, in Yale, Vol. 14 (1976); also discussed in Geoffrey Bullough, 'More in Valencia: A Holograph Manuscript of the Latin "Passion"', *The Tablet*, 217 (21 December 1963), 1379-80; G. Marc'hadour, 'Au pays de J.L. Vivès: la plus noble relique de Thomas More', *Moreana*, Nos. 9 (1966), 93-6, and 10 (1966), 85-6; Clarence H. Miller, 'The Holograph of More's *Expositio Passionis*: A Brief History', *Moreana*, Nos. 15-16 (1967), 372-9; J.B. Trapp, 'The Holograph of More's *Expositio Passionis*: A Postscript', *Moreana*, No. 18 (1968), 59-63. Facsimiles of ff. 158 and 159v also in *Thomas More's Prayer Book* (Yale, 1969), pp. xxx, xxxii, and f. 83v in Petti, *English Literary Hands*, No. 18.

Patriarca (Royal College of Corpus Christi), Valencia, Spain, MS in the Chapel of the Relics.

MrT 20 -----

Copy, in the same hand as MrT 44, with some corrections possibly in another hand, in a MS volume of More's works probably produced by members of the More circle; c. 1550-7.

This MS collated in Yale; facsimile of f. 327v in Yale, Vol. 13, facing p. xxiv.

British Library, Royal MS 17 D. XIV, ff. 325-75v.

MrT 21 -----

Copy in a MS volume of More's works probably produced for a man of wealth or high position; c. 1553-7.

This MS collated in Yale.

Bodleian, MS Bodl. 431, ff. 150-224v.

MrT 22 *Devout Instructions, Meditations and Prayers.*

Copy of More's English 'godly instruccion' (beginning 'Beare no malice nor euill will...') in a theological miscellany compiled by Robert Parkyn (d. 1570), curate of Adwick-le-Street, Yorkshire; c. 1551.

Devout Instructions &c. first pub. in *Workes* (London, 1557), pp. 1405-18 (this prayer on p. 1405); Yale, Vol. 13 (1976), (pp. 207-8). This MS collated in Yale.

Bodleian, MS Lat. th. d. 15, f. 118.

*MrT 23 -----

Autograph devotional notes in Latin out of which was apparently assembled the Latin 'godly instruccion' (beginning 'Vita per offensam dei seruata erit...') printed in 1557; written in the last gathering of the Valencia MS of *De tristitia Christi* (see MrT 19); [17 April 1534 - 12 June 1535].

Workes (1557), pp. 1405-7. Edited from this MS in Yale, Vol. 13, pp. 209-11. Facsimiles of ff. 158, 159v, in *Thomas More's Prayer Book* (Yale, 1969), pp. xxx, xxxii; ff. 156v-161v in Yale, Vol. 14, Part I, and see Part II, 744-5.

Patriarca (Royal College of Corpus Christi), Valencia, Spain, MS in the Chapel of the Relics, ff. 156v-61v.

MrT 24 -----

Copy of the Latin 'godly instruccion' (beginning 'Vita per offensam dei seruata erit...') in a MS also containing other works of More (see MrT 11); end 16th-early 17th century.

This MS collated in Yale, Vol. 13; discussed in Clarence H. Miller, 'A Vatican Manuscript containing Three Brief Works by St. Thomas More', *Moreana*, No. 26 (1970), 41-4.

Vatican Library, MS Barbarinus latinus 2567, f. 52r-v.

*MrT 25 -----

Autograph marginalia in More's Prayer Book (see MrT 46) denoting his arrangement of verses of the Psalms to form what was eventually his 'deuoute prayer, collected oute of the psalmes of Dauid' (beginning 'Domine quid multiplicati sunt qui tribulant me?'), probably written while he was a prisoner in the Tower of London; [17 April 1534 - 12 June 1535].

Workes (1557), pp. 1408-16; Yale, Vol. 13, pp. 214-25. The annotated pages reproduced in *Thomas More's Prayer Book* (Yale, 1969), and see pp. xxxi-xxxiv; discussed in Yale, Vol. 13, p. clviii seq.

Yale, MS Vault Shelves/More.

*MrT 26 -----

Autograph of More's English 'godly meditacion' (beginning 'Gyve me thy grace good lord...') inscribed in his Prayer Book (see MrT 46) probably while he was a prisoner in the Tower of London; [17 April 1534 - 12 June 1535].

Workes (1557), pp. 1416-17. This MS reproduced, with a transcript, in *Thomas More's Prayer Book* (Yale, 1969), pp. 3-21, 185-7; also discussed, with facsimiles, in G. Marc'hadour, 'A Godly Meditation', *Moreana*, No. 5 (1965), 53-72.

Yale, MS Vault Shelves/More.

MrT 27 -----

Copy of More's English 'godly meditacion' (beginning 'Gyve me thy grace good lord...') in a theological miscellany compiled by Robert Parkyn; c. 1551.

This MS collated in Yale.

Bodleian, MS Lat. th. d. 15, f. 118v.

MrT 28 -----

Copy of More's English 'deuoute prayer' (beginning 'O Holy Trinitie, the father, the sonne, and the holy ghost...') in a theological miscellany compiled by Robert Parkyn; c. 1551.

Workes (1557), pp. 1417-18; Yale, Vol. 13, pp. 228-31. This MS collated in Yale.

Bodleian, MS Lat. th. d. 15, f. 116v seq.

MrT 29 *A Dialogue of Comfort.*

Copy, with alterations and additions in another hand, and marginal annotations in later hands (possibly including that of the editor William Rastell); probably once owned by Sir Geoffrey Pole (d. 1558); c. 1540-50.

First pub. London, 1553. Edited from this MS (with several facsimile examples) in Yale, Vol. 12 (1976).

Bodleian, MS CCC. 37.

MrT 30 -----

Copy in a MS volume of More's works probably produced by members of the More circle; c. 1550-7.

This MS collated in Yale, with a facsimile of f. 180v in plate VIII after p. 320.

British Library, Royal MS 17 D. XIV, ff. 5-192.

--- *Expositio passionis.*

See MrT 19-21.

MrT 31 *The History of King Richard III.*

Copy of the Latin version (*Historia Richardis Regis Tertii*); incomplete; c. 1500-50.

English version first pub. in *The chronicle of Ihon Hardyng* (London, 1543); Latin version first pub. in *Thomae Mori...omnia...latina opera* (Louvain, 1565); Yale, Vol. 2 (1963). Printed from this MS in Yale, pp. 94-149, with a facsimile of f. 25v as the frontispiece.

College of Arms, MS Arundel 43.

MrT 32 -----

Copy of the Latin version, transcribed from More's *Latina opera* (Louvain, 1565), in a volume of state letters and speeches; c. 1575-1600.

This MS collated in Yale.

Bodleian, MS Tanner 302, ff. 87-110v.

MrT 33 -----

Copy of the opening pages of the Latin version in a volume of historical documents; c. 1550-75.

This MS collated in Yale.

British Library, Harley MS 902, ff. 158-62.

--- -----

See also INTRODUCTION.

--- *Instructions and Prayers.*

See MrT 22-8.

MrT 34 *The Life of John Picus, Earl of Mirandula.*

Copy of More's English verse translation of a prayer by Pico della Mirandola (beginning 'O holly gode of dreydfull maieste'), in a theological miscellany compiled by Robert Parkyn (d. 1570), curate of Adwick-le-Street, Yorkshire; c. 1551.

First pub. London, [1510?]; Yale, Vol. 1.

Bodleian, MS Lat. th. d. 15, f. 119.

--- -----

See also INTRODUCTION.

MrT 35 *The Supplication of Souls.*

Exemplum of the second edition (London, 1529) with MS annotations and emendations apparently made by William Rastell, used as the printer's copy of this work in Rastell's edition of More's *Workes* (1557); c. 1557.

First pub. [London, 1529]; Yale, Vol. 7. This item discussed in Yale, Vol. 12 (1976), p. xlviii, with facsimile examples in plate X after p. 320.

Yale, If.M81.*S529.

The Supplication of Souls

MrT 36 -----

Copy of the second book in a MS volume of More's works apparently transcribed from *Workes* (1557); mid-16th century.

Bodleian, MS Ballard 72, ff. 1-51.

MrT 37 *Translations of Lucian.*

Printed exemplum of *Luciani Erasmo interprete dialogi &c.* (Paris, 1514), containing Erasmus's autograph annotations, which may have been partly suggested to him by More; used as the copy-text for *Luciani cynicus &c.* (Basle, 1517); c. 1517.

More's translations of Lucian first pub. Paris, 1506; Yale, Vol. 3, Part I (1974), with facsimiles of these annotations facing pp. lx, lxii.

University of Basle, Switzerland, A N V 80.

MrT 38 *A Treatise to Receive the Blessed Body.*

Copy, with some corrections possibly in another hand, in a MS volume of More's works probably produced by members of the More circle; c. 1550-7.

First pub. in *Workes* (London, 1557), pp. 1264-9; Yale, Vol. 13 (1976). This MS collated in Yale.

British Library, Royal MS 17 D. XIV, ff. 315-24.

MrT 39 -----

Copy in a theological miscellany compiled by Robert Parkyn (d. 1570), curate of Adwick-le-Street, Yorkshire; 19-20 July 1555.

This MS collated in Yale.

Aberdeen University Library, MS 185, ff. 217-20.

MrT 40 -----

Copy in a MS volume of More's works probably produced for a man of wealth or high position; c. 1553-7.

This MS collated in Yale.

Bodleian, MS Bodl. 431, ff. 138-46v.

MrT 41 -----

Copy in a MS volume of theological works; 16th century.

This MS collated in Yale.

Bodleian, MS Rawl. C. 587, ff. 4-13v.

MrT 42 -----

Copy in a composite volume of theological works; 1575.

This MS collated in Yale.

British Library, Harley MS 6208, ff. 43-50.

MrT 43 -----

Copy in a MS volume of Catholic treatises; incomplete; c. 1576.

This MS collated in Yale.

Manhattan College, [no ref. number], ff. 59v-65v.

MrT 44 *A Treatise upon the Passion.*

Copy, in the same hand as MrT 20, with some corrections possibly in another hand; lacking the brief introduction and imperfect at the end; in a MS volume of More's works probably produced by members of the More circle; c. 1550-7.

First pub. in *Workes* (London, 1557), pp. 1270-1349; Yale, Vol. 13 (1976). This MS collated in Yale, with a facsimile of f. 314v facing p. 160.

British Library, Royal MS 17 D. XIV, ff. 193-314v.

MrT 45 -----

Copy, untitled, in a MS volume of More's works probably produced for a man of wealth or high position; c. 1553-7.

This MS collated in Yale, with facsimiles of ff. 37 and 149 facing pp. 51 and xxvii.

Bodleian, MS Bodl. 431, ff. 1-137, 148-9.

--- *Utopia.*

See INTRODUCTION.

MISCELLANEOUS

*MrT 46 *Prayer Book.*

More's prayer book, consisting of two incomplete printed books (a Latin Book of Hours, 1530, and a liturgical Latin Psalter, 1522) bound together and containing his autograph annotations, including the English prayer known as 'A Godly Meditation' (see MrT 26); used and probably annotated by More while he was a prisoner in the

Prayer Book

Tower of London (17 April 1534 - 6 July 1535, but before 12 June 1535 when he was denied writing materials).

Published in facsimile as *Thomas More's Prayer Book* (Yale, 1969). See also MrT 25.

Yale, MS Vault Shelves/More.

MrT 47 -----

A prayer book used by the More family, consisting of a MS Book of Hours (c. 1490) with entries recording family events between 1531 and 1561 chiefly in the hand of More's son, John (c.1510-57), the entry for 1531 possibly in Sir Thomas's autograph.

This item discussed in H. Schulte Herbrüggen, 'A Prayer-Book of Sir Thomas More', *TLS* (15 January 1970), p. 64.

Dioclesan Museum, Bamberg, West Germany.

Thomas Nashe

1567-1601?

ABBREVIATIONS

McKerrow *The Works of Thomas Nashe*, ed. Ronald B. McKerrow, 5 vols (Oxford, 1904-10; reprinted, revised by F. P. Wilson, 1958).

For abbreviations used throughout Volume I, see p.xi.

INTRODUCTION

There are four known examples of Nashe's handwriting. One is his signature in the Admission Book (1584) of St John's College, Cambridge; it is reproduced in Greg, *English Literary Autographs*, plate XX(e). Another example is his undergraduate verses on Ecclesiasticus (NaT 7). A third example is a letter sent to William Cotton, c. September 1596, now in the British Library (Cotton MS Julius C. III, f. 280); part of this letter is reproduced in McKerrow, V, frontispiece (text on pp. 192-6), in Greg, plate XX(a-c), and in Petti, *English Literary Hands*, No. 33. For a fourth example, some annotations in a printed exemplum of Leland's *poemata*, including quotations from *Doctor Faustus*, see CHRISTOPHER MARLOWE, MrC 20.

The *Index* records early MS copies of two other poems usually attributed to Nashe, notably the bawdy piece *The choise of valentines* (NaT 1-6). The only other MS of works by this prolific writer to be found is a series of very brief extracts from his prose works in a miscellany compiled by Edward Pudsey (1573-1613), now in the Bodleian (MS Eng. poet. d. 3, f. 21r-v). These extracts are from *Christs Teares over Ierusalem* (1593), *Have With You to Saffron-Walden* (1596), *Nashes Lenten Stuffe* (1599), *Pierce Penilesse* (1592), and *Summers Last Will and Testament* (1600).

PB.

ARRANGEMENT

Verse NaT 1-17.

Thomas Nashe

VERSE

NaT 1 *The choise of valentines* ('It was the merie moneth of Februarie').

Copy, headed 'The choosing of valentines', with a dedicatory sonnet 'To the right Honorable the lord S.' (beginning 'Pardon sweete flower of matchless Poetrie'), in a verse miscellany bound up in a composite volume of state papers; early 17th century.

Lines 1-17 first pub. (from this MS) in *The Complete Works of Thomas Nashe*, ed. A.B. Grosart (London, 1883-4), I, lx-lxi; printed complete from this MS, London, 1899, ed. John S. Farmer (privately printed), and in McKerrow, III, 402-14.

Inner Temple Library, Petyt MS 538, Vol. 43, ff. 295v-8v.

NaT 2 -----

Copy, headed 'Nash his Dildo', with the dedicatory sonnet, in a MS volume of amatory poems; early 17th century.

This MS collated in Farmer and in McKerrow.

Bodleian, MS Rawl. poet. 216, ff. 96-106v, 94.

NaT 3 -----

Copy, headed 'Gnash his valentine' and here beginning 'In the merrie Moneth of ffebruary', in a miscellany once owned by Margaret Bellasys, probably the daughter of Thomas, first Lord Fauconberg (1577-1653); c. 1630.

This MS not recorded by editors.

British Library, Add. MS 10309, ff. 135v-9v.

NaT 4 -----

Copy, headed 'Nashes Dilldo', with the dedicatory sonnet (here 'To the right Honourable Lord Strainge'), in a verse miscellany; early-mid-17th century.

This MS not recorded by editors.

Folger, MS V. a. 399, ff. 53v-7.

NaT 5 -----

Copy of an abbreviated and untitled 162-line version, beginning 'ffaire was the morne & brightsome was the day', with the dedicatory sonnet, in a verse miscellany probably compiled by a member of an Inn of Court; c. 1598-1600s.

This MS discussed in James L. Sanderson, 'An Unnoted Text of Nashe's "The Choise of Valentines"', *ELN*, 1 (1964), 252-3.

Rosenbach Foundation, MS 1083/15, ff. 9v-11v.

NaT 6 -----

Copy of an abbreviated 161-line version, partly written in cryptography, headed 'Lector abj si to scelerjs contagio vexat | At tibi si mens sit sanctificata venj.', with the dedicatory sonnet, in a verse miscellany; c. 1620.

This MS collated in McKerrow.

Victoria and Albert Museum, Dyce Collection, Cat. No. 44 (Pressmark 25. F. 39), ff. 2-4.

*NaT 7 *Latin Verses on Ecclesiasticus 41.1* ('Quos mala nulla premunt, quos nulla pericula cingunt').

Autograph fair copy, headed 'Eccle. cap. 41. ver. 1°', in a MS volume of eleven Latin poems on the same subject made by scholars of St John's College, Cambridge; 1585.

First pub. (from this MS) in McKerrow (1905), III, 298-9. Facsimiles in McKerrow and in Greg, *English Literary Autographs*, plate XX(d).

Public Record Office, SP.15/29/167.

NaT 8 *Verses from 'Astrophel and Stella'* ('If flouds of teares could clense my follies past').

Copy of a version comprising lines 7-12 (here beginning 'I se my hopes must wether in the budde'), lines 1-6, and an additional six-line stanza beginning 'Prayse blyndnes (eyes) for seeinge is deceyte', in a verse miscellany bound with a volume of printed works by Nicholas Breton; early 17th century.

First pub. in 'Poems and Sonets of sundrie other Noble men and Gentlemen' appended to Sir Philip Sidney, *Astrophel and Stella* (London, 1591); McKerrow, III, 396 (in poems of doubtful authorship); Doughtie, *Lyrics from English Airs*, pp. 104-5. Printed from this MS in G.L., 'Poem attributed to Thomas Nash', *The Shakespeare Society's Papers*, I (London, 1844), 76-9; collated in Doughtie, pp. 480-2; recorded in McKerrow.

Bodleian, Tanner 221, MS, fol. 2.

NaT 9 -----

Copy in a verse miscellany; c. 1596-1601.

This MS collated in Doughtie, pp. 480-2; recorded in McKerrow.

British Library, Harley MS 6910, f. 156r-v.

Verses from 'Astrophel and Stella'

NaT 10 -----

Copy in a four-part musical setting by John Dowland in a MS songbook once owned by one Thomas Myriell; early 17th century.

This setting first pub. in John Dowland, *The Second Booke of Songs or Ayres* (London, 1600). This MS collated in Doughtie, pp. 480-2.

Bibliothèque Royale, Brussels, MS II. 4. 109 (Fétis 3095), pp. 24-5.

NaT 11 -----

Copy of the incipit with a musical setting written in the counter-tenor MS part book of the 'St Andrews Psalter'; early 17th century.

This MS recorded (but not seen) in Doughtie (p. 481).

British Library, Add. MS 33933, f. 85v.

NaT 12 -----

Copies of two versions in one of the musical settings by John Dowland, in a MS songbook compiled by Robert Taitt, schoolmaster of Lauder, Berwickshire; [1676-89].

This MS collated in Doughtie, pp. 480-2.

Clark Library, Los Angeles, T135Z.B724 1677-89 Bound, Cantus 70, ff. 74', 86-7.

NaT 13 -----

Copies in a musical setting, written in two MS part books of the 'St Andrews Psalter'; early 17th century.

This MS recorded (but not seen) in Doughtie (p. 481).

Edinburgh University Library, MS La. III. 483, Tenor, p. 184; Bassus, p. 200.

NaT 14 -----

Copy in a musical setting in a MS music book partly compiled by John Skene of Hallyards; c. 1620-35.

This MS recorded (but not seen) in Doughtie (p. 481).

National Library of Scotland, Adv. MS. 5. 2. 15, p. 114.

NaT 15 -----

Copy of a four-stanza version in a musical setting in a MS songbook; early 17th century.

This MS collated in Doughtie, pp. 480-2.

St Michael's College, Tenbury Wells, MS 1019, f. 1.

NaT 16 -----

Copy of a three-stanza version in one of the musical settings by John Dowland in a transcript of the first edition (Aberdeen, 1662) of John Forbes, *Cantus, Songs and Fancies*; c. 1662.

This MS not recorded by editors.

Sandeman Library, Perth, N16 (No. xiii).

NaT 17 -----

Copy in a verse miscellany; c. 1620.

This MS not recorded by editors.

Victoria and Albert Museum, Dyce Collection, Cat. No. 44 (Pressmark 25. F. 39), f. 107v.

PROSE

See INTRODUCTION.

MARGINALIA IN PRINTED BOOKS AND MANUSCRIPTS

See CHRISTOPHER MARLOWE, MrC 20.

George Peele

1556-96

ABBREVIATIONS

Yale *The Life and Works of George Peele*, general editor Charles Tyler Prouty, 3 vols (New Haven, 1952-70). Volume I: David H. Horne, *The Life and Minor Works of George Peele* (1952); Volumes II and III: *The Dramatic Works of George Peele*, ed. Frank S. Hook, John Yoklavich, R. Mark Benbow, and Elmer Blistein (1961, 1970).

For abbreviations used throughout Volume I, see p.xi.

INTRODUCTION

Only two autographs of George Peele are known. One is the important but unfortunately damaged autograph of *Anglorum Feriae* (PIG 1). The other is a letter of 17 January 1595/6 to Lord Burghley, now in the British Library (Lansdowne MS 99, f. 151). The letter is reproduced in Greg, *English Literary Autographs*, plate XVI; in *Shakespeare's England* (Oxford, 1917), I, facing p. 290; and in Yale, I, 106.

In addition to the important playhouse 'plot' of *The Battle of Alcazar* (PIG 22), the *Index* records only a few early copies of poems by Peele and certain extracts from his works in miscellanies. The extracts include ones from Peele's lost 'Pastoral' *The Hunting of Cupid* (PIG 3-7). The canon is based on the Yale edition. It includes the well-known 'Sonet' beginning 'His Golden lockes, Time hath to Silver turn'd' (PIG 10-21), which was appended to the first edition of *Polyhymnia*, although evidence tends to support Sir Henry Lee's authorship. Except where otherwise stated, the MSS recorded have not been previously noted by editors. For a list of documents relating to Peele's life and works, see Yale, I, 283-6.

PB.

ARRANGEMENT

See also Addenda to Part 2, p. 632

George Peele

VERSE

(1) POEMS BY PEELE

*P1G 1 *Anglorum Feriae* ('Descende ye sacred daughters of King Jove').

Autograph; imperfect (damaged in the 19th century by a corrosive substance); 1595.

No contemporary publication known; first printed (from this MS) by W. Stevenson Fitch of Ipswich [privately printed, c. 1830]; printed from this MS by D.H. Horne in Yale, I, 265-76; facsimile of f. 10v in Croft, *Autograph Poetry*, I, 16.

British Library, Add. MS 21432.

P1G 2 *The Honour of the Garter* ('About the time when Vesper in the West').

Copy of an adaptation of Peele's poem (without the prologue), entitled 'The Honour of the Garter. Displaied in a Poeme gratulatory: Entitled to the right honorable and worthy, Sir Robert Karre knight, viscount Rochester, Created Knight of that Order, and install'd att windsore. Anno regni Iacobi 9. Anno Dom: 1611'; once owned by one Edward Webbe; c. 1611.

First pub. London, [1593]; ed. D.H. Horne in Yale, I, 245-59. This MS recorded in Horne, p. 174.

Bodleian, MS Rawl. B. 30.

P1G 3 *The Hunting of Cupid.*

Extracts from Peele's lost 'Pastoral', here beginning 'On the snowie browes of albion. sweet woodes sweet running', in a miscellany compiled by William Drummond of Hawthornden; [1609].

Probably pub. c. 1581-91 but complete text now lost. Drummond's extracts (91 lines) first pub. in *The Works of George Peele*, ed. Alexander Dyce, 2 vols (London, 1828); printed, with a facsimile, in W.W. Greg, 'The Hunting of Cupid, a lost play by George Peele', *Collections*, I, Parts IV and V, Malone Society (Oxford, 1911), 307-14; printed by D.H. Horne in Yale, I, 204-8. For an argument that the work was probably not a play, as has been traditionally supposed, but a pastoral poem or entertainment, see John P. Cutts, 'Peele's *Hunting of Cupid*', *SR*, 5 (1958), 121-32.

National Library of Scotland, MS 2059 (Hawthornden Vol. VII), ff. 352-3.

P1G 4 ----- Song: 'What thing is love for (wel I wot) love is a thing'.

Copy of an 11-line version, untitled, ascribed to 'G. Peelle', and here beginning 'What thinge is loue? for since loue is a thinge', in a miscellany compiled by a Cambridge student, possibly Sir John Finett (1571-1641) of Fordwich, Kent; c. 1586-91.

Horne, lines 12-20, 25-6. This song pub. separately, in an eight-line version, in *The Wisdom of Doctor Dodypoll* (London, 1600), and in John Bartlet, *A Book of Ayres* (London, 1606). Printed from this MS in Greg, p. 313; recorded in Horne, pp. 153-276.

Bodleian, MS Rawl. poet. 85, f. 13.

P1G 5 ----- -----

Copy of an 11-line version, headed 'A Discription of loue' and here beginning 'What thinge is loue for sure loue is a thinge', in a composite volume of verse and prose; early 17th century.

This MS collated in Doughtie, *Lyrics from English Airs*, pp. 546-7.

Bodleian, MS Rawl. poet. 172, f. 2v.

P1G 6 ----- -----

Copy of an 11-line version, untitled and here beginning 'What thinge is loue? for sure loue is a thinge', in a verse miscellany compiled by the antiquary St Loe Kniveton of Gray's Inn; c. 1585-90s.

British Library, Harley MS 7392, f. 69.

P1G 7 ----- Song: 'Melampus, when will Love be void of feares?'.

Copy of the song of Coridon and Melampus in a miscellany compiled by William Drummond of Hawthornden; c. 1620s.

This song pub. separately in *Englands Helicon* (London, 1600); Horne, p. 207.

National Library of Scotland, MS 2060 (Hawthornden Vol. VIII), f. 236.

P1G 8 *Polyhymnia* ('Therefore, when thirtie two were come and gone').

Copy in two hands; c. 1590-1625.

First pub. London, 1590; ed. D.H. Horne in Yale, I, 231-43. This MS collated in *The Works of George Peele*, ed. Alexander Dyce, 2 vols (London, 1828), and in Horne.

St John's College, Oxford, MS 216.

P1G 9 -----

Extract in a composite volume of MSS collected by William Parkhurst (fl. 1604-67), among the papers of the Finch family of Burley-on-the Hill, Rutland; 1600s-41.

Leicestershire Record Office, DG. 7/Lit. 2, f. 320.

Polyhymnia

--- -----

See also PlG 10-21.

(2) POEMS OF DOUBTFUL AUTHORSHIP

PlG 10 *A Sonet* ('His Golden lockes, Time hath to Silver turn'd').

Copy, headed 'Sr H. lea', in a verse miscellany compiled by John Harington of Stepney (1520?-82) and his son Sir John Harington of Kelston (1560-1612); late 16th century.

First pub. as an appendix to *Polyhymnia* (London, 1590); ed. D.H. Horne in Yale, I, 244. The sonnet probably written by Sir Henry Lee: see Horne, pp. 169-70, and Thomas Clayton, '"Sir Henry Lee's Farewell to the Court": The Texts and Authorship of "His Golden Locks Time Hath to Silver Turned"', *ELR*, 4 (1974), 268-75. This text collated in Clayton from a 19th-century transcript in the British Library (Add. MS 28635, f. 88v), which is also recorded in Horne, p. 170; printed from the Arundel MS in Ruth Hughey, *Arundel Harington MS*, I, No. 199, pp. 243-4, and collated II, 322-7.

Owned by the Duke of Norfolk, Arundel Castle, MSS (Special Press), 'Harrington MS. Temp. Eliz.', f. 147v.

PlG 11 -----

Copy of the incipit, here 'His golden locks', in a musical setting by John Dowland, in a MS virginal book compiled by 'R. Cr.' (? R. Creighton); c. 1635-8.

This setting first pub. in John Dowland, *First Booke of Songes or Ayres* (London, 1597).

Bibliothèque Nationale, Paris, Département de la Musique, MS Conservatoire Rés. 1186, f. 11.

PlG 11.5 See Addenda, p. 632.

PlG 12 -----

Copy, headed 'Certain verses causd to bee songe to the Queenes Matie by Sr Hen: Lea K^t when hee yealded vp his Helmit & Launce to the Earle of Cumberland at The tilt yard An. do: 1590', in a verse miscellany once owned by one Peter Daniell; c. 1630s-40s.

This MS collated in Clayton.

Bodleian, MS Eng. poet. c. 50, f. 59.

PlG 13 -----

Copy in a musical setting by John Dowland, in a MS songbook compiled by Thomas Hamond (d. 1662) of Suffolk; c. 1630.

This MS collated in Clayton.

Bodleian, MS Mus. f. 7-10: f. 8, fol. 10v.

PlG 14 -----

Copy of the last stanza (beginning 'And when he saddest sits in homely Cell') written as the last stanza of a poem headed 'In yeeldinge up his Tilt staff: hee sayd', beginning 'Tymes eldest sonne, old age the heire of ease', and subscribed 'q^d Sr Henry Leigh', in a verse miscellany compiled by John Lilliat (c.1550-c.1599); [1590-9].

This MS recorded in Horne, p. 170.

Bodleian, MS Rawl. poet. 148, f. 75v.

PlG 15 -----

Copy, untitled and endorsed 'The following Lines I found on the fly leaf of Mornay's Work "of the trewe Relligion"' [translated by Sir Philip Sidney and Arthur Golding (1587)], in a composite volume of MSS; c. 1590s.

This MS collated in Clayton and in Hughey; recorded in Horne, pp. 169-70.

British Library, Add. MS 33963, f. 109.

PlG 16 -----

Copy of lines 1-5, untitled, written at the end of a stave of music in a MS volume of musical pieces; late 16th-early 17th century.

This MS collated in Clayton and in Hughey.

British Library, Add. MS 36526A, f. 9.

PlG 17 -----

Copy made by Oliver St John, first Earl of Bolingbroke (1584-1646), headed 'Sr Henrye Lee', written on a flyleaf in a MS copy of a letter of the Earl of Essex together with a Jacobean treatise; early 17th century.

This MS collated in Clayton and in Hughey.

British Library, Stowe MS 276, f. 2.

PlG 18 -----

Copy, headed 'Panegyricks | Sr Henry Lea his Farewell to the Court', in a verse miscellany; c. 1630.

This MS collated in Clayton and in Hughey.

Folger, MS V. a. 103, Part I, f. 52.

PlG 19 -----

Copy in the hand of Simon Willis, a secretary (until 1602) of Sir Robert Cecil, Earl of Salisbury (1563?-1612), in a volume of state letters compiled for Cecil; [1590-1602].

Owned by the Marquess of Salisbury, Hatfield House, Cecil Papers 286, f. [32].

A Sonet ('His Golden lockes')

PlG 20 -----

Copy, untitled, on a single leaf, among the papers of the Cranfield family; end 16th-early 17th century.

This MS collated in Clayton.

Kent Archives Office, U269 F36.

PlG 21 -----

Copy, headed 'Sr Henry Lea his Farewell to the Court', in a verse miscellany; c. 1630.

University of Nottingham, Portland MS Pw V 37, p. 107.

DRAMATIC WORKS

PlG 22 *The Battle of Alcazar.*

Copy of 'The Plott of the Battell of Alcazar' made by a playhouse scribe; prepared for a revival of the play by the Admiral's Company; c. 1598-9.

First acted 1589; first pub. London, 1594; ed. John Yoklavich in Yale, II, 294-347. The 'Plott' first pub. by W.W. Greg in *Henslowe Papers* (London, 1907), pp. 138-41. Revised transcripts and facsimiles in Greg, *Two Elizabethan Stage Abridgements: The Battle of Alcazar and Orlando Furioso*, Malone Society (Oxford, 1922); Greg, *Dramatic Documents*, I, 44-59, and II, plate VI; Yoklavich, facing p. 280.

British Library, Add. MS 10449, f. 3.

PlG 23 *Edward I.*

Exemplum of the edition of 1593 with the text of some damaged leaves supplied in MS, transcribed from the edition of 1599; 17th century.

First pub. London, 1593; ed. Frank S. Hook in Yale, II, 1-212. This item recorded in Yale, III, 445.

National Library of Scotland, Bute 414.

--- *The Hunting of Cupid.*

See PlG 3-7.

PlG 24 *The Old Wives Tale.*

Misquotation from the play in a miscellany once owned by Elizabeth Clarke and Chatham Hordinant; c. 1595.

First pub. London, 1595; ed. Frank S. Hook in Yale, III, 385-421. Formerly MS 1072.1, this MS recorded in De Ricci, I, 367.

Folger, MS X. d. 177.

George Puttenham

d. 1590

For abbreviations used throughout Volume I, see p.xi.

INTRODUCTION

George Puttenham has commonly been accepted as the author of *The Arte of English Poesie* (London, 1589) on the basis of a reference in Edmond Bolton's *Hypercritica* (written c. 1621): 'the Arte of English Poetry [is] the Work (as the Fame is) of one of [Queen Elizabeth's] Gentlemen Pensioners, Puttenham'. His brother Richard, and John, Lord Lumley (1534?—1609), have been advanced as less plausible candidates: see Sidney Lee's account in the *DNB*; B. M. Ward, 'The Authorship of the *Arte of English Poesie*: A Suggestion', *RES*, 1 (1925), 284-308; and Roderick L. Eagle, '"The Arte of English Poesie" (1589)', *N & Q*, 201 (May 1956), 188-90.

Of various other works which the author of the *Arte* claims to have written, only his *Partheniades* (PtG 1) has been identified or is known to have survived. A prose defence of Queen Elizabeth's execution of Mary Queen of Scots is, however, specifically ascribed to George Puttenham in two contemporary copies (PtG 3-4) and the work is certainly one which might have been written by a gentleman pensioner of Elizabeth's.

There is no known specimen of Puttenham's hand, and it is unlikely that any of the MSS recorded in the *Index* is autograph.

PB.

ARRANGEMENT

Verse	PtG 1
Prose	PtG 2-5.

George Puttenham

VERSE

PtG 1 *Partheniades* ('Gracious Princesse, Where princes are in place').

Copy of 17 poems presented to Queen Elizabeth on 1 January 1578/9, headed 'The principall addresse in nature of a New yeares gifte, seeminge therebye the Author intended not to have his name knowne', in a composite volume of heraldic and historical MSS (see CmW 151); c. 1579.

Extracts first pub. in *The Arte of English Poesie* (London, 1589); first pub. complete (from this MS) in *Ancient Critical Essays upon English Poets and Poesy*, ed. Joseph Haslewood, 2 vols (London, 1811-15), I, xviii-xxxviii.

British Library, Cotton MS Vespasian E. VIII, ff. 169-78.

PROSE

PtG 2 *An Apology or True Defence of Her Majesty's Honourable and Good Renown.*

Copy, untitled, here beginning 'Ther hathe not hapened since the memory of man...'; 17 leaves; late 16th century.

Believed to be unpublished. This MS formerly Phillipps MS 22357.

Bibliothèque Nationale, Paris, fonds anglais n° 165.

PtG 3 -----

Copy, untitled, here beginning 'There hath not happened since the memorie of man...'; inscribed by Robert Beale (1541-1601), Clerk of the Council to Queen Elizabeth, 'A discours touching the Just Execution of ye Scotishe Queen | It is thoght that this book was mad by George Puttēham', in a composite volume of state papers (chiefly relating to Mary Queen of Scots) collected by Beale; late 16th century.

Formerly Yelverton MS 31, this MS recorded in *HMC*, 2nd Report (1871), Appendix, p. 41.

British Library, Add. MS 48027, ff. 451-76.

PtG 4 -----

Copy, headed 'An apologie, or true defence of her ma^ts: hono^r: and good renowne against all such as have unduelie sought or shall seek to blemish the same...in any parte of her ma^ts: proceedings against the late Scotish Queene... Written by George Puttenham', here beginning 'There hath not happened since the memory of man...'; 136 pages plus blank leaves; late 16th century.

British Library, Harley MS 831.

PtG 5 -----

Copy, here beginning 'There hath not happened since the memorye of man...', ascribed to Queen Elizabeth, with comments on the treatise in a different hand; late 16th century?

Formerly Mostyn MS 261, this MS recorded in *HMC*, 4th Report (1874), Appendix, p. 361.

Sotheby's, 13 July 1920, Lot 35, sold to Maggs; unlocated.

Sir Walter Ralegh

1554-1618

ABBREVIATIONS

Edwards   Edward Edwards, *The Life of Sir Walter Ralegh. . .together with his Letters*, 2 vols (London, 1868).

Hannah (1845)   *Poems by Sir Henry Wotton, Sir Walter Raleigh and others*, ed. John Hannah (London, 1845).

Hannah (1870)   *The Courtly Poets from Raleigh to Montrose*, ed. John Hannah (London, 1870).

Latham   *The Poems of Sir Walter Ralegh*, ed. Agnes M.C. Latham [first pub. 1929], revised edition (London, 1951; reprinted 1962).

Lefranc (1968)   Pierre Lefranc, *Sir Walter Ralegh écrivain* (Paris, 1968).

Works (1829)   *The Works of Sir Walter Ralegh, Kt.*, 8 vols (Oxford, 1829; reprinted New York, 1965).

For abbreviations used throughout Volume I, see p.xi.

INTRODUCTION

Many autographs of Sir Walter Ralegh have survived. Of special literary as well as historical interest are the following: the autograph fragments of his *Cynthia* poems (RaW 8-9, 146, 188); a notebook which he kept during his imprisonment in the Tower (RaW 728) containing another *Cynthia* poem (RaW 200) and material used for *The History of the World*; some fragmentary notes for his lost *Of the Art of Warre by Sea* (RaW 692); and the original journal compiled during his second voyage to Guiana (RaW 726). A political memorandum on the succession to Queen Elizabeth is also in his hand (RaW 698); so too is his *Considerations concerning Reprysalles* (RaW 571), a memorandum previously known only from the unreliable testimony of the forger John Payne Collier but of which the authenticity can now be confirmed. In addition, some of his autograph scientific papers are extant (RaW 711, 713), various state or legal documents are wholly or partly in his hand, a few printed books bear his signature, and a substantial number of his original letters survive.

Late 16th and 17th-century MS copies of Ralegh's works abound. The only ones clearly made at his direction are certain copies of *A Dialogue between a Counsellor of State and a Justice of the Peace* (RaW 572) and of the discourses, usually attributed to him, on the proposed marriages of Prince Henry (RaW 621) and Princess Elizabeth (RaW 648); these copies form part of a volume of tracts once in his possession (RaW 727). It is likely, however, that the extant copies of *Of the Voyage for Guiana* (RaW 694) and his memorial on the conduct of the war (RaW 695) were made for him, and some early texts such as the Lambeth MS of *The Discovery of Guiana* (RaW 676) and certain tracts in the Public Record Office (RaW 597-8) may well have been produced by or for people in his immediate circle. Whatever the precise line of descent from the author's autographs, there can be no doubt about the importance of the MS texts in general since the majority of Ralegh's works were not published until long after his death.

Canon

Since so few of his works were published in his lifetime, and since many anonymous poems and tracts were posthumously attributed to him, the canon is highly problematical. The 'standard' collected edition of his *Works* (1829) is very much open to amendment. A project for a Clarendon Press edition of the complete works, under the general editorship of Pierre Lefranc, was begun in 1970 under the auspices of the Canada Council, but this project is now defunct. Individual editors hope, however, to publish particular works in due course. In the meantime several published discussions of the canon are to be found — notably Pierre Lefranc's 1968 survey of Ralegh studies, and articles by Ernest Strathmann (see *NCBEL*, I, cols. 2214-19). Although the uncertainty of so many attributions is likely to leave the canon subject to debate, the canon accepted in the Index is based on a broad consensus of currently available scholarly opinion.

Verse

Until Professor Lefranc completes his new edition of the poems, the standard edition of Ralegh's verse remains Latham (1951). The first series of entries, under the heading 'Poems generally attributed to Ralegh' (RaW 1-359), consists chiefly of those poems printed in full by Miss Latham in the main body of her text (pp. 1-84), but incorporates recent additions to the canon and, with due cross-references, omits certain poems whose authenticity has been seriously questioned by scholars. The entries include most of her 'conjectural "Ralegh Group" in "The Phoenix Nest"' (pp. 73-84); for a more recent discussion of the authorship of these poems see Michael Rudick, 'The "Ralegh Group" in *The Phoenix Nest*', *SB*, 24 (1971), 131-7. Miss Latham records (but does not usually collate) many early MS copies of Ralegh's poems; many more (not previously noted unless otherwise stated) are recorded in the entries below. As well as the *Cynthia* poem found in Ralegh's notebook (RaW 200-2), the full text of *'Fortune hath taken thee away my love'* (RaW 133-5) can be added to Miss Latham's version of the canon; only six lines, quoted in Puttenham's *Arte of English Poesie*, were previously known. The full text of an answering poem by Queen Elizabeth has also been discovered (see RaW 135). Another version (the earliest known text) of Ralegh's *Petition to the Queen*, a poem based on verses in the *Cythia* poems, has been also located (RaW 294).

The second series of entries, under the heading 'Poems doubtfully ascribed to Ralegh' (RaW 360-542), consists chiefly of those poems recorded (but for the most part not printed) by Miss Latham in her Appendix (pp. 163-74). Although ascription to Ralegh of most of these poems has no authority, the poems are included, despite their uncertainty, since they will probably continue to play a part in Ralegh studies. It is also possible that previously unknown copies now recorded may shed light on the matter. In view of the consistent attribution to Ralegh of the bawdy verse on the Lady Bendbow (RaW 412-27), for instance, this quip must merit serious consideration for inclusion in the canon.

The section on doubtful poems is increased by the addition of poems formerly attributed to Ralegh (such as *The passionate mans Pilgrimage*, RaW 438-52) but now considered probably unauthentic. Conversely, two of Miss Latham's poems are excluded from the canon altogether. One is the poem *'Would I were chaung'd into that golden showre'* (Latham, pp. 81-2), which is assigned in Lefranc (1968), p. 95, to Sir Arthur Gorges and is printed in *The Poems of Sir Arthur Gorges*, ed. Helen E. Sandison (Oxford, 1953), No. 46. The poem is to be found in a volume of Gorges's verse in the British Library (Egerton MS 3165, f. 43); also in Harley MS 7392, f. 36v, and in Bodleian, MS Rawl. poet. 85, f. 46. The other excluded poem is *'Thou sentst to me a heart was crowned'*, which is ascribed to Ralegh in two miscellanies written in the same hand — one in the Folger (MS V. a. 103, Part I, f. 41), the other at the University of Nottingham (Portland MS Pw V 37, p. 78). This poem is mentioned by Miss Latham in her Appendix, p. 173. It is more generally assigned to Sir Robert Ayton and is printed in *The English and Latin Poems of Sir Robert Ayton*, ed. Charles B. Gullans, STS, 4th Ser. 1 (Edinburgh, 1963), pp. 181-2. Gullans records (pp. 291-5) fourteen MS copies of the poem, to which number may be added the following: Bodleian (MS Mus. Sch. F. 575, p. 6); Carlisle Cathedral (Dean & Chapter of Carlisle MSS, Box B1, Altus, p. 112); Folger (MS V. a. 245, f. 17); Harvard (MS Eng 966.6, f. 133v); New York Public Library, Music Division (Drexel MS 4257, No. 18); and Yale, Osborn Collection (b 4, f. 6v; b 197, p. 38; b 200, p. 86; and b 213, pp. 11-12). Another poem probably by Ayton, *'Wrong not, deare Empresse of my Heart'*, is, however, included in the entries (RaW 500-42) since for some reason it became closely linked with Ralegh's poem beginning 'Our Passions are most like to Floods and streames' (RaW 320-38) (the two are printed as one poem in Latham) and since MSS which throw light on the textual history of one poem will be of obvious relevance to that of the other.

Other poems are to be found ascribed to Ralegh in MS sources — usually poems normally assigned to other authors (for instance, Edward Dyer's *'The lowest Trees haue tops'* and Henry Wotton's verses *Upon the Sudden Restraint of the Earl of Somerset*), — but no attempt has been made to account for the complete Ralegh apocrypha. For a couplet beginning 'Pray for thy fayth that it may fayle thee neeuer', which is copied out and ascribed to 'Walter Wrawleigh' by Charles Stanhope, second Baron Stanhope (1595-1675), in a volume of Jonson's *Workes* (1640), see James M. Osborn, 'Ben Jonson and the Eccentric Lord Stanhope', *TLS* (4 January 1957), p. 16.

Besides those MSS recorded in the entries, a number of later transcripts are to be found. Ralegh's celebrated epigram *'Euen such is tyme'* is copied in 18th-century miscellanies in, for instance, the Bodleian (MSS Rawl. C. 986, f. 15; Rawl. D. 383, f. 140; Rawl. D. 1334, f. 29 rev.); Cambridge University Library (MS Mm. 1. 45, p. 210); and the Folger (MS W. b. 455, p. 25). Early brass or marble monuments bearing the epigram can be found in the Parish Churches at Ross, Herefordshire (Thomas Baker, d. 1622), at Isel, Cumbria (Wilfred Lawson, d. 1632), and at Sanderstead, now part of Greater London (Henry Mellish, d. 1677): see W.A. Thorpe in *TLS* (12 October 1951), p. 645, and H. G. Carter in *TLS* (12 November 1951), p. 693. An 18th-century copy of *The Nimphs reply to the Sheepheard*, headed 'The Milk-maid's mother's answer to Mr. Marlow's Milk-maid's song', is in the British Library (Stowe MS 972, f. 6). The doubtful poem *'ICUR, good Mounser Carr'* is copied in an 18th-century miscellany in the British Library (Harley MS 7316, f. 4v), and a copy of the doubtful poem *'Say not you love, unless you do'* is in one of Thomas Hearne's diaries (No. 30, p. 229) in the Bodleian. A collection of transcripts of Ralegh's poems made from various sources in the 1890s by one Abram E. Cutter is in the Boston Public Library (H. 80. 107-109). John Hannah's annotated exemplum of his 1845 edition of Ralegh's poems is now in the Bodleian (13. θ. 132).

Additional texts are also to be found of the epitaph (doubtfully attributed to Ralegh) on the Earl of Leicester, *'Here lyes the noble warryor that never bludyed sword'*, for it is cited in the pro-Catholic tract (probably by Richard Verstegan) *A Declaration of the True Causes of the Great Troubles*: see E.A. Strathmann in *MLN*, 60 (1945), 111-14. The numerous extant copies of this tract — sometimes entitled *Cecil's Commonwealth* — include MSS at All Souls College, Oxford (MS 155, ff. 217-38v); in the Bodleian (MS CCC. 200, ff. 30-79); in the British Library (Add. MS 48122 (Yelverton MS 129, recorded in *HMC*, 2nd Report (1871), Appendix, p. 44); Harley MS 6807, ff. 144-69); in the Huntington (HM 267); in the University of London Library (MS 312, ff. 153-91v); in the Osborn Collection at Yale (fb 40 (the Eaton Hall MS recorded in *HMC*, 3rd Report (1872), Appendix, p. 215)); and a MS on temporary deposit in the Fitzwilliam Museum, Cambridge (Bradfer-Lawrence 48, item 1). Miss Latham notes (p.172) that Sir Walter Scott quoted the epitaph in *Kenilworth* (1821), his text deriving from a copy among the Drummond Papers, most of which are now in the National Library of Scotland (MSS 2053-67).

Prose

The entries devoted to Ralegh's prose works (RaW 543-

710) include those tracts, histories, and notable political, military, and naval memoranda generally accepted as Ralegh's by modern scholars. For tracts and memorials which have been added to the canon since 1829, see RaW 571, 604, 692-5, 698. The entries include *Observations concerning the Royal Navy and Sea-Service* (RaW 683-91), which is sometimes found appended to Sir Arthur Gorges's *Islands Voyage* (or in one case to his *Observations...for a Sea fight*) but which seems to be of Ralegh's authorship. Additional copies of Gorges's *Islands Voyage* without Ralegh's *Observations* can be found in the Public Record Office (SP. 15/36/94) and in the Berkshire Record Office (Trumbull Add. 22). Ralegh's *Orders to be observed by the Commanders of the Fleet with Land Companies, 3 May 1617* (RaW 701-8) was incorporated in Gorges's *A forme of orders...in conducting a Fleet through the Narrow Seas*, so copies of the latter are also included in the entries for Ralegh's work (RaW 705-8). Ralegh's *Opinion upon the Articles propounded by the Earl of Essex...in 1596* is included (RaW 699-700). Other related MSS, such as copies of Essex's articles and the opinions of other commanders, are to be found, for instance, in the Public Record Office (SP. 12/260/82-83, 12/260/93, 12/260/101, 12/265/2) and the Huntington (EL 1612, pp. 37-8). For naval documents relating to Essex and Ralegh in 1597, see the account of miscellaneous papers below. Some of the MSS of Ralegh's prose works are mentioned in footnotes in Lefranc (1968), and that work offers an analysis (pp. 584-5) of the MS volume of tracts chiefly by Ralegh in Dr Williams's Library (MS Jones B. 60). But unless otherwise stated, the MSS recorded in the entries have not been printed, collated, or discussed in any published work to date.

Besides the MS texts recorded in the entries, many extracts from Ralegh's histories and tracts were copied, usually from printed sources, in miscellanies. *The History of the World* (1614), with its providential view of history, was an especially popular and influential book in the 17th century (it was a favourite book of Oliver Cromwell, for instance). Among those MSS known to contain extracts from it are the following:

> Bodleian (MSS Eng. misc. e. 226, f. 12; Eng. poet. e. 57, f. 15v; Eng. poet. f. 10, fol. 70; Rawl. D. 267, ff. 1-33; Rawl. D. 368, pp. 1-12); British Library (Add. MS. 36354, p. 114 (Milton's commonplace book)); Chetham's Library, Manchester (Mun. A 6. 33, pp. 264-5 et passim); Gonville and Caius College, Cambridge (MS 291/274, pp. 403-4); Hertfordshire Record Office (D/EP F11, passim); Inner Temple Library (Miscellaneous MS 38, passim); University College London (MSS Ogden 7/21, f. [27]; 7/33, passim; 7/37, f. [1 rev. seq.]; 7/38, f. [2r-v rev.]); an unlocated miscellany of James Earl, of Derby, formerly among the Webb MSS at Hardwick Vicarage, Hereford (recorded in *HMC*, 7th Report, Part I (1879), Appendix, p. 682); and John Evans's miscellany *Hesperides, or the Muses' Garden* (see WILLIAM SHAKESPEARE, INTRODUCTION).

A Latin translation of a passage from *The History of the World*, made in the 1630s by Thomas Egerton, younger son of John, first Earl of Bridgewater (1579-1649), is found in the Ellesmere MS (item 18) owned by Sir Geoffrey Keynes (*Bibliotheca Bibliographici*, No. 1862, and see *TLS* (28 May 1954), p. 351). Extracts from Ralegh's *Instructions to his Son and to Posterity* occur in miscellanies in the British Library (Harley MS 6534, ff. 102-3); in the Folger (MS V. b. 110, pp. 490-5); and at University College London (MS Ogden 7/7, ff. 14-16v). A miscellany in the British Library (Harley MS 980) contains extracts from Ralegh's *Apology for his Voyage to Guiana* (f. 142v) and from his *Dialogue between a Counsellor of State and a Justice of the Peace* (f. 15r-v). An early 18th-century receipt book of the Malet family (Folger, MS W. a. 303) contains (pp. 29-30) brief extracts from Ralegh's *Discourse of...War*, allegedly taken from a MS then in Northamptonshire. Some notes from Ralegh's *Remains* (London, 1657) and from other works by him are found in the Bodleian (MSS Ashmole 816, ff. 3-4, and Rawl. D. 1372, ff. 55-7v).

Apocryphal tracts

Those prose works which have been spuriously attributed to Ralegh in the past — some, perhaps, simply because copies were found among his papers — and of which MS texts are known, can be listed as follows:

(1) *A Breviary of the History of England, with the Reign of King William I* (London, 1693); *Works* (1829), VIII, 508-37. See SAMUEL DANIEL, DaS 31-9.

(2) *The Cabinet-Council: containing the Chief Arts of Empire and Mysteries of State* (London, 1658); *Works* (1829), VIII, 35-150. By 'T. B.', possibly Thomas Bedingfield: see Ernest A. Strathmann, 'A Note on the Ralegh Canon', *TLS* (13 April 1956), p. 228, and Lefranc (1968), p. 64. MS texts: owned by the Duke of Northumberland, Alnwick Castle (recorded in *HMC*, 3rd Report (1872), Appendix, p. 120); Bodleian (MS Don. d. 93); British Library (Add. MS 27320; Add. MS 33359; Hargrave MS 280; Harley MS 1853, ff. 39-89v; Harley MS 1889); Huntington (EL 1174); and Wadham College, Oxford (MS 26).

(3) *A Discourse concerneinge peace or warre with Spain*. Unpublished tract, beginning 'By the relation of the Spanish project agt. this State of England most illustrious Prince...'. Ascribed to Ralegh in Bodleian, MS Carte 96, ff. 82-94. See Lefranc (1968), p. 64.

(4) *A Discourse of Sea-ports, principally of the Port and Haven of Dover* (London, 1700). By Thomas Digges or Sir Dudley Digges?: see Ernest A Strathmann in *TLS* (1956), p. 228, and Lefranc (1968), p. 65. MS texts: Bodleian (MS Eng. misc. c. 144, pp. 338-57) and British Library (Sloane MS 3828, ff. 181-5).

(5) *A Discourse of Tenures, which were before the Conquest* (London, 1761); *Works* (1829), VIII, 592-626. Comprises extracts from a work by Sir Roger Owen, of which there are numerous MS texts: see Ernest A. Strathmann, 'Ralegh's *Discourse of Tenures* and Sir Roger Owen', *HLQ*, 20 (1957), 219-32, and Lefranc (1968), p. 65.

(6) *The Life and Death of Mahomet* (London, 1637). A synopsis of a translation (or a translation of a synopsis) of a work by Miguel de Luna: see Lefranc (1968), pp. 65-6. MS texts: Trinity College, Dublin (MS 732, ff. 102-32v); National Library of Wales (Brogyntyn (1938 deposit) MS 13 (=Brogyntyn MS 29), pp. 119-79, recorded

in *HMC*, 2nd Report (1871), Appendix, p. 85); unlocated Phillipps MS 8455, sold at Sotheby's, 15 June 1896, Lot 982, to W. Flower; and an unlocated folio volume of tracts attributed to Ralegh formerly among the Finch MSS and recorded in *HMC*, 7th Report (1879), Appendix, p. 516 (possibly destroyed in a fire in 1908).

(7) *A Military Discourse* (London, 1734). By Sir Thomas Wilford?: see Lefranc (1968), pp. 64-5. MS texts: Bodleian (MSS Rawl. C. 680, ff. 111-49; Tanner 103, ff. 7-17); British Library (Add. MS 48162 (Yelverton MS 174, recorded in *HMC*, 2nd Report (1871), Appendix, p. 46); Hargrave MS 168, ff. 307-62v; Harley MS 132; Harley MS 4685, ff. 1-28); owned by Bent E. Juel-Jensen, Oxford (the Harvey MS recorded in *HMC*, 1st Report (1870), Appendix, p. 62); University of Michigan, William L. Clements Library (Hubert S. Smith Collection); and a MS advertised in Maggs Brothers catalogue No. 590 (1933), item 252, owned in 1935 by Hamilton Cottier, Princeton, and of which a photocopy is preserved in Princeton University Library (AM 20450).

(8) *Observations concerning the Causes of the Magnificence and Opulence of Cities* (London, 1651); *Works* (1829), VIII, 541-7. A translation of parts of a work by Giovanni Botero: see Lefranc (1968), p. 66. A MS text was in the lost Finch volume (see No. 6 above).

(9) *Observations touching Trade and Commerce with the Hollander* (London, 1653); *Works* (1829), VIII, 351-76. By John Keymer: see Adolf Buff, 'Who is the author of the tract intitled "Some observations touching trade with the Hollander"?', *ES*, 1 (1877), 187-212, and Lefranc (1968), p. 64. One copy is in Ralegh's extant volume of MS tracts (see RaW 727). Other MS texts: British Library (Add. MS 41614, ff. 220-9 (formerly Leconfield MS 115 at Petworth House, recorded in *HMC*, 6th Report (1877), Appendix, p. 312); Add. MS 48063, ff. 253-60 (Yelverton MS 69, recorded in *HMC*, 2nd Report (1871), Appendix, p. 43); Cotton MS Titus B. V, ff. 231-44v; Harley MS 5111, ff. 36-42v; Harley MS 6273, ff. 151-63; Lansdowne MS 216, ff. 133v-44; Lansdowne MS 798, ff. 78-104v; Lansdowne MS 811, ff. 7-16; Sloane MS 2179, ff. 24-31v); owned by Agnes Latham, Pickering; Northamptonshire Record Office (the Isham MS recorded in *HMC*, 3rd Report (1872), Appendix, p. 253); and Public Record Office (SP.14/118/114 and 115).

(10) *The Present Stat of Thinges as they now Stand betweene the three great Kingedomes, Fraunce, England, and Spaine*. Ascribed to Ralegh in British Library, Harley MS 354, ff. 36-42; printed from this MS in Lefranc (1968), pp. 590-5, and discussed pp. 586-90; the attribution subsequently doubted by Professor Lefranc (privately communicated by letter). Additional MS texts: Bibliothèque Nationale, Paris (fonds anglais n° 146, pp. 6-9); British Library (Cotton MS Vitellius C. XVI, ff. 390v-4v; Harley MS 787, ff. 5-9; Harley MS 1305, ff. 24-7v; Harley MS 6798, ff. 299v-306v; Sloane MS 23, ff. 1-7v); Folger (MSS G. a. 1, ff. 58-75; V. b. 173, ff. 26-35v); University of London Library (MS 20, ff. 199v-210, ascribed to Ralegh); and National Library of Wales (Castell Gorfod MS 1, ff. 24v-32v, dated 1623).

(11) *The Prince, or Maxims of State* (London, 1642); *Works* (1829), VIII, 1-34. See Lefranc (1968), pp. 67-70. A MS text was in the lost Finch volume (see No. 6 above).

(12) *The Scepticke* (London, 1651); *Works* (1829), VIII, 548-56. A translation of extracts from the *Hypotyposes* of Sextus Empiricus: see Lefranc (1968), pp. 66-7. MS texts: British Library (Harley MS 7017, ff. 25-33; Lansdowne MS 254, ff. 353-65); Trinty College, Dublin (MS 532, ff. 130-45); Dr Williams's Library (MS Jones B. 60, pp. 151-68); and the lost Finch volume (see No. 6 above). These MSS are discussed in R.H. Popkin, 'A Manuscript of Ralegh's "The Scepticke"', *PQ*, 36 (1957), 253-9, and in S.E. Sprott, 'Ralegh's "Sceptic" and the Elizabethan Translation of Sextus Empiricus', *PQ*, 42 (1963), 166-75.

(13) *A Treatise of the Soul*. Ascribed to Ralegh in Bodleian, MS Ashmole 1149, Part III; printed from this MS in *Works* (1829), VIII, 571-9. See Lefranc (1968), pp. 57-8.

Another work attributed to Ralegh is an *Estimate of Spaine & Portugale as they flourisht in the Yeare 1582*. A forty-four-page late 16th-century transcript, ascribed to Ralegh apparently in a 17th-century hand on the back cover, was sold at Christie's, 28 November 1960, Lot 127, and is now at the Riveredge Foundation, Calgary, Canada (No. R.256.16); microfilms and other reproductions are in the British Library (RP 235 and RP 268) and in the Folger (Film Acc. 256 and PR. 1405. E7). This treatise, which lists the revenues of the Spanish nobles and clergy and, among other matters, gives an account of the provinces, cities and shipping of Spain, can possibly be identified with the 'lost' work *Of the present state of Spain, with a most accurate Account of his Catholique Majesties Power and Riches; with the Names and Worth of the most considerable Persons in that Kingdom*. The latter was mentioned in the late 17th century by John Shirley and Anthony Wood as 'a MS going about from hand to hand, said to have been written by our author [Ralegh]' (see Lefranc (1968), p. 72). Since, however, the attribution here is uncertain, and since the surviving treatise is a very mediocre work, quite uncharacteristic of Ralegh, its only likely connection with him is that he may once have had a copy among his papers. It may be noted that various other contemporary tracts on the wealth and power of Spain are to be found (for instance, among the Cotton MSS in the British Library), including examples in a MS volume owned by Ralegh (see RaW 727). For other lost works — notably discourses which he himself claimed to have written on the Spanish faction in Scotland, on the West Indies, and on how war might be made against Spain and the Indies — see Lefranc (1968), pp. 70-4. For an apocryphal work, *Tubus Historicus*, which survives only in a printed edition, and for certain 'works' by Ralegh which are really parts of his *History of the World*, see Lefranc (1968), pp. 63-4.

Marginalia in printed books and manuscripts

A notable omission from the entries is a section on Ralegh's marginalia in printed books and MSS. Ralegh once possessed a library of at least several hundred volumes. The titles of more than 500 books are listed in his notebook (RaW 728), a list printed and discussed in

Walter Oakeshott, 'Sir Walter Ralegh's Library', *The Library*, 5th Ser. 23 (1968), 285-327. Attempts to identify extant volumes from Ralegh's library, however, have yielded few results, and indeed speculation about possible ownership and the patent misidentification of marginalia allegedly in Ralegh's hand have led to some confusion. On the basis of MS annotations mistakenly thought to be in Ralegh's hand, his ownership has been claimed, for instance, for extant volumes of Pierre d'Ailly, *Imago mundi* (Louvain, [1483]), of J.J. Wecker, *De secretis libri xvii* (Basle, 1587), and of Diego de Torres, *Relación del origen y sucesso de los Xarifes* (Seville, 1586) (see Walter Oakeshott's article cited and the arguments advanced in his articles in *BC*, 15 (Spring 1966), 12-18, and in *The Library* (1971), 1-21). An exemplum of the 1617 folio of Spenser's works, formerly belonging to Dr Oakeshott, was once owned and annotated by Ralegh's wife and by his son, Carew (see Walter Oakeshott, 'Carew Ralegh's Copy of Spenser', *The Library*, 5th Ser. 26 (1971), 1-21), but the claim that certain interesting pencil notes in the volume against passages referring to Ralegh (illustrated in the article cited) were probably made by Ralegh himself is untenable on purely palaeographical grounds: the hand belongs to a later period in the 17th century, possibly even the 18th century. Dr Oakeshott also claims that the cipher in an exemplum of *The History of the World* (1614) now in the Hyde Collection, Somerville, is 'certainly in his hand' (*The Library* (1968), 293); however, the cipher 'WR' proves to be only an idle jotting made by a reader in the margin of the page containing the verses on Ralegh's portrait, an inscription repeated after the title of the poem, perhaps in another hand. (A similar doodle, the letter 'R' repeated several times, occurs, for instance, in the margin of the Arundel MS copy of Ralegh's 'A quip for Cupide' (RaW 124)). Another printed work by Ralegh, an exemplum of *The Discovery of Guiana* (1595) formerly owned by Dr Oakeshott, has, he claims (*loc. cit.*, p. 293), 'an *ex dono* cipher' possibly in the author's hand. Dr Oakeshott's own reservations about the positive identification of this hand, and the evident lack of a clear signature in the volume, do not support the likelihood of Ralegh's ownership. One other volume, as Dr Oakeshott rightly observes (*The Library* (1968), pp. 292, 326), has been claimed as Ralegh's on the basis of a probable forgery (see Fred Sorenson in *N & Q*, 166 (10 February 1934), 102-3). The volume, Robert Gray's *A Good Speed to Virginia* (London, 1609), now in the Newberry Library, Chicago, has on the title page the partly obliterated signature 'W. Ralegh' followed by the words 'Turr Lond'. The last two words do indeed appear to be in a 17th-century hand, but the 'signature' (which has been clearly tampered with) is not Ralegh's and is very likely the work of John Payne Collier, who once apparently owned the volume.

Other spurious or, at best, unauthenticated items may be mentioned. A MS volume which was catalogued by Sir Thomas Phillipps (MS 9290) as 'Sir Walter Raleigh's Prayers, found at Fardel, Co. Devon' is now in the Devon Record Office, Exeter (MS 44). The attribution rests on an inscription on a flyleaf (? in an 18th-century hand), 'This book is an original manuscript of S[r] Walter Raleigh found at Fardel in Devonshire the seat of his father...', but the volume (a small prayer book of over 250 pages) bears no trace of Ralegh's own hand; neither does it seem likely that it belonged to his father (d. 1581), for the hand appears to date from the early 17th century. An exemplum of Peter Martyr, *The History of travayle in the West and East Indies* (London, 1577), formerly in the Grenville Kane Collection at Princeton, was catalogued as having some annotations 'possibly' in Ralegh's hand, but no signature is mentioned; it is impossible to comment further on this doubtful item since the volume was stolen from Princeton University Library in 1973. Another unlocated volume allegedly annotated by Ralegh is an exemplum of Jan Jantzoon Orlers and Henry de Haestens, *Description et représentation de toutes les victoires de son excellence, le prince de Nassau* (Leiden, 1612); this volume, supposedly containing Ralegh's pencil notes in French, was once owned (and quoted) by William Oldys (1696-1761): see *Works* (1829), I, 245 seq. It is not impossible that this item was authentic: the work contains an account of the action at Cadiz, which would have been of obvious interest to Ralegh, and Oldys, author of a Life of Ralegh, would probably have been familiar with his autograph. In *N & Q*, 166 (24 February 1934), 138-9, William Jaggard supplies some not particularly helpful information about one other unlocated volume perhaps owned by Ralegh: 'My old friend, the late Gordon Duff (Librarian of the Rylands Library 1893-1900) once showed me, in his private collection, a volume (title forgotten) from Ralegh's library. On the side, in blind relief, was stamped the coat-of-arms reproduced in the late Dr. Brushfield's "Ralegh Bibliography"'. Gordon Duff's library was sold at Sotheby's, 16-19 March 1925.

A case for Ralegh's possible ownership of certain other items is provided by evidence of provenance. A Spanish document of 1577 relating to Cristoval Palomeque was given to the Bodleian in 1622 by Carew Ralegh (present pressmark MS Bodl. 909). Dr Oakeshott (*The Library* (1968), 293) plausibly suggests that this document may well have been captured by Sir Walter on his last voyage. An exemplum of Laurence Humphrey, *Jesuitismi*, 2 vols (London, 1584), now at Yale (Mhc5 H885 J4), has on the title page of the second volume the partly cropped inscription, 'Excellēti & Generoso viro D. Gual. Rau[ ] Laur. Humfred[us] D.D.'. Though this defective inscription is less than conclusive, and the volumes bear no traces of Ralegh's hand, they may have been presented to him by the author.

To the account of Ralegh's library given in his notebook may be added certain other references. Ralegh, like many other intellectual figures of the time (e.g. Bacon, Camden, and Jonson), made use of the library of Sir Robert Cotton (1571-1631). An autograph letter to Cotton, now in the British Library (Cotton MS Julius C. III, f. 311), includes a brief list of titles and asks Cotton, 'if yow haue any of thes old books or any manuscrips' relating to 'our Brittan antiquites', whether Ralegh might borrow them (see Edwards, No. CXL). The Cotton library, perhaps the single most important collection of MSS preserved in the British Library, presents serious possibilities for research connected with Ralegh and his sources, as with other members of Cotton's circle. Another relevant library is that of Henry Percy, ninth Earl of Northumberland (1564-1632), who was Ralegh's fellow prisoner in the Tower from 1605 and with whom he obviously shared common intellectual interests and pursuits. Percy's library at Alnwick Castle, seat of the present Duke of Northumberland, is largely preserved. He also lived, between 1621 and 1632, at Petworth House, Sussex, later seat of the Earl of Leconfield and now the seat of Lord Egremont. A substantial portion of the Leconfield library (including books and MSS with Percy's armorial crest) is preserved at Petworth, though a number of volumes were sold at Sotheby's, 23 April 1928. For some account of the Percy library, see G.R. Batho, 'The Library of the "Wizard" Earl: Henry Percy, Ninth Earl of Northumberland (1564-1632)', *The Library*, 5th Ser. 15 (1960), 246-61.

The most famous of Ralegh's books, though not mentioned in any of his lists, is obviously the Bible in which, according to so many early texts, he inscribed '*Euen such is tyme*' and which he left in the Gatehouse Prison at Westminster before his execution. It is scarcely to be hoped that this volume could have survived. A MS volume of material relating to the trials for the Overbury murder, now in the University of London Library (MS 313), contains (f. 15) this interesting note concerning another Bible: 'Sir Walter Rawleye sent a bible to Earle Somersett being in the tower he desiring to haue a Bible with a leafe turned downe at the *xxiiii*[th] Chapter of Ecclesiasticus verse *xiiii*[th] *Remember thy father and mother &c* and soe to the end of the Chapter'. Sir Robert Carr, Earl of Somerset, was committed to the Tower in 1615; he and his wife, Frances Howard, occupied Ralegh's rooms and adjoining apartments (in the upper story of the Bloody Tower) for some years after Ralegh's release in March 1615/16. It would be an extraordinary irony if a particular Bible was passed between the two prisoners and was the one in which Ralegh finally wrote '*Euen such is tyme*' (though this is unlikely).

As for Ralegh's extant volumes, the following is a list of the only books known to me — apart from his volume of MS tracts (RaW 727) — for which there is clear evidence of Ralegh's ownership:

(1) Fernando Colombo, *Historie* (Venice, 1571); at the University of Glasgow (Hunterian Collection, K.8.18.). Ralegh's signature, 'W Ralegh', at the foot of the title page.

(2) *Rerum Britannicarum*, ed. Hieronymus Commelin (Heidelberg, 1587); in Cambridge University Library (L*.9. 4). Ralegh's signature, 'W Ralegh. T.', at the top of the title page. This volume possibly noted in Ralegh's list of books (Oakeshott's No. 305).

(3) *Historiae fragmentum certaminis beatique exitus gloriosi & inclyti martyris Ballazaris Gerardi* (Paris, 1584); bound in a composite volume of pamphlets (of a similar nature) owned by the Marquess of Salisbury, Hatfield House. No signature, but on a slip pasted over a hole cut out beneath the title is a note in Ralegh's hand: 'In this place was the name of the Spanish Emb: who was afterward ashamed of his Martir'.

(4) Francesco Patrizi, *Militia Romana* (Ferrara, 1583); at Worcester College, Oxford. Ralegh's signature, 'W Ralegh' (heavily deleted), at the foot of the title page and his autograph motto, 'Amore et virtute', at the top. Facsimile of this page in Walter Oakeshott, *The Queen and the Poet* (London, 1960), facing p. 150.

(5) Bernardino Rocca, *De' discorsi di guerra* (Venice, 1582); at the Royal College of Physicians (Dorchester Library, D 32 b/5; Accession No. 7881). Ralegh's signature, 'W Ralegh', on the title page (midway down on either side) and his autograph motto, 'Medium Medijs', at the bottom; also the signature of his cousin, George Carew, Baron Carew of Clopton (1555-1629). This volume recorded by W.R.B. Prideaux in *N&Q*, 9th Ser. 7 (5 January 1901), 7. It is noted in Ralegh's list of books (Oakeshott's No. 507, with a reference to this volume mistakenly printed under No. 506).

(6) Torquato Tasso, *Rime, et prose. Parte prima* (Ferrara, 1583); at Yale (1975 380). Ralegh's signature, 'W Ralegh' (struck through), on the title page (part way down on either side) and his autograph motto, 'Medium Medijs', at the bottom; also the signature of one 'L. Berard'.

(7) A 15th-century, French, illuminated MS book of hours; in the Bodleian (MS Add. A. 185). Ralegh's signature, 'W Ralegh', at the top of fol. 1. This volume briefly discussed in Rosemond Tuve, 'Spenser and some Pictorial Conventions', *SP*, 37 (1940), 149-76 (p. 151), and in G.A. Wilkes, 'The Authorship of "The Passionate Mans Pilgrimage"', *N & Q*, 202 (August 1957), 335-6.

(8) *Roteiro de Dom. Joham de Castro, da viagee que os Portugueses fizeram desa India ate Soez*: a large calligraphic MS of 92 leaves, with coloured maps and drawings, transcribed by one Gaspar Aloisius in 1543; now in the British Library (Cotton MS Tiberius D. IX). No trace of Ralegh's hand, but there can be little doubt that this is the MS mentioned in *Purchas his Pilgrimes* (1625) as the 'originall. . .reported to have beene bought by Sir Walter Raleigh, at sixtie pounds, and by him caused to be done into English, out of the Portugall' (Glasgow edition (1905-7), VII, 236). Ralegh himself refers in *The History of the World* (II. iii. 8) to 'the report of Castro, a principal Commander under Gama (which Discourse I gave Mr. Hacluit to publish)'. The possibility that Ralegh's friend, Sir Robert Cotton, could have owned a second (and obviously very expensive) contemporary Portuguese copy of this rare work is extremely remote, whereas, on the contrary, some of Ralegh's MSS (e.g. RaW 692 and 726) are known to have passed into Cotton's collection. The text corresponds fairly closely with the English translation printed by Purchas (Glasgow edition, VII, 236-309), a translation 'which yet in part was done, as I thinke, and many marginall notes added by Sir Walter Raleigh himselfe'.

Maps

To this list may be added three MS maps of Guiana which belonged to Ralegh. One, in the British Library (Add. MS 17940A), was perhaps drawn for him by Thomas Harriot (1560-1621). The names appear to be in Ralegh's own hand. This map has been often reproduced: in T.N. Brushfield, *A Bibliography of Sir Walter Ralegh Knt.* (Exeter, 1908), p. 29; in *Geographical Journal*, 44 (1914), facing p. 181; in Ralegh, *Selections*, ed. G.E. Hadow (Oxford, 1917), after p. 200; in John Winton, *Sir Walter Ralegh* (London, 1975), p. 172; and, on large folded leaves, in Richard Hakluyt, *Principal Navigations of the English Nation* (Glasgow edition, 1903-5), X, after p. 384, and in Ralegh, *The Discoverie of...Guiana*, ed. V.T. Harlow (London, 1928), facing p. 1. A second map, on vellum, perhaps also drawn by Harriot or else by Thomas Hood, was evidently presented to Ralegh's friend Henry Percy, Earl of Northumberland. Formerly among the Leconfield MSS at Petworth House, this map was owned after 1928 by Boies Penrose (who died in 1976), at Barbados Hill, Devon, Pennsylvania, and is now owned by the present Duke of Northumberland at Alnwick Castle. It is reproduced in Penrose's *Travel and Discovery in the Renaissance* (Cambridge, 1952), facing p. 108. A third map, probably drawn by Robert Tatton, is to be found in the Archivo General, Simancas, Spain (Mapas, Planos y Dibujos, IV-56). It was first recorded in James Augustus St John, *Life of Sir Walter Raleigh* (London, 1868), I, 241, and is discussed, with a facsimile example, in R.A. Skelton, 'Ralegh as Geographer', *The Virginia Magazine of History and Biography*, 71 (1963), 131-49 (p. 141 and after p. 142). The map bears three or four inscriptions in Ralegh's hand, in French, indicating to the French ships where they were supposed to find him (in 1617). This feature explains how the map came to be in Spanish archives, for it was clearly given by Ralegh to one of his French agents, probably Antoine Belle, who subsequently disclosed the arrangements to the Spaniards. A fourth extant map of Guiana, which could conceivably have been owned by Ralegh, is a sketch among the papers of his great enemy, Count Gondomar. The sketch was reproduced in C. Pérez Bustamente, *El Conde de Gondomar y su intervención en el proceso, prisión y muerte de Sir Walter Raleigh* (Santiago,1928), after p. xxiv, and is probably now among the incompletely catalogued Gondomar papers in the Biblioteca de Palacio, Madrid. It was perhaps given to King James, who may have passed it on to Gondomar, before Ralegh's last voyage, as a gesture of appeasement. As such, it is another tangible reminder of one of the main reasons why the expedition was doomed from the start.

Clearly Ralegh owned many more maps and geographical documents, notably 'a great manuscript booke in pchment nere a yard square containing the discriptions of all contries in the world' which Sir Thomas Wilson described in a letter to King James (Public Record Office, SP.14/103/67, quoted by Walter Oakeshott in *The Library* (1968), 326). For some indication of the nature and disposal of Ralegh's maps (and of his mathematical instruments and books and papers in general), see Edwards, II, 413-14, 420-4; R.A. Skelton, *loc. cit.*; Oakeshott, *The Library* (1968), 285-327; and Lefranc (1968)), pp. 42-4. It is clear that steps were taken to confiscate Ralegh's possessions of this kind for the Royal collection, but Lady Ralegh seems to have petitioned successfully to retain them. However, a number of Ralegh's books and MSS probably perished in 1623, in a fire which destroyed the London house of Sir William Cockayne (who owned a trunk-full of them) and also the neighbouring house of Lady Ralegh herself. One other tantalising possibility is that Lady Ralegh took steps earlier to secure some of them against possible seizure by the government, perhaps also at the time when Ralegh was first arrested, in 1603. In an age without bank vaults and safes, one place to hide things was behind the panelling, in the secret niches which are a common feature of great Elizabethan houses, including Sherborne Castle.

Miscellaneous

The entries devoted to miscellaneous items (RaW 711-822) include Ralegh's journal (RaW 726), his extant notebook (RaW 728), his volume of MS tracts (RaW 727), and a few other items of special interest.

Ralegh's scientific papers — both those in his own hand and some early copies of receipts attributed to him — are recorded (RaW 711-25). For a discussion of the most famous of his receipts, his 'great Cordiall', see John Knott, 'Sir Walter Raleigh's "Royal Cordial"', *Dublin Journal of Medical Science*, 121 (1906), 63-70, 131-43. For some account of Ralegh's general activities in the field of chemistry and medicine, see Lefranc (1968), pp. 678-82, and John William Shirley, 'The Scientific Experiments of Sir Walter Ralegh, the Wizard Earl, and the Three Magi in the Tower 1603-1617', *Ambix*, 4 (1949), 52-66.

The miscellaneous entries also include certain memorials arising from Ralegh's final arraignment and execution. Of the two brief items which Edwards called Ralegh's 'testamentary notes' (RaW 729-36), the first is a note of some last wishes regarding purely practical matters, and the second is a list of points which Ralegh prepared for his own defence, a list which survives in several early transcripts. An unpublished item included is a prayer, described in one MS source as 'A Speech found in Sir Walter Rawleighes pockett after his Execution Written by him in the Gatehouse ye night befores dea[th]' (RaW 737-8). Although the precise details of this description need not be taken literally, for similar claims were made about various poems and letters of Ralegh, it seems quite possible that this 'Speech' is a genuine composition of Ralegh's, perhaps a pious confession prepared by him for circulation in case he was not allowed to speak on the scaffold (a suggestion made to me in a private letter by Professor Lefranc). The final entries (RaW 739-822) record extant texts of the celebrated speech which Ralegh actually made on the scaffold. The number of surviving copies of the speech and of accounts of the execution containing summaries thereof testifies to the interest which this event commanded in the 17th century; it can only be imagined how many MS texts must once have been in existence. No attempt is made here to date the various MSS narrowly. Perhaps some of the extant copies were produced and sold by professional scribes within days of the execution; transcripts of the speech continued to be made, however, until well into the middle of the 17th century. A few independent accounts of the speech found in contemporary letters provide additional witnesses to the text (see RaW 817-22), and it is conceivable (if not probable) that one item — a note of the main points in the speech made by Ralegh's friend Thomas Harriot (RaW 816) — was jotted down at the execution itself.

A few additional items relating to the execution may be mentioned. In a letter of 7 November 1618 to Sir Dudley Carleton (Public Record Office, SP.14/103/73), John Chamberlain describes Ralegh's deportment the night before his execution; the text is printed in *The Letters of*

John Chamberlain, ed. N. E. McClure (Philadelphia, 1939), II, 179-82. In another letter to Carleton, also written on 7 November 1618 (Public Record Office, SP.14/103/74), John Pory describes Ralegh's manner on the morning of his death; this letter is printed in William S. Powell, 'John Pory on the Death of Sir Walter Ralegh', *WMQ*, 3rd Ser. 9 (1952), 532-8 (pp. 537-8). In a letter of 9 November 1618 to Sir John Isham, Dr Robert Tounson, Dean of Westminster (who accompanied Ralegh to the scaffold), describes Ralegh's manner and state of mind before the execution; this letter is now preserved in the Northamptonshire Record Office (I.C. 152), and the text is printed in *Works* (1829), VIII, 780-3, and in Edwards, II, 489-92. An account of 'The vntimely and vnfortunate death of S[r] walter Rawleighe knt. 1618', which notes the reasons for his execution and includes poems on his death, is among the Hopkinson MSS in Bradford Central Library (Vol. 27, ff. 127v-9v). Brief notes on the execution written c. 1655 by Sir Francis Fane are in the Shakespeare Birthplace Trust Record Office (ER 93/1, p. 180).

Many MS texts exist both of the answers Ralegh made to the charges brought against him in 1618 and of accounts of his original full trial at Winchester in 1603. Among the known MS accounts of one or both of these proceedings are the following:

All Souls College, Oxford (MS 155, ff. 293-4v); a MS owned by the Duke of Bedford, Bedford Office, London (Woburn MSS HMC No. 195); Bibliothèque Nationale, Paris (fonds anglais n° 149, ff. 75-93); Bodleian (MSS Bodl. 966, p. 253; Carte 77, f. 60r-v; Perrott 4, ff. 3-11; Tanner 299, f. 26); Bradford Central Library (Hopkinson MSS, Vol. 27, ff. 62-3); British Library (Add. MS 30663, ff. 481-6v; Cotton MS Titus C. VII, ff. 85-92v; Harley MS 39, f. 360r-v; Harley MS 968; Harley MS 1576, f. 212r-v; Sloane MS 3079; Stowe MS 180, f. 9r-v); Cambridge University Library (MSS Add. 335, f. 50; Ee. 5. 23, pp. 462-4); Cheshire Record Office (DLT/B8, pp. 21-34 (the Tabley MS recorded in *HMC*, 1st Report (1870), Appendix, pp. 47-8)); Chester City Record Office (CR 63/2/19, f. 16r-v (the Davenport of Bramhall MS recorded in *HMC*, 12th Report, Appendix IX (1891), pp. 545-52)); University of Chicago (MS 824, ff. 7-28); Derbyshire Record Office (D 258/67/31/2); East Sussex Record Office (RAF/F/13/1, pp. 99-100); Edinburgh University Library (MSS La. III. 493, ff. 29, 32; La. III. 501, f. 65); Folger (MS V. a. 130); Harvard (MS Eng 1021); Inner Temple Library (Petyt MS 538, Vol. 36, ff. 273-314); University of Kansas (MS D153, item 2); two MSS owned by Agnes Latham, Pickering; Lincoln's Inn Library (MS Maynard LIX, item 15); National Library of Scotland (MS 5444); National Library of Wales (Brogyntyn (1938 deposit) MS 13 (=Brogyntyn MS 29), pp. 1-29); University of North Carolina (CSWR A31, A32, A84); Pforzheimer Library (MS 112, ff. 1-47v (the Alfred Morrison MS recorded in *HMC*, 9th Report, Appendix, Part II (1884), p. 408)); The Queen's College, Oxford (MSS 32, ff. 13-14; 121, pp. 511-12); Trinity College, Cambridge (MS R. 5. 12 (James 707), ff. 160v-4v); University College London (MSS Ogden 7/45; 7/52, ff. [5-9v]); Yale, Osborn Collection (212/3, item 5 (the John Loveday MS sold at Sotheby's, 19 February 1963, Lot 393)); also the unlocated Finch volume recorded in *HMC*, 7th Report (1879), Appendix, p. 516.

Some notes of earlier speeches by Ralegh, in Parliament in 1601, can be found in a parliamentary journal in the Bodleian (MS Rawl. A. 100).

A number of other miscellaneous documents are of interest. A plan for Munster in the hand of Lord Burghley, 25 October 1582, with autograph revisions by Ralegh, is in the Public Record Office (SP.63/96/30), and was printed in Sir John Pope-Hennessy, *Sir Walter Ralegh in Ireland* (London, 1883), pp. 227-32. A questionnaire, of 12 May 1589, submitted to 'undertakers' in Munster and containing Ralegh's autograph answers, is also in the Public Record Office (SP.63/144/27); so is a paper signed by Ralegh recording the names of his tenants in Munster, September [1589] (SP.63/144/28). A copy of Ralegh's instructions for the Muster Masters of Cornwall, [1587 or '88?] is likewise in the Public Record Office (SP.12/265/113). A signed petition to Lord Burghley, [1588 or '89], concerning the reform of abuses in the wine-licenses, is now in the New York Public Library, Manuscripts Division (Montague Collection, No. 1307). Contemporary transcripts of two joint memoranda from Cecil, Ralegh, and other commissioners concerning the Great-Carrack, 21 and 24 September 1592, are owned by the Marquess of Salisbury, Hatfield House (Cecil Papers 168/134-5). Various joint letters to the Privy Council or to individuals such as Burghley, Cecil, and Lord Howard were written and signed by Essex, Ralegh, and other naval commanders in July and August 1597. Four despatches of this kind signed by Ralegh are in the Public Record Office (SP.12/264/11; 12/264/12; 12/264/13(i); 12/264/60), and another is owned by the Marquess of Salisbury, Hatfield House (Cecil Papers 54/27). A similar joint letter from Howard, Ralegh, and Mountjoy to Essex, 5 November 1597, is now in the Warwickshire Record Office, among the papers of the Earl of Aylesford, of Packington Hall (Essex Letter Book, No. 58). An autograph memorandum (to Cecil?), [c. 20 March?] 1601/2, on the case of Kettleby v. Kettleby, is owned by the Marquess of Salisbury, Hatfield House (Cecil Papers, Petitions 2237a); so is an autograph memorandum, [April 1602], annotated by Cecil, concerning prizes taken by the *Refusal* commanded by Sir John Gilbert the Younger (Cecil Papers, Petitions 2237).

A document signed by Ralegh concerning the sale of land in Derbyshire formerly owned by the conspirator Anthony Babington, dated 18 March 1587, was in 1942 in the possession of Mr Francis Blom of New Orleans; a photograph is in the Folger (PR 1405 R2). The seal and signature on this document, which was formerly owned by E. Basil Jupp, F.S.A., are reproduced in *Miscellanea Genealogica et Heraldica*, ed. Joseph Jackson Howard, II (London, 1876), 155. Another signed document concerning the sale of land in Derbyshire formerly owned by Babington, dated 1 August 1587, was sold at Sotheby's, 27 October 1970, Lot 368, and subsequently exported; a photocopy is in the British Library (RP 546). A warrant signed by Ralegh and his brother Carew, 28 September 1587, appointing a deputy steward of the Manor of Mere is preserved in the Wiltshire Record Office (WRO 150). A signed patent for the stewardship of the Manor of Gillingham, 30 June 1588 — a document endorsed by one 'Rand[olph] Baron', who refers to Ralegh as 'my master' — was recorded in the printed catalogue of the R.B. Adam Library (1929), III, 201, and is now in the Hyde

Collection, Somerville, New Jersey (*Life*, I, 3, 226). A signed indenture leasing lands in Munster to Thomas Colthurst, 8 September 1589, was sold at Sotheby's, 14 March 1979, Lot 434, to Batchelder (a reduced facsimile is in the sale catalogue). A signed mandate to the steward of the Manor of Trematon, Cornwall, 25 June 1591, is preserved in Chetham's Library, Manchester (Mun. A 1. 2). A signed warrant appointing John Meere as Keeper of Sherborne, 28 August 1592, is in the Public Record Office (SP.12/242/124). An authorisation of payment for arrows for the Queen's guards, signed by both the Queen and Ralegh, 31 December 1593, is now in the Arents Collection in the New York Public Library. An autograph warrant concerning the delivery of timber cut in Ireland, 29 August 1599, is preserved by the Historical Society of Pennsylvania (Case 10, Box 34, pp. [D-E]). A legal transcript of a warrant appointing John Foster bailiff of Sherborne, 12 September 1599, is in the Public Record Office (E. 143/7). An autograph declaration to Sir Robert Carr of good usage for Sherborne, December 1609, also signed by Lady Ralegh and Walter Ralegh the Younger, is owned by the Duke of Bedford, Bedford Office, London. Two signed certificates of service for one John Duckett, disabled by war-wounds, [1613?], are in the Wiltshire Record Office, (in the Great Rolls, Quarter Sessions: Easter 1613, No. 187, and Autograph Book, f. 13). Two Wills made by Ralegh are still preserved at Sherborne: one, of 8 July 1597 (the chief interest of which lies in its disclosure that he had an illegitimate child in Ireland) is discussed in Agnes M.C. Latham, 'Sir Walter Ralegh's Will', *RES*, NS 22 (1971), 129-36; the other, of 20 January 1602/3, is reproduced in a reduced facsimile in John Winton, *Sir Walter Ralegh* (London, 1975), p. 343. A signature and autograph inscription of Ralegh, 'Opus peragunt labor et amor', can also be found in the autograph album of Captain Francis Segar, now in the Huntington (HM 743, f. 110v).

Among the various other documents relating to Ralegh in the public records and elsewhere, a number concern his voyages, especially his second expedition to Guiana in 1617. A 'Cashe Booke for the Voyage Sett fforthe By the Right Worshipfull Sir Walter Rawlighe and others in anno 1592' (a voyage from which he was recalled by the Queen) is among the papers of the Myddelton family, now in the National Library of Wales (Chirk MS F. 12629); it is discussed in G. M. Griffiths, 'An Account Book of Raleigh's Voyage, 1592', *NLWJ*, 7 (1951-2), 347-53. Brief descriptions of the same voyage appear in various volumes of maritime tracts, including one owned by Lord Egremont at Petworth House (HMC MS 59, pp. 20-1) and another owned by the Marquess of Bath at Longleat House (recorded in *HMC*, 3rd Report (1872), Appendix, p. 183). A contemporary transcript of the official account of the Islands Voyage in 1597, the original of which was signed by Ralegh and the Council of War, is in the British Library (Harley MS 36, ff. 323-8); this account was printed in 1625 in *Purchas his Pilgrimes* (Glasgow edition (1905-7), XX, 24-33). Spanish documents concerning Ralegh's 'piracies' are preserved in the Archivo General, Simancas ('Secretaria de Estado. Documentos relativos a Inglaterra', Legajos 2.514, 2.850, & 7.030 (Libro 373)) and among other state papers. Transcripts of various documents in the Spanish archives relating to Ralegh's voyages were made at the end of the 19th century at the time of the Guiana-Venezuela Boundary Dispute and are now in the British Library (Add. MSS 36316-7, 36320). A number of relevant Spanish documents are printed in C. Pérez Bustamente, *El Conde de Gondomar y su intervención en el proceso, prisión y muerte de Sir Walter Raleigh* (Santiago, 1928) and Don Antonio Ballesteros y Beretta, *Correspondencia oficial de Don Diego Sarmiento de Acuña, Conde de Gondomar* (Madrid, 1943). Certain documents relating to the 1617 voyage are printed in V.T. Harlow, *Ralegh's Last Voyage* (London, 1932). Others are discussed and quoted from transcripts in her own possession by Agnes Latham in 'Sir Walter Ralegh's Gold Mine: New Light on the Last Guiana Voyage', *E & S*, NS 4 (1951), 94-111. Some documents in the Public Record Office relating to Ralegh's finances are discussed in John W. Shirley, 'Sir Walter Raleigh's Guiana Finances', *HLQ*, 13 (1949-50), 55-69. Ralegh's own estimate of his expenses for the expedition is preserved in a transcript in the Folger (MS G. b. 10, ff. 111-12v); the text of this memorandum is printed in Ernest A. Strathmann, 'Ralegh Plans his Last Voyage', *MM*, 50 (1964), 261-70. A signed agreement (26 March 1617) between Ralegh and Charles Howard, Earl of Nottingham, concerning the voyage is preserved in the Arents Collection in the New York Public Library; a reduced facsimile appears in Sotheby's sale catalogue, 5 July 1955, Lot 981. A document signed on the same day, covenanting to pay a share of the profits to Sir Arthur Ingram, is on temporary deposit in the Fitzwilliam Museum, Cambridge (Bradfer-Lawrence 60). Copies of James I's commission to Ralegh for the expedition are to be found among various state papers, including MSS in the Bodleian (MS North a. 6, ff. 1-16) and at the University of North Carolina (CSWR A28 and A29).

Letters

It remains to note the most substantial body of original Ralegh MSS: his letters. Edwards prints the text of 166 letters of Ralegh, perhaps as many as 125 of which survive in the originals (some in Ralegh's own hand, some written by his amanuenses). Most are now in the British Library and the Public Record Office or among the Cecil Papers at Hatfield House. Facsimile examples of letters in the British Library are to be found in Greg, *English Literary Autographs*, plates LXXIV-LXXV, in *Facsimiles of Royal, Historical, and Literary Autographs in the British Museum* (1899), plate 20, and in Sir Henry James, *Facsimiles of National Manuscripts from William the Conqueror to Queen Anne*, 4 vols (Southampton, 1865-8), III, plate XC; IV, plate XIX. A letter in the Bodleian (MS Tanner 79, f. 117) is reproduced in Edwards, II, frontispiece, and one in the Public Record Office is reproduced in Ralegh, *Selections*, ed. G.E. Hadow (Oxford, 1917), facing p. 34. Lefranc (1968) supplies (pp. 579-83) a list of 64 additional letters found in numerous other repositories. One, now in the Pforzheimer Library (MS 106), is reproduced in *The Carl H. Pforzheimer Library: English Literature 1475-1700* (New York, 1940), III, facing p. 853. Lefranc also establishes the inauthenticity of certain letters which have been attributed to Ralegh in other sources. Ralegh's complete letters are currently being edited by Agnes Latham.

The following two checklists (i-xvi, 1-7) of letters which have come to light in the last ten years or so may serve as a supplement to Edwards and Lefranc (1968). The two lists are largely based on information provided by Miss Latham, information which in turn is greatly indebted to recent research by Professor Lefranc.

The following are letters previously known, but, for the most part, only from transcripts:

(i) 26 July 1584: To Richard Duke (Edwards, No. X). Original in the Devon Record Office, Exeter (2850/Z3).

(ii) 27 February 1587/8: To Sir John Gilbert the Elder (Lefranc, No. 8). Original sold at Christie's, 2 April 1975, Lot 149 (facsimile in the sale catalogue, frontispiece); later item 88 in catalogue No. 21 (October 1975) of John Wilson (and facsimile in catalogue); now privately owned in Venezuela; a photocopy is in the British Library (RP 1213).

(iii) 10 February [1591/2]: To Sir John Gilbert the Elder (Lefranc, No. 15). Original with the Historical Society of Pennsylvania (Case 12, Box 15).

(iv) 3 [March 1591/2]: To Sir John Gilbert the Elder (Edwards, No. LII). Original with the Maine Historical Society (John S.H. Fogg Autograph Collection, Vol. 14).

(v) [13] September [1592]: To Lord Burghley (Edwards, No. XXVIII). Original owned by the Marquess of Bath, Longleat House (Portland Papers, I, f. 149).

(vi) 16 September 1592: To Lord Burghley (Edwards, No. XXIX). Original owned by the Marquess of Bath, Longleat House (Portland Papers, I, f. 151).

(vii) 17 September 1592: To Lord Burghley and Lord Howard (Edwards, No. XXX). Original owned by the Marquess of Bath, Longleat House (Portland Papers, I, f. 153).

(viii) [c. 23 June] 1596: To Sir Arthur Gorges (Lefranc, No. 29). Original still unlocated, but another early transcript, corrected in a second hand, is in the Folger (MS V. b. 214, ff. 106v-9).

(ix) [late April] 1602: To Sir John Gilbert the Younger (Edwards, No. LXXXIII). Original in the New York Public Library, Arents Collection (Acc. 5851).

(x) 21 January 1603/4: To King James (Edwards, No. CXXIX). The original, printed by Edwards, is owned by the Marquess of Salisbury, Hatfield House (Cecil Papers 102/111); an autograph copy is also preserved in the Somerset Record Office (DD/MI 18/82 [ii]).

(xi) [before July] 1611: To some lords of the Privy Council (Edwards, No. CXLVIII). Copy in Ralegh's 'miscellany' (RaW 727), f. 135v.

(xii) [after July] 1611: To King James (Lefranc, No. 53). Copy in Ralegh's 'miscellany' (RaW 727), f. 136.

(xiii) [1611]: To Sir Robert Cecil (Lefranc, No. 54). Copy in Ralegh's 'miscellany' (RaW 727), f. 138.

(xiv) July 1615: To Sir Ralph Winwood (Lefranc, No. 57). Copy in Ralegh's 'miscellany' (RaW 727), f. 137.

(xv) 17 March 1615/16: To Sir George Villiers (Edwards, No. CL). Original still unlocated, but an early transcript is owned by the Marquess of Bath, Longleat House (Portland Papers, II, f. 9).

(xvi 1617: To Sir Ralph Winwood (Lefranc, No. 61). The previously unlocated 'Wilson' MS is a later transcript, not the original letter, and is now in Bradford Central Library (Hopkinson MSS, Vol. 19, f. 81r-v). It is, however, not an unpublished letter to Winwood but Edwards No. CXLIX, the text of which Edwards printed from a curtailed version in Ralegh's *Remains* (1657) and which he tentatively dated 1615-16.

The following are letters not recorded in Edwards or Lefranc (1968), and are in addition to miscellaneous documents noted above (certain of which might be regarded as letters):

(1) September 1590: To James Bisse and the Chapter of Wells Cathedral. Original in Somerset Record Office (DD. C/1878. Box 2).

(2) 28 April 1594: To Master Pytt, Teller of the Exchequer. Original at University of Basle, Switzerland (Autographen-Sammlung Geigy-Hagenbach, No. 299).

(3) c. 6 April 1595: To Antonio de Berrío, Governor of Guiana. Quotation, apparently verbatim, from this letter (original unlocated) in a letter of Berrío, 9 July 1595, in the Archivo General de Indias, Seville, Spain (AG1, Sto Domingo 180); printed in Pablo Ojer, *La formación del oriente venezolana* (Caracas, 1966), I, 543.

(4) 1 September 1600: To Thomas Reynell, Christopher and Robert Hamlyn, and John Sweete, steward of the Stannary Court. Original in the New York Public Library, Arents Collection (Acc. 5682); printed in Sotheby's sale catalogue, 14 December 1906, Lot 451.

(5) September 1601: To the Justices of Jersey. Original at Harvard (fMS 870 [5A-B]); printed in P. Ahier, *The Governorship of Sir Walter Ralegh in Jersey* (St Helier, 1971), p. 27.

(6) 13 December 1601: To the Bailiff and Justices of Jersey. Original owned by Major I.F. Hyne, Baldock, Hertfordshire; printed in P. Ahier, *op. cit.*, p.196.

(7) May [1603]: To Adrian Gilbert. Quotation, apparently verbatim, from this letter (original unlocated) in a report of a judgement in Chancery, 17 June 1613, in the Public Record Office (C.38/19); printed in Cecil Monro, *Acta Cancellariae* (London, 1847), p. 86.

Seventeenth-century transcripts of Ralegh's letters abound, especially of those arising from his troubles in 1603 and 1617-18. Such copies have obvious editorial value when the originals are damaged or no longer exist; more especially they witness to the extent of contemporary and posthumous interest in Ralegh. Among the innumerable transcripts of letters by Ralegh which are not specifically recorded in Edwards or Lefranc (1968) are the following:

All Souls College, Oxford (MS 155, f. 353r-v); Balliol College, Oxford (MS 270, f. 75); a MS owned by the Duke of Bedford, Bedford Office, London (Woburn MSS HMC No. 261, pp. 519-60); Bibliothèque

Nationale, Paris (fonds anglais n° 146, pp. 166-75; n° 149, ff. 93v-102); Bodleian (MSS Ashmole 781; Ashmole 830; Ballard 11; Carte 77, ff. 43-6; Eng. hist. c. 272, pp. 44-6 (Gurney MS XXV recorded in *HMC*, 12th Report, Appendix IX (1891), p. 146); Eng. hist. d. 138 (Mostyn MS 142 recorded in *HMC*, 4th Report (1874), Appendix, p. 353); Jesus College 83, f. 64 seq.; Lyell empt. 19, f. 10; Rawl. B. 151, f. 1v; Rawl. D. 589; Rawl. D. 924; Tanner 74, 75, 82, 149, 278, 290, and 299; University College 152, ff. 43, 151-9); Bradford Central Library (Hopkinson MSS, Vol. 19, ff. 81-8v; Vol. 44, pp. 388-401); British Library (Add. MSS 4106, f. 81; 4108, ff. 111-14v; 11308, f. 135; 22587, f. 8; 22601, f. 17v; 25707, ff. 138, 147; 29598, f. 2; 40838, ff. 31-6; 44848, ff. 164-9; 52585, ff. 41v-2; Cotton MS Otho E. VII, f. 208; Egerton MS 2884, f. 12; Hargrave MS 226, ff. 261-9v; Harley MSS 39, ff. 351v-60, 369-72; 703, f. 162v; 787, f. 59; 852, ff. 21-3v; 1221, f. 95v; 1576, ff. 94v-5v, 209v-13; 1893, f. 80r-v; 3787, f. 183; 4761, ff. 13-25v; 4808, p. 106; 6038, ff. 31-4; 6242, f. 90; 6908, ff. 92-90 rev.; Sloane MSS 3079, f. 42; 3272, f. 46; 3520; Stowe MS 180, f. 26); Cambridge University Library (MSS Add. 79, ff. 64v-5v; Ee. 5. 23, pp. 427-9, 436-7. 446-50, 452-3); Cheshire Record Office (DLT/B8, pp. 199-203, 300-1 (the Tabley MS recorded in *HMC*, 1st Report (1870), Appendix, pp. 47-8)); Chester City Record Office (CR 63/2/19, ff. 15-17 (the Davenport of Bramhall MS recorded in *HMC*, 12th Report, Appendix IX (1891), pp. 545-52)); Chetham's Library, Manchester (Mun. A 4. 15, printed in Grosart, *The Dr Farmer MS* (1873)); University of Chicago (MS 824, f. 26); Derbyshire Record Office (D 258/31/73; D 258/67/6b & 6c); Downing College, Cambridge (Bowtell Collection, MS 'Wickstede Thesaurus', Part II, f. 40); East Sussex Record Office (RAF/F/13/1, pp. 7, 19-21, 39, 66-71, 73-4); Edinburgh University Library (MS La. III. 501, ff. 66v-7); Essex Record Office (D/DSh Z1, f. 36r-v); Folger (MSS G. b. 7; J. a. 2; L. a. 758; V. a. 130; V. a. 239; V. a. 339; V. a. 418; V. b. 214; V. b. 234; V. b. 303; X. c. 45; X. d. 241 (a & c); Z. e. 1 (the Cholmondely MS recorded in *HMC*, 5th Report (1876), Appendix, pp. 354-5)); Harvard (MSS Eng 628, p. 362; Eng 1021); Huntington (EL 2805; EL 6232; HM 267; HM 36836, pp. 102-27); Inner Temple Library (Petyt MS 538, Vols. 36 and 51); University of Kansas (MSS D153, item 2; 4A:1, p. 18; also a 19th-century transcript in MS 153: 10, pp. [32-40]); Kent Archives Office (U 951 Z6, pp. 1-18, 87-93); three MSS owned by Agnes Latham, Pickering (including the Bacon Frank MS B. 3 recorded in *HMC*, 6th Report (1877), Appendix, p. 459, and the Richard Tichborne MS described by C. Deedes in *N & Q*, 8th Ser. 3 (24 June 1893), 481-2, and 4 (8 July 1893), 21-2); Leicestershire Record Office (DG. 7/Lit. 2, ff. 250-1v); a MS owned by the Marquess of Bath, Longleat House (MS Miscellaneous, p. 277); National Library of Scotland (Adv. MS 33. 7. 19, ff. 7-13); National Library of Wales (Brogyntyn (1938 deposit) MS 13 (=Brogyntyn MS 29), pp. 31-4 (recorded in *HMC*, 2nd Report (1871), Appendix, p. 85); Carreglwyd, ser. ii, no. 346; Castell Gorfod MS 1, ff. 7v-24); National Maritime Museum (MS LEC/6 (Leconfield MS 34 recorded in *HMC*, 6th Report (1877), Appendix, p. 304)); Northamptonshire Record Office (F.H. 3641/4 & 5; I.C. 3494; I.C. 3497); University of Nottingham (Clifton MSS Cl LP 5/2, pp. 1-2, and 5/4); two MSS owned by Lord Egremont, Petworth House (HMC MSS 60, pp. 112-23, and 61, pp. 374-95): Pierpont Morgan Library (MA 664, pp. 214-18); Public Record Office (SP.14/96/70 & 71); The Queen's College, Oxford (MSS 32, ff. 9, 16v-18; 121, pp. 499-511); Somerset Record Office (DD/MI 18/81 (among the Mildmay MSS recorded in *HMC*, 7th Report (1879), Appendix, p. 592)); Trinity College, Cambridge (MS R. 5. 12 (James 707), ff. 164v-71v, 175v-7v); Trinity College, Dublin (MSS 672, p. 188; 862); University College London (MS Ogden 7/37); Wiltshire Record Office (413/445, f. [41r-v]; 865/500, ff. [28-30]); Yale, Osborn Collection (212/3, item 6 (Loveday MS); fb 155, f. 379 (Braye MS recorded in *HMC* 15, 10th Report, Appendix VI (1887), p. 122); P.B. VI/107, f. 415 (Gurney MS XXXIII recorded in *HMC*, 12th Report, Appendix IX (1891), p. 161)); Yorkshire Archaeological Society, Leeds (MD 59/22, [no item number]); also the lost Finch volume recorded in *HMC*, 7th Report (1879), Appendix, p. 516; the unlocated Phillipps MS 11138; and MSS sold at Sotheby's, 4-5 July 1955, Lots 982 (to Maggs) and 983 (to Quaritch), and 2 March 1965, Lot 423 (to F. Edwards).

Ralegh's letter of 1618 to his cousin George, Lord Carew of Clopton (beginning 'Because I know not whether I shall live . . .'), was widely circulated in transcripts as his 'short Apology for his last action at Guiana'. The text is printed in Edwards (No. CLX) from an imperfect MS in the British Library (Cotton MS Vitellius C. XVII, ff. 439-40). Edwards took this MS to be the original letter, written by an amanuensis with Ralegh's minor autograph corrections, but this assumption is open to question. For her edition Miss Latham proposes to use as copy-text MS Carte 77, ff. 41-2, in the Bodleian. Among the other extant transcripts of the letter are the following:

Bodleian (MSS Eng. hist. d. 138, f. 8 (Mostyn MS 142); Eng. hist. c. 121, ff. 7-8; Rawl. D. 180, ff. 42-5; Rawl. D. 589; Tanner 74, f. 140; Tanner 265; Tanner 269, f. 9); British Library (Add. MSS 22587, ff. 5-7; 34631, f. 55; 40838, ff. 49-51; Harley MS 1327, f. 60v; Harley MS 1576, f. 211r-v)); Cheshire Record Office (DLT/B8, pp. 279-82 (Tabley MS)); Folger (MSS V. a. 418, ff. 8-10; Z. e. 1 (10) (Cholmondely MS)); Gonville and Caius College, Cambridge (MS 73/40, ff. 204-5); House of Lords Record Office (Historical Collections, No. 53 (the Eaton Hall MS recorded in *HMC*, 3rd Report (1872), Appendix, p. 214)); Inner Temple Library (Petyt MS 538, Vol. 18); Leeds Archives Department (MX 269, ff. [13v-15]); Leicestershire Record Office (DG. 7/Lit. 2, ff. 92-3v); Public Record Office (SP.14/98/88); Staffordshire Record Office (D 1721/3/186); Dr Williams's Library (MS Jones B. 60, pp. 213-19); and Wiltshire Record Office (413/445, ff. [42-4]).

The autograph and some proof sheets of the Life of Ralegh written before 1751 by Thomas Birch, together with some supplementary material, including transcripts of letters of Ralegh, are to be found in the British Library (Add. MS 4231).

PB.

ARRANGEMENT

Verse:	(1) Poems generally attributed to Ralegh	RaW 1-359
	(2) Poems doubtfully ascribed to Ralegh	RaW 360-542
Prose		RaW 543-710
Miscellaneous		RaW 711-822.

See also Addenda to Part 2, p. 632

FACSIMILE XXVIII — Sir Walter Ralegh: The last nine lines of *The 11th: and last booke of the Ocean to Scinthia* and the first twenty-one lines of *The end of the boockes, of the Oceans love to Scinthia, and the beginninge of the 12 boock, entreatinge of Sorrow*, c.1592-1618 (RaW 8 and 9). Hatfield House, Cecil Papers 144/247 recto. Reproduced by courtesy of The Marquess of Salisbury.

my steapps ar backwarde, gasinge on my loss,
my minds affection, and my sowles sole love,
not mixte with fances chafe, or fortunes dross,
to god I leve it, who first gave it me,
and I her gave, and she returnd agayne,
as it was herrs, so lett his mercies bee,
of my last cumforts the essentiall meane;

But be it so, or not, th'effects, ar past,
her love hath end; my woe must ever last.

The end of the boockes, of the Oceans love to Scinthia, and the beginninge of the 22 boock, entreatinge of Sorrow.

My dayes delights, my springetyme ioies fordunn,
which in the dawne, and risinge soonn of youth
had their creation, and weare first begunn,

do in the yeveninge, and the winter sadd
present my minde, which takes my tymes accompt
the greif remayninge of the ioy it had.

my tymes that then rann ore them sealves in thes
and now runn out in others happines
bringe unto thos new ioyes, and new borne dayes,

so could shee not, if shee weare not the soonn
which sees the birth, and buriall, of all elce,
and holds that poure, with which shee first begunn;

levinge each withered boddy to be torne
by fortune, and by tymes tempestius,
which by her vertu, once faire frute have borne,

knowinge shee cann renew, and cann create
green from the grounde, and floures, yeven out of stone,
by vertu lastinge over tyme and date,

Sir Walter Ralegh

VERSE

(1) POEMS GENERALLY ATTRIBUTED TO RALEGH

RaW 1 *'A Secret murder hath bene done of late'.*

Copy, subscribed 'finis: Goss:', in a miscellany compiled by a Cambridge student, possibly Sir John Finett (1571-1641) of Fordwich, Kent; c. 1586-91.

First pub. in *The Phoenix Nest* (London, 1593); Latham, pp. 78-9. This MS collated in *The Phoenix Nest*, ed. H.E. Rollins (Cambridge, Mass., 1931), p. 173; recorded in Latham, p. 159.

Bodleian, MS Rawl. poet. 85, f. 108v.

RaW 2 *The Advice* ('Many desire, but few or none deserve').

Copy, subscribed 'Finis written to M[rs]. A.V.', in a miscellany compiled by a Cambridge student, possibly Sir John Finett (1571-1641) of Fordwich, Kent; c. 1586-91.

First pub. in *Le Prince d'Amour* (London, 1660); Latham, pp. 14-15. This MS recorded in Latham, p. 110.

Bodleian, MS Rawl. poet. 85, f. 116.

RaW 3 -----

Copy, headed 'To A. Vauas', in a miscellany compiled by someone connected with the Court; c. 1605.

This MS recorded in Latham, p. 110.

British Library, Add. MS 22601, f. 71.

RaW 4 *'As you came from the holy land'.*

Copy, with corrections in a different ink, ascribed to 'S[r]. W. R:', together with a deleted version, in a miscellany compiled by a Cambridge student, possibly Sir John Finett (1571-1641) of Fordwich, Kent; c. 1586-91.

First pub. in Thomas Deloney, *The Garland of Good-Will* (London, 1596?; first extant edition 1628). Printed from this MS in Latham, pp. 22-3.

Bodleian, MS Rawl. poet. 85, f. 123r-v.

RaW 5 -----

Copy in a MS volume of ballads (the 'Percy Folio'); mid-17th century.

Printed from this MS in *Bishop Percy's Folio Manuscript*, ed. John W. Hales, Frederick J. Furnivall, et al., 4 vols (London, 1867-8); this publication mentioned in Latham, p. 120.

British Library, Add. MS 27879, f. 251r-v.

RaW 6 -----

Copy on a leaf inserted in a verse miscellany owned by Edward Denny, Charles Cokes, and others; c. 1595.

Printed from this MS in Josephine Waters Bennett, 'Early Texts of Two of Ralegh's Poems from a Huntington Library Manuscript', *HLQ*, 4 (1940-1), 469-75 (pp. 473-4); recorded in Latham, p. 120.

Huntington, HM 198, Part I, f. 4.

RaW 7 -----

Copy in a miscellany; late 17th century.

Yale, Osborn Collection, b 213, pp. 34-7.

--- -----

See also BEAUMONT & FLETCHER, INTRODUCTION.

--- *Conjectural First Draft of the Petition to Queen Anne* ('My dayes delight, my spring tyme ioyes foredun').

See RaW 295.

--- *Cynthia.*

See RaW 8-9, 146, 188; also 133-5, 200-2.

*RaW 8 *The 11th: and last booke of the Ocean to Scinthia* ('Sufficeth it to yow my ioyes interred').

Autograph.

First pub. (from this MS) in Hannah (1870); printed from this MS in Latham, pp. 25-43. Facsimiles of first page in Philip Edwards, *Sir Walter Ralegh* (London, 1953), facing p. 96, and in John Winton, *Sir Walter Ralegh* (London, 1975), facing p. 122. See also FACSIMILE XXVIII.

Owned by the Marquess of Salisbury, Hatfield House, Cecil Papers 144/240-7.

*RaW 9 *The end of the bookes, of the Oceans love to Scinthia, and the beginninge of the 12 Boock, entreatinge of Sorrow* ('My dayes delights, my springetyme ioies fordvnn').

Autograph.

First pub. (from this MS) in Hannah (1870); printed from this MS in Latham, p. 44. See FACSIMILE XXVIII.

Owned by the Marquess of Salisbury, Hatfield House, Cecil Papers 144/247r-v.

--- *Epitaph on the Earl of Salisbury* ('Here lies Hobinall, our Pastor while ere').

See RaW 360-80.

An Epitaph upon the right Honorable sir Philip Sidney knight

RaW 10 *An Epitaph upon the right Honorable sir Philip Sidney knight: Lord governor of Flushing* ('To praise thy life, or waile thy woorthie death').

Copy, headed 'Sr Wallter Rawleys epitaphe on Sr Phillip Sydney', the heading and lines 1-2 in the hand of Sir John Harington, in a verse miscellany compiled by John Harington of Stepney (1520?-82) and his son Sir John Harington of Kelston (1560-1612); late 16th century.

First pub. in *The Phoenix Nest* (London, 1593); Latham, pp. 5-7. Printed from this MS in Hughey, *Arundel Harington MS*, I, No. 225, pp. 255-7; recorded in Latham, pp. 97-8.

Owned by the Duke of Norfolk, Arundel Castle, MSS (Special Press), 'Harrington MS. Temp. Eliz.', f. 156r-v.

RaW 11 *'Euen such is tyme which takes in trust'.*

Copy, with a sidenote 'At Sr Walter Rawleigh deathe', among the papers of the Trevor Wingfield family and possibly deriving from the papers of the Boteler family of Biddenham; early-mid-17th century.

First pub. in Richard Brathwayte, *Remains after Death* (London, 1618); Latham, p. 72. This poem is ascribed to Ralegh in most MS copies and is often appended to copies of his speech on the scaffold (see RaW 739-822).

Bedfordshire Record Office, TW 1145.

RaW 12 -----

Copy, headed 'These verses following were made by S^r. Walter Rauleigh the night before he dyed and left att the Gate howse', among some documents relating to Ralegh in a French composite volume of state papers; early-mid-17th century.

Printed from this MS in Latham.

Bibliothèque Nationale, Paris, Cinq cents de Colbert n° 467, f. 68v.

RaW 13 -----

Copy in the hand of Sir Richard Napier, in his notebook recording his medical practice from 19 August 1618 to 17 May 1619.

Bodleian, MS Ashmole 230, f. 343v.

RaW 14 -----

Copy in a miscellany compiled by one John Stansby; c. 1669.

Bodleian, MS Ashmole 1463, p. 13.

RaW 15 -----

Copy in a scribal hand in a MS book of memorials of English affairs to 1625 compiled by William Fulman (1632-88); mid-17th century.

Bodleian, MS CCC. 297, f. 172v.

RaW 16 -----

Copy in a miscellany of English and Welsh poems compiled by Richard Roberts, Justice of the Peace; c. 1620s.

Bodleian, MS Don. c. 54, f. 3v.

RaW 17 -----

Second copy in Richard Roberts's miscellany; c. 1620s.

Bodleian, MS Don. c. 54, f. 11.

RaW 18 -----

Copy, headed 'verses written by S^r walter Raleigh but twoe howers before his death', in a volume of historical papers once owned by Sir Henry Spelman (1564?-1641); [1626-9].

Formerly Gurney MS XXXV at Keswick Hall, Norfolk, this MS recorded in *HMC*, 12th Report, Appendix IX (1891), p. 145; recorded in Latham, pp. 153-4, 156.

Bodleian, MS Eng. hist. c. 272, p. 50.

RaW 19 -----

Copy, headed 'Rawleighs Meditation', in a verse miscellany once owned by one Peter Daniell; c. 1630s-40s.

Bodleian, MS Eng. poet. c. 50, f. 31v.

RaW 20 -----

Copy in a composite volume of family papers collected by Hannibal Baskervile of Sunningwell, Berkshire; early-mid-17th century.

Bodleian, MS Rawl. D. 859, f. 85v.

RaW 21 -----

Copy, here ascribed to 'John Cooke', in a composite volume of verse and prose owned c. 1669 by one John Cooke of Bury St Edmunds, Suffolk; 17th century.

Bodleian, MS Rawl. poet. 26, f. v.

'Euen such is tyme which takes in trust'

RaW 22 -----

Second copy, headed 'Sr Walter Raleigh's Epitaph on his owne death - Novemb: 1618', in John Cooke's MS volume; c. 1620s-30s.

This MS recorded in Latham, p. 153.

Bodleian, MS Rawl. poet. 26, f. 2.

RaW 23 -----

Third copy, headed 'His owne Epitaph', in John Cooke's MS volume; c. 1620s-30s.

This MS recorded in Latham, p. 153.

Bodleian, MS Rawl. poet. 26, f. 69v.

RaW 24 -----

Copy in a verse miscellany compiled by one John Hooper of Devon; c. 1660s.

Bodleian, MS Rawl. poet. 208, f. 3.

RaW 25 -----

Copy in a volume of state papers; early-mid-17th century.

This MS recorded in Latham, p. 153.

Bodleian, MS Tanner 74, f. 144v.

RaW 26 -----

Copy, headed 'Verses found in S^{r}: Walter Raleighs Bible in the Gate howse', in a volume of state papers; mid-17th century.

This MS recorded in Latham, p. 153.

Bodleian, MS Tanner 82, f. 244.

RaW 27 -----

Copy, headed 'Sr Walter Rauleighs Epitaph made by himselfe, & giuen to one of his the night before his sufferinge', in a volume of letters and tracts compiled by Archbishop William Sancroft (1617-93); mid-late 17th century.

Bodleian, MS Tanner 299, f. 28v.

RaW 28 -----

Copy in the hand of John Aubrey (1626-97), headed 'These lines Sir Walter Ralegh wrote in his Bible, the night before he was beheaded', in Aubrey's volume of letters written to Anthony Wood; [1657-95].

This MS recorded in Latham, p. 153.

Bodleian, MS Wood. F. 39, f. 223v.

RaW 29 -----

Copy, headed 'His Epitaph, made by himselfe' and here beginning 'O cruell time, which takes in trust', in a volume of transcripts of historical documents made by the Yorkshire antiquary John Hopkinson (1610-80) chiefly from papers belonging to John Savile, Baron of Pontefract, and Edward Taylor, of Furnivall's Inn, Holborn; 1674.

Bradford Central Library, Hopkinson MSS, Vol. 27, f. 129.

RaW 30 -----

Copy, headed 'Epitaph vpon Sr Walter Rawleigh made by himselfe' and here beginning 'O cruell tyme, wch takes in trust', in a verse miscellany compiled by John Hopkinson; mid-17th century.

Bradford Central Library, Hopkinson MSS, Vol. 34, p. 35.

RaW 31 -----

Copy, headed 'Verses found in Sr Walter Raleighs Bible in ye Ga[te]house', in a volume of state letters once owned by John Hopkinson; mid-17th century.

Bradford Central Library, Hopkinson MSS, Vol. 44, p. 401.

RaW 32 -----

Copy, headed 'Nox ante obitum. S^{r}. W.R. 29 october. 1618', in a miscellany once owned by Margaret Bellasys, probably the daughter of Thomas, first Lord Fauconberg (1577-1653); c. 1630.

This MS recorded in Latham, p. 153.

British Library, Add. MS 10309, f. 141.

RaW 33 -----

Copy, headed 'S^{r}. Walter Raliegh the night before his death', transcribed from *Reliquiae Wottonianae* (London, 1651), in a verse miscellany probably compiled by Marmaduke Rawdon (c.1610-68) of Hoddesdon, Hertfordshire; c. 1662.

This MS recorded in Latham, p. 153. See also RaW 101.

British Library, Add. MS 18044, f. 153v.

RaW 34 -----

Copy, headed 'Another', in a verse miscellany compiled by Daniel Leare (a distant cousin of William Strode) probably while at Christ Church, Oxford; c. 1631-3.

'Euen such is tyme which takes in trust'

This MS recorded in Latham, p. 153.

British Library, Add. MS 30982, f. 21v.

RaW 35 -----

Second copy, headed 'on S^{r}: Water Rawly', in Daniel Leare's miscellany; c. 1631-3.

This MS recorded in Latham, p. 153.

British Library, Add. MS 30982, f. 148v rev.

RaW 36 -----

Copy, headed 'By Sir Walter Rawleigh a little before he was ledd from the Gatehouse', in a volume of state papers constituting Volume LXVIII of the Vernon Papers principally collected by James Vernon (1646-1727) and his son Edward; mid-17th century.

British Library, Add. MS 40838, f. 30v.

RaW 37 -----

Copy, headed 'Verses found in Sr Walter Raleighs Bible in the Gatehowse', in a volume of state papers; mid-17th century.

British Library, Add. MS 44848, f. 167v.

RaW 38 -----

Copy, headed 's Walter Rawley his Epitaph', in a miscellany compiled by one Richard Waferer; c. 1620.

British Library, Add. MS 52585, f. 56v.

RaW 39 -----

Copy, headed 'This Epetath followinge was writtene by S^{r} walter Ralegh the Night before he died', in a volume of state papers and tracts; early-mid-17th century.

British Library, Harley MS 39, f. 368v.

RaW 40 -----

Copy in a volume of state papers compiled for Sir Walter Covert, High Sheriff and Deputy Lieutenant in Sussex; early-mid-17th century.

British Library, Harley MS 703, f. 162v.

RaW 41 -----

Copy in a volume of state papers; early-mid-17th century.

This MS recorded in Latham, p. 153.

British Library, Harley MS 1576, f. 2.

RaW 42 -----

Copy, headed 'Verses found in Sr Walter Rayleighs Bible in the Gatehouse', in a volume of state letters; early-mid-17th century.

British Library, Harley MS 4761, f. 22.

RaW 43 -----

Copy, headed 'By S^{r} W: Rawleigh the morn a little before he was ledd from ye Gatehouse', in a composite volume of letters and papers collected by the Duke of Ormonde; early-mid-17th century.

British Library, Harley MS 7056, f. 50v.

RaW 44 -----

Copy, headed 'S^{r} W: Raleigh de seipso', among poems appended to a MS volume of poems by William Browne of Tavistock, possibly compiled by a member of an Inn of Court; c. 1637-50.

This MS recorded in Latham, p. 153.

British Library, Lansdowne MS 777, f. 64.

RaW 45 -----

Copy on a leaf pasted in at the end of a volume of alchemical treatises; 17th century.

This MS recorded in Latham, p. 153.

British Library, Sloane MS 1842, f. 117.

RaW 46 -----

Copy, headed 'The verses following were made by Sir Walter Rawleigh the night before his death at the gate house', in a volume of state papers; early-mid-17th century.

British Library, Stowe MS 141, f. 74v.

RaW 47 -----

Copy, headed 'Verses made by Sr Walt^{r} Rawly at his beheading', in a miscellany; c. 1620s-43.

Cambridge University Library, MS Add. 7196, f. [20 rev.].

RaW 48 -----

Copy in a volume of state tracts and letters; early-mid-17th century.

Cambridge University Library, MS Mm. 6. 33, f. 185v.

'Euen such is tyme which takes in trust'

RaW 49 -----

Copy in a miscellany probably compiled by someone connected with an Inn of Court; c. 1620s.

Cat. No. 8012; printed from this MS in Grosart, *The Dr Farmer MS* (1873), II, 191; recorded in Latham, p. 153.

Chetham's Library, Manchester, Mun. A 4. 15, p. 162.

RaW 50 -----

Copy, headed 'Sir W. Rawleighs Epitaph made by himselfe', in a volume of works by or relating to Ralegh owned in 1674 by one Andrew Card; c. 1674.

University of Chicago, MS 824, f. 27v.

RaW 51 -----

Copy, subscribed 'made by himselfe, the night before his execution', among the papers of the Gell family, formerly of Hopton Hall, Derbyshire; early-mid-17th century.

Derbyshire Record Office, D 258/67/6b, f. [3v].

RaW 52 -----

Copy, headed 'Sir Walter Rawleys Epitaph written by himselfe the night before his execution', among the papers of the Gell family; early-mid-17th century.

Derbyshire Record Office, D 258/67/33a.

RaW 53 -----

Second copy (not in the same hand as RaW 52), among the papers of the Gell family; 17th century.

Derbyshire Record Office, D 258/67/33a.

RaW 54 -----

Copy in a miscellany of verse and prose; c. 1630.

Edinburgh University Library, MS La. III. 493, f. 32.

RaW 55 -----

Copy, headed 'his Epith.', in a volume of scullery and kitchen accounts (probably connected with the Royal establishment) kept by one David Young, servant of the Scullery; c. 1628-38.

Edinburgh University Library, MS La. III. 501, f. 67.

RaW 56 -----

Copy, headed 'The night before hee died', in a miscellany belonging to the Smyth family of Hill Hall, Essex; early-mid-17th century.

Essex Record Office, D/DSh Z1, f. 38v.

RaW 57 -----

Copy, headed 'This Epitath ffollowinge was wrytten, by S^{r}: Walter; Ralegh the night before he dyed', in a volume of state letters and tracts; early-mid-17th century.

Folger, MS G. b. 9, f. 170r-v.

RaW 58 -----

Copy, headed 'Verses found in Sir Walter Rawleighs Bible in the gate howse', in a miscellany of verse and dramatic works compiled in Cambridge; early-mid-17th century.

Folger, MS J. a. 2, f. 87.

RaW 59 -----

Copy, headed 'Verses found in Sir Walter Raleighs Bible in the Gatehowse', in a volume of state letters; mid-17th century.

Folger, MS V. a. 239, p. 704.

RaW 60 -----

Copy in a verse miscellany probably compiled by a member of an Inn of Court; mid-17th century.

Formerly MS 2073.4, this MS recorded in Latham, p. 154.

Folger, MS V. a. 262, p. 54.

RaW 61 -----

Second copy in a verse miscellany probably compiled by a member of an Inn of Court; mid-17th century.

This MS recorded in Latham, p. 154.

Folger, MS V. a. 262, p. 136.

RaW 62 -----

Copy in a miscellany later owned by one Joseph Hall; c. 1630s-50.

Formerly MS 2071.7, this MS recorded in Latham, p. 154.

Folger, MS V. a. 339, f. 204v.

'Euen such is tyme which takes in trust'

RaW 63 -----

Copy, headed 'Sr Walter Rawlighes verses the nighte before he was beheaded in London 1619', in a miscellany; c. 1630.

Formerly MS 452.5, this MS recorded in Latham, p. 154.

Folger, MS V. a. 345, p. 31.

RaW 64 -----

Copy, headed 'Verses made by himselfe', in a volume of documents by or relating to Ralegh; early-mid-17th century.

Folger, MS V. a. 418, f. 4v.

RaW 65 -----

Copy, headed 'Verses found in Sir Walter Raleighs Bible in the Gate house', in a volume of state letters; c. 1675.

Formerly MS F. 2. 20. 46, this MS recorded in Latham, p. 154.

Folger, MS V. b. 234, pp. 675-6.

RaW 66 -----

Copy, headed 'The wourdes vnderwritten he wrote the nighte before he suffred', in a volume of state papers possibly compiled in part by or for one Thomas Gee; early-mid-17th century.

This MS formerly Phillipps MS 7511: see RaW 782.

Folger, MS V. b. 303, p. 229.

RaW 67 -----

Copy in a volume of state tracts; early-mid-17th century.

Gonville and Caius College, Cambridge, MS 73/40, f. 215v.

RaW 68 -----

Copy, headed 'Sr Walter Rawleigh hys verses written in his byble a lyttell before his deathe' and here beginning 'Yeouen suche ys tyme wch takes in haste', in a miscellany of verse and prose; c. 1620.

Formerly owned by Percy Dobell, this MS recorded in Latham (1929), p. 166, and in Latham (1951), p. 154.

Harvard, MS Eng 628, p. 385.

RaW 69 -----

Copy on a single small leaf; 17th century.

Historical Society of Pennsylvania, Ag. E.83/044.

RaW 70 -----

Copy, headed 'Verses found in S^{r}. Walter Raleigh's Bible in the Gatehouse', in a volume of state letters once owned by the antiquary Michael Lort (1725-90); early-mid-17th century.

This MS sold at Sotheby's, 24 October 1972, Lot 383.

Huntington, HM 36836, p. 127.

RaW 71 -----

Copy, written on the back of a letter of 27 October 1618 from Richard Blackall to Sir Lionel Cranfield; c. 1618.

Among the MSS of the Earl de la Warr of Knole Park, Kent, this MS recorded (as A 10) in *HMC*, 4th Report (1874), Appendix, p. 314.

Kent Archives Office, EN. M1012.

RaW 72 -----

Copy, headed 'part of an Epytaph made by S^{r} water Raugley beefore he sufferd', in a miscellany compiled by Sir Roger Twysden (1597-1672); c. 1618-26.

Kent Archives Office, U48 Z1, p. [2].

RaW 73 -----

Copy in a small volume of documents by or relating to Ralegh; 17th century.

Owned by Agnes Latham, Pickering, MS, f. 22.

RaW 74 -----

Copy, indexed (f. 13v) as 'Verses made by Sir Walter Rawleigh', in a miscellany compiled by one Jo. Tempest; mid-17th century.

University of Leeds, Brotherton Collection, MS Lt. q. 9, f. 17.

RaW 75 -----

Copy transcribed by the botanist John Goodyer on the back of a draft letter dated from his lodgings at the Red Lyon in Fleet Street, London, 7 November 1618, in a volume of Goodyer's papers.

Printed from this MS in R.T. Gunther, *Early British Botanists and their Gardens* (Oxford, 1922), p. 32; recorded in Latham, p. 156.

Magdalen College, Oxford, MS 324, f. 2.

'Euen such is tyme which takes in trust'

RaW 76 -----

Copy, headed 'Epitaphe S^r W R. by himselfe', in a miscellany compiled by William Drummond of Hawthornden; c. 1620s.

Printed from this MS in David Laing, 'Extracts from the Hawthornden Manuscripts', *Transactions of the Society of Antiquaries of Scotland*, 4 (1833), 225-40 (p. 238); recorded in Latham, p. 153.

National Library of Scotland, MS 2060 (Hawthornden Vol. VIII), f. 2.

RaW 77 -----

Copy in a composite volume of verse and dramatic works compiled by members of the Salusbury family of Llewenni, Denbighshire; early-mid-17th century.

National Library of Wales, NLW. MS 5390D, p. 334 rev.

RaW 78 -----

Second copy (not in the same hand as RaW 77), subscribed 'Sr wa: Rawghleygh knt wrytten ye daye hee died', in a composite miscellany of the Salusbury family; early-mid-17th century.

National Library of Wales, NLW. MS 5390D, p. 334 rev.

RaW 79 -----

Copy, on a slip pasted on the second leaf of a copy of Ralegh's speech on the scaffold (see RaW 791); early-mid-17th century.

This MS sold at Sotheby's, 5 July 1955 (André de Coppet sale), Lot 984.

New York Public Library, Arents Collection, Acc. 7482.

RaW 80 -----

Copy, among the papers of the Isham family of Lamport Hall, Northamptonshire; early-mid-17th century.

Northamptonshire Record Office, I.C. 3495.

RaW 81 -----

Copy, among the papers of the Isham family of Lamport Hall, Northamptonshire; early-mid-17th century.

Northamptonshire Record Office, I.C. 4774.

RaW 82 -----

Copy on a single leaf among the collections of the Duke of Portland, of Welbeck Abbey, Nottinghamshire; early-mid-17th century.

University of Nottingham, Portland MS Pw V 359.

RaW 83 -----

Copy, headed 'Verses found in Sr Walter Raleighs Bible att the Gatehowse' and concluding with two lines in Latin, in a volume of state letters; mid-17th century.

Owned by Lord Egremont, Petworth House, HMC MS 61, p. 391.

RaW 84 ----

Copy in the hand of one Humphrey Holden, headed 'S^r. Walter Rawleigh wrote these verses ye night before his Execution. Oct 28 1618', written on the first unsigned leaf in a printed exemplum of Ralegh's *The History of the World* (London, 1614); 17th century.

Printed from this MS in *The Carl H. Pforzheimer Library: English Literature 1475-1700* (New York, 1940), III, 846. Facsimile in Henry Stevens, Son, & Stiles, catalogue No. 177 (1927), plate XII.

Pforzheimer Library.

RaW 85 -----

Copy, headed 'These ensueing verses are sayd to bee written, by S^r. Walter Raleigh, in the prison of the Gatehouse, the same morneing hee suffered', in a volume of accounts of Ralegh's arraignment and execution; early-mid-17th century.

Formerly in the Alfred Morrison collection, this MS recorded in *HMC*, 9th Report, Appendix, Part II (1884), p. 408; partly collated in *The Carl H. Pforzheimer Library: English Literature 1475-1700* (New York, 1940), III, 858.

Pforzheimer Library, MS 112, f. 54.

RaW 86 -----

Copy, headed 'Upon Sr Walter Rawleigh made by himself before he was beheaded', written in a verse miscellany used by members of the Holgate family of Saffron Walden, Essex; c. 1687.

Pierpont Morgan Library, MA 1057, p. 217.

'Euen such is tyme which takes in trust'

RaW 87 -----

Copy, headed 'Verses found in S[r]. Walter Raleighs Bible in y[e] Gatehouse', in a volume of letters and state papers; mid-17th century.

Pierpont Morgan Library, MA 1162, p. 458.

RaW 88 -----

Copy, endorsed 'des carmes faits par S[r] walt: Rawleigh le iour deuant qu'il fut execute A[o]. dni. 1618. Nouemb.', together with copies of two letters of Ralegh, in a collection of state papers; early-mid-17th century.

This MS recorded in Latham, p. 154.

Public Record Office, SP.14/96/71.

RaW 89 -----

Copy, headed 'Made by s[r] W: Raleigh the morning before his death and deliuerd to the deane of Westminster a littell before his ende'; early-mid-17th century.

This MS recorded in Latham, p. 154.

Public Record Office, SP.14/103/51v.

RaW 90 [entry deleted].

RaW 91 -----

Copy in a composite volume of state papers; mid-17th century.

The Queen's College, Oxford, MS 121, p. 518.

RaW 92 -----

Copy, headed 'S[r] Walter Raleigh the night before his death', in a verse miscellany entitled *Recueil Choisi De Pieces fugitives En Vers Anglois*; c. 1713.

Formerly Phillipps MS 9500, this MS recorded in Latham, p. 154.

Rosenbach Foundation, MS 239/16, p. 6.

RaW 93 -----

Copy, headed 'S[r] Walter Rawleighs Epitaph: by himselfe made', in a verse miscellany compiled by one Robert Bishop; c. 1630.

Formerly Rosenbach 187, this MS recorded in Latham, p. 154.

Rosenbach Foundation, MS 1083/16, p. 109.

RaW 94 -----

Copy, headed 'The morneing before his execucon', in a verse miscellany owned and possibly compiled by John Pike of Cambridge; c. 1636-40s.

St John's College, Cambridge, MS S. 32 (James 423), f. 34v.

RaW 95 -----

Copy, headed 'His last verses', in a volume of state papers; early-mid-17th century.

Trinity College, Cambridge, MS O. 5. 21 (James 1302), (20), f. [5].

RaW 96 -----

Copy in a volume of works chiefly by Ralegh; early-mid-17th century.

Dr Williams's Library, MS Jones B. 60, p. 267.

RaW 97 -----

Second copy in a volume of works chiefly by Ralegh; early-mid-17th century.

Dr Williams's Library, MS Jones B. 60, p. 282.

RaW 98 -----

Copy, headed '1618 - S[r] Walter Rawley, nox ante obitum', in a letterbook of Sir Francis Castillion (1561-1638); 1620s-30s.

Yale, Osborn Collection, fb 69, p. 208.

RaW 99 -----

Copy, headed 'S[r] W. Rawleigh's Epitaph on Himself', in a volume of epitaphs; c. 1694.

Yale, Osborn Collection, fb 143, p. 14.

RaW 100 -----

Copy, headed 'S[r]. Walter Rawleighs Epitaph in his Bible...', on one of five leaves detached from a composite volume of state papers once belonging to Sir Henry Spelman (1564?-1641); early-mid-17th century.

Formerly part of Gurney MS XXXIII at Keswick Hall, Norfolk, this MS recorded in *HMC*, 12th Report, Appendix IX (1891), p. 161. See also RaW 811.

Yale, Osborn Collection, PB VI/107, f. 414.

'Euen such is tyme which takes in trust'

RaW 101 -----

Copy, headed 'S[r] walter Rawleighs Epitaph made by himselfe', in a miscellany compiled by members of the family of Sir Marmaduke Rawdon (1582-1646) of Hoddesdon, Hertfordshire; mid-17th century.

See also RaW 33.

York Minster, MS Add. 122, f. 34.

RaW 102 -----

Copy, headed 'S[r] Walter Rawleigh His Verses, wrytten in a voide place of his Bible the night before his death, in the Gatehouse', apparently appended to a printed exemplum of *Newes from London* (November 1618) among the papers of the Trevelyan family of Trevelyan, near Lostwithiel, Cornwall; c. 1618.

This item printed in *Trevelyan Papers*, ed. John Payne Collier, III, Camden Society 105 (London, 1872), 154-5.

The Trevelyan Papers are now in the Somerset Record Office, but this item cannot at present be located.

RaW 103 -----

Copy, here beginning 'Even so dooth tyme take up withe truste', in a miscellany compiled by Adam Winthrop (1548-1623); [1618-23].

Printed from this MS in *Proceedings of the Massachusetts Historical Society*, 1st Ser. 13 (1873), 98; this publication recorded in Latham, p. 154.

Formerly (but no longer) owned by the Massachusetts Historical Society; unlocated.

RaW 104 [entry deleted].

RaW 105 [entry deleted].

--- -----

See also RaW 302, 304 and INTRODUCTION.

RaW 106 *The Excuse* ('Calling to minde mine eie long went about').

Copy, ascribed to 'S[r] Wa: Raleigh', in a miscellany; c. 1621-31.

First pub. in *The Phoenix Nest* (London, 1593); Latham, p. 10. This MS collated in *The Phoenix Nest*, ed. H.E. Rollins (Cambridge, Mass., 1931), pp. 178-9; recorded in Latham, p. 101.

Bodleian, MS Ashmole 781, p. 138.

RaW 107 -----

Copy in a verse miscellany; early 17th century.

This MS recorded in Latham, p. 102.

Bodleian, MS Rawl. poet. 31, f. 2.

RaW 108 -----

Copy, headed 'A Fancy', in a verse miscellany belonging to the Paulet family and owned in 1659 by one Egigius Frampton; mid-17th century.

This MS recorded in Latham, p. 102.

Bodleian, MS Rawl. poet. 84, f. 58.

RaW 109 -----

Copy in a miscellany compiled by a Cambridge student, possibly Sir John Finett (1571-1641) of Fordwich, Kent; c. 1586-91.

This MS collated in Rollins, pp. 178-9; recorded in Latham, p. 102.

Bodleian, MS Rawl. poet. 85, f. 104v.

RaW 110 -----

Copy, headed 'A ffancy', in a verse miscellany; c. 1640.

This MS collated in Rollins, pp. 178-9; recorded in Latham, p. 102.

Bodleian, MS Rawl. poet. 153, f. 20.

RaW 111 -----

Copy, headed 'To his Loue' and ascribed to 'S[r] walt: Raleigh', ir a verse miscellany probably compiled by a Cambridge man; c. 1630s.

This MS collated in Rollins, pp. 178-9; recorded in Latham, p. 101.

British Library, Add. MS 15227, f. 88v.

RaW 112 -----

Copy, untitled, in a verse miscellany; c. 1620-33.

This MS collated in Rollins, pp. 178-9; recorded in Latham, p. 102.

British Library, Harley MS 4064, f. 232v.

The Excuse

RaW 113 -----

Copy, untitled, in a verse miscellany; c. 1596-1601.

This MS collated in Rollins, pp. 178-9; recorded in Latham, p. 102.

British Library, Harley MS 6910, f. 142v.

RaW 114 -----

Copy, untitled and ascribed to 'RA[legh]', in a verse miscellany compiled by the antiquary St Loe Kniveton of Gray's Inn; c. 1585-90s.

This MS recorded in Latham, p. 102.

British Library, Harley MS 7392, ff. 36v-7.

RaW 115 -----

Copy, untitled, in a verse miscellany; c. 1637.

British Library, Stowe MS 962, f. 85v.

RaW 116 -----

Copy, ascribed to 'W.R.', in a verse miscellany compiled by Henry Stanford, household tutor in the Carey family; c. 1585-98.

This MS recorded in Latham, p. 102.

Cambridge University Library, MS Dd. 5. 75, f. 27.

RaW 117 -----

Copy, untitled and ascribed to 'S^{r} Wa: Raleighe', in a group of poems in the middle of a volume of state letters and speeches; among the papers of the Fuller family of Brightling Park and possibly once owned by Ambrose Trayton of Lewes, Esquire of the Body to James I and Charles I; c. 1614-20s.

East Sussex Record Office, RAF/F/13/1, [no page number].

RaW 118 -----

Copy in a verse miscellany owned before 1610 by Anne Cornwallis, afterwards Countess of Argyll; c. 1590s.

Formerly MS 1.112, this MS recorded in Latham, p. 102.

Folger, MS V. a. 89, p. 19.

RaW 119 -----

Copy, headed 'Sr W. R: A Lover to his Mistresse', in a verse miscellany; c. 1630.

Formerly MS 1.28, this MS recorded in Latham, p. 102.

Folger, MS V. a. 103, Part I, f. 29r-v.

RaW 120 -----

Copy, headed 'A Fancy', in a verse miscellany compiled by an Oxford man and once owned by one Stephen Welden; mid-17th century.

Formerly MS 452.4, this MS recorded in Latham, p. 102.

Folger, MS V. a. 162, f. 89v.

RaW 121 -----

Copy, headed 'A fancy' and here beginning 'Callinge to minde eyes went longe aboute', in a verse miscellany owned and probably compiled by Hugh Barrow (b. 1617/18) of Brasenose College, Oxford; c. 1638.

Formerly Rosenbach 192, this MS recorded in Latham, p. 102.

New York Public Library, Arents Collection, Cat. No. S288, pp. 106-7.

RaW 122 -----

Copy, headed 'A Lover on his Mistresse', in a verse miscellany; c. 1630.

University of Nottingham, Portland MS Pw V 37, p. 59.

RaW 123 -----

Copy, headed 'A Fancie' and here beginning 'Calling to minde mine eyes about', in a miscellany; mid-17th century.

Yale, Osborn Collection, b 205, f. 27v.

RaW 124 *A Farewell to false Love* ('Farewell false loue, the oracle of lies').

Copy, headed 'A quip for Cupide', the heading and lines 1-7 in the hand of Sir John Harington, in a verse miscellany compiled by John Harington of Stepney (1520?-82) and his son Sir John Harington of Kelston (1560-1612); late 16th century.

First pub. (in a musical setting) in William Byrd, *Psalmes, Sonets & songs* (London, 1588); Latham, pp. 7-8. Printed from this MS in Hughey, *Arundel Harington MS*, I, No. 235, pp. 274-5.

Owned by the Duke of Norfolk, Arundel Castle, MSS (Special Press), 'Harrington MS. Temp. Eliz.', f. 162v.

RaW 124.5 See Addenda, p. 632.

RaW 125 -----

Copy in a miscellany compiled by a Cambridge

student, possibly Sir John Finett (1571-1641) of Fordwich, Kent; c. 1586-91.

Printed from this MS in *The Complete Works of John Lyly*, ed. R. Warwick Bond (Oxford, 1902), III, 471-2; collated in Hughey, II, 384-5; recorded and the last stanza printed in Latham.

Bodleian, MS Rawl. poet. 85, f. 48r-v.

RaW 126 -----

Copy of the incipit (here 'Fairweill fals loue') in a musical setting in a Scottish MS songbook compiled by David Melvill; early 17th century.

British Library, Add. MS 36484, f. 53.

RaW 127 -----

Copy, untitled and ascribed to 'RA[legh]', in a verse miscellany compiled by the antiquary St Loe Kniveton of Gray's Inn; c. 1585-90s.

This MS collated in Hughey, II, 384; recorded in Latham, p. 100.

British Library, Harley MS 7392, f. 37r-v.

RaW 128 -----

Copy of the final couplet, beginning 'False Loue; Desyre; and Bewty frayll adewe', in St Loe Kniveton's miscellany; c. 1585-90s.

This MS recorded in Latham, p. 100.

British Library, Harley MS 7392, f. 28.

RaW 129 -----

Copy of six lines only in a verse miscellany owned before 1610 by Anne Cornwallis, afterwards Countess of Argyll; c. 1590s.

Formerly MS 1.112, this MS collated in Hughey, II, 384; recorded in Latham, p. 100.

Folger, MS V. a. 89, p. 10.

RaW 130 -----

Copy of a three-stanza version, ascribed to 'Mr Rawleigh', in a miscellany of verse and dramatic works; c. 1577-84.

The text accompanied by a companion poem by Sir Thomas Heneage (d. 1595) beginning 'Most welcome love thou mortall foe to lies'. Printed from this MS in Bertram Dobell, 'Poems by Sir Thomas Heneage and Sir Walter Raleigh', *The Athenaeum* (14 September 1901), p. 349; collated from this publication in Hughey, II, 384, and recorded in Latham, p. 100. A microfilm of the MS is in the British Library (RP 349).

Harvard, fMS Eng 1285, f. 72v.

RaW 131 -----

Copy of a four-stanza version in a small verse miscellany owned in 1781 by Rev. John Williams of Llanrwst; early 17th century.

National Library of Wales, NLW. MS 473B, ff. 9v-10.

RaW 132 -----

Copy of a four-stanza version in a collection of state papers; late 16th century.

This MS recorded in Pierre Lefranc, 'A Miscellany of Ralegh Material', *N & Q*, 202 (January 1957), 24-6.

Public Record Office, SP.46/126, f. 123v.

RaW 133 *'Fortune hath taken thee away my love'.*

Copy, here beginning 'Fortune hathe taken away my love', on f. 116 in a miscellany compiled by someone in the service of Henry Stanley, fourth Earl of Derby (1531-93), possibly Martin Heton, later Bishop of Ely (1552-1609), with later annotations in the hand of William Oldys (1696-1761); c. 1585-7.

Six lines cited in George Puttenham, *The Arte of English Poesie* (London, 1589), reprinted in Latham, p. 9. First pub. as a broadside, London, 1592 (?): see *TLS* (12 September 1968), p. 1032. This poem is related to the song '*Fortune my foe*': see *TLS* (30 May 1968), p. 553. Walter Oakeshott, *The Queen and the Poet* (London, 1960), prints the lines beginning 'In vain mine Eyes, in vain ye waste your tears' (p. 154) as if a separate poem but reproduces a facsimile of this MS (formerly Phillipps MS 3602) facing p. 157. Facsimile of first two stanzas also in Sotheby's sale catalogue, 27 June 1977, p. 63.

Sotheby's, 30 November 1971, Lot 527, and 27 June 1977, Lot 4941; owned (1978) by A.G. Thomas, London.

RaW 134 -----

Copy in a miscellany of verse and prose once owned by one Robert Thornton; c. 1580s-90s.

Printed from this MS in L.G. Black, 'A Lost Poem by Queen Elizabeth I', *TLS* (23 May 1968), p. 535.

Marsh's Library, Dublin, MS Z 3. 5. 21, f. 30v.

RaW 135 -----

Copy (in six four-line stanzas), headed 'A sonnett', in a miscellany of poems and state papers; among the papers of the Troyte-Bullock family, formerly of Zeals House, Mere, and probably deriving from the papers of the Chafyn family of Bulford and Chisenbury or the Reymes family of Waddon, near Dorchester; c. 1620s.

'Fortune has taken thee away my love'

The text accompanied by 'An aunswer' (in six four-line stanzas), beginning 'Ah silly pugg wert thou so sort afrayd'; this answer printed in Black, *loc. cit.*, from a 21-line text in the Inner Temple Library (Petyt MS 538, Vol. 10, f. 3) and attributed to Queen Elizabeth.

Wiltshire Record Office, 865/500, f. [27].

RaW 136 *'Hir face, Hir tong, Hir wit'.*

Copy of the first stanza, headed 'To his M[ris]', in a verse miscellany compiled by an Oxford man, possibly a member of Wadham College, and later used by William Fulman (1632-88); c. late 1630s.

First pub. in *Brittons Bowre of Delights* (London, 1591); Latham, p. 80. This poem perhaps written jointly by Ralegh and Sir Arthur Gorges: see Lefranc (1968), p. 95.

Bodleian, MS CCC. 328, f. 74v.

RaW 137 -----

Copy of a two-stanza version, here beginning 'Your face; your tongue; your witt', in a miscellany compiled partly by the Oxford printer Christopher Wase (1627-90); mid-17th century.

This MS collated in *The Phoenix Nest*, ed. E.H. Rollins (Cambridge, Mass., 1931), pp. 174-5; recorded in Latham, p. 160.

Bodleian, MS Rawl. poet. 117, f. 161 rev.

RaW 138 -----

Second copy of a two-stanza version, also beginning 'Your face; your tongue; your witt', in Christopher Wase's miscellany; mid-17th century.

This MS collated in Rollins, pp. 174-5; recorded in Latham, p. 160.

Bodleian, MS Rawl. poet. 117, f. 168v rev.

RaW 139 -----

Copy of a six-stanza version, headed 'Vnto his Loue', in a verse miscellany probably compiled by a Cambridge man; c. 1630s.

This MS collated in Rollins, pp. 174-5; recorded in Latham, p. 160.

British Library, Add. MS 15227, ff. 84v-5.

RaW 140 -----

Copy of a two-stanza version, headed 'To his Mistresse' and here beginning 'Y[r] Face, y[r] Tongue, y[r] witt', in a verse miscellany; c. 1630s.

This MS collated in Rollins, pp. 174-5; recorded in Latham, p. 160.

British Library, Add. MS 22118, f. 34.

RaW 141 -----

Copy of a six-stanza version made by an amanuensis of Sir Arthur Gorges (1557-1625), in a MS volume of Gorges's own poems; c. 1589-1625.

Printed from this MS in *The Poems of Sir Arthur Gorges*, ed. H.E. Sandison (Oxford, 1953), pp. 77-8; recorded in Latham, p. 160.

British Library, Egerton MS 3165, f. 61.

RaW 142 -----

Copy of a six-stanza version, ascribed to 'Raley', in a verse miscellany compiled by the antiquary St Loe Kniveton of Gray's Inn; c. 1585-90s.

Printed from this MS in Sandison, pp. 210-11; recorded in Latham, p. 160.

British Library, Harley MS 7392, f. 66v.

RaW 143 -----

Copy of a six-stanza version, here beginning 'Your face your tongue your witte', in a verse miscellany compiled by Henry Stanford, household tutor in the Carey family; c. 1585-98.

Printed from this MS in Sandison, p. 211; recorded in Latham, p. 160.

Cambridge University Library, MS Dd. 5. 75, f. 36.

RaW 144 -----

Copy of the first stanza in a miscellany; c. 1630s.

This MS collated in Doughtie, *Lyrics from English Airs*, p. 450.

John Rylands University Library of Manchester, Rylands English MS 410, f. 21.

RaW 145 -----

Copy, headed 'A Propheticall Poesie' and here beginning 'Your face, your toungue, your wit', in a miscellany compiled by one John Moulton; c. 1625.

This MS recorded (but not seen) in Rollins, p. 175; first stanza printed in Sandison, p. 210.

Colbeck, Radford & Co., catalogue No. 9 (1930), item 192; unlocated.

'If Synthia be a Queene, a princes, and supreame'

*RaW 146 *'If Synthia be a Queene, a princes, and supreame'.*

Autograph.

First pub. (from this MS) in Hannah (1870); printed from this MS in Latham, p. 24.

Owned by the Marquess of Salisbury, Hatfield House, Cecil Papers 144/238.

--- *'In vain mine Eyes, in vain ye waste your tears'.*

See RaW 133-5.

RaW 147 *The Lie* ('Goe soule the bodies guest').

Copy, headed in a different ink 'Satyr on all things', in a volume of miscellaneous verse and prose transcribed from the papers of Sir Christopher Yelverton (1535?-1612); early 17th century.

First pub. in Francis Davison, *A Poetical Rapsodie* (London, 1611); Latham, pp. 45-7. This poem is attributed to Richard Latworth (or Latewar) in Lefranc (1968), pp. 85-94, but see Stephen J. Greenblatt, *Sir Walter Ralegh* (New Haven & London, 1973), pp. 171-6; see also Karl Josef Höltgen, 'Richard Latewar Elizabethan Poet and Divine', *Anglia*, 89 (1971), 417-38 (p. 430). Latewar's 'answer' to this poem is printed in Höltgen, pp. 435-8. Some texts are accompanied by other answers. This MS recorded in Latham, p. 131.

All Souls College, Oxford, MS 155, ff. 18v-19v.

RaW 148 -----

Copy, untitled, in a volume of state letters and tracts; early-mid-17th century.

Bibliothèque Nationale, Paris, fonds anglais n° 149, f. 73.

RaW 149 -----

Copy in a miscellany compiled by one Ann Bowyr; early-mid-17th century.

Bodleian, MS Ashmole 51, f. 6.

RaW 150 -----

Copy of lines 1-54, headed 'Sr Walter Rawleighes farewell', in a verse miscellany; c. 1630s.

This MS recorded in Latham, p. 129.

Bodleian, MS Douce f. 5, fols. 11-12.

RaW 151 -----

Copy of lines 1-54 in a miscellany compiled by Edward Pudsey (1573-1613); imperfect, lacking the ending; 1600s.

This MS recorded in Latham, p. 131.

Bodleian, MS Eng. poet. d. 3, f. 2v.

RaW 152 -----

Copy in a verse miscellany; c. 1640.

Bodleian, MS Firth e. 4, pp. 3-5.

RaW 153 -----

Copy, with two additional stanzas, headed 'D^r^. Latworthe lye to all estates', in a composite volume of verse and prose; early 17th century.

This MS recorded in Latham, pp. 129, 134-5, and in Höltgen, p. 435.

Bodleian, MS Rawl. poet. 172, f. 12v.

RaW 154 -----

Copy, headed 'W R farewell made by D: Lat:', in a miscellany compiled by an Oxford man; early 17th century.

The text accompanied by Latewar's answer. Printed from this MS in Höltgen, pp. 435-8; recorded in Latham, pp. 129-30.

Bodleian, MS Rawl. poet. 212, ff. 88-90.

RaW 155 -----

Copy in a composite volume of verse partly collected by Archbishop William Sancroft (1617-93); early-mid-17th century.

This MS recorded in Latham, p. 131.

Bodleian, MS Tanner 306, f. 188.

RaW 156 -----

Copy in a verse miscellany compiled by the Yorkshire antiquary John Hopkinson (1610-80); mid-17th century.

Bradford Central Library, Hopkinson MSS, Vol. 34, pp. 9-11.

RaW 157 -----

Copy, with two additional stanzas, in the hand of Rev. William Cole (1714-82), transcribed from an earlier MS, headed 'A Lye to the World, or The Farewell', an ascription to 'Sir Wa: Ralegh' deleted and replaced by 'By the royall Earle of Essex', in Volume XXXI of Cole's miscellaneous collections; 18th century.

This MS recorded in Latham, pp. 129, 134-5.

British Library, Add. MS 5832, ff. 218-19.

RaW 158 -----

Transcript, made from an unidentified source, sent by Matthew Ogle to Richard Brinsley Sheridan in 1803 as 'a copy of the vigorous verses written by the great Sir Walter Raleigh, after his condemnation', headed 'The Souls Errand', in a composite volume of papers connected with Sheridan; 1803.

This MS recorded in Latham, p. 130.

British Library, Add. MS 29764, f. 9.

RaW 159 -----

Copy, with two additional stanzas, in a volume of miscellaneous papers; late 16th-early 17th century.

This MS recorded in Latham, pp. 131, 134-5.

British Library, Harley MS 2296, f. 135.

RaW 160 -----

Copy, untitled, in a verse miscellany; c. 1596-1601.

This MS recorded in Latham, p. 131.

British Library, Harley MS 6910, ff. 141v-2.

RaW 161 -----

Copy, headed 'Satira Volans' and here ascribed to 'Doctor Latworth', in a verse miscellany compiled by a Cambridge man; c. 1630.

A 19th-century transcript of this MS is in the Bodleian, MS Firth d. 7, f. 146.

Cambridge University Library, MS Add. 4138, f. 46r-v.

RaW 162 -----

Copy, ascribed to 'Wa: Raleigh', with an additional stanza, in a miscellany probably compiled by someone connected with an Inn of Court; c. 1620s.

Cat. No. 8012; printed from this MS in Grosart, *The Dr Farmer MS* (1873), I, 114-17, with a facsimile of two pages; recorded in Latham, pp. 129, 134.

Chetham's Library, Manchester, Mun. A 4. 15, p. 103 seq.

RaW 163 -----

Copy, headed 'Satyra Volans. A flying satyre made by Dr Lateware. S^t^. Johns', in a verse miscellany; c. 1630.

Formerly MS 1.28, this MS recorded in Latham and Höltgen, p. 435.

Folger, MS V. a. 103, Part I, f. 67r-v.

RaW 164 -----

Copy, untitled and ascribed to 'Sir Walter Rawley', in a miscellany; c. 1630.

Formerly MS 452.5, this MS recorded in Latham, p. 129.

Folger, MS V. a. 345, pp. 176-7.

RaW 165 -----

Copy, with corrections in another hand, here ascribed to 'Anne Southwell', in a verse miscellany entitled *The Workes of the Lady Ann Southwell* assembled from the papers of Lady Ann Southwell (1573-1636), daughter of Sir Thomas Harris of Cornworthy, Devon; mid-17th century.

Formerly MS 1669.1, this MS recorded in Latham, p. 130.

Folger, MS V. b. 198, f. 2.

RaW 166 -----

Copy, untitled, on a leaf inserted in a verse miscellany owned by Edward Denny, Charles Cokes, and others; 1595.

Printed from this MS in Josephine Waters Bennett, 'Early Texts of Two of Ralegh's Poems from a Huntington Library Manuscript', *HLQ*, 4 (1940-1), 469-75 (pp. 471-2); recorded in Latham, p. 131.

Huntington, HM 198, Part I, f. 1.

RaW 167 -----

Copy, headed 'Satyra volans', in a composite verse miscellany including a section once owned by one David Williams, used c. 1666-74 by members of the Lloyd family of Llwydiarth; early-mid-17th century.

National Library of Wales, Sotheby MS B2, pp. 131-3.

RaW 168 -----

Copy, headed 'Satyre volans. Or a flying Satyre made by Dr Latewarr of St Johns', in a verse miscellany; c. 1630.

This MS recorded (as MS Taverham) in Latham,

p. 129, and in Höltgen, p. 435.

University of Nottingham, Portland MS Pw V 37, pp. 138-9.

RaW 169 -----

Copy, untitled, in a verse miscellany used by members of the Holgate family of Saffron Walden, Essex; c. 1630s.

Pierpont Morgan Library, MA 1057, p. 42.

RaW 170 -----

Copy, with two additional stanzas, on two leaves; c. 1605.

Once owned by W.A. White, this MS formerly but no longer believed to be autograph; collated and additional stanzas printed in Samuel Tannenbaum, 'Unfamiliar Versions of Some Elizabethan Poems', *PMLA*, 45 (1930), 809-21 (pp. 810-14); recorded in Latham, pp. 130, 134-5.

Princeton, Robert H. Taylor Collection.

RaW 171 -----

Copy, ascribed to 'Sr W.R.', in a verse miscellany, c. 1634.

Formerly Rosenbach 189, this MS recorded in Latham, pp. 130-1.

Rosenbach Foundation, MS 239/27, pp. 175-7.

RaW 172 -----

Copy, headed 'Sir Walter Wrayly his lye', in a verse miscellany probably compiled by a member of an Inn of Court; c. 1598-1600s.

Formerly Rosenbach 186, and once owned by John Payne Collier; printed from this MS in Tannenbaum, pp. 811-13; recorded in Latham, p. 129.

Rosenbach Foundation, MS 1083/15, ff. 16v-17.

RaW 173 -----

Copy of lines 1-6, untitled, in a verse miscellany compiled by John Cruso (1618-81) of Gonville and Caius College, Cambridge; c. 1630s.

St John's College, Cambridge, MS U. 26 (James 548), p. 43.

RaW 174 -----

Copy, untitled, in a MS volume of poems chiefly by Donne, among the family papers of the Earl of Dalhousie; c. 1620-5.

Scottish Record Office, GD45/26/95/1, ff. 57v-8.

RaW 175 -----

Copy, untitled, probably transcribed from RaW 174, in a MS volume of poems chiefly by Donne, among the family papers of the Earl of Dalhousie and once owned by Andrew Ramsey; c. 1622-9.

Scottish Record Office, GD45/26/95/2, f. 30r-v.

RaW 176 -----

Copy, untitled, in a verse miscellany appended to a MS volume of poems by Donne; c. 1630s.

Formerly MS G.2.21, this MS recorded in Latham, p. 131.

Trinity College, Dublin, MS 877, ff. 216-17v.

RaW 177 -----

Copy in a volume of works chiefly by Ralegh; early-mid-17th century.

Dr Williams's Library, MS Jones B. 60, pp. 257-60.

RaW 178 *Like to a Hermite poore* ('Like to a Hermite poore in place obscure').

Copy in a verse miscellany compiled by John Harington of Stepney (1520?-82) and his son Sir John Harington of Kelston (1560-1612); late 16th century.

First pub. in *Brittons Bowre of Delights* (London, 1591); Latham, pp. 11-12. Printed from this MS in Hughey, *Arundel Harington MS*, I, No. 194, pp. 240-1; a 19th-century transcript (British Library, Add. MS 28635, f. 86v) recorded in Latham, p. 104.

Owned by the Duke of Norfolk, Arundel Castle, MSS (Special Press), 'Harrington MS. Temp. Eliz.', f. 145v.

RaW 179 -----

Copy in a miscellany compiled by a Cambridge student, possibly Sir John Finett (1571-1641) of Fordwich, Kent; c. 1586-91.

This MS collated in Hughey, II, 314; recorded in Latham, p. 104.

Bodleian, MS Rawl. poet. 85, f. 25v.

RaW 179.5 See Addenda, p. 632.

RaW 180 -----

Copy, headed 'Incerti Authoris', in a miscellany compiled by Sir Edward Hoby (1560-1617); c. 1580s-90s.

This MS collated in Hughey, II, 313-14; recorded in Latham, p. 104.

British Library, Add. MS 38823, f. 58v.

Like to a Hermite poore

RaW 181 -----

Copy in a verse miscellany; c. 1596-1601.

This MS collated in Hughey, II, 314; recorded in Latham, p. 104.

British Library, Harley MS 6910, f. 139v.

RaW 182 -----

Copy, headed 'S[r] Walter Rayleyes last Eligie', in a verse miscellany owned in 1623 and probably compiled by one Richard Jackson; c. 1620s-30s.

This MS recorded in Latham, p. 104.

Edinburgh University Library, MS H.-P. Coll. 401, f. 102.

RaW 183 -----

Copy, headed 'The despairing Lover', in a verse miscellany; c. 1630s-40s.

Edinburgh University Library, MS La. III. 436, pp. 114-15.

RaW 184 -----

Copy in a miscellany owned by James Bateman (b. 1633/4) of Christ's College, Cambridge, by Robert Pierrepont (either the son of Col. Francis Pierrepont, M.P. (d. 1659), or the third Earl of Kingston (1650/1-82)) of Holme-Pierrepoint, Nottinghamshire, and by the poet John Oldham (1653-83); c. 1650s-60s.

Formerly MS 621.2, this MS collated in Hughey, II, 314; recorded in Latham, p. 104.

Folger, MS V. a. 169, Part II, f. 10v.

RaW 185 -----

Copy in a musical setting in a MS music book owned (in 1659) and partly compiled by the composer John Gamble; c. 1630s-50s.

A musical setting first pub. in Alfonso Ferrabosco, *Ayres* (London, 1609); a setting by Nicholas Lanier first pub. in John Playford, *Select Musicall Ayres* (London, 1652). This MS collated in Hughey, II, 316.

New York Public Library, Music Division, Drexel MS 4257, No. 15.

RaW 186 -----

Copy, headed 'Cant: 3', in a verse miscellany compiled by Herbert Aston, son of Sir Walter Aston (1584-1639) of Tixall, Staffordshire; imperfect; c. 1634.

Yale, Osborn Collection, b 4, f. 2v.

RaW 186.5 See Addenda, p. 632.

RaW 187 -----

Copy in a verse miscellany owned in 1662 by William Turner and afterwards by Catherine Gage, Lady Aston (d. 1720), of Tixall, Staffordshire; 17th century.

Printed from this MS in Arthur Clifford, *Tixall Poetry* (Edinburgh, 1813), pp. 115-16; recorded in Latham, p. 104.

Unlocated.

*RaW 188 *'My boddy in the walls captived'.*

Autograph.

First pub. (from this MS) in Hannah (1870); printed from this MS in Latham, pp. 24-5. Facsimiles in T.N. Brushfield, *A Bibliography of Sir Walter Ralegh Knt*, 2nd edition (Exeter, 1908), facing p. 143; Flower & Munby, *English Poetical Autographs*, plate 2; Croft, *Autograph Poetry*, I, 13.

Owned by the Marquess of Salisbury, Hatfield House, Cecil Papers 144/239v.

--- *'Nature that washt her hands in milke'.*

See RaW 297-304.

RaW 189 *The Nimphs reply to the Sheepheard* ('If all the world and loue were young').

Copy of lines 1-16, 21-4, headed 'The Aunswere' and here beginning 'If that the Worlde and Loue were yong', in a volume of alchemical papers compiled by Simon Forman (1552-1611); c. 1598.

One stanza pub. in *The Passionate Pilgrime* (London, 1599); first pub. complete in *Englands Helicon* (London, 1600); Latham, pp. 16-17. For the companion poem by Marlowe, which accompanies most of the texts of Ralegh's 'reply', see MrC 10-19. This MS recorded in Latham, p. 112; facsimile in John Bakeless, *The Tragicall History of Christopher Marlowe* (Cambridge, Mass., 1942), II, facing p. 184.

Bodleian, MS Ashmole 1486, II, f. 6v.

RaW 190 -----

Copy in a verse miscellany compiled by John Lilliat (c.1550-c.1599); c. 1589-99.

This MS recorded in Latham, p. 112.

Bodleian, MS Rawl. poet. 148, ff. 96v-7.

RaW 191 -----

Copy, untitled, in a miscellany compiled by one Richard Waferer; c. 1620.

British Library, Add. MS 52585, f. 63v.

The Nimphs reply to the Sheepheard

RaW 192 -----

Quotation from the poem scribbled inside the lower cover of a calf binding; mid-17th century.

Folger, MS V. a. 150.

RaW 193 -----

Copy, headed 'The milke maids mothers answer', in a miscellany owned by James Bateman (b. 1633/4) of Christ's College, Cambridge, by Robert Pierrepont (either the son of Col. Francis Pierrepont, M.P. (d. 1659), or the third Earl of Kingston (1650/1-82)) of Holme-Pierrepoint, Nottinghamshire, and by the poet John Oldham (1653-83); c. 1650s-60s.

Formerly MS 621.1, this MS recorded in Latham, p. 112.

Folger, MS V. a. 169, Part II, f. 2v-3.

RaW 194 -----

Copy in a miscellany possibly once owned by John Thornborough, Bishop of Limerick (1551-1641); late 16th-early 17th century.

Formerly MS 297.3 and V.b.75, this MS recorded in Latham, p. 112; facsimile in A.D. Wraight and V.F. Stern, *In Search of Christopher Marlowe* (London, 1965), p. 130.

Folger, MS Z. e. 28, f. 101.

RaW 195 -----

Copy of lines 1-6, headed 'The Answer by S[r] Arthur' and apparently transcribed from an early MS source, written on a blank leaf in a printed exemplum of Ralegh's *The History of the World* (London, 1614); late 18th-early 19th century.

Printed from this MS in Susanne Woods, '"The Passionate Sheepheard" and "The Nimphs Reply": A Study of Transmission', *HLQ*, 34 (1970), 25-33 (p. 26).

Huntington, RB 69107.

RaW 196 -----

Copy, untitled and here beginning 'If now the worlde and loue weare young', in a composite verse miscellany including a section once owned by one David Williams, used c. 1666-74 by members of the Lloyd family of Llwydiarth; early 17th century.

National Library of Wales, Sotheby MS B2, pp. 151-2.

RaW 197 -----

Copy of a three-stanza version, headed 'Response' and beginning 'But if the world & love were sound', on a single leaf in a collection of state papers; c. 1600-10.

Printed from this MS in Curt F. Bühler, 'Four Elizabethan Poems', *Joseph Quincy Adams Memorial Studies* (Washington, D.C., 1948), 695-706 (pp. 696-7); recorded in Latham, p. 112.

Pierpont Morgan Library, R-V. R. of E. (Eliz. 1), No. 48.

RaW 198 -----

Copy, headed 'Her Answeare' and here beginning 'If that the world & Loue weare young', in a verse miscellany probably compiled by a member of an Inn of Court; c. 1598-1600s.

Formerly Rosenbach 186, printed from this MS in Samuel A. Tannenbaum, 'Unfamiliar Versions of Some Elizabethan Poems', *PMLA*, 45 (1930), 809-21 (pp. 816-17); recorded in Latham, p. 112.

Rosenbach Foundation, MS 1083/15, f. 29r-v.

RaW 199 -----

Copy of a five-stanza version, headed 'Respon:' and here beginning 'If now the world & love were younge', in a miscellany of poems and state papers; among the papers of the Troyte-Bullock family, formerly of Zeals House, Mere, and probably deriving from the papers of the Chafyn family of Bulford and Chisenbury or the Reymes family of Waddon, near Dorchester; c. 1620s.

Wiltshire Record Office, 865/500, f. [11v].

--- -----

See also INTRODUCTION.

*RaW 200 *'Now we have present made'.*

Autograph in one of Ralegh's notebooks (see RaW 728); c. 1603-18.

First pub. (from this MS) in Walter Oakeshott, 'An Unknown Ralegh MS', *The Times* (29 November 1952), p. 7; also printed in George Seddon, 'A Newly Discovered and Unknown Poem in Sir Walter Raleigh's Autograph', *ILN* (28 February 1953), p. 330 (with a facsimile), and in Walter Oakeshott, *The Queen and the Poet* (London, 1960), pp. 205-6 (with a facsimile facing p. 141). Facsimile of last two stanzas also in Petti, *English Literary Hands*, No. 48.

British Library, Add. MS 57555, f. 172v.

RaW 201 -----

Copy on one side of two conjugate leaves; endorsed in a contemporary hand 'Verses 1602'.

Printed from this MS in Lefranc (1968), p. 603.

Owned by the Marquess of Salisbury, Hatfield House, Cecil Papers 140/132.

'Now we have present made'

RaW 202 -----

Copies in a musical setting, in five MS part books; early 17th century.

This MS collated in Oakeshott, *The Queen and the Poet*, pp. 205-6.

St Michael's College, Tenbury Wells, MS 1163-7.

--- *The Ocean to Cynthia.*

See RaW 8-9, 146, 188; also 133-5, 200-2.

RaW 203 *On the Cardes, and Dice* ('Beefore the sixt day of the next new year').

Copy, headed 'S[r] Water Rawleighs Prophecy on cards & dice', in a verse miscellany compiled by an Oxford man; mid-17th century.

First pub. as 'A Prognostication upon Cards and Dice' in *Poems of Lord Pembroke and Sir Benjamin Ruddier* (London, 1660); Latham, p. 48. Formerly Corpus Christi College, MS E.i.33, this MS recorded in Latham, p. 139.

Bodleian, MS CCC. 176, f. 21v.

RaW 204 -----

Copy of a version of lines 1-12, here beginning 'The first day of the next new year', in a miscellany; 17th century.

Bodleian, MS Eng. misc. f. 49, fol. 20v.

RaW 205 -----

Second copy of a version of lines 1-12, also beginning 'The first day of the next new year', in a miscellany; 17th century.

Bodleian, MS Eng. misc. f. 49, fol. 70.

RaW 206 -----

Copy, headed 'A prognostication vpon cardes & dice', in a verse miscellany compiled by an Oxford man and once owned by one Henry Lawson; c. 1630s.

This MS recorded in Latham, p. 139.

Bodleian, MS Eng. poet. e. 14, f. 77.

RaW 207 -----

Copy, ascribed in another hand to 'S[r] Wal: R.', in a verse miscellany probably compiled by a member of New College, Oxford; c. 1620s-30s.

Printed from this MS in Latham.

Bodleian, MS Malone 19, p. 55.

RaW 208 -----

Copy, headed 'A Prophesie', in a verse miscellany belonging to the Paulet family and owned in 1659 by one Egigius Frampton; mid-17th century.

This MS recorded in Latham, p. 139.

Bodleian, MS Rawl. poet. 84, f. 68.

RaW 209 -----

Copy, headed 'A rimeing prophecye alludeing to the Cards and Dice in Christenmas', in a verse miscellany compiled by the Yorkshire antiquary John Hopkinson (1610-80); mid-17th century.

Bradford Central Library, Hopkinson MSS, Vol. 34, p. 107.

RaW 210 -----

Copy, headed 'A Prophecie', in a miscellany once owned by Margaret Bellasys, probably the daughter of Thomas, first Lord Fauconberg (1577-1653); c. 1630.

This MS recorded in Latham, p. 139.

British Library, Add. MS 10309, f. 147v.

RaW 211 -----

Copy, headed 'A Prophesie to come to pase the next yeare', in a verse miscellany once owned by one W. Allen; c. 1630s.

This MS recorded in Latham, p. 139.

British Library, Egerton MS 923, f. 9v.

RaW 212 -----

Copy, headed 'A Prophesie of then future Warres in this Kingdome', in a heraldic miscellany compiled by William Penson, Chester Herald; early-mid-17th century.

This MS recorded in Latham, p. 139.

British Library, Harley MS 1107, f. 92v.

RaW 213 -----

Copy, headed 'A Prophesy giuen to the king 1618', in a miscellany once owned by Thomas Martin (1697-1771) of Palgrave; c. 1620s.

Cat. No. 8011, this MS recorded in Latham, p. 139.

Chetham's Library, Manchester, Mun. A 4. 16, p. 40.

RaW 214 -----

Copy, untitled, in a verse miscellany compiled by an Oxford man, possibly a member of Christ Church; c. late 1630s.

Folger, MS V. a. 97, p. 202.

RaW 215 -----

Copy, headed 'S[r]. Walter Ralegh's prophecie of Cardes & Dice', in a miscellany compiled by Matthew Day of Windsor; c. 1633-4.

Formerly MS 452.1, this MS recorded in Latham, p. 139.

Folger, MS V. a. 160, p. 23 (2nd series).

RaW 216 -----

Copy in a verse miscellany compiled by an Oxford man and once owned by one Stephen Welden; mid-17th century.

Formerly MS 452.4, this MS recorded in Latham, p. 139.

Folger, MS V. a. 162, f. 65v.

RaW 217 -----

Copy, headed 'Sir Walter Raleighs prophecie of the sports and games of christmas', in a verse miscellany probably compiled by a member of an Inn of Court; mid-17th century.

Formerly MS 2073.4, this MS recorded in Latham, p. 139.

Folger, MS V. a. 262, p. 58.

RaW 218 -----

Copy, headed 'A profesie' and here beginning 'The first day of the nex new yere', in a miscellany later owned by one Joseph Hall; c. 1630s-50.

Formerly MS 2071.7, this MS recorded in Latham, p. 139.

Folger, MS V. a. 339, f. 274v.

RaW 219 -----

Copy, untitled, in a verse miscellany compiled by one or two Oxford men, possibly connected with New College, Oxford, and afterwards with the Inns of Court; 1630s.

Harvard, MS Eng 686, f. 75.

RaW 220 -----

Copy, headed 'S[r] Walter Rauleighs prophecy of Cards, & Dice at Christmas' and here beginning 'Before y[e] sixt of y[e] Next yeare', in a miscellany compiled by an Oxford man, possibly a member of Brasenose College; c. late 1630s.

Huntington, HM 116, p. 97.

RaW 221 -----

Copy, headed 'Aenigma on the Cardes', in a verse miscellany of Welsh origin bound with a miscellany owned by one Edward Lewis; c. 1630s.

National Library of Wales, NLW. MS 12443A, Part ii, pp. 19-20.

RaW 222 -----

Copy, headed 'An old and true Prophesy' and ascribed to 'S[r] W.R.', in a verse miscellany; c. 1630.

Printed from this MS in H. Harvey Wood, 'A Seventeenth-Century Manuscript of Poems by Donne and Others', *E & S*, 16 (1930), 179-90 (p. 182); recorded (as MS Taverham) in Latham, p. 139.

University of Nottingham, Portland MS Pw V 37, p. 170.

RaW 223 -----

Copy, headed 'An old Prophecye', in a verse miscellany; c. 1638-45.

Formerly Rosenbach 193, this MS recorded in Latham, p. 139.

Rosenbach Foundation, MS 239/22, p. 26.

RaW 223.5 See Addenda, p. 632.

RaW 224 *On the Life of Man* ('What is our life? a play of passion').

Copy, headed 'Mans life', in a verse miscellany once owned by Elizabeth Lane and John Finch; c. 1630s.

First pub. (in a musical setting) in Orlando Gibbons, *The First Set of Madrigals and Mottets* (London, 1612); Latham, pp. 51-2.

Aberdeen University Library, MS 29, p. 141.

RaW 225 -----

Copy in the hand of Elias Ashmole (1617-92) in a composite volume of verse collected by him; mid-17th century.

This MS recorded in Latham, p. 144.

Bodleian, MS Ashmole 36/37, f. 35.

RaW 226 -----

Copy in a verse miscellany compiled by Nicholas Burghe (d. 1670); c. 1638.

This MS recorded in Latham, p. 144.

Bodleian, MS Ashmole 38, p. 154.

On the Life of Man

RaW 227 -----

Copy, headed 'On mans life', in a verse miscellany partly compiled by Elias Ashmole; c. 1630s-40s.

This MS recorded in Latham, p. 144.

Bodleian, MS Ashmole 47, ff. 51v-2.

RaW 228 -----

Copy, headed 'On ye brittlety of man's life', in a verse miscellany compiled by an Oxford man; mid-17th century.

Bodleian, MS CCC. 176, f. 7v.

RaW 229 -----

Copy, headed 'Of mans Life', in a verse miscellany compiled by an Oxford man, possibly a member of Wadham College, and later used by William Fulman (1632-88); c. late 1630s.

Bodleian, MS CCC. 328, f. 19.

RaW 230 -----

Copy in a miscellany of English and Welsh poems compiled by Richard Roberts, Justice of the Peace; c. 1620s.

Bodleian, MS Don. c. 54, f. 3v.

RaW 231 -----

Second copy in Richard Roberts's miscellany; c. 1620s.

Bodleian, MS Don. c. 54, f. 11.

RaW 232 -----

Copy in a musical setting in a MS songbook; c. 1640s.

This MS collated in John P. Cutts, 'A Bodleian Song-Book: Don. C. 57', *M & L*, 34 (1953), 192-211 (p. 202).

Bodleian, MS Don. c. 57, f. 38v.

RaW 233 -----

Copy in a verse miscellany; c. 1630s.

This MS recorded in Latham, p. 144.

Bodleian, MS Douce f. 5, fol. 5.

RaW 234 -----

Copy in a verse miscellany compiled by an Oxford man and once owned by one Henry Lawson; c. 1630s.

This MS recorded in Latham, p. 144.

Bodleian, MS Eng. poet. e. 14, f. 101.

RaW 235 -----

Copy in a verse miscellany owned in 1619 and possibly compiled by Simon Sloper (b. 1596/7) of Magdalen Hall, Oxford; c. 1620s.

Bodleian, MS Eng. poet. f. 10, fol. 92v.

RaW 236 -----

Copy in a verse miscellany compiled by Robert Codrington (1602-65); c. 1638.

Bodleian, MS Eng. poet. f. 27, p. 91.

RaW 237 -----

Copy in a musical setting by Orlando Gibbons, possibly in the hand of Edmond Stapley, in a MS songbook compiled by Thomas Hamond (d. 1662) of Suffolk; c. 1630s-56.

Bodleian, MS Mus. f. 11-15: f. 11, fol. 33.

RaW 238 -----

Copy in a miscellany compiled by a member of St John's College, Oxford; c. 1680-90.

This MS recorded in Latham, p. 144.

Bodleian, MS Rawl. poet. 65, f. 92.

RaW 239 -----

Copy, untitled, in a miscellany compiled partly by the Oxford printer Christopher Wase (1627-90); mid-17th century.

This MS recorded in Latham, p. 144.

Bodleian, MS Rawl. poet. 117, f. 271 rev.

RaW 240 -----

Copy in a composite volume of verse and prose; early 17th century.

This MS recorded in Latham, p. 144.

Bodleian, MS Rawl. poet. 172, f. 8.

On the Life of Man

RaW 241 -----

Copy, headed 'Upon the life of man', in a verse miscellany compiled by the Yorkshire antiquary John Hopkinson (1610-80); mid-17th century.

Bradford Central Library, Hopkinson MSS, Vol. 34, p. 31.

RaW 242 -----

Copy, headed 'Vita Fabula' and here ascribed to 'Tho: Dod, Jesu', in a verse miscellany possibly compiled by a Cambridge man; c. 1630s.

This MS recorded in Latham, p. 144.

British Library, Add. MS 15227, f. 14v.

RaW 243 -----

Copy, headed 'Sr Walter Raleigh of life and death', in a verse miscellany probably compiled by Marmaduke Rawdon (c.1610-68) of Hoddesdon, Hertfordshire; c. 1662.

This MS recorded in Latham, p. 144.

British Library, Add. MS 18044, f. 154v.

RaW 244 -----

Copy, untitled, transcribed from RaW 245, in a verse miscellany possibly compiled by a member of an Inn of Court; c. 1630s.

This MS the Pickering MS printed in Hannah (1845), pp. 81-2; recorded in Latham, p. 144.

British Library, Add. MS 21433, f. 113v.

RaW 245 -----

Copy, untitled, in a miscellany possibly compiled by a member of an Inn of Court; c. 1620s-30s.

This MS recorded in Latham, p. 144.

British Library, Add. MS 25303, f. 118v.

RaW 246 -----

Copy, untitled, in a composite volume of verse belonging to the Skipwith family of Cotes, Leicestershire; early-mid-17th century.

This MS recorded in Latham, p. 144.

British Library, Add. MS 25707, f. 7v.

RaW 247 -----

Copy, headed 'Song', in a verse miscellany compiled by Daniel Leare (a distant cousin of William Strode) probably while at Christ Church, Oxford; c. 1631-3.

This MS recorded in Latham (1929), p. 162.

British Library, Add. MS 30982, f. 139 rev.

RaW 248 -----

Copy in a verse miscellany once owned by one W. Allen; c. 1630s.

This MS recorded in Latham, p. 144.

British Library, Egerton MS 923, f. 8.

RaW 249 -----

Copy, untitled, in a verse miscellany; c. 1630.

This MS recorded in Latham, p. 144.

British Library, Egerton MS 2230, f. 7v.

RaW 250 -----

Copy, headed 'De brevitate vitae', in a miscellany once owned by Sir Thomas Meres (1634-1715) of Kirton, Lincolnshire; c. 1640s.

British Library, Egerton MS 2725, f. 60v.

RaW 251 -----

Copy in a verse miscellany compiled by Arthur Capell; mid-17th century.

This MS recorded in Latham, p. 144.

British Library, Harley MS 3511, f. 1r-v.

RaW 252 -----

Copy, headed 'On the brevity of mans life', in a verse miscellany compiled by one Thomas Crosse; c. 1630s.

This MS recorded in Latham, p. 144.

British Library, Harley MS 6057, f. 14v.

RaW 253 -----

Copy, headed 'Verses syr Walt. Rauleigh made the same morning he was executed', in a composite volume of verse; early-mid-17th century.

This MS recorded in Latham, p. 144.

British Library, Harley MS 7332, f. 215.

RaW 254 -----

Copy, untitled, in a volume of state papers; early-mid-17th century.

This MS recorded in Latham, p. 144.

British Library, Lansdowne MS 498, f. 60.

On the Life of Man

RaW 255 -----

Copy, among poems appended to a MS volume of poems by William Browne of Tavistock, possibly compiled by a member of an Inn of Court; c. 1637-50.

This MS recorded in Latham, p. 144.

British Library, Lansdowne MS 777, f. 70.

RaW 256 -----

Copy, ascribed to Ralegh, in a miscellany probably compiled by a Cambridge man; c. 1627.

This MS recorded in Latham, p. 144.

British Library, Sloane MS 1489, f. 21v.

RaW 257 -----

Copy, headed 'Mans life', in a verse miscellany probably compiled by one 'I.A.' of Christ Church, Oxford, and later owned by Robert Killigrew; c. early 1630s.

This MS recorded in Latham, p. 144.

British Library, Sloane MS 1792, f. 56.

RaW 258 -----

Second copy in the verse miscellany of 'I.A.' and Robert Killigrew; c. early 1630s.

This MS recorded in Latham, p. 144.

British Library, Sloane MS 1792, f. 113.

RaW 259 -----

Copy, headed 'ffŭnerall Verses', in a miscellany compiled by one Thomas Smyth; c. 1630.

Chetham's Library, Manchester, Mun. A 3. 47, f. [30v].

RaW 260 -----

Copy, headed 'On Man', in a verse miscellany compiled by an Oxford man, possibly a member of Christ Church; c. late 1630s.

Formerly MS 1.27, this MS recorded in Latham, p. 144.

Folger, MS V. a. 97, p. 7.

RaW 261 -----

Copy, untitled, in a verse miscellany compiled by an Oxford man and once owned by one Stephen Welden; mid-17th century.

Formerly MS 452.4, this MS recorded in Latham, p. 144.

Folger, MS V. a. 162, f. 32.

RaW 262 -----

Copy of a variant version, headed 'On Man', here beginning 'What is our Life, but a play of derision' and ascribed to 'W.S.', in a verse miscellany compiled by an Oxford man; c. 1630s.

Formerly MS 646.4, this MS recorded in Latham, p. 144.

Folger, MS V. a. 170, p. 44.

RaW 263 -----

Copy in a verse miscellany; c. 1630s.

Folger, MS V. a. 245, f. 41v.

RaW 264 -----

Copy in a verse miscellany probably compiled by a member of an Inn of Court; mid-17th century.

Formerly MS 2073.4, this MS recorded in Latham, p. 144.

Folger, MS V. a. 262, p. 82.

RaW 265 -----

Copy, headed 'Sr Walter Raughly on mans life', in a verse miscellany; c. 1640.

Formerly MS 2073.3, this MS recorded in Latham, p. 144.

Folger, MS V. a. 319, f. 2.

RaW 266 -----

Copy, headed 'Life's description', in a miscellany later owned by one Joseph Hall; c. 1630s-50.

Formerly MS 2071.7, this MS recorded in Latham, p. 144.

Folger, MS V. a. 339, f. 18.

RaW 267 -----

Copy, headed 'Of man', in a miscellany; c. 1630.

Formerly MS 452.5, this MS recorded in Latham, p. 144.

Folger, MS V. a. 345, p. 14.

On the Life of Man

RaW 268 -----

Copy in a verse miscellany compiled by one or two Oxford men, possibly connected with New College and afterwards with the Inns of Court; 1630s.

Harvard, MS Eng 686, f. 17.

RaW 269 -----

Second copy in a verse miscellany compiled by one or two Oxford men, possibly connected with New College and afterwards with the Inns of Court; 1630s.

Harvard, MS Eng 686, f. 67v.

RaW 270 -----

Copy, untitled but subscribed 'by one ready to dye', in a miscellany compiled by or for Sir Henry Cholmley, brother of Sir Hugh Cholmley (1600-57); c. 1624-41.

Harvard, MS Eng 703, f. 15v.

RaW 271 -----

Copy, untitled, in a miscellany; c. 1630s.

John Rylands University Library of Manchester, Rylands English MS 410, f. 20.

RaW 272 -----

Copy, headed 'Mans life', in a verse miscellany compiled by one Edward Hyde, possibly the future first Earl of Clarendon (1609-74); c. 1630s.

Owned by Sir Geoffrey Keynes, *Bibliotheca Bibliographici* No. 1863, f. 2.

RaW 273 -----

Copy, untitled and here subscribed 'Tho: Harding', in a verse miscellany possibly once owned by Sir John Reresby (d. 1646); among the papers of the Savile family, formerly of Methley Hall, near Pontefract; c. 1630s.

Leeds Archives Department, MX 237, f. 7v.

RaW 274 -----

Copy in the hand of William Parkhurst (fl. 1604-67), untitled, in a composite volume of MSS collected by Parkhurst; among the papers of the Finch family of Burley-on-the-Hill, Rutland; 1600s-41.

Printed from this MS in *The Poems of John Donne*, ed. Herbert J.C. Grierson (Oxford, 1912), I, 441; recorded in Latham, p. 144.

Leicestershire Record Office, DG. 7/Lit. 2, f. 342v.

RaW 275 -----

Copy, headed 'Of mans Life', in a verse miscellany once owned by Elizabeth Herrick (1684-1745) and William Herrick (1689-1773); c. 1630.

Leicestershire Record Office, DG. 9/2796, p. 67.

RaW 276 -----

Copy, ascribed to Ralegh, in a miscellany of verse and prose once owned by one Robert Thornton; c. 1580s-90s.

This MS recorded in Latham, p. 144.

Marsh's Library, Dublin, MS Z 3.5.21, f. 126.

RaW 277 -----

Copy in a verse miscellany of Welsh origin bound with a miscellany owned by one Edward Lewis; c. 1630s.

National Library of Wales, NLW. MS 12443A, Part ii, pp. 9-10.

RaW 278 -----

Copy of lines 1-8, headed 'On Man' and here ascribed to Benjamin Stone, in a verse miscellany; c. 1630.

This MS recorded (as MS Taverham) in Latham, p. 144.

University of Nottingham, Portland MS Pw V 37, p. 169.

RaW 279 -----

Copy, headed 'Of Man', in a verse miscellany used by members of the Holgate family of Saffron Walden, Essex; c. 1630s.

Pierpont Morgan Library, MA 1057, p. 45.

RaW 280 -----

Copy, untitled, in a verse miscellany; c. 1630.

Rosenbach Foundation, MS 239/23, p. 182.

RaW 281 -----

Copy, headed 'On the shortnesse of mans life', in a verse miscellany; c. 1634.

Formerly Rosenbach 189, this MS recorded in Latham, p. 144.

Rosenbach Foundation, MS 239/27, p. 187.

On the Life of Man

RaW 282 -----

Copy, headed 'On life' and here ascribed to 'John Donne', in a miscellany compiled by or for Sir Thomas Finch, Viscount Maidstone and Earl of Winchelsea; c. 1634.

Formerly Rosenbach 190, this MS recorded in Latham, p. 144.

Rosenbach Foundation, MS 243/4, p. 49.

RaW 283 -----

Copy, headed 'On Mans Life', in a verse miscellany compiled by one Robert Bishop; c. 1630.

Formerly Rosenbach 187, this MS recorded in Latham, p. 144.

Rosenbach Foundation, MS 1083/16, p. 5.

RaW 284 -----

Copy, headed 'On mans life' and here beginning 'Mans life is but a play of passion', in a verse miscellany owned in 1642 by one Horatio Carey; c. 1638-42.

Formerly Rosenbach 194, this MS recorded in Latham, p. 144.

Rosenbach Foundation, MS 1083/17, f. 80v.

RaW 285 -----

Copy, headed 'On Mans life', in a verse miscellany owned and possibly compiled by John Pike of Cambridge; c. 1636-40s.

St John's College, Cambridge, MS S. 32 (James 423), f. 4.

RaW 286 -----

Copy, untitled, in a verse miscellany once owned by Sir Henry Spelman (1564?-1641); c. 1630s.

South African Library, Cape Town, MS Grey 7 a 29, p. 139.

RaW 287 -----

Copy, untitled and subscribed 'g s.', in a miscellany owned and partly compiled by Robert Herrick; c. 1612-23.

This MS reproduced, with a transcript, in Norman K. Farmer, Jr., 'Poems from a Seventeenth-Century Manuscript with the Hand of Robert Herrick', *TQ*, 16, No. 4 (Supplement) (Winter 1973), (pp. 94-5), and see P.J. Croft, 'Errata in "Poems from a Seventeenth-Century Manuscript"', *TQ*, 19, No. 1 (Spring 1976), 160-73 (p. 167).

University of Texas at Austin, Ms File/(Herrick, R)/Works B, p. 113.

RaW 288 -----

Copy, headed 'Epitaphium', in a verse miscellany; c. 1620.

Victoria and Albert Museum, Dyce Collection, Cat. No. 44 (Pressmark 25. F. 39), f. 70v.

RaW 289 -----

Copy, headed 'Mans Life', in a verse miscellany connected with Christ Church, Oxford, owned and perhaps partly compiled by George Morley, later Bishop of Winchester (1598-1684); 1620s-30s.

Westminster Abbey, MS 41, f. 32r-v.

RaW 290 -----

Copy, headed 'One Mans life', in a verse miscellany; c. 1640.

Yale, Osborn Collection, b 62, pp. 46-7.

RaW 291 -----

Copy, headed 'On mans life', in a miscellany; mid-17th century.

Yale, Osborn Collection, b 200, pp. 112-13.

RaW 292 -----

Copy, headed 'Vita est tanquam fabula', in a miscellany; mid-17th century.

Yale, Osborn Collection, b 205, f. 44.

RaW 293 -----

Copy in a miscellany; early 17th century.

Yale, Osborn Collection, b 208, p. 59.

--- *'Our Passions are most like to Floods and streames'.*

See RaW 320-38.

--- *The passionate mans Pilgrimage* ('Giue me my Scallop shell of quiet').

See RaW 438-52.

RaW 294 *Petition to the Queen* ('My dayes delight, my spring tyme ioyes foredun').

Copy of an early 78-line version, untitled and beginning with the first two stanzas of the last book of *Cynthia* (see RaW 9), on a single leaf among the papers of the Mildmay family of Hazelgrove House, Somerset, and deriving from the papers of the Harvey family; c. 1620.

This version first pub. (from this MS) in Pierre Lefranc, 'Une nouvelle version de la "Petition to Queen Anne" de Sir Walter Ralegh', *Annales de la Faculté des Lettres et Sciences Humaines de Nice*, 34 (1978), 57-67. This MS recorded in *HMC*, 7th Report (1879), Appendix, p. 592.

Somerset Record Office, DD/MI 18/88.

RaW 295 -----

Copy of an intermediate 51-line version, untitled and beginning with the first two stanzas of the last book of *Cynthia* (see RaW 9), in a composite volume of verse collected by Peter Le Neve (1661-1729), his brother Oliver, and Thomas Martin (1697-1771) of Palgrave; early-mid-17th century.

This version first pub. (from this MS) in Agnes M.C. Latham, 'Sir Walter Ralegh's *Cynthia*', *RES*, 4, No. 14 (April 1928), 129-34 (pp. 133-4); printed from this MS in Latham (1951), pp. 68-9, as 'Conjectural First Draft of the Petition to Queen Anne'.

British Library, Add. MS 27407, f. 130r-v.

RaW 296 *Petition to the Queen* ('O Had Truth Power the guiltlesse could not fall').

Copy of a shortened, 36-line version of the petition (see RaW 294-5), headed 'S.W. Raghlies Petition to the Queene. 1618', in a miscellany compiled by William Drummond of Hawthornden; c. 1620s.

First pub. (from this MS) in David Laing, 'Extracts from the Hawthornden Manuscripts', *Transactions of the Society of Antiquaries of Scotland*, 4 (1833), 225-40 (pp. 236-7); printed from this MS under Drummond's title in Latham, pp. 70-1.

National Library of Scotland, MS 2060 (Hawthornden Vol. VIII), ff. 12-13.

RaW 297 *A Poem of Sir Walter Rawleighs* ('Nature that washt her hands in milke').

Copy, untitled, in a verse miscellany once owned by one Peter Daniell; c. 1630s-40s.

First pub. in A.H. Bullen, *Speculum Amantis* (London, 1889), pp. 76-7; Latham, pp. 21-2.

Bodleian, MS Eng. poet. c. 50, f. 109.

RaW 298 -----

Copy of lines 1-12, 19-24, in a musical setting by John Wilson, in his corrected MS volume of his own songs; possibly in Wilson's autograph or else in the hand of someone similarly associated with Edward Lowe (c.1610-82); c. 1656.

Printed from this MS in Norman Ault, *A Treasury of Unfamiliar Lyrics* (London, 1938), p. 185; recorded in Latham, pp. 119-20.

Bodleian, MS Mus. b. 1, f. 77r-v.

RaW 299 -----

Copy, untitled, in a composite volume of verse belonging to the Skipwith family of Cotes, Leicestershire; early-mid-17th century.

This MS recorded in Latham, pp. 119-20.

British Library, Add. MS 25707, f. 92v.

RaW 300 -----

Copy in a verse miscellany compiled by Peter Calfe (1610-67); c. 1641.

Printed from this MS in Bullen (1889) and in Latham.

British Library, Harley MS 6917, f. 48r-v.

RaW 301 -----

Copy of lines 1-12, 19-24, headed 'Sonnett', in a verse miscellany probably compiled by Francis Baskerville of Malmesbury, Wiltshire, and owned in 1663 by William Wallrond; c. 1633.

This MS recorded in Latham, pp. 119-20.

British Library, Sloane MS 1446, f. 51v.

RaW 302 -----

Copy, headed 'S. W. R. On his Mistresse Serena', concluding with the final couplet of *'Euen such is tyme'* (here beginning 'But from this Grave, and Earth, and dust') with a marginal note, 'This last staffȩ was saide to bee made by Sr Walter Raleigh a little before his death, wth the additio of these two last verses', in a verse miscellany; c. 1630.

Formerly MS 1.28, this MS recorded in Latham, pp. 119-20.

Folger, MS V. a. 103, Part I, f. 29v.

RaW 303 -----

Copy, untitled, in a verse miscellany owned in 1640 by Anthony St John (1618-73) and Ann St John, of Bletsoe, Bedfordshire; c. 1630s.

Harvard, fMS Eng 626, f. 63r-v.

RaW 304 -----

Copy, headed 'Sr W. R. On his Mistresse Serena', concluding with the final couplet of *'Euen such is tyme'* (here beginning 'But from this Earth, and Grave, and Dust') with the marginal note,

A Poem of Sir Walter Rawleighs

'This last staffe was said to bee made by S[r] W.R. a little before his death, wth the addition of these two Verses', in a verse miscellany; c. 1630.

This MS recorded (as MS Taverham) in Latham, pp. 119-20.

University of Nottingham, Portland MS Pw V 37, p. 60.

RaW 305 *A Poem put into my Lady Laiton's pocket by Sir W. Rawleigh* ('Lady farwell whom I in Sylence serve').

Copy, untitled, in a verse miscellany compiled by the antiquary St Loe Kniveton of Gray's Inn; c. 1585-90s.

First pub. in Hannah (1870), p. 57. Printed from this MS in Latham, pp. 4-5.

British Library, Harley MS 7392, f. 65v.

RaW 306 -----

Copy of the first stanza, heavily scribbled over, in a miscellany probably compiled by someone connected with an Inn of Court; c. 1620s.

Cat. No. 8012; printed from this MS in Hannah and in Grosart, *The Dr Farmer MS* (1873), I, 96; recorded in Latham, p. 96.

Chetham's Library, Manchester, Mun. A 4. 15, p. 85.

--- *S.W. Raghlies Petition to the Queene 1618* ('O Had Truth Power the guiltlesse could not fall').

See RaW 296.

RaW 307 *Sir W. Raleigh, On the Snuff of a Candle the night before he died* ('Cowards fear to Die, but Courage stout').

Copy, transcribed from an edition of Ralegh's *Remains*, in a miscellany compiled by one John Stansby; c. 1669.

First pub. in *Remains* (London, 1657); Latham, p. 72. This MS recorded in Latham, pp. 156-7.

Bodleian, MS Ashmole 1463, p. 13.

RaW 308 -----

Copy in a miscellany probably compiled by members of the Cartwright family of Aynho, Northamptonshire; mid-17th century.

Bodleian, MS Don. e. 6, f. 16v.

RaW 309 -----

Copy, transcribed from an edition of Ralegh's *Remains*, in a verse miscellany probably compiled by Marmaduke Rawdon (c.1610-68) of Hoddesdon, Hertfordshire; c. 1662.

This MS recorded in Latham, p. 156.

British Library, Add. MS 18044, f. 156.

RaW 310 -----

Copy in a volume of state papers and tracts; early-mid-17th century.

British Library, Harley MS 39, f. 368v.

RaW 311 -----

Copy, headed 'Rawleigh one a Candle snuffe', in a verse miscellany; c. 1637.

British Library, Stowe MS 962, f. 132.

RaW 312 -----

Copy in a volume of works by or relating to Ralegh owned in 1674 by one Andrew Card; c. 1674.

University of Chicago, MS 824, f. 27v.

RaW 313 -----

Copy in a volume of state letters and tracts; early-mid-17th century.

Folger, MS G. b. 9, f. 170v.

RaW 314 -----

Copy in a verse miscellany entitled *Recueil Choisi De Pieces fugitives En Vers Anglois*; c. 1713.

Formerly Phillipps MS 9500, this MS recorded in Latham, p. 157.

Rosenbach Foundation, MS 239/16, p. 7.

RaW 315 -----

Copy in a volume of works chiefly by Ralegh; early-mid-17th century.

Dr Williams's Library, MS Jones B. 60, p. 267.

RaW 316 *Sir Walter Rauleigh to his sonne* ('Three thinges there bee that prosper up apace').

Copy of lines 1-12, headed 'Sir Walter Rauleigh to his sonne', in a verse miscellany probably compiled by a member of New College, Oxford; c. 1620s-30s.

First pub. in Latham (1929), p. 102; Latham (1951), p. 49, recording this MS on p. 140.

Bodleian, MS Malone 19, p. 138.

RaW 317 -----

Copy, untitled, in a composite volume of verse among the 'Conway Papers' chiefly descended from Sir Edward Conway, Viscount Conway (d. 1631) of Conway Castle; early 17th century.

Printed from this MS in Latham.

British Library, Add. MS 23229, f. 107.

RaW 318 -----

Copy of lines 1-12, headed 'S^{r}: Walter Rawley to his sonne', in a verse miscellany compiled by an Oxford man and once owned by one Stephen Welden; mid-17th century.

Formerly MS 452.4, this MS recorded in Latham, p. 140.

Folger, MS V. a. 162, f. 38v.

RaW 319 -----

Copy, headed 'Sr Walter Rawleigh to his sonne, Waltr.', in a verse miscellany compiled by one or two Oxford men, possibly connected with New College and afterwards with the Inns of Court; 1630s.

Harvard, MS Eng 686, f. 16.

RaW 320 *Sir Walter Ralegh to the Queen* ('Our Passions are most like to Floods and streames').

Copy, headed 'W: R: To his Mistris', here beginning 'Passions are likened best to floods, and streames', and prefixed to *'Wrong not, deare Empresse of my Heart'* (see RaW 500), in a verse miscellany once owned by Elizabeth Lane and John Finch; c. 1630s.

First pub., prefixed to *'Wrong not, deare Empresse of my Heart'* (see RaW 500-42) and headed 'To his Mistresse by Sir Walter Raleigh', in *Wits Interpreter* (London, 1655); printed in this form in Latham, p. 18. For a discussion of the authorship and different texts of this poem see Charles B. Gullans, 'Raleigh and Ayton: the disputed authorship of Wrong not sweete empresse of my heart', *SB*, 13 (1960), 191-8, reprinted in *The English and Latin Poems of Sir Robert Ayton*, ed. Gullans, STS, 4th Ser. 1 (Edinburgh & London, 1963), pp. 318-26.

Aberdeen University Library, MS 29, p. 171.

RaW 321 -----

Copy, untitled and here beginning 'Passions are likened best to floods & streames', in a miscellany; c. 1630.

Formerly Long Island Historical Society MS 22, this MS recorded in De Ricci, II, 1200.

Bodleian, MS Eng. poet. e. 112, f. 79.

RaW 322 -----

Copy, untitled and here beginning 'Passions are likened best to flouds & streames', in a verse miscellany; c. 1625-31.

This MS recorded in Gullans.

Bodleian, MS Malone 16, p. 17.

RaW 323 -----

Copy, headed 'Of Passions', in a verse miscellany probably compiled by a member of New College, Oxford; c. 1620s-30s.

This MS recorded in Latham, p. 116, and in Gullans.

Bodleian, MS Malone 19, p. 44.

RaW 324 -----

Copy, here beginning 'Passions are like to floods & streames', in a miscellany compiled by William Eliot (a nephew of Sir Simonds D'Ewes), bound in a composite volume; c. 1640-55.

This MS recorded in Gullans.

Bodleian, MS Rawl. poet. 116, f. 53v.

RaW 325 -----

Copy, headed 'Sir Walter Ralegh to Queene Elizabeth' and prefixed to *'Wrong not, deare Empresse of my Heart'* (see RaW 508), in a verse miscellany; c. 1630s.

Printed from this MS in Gullans, p. 325; recorded in Latham, p. 115.

Bodleian, MS Rawl. poet. 160, f. 117.

RaW 326 -----

Copy, untitled, here beginning 'Passions are likened best to flouds and streames', prefixed to *'Wrong not, deare Empresse of my Heart'* which is subscribed 'S^{r} W: R:' (see RaW 510), transcribed from RaW 328, in a verse miscellany possibly compiled by a member of an Inn of Court; c. 1630s.

This MS the Pickering MS printed in Hannah (1845), pp. 132-4; recorded in Latham, p. 115, and in Gullans.

British Library, Add. MS 21433, f. 112v.

Sir Walter Ralegh to the Queen

RaW 327 -----

Copy, headed 'S^{r}. Walter Ralegh to ye Queen', prefixed to *'Wrong not, deare Empresse of my Heart'* (see RaW 511), in a verse miscellany; mid-17th century.

Printed from this MS in Latham; recorded in Gullans.

British Library, Add. MS 22602, f. 30v.

RaW 328 -----

Copy, untitled, here beginning 'Passions are likened beste to flouds & streams', prefixed to *'Wrong not, deare Empresse of my Heart'* (see RaW 513) which is subscribed 'S^{r} W R ', in a miscellany possibly compiled by a member of an Inn of Court; c. 1620s-30s.

This MS recorded in Latham, p. 115, and in Gullans.

British Library, Add. MS 25303, f. 118.

RaW 329 -----

Copy, untitled, here beginning 'Passions are likned unto floods & streames', and subscribed 'Th: C:', in a verse miscellany compiled by one Thomas Crosse; c. 1630s.

This MS recorded in Latham, p. 115, and in Gullans.

British Library, Harley MS 6057, f. 9.

RaW 330 -----

Copy, headed 'A Louer' and here beginning 'Passions are likned best to flouds of streames', in a verse miscellany compiled by an Oxford man, possibly a member of Christ Church; c. late 1630s.

Formerly MS 1.27, this MS recorded in Latham, p. 116, and in Gullans.

Folger, MS V. a. 97, p. 43.

RaW 331 -----

Copy, headed 'S^{r} Wa: Ral: To the sole Governesse of His Affections', here beginning 'Passions are likned best to flouds and streames', and prefixed to *'Wrong not, deare Empresse of my Heart'* (see RaW 525), in a verse miscellany; c. 1630.

Formerly MS 1.28, this MS recorded in Latham, p. 115, and in Gullans.

Folger, MS V. a. 103, Part I, f. 30.

RaW 332 -----

Copy, headed 'Of Passions' and here beginning 'Passions are likened best to flouds & streames', in a verse miscellany compiled by one or two Oxford men, possibly connected with New College and afterwards with the Inns of Court; 1630s.

Harvard, MS Eng 686, f. 11r-v.

RaW 333 -----

Copy, headed 'Sr Gwalter Raleigh to ye sole Governours of his Affection', here beginning 'Passions are likn'd best to flouds & streams', and prefixed to *'Wrong not, deare Empresse of my Heart'* (see RaW 527), in a miscellany compiled by an Oxford man, possibly a member of Brasenose College; c. late 1630s.

This MS recorded in Gullans.

Huntington, HM 116, p. 16.

RaW 334 -----

Copy, untitled and here beginning 'Passions are likned best to flouds & streams', in a verse miscellany owned by Edward Denny, Charles Cokes, and others; c. 1630s.

This MS recorded in Gullans.

Huntington, HM 198, Part I, p. 165.

RaW 335 -----

Copy, headed 'To the sole Governes of his affections', here beginning 'Passions are likened best to Flouds and Streames', and prefixed to *'Wrong not, deare Empresse of my Heart'* (see RaW 535), in a verse miscellany; c. 1630.

University of Nottingham, Portland MS Pw V 37, p. 61.

RaW 336 -----

Copy, headed 'Sr Walter Rawleigh to his M^{rs}', here beginning 'Passions are likened to floods & streams', and prefixed to *'Wrong not, deare Empresse of my Heart'* (see RaW 537), in a verse miscellany; c. 1634.

Formerly Rosenbach 189, this MS recorded in Latham, pp. 115-16.

Rosenbach Foundation, MS 239/27, p. 50.

RaW 337 -----

Copy, headed 'Sr Walter Rawly: to the Queene', here beginning 'Passions are most like to shades and dreames', and prefixed to *'Wrong not, deare Empresse of my Heart'* (see RaW 538), in a miscellany partly compiled by one Robert Berkeley; c. 1640.

Formerly Rosenbach 195, this MS recorded in Latham, p. 116.

Rosenbach Foundation, MS 240/2, pp. 5, 7.

RaW 338 -----

Copy, headed 'On a passionate lover' and here beginning 'Passions best likned are to floods & streames', in a miscellany; mid-17th century.

Yale, Osborn Collection, b 205, f. 31.

--- *A songe made by Sir Walter Rawley* ('What teares (Deare Prince) can serue to water all').

See RaW 483-5.

RaW 339 *'Sweete ar the thoughtes, wher Hope persuadeth Happe'.*

Copy, ascribed to 'RA[legh]', in a verse miscellany compiled by the antiquary St Loe Kniveton of Gray's Inn; c. 1585-90s.

First pub. (from this MS) in Hoyt T. Hudson, 'Notes on the Ralegh Canon', *MLN*, 46 (1931), 386-9 (p. 387); printed from this MS in Latham, p. 4.

British Library, Harley MS 7392, f. 36.

RaW 340 *'The word of deniall, and the letter of fifty'.*

Copy, headed 'Sr Walter Rawleigh to Bp. Nowell', in a verse miscellany; c. 1630s.

First pub. in *Works* (1829), VIII, 736; Latham, pp. 47-8. This MS recorded in Latham, p. 138.

Bodleian, MS Douce f. 5, fol. 31.

RaW 341 -----

Copy in a verse miscellany probably compiled by a member of New College, Oxford; c. 1620s-30s.

This MS recorded in Latham, p. 138.

Bodleian, MS Malone 19, p. 53.

RaW 342 -----

Copy in a verse miscellany belonging to the Paulet family and owned in 1659 by one Egigius Frampton; mid-17th century.

This MS recorded in Latham, p. 138.

Bodleian, MS Rawl. poet. 84, f. 72v.

RaW 343 -----

Copy in a miscellany compiled partly by the Oxford printer Christopher Wase (1627-90); mid-17th century.

This MS recorded in Latham, p. 138.

Bodleian, MS Rawl. poet. 117, f. 271 rev.

RaW 344 -----

Copy in a verse miscellany compiled by John Lilliat (c.1550-c.1599); c. 1589-99.

Bodleian, MS Rawl. poet. 148, f. 1.

RaW 345 -----

Copy in a diary compiled by John Manningham of the Middle Temple; 30 December 1602.

Printed from this MS in Latham.

British Library, Harley MS 5353, f. 83.

RaW 346 -----

Copy in a miscellany probably compiled by a Cambridge man; c. 1627.

This MS recorded in Latham, p. 138.

British Library, Sloane MS 1489, f. 16v.

RaW 347 -----

Copy in a verse miscellany owned in 1623 and probably compiled by one Richard Jackson; c. 1620s-30s.

Edinburgh University Library, MS H.-P. Coll. 401, f. 62v.

RaW 348 -----

Copy, headed 'S^r: W.R. On D^r. Noell', in a verse miscellany; c. 1630.

Formerly MS 1.28, this MS recorded in Latham, p. 138.

Folger, MS V. a. 103, Part I, f. 68.

RaW 349 -----

Copy, headed 'Rawleys reply on Noel', in a verse miscellany compiled by an Oxford man and once owned by one Stephen Welden; mid-17th century.

Formerly MS 452.4, this MS recorded in Latham, p. 138.

Folger, MS V. a. 162, f. 64.

'The word of deniall, and the letter of fifty'.

RaW 350 -----

Copy, headed 'Rawley upon Noell', in a verse miscellany; c. 1640.

Formerly MS 2073.3, this MS recorded in Latham, p. 138.

Folger, MS V. a. 319, f. 13v.

RaW 351 -----

Copy, headed 'On the Lord Noel', in a miscellany; c. 1630.

Formerly MS 452.5, this MS recorded in Latham, p. 138.

Folger, MS V. a. 345, p. 277.

RaW 352 -----

Copy in a verse miscellany compiled by one or two Oxford men, possibly connected with New College and afterwards with the Inns of Court; 1630s.

Harvard, MS Eng 686, f. 17v.

RaW 353 -----

Copy, headed 'On D[r] Noell', in a verse miscellany; c. 1630.

University of Nottingham, Portland MS Pw V 37, p. 140.

RaW 354 -----

Copy, headed 'S[r] Walter Rawleigh of H. Noell Courtier', in a verse miscellany compiled by one Robert Bishop; c. 1630.

Formerly Rosenbach 187, this MS recorded in Latham, p. 138.

Rosenbach Foundation, MS 1083/16, p. 195.

--- *These verses following were made by Sir Walter Rauleigh the night before he dyed and left att the Gate howse* ('Euen such is tyme which takes in trust').

See RaW 11-103.

RaW 355 *'Those eies that holds the hand of every hart'.*

Copy in a miscellany compiled by a Cambridge student, possibly Sir John Finett (1571-1641) of Fordwich, Kent; c. 1586-91.

First pub. in *Brittons Bowre of Delights* (London, 1591); Latham, p. 83. This MS collated in *The Phoenix Nest*, ed. H.E. Rollins (Cambridge, Mass., 1931), p. 183; recorded in Latham, p. 162.

Bodleian, MS Rawl. poet. 85, f. 24v.

RaW 356 -----

Copy in a verse miscellany owned in 1596 by one Anthony Babington of Warington; c. 1596.

Printed from this MS in *The Works in Verse and Prose of Nicholas Breton*, ed. A.B. Grosart (Edinburgh, 1879), I (d), p. 12; collated in Rollins, p. 183; recorded in Latham, p. 162.

British Library, Add. MS 34064, f. 7v.

RaW 357 *To his Love when hee had obtained Her* ('Now Serena bee not coy').

Copy in a verse miscellany; c. 1630.

First pub. in H. Harvey Wood, 'A Seventeenth-Century Manuscript of Poems by Donne and Others', *E & S*, 16 (1930), 179-90 (pp. 181-2). Formerly MS 1.28; printed from this MS in Latham, p. 20.

Folger, MS V. a. 103, Part I, f. 30v.

RaW 358 -----

Copy in a verse miscellany; c. 1630.

Printed from this MS in Harvey Wood; recorded (as MS Taverham) in Latham, pp. 118-19.

University of Nottingham, Portland MS Pw V 37, p. 62.

--- *Vertue the best monument* ('Not Caesars birth made Caesar to suruiue').

See RaW 497.

RaW 359 *Who list to heare* ('Who list to heare the sum of sorrowes state').

Copy in a miscellany later owned by one Joseph Hall; c. 1630s-50.

First pub. in *The Phoenix Nest* (London, 1593); Latham, pp. 83-4.

Folger, MS V. a. 339, f. 199.

--- *'Would I were chaung'd into that golden showre'.*

See INTRODUCTION.

(2) POEMS DOUBTFULLY ASCRIBED TO RALEGH

--- [*Epitaph on the Earle of Leicester*] ('Here lyes the noble warryor').

See RaW 384-9.5.

RaW 360 *Epitaph on the Earl of Salisbury* ('Here lies Hobinall, our Pastor while ere').

Copy, here beginning 'Here lies Robert our shepherd whilom', as given to John Aubrey (1626-97) by 'Sir Thomas Malett...who knew S[r] W. Raleigh', in Aubrey's autograph of the first part of *Brief Lives*; incomplete; 1679-80.

First pub. in Francis Osborne, *Traditionall Memoyres on the raigne of King Iames* (London, 1658); Latham, p. 53; of doubtful authorship according to Latham, p. 146, and Lefranc (1968), p. 84. This MS recorded in Latham, p. 146.

Bodleian, MS Aubrey 6, f. 78v.

RaW 361 -----

Copy, headed 'Vpon S[r] R.C. Lord Treasurer', in a verse miscellany compiled by an Oxford man and once owned by one Henry Lawson; c. 1630s.

This MS recorded in Latham, p. 146.

Bodleian, MS Eng. poet. e. 14, f. 79.

RaW 362 -----

Copy, headed 'Upon S[r] Robert Cecill Earle of Salisbury and L[d] Treasurer' and ascribed to 'S[r] Walter Raleigh', in a composite volume of verse and prose owned c. 1669 by one John Cooke of Bury St Edmunds, Suffolk; c. 1620s-30s.

This MS recorded in Latham, p. 146.

Bodleian, MS Rawl. poet. 26, f. 78.

RaW 363 -----

Copy in a volume of letters and tracts compiled by Archbishop William Sancroft (1617-93); mid-late 17th century.

Bodleian, MS Tanner 299, f. 12v.

RaW 364 -----

Copy, headed 'In obitum Ro: Cecillij', in a verse miscellany among the papers of the Stanhope family of Horsforth, near Leeds; c. late 1620s.

Bradford Central Library, Spencer-Stanhope MSS, Calendar No. 2795 (Bundle 10, No. 34), f. [6].

RaW 365 -----

Copy, untitled and here beginning 'Heere lyes Hobbinoll our shepheard while ere', in a verse miscellany; c. 1630.

British Library, Egerton MS 2230, f. 34.

RaW 366 -----

Copy, untitled and here beginning 'Heere Hobbinoll lyes our Shepeheard whilere', in a composite volume of MSS; mid-17th century.

British Library, Harley MS 1221, f. 74.

RaW 367 -----

Copy, untitled and here beginning 'Here Hobbinoll lies our shepheard whilere', in a verse miscellany bound in a composite volume of MSS; mid-17th century.

British Library, Harley MS 6038, f. 18.

RaW 368 [Entry deleted].

RaW 369 [Entry deleted].

RaW 370 -----

Copy, headed 'Upon Cicells Death' and here beginning 'Here lies Hobbinall o[r] Shepherd whileare', in a miscellany later owned by one Joseph Hall; c. 1630s-50.

Formerly MS 2071.7, this MS recorded in Latham, p. 146.

Folger, MS V. a. 339, f. 258.

RaW 371 -----

Copy, headed 'In obitum Ro: Ceciliij.', here beginning 'Here lyes old Hobinol our shephard while heere', and ascribed to 'S[r] wall. Rawleigh', in a miscellany; c. 1630.

Formerly MS 452.5, this MS recorded in Latham, p. 146.

Folger, MS V. a. 345, p. 110.

Epitaph on the Earl of Salisbury

RaW 372 -----

Copy, under a general heading 'Epitaphes and verses of my Lord Tresorer Cicill' and here beginning 'Hear Hobbinole lyeth a sheppard whyle eere', in a volume chiefly of transcripts of correspondence of John Holles, first Earl of Clare (1587-1637), and his son John, second Earl of Clare (1595-1666); among the collections of the Duke of Portland, of Welbeck Abbey; c. 1620.

University of Nottingham, Portland MS Pw V 2, p. 145.

RaW 373 -----

Copy of a version headed 'A Sarisbury Sheaphard' and here beginning 'Heare lies our sheaphard a while, soe deare', in a verse miscellany compiled by one Robert Bishop; c. 1630.

Rosenbach Foundation, MS 1083/16, f. 90.

RaW 374 -----

Copy, untitled and here beginning 'Here lyes Hobbynoll o^r shepheard whileere', with two other poems on Cecil's death, on a single leaf in a collection of unbound papers on affairs of state; early-mid-17th century.

St John's College, Cambridge, MS K. 56 (James 542), No. 73.

RaW 375 -----

Copy in the hand of Robert Herrick, the first three words in another hand, here beginning 'Here lies Hobinall our Shepheard whileare', in a miscellany once owned and partly compiled by Herrick; c. 1612-23.

This MS reproduced in facsimile, with a transcript, in Norman K. Farmer, Jr., 'Poems from a Seventeenth-Century Manuscript with the Hand of Robert Herrick', *TQ*, 16, No. 4 (Supplement) (Winter 1973), (pp. 40-1), and see P.J. Croft, 'Errata In "Poems from a Seventeenth-Century Manuscript"', *TQ*, 19, No. 1 (Spring 1976), 160-73 (p. 162).

University of Texas at Austin, Ms File/(Herrick, R)/Works B, p. 73.

RaW 376 -----

Copy, untitled and here beginning 'Heere Hobinol lyes oure shepheard while ere', in a verse miscellany; c. 1620.

Victoria and Albert Museum, Dyce Collection, Cat. No. 44 (Pressmark 25. F. 39), f. 71.

RaW 377 -----

Copy, headed 'On Sr Rob: Cicil' and inscribed 'S^r W: Raleigh in ye Tower', here beginning 'Heere lieth Hobinol our Sheapheard while ere', in a fragment of a miscellany among the papers of the Newdegate family of Arbury Hall, Nuneaton; c. 1620s-30s.

Warwickshire Record Office, CR 136/B3468, p. 73.

RaW 378 -----

Copy, under a general heading 'Scurrallous epitaphes' and here beginning 'Heare lyeth Hobinoll our shepherd whileare', in a miscellany of poems and state papers; among the papers of the Troyte-Bullock family, formerly of Zeals House, Mere, and probably deriving from the papers of the Chafyn family of Bulford and Chisenbury or the Reymes family of Waddon, near Dorchester; c. 1620s.

Wiltshire Record Office, 865/500, f. [32v].

RaW 379 -----

Copy in a miscellany entitled *A Collection of Witt and Learning*; c. 1677-81.

Yale, Osborn Collection, b 54, p. 880.

RaW 380 -----

Copy on a single leaf; early-mid-17th century.

Yale, Osborn Collection, PB VI/84.

RaW 381 *'Fayne woulde I but I dare not'.*

Copy, ascribed in a different ink to 'W.R.', in a miscellany compiled by a Cambridge student, possibly Sir John Finett (1571-1641) of Fordwich, Kent; c. 1586-91.

First pub. (from this MS) in *Works* (1829), VIII, 732-3; printed from this MS in Latham (1929), pp. 72-3; listed but not printed in Latham (1951), pp. 172-3. This MS recorded in Latham.

Bodleian, MS Rawl. poet. 85, ff. 43v-4.

RaW 382 -----

Copy of a twelve-line version in a verse miscellany; c. 1596-1601.

This MS recorded in Latham.

British Library, Harley MS 6910, f. 154r-v.

'Fayne woulde I but I dare not'

RaW 383 -----

Copy, headed 'Ferenda Natura' and here ascribed to 'DY[er]', with an additional couplet as 'Lenuoy', in a verse miscellany compiled by the antiquary St Loe Kniveton of Gray's Inn; c. 1585-90s.

This MS recorded in Latham.

British Library, Harley MS 7392, f. 22r-v.

RaW 384 *'Here lyes the noble warryor that never bludyed sword'.*

Copy, headed 'On S[r] Robert Dudley Earle of warwicke and Leicester', and here beginning 'Here lies the souldier that neuer drewe his sword', in a verse miscellany compiled by Nicholas Burghe (d. 1670); c. 1638.

First pub. in Richard Verstegan, *A Declaration of the True Causes of the Great Troubles* (London, 1592); listed but not printed in Latham, p. 172. This MS recorded in Latham.

Bodleian, MS Ashmole 38, p. 181.

RaW 385 -----

Copy of a twelve-line version, headed 'Epitaphium' and here beginning 'Heere lyes the valiant soldier | that nev[r] drewe his sword', at the end of a MS copy of *Leicester's Commonwealth*; late 16th-early 17th century.

Printed from this MS in D.C. Peck, 'Another Version of the Leicester Epitaphium', *N & Q*, 221 (May-June 1976), 227-8.

British Library, Stowe MS 156, f. 204v.

RaW 386 -----

Copy of an eight-line version, headed 'Epitaph E. Lester' and here beginning 'Heir Lyes ane waliant Wariour | Who never drew his sworde', in a verse miscellany; c. 1630s-40s.

Edinburgh University Library, MS La. III. 436, p. 99.

RaW 387 -----

Copy, headed 'epetaphe', here beginning 'Heere lies the woorthy warrier', and ascribed to 'Wa. Ra.', in a miscellany; early 17th century.

Printed from this MS in Ernest A. Strathmann, 'An Epitaph attributed to Ralegh', *MLN*, 60 (1945), 111-14; recorded in Latham.

Huntington, El 6183 in EL 6162, f. 8a[v] rev.

RaW 388 -----

Copy of an eight-line version, here beginning 'Here lyes the woorthie warrior', in a composite volume of state tracts; early 17th century.

Huntington, HM 267, No. 2, f. 15.

RaW 389 -----

Copy of a four-line version, headed 'An Epitaph of the E: of Leicester' and here beginning 'Here lyeth that noble souldier y[t] neu[r] brandeth sword', at the end of a MS copy of *Leicester's Commonwealth*; early 17th century.

This MS formerly Phillipps MS 8989.

University of London Library, MS 312, f. 105v.

RaW 389.5 See Addenda, p. 632.

--- -----

See also INTRODUCTION.

RaW 390 *'ICUR, good Mounser Carr'.*

Copy in a miscellany of English and Welsh poems compiled by Richard Roberts, Justice of the Peace; c. 1620s.

First pub. in *Love-Poems and Humourous Ones*, ed. Frederick J. Furnivall, The Ballad Society (Hertford, 1874; reprinted New York, 1977), p. 20; listed but not printed in Latham, p. 174.

Bodleian, MS Don. c. 54, f. 22v.

RaW 391 -----

Copy in a verse miscellany; c. 1630s.

Bodleian, MS Douce f. 5, fol. 34v.

RaW 392 -----

Copy, headed 'S[r] Walter Raleigh to y[e] L[d]. Carr', in a verse miscellany compiled by an Oxford man and once owned by one Henry Lawson; c. 1630s.

This MS recorded in Latham.

Bodleian, MS Eng. poet. e. 14, f. 49.

RaW 393 -----

Copy in a volume of miscellaneous verse and prose; early 17th century.

Edited partly from this MS in Beatrice White, *Cast of Ravens* (London, 1965), p. 227.

Bodleian, MS Rawl. D. 1048, f. 64v.

RaW 394 -----

Copy, headed 'On the Earle of Sōmsett', in a verse miscellany; c. 1630s.

Bodleian, MS Rawl. poet. 160, f. 162v.

'ICUR, good Mounser Carr'

RaW 395 -----

Copy in a book of jests compiled by Archbishop William Sancroft (1617-93); mid-late 17th century.

Bodleian, MS Sancroft 53, p. 48.

RaW 396 -----

Second copy, deleted, in Archbishop Sancroft's book of jests; mid-late 17th century.

Bodleian, MS Sancroft 53, p. 58.

RaW 397 -----

Copy, headed 'In Robertum Car, comitem Somersetensem, postquam Essex: vxorem dixit', in a verse miscellany probably compiled by a Cambridge man; c. 1630s.

Edited partly from this MS in Beatrice White.

British Library, Add. MS 15227, f. 42v.

RaW 398 -----

Copy in a volume of papers relating to the murder of Sir Thomas Overbury compiled by Nicholas Oldisworth; 1637.

Edited partly from this MS in Beatrice White.

British Library, Add. MS 15476, f. 1.

RaW 399 -----

Copy in a verse miscellany compiled by Daniel Leare (a distant cousin of William Strode) probably while at Christ Church, Oxford; c. 1631-3.

British Library, Add. MS 30982, f. 22.

RaW 400 -----

Copy in a composite volume of MSS; mid-17th century.

Printed from this MS in John Wardroper, *Love and Drollery* (London, 1969), p. 268.

British Library, Harley MS 1221, f. 91.

RaW 401 -----

Copy in a MS volume of works chiefly by Jonson and Donne compiled for the Cavendish family, probably for Sir William Cavendish, first Earl of Newcastle (1592-1676); c. 1620s-30s.

British Library, Harley MS 4955, f. 81.

RaW 402 -----

Copy in a miscellany probably compiled by a Cambridge man; c. 1627.

British Library, Sloane MS 1489, f. 9v.

RaW 403 -----

Copy in a verse miscellany bound with a collection of printed amatory poems and pamphlets; early 17th century.

Printed from this MS in Furnivall (1874).

British Library, Department of Printed Books, C. 39. a. 37, f. 12.

RaW 404 -----

Copy, deleted, in a verse miscellany compiled by a Cambridge man; c. 1630.

A 19th-century transcript of this MS is in the Bodleian, MS Firth d. 7, f. 152.

Cambridge University Library, MS Add. 4138, f. 47.

RaW 405 -----

Copy in a miscellany once owned by Thomas Martin (1697-1771) of Palgrave; c. 1620s.

Chetham's Library, Manchester, Mun. A 4. 16, p. 37.

RaW 406 -----

Copy in a verse miscellany owned in 1623 and probably compiled by one Richard Jackson; c. 1620s-30s.

Edinburgh University Library, MS H.-P. Coll. 401, f. 43* [bis].

RaW 407 -----

Copy, headed 'On my Lord Carre', in a verse miscellany compiled by an Oxford man and once owned by one Stephen Welden; mid-17th century.

Folger, MS V. a. 162, f. 35.

RaW 408 -----

Copy in a miscellany of verse and prose; c. 1620.

Harvard, MS Eng 628, p. 319.

RaW 409 -----

Copy, headed 'On the late Earle of Somersett', written in a verse miscellany probably compiled by a member of an Inn of Court; c. 1630.

Rosenbach Foundation, MS 1083/15, f. 70v.

RaW 410 -----

Copy, headed 'On the late Earle of Somersett', in a verse miscellany compiled by one Robert Bishop; c. 1630.

Rosenbach Foundation, MS 1083/16, p. 172.

RaW 410.5 See Addenda, p. 632.

RaW 411 -----

Copy in a bundle of unbound verses and songs among the papers of the Sanford family of Somerset; early-mid-17th century.

Somerset Record Office, DD/SF C/2635, Box 1, [no item number].

RaW 411.5 See Addenda, p. 632.

--- -----

See also INTRODUCTION.

RaW 412 *'I cannot bend the bow'.*

Copy, headed 'S^{r}: Walter Rawleigh to my Lady Bentbowe', written in a MS journal of proceedings in Parliament from January to March 1628/9, owned on 1 May 1629 by one Arthur Langford; among the papers of the Trumbull family of Easthampstead Park; c. 1630.

Believed to be unpublished; listed but not printed in Latham, pp. 173-4.

Berkshire Record Office, Trumbull Add. MS 51, f. [61].

RaW 413 -----

Copy, headed 'Rawly to ye Lady Bendbow', in a verse miscellany later used by William Fulman (1632-88); c. 1630.

Bodleian, MS CCC. 327, f. 27v.

RaW 414 -----

Copy, headed 'A ridle proposed to by Lady bendbow', in a verse miscellany compiled by an Oxford man and once owned by one Henry Lawson; c. 1630s.

Bodleian, MS Eng. poet. e. 14, f. 85.

RaW 415 -----

Copy in a verse miscellany probably compiled by a member of New College, Oxford; c. 1620s-30s.

Bodleian, MS Malone 19, p. 44.

RaW 416 -----

Copy, headed 'Sr Walter Raleigh to ye Lady Bend-bow', in a composite volume of verse and prose owned c. 1669 by one John Cooke of Bury St Edmunds, Suffolk; c. 1620s-30s.

This MS recorded in Latham.

Bodleian, MS Rawl. poet. 26, f. 2.

RaW 417 -----

Copy, untitled and here beginning 'There is a bowe wherin to shoote I sue', in a miscellany compiled partly by the Oxford printer Christopher Wase (1627-90); mid-17th century.

The text followed by a six-line 'Answer', beginning 'You bended have the bowe wherin to shute you sue'.

Bodleian, MS Rawl. poet. 117, f. 17.

RaW 418 -----

Copy, untitled and here beginning 'The bow is not yet bent, wherin to shoot I sue', in a verse miscellany compiled by John Lilliat (c.1550-c.1599); c. 1589-99.

The text followed by a six-line 'Answer', beginning 'The man that sued to shoote, in this well bended Bow'.

Bodleian, MS Rawl. poet. 148, f. 4.

RaW 419 -----

Copy, headed 'Sr Watter Rawleigh to the Lady Bendbow', in a verse miscellany; c. 1630s.

British Library, Egerton MS 923, f. 44v.

RaW 419.5 See Addenda, p. 632.

RaW 420 -----

Copy of a six-line version, headed 'To his loue' and here beginning 'There is a bow wherein to shoote I sue', in a miscellany compiled by Matthew Day of Windsor; c. 1633-4.

The text followed by 'Her answere', beginning 'You bended have the bow'.

Folger, MS V. a. 160, p. 1 (2nd series).

RaW 421 -----

Copy, headed 'On the lady Bendbow', in a verse miscellany compiled by an Oxford man and once owned by one Stephen Welden; mid-17th century.

Folger, MS V. a. 162, f. 37.

RaW 422 -----

Copy, headed 'Sir W. Ralegh to the Lady Bendbow' and here beginning 'In vayne I bend the bow wherein to shoote I sue', in a verse miscellany probably compiled by a member of an Inn of Court; mid-17th century.

Formerly MS 2073.4, this MS recorded in Latham.

Folger, MS V. a. 262, p. 81.

'I cannot bend the bow'

RaW 423 -----

Copy, headed 'A ridle proposed by Sr Walter Rawley to ye Lady Bendbow', in a verse miscellany; c. 1640.

Formerly MS 2073.3, this MS recorded in Latham.

Folger, MS V. a. 319, f. 31.

RaW 424 -----

Copy, headed 'A Riddle upon the Lady Bendbow', in a verse miscellany compiled by one or two Oxford men, possibly connected with New College and afterwards with the Inns of Court; 1630s.

Harvard, MS Eng 686, f. 32.

RaW 425 -----

Copy, headed 'A riddle propounded by Sr Walter Raughly to ye Lady Bend-bow', in a miscellany compiled by an Oxford man, possibly a member of Brasenose College; c. late 1630s.

Huntington, HM 116, p. 77.

RaW 426 -----

Copy, headed 'A Rose to his m^rs^' and here beginning 'ffaine would I bend ye bowe whearin to shoote I sue', in a verse miscellany probably compiled by a member of an Inn of Court; c. 1598-1600s.

Rosenbach Foundation, MS 1083/15, f. 51.

RaW 427 -----

Copy, headed 'Rawleigh to ye Lady Bendbow', in a miscellany; mid-17th century.

Yale, Osborn Collection, b 200, p. 412.

--- *The Lie* ('Goe soule the bodies guest').

See RaW 147-77.

RaW 428 *'Like to a Ring without a finger'.*

Copy, headed 'Canto', in a composite volume of verse collected by Peter Le Neve (1661-1729), his brother Oliver, and Thomas Martin (1697-1771) of Palgrave; 17th century.

First pub. (from this MS) in Latham (1951), pp. 165-7, as 'A poem doubtfully ascribed to Ralegh'.

British Library, Add. MS 27406, f. 107v.

RaW 429 -----

Copy of lines 1-32, 49-80, plus four additional stanzas, in a verse miscellany once owned by one W. Allen; c. 1630s.

This MS recorded and additional stanzas printed in Latham, pp. 169-70.

British Library, Egerton MS 923, f. 1.

RaW 430 -----

Copy in a verse miscellany; c. 1690-1730.

Folger, MS V. a. 308, f. 34v.

RaW 431 -----

Copy of lines 1-64, headed 'Canto' and ascribed in another hand to 'W.R.', in a miscellany later owned by one Joseph Hall; c. 1630s-50.

Formerly MS 2071.7, this MS recorded in Latham, pp. 167-9.

Folger, MS V. a. 339, ff. 224v-5.

RaW 432 -----

Copy in a verse miscellany once owned by one Edward Lewis and bound with another miscellany of Welsh origin; c. 1630s.

National Library of Wales, NLW. MS 12443A, Part i, pp. 33-5.

RaW 433 -----

Copy of lines 1-16 in a verse miscellany owned and possibly compiled by John Pike of Cambridge; c. 1636-40s.

St John's College, Cambridge, MS S. 32 (James 423), f. 21.

RaW 434 *'Now what is Loue, I praie thee tell'.*

Copy of a version in 19 stanzas in a miscellany compiled by someone connected with the Court; c. 1605.

First pub. in *The Phoenix Nest* (London, 1593); first and last stanzas also a song in Thomas Heywood, *The Rape of Lucrece* (London, 1608); listed but not printed in Latham, p. 171; printed in Doughtie, *Lyrics from English Airs*, pp. 156-7. Ralegh's possible authorship also discussed and largely supported in Walter Oakeshott, *The Queen and the Poet* (London, 1960), p. 161; Lefranc (1968), pp. 78-9, 83; and Michael West, 'Raleigh's disputed Authorship of "A Description of Loue"', *ELN*, 10 (1972-3), 92-9. This MS collated, and the additional stanzas printed, in Doughtie, pp. 504-10; recorded in Latham.

British Library, Add. MS 22601, ff. 104-6.

'Now what is Loue, I praie thee tell'

RaW 435 -----

Copy in a musical setting in a MS songbook; early 17th century.

This MS collated in Doughtie, pp. 504-10.

Christ Church, Oxford, MS Mus. 439, p. 35.

RaW 436 -----

Copy, headed 'Tam arte quam Marte', in a verse miscellany; early-mid-17th century.

This MS collated in Doughtie, pp. 503-10.

Folger, MS V. a. 399, f. 10r-v.

RaW 437 -----

Copy of a version in 15 stanzas in a verse miscellany probably compiled by a member of an Inn of Court; c. 1598-1600s.

Extracts from this MS printed in John Payne Collier, *An Old Man's Diary* (London, 1871), Part i, pp. 39-40. Formerly Rosenbach 186, this MS collated in Doughtie, pp. 504-10; recorded in Latham.

Rosenbach Foundation, MS 1083/15, ff. 49v-50v.

RaW 438 *The passionate mans Pilgrimage* ('Giue me my Scallop shell of quiet').

Copy, headed 'Verses Made by S^{r} walter Raleigh the night before hee was beheaded', in a verse miscellany compiled by Nicholas Burghe (d. 1670); c. 1638.

First pub. with *Daiphantvs or The Passions of Loue* (London, 1604); Latham, pp. 49-51. This poem rejected from the canon and attributed to an anonymous Catholic poet in Philip Edwards, 'Who Wrote *The Passionate Man's Pilgrimage*?', *ELR*, 4 (1974), 83-97. This MS recorded in Latham, pp. 141-2.

Bodleian, MS Ashmole 38, p. 59.

RaW 439 -----

Copy, headed 'verses written by S^{r} walter Raleigh in the gatehouse att westm^{r} the evening before he died', in a volume of historical papers once owned by Sir Henry Spelman (1564?-1641); [1626-9].

This MS recorded in Latham, pp. 141-2.

Bodleian, MS Eng. hist. c. 272, p. 49.

RaW 440 -----

Copy, headed 'Sir Walter Raleighs Pilgrimage', in a verse miscellany; c. 1630s.

This MS recorded in Latham, pp. 141-2.

Bodleian, MS Rawl. poet. 160, f. 57r-v.

RaW 441 -----

Copy, headed 'Sr Walter Railieghs Pilgrim', probably transcribed from an edition of Ralegh's *Remains*, in a verse miscellany probably compiled by Marmaduke Rawdon (c.1610-68) of Hoddesdon, Hertfordshire; c. 1662.

This MS recorded in Latham, pp. 141-3.

British Library, Add. MS 18044, ff. 155-6.

RaW 442 -----

Copy, headed 'Sr Walter Rawleighs Pilgrimage', transcribed from RaW 443, in a verse miscellany possibly compiled by a member of an Inn of Court; c. 1630s.

This MS the Pickering MS collated in Hannah (1845), pp. 105-8; recorded in Latham, pp. 141-2.

British Library, Add. MS 21433, ff. 82-3.

RaW 443 -----

Copy, headed 'Sr Walter Rawleighs Pilgrimage', in a miscellany possibly compiled by a member of an Inn of Court; c. 1620s-30s.

This MS recorded in Latham, pp. 141-2.

British Library, Add. MS 25303, ff. 71v-2.

RaW 444 -----

Copy, headed 'Sr Walter Rawleighes Pilgrimage', in a verse miscellany compiled by one Thomas Crosse; c. 1630s.

This MS recorded in Latham, pp. 141-2.

British Library, Harley MS 6057, f. 22v.

RaW 445 -----

Copy, headed 'Sir Walter Raw.'s Pilgrimage', in a volume of works by or relating to Ralegh owned in 1674 by one Andrew Card; c. 1674.

University of Chicago, MS 824, f. 27r-v.

RaW 446 -----

Copy, headed 'Sr Walter Rawleighs Pilgrimage', in a verse miscellany of Welsh origin bound with a miscellany owned by one Edward Lewis; c. 1630s.

National Library of Wales, NLW. MS 12443A, Part ii, pp. 237-8.

The passionate mans Pilgrimage

RaW 447 -----

Copy, headed 'S[r] Walter Raleigh his Pilgrimage; Or A Preparative made by Himselfe, the Night before hee was beheaded', in a verse miscellany; c. 1630.

University of Nottingham, Portland MS Pw V 37, pp. 191-2.

RaW 448 -----

Copy, headed 'Verses that S[r] Wal: Rawly made a little beefore hee was beeheaded, his Farewell to the world', in a miscellany partly compiled by one Robert Berkeley; c. 1640.

Formerly Rosenbach 195, this MS recorded in Latham, pp. 141-2.

Rosenbach Foundation, MS 240/2, pp. 35, 37.

RaW 449 -----

Copy, headed 'By S[r] Wa: Raleigh the night before his execucon', in a verse miscellany owned and possibly compiled by John Pike of Cambridge; c. 1636-40s.

St John's College, Cambridge, MS S. 32 (James 423), f. 33v-4v.

RaW 450 -----

Copy, headed 'The Lo: Straford his Pilgrymage', in a volume of state papers; mid-17th century.

Formerly MS F.1.20, this MS recorded in Latham, p. 141.

Trinity College, Dublin, MS 806, ff. 538v, 485.

RaW 451 -----

Copy, headed 'Sir Walter Raleighes Pilgrimage', in a MS volume of works chiefly by Ralegh; early-mid-17th century.

Dr Williams's Library, MS Jones B. 60, pp. 265-7.

RaW 452 -----

Copy, headed 'S[r] W: Ralegs Pilgrimage', in a verse miscellany compiled by Tobias Alston (1620-c.1639) of Sayham Hall, near Sudbury, Suffolk; c. 1639.

Yale, Osborn Collection, b 197, pp. 25-6.

RaW 453 *'Say not you love, unless you do'.*

Copy, headed 'Two Louers dialogue', in a verse miscellany once owned by Elizabeth Lane and John Finch; c. 1630s.

First pub. in *Inedited Poetical Miscellanies, 1584-1700*, ed. W.C. Hazlitt ([London], 1870), p. [179]; listed but not printed in Latham, p. 174.

Aberdeen University Library, MS 29, p. 186.

RaW 453.5 See Addenda, p. 632.

RaW 454 -----

Copy, here ascribed to 'D: Donn', in a verse miscellany compiled by Nicholas Burghe (d. 1670); c. 1638.

Bodleian, MS Ashmole 38, p. 152.

RaW 455 -----

Copy, headed 'A Gentlewoman to a gentleman', in a verse miscellany partly compiled by Elias Ashmole (1617-92); c. 1630s-40s.

This MS recorded in Latham.

Bodleian, MS Ashmole 47, f. 54v.

RaW 456 -----

Copy, headed 'A Gentlewoman to A Gentleman', in a verse miscellany compiled by an Oxford man; mid-17th century.

Bodleian, MS CCC. 176, f. 32v.

RaW 457 -----

Copy, headed 'A conference betwixt 2 lovers', in a verse miscellany; c. 1630s.

This MS recorded in Latham.

Bodleian, MS Douce f. 5, fol. 18v.

RaW 458 -----

Copy, headed 'Of loue' and here beginning 'Loue, or doe not say doe', in a verse miscellany compiled by an Oxford man and once owned by one Henry Lawson; c. 1630s.

Bodleian, MS Eng. poet. e. 14, f. 82.

RaW 459 -----

Copy, headed 'A Dialogue between a man and woman', in a verse miscellany compiled by Robert Codrington (1602-65); c. 1638.

Bodleian, MS Eng. poet. f. 27, p. 213.

RaW 460 -----

Copy, headed 'A Lady to her Louer', transcribed from RaW 461, in a verse miscellany possibly compiled by a member of an Inn of Court; c. 1630s.

British Library, Add. MS 21433, f. 95r-v.

'Say not you love, unless you do'

RaW 461 -----

Copy, headed 'A ladye to hyr Louer', in a miscellany possibly compiled by a member of an Inn of Court; c. 1620s-30s.

British Library, Add. MS 25303, f. 90.

RaW 462 -----

Copy, headed 'Sr Walter Ralegh & a Lady', in a miscellany compiled by Anthony Scattergood (1611-87) of Trinity College, Cambridge; c. 1632-40.

Printed from this MS in Hazlitt (1870).

British Library, Add. MS 44963, f. 37v.

RaW 462.5 See Addenda, p. 633.

RaW 463 -----

Copy, headed 'On 2 louers A dialogue', in a verse miscellany probably compiled by one 'I.A.' of Christ Church, Oxford, and later owned by Robert Killigrew; c. early 1630s.

British Library, Sloane MS 1792, f. 76.

RaW 464 -----

Copy, headed 'his M^rs', in a miscellany; c. 1620s-43.

Cambridge University Library, MS Add. 7196, f. [5v rev.].

RaW 465 -----

Copy, headed 'Dialogue', in a verse miscellany owned in 1623 and probably compiled by one Richard Jackson; c. 1620s-30s.

Edinburgh University Library, MS H.-P. Coll. 401, f. 12.

RaW 466 -----

Copy, headed 'A Lady to D^r. Donne', in a verse miscellany compiled by an Oxford man; c. 1630s.

Folger, MS V. a. 170, p. 49.

RaW 467 -----

Second copy, headed 'A dialogue. J.D', in a verse miscellany compiled by an Oxford man; c. 1630s.

Folger, MS V. a. 170, p. 175.

RaW 468 -----

Copy, headed 'A Dialogue', in a verse miscellany; c. 1630s.

Folger, MS V. a. 245, f. 43.

RaW 469 -----

Copy, headed 'A conference between two Louers', in a verse miscellany; c. 1640.

Folger, MS V. a. 319, f. 42v.

RaW 470 -----

Copy, headed 'two Louers', in a verse miscellany; mid-17th century.

Folger, MS V. a. 322, p. 1*.

RaW 471 -----

Copy, headed 'A conference betwixt 2 louers', deleted, in a miscellany; c. 1630.

Folger, MS V. a. 345, p. 27.

RaW 472 -----

Copy in a verse miscellany compiled by one or two Oxford men, possibly connected with New College and afterwards with the Inns of Court; 1630s.

Harvard, MS Eng 686, f. 87v.

RaW 473 -----

Copy, headed 'A Gentlewoman to Doctour Dun', in a miscellany compiled by an Oxford man, possibly a member of Brasenose College; c. late 1630s.

Huntington, HM 116, p. 12.

RaW 474 -----

Copy, headed 'A ladyes speech to her suitour', in a miscellany; c. 1630s.

John Rylands University Library of Manchester, Rylands English MS 410, f. 22v.

RaW 475 -----

Copy in a verse miscellany possibly once owned by Sir John Reresby (d. 1646); among the papers of the Savile family, formerly of Methley Hall, near Pontefract; c. 1630s.

Leeds Archives Department, MX 237, f. 8v.

'Say not you love, unless you do'

RaW 476 -----

Copy, headed 'Doctor Dunns Answer to a ladie', in a verse miscellany; c. 1643-50s.

University of Newcastle upon Tyne, MS Bell/White 25, f. 38.

RaW 476.3, 476.5, 476.8 See Addenda, p. 633.

RaW 477 -----

Copy, headed 'A dialogue', in a verse miscellany; c. 1640.

Yale, Osborn Collection, b 62, p. 16.

--- -----

See also INTRODUCTION.

RaW 478 *'Shall I, like an hermit, dwell'.*

Copy in a musical setting by Robert Johnson in a MS songbook; c. 1640s.

First pub. in *The London Magazine* (1734), p. 444; listed but not printed in Latham, p. 173. Printed from this MS in Norman Ault, *A Treasury of Unfamiliar Lyrics* (London, 1938), p. 124.

Bodleian, MS Don. c. 57, f. 36v.

RaW 479 -----

Copy in a MS volume of poems chiefly by Donne; c. 1620s.

Harvard, MS Eng 966.7, f. 16v.

RaW 480 -----

Copy of a four-stanza version in a musical setting by Robert Johnson in a MS music book owned (in 1659) and partly compiled by the composer John Gamble; c. 1630s-50s.

New York Public Library, Music Division, Drexel MS 4257, No. 259.

RaW 481 -----

Copy, allegedly in the hand of Sir Henry Goodyer (1571-1627), in a MS collection of poems once owned by Sir Kenelm Digby (1603-65); early 17th century.

Printed from this MS in *Poems from Sir Kenelm Digby's Papers, in the possession of Henry A. Bright*, Roxburghe Club (London, 1877), pp. 32-3; the hand identified as Goodyer's by Sir George Warner (pp. 34-6).

Unlocated.

RaW 482 *'So lies my lovinge heart conceald'.*

Copy, ascribed in another hand to 'W.R.', in a miscellany later owned by one Joseph Hall; c. 1630s-50s.

First pub. (from this MS) in Latham (1951), p. 169, as a doubtfully ascribed fragment.

Folger, MS V. a. 339, f. 207.

RaW 483 *A songe made by Sir Water Rawley* ('What teares (Deare Prince) can serue to water all').

Copy of the first stanza in a musical setting by Robert Ramsey in a MS songbook; c. 1640s.

First pub. in Latham (1929); Latham (1951), p. 52; of doubtful authorship according to Latham, pp. 145-6, and Lefranc (1968), p. 84. Edited from this MS in *English Songs 1625-1660*, ed. Ian Spink, Musica Britannica XXXIII (London, 1971), No. 12.

Bodleian, MS Don. c. 57, f. 20.

RaW 484 -----

Copy in a musical setting by Robert Ramsey in a MS songbook chiefly compiled by one 'T.C.'; c. 1656-9.

This MS recorded in Spink.

British Library, Add. MS 11608, f. 26.

RaW 485 -----

Copy in a verse miscellany; c. 1630s.

Printed from this MS in Latham.

British Library, Add. MS 22118, f. 31.

RaW 486 *'The state of Fraunce as nowe it standes'.*

Copy in a miscellany compiled by a Cambridge student, possibly Sir John Finett (1571-1641) of Fordwich, Kent; c. 1586-91.

First pub. in *A Catalogue of the Harleian Manuscripts in the British Museum* (London, 1808), III, 78; listed but not printed in Latham, p. 172. This MS collated in Steven W. May, '"The French Primero": A Study in Renaissance Textual Transmission and Taste', *ELN*, 9 (1971-2), 102-8.

Bodleian, MS Rawl. poet. 85, f. 104.

RaW 487 -----

Copy, headed 'The French Primero', in a notebook compiled by Sir Stephen Powle, Clerk of the Crown; c. 1606-9.

This MS collated in May.

Bodleian, MS Tanner 169, f. 70v.

RaW 488 -----

Copy, headed 'The State of Fraunce translated oute of frenche into Englyshe Anno domini 1585', in a miscellany chiefly of heraldic and historical collections compiled by Robert Commaundre, Rector of Tarporley, Cheshire (d. 1613); late 16th-early 17th century.

This MS collated in May.

British Library, Egerton MS 2642, ff. 232v, 236.

RaW 488.5 See Addenda, p. 633.

RaW 489 -----

Copy, subjoined to 'A coppy of a lettre sent by the great lord to the King of Novarr. translated out of greek into ffrenshe and soe into English', in a composite volume of tracts and papers; late 16th-early 17th century.

Printed from this MS in *Catalogue of Harleian Manuscripts* (1808); collated in May; recorded in Latham.

British Library, Harley MS 3787, f. 214v.

RaW 490 -----

Copy in a verse miscellany compiled by the antiquary St Loe Kniveton of Gray's Inn; c. 1585-90s.

This MS collated in May; recorded in Latham.

British Library, Harley MS 7392, f. 62v.

RaW 491 -----

Copy in a verse miscellany compiled by Henry Stanford, household tutor in the Carey family; c. 1585-98.

Printed from this MS in May.

Cambridge University Library, MS Dd. 5. 75, f. 29.

RaW 492 -----

Copy in a verse miscellany owned before 1610 by Anne Cornwallis, afterwards Countess of Argyll; c. 1590s.

This MS collated in May; recorded in Latham.

Folger, MS V. a. 89, pp. 32-3.

RaW 493 -----

Copy, headed 'Tempore Hen: 3', in a MS volume of poems by Donne once owned by John Egerton, first Earl of Bridgewater (1579-1649); c. 1622-3.

This MS recorded (but not seen) in May.

Huntington, EL 6893, f. 48v.

RaW 494 -----

Copy in a miscellany once owned by one Robert Thornton; c. 1580s-90s.

This MS collated in May.

Marsh's Library, Dublin, MS Z 3.5.21, f. 22.

RaW 495 -----

Copy, endorsed 'Verses of the Civill Vprores in Fraunc', on a single leaf among the papers of the Clifton family of Clifton Hall, Nottinghamshire; early-mid-17th century.

University of Nottingham, Clifton MS Cl LM 19.

RaW 496 -----

Copy, headed in a later hand 'On the State of France under ye Administration of ye Guises by Sr Walter Rawleigh', in a collection of state papers; c. 1600-10.

Printed from this MS in Curt F. Bühler, 'Four Elizabethan Poems', *Joseph Quincy Adams Memorial Studies* (Washington, D.C., 1948), 695-706 (pp. 700-1); collated in May; recorded in Latham.

Pierpont Morgan Library, R-V. R. of E. (Eliz. 1), No. 48.

RaW 496.5 See Addenda, p. 633.

--- *'Thou sentst to me a heart was crowned'*.

See INTRODUCTION.

RaW 497 *Vertue the best monument* ('Not Caesars birth made Caesar to suruiue').

Copy, ascribed to 'Sr Walt: Raleighe', in a verse miscellany probably compiled by Francis Baskerville of Malmesbury, Wiltshire, and owned in 1663 by William Wallrond; c. 1633.

First pub. (from this MS) in Latham (1929); Latham (1951), p. 53; of doubtful authorship according to Latham, p. 147, and Lefranc (1968), p. 84.

British Library, Sloane MS 1446, f. 24v.

RaW 498 *'When first this circell Round, this buildinge faire'*.

Copy, headed 'Certaine hellish verses devysed by that Atheist and traitor Ralegh as it is said', in a collection of state papers; 1603.

First pub. as part of the anonymous play *The First Part of the Tragicall Raigne of Selimus* (London, 1594); listed but not printed in Latham, p. 173. Printed from this MS in *HMC*, 2nd Report (1871), Appendix, p. 52, and in Jean Jacquot, 'Ralegh's "Hellish Verses" and the "Tragicall Raigne of Selimus"', *MLR*, 48 (1953), 1-9.

Owned by the Marquess of Bath, Longleat House, Portland Papers, I, f. 191.

RaW 499 -----

Copy, headed 'Certaine hellish verses devised by that Atheist and traitour Rawley as yt is said', in Volume II of a collection of state papers formerly owned by the Malet family of Wilbury, Wiltshire; [1603].

This MS recorded in *HMC*, 5th Report (1876), Appendix, p. 311, and in Latham and in Jacquot.

British Library, Add. MS 32092, f. 201.

RaW 500 *'Wrong not, deare Empresse of my Heart'.*

Copy, prefixed by 'Passions are likened best to floods, and streames' (see RaW 320), in a verse miscellany once owned by Elizabeth Lane and John Finch; c. 1630s.

First pub. in *Wits Interpreter* (London, 1655), printed twice, the first version prefixed by 'Our Passions are most like to Floods and streames' (see RaW 320-38) and headed 'To his Mistresse by Sir Walter Raleigh'; printed with the prefixed stanza in Latham, pp. 18-19; printed in *The English and Latin Poems of Sir Robert Ayton*, ed. Charles B. Gullans, STS, 4th Ser. 1 (Edinburgh & London, 1963), pp. 197-8. This poem probably written by Sir Robert Ayton: for a discussion of the authorship and the different texts see Gullans, pp. 318-26 (also printed in *SB*, 13 (1960), 191-8).

Aberdeen University Library, MS 29, pp. 171-2.

RaW 501 -----

Copy of stanzas 1-7, subscribed 'Lo: Walden', now in an illegible state, in a miscellany; c. 1621-31.

This MS recorded in Latham, p. 116, and in Gullans.

Bodleian, MS Ashmole 781, p. 143.

RaW 502 -----

Copy of stanzas 1-7, headed 'To his M^{rs}' and here beginning 'Wronge not deare M^{rs} of my harte', in a verse miscellany later used by William Fulman (1632-88); c. 1630.

This MS recorded in Gullans.

Bodleian, MS CCC. 327, ff. 10v-11.

RaW 503 -----

Copy, headed 'A paradox y^{t} silence is ye best suiter', in a verse miscellany compiled by an Oxford man, possibly a member of Wadham College, and later used by William Fulman (1632-88); c. late 1630s.

This MS collated in Gullans.

Bodleian, MS CCC. 328, f. 78r-v.

RaW 504 -----

Copy of stanzas 1, 3, 4, 2 and 7 in a verse miscellany compiled by the Yorkshire antiquary John Hopkinson (1610-80); c. 1647.

This MS recorded in Gullans.

Bodleian, MS Don. d. 58, f. 22v.

RaW 505 -----

Copy of stanzas 1, 3, 4, 2 and 7, headed 'A Song', in a verse miscellany compiled by an Oxford man and once owned by one Henry Lawson; c. 1630s.

This MS recorded in Latham, p. 116, and in Gullans.

Bodleian, MS Eng. poet. e. 14, f. 19.

RaW 506 -----

Copy in a MS volume of poems chiefly by Donne compiled by Henry Champernowne (1600-56) of Dartington, Devon; c. 1623.

This MS recorded in Latham, p. 116.

Bodleian, MS Eng. poet. f. 9, p. 6.

RaW 507 -----

Copy, headed 'The silent wooer', in a verse miscellany compiled by Robert Codrington (1602-65); c. 1638.

Bodleian, MS Eng. poet. f. 27, pp. 150-1.

RaW 508 -----

Copy, prefixed by 'Our passions are most like to floods & streames' (see RaW 325), in a verse miscellany; c. 1630s.

Printed from this MS in Norman Ault, *Elizabethan Lyrics*, 4th edition (London, 1966), pp. 284-5; collated in Gullans; recorded in Latham, p. 115.

Bodleian, MS Rawl. poet. 160, f. 117.

RaW 509 -----

Copy, with corrections in the hand of Sir John Ayton, in his MS volume of poems by his uncle Sir Robert Ayton; c. 1660s.

Printed from this MS in *The Oxford Book of Seventeenth Century Verse* (Oxford, 1958), pp. 85-6; collated in Gullans; recorded in Latham, p. 116.

British Library, Add. MS 10308, ff. 9v-10.

'Wrong not, deare Empresse of my Heart'

RaW 510 -----

Copy, prefixed by 'Passions are likened best to flouds and streames' (see RaW 326) and subscribed 'S^{r} W: R:', transcribed from RaW 513, in a verse miscellany possibly compiled by a member of an Inn of Court; c. 1630s.

This MS collated in Gullans; recorded in Latham, p. 115.

British Library, Add. MS 21433, ff. 112v-13v.

RaW 511 -----

Copy, prefixed by 'Our Passions are most like to Floods and streames' (see RaW 327), in a verse miscellany; mid-17th century.

Printed from this MS in Latham; collated in Gullans.

British Library, Add. MS 22602, ff. 30v-1.

RaW 512 -----

Copy in a composite volume of verse among the 'Conway Papers' chiefly descended from Sir Edward Conway, Viscount Conway (d. 1631) of Conway Castle; early 17th century.

This MS collated in Gullans; recorded in Latham, p. 116.

British Library, Add. MS 23229, f. 54r-v.

RaW 513 -----

Copy, prefixed by 'Passions are likened beste to flouds & streams' (see RaW 328) and subscribed 'S^{r} W R ', in a miscellany possibly compiled by a member of an Inn of Court; c. 1620s-30s.

This MS collated in Gullans; recorded in Latham, p. 115.

British Library, Add. MS 25303, f. 118r-v.

RaW 514 -----

Copy in Scottish orthography, subscribed 'finis quod sumbodie', in a composite volume of verse and prose collected by Peter Le Neve (1661-1729), his brother Oliver, and Thomas Martin (1697-1771) of Palgrave; early 17th century.

This MS collated in Gullans; recorded in Latham, p. 116.

British Library, Add. MS 27407, f. 129.

RaW 515 -----

Copy in a MS volume of poems by Sir Robert Ayton; c. 1670s.

This MS collated in Gullans; recorded in Latham, p. 116.

British Library, Add. MS 28622, f. 18r-v.

RaW 516 -----

Copy of stanzas 1, 3, 4, 6-8 in a composite volume of verse and prose; late 17th century.

This MS recorded in Latham, p. 116, and in Gullans.

British Library, Egerton MS 2560, f. 114.

RaW 517 -----

Copy of stanzas 1, 3, 4, 6-8, in a verse miscellany compiled by Arthur Capell; mid-17th century.

This MS recorded in Latham, p. 116, and in Gullans.

British Library, Harley MS 3511, ff. 12v-13.

RaW 518 -----

Copy, headed 'An Ode', in a verse miscellany compiled by one Thomas Crosse; c. 1630s.

This MS collated in Gullans; recorded in Latham, p. 115.

British Library, Harley MS 6057, f. 18.

RaW 519 -----

Copy, headed 'To his Mistresse' and ascribed to 'S^{r}: Walter Rawleigh', among poems appended to a MS volume of poems by William Browne of Tavistock, probably compiled by a member of an Inn of Court; c. 1637-50.

This MS collated in Gullans; recorded in Latham, p. 115.

British Library, Lansdowne MS 777, f. 63r-v.

RaW 520 -----

Copy of stanzas 1-7, headed 'The Lord Walden to ye princesse Eliz:' and here beginning 'Wrong not dear mistress of my heart', in a verse miscellany; c. 1637.

This MS recorded in Gullans.

British Library, Stowe MS 962, f. 185r-v.

RaW 521 -----

Copy, ascribed to 'W: R:', in a miscellany; c. 1620s-43.

Cambridge University Library, MS Add. 7196, f. [5r-v rev.].

'Wrong not, deare Empresse of my Heart'

RaW 522 -----

Copy of stanzas 1-7, here beginning 'Wrong (not dear m^{rs}: of my heart' and set out as two poems, in a miscellany owned in the late 17th century by one John Peck; mid-17th century.

This MS recorded in Gullans.

Cambridge University Library, MS Ee. 5. 23, pp. 6-7.

RaW 523 -----

Copy, headed 'Songe', in a verse miscellany; c. 1630s-40s.

This MS collated in Gullans.

Edinburgh University Library, MS La. III. 436, pp. 20-1.

RaW 524 -----

Copy, ascribed to 'S^{r}: Walter Raleigh', in a verse miscellany owned in 1691 by one Thomas White; c. 1640.

Formerly MS 1.21, this MS collated in Gullans; recorded in Latham, p. 115.

Folger, MS V. a. 96, ff. 62-3.

RaW 525 -----

Copy, prefixed by 'Passions are likned best to flouds and streames' (see RaW 331), in a verse miscellany; c. 1630.

Formerly MS 1.28, this MS collated in Gullans; recorded in Latham, p. 115.

Folger, MS V. a. 103, Part I, f. 30.

RaW 526 -----

Copy, headed 'A silent wooer', in a miscellany; c. 1630.

Formerly MS 452.5, this MS collated in Gullans; recorded in Latham, p. 116.

Folger, MS V. a. 345, pp. 90-1.

RaW 527 -----

Copy of lines 1-2, 5-28, 31-2, prefixed by 'Passions are likn'd best to flouds & streams' (see RaW 333), in a miscellany compiled by an Oxford man, possibly a member of Brasenose College; c. late 1630s.

This MS recorded in Gullans.

Huntington, HM 116, pp. 17-18.

RaW 528 -----

Copy in a MS volume of poems chiefly by Donne once owned by one Meriall Tracy; c. 1620-33.

This MS recorded in Gullans.

Huntington, HM 198, Part II, ff. 52v-3.

RaW 529 -----

Copy in the hand of William Parkhurst (fl. 1604-67) in a composite volume of MSS collected by him; among the papers of the Finch family of Burley-on-the-Hill, Rutland; 1600s-41.

Leicestershire Record Office, DG. 7/Lit. 2, f. 351.

RaW 530 -----

Copy, transcribed from an early MS source, in a collection of transcripts of ballads made chiefly by Robert Jamieson (1780?-1844); c. 1800.

This MS recorded in G. Neilson, 'A Bundle of Ballads', *E & S*, 7 (1921), 108-42 (p. 111).

Mitchell Library, Glasgow, 308897, p. 19.

RaW 531 -----

Copy of a sixteen-line version in a musical setting in a MS songbook ('Earl Ferrers' MS'); c. 1640.

Printed partly from this MS in John P. Cutts, 'Drexel Manuscript 4041', *MD*, 18 (1964), 151-202 (p. 181).

New York Public Library, Music Division, Drexel MS 4041, No. 58, f. 42v.

RaW 532 -----

Second copy of a sixteen-line version in a musical setting in 'Earl Ferrers' MS'; c. 1640.

Printed partly from this MS in Cutts, p. 181.

New York Public Library, Music Division, Drexel MS 4041, No. 65, f. 46.

RaW 533 -----

Copy in a musical setting in a MS songbook once owned by a certain Anne Twice; c. 1620.

This MS collated in John P. Cutts, '"Songs vnto the Violl and Lute"--Drexel MS 4175', *MD*, 16 (1962), 72-92 (pp. 85-6).

New York Public Library, Music Division, Drexel MS 4175, No. xxviii.

'Wrong not, deare Empresse of my Heart'

RaW 534 -----

Copy of a garbled version in a musical setting in a MS music book owned (in 1659) and partly compiled by the composer John Gamble; c. 1630s-50s.

This MS recorded in Cutts, *MD*, 16 (1962), 85.

New York Public Library, Music Division, Drexel MS 4257, No. 211.

RaW 535 -----

Copy, prefixed by 'Passions are likened best to Flouds and Streames' (see RaW 335), in a verse miscellany; c. 1630.

University of Nottingham, Portland MS Pw V 37, p. 61.

RaW 536 -----

Copy in a verse miscellany used by members of the Holgate family of Saffron Walden, Essex; c. 1630s.

Pierpont Morgan Library, MA 1057, pp. 134-5.

RaW 537 -----

Copy, prefixed by 'Passions are likened to floods & streams' (see RaW 336), in a verse miscellany; c. 1634.

Formerly Rosenbach 189, this MS recorded in Latham, pp. 115-16; recorded (but not seen) in Gullans.

Rosenbach Foundation, MS 239/27, pp. 50-1.

RaW 538 -----

Copy, prefixed by 'Passions are most like to shades and dreames' (see RaW 337), in a miscellany partly compiled by one Robert Berkeley; c. 1640.

Formerly Rosenbach 195, this MS recorded in Latham, p. 116; recorded (but not seen) in Gullans.

Rosenbach Foundation, MS 240/2, p. 5.

RaW 539 -----

Copy, headed 'A Songe', in a miscellany compiled by or for Sir Thomas Finch, Viscount Maidstone and Earl of Winchelsea; c. 1634.

Formerly Rosenbach 190, this MS recorded in Latham, p. 116; recorded (but not seen) in Gullans.

Rosenbach Foundation, MS 243/4, p. 7.

RaW 540 -----

Copy, headed 'Sonnett: to his Dearest', in a verse miscellany compiled by one Robert Bishop; c. 1630.

Formerly Rosenbach 187, this MS recorded in Latham, p. 116; recorded (but not seen) in Gullans.

Rosenbach Foundation, MS 1083/16, pp. 49-50.

RaW 541 -----

Copy, here ascribed to 'Lo: Wal.', in a verse miscellany compiled by Tobias Alston (1620-c.1639) of Sayham Hall, near Sudbury, Suffolk; c. 1639.

Yale, Osborn Collection, b 197, p. 212.

RaW 542 -----

Copy, headed 'To his Mistresse', in a miscellany; mid-17th century.

Yale, Osborn Collection, b 200, pp. 78-9.

PROSE

RaW 543 *Apology for his Voyage to Guiana.*

Copy in a volume of tracts and letters relating to seafaring once owned and annotated by Francis Russell, fourth Earl of Bedford (1593-1641); early-mid-17th century.

First pub. in *Judicious and Select Essays and Observations* (London, 1650); *Works* (1829), VIII, 477-97; edited by V.T. Harlow in *Ralegh's Last Voyage* (London, 1932), pp. 316-34.

Owned by the Duke of Bedford, Bedford Office, London, Woburn MSS HMC No. 261, pp. 445-518.

RaW 544 -----

Copy in three or four hands, in a composite volume of historical and state papers collected by Elias Ashmole (1617-92); early-mid-17th century.

Bodleian, MS Ashmole 830, ff. 87-103v.

RaW 545 -----

Copy in a volume of four works by Ralegh; early-mid-17th century.

Formerly Mostyn MS 142, this MS recorded in *HMC*, 4th Report (1874), Appendix, p. 353; printed from this MS in Harlow, pp. 316-34.

Bodleian, MS Eng. hist. d. 138, ff. 8-40.

RaW 546 -----

Copy in a volume of state papers; early-mid-17th century.

Bodleian, MS Jesus College, 83, ff. 60-8v.

Apology for his Voyage to Guiana

RaW 547 -----

Copy in a volume of state papers; early-mid-17th century.

Bodleian, MS Rawl. D. 180, ff. 25-41.

RaW 548 -----

Copy in a volume of letters and tracts compiled by Archbishop William Sancroft (1617-93); mid-late 17th century.

Bodleian, MS Tanner 299, ff. 15-24v.

RaW 549 -----

Copy in a volume of state papers constituting Volume LXVIII of the Vernon Papers principally collected by James Vernon (1646-1727) and his son Edward; mid-17th century.

British Library, Add. MS 40838, ff. 36v-48v.

RaW 550 -----

Copy; early-mid-17th century.

British Library, Sloane MS 760.

RaW 551 -----

Copy in a volume of state papers; early-mid-17th century.

British Library, Sloane MS 1856, ff. 63-71.

RaW 552 -----

Copy in a volume of state tracts and letters once owned by the antiquary Sir Peter Leycester (1614-78); early-mid-17th century.

Among the Tabley House MSS, this MS recorded in *HMC*, 1st Report (1870), Appendix, pp. 47-8.

Cheshire Record Office, DLT/B8, pp. 283-300.

RaW 553 -----

Copy among the papers of the Gell family, formerly of Hopton Hall, Derbyshire; early-mid-17th century.

This MS recorded in *HMC*, 9th Report, Part II (1884), Appendix, p. 386.

Derbyshire Record Office, D 258/67/6c.

RaW 554 -----

Copy in a volume of state tracts; early-mid-17th century.

Gonville and Caius College, Cambridge, MS 73/40, ff. 205-13v.

RaW 555 -----

Copy, bound with two other tracts; early-mid-17th century.

Inner Temple Library, Petyt MS 526, ff. 43-50.

RaW 556 -----

Copy, the third item in a volume of tracts by Ralegh; early-mid-17th century.

Institution of Electrical Engineers, London, (among the MSS of Silvanus Phillips Thompson, [no ref. number]).

RaW 556.5 See Addenda, p. 633.

RaW 557 -----

Copy in a volume of transcripts of Ralegh's last letters, among the papers of the Knatchbull family of Mersham-le-Hatch and related families; early-mid-17th century.

Kent Archives Office, U951 Z6, pp. 19-86.

RaW 558 -----

Copy in a volume of miscellaneous verse and prose among the collections of Archbishop Thomas Tenison (1636-1715); 17th century.

Lambeth Palace, MS 806, No. 16.

RaW 559 -----

Copy in a volume of transcripts of letters by Ralegh and other state papers; mid-17th century.

Formerly owned by F. Bacon Frank of Campsall Hall, Yorkshire, this MS recorded in *HMC*, 6th Report (1877), Appendix, p. 459.

Owned by Agnes Latham, Pickering, Bacon Frank MS, pp. 133-58.

RaW 560 -----

Copy in a composite volume of MSS belonging to the Fairfax family; eight leaves; imperfect, lacking beginning and end; early-mid-17th century.

Formerly among the Ingilby MSS at Ripley Castle, Yorkshire, this MS recorded in *HMC*, 6th Report (1877), Appendix, p. 362.

National Maritime Museum, MS AND/25, No. 13a.

RaW 561 -----

Copy; early-mid-17th century.

University of North Carolina, CSWR A30, pp. 5-23.

Apology for his Voyage to Guiana

RaW 562 -----

Copy among the papers of the Clifton family of Clifton Hall, Nottinghamshire; early-mid-17th century.

This MS recorded in *HMC*, 55, Various Collections, VII (1914), p. 395.

University of Nottingham, Clifton MS Cl LP 5/1.

RaW 563 -----

Copy; eight leaves; imperfect, lacking the beginning; c. 1618?

Public Record Office, SP.14/98/48.

RaW 564 -----

Copy, possibly transcribed from RaW 563; seven leaves; imperfect, lacking the beginning; 17th century.

Public Record Office, SP.14/98/49.

RaW 565 -----

Copy apparently transcribed by one A. Throkmorton for an aristocratic friend, with Throkmorton's accompanying letter (on f. 1r-v) dated 31 October 1618; in a volume of state tracts; [1618].

St John's College, Cambridge, MS I. 4. (James 305), ff. [2-11v].

RaW 566 -----

Copy in a composite volume of state papers; early-mid-17th century.

Trinity College, Cambridge, MS R. 5. 12 (James 707), ff. 172-5v.

RaW 567 -----

Copy in a volume of works chiefly by Ralegh; early-mid-17th century.

Dr Williams's Library, MS Jones B. 60, pp. 169-211.

RaW 568 -----

Copy in a volume of state tracts once owned by Sir Richard Grosvenor (1585-1645); c. 1640.

Formerly owned by the Duke of Westminster, Eaton Hall, Cheshire, this MS recorded in *HMC*, 3rd Report (1872), Appendix, p. 215; a microfilm is in the British Library (RP 83).

Yale, Osborn Collection, fb 40, pp. 513-44.

RaW 569 -----

Copy in a folio volume of tracts attributed to Ralegh; 17th century.

Formerly among the Finch MSS at Burley-on-the-Hill, Rutland, this MS recorded in *HMC*, 7th Report (1879), Appendix, p. 516.

Unlocated (not with the Finch MSS in the Leicestershire Record Office and possibly destroyed in a fire in 1908).

RaW 570 -----

Three-page abstract of the tract, headed 'Out of the Apologie of Sr Walter Ralegh after his unfortunate sucesse in Guiaiana. 1618' and here beginning 'My ill success was not without example...', in a volume of state papers; early 17th century.

British Library, Cotton MS Titus C. VII, ff. 96-7.

--- -----

See also INTRODUCTION.

--- *A Breviary of the History of England, with the Reign of King William I.*

See SAMUEL DANIEL, DaS 31-9.

--- *The Cabinet-Council: containing the chief Arts of Empire and Mysteries of State.*

See INTRODUCTION.

*RaW 571 *Considerations concerning Reprysalles.*

Autograph memorandum on one leaf; untitled; endorsed by Secretary Thomas Windebank; c. February 1602/3.

First pub. (from this MS) in John Payne Collier, 'Sir Walter Raleigh. Additional Papers', *N & Q*, 3rd Ser. 5 (12 March 1864), 207-8. Discussed (when the MS was unlocated) in Lefranc (1968), p. 52, and the MS subsequently rediscovered by Pierre Lefranc.

Public Record Office, SP.12/253/117.

*RaW 572 *A Dialogue between a Counsellor of State and a Justice of the Peace.*

Copy, with a few minor autograph corrections and additions in the dedicatory epistle to King James, in a volume of tracts owned by Ralegh (see RaW 727); c. 1615.

First pub. as *The Prerogative of Parliaments*

in England ('Midelburge' and 'Hamburg' [i.e. London], 1628); *Works* (1829), VIII, 151-221.

On temporary loan to the Fitzwilliam Museum, Cambridge: Bradfer-Lawrence 61, ff. 148-70v.

RaW 573 -----

Copy in a volume of state papers; early-mid-17th century.

Bodleian, MS Jones 56, ff. 36v-46v.

RaW 574 -----

Copy in a volume of state tracts; early-mid-17th century.

Bodleian, MS Tanner 103, ff. 213-20.

RaW 575 -----

Copy in a volume of Ralegh's works constituting Volume XXI of the collections of Macvey Napier (1776-1847); imperfect; early-mid-17th century.

British Library, Add. MS 34631, ff. 20-46v.

RaW 576 -----

Two-leaf fragment of a copy, in a composite volume of state papers and tracts; early-mid-17th century.

British Library, Harley MS 248, ff. 107-8v.

RaW 577 -----

Fragment of a copy, comprising only the last portion, in a composite volume of tracts; early-mid-17th century.

British Library, Harley MS 4685, ff. 115-26v.

RaW 578 -----

Copy; early-mid-17th century.

British Library, Harley MS 6191.

RaW 579 -----

Copy in a volume of state tracts; early-mid-17th century.

British Library, Lansdowne MS 806, ff. 28-39.

RaW 580 -----

Copy in Volume XI of a collection of state papers assembled by Sir Thomas Edmondes (1563?-1633); [1615-33].

British Library, Stowe MS 177, ff. 138-70.

RaW 581 -----

Copy in a composite volume of state tracts once owned by John Patrick (1632-95); mid-17th century.

Cambridge University Library, MS Add. 27, ff. i, 1-18v.

RaW 582 -----

Copy in a composite volume of tracts; early-mid-17th century.

Cambridge University Library, MS Dd. 3. 85, (1).

RaW 583 -----

Copy; early-mid-17th century.

Cambridge University Library, MS Mm. 5. 8.

RaW 584 -----

Copy in a volume of tracts; early-mid-17th century.

University of Chicago, MS 870, ff. 1-53v.

RaW 585 -----

Copy; early-mid-17th century.

This MS formerly Phillipps MS 34507 and once owned by T.N. Brushfield.

Devon Record Office, Exeter, MS 36.

RaW 586 -----

Copy of the dedicatory epistle to King James and of the beginning of the dialogue in a volume of collections relating to parliament compiled by one 'W.L.'; subscribed in another hand 'Perlegi et pro Libitu Excerpsi Aug. 5. 1697. W.K.'; incomplete; mid-17th century.

Exeter College, Oxford, MS 139, ff. 190v-2.

RaW 587 -----

Copy in a volume of state papers compiled by Sir Roger Twysden (1597-1672); inscribed by Twysden 'The lady Raleigh did assure me this was her husbands doeing i Rog: Twysden: 1622'.

Folger, MS G. b. 7, ff. 47-73.

RaW 588 -----

Copy in a volume of state letters and tracts; early-mid-17th century.

This MS sold at Sotheby's, 4 July 1955 (André de Coppet sale), Lot 950.

Folger, MS G. b. 9, ff. 1-61v.

A Dialogue between a Counsellor of State and a Justice of the Peace

RaW 589 -----

Copy; early-mid-17th century.

Folger, MS V. b. 230.

RaW 590 -----

Copy; early-mid-17th century.

This MS sold at Sotheby's, 2 March 1965, Lot 311.

Folger, MS V. b. 276.

RaW 591 -----

Copy in a composite volume of state tracts, once owned by John Egerton, first Earl of Bridgewater (1579-1649); incomplete; early-mid-17th century.

Huntington, EL 7976, No. 5.

RaW 592 -----

Copy among the papers of the De L'Isle (Sidney) family of Penshurst Place; early-mid-17th century.

This MS recorded in *HMC*, 3rd Report (1872), Appendix, p. 230.

Kent Archives Office, U 1475 Z7.

RaW 593 -----

Copy; 60 leaves numbered 1-116; early-mid-17th century.

Owned by Agnes Latham, Pickering.

RaW 594 -----

Copy among the papers of the Hatton family, formerly of Holdenby and Kirby Hall, Northamptonshire; early-mid-17th century.

This MS recorded in *HMC*, 1st Report (1870), Appendix, p. 32.

Northamptonshire Record Office, F.H. 71.

RaW 595 -----

Copy of part of the work among the papers of the Clifton family of Clifton Hall, Nottinghamshire; early-mid-17th century.

University of Nottingham, Clifton MS Cl LP 5/2, pp. 3-13.

RaW 596 -----

Copy, once owned by, and some passages marked in the hand of, Sir John Eliot (1592-1632); [1615-32].

This MS recorded in *HMC*, 1st Report (1870), Appendix, p. 42.

Owned by Lord Eliot, Port Eliot, Cornwall (possession confirmed by letter 9 September 1975).

RaW 597 -----

Copy; this or RaW 598 possibly submitted by Ralegh to James I; c. 1615.

Public Record Office, SP.14/84/44.

RaW 598 -----

Copy; this or RaW 597 possibly submitted by Ralegh to James I; c. 1615.

Public Record Office, SP.14/85.

RaW 599 -----

Copy in a volume of tracts once owned by Thomas Wentworth, first Earl of Strafford (1593-1641); c. 1617.

Sheffield Central Library, Wentworth Woodhouse Muniments, MSS and Treatises 1, ff. 95-130.

RaW 600 -----

Copy in a miscellany; late 17th century.

Yale, Osborn Collection, b 52/2, pp. 1-108.

RaW 601 -----

Copy in a folio volume also containing a copy of a letter from Ralegh to the King and a late 17th-century tract 'Of the Antiquitie of Parliament'; 17th century.

Formerly among the MSS of the Winnington family of Stanford Court, Worcestershire, this MS recorded in *HMC*, 1st Report (1870), Appendix, p. 53.

Unlocated (Stanford Court destroyed by fire in 1882).

RaW 602 -----

Copy in a composite volume of tracts lettered 'Liber B' once owned by Charles Fairfax; 17th century.

This MS formerly Phillipps MS 11138.

Sotheby's, 8 June 1898, Lot 406, sold to Downing; unlocated.

A Dialogue between a Counsellor of State and a Justice of the Peace

RaW 603 -----

Extract from an early version of Ralegh's dedicatory epistle to the King, in a volume of works chiefly by Ralegh; early-mid-17th century.

Dr Williams's Library, MS Jones B. 60, pp. 235-6.

--- -----

See also INTRODUCTION.

RaW 604 *A Dialogue between a Jesuit and a Recusant.*

Copy in a composite volume of state tracts once owned by John Patrick (1632-95); incomplete, ending at p. 62 of the published version; mid-17th century.

First pub. in *An Abridgement of Sir Walter Raleigh's History of the World* (London, 1700); authorship discussed in Lefranc (1968), pp. 59-62.

Cambridge University Library, MS Add. 27, ff. 29-62v.

--- *A Discourse concerneinge peace or warre with Spain.*

See INTRODUCTION.

--- *A Discourse of Sea-ports, principally of the Port and Haven of Dover.*

See INTRODUCTION.

--- *A Discourse of Tenures, which were before the Conquest.*

See INTRODUCTION.

RaW 605 *A Discourse of the Invention of Ships, Anchors, Compass, &c.*

Copy in a volume of tracts and letters relating to seafaring once owned and annotated by Francis Russell, fourth Earl of Bedford (1593-1641); early-mid-17th century.

First pub. in *Judicious and Select Essayes and Observations* (London, 1650); *Works* (1829), VIII, 317-34. This MS recorded in *HMC*, 2nd Report (1871), Appendix, p. 4.

Owned by the Duke of Bedford, Bedford Office, London, Woburn MSS HMC No. 261, pp. 19-64.

RaW 606 -----

Copy in a volume of state papers; early-mid-17th century.

British Library, Sloane MS 1856, ff. 50v-6v.

RaW 607 -----

Copy in a volume of state tracts once owned by Sir Richard Grosvenor (1585-1645); c. 1634.

Formerly owned by the Duke of Westminster, Eaton Hall, Cheshire, this MS recorded in *HMC*, 3rd Report (1872), Appendix, p. 211; a microfilm is in the British Library (RP 170).

Harvard, MS Eng 1266 (27), v. 1, ff. 45-63.

RaW 608 -----

Copy, the first item in a volume of tracts by Ralegh; early-mid-17th century.

Institution of Electrical Engineers, London, (among the MSS of Silvanus Phillips Thompson, [no ref. number]).

RaW 609 -----

Copy in a volume of works chiefly by Ralegh; early-mid-17th century.

Dr Williams's Library, MS Jones B. 60, pp. 65-99.

RaW 610 -----

Copy, complete in 17 folios apparently in original vellum binding (though the title page also includes the title of Ralegh's 'Discourse of...War'); early-mid-17th century.

Formerly Leconfield MS 41 at Petworth House, Sussex, this MS recorded in *HMC*, 6th Report (1877), Appendix, p. 304.

Yale, MS 566.

RaW 611 *A Discourse of the Original and Fundamental Cause of Natural, Arbitrary, Necessary, and Unnatural War.*

Copy in a volume of tracts and letters relating to seafaring once owned and annotated by Francis Russell, fourth Earl of Bedford (1593-1641); early-mid-17th century.

First pub. (in part) in *Judicious and Select Essays and Observations* (London, 1650); pub. complete in *Three Discourses of Sir Walter Ralegh* (London, 1702); *Works* (1829), VIII, 253-97.

Owned by the Duke of Bedford, Bedford Office, London, Woburn MSS HMC No. 261, pp. 65-138.

RaW 612 -----

Copy, untitled, in a volume of works by Ralegh constituting Volume XXI of the collections of Macvey Napier (1776-1847); imperfect; early-mid-17th century.

British Library, Add. MS 34631, ff. 2-19v.

A Discourse of the Original and Fundamental Cause of...War

RaW 613 -----

Copy in a volume of state tracts; late 17th century.

British Library, Harley MS 6274, ff. 149-85v.

RaW 614 -----

Copy in a volume of state papers; early-mid-17th century.

British Library, Lansdowne MS 211, ff. 309-43.

RaW 615 -----

Copy in a volume of state papers; early-mid-17th century.

British Library, Sloane MS 1856, ff. 57-62v.

RaW 616 -----

Copy in a volume of state tracts once owned by Sir Richard Grosvenor (1585-1645); c. 1634.

Formerly owned by the Duke of Westminster, Eaton Hall, Cheshire, this MS recorded in *HMC*, 3rd Report (1872), Appendix, p. 211; a microfilm is in the British Library (RP 170).

Harvard, MS Eng 1266 (28), v. 1, ff. 1-30.

RaW 617 -----

Copy, the second item in a volume of tracts by Ralegh; early-mid-17th century.

Institution of Electrical Engineers, London, (among the MSS of Silvanus Phillips Thompson [no ref. number]).

RaW 618 -----

Copy in a volume of state tracts; early-mid-17th century.

Trinity College, Dublin, MS 732, ff. 68-83.

RaW 619 -----

Copy in a volume of works chiefly by Ralegh; early-mid-17th century.

Dr Williams's Library, MS Jones B. 60, pp. 103-50.

RaW 620 -----

Copy; folio; 17th century.

Formerly among the MSS of the Duke of Marlborough at Blenheim Palace, this MS recorded in *HMC*, 8th Report (1881), Appendix, p. 25.

Unlocated.

--- -----

See also RaW 610 and INTRODUCTION.

RaW 621 *A Discourse touching a Marriage between Prince Henry and a Daughter of Savoy.*

Copy in a volume of tracts once owned by Ralegh (see RaW 727); c. 1611-15.

First pub. in *The Interest of England with regard to Foreign Alliances, explained in two discourses:...2) Touching a Marriage between Prince Henry of England and a Daughter of Savoy* (London, 1750); *Works* (1829), VIII, 237-52. Ralegh's authorship is not certain.

On temporary loan to the Fitzwilliam Museum, Cambridge: Bradfer-Lawrence 61, ff. 105-9v.

RaW 622 -----

Copy in a composite volume of state papers; first leaf imperfect; early-mid-17th century.

Bodleian, MS Carte 77, ff. 89-102.

RaW 623 -----

Copy, headed 'A politick dispute about the happiest match for the noble and most hopefull prince Charles', in a volume of state tracts; early-mid-17th century.

Bodleian, MS Rawl. D. 1208, ff. 32-45.

RaW 624 -----

Copy, headed 'A politique dispute about ye happiest marriage for the noble prince Charles', in a composite volume of state letters and tracts; early-mid-17th century.

Bodleian, MS Tanner 303, ff. 1-14.

RaW 625 -----

Copy in a volume of state papers and tracts compiled chiefly by Ralph Starkey (d. 1628); c. 1624-8.

British Library, Add. MS 4149, ff. 193-203v.

RaW 626 -----

Copy, bound with Thomas Birch's papers for his Life of Ralegh; 18th century.

British Library, Add. MS 4231, ff. 98-106v.

RaW 627 -----

Copy, headed 'A politique dispute about ye happiest match for ye Noble prince Charles', in a volume of state tracts compiled by John Scudamore, first Viscount

Scudamore (1601-71), constituting Volume IV of the Scudamore Papers; early-mid-17th century.

British Library, Add. MS 45143, ff. 10-15.

RaW 628 -----

Copy, headed 'A Politique discourse by way of Disput about ye happiest mariage for ye Noble Prince Henry written by Sr Arthure Gorge in Ano. 1611', the ascription emended to 'by Sr Walter Rauleghe', in a composite volume of state tracts; imperfect; early 17th century.

This MS formerly divided between Vitellius C. XVI and XVII but now united.

British Library, Cotton MS Vitellius C. XVI, ff. 529-38.

RaW 629 -----

Copy in a volume of miscellaneous tracts; early-mid-17th century.

British Library, Harley MS 6273, ff. 139-50v.

RaW 630 -----

Copy in a volume of state papers; early-mid-17th century.

British Library, Harley MS 6845, ff. 210-15.

RaW 631 -----

Copy in a volume of state tracts; late 17th century.

British Library, Lansdowne MS 213, ff. 101-10.

RaW 632 -----

Copy, headed 'A politique dispute about the happiest mariage for the noble Prince Charles', in a volume of state papers; early-mid-17th century.

British Library, Lansdowne MS 498, ff. 53-9v.

RaW 633 -----

Copy, headed 'A Politique dispute aboute the happiest Mariag for the Noble Prince Charles', in a composite volume of state tracts; imperfect; early-mid-17th century.

British Library, Lansdowne MS 806, ff. 167-90v.

RaW 634 -----

Copy; early-mid-17th century.

British Library, Sloane MS 713.

RaW 635 -----

Copy, headed 'A Politique dispute aboute the happiest Match for the noble and most hopefull Prince Charles', in a volume of state tracts and letters; early-mid-17th century.

Cambridge University Library, MS Mm. 6. 33, ff. 167-80v.

RaW 636 -----

Copy in a volume of state tracts and letters once owned by the antiquary Sir Peter Leycester (1614-78); early-mid-17th century.

Among the Tabley House MSS, this MS recorded in *HMC*, 1st Report (1870), Appendix, pp. 47-8.

Cheshire Record Office, DLT/B8, pp. 35-48.

RaW 637 -----

Copy in a volume of state letters and tracts; early-mid-17th century.

Folger, MS G. b. 9, ff. 295v-310v.

RaW 638 -----

Copy, with some marginal annotations, one initialled 'A ( ) H ( )', in a volume of state papers; early-mid-17th century.

Inner Temple Library, Petyt MS 538, Vol. 43, ff. 84-103.

RaW 639 -----

Copy; early-mid-17th century.

This MS recorded in *BC*, 15 (Summer 1966), p. 163.

Owned by Bent E. Juel-Jensen, Oxford.

RaW 640 -----

Copy in a volume of state papers; early-mid-17th century.

This MS recorded in *HMC*, 3rd Report (1872), Appendix, p. 185.

Owned by the Marquess of Bath, Longleat House, MS 114, pp. 342-76.

RaW 641 -----

Copy, with marginal annotations in another hand, headed 'A politiqe Dispute about the happiest match for the noble Prince [Charles *deleted*] Henry', in a volume of state tracts; early-mid-17th century.

Among the Ormsby-Gore MSS, this MS recorded in *HMC*, 2nd Report (1871), Appendix, p. 85.

National Library of Wales, Brogyntyn (1938 deposit) MS 14 (=Brogyntyn MS 30), pp. 73-93.

RaW 642 -----

Copy; early-mid-17th century.

New York Public Library, Manuscripts Division, Miscellaneous Papers, [no ref. number].

RaW 643 -----

Copy; early-mid-17th century.

University of North Carolina, CSWR A36.

RaW 644 -----

Copy among the papers of the Hatton family, formerly of Holdenby and Kirby Hall, Northamptonshire; early-mid-17th century.

See also RaW 658.

Northamptonshire Record Office, F.H. 91, ff. 7v-14.

RaW 645 -----

Copy, headed 'A Politique Dispute aboute the Happiest Marriage for the Most Noble Prince Charles'; early 17th century.

Public Record Office, SP.14/72/130.

RaW 646 -----

Copy in a volume of state tracts; early-mid-17th century.

Trinity College, Dublin, MS 545, ff. 1-10.

RaW 647 -----

Copy, headed 'A politicke dispute about the happiest Match for the noble Prince Charles', in a volume of state tracts; early-mid-17th century.

Yale, Osborn Collection, fb 23, ff. 287-98.

RaW 648 *A Discourse touching a Match between the Lady Elizabeth and the Prince of Piedmont.*

Copy in a volume of tracts once owned by Ralegh (see RaW 727); c. 1611-15.

First pub. in *The Interest of England with regard to Foreign Alliances, explained in two discourses: 1) Concerning a match propounded by the Savoyan, between the Lady Elizabeth and the Prince of Piedmont* (London, 1750); *Works* (1829), VIII, 223-36. Ralegh's authorship is not certain.

On temporary loan to the Fitzwilliam Museum, Cambridge: Bradfer-Lawrence 61, ff. 99-105.

RaW 649 -----

Copy in a volume of state papers and tracts compiled chiefly by Ralph Starkey (d. 1628); c. 1624-8.

British Library, Add. MS 4149, ff. 184-92v.

RaW 650 -----

Copy, bound with Thomas Birch's papers for his Life of Ralegh; 18th century.

British Library, Add. MS 4231, ff. 89-97v.

RaW 651 -----

Copy of an abridged version, headed 'An opinion of y[e] match propounded by y[e] Embassadour of Savoy betweene y[e] Lady Elizabeth his Ma[ties] eldest (and now only daughter)', in a volume of transcripts of papers of Sir Charles Cornwallis (d. 1629) probably made for his son Charles; early-mid-17th century.

British Library, Add. MS 39853, ff. 25-6.

RaW 652 -----

Copy in a composite volume of state papers; imperfect; early 17th century.

British Library, Cotton MS Vitellius C. XVI, ff. 395-403v.

RaW 653 -----

Second copy in a composite volume of state papers; imperfect; early 17th century.

British Library, Cotton MS Vitellius C. XVI, ff. 541-5.

RaW 654 -----

Copy in a volume of miscellaneous tracts; imperfect; early-mid-17th century.

British Library, Harley MS 6273, ff. 128-38.

RaW 655 -----

Copy in a volume of state papers; early-mid-17th century.

British Library, Harley MS 6845, ff. 198-206.

A Discourse touching a Match between the Lady Elizabeth and the Prince of Piedmont

RaW 656 -----

Copy in a volume of state letters and tracts; early-mid-17th century.

Folger, MS G. b. 9, ff. 283-95.

RaW 657 -----

Copy in a volume of tracts once owned by Sir Thomas Clarke (1703-64); 17th century.

Lincoln's Inn Library, Misc. MS 218, (6).

RaW 658 -----

Copy among the papers of the Hatton family, formerly of Holdenby and Kirby Hall, Northamptonshire; early-mid-17th century.

This MS recorded in *HMC*, 1st Report (1870), Appendix, p. 32.

Northamptonshire Record Office, F.H. 91, ff. 1-7.

RaW 659 *A Discourse touching a War with Spain, and of the Protecting of the Netherlands.*

Copy in a volume of state tracts; early 17th century.

First pub. in *Three Discourses of Sir Walter Ralegh* (London, 1702); *Works* (1829), VIII, 299-316. Formerly Yelverton MS 68, this MS recorded in *HMC*, 2nd Report (1871), Appendix, p. 43.

British Library, Add. MS 48062, ff. 370-85.

RaW 660 -----

Copy in a volume of state papers; early-mid-17th century.

British Library, Harley MS 444, ff. 104-19.

RaW 661 -----

Copy in a composite volume of MSS; early-mid-17th century.

British Library, Sloane MS 63, ff. 58-69.

RaW 662 -----

Copy in a volume of state tracts; c. 1630s.

Cambridge University Library, MS Ee. 2. 32, ff. 109-27.

RaW 663 -----

Copy in a composite volume of state tracts; early-mid-17th century.

Cambridge University Library, MS Mm. 4. 24, ff. 60-6.

RaW 664 -----

Copy among the papers of the Gell family, formerly of Hopton Hall, Derbyshire; c. 1602-25.

This MS recorded in *HMC*, 9th Report, Part II (1884), Appendix, p. 386.

Derbyshire Record Office, D258/34/37.

RaW 665 -----

Copy in a volume of state papers; early-mid-17th century.

Folger, MS V. b. 151, ff. 63-73.

RaW 666 -----

Copy in a composite volume of state tracts, once owned by John Egerton, first Earl of Bridgewater (1579-1649); early-mid-17th century.

Huntington, EL 7976, No. 3.

RaW 667 -----

Copy; early 17th century.

Formerly owned by the Sotheby family at Ecton Hall, Northamptonshire, this MS described in Howard H. Peckham, *Guide to the Manuscript Collections in the William L. Clements Library* (Ann Arbor & London, 1942), p. 211, No. 130.

University of Michigan, William L. Clements Library.

RaW 668 -----

Copy; early 17th century.

Public Record Office, SP.14/205/43.

RaW 669 -----

Copy, headed 'Of Spaine & ye Netherlands', in a composite volume of tracts collected in 1674 by one John Witham; early-mid-17th century.

Rosenbach Foundation, MS 239/4/4.

RaW 670 -----

Copy in a volume of state tracts; early-mid-17th century.

Trinity College, Dublin, MS 861, ff. 239-64v.

A Discourse touching a War with Spain, and of the Protecting of the Netherlands

RaW 671 -----

Copy in a volume of works chiefly by Ralegh; early-mid-17th century.

Dr Williams's Library, MS Jones B. 60, pp. 33-63.

RaW 672 -----

Copy in a volume of state tracts; early-mid-17th century.

Formerly owned by the Duke of Westminster, Eaton Hall, Cheshire, this MS recorded in *HMC*, 3rd Report (1872), Appendix, p. 212; a microfilm is in the British Library (RP 45).

Yale, Osborn Collection, fb 178, ff. 1-16v.

RaW 673 -----

Copy, the first item in a volume of state tracts and papers; 17th century.

Formerly Mostyn MS 139, this MS recorded in *HMC*, 4th Report (1874), Appendix, p. 352.

Sotheby's, 13 July 1920, Lot 72, sold to Sumner; unlocated.

RaW 674 -----

Copy in a folio volume of tracts attributed to Ralegh; 17th century.

Formerly among the Finch MSS at Burley-on-the-Hill, Rutland, this MS recorded in *HMC*, 7th Report (1879), Appendix, p. 516.

Unlocated (not with the Finch MSS in the Leicestershire Record Office and possibly destroyed in a fire in 1908).

RaW 675 -----

Copy; 4to; 17th century.

This MS formerly Phillipps MS 4855 (described as 'Sir Walter Raleigh's Discourse on Spain. 1602').

Unlocated.

RaW 676 *The Discovery of Guiana.*

Copy of an early version in a volume of state papers; c. 1596.

First pub. as *The Discoverie of the Large, Rich and Bewtiful Empire of Guiana* (London, 1596); *Works* (1829), VIII, 377-476; ed. V.T. Harlow (London, 1928).

Lambeth Palace, MS 250, ff. 315-37v.

RaW 677 -----

Synopsis of the work in a small volume of works by Ralegh inscribed 'Liber Richardi [? Larmaxe:] Oxoniae. 1618'.

British Library, Sloane MS 3272, ff. 1-21.

RaW 678 *The History of the World.*

Copy of the Preface transcribed from a printed source by Elias Ashmole (1617-92); mid-late 17th century.

First pub. London, 1614; *Works* (1829), Vols. II-VII.

Bodleian, MS Ashmole 787.

RaW 679 -----

Copy of an abridged version, with two prefatory poems in praise of Ralegh, once owned by Robert Greville, fourth Lord Brooke (c.1638-77) of Warwick Castle; 212 pages; mid-17th century.

This MS or one similar to it used by Laurence Echard as the basis for his *Abridgment of Sir Walter Raleigh's History of the World* (London, 1700). This MS sold at Sotheby's, 11 May 1970, Lot 146; a microfilm is in the British Library (RP 880).

University of North Carolina, CSWR A96.

--- -----

See also RaW 728 and INTRODUCTION.

RaW 680 *Instructions to his Son and to Posterity.*

Copy of chapters I-IX, headed 'Sir Walter Rawleigh to his sonne', with a transcript of a related letter of Ralegh's to his son, in a volume of state papers; early-mid-17th century.

First pub. London, 1632; *Works* (1829), VIII, 557-70; edited by Louis B. Wright in *Advice to a Son* (Ithaca, 1962), pp. 15-32. This MS discussed and the letter printed in Agnes Latham, 'Sir Walter Ralegh's Instructions to his Son', *Elizabethan and Jacobean Studies Presented to Frank Percy Wilson* (Oxford, 1969), 199-218 (pp. 206-8).

British Library, Add. MS 22587, ff. 11-16.

RaW 681 -----

Copy of Ralegh's letter to his son (see RaW 680), in a volume of state papers; early-mid-17th century.

This MS recorded in Latham, *loc. cit.*, p. 207.

Inner Temple Library, Petyt MS 538, Vol. 18, f. 215.

Instructions to his Son and to Posterity

RaW 682 -----

Copy, the first item in a 4to volume of tracts; 17th century.

This MS formerly Phillipps MS 8455.

Sotheby's, 15 June 1896, Lot 982, sold to W. Flower; unlocated.

--- -----

See also INTRODUCTION.

--- *A Journal of Ralegh's Second Voyage to Guiana.*

See RaW 726.

--- *The Life and Death of Mahomet.*

See INTRODUCTION.

--- *A Military Discourse.*

See INTRODUCTION.

--- *Observations concerning the Causes of the Magnificence and Opulence of Cities.*

See INTRODUCTION.

RaW 683 *Observations concerning the Royal Navy and Sea-Service.*

Copy in a volume of tracts and letters relating to seafaring once owned and annotated by Francis Russell, fourth Earl of Bedford (1593-1641); early-mid-17th century.

First pub. in *Judicious and Select Essayes and Observations* (London, 1650); *Works* (1829), VIII, 335-50. These notes probably written by Ralegh but usually appended to Sir Arthur Gorges, *A larger Relation of the...Iland Voyage* (printed in *Purchas his Pilgrimes* (London, 1625); Glasgow edition, XX (1907), 34-129): see Helen Estabrook Sandison, 'Manuscripts of the "Islands Voyage" and "Notes on the Royal Navy"', *Essays and Studies in Honor of Carleton Brown* (New York, London & Oxford, 1940), 242-52, and Lefranc (1968), pp. 53, 58-9.

Owned by the Duke of Bedford, Bedford Office, London, Woburn MSS HMC No. 261, pp. 388-429.

RaW 684 -----

Copy, appended to a copy of Gorges's *Islands Voyage*, in a volume of tracts relating to seafaring; c. 1640.

The previously unpublished introduction in this MS printed in Sandison.

Bodleian, MS Ballard 52, ff. 125-36v.

RaW 685 -----

Copy, ascribed to Ralegh, in a volume of naval documents; c. 1640.

British Library, Add. MS 9298, ff. 39-54v.

RaW 686 -----

Copy, here ascribed to Gorges; early-mid-17th century.

British Library, Harley MS 4311.

RaW 687 -----

Copy, appended to a copy of Gorges's *Observations and overtures for a Sea fight*, in a volume of state tracts; late 17th century.

British Library, Lansdowne MS 213, ff. 49-56v.

RaW 688 -----

Copy, ascribed to Ralegh, with 'An Index of the particular heads contained in the discourse', in a volume of state tracts; early-mid-17th century.

Inner Temple Library, Petyt MS 538, Vol. 37, ff. 1-17.

RaW 689 -----

Copy among the papers of Edward, Lord Herbert of Cherbury, formerly at Powis Castle; imperfect; early-mid-17th century.

National Library of Wales, Powis MSS (1959 deposit), Series II, Packet XI, 'Historical Papers, James I', No. 23.

RaW 690 -----

Copy, appended to a presentation copy of Gorges's *Islands Voyage*; c. 1612-19.

Formerly Leconfield MS 83 at Petworth House, Sussex, this MS recorded in *HMC*, 6th Report (1877), Appendix, p. 308; discussed in Sandison.

Sotheby's, 24 April 1928, Lot 105, sold to Rosenbach; reported in Sandison to be in the Harmsworth Trust Library at Bexhill; unlocated.

RaW 691 -----

Copy in a folio volume of tracts attributed to Ralegh; 17th century.

Formerly among the Finch MSS at Burley-on-the-Hill, Rutland, this MS recorded in *HMC*, 7th

Report (1879), Appendix, p. 516.

Unlocated (not with the Finch MSS in the Leicestershire Record Office and possibly destroyed in a fire in 1908).

--- -----

See also INTRODUCTION.

--- *Observations touching Trade and Commerce with the Hollander.*

See INTRODUCTION.

*RaW 692 *Of the Art of Warre by Sea.*

Two fragments of autograph notes for the work, consisting of lists of topics and chapter headings, the second for 'The pface'; bound in a composite volume of state papers.

No complete text of this treatise known; these fragments first pub. in Lefranc (1968), pp. 597-9.

British Library, Cotton MS Titus B. VIII, ff. 226, 228.

RaW 693 -----

Copy of notes belonging to the *Art of Warre by Sea*, consisting of later additions to the treatise, in a group headed 'Fragments of S^r^. Walter Raleighes' transcribed from Ralegh's autograph papers or from an early copy of them; in a volume of works chiefly by Ralegh; early-mid-17th century.

These notes first pub. in Lefranc (1968), pp. 599-601.

Dr Williams's Library, MS Jones B. 60, pp. 230-4.

--- *Of the present state of Spain.*

See INTRODUCTION.

RaW 694 *Of the Voyage for Guiana.*

Copy, perhaps made for Ralegh; c. 1595-6.

First pub. (from this MS) in *The Discoverie of...Guiana*, ed. Sir Robert H. Schomburgk, Hakluyt Society, 1st Ser. 3 (London, 1848); edited by V.T. Harlow in *The Discoverie of...Guiana* (London, 1928), pp. 138-49.

British Library, Sloane MS 1133.

RaW 695 [*On the Conduct of the War*].

Copy of an untitled tract beginning 'Whosoev^r^ attendeth ye approach [of an Invador]...', in a volume of state papers; imperfect; c. 1596-7.

First pub. (from this MS) in Pierre Lefranc, 'Un inédit de Ralegh sur la conduite de la guerre (1596-1597)', *EA*, 8 (1955), 193-211; recorded in T.N. Brushfield, *A Bibliography of Sir Walter Ralegh* (Exeter, 1908), No. 249, as 'A Discourse on the Defence of a Country, the conduct of a Fleet and Army, &c.'.

British Library, Cotton MS Otho E. XI, ff. 377-81v.

RaW 696 *On the Seat of Government.*

Copy, headed 'An impfect discourse of S^r^: Walter Raleighs'; 4 pages; in a volume of state letters and tracts, among the papers of the Finch-Hatton family; early-mid-17th century.

First pub. together with *Sir Walter Raleigh's Scepticke* (London, 1651); *Works* (1829), VIII, 538-40.

Northamptonshire Record Office, F.H. 3641/3.

RaW 697 -----

Copy in a volume of works chiefly by Ralegh; early-mid-17th century.

Dr Williams's Library, MS Jones B. 60, pp. 17-22.

*RaW 698 [*On the Succession*].

Autograph untitled memorandum beginning 'first ther is no good subiect that ought to doubt of her Maiesties care and providence...', addressed to Queen Elizabeth and submitted by Ralegh to Sir Robert Cecil; endorsed in a contemporary hand 'Reasons why Q. Eliz. sh^d^ not name her Successor'; [February 1592/3].

First pub. (from this MS) in Pierre Lefranc, 'Un inédit de Ralegh sur la succession', *EA*, 13 (1960), 38-46. Ralegh's letter accompanying this memorandum is Cecil Papers 83/35 (also printed in Lefranc).

Owned by the Marquess of Salisbury, Hatfield House, Cecil Papers 139/139-40v.

RaW 699 *Opinion upon the Articles propounded by the Earl of Essex upon the Alarum given by the Spaniards in 1596.*

Copy, with a copy of Essex's articles; c. 1596.

First pub. in *Opinions delivered by the Earl of Essex*, [*&c.*]...*on the Alarm of an Invasion from Spain in the Year 1596* (London, n.d.) [the exemplum in the Public Record Office, SP.9/52/25, bears the MS date '1803']; *Works* (1829), VIII, 675-81.

Bodleian, MS Tanner 235, ff. 18-22.

Opinion upon the Articles propounded by the Earl of Essex

RaW 700 -----

Copy in a volume of state tracts; early-mid-17th century.

Yale, Osborn Collection, fb 23, ff. 196-9v.

--- -----

See also INTRODUCTION.

RaW 701 *Orders to be observed by the Commanders of the Fleet with Land Companies. 3 May 1617.*

Copy in a composite volume of historical and state papers collected by Elias Ashmole (1617-92); early-mid-17th century.

First pub. in *Newes of Sir Walter Rauleigh* (London, 1618); *Works* (1829), VIII, 682-8; edited by V.T. Harlow in *Ralegh's Last Voyage* (London, 1932), pp. 121-6.

Bodleian, MS Ashmole 830, ff. 109-10v.

RaW 702 -----

Copy; c. 1617?

This MS recorded in *HMC*, 6th Report (1877), Appendix, p. 328.

Owned by Sir Richard Graham, Norton Conyers, Yorkshire (possession confirmed by letter 10 September 1975).

RaW 703 -----

Copy on two leaves in a composite volume of maritime documents; c. 1617?

National Maritime Museum, REC/1/50, [no page numbers].

RaW 704 -----

Copy; [1617].

Printed from this MS in Sir Julian Corbett, 'The Elizabethan Origin of Ralegh's Instructions', *Fighting Instructions, 1530-1816*, Navy Record Society (London, 1905), 27-45.

Public Record Office, SP.14/92/9.

RaW 705 -----

MS of Sir Arthur Gorges's 'A forme of Orders and dire[c]tions to bee given by an Admirall, in conducting a Fleet through the Narrow Seas...', a work which incorporates Ralegh's orders, appended to Gorges's *Observations and overtures for a Sea fight*; in the hand of an amanuensis, with Gorges's autograph revisions; [1619].

Printed from this MS, and the relation between Ralegh's orders and Gorges's version discussed, in Helen E. Sandison, 'Ralegh's Orders once more', *MM*, 20 (1934), 323-30.

British Library, Stowe MS 426, ff. 30v-6.

RaW 706 -----

Copy of Gorges's 'forme of orders' (see RaW 705), appended to a presentation copy of his *Observations and overtures for a Sea fight*; c. 1619.

Formerly Leconfield MS 48 at Petworth House, Sussex, this MS recorded in *HMC*, 6th Report (1877), Appendix, p. 305; recorded in Sandison, p. 328, and in Helen E. Sandison, 'Manuscripts of the "Islands Voyage" and "Notes on the Royal Navy"', *Essays and Studies in Honor of Carleton Brown* (New York, London & Oxford, 1940), 242-52 (p. 244).

National Maritime Museum, MS LEC/8, p. 35 seq.

RaW 707 -----

Copy of Gorges's 'forme of orders' (see RaW 705), appended to a copy of his *Observations and overtures for a Sea fight*, in a volume of state tracts; late 17th century.

This MS discussed in Sandison, *MM*, 20, 323-4.

British Library, Lansdowne MS 213, ff. 46-8v.

RaW 708 -----

Copy of Gorges's 'forme of orders' (see RaW 705), appended to a copy of his *Observations and overtures for a Sea fight*; c. 1619.

This MS recorded in Sandison, *MM*, 20, 328.

Public Record Office, SP.14/17/103.

--- *The Prerogative of Parliaments in England, Proved in a Dialogue between a Counsellor of State and a Justice of the Peace.*

See RaW 572-603.

--- *The Present Stat of Thinges as they now Stand betweene the three great Kingedomes, Fraunce, England, and Spaine.*

See INTRODUCTION.

--- *The Prince, or Maxims of State.*

See INTRODUCTION.

RaW 709 *A Relation of the Action at Cadiz.*

Copy, inscribed 'Transcrib'd from a MS. in y[e] Hande of his Grandchild, M[r] Raleigh', in a volume of state tracts; mid-17th century.

First pub. in *An Abridgement of Sir Walter Raleigh's History of the World* (London, 1700); *Works* (1829), VIII, 667-74.

Bodleian, MS Tanner 278, ff. 240-4.

A Relation of the Action of Cadiz

RaW 710 -----

Copy, headed 'Sir Walter Raleighs letter to the Earle of Northumberland being a true Relation of the taking of Cales', in a volume of works chiefly by Ralegh; early-mid-17th century.

Dr Williams's Library, MS Jones B. 60, pp. 1-15.

--- *The Scepticke.*

See INTRODUCTION.

--- *A Speech found in Sir Walter Rawleighes pockett after his Execution Written by him in the Gatehouse ye night befores dea[th].*

See RaW 737-8.

--- *Speech on the Scaffold.*

See RaW 739-822.

--- [*Testamentary Notes*].

See RaW 729-36.

--- *A Treatise of the Soul.*

See INTRODUCTION.

MARGINALIA IN PRINTED BOOKS AND MANUSCRIPTS

See INTRODUCTION.

MISCELLANEOUS

*RaW 711 [*Chemical and Medical Receipts*].

Autograph notebook of chemical and medical receipts, including Ralegh's 'great Cordiall', and accounts of experiments; 70 pages, with Ralegh's writing on 53 pages.

This MS discussed in Lefranc (1968), p. 682; facsimile of the words 'Our great Cordiall' in Walter Oakeshott, 'Carew Ralegh's Copy of Spenser', *The Library*, 5th Ser. 26 (1971), 1-21 (plate V(c)).

British Library, Sloane MS 359.

RaW 712 -----

Copy of Ralegh's receipts, allegedly 'transcribed out of Sr Walter Raleghs booke of receipts written with his owne hand, and...done according to the originall in everie sillable'; the copyist claiming that 'This that followeth S^r W:R: wrote with his owne hand and gave it to mee, to teach me to make the Magister of Pearles'; 36 pages; bound in a composite volume of cookery and receipt books collected in the late 18th-early 19th century by James Shrowl; c. 1620s.

A transcript of portions of this MS made after 1914 by John E. Hodgkin is in his book of notes on his collection of cookery books, now at the University of Leeds (MS 45, ff. 61-74).

Wellcome Historical Medical Library, London, MS 749/13.

*RaW 713 -----

Autograph eight-line receipt on a single leaf; headed in another hand 'To keepe beefe at sea'; inscribed in other hands 'Autographum Walt. Ralegh. in Turri Londinensi don. d^r. Kileigrew' and 'To my hono^ble: and mutche respected frend S^r walter Raleighe knight these'; in a composite autograph album.

This MS recorded in Lefranc (1968), p. 681. See also RaW 723 (concerning Sir Robert Killigrew (1579-1633)).

British Library, Add. MS 12097, f. 13.

RaW 714 -----

A list of chemical symbols used by Ralegh, headed 'Clavis Adversariorum Equitis Walteri Rhalegh'; 1592.

This MS recorded in Lefranc (1968), p. 678.

Public Record Office, SP.12/240/149.

RaW 715 -----

A list of chemical symbols used by Ralegh, headed 'Alphabetum seu clavis chemicus N.S. Gwalteri Ralegh, equitis', in a volume of chemical and medical collections compiled by Theodore Turquet de Mayerne; 17th century.

This MS recorded in Lefranc (1968), p. 678.

British Library, Sloane MS 2046, f. 110.

RaW 716 -----

Copy of Ralegh's receipt to make quicksilver, in a volume of alchemical papers compiled by Thomas Robson; 1611-12.

This MS recorded in Lefranc (1968), p. 680.

Bodleian, MS Ashmole 1407, II, ff. 35v-6.

RaW 717 -----

Two copies of Ralegh's receipt to make quicksilver, in a volume of alchemical papers compiled by Thomas Robson; 1615.

This MS recorded in Lefranc (1968), p. 680.

Bodleian, MS Ashmole 1424, ff. 49v-50, 57v-8.

[*Chemical and Medical Receipts*]

RaW 718 -----

Copy of Ralegh's receipt to make quicksilver, in a volume of chemical tracts and receipts compiled by Robert Garland; 1596.

This MS recorded in Lefranc (1968), p. 680.

Bodleian, MS Ashmole 1486, I, f. 24v.

RaW 719 -----

Copy of Ralegh's receipts for the stone, dropsy, &c., in a notebook compiled by Sir Stephen Powle, Clerk of the Crown; [1613-14].

This MS recorded in Lefranc (1968), p. 680 seq.

Bodleian, MS Tanner 169, ff. 139-42.

RaW 720 -----

Copy of 'A present Metson for the Agewe' ascribed to 'Si^{r} water Raylishe 1616' (this ascription deleted) in a navigational notebook possibly associated with the East India Company; c. 1616.

This MS (formerly owned by Boies Penrose) offered for sale at Sotheby's, 24 July 1978, Lot 97.

British Library, Egerton MS 3801, f. [33v].

RaW 721 -----

Copy of a receipt by Ralegh on p. 362 of a 17th-century transcript of a book of medical prescriptions compiled in the 16th century by Sir Samuel Sandys of Ombersley, Worcestershire, son of Edwin Sandys (d. 1558); from the papers of the Shirley family of Ettington Park, near Stratford-upon-Avon.

This MS recorded in *HMC*, 5th Report (1876), Appendix, p. 365 (No. 33).

Sotheby's, 29 April 1947, Lot 333, sold to Myers.

RaW 722 -----

Copy of a receipt for 'An Excellent Cordiall jelly a Comforter of the harte and helpe to digesture, of Sir walter raleigh', in a volume of chemical receipts; c. 1625-1700.

Folger, MS V. a. 361, f. 38.

RaW 723 -----

Copy of 'Sr Walter Raleighs Great Cordiall Sr Robert Killigrews way' in a book of medical receipts and prescriptions, in the Cole Park Collection deriving from the papers of the Lovell, Willes, and Harvey families; late 17th century.

See also RaW 713.

Wiltshire Record Office, 161/90A, p. 135 (bis).

RaW 724 -----

Copy of 'Sir Walter Rawleigh's Cordial' in a volume of cookery receipts; sm. 4to; 2nd half 17th century.

Sotheby's, 9 May 1961, Lot 282, sold to Dawson.

RaW 725 -----

Copy of 'Sir Walter Rawleigh's great Cordiall' in a receipt book of one 'M^{ris} Gratia Bartlet'; 1694.

Sotheby's, 22 February 1972, Lot 544; owned (1979) by Lady Poole, London.

*RaW 726 *A Journal of Ralegh's Second Voyage to Guiana.*

Ralegh's autograph journal compiled on his last voyage to Guiana; bound in a composite volume of state papers; 19 August 1617 - 13 February 1617/18.

First pub. (from this MS) in *The Discoverie of...Guiana*, ed. Sir Robert H. Schomburgk, Hakluyt Society, 1st Ser. 3 (London, 1848), 177-208. Facsimile examples in *Facsimiles of Royal, Historical and Literary Autographs in the British Museum* (1899), plate 28; Walter Oakeshott, 'Carew Ralegh's Copy of Spenser', *The Library*, 5th Ser. 26 (1971), 1-21 (plate V(d-e)); Petti, *English Literary Hands*, No. 49.

British Library, Cotton MS Titus B. VIII, ff. 162-75.

*RaW 727 [*Miscellany*].

A MS volume owned by Ralegh, consisting of copies of various tracts on Spain and on political and military affairs, including three of his own works (see RaW 572, 621, 648), his proposal for an agreement with the Lords in 1611 for the voyage to Guiana, and copies of three of his own letters, with a number of minor autograph annotations throughout the volume; c. 1611-15.

This MS analysed in Phyllis M. Giles, 'A Handlist of the Bradfer-Lawrence Manuscripts deposited on loan at the Fitzwilliam Museum', *Transactions of The Cambridge Bibliographical Society*, 6, Part 2 (1973), 86-99 (p. 96). See also INTRODUCTION.

On temporary loan to the Fitzwilliam Museum, Cambridge: Bradfer-Lawrence 61.

*RaW 728 [*Notebook*].

An autograph notebook compiled during Ralegh's imprisonment in the Tower of London; containing a glossary of geographical notes (used for his *History of the World*), several annotated ink and watercoloured maps, a list of his books (partly in the hand of an amanuensis), and the text of possibly the last poem in the *Cynthia* series (see RaW 200); [1603-18].

Formerly Phillipps MS 6339, this MS described by Walter Oakeshott (with a facsimile example) in 'An Unknown Raleigh MS', *The Times* (29 November 1952), p. 7; in *The Queen and the Poet* (London, 1960) (with facsimile examples facing pp. 119, 223); and in 'Sir Walter Ralegh's Library', *The Library*, 5th Ser. 23 (1968), 285-327 (with facsimile examples after p. 288, but plates I and II are not in Ralegh's hand). Facsimile examples also in Philip Edwards, *Sir Walter Ralegh* (London, 1953), facing p. 97; Sotheby's sale catalogue, 30 November 1971, Lot 526; John Winton, *Sir Walter Ralegh* (London, 1975), facing p. 288; and Petti, *English Literary Hands*, Nos. 47-8.

British Library, Add. MS 57555.

RaW 729 *Ralegh's First Testamentary Note.*

Copy of Ralegh's memorandum concerning his estate, last wishes, &c as delivered to Sir Thomas Wilson, in Wilson's hand; c. 1618.

Printed from this MS in Edwards (1868), II, 493-4.

Public Record Office, SP.14/103/37.

RaW 730 *Ralegh's Second Testamentary Note.*

Copy of Ralegh's list of points in his own defence, beginning 'I did neuer receive Advise from my Lord Carew to make any escape...' and subscribed 'Att my Death. W: Raleigh', in a volume of state papers; c. 1618.

Pub. in *The Works of Sir Walter Ralegh*, ed. Thomas Birch (London, 1751), II, 280-1; *Works* (1829), VIII, 563. Printed from this MS in Edwards (1868), II, 494-5.

British Library, Cotton MS Titus C. VII, f. 93.

RaW 731 -----

Copy in a volume of state papers possibly compiled in part by or for one Thomas Gee; early-mid-17th century.

This MS Phillipps MS 7511. See RaW 782.

Folger, MS V. b. 303, pp. 229-30.

RaW 732 -----

Copy, headed 'An answere made by S^r: walter Rawleigh at his death to the false accusations, y^t a repriued and infamous fellow called Lewds stukleye charged him wth all...[&c]', in a volume of essays and letters, among the papers of the Savile family, formerly of Methley Hall, near Pontefract; early-mid-17th century.

Leeds Archives Department, MX 269, f. [15v].

RaW 732.3, 732.5, 732.8 See Addenda, p. 633.

RaW 733 -----

Copy of the text in a French translation, on a single leaf bound with other documents relating to Ralegh in a composite volume of French state papers; early-mid-17th century.

Bibliothèque Nationale, Paris, Cinq cents de Colbert n° 467, f. 72.

RaW 734 -----

Copy of the text in a French translation, headed 'Confession du Cheuallier Raulegh executé à Londres', in a French volume of state papers; 17th century.

Bibliothèque Nationale, Paris, Cinq cents de Colbert n° 488, ff. 167-8.

RaW 735 -----

Copy of the text in a French translation, headed 'Escript et confession de Raulegh', in a French volume of state papers; 17th century.

Bibliothèque Nationale, Paris, fonds français n° 5812, ff. 82-3.

RaW 736 -----

Copy of the text in a French translation, headed 'Confession du Sr Walter Raley a l'Instan de sa mors', in a volume of transcripts of state papers made at the direction of Jean Baptiste Colbert (d. 1683), minister of Louis XIV; late 17th century.

British Library, Add. MS 30663, f. 480r-v.

RaW 737 *A Speech found in Sir Walter Rawleighes pockett after his Execution Written by him in the Gatehouse ye night befores dea[th].*

Copy of a prayer, beginning 'I owe to god a death because his sonne died for me...' and ending '...I am willing help my vnwillingnes finis Walter Rawleigh', on a single leaf in a composite volume of MSS; c. 1618?

Unpublished. See INTRODUCTION. A transcript of this MS made by Thomas Baker (1656-1740) is in Cambridge University Library, MS Mm. 1. 45, p. 211.

British Library, Harley MS 3787, f. 182r-v.

RaW 738 -----

Copy, headed 'A prayer' and unsigned, in a volume of miscellaneous verse and prose (which includes other letters and poems of Ralegh) transcribed from the papers of Sir Christopher Yelverton (1535?-1612); early 17th century.

All Souls College, Oxford, MS 155, ff. 144v-5.

Speech on the Scaffold (29 October 1618)

RaW 739 *Speech on the Scaffold (29 October 1618).*

Copy in a volume of state tracts; early-mid-17th century.

Transcripts of Ralegh's speech have been printed in his *Remains* (London, 1657); *Works* (1829), I, 558-64, 691-6; VIII, 775-9; and elsewhere. Copies range from verbatim transcripts to summaries of the speech, they usually form part of an account of Ralegh's execution, they have various headings, and the texts differ considerably.

Balliol College, Oxford, MS 270, pp. 165-7.

RaW 740 -----

Copy among the papers of the Trevor Wingfield family and possibly deriving from the papers of the Boteler family of Biddenham; early-mid-17th century.

Bedfordshire Record Office, TW 1145.

RaW 741 -----

Copy in a volume of state letters and tracts; early-mid-17th century.

Bibliothèque Nationale, Paris, fonds anglais n°. 149, ff. 102v-4.

RaW 742 -----

Copy in the hand of Elias Ashmole (1617-92), in a composite volume of historical and state papers collected by him; mid-17th century.

Bodleian, MS Ashmole 830, ff. 114-15v.

RaW 743 -----

Copy in the hand of William Fulman (1632-88) in his MS book of memorials of English affairs to 1625; mid-late 17th century.

Bodleian, MS CCC. 297, ff. 166-9v.

RaW 744 -----

Copy in a scribal hand in William Fulman's book of memorials of English affairs to 1625; mid-17th century.

Bodleian, MS CCC. ff. 170-2.

RaW 745 -----

Copy in a volume of state papers; early-mid-17th century.

Bodleian, MS Eng. hist. c. 319, ff. 19-22.

RaW 746 -----

Copy in two hands, in a volume of state papers; early-mid-17th century.

Bodleian, MS Jesus College 83, ff. 68v-70.

RaW 747 -----

Copy in a volume of state papers; early-mid-17th century.

Bodleian, MS Rawl. D. 180, ff. 46-52.

RaW 748 -----

Copy, with annotations in the hand of someone apparently present at the execution, in a volume of miscellaneous family papers assembled by Hannibal Baskervile of Sunningwell, Berkshire; c. 1618.

Bodleian, MS Rawl. D. 859, ff. 84-5v.

RaW 749 -----

Copy in a volume of state papers; early-mid-17th century.

Bodleian, MS Tanner 74, ff. 148-50.

RaW 750 -----

Copy in a volume of letters and tracts compiled by Archbishop William Sancroft (1617-93); mid-late 17th century.

Printed from this MS in *Works* (1829), VIII, 775-80, and in Edwards (1868), I, 698-706.

Bodleian, MS Tanner 299, ff. 26v-8v.

RaW 751 -----

Copy, with alterations, in a composite volume of state papers collected by Thomas Birch (1705-66); early-mid-17th century.

British Library, Add. MS 4106, ff. 82-3v.

RaW 752 -----

Copy in a volume of works by Ralegh constituting Volume XXI of the collections of Macvey Napier (1776-1847); early-mid-17th century.

British Library, Add. MS 34631, ff. 61-3v.

RaW 753 -----

Copy of a version allegedly 'written by m[r] Al: S. to the L.A:', in a volume of state papers constituting Volume LXVIII of the Vernon Papers principally collected by James Vernon (1646-1727) and his son Edward; mid-17th century.

See also RaW 803.

British Library, Add. MS 40838, ff. 27v-30.

RaW 754 -----

Copy (the speech here dated 1605) in a volume of state papers; mid-17th century.

British Library, Add. MS 44848, ff. 267-9v.

RaW 755 -----

Fragment of a copy, inserted in a MS volume of poems by Sir Arthur Gorges (1557-1625) originally compiled by Gorges; c. 1618.

British Library, Egerton MS 3165, f. 115.

RaW 756 -----

Copy in a volume of state papers and tracts; early-mid-17th century.

British Library, Harley MS 39, ff. 361-8v.

RaW 757 -----

Copy in a composite volume of MSS; early-mid-17th century.

British Library, Harley MS 791, ff. 49v-50v.

RaW 758 -----

Copy in a volume of state tracts; early-mid-17th century.

British Library, Harley MS 852, ff. 29-32.

RaW 759 -----

Copy in a volume of state letters and tracts; early-mid-17th century.

British Library, Harley MS 1327, f. 56r-v.

RaW 760 -----

Copy in a composite volume of state papers; early-mid-17th century.

British Library, Harley MS 1576, ff. 93-4.

RaW 761 -----

Copy in a volume of state tracts; incomplete; early-mid-17th century.

British Library, Harley MS 1893, f. 81.

RaW 762 -----

Copy in a volume of state tracts; early-mid-17th century.

British Library, Harley MS 6353, ff. 80-6.

RaW 763 -----

Copy of 'S[r] Walter Rawleighs Wordes at his Death, taken exactly by Tho: Aylsbury Esqr. [Sir Thomas Aylesbury (1576-1657)] 1618', in a composite volume of letters and papers collected by the Duke of Ormonde; early-mid-17th century.

British Library, Harley MS 7056, ff. 49-50v.

RaW 764 -----

Copy in a volume of state papers; imperfect, lacking the beginning; early-mid-17th century.

British Library, Stowe MS 141, f. 74r-v.

RaW 765 -----

Second copy, untitled, in a volume of state papers; early-mid-17th century.

British Library, Stowe MS 141, f. 75r-v.

RaW 766 -----

Copy in a volume of state papers; early-mid-17th century.

British Library, Stowe MS 180, ff. 47-8v.

RaW 767 -----

Copy, untitled, in a composite volume of tracts; 6 leaves; early-mid-17th century.

Cambridge University Library, MS Dd. 3. 87, (18).

RaW 768 -----

Copy in a miscellany owned in the late 17th century by one John Peck; early-mid-17th century.

Cambridge University Library, MS Ee. 5. 23, pp. 464-7.

RaW 769 -----

Copy in a volume of state tracts and letters; early-mid-17th century.

Cambridge University Library, MS Mm. 6. 33, ff. 181-5v.

Speech on the Scaffold (29 October 1618)

RaW 770 -----

Copy in a volume of state tracts and letters once owned by the antiquary Sir Peter Leycester (1614-78); early-mid-17th century.

Among the Tabley House MSS, this MS recorded in *HMC*, 1st Report (1870), Appendix, p. 48.

Cheshire Record Office, DLT/B8, pp. 302-6.

RaW 771 -----

Copy of an account of Ralegh's last 'speeches' here beginning 'This daie whether the sunne refused to be a beholder or in pittie withdrew himselfe...', in a volume of state tracts and letters once owned by Sir Peter Leycester; early-mid-17th century.

See RaW 770.

Cheshire Record Office, DLT/B8, pp. 306-12.

RaW 772 -----

Copy in a volume of works by or relating to Ralegh owned in 1674 by one Andrew Card; c. 1674.

University of Chicago, MS 824, ff. 28-9.

RaW 773 -----

Copy among the papers of the Gell family, formerly of Hopton Hall, Derbyshire; early-mid-17th century.

This MS recorded in *HMC*, 9th Report, Part II (1884), Appendix, p. 386b.

Derbyshire Record Office, D258/67/6b, ff. [1-3].

RaW 774 -----

Copy among the papers of the Gell family; early-mid-17th century.

Derbyshire Record Office, D258/67/33b.

RaW 775 -----

Copy in a volume of state letters and speeches, among the papers of the Fuller family of Brightling Park and possibly once owned by Ambrose Trayton of Lewes, Esquire of the Body to James I and Charles I; c. 1620s.

East Sussex Record Office, RAF/F/13/1, pp. 101-4.

RaW 776 -----

Copy in a miscellany of verse and prose; c. 1630.

Edinburgh University Library, MS La. III. 493, ff. 32-3v.

RaW 777 -----

Copy in a volume of scullery and kitchen accounts (probably connected with the Royal establishment) apparently kept by David Young, servant of the Scullery; c. 1628-38.

Edinburgh University Library, MS La. III. 501, ff. 65-6v.

RaW 778 -----

Copy in a miscellany belonging to the Smyth family of Hill Hall; early-mid-17th century.

Essex Record Office, D/DSh Z1, ff. 37-8v.

RaW 779 -----

Copy in a volume of state papers compiled by Sir Roger Twysden (1597-1672); 1620s.

Folger, MS G. b. 7, ff. 135-8v.

RaW 780 -----

Copy in a volume of state letters and tracts; early-mid-17th century.

This MS sold at Sotheby's, 4 July 1955 (André de Coppet sale), Lot 950.

Folger, MS G. b. 9, ff. 161-70v.

RaW 781 -----

Copy in a volume of documents by or relating to Ralegh; early-mid-17th century.

Folger, MS V. a. 418, ff. 1-4v.

RaW 782 -----

Copy in a volume of state papers possibly compiled in part by or for one Thomas Gee; early-mid-17th century.

Formerly Phillipps MS 7511, this MS sold at Sotheby's, 26 June 1967, Lot 596, when it was incorrectly described as a commonplace book of Sir Thomas Crewe, Speaker of the House of Commons (d. 1634). A microfilm is in the British Library (RP 154).

Folger, MS V. b. 303, pp. 229-33.

RaW 783 -----

Copy in the hand of John Smyth (1567-1640) of Nibley, Gloucestershire, transcribed for Lady Berkeley, in a volume of historical papers compiled by Smyth; [1618-40].

Formerly among the Cholmondeley MSS at Condover Hall, Salop, this MS recorded in *HMC*, 5th Report (1876), Appendix, pp. 354-5.

Folger, MS Z. e. 1 (11).

Speech on the Scaffold (29 October 1618)

RaW 784 -----

Copy in a volume of state tracts; early-mid-17th century.

Gonville and Caius College, Cambridge, MS 73/40, ff. 214-15.

RaW 785 -----

Copy in a miscellany of verse and prose; c. 1620.

Harvard, MS Eng 628, pp. 387-9.

RaW 786 -----

Copy in a volume of state papers; early-mid-17th century.

Inner Temple Library, Petyt MS 538, Vol. 18, f. 240.

RaW 787 -----

Copy on two leaves and in two hands, the second leaf evidently a later replacement for a lost or damaged original; early-mid-17th century.

This MS recorded in *HMC*, 14th Report, Appendix IV (1894), p. 24.

Owned by Lord Kenyon, Kenyon MSS HMC. 43 (possession confirmed by letter 9 September 1975).

RaW 788 -----

Copy in a small volume of documents by or relating to Ralegh; 17th century.

Owned by Agnes Latham, Pickering, MS, ff. 20-2.

RaW 789 -----

Copy in a volume of legal and state papers once owned by one Richard Tichborne; early-mid-17th century.

This MS recorded in C. Deedes, 'Unpublished Letters of Sir Walter Ralegh', *N & Q*, 8th Ser. 3 (24 June 1893), 481-2.

Owned by Agnes Latham, Pickering, Tichborne MS, ff. 34-7v.

RaW 790 -----

Copy in a volume of state letters; early-mid-17th century.

National Library of Scotland, Adv. MS 33. 7. 19, ff. 13v-16.

RaW 791 -----

Copy on two conjugate leaves; early-mid-17th century.

This MS sold at Sotheby's, 5 July 1955 (André de Coppet sale), Lot 984.

New York Public Library, Arents Collection, Acc. 7482.

RaW 792 -----

Copy in the hand of one Henry Bull, Jr., written at the end of his copy of an account of Ralegh's trial in 1603, bound with a MS 'booke of memorable accidents and famous arraignements' compiled in 1614 by William Bull of the Middle Temple; early-mid-17th century.

University of North Carolina, CSWR A32, pp. 267-72.

RaW 793 -----

Copy among the papers of the Isham family of Lamport Hall; early-mid-17th century.

Northamptonshire Record Office, I.C. 3495.

RaW 794 -----

Copy among the papers of the Isham family of Lamport Hall; early-mid-17th century.

Northamptonshire Record Office, I.C. 3496.

RaW 795 -----

Copy among the papers of the Clifton family of Clifton Hall, Nottinghamshire; early-mid-17th century.

This MS recorded in *HMC*, 55, Various Collections, VII (1914), p. 269.

University of Nottingham, Clifton MS Cl LP 5/5.

RaW 796 -----

Copy in a volume of accounts of Ralegh's arraignment and execution; early-mid-17th century.

Formerly in the Alfred Morrison collection, this MS recorded in *HMC*, 9th Report, Appendix, Part II (1884), p. 408.

Pforzheimer Library, MS 112, ff. 49-54.

RaW 797 -----

Copy probably made by Edmund Elms of Lilliford, Clerk of the City of London, in a collection of state papers; c. 1618?

Speech on the Scaffold (29 October 1618)

This MS printed in R.H. Bowers, 'Ralegh's Last Speech: The "Elms" Document', *RES*, NS 21 (1951), 209-16.

Pierpont Morgan Library, R-V. R. of E. (Eliz. 1), No. 49.

RaW 798 -----

Copy (incorrectly stated to be made by Serjeant Fleetwood), in a collection of state papers; c. 1618?

This MS described in Bowers, pp. 210-11 (see RaW 797).

Pierpont Morgan Library, R-V. R. of E. (Eliz. 1), No. 50.

RaW 799 -----

Copy; early-mid-17th century.

Princeton, MA 20450 General MSS [Misc.].

RaW 800 -----

Copy; five pages; early-mid-17th century.

Public Record Office, SP.14/103/52.

RaW 801 -----

Copy; seven leaves; early-mid-17th century.

Public Record Office, SP.14/103/53.

RaW 802 -----

Copy in a volume of state papers; early-mid-17th century.

The Queen's College, Oxford, MS 32, ff. 14-16v.

RaW 803 -----

Copy, allegedly 'Tooke by M^r^. Alsb^r^: sec^tie^: to ye L^d^. Ad^ll^' [i.e. Lord Arundel], in a composite volume of state papers; early-mid-17th century.

See also RaW 753.

The Queen's College, Oxford, MS 121, pp. 512-17.

RaW 804 -----

Copy, with corrections and additions, on two conjugate leaves among the papers of the Mildmay family of Hazelgrove House, Somerset, and deriving from the papers of the Harvey family; early-mid-17th century.

This MS recorded in *HMC*, 7th Report (1879), Appendix, p. 592.

Somerset Record Office, DD/MI 18/82.

RaW 805 -----

Copy on two conjugate leaves among the papers of the Sanford family of Somerset; early-mid-17th century.

Somerset Record Office, DD/SF C/2635, Box 1, [no item number].

RaW 806 -----

Copy among the papers of the Bagot family of Blithfield, Staffordshire; early-mid-17th century.

Staffordshire Record Office, D 1721/3/186.

RaW 807 -----

Copy, with annotations in a later hand, in a volume of state papers; early-mid-17th century.

Trinity College, Cambridge, MS O. 5. 21 (James 1302), (20).

RaW 808 -----

Copy in a volume of works chiefly by Ralegh; early-mid-17th century.

Dr Williams's Library, MS Jones B. 60, pp. 269-82.

RaW 809 -----

Copy in a volume chiefly of transcripts of correspondence of John Holles, second Earl of Clare (1595-1666); c. 1629-32.

Yale, Osborn Collection, b 32, pp. 145-53.

RaW 810 -----

Copy in a miscellany compiled by Adam Winthrop (1548-1623); [1618-23].

Printed from this MS in *Proceedings of the Massachusetts Historical Society*, 1st Ser. 13 (1873), 83-98 (pp. 94-8).

Formerly (but no longer) owned by the Massachusetts Historical Society; unlocated.

Speech on the Scaffold (29 October 1618)

RaW 811 -----

Copy on leaves detached from a composite volume of state papers once belonging to Sir Henry Spelman (1564?-1641); early-mid-17th century.

Formerly part of Gurney MS XXXIII at Keswick Hall, Norfolk, this MS recorded in *HMC*, 12th Report, Appendix IX (1891), p. 161. This MS part of eight leaves sold at Sotheby's, 31 March 1936, Lot 188, to Last, five of which are now in the Osborn Collection at Yale (see RaW 100).

Unlocated.

RaW 812 -----

Copy on pp. 275-8 of a volume of state papers; 17th century.

Formerly Gurney MS XXXIV at Keswick Hall, Norfolk, this MS recorded in *HMC*, 12th Report, Appendix IX (1891), p. 162.

Unlocated.

RaW 813 -----

Copy of the speech in a Spanish translation, with alterations in a different ink, headed 'La suma de lo que dixo Don Gualtero Ralegh estando sobre el cadahalso antes que le degollassen', in a composite volume of Spanish papers relating to the affairs of Spain in 1613-19; 17th century.

British Library, Add. MS 14015, ff. 134-5v.

RaW 814 -----

Copy of the speech in a French translation, headed 'Dernieres parolles du Cheualier Raulegh, traduittes d'Anglois mot à mot', bound with other documents relating to Ralegh in a composite volume of French state papers; early-mid-17th century.

Bibliothèque Nationale, Paris, Cinq cents de Colbert n° 467, ff. 67-8v.

RaW 815 -----

Copy of the speech in a French translation, headed 'Dernieres parolles du Chevaleir Raileigh Traduites d'Anglois mot a mot', in a volume of transcripts of state papers made at the direction of Jean Baptiste Colbert (d. 1683), minister of Louis XIV; late 17th century.

British Library, Add. MS 30663, ff. 489-93.

RaW 816 -----

Brief notes of the main points in Ralegh's speech in the hand of the mathematician Thomas Harriot (1560-1621), on a single leaf among his miscellaneous collections; these notes possibly jotted down at the execution itself; [1618].

This MS printed and discussed in B.J. Sokol, 'Thomas Hariot's Notes on Sir Walter Raleigh's Address from the Scaffold', *Manuscripts*, 26, No. 3 (Summer 1974), 198-206.

British Library, Add. MS 6789, f. 533.

RaW 817 -----

Account of Ralegh's speech and execution in a letter written by Thomas Lorkin to Sir Thomas Puckering; bound in a composite volume of state letters; 3 November 1618.

This MS printed in V.T. Harlow, *Ralegh's Last Voyage* (London, 1932), pp. 311-14.

British Library, Harley MS 7002, f. 420.

RaW 818 -----

Account of Ralegh's speech in a letter written by John South to an unidentified person; c. 30 October 1618.

Folger, MS X. d. 241, ff. 4d-5.

RaW 819 -----

Account of Ralegh's speech and execution in a letter written by John Chamberlain to Sir Dudley Carleton; 31 October 1618.

This MS printed in *The Letters of John Chamberlain*, ed. Norman Egbert McClure (Philadelphia, 1939), II, 175-9. Extracts from this letter appear in SP.14/103/59-60.

Public Record Office, SP.14/103/58.

RaW 820 -----

Account of Ralegh's execution and speech in a letter written by John Pory (1572-1635) to Sir Dudley Carleton; 31 October 1618.

This MS printed in William S. Powell, 'John Pory on the Death of Sir Walter Raleigh', *WMQ*, 3rd Ser. 9 (1952), 532-8 (pp. 534-7).

Public Record Office, SP.14/103/61.

RaW 821 -----

Account in Spanish of Ralegh's execution, in a letter written by Juan Bautista van Male to the Count of Gondomar, in a composite volume of Gondomar's diplomatic correspondence; 14 November 1618.

Speech on the Scaffold (29 October 1618)

This MS printed in F.J. Sánchez Cantón, 'Cóme se enteró el Conde de Gondomar de la ejecución de Sir Walter Ralegh', *Real Academia de la Historia, Boletín* 113 (1943), 123-9.

Biblioteca de Palacio, Madrid, MS 2160, no. 57.

RaW 822 -----

Account in Spanish of Ralegh's speech and execution, in a letter written by the Spanish agent Ulloa to King Philip; 1618.

This account printed (in an English translation) in Martin A.S. Hume, *Sir Walter Ralegh* (London, 1897), pp. 414-16; reprinted from this publication in V.T. Harlow, *Ralegh's Last Voyage* (London, 1932), pp. 314-15.

Hume's source, presumably in the Spanish archives, is unlocated; it is not at Simancas and cannot be identified in the archives of the Biblioteca de Palacio, Madrid, although it may be among uncatalogued papers.

--- -----

See also INTRODUCTION.

Thomas Sackville
Earl of Dorset

1536-1608

For abbreviations used throughout Volume I, see p.xi.

INTRODUCTION

Sackville's reputation as a poet rests solely on the *Induction* and *Complaint of Buckingham* which he contributed to *A Myrrour for Magistrates*. By good fortune the original MS of an enlarged version of this composition survives (SaT 1); it is among the earliest poetical autographs recorded in the *Index*.

Sackville collaborated with Thomas Norton on the tragedy of *Gorboduc*, but this is represented in the *Index* only by a MS extract from a printed source (SaT 2). A poem *On Sir Philip and Sir Thomas Hobby* (beginning 'Two woorthie knightes, and Hobbyes both by name') was printed in John Payne Collier, 'On Norton and Sackville, the authors of "Gorboduc", the earliest blank verse Tragedy in our language', *The Shakespeare Society's Papers*, IV (London, 1849), 123-8. Collier claimed that he found the poem in Sackville's autograph in a 'friend's portfolio', but the MS has never come to light since then and it is now quite impossible to test this claim.

Many other autographs of Sackville survive in the form of letters, official papers and signed legal documents, but these have not been included in the *Index*. His papers can be found chiefly in the British Library (Additional, Cotton, Harley and Lansdowne MSS), the Public Record Office, the Folger and Pierpont Morgan Libraries, the Robert H. Taylor Collection at Princeton, and in various collections recorded in the *HMC* reports. Other documents of Sackville have appeared from time to time in booksellers' catalogues. Some of his letters are printed in *The Works of Thomas Sackville*, ed. Reginald W. Sackville-West (London, 1859), and a number are cited in Paul Bacquet, *Un contemporain d'Elisabeth I: Thomas Sackville* (Geneva, 1966). Sackville's letter to Lord Burghley, 30 November 1586 (Lansdowne MS 50, f. 67), is reproduced in Greg, *English Literary Autographs*, plate XXXIII(b).

PB.

ARRANGEMENT

Thomas Sackville Earl of Dorset

VERSE

SaT 1 *The Complaint of Henry Duke of Buckingham* ('Who trustes to much in honours highest trone').

MS, mainly a fair copy with revisions, partly a first draft, of a 192-stanza poem incorporating *The Induction* and *The Complaint of Henry Duke of Buckingham* (published in 1563), plus an unfinished draft of what is possibly an Epilogue to the poem (beginning 'Be this phaeton whirled within his cart'); chiefly autograph, partly in the hand of an amanuensis; c. 1557.

The Induction and *The Complaint of...Buckingham* first pub. in *A Myrrour for Magistrates*, 2nd edition (London, 1563). Additional passages in this MS first pub. in Marguerite Hearsey, 'The MS. of Sackville's Contribution to the *Mirror for Magistrates*', *RES*, 8 (1932), 282-90. The whole MS edited, with facsimiles of three pages, by Marguerite Hearsey (New Haven, 1936). Facsimiles of two pages in Croft, *Autograph Poetry*, I, 10-11.

St John's College, Cambridge, MS L. 7 (James 364).

--- *The Induction* ('The wrathfull winter proching on apace').

See SaT 1.

--- *On Sir Philip and Sir Thomas Hobby* ('Two woorthie knightes, and Hobbyes both by name').

See INTRODUCTION.

DRAMATIC WORKS

SaT 2 *Gorboduc or Ferrex and Porrex.*

Extracts transcribed from a printed edition in a miscellany compiled by William Briton (1564-1637) of Kelston, Somerset; c. 1586-96.

First pub. London, 1565; ed. Irby B. Cauthen, Jr. (University of Nebraska Press, 1970). This MS recorded in *The Poems of Sir Philip Sidney*, ed. William Ringler (Oxford, 1962), p. 541.

Owned by Arthur A. Houghton, Jr., MS, ff. 89v-90v (to be sold at Christie's, 1980).

MARGINALIA IN PRINTED BOOKS AND MANUSCRIPTS

SaT 3 Fabyan, Robert. *The Chronicle of Fabyan* (London, 1542).

Autograph notes.

Pierpont Morgan Library, W. 3. D. os.

William Shakespeare

1564-1616

ABBREVIATIONS

Evans, *PQ*, 41 (1962) G. Blakemore Evans, 'The Douai Manuscript — Six Shakespearean Transcripts (1694-95)', *Philological Quarterly*, 41 (1962), 158-72.

Savage, *Shakespearean Extracts* *Shakespearean Extracts from "Edward Pudsey's Booke" ... collected by Richard Savage* (Stratford-on-Avon, [1887]).

For abbreviations used throughout Volume I, see p.xi.

INTRODUCTION

There are six genuine autograph signatures of Shakespeare. Three signatures (the last preceded by the words 'By me') are on his Will, of 25 March 1616, in the Public Record Office (PROB 1/4); another is attached to the deposition in the case of Belott versus Mountjoy, 11 May 1612, in the Public Record Office (Court of Requests, Documents of Shakespearian Interest, Req. 4/1); and two more are attached to the conveyance and mortgage of the Blackfriars gate-house, 10 and 11 March 1612/13, in the Guildhall Library and the British Library (Egerton MS 1787) respectively. These signatures have been often reproduced in facsimile: they are discussed, for example, in R. C. Bald, '*The Booke of Sir Thomas Moore* and its Problems', *SS*, 2 (1949), 44-65. Both signatures and documents to which they are affixed, together with many other documents relating to Shakespeare's life, are reproduced in S. Schoenbaum, *William Shakespeare: A Documentary Life* (Oxford, 1975).

On the basis of these signatures the celebrated 'Hand D' in the MS of *Sir Thomas More* (ShW 88) has been attributed to Shakespeare, an attribution which is now virtually certain. For the latest evidence of authenticity in a long line of palaeographical discussions, see Giles Dawson's article in *TLS* (22 April 1977), p. 484.

No other genuine specimens of Shakespeare's handwriting are known, although various 'discoveries' have been claimed over the years, one of the most interesting of which is perhaps the series of annotations in a printed exemplum of *Halle's Chronicle* (1550) discovered by Alan Keen: see Alan Keen and Roger Lubbock, *The Annotator* (London, 1954). Nor are there any transcripts of Shakespeare's works which could have his authority. For this reason, with certain obvious exceptions, MS texts have commanded relatively little attention from scholars despite the magnitude of the Shakespeare industry. A considerable number of MS texts of various kinds are recorded in the entries below and they have not been noted by editors unless otherwise stated.

Among the most important items are marked proof sheets for the First Folio of Shakespeare's *Works* (London, 1623); five examples have so far been discovered (ShW 36, 53-4, 70, 84). Several notable 17th-century MS acting versions of plays are recorded (ShW 38, 40, 48, 51-2, 59, 64, 85, 106), and also the Peacham document of *Titus Andronicus* (ShW 104), which must be the earliest illustration of a Shakespearian performance.

Various extracts from the plays in 17th-century miscellanies are likewise recorded. The earliest quotations would appear to be those in a miscellany compiled by Edward Pudsey (1573-1613), a native of Derbyshire, who lived part of his life in London and died in Tewkesbury, Gloucestershire. Pudsey copied extracts from eight of Shakespeare's plays; all were evidently transcribed from the early Quartos except *Othello* (ShW 73), which was not printed until 1622 and which must have been quoted by Pudsey from memory or from notes he made during an early performance. All the Shakespearian texts except *Othello* were printed from Pudsey's miscellany in 1887 in Richard Savage's *Shakespearean Extracts*. The miscellany was subsequently bought by the Shakespearian scholar and collector James Orchard Halliwell-Phillipps (1820-89), and after his death was acquired by the Bodleian (pressmark MS Eng. poet. d. 3). It was then discovered that the miscellany lacked several of its original leaves, including the extracts from *Hamlet*, *Much Ado about Nothing*, *Richard II*, *Richard III*, and part of *Romeo and Juliet*; these leaves were only rediscovered in 1977 among Savage's papers at the Shakespeare Birthplace Trust Record Office (ER 82). The main Bodleian portion of the miscellany has been fully edited, and the known facts about Pudsey's life established, in Juliet Mary Gowan, *An Edition of Edward Pudsey's Commonplace Book (c.1600-1615) from the Manuscript in the Bodleian Library* (unpub. M. Phil., University of London, 1967). Miss Gow n (now Mrs Akehurst) has also examined the Stratford fragment and it was she who identified the previously unrecognised and unprinted extracts from *Othello*.

Among other miscellanies with extracts from Shakespeare one stands out as having special interest. In an article on 'An Unknown Shakespearian Commonplace

Book' in *The Library* (1973), Gunnar Sorelius described the remains he had discovered of a MS compilation of c.1660 containing literally hundreds of quotations from Shakespeare. The original MS was once owned by James Orchard Halliwell-Phillipps, who had chosen to cut it up into many scores of small strips (along with other MSS, incunabula, early play texts, etc.) which he distributed among his immense collection of scrapbooks. The main set of scrapbooks, his *Notes upon the Works of Shakespeare*, was designed to illustrate words and phrases in Shakespeare as a supplement to Halliwell-Phillipps's own edition of the *Works* (16 vols, 1853-65); it consists of 128 volumes (each 17 cm x 12.5 cm), arranged according to play, and is preserved in the Shakespeare Centre at Stratford-upon-Avon (see ShW 113). Two other scrapbooks which Gunnar Sorelius found contained cuttings from the same MS are preserved in the Folger; they include the first page of the MS bearing the title 'Hesperides or the Muses Garden' and the complete index to the MS (see ShW 114). It was possible to deduce from the various fragments so discovered that the original MS was a large commonplace book of at least 1028 numbered pages, each measuring about 20.3 x 15.8 cm, containing quotations from some 302 miscellaneous works, including 36 plays of Shakespeare. The MS was neatly written in double columns and arranged alphabetically under headings (such as 'Abasement', 'Friendship', 'Remembering', 'Treacherous', etc.). The compiler's identity was not known, however, nor was the fate of the rest of the MS containing non-Shakespearian matter.

The last problem remains unsolved, but research for the *Index* has been able to establish the exact identity and text of the work. In the Stationers' Register, under the date 16th of August 1655, appears the following entry for 'Master Mosely':

> . . . a booke entituled Hesperides, or the Muses' Garden stored wth the choicest flowers of language and learning, in philosophy, history, cosmography, intermixed wth the sweets of poetry, wherein ye ceremonious courtier & passionat amorist may gather rarities suitable to their ffancies being upon twelve hundred heads alphabetically digested by John Evans, Gent.

Of the named compiler nothing more can be said; various John Evanses graduated from the universities and one John Evans, M.A., produced the early spelling-dictionary *The Palace of profitable Pleasure* (London, for W. Stansby, 1621). *Hesperides* evidently remained unpublished. In a list of books 'printed for Humphrey Moseley, at the Princes Armes in St. Pauls Church-yard', a list which is preserved in the Bodleian (Don. f. 144) and which can be dated no earlier than 1659, a largely similar description of '*Hesperides*, or the Muses Garden' appears as item 341; it immediately follows the heading 'These Books I purpose to Print, Deo Volente'. Moseley's death on 31 January 1660/1 must have sealed the fate of the work. Halliwell-Phillipps's dissections would have done almost as much for the unpublished MS, but a second and almost perfect MS copy of *Hesperides* can fortunately be identified as MS V. b. 93 in the Folger (see ShW 115). Comparison between this MS and some of the Halliwell-Phillipps fragments shows that both are written in the same scribal hand, though possibly at different periods. The Folger MS (V. b. 93) would appear to be the same work as the fragments but probably in an enlarged version. The index in MS V. a. 75 lists 302 titles (from which, as Dr Sorelius noted, the works of Beaumont and Fletcher are conspicuously absent); the index in MS V. b. 93 (less neatly written but more consistently arranged) lists 358 titles, including all those found in V. a. 75 and, among other works, 39 titles for Beaumont and Fletcher. Thus it now becomes possible to comprehend virtually in its entirety an anthology containing one of the earliest truly extensive collections of quotations from Shakespeare. The quotations derive from the First Folio, as Gunnar Sorelius noted, but, as part of a systematically arranged commonplace book, they can arguably shed light on the way Shakespeare was interpreted in the mid-17th century, and they have the additional interest of having been produced for one of the most notable publishers of the time.

In a different connection, certain other miscellanies are of interest because they contain texts of Shakespeare's poems, particularly of the Sonnets. The last editor to leave evidence of having taken pains to find and collate MS versions of the Sonnets was Tucker Brooke in 1936. Tucker Brooke listed (pp. 66-9) a number of MS texts but dismissed their value by saying 'None appear to be earlier than the Quarto, and none improve its text at any point'. He noted characteristically (p. 245) that the MS copies of Sonnet 2 ('When forty winters shall besiege thy brow') 'give the text in various states of corruption', an assumption never questioned by other editors. It is, however, known that at least some of the Sonnets had a MS circulation in the 1590s: among the works of the 'mellifluous & hony-tongued Shakespeare' which Francis Meres praises in *Palladis Tamia* (London, 1598), pp. 281-2, are 'his sugred Sonnets among his priuate friends'. It is at least a possibility that certain of the texts found in miscellanies of the 1620s and '30s ultimately derive from early MS copies of individual sonnets and have no connection whatever with the 1609 edition. It is also interesting that one textual tradition of Sonnet 2 relates to a song version (see ShW 14), perhaps a lost setting written in the 1620s. The extant MS texts of this particular sonnet are discussed in Mary Hobbs, 'Shakespeare's Sonnet II — "A Sugred Sonnet"?', *N & Q* (forthcoming, April 1979).

Another group of Shakespearian texts found in MS sources is of songs from the plays. Like those in other contemporary plays, Shakespeare's songs sometimes circulated as independent pieces, the most interesting texts being those which preserve early — if not the original — musical settings. The important subject of music in Shakespeare's plays lies largely outside the scope of the *Index*. There are, for instance, many copies of the words or music of songs which are only cited in the plays. A few examples may be given. Silence's song 'Do me right' in *2 Henry IV* (V, iii, 72-4) is the refrain from the popular Elizabethan song 'Monser myngo for qualifying does passe'. Versions appear in the Bodleian (MS Mus. Sch. f. 17-19: f. 19, fol. 50v), the British Library (Add. MS 24665, f. 36r-v), Carlisle Cathedral Library (Dean & Chapter of Carlisle MSS, Box B1, Altus, pp. 22-3; Bassus, pp. 20-1), Christ Church, Oxford (MS Mus. 439, ff. 37v-8), and the National Library of Scotland (Adv. MS 5. 2. 14, f. 25v, and MS 9447 (Panmure 10), ff. 138-40). Most of these versions are discussed in John P. Cutts, 'The Original Music of a Song in *2 Henry IV*', *SQ*, 7 (1956), 385-92, and in Frederick W. Sternfeld, 'Lasso's Music for Shakespeare's "Samingo"', *SQ*, 9 (1958), 105-16; the Carlisle text is printed in Cutts, *Bishop Smith's Part-Song Books in Carlisle Cathedral Library* (American Institute of Musicology, 1972), pp. 45-6. The Fitzwilliam Virginal Book (Fitzwilliam Museum, Cambridge, MU. 52. D. 29, No. 297, p. 416) contains music only for Autolycus's song 'Jog on, jog on, thy foot-path way' in *The Winter's Tale* (IV, iii, 120-3) and (No. 66, p. 125) for the Clown's song 'O mistress mine, where are you roaming?' in *Twelfth Night* (II, iii, 41-6, 49-54). The song 'Farewell, dear heart' cited by Sir Toby Belch (*Twelfth Night*, II, iii, 105) appears in Trinity College, Dublin (MS 412, ff. 58v-9), and is printed in J. Stafford Smith, *Musica Antiqua* (London, 1812), II, 204-5. The complete text of the song 'The god of love' cited by Benedick in *Much Ado about Nothing* (V, ii, 26-9) is preserved in the 'Braye MS' in the Osborn Collection at Yale (Music MS 13): see James M. Osborn, 'Benedick's Song in "Much Ado"', *The Times* (17 November 1958), p. 11. The possible connection between Edgar's 'Tom o' Bedlam' song in *King Lear* and other MS Bedlamite verses is explored in Robert Graves, *Loving Mad Tom* (1927; reprinted Welwyn Garden City, 1969), and in Stanley Wells, 'Tom o' Bedlam's Song and *King Lear*', *SQ*, 12 (1961), 311-15. These and similar items, such as Ophelia's songs in *Hamlet*, are the subject of much discussion by musicologists. For a brief list of settings of 'Shakespearian' songs and of some important critical studies, see Vincent Duckles, 'The Music for the Lyrics in Early Seventeenth-Century English Drama: A Bibliography of the Primary Sources', *Music in English Renaissance Drama*, ed. John H. Long (Lexington, 1968), 117-60 (pp. 151-6).

Entries are not given to prompt books of Shakespeare's plays (unless they also happen to be MSS). A descriptive catalogue of Shakespeare prompt books from the early 17th century to 1961 is available in Charles H. Shattuck, *The Shakespeare Promptbooks* (Urbana & London, 1965); a supplementary list appears in *Theatre Notebook*, 24 (1969), 5-17. The largest extant collection of examples dating from the 17th century is of those used at Joseph Ashbury's Smock Alley Theatre in Dublin in the 1670s and '80s; all the texts belong to a Third Folio (1663). The Folger has the Smock Alley prompt books of *The Comedy of Errors*, *Henry VIII*, *King Lear*, *Macbeth*, *The Merry Wives of Windsor* (also a MS portion written to replace missing pages: see ShW 65), *Othello*, *Timon of Athens*, *Twelfth Night*, *The Winter's Tale*, and a half-leaf fragment of the prompt book of *1 Henry IV*. Edinburgh University Library has the Smock Alley prompt books of *Hamlet* (JY 442) and *A Midsummer Night's Dream* (JY 441), and the last page of the prompt book of *Macbeth* (JY 442). The Smock Alley prompt book of *Julius Caesar*, formerly in the Shakespeare Memorial Library, Birmingham, was destroyed by fire in 1879, but a few lines belonging to it are written on the first page of the *Macbeth* prompt book in Edinburgh and the cast list is written on the last page of the *Timon* prompt book in the Folger. The Smock Alley prompt books of *Henry IV, Parts I and II* were found by Gunnar Sorelius to have suffered the same fate as the *Hesperides* miscellany; they were cut up and pasted in Halliwell-Phillipps's Shakespearian scrapbooks, those now in the Shakespeare Centre at Stratford: see Gunnar Sorelius, 'The Smock Alley Prompt-Books of 1 and *2 Henry IV*', *SQ*, 22 (1971), 111-28. The Smock Alley prompt books in general are discussed in R. C. Bald, 'Shakespeare on the Stage in Restoration Dublin', *PMLA*, 56.i (1941), 369-78, and full-scale facsimile editions of the *Hamlet* and *Macbeth* prompt books have been produced by G. Blakemore Evans in his series *Shakespearean Prompt-Books of the Seventeenth Century* (Bibliographical Society of the University of Virginia, Charlottesville), Vols IV (1966) and V (1970).

The second most notable group of early prompt books is found in an exemplum of the First Folio at the University of Padua (RARI N.S.1), in which *Macbeth*, *Measure for Measure*, and *The Winter's Tale* have been prepared for theatrical use (c.1640). These texts are discussed in Leslie F. Casson, 'Notes on a Shakespeare First Folio in Padua', *MLN*, 51 (1936), 417-23, and in G. Blakemore Evans, 'New Evidence on the Provenance of the Padua Prompt-Books of Shakespeare's *Macbeth*, *Measure for Measure*, and *Winter's Tale*', *SB*, 20 (1967), 239-42. They are all edited in facsimile in Blakemore Evans's prompt book series, Vols I (1960) and II (1963). In Vol III of his series (1964) Blakemore Evans edits in facsimile the prompt books of *The Comedy of Errors* and *A Midsummer Night's Dream* which were used c.1672 in the Hatton Garden 'Nursery' and which are now in Edinburgh University Library (JY 438 and JY 439). Other 17th-century prompt books of unknown provenance are to be found in the Boston Public Library, Massachusetts (G. 17b. 21: *The Merry Wives of Windsor*), the Folger (TN, Second Folio: *Twelfth Night*), the Huntington (RB 69317 and 69337: *2 Henry IV* and *Othello*), the University of Michigan (*The Merchant of Venice*), the Victoria and Albert Museum (Dyce Collection, Cat. No. 8980: *Much Ado about Nothing*), and the Elizabethan Club at Yale (No. 191: *Romeo and Juliet*).

One additional item of interest is the account written by Simon Forman (1552-1611) of the performances of *The Winter's Tale*, *Cymbeline*, and *Macbeth* (also a play on Richard II) which he saw at the Globe probably in April and May of 1611 (though *Macbeth* is dated 1610). His original account is in the Bodleian (MS Ashmole 208, ff. 201-7v). This account is printed, with facsimiles, in Halliwell-Phillipps's edition of Shakespeare (1853-65), VIII, 41; IX, 8; XIV, 61; XV, 417. A facsimile of f. 206 (the account of *Cymbeline*) appears in S. Schoenbaum, *William Shakespeare: A Documentary Life* (1975), p. 215.

All quotations and line references cited are taken from the *New Cambridge Shakespeare*, original editor John Dover Wilson, 39 vols (Cambridge, 1921-). The various poems and plays which constitute the Shakespeare 'apocrypha' are not included. For certain later adaptations of the plays (such as Davenant's *Macbeth*) see Volume II of the *Index*. Shakespeare's contribution to *The Passionate Pilgrim* (London, 1599) is taken to be poems 1, 2, 3, 5, and 16; for certain other poems see RICHARD BARNFIELD, CHRISTOPHER MARLOWE, and SIR WALTER RALEGH.

PB.

ARRANGEMENT

Verse	ShW 1-35
Dramatic works: (1) Individual plays	ShW 36-112
(2) Miscellaneous extracts	ShW 113-17.

See also Addenda to Part 2, p. 633

William Shakespeare

VERSE

ShW 1 *A Lover's Complaint* ('From off a hill whose concave womb reworded').

Copy of part of lines 41-2, here beginning '...lets not bounty fall', partly erased, scribbled inside the detached cover of a book; mid-17th century.

First pub. in *Sonnets* (London, 1609).

Folger, MS V. a. 150.

--- *The Passionate Pilgrim.*

See INTRODUCTION; ShW 30; RICHARD BARNFIELD, INTRODUCTION; MrC 10-19; and RaW 189-99.

ShW 2 *The Rape of Lucrece* ('From the besieged Ardea all in post').

Extracts, comprising lines 365-71, 386-99, 419-20, beginning 'Into ye chamber wickedly he stalkes', in a composite volume of verse collected by Peter Le Neve (1661-1729), his brother Oliver, and Thomas Martin (1697-1771) of Palgrave; c. 1630.

First pub. London, 1594.

British Library, Add. MS 27406, f. 74.

ShW 2.5 See Addenda, p. 633.

ShW 3 -----

Copy of lines 869-910, beginning 'Unruly blasts wait on the tender spring', in a miscellany compiled by one Richard Waferer; c. 1620.

British Library, Add. MS 52585, ff. 54v-5.

ShW 4 -----

Copy of lines 958-9, beginning 'To cheer the ploughman with increaseful crops', in a miscellany compiled by John Abbott (b. 1653/4) of St John's College, Oxford; c. 1670s.

Bodleian, MS Rawl. D. 954, f. 41v.

ShW 5 -----

Copy of line 1086 and part of line 1087, here given as 'reuealing day through euery Crany peepes and see', written on the title page of a MS volume of prose works connected with the Court or state affairs; c. 1597.

This MS reproduced in Frank J. Burgoyne, *Collotype Facsimile & Type Transcript of an Elizabethan Manuscript Preserved at Alnwick Castle, Northumberland* (London, 1904).

Owned by the Duke of Northumberland, Alnwick Castle, MS 525 (Safe 4).

ShW 6 *Sonnets.*

Three pages of miscellaneous quotations from the *Sonnets* (including ShW 7, 22, 23, 27), headed 'Shakespeare', in a verse miscellany once owned by one 'E.H.'; c. 1660.

First pub. London, 1609; 2nd edition in *Poems Written by Wil. Shake-speare. Gent.* (London, 1640); ed. R.M. Alden (Boston & New York, 1916); ed. Tucker Brooke (London, 1936); ed. H.E. Rollins, New Variorum edition (Philadelphia & London, 1944); ed. Stephen Booth (New Haven & London, 1977). Formerly MS 267.1, this MS analysed in Tucker Brooke, pp. 68-9. Facsimile of f. 22 in Bertram Dobell sale catalogue, June 1902.

Folger, MS V. a. 148, Part I, ff. 22-3.

ShW 7 *Sonnet 1* ('From fairest creatures we desire increase').

Copy of a composite version made up of lines 5-14 of Sonnet 1, here beginning 'Thou Contracted to thine owne bright eys', together with lines 1-4 of Sonnet 2 and line 5 of Sonnet 54, headed 'Cruel', in a verse miscellany once owned by one 'E.H.' (see ShW 6); c. 1660.

Printed from this MS in Alden, p. 23; recorded in Tucker Brooke, p. 66. Facsimile in Dobell sale catalogue, June 1902.

Folger, MS V. a. 148, Part I, f. 22.

ShW 8 *Sonnet 2* ('When forty winters shall besiege thy brow').

Copy, headed 'Spes Altera' and here beginning 'When threescore winters shall besiege thy brow', in a miscellany once owned by Margaret Bellasys, probably the daughter of Thomas, first Lord Fauconberg (1577-1653); c. 1630.

British Library, Add. MS 10309, f. 143.

ShW 9 -----

Copy, headed 'Spes Altera', transcribed from ShW 10, in a verse miscellany possibly compiled by a member of an Inn of Court; c. 1630s.

This MS recorded in Tucker Brooke, p. 66.

British Library, Add. MS 21433, f. 114v.

ShW 10 -----

Copy, headed 'Spes altera', in a miscellany possibly compiled by a member of an Inn of Court; c. 1620s-30s.

This MS recorded in Tucker Brooke, p. 66.

British Library, Add. MS 25303, f. 119v.

Sonnet 2

ShW 11 -----

Copy, headed 'To one that would dy a maide', in a verse miscellany compiled by Daniel Leare (a distant cousin of William Strode), probably while at Christ Church, Oxford; c. 1631-3.

This MS recorded in Tucker Brooke, p. 66.

British Library, Add. MS 30982, f. 18.

ShW 12 -----

Copy, headed 'To one that would die a Mayd', in a verse miscellany probably compiled by one 'I.A.' of Christ Church, Oxford, and later owned by Robert Killigrew; c. early 1630s.

Printed from this MS in C.C. Stopes, 'An Early Variant of a Shakespeare Sonnet', *The Athenaeum* (26 July 1913), p. 89, and in Alden, pp. 21-2; recorded in Tucker Brooke, p. 66.

British Library, Sloane MS 1792, f. 45.

ShW 13 -----

Copy, headed 'To one that would dye a Mayd', in a verse miscellany compiled by an Oxford man; c. 1630s.

Printed from this MS in Bertram Dobell, 'An Early Variant of a Shakespeare Sonnet', *The Athenaeum* (2 August 1913), p. 112, and in Alden, p. 22; recorded in Tucker Brooke, p. 67 (e).

Folger, MS V. a. 170, pp. 163-4.

ShW 14 -----

Copy, headed 'Spes Altera A song', in a miscellany; c. 1630.

Formerly MS 452.5, this MS recorded in Tucker Brooke, p. 67.

Folger, MS V. a. 345, p. 145.

ShW 15 -----

Copy, headed 'A Lover to his Mistres' and ascribed to 'W.S.', in a verse miscellany; c. 1630.

Printed from this MS in H. Harvey Wood, 'A Seventeenth-Century Manuscript of Poems by Donne and Others', *E & S*, 16 (1930), 179-90 (p. 180).

University of Nottingham, Portland MS Pw V 37, p. 69.

ShW 16 -----

Copy, headed 'The Benefitt of Mariage' and here beginning 'When forty yeares shall beseig thy browe', in a verse miscellany owned in 1642 by one Horatio Carey; c. 1638-42.

This MS recorded in Tucker Brooke, p. 67 (g).

Rosenbach Foundation, MS 1083/17, ff. 132v-3.

ShW 17 -----

Copy, untitled and ascribed to 'W. Shakspere', in a verse miscellany; c. 1630s-40s.

This MS collated in H.T. Price, 'An Early Variant of a Shakespeare Sonnet', *The Athenaeum* (6 September 1913), p. 230, and printed in Alden, p. 22; recorded in Tucker Brooke, p. 67.

St John's College, Cambridge, MS S. 23 (James 416), f. 38r-v.

ShW 18 -----

Copy, headed 'To one y^t would dye a Mayd', in a verse miscellany connected with Christ Church, Oxford, owned and perhaps partly compiled by George Morley, later Bishop of Winchester (1598-1684); 1625-30s.

Westminster Abbey, MS 41, f. 49.

ShW 19 -----

Copy, headed 'To one that would die a maide', in a miscellany; mid-17th century.

This MS recorded in *BC*, 8 (Winter 1959), p. 387.

Yale, Osborn Collection, b 205, f. 54v.

ShW 20 *Sonnet 8* ('Music to hear, why hear'st thou music sadly?').

Copy, headed 'In laudem Musice et opprobrium Contemporij eiusdem', in a miscellany; c. 1630.

Printed from this MS in Alden, pp. 33-4, and in *The Shakespeare Allusion-Book* (London, 1932), I, 211; recorded in Tucker Brooke, p. 67.

British Library, Add. MS 15226, f. 4v.

ShW 21 *Sonnet 32* ('If thou survive my well-contented day').

Copy in a verse miscellany compiled by an Oxford man and once owned by one Stephen Welden; mid-17th century.

Formerly MS 452.4, this MS collated in Tucker Brooke, p. 67.

Folger, MS V. a. 162, f. 26.

ShW 22 *Sonnet 33* ('Full many a glorious morning have I seen').

Copy in a verse miscellany once owned by one 'E.H.' (see ShW 6); c. 1660.

Formerly MS 267.1, this MS recorded in Tucker Brooke, p. 67.

Folger, MS V. a. 148, Part I, f. 23.

ShW 23 *Sonnet 68* ('Thus is his cheek the map of days outworn').

Copy in a verse miscellany once owned by one 'E.H.' (see ShW 6); c. 1660.

Formerly MS 267.1, this MS recorded in Tucker Brooke, p. 67.

Folger, MS V. a. 148, Part I, f. 22v.

ShW 24 *Sonnet 71* ('No longer mourn for me when I am dead').

Copy in a verse miscellany compiled by an Oxford man and once owned by one Stephen Welden; mid-17th century.

Formerly MS 452.4, this MS collated in Tucker Brooke, p. 67 (as his sonnet 75).

Folger, MS V. a. 162, f. 12v.

ShW 25 *Sonnet 106* ('When in the chronicle of wasted time').

Copy, headed 'On his Mistris Beauty' and here beginning 'When in the Annalls of all wastinge Time', in a verse miscellany used by members of the Holgate family of Saffron Walden, Essex; c. 1630s.

Printed from this MS in Rollins, p. 260. Facsimile in *Autograph Letters & Manuscripts: Major Acquisitions of the Pierpont Morgan Library 1924-1974* (New York, 1974), plate 12.

Pierpont Morgan Library, MA 1057, p. 96.

ShW 26 -----

Copy, headed 'On his M[ris] Beauty' and here beginning 'When in the Annales of all-wasting time', with 18 additional lines, in a verse miscellany compiled by one Robert Bishop; c. 1630.

This MS recorded in Tucker Brooke, p. 67.

Rosenbach Foundation, MS 1083/16, pp. 256-7.

ShW 27 *Sonnet 107* ('Not mine own fears, nor the prophetic soul').

Copy, headed 'A Monument', in a verse miscellany once owned by one 'E.H.' (see ShW 6); c. 1660.

Formerly MS 267.1, this MS collated in Alden, p. 252, and in Tucker Brooke, p. 67. Facsimile in Dobell sale catalogue, June 1902.

Folger, MS V. a. 148, Part I, f. 22.

ShW 28 *Sonnet 116* ('Let me not to the marriage of true minds').

Copy, here beginning 'Selfe blinding error seazeth all those mindes', in a musical setting by Henry Lawes, in a MS music book owned (in 1659) and partly compiled by the composer John Gamble; c. 1630s-50s.

Printed from this MS, with a facsimile, in Willa McClung Evans, 'Lawes' Version of Shakespeare's Sonnet CXVI', *PMLA*, 51.i (1936), 120-2, and in Evans, *Henry Lawes* (New York & London, 1941), pp. 43-4.

New York Public Library, Music Division, Drexel MS 4257, No. 33.

ShW 29 *Sonnet 128* ('How oft when thou, my music, music play'st').

Copy in a composite volume of verse; c. 1625-40s.

Bodleian, MS Rawl. poet. 152, f. 34.

ShW 30 *Sonnet 138* ('When my love swears that she is made of truth').

Copy in a miscellany later owned by one Joseph Hall; c. 1630s-50.

Sonnet 138 first pub. as poem 1 in *The Passionate Pilgrime* (London, 1599). Formerly MS 2071.7, this MS recorded in Rollins, p. 354.

Folger, MS V. a. 339, f. 197v.

ShW 31 *Venus and Adonis* ('Even as the sun with purple-coloured face').

Copy of lines 17-18 (beginning 'Here come and sit, where never serpent hisses') in a four-line version headed 'Kessing: a song' and beginning 'Come sweet sit heere where neuer serpent hisses', in a verse miscellany compiled by one Robert Bishop; c. 1630.

First pub. London, 1593.

Rosenbach Foundation, MS 1083/16, p. 279.

ShW 32 -----

Copy of lines 131-2, beginning 'Fair flowers that are not gather'd in their prime', inscribed in a 13th-century MS volume of Latin treatises; early 17th century.

Printed from this MS in *The Shakespeare Allusion-Book* (London, 1932), I, 216.

British Library, Royal MS 8 A. XXI, f. 153v.

Venus and Adonis

ShW 33 -----

Copy of lines 517-22, beginning 'A thousand kisses buys my heart from me', in a musical setting, in a MS songbook compiled by one Giles Earle; c. 1615-26.

Printed from this MS in John P. Cutts, '"Venus and Adonis" in an Early Seventeenth-Century Song-Book', *N & Q*, 208 (August 1963), 302-3.

British Library, Add. MS 24665, f. 75r-v.

ShW 34 -----

Copy of lines 529-34, headed 'Another' [on Night] and here beginning 'Now the worlds comforter with weary gate', in a verse miscellany; c. 1634.

These lines pub. as a separate poem in *Englands Parnassus* (London, 1600).

Rosenbach Foundation, MS 239/27, p. 166.

ShW 35 -----

Copy of lines 529-34, headed 'Goodnight to yoủ' and here beginning 'Now the worlds Comforter w[t] weary gate', in a verse miscellany compiled by one Robert Bishop; c. 1630.

Rosenbach Foundation, MS 1083/16, p. 175.

DRAMATIC WORKS

(1) INDIVIDUAL PLAYS

ShW 36 *Antony and Cleopatra.*

Proof sheet, with MS markings calling for nineteen corrections, of sig. xx6^v (p. 352) belonging to an exemplum of the First Folio (1623) but now a disjunct single leaf.

First pub. in the First Folio (London, 1623). This item (first discovered by J.O. Halliwell-Phillipps) described, with facsimiles, in Edwin Eliott Willoughby, *The Printing of the First Folio of Shakespeare* (Oxford Bibliographical Society, 1932), and in Charlton Hinman, *The Printing and Proof-Reading of the First Folio of Shakespeare*, 2 vols (Oxford, 1963), I, 317-19 and facing p. 234.

Folger, STC 22273, Frag. (Halliwell-Phillipps).

ShW 37 -----

Extracts in a miscellany; late 17th century.

British Library, Lansdowne MS 1185, ff. 26v-36.

ShW 38 *As You Like It.*

Copy, untitled, a text derived from the Second Folio (London, 1632), used for amateur staging by one of the English colleges at Douai; 9 March 1694/5.

First pub. in the First Folio (London, 1623). This MS described in Evans, *PQ*, 41 (1962).

Bibliothèque Municipale, Douai, France, MS 787, ff. 32v-65v.

ShW 39 ----- V, iii, 15-38. Song: 'It was a lover and his lass'.

Copy of the Pages' song in a musical setting by Thomas Morley, in a MS songbook possibly compiled by one William Stirling with later additions by John Leyden (1775-1811); c. 1639.

This setting first pub. in Thomas Morley, *First Book of Ayres* (London, 1600). Printed from this MS in Nelly Diem, *Beiträge zur Geschichte der Schottischen Musik im XVII Jahrhundert* (Zürich & Leipzig, 1919), p. 97; discussed in Edmund H. Fellowes, '"It was a Lover and his Lass": Some Fresh Points of Criticism', *MLR*, 41 (1946), 202-6; and in Doughtie, *Lyrics from English Airs*, pp. 496-7.

National Library of Scotland, Adv. MS 5. 2. 14, f. 18r-v.

ShW 40 *The Comedy of Errors.*

Copy, a text derived from the Second Folio (London, 1632), with stage directions in another hand; used for amateur staging by one of the English colleges at Douai; 1694.

First pub. in the First Folio (London, 1623). This MS described in Evans, *PQ*, 41 (1962).

Bibliothèque Municipale, Douai, France, MS 787, ff. 66v-93v.

ShW 41 -----

Brief quotations, including Aegeon's lines beginning 'Yet this my comfort: when your words are done' (I, i, 27-8), in a miscellany; c. 1700.

University of Leeds, Brotherton Collection, MS Lt. 48, f. [32 rev].

ShW 42 *Cymbeline*, II, iii, 19-27. Song: 'Hark, hark, the lark at heaven's gate sings'.

Copy in a musical setting possibly by Robert Johnson, in a MS songbook; c. 1640s.

First pub. in the First Folio (London, 1623). Printed from this MS, with a facsimile, in

Willa McClung Evans, 'Shakespeare's "Harke harke ye larke"', *PMLA*, 60. i (1945), 95-101; also discussed in George A. Thewlis, 'Some Notes on a Bodleian Manuscript', *M & L*, 22 (1941), 32-5, and printed in Cutts, *Musique de la troupe de Shakespeare*, p. 6.

Bodleian, MS Don. c. 57, f. 40v.

ShW 43 ----- -----

Copy, transcribed from the Folio of 1664, in a MS book of jests compiled by Archbishop William Sancroft (1617-93); late 17th century.

Bodleian, MS Sancroft 53, p. 43.

ShW 44 *Hamlet.*

Excerpts, with comments on the play, in a miscellany compiled by Abraham Wright (1611-90); c. 1640.

First pub. London, 1603. These extracts and comments printed in James G. McManaway, 'Excerpta quaedam per A.W. adolescentem', *Studies in Shakespeare, Bibliography and Theater* (New York, 1969), 279-91 (pp. 286-9); and in Arthur C. Kirsch, 'A Caroline Commentary on the Drama', *MP*, 66 (1968-9), 256-61 (pp. 257-8).

British Library, Add. MS 22608, f. 85r-v.

ShW 45 -----

Extracts on both sides of one of four leaves now detached from a miscellany compiled by Edward Pudsey (1573-1613); 1600s.

Printed from this MS in Savage, *Shakespearean Extracts*, pp. 51-80.

Shakespeare Birthplace Trust Record Office, ER 82.

ShW 46 -----

Extracts from Polonius's speech to Laertes (I, iii, 59-69, 75-8), headed 'Advice to a Young man', here beginning 'Give thy thoughts noe tongue', and subscribed 'Sh:', among miscellaneous notes written at the end of a MS volume of works by or relating to Sir Walter Ralegh, owned in 1674 by one Andrew Card; c. 1684.

University of Chicago, MS 824, f. 113.

ShW 47 -----

Copy of Hamlet's soliloquy 'To be, or not to be, that is the question' (III, i, 56-88) in a musical setting by Cesare Morelli, in a MS volume of music compiled by Morelli for Samuel Pepys; c. 1680-93.

Printed from this MS in Macdonald Emslie, 'Pepys' Shakespeare Song', *SQ*, 6 (1955), 159-70.

Magdalene College, Cambridge, Pepys Library, MS 2591, ff. 37-40.

ShW 48 *Henry IV, Parts I and II.*

MS of a play adapted from Shakespeare's two plays by Sir Edward Dering (1598-1644) of Surrenden, Kent, probably written for a private theatrical performance; partly in Dering's hand, partly in the hand of an amanuensis with Dering's corrections and revisions; the text based on the Fifth Quarto of *1 Henry IV* (1613) and a 1600 Quarto of *2 Henry IV*; c. 1620s.

1 Henry IV first pub. London, 1598; *2 Henry IV* first pub. London, 1600. Printed from this MS, with facsimile examples, in *Shakespeare's Play of King Henry the Fourth Printed from a Contemporary Manuscript*, ed. James Orchard Halliwell, Shakespeare Society (London, 1845); collated in *Henry IV, Part I*, ed. Samuel Burdett Hemingway (Philadelphia & London, 1936), pp. 495-501, and in *Henry IV, Part II*, ed. Matthias A. Shaaber (Philadelphia & London, 1940), pp. 645-50; discussed in G. Blakemore Evans, 'The "Dering MS" of Shakespeare's *Henry IV* and Sir Edward Dering', *JEGP*, 54 (1955), 498-503. Facsimile of one page in Giles E. Dawson and Laetitia Kennedy-Skipton, *Elizabethan Handwriting 1500-1650* (London, 1968), plate 39.

Folger, MS V. b. 34.

ShW 49 *Henry IV, Part I.*

Copy of Prince Hal's speech beginning 'I know you all, and will awhile uphold' (I, ii, 187-209), headed 'The Prince of Walles his speech. 165' and written out as prose, in a composite volume of MSS; 14 April 1628.

Printed from this MS in *The Shakespeare Allusion-Book* (London, 1932), I, 336.

British Library, Egerton MS 2446, f. 13.

ShW 50 *Henry V.*

Extracts in a miscellany perhaps partly compiled by one William How; mid-17th century.

First pub. London, 1600.

Folger, MS V. a. 87, f. 6.

ShW 51 *Julius Caesar.*

Copy, a text derived from the Second Folio (London, 1632), with stage directions in another hand; used for amateur staging by one of the English colleges at Douai; 1694.

Julius Caesar

First pub. in the First Folio (London, 1623). This MS described in Evans, *PQ*, 41 (1962).

Bibliothèque Municipale, Douai, France, MS 787, ff. 131-70v.

ShW 52 -----

Copy of a text (possibly a prompt book) derived from the Second Folio (London, 1632), possibly related to ShW 51, in a miscellany; imperfect, lacking most of the last scene; c. 1690s.

This MS described in G. Blakemore Evans, 'Shakespeare's *Julius Caesar* -- A Seventeenth-Century Manuscript', *JEGP*, 41 (1942), 401-17.

Folger, MS V. a. 85, pp. 74-140.

ShW 53 *King Lear*.

Proof sheet, with MS markings calling for five corrections, of sig. qq6^{v} (p. 292) in an exemplum of the First Folio (1623).

First pub. London, 1608. This item discussed, with a facsimile, in Charlton Hinman, 'Mark III: New Light on the Proof-Reading for the First Folio of Shakespeare', *SB*, 3 (1950-1), 145-53.

Folger, STC 22273, No. 48.

ShW 54 -----

Proof sheet, with MS markings calling for ten corrections, of sig. rr3^{r} (p. 297) in an exemplum of the First Folio (1623).

This item discussed, with facsimiles, in James G. McManaway, 'Another Discovery of a Proof Sheet in Shakespeare's First Folio', *HLQ*, 41 (1977-8), 19-26.

Huntington, RB 56422.

ShW 55 *Love's Labours Lost*.

Extracts in a miscellany; late 17th century.

First pub. London, 1598.

British Library, Lansdowne MS 1185, ff. 14v-16.

ShW 56 -----

Copy of Longaville's couplet beginning 'Fat paunches have lean pates; and dainty bits' (I, i, 26-7), in a miscellany compiled by John Abbott (b. 1653/4) of St John's College, Oxford; c. 1670s.

Bodleian, MS Rawl. D. 954, f. 44v.

ShW 57 -----

Copy of Longaville's couplet (I, i, 26-7) in a miscellany compiled partly by the Oxford printer Christopher Wase (1627-90); mid-17th century.

Bodleian, MS Rawl. poet. 117, f. 276 rev.

ShW 58 -----

Copy of Armado's couplet beginning 'The Fox, the Ape, and the Humble-bee' (III, i, 84-5), in a verse miscellany probably compiled by a member of Christ Church, Oxford; c. 1630s-40s.

Bodleian, MS Eng. poet. e. 97, p. 180.

ShW 59 *Macbeth*.

Copy, a text derived from the Second Folio (London, 1632), used for amateur staging by one of the English colleges at Douai; 1694.

First pub. in the First Folio (London, 1623). This MS described in Evans, *PQ*, 41 (1962).

Bibliothèque Municipale, Douai, France, MS 787, ff. 171-209.

--- ----- III, v, 34. Song: 'Come away, come away, &c.'

See THOMAS MIDDLETON, MiT 32-3.

ShW 60 *Measure for Measure*.

Copy of two of the Duke's speeches (III, ii, 178-81, beginning 'No might nor greatness in mortality', and III, ii, 253-66, beginning 'He, who the sword of heaven will bear'), in a miscellany; c. 1700.

First pub. in the First Folio (London, 1623).

University of Leeds, Brotherton Collection, MS Lt. 48, ff. [17v, 20].

--- ----- IV, i, 1-6. Song: 'Take, oh take those lips away'.

See BEAUMONT and FLETCHER, *The Bloody Brother*, V, ii. Song: 'Take, oh, take those lips away' (B&F 15-26), of which Shakespeare's song forms the first stanza.

ShW 61 *The Merchant of Venice*.

Extracts in a miscellany compiled by Edward Pudsey (1573-1613); 1600s.

First pub. London, 1600. Printed from this MS in Savage, *Shakespearean Extracts*, pp. 1-6.

Bodleian, MS Eng. poet. d. 3, f. 41.

The Merchant of Venice

ShW 62 -----

Extracts in a miscellany; late 17th century.

British Library, Lansdowne MS 1185, ff. 16-20.

ShW 63 -----

Extracts in a miscellany perhaps partly compiled by one William How; mid-17th century.

Folger, MS V. a. 87, ff. 5v-6.

ShW 64 *The Merry Wives of Windsor.*

Copy, probably an acting version prepared for a private performance; c. 1660.

First pub. London, 1602. This MS described in James Orchard Halliwell, *An Account of the Only Known Manuscript of Shakespeare's Plays* (London, 1843).

Folger, MS V. a. 73.

ShW 65 -----

Copy of part of Act III, v, and Act IV, i-v, on eight leaves; written to supply the missing text in a prompt book prepared for use by the Smock Alley Theatre, Dublin; c. 1680.

The rest of the prompt book (part of a Third Folio) also in the Folger: see INTRODUCTION.

Folger, MS V. b. 240.

ShW 66 -----

Extracts in a miscellany; late 17th century.

British Library, Lansdowne MS 1185, ff. 21v-5.

ShW 67 *Much Ado about Nothing.*

Extracts in a miscellany; late 17th century.

First pub. London, 1600.

British Library, Lansdowne MS 1185, ff. 20-1v.

ShW 68 -----

Extracts on one of four leaves now detached from a miscellany compiled by Edward Pudsey (1573-1613); 1600s.

Printed from this MS in Savage, *Shakespearean Extracts*, pp. 32-50.

Shakespeare Birthplace Trust Record Office, ER 82.

ShW 69 ----- II, iii, 61-76. Song: 'Sigh no more, ladies, sigh no more'.

Copies of Balthazar's song in a musical setting by Thomas Ford (c.1580-1648), in three MS music part books; early-mid 17th century.

This version printed in John H. Long, *Shakespeare's Use of Music*, I, (Gainesville, Florida, 1955), 132-3.

Christ Church, Oxford, MSS Mus. 736-7, ff. 3-4; 738, f. 3r-v.

ShW 70 *Othello.*

Proof sheet, with MS markings calling for nine corrections, of sig. vv3^{r} (p. 333) in an exemplum of the First Folio (1623).

First pub. London, 1622. This item discussed, with a facsimile, in Charlton Hinman, 'A Proof-Sheet in the First Folio of Shakespeare', *The Library*, 4th Ser. 23 (1943), 101-7.

Folger, STC 22273, No. 47.

ShW 71 -----

Excerpts, with comments on the play, in a miscellany compiled by Abraham Wright (1611-90); c. 1640.

These extracts and comments printed in James G. McManaway, 'Excerpta quaedam per A.W. adolescentem', *Studies in Shakespeare, Bibliography and Theater* (New York, 1969), 279-91 (pp. 286-9), and in Arthur C. Kirsch, 'A Caroline Commentary on the Drama', *MP*, 66 (1968-9), 256-61 (p. 257).

British Library, Add. MS 22608, ff. 83-4v.

ShW 72 -----

Extracts relating to marriage, transcribed from a printed source, in a verse miscellany used by members of the Holgate family of Saffron Walden, Essex; c. 1687.

Pierpont Morgan Library, MA 1057, pp. 219-20.

ShW 73 -----

Extracts copied after an early performance of the play on one of four leaves now detached from a miscellany compiled by Edward Pudsey (1573-1613); written without heading directly after extracts from *Richard III* (see ShW 83); c. 1604-9.

This MS discussed in Philip Howard, 'Purple passages from the early days of Othello', *The Times* (25 June 1977), p. 14.

Shakespeare Birthplace Trust Record Office, ER 82.

Othello

ShW 74 -----

Two quotations (I, i, 41-58, Iago's speech beginning 'O, sir, content you', and I, iii, 202-9, Duke of Brabantio's speech beginning 'When remedies are past, the griefs are ended'), transcribed from the edition of 1622, in a miscellany compiled in the North Riding of Yorkshire and once owned by one Henry Danby; early 17th century.

Sotheby's, 29 October 1975, Lot 150, sold to Kleinmann; unlocated.

ShW 75 -----

Copy of Iago's lines beginning 'She that was ever fair, and never proud' (II, i, 148-58), transcribed from the Folio of 1664, in a MS book of jests compiled by Archbishop William Sancroft (1617-93); late 17th century.

Bodleian, MS Sancroft 53, p. 43.

ShW 76 ----- IV, iii, 40-8. Song: 'The poor soul sat sighing by a sycamore tree'.

Copy of Desdemona's willow song in a five-strophe version in a musical setting, in a MS songbook owned in 1630 by one Hugh Floyd; c. 1614-30.

Printed from this MS in Cutts, *Musique de la troupe de Shakespeare*, pp. 1-2, 115-19, and in F.W. Sternfeld, *Music in Shakespearean Tragedy* (London, 1963), 39-44 (with facsimiles). Musical settings for this song but without words appear in Folger MS V. a. 159, f. 19, and Trinity College, Dublin, MS 410, p. 26, and there is a related MS song on the flyleaf of New York Public Library, Music Division, Drexel 4183 (these are all printed, with facsimiles, in Sternfeld, pp. 44-52).

British Library, Add. MS 15117, f. 18.

ShW 77 *Pericles.*

Several brief quotations on a slip of paper once used as a bookmark, in a composite volume of MSS; early-mid-17th century.

First pub. London, 1609.

British Library, Add. MS 41063, f. 87.

ShW 78 -----

Extracts in a miscellany perhaps partly compiled by one William How; mid-17th century.

Folger, MS V. a. 87, ff. 4v-5v.

ShW 79 *Richard II.*

Extracts in a miscellany later owned by one Joseph Hall; c. 1630s-50.

First pub. London, 1597.

Folger, MS V. a. 339, ff. 199v-201v.

ShW 80 -----

Extracts on one of four leaves now detached from a miscellany compiled by Edward Pudsey (1573-1613); 1600s.

Printed from this MS in Savage, *Shakespearean Extracts*, pp. 23-7.

Shakespeare Birthplace Trust Record Office, ER 82.

ShW 81 *Richard III.*

Several brief quotations on a slip of paper once used as a bookmark, in a composite volume of MSS; early-mid-17th century.

First pub. London, 1597.

British Library, Add. MS 41063, f. 87.

ShW 82 -----

Extracts in a miscellany; late 17th century.

British Library, Lansdowne MS 1185, ff. 2-3v.

ShW 83 -----

Extracts on one of four leaves now detached from a miscellany compiled by Edward Pudsey (1573-1613); 1600s.

Printed from this MS in Savage, *Shakespearean Extracts*, pp. 28-31.

Shakespeare Birthplace Trust Record Office, ER 82.

ShW 84 *Romeo and Juliet.*

Proof sheet, with MS markings calling for two corrections, of sig. ff6^r (p. 71) in an exemplum of the First Folio (1623).

First pub. London, 1597. This item discussed, with a facsimile, in Charlton Hinman, 'The Proof-Reading of the First Folio Texts of *Romeo and Juliet*', *SB*, 6 (1954), 61-70.

Folger, STC 22273, No. 50.

ShW 85 -----

Copy, untitled, a text derived from the Second Folio (London, 1632), with stage directions in another hand; used for amateur staging by one of the English colleges at Douai; 1694.

This MS described in Evans, *PQ*, 41 (1962).

Bibliothèque Municipale, Douai, France, MS 787, ff. 94v-130v.

Romeo and Juliet

ShW 86 -----

Extracts in a miscellany compiled by Edward Pudsey (1573-1613); 1600s.

Printed from this MS in Savage, *Shakespearean Extracts*, pp. 10-22. See also ShW 87.

Bodleian, MS Eng. poet. d. 3, f. 86v.

ShW 87 -----

Extracts on one of four leaves now detached from a miscellany compiled by Edward Pudsey; 1600s.

This MS continues the text from ShW 86 as printed in Savage.

Shakespeare Birthplace Trust Record Office, ER 82.

*ShW 88 *Sir Thomas More.*

MS, entitled 'The Booke of Sir Thomas Moore', of a play originally by Anthony Munday and chiefly in his autograph, with additions in five other hands, one of which (contributing one scene on ff. 8-9 and generally known as 'Hand D') has been identified as Shakespeare's autograph; c. mid-1590s.

First pub. (from this MS) London, 1844, ed. Alexander Dyce, Shakespeare Society; ed. W.W. Greg, Malone Society (Oxford, 1911; reprinted 1961); reproduced by John S. Farmer, Tudor Facsimile Texts (London, 1910). Discussed, with facsimile examples, in Malone Society edition; Greg, *Dramatic Documents*, I, 224-5; II, plate 2; R.C. Bald, 'The Booke of Sir Thomas Moore and its Problems', *SS*, 2 (1949), 44-65; Peter W.M. Blayney, '*The Booke of Sir Thomas Moore* Re-Examined', *SP*, 69 (1972), 167-91; Croft, *Autograph Poetry*, I, 23; Michael L. Hays, 'Shakespeare's Hand in *Sir Thomas More*: Some Aspects of the Paleographic Argument', *SSt*, 8 (1975), 241-53; Paul Ramsey, 'Shakespeare and *Sir Thomas More* Revisited: or, A Mounty on the Trail', *PBSA*, 70 (1976), 333-46; Giles E. Dawson, 'Theobald, table/babbled, and Sir Thomas More', *TLS* (22 April 1977), p. 484; Petti, *English Literary Hands*, No. 36; and elsewhere (see *NCBEL*, I, cols. 1551-2). See also THOMAS DEKKER (DkT 45) and THOMAS HEYWOOD (HyT 12).

British Library, Harley MS 7368.

ShW 89 *The Tempest.*

Extracts in a miscellany; late 17th century.

First pub. in the First Folio (London, 1623).

British Library, Lansdowne MS 1185, ff. 25v-6.

ShW 90 ----- I, ii, 400-9. Song: 'Full fathom five thy father lies'.

Copy of Ariel's song in a musical setting by Robert Johnson (as edited by John Wilson) in the hand of Edward Lowe (c.1610-82), on a leaf detached from one of Lowe's MS songbooks (1st treble part); c. 1676.

Johnson's setting first pub. in John Wilson, *Cheerfull Ayres* (Oxford, 1659). Printed from this MS in Cutts, *Musique de la troupe de Shakespeare*, p. 24; discussed in Cutts, 'Seventeenth-Century Songs and Lyrics in Edinburgh University Library Music MS Dc. 1. 69', *MD*, 13 (1959), 169-94.

Birmingham Reference Library, Shakespeare Library, Acc. No. 57316, Location No. S747.01.

ShW 91 ----- -----

Copy in a musical setting by Robert Johnson (as edited by John Wilson), in a MS songbook (2nd treble part) compiled by Edward Lowe; c. 1650s.

Bodleian, MS Mus. d. 238, p. 87.

ShW 92 --- - -----

Copy in a verse miscellany once owned by Francis Norreys (? Sir Francis Norris (1609-69)) and Henry Balle; mid-17th century.

This MS recorded in *The Shakespeare Allusion-Book* (London, 1932), I, 425-6.

British Library, Egerton MS 2421, f. 6v.

ShW 93 ----- -----

Copies in a musical setting by Robert Johnson (as edited by John Wilson), on leaves detached from four MS music part books compiled by John Playford (1623-86?); c. 1660.

Formerly MS 747, this MS recorded in Cutts, *Musique de la troupe de Shakespeare*, pp. 129, 131. The part books to which these leaves belong are at the University of Glasgow (MSS R. d. 58-61), and nine leaves are at the Shakespeare Centre, Stratford-upon-Avon (Halliwell-Phillipps, 'Notes upon the Works of Shakespeare', *Henry V* and *Twelfth Night*).

Folger, MS V. a. 411, ff. 9v, 10, 11, 12v.

ShW 94 ----- -----

Copy (words only) in a MS songbook ('Earl Ferrers' MS'); c. 1640.

This MS recorded in Cutts, *Musique de la troupe de Shakespeare*, pp. 131-2.

New York Public Library, Music Division, Drexel MS 4041, No. 90, ff. 67v-8.

ShW 94.5 See Addenda, p. 633.

The Tempest

ShW 95 ----- II, ii, 48-56. Song: 'The master, the swabber, the bos'n, and I'.

Copy of Stephano's song in a verse miscellany once owned by Francis Norreys (? Sir Francis Norris (1609-69)) and Henry Balle; mid-17th century.

This MS recorded in *The Shakespeare Allusion-Book*, I, 425-6.

British Library, Egerton MS 2421, f. 6v.

ShW 96 ----- II, ii, 185-90. Song: 'No more dams I'll make for fish'.

Copy of Caliban's song in a verse miscellany once owned by Francis Norreys (? Sir Francis Norris (1609-69)) and Henry Balle; mid-17th century.

This MS recorded in *The Shakespeare Allusion-Book*, I, 425-6.

British Library, Egerton MS 2421, f. 6v.

ShW 97 ----- IV, i, 106-17. Song: 'Honour, riches, marriage-blessing'.

Copy of the song sung by Juno and Ceres in a verse miscellany once owned by Francis Norreys (? Sir Francis Norris (1609-69)) and Henry Balle; mid-17th century.

This MS recorded in *The Shakespeare Allusion-Book*, I, 425-6.

British Library, Egerton MS 2421, f. 7.

ShW 98 ----- V, i, 88-94. Song: 'Where the bee sucks, there suck I'.

Copy of Ariel's song in a musical setting by Robert Johnson (as edited by John Wilson), together with a leaf containing three additional stanzas, both in the hand of Edward Lowe; these leaves detached from one of Lowe's MS songbooks (1st treble part); the second leaf endorsed by Lowe 'this I had of Madam Trumball at Chalfont 27 Sept. 1676'.

Johnson's setting first pub. in John Wilson, *Cheerfull Ayres* (Oxford, 1659). Printed from this MS in Cutts, *Musique de la troupe de Shakespeare*, p. 25; discussed in Cutts, 'Seventeenth-Century Songs and Lyrics in Edinburgh University Library Music MS. Dc. 1. 69', *MD*, 13 (1959), 169-94.

Birmingham Reference Library, Shakespeare Library, Acc. No. 57316, Location No. S747.01.

ShW 99 ----- -----

Copy in a musical setting by Robert Johnson (as edited by John Wilson) in a MS songbook; c. 1640s.

This MS reproduced in John H. Long, *Shakespeare's Use of Music*, II (Gainesville, 1961), 147; collated in Cutts, *Musique de la troupe de Shakespeare*, pp. 132-3.

Bodleian, MS Don. c. 57, f. 75.

ShW 100 ----- -----

Copy in a musical setting by Robert Johnson (as edited by John Wilson), in a MS songbook (2nd treble part) compiled by Edward Lowe; c. 1650s.

Bodleian, MS Mus. d. 238, p. 88.

ShW 101 ----- -----

Copy in a verse miscellany once owned by Francis Norreys (? Sir Francis Norris (1609-69)) and Henry Balle; mid-17th century.

This MS recorded in *The Shakespeare Allusion-Book*, I, 425-6.

British Library, Egerton MS 2421, f. 7.

ShW 102 ----- -----

Copy in a verse miscellany; late 17th century.

British Library, Harley MS 3991, ff. 83v-4.

ShW 103 ----- -----

Copies in a musical setting by Robert Johnson (as edited by John Wilson), on leaves detached from four MS music part books compiled by John Playford (1623-86?); c. 1660.

Formerly MS 747, this MS recorded in Cutts, *Musique de la troupe de Shakespeare*, pp. 129, 132, and see ShW 93.

Folger, MS V. a. 411, ff. 9v, 10v, 11v, 13v.

ShW 103.5 See Addenda, p. 633.

ShW 104 *Titus Andronicus*.

Drawing of a scene and the text of speeches by Tamora, Titus and Aaron (I, i, 104-20; V, i, 125-44; I, i, 121, 125), on a single leaf, signed 'Henricus Peacham' and endorsed in another hand 'Henrye Peachams Hande 1595'; the text possibly not in the same hand as the drawing but perhaps copied later from the First Folio (1623).

First pub. London, 1594. This MS discussed in E.K. Chambers, 'The First Illustration to "Shakespeare"', *The Library*, 4th Ser. 5 (1924-5), 326-30, and in John Dover Wilson, '"Titus Andronicus" on the Stage in 1595', *SS*, 1 (1948), 17-22. Facsimiles in Chambers; W. Moelwyn Merchant, *Shakespeare and the Artist* (London, 1959), facing p. 16; S. Schoenbaum, *William Shakespeare: A Documentary Life* (Oxford, 1975), p. 122.

Owned by the Marquess of Bath, Longleat House, Harley Papers, Vol. I, f. 159v.

Titus Andronicus

ShW 105 -----

Extracts in a miscellany compiled by Edward Pudsey (1573-1613); 1600s.

Printed from this MS in Savage, *Shakespearean Extracts*, pp. 8-9.

Bodleian, MS Eng. poet. d. 3, f. 86v.

ShW 106 *Twelfth Night.*

Copy, untitled, a text derived from the Second Folio (London, 1632), with stage directions in another hand; used for amateur staging by one of the English colleges at Douai; 13 June 1694.

First pub. in the First Folio (London, 1623). This MS described in Evans, *PQ*, 41 (1962).

Bibliothèque Municipale, Douai, France, MS 787, ff. 1v-31.

ShW 107 -----

Extracts in a miscellany compiled partly by the Oxford printer Christopher Wase (1627-90); mid-17th century.

Bodleian, MS Rawl. poet. 117, f. 162 rev.

ShW 108 -----

Extracts in a miscellany; late 17th century.

British Library, Lansdowne MS 1185, ff. 36-40v.

ShW 109 *The Winter's Tale*, IV, iv, 218-30. Song: 'Lawn as white as driven snow'.

Copy of Autolycus's song in a musical setting, in a MS songbook (2nd treble part) compiled by Edward Lowe (c. 1610-82); c. 1650s.

First pub. in the First Folio (London, 1623); this setting first pub. in John Wilson, *Cheerfull Ayres* (Oxford, 1659).

Bodleian, MS Mus. d. 238, pp. 114-15.

ShW 110 ----- -----

Copy in a musical setting in a MS music book; c. 1675.

Folger, MS V. a. 437, ff. 1-6.

ShW 111 ----- IV, iv, 294-309. Song: 'Get you hence, for I must go'.

Copy of the song sung by Autolycus, Dorcas and Mopsa, with a second verse, in a musical setting possibly by Robert Johnson, in a MS songbook ('Earl Ferrers' MS'); c. 1640.

Printed from this MS in John P. Cutts, 'An Unpublished Contemporary Setting of a Shakespeare Song', *SS*, 9 (1956), 86-9, and in Cutts, *Musique de la troupe de Shakespeare*, p. 19.

New York Public Library, Music Division, Drexel MS 4041, No. 142, ff. 131v-3v.

ShW 112 ----- -----

Copy in a musical setting possibly by Robert Johnson, in a MS songbook once owned by a certain Anne Twice; c. 1620.

Printed from this MS in Cutts, *Musique de la troupe de Shakespeare*, pp. 17-18. Facsimile in John H. Long, *Shakespeare's Use of Music*, II (Gainesville, 1961), 138-9.

New York Public Library, Music Division, Drexel MS 4175, No. lix.

(2) MISCELLANEOUS EXTRACTS

ShW 113 [*Extracts*].

Cuttings from a miscellany of at least 1028 pages entitled *Hesperides, or the Muses Garden* compiled by one John Evans for the publisher Humphrey Moseley, containing innumerable quotations from Shakespeare; now pasted in 61 of a collection of 128 Shakespearian scrapbooks formed by James Orchard Halliwell-Phillipps (1820-89); c. 1655-9.

These cuttings from the same MS as ShW 114 and also in the same hand as ShW 115; discussed in Gunnar Sorelius, 'An Unknown Shakespearian Commonplace Book', *The Library*, 5th Ser. 28 (1973), 294-308, and see also INTRODUCTION. Facsimile examples of this MS in *The Works of William Shakespeare*, ed. James O. Halliwell, 16 vols (London, 1853-65), I, 395; II, facing p. 177; III, facing pp. 51, 133; IV, facing p. 184; V, facing p. 308; VI, facing p. 471; VII, facing p. 128.

Shakespeare Centre, Stratford-upon-Avon, Halliwell-Phillipps, 'Notes upon the Works of Shakespeare'.

ShW 114 -----

Fragments from the same MS as ShW 113, including (V. a. 75) a six-page 'Catalogue of the Bookes from whence these Collections were extracted' (size c. 20.6 x 15.5 cm); one fragment in four leaves, the other two items consisting of cuttings pasted in two scrapbooks (of fifteen leaves and eighteen leaves respectively), all once owned by James Orchard Halliwell-Phillipps; c. 1655-9.

See ShW 113. These three items recorded as Nos. 133, 173, and 313 in James O. Halliwell,

[*Extracts*]

A Brief Hand-list of Books, Manuscripts, etc. illustrative of the Life and Writings of Shakespeare; collected between the years 1842 and 1859 (London, 1859).

Folger, MSS V. a. 75, V. a. 79, V. a. 80.

ShW 115 -----

An untitled miscellany containing innumerable quotations from Shakespeare, and with a six-page index at the end, all in the same hand as ShW 113-14 and apparently a duplicate, with additions, of the MS from which those cuttings were taken; 900 pages (size c. 29.6 x 18.8 cm), of which pp. 1-4, 379-80, 667-8, 715-20, and 785-8 are missing; c. 1655-9.

See INTRODUCTION.

Folger, MS V. b. 93.

ShW 116 -----

Quotations from Shakespeare (including *Henry VI*, *King Lear*, and *A Midsummer Night's Dream*) in a miscellany compiled by Archbishop William Sancroft (1617-93); late 17th century.

Bodleian, MS Sancroft 97, pp. 79-82.

ShW 117 -----

Brief quotations from Shakespeare (including *All's Well that Ends Well*, *Henry IV*, *King John*, and *Troilus and Cressida*) in a miscellany; late 17th century.

See also ShW 37, 55, 62, 66, 82, 89, 108.

British Library, Lansdowne MS 1185, ff. 4-14.

Sir Philip Sidney

1554-86

ABBREVIATIONS

Duncan-Jones & Van Dorsten *Miscellaneous Prose of Sir Philip Sidney*, ed. Katherine Duncan-Jones and Jan Van Dorsten (Oxford, 1973).

Feuillerat *The Prose Works of Sir Philip Sidney*, ed. Albert Feuillerat, 4 vols (Cambridge, 1912-26; reprinted 1963).

Osborn, *Young Philip Sidney* James M. Osborn, *Young Philip Sidney 1572-1577* (New Haven & London, 1972).

Ringler *The Poems of Sir Philip Sidney*, ed. William A. Ringler, Jr. (Oxford, 1962).

Robertson Sir Philip Sidney, *The Countess of Pembroke's Arcadia (The Old Arcadia)*, ed. Jean Robertson (Oxford, 1973)

For abbreviations used throughout Volume I, see p.xi.

INTRODUCTION

Of all Sidney's literary works, only three pieces are preserved in his autograph: *Certain Sonnets* No. 6 (SiP 31), the prose *Defence of the Earl of Leicester* (SiP 172), and the prose *Discourse on Irish Affairs* (SiP 180). His hand can be found elsewhere, however, in many surviving letters. A considerable number of Sidney's letters are preserved in the Public Record Office and in the British Library; a number are in the private muniments of great houses such as Hatfield House, Longleat House, Rousham House, and Sidney's own family seat, Penshurst Place; a number sent to foreign correspondents are in continental archives, and a certain number have been dispersed to various collections in Britain, Europe, and America. One hundred and fifteen of Sidney's letters are printed, chiefly from the originals, in Feuillerat (III, 75-184). Sixteen additional letters, as well as seventy-three letters sent to Sidney by correspondents, are recorded in Charles S. Levy, 'A Supplementary Inventory of Sir Philip Sidney's Correspondence', *MP*, 67 (1969-70), 177-81. Levy's item 'M', a letter in French to Lord Willoughby de Eresby, 14 July 1586, is now in the Lincolnshire Archives Office (6 Ancaster Vol. II/11). Three of the additional letters found in continental archives are printed by Levy in 'An Unpublished Letter to Sir Philip Sidney', *N & Q*, 211 (July 1966), 248-51, and in 'The Sidney-Hanau Correspondence', *ELR*, 2 (1972), 19-28. Another of the additional letters, now at Harvard, is printed in William H. Bond, 'A Letter from Sir Philip Sidney to Christopher Plantin', *HLB*, 8 (1954), 233-5. One more letter of Sidney's, written to Edward Denny, is preserved in a transcript now in the Bodleian (MS Don. d. 152); the text is printed by John Buxton, with facsimiles, in 'An Elizabethan reading-list: An Unpublished Letter from Sir Philip Sidney', *TLS* (24 March 1972), pp. 343-4 (and see ensuing correspondence on pp. 366, 394, 421, and 495), and in 'A New Letter from Sir Philip Sidney', *ELR*, 2 (1972), after p. 28, and it is also printed in Osborn, *Young Philip Sidney*, pp. 535-40. The text of some ninety-six letters sent to Sidney by Hubert Languet (1518-81) is to be found in *H. Langueti epistolae ad P. Sydnaeum* (Frankfurt, 1633; Leiden, 1646); fifty-three of these letters are translated in *The Correspondence of Sir Philip Sidney and Hubert Languet*, ed. Steuart A. Pears (London, 1845; reprinted 1971). One other related item, now at Harvard, is transcribed in William H. Bond, 'A Letter of Languet about Sidney', *HLB*, 9 (1955), 105-9. Seventy-six additional letters sent to Sidney by various correspondents were sold at Sotheby's, 26 June 1967, Lots 741-2. Eleven of those letters, written by Canon Robert Dorsett, are now at Christ Church, Oxford; the remaining sixty-five (formerly constituting Phillipps MS 11762) are in the Osborn Collection at Yale, and a microfilm of them is in the British Library (RP 125). They have been discussed and cited by James M. Osborn in 'New Light on Sir Philip Sidney', *TLS* (30 April 1970), pp. 487-8, and in *Young Philip Sidney*. Facsimiles of various letters of Sidney are to be found in Feuillerat, III, frontispiece; *Facsimiles of Royal, Historical, and Literary Autographs in the British Museum* (1899), plate 19; Greg, *English Literary Autographs*, plate XLI; *The Library*, 5th Ser. 21 (1966), after p. 326 (plate XII); Ann Morton, *Men of Letters*, Public Record Office Museum Pamphlets No. 6 (London, 1974), plate I; 'Robert H. Taylor Collection', *PULC*, 38 (1977), facing p. 132; Petti, *English Literary Hands*, No. 27; and (Sidney's last letter, written on his death-bed) in Sir Henry James, *Facsimiles of National Manuscripts from William the Conqueror to Queen Anne*, 4 vols (Southampton, 1865-8), III, plate LXXXVII. The complete Sidney correspondence is currently being edited for the Oxford University Press by Charles S. Levy and Roger Kuin.

Sidney's letter to Queen Elizabeth on the proposed Alençon marriage may properly be regarded as a political discourse and so is included in the entries (SiP 181-215). The original letter sent to the Queen is no longer among the state papers but many transcripts were made and the work was a popular choice for 17th-century anthologies of state letters. One other letter of Sidney's, a personal letter to his brother, Robert, on the subject of travel (Feuillerat, III, 124-7), achieved an almost comparable popularity. Again, the original letter has not survived, but copies can be found in the Bodleian (MSS Rawl. D. 924, f. 14; Tanner 169, f. 60v; University College 152, pp. 6-12); the British Library (Add. MS 4160, No. 39; Harley MS 444, f. 14; Harley MS 3638, f. 100); Cambridge University Library (MSS Add. 7958, ff. 12v-14v; Ee. 2. 32, f. 99; Ee. 5. 23, p. 438); the Cheshire Record Office (DLT/B8, pp. 96-9 (the Tabley House MS recorded in *HMC*, 1st Report (1870), Appendix, pp. 47-8)); the East Sussex Record Office (RAF/F/13/1, pp. 46-8); the University of London Library (MS 20, ff. 261v-5); the Northamptonshire Record Office (F.H. 2381); Trinity College, Dublin (MS 802, No. 2); in a MS owned by the Marquess of Bute (D 18, f. 53); in a MS owned by Bent E. Juel-Jensen, Oxford (recorded in *BC*, 15 (Summer 1966), 156); and in Mostyn MS 139, recorded in *HMC*, 4th Report (1874), Appendix, p. 352, and sold at Sotheby's, 13 July 1920, Lot 72, to Sumner.

A few other miscellaneous documents can be found bearing Sidney's signature. For instance, a document of 1577 is at Colorado College, and a document dated 26 January 1573 is in the Hyde Collection, Somerville, New Jersey (*Letters*, III, 116); this last item was reproduced in the printed catalogue of the R. B. Adam Library (London & New York, 1929), III, facing p. 221. There are also one or two printed books once owned by Sidney and bearing his inscriptions (that is, in addition to SiP 31). An exemplum of Matteo Bandello, *Histoires tragiques*, translated by Pierre Boisteau and François de Belleforest (Lyons, 1561), now in the Hugh Walpole Collection at King's School, Canterbury, has brief inscriptions by Sidney and by his friend Fulke Greville made when they were both schoolboys; these inscriptions are reproduced and discussed in Jean Robertson, 'Sidney and Bandello', *The Library*, 5th Ser. 21 (1966), 326-8. An exemplum of Francesco Guicciardini, *La historia d'Italia* (Venice, 1569), now in the Widener Library at Harvard, is inscribed 'Philippo Sidneio, Patauij. 20. Junij 1574'; it is discussed in William L. Godshalk, 'A Sidney Autograph', *BC*, 13 (Spring 1964), 65, and the inscription is reproduced in W. C. Hazlitt, *A Roll of Honour* (London, 1908), p. 214. One other volume indirectly connected with Sidney is an exemplum of Thomas Cranmer, *Defensio verae et catholicae doctrine de sacramento* (Emden, 1557) once owned by Thomas Ashton (d.1578), who was Sidney's headmaster at Shrewsbury School. The volume, now preserved at Shrewsbury School, is inscribed 'Thomae Martialis et amicorum Salopiae ex Libris Thomae Astoni Ludimagistri Philippi Sidnei'.

The canon of Sidney's verse accepted in the *Index* is based entirely on Ringler. Thirty poems classified in Ringler as 'Wrongly attributed poems' (pp. 349-53) have been excluded, although MS texts of certain of these poems are to be found in addition to those mentioned in Ringler. For instance, copies of Ringler's AT 19 and 21 ('*Philisides, the Shepherd good and true*' and '*Singe neighbours singe, here yow not Say*') appear in the important Ottley MS in the National Library of Wales (see SiP 100), together with a related poem beginning 'Waynd from the hope wch made affection glad'. For an argument that a poem beginning 'Blushe Phebus blushe thy glorye is forlorne', found in the Arundel Harington MS (f. 144), may belong to *Astrophil and Stella*, see Jean Robertson in *RES*, NS 13 (1962), 403-6. Another poem which is ascribed to Sidney but which seems to have escaped the attention of editors is a lengthy poem headed *Sr Philip Sidney to the Lady Penelope Rich* (beginning 'If yet a choyce more worthy, cause more new'). It appears in a miscellany compiled by Henry Champernowne (1600-59), now in the Bodleian (MS Eng. poet. f. 9, pp. 224-31), where the text is followed shortly afterwards (p. 234 seq.) by an answering poem, *The Lady Penelope Rich to S^r^. Phillipe Sidney* (beginning 'Martyrd in thought but martyr'd more in soule'). It seems likely that they are early 17th-century compositions featuring Sidney and Lady Rich as *personae*, especially since the poems are accompanied by an introduction and a series of notes explaining the allusions and who the protagonists were.

Besides the extant scribal transcripts of *Astrophil and Stella*, of *Certain Sonnets*, and of one or two additional poems, the entries include MS copies of the translation of the Psalms made by Sidney and his sister, Mary Herbert, Countess of Pembroke (1561-1621) (SiP 72-88), although Sidney was responsible for translating only the first forty-three Psalms. Various other copies are to be found of individual Psalms translated by his sister: for instance, copies in All Souls College, Oxford (MS 155, ff. 123-7), the Inner Temple Library (Petyt MS 538, Vol. 43, f. 284 seq.), the University of Nottingham (Clifton MS Cl LM 50), and, with musical settings, in the British Library (Add. MS 15117, ff. 4v, 5v).

As for Sidney's *magnum opus*, his 'trifle' *Arcadia*, no example is known of the 'loose sheets of paper' which he says he wrote chiefly in his sister's presence, 'the rest by sheets sent unto you as fast as they were done' (Robertson, p. 3). At his death he ordered the work to be burnt, but it is hardly likely that the loss of his 'sheets' would have been occasioned by the observance of such instructions. Many copies of the work at various stages of completion or revision were made before the posthumous publication of the first edition (1590). The work afterwards achieved considerable popularity in the 17th century and is often found quoted in miscellanies. Besides those MSS recorded in the entries below, extracts are to be found, for instance, in MSS in the Bodleian (MSS CCC. 263, ff. 115-19v; Sancroft 29); in the British Library (Add. MS 36354, pp. 16*, 17, 187-8 (John Milton's commonplace book); Harley MS 677, ff. 85v-6); in the East Sussex Record Office (FRE 686, pp. 1-15, 61 seq.); in the Folger (MS V. b. 83, ff. 15-30); and in a miscellany of Judge John Saffin of New England, now in the Rhode Island Historical Society (printed in *John Saffin his Book (1665-1708)*, ed. Caroline Hazard (New York, 1928), and discussed in Jessie A. Coffee, 'Arcadia to America: Sir Philip Sidney and John Saffin', *AL*, 45 (1973-4), 100-4). Extracts from *Arcadia* — as well as from *Astrophil and Stella, Certain Sonnets, A Defence of Poetry*, and *The Lady of May* — also appear in John Evans's miscellany *Hesperides, or the Muses' Garden* (c. 1655), for details of which see WILLIAM SHAKESPEARE, INTRODUCTION. A new edition of the version of *Arcadia* published in 1590 (the '*New*

Arcadia') is currently being prepared for the Oxford University Press by Victor Skretkowicz.

Various other items connected with *Arcadia* are to be found. An exemplum of the edition of 1613 in the Widener Library at Harvard has on the title page the inscription 'This was the Countess of pembrokes owne booke given me by the Countess of Montgomery her daughter 1625', beneath which has been added in a later hand the signature 'Ancram'. The authenticity of the inscription has been called into question (see Bent Juel-Jensen in *BC*, 11 (Winter 1962), 474), yet it seems unlikely that the inscription is a forgery; rather it is true to say that this title page belongs to a different volume and has at some time been bound into the Widener exemplum, which is therefore not the one owned by the Countess of Pembroke. Another exemplum of the 1613 edition at Harvard (in the Houghton Library, 14457.23.8.7*) has extensive 17th-century MS annotations which were formerly but no longer ascribed to Gabriel Harvey: see William L. Godshalk, 'Gabriel Harvey and Sidney's *Arcadia*', *MLR*, 59 (1964), 497-9. An exemplum of the edition of 1598 preserved in the Royal Library, Windsor (III.33.K), is one originally bound for Queen Elizabeth I; the title page bears the signature 'Charles Plessington'. Numerous quotations from the edition of 1590 appear in John Hoskyns's treatise *Directions for Speech and Style exemplified out of Arcadia*, early MS copies of which are in the Bodleian (MS Ash. Mus. d. 1) and in the British Library (Add. MS 15230; Harley MS 850; and Harley MS 4604). This work, written in 1590, is edited by H. H. Hudson (Princeton, 1935) and by Louise Brown Osborn in *The Life, Letters, and Writings of John Hoskyns 1566-1638* (New Haven, 1937), pp. 114-66. A French translation of at least Book II of *Arcadia* was made c. 1607-10 by Jean Loiseau de Tourval; part of a MS text is preserved in the Bodleian (MS Rawl. D. 920, ff. 365-82), and is printed in Albert W. Osborn, *Sir Philip Sidney en France* (Paris, 1932), Appendice, pp. i-xlii. Extracts from a German translation appear in a 17th-century miscellany in the Österreichische Nationalbibliothek, Vienna (Cod. 15.414,5, fol. 26v-9v). An anonymous MS play entitled *Loves Changelinges change* in the British Library (Egerton MS 1994, ff. 293-316) is a dramatic adaptation of *Arcadia*; individual poems are recorded in the entries (SiP 111, 117, 120). The complete play has been edited by Felicina Rota in *L'Arcadia di Sidney e il teatro* (Bari, 1966) and by John P. Cutts (Fennimore, 1974). A MS index to *Arcadia*, probably made in the 1640s, is owned by John Buxton and is discussed by him in 'Sidney and Theophrastus', *ELR*, 2 (1972), 79-82. The index is in two parts, the first entitled *Sr Philip Sydneys exact Characters where-in hee is both painter & poet; the owtward Character poynting at the painter, the inward description at the poet*; the second entitled *A Clavis opening ye names and referring to the Characters*. This MS is in the same hand as a MS satirical poem based on *Arcadia* entitled *A Draught of Sir Philip Sidney's Arcadia* (beginning 'Hee that would read and understand'), also owned by John Buxton. The poem was privately printed at the New Bodleian Library, Oxford, 1961, and reprinted in *Historical Essays 1600-1750 Presented to David Ogg* (London, 1963), pp. 60-77.

Sidney's prose works other than *Arcadia* have been most recently edited in Duncan-Jones & Van Dorsten (1973). This edition also includes (pp. 147-52) the text of Sidney's Will (proved 19 June 1589), which is preserved in a scribal copy in the Public Record Office (PROB 11/74, ff. 55-6), and (pp. 166-72) the account, probably by George Gifford, of *The Manner of Sir Philip Sidney's Death*. MS copies of this account are preserved in the British Library (Cotton MS Vitellius C. 17, ff. 382-7) and in the possession of Bent E. Juel-Jensen, Oxford; the second of these copies is the John Harvey MS recorded in *HMC*, 1st Report (1870), Appendix, p. 62, and this text was printed at the New Bodleian Library, 1959. For the *Life of Sidney* by Fulke Greville, see GrF 24-6. Duncan-Jones & Van Dorsten reject from the canon (p. 159) the essay *Valour Anatomized in a Fancie* which is attributed to Sidney in *Cottoni Posthuma* (London, 1651) and which is included in Feuillerat (III, 308-10) as a doubtful work. Sidney's editors have failed to notice that this essay is, in fact, John Donne's *Essay of Valour* (see DnJ 4066-7), and that the ascription to Sidney of this cynical argument on the value of honour and valour as ploys to seduce women is probably a deliberate satirical device.

Numerous quotations taken from a MS of Sidney's *Defence of Poetry* appear in the *Analysis tractationis de poesi contextae a nobilissimo viro Philippo Sidneio Equite Auratu* written by William Temple (1555-1627), Sidney's secretary in Flushing. A MS of this work, partly in Temple's autograph, is among the MSS of the Viscount De L'Isle at Penhurst Place; it is discussed in J. P. Thorne, 'A Ramistical Commentary on Sidney's *An Apologie for Poetrie*', *MP*, 54 (1957), 158-64. An early 17th-century Spanish version of *A Defence of Poetry*, possibly by Don Juan de Bustamente, is preserved in a MS in the Biblioteca Nacional, Madrid (MS 3908); it is edited by Dwight O. Chambers as *Deffensa de Poesia: A Spanish Version* (n.p., 1968), and by Benito Brancaforte as *Deffensa de la Poesia: A 17th Century Anonymous Spanish Translation of Philip Sidney's 'Defence of Poesie'* (Chapel Hill, 1977).

A few other miscellaneous items of interest may be mentioned. Sidney's 'passport' has been discovered at New College, Oxford (MS 328 (II)); the text is printed, with a facsimile, in John Buxton and Bent Juel-Jensen, 'Sir Philip Sidney's First Passport Rediscovered', *The Library*, 5th Ser. 25 (1970), 42-6. Sidney's horoscope is preserved in the Bodleian (MS Ashmole 356, item 5); it is printed and discussed by James M. Osborn in 'Mica mica parva stella: Sidney's horoscope', *TLS* (1 January 1971), pp. 17-18 (and see correspondence, p. 69), and in *Young Philip Sidney*, pp. 517-22. This last publication also includes the texts (p. 523) of Sidney's patent to bear arms in Italy in 1574 (now in the Venetian archives) and (pp. 525-8) of the instructions for Sidney's embassy, 7 February 1576/7 (now in the British Library, Harley MS 36, ff. 295-8). The Inquisition Post Mortem taken on Sidney's estate, 8 July 1588, is among the Inquisitions in the Public Record Office, but an official transcript (a roll of 63 leaves) made in 1607, and now in the Osborn Collection at Yale (fb 109), bears witness to the complex problems of Sidney's estate which continued to vex his heirs during ensuing generations.

Most of the MSS described in the entries below have been known to editors (notably Ringler), but where no reference is given the MSS are hitherto unrecorded.

PB.

ARRANGEMENT

See also Addenda to Part 2, p. 633

Sir Philip Sidney

VERSE

(1) POEMS BY SIDNEY NOT IN *ARCADIA*

SiP 1 *Astrophil and Stella.*

Copy of sonnets 1-20, 105-8, and songs viii and xi, untitled, in a miscellany; c. late 1580s.

First pub. London, 1591; Ringler, pp. 163-237. This MS (the 'Bright MS') collated in Ringler and described pp. 538-9.

British Library, Add. MS 15232, ff. 21-38.

SiP 2 -----

Copy of sonnets 1-66, 87-108, and songs i, ix-xi, transcribed by or for Sir Edward Dymoke (c.1559-1624) of Scrivelsby and Kyme, Lincolnshire, with later annotations by William Drummond of Hawthornden; untitled; imperfect; c. late 1580s-early 1590s.

This MS collated in Ringler and described pp. 539-40.

Edinburgh University Library, MS De. 5. 96.

SiP 3 -----

Copy of sonnets 1-23, 26-7, 29-34, 36, 38-9, 41-4, 47-108 (in an irregular order), headed 'Sonnetts wrytten by Sr Phillipp Sydney Knight', in a miscellany compiled by William Briton (1564-1637) of Kelston, Somerset; c. 1586-96.

This MS collated in Ringler and described pp. 540-2.

Owned by Arthur A. Houghton, Jr., MS, ff. 91-103 (to be sold at Christie's, 1980).

SiP 4 -----

Notes from *Astrophil and Stella* in Volume X of the miscellaneous collections of Brian Twyne (1579?-1644); early 17th century.

Bodleian, MS CCC. 263, f. 120.

--- -----

See also INTRODUCTION.

SiP 5 ----- *Sonnet 1* ('Loving in truth, and faine in verse my love to show').

Copy in the hand of Sir John Harington, headed 'Sonnettes of Sr Phillip Sydneys [vppon *deleted*] to ye Lady Ritch', in a verse miscellany compiled by John Harington of Stepney (1520?-82) and his son Sir John Harington of Kelston (1560-1612); late 16th century.

Printed from this MS in Hughey, *Arundel Harington MS*, I, No. 223, pp. 254-5; collated in Ringler.

Owned by the Duke of Norfolk, Arundel Castle, MSS (Special Press), 'Harrington MS. Temp. Eliz.', f. 155.

SiP 6 ----- *Sonnet 37* ('My mouth doth water, and my breast doth swell').

Copy of lines 5-9, 12-14, headed 'Ladie Rich' and beginning 'Towardes Aurora's Court a Nymph doth dwell', in a composite volume of verse and prose; early 17th century.

This MS recorded in Ringler, p. 473.

Bodleian, MS Rawl. poet. 172, f. 15v.

SiP 7 ----- *Song ii* ('Have I caught my heav'nly jewell').

Copy in a musical setting in a MS songbook owned in 1630 by one Hugh Floyd; c. 1614-30.

Ringler, pp. 202-3. Printed from this MS in John P. Cutts, 'Falstaff's "Heauenlie Iewel": Incidental Music for *The Merry Wives of Windsor*', *SQ*, 11 (1960), 89-92; recorded in Ringler, p. 480.

British Library, Add. MS 15117, f. 19.

SiP 8 ----- *Song iv* ('Onely joy, now here you are').

Copy in a miscellany compiled by a Cambridge student, possibly Sir John Finett (1571-1641) of Fordwich, Kent; c. 1586-91.

Ringler, pp. 210-11. This MS collated in Ringler.

Bodleian, MS Rawl. poet. 85, f. 42r-v.

SiP 9 ----- *Song vi* ('O you that heare this voice').

Copies in a musical setting by William Byrd in five MS music part books; early 17th century.

Ringler, pp. 215-17; Byrd's setting first pub. in his *Psalmes, Sonets, & songs of sadnes and pietie* (1588). These MSS recorded in Ringler, pp. 447, 566.

British Library, Add. MSS 29401-5, ff. 8v-9.

SiP 10 ----- -----

Copy in a musical setting by William Byrd in a MS volume of musical pieces once owned by one Edward Paston; c. 1611.

This MS recorded in Ringler, pp. 447, 566.

British Library, Add. MS 31992, f. 37v.

SiP 11 ----- *Song viii* ('In a grove most rich of shade').

Copy of lines 1-36, 41-104, in a miscellany compiled by a Cambridge student, possibly Sir John Finett (1571-1641) of Fordwich, Kent; c. 1586-91.

Ringler, pp. 217-21. This MS collated in Ringler.

Bodleian, MS Rawl. poet. 85, ff. 34v-6v.

SiP 12 ----- -----

Copy in a verse miscellany; c. 1596-1601.

This MS collated in Ringler.

British Library, Harley MS 6910, ff. 171-2v.

SiP 13 ----- *Song ix* ('Go my flocke, go get you hence').

Copy in a verse miscellany compiled by Henry Stanford, household tutor in the Carey family; c. 1585-98.

Ringler, pp. 221-2. This MS collated in Ringler.

Cambridge University Library, MS Dd. 5. 75, f. 47r-v.

SiP 14 ----- -----

Copy of a version beginning 'I never laie me downe to rest', in a musical setting in a MS songbook; early 17th century.

This MS recorded in Ringler, pp. 486, 566.

Christ Church, Oxford, MS Mus. 439, f. 9.

SiP 15 ----- *Song x* ('O deare life, when shall it be').

Copy in the hand of Sir John Harington, subscribed 'Sr Phillip Syd: to the bewty of the worlde', in a verse miscellany compiled by John Harington of Stepney (1520?-82) and his son Sir John Harington of Kelston (1560-1612); late 16th century.

Ringler, pp. 225-7. Printed from this MS in Hughey, *Arundel Harington MS*, I, No. 71, pp. 116-17; collated in Ringler.

Owned by the Duke of Norfolk, Arundel Castle, MSS (Special Press), 'Harrington MS. Temp. Eliz.', f. 36v.

SiP 16 ----- -----

Copy of lines 1-20, 25-48, here ascribed to [Nicholas] 'Britton', in a miscellany compiled by a Cambridge student, possibly Sir John Finett (1571-1641) of Fordwich, Kent; c. 1586-91.

This MS collated in Ringler.

Bodleian, MS Rawl. poet. 85, ff. 107v-8.

SiP 17 ----- -----

Copies in a musical setting by William Byrd in five MS music part books; early 17th century.

Byrd's setting first pub. in his *Songs of sundrie natures* (1589). This MS recorded in Ringler, pp. 447, 566.

British Library, Add. MSS 29401-5, ff. 3v-4.

SiP 18 ----- -----

Copy in a musical setting by William Byrd in a MS volume of musical pieces once owned by one Edward Paston; c. 1611.

This MS recorded in Ringler, pp. 447, 566.

British Library, Add. MS 31992, f. 36.

SiP 19 *Certain Sonnets*.

Copy of sonnets 1-4, 6-24, 26-8, and 31 (in an irregular order), headed 'Certein lowse Sonnettes and songes', appended to a MS copy of *Arcadia* (see SiP 92); imperfect; c. 1580-90.

First pub. in *Arcadia* (London, 1598); Ringler, pp. 133-62. This MS collated in Ringler.

Bodleian, MS e. Mus. 37, ff. 237-46.

SiP 20 -----

Copy of sonnets 3-32, headed 'Dyuers and sondry Sonettes', appended to a MS copy of *Arcadia* (the 'Clifford MS': see SiP 97); late 16th century.

This MS collated in Ringler.

Folger, MS H. b. 1, ff. 216v-26v.

SiP 21 -----

Copy of sonnets 8 (lines 1, 4-10), 9 (lines 1-7), 10 (lines 1-4), 11 (lines 1-8), 12 (lines 7-9, 16), 15, 16, 17 (lines 11-12, 14-15, 17-20, 27-45, 48-52), 18 (lines 3-4, 13-14), 19 (lines 3-4, 6), 21, 22 (lines 9-10, 62-3, 65-8), 23 (lines 16-20, 25-6, 29-32), 24 (lines 6-7, 12-13, 15-16, 22-7), 26 (lines 16-22, 27-33), 27, 30 (lines 4-6, 12-16, 23-6), 31, transcribed from a printed edition, in a miscellany compiled by William Drummond of Hawthornden; c. 1606-9.

This MS recorded in Ringler, p. 560.

National Library of Scotland, MS 2059 (Hawthornden Vol. VII), ff. 292-4, 295v-6.

Certain Sonnets

SiP 22 -----

Copy of sonnets 1-2, 13-25, 31, 32 (in an irregular order), with other poems of Sidney (see SiP 100), on six folio leaves, in an unbound collection of miscellaneous literary papers assembled by Adam Ottley (1685-1752), Registrar of the diocese of St David's, Wales; c. 1580s.

This MS described and collated in Peter Beal, 'Poems by Sir Philip Sidney: The Ottley Manuscript', *The Library*, 5th Ser. 33 (1978), 284-95.

National Library of Wales, Ottley (unnumbered bundle of literary papers).

--- -----

See also INTRODUCTION.

SiP 23 ----- *Sonnet 1* ('Since shunning paine, I ease can never find').

Copy in a verse miscellany compiled by John Harington of Stepney (1520?-82) and his son Sir John Harington of Kelston (1560-1612); late 16th century.

Printed from this MS in Hughey, *Arundel Harington MS*, I, No. 176, p. 214; collated in Ringler.

Owned by the Duke of Norfolk, Arundel Castle, MSS (Special Press), 'Harrington MS. Temp. Eliz.', f. 130.

SiP 24 ----- *Sonnet 3* ('The fire to see my wrongs for anger burneth').

Copy in a verse miscellany compiled by John Harington of Stepney (1520?-82) and his son Sir John Harington of Kelston (1560-1612); late 16th century.

Printed from this MS in Hughey, *Arundel Harington MS*, I, No. 67, pp. 111-12 (where the hand is mistakenly described as that of Sir John Harington); collated in Ringler.

Owned by the Duke of Norfolk, Arundel Castle, MSS (Special Press), 'Harrington MS. Temp. Eliz.', f. 34.

SiP 25 ----- -----

Copy in a miscellany compiled by a Cambridge student, possibly Sir John Finett (1571-1641) of Fordwich, Kent; c. 1586-91.

This MS collated in Ringler.

Bodleian, MS Rawl. poet. 85, f. 9v.

SiP 26 ----- -----

Copy in a verse miscellany compiled by the antiquary St Loe Kniveton of Gray's Inn; c. 1585-90s.

This MS collated in Ringler.

British Library, Harley MS 7392, f. 39.

SiP 27 ----- -----

Copy in a verse miscellany compiled by Henry Stanford, household tutor in the Carey family; c. 1585-98.

This MS collated in Ringler.

Cambridge University Library, MS Dd. 5. 75, f. 27.

SiP 28 ----- -----

Copy of the incipit, in the same hand as SiP 176, in a MS copy of the *New Arcadia* (see SiP 103); c. 1584.

This MS collated in Ringler.

Cambridge University Library, MS Kk. 1. 5 (2).

SiP 29 ----- -----

Copy, appended to a MS copy of the *Old Arcadia* (see SiP 102); late 16th century.

This MS collated in Ringler.

St John's College, Cambridge, MS I. 7 (James 308), f. 241v.

SiP 30 ----- *Sonnet 5* ('O my thoughtes' sweete foode, my onely owner').

Copy, appended to a MS copy of the *Old Arcadia* (see SiP 102); late 16th century.

This MS collated in Ringler.

St John's College, Cambridge, MS I. 7 (James 308), f. 241r-v.

*SiP 31 ----- *Sonnet 6* ('Sleepe Babie mine, Desire, nurse Beautie singeth').

Autograph, written on the last page of a printed exemplum of Jean Bouchet, *Les annales d'Aquitaine. faicts & gestes en sommaire des roys de France, & d'Angleterre* (Poitiers, 1557).

This MS reproduced in Croft, *Autograph Poetry*, I, 14.

Bibliotheca Bodmeriana, Cologny-Geneva, Switzerland.

Certain Sonnets. Sonnet 6

SiP 32 ----- -----

Copy, appended to a MS copy of the *Old Arcadia* (see SiP 102); late 16th century.

This MS collated in Ringler.

St John's College, Cambridge, MS I. 7 (James 308), f. 241.

SiP 33 ----- *Sonnets 8-11* ('The scourge of life, and death's extreame disgrace').

Copy of four sonnets, headed 'These 4 Sonnets followinge wer made by S^r^: P: Sidney when his Ladye hadd a payne [the small pox *added in another hand*] in her face', in a miscellany compiled by a Cambridge student, possibly Sir John Finett (1571-1641); c. 1586-91.

This MS collated in Ringler.

Bodleian, MS Rawl. poet. 85, ff. 55-6.

SiP 34 ----- *Sonnet 12* ('You better sure shall live, not evermore').

Copy, headed 'A translation of Horace his 10th Ode of ye second booke ab Licinium', on a leaf inserted in a printed exemplum of *Arcadia* (London, 1598); 17th century.

Bodleian, Godwyn folio 276, after p. 476.

SiP 35 ----- *Sonnet 15* ('Like as the Dove which seeled up doth flie').

Copy, transcribed from the edition of 1598, in a verse miscellany compiled by John Lilliat (c.1550-c.1599); c. 1599.

This MS recorded in Ringler, pp. 424, 558.

Bodleian, MS Rawl. poet. 148, f. 86.

SiP 36 ----- -----

Copy, headed 'Uppon the Deuise of a sealed Doue W^th^ these of Petrarch...', in a miscellany once owned by one Robert Thornton; c. 1580s-90s.

This MS collated in Ringler.

Marsh's Library, Dublin, MS Z 3. 5. 21, f. 17v.

SiP 37 ----- *Sonnet 16* ('A Satyre once did runne away for dread').

Copy in a miscellany compiled by a Cambridge student, possibly Sir John Finett (1571-1641) of Fordwich, Kent; c. 1586-91.

This MS collated in Ringler.

Bodleian, MS Rawl. poet. 85, f. 8v.

SiP 38 ----- -----

Copy in a verse miscellany compiled by the antiquary St Loe Kniveton of Gray's Inn; c. 1585-90s.

This MS collated in Ringler.

British Library, Harley MS 7392, f. 25r-v.

SiP 39 ----- -----

Copy in a verse miscellany owned before 1610 by Anne Cornwallis, afterwards Countess of Argyll; c. 1590s.

This MS collated in Ringler.

Folger, MS V. a. 89, p. 23.

SiP 40 ----- *Sonnet 19* ('If I could thinke how these my thoughts to leave').

Copy in a miscellany compiled by a Cambridge student, possibly Sir John Finett (1571-1641) of Fordwich, Kent; c. 1586-91.

This MS collated in Ringler.

Bodleian, MS Rawl. poet. 85, f. 11v.

SiP 41 ----- -----

Copy in a verse miscellany compiled by the antiquary St Loe Kniveton of Gray's Inn; c. 1585-90s.

This MS collated in Ringler.

British Library, Harley MS 7392, f. 38v.

SiP 42 ----- -----

Copy in a miscellany once owned by one Robert Thornton; c. 1580s-90s.

This MS collated in Ringler.

Marsh's Library, Dublin, MS Z 3. 5. 21, f. 19v.

SiP 43 ----- -----

Copy, appended to a MS copy of the *Old Arcadia* (see SiP 102); late 16th century.

This MS collated in Ringler.

St John's College, Cambridge, MS I. 7 (James 308), f. 241.

SiP 44 ----- *Sonnet 21* ('Finding those beames, which I must ever love').

Copy in a miscellany compiled by a Cambridge student, possibly Sir John Finett (1571-1641) of Fordwich, Kent; c. 1586-91.

This MS collated in Ringler.

Bodleian, MS Rawl. poet. 85, f. 12.

SiP 45 ----- *Sonnet 22. The 7. Wonders of England* ('Neere Wilton sweete, huge heapes of stones are found').

Copy, headed 'loue fashyoned to 7: Wonders of Englande', in a miscellany compiled by a Cambridge student, possibly Sir John Finett (1571-1641) of Fordwich, Kent; c. 1586-91.

This MS collated in Ringler.

Bodleian, MS Rawl. poet. 85, ff. 102-3v.

SiP 46 ----- -----

Copy in a miscellany once owned by one Robert Thornton; c. 1580s-90s.

This MS collated in Ringler.

Marsh's Library, Dublin, MS Z 3. 5. 21, ff. 18v-19v.

SiP 47 ----- *Sonnet 23* ('Who hath his fancie pleased').

Copy in a miscellany compiled by a Cambridge student, possibly Sir John Finett (1571-1641) of Fordwich, Kent; c. 1586-91.

This MS collated in Ringler.

Bodleian, MS Rawl. poet. 85, ff. 12v-13.

SiP 48 ----- -----

Copy of lines 1-32 in a verse miscellany; c. 1596-1601.

This MS collated in Ringler.

British Library, Harley MS 6910, f. 149.

SiP 49 ----- -----

Copy in a verse miscellany compiled by the antiquary St Loe Kniveton of Gray's Inn; c. 1585-90s.

This MS collated in Ringler.

British Library, Harley MS 7392, f. 70v.

SiP 50 ----- -----

Copy, headed 'To the tune of Wyllielmus Van Nassann, Ec.', in a miscellany once owned by one Robert Thornton; c. 1580s-90s.

This MS collated in Ringler.

Marsh's Library, Dublin, Z 3. 5. 21, f. 18.

SiP 51 ----- *Sonnet 25* ('When to my deadlie pleasure').

Copy of lines 27-34, here beginning 'Thus do I fall to ryse thus', in a miscellany compiled by a Cambridge student, possibly Sir John Finett (1571-1641) of Fordwich, Kent; c. 1586-91.

This MS collated in Ringler.

Bodleian, MS Rawl. poet. 85, f. 65v.

SiP 52 ----- -----

Copy of a six-line paraphrase of lines 30-4, beginning 'Sweet I cannot be from you', in a miscellany once owned by Margaret Bellasys, probably the daughter of Thomas, first Lord Fauconberg (1577-1653); c. 1630.

Printed from this MS in Ringler, p. 431.

British Library, Add. MS 10309, f. 45v.

SiP 53 ----- *Sonnet 27* ('Al my sense thy sweetnesse gained').

Copy in a verse miscellany compiled by John Harington of Stepney (1520?-82) and his son Sir John Harington of Kelston (1560-1612); late 16th century.

Printed from this MS in Hughey, *Arundel Harington MS*, I, No. 192, pp. 239-40; collated in Ringler.

Owned by the Duke of Norfolk, Arundel Castle, MSS (Special Press), 'Harrington MS. Temp. Eliz.', f. 145.

SiP 54 ----- *Sonnet 30* ('Ring out your belles, let mourning shewes be spread').

Copy in a verse miscellany compiled by John Harington of Stepney (1520?-82) and his son Sir John Harington of Kelston (1560-1612); late 16th century.

Printed from this MS in Hughey, *Arundel Harington MS*, I, No. 196, pp. 241-2; collated in Ringler.

Owned by the Duke of Norfolk, Arundel Castle, MSS (Special Press), 'Harrington MS. Temp. Eliz.', f. 146.

SiP 55 ----- -----

Copy, endorsed by Edward Bannister 'A Dyttye mad by S^r phillip sydnye gevene me Att pvtteny In svrrye Decembris X^o Ann^o 1584', with the name of the donor 'S^r phillyppe Sydnye', in a composite volume of verse compiled chiefly by members of the Caryll family.

This MS collated in Ringler.

British Library, Add. MS 28253, f. 3r-v.

Certain Sonnets. Sonnet 30

SiP 56 ----- -----

Copy in a verse miscellany compiled by the antiquary St Loe Kniveton of Gray's Inn; c. 1585-90s.

This MS collated in Ringler.

British Library, Harley MS 7392, f. 35r-v.

SiP 57 ----- -----

Copy in a verse miscellany compiled by Henry Stanford, household tutor in the Carey family; c. 1585-98.

This MS collated in Ringler.

Cambridge University Library, MS Dd. 5. 75, f. 27.

SiP 58 ----- -----

Copy, appended to a MS copy of the *Old Arcadia* (see SiP 102); late 16th century.

This MS collated in Ringler.

St John's College, Cambridge, MS I. 7 (James 308), f. 242.

SiP 59 ----- *Sonnet 32* ('Leave me o Love, which reachest but to dust').

Copy in a miscellany compiled by Edward Pudsey (1573-1613); 1600s.

This MS recorded in Ringler, p. 557.

Bodleian, MS Eng. poet. d. 3, f. 1.

SiP 60 ----- -----

Copy of lines 1-4 written in a later hand (probably that of a vicar) in a miscellany originally compiled by Edward Pudsey; 17th century.

Bodleian, MS Eng. poet. d. 3, f. 36.

SiP 61 ----- -----

Copy made by Sir James Murray of Tibbermure or by someone in his household, written at the end of a 15th century MS of John Lydgate's *Destruction of Troy*; c. 1612.

This MS recorded in Ringler, p. 554.

Cambridge University Library, MS Kk. 5. 30 (II), ff. 71v-2.

SiP 62 ----- -----

Copy, here ascribed to 'Sir ffrancis Bacon', in a miscellany of Scottish provenance compiled by Gideon and Jean Rutherford; c. 1690-1725.

This MS recorded in Ringler, p. 561.

Folger, MS V. a. 255, f. 7.

SiP 63 *The Epitaph* ('His being was in her alone').

Copy of lines 1-2 in a miscellany probably compiled by members of the Cartwright family of Aynho, Northamptonshire; mid-17th century.

First pub. in *Arcadia* (London, 1593), a blank space having been left for this epitaph in the edition of 1590; Ringler, p. 241.

Bodleian, MS Don. e. 6, f. 28.

SiP 64 -----

Copy, written in an exemplum of John Stanbridge's *Pervula* printed by Wynkyn de Woorde [1495?]; 17th century.

This MS recorded in Ringler, p. 493.

Bodleian, Douce D 238 (3), sig. A6.

SiP 65 -----

Copy of lines 1-2 in a miscellany compiled by John Abbot (b. 1653/4) of St John's College, Oxford; c. 1670s.

Bodleian, MS Rawl. D. 954, f. 26.

SiP 66 -----

Copy written in a printed exemplum of *Arcadia* (London, 1590) to fill the blank space left for this epitaph; end 16th-17th century.

This MS recorded in Ringler, p. 493.

Owned by Arthur A. Houghton, Jr. (and to be sold at Christie's, 1980).

SiP 67 -----

Copy written in a printed exemplum of *Arcadia* (London, 1590) to fill the blank space left for this epitaph; end 16th-17th century.

This MS recorded in Ringler, p. 493.

Huntington, RB 69441.

SiP 68 -----

Copy written in a printed exemplum of *Arcadia* (London, 1590) to fill the blank space left for this epitaph; end 16th-17th century.

This MS recorded in Ringler, p. 493.

Huntington, RB 69442.

The Epitaph

SiP 69 -----

Copy, headed 'On Argalus and Parthenia, Epitaph', in a miscellaneous collection of unbound verse belonging to the Aston family of Tixall, Staffordshire; 17th century?

Printed from this MS in Arthur Clifford, *Tixall Poetry* (Edinburgh, 1813), p. 276.

Unlocated.

--- *The Lady of May.*

See SiP 216-19.

SiP 70 *'Me thought some staves he mist: if so, not much amisse'.*

Copy, in the same hand as SiP 176, in a MS copy of the *New Arcadia* (see SiP 103); c. 1584.

First pub. in *Arcadia* (London, 1590); Ringler, p. 241. This MS collated in Ringler.

Cambridge University Library, MS Kk. 1. 5 (2), f. 127v.

SiP 71 *'Miso mine owne pigsnie, thou shalt heare news o' Damaetas'.*

Copy, in the same hand as SiP 176, in a MS copy of the *New Arcadia* (see SiP 103); c. 1584.

First pub. in *Arcadia* (London, 1590); Ringler, p. 241. This MS collated in Ringler.

Cambridge University Library, MS Kk. 1. 5 (2).

SiP 72 *The Psalms of David.*

Copy of Psalms 1-150; early 17th century.

Psalms 1-43 translated by Sidney; Psalms 44-150 translated by his sister, the Countess of Pembroke. First pub. complete London, 1823, ed. S.W. Singer. Psalms 1-43, without the Countess of Pembroke's revisions, printed in Ringler, pp. 265-337; Psalms 1-150 in her revised form printed in *The Psalms of Sir Philip Sidney and the Countess of Pembroke*, ed. J.C.A. Rathmell (New York, 1963). This MS described in Ringler, p. 548; facsimile of title page in Rathmell, p. xxxiii.

Bodleian, MS Rawl. poet. 24.

SiP 73 -----

Copy of Psalms 1-87, 102-30, transcribed by Dr Samuel Woodford from the Countess of Pembroke's heavily revised working copy; untitled; imperfect; 1694/5.

Psalms 1-43 printed from this MS in Ringler and described pp. 547-8.

Bodleian, MS Rawl. poet. 25.

SiP 74 -----

Copy of Psalms 1-26, 51, 58, 68-71, 73-8, 80, 83-6, 88-9, 91, 93, 96, 98-100, 102, 104-5, 108-13, 117, 120-7, 129-34, 137-8, 142-3, 147, 149, 150 (in an irregular order), with second versions of Psalms 75, 89 and 122; a copy made for Sir John Harington, with a few corrections in his hand; untitled; late 16th century.

This MS described in Ringler, p. 550.

British Library, Add. MS 12047.

SiP 75 -----

Copy of Psalms 1-150, with a few alterations in a different ink; early 17th century.

This MS described in Ringler, pp. 549-50.

British Library, Add. MS 12048.

SiP 76 -----

Copy of Psalms 1-6, 8-148, made for Sir John Harington, with a few corrections in his hand; untitled; imperfect; constituting Volume VII of the Harington Papers; late 16th century.

This MS collated in Ringler and described pp. 551-2.

British Library, Add. MS 46372.

SiP 77 -----

Copy of Psalms 1-150 in a calligraphic hand, signed 'W.H.'; early 17th century.

This MS sold at Sotheby's, 24 November 1969, Lot 135; described in G.F. Waller, 'The Text and Manuscript Variants of the Countess of Pembroke's Psalms', *RES*, NS 26 (1975), 1-18. A microfilm is in the British Library (RP 412).

Owned before 1976 by Mr John Goelet when it was on deposit at Harvard (*69M-142); unlocated.

SiP 78 -----

Copy of Psalms 1-150 in two or more hands, untitled, once owned by one Henry Platt; c. 1605-20.

This MS described in Cecil C. Seronsy, 'Another Huntington Manuscript of the Sidney Psalms', *HLQ*, 29 (1965-6), 109-16.

Huntington, EL 11637.

SiP 79 -----

Copy of Psalms 1-150; early 17th century.

This MS described in Ringler, p. 552.

Huntington, HM 100.

SiP 80 -----

Copy of Psalms 1-150; early 17th century.

This MS described in Ringler, p. 552.

Huntington, HM 117.

SiP 81 -----

Copy of Psalms 1-150 in a calligraphic hand, untitled, with a dedicatory poem to Queen Elizabeth and a poem on Sidney by his sister; once in the library of Sir Walter Aston (1583-1639) of Tixall, Staffordshire; early 17th century.

This MS described by B.E. Juel-Jensen in *BC*, 15 (Summer (1966), 156 (with a facsimile of two pages in plate 3), and in *BC*, 18 (Summer 1969), 222-3; described in Ringler, pp. 550-1.

Owned by Bent E. Juel-Jensen, Oxford.

SiP 82 -----

Copy of Psalms 1-150; 18th century.

National Library of Wales, Peniarth MS 374B.

SiP 83 -----

Copy of Psalms 1-150, with a second version of Psalms 75 and 131, once owned by Sir Kenelm Digby (1603-65); early 17th century.

This MS described in Ringler, p. 552.

Bibliothèque des Universités de Paris à la Sorbonne, MS 1110.

SiP 84 -----

Copy of Psalms 4-150, transcribed from the Countess of Pembroke's working copy by John Davies (1565-1618) of Hereford; imperfect; lacking title; late 16th century.

Printed from this MS in Rathmell; collated in Ringler and described pp. 546-7. Facsimile of Psalm 117 in John Buxton, *Sir Philip Sidney and the English Renaissance*, revised edition, (London, 1964), after p. 156.

Owned by the Viscount De L'Isle, Penshurst Place.

SiP 85 -----

Copy of Psalms 1-150; early 17th century.

This MS described in Ringler, p. 549.

The Queen's College, Oxford, MS 341.

SiP 86 -----

Copy of Psalms 1-150, with some corrections in another hand; late 16th century.

This MS described in Ringler, p. 549.

Trinity College, Cambridge, MS O. 1. 51 (James 1075).

SiP 87 -----

Copy of Psalms 1-150; early 17th century.

This MS described in Ringler, p. 549.

Trinity College, Cambridge, MS R. 3. 16 (James 596).

SiP 88 -----

Copy of Psalms 17-150; imperfect; lacking title; early 17th century.

This MS described in Ringler, pp. 548-9.

Wadham College, Oxford, MS 25.

(2) POEMS OF UNCERTAIN AUTHORSHIP

SiP 89 *'The darte, the beames, the stringe so stronge I prove'.*

Copy, ascribed to 'S P S.', in a miscellany compiled by a Cambridge student, possibly Sir John Finett (1571-1641) of Fordwich, Kent; c. 1586-91.

First pub. in [Philip Bliss], *Bibliographical Miscellanies* (Oxford, 1813), p. 63. Printed from this MS in Ringler, pp. 344-5.

Bodleian, MS Rawl. poet. 85, f. 9.

SiP 90 -----

Copy in a verse miscellany compiled by the antiquary St Loe Kniveton of Gray's Inn; c. 1585-90s.

This MS collated in Ringler.

British Library, Harley MS 7392, f. 66.

SiP 91 *Inscription on Sidney's portrait at Longleat, 1577* ('Who gives him selfe, may well his picture give').

Two copies in a miscellany compiled by William Drummond of Hawthornden; c. 1620s.

First pub. in A.C. Judson, *Sidney's Appearance* (Bloomington, Indiana, 1958), p. 51; Ringler, p. 345. These copies recorded in Ringler, p. 518 (with one folio incorrectly cited as f. 9v).

National Library of Scotland, MS 2060 (Hawthornden Vol. VIII), ff. 48v, 128.

VERSE AND PROSE

THE COUNTESS OF PEMBROKE'S ARCADIA

(1) THE COMPLETE TEXT OR LARGE SELECTIONS

SiP 92 *The Old Arcadia.*

Copy of the complete text in two hands; c. 1580-90.

The revised version of *Arcadia* (the New Arcadia) first pub. London, 1590; the original version (the Old Arcadia) first pub. in Feuillerat, IV (1926); the complete Old Arcadia edited by Jean Robertson (Oxford, 1973); the poems printed in Ringler, pp. 7-131. This MS collated in Robertson and the poems collated in Ringler; described in Ringler, p. 529.

Bodleian, MS e. Mus. 37, ff. 1-236v.

SiP 93 -----

Copy of the complete text, once owned by the Thelwall family; imperfect; late 16th century.

This MS collated in Robertson and the poems collated in Ringler; described in Ringler, p. 525.

Bodleian, MS Jesus College 150.

SiP 94 -----

Copy of an almost complete text, made for, and partly in the hand of, Sir John Harington; headed 'A treatis made by Sr Phillip Sydney Knyght of certeyn accidents in Arcadia. made in the yeer 1580 and emparted to some few of his frends, in his lyfe tyme and to more sence his vnfortunat deceasse'; lacking the last leaf; c. 1590.

Formerly Phillipps MS 9610; this MS collated in Robertson and the poems collated in Ringler; described in Ringler, pp. 526-7. The identification of Harington's hand established by P.J. Croft in a seminar paper to be given at the Clark Library, Los Angeles, April 1980 (publication forthcoming).

British Library, Add. MS 38892.

SiP 95 -----

Copy of the complete text; untitled; late 16th century.

This MS (the 'Davies MS') collated in Robertson and the poems collated in Ringler; described in Ringler, p. 526.

British Library, Add. MS 41204.

SiP 96 -----

Copy of 66 poems from *Arcadia* and two prose passages from Book II; untitled; c. 1580-2.

This MS (the 'Lee MS') collated in Robertson and the poems collated in Ringler; described in Ringler, pp. 527-8.

British Library, Add. MS 41498.

SiP 97 -----

Copy of the complete text, once owned by the Clifford family; late 16th century.

Printed from this MS in Feuillerat; collated in Robertson and the poems collated in Ringler; described in Ringler, p. 527.

Folger, MS H. b. 1, ff. 1-216.

SiP 98 -----

Copy of the complete text, untitled, probably once owned by Sir Lionel Tollemache (1562-1612) of Helmingham Hall, Suffolk; imperfect; late 16th century.

This MS collated in Robertson and described p. xlii; described in Ringler, pp. x-xii. Facsimile of f. 61 in Sotheby's sale catalogue, 6 June 1961, Lot 21. A complete microfilm is in the British Library (M/623).

Owned by Arthur A. Houghton, Jr., MS, ff. 1-152v (to be sold at Christie's, 1980).

SiP 99 -----

Copy of most of the text in several hands; once owned by Robert Walker, Treasurer to Sir Henry Sidney from 1575 to c. 1581; imperfect; late 16th century.

This MS (the 'Ashburnham MS') collated in Robertson and the poems collated in Ringler; described in Ringler, p. 528.

Huntington, HM 162.

SiP 100 -----

Copy of 24 of the poems (Nos. 2, 3, 11, 12, 13 [Lines 116-21, 123, 125, 129, 131-2, 136-7, 141], 14-22, 27, 28 [lines 37-48], 31, 33-5, 38, 60, 62, 77, in an irregular order) and also the 'Nota' on rules of verse (here beginning 'Rules in mesured verses in English wch I observe'), with other poems of Sidney (see SiP 22), on six folio leaves, in an unbound collection of miscellaneous literary papers assembled by Adam Ottley (1685-1752), Registrar of the diocese of St David's, Wales; c. 1580s.

The 'Nota' printed (from SiP 102) in Ringler, p. 391, and in Robertson, pp. 80-1. This MS described and collated, with facsimiles of one page, in Peter Beal, 'Poems by Sir Philip Sidney: The Ottley Manuscript', *The Library*, 5th Ser. 33 (1978), 284-95.

National Library of Wales, Ottley (unnumbered bundle of literary papers).

The Old Arcadia

SiP 101 -----

Copy of the complete text in two or more hands, probably transcribed from SiP 98; untitled; late 16th century.

This MS collated in Robertson and the poems collated in Ringler; described in Ringler, pp. 525-6.

The Queen's College, Oxford, MS 301.

SiP 102 -----

Copy of the complete text, with some corrections in a later hand; c. 1581-2.

Printed from this MS in Robertson; the poems collated in Ringler; described in Ringler, pp. 528-9.

St John's College, Cambridge, MS I. 7 (James 308), ff. 1-239v.

SiP 103 *The New Arcadia.*

Copy of the prose text (incomplete) and 17 of the poems (Nos. 2-5, 8 [beginning only], 14-17, 20-2, 25, 26 [lines 1-4], 30 [lines 5-37], 62 [lines 1-8], 74 [lines 1-6]), in the same hand as SiP 176; untitled; 208 leaves; bound in a composite volume of MSS; c. 1584.

This MS collated in Robertson and the poems collated in Ringler; described in Ringler, pp. 529-31.

Cambridge University Library, MS Kk. 1. 5 (2).

SiP 104 -----

Substantial prose extracts from Books I-V and 19 of the poems (Nos. 3, 8, 9 [lines 121-37], 10 [lines 67-85, 89-96], 21, 25, 27, 40, 41, 43, 46, 52, 54, 59, 60, 65, 69, 72 [lines 1-20], 75 [lines 79-93], in an irregular order), transcribed from a printed source, in a miscellany compiled by William Drummond of Hawthornden; c. 1606-9.

This MS recorded in Ringler, p. 560.

National Library of Scotland, MS 2059 (Hawthornden Vol. VII), ff. 6v, 36-8, 39-42, 236v-91v.

SiP 105 -----

Epitome of Books I-III, with ten of the poems, based on the edition of 1627; entitled 'The History of Arcadia'; 17th century.

This MS recorded in Ringler, p. 531.

Owned by the Viscount De L'Isle, Penshurst Place.

SiP 106 -----

Prose extracts and part of lines 1-6 of poem No. 77, headed 'A Sonet of Death. by S. P.S.', transcribed from a printed source, in a miscellany; imperfect; mid-17th century.

This MS recorded in Ringler, p. 554.

British Library, Add. MS 12515, ff. 17-24.

SiP 107 -----

Prose extracts with three of the poems (Nos. 17, 20 and 62 [lines 35-6, 95-6, 125-6, 123-4, 73-6, 65-6, 37-8, 21-2]), transcribed from a printed source, in a miscellany; mid-17th century.

This MS recorded in Ringler, p. 557.

British Library, Sloane MS 1925.

SiP 108 See Addenda, p. 634.

SiP 109 [entry deleted].

--- -----

See also INTRODUCTION.

(2) INDIVIDUAL POEMS
[in addition to those in SiP 92-108]

SiP 110 *Old Arcadia. Book I, No. 2* ('Transformed in shew, but more transformed in minde').

Copy, transcribed from the edition of 1593, in a verse miscellany owned in 1596 by one Anthony Babington of Warrington; c. 1596.

Ringler, pp. 11-12; Robertson, pp. 28-9. This MS recorded in Ringler, p. 555, and in Robertson, p. 423.

British Library, Add. MS 34064, f. 28.

SiP 111 -----

Copy in an anonymous MS play entitled *Loves Changelinges change*, bound in a composite volume of MS plays; c. 1630-40?

Printed from this MS in John P. Cutts, 'More Manuscript Versions of Poems by Sidney', *ELN*, 9 (1971-2), 3-12 (pp. 4-5).

British Library, Egerton MS 1994, f. 298.

SiP 112 ----- -----

Copy in a verse miscellany compiled by Henry Stanford, household tutor in the Carey family; c. 1585-98.

This MS collated in Ringler and in Robertson.

Cambridge University Library, MS Dd. 5. 75, f. 38.

Old Arcadia. Book I, No. 3

SiP 113 ----- *Book I, No. 3* ('What length of verse can serve brave Mopsa's good to show').

Copy, transcribed from a printed source, in a miscellany compiled by an Oxford man and once owned by one William Bloys; c. 1630s-40s.

Ringler, p. 12; Robertson, pp. 30-1. This MS recorded in Ringler, p. 558, and in Robertson, p. 424.

Bodleian, MS Rawl. poet. 142, f. 26v.

SiP 114 ----- -----

Copy in a verse miscellany; c. 1596-1601.

This MS collated in Ringler and in Robertson.

British Library, Harley MS 6910, f. 145v.

SiP 115 ----- -----

Copy in a verse miscellany compiled by the antiquary St Loe Kniveton of Gray's Inn; c. 1585-90s.

This MS collated in Ringler and in Robertson.

British Library, Harley MS 7392, f. 75.

SiP 116 ----- -----

Copy in a verse miscellany compiled by Henry Stanford, household tutor in the Carey family; c. 1585-98.

This MS collated in Ringler and in Robertson.

Cambridge University Library, MS Dd. 5. 75, f. 37v.

SiP 117 ----- *Book I, No. 4* ('Come shepheard's weedes, become your master's minde').

Copy of an abridged version beginning 'These weedes will beecome my mind', in an anonymous MS play entitled *Loves Changelinges change*, bound in a composite volume of MS plays; c. 1630-40?

Ringler, p. 13; Robertson, p. 40. Printed from this MS in John P. Cutts, 'More Manuscript Versions of Poems by Sidney', *ELN*, 9 (1971-2), 3-12 (p. 5).

British Library, Egerton MS 1994, f. 300.

SiP 118 ----- *Book I, No. 5* ('Now thanked be the great God Pan').

Copy of the first stanza in a musical setting in a Scottish MS book of roundels compiled by David Melvill; 1612.

Ringler, p. 13; Robertson, p. 51; this setting first pub. in Thomas Ravenscroft, *Pammelia* (London, 1609). Printed from this MS in *The Melvill Book of Roundels*, ed. Granville Bantock and H. Orsmond Anderton, Roxburghe Club (London, 1916), No. 68, pp. 27, 139-41; discussed in John P. Cutts, 'Dametas' Song in Sidney's Arcadia', *RN*, 11 (1958), 183-8; recorded in Ringler, p. 567, and in Robertson, p. 427.

Library of Congress, Music Division, PR1105.R7 1916c.

SiP 119 ----- -----

Copy of the incipit in a musical setting, written in one of the MS part books of the 'St Andrews Psalter'; early 17th century.

Trinity College, Dublin, MS 412, f. 28v.

SiP 120 ----- *First Eclogues No. 6* ('We love, and have our loves rewarded').

Copy of a two-stanza version beginning 'wee loue and are beelovd againe' in an anonymous MS play entitled *Loves Changelinges change*, bound in a composite volume of MS plays; c. 1630-40?

Ringler, p. 14; Robertson, pp. 57-8. Printed from this MS in John P. Cutts, 'More Manuscript Versions of Poems by Sidney', *ELN*, 9 (1971-2), 3-12 (pp. 5-6).

British Library, Egerton MS 1994, f. 300v.

SiP 121 ----- *First Eclogues, No. 7* ('Come Dorus, come, let songs thy sorowes signifie').

Copy of lines 152-6, here beginning 'My earthy moulde doth melt in watry teares', in a miscellany compiled by a Cambridge student, possibly Sir John Finett (1571-1641) of Fordwich, Kent; c. 1586-91.

Ringler, pp. 14-20; Robertson, pp. 58-64. This MS collated in Ringler and in Robertson.

Bodleian, MS Rawl. poet. 85, f. 65v.

SiP 122 ----- *First Eclogues, No. 13* ('Lady, reservd by the heav'ns to do pastors' company honnor').

Copy of lines 113-39, 141-4, 146-54, beginning 'And when I meete these trees, in the earth's faire lyvery clothed', in a miscellany compiled by a Cambridge student, possibly Sir John Finett (1571-1641) of Fordwich, Kent; c. 1586-91.

Ringler, pp. 31-7; Robertson, pp. 82-8. This MS collated in Ringler and in Robertson.

Bodleian, MS Rawl. poet. 85, f. 22r-v.

SiP 123 ----- *Book II, No. 14* ('In vaine, mine Eyes, you labour to amende').

Copy, transcribed from the edition of 1593, in a verse miscellany owned in 1596 by one Anthony Babington of Warrington; c. 1596.

Ringler, p. 38; Robertson, p. 93. This MS recorded in Ringler, p. 555, and in Robertson, p. 437.

British Library, Add. MS 34064, f. 28v.

SiP 124 ----- *Book II, No. 15* ('Let not old age disgrace my high desire').

Copy in a composite volume of verse and prose; early 17th century.

Ringler, pp. 38-9; Robertson, p. 95. This MS recorded in Ringler, pp. 558-9, and in Robertson, p. 437.

Bodleian, MS Rawl. poet. 172, f. 6.

SiP 125 ----- -----

Copy, headed 'An old man fallen in love with a yonge maiden', transcribed from the edition of 1593, in a verse miscellany owned in 1596 by one Anthony Babington of Warrington; c. 1596.

This MS recorded in Ringler, p. 555, and in Robertson, p. 437.

British Library, Add. MS 34064, ff. 26v-8.

SiP 126 ----- -----

Copy of lines 1-8, 13-14, in a verse miscellany; c. 1596-1601.

This MS collated in Ringler and in Robertson.

British Library, Harley MS 6910, f. 154v.

SiP 126.5 See Addenda, p. 634.

SiP 127 ----- *Book II, No. 16* ('Since so mine eyes are subject to your sight').

Copy in a verse miscellany compiled by an Oxford man and once owned by one Henry Lawson; c. 1630s.

Ringler, p. 39; Robertson, p. 99.

Bodleian, MS Eng. poet. e. 14, f. 9.

SiP 128 ----- -----

Copy, transcribed from the edition of 1593, in a verse miscellany owned in 1596 by one Anthony Babington of Warrington; c. 1596.

This MS recorded in Ringler, p. 555, and in Robertson, p. 437.

British Library, Add. MS 34064, f. 28.

SiP 129 ----- *Book II, No. 17* ('My sheepe are thoughts, which I both guide and serve').

Copy in a miscellany later owned by one Joseph Hall; c. 1630s-50.

Ringler, p. 39; Robertson, p. 107. This MS recorded in Ringler, p. 561, and in Robertson, p. 438.

Folger, MS V. a. 339, f. 187.

SiP 130 ----- -----

Copy in a miscellany once owned by one Robert Thornton; c. 1580s-90s.

This MS collated in Ringler and in Robertson.

Marsh's Library, Dublin, MS Z 3. 5. 21, f. 17v.

SiP 131 ----- *Book II, No. 21* ('Over these brookes trusting to ease mine eyes').

Copy in a miscellany compiled by a Cambridge student, possibly Sir John Finett (1571-1641) of Fordwich, Kent; c. 1586-91.

Ringler, pp. 41-2; Robertson, p. 118. This MS collated in Ringler and in Robertson.

Bodleian, MS Rawl. poet. 85, f. 23v.

SiP 132 ----- -----

Copy, transcribed from the edition of 1598, in a verse miscellany compiled by John Lilliat (c.1550-c.1599); c. 1599.

This MS recorded in Ringler, p. 558, and in Robertson, p. 440.

Bodleian, MS Rawl. poet. 148, ff. 99v-100.

SiP 133 ----- -----

Copy, transcribed from the edition of 1593, in a verse miscellany owned in 1596 by one Anthony Babington of Warrington; c. 1596.

This MS recorded in Ringler, p. 555, and in Robertson, p. 440.

British Library, Add. MS 34064, f. 28v.

SiP 134 ----- -----

Copy, transcribed from a printed source, in a verse miscellany compiled by Arthur Capell; mid-17th century.

This MS recorded in Ringler, p. 556, and in Robertson, p. 440.

British Library, Harley MS 3511, ff. 74v-5.

Old Arcadia. Book II, No. 22

SiP 135 ----- *Book II, No. 22* ('Wyth two strange fires of equall heate possest').

Copy in a miscellany compiled by a Cambridge student, possibly Sir John Finett (1571-1641) of Fordwich, Kent; c. 1586-91.

Ringler, p. 42; Robertson, p. 123. This MS collated in Ringler and in Robertson.

Bodleian, MS Rawl. poet. 85, f. 23.

SiP 136 ----- *Second Eclogues, No. 27* ('Thou Rebell vile, come, to thy master yelde').

Copy, headed 'The Scyrmish betwixt Reasons and Passion', transcribed from the edition of 1593, in a verse miscellany owned in 1596 by one Anthony Babington of Warrington; c. 1596.

Ringler, pp. 46-7; Robertson, pp. 135-6. This MS recorded in Ringler, p. 555, and in Robertson, p. 443.

British Library, Add. MS 34064, f. 27r-v.

SiP 137 ----- *Second Eclogues, No. 33* ('Reason, tell me thy mind, if here be reason').

Copy in a miscellany compiled by a Cambridge student, possibly Sir John Finett (1571-1641) of Fordwich, Kent; c. 1586-91.

Ringler, pp. 67-8; Robertson, pp. 165-6. This MS collated in Ringler and in Robertson.

Bodleian, MS Rawl. poet. 85, f. 24.

SiP 138 ----- *Second Eclogues, No. 34* ('O sweet woods the delight of solitarines!').

Copy of lines 1-2 as the first two lines of a song (here first stanza only) by John Dowland, in a miscellany compiled by John Ramsey (b. 1578) of Peterhouse, Cambridge; early 17th century.

Ringler, pp. 68-9; Robertson, pp. 166-7; Dowland's song (in a musical setting) pub. in *The Second Booke of Songs or Ayres* (London, 1600). This MS recorded in Robertson, p. 447.

Bodleian, MS Douce 280, f. 69.

SiP 139 ----- -----

Copy of lines 1-2 in the song version of John Dowland (first stanza only) (see SiP 138), in a musical setting by Henry Lawes in Lawes's autograph songbook; mid-17th century.

This MS recorded in Ringler, p. 566, and in Robertson, p. 447; facsimiles in Willa McClung Evans, *Henry Lawes* (New York & London, 1941), p. 20, and in Pamela J. Willetts, *The Henry Lawes Manuscript* (London, 1969), plate XIII.

British Library, Add. MS 53723, f. 11v.

SiP 140 ----- *Book III, No. 35* ('Sweete glove the wittnes of my secrett blisse').

Copy in a verse miscellany compiled by Henry Stanford, household tutor in the Carey family; c. 1585-98.

Ringler, p. 70; Robertson, p. 169. This MS collated in Ringler and in Robertson.

Cambridge University Library, MS Dd. 5. 75, f. 36v.

SiP 141 ----- *Book III, No. 38* ('Phaebus farewell, a sweeter Saint I serve').

Copy in a miscellany compiled by a Cambridge student, possibly Sir John Finett (1571-1641) of Fordwich, Kent; c. 1586-91.

Ringler, p. 72; Robertson, p. 177. This MS collated in Ringler and in Robertson.

Bodleian, MS Rawl. poet. 85, f. 5v.

SiP 142 ----- *Book III, No. 41* ('Like those sicke folkes, in whome strange humors flowe').

Copy in a miscellany compiled by a Cambridge student, possibly Sir John Finett (1571-1641) of Fordwich, Kent; c. 1586-91.

Ringler, p. 74; Robertson, p. 181. This MS collated in Ringler and in Robertson.

Bodleian, MS Rawl. poet. 85, f. 21v.

SiP 143 ----- -----

Copy in a verse miscellany compiled by Henry Stanford, household tutor in the Carey family; c. 1585-98.

This MS collated in Ringler and in Robertson.

Cambridge University Library, MS Dd. 5. 75, f. 26v.

SiP 144 ----- *Book III, No. 42* ('Howe is my Sunn, whose beames are shining bright').

Copy of lines 1-8 in a verse miscellany compiled by Henry Stanford, household tutor in the Carey family; c. 1585-98.

Ringler, p. 74; Robertson, pp. 181-2. This MS collated in Ringler and in Robertson.

Cambridge University Library, MS Dd. 5. 75, f. 26v.

SiP 145 ----- *Book III, No. 45* ('My true love hath my hart, and I have his').

Copy in a musical setting in a MS songbook owned in 1630 by one Hugh Floyd; c. 1614-30.

Ringler, pp. 75-6; Robertson, pp. 190-1. This

MS recorded in Ringler, p. 566, and in Robertson, p. 452.

British Library, Add. MS 15117, f. 18v.

SiP 146 ----- -----

Copy in a verse miscellany compiled by the antiquary St Loe Kniveton of Gray's Inn; c. 1585-90s.

This MS collated in Ringler and in Robertson.

British Library, Harley MS 7392, f. 68.

SiP 147 ----- *Book III, No. 47* ('Do not disdaine, o streight up raised Pine').

Copy, transcribed from the edition of 1593, in a verse miscellany owned in 1596 by one Anthony Babington of Warrington; c. 1596.

Ringler, p. 77; Robertson, p. 198. This MS recorded in Ringler, p. 555, and in Robertson, p. 453.

British Library, Add. MS 34064, f. 29.

SiP 148 ----- *Book III, No. 48* ('Sweete roote say thou, the roote of my desire').

Copy in a verse miscellany compiled by Henry Stanford, household tutor in the Carey family; c. 1585-98.

Ringler, p. 77; Robertson, p. 198. This MS collated in Ringler and in Robertson.

Cambridge University Library, MS Dd. 5. 75, f. 26v.

SiP 149 ----- *Book III, No. 51* ('Locke up, faire liddes, the treasures of my harte').

Copy in a verse miscellany compiled by John Harington of Stepney (1520?-82) and his son Sir John Harington of Kelston (1560-1612); late 16th century.

Ringler, p. 79; Robertson, pp. 200-1. Printed from this MS in Hughey, *Arundel Harington MS*, I, No. 191, p. 239; collated in Ringler and in Robertson.

Owned by the Duke of Norfolk, Arundel Castle, MSS (Special Press), 'Harrington MS. Temp. Eliz.', f. 145.

SiP 150 ----- -----

Copy in a miscellany compiled by a Cambridge student, possibly Sir John Finett (1571-1641) of Fordwich, Kent; c. 1586-91.

This MS collated in Ringler and in Robertson.

Bodleian, MS Rawl. poet. 85, f. 9.

SiP 151 ----- -----

Copy in a verse miscellany compiled by the antiquary St Loe Kniveton of Gray's Inn; c. 1585-90s.

This MS collated in Ringler and in Robertson.

British Library, Harley MS 7392, f. 38v.

SiP 152 ----- -----

Copy in a verse miscellany compiled by Henry Stanford, household tutor in the Carey family; c. 1585-98.

This MS collated in Ringler and in Robertson.

Cambridge University Library, MS Dd. 5. 75, f. 26.

SiP 153 ----- *Book III, No. 54* ('My Lute within thy selfe thy tunes enclose').

Copy in a musical setting by Henry Lawes, in Lawes's autograph songbook; mid-17th century.

Ringler, p. 81; Robertson, pp. 210-11. This MS recorded in Ringler, p. 566, and in Robertson, p. 455.

British Library, Add. MS 53723, f. 3v.

SiP 154 ----- *Book III, No. 60* ('Vertue, beawtie, and speach, did strike, wound, charme').

Copy in a verse miscellany compiled by the antiquary St Loe Kniveton of Gray's Inn; c. 1585-90s.

Ringler, p. 84; Robertson, pp. 229-30. This MS collated in Ringler and in Robertson.

British Library, Harley MS 7392, f. 66.

SiP 155 ----- *Book III, No. 62* ('What toong can her perfections tell').

Copy, headed 'In com̄endation of a beautifull lady', in a verse miscellany compiled by an Oxford man, possibly a member of Wadham College, and later used by William Fulman (1632-88); c. late 1630s.

Ringler, pp. 85-90; Robertson, pp. 238-42. This MS recorded in Ringler, p. 559, and in Robertson, p. 459.

Bodleian, MS CCC. 328, ff. 85-6v.

SiP 156 ----- -----

Copy, transcribed from the edition of 1593, in a verse miscellany owned in 1596 by one Anthony Babington of Warrington; c. 1596.

Old Arcadia. Book III, No. 62

This MS recorded in Ringler, p. 555, and in Robertson, p. 459.

British Library, Add. MS 34064, ff. 29-31.

SiP 157 ----- -----

Copy in a verse miscellany compiled by Henry Stanford, household tutor in the Carey family; c. 1585-98.

This MS collated in Ringler and in Robertson.

Cambridge University Library, MS Dd. 5. 75, ff. 26, 36v-7.

SiP 158 ----- -----

Copy, headed 'In prayse of bewty', transcribed from a printed source, in a verse miscellany compiled by an Oxford man and once owned by one Stephen Welden; mid-17th century.

Formerly MS 452.4, this MS recorded in Ringler, p. 560, and in Robertson, p. 459.

Folger, MS V. a. 162, ff. 95-6v.

SiP 159 ----- -----

Copy of lines 1-4 in a composite volume of verse collected by Peter Le Neve (1661-1729), his brother Oliver, and Thomas Martin (1697-1771) of Palgrave; 17th century.

This MS recorded in Ringler, p. 555, and in Robertson, p. 459.

British Library, Add. MS 27406, f. 117.

SiP 160 ----- -----

Copy of lines 75-6, headed 'On a Mayden' and beginning 'A prettie seale of virgine waxe', in a composite volume of verse collected by Elias Ashmole (1617-92); mid-17th century.

Bodleian, MS Ashmole 36/37, f. 143v.

SiP 161 ----- -----

Copy of a version of lines 75-6, headed 'A maiden' and here beginning 'Aprills seale of virgin wax', in a verse miscellany compiled by an Oxford man and once owned by one Henry Lawson; c. 1630s.

Bodleian, MS Eng. poet. e. 14, f. 70.

SiP 162 ----- -----

Copy of lines 75-6, headed 'A Mayden' and here beginning 'A pretty seale of Virgin wax', in a verse miscellany compiled by one Robert Bishop; c. 1630.

Rosenbach Foundation, MS 1083/16, p. 22.

SiP 163 ----- -----

Copy of lines 143-6, beginning 'The inke immortall fame dooth lende', in a verse miscellany once owned by Francis Norreys (? Sir Francis Norris (1609-69)) and Henry Balle; imperfect; mid-17th century.

This MS collated in Ringler and in Robertson.

British Library, Egerton MS 2421, f. 46v rev.

SiP 164 ----- *Third Eclogues, No. 64* ('A neighbor mine not long agoe there was').

Copy in a verse miscellany; c. 1596-1601.

Ringler, pp. 94-7; Robertson, pp. 249-53. This MS collated in Ringler and in Robertson.

British Library, Harley MS 6910, ff. 173v-5.

SiP 165 ----- *Book IV, No. 68* ('Who hath his hire, hath well his labour plast').

Copy, transcribed from the edition of 1598, in a verse miscellany compiled by John Lilliat (c.1550-c.1599); c. 1599.

Ringler, p. 108; Robertson, p. 265. This MS recorded in Ringler, p. 558, and in Robertson, p. 466.

Bodleian, MS Rawl. poet. 148, f. 5v.

SiP 166 ----- *Fourth Eclogues, No. 71* ('Yee Gote-heard Gods, that love the grassie mountaines').

Copy in a miscellany compiled by a Cambridge student, possibly Sir John Finett (1571-1641) of Fordwich, Kent; c. 1586-91.

Ringler, pp. 111-13; Robertson, pp. 328-30. This MS collated in Ringler and in Robertson.

Bodleian, MS Rawl. poet. 85, ff. 20-1v.

SiP 167 ----- *Fourth Eclogues, No. 74* ('Unto the caitife wretch, whom long affliction holdeth').

Copy in a verse miscellany compiled by John Harington of Stepney (1520?-82) and his son Sir John Harington of Kelston (1560-1612); late 16th century.

Ringler, pp. 122-4; Robertson, pp. 341-4. Printed from this MS in Hughey, *Arundel Harington MS*, I, No. 229, pp. 258-61; collated in Ringler and in Robertson.

Owned by the Duke of Norfolk, Arundel Castle, MSS (Special Press), 'Harrington MS. Temp. Eliz.', ff. 157-8v.

SiP 168 ----- *Book V, No. 77* ('Since nature's works be good, and death doth serve').

Copy, headed 'Verses ag^{t} feare of Death: made by Sir ph: sidney', transcribed from a printed source, in a miscellany compiled by one Gilbert Frevile of Bishop Middleham, County Durham; c. 1630.

Ringler, p. 131; Robertson, pp. 373-4. This MS recorded in Ringler, p. 556, and in Robertson, p. 480.

British Library, Egerton MS 2877, f. 105.

PROSE

SiP 169 *Certain notes concerning the present state of the Prince of Orange and the provinces of Holland and Zeeland, as they were in the month of May 1577.*

Copy in a volume of state papers; [1577].

First pub. in Baron Kervynde Lettenhove, *Relations politiques des Pays-Bas et de l'Angleterre sous le règne de Philippe II*, Vol. IX (Brussels, 1890). Printed from this MS and attributed to Sidney in Osborn, *Young Philip Sidney*, pp. 482-90; also discussed by James M. Osborn in *TLS* (30 April 1970), pp. 487-8.

British Library, Cotton MS Galba C. VI, Part I, ff. 52-5.

SiP 170 -----

Copy; [1577].

The text corrected from this MS in Osborn.

Public Record Office, SP.70/145/1225.

SiP 171 -----

Copy; [1577].

Printed from this MS in Lettenhove; the text corrected from this MS in Osborn.

Public Record Office, SP.70/145/1226.

*SiP 172 *Defence of the Earl of Leicester.*

Autograph draft, with revisions; untitled; c. 1585.

First pub. in Arthur Collins, *Letters and Memorials of State of the Sidney Family* (London, 1746), I, 62-8; Feuillerat, III, 61-71. Printed from this MS in Duncan-Jones & Van Dorsten, pp. 129-41. Facsimile pages in Ringler, facing p. lxiii; *The Pierpont Morgan Library: A Review of Acquisitions 1949-1968* (New York, 1969), plate 31; *Autograph Letters & Manuscripts: Major Acquisitions of the Pierpont Morgan Library 1924-1974* (New York, 1974), plate 8.

Pierpont Morgan Library, MA 1475.

SiP 173 -----

Copy, in the same hand as SiP 184, probably transcribed from SiP 172, untitled, headed in another hand 'Apologie par le feu renõme Cheualeir Ph. Sidney põ le Cõte de Leycester sõ oncle 1582', in a volume of documents relating to diplomatic relations between England and France; late 16th-early 17th century.

This MS collated in Feuillerat, III, 333-4, and in Duncan-Jones & Van Dorsten.

Bibliothèque Nationale, Paris, Cinq cents de Colbert n° 466, ff. 111-16.

SiP 174 -----

Copy, probably transcribed from SiP 172, perhaps by Arthur Collins, among the papers of the Sidney (De L'Isle) family of Penshurst Place; early 18th century.

Printed from this MS in Feuillerat; collated in Duncan-Jones & Van Dorsten.

Kent Archives Office, U 1475 Z3.

SiP 175 *A Defence of Poetry.*

Copy, once owned by Robert Sidney (1563-1626), with some corrections on the last leaf in his hand; 16 leaves; late 16th century.

First pub. London, 1595; Feuillerat, III, 1-46. Edited from this MS in Duncan-Jones & Van Dorsten, pp. 73-121; collated in Feuillerat, III, 317-25. A microfilm is at the University of Birmingham, Shakespeare Institute (Mic. S82).

Owned by the Viscount De L'Isle, Penshurst Place, MS 1226.

SiP 176 -----

Copy, in the same hand as SiP 103, untitled, bound up with a miscellany compiled by Francis Blomefield (1705-52), Rector of Fersfield, Norfolk; indexed by Blomefield in 1726 as 'A treatise of Horsman shipp. (Not so.). Tis a defence of Neglected Poetry, in 19 fol:'; c. 1584.

Printed from this MS, with a facsimile of the first page, in *The Norwich Sidney Manuscript: The Apology for Poetry*, ed. Mary R. Mahl (Northridge, California, 1969); discussed by Mary Mahl in *TLS* (21 December 1967), p. 1245, in 'The Norwich Sidney Manuscript: Adventures of a Literary Detective', *Coranto*, 8 (1972), 18-32, and in 'Sir Philip Sidney's Scribe: The *New Arcadia* and the *Apology for Poetry*', *ELN*, 10 (1972-3), 90-1; collated in Duncan-Jones & Van Dorsten.

Norfolk Record Office, MS 10837 P138B.

A Defence of Poetry

SiP 177 -----

Extracts in Volume X of the miscellaneous collections of Brian Twyne (1579?-1644); early 17th century.

Bodleian, MS CCC. 263, ff. 114v-15.

SiP 178 -----

Extracts, headed 'Apolog: of Poetry. s[r] P.S.', in a miscellany compiled by Edward Pudsey (1573-1613); 1600s.

This MS recorded in Ringler, p. 557.

Bodleian, MS Eng. poet. d. 3, f. 73r-v.

SiP 179 -----

Extracts in a miscellany owned by William Drake (1606-69) of Shardeloes, near Amersham, Buckinghamshire; c. 1659.

University College London, MS Ogden 7/13, ff. [33-7].

--- -----

See also INTRODUCTION.

*SiP 180 *Discourse on Irish Affairs.*

Autograph, untitled, in a composite volume of historical tracts and documents; incomplete; [1577].

First pub. (from this MS) in Feuillerat, III (1923), 46-50; printed from this MS in Duncan-Jones & Van Dorsten, pp. 8-12.

British Library, Cotton MS Titus B. XII, ff. 564-5.

SiP 181 *A Letter to Queen Elizabeth touching her Marriage with Monsieur.*

Copy in a volume of miscellaneous verse and prose transcribed from the papers of Sir Christopher Yelverton (1535?-1612); early 17th century.

First pub. in *Scrinia Caeciliana or Supplement of the Cabala* (London, 1663); Feuillerat, III, 51-60; Duncan-Jones & Van Dorsten, pp. 46-57.

All Souls College, Oxford, MS 155, ff. 306-12v.

SiP 182 -----

Copy in a MS volume of prose works connected with the Court or state affairs; imperfect; c. 1597.

This MS reproduced in *Collotype Facsimile & Type Transcript of an Elizabethan Manuscript preserved at Alnwick Castle, Northumberland*, ed. Frank J. Burgoyne (London, 1904); collated in Feuillerat, III, 326 seq.; recorded in Duncan-Jones & Van Dorsten, p. 38.

Owned by the Duke of Northumberland, Alnwick Castle, MS 525 (Safe 4), ff. 55-61.

SiP 183 -----

Copy, untitled, in a volume of transcripts of state letters; incomplete, skipping a leaf; early 17th century.

Owned by Peter Beal, Leeds, 'Elizabethan MSS', pp. 1028-35.

SiP 184 -----

Copy, in the same hand as SiP 173, in a volume of documents relating to diplomatic relations between England and France; late 16th-early 17th century.

Printed from this MS in Feuillerat; collated in Duncan-Jones & Van Dorsten.

Bibliothèque Nationale, Paris, Cinq cents de Colbert n° 466, ff. 89-95.

SiP 185 -----

Copy in a composite volume of political papers and speeches collected by Elias Ashmole (1617-92); late 16th-early 17th century.

This MS collated in Feuillerat, III, 326 seq.; recorded in Duncan-Jones & Van Dorsten, p. 37.

Bodleian, MS Ashmole 800, ff. 1-4.

SiP 186 -----

Copy in a volume of tracts and sermons; late 16th-early 17th century.

This MS collated in Feuillerat, III, 326 seq., and in Duncan-Jones & Van Dorsten.

Bodleian, MS Douce 46, ff. 2-15.

SiP 187 -----

Copy in a volume of tracts and papers relating to France; early 17th century.

This MS formerly Phillipps MS 11931.

Bodleian, MS Eng. hist. f. 8, fols. 91-8.

SiP 188 -----

Copy in a volume of transcripts of historical documents made by Robert Horn of Shropshire; c. 1618-30s.

This MS collated in Feuillerat, III, 326 seq.; recorded in Duncan-Jones & Van Dorsten, p. 38.

Bodleian, MS Rawl. B. 151, ff. 3-6.

A Letter to Queen Elizabeth touching her Marriage with Monsieur

SiP 189 -----

Copy in a volume of transcripts of historical documents made by the Yorkshire antiquary John Hopkinson (1610-80); 1660.

Formerly among the MSS of Matthew Wilson at Eshton Hall, Yorkshire, this MS recorded in *HMC*, 3rd Report (1872), Appendix, p. 297; recorded (but not seen) in Feuillerat, III, 326.

Bradford Central Library, Hopkinson MSS, Vol. 18, ff. 93-9v.

SiP 190 -----

Copy in a volume of state papers; imperfect; late 16th-early 17th century.

This MS collated in Feuillerat, III, 325 seq.; recorded in Duncan-Jones & Van Dorsten, p. 37.

British Library, Add. MS 33271, ff. 32-4 (f. 33 is reversed).

SiP 191 -----

Copy, untitled, in a volume of miscellaneous tracts owned by Sir John Harington (constituting Volume I of the Harington Papers: see HrJ 340); late 16th century.

British Library, Add. MS 46366, ff. 100-6.

SiP 192 -----

Copy in a composite volume of state papers collected by Robert Beale, Clerk of the Council to Queen Elizabeth (1541-1601); late 16th century.

Formerly Yelverton MS 31, this volume recorded in *HMC*, 2nd Report (1874), Appendix, p. 41.

British Library, Add. MS 48027, ff. 230-5v.

SiP 193 -----

Copy in two hands in a volume of state papers; mid-17th century.

This MS collated in Feuillerat, III, 325 seq.; recorded in Duncan-Jones & Van Dorsten, p. 38.

British Library, Hargrave MS 226, ff. 270-82v.

SiP 194 -----

Copy in a volume of state papers; early-mid-17th century.

This MS collated in Feuillerat, III, 325 seq.; recorded in Duncan-Jones & Van Dorsten, p. 38.

British Library, Harley MS 444, ff. 3-14.

SiP 195 -----

Copy in a volume of state papers; early 17th century.

Printed from this MS in Duncan-Jones & Van Dorsten; collated in Feuillerat, III, 325 seq.

British Library, Harley MS 1323, ff. 43-56v.

SiP 196 -----

Copy of part of the letter in a volume of state papers; imperfect; early-mid-17th century.

This MS collated in Feuillerat, III, 325 seq.; recorded in Duncan-Jones & Van Dorsten, p. 38.

British Library, Harley MS 6845, ff. 196-7.

SiP 197 -----

Notes taken from the letter in a volume of state papers; late 16th century.

This MS recorded in Feuillerat, III, 325.

British Library, Lansdowne MS 94, ff. 54-6v.

SiP 198 -----

Copy; early 17th century.

This MS collated in Feuillerat, III, 325 seq.; recorded in Duncan-Jones & Van Dorsten, p. 38.

British Library, Sloane MS 24.

SiP 199 -----

Copy, untitled, in a composite volume of MSS; late 16th-early 17th century.

This MS collated in Feuillerat, III, 326 seq.; recorded in Duncan-Jones & Van Dorsten, p. 38.

Cambridge University Library, MS Kk. 1. 3. 4, ff. 2v-6v.

SiP 200 -----

Copy in a volume of state letters and tracts once owned by the antiquary Sir Peter Leycester (1614-78); early-mid-17th century.

Among the Tabley House MSS, this MS recorded in *HMC*, 1st Report (1870), Appendix, pp. 47-8; recorded (but not seen) in Feuillerat, III, 326.

Cheshire Record Office, DLT/B8, pp. 185-6.

SiP 201 -----

Copy in a volume of state papers; early-mid-17th century.

Folger, MS V. b. 151, ff. 57-62.

A Letter to Queen Elizabeth touching her Marriage with Monsieur

SiP 202 -----

Copy; mid-17th century.

This MS recorded in Duncan-Jones & Van Dorsten, p. 38.

Folger, MS X. d. 210.

SiP 203 -----

Copy in a miscellany; early 17th century.

Formerly Phillipps MS 10665; this MS recorded in Duncan-Jones & Van Dorsten, p. 38.

Huntington, HM 102, ff. 1-5v.

SiP 204 -----

Copy in a volume of state papers; early-mid-17th century.

This MS collated in Feuillerat, III, 326 seq.; recorded in Duncan-Jones & Van Dorsten, p. 38.

Inner Temple Library, Petyt MS 538, Vol. 51, ff. 110-18.

SiP 205 -----

Copy; early 17th century?

Sold at Sotheby's, 10 April 1962, Lot 467, this MS recorded in *BC*, 15 (Summer 1966), 156, and in Duncan-Jones & Van Dorsten, p. 38.

Owned by Bent E. Juel-Jensen, Oxford.

SiP 206 -----

Copy in a composite volume of state tracts; mid-17th century.

Formerly Mostyn MS 177, this volume recorded in *HMC*, 4th Report (1874), Appendix, p. 355. See also WoH 299 and note that the same hand also occurs in Vols. III and V of the Acland-Hood MSS recorded in SiP 211.

University of Kansas, MS E205, ff. 44-59.

SiP 207 -----

Copy in a volume of state letters and poems belonging to the Sotheby family of London; early 17th century.

University of Kansas, MS 4A:1, pp. 38-48.

SiP 208 -----

Copy in a composite volume of MSS collected by William Parkhurst (fl. 1604-67); among the papers of the Finch family of Burley-on-the-Hill, Rutland; 1600s-41.

This MS recorded (but not seen) in Feuillerat, III, 326.

Leicestershire Record Office, DG. 7/Lit. 2, ff. 237-41.

SiP 209 -----

Copy in a volume of state tracts; mid-17th century.

This MS formerly Phillipps MS 10464.

University of London Library, MS 308, ff. 230-43.

SiP 210 -----

Copy; 17th century?

This MS recorded in Feuillerat, III, 326, and in Duncan-Jones & Van Dorsten, p. 38.

Owned by the Viscount De L'Isle, Penshurst Place, Sidney Papers B.

SiP 211 -----

Copy in a composite volume of state tracts; mid-17th century.

This MS among the MSS of Sir Alexander Acland-Hood of St Audries, recorded in *HMC*, 6th Report (1877), Appendix, p. 350; recorded (but not seen) in Feuillerat, III, 326. See also WoH 258.

Somerset Record Office, DD/AH Box 51, Vol. I, ff. 48-60v.

SiP 212 -----

Copy in a composite volume of MSS; early 17th century.

This MS collated in Feuillerat, III, 326 seq.; recorded in Duncan-Jones & Van Dorsten, p. 38.

Trinity College, Dublin, MS 588, ff. 2-16.

SiP 213 -----

Copy in a volume of state tracts; early-mid-17th century.

This MS collated in Feuillerat, III, 326 seq.; recorded in Duncan-Jones & Van Dorsten, p. 38.

Trinity College, Dublin, MS 732, ff. 34-45.

SiP 214 -----

Copy in a volume of state papers; early 17th century.

This MS collated in Feuillerat, III, 326 seq.; recorded in Duncan-Jones & Van Dorsten, p. 38.

Trinity College, Dublin, MS 802, ff. 1-10.

A Letter to Queen Elizabeth touching her Marriage with Monsieur

SiP 215 -----

Copy, with one other tract (see PtG 5); late 16th century?

Formerly Mostyn MS 261, this MS recorded in *HMC*, 4th Report (1874), Appendix, p. 361.

Sotheby's, 13 July 1920, Lot 35, sold to Maggs; unlocated.

DRAMATIC WORKS

SiP 216 *The Lady of May*.

Copy, untitled, appended to a MS copy of *Arcadia* (see SiP 98) probably once owned by Sir Lionel Tollemache (1562-1612) of Helmingham Hall, Suffolk; late 16th century.

First pub. in *Arcadia* (London, 1598); Duncan-Jones & Van Dorsten, pp. 21-32; verse portions in Ringler, pp. 3-5. Printed from this MS in Robert Kimbrough and Philip Murphy, 'The Helmingham Hall Manuscript of Sidney's *The Lady of May*: A Commentary and Transcription', *RD*, NS 1 (1968), 103-19; collated in Duncan-Jones & Van Dorsten; recorded in Ringler, pp. x-xii. A microfilm is in the British Library (M/623).

Owned by Arthur A. Houghton, Jr., MS, ff. 154v-8 (to be sold at Christie's, 1980).

SiP 217 -----

Substantial extracts, transcribed from a printed source, in a miscellany compiled by William Drummond of Hawthornden; c. 1606-9.

This MS recorded in Ringler, pp. 361, 560, and in Duncan-Jones & Van Dorsten, p. 20.

National Library of Scotland, MS 2059 (Hawthornden Vol. VII), ff. 294v-5, 296v-9v.

SiP 218 -----

Notes taken from one of Rhombus's speeches, in Volume X of the miscellaneous collections of Brian Twyne (1579?-1644); early 17th century.

This MS recorded in Ringler, p. 361, and in Duncan-Jones & Van Dorsten, p. 20.

Bodleian, MS CCC. 263, f. 120.

SiP 219 -----

Extracts, transcribed from a printed source, in a miscellany; c. 1672.

This MS recorded in Ringler, p. 361, and in Duncan-Jones & Van Dorsten, p. 20.

British Library, Sloane MS 161, ff. 29-30.

--- -----

See also INTRODUCTION.

MARGINALIA IN PRINTED BOOKS AND MANUSCRIPTS

--- See SiP 31 and INTRODUCTION.

John Skelton

1460?-1529

ABBREVIATIONS

Canon Robert S. Kinsman and Theodore Yonge, *John Skelton: Canon and Census*, Renaissance Society of America, Bibliographies and Indexes No. 4 (Darien, Connecticut, 1967).

Dyce *The Poetical Works of John Skelton*, ed. Alexander Dyce, 2 vols (London, 1843).

For abbreviations used throughout Volume I, see p.xi.

INTRODUCTION

Only two MSS are known to contain Skelton's handwriting. One is his autograph of a congratulatory poem on the accession of Henry VIII (SkJ 6); the other is a medieval MS chronicle containing Skelton's annotations (SkJ 30). In addition to these MSS, there exist contemporary scribal copies of Skelton's translation of Diodorus Siculus (SkJ 28) and of his *Speculum principis* (SkJ 29), the latter probably his presentation copy to Henry VIII. Various poems attributed to Skelton are found in complete or partial transcripts in early miscellanies.

The standard edition of Skelton, from which titles and first lines are cited in the *Index*, remains Dyce. The canon, however, is still open to amendment. The latest assessment of it is by Robert Kinsman and Theodore Yonge in *Canon* (1967). The distinction made in the *Index* between works evidently by Skelton and works of doubtful authorship is based on the classification in *Canon* except for the poem *'Wofully araid'*, which is here treated as a doubtful item (SkJ 23-7) rather than as a definitely 'lost' work.

Kinsman and Yonge firmly reject from the canon the following poems which have at various times been attributed to Skelton and which exist in MSS:

(1) *Elegy on King Henry the Seventh* ('O wauering worlde all wrapped in wretchidnes'). *Canon*, R60, pp. 19-20. Printed in Dyce, II, 399-400. See STEPHEN HAWES, HaS 3.

(2) *'Hoyda joly rutterkin hoyda'*. *Canon*, R62, p. 20. Printed in Sir John Hawkins, *A General History of the Science and Practice of Music* (London, 1776), III, 2. In a musical setting by William Cornish in the Fairfax MS in the British Library (Add. MS 5465, ff. 101v-4), printed in *Early Tudor Songs and Carols*, ed. John Stevens, Musica Britannica XXXVI (London, 1975), pp. 132-4.

(3) *The Image of Ypocresye. Canon*, R64, p. 21. Printed in Dyce, II, 413-47. In the British Library (Lansdowne MS 794, ff. 2-153). Thomas Martin's transcript (1738) (Phillips MS 9261) is in Cambridge University (MS Add. 3309).

(4) *The Maner of the World Now a Dayes* ('So many poynted caps'). *Canon*, R65, p. 21. Printed London, [c. 1562]; Dyce, I, 148-54. A 120-line version is in a cartulary book of Missenden Abbey, Buckinghamshire, in the British Library (Sloane MS 747, ff. 88v-9).

(5) *'Masteres Anne'. Canon*, R66, p. 21. Printed in *The Romans of Partenay*, ed. Walter W. Skeat, EETS 22 (London, 1866), p. vi. In Trinity College, Cambridge (MS R. 3. 17 (James 597)).

(6) *'Non meministi'. Canon*, R67, pp. 21-2. Printed by Ian A. Gordon in *TLS* (20 September 1934), p. 636. In the British Library (Egerton MS 2642, f. 250v).

(7) *'Petevelly constrayned am Y'. Canon*, R68, p. 22. printed in Ewald Flügel, 'Liedersammlungen des XVI. Skelton', *Athenaeum* (29 November 1873), p. 697, from a MS bound with a printed exemplum of Pseudo-Boethius, *De disciplina scholarium cum notabili commento* (Deventer, 1496), now in the Robert H. Taylor Collection at Princeton ([no ref. number], pp. 5-6, and see also SkJ 27). A longer version, beginning 'Thofe I doo syng my hert doth wepe', is printed in Ewald Flügel, 'Liedersammlungen des XVI. Jahrhunderts, besonders aus der Zeit Heinrich's VIII', *Anglia*, 12 (1889), 225-72 (pp. 266-7), from a MS copy with a musical setting by Robert Cooper in the British Library (Royal MS App. 58, ff. 17v-19).

(8) *The Recule ageinst Gaguyne of the Frenshe Nacyoun. Canon*, L106, p. 30. A lost piece; doubtfully identified in Friedrich Brie, 'Skelton-Studien', *ES*, 37 (1907), 1-86 (pp. 31-2), with seven lines beginning 'How darest thou swere or be so bold also' in Trinity College, Cambridge (MS O. 2. 53 (James 1157), f. 66).

(9) *Vexilla regis. Canon*, L117, p. 32. A lost piece; doubtfully identified in Dyce (I, 144-6; II, 199) with verses beginning 'Now synge we, as we were wont', first printed in *Christmas Carolles* [c. 1550] and existing in the following MS versions: British Library (Add. MS

37049, f. 67v; Arundel MS 285, ff. 164v-8, printed in Carlton Brown, *Religious Lyrics of the XVth Century* (Oxford, 1939), pp. 151-6); and Edinburgh University Library (MS Borl. 205, f. 201, printed in *Pieces from the Makculloch and the Gray MSS*, ed. George Stevenson, STS 65 (Edinburgh & London, 1918), pp. 35-6).

(10) *Vox Populi, Vox Dei* ('I pray yow, be not wrothe'). *Canon*, R70, pp. 22-3. Printed in Dyce, II, 400-13. In the British Library (Harley MS 367, ff. 130-43v) and Cambridge University Library (MS Nn. 4. 5).

One other piece which may be connected with Skelton but which has not been given an entry in the *Index* is William Cornish's *A Treatise bitwene Trouth and Information* ('The knowlege of God passyth comparison'), first printed in *Pithy pleasaunt and profitable workes of maister Skelton* (London, 1568). The poem is reprinted in Nan Cooke Carpenter, 'Skelton's Hand in William Cornish's Musical Parable', *CL*, 22 (1970), 157-72. 'The poem is obviously not Skelton's', Ms Carpenter observes, 'but there are signs that the laureate probably had a hand in its composition'. An early copy is in the British Library (Royal MS 18 D. II, ff. 163-4).

Early 19th-century copies of various poems by Skelton can be found in the Bodleian (MS Eng. misc. e. 573, made by Richard Heber (1774-1833)) and in the Folger (MS N. b. 49 (Phillipps MS 10112), made by Joseph Haslewood (1769-1833)). Copies made by Joseph Hunter (1783-1861) of three prayers doubtfully attributed to Skelton (see SkJ 19-20) are in the British Library (Add. MS 24542). There is also a four-line quotation from Skelton's *Why Come ye nat to Courte* (lines 753-6) in a notebook compiled by Thomas Plume (1630-1704) in the Plume Library, Maldon (MS 25): see Andrew Clark, 'Dr. Plume's Pocket-Book', *The Essex Review*, 14 (1905), 9-20 (p. 14).

A MS household book which throws some light on Skelton's relationship with the Howard family was transcribed in *The Works of Henry Howard, Earl of Surrey, and Sir Thomas Wyatt*, ed. G. F. Nott, 2 vols (London, 1815-16), I, Appendix II, pp. iii-vi. The MS is now at the University of California at Berkeley and is discussed in Melvin J. Tucker, 'California MS. AC 523, formerly Phillipps MS. 3841', *N & Q*, 209 (October 1964), 374-6.

PB.

ARRANGEMENT

See also Addenda to Part 2, p.634

John Skelton

VERSE

(1) POEMS BY SKELTON

SkJ 1 *Colyn Cloute* ('What can it auayle').

Copy of a 1107-line version, plus a Latin epilogue (see SkJ 3), in a miscellany compiled by one John Colyns of the parish of St Mary Woolchurch, London; c. 1530.

Canon, C12, p. 5; first pub. London, [c. 1530]; Dyce, I, 311-60. This MS collated in Dyce.

British Library, Harley MS 2252, ff. 147-53.

SkJ 2 -----

Copy of lines 462-80, beginning 'Som men thynke that ye' and subscribed 'The profecy of Skylton, 1529', in a composite volume of verse and prose; 16th century.

Printed from this MS in Dyce, I, 329.

British Library, Lansdowne MS 762, ff. 75-6.

SkJ 3 *'Colinus Cloutus, quanquam mea carmina multis'.*

Copy of a Latin epilogue to *Colyn Cloute* (see SkJ 1) in a miscellany compiled by one John Colyns of the parish of St Mary Woolchurch, London; c. 1530.

Canon, C11, p. 5; first pub. (?) (from this MS) in Dyce (1843), I, 360.

British Library, Harley MS 2252, f. 153v.

SkJ 4 *Epigramma ad tanti principis maiestatem in sua puericia* ('Si quid habes, mea musa, dei resonantis amenam').

Fair copy on vellum, headed 'Ad tanti principis maiestatem in sua puericia, quando erat insignitus Dux Eboraci, etc., Skeltonis Laureatus hoc Epigramma et.', appended to the MS of *Speculum principis* probably presented by Skelton to Henry VIII (see SkJ 29); c. 1509-10.

Canon, C51, p. 15; first pub. (from this MS) in F.M. Salter, 'Skelton's *Speculum Principis*', *Speculum*, 9 (1934), 25-37 (pp. 36-7).

British Library, Add. MS 26787, ff. 24v-6v.

SkJ 5 *Garlande of Laurell* ('Arectyng my syght towarde the zodyake').

Copy in a volume of miscellaneous tracts; imperfect; late 15th-early 16th century.

Canon, C27, p. 9; first pub. in an incomplete version [London], 1523; complete in *Pithy pleasaunt and profitable workes of maister Skelton* (London, 1568); Dyce, I, 361-427. This MS collated in Dyce.

British Library, Cotton MS Vitellius E. X, ff. 208-25v.

--- *'I, liber, et propera, regem tu pronus adora'.*

[Dyce, I, 147].

See SkJ 30.

*SkJ 6 *A Lawde and Prayse Made for Our Souereigne Lord the Kyng* ('The Rose both White and Rede').

Autograph; probably presented to Henry VIII; [1509].

Canon, C35, p. 11; first pub. (from this MS) in Dyce (1843), I, ix-xi. Facsimiles in Maurice Pollet, *John Skelton* (trans. John Warrington, London, 1971), after p. 62; Croft, *Autograph Poetry*, I, 6-8.

Public Record Office, E. 36/228, ff. 7-8.

SkJ 7 *Manerly Margery Mylk and Ale* ('Ay, besherewe yow, be my fay').

Copy, untitled, in a musical setting by William Cornish in a MS songbook apparently written for Robert Fairfax, organist of St Albans; c. 1500.

Canon, C37, p. 11; first pub. (from this MS) in Sir John Hawkins, *A General History of the Science and Practice of Music* (London, 1776), III, 2; printed from this MS in Dyce, I, 28-9, and in *Early Tudor Songs and Carols*, ed. John Stevens, Musica Britannica XXXVI (London, 1975), pp. 128-30.

British Library, Add. MS 5465, ff. 96v-9.

SkJ 8 *Palinodium* ('Iam nunc pierios cantus et carmina laudis').

Fair copy on vellum, headed 'Ad serenissimam iam nunc suam maiestatem regiam, Skeltonidis Laureati non ignobile palinodium, etc.', appended to the MS of *Speculum principis* probably presented by Skelton to Henry VIII (see SkJ 29); c. 1509-10.

Canon, C51, p. 15; first pub. (from this MS) in F.M. Salter, 'Skelton's *Speculum Principis*', *Speculum*, 9 (1934), 25-37 (p. 37).

British Library, Add. MS 26787, ff. 27-8v.

SkJ 9 *Poems against Garnesche* ('Sithe ye haue me chalyngyd, Master Garnesche').

Copy in a composite volume of MSS collected by John Stow (1525?-1605); imperfect; mid-16th century.

Canon, C2, p. 3; first pub. (from this MS) in Dyce (1843), I, 116-31.

British Library, Harley MS 367, ff. 101-9v.

--- *Poeta Skelton laureatus libellum suum metrice alloquitur* ('Ad dominum properato meum, mea pagina, Percy').

See SkJ 12.

SkJ 10 *Speke, Parrot* ('My name is Parrot, a byrd of paradyse').

Copy of lines 1-59, 230-513, in a miscellany compiled by one John Colyns of the parish of St Mary Woolchurch, London; c. 1530.

Canon, C41, p. 12; lines 3-237 first pub. in *Certaine bokes cōpyled by mayster Skeltō* (London, [c. 1545]); a text of 513 lines first pub. (partly from this MS) in Dyce (1843), II, 1-25.

British Library, Harley MS 2252, ff. 133*v-140.

--- *Tetrastichon Skelton, laureati ad Magistrum Rukshaw, sacrae theologiae egregium professorem* ('Accipe nunc demum, doctor celeberrime Rukshaw').

See SkJ 12.

--- *'That ever England had'.*

See SkJ 30.

SkJ 11 *The Tunnyng of Elynour Rummyng* ('Tell you I chyll').

Attempted MS facsimile of a 16th century printed edition; owned in 1693 by one William Daniel; mid-17th century.

Canon, C42, p. 12; first pub. [c. 1520]; Dyce, I, 95-115.

British Library, Add. MS 28504.

SkJ 12 *Vpon the doulourus dethe and muche lamentable chaunce of the most honorable Erle of Northumberlande* ('I wayle, I wepe, I sobbe, I sigh ful sore').

Fair copy on vellum, preceded by a dedication, 'Poeta Skelton laureatus libellum suum metrice alloquitur' (beginning 'Ad dominum properato meum, mea pagina, Percy', and ending with 'Tetrastichon Skelton. laureati ad Magistrum Rukshaw', beginning 'Accipe nunc demum, doctor celeberrime Rukshaw'), in a composite volume of MSS once owned by Henry Fitzalan, twelfth Earl of Arundel (1511?-80), nephew of the fifth Earl of Northumberland; c. 1516-23.

Canon, C18, pp. 6-7; first pub. in *Pithy pleasaunt and profitable workes of maister Skelton* (London, 1568); Dyce, I, 6-14. This MS collated in Dyce.

British Library, Royal MS 18 D. II, ff. 165-6v.

SkJ 13 *Why Come ye nat to Courte?* ('All noble men, of this take hede').

Copy of the introductory lines and lines 838-1248 in a verse miscellany; c. 1537.

Canon, C46 & C5, pp. 13-14, 4; first pub. London, [c. 1545]; Dyce, II, 26-67. Printed from this MS in Julius Zupitza, 'Handschriftliche Bruchstücke von John Skeltons *Why come ye nat to court?*', *Archiv*, 85 (1890), 429-36.

Bodleian, MS Rawl. C. 813, ff. 36-43v.

--- -----

See also INTRODUCTION.

(2) POEMS OF DOUBTFUL AUTHORSHIP

SkJ 14 *How euery thing must haue a tyme* ('Tyme is a thing that no man may resyst').

Copy of a five-stanza version (plus a two-line burden) in a miscellany chiefly of heraldic and historical collections compiled by Robert Commaundre, Rector of Tarporley, Cheshire (d. 1613); late 16th-early 17th century.

Canon, D52, p. 16; first pub. in *Certaine bokes cōpyled by mayster Skeltō* (London, [c. 1545]); Dyce, I, 137-8. This MS recorded in *Canon*.

British Library, Egerton MS 2642, f. 250v.

SkJ 15 -----

Copy of the poem as stanzas 6 and 9-11 of a thirteen-stanza poem beginning 'O god that in tyme all thingis did begin', in a MS volume of Scottish poetry compiled by George Bannatyne; c. 1568.

Printed from this MS in *The Bannatyne Manuscript*, ed. J. Barclay Murdoch, II, Hunterian Club (Glasgow, 1896), 227-30; *The Bannatyne Manuscript*, ed. W. Tod Ritchie, II, STS, NS 22 (Edinburgh & London, 1928), 208-11; recorded in *Canon*.

National Library of Scotland, Adv. MS 1. 1. 6, Vol. II, ff. 82-3 (pp. 225-7).

SkJ 16 *Of the Death of the Noble Prince, Kynge Edwarde the Forth* ('Miseremini mei, ye that be my frendis!').

Of the Death of the Noble Prince, Kynge Edwarde the Forth

Copy, subscribed 'A lamentable of kyng Edward ye iiij', in a MS also containing copies of Mandeville's Travels and other works; from the papers of the Richardson-Currer family of Eshton Hall, near Skipton, Yorkshire; c. 1487.

Canon, D53, pp. 16-17; first pub. (lacking lines 37-48) in *Certaine bokes cōpyled by mayster Skeltō* (London, [c. 1545]); complete in Dyce (1843), I, 1-5. This MS the Miss Richardson-Currer MS collated in Dyce; printed in Robert S. Kinsman, '"A lamentable of Kyng Edward the IIII"', *HLQ*, 29 (1966), 95-108.

Corning Museum of Glass, [no ref. number].

SkJ 17 -----

Copy, headed 'the Epitaphy of kynge Edward ye fowrthe', in a MS volume of poems by John Lydgate and others compiled by or for John Stow (1525?-1605); c. 1558.

This MS collated in Kinsman.

British Library, Add. MS 29729, ff. 8-9.

SkJ 18 -----

Copy, untitled, in a MS volume of poems by John Lydgate and others; c. 1575.

Printed from this MS in Carleton Brown, *Religious Lyrics of the XVth Century* (Oxford, 1939), pp. 250-3; collated in Kinsman.

British Library, Harley MS 4011, ff. 169v-70v.

--- *On Tyme* ('Tyme is a thing that no man may resyst').

See SkJ 14-15.

SkJ 19 [*Prayers*].

Copy of three prayers -- 'to the Father of Heauen' (beginning 'O Radiant Luminary of lyght intermynable'), 'To the Seconde Parson' (beginning 'O Benygne Jesu, my souerayne Lord and Kynge'), and 'To the Holy Gooste' (beginning 'O Firy feruence, inflamed wyth all grace') -- written on the end-papers of a 14th century MS *Registrum brevium cancellariae*; late 15th century.

Canon, D54, p. 17; first pub. in *Certaine bokes cōpyled by mayster Skeltō* (London, [c. 1545]); Dyce, I, 139-40. This MS recorded in *Canon*.

British Library, Add. MS 20059, ff. 100v-1.

SkJ 20 -----

Copy of three prayers ('to the Father of Heauen', 'To the Seconde Parson', and 'To the Holy Gooste') in a MS prayer book (Sarum use) owned by one Robert Cooke; 1583.

This MS sold at Sotheby's, 8 July 1957, Lot 78; recorded in De Ricci, *Supplement*, p. 406.

Owned by Robert S. Pirie, Hamilton, Massachusetts.

--- -----

See also INTRODUCTION.

SkJ 21 *'Qui trahis ex domiti ramum pede diue leonis'*.

Copy of Latin verses ascribed to Skelton on a sheet of parchment inserted in a MS law book once owned by Walter and Margery Ashwell; mid-16th century.

Canon, D55, p. 17; first pub. (from this MS) in Friedrich Brie, 'Skelton-Studien', *ES*, 37 (1907), 1-86 (p. 28).

Cambridge University Library, MS Ee. 5. 18, f. 52a.

SkJ 22 *'Salve plus decies quam sunt momenta dierum!'*.

Copy in a volume of historical collections compiled by Sir James Ware (1594-1666); c. 1580s.

Canon, D56, p. 17; first pub. in *Pithy pleasaunt and profitable workes of maister Skelton* (London, 1568); Dyce, I, 177. This MS collated in Dyce.

British Library, Add. MS 4787, f. 224.

SkJ 22.3, 22.5, 22.8 See Addenda, p. 634.

--- *To the Father of Heauen* ('O Radiant Luminary of lyght intermynable').

See SkJ 19-20.

--- *To the Holy Gooste* ('O Firy feruence, inflamed wyth all grace').

See SkJ 19-20.

--- *To the Seconde Parson* ('O Benygne Jesu, my souerayne Lord and Kynge').

See SkJ 19-20.

SkJ 23 *'Wofully araid'*.

Copy of a 62-line version in a four-part musical setting by William Cornish, in a MS songbook apparently written for Robert Fairfax, organist of St Albans; c. 1500.

Skelton wrote a 'Wofully araid' but it is uncertain whether his version can be identified with any extant poem incorporating these words: see *Canon*, L118, pp. 32-3. Printed from this MS in Dyce (1843), I, 141-3, and in *Early Tudor Songs and Carols*, ed. John Stevens, Musica Britannica XXXVI (London, 1975), pp. 92-7.

British Library, Add. MS 5465, ff. 63v-7.

'Wofully araid'

SkJ 24 -----

Copy of a 62-line version in a three-part musical setting by John Browne, in a MS songbook apparently written for Robert Fairfax, organist of St Albans; c. 1500.

This MS collated in Dyce; printed in Stevens, pp. 104-9.

British Library, Add. MS 5465, ff. 73v-7.

SkJ 25 -----

Copy of a shorter version in the form of a prayer, on vellum in a devotional miscellany; late 15th century.

Printed from this MS in Carleton Brown, *Religious Lyrics of the XVth Century* (Oxford, 1939), pp. 156-8.

British Library, Harley MS 4012, f. 109r-v.

SkJ 26 -----

Copy of the first two stanzas written on the last page of a 15th-century MS of offices of the dead, &c; late 15th-16th century.

Printed from this MS in Quaritch catalogue of Illuminated and other MSS (1931), item 66, and catalogue 474 (1933), item 148.

Bodleian, MS Lyell 24, f. 100.

SkJ 27 -----

Copy of a longer version in the hand of one John Symson, ascribed to Skelton, in a MS miscellany bound up with a printed exemplum of Pseudo-Boethius, *De disciplina scholarium cum notabili commento* (Deventer, 1496); 1521.

This MS the Heber MS collated in Dyce; printed in Walter De Gray Birch, 'A New Poem by John Skelton', *Athenaeum* (29 November 1873), p. 697.

Princeton, Robert H. Taylor Collection, [no ref. number], pp. 3-5.

PROSE

SkJ 28 *The Bibliotheca Historica of Diodorus Siculus.*

Copy of Skelton's English translation of Diodorus Siculus from the Latin version of Poggio Bracciolini in three scribal hands, with annotations in later hands; once owned by Robert Pen, a Gentleman of the Chapel under Henry VII and Henry VIII; imperfect; early 16th century.

Canon, C50, pp. 14-15; first pub. (from this MS) London, 1956-7, ed. F.M. Salter and H.L.R. Edwards, 2 vols, EETS, 233 and 239, with reduced facsimiles of ff. 73 and 247 in Vol. I, frontispiece.

Corpus Christi College, Cambridge, MS 357.

--- [*Complaint*].

See SkJ 29.

SkJ 29 *Speculum principis.*

Fair copy on vellum, followed by Latin verses (see SkJ 4 and 8) and Skelton's 'complaint' to the King (headed 'Skeltonis Laureatus, didasculus quondam Regius, etc., tacitus secum in soliloquio ceu vir totus obliuioni datus aut tanquam mortuus a corde, etc.'); probably presented by Skelton to Henry VIII; imperfect and lacking title; c. 1509-10.

Canon, C51, p. 15; first pub. (from this MS) in F.M. Salter, 'Skelton's *Speculum Principis*', *Speculum*, 9 (1934), 25-37. Facsimiles of parts of ff. 2 and 29 in Petti, *English Literary Hands*, Nos. 14, 15 (where it is suggested that the MS is autograph, but see P.J. Croft's review in *TLS* (24 February 1978), p. 241).

British Library, Add. MS 26787.

MARGINALIA IN PRINTED BOOKS AND MANUSCRIPTS

*SkJ 30 *Chronique de Rains.*

A 13th-century MS chronicle of the life of Richard Coeur de Lion with Skelton's autograph annotations and dedications, including ten Latin hexameters beginning 'I, liber, et propera, regem tu pronus adora' and an English verse beginning 'That ever Englond had'; presented by Skelton to Henry VIII; [1511-12].

Canon, C31, pp. 9-10. Parts of the dedications pub. from this MS in James Nasmith, *Catalogus librorum manuscriptorum quos Collegio Corporis Christi legavit Matthaeus Parker* (Cambridge, 1777), p. 400, and in Dyce, I, 147; see also H.L.R. Edwards, 'The Dating of Skelton's Later Poems', *PMLA*, 53.i (1938), 601-19. Facsimile of part of f. 1v in Petti, *English Literary Hands*, No. 16.

Corpus Christi College, Cambridge, MS 432.

Robert Southwell, S.J.

c.1561-95

ABBREVIATIONS

Brown *The Poems of Robert Southwell, S. J.*, ed. James H. McDonald and Nancy Pollard Brown (Oxford, 1967).

Brown, *Two Letters* Robert Southwell, *Two Letters and Short Rules of a Good Life*, ed. Nancy Pollard Brown (Charlottesville, 1973).

Grosart *The Complete Poems of Robert Southwell, S. J.*, ed. Alexander B. Grosart (London, 1872).

McDonald James H. McDonald, *The Poems and Prose Writings of Robert Southwell, S. J.: A Bibliographical Study* (Oxford, 1937).

Trotman *The Triumphs over Death, by the Ven. Robert Southwell*, ed. John William Trotman (London, 1914).

For abbreviations used throughout Volume I, see p.xi.

INTRODUCTION

A small volume of autograph papers of Robert Southwell is preserved at Stonyhurst College, Lancashire (MS A. v. 4). It contains a rough draft of the *Peeter Playnt* (SoR 170), which is a forerunner of *Saint Peters Complaint*, and various devotional works in verse and prose, chiefly in Latin. Many of them remain unpublished, including an English prose piece — later developed into *Mary Magdalen's Funeral Tears* (see SoR 313) — of which the first page is reproduced in FACSIMILE XXIX. The collection is analysed in McDonald, pp. 12-14. One other autograph item of considerable interest is a Latin notebook compiled during Southwell's Jesuit training in Rome, an item which, however, cannot at present be located (see SoR 342). There are, besides, a number of extant letters. A list of thirty letters, mainly autograph, is printed in McDonald, pp. 63-4. Most are preserved at Stonyhurst (though No. 21 in McDonald's list has been removed to the English Province of the Society of Jesus, London). A facsimile of one of them, written to John Deckers in 1580 and ending with a rhythmical prayer to Our Lady, is reproduced in *Publications of the Catholic Record Society*, 5 (1908), p. 295. Thirteen additional letters written to Fr Claudius Aquaviva were discovered some years ago by Fr Philip Caraman in the Jesuit Archives in Rome (Fondo Gesuitico 651). These letters are quoted in Fr Christopher Devlin, *The Life of Robert Southwell, Poet and Martyr* (London, 1956). Letters to Aquiviva from Southwell's fellow priest Henry Garnet, preserved in the same collection, were used in Fr Caraman's biography of Garnet (London, 1964).

The early editions of *Saint Peters Complaint, with other Poemes* (first published in London, 1595; second edition in the same year) are supplemented by five main MS collections of Southwell's English poems. These collections, none of which is autograph, are all described in McDonald and in Brown:

(1) Stonyhurst College, MS A. v. 27. The WALDEGRAVE MS. A MS volume of Southwell's English verse and some prose works, in a single hand but for one poem and some corrections in a second hand; bearing the childish signature of 'iereneme WalDegrave' (? the future nun Dame Hieronima Waldegrave, c. 1603-35) and once in the possession of the Waldegrave family of Essex; 80 leaves; c. 1592-1609. Described in McDonald, pp. 19-22, and in Brown, pp. xxxvii-xl. This MS, which Professor Brown regards as the most reliable MS text of the poems, can probably be identified with the 'lost' Bury St Edmunds MS recorded in McDonald, pp. 25-7: see Brown, pp. xxxix-xl.

(2) Bodleian, MS Eng. poet. e. 113. The VIRTUE AND CAHILL MS (formerly in the Virtue and Cahill Library in the Roman Catholic See of Portsmouth). A MS volume of Southwell's English verse and some prose works in a single hand, bound with pp. 1-34 of a printed exemplum of *Saint Peters Complaint, with other Poemes* (London, 1595); bearing the signatures of several 17th-century owners, including members of the Champney family; 75 MS leaves; early 17th century. Described in McDonald, pp. 22-3, and in Brown, pp. xl-xliii.

(3) British Library, Add. MS 10422. A MS volume of Southwell's English verse and some prose works in a single hand; 110 leaves; early 17th century. Once owned by Richard Heber (1773-1833). Described in McDonald, pp. 23-5, and in Brown, pp. xliii-xlv.

(4) British Library, Harley MS 6921. The CAVENDISH MS. A MS volume of Southwell's English verse in a single hand, owned in 1620 and possibly compiled by a certain Charles Cavendish (? Charles Cavendish, d. 1654, brother of William, first Duke of Newcastle); 44 leaves plus 14 blanks. Described in McDonald, pp. 27-9, and in Brown, pp. xlvi-xlvii.

(5) Folger, STC 22957. The HARMSWORTH MS (formerly owned by Sir Leicester Harmsworth). A MS volume of religious poems chiefly by Southwell in a single hand, bound with a printed exemplum of *Saint Peters Complaint, with other Poemes* (London, 1595) in which the same hand has made corrections; 88 MS leaves; early 17th century. Described in McDonald, pp. 39-59, and in Brown, pp. xlvii-li.

These MSS are all collated in Brown, whose text is usually based on the earliest printed editions.

Two miscellanies which contain a large number of poems by Southwell can be added to this list.

(i) Bodleian, MS Eng. poet. b. 5. A verse miscellany compiled by Thomas Fairfax (d. 1691), yeoman of Wootton Wawen in Warwickshire; dating chiefly 1651-2, with some later entries for 1654 and 1657. Described in F. M. McKay, 'A Seventeenth-Century Collection of Religious Poetry', *BLR*, 8, No. 4 (April 1970), 185-91. Fairfax's texts derive from MS sources and are collated in Brown.

(ii) Syracuse University, George Arents Research Library, [no ref. number]. A miscellany compiled by Thomas Read, a student of Magdalen College, Oxford; dated 1624. This MS is recorded in Brown, p. li, but is not collated in that edition since Read's texts evidently derive from printed sources.

The canon of Southwell's English poems accepted in the *Index* is based on Brown with the single addition of the autograph 'Amemmon' fragment (SoR 236). The 'English poems of doubtful authorship' (SoR 261-83) are poems so classified in Brown, including the three poems from *Moeoniae* (see Brown, pp. lxxxi-lxxxii, 153). Various other doubtful poems mentioned in McDonald are excluded. A 19th-century copy of *Losse in delaies* in the Bodleian (MS Eng. letters d. 103, p. 141 rev.) has also been excluded.

The poem *A Foure-fold Meditation: of the foure last things* ('O wretched man, which louest earthlie thinges') has sometimes been attributed to Southwell but is more commonly ascribed to Philip Howard, first Earl of Arundel (1557-95), with whom Southwell was acquainted (see McDonald, pp. 6-7, 121-2). MS copies of this poem are in the Bodleian (MS Rawl. poet. 219; MS Tanner 118, ff. 44-53 (stanzas 37-48 misplaced in MS Tanner 80, f. 155r-v); the Folger (STC 22957 (the Harmsworth MS); MS V. a. 198, ff. 30-44v; MS Z. e. 28 (formerly among the Carew MSS at Crowcombe Court, Somerset, recorded in *HMC*, 4th Report (1874), Appendix, p. 372)); Harvard (MS Eng 749, ff. 101-16v); and Oscott College, Sutton Coldfield (Shelf RNN3 (Peter Mowle's miscellany), pp. 109-24).

The Latin poems included in the *Index* (SoR 284-92) have been printed (but with inaccuracies of transcription) in Grosart (1872). The titles and first lines of these poems are cited in the entries from the MSS themselves.

The English and Latin prose works included in the *Index* (SoR 293-325, 326-38) are all attributed to Southwell by McDonald. (See McDonald, pp. 16-18, 121-3, for other works spuriously attributed to Southwell.) The recorded items include some notes and prayers for which headings have been supplied (SoR 321, 334, 336, 337, 338). Southwell's *Epistle unto his Father* of 22 October 1589 (SoR 296-306) has been included since it is, in effect, a prose tract in epistolary form; so are the consolatory letter of 30 September 1591 to the Earl of Arundel, published in 1595 as *The Triumphs over Death* (SoR 322-5), and the important *Letter to Sir Robert Cecil* of 6 April 1593 (SoR 312), published by Professor Brown in 1973. *The Author to his loving Cosen* (SoR 293-5) is the dedicatory epistle prefacing the English poems. Two other letters, which are not included in the entries — one addressed to his father, the other to an unnamed kinsman — are preserved in copies in two of the MS collections of Southwell's poems: viz. in Bodleian, MS Eng. poet. e. 113 (the Virtue and Cahill MS), ff. 61v-2, 62v, and in British Library, Add. MS 10422, ff. 83-4, 84v-5. These letters are printed from the Bodleian MS in Brown, *Two Letters*, pp. 99-101, and from the British Library MS in Trotman, pp. 65, 68.

Two additional prose works are included as 'Works of doubtful authorship'. They are so classified by Professor Brown and Fr Cyprian Lynch, who are currently editing Southwell's prose works and who have kindly communicated their views by letter to the Compiler. One doubtful work is an English translation of Diego de Estella's *Meditaciones devotissimas del amor de Dios*, published as *The Hundred Meditations of the Love of God* (SoR 339-40). This has traditionally formed part of the Southwell canon (see McDonald, pp. 15-16), but it appears that the translation is based not on an Italian version as was once believed but on the original Spanish (first published in Salamanca, 1576), and there is no evidence that Southwell had any command of this language. A second doubtful work, headed *Meditationes de Attributis Divinis ad amorem Dei excitantes*, is ascribed to Southwell in a MS source (SoR 341), but this attribution may well be no more than the assumption of a pious copyist.

A versification of *Mary Magdalen's Funeral Tears* was made by Gervase Markham and published in 1601 under the title *Marie Magdalens Lamentations for the losse of her Master Iesus*. A MS copy of this poem, probably transcribed from a printed source, is in the Bodleian (MS Eng. poet. e. 2); it is recorded in F. N. L. Poynter, *A Bibliography of Gervase Markham 1568?-1637*, Oxford Bibliographical Society, NS 11 (1962), p. 49. Another early copy, made by Julian Crewe, can be found in the Chester City Record Office (CR 63/2/697).

PB.

ARRANGEMENT

FACSIMILE XXIX — Robert Southwell: First page of a draft later developed into *Mary Magdalen's Funeral Tears* (inscribed at the top in a later hand), c.1580 (SoR 313). Stonyhurst College, MS A. v. 4, folio 56 recto. Reproduced by permission of The Rector, Stonyhurst College.

B. P. Roberti
Southwelli Martyris.
autographum.

In this present solemnity havynge to speake in this audience
of these mysteries we ar put in mynde how that Mary
Magdalen lovynge our lord above all creatures whom surpassed many in love so she the most
his owne disciples faintly had followed him goynge unto deathe
kindled with the sparkles of inward love burnynge with most earnest desyre and incessantly weepynge never departed
from his tombe. For Marye as the Evangelist reporteth
did stand without at the tombe weepynge
We have heard of marie at the tombe without standynge but
now also let us hear of her weepynge lett us see if we be able to perceive
where she did stande up. and let us see why so many teares trickled downe
lett us take some profit by her standynge some profit
lett us take by her weepynge Love was the cause of
her standynge and sorow enforced her to weepynge
She did stand and looke about her whether she could
happely see him that was deere unto her She did weepe
because she doubted that she had been robbed of Christ whom
she so sorowfully sought Her griefe was renewed in that
first she bewayled his takynge departure out of lyfe and she bewayled now
his takynge away of the grave this griefe was the greater
because it had no cure nor consolation The first cause of
her anguish was for that she had lost the enioyynge of him alyve
but this conceyte had a comfort because she hoped to have
enioyed him dead But for this sorow no salve
she not fyndynge because his dead body [illegible] she fyndyng
not She found lost the love of her lord in her harte [illegible]
as she found not his body [illegible]
[illegible] She was come unto the [illegible] tombe
with spyces and ointmentes that as before she had anoynted his
his feete with precious oyntementes so now his hole body
she myght anoynt with oyntementes and embalme
with spyces. And as before she had shed many a teare

Robert Southwell

VERSE

(1) ENGLISH POEMS BY SOUTHWELL

SoR 1 *At home in Heaven* ('Faire soule, how long shall veyles thy graces shroud?').

Copy in the Waldegrave MS; c. 1592-1609.

First pub. in *Saint Peters Complaint*, 2nd edition (London, 1595); Brown, pp. 55-6.

Stonyhurst College, MS A. v. 27, ff. 66-7.

SoR 2 -----

Copy in the Virtue and Cahill MS; early 17th century.

Bodleian, MS Eng. poet. e. 113, f. 40r-v.

SoR 3 -----

Copy in a MS volume of Southwell's works; early 17th century.

British Library, Add. MS 10422, ff. 37-8.

SoR 4 -----

Copy in the Cavendish MS; [1620].

British Library, Harley MS 6921, f. 34r-v.

SoR 5 -----

Copy in the Harmsworth MS; early 17th century.

Folger, STC 22957, ff. 35v-6v.

SoR 6 -----

Copy in Thomas Read's miscellany; [1624].

This MS not collated in Brown.

Syracuse University, George Arents Research Library, [no ref. number], p. 29.

SoR 7 *The burning Babe* ('As I in hoarie Winters night').

Copy in the Waldegrave MS; c. 1592-1609.

First pub. in *Saint Peters Complaint* (London, 1602); Brown, pp. 15-16.

Stonyhurst College, MS A. v. 27, f. 46.

SoR 8 -----

Copy in the Virtue and Cahill MS; early 17th century.

Bodleian, MS Eng. poet. e. 113, ff. 9v-10.

SoR 9 -----

Copy, with corrections in two later hands, in a MS volume of Southwell's works; early 17th century.

British Library, Add. MS 10422, f. 10v.

SoR 10 -----

Copy in the Cavendish MS; [1620].

British Library, Harley MS 6921, ff. 9v-10.

SoR 11 -----

Copy in the Harmsworth MS; early 17th century.

Folger, STC 22957, f. 11r-v.

SoR 12 -----

Copy in Thomas Fairfax's miscellany; c. 1651-4.

Bodleian, MS Eng. poet. b. 5, p. 52.

SoR 13 *A childe my Choyce* ('Let folly praise that fancie loves, I praise and love that child').

Copy in the Waldegrave MS; c. 1592-1609.

First pub. in *Saint Peters Complaint*, 1st edition (London, 1595); Brown, p. 13.

Stonyhurst College, MS A. v. 27, f. 45.

SoR 14 -----

Copy in the Virtue and Cahill MS; early 17th century.

Bodleian, MS Eng. poet. e. 113, f. 8.

SoR 15 -----

Copy in a MS volume of Southwell's works; early 17th century.

British Library, Add. MS 10422, f. 9.

SoR 16 -----

Copy in the Cavendish MS; [1620].

British Library, Harley MS 6921, ff. 7v-8v.

A childe my Choyce

SoR 17 -----

Copy in Thomas Fairfax's miscellany; c. 1651-4.

Bodleian, MS Eng. poet. b. 5, p. 91.

SoR 18 -----

Copy of lines 5-16, beginning 'Loves sweetest mark, Lawdes highest theme, mans most desired light' and headed 'Of Xt', in Thomas Read's miscellany; [1624].

This MS not collated in Brown.

Syracuse University, George Arents Research Library, [no ref. number], p. 25.

SoR 19 -----

Copy in a miscellany of religious verse compiled by Constance, daughter of Sir Walter Aston (1584-1639) of Tixall, Staffordshire; c. 1630s.

This MS not recorded in Brown.

Huntington, HM 904, f. 35r-v.

SoR 20 *Christs bloody sweat* ('Fat soile, full spring, sweete olive, grape of blisse').

Copy in the Waldegrave MS; c. 1592-1609.

First pub. (lines 1-12) in *Moeoniae* (London, 1595); Brown, pp. 18-19.

Stonyhurst College, MS A. v. 27, ff. 47v-8.

SoR 21 -----

Copy in the Virtue and Cahill MS; early 17th century.

Bodleian, MS Eng. poet. e. 113, f. 12v.

SoR 22 -----

Copy in a MS volume of Southwell's works; early 17th century.

British Library, Add. MS 10422, ff. 12v-13.

SoR 23 -----

Copy in the Cavendish MS; [1620].

British Library, Harley MS 6921, ff. 11v-12.

SoR 24 -----

Copy of a 36-line version in the Harmsworth MS; early 17th century.

Folger, STC 22957, ff. 13v-14.

SoR 25 -----

Copy in Thomas Fairfax's miscellany; c. 1651-4.

Bodleian, MS Eng. poet. b. 5, p. 81.

SoR 26 -----

Copy in Thomas Read's miscellany; [1624].

This MS not collated in Brown.

Syracuse University, George Arents Research Library, [no ref. number], p. 33.

SoR 27 *Christs sleeping friends* ('When Christ with care and pangs of death opprest').

Copy in the Waldegrave MS; c. 1592-1609.

First pub. in *Moeoniae* (London, 1595); Brown, pp. 19-21.

Stonyhurst College, MS A. v. 27, ff. 48-9.

SoR 28 -----

Copy in the Virtue and Cahill MS; early 17th century.

Bodleian, MS Eng. poet. e. 113, f. 13r-v.

SoR 29 -----

Copy in a MS volume of Southwell's works; early 17th century.

British Library, Add. MS 10422, ff. 13-14.

SoR 30 -----

Copy in the Cavendish MS; [1620].

British Library, Harley MS 6921, ff. 12-13.

SoR 31 -----

Copy in the Harmsworth MS; early 17th century.

Folger, STC 22957, ff. 14-15v.

SoR 32 -----

Copy in Thomas Fairfax's miscellany; c. 1651-4.

Bodleian, MS Eng. poet. b. 5, p. 81.

SoR 33 -----

Copy in Thomas Read's miscellany; [1624].

This MS not collated in Brown.

Syracuse University, George Arents Research Library, [no ref. number], p. 33.

SoR 34 *Content and rich* ('I dwell in graces courte').

Copy in the Waldegrave MS; c. 1592-1609.

First pub. in *Saint Peters Complaint*, 1st edition (London, 1595); Brown, pp. 67-9.

Stonyhurst College, MS A. v. 27, ff. 72v-3v.

SoR 35 -----

Copy in the Virtue and Cahill MS; early 17th century.

Bodleian, MS Eng. poet. e. 113, ff. 48v-50.

SoR 36 -----

Copy in a MS volume of Southwell's works; early 17th century.

British Library, Add. MS 10422, ff. 45-6v.

SoR 37 -----

Copy in the Cavendish MS; [1620].

British Library, Harley MS 6921, ff. 41-2.

SoR 38 -----

Copy in Thomas Read's miscellany; [1624].

This MS not collated in Brown.

Syracuse University, George Arents Research Library, [no ref. number], p. 26.

SoR 39 -----

Copy, headed 'The contented man', in a verse miscellany owned in 1668 by one H. Packwood; late 17th century.

This MS not recorded in Brown.

British Library, Add. MS 29921, f. 69v.

SoR 40 *Davids Peccavi* ('In eaves, sole Sparrowe sits not more alone').

Copy in the Waldegrave MS; c. 1592-1609.

First pub. in *Saint Peters Complaint* (London, 1602); Brown, pp. 35-6.

Stonyhurst College, MS A. v. 27, f. 56v.

SoR 41 -----

Copy in the Virtue and Cahill MS; early 17th century.

Bodleian, MS Eng. poet. e. 113, f. 24r-v.

SoR 42 -----

Copy in a MS volume of Southwell's works; early 17th century.

British Library, Add. MS 10422, ff. 23v-4.

SoR 43 -----

Copy in the Cavendish MS; [1620].

British Library, Harley MS 6921, f. 22r-v.

SoR 44 -----

Copy in the Harmsworth MS; early 17th century.

Folger, STC 22957, ff. 23v-4v.

SoR 45 *Decease release. Dum morior orior* ('The pounded spice both tast and sent doth please').

Copy in the Waldegrave MS; c. 1592-1609.

First pub. in *St. Peter's Complaint, and other Poems; by the Rev. Robert Southwell*, ed. W.J. Walter (London, 1817). Printed from this MS in Brown, pp. 47-8.

Stonyhurst College, MS A. v. 27, f. 62r-v,

SoR 46 -----

Copy in the Virtue and Cahill MS; early 17th century.

Bodleian, MS Eng. poet. e. 113, f. 33r-v.

SoR 47 -----

Copy in a MS volume of Southwell's works; early 17th century.

Printed from this MS in Walter.

British Library, Add. MS 10422, ff. 31v-2.

SoR 48 -----

Copy in the Cavendish MS; [1620].

British Library, Harley MS 6921, ff. 29-30.

SoR 49 -----

Copy in the Harmsworth MS; early 17th century.

Folger, STC 22957, ff. 38v-9v.

SoR 50 -----

Copy, endorsed 'Des vers de Mr. Southwell de la reyne d'Escosse: l'an 1596, reçeus au moi de feuvrier. Sa vertu m'attire', in Volume IX of the papers of Anthony Bacon (1558-1601); [1596/7].

This MS recorded in Brown, p. lxxx, but not collated; also described in Louise Imogen Guiney, *Recusant Poets* (London & New York, 1938), p. 247.

Lambeth Palace, MS 655, f. 112.

--- *Epitaph on Lady Margaret Sackville* ('Of Howards stemme a glorious branch is dead').

See SoR 322-5.

SoR 51 *Fortunes Falsehoode* ('In worldly meriments lurketh much miserie').

Copy in the Waldegrave MS; c. 1592-1609.

First pub. in *Saint Peters Complaint*, 1st edition (London, 1595); Brown, pp. 65-6.

Stonyhurst College, MS A. v. 27, f. 71r-v.

SoR 52 -----

Copy in the Virtue and Cahill MS; early 17th century.

Bodleian, MS Eng. poet. e. 113, f. 47r-v.

SoR 53 -----

Copy in a MS volume of Southwell's works; early 17th century.

British Library, Add. MS 10422, ff. 43v-4.

SoR 54 -----

Copy in the Cavendish MS; [1620].

British Library, Harley MS 6921, ff. 39v-40.

SoR 55 -----

Exemplum of *Saint Peters Complaint*, 1st edition (1595), with MS corrections in the text of 'Fortunes Falsehoode' made by the compiler of the 'Harmsworth MS'; early 17th century.

Folger, STC 22957, pp. 41-2.

SoR 56 -----

Copy in Thomas Read's miscellany; [1624].

This MS not collated in Brown.

Syracuse University, George Arents Research Library, [no ref. number], p. 24.

SoR 57 *From Fortunes reach* ('Let fickle fortune runne her blindest race').

Copy in the Waldegrave MS; c. 1592-1609.

First pub. in *Saint Peters Complaint*, 2nd edition (London, 1595); Brown, pp. 66-7.

Stonyhurst College, MS A. v. 27, f. 72.

SoR 58 -----

Copy in the Virtue and Cahill MS; early 17th century.

Bodleian, MS Eng. poet. e. 113, f. 48.

SoR 59 -----

Copy in a MS volume of Southwell's works; early 17th century.

British Library, Add. MS 10422, ff. 44v-5.

SoR 60 -----

Copy in the Cavendish MS; [1620].

British Library, Harley MS 6921, f. 40v.

SoR 61 -----

Copy in the Harmsworth MS; early 17th century.

Folger, STC 22957, ff. 37v-8.

SoR 62 -----

Copy in Thomas Fairfax's miscellany; c. 1651-4.

Bodleian, MS Eng. poet. b. 5, p. 53.

SoR 63 -----

Copy in Thomas Read's miscellany; [1624].

This MS not collated in Brown.

Syracuse University, George Arents Research Library, [no ref. number], pp. 30-1.

SoR 64 -----

Copy of lines 1-6, untitled, in a composite volume of verse and prose; early 17th century.

This MS not recorded in Brown.

British Library, Lansdowne MS 762, f. 88.

SoR 65 *A holy Hymne* ('Praise, O Sion, praise thy Saviour').

A holy Hymne

Copy, headed 'Saint Thomas of Aquines Hymne read on corpus christy daye. Lauda Sion saluatorem', in the Waldegrave MS; c. 1592-1609.

First pub. in *Moeoniae* (London, 1595); Brown, pp. 23-6.

Stonyhurst College, MS A. v. 27, ff. 50v-1v.

SoR 66 -----

Copy, headed 'Saint Thomas of Aquines Hymne. read on corpus christy daye', in the Virtue and Cahill MS; early 17th century.

Bodleian, MS Eng. poet. e. 113, ff. 16-17.

SoR 67 -----

Copy, headed 'Saint Thomas of Aquines hym̄e redd on Corpus xpi day. Lauda Syon Sal.', in a MS volume of Southwell's works; early 17th century.

British Library, Add. MS 10422, ff. 16-17.

SoR 68 -----

Copy, headed 'Sainte thomas of Aquines Hymne redd on corpus christie daye Lauda syon saluatorem', in the Cavendish MS; [1620].

British Library, Harley MS 6921, ff. 15-16v.

SoR 69 -----

Copy, headed 'St. Thomas of Aquines hymne read on Corpus Christi daye: Lauda Sion Salvatorem', in the Harmsworth MS; early 17th century.

Folger, STC 22957, ff. 17v-19v.

SoR 70 *I dye alive* ('O life what lets thee from a quicke decease?').

Copy in the Waldegrave MS; c. 1592-1609.

First pub. in *Saint Peters Complaint*, 2nd edition (London, 1595); Brown, pp. 52-3. Facsimile of stanza 3 of this MS in Grosart (4° edition), facing p. 84. For an account of Grosart's misreadings see Pierre Janelle, *Robert Southwell the Writer* (London, 1935), pp. 304-5.

Stonyhurst College, MS A. v. 27, f. 65.

SoR 71 -----

Copy in the Virtue and Cahill MS; early 17th century.

Bodleian, MS Eng. poet. e. 113, f. 37v.

SoR 72 -----

Copy in a MS volume of Southwell's works; early 17th century.

British Library, Add. MS 10422, f. 35v.

SoR 73 -----

Copy, with the second stanza first (beginning 'I live, but such a life as ever dies'), in the Cavendish MS; [1620].

British Library, Harley MS 6921, f. 32v.

SoR 74 -----

Copy in the Harmsworth MS; early 17th century.

Folger, STC 22957, f. 34.

SoR 75 -----

Copy in Thomas Read's miscellany; [1624].

This MS not collated in Brown.

Syracuse University, George Arents Research Library, [no ref. number], p. 28.

SoR 76 *I dye without desert* ('If orphane Childe enwrapt in swathing bands').

Copy in the Waldegrave MS; c. 1592-1609.

First pub. in *St. Peter's Complaint, and other Poems; by the Rev. Robert Southwell*, ed. W.J. Walter (London, 1817). Printed from this MS in Brown, pp. 48-9.

Stonyhurst College, MS A. v. 27, ff. 62v-3.

SoR 77 -----

Copy in the Virtue and Cahill MS; early 17th century.

Bodleian, MS Eng. poet. e. 113, f. 34r-v.

SoR 78 -----

Copy in a MS volume of Southwell's works; early 17th century.

Printed from this MS in Walter.

British Library, Add. MS 10422, ff. 32v-3.

SoR 79 -----

Copy in the Cavendish MS; [1620].

British Library, Harley MS 6921, f. 30r-v.

SoR 80 -----

Copy in the Harmsworth MS; early 17th century.

Folger, STC 22957, ff. 39v-40v.

SoR 81 *Josephs Amazement* ('When Christ by growth disclosed his descent').

Copy in the Waldegrave MS; c. 1592-1609.

First pub. in *Saint Peters Complaint* (London, 1602); Brown, pp. 21-3.

Stonyhurst College, MS A. v. 27, ff. 49-50v.

SoR 82 -----

Copy in the Virtue and Cahill MS; early 17th century.

Bodleian, MS Eng. poet. e. 113, ff. 14-15v.

SoR 83 -----

Copy in a MS volume of Southwell's works; early 17th century.

British Library, Add. MS 10422, ff. 14-16.

SoR 84 -----

Copy in the Cavendish MS; [1620].

British Library, Harley MS 6921, ff. 13-14v.

SoR 85 -----

Copy in the Harmsworth MS; early 17th century.

Folger, STC 22957, ff. 15v-17v.

SoR 86 *Lewd Love is Losse* ('Misdeeming eye that stoupest to the lure').

Copy in the Waldegrave MS; c. 1592-1609.

First pub. in *Saint Peters Complaint*, 2nd edition (London, 1595); Brown, pp. 62-3.

Stonyhurst College, MS A. v. 27, ff. 69v-70v.

SoR 87 -----

Copy in the Virtue and Cahill MS; early 17th century.

Bodleian, MS Eng. poet. e. 113, f. 45r-v.

SoR 88 -----

Copy in a MS volume of Southwell's works; early 17th century.

British Library, Add. MS 10422, ff. 41v-2v.

SoR 89 -----

Copy in the Cavendish MS; [1620].

British Library, Harley MS 6921, f. 38r-v.

SoR 90 -----

Copy in the Harmsworth MS; early 17th century.

Folger, STC 22957, ff. 36v-7v.

SoR 91 -----

Copy in Thomas Read's miscellany; [1624].

This MS not collated in Brown.

Syracuse University, George Arents Research Library, [no ref. number], p. 30.

SoR 92 *Life is but Losse* ('By force I live, in will I wish to die').

Copy in the Waldegrave MS; c. 1592-1609.

First pub. in *Saint Peters Complaint*, 2nd edition (London, 1595); Brown, pp. 50-1.

Stonyhurst College, MS A. v. 27, f. 64r-v.

SoR 93 -----

Copy in the Virtue and Cahill MS; early 17th century.

Bodleian, MS Eng. poet. e. 113, f. 36r-v.

SoR 94 -----

Copy in a MS volume of Southwell's works; early 17th century.

British Library, Add. MS 10422, f. 34r-v.

SoR 95 -----

Copy in the Cavendish MS; [1620].

British Library, Harley MS 6921, ff. 31-2.

SoR 96 -----

Copy in the Harmsworth MS; early 17th century.

Folger, STC 22957, ff. 32-3.

SoR 97 -----

Copy in Thomas Read's miscellany; [1624].

This MS not collated in Brown.

Syracuse University, George Arents Research Library, [no ref. number], p. 28.

SoR 98 *Lifes death loves life* ('Who lives in love, loves least to live').

Copy in the Waldegrave MS; c. 1592-1609.

Lifes death loves life

First pub. in *Saint Peters Complaint*, 2nd edition (London, 1595); Brown, pp. 54-5.

Stonyhurst College, MS A. v. 27, ff. 65v-6.

SoR 99 -----

Copy in the Virtue and Cahill MS; early 17th century.

Bodleian, MS Eng. poet. e. 113, f. 39r-v.

SoR 100 -----

Copy in a MS volume of Southwell's works; early 17th century].

British Library, Add. MS 10422, ff. 36v-7.

SoR 101 -----

Copy in the Cavendish MS; [1620].

British Library, Harley MS 6921, ff. 33v-4.

SoR 102 -----

Copy in the Harmsworth MS; early 17th century.

Folger, STC 22957, f. 35r-v.

SoR 103 -----

Copy in Thomas Fairfax's miscellany; c. 1651-4.

Bodleian, MS Eng. poet. b. 5, p. 21.

SoR 104 -----

Copy in Thomas Read's miscellany; [1624].

This MS not collated in Brown.

Syracuse University, George Arents Research Library, [no ref. number], p. 29.

SoR 105 -----

Copy in a miscellany of religious verse compiled by Constance, daughter of Sir Walter Aston (1584-1639) of Tixall, Staffordshire; c. 1630s.

This MS not recorded in Brown.

Huntington, HM 904, ff. 35v-6.

SoR 106 *Looke home* ('Retyred thoughts enjoy their owne delights').

Copy in the Waldegrave MS; c. 1592-1609.

First pub. in *Saint Peters Complaint*, 1st edition (London, 1595); Brown, p. 57.

Stonyhurst College, MS A. v. 27, f. 67r-v.

SoR 107 -----

Copy in the Virtue and Cahill MS; early 17th century.

Bodleian, MS Eng. poet. e. 113, f. 41.

SoR 108 -----

Copy in a MS volume of Southwell's works; early 17th century.

British Library, Add. MS 10422, f. 38r-v.

SoR 109 -----

Copy in the Cavendish MS; [1620].

British Library, Harley MS 6921, f. 35.

SoR 110 -----

Copy of lines 1-18 in a verse miscellany; c. 1596-1601.

This MS recorded in Brown, p. 146.

British Library, Harley MS 6910, f. 126.

SoR 111 *Losse in delaies* ('Shun delaies, they breede remorse').

Copy in the Waldegrave MS; c. 1592-1609.

First pub. in *Saint Peters Complaint*, 1st edition (London, 1595); Brown, pp. 58-9.

Stonyhurst College, MS A. v. 27, f. 68r-v.

SoR 112 -----

Copy in the Virtue and Cahill MS; early 17th century.

Bodleian, MS Eng. poet. e. 113, f. 42r-v.

SoR 113 -----

Copy in a MS volume of Southwell's works; early 17th century.

British Library, Add. MS 10422, ff. 39v-40.

SoR 114 -----

Copy in the Cavendish MS; [1620].

British Library, Harley MS 6921, f. 36r-v.

SoR 115 -----

Exemplum of *Saint Peters Complaint*, 1st edition (1595), with a MS correction in the text of

Losse in delaies made by the compiler of the Harmsworth MS; early 17th century.

Folger, STC 22957, pp. 51-2.

SoR 116 -----

Copy in Thomas Fairfax's miscellany; c. 1651-4.

Bodleian, MS Eng. poet. b. 5, p. 43.

SoR 117 -----

Copy in Thomas Read's miscellany; [1624].

This MS not collated in Brown.

Syracuse University, George Arents Research Library, [no ref. number], p. 27.

SoR 118 *Loves Garden grief* ('Vaine loves avaunt, infamous is your pleasure').

Copy in the Waldegrave MS; c. 1592-1609.

First pub. in *Saint Peters Complaint*, 2nd edition (London, 1595); Brown, p. 64.

Stonyhurst College, MS A. v. 27, ff. 70v-1.

SoR 119 -----

Copy in the Virtue and Cahill MS; early 17th century.

Bodleian, MS Eng. poet. e. 113, f. 46r-v.

SoR 120 -----

Copy in a MS volume of Southwell's works; early 17th century.

British Library, Add. MS 10422, ff. 42v-3v.

SoR 121 -----

Copy in the Cavendish MS; [1620].

British Library, Harley MS 6921, f. 39r-v.

SoR 122 -----

Copy in the Harmsworth MS; early 17th century.

Folger, STC 22957, ff. 40v-1v.

SoR 123 -----

Copy in Thomas Read's miscellany; [1624].

This MS not collated in Brown.

Syracuse University, George Arents Research Library, [no ref. number], p. 30.

SoR 124 *Loves servile lot* ('Love mistris is of many mindes').

Copy in the Waldegrave MS; c. 1592-1609.

Lines 1-48 first pub. in *Saint Peters Complaint*, 1st edition (London, 1595); lines 49-76 in 2nd edition (1595); Brown, pp. 60-2.

Stonyhurst College, MS A. v. 27, ff. 68v-9v.

SoR 125 -----

Copy in the Virtue and Cahill MS; early 17th century.

Bodleian, MS Eng. poet. e. 113, ff. 43-4v.

SoR 126 -----

Copy in a MS volume of Southwell's works; early 17th century.

British Library, Add. MS 10422, ff. 40v-1v.

SoR 127 -----

Copy in the Cavendish MS; [1620].

British Library, Harley MS 6921, ff. 36v-8.

SoR 128 -----

Copy in Thomas Read's miscellany; [1624].

This MS not collated in Brown.

Syracuse University, George Arents Research Library, [no ref. number], pp. 27-8.

SoR 129 *Mans civill warre* ('My hovering thoughts would flie to heaven').

Copy in the Waldegrave MS; c. 1592-1609.

First pub. in *Moeoniae* (London, 1595); Brown, pp. 49-50.

Stonyhurst College, MS A. v. 27, f. 63v.

SoR 130 -----

Copy in the Virtue and Cahill MS; early 17th century.

Bodleian, MS Eng. poet. e. 113, f. 35r-v.

SoR 131 -----

Copy in a MS volume of Southwell's works; early 17th century.

British Library, Add. MS 10422, f. 33r-v.

Mans civill warre

SoR 132 -----

Copy in the Cavendish MS; [1620].

British Library, Harley MS 6921, ff. 30v-1.

SoR 133 -----

Copy in the Harmsworth MS; early 17th century.

Folger, STC 22957, ff. 31v-2.

SoR 134 -----

Copy in Thomas Fairfax's miscellany; c. 1651-4.

Bodleian, MS Eng. poet. b. 5, p. 15.

SoR 135 -----

Copy in Thomas Read's miscellany; [1624].

This MS not collated in Brown.

Syracuse University, George Arents Research Library, [no ref. number], p. 36.

SoR 136 *Marie Magdalens complaint at Christs death* ('Sith my life from life is parted').

Copy in the Waldegrave MS; c. 1592-1609.

First pub. in *Saint Peters Complaint*, 1st edition (London, 1595); Brown, pp. 45-6.

Stonyhurst College, MS A. v. 27, ff. 61v-2.

SoR 137 -----

Copy in the Virtue and Cahill MS; early 17th century.

Bodleian, MS Eng. poet. e. 113, f. 32r-v.

SoR 138 -----

Copy in a MS volume of Southwell's works; early 17th century.

British Library, Add. MS 10422, ff. 30v-1.

SoR 139 -----

Copy in the Cavendish MS; [1620].

British Library, Harley MS 4961, ff. 28v-9.

SoR 140 -----

Exemplum of *Saint Peters Complaint*, 1st edition (1595), with a MS correction in the text of *Marie Magdalens complaint* made by the compiler of the Harmsworth MS; early 17th century.

Folger, STC 22957, pp. 37-8.

SoR 141 -----

Copy of line 25, here 'With my loue my life was rested' and untitled, in a musical setting by Thomas Morley in a MS virginal book compiled by 'R. Cr.' (? R. Creighton); c. 1638.

This setting first pub. in Thomas Morley, *First Booke of Ayres* (London, 1600); see Doughtie, *Lyrics from English Airs*, pp. 138, 494-6. This MS not recorded in Brown.

Bibliothèque Nationale, Paris, Département de la Musique, MS Conservatoire Rés. 1186, f. 23.

SoR 142 -----

Copy of line 25, here 'With my loue my life was nestled' and untitled, in a musical setting by Thomas Morley in a MS virginal book compiled by 'R. Cr.' (? R. Creighton); c. 1638.

This MS not recorded in Brown.

Bibliothèque Nationale, Paris, Département de la Musique, MS Conservatoire Rés. 1186, f. 57r-v.

SoR 143 -----

Copy of lines 25-30, 19-24, 13-18, untitled, in a verse miscellany compiled by John Hopkinson (1610-80); c. 1647.

This MS not recorded in Brown.

Bodleian, MS Don. d. 58, f. 23.

SoR 144 -----

Copy of lines 25-30, headed 'I live where I love' and here beginning 'With my hart my love was nesled', followed by five new stanzas, in a MS volume of ballads (the 'Percy Folio'); mid-17th century.

Printed from this MS in *Bishop Percy's Folio Manuscript*, ed. John W. Hales, Frederick J. Furnivall, et al., 4 vols (London, 1867-8); not recorded in Brown.

British Library, Add. MS 27879, f. 144.

SoR 145 -----

Copy of lines 25-30, 19-24, 18-18, untitled, in a musical setting by Thomas Morley in a MS songbook; early 17th century.

Printed from this MS in John P. Cutts, *Seventeenth Century Songs and Lyrics* (Columbia, Mo., 1959), p. 423; not recorded in Brown.

Christ Church, Oxford, MS Mus. 439, p. 37.

SoR 146 -----

Copy of line 25, here 'With my love my lyf was nestled' and untitled, in a musical setting by

Thomas Morley, written in the bass MS part book of the 'St Andrews Psalter'; early 17th century.

This MS not recorded in Brown.

Edinburgh University Library, MS La. III. 483, Bassus, p. 188.

SoR 147 -----

Copy of line 25 seq, here beginning 'With my Love, my life was nested' and untitled, in a musical setting, in a MS copy of the first edition (Aberdeen, 1662) of John Forbes's *Cantus, Songs and Fancies*; c. 1662.

This MS not recorded in Brown.

Sandeman Library, Perth, N16 (No. xliii).

SoR 148 -----

Copy of line 25, untitled, in a musical setting by Thomas Morley, written in a MS part book of the 'St Andrews Psalter'; early 17th century.

This MS not recorded in Brown.

Trinity College, Dublin, MS 412, f. 23.

SoR 149 *Mary Magdalens blush* ('The signs of shame that staine my blushing face').

Copy in the Waldegrave MS; c. 1592-1609.

First pub. in *Saint Peters Complaint*, 1st edition (London, 1595); Brown, pp. 32-3.

Stonyhurst College, MS A. v. 27, f. 55r-v.

SoR 150 -----

Copy in the Virtue and Cahill MS; early 17th century.

Bodleian, MS Eng. poet. e. 113, f. 23r-v.

SoR 151 -----

Copy in a MS volume of Southwell's works; early 17th century.

British Library, Add. MS 10422, ff. 21v-2.

SoR 152 -----

Copy in the Cavendish MS; [1620].

British Library, Harley MS 6921, ff. 20v-2.

SoR 153 -----

Exemplum of *Saint Peters Complaint*, 1st edition (1595), with a MS correction in the text of *Mary Magdalens blush* made by the compiler of the Harmsworth MS; early 17th century.

Folger, STC 22957, pp. 35-6.

SoR 154 *New heaven, new warre* ('Come to your heaven you heavenly quires').

Copy in the Waldegrave MS; c. 1592-1609.

First pub. in *Saint Peters Complaint* (London, 1602); Brown, pp. 13-15.

Stonyhurst College, MS A. v. 27, ff. 45-6.

SoR 155 -----

Copy in the Virtue and Cahill MS; early 17th century.

Bodleian, MS Eng. poet. e. 113, ff. 8v-9.

SoR 156 -----

Copy in a MS volume of Southwell's works; early 17th century.

British Library, Add. MS 10422, ff. 9v-10v.

SoR 157 -----

Copy in the Cavendish MS; [1620].

British Library, Harley MS 6921, ff. 8v-9v.

SoR 158 -----

Copy in the Harmsworth MS; early 17th century.

Folger, STC 22957, f. 10.

SoR 159 *New Prince, new pompe* ('Behold a silly tender Babe').

Copy in the Waldegrave MS; c. 1592-1609.

First pub. in *Saint Peters Complaint* (London, 1602); Brown, pp. 16-17.

Stonyhurst College, MS A. v. 27, f. 46v.

SoR 160 -----

Copy in the Virtue and Cahill MS; early 17th century.

Bodleian, MS Eng. poet. e. 113, ff. 10v-11.

SoR 161 -----

Copy in a MS volume of Southwell's works; early 17th century.

British Library, Add. MS 10422, f. 11r-v.

New Prince, new pompe

SoR 162 -----

Copy in the Cavendish MS; [1620].

British Library, Harley MS 6921, f. 10v.

SoR 163 -----

Copy in the Harmsworth MS; early 17th century.

Folger, STC 22957, f. 12r-v.

SoR 164 -----

Copy in Thomas Fairfax's miscellany; c. 1651-4.

Bodleian, MS Eng. poet. b. 5, p. 51.

SoR 165 *Of the Blessed Sacrament of the Aulter* ('In paschall feast the end of auncient rite').

Copy in the Waldegrave MS; c. 1592-1609.

First pub. as 'The Christians Manna' in *S. Peters Complaint and Saint Mary Magdalens Fvnerall Teares* ([St Omers], 1616). Printed from this MS in Brown, pp. 26-8.

Stonyhurst College, MS A. v. 27, ff. 51v-3.

SoR 166 -----

Copy in the Virtue and Cahill MS; early 17th century.

Bodleian, MS Eng. poet. e. 113, ff. 17-19.

SoR 167 -----

Copy in a MS volume of Southwell's works; early 17th century.

Printed from this MS in *St. Peter's Complaint, and other Poems; by the Rev. Robert Southwell*, ed. W.J. Walter (London, 1817).

British Library, Add. MS 10422, ff. 17v-19.

SoR 168 -----

Copy in the Cavendish MS; [1620].

British Library, Harley MS 6921, ff. 16v-18.

SoR 169 -----

Copy in the Harmsworth MS; early 17th century.

Folger, STC 22957, ff. 19v-20v.

*SoR 170 *[The] Peeter Playnt* ('That sturdy peter...an... did boaste').

Autograph first draft of a verse translation of part of Luigi Tansillo's *Le Lagrime di San Pietro*, in a bound collection of Southwell's autograph papers.

First pub. (from this MS) in Grosart (1872); transcribed more accurately in Mario Praz, 'Robert Southwell's "Saint Peter's Complaint" and its Italian Source', *MLR*, 19 (1924), 273-90; also in McDonald, pp. 144-7, and in Brown, pp. 103-7. Facsimiles of f. 50 in Brown, frontispiece, and Croft, *Autograph Poetry*, I, 19; and f. 51 in Petti, *English Literary Hands*, No. 29.

Stonyhurst College, MS A. v. 4, ff. 50-1v.

SoR 171 *A Phansie turned to a sinners complaint* ('Hee that his mirth hath lost').

Copy in the Waldegrave MS; c. 1592-1609.

First pub. in *Saint Peters Complaint* (London, 1602); Brown, pp. 36-40.

Stonyhurst College, MS A. v. 27, ff. 57-8v.

SoR 172 -----

Copy in the Virtue and Cahill MS; early 17th century.

Bodleian, MS Eng. poet. e. 113, ff. 25-8.

SoR 173 -----

Copy in a MS volume of Southwell's works; early 17th century.

British Library, Add. MS 10422, ff. 24-6v.

SoR 174 -----

Copy in the Cavendish MS; [1620].

British Library, Harley MS 6921, ff. 23-5v.

SoR 175 -----

Copy in the Harmsworth MS; early 17th century.

Folger, STC 22957, ff. 24v-8.

SoR 176 *The prodigall childs soule wracke* ('Disankerd from a blisfull shore').

Copy in the Waldegrave MS; this poem in the hand of a second scribe responsible only for corrections elsewhere in the MS; c. 1592-1609.

First pub. in *Moeoniae* (London, 1595); Brown, pp. 43-5.

Stonyhurst College, MS A. v. 27, ff. 60v-1.

The prodigall childs soule wracke

SoR 177 -----

Copy in the Virtue and Cahill MS; early 17th century.

Bodleian, MS Eng. poet. e. 113, ff. 30v-1v.

SoR 178 -----

Copy in a MS volume of Southwell's works; early 17th century.

British Library, Add. MS 10422, ff. 29-30.

SoR 179 -----

Copy in the Cavendish MS; [1620].

British Library, Harley MS 6921, ff. 27-8v.

SoR 180 -----

Copy in the Harmsworth MS; early 17th century.

Folger, STC 22957, ff. 29v-31.

SoR 181 -----

Copy in Thomas Fairfax's miscellany; c. 1651-4.

Bodleian, MS Eng. poet. b. 5, p. 16.

SoR 182 -----

Copy in Thomas Read's miscellany; [1624].

This MS not collated in Brown.

Syracuse University, George Arents Research Library, [no ref. number], p. 36.

SoR 183 -----

Copy in a miscellany of religious verse compiled by Constance, daughter of Sir Walter Aston (1584-1639) of Tixall, Staffordshire; c. 1630s.

This MS not recorded in Brown.

Huntington, HM 904, ff. 22v-3v.

SoR 184 *S. Peters afflicted minde* ('If that the sicke may grone').

Copy in the Waldegrave MS; c. 1592-1609.

First pub. in *Moeoniae* (London, 1595); Brown, p. 31.

Stonyhurst College, MS A. v. 27, f. 54v.

SoR 185 -----

Copy in the Virtue and Cahill MS; early 17th century.

Bodleian, MS Eng. poet. e. 113, f. 21.

SoR 186 -----

Copy in a MS volume of Southwell's works; early 17th century.

British Library, Add. MS 10422, f. 21.

SoR 187 -----

Copy in the Cavendish MS; [1620].

British Library, Harley MS 6921, f. 20.

SoR 188 -----

Copy in the Harmsworth MS; early 17th century.

Folger, STC 22957, ff. 20v-2.

SoR 189 -----

Copy in Thomas Fairfax's miscellany; c. 1651-4.

Bodleian, MS Eng. poet. b. 5, p. 17.

SoR 190 -----

Copy in Thomas Read's miscellany; [1624].

This MS not collated in Brown.

Syracuse University, George Arents Research Library, [no ref. number], p. 34.

SoR 191 *Saint Peters Complaynte* ('How can I live, that have my life deny'de?').

Copy in the Waldegrave MS; c. 1592-1609.

This version first pub. (from this MS) in McDonald (1937), pp. 141-3; printed from this MS in Brown, pp. 29-31.

Stonyhurst College, MS A. v. 27, ff. 53-4v.

SoR 192 -----

Copy in the Virtue and Cahill MS; early 17th century.

Bodleian, MS Eng. poet. e. 113, ff. 19v-20.

SoR 193 -----

Copy in a MS volume of Southwell's works; early 17th century.

British Library, Add. MS 10422, ff. 19v-21.

Saint Peters Complaynte

SoR 194 -----

Copy in the Cavendish MS; [1620].

British Library, Harley MS 6921, ff. 18v-19v.

SoR 195 -----

Copy of lines 5-72, beginning 'O synne of synnes, of evells the very worste', made by the compiler of the Harmsworth MS on the final blank leaf of an exemplum of *Saint Peters Complaint*, 1st edition (1595); imperfect and lacking title; early 17th century.

Folger, STC 22957, f. 1r-v.

SoR 196 *Saint Peters Complaint* ('Launche foorth my Soul into a maine of teares').

Copy, complete with 'The Author to the Reader' (beginning 'Deare eie that daynest to let fall a looke'), in a MS volume of Southwell's works; early 17th century.

First pub. London, 1595; Brown, pp. 75-100.

British Library, Add. MS 10422, ff. 47-64v.

SoR 197 -----

Exemplum of the first edition (1595) with MS corrections made by the compiler of the Harmsworth MS; early 17th century.

Folger, STC 22957, pp. 1-34.

SoR 198 -----

Copy, complete with 'The Author to the Reader', in a miscellany of religious verse and prose compiled by Peter Mowle of Attleborough, Norfolk; c. 1592-1605.

This MS collated in Brown.

Oscott College, Sutton Coldfield, Shelf RNN3, pp. 140-56.

SoR 199 -----

Copy, with 12 lines of 'The Author to the Reader' arranged in the sequence lines 7, 9, 8, 10-12, 20-1, 23-4, 3-4 (beginning 'If equities even-hand the ballance held'), in Thomas Read's miscellany; [1624].

This MS not collated in Brown.

Syracuse University, George Arents Research Library, [no ref. number], pp. 44-51.

SoR 200 *S. Peters remorse* ('Remorse upbraids my faults').

Copy in the Waldegrave MS; c. 1592-1609.

First pub. in *Moeoniae* (London, 1595); Brown, pp. 33-5.

Stonyhurst College, MS A. v. 27, ff. 55v-6.

SoR 201 -----

Copy in the Virtue and Cahill MS; early 17th century.

Bodleian, MS Eng. poet. e. 113, ff. 21v-2v.

SoR 202 -----

Copy in a MS volume of Southwell's works; early 17th century.

British Library, Add. MS 10422, ff. 22-3.

SoR 203 -----

Copy in the Cavendish MS; [1620].

British Library, Harley MS 6921, ff. 21-2.

SoR 204 -----

Copy in the Harmsworth MS; early 17th century.

Folger, STC 22957, ff. 22-3v.

SoR 205 -----

Copy in Thomas Read's miscellany; [1624].

This MS not collated in Brown.

Syracuse University, George Arents Research Library, [no ref. number], p. 34.

SoR 206 *Scorne not the least* ('Where wards are weake, and foes encountring strong').

Copy in the Waldegrave MS; c. 1592-1609.

First pub. in *Saint Peters Complaint*, 1st edition (London, 1595); Brown, pp. 69-70.

Stonyhurst College, MS A. v. 27, ff. 73v-4.

SoR 207 -----

Copy in the Virtue and Cahill MS; early 17th century.

Bodleian, MS Eng. poet. e. 113, f. 50v.

SoR 208 -----

Copy in a MS volume of Southwell's works; early 17th century.

British Library, Add. MS 10422, ff. 46v-7.

Scorne not the least

SoR 209 -----

Copy in the Cavendish MS; [1620].

British Library, Harley MS 6921, f. 42r-v.

SoR 210 -----

Exemplum of *Saint Peters Complaint*, 1st edition (1595), with MS corrections in the text of *Scorne not the least* made by the compiler of the Harmsworth MS; early 17th century.

Folger, STC 22957, p. 43.

SoR 211 -----

Copy in Thomas Read's miscellany; [1624].

This MS not collated in Brown.

Syracuse University, George Arents Research Library, [no ref. number], p. 24.

SoR 212 -----

Copy of lines 1-18 in a miscellany compiled by someone connected with the Court; c. 1605.

This MS recorded in Brown, p. 152. See also SoR 241.

British Library, Add. MS 22601, f. 71v.

SoR 213 -----

Copy, untitled, in a verse miscellany; c. 1596-1601.

This MS recorded in Brown, p. 152.

British Library, Harley MS 6910, ff. 126v-7.

SoR 214 *Seeke flowers of heaven* ('Soare up my soule unto thy rest')

Copy in the Waldegrave MS; c. 1592-1609.

First pub. in *Moeoniae*, 1st ed. (London, 1595); Brown, p. 52.

Stonyhurst College, MS A. v. 27, ff. 64v-5.

SoR 215 -----

Copy in the Virtue and Cahill MS; early 17th century.

Bodleian, MS Eng. poet. e. 113, f. 37.

SoR 216 -----

Copy in a MS volume of Southwell's works; early 17th century.

British Library, Add. MS 10422, f. 35.

SoR 217 -----

Copy in the Cavendish MS; [1620].

British Library, Harley MS 6921, f. 32r-v.

SoR 218 -----

Copy in the Harmsworth MS; early 17th century.

Folger, STC 22957, ff. 33-4v.

SoR 219 -----

Copy in Thomas Fairfax's miscellany; c. 1651-4.

Bodleian, MS Eng. poet. b. 5, p. 14.

SoR 220 -----

Copy in Thomas Read's miscellany; [1624].

This MS not collated in Brown.

Syracuse University, George Arents Research Library, [no ref. number], p. 37.

SoR 221 *The Sequence on the Virgin Mary and Christ* ('Our second Eve puts on her mortall shroude').

Copy of the sequence of fourteen poems in the Waldegrave MS; c. 1592-1609.

Poems vi & xii first pub. in *Saint Peters Complaint*, 1st edition (London, 1595); poems i-v, vii-xi first pub. in *Moeoniae* (London, 1595); poems xiii & xiv first pub. in *The Poetical Works of the Rev. Robert Southwell*, ed. W.B. Turnbull (London, 1856); Brown, pp. 3-12.

Stonyhurst College, MS A. v. 27, ff. 39v-44v.

SoR 222 -----

Copy of the sequence of fourteen poems in the Virtue and Cahill MS; early 17th century.

Bodleian, MS Eng. poet. e. 113, ff. 1-7v.

SoR 223 -----

Copy of the sequence of fourteen poems in a MS volume of Southwell's works; early 17th century.

Poems xiii & xiv printed from this MS in Turnbull.

British Library, Add. MS 10422, ff. 2-8v.

SoR 224 -----

Copy of the sequence of fourteen poems in the Cavendish MS; [1620].

British Library, Harley MS 6921, ff. 2-7v.

The Sequence on the Virgin Mary and Christ

SoR 225 -----

Copy of the sequence of fourteen poems in the Harmsworth MS; early 17th century.

Folger, STC 22957, ff. 3v-9v.

SoR 226 -----

Copy of the sequence of fourteen poems in Thomas Fairfax's miscellany; c. 1651-4.

Bodleian, MS Eng. poet. b. 5, pp. 76-83.

SoR 227 -----

Copy of poems i-xii in Thomas Read's miscellany; [1624].

This MS not collated in Brown.

Syracuse University, George Arents Research Library, [no ref. number], pp. 31-3, 25.

SoR 228 ----- *vi. The Nativitie of Christ* ('Beholde the father, is his daughters sonne').

Copy of lines 1-4, headed 'Upon Christ', in a verse miscellany compiled by an Oxford man, possibly a member of Wadham College, and later used by William Fulman (1632-88); c. late 1630s.

This MS not recorded in Brown.

Bodleian, MS CCC, 328, f. 46.

SoR 229 ----- -----

Copy, headed 'Upon Christ', in a miscellany compiled by John Ramsey (b. 1578) of Peterhouse, Cambridge; early 17th century.

This MS not recorded in Brown.

Bodleian, MS Douce, 280, f. 180v.

SoR 230 ----- -----

Copy, headed 'Upon Christ', in a miscellany compiled by John Abbott (b. 1653/4) of St John's College, Oxford; c. 1670s.

This MS not recorded in Brown.

Bodleian, MS Rawl. D. 954, f. 40v.

SoR 231 *Sinnes heavie loade* ('O Lord my sinne doth over-charge thy brest').

Copy in the Waldegrave MS; c. 1592-1609.

First pub. in *Saint Peters Complaint* (London, 1602); Brown, pp. 17-18.

Stonyhurst College, MS A. v. 27, f. 47r-v.

SoR 232 -----

Copy in the Virtue and Cahill MS; early 17th century.

Bodleian, MS Eng. poet. e. 113, ff. 11v-12.

SoR 233 -----

Copy in a MS volume of Southwell's works; early 17th century.

British Library, Add. MS 10422, ff. 11v-12v.

SoR 234 -----

Copy in the Cavendish MS; [1620].

British Library, Harley MS 6921, f. 11r-v.

SoR 235 -----

Copy in the Harmsworth MS; early 17th century.

Folger, STC 22957, ff. 12v-13.

*SoR 236 *'The shippe that frō the port dothe sayle'.*

Autograph fragment, consisting of seven lines of verse (with revisions) preceded by the words 'I goe...Amemmon', on a single leaf also containing a transcript in a later hand, in a bound collection of Southwell's autograph papers; c. 1580.

First pub. (from this MS) in McDonald (1937), p. 159.

Stonyhurst College, MS A. v. 4, f. 61.

SoR 237 *Time goe by turnes* ('The lopped tree in time may grow againe').

Copy in the Waldegrave MS; c. 1592-1609.

First pub. in *Saint Peters Complaint*, 1st edition (London, 1595); Brown, pp. 57-8.

Stonyhurst College, MS A. v. 27, f. 67v.

SoR 238 -----

Copy in the Virtue and Cahill MS; early 17th century.

Bodleian, MS Eng. poet. e. 113, f. 41v.

SoR 239 -----

Copy in a MS volume of Southwell's works; early 17th century.

British Library, Add. MS 10422, ff. 38v-9.

SoR 240 -----

Copy in the Cavendish MS; [1620].

British Library, Harley MS 6921, f. 35v.

SoR 241 -----

Copy of lines 7-12, beginning 'The sea of fortune doth not ever flowe', added as the concluding stanza to a copy of the first three stanzas of *Scorne not the least* (see SoR 212), in a miscellany compiled by someone connected with the Court; c. 1605.

This MS recorded in Brown, p. 146.

British Library, Add. MS 22601, f. 71v.

SoR 242 -----

Copy, untitled, in a verse miscellany; c. 1596-1601.

This MS recorded in Brown, p. 146.

British Library, Harley MS 6910, f. 124.

SoR 243 *To the Reader* ('Deare eye that doest peruse my muses style').

Copy in the Waldegrave MS; c. 1592-1609.

First pub. in *Saint Peters Complaint*, 1st edition (London, 1595); Brown, p. 2.

Stonyhurst College, MS A. v. 27, f. 39.

SoR 244 -----

Copy in a MS volume of Southwell's works; imperfect; early 17th century.

British Library, Add. MS 10422, f. 1.

SoR 245 -----

Copy in the Cavendish MS; [1620].

British Library, Harley MS 6921, f. 2.

SoR 246 -----

Exemplum of *Saint Peters Complaint*, 1st edition (1595), with MS corrections in the text of *To the Reader* made by the compiler of the Harmsworth MS; early 17th century.

Folger, STC 22957, sig. A3.

SoR 247 -----

Copy in Thomas Fairfax's miscellany; c. 1651-4.

Bodleian, MS Eng. poet. b. 5, p. vii.

SoR 248 -----

Copy of lines 3-10, 17-18, beginning 'Give sobrest countnance leave sometime to smyle', in Thomas Read's miscellany; [1624].

This MS not collated in Brown.

Syracuse University, George Arents Research Library, [no ref. number], p. 44.

SoR 249 *A vale of teares* ('A vale there is enwrapt with dreadfull shades').

Copy in the Waldegrave MS; c. 1592-1609.

First pub. in *Moeoniae* (London, 1595); Brown, pp. 41-3.

Stonyhurst College, MS A. v. 27, ff. 59-60.

SoR 250 -----

Copy in the Virtue and Cahill MS; early 17th century.

Bodleian, MS Eng. poet. e. 113, ff. 28v-30.

SoR 251 -----

Copy in a MS volume of Southwell's works; early 17th century.

British Library, Add. MS 10422, ff. 26v-8v.

SoR 252 -----

Copy in the Cavendish MS; [1620].

British Library, Harley MS 6921, ff. 25v-7.

SoR 253 -----

Copy in the Harmsworth MS; early 17th century.

Folger, STC 22957, ff. 28-9v.

SoR 254 -----

Copy in Thomas Read's miscellany; [1624].

This MS not collated in Brown.

Syracuse University, George Arents Research Library, [no ref. number], p. 35.

SoR 255 *What joy to live?* ('I wage no warre yet peace I none enjoy').

Copy in the Waldegrave MS; c. 1592-1609.

First pub. in *Saint Peters Complaint*, 2nd edition (London, 1595); Brown, pp. 53-4.

Stonyhurst College, MS A. v. 27, f. 65r-v.

What joy to live?

SoR 256 -----

Copy in the Virtue and Cahill MS; early 17th century.

Bodleian, MS Eng. poet. e. 113, f. 38r-v.

SoR 257 -----

Copy in a MS volume of Southwell's works; early 17th century.

British Library, Add. MS 10422, f. 36r-v.

SoR 258 -----

Copy in the Cavendish MS; [1620].

British Library, Harley MS 6921, f. 33r-v.

SoR 259 -----

Copy in the Harmsworth MS; early 17th century.

Folger, STC 22957, ff. 34-5.

SoR 260 -----

Copy in Thomas Read's miscellany; [1624].

This MS not collated in Brown.

Syracuse University, George Arents Research Library, [no ref. number], p. 29.

(2) ENGLISH POEMS OF DOUBTFUL AUTHORSHIP

SoR 261 *The Annuntiation altered from that before* ('Spel Eva backe, and Ave shall you find').

Copy in the Harmsworth MS; early 17th century.

First pub. (from this MS) in McDonald (1937), pp. 57-8; printed from this MS in Brown, p. 117.

Folger, STC 22957, f. 49v.

SoR 262 *Beatus vir qui non abiit etc.* ('O happie wight that hath not raun'gd astray').

Copy in the Harmsworth MS; early 17th century.

First pub. (from this MS) in McDonald (1937), p. 51; printed from this MS in Brown, pp. 110-11.

Folger, STC 22957, f. 43r-v.

SoR 263 *Christ upon the Crosse to man* ('Behold I fainte and fade away').

Copy in the Harmsworth MS; early 17th century.

First pub. (from this MS) in McDonald (1937), pp. 53-4; printed from this MS in Brown, pp. 113-14.

Folger, STC 22957, ff. 45v-6.

SoR 264 *Christes answere* ('Withdraw thy tender eies a while').

Copy in the Harmsworth MS; early 17th century.

First pub. (from this MS) in McDonald (1937), p. 53; printed from this MS in Brown, p. 113.

Folger, STC 22957, f. 45r-v.

SoR 265 *The Complaint of the B. Virgin having lost her Sonne in Hierusalem* ('How may I live, since that my life is gone?').

Copy in the Harmsworth MS; early 17th century.

First pub. (from this MS) in McDonald (1937), pp. 54-7; printed from this MS in Brown, pp. 114-17.

Folger, STC 22957, ff. 46v-9v.

SoR 266 -----

Copy of lines 1-42 in Thomas Fairfax's miscellany; c. 1651-4.

Bodleian, MS Eng. poet. b. 5, p. 84.

SoR 267 *Conceptio B. Virginis sub porta aurea* ('A golden gate was her conceaving place').

Copy in the Harmsworth MS; early 17th century.

First pub. (from this MS) in McDonald (1937), p. 42; printed from this MS in Brown, p. 108.

Folger, STC 22957, f. 2.

SoR 268 *Man to the wound in Christs side* ('O pleasant port, O place of rest').

Copy in the Harmsworth MS; early 17th century.

First pub. in *Moeoniae* (London, 1595); Brown, pp. 72-3.

Folger, STC 22957, f. 46r-v.

SoR 269 -----

Copy in Thomas Fairfax's miscellany; c. 1651-4.

Bodleian, MS Eng. poet. b. 5, p. 15.

SoR 270 -----

Second copy in Thomas Fairfax's miscellany; c. 1651-4.

Bodleian, MS Eng. poet. b. 5, p. 85.

Man to the wound in Christs side

SoR 271 -----

Copy in Thomas Read's miscellany; [1624].

This MS not collated in Brown.

Syracuse University, George Arents Research Library, [no ref. number], p. 34.

SoR 272 -----

Copy in a miscellany of religious verse compiled by Constance, daughter of Sir Walter Aston (1584-1639) of Tixall, Staffordshire; c. 1630s.

This MS not recorded in Brown.

Huntington, HM 904, ff. 23v-4.

SoR 273 *Optima Deo* ('Behold how first the modest Rose doth prie').

Copy in the Harmsworth MS; early 17th century.

First pub. (from this MS) in McDonald (1937), p. 50; printed from this MS in Brown, pp. 109-10.

Folger, STC 22957, f. 42r-v.

--- *Our Ladie to Christ upon the Crosse* ('What mist hath dimd that glorious face?').

See SoR 283.

SoR 274 *Praesentatio B. Virginis* ('A glorious temple wrought with secret art').

Copy in the Harmsworth MS; early 17th century.

First pub. (from this MS) in McDonald (1937), p. 43; printed from this MS in Brown, pp. 108-9.

Folger, STC 22957, f. 2r-v.

SoR 275 *S. Peters complaint* ('How can I live, that have forsaken life').

Copy in the Harmsworth MS; early 17th century.

First pub. (from this MS) in McDonald (1937), pp. 51-2; printed from this MS in Brown, pp. 111-12.

Folger, STC 22957, ff. 43v-4v.

SoR 276 *Ubi est Deus meus?* ('Alas I live without my life').

Copy in the Harmsworth MS; early 17th century.

First pub. (from this MS) in McDonald (1937), pp. 49-50; printed from this MS in Brown, p. 109.

Folger, STC 22957, ff. 41v-2.

SoR 277 *Unworthy receaving* ('I freeze in fire, I thirst amiddest the crystal streames').

Copy in the Harmsworth MS; early 17th century.

First pub. (from this MS) in McDonald (1937), pp. 50-1; printed from this MS in Brown, p. 110.

Folger, STC 22957, ff. 42v-3.

SoR 278 *Upon the Image of death* ('Before my face the picture hangs').

Copy in the Harmsworth MS; early 17th century.

First pub. in *Moeoniae* (London, 1595); Brown, pp. 73-4.

Folger, STC 22957, f. 50r-v.

SoR 279 -----

Copy in Thomas Fairfax's miscellany; c. 1651-4.

Bodleian, MS Eng. poet. b. 5, p. 21.

SoR 280 -----

Copy in Thomas Read's miscellany; [1624].

This MS not collated in Brown.

Syracuse University, George Arents Research Library, [no ref. number], p. 35.

SoR 281 *The virgin Mary to Christ on the Crosse* ('What mist hath dimd that glorious face').

Copy in Thomas Fairfax's miscellany; c. 1651-4.

First pub. in *Moeoniae* (London, 1595); Brown, pp. 71-2.

Bodleian, MS Eng. poet. b. 5, p. 85.

SoR 282 -----

Copy in Thomas Read's miscellany; [1624].

This MS not collated in Brown.

Syracuse University, George Arents Research Library, [no ref. number], p. 33.

SoR 283 -----

Copy of a version headed 'Our Ladie to Christ upon the Crosse' in the Harmsworth MS; early 17th century.

Printed from this MS in Brown, pp. 112-13.

Folger, STC 22957, ff. 44v-5.

(3) LATIN POEMS BY SOUTHWELL

*SoR 284 *Ad deū in aff. Elegia* ('Tu tacitas nosti lachrimas tu saucia cernis').

Autograph draft, in a bound collection of Southwell's autograph papers; c. 1580.

First pub. (from this MS) in Grosart (1872), p. 212.

Stonyhurst College, MS A. v. 4, f. 22.

*SoR 285 *Ad S. Catherinā uirg. et mar* ('Tu Catherina mei solatrix vnica luctus').

Autograph draft, in a bound collection of Southwell's autograph papers; c. 1580.

First pub. (from this MS) in Grosart (1872), p. 213.

Stonyhurst College, MS A. v. 4, f. 22r-v.

--- *'Clara Ducum soboles, superis nova sedibus hospes'.*

See SoR 322-5.

*SoR 286 *Elegia 7* ('Ex luctu populus redditur ipse chalybs').

Autograph draft of the last part of what would have been 'Elegia 7', in a bound collection of Southwell's autograph papers; imperfect, lacking the beginning; c. 1580.

First pub. (from this MS) in Grosart (1872), pp. 206-7.

Stonyhurst College, MS A. v. 4, f. 26r-v.

*SoR 287 *Elegia 8* ('Dic vbi nunc quod amo est! vbinam quod semper amavi?').

Autograph draft, in a bound collection of Southwell's autograph papers; c. 1580.

First pub. (from this MS) in Grosart (1872), pp. 208-10.

Stonyhurst College, MS A. v. 4, ff. 26v-7v.

*SoR 288 *Elegia 9* ('Quid conclamato iacis irrita vota sepulchro?').

Autograph draft, in a bound collection of Southwell's autograph papers; imperfect, lacking the ending; c. 1580.

First pub. (from this MS) in Grosart (1872), pp. 210-11.

Stonyhurst College, MS A. v. 4, f. 27v.

*SoR 289 *Filij Prodigi porcos pascentis ad Patrē Epistola* ('Si tam longinquis rogites quis scripsit ab oris').

Autograph draft, in a bound collection of Southwell's autograph papers; c. 1580.

First pub. (from this MS) in Grosart (1872), pp. 199-205.

Stonyhurst College, MS A. v. 4, ff. 14-18.

*SoR 290 *In festum pentecostes A° D. 1.5.80. 21. Maij* ('Postquam tartarei spolijs ditatus Auerni').

Autograph draft, in a bound collection of Southwell's autograph papers; 21 May 1580.

First pub. (from this MS) in Grosart (1872), pp. 214-15.

Stonyhurst College, MS A. v. 4, ff. 22v-3.

*SoR 291 *In renouationem uotorum festis Natalis Domini* ('Vita uenit uitae cū uotis obuius ito').

Autograph draft, in a bound collection of Southwell's autograph papers; c. 1580.

First pub. (from this MS) in Grosart (1872), p. 214.

Stonyhurst College, MS A. v. 4, f. 22v.

*SoR 292 *Poēma de Assumptione B.M.V.* ('Cum caelum et tellus, et uasti machina mūdi').

Autograph draft, signed 'Robertus Southwellus', in a bound collection of Southwell's autograph papers; c. 1580.

First pub. (from this MS) in Grosart (1872), pp. 191-9. Facsimile of part of f. 8 in Grosart (4° edition), facing p. 84.

Stonyhurst College, MS A. v. 4, ff. 4-8.

PROSE

(1) ENGLISH WORKS BY SOUTHWELL

SoR 293 *The Author to his loving Cosen.*

Copy of the dedication of Southwell's poems in the Cavendish MS; [1620].

First pub. in *Saint Peters Complaint*, 1st edition (London, 1595); Brown, pp. 1-2. This MS collated in Brown.

British Library, Harley MS 6921, f. 1r-v.

The Author to his loving Cosen

SoR 294 -----

Exemplum of *Saint Peters Complaint*, 1st edition (1595), with MS corrections in the text of Southwell's dedicatory epistle made by the compiler of the Harmsworth MS; early 17th century.

This MS collated in Brown.

Folger, STC 22957, sig. A2-A2v.

SoR 295 -----

Copy of the dedication of Southwell's poems in the Waldegrave MS; c. 1592-1609.

This MS collated in Brown.

Stonyhurst College, MS A. v. 27, f. 38r-v.

SoR 296 *An Epistle unto his Father (22 October 1589).*

Copy in a MS volume of miscellaneous verse and prose transcribed from the papers of Sir Christopher Yelverton (1535?-1612); early 17th century.

First pub. as 'An Epistle of a Religious Priest unto his Father' in *A Short Rule of Good Life* ([London?, 1596-7?]); Trotman, pp. 36-64; Brown, *Two Letters*, pp. 1-20. This MS not recorded by editors.

All Souls College, Oxford, MS 155, ff. 295-306.

SoR 297 -----

Copy in the Virtue and Cahill MS; early 17th century.

This MS collated in Brown, *Two Letters*.

Bodleian, MS Eng. poet. e. 113, ff. 52-61.

SoR 298 -----

Copy, untitled, endorsed on f. 226v 'To his very louing Freind Mr Clement Knight bookseller at his shopp nere Paules church giue theise', in a composite volume of theological works; imperfect; early 17th century.

Apparently printed from this MS in *St. Peter's Complaint, and other Poems; by the Rev. Robert Southwell*, ed. W.J. Walter (London, 1817); not recorded by other editors.

Bodleian, MS Tanner 279, ff. 221-5.

SoR 299 -----

Copy in a MS volume of Southwell's works; early 17th century.

Printed chiefly from this MS in Trotman; collated in Brown, *Two Letters*.

British Library, Add. MS 10422, ff. 65-82.

SoR 300 -----

Copy, transcribed from the first edition of *A Short Rule of Good Life*, in a bound collection of papers of the Williams (alias Cromwell) family of Huntingdonshire; imperfect; 1607.

This MS collated in Trotman; described in McDonald, pp. 11-12; recorded in Brown, *Two Letters*, p. xlvii.

British Library, Add. MS 34395, ff. 36-42v.

SoR 301 -----

Copy of the last 23 lines, bound in a collection of correspondence of Sir Robert Southwell (1635-1702); probably transcribed from the original letter, or an early copy of it, which was among the papers of the Southwell family; imperfect; 17th century.

This MS recorded in McDonald, p. 11; not collated by editors.

British Library, Add. MS 38015, f. 1.

SoR 302 -----

Copy in a composite volume of historical papers; early 17th century.

This MS not recorded by editors.

British Library, Stowe MS 152, ff. 25-8.

SoR 303 -----

Copy, transcribed from the first edition of *A Short Rule of Good Life*, in a MS volume of Southwell's works; c. 1608-12.

Printed from this MS in Brown, *Two Letters*. Microfilm in the British Library (M/714).

Folger, MS V. a. 421, ff. 1-14.

SoR 304 -----

Copy in a miscellany of religious verse and prose compiled by Peter Mowle of Attleborough, Norfolk; c. 1589-97.

This MS collated in Trotman and in Brown, *Two Letters*.

Oscott College, Sutton Coldfield, Shelf RNN3, pp. 100-8.

SoR 305 -----

Copy in the Waldegrave MS; c. 1592-1609.

This MS collated in Trotman and in Brown, *Two Letters*.

Stonyhurst College, MS A. v. 27, ff. 4-18.

An Epistle unto his Father (22 October 1589)

SoR 306 -----

Copy, lacking the title page, in a MS volume containing also *A Short Rule of Good Life* (SoR 319) and an account of the death of Margaret Clitheroe; end 16th-early 17th century.

This MS not recorded by editors.

York Minster, MS Add. 151, pp. 68-81.

SoR 307 *An Humble Supplication to Her Majesty.*

Copy transcribed for Sir Thomas Egerton (1540?-1617); c. 1590s.

First pub. (by a secret English press) '1595' [for 1600?]; ed. R.C. Bald (Cambridge, 1953). This MS collated in Bald.

Huntington, EL 2089.

SoR 308 -----

Copy, apparently transcribed from the edition of '1595', in a composite volume of state tracts; c. 1590s.

This MS recorded in Bald, pp. 47-8.

Inner Temple Library, Petyt MS 538, Vol. 10, ff. 129-40.

SoR 309 -----

Copy in a composite volume of state tracts; c. 1590s.

Printed from this MS in Bald; described in McDonald, p. 16.

Inner Temple Library, Petyt MS 538, Vol. 36, ff. 56-77v.

SoR 310 -----

Copy; 37 pages; incomplete; c. 1600.

This MS not recorded in Bald.

Pierpont Morgan Library, MA 291.

SoR 311 -----

Exemplum of the edition of '1595' with MS corrections made by two hands from a MS source; c. 1600s.

This item collated in Bald.

British Library, Department of Printed Books, 3935. aa. 33.

--- *The Hundred Meditations of the Love of God.*

See SoR 339-40.

SoR 312 *Letter to Sir Robert Cecil.*

Copy of Southwell's letter from the Tower, 6 April 1593, in a MS volume of works by Southwell; c. 1608-12.

First pub. (from this MS) in Brown, *Two Letters* (1973), pp. 75-85, with a facsimile of f. 54 as the frontispiece. Microfilm in the British Library (M/714).

Folger, MS V. a. 421, ff. 54-61v.

*SoR 313 *Mary Magdalen's Funeral Tears.*

Autograph draft of an English translation by Southwell of a 13th-century Latin homily (formerly attributed to Origen), intended to be read as a sermon; here beginning 'In this psent solemnity hauynge to speake in this audience of y^{r} charityes...'; unfinished; a work later expanded into *Mary Magdalen's Funeral Tears*; in a bound collection of Southwell's autograph papers; c. 1580.

Marie Magdalens Funerall Teares first pub. London, 1591; facsimile edition of exemplum in the Huntington pub. New York, 1975. This MS unpublished; discussed in Pierre Janelle, *Robert Southwell the Writer* (London, 1935), pp. 184-5. See FACSIMILE XXIX.

Stonyhurst College, MS A. v. 4, ff. 56-60, 62.

*SoR 314 -----

Autograph draft of the beginning of Southwell's English translation of the 13th-century Latin homily; here beginning 'As she surpassed many in loue so she passed most christs oune disciples in loyalty...'; unfinished; a work later expanded into *Mary Magdalen's Funeral Tears*; in a bound collection of Southwell's autograph papers; c. 1580.

See SoR 313.

Stonyhurst College, MS A. v. 4, f. 61v.

--- -----

See also INTRODUCTION.

SoR 315 *A Short Rule of Good Life.*

Copy, entitled 'A short rule of good life to derecte the devowte Christian', in one or possibly two hands, with corrections, once owned by one James Cleasbie; 95 leaves; in a composite volume of religious tracts; end 16th-early 17th century.

First pub. [London?, 1596-7?]; Brown, *Two Letters*, pp. 21-73. This MS not recorded in Brown.

Durham Cathedral, Hunter MS 108, item 2.

A Short Rule of Good Life

SoR 316 -----

Copy of a version transcribed from the first edition, with changes made by an Anglican editor, in a MS volume of works by Southwell; c. 1608-12.

Printed from this MS in Brown, *Two Letters*. Microfilm in the British Library (M/714).

Folger, MS V. a. 421, ff. 15-53.

SoR 317 -----

Copy in a composite volume of theological and historical tracts; end 16th-early 17th century.

This MS not recorded in Brown.

Gonville and Caius College, Cambridge, MS 218/233, pp. 115-245.

SoR 318 -----

Copy; end 16th-early 17th century.

This MS collated in Brown, *Two Letters*.

Jesuit House of Studies, Milltown Park, Dublin.

SoR 319 -----

Copy in a MS volume containing also the *Epistle unto his Father* (SoR 306) and an account of the death of Margaret Clitheroe; end 16th-early 17th century.

This MS not recorded in Brown.

York Minster, MS Add. 151, pp. 1-48.

SoR 320 -----

Extracts transcribed from the first edition in a bound collection of papers of the Williams (alias Cromwell) family of Huntingdonshire; c. 1607-30.

This MS recorded in Brown, *Two Letters*, p. xlvii.

British Library, Add. MS 34395, ff. 43-5v.

*SoR 321 [*A Soliloquy*].

Autograph copy of a Euphuistic prose recollection, beginning 'Alas whre doe I lament his losse...', in a bound collection of Southwell's autograph papers; c. 1580.

First pub. (from this MS) in Trotman (1914), pp. 69-70.

Stonyhurst College, MS A. v. 4, f. 37.

SoR 322 *The Triumphs over Death.*

Copy, headed 'A letter consolatorye for the death of a nobleman his sister', complete with dedicatory epistle to Philip Howard, Earl of Arundel, the 'Epitaph on Lady Margaret Sackville' (beginning 'Of Howards stemme a glorious branch is dead') and the Latin epitaph 'Clara Ducum soboles, superis nova sedibus hospes', in the Virtue and Cahill MS; early 17th century.

First pub. London, 1595; Trotman, pp. 1-35. The 'Epitaph on Lady Margaret Sackville' also printed and collated with the main MS copies in Brown, pp. 101-2, and the Latin epitaph printed in Brown, pp. 171-2. This MS not recorded in Trotman; recorded in Brown, p. xli.

Bodleian, MS Eng. poet. e. 113, ff. 63-74v.

SoR 323 -----

Copy, complete with dedicatory epistle, the 'Epitaph on Lady Margaret Sackville' and the Latin epitaph, in a MS volume of Southwell's works; early 17th century.

Printed chiefly from this MS in Trotman.

British Library, Add. MS 10422, ff. 86-109.

SoR 324 -----

Copy, complete with dedicatory epistle, the 'Epitaph on Lady Margaret Sackville' and the Latin epitaph, in the Waldegrave MS; c. 1592-1609.

This MS collated in Trotman.

Stonyhurst College, MS A. v. 27, ff. 20-36.

SoR 325 -----

MS abridgement, headed 'Comfortes for the afflicted of thē that haue lost a sister or such like', with lines 5-6, 13-18 of the 'Epitaph on Lady Margaret Sackville', here beginning 'Fame, honor, grace, gaue aire vnto his breath', and lines 3-4, 9-10 of the Latin epitaph, here beginning 'Dotibus ornauit, superauit moribus ortū', in Thomas Read's miscellany; [1624].

This MS not recorded by editors.

Syracuse University, George Arents Research Library, [no ref. number], pp. 37-44.

(2) LATIN WORKS BY SOUTHWELL

*SoR 326 *Ad omnia accomodata precatio.*

Autograph draft of a prayer beginning 'O dulcissime Jesu Christe ecce nūc venit occasio...', in a bound collection of Southwell's autograph papers; c. 1580.

Unpublished. This MS recorded in McDonald, p. 13.

Stonyhurst College, MS A. v. 4, f. 41r-v.

*SoR 327 *Ante Missam precatio.*

Autograph draft of a prayer beginning 'Cum tu dulcissime Jesu temetipsum spinis coronatū...', in a bound collection of Southwell's autograph papers; c. 1580.

Unpublished. This MS recorded in McDonald, p. 13.

Stonyhurst College, MS A. v. 4, ff. 42v-3.

*SoR 328 *Ante orationem precatio.*

Autograph draft of a prayer beginning 'Cum tu amātisse Jesu humanam naturā assūpteris...', in a bound collection of Southwell's autograph papers; c. 1580.

Unpublished. This MS recorded in McDonald, p. 13.

Stonyhurst College, MS A. v. 4, ff. 41v-2.

*SoR 329 *Ante studia precatio.*

Autograph draft of a prayer beginning 'O benignissime Jesu qui vt ignaros viam salutis doceres...', in a bound collection of Southwell's autograph papers; c. 1580.

Unpublished. This MS recorded in McDonald, p. 13.

Stonyhurst College, MS A. v. 4, ff. 43-4.

*SoR 330 *Antequam cum externis aut etiam domesticis loquaris prec.*

Autograph draft of a prayer beginning 'O bone Jesu qui semper mecā es...', in a bound collection of Southwell's autograph papers; c. 1580.

Unpublished. This MS recorded in McDonald, p. 13.

Stonyhurst College, MS A. v. 4, f. 44r-v.

SoR 331 *Exercitia et Devotiones.*

Copy, allegedly transcribed from Southwell's autograph; 73 leaves; 11 February 1607.

First pub. (from this MS) in *Spiritual Exercises and Devotions of Blessed Robert Southwell, S.J.*, ed. J.M. de Buck, S.J. (London, 1931). This MS recorded in McDonald, p. 14.

Bibliothèque Royale, Brussels, fonds générals, inventaire n°. 5618, catalogue n°. 2262.

SoR 332 -----

Copy in a small MS volume of religious writings; 82 leaves; [1609-22].

This MS collated in de Buck and described pp. 9-11.

In 1931 this MS was in the Jesuit Résidence in Ghent, Belgium, but is no longer there, nor apparently in any other libraries and archives in Ghent. Unless destroyed in World War II it may have been transferred to other Belgian Jesuit archives.

SoR 333 -----

Copy in a MS book of devotional meditations compiled by an unidentified Jesuit in Louvain; c. 1614.

Formerly in the Phillipps collection; this MS recorded in de Buck, pp. 14-15, (but not seen by him). See also SoR 341.

Folger, MS V. a. 214 (last item).

*SoR 334 [*Meditatio*].

Autograph draft of a meditation beginning 'Omnia te in cruce dereliquerunt...', in a bound collection of Southwell's autograph papers; c. 1580.

Unpublished. This MS recorded in McDonald, p. 13.

Stonyhurst College, MS A. v. 4, f. 36r-v.

--- *Meditationes de Attributis Divinis ad amorem Dei excitantes.*

See SoR 341.

*SoR 335 *Meditoes in aduentu.*

Autograph theological notes in a bound collection of Southwell's autograph papers; c. 1580.

Unpublished. This MS recorded in McDonald, p. 13.

Stonyhurst College, MS A. v. 4, ff. 28-34.

*SoR 336 [*Notae theologicae*].

Autograph notes of a treatise on dogmatic theology, in a bound collection of Southwell's autograph papers; c. 1580.

Unpublished. This MS recorded in McDonald, p. 12.

Stonyhurst College, MS A. v. 4, ff. 1-3v.

--- *On Christ's condemnation to death and the injustice of such a sentence.*

See SoR 342.

*SoR 337 [*Precatio*].

Autograph draft of a prayer beginning 'Domine Jesu Christe fateor me indignū esse qui oculos meos ad te attollam...', in a bound collection of Southwell's autograph papers; c. 1580.

Unpublished. This MS recorded in McDonald, p. 13.

Stonyhurst College, MS A. v. 4, ff. 44v-6.

*SoR 338 [*Precatio*].

Autograph draft of a prayer beginning 'O dulcissime et suauissime Jesu...', in a bound collection of Southwell's autograph papers; c. 1580.

Unpublished. This MS recorded in McDonald, p. 13.

Stonyhurst College, MS A. v. 4, ff. 39-40.

--- [*Precatio ad Virginem*].

See INTRODUCTION.

(3) WORKS OF DOUBTFUL AUTHORSHIP

SoR 339 *The Hundred Meditations of the Love of God.*

Transcript of an early copy of an English translation of Diego de Estella's *Meditaciones devotissimas del amor de Dios*, the early copy allegedly transcribed from 'ye originall... written wth Mr Robert Southwells owne hand' and with a dedication by the early copyist to Lady Beauchamp; 408 leaves (plus blanks); early 19th century.

First pub. (from this MS) London, 1873, ed. John Morris, S.J. This MS described in McDonald, pp. 15-16. See INTRODUCTION.

Stonyhurst College, MS B. vi. 1.

SoR 340 -----

Copy; early 17th century.

This MS recorded in Brown, p. xx.

English Province of the Society of Jesus, London, 7/1/1.

SoR 341 *Meditationes de Attributis Divinis ad amorem Dei excitantes.*

Copy of a Latin devotional work here ascribed to Southwell, in a MS book of devotional meditations compiled by an unidentified Jesuit in Louvain; c. 1614.

Unpublished. See also SoR 333 and INTRODUCTION.

Folger, MS V. a. 214, item 1.

MISCELLANEOUS

*SoR 342 [*Notebook*].

Autograph booklet of notes and memoranda, comprising two MSS containing copies of Jesuit rules and spiritual exercises, a calendar of duties, and a Latin devotional tract 'On Christ's condemnation to death and the injustice of such a sentence', compiled while Southwell was a novice or scholastic in Rome; 96 pages, 16mo; [1580-1].

This MS unpublished; described in H[erbert] T[hurston, S.J.], 'An Autograph Manuscript of the Venerable Robert Southwell, S.J.', *The Month*, 193, No. 718 (April 1924), p. 353; in *Spiritual Exercises and Devotions of Blessed Robert Southwell, S.J.*, ed. J.-M. de Buck, S.J. (London, 1931), pp. 29-31; and in McDonald, pp. 14-15.

Owned in 1930 by the Viscount Southwell (d. 1944) and temporarily deposited in St Joseph's Church, Newbury, Berkshire. A typescript summary and partial transcript of the MS made in London in 1930 by or for Fr C.A. Newdigate, S.J., and now preserved in the custody of Patrick C. Barry, in the Office of the Vice-Postulation for the Cause of the English and Welsh Martyrs, in the English Province of the Society of Jesus, London. The MS is not in the possession of the present Viscount Southwell (confirmed by letter 15 July 1975), nor preserved at Newbury (confirmed 1978); unlocated.

Edmund Spenser

1552?-99

ABBREVIATIONS

Variorum *The Works of Edmund Spenser: A Variorum Edition*, ed. Edwin Greenlaw, Charles Grosvenor Osgood, Frederick Morgan Padelford, Ray Heffner, Henry Gibbons Lotspeich, Rudolf Gottfried, et al., 9 vols + Index + A. C. Judson, *Life of Spenser* (Baltimore, 1932-58; reprinted in 11 vols 1966).

For abbreviations used throughout Volume I, see p.xi.

INTRODUCTION

None of Spenser's literary works is preserved in his autograph. His hand survives, however, in a number of documents and letters, some relating to his private affairs but most written in his official capacity as secretary in Ireland to Lord Grey and afterwards to Sir John Norris. Some sixty documents of this kind have so far been identified, nearly all among the Irish State Papers in the Public Record Office. Many other official papers — perhaps three dozen or more — bear his additions or endorsements. A few documents in his hand are in the British Library (Add. MS 19869; Add. MS 33924, f. 6; Cotton MS Titus B. XIII, f. 364) and some similar examples are among the Cecil Papers at Hatfield House. A document which Spenser wrote as secretary to John Young, Bishop of Rochester — a brief receipt for rent of the parsonage of Kirtling, signed 'John Roffens', 23 November 1578 — is now at the University of Kansas (MS uncat North 2C:2:1); a microfilm (from which this identification was made) is in the British Library (RP 367). The main documents in Spenser's hand are indexed and discussed at length, with facsimile examples, in Roland M. Smith, 'Spenser's Scholarly Script and "Right Writing"', *Studies in Honor of T. W. Baldwin*, ed. Don Cameron Allen (Urbana, 1958), pp. 66-111. For other discussions and facsimiles see particularly Hilary Jenkinson, 'Elizabethan Handwritings: A Preliminary Sketch', *The Library*, 4th Ser. 3 (1922-3)), 1-34 (pp. 33-4); Henry R. Plomer, 'Edmund Spenser's Handwriting', *MP*, 21 (November 1923), 201-7; Greg, *English Literary Autographs*, plates XXXIX-XL; Raymond Jenkins, 'Spenser's Hand', *TLS* (7 January 1932), p. 12; Jenkins, '*Newes out of Munster*, A Document in Spenser's Hand', *SP*, 32 (1935), 125-30; Jenkins, 'Spenser with Lord Grey in Ireland', *PMLA*, 52.i (1937), 338-53; Jenkins, 'Spenser: The Uncertain Years 1584-1589', *PMLA*, 53.i (1938), 350-62; *Facsimiles of Royal, Historical, and Literary Autographs in the British Museum* (1899), plate 92; and Petti, *English Literary Hands*, Nos. 25-6.

An additional autograph can now be identified, one which approximates most closely to a 'literary' autograph. It is Spenser's transcript of a letter in Latin from Erhardus Stibarus to Erasmus Neustetter, followed by two Latin Poems, perhaps belonging to a volume of Petrus Lotichius's *Poemata* (see SpE 65 and FACSIMILE XXX). This letter is on the subject of poetry and would be of obvious interest to Spenser. The single leaf containing the transcript was until recently bound in a printed exemplum of Georgius Sabinus, *Poemata* (Leipzig, 1563), and attention was drawn to it in connection with Spenser since the volume bears on the title page his motto 'Immerito'. The leaf was evidently inserted in the volume (which has a modern binding) by a later owner, however, and was not an integral part of it. Of the volume itself (Folger, MS V. a. 341), it can be said that the inscribed motto, 'Immerito', is not in a script which can be recognised as Spenser's though it may be genuine: he may conceivably have adopted a rather larger and more angular italic for inscriptions, alternatively it may be in the hand of a scribe. The title page also bears the slightly cropped inscription, 'Donū amiciss. viri Johannis Capelli'. This is in a hand similar to Spenser's but is not necessarily his (being slightly more angular than his known italic). The volume must remain classified as one possibly presented to Spenser by one John Capell, though the marginal annotations found in the main body of the text are in a contemporary hand which is not Spenser's. The only other printed volume which is recorded as possibly belonging to him (since the title page bears an inscription in Greek meaning 'the author to himself') is the Frank Hogan exemplum of *The Faerie Queene* (1590), a volume at present unlocated (see SpE 1). A small slip with the words 'Spenser [?] owes this booke' was recorded as a Spenser autograph in the printed catalogue of the R. B. Adam Library (1929), III, 225, but this inscription, now in the Hyde Collection (*Life*, II, 1, 42), is not in the hand of Edmund Spenser the poet.

Various early MS copies of, or extracts from, Spenser's poems are recorded in the entries below (also one copy, SpE 32, which is written in a 17th-century miscellany but which later inspection reveals to be a 19th-century transcript). Transcripts of poems from *Complaints* account for a number of entries. It is known that such copies were in circulation before 1591: the printer, William Ponsonby, tells the reader how he endeavoured to get hold of 'such smale Poemes of the same Authors; as I heard were disperst abroad in sundrie hands, and not easie to bee come by, by himselfe; some of them hauing bene diuerslie imbeziled and purloyned from him, since his departure ouer Sea'. It seems likely, however, that most of the extant MS texts are of later date and transcribed from Ponsonby's edition; their *raison d'être* is not immediately apparent. The only other poem by Spenser which seems to have had a relatively wide circulation in manuscript is Sonnet VIII of the *Amoretti* (SpE 2-7).

A few MS extracts from Spenser's poems are to be found which are not included in the entries. Sir Kenelm Digby's *Observations on the 22. Stanza in the 9th. Canto of the 2d. book of Spensers Faery queen*, one of the earliest commentaries on Spenser (written in 1628), was first published in London, 1643; the text is printed in Variorum, II, 472-8. This work (which, of course, quotes the relevant passage by Spenser) also survives in various MS texts, including MSS in the Bodleian (MSS Perrott 7, ff. 36-47v; Tanner 82, ff. 313v-26), in the British Library (Add. MS 44848, f. 235 seq.; Egerton MS 2725, f. 117v seq.; Harley MS 7375), in the Folger (MSS V. a. 239, p. 895 seq.; V. b. 234, p. 961 seq.), and in a MS owned by Lord Egremont, Petworth House (HMC MS 61, pp. 527-49). This commentary is to be distinguished from a brief discourse *Concerning Spenser* which survives in Digby's autograph in the British Library (Add. MS 41846, ff. 108-11) and which is printed in E.W. Bligh, *Sir Kenelm Digby and his Venetia* (London, 1932), pp. 277-80; another text is in Harley MS 4153, ff. 1-5v. The poet John Lane quotes from *The Faerie Queene* (Book IV, Canto II, stanzas 31-5) in his continuation of Chaucer's *Squire's Tale*, MS texts of which are in the Bodleian (MS Douce 170, f. v, dated 1615) and in the Plume Library, Maldon (MS 0. 3. 17, pp. vi-vii, dated 1616); a revised version of this work, of 1630, is also in the Bodleian (MS Ashmole 53). *The Faerie Queene* is briefly quoted by Dr William Balam (1651-1726) in a letter in the Bodleian (MS Rawl. letters 93, f. 311). John Shrimpton quotes lines 36-42 of *The Ruines of Time* in his MS *History of St Albans* (c. 1640), now in the Bodleian (MS Gough Herts 3, f. 56). There is also to be found an unpublished *Supplement of the Faery Queene*, a work of 376 leaves written in 1635 apparently by Ralph Knevett (1600-71), and now in Cambridge University Library (MS Ee. 3. 53).

At least two independent Latin versions of *The Shepheardes Calender* are preserved in MSS. The text of one, made by John Dove (c. 1584), is now at Gonville and Caius College, Cambridge (MS 547/595). A second Latin version was made c. 1608 by Theodore Bathurst and was published in the 1653 edition of Spenser's poems. A MS text containing a draft dedication in Bathurst's autograph is preserved at Pembroke College, Cambridge, and other MS copies are in the British Library (Department of Printed Books, 1077. e. 52 and C. 117. b. 10), in the Pforzheimer Library (MS 116), and in the Folger (MS J. a. 2). The first three of those MSS are each bound with a printed exemplum of *The Shepheardes Calender* (London, 1597), and the fourth was formerly bound with an exemplum of that edition; the fifth is in a Cambridge dramatic and verse miscellany (c. 1615-30). The first three MSS are discussed in Leicester Bradner, 'The Latin Translations of Spenser's Shepheardes Calender', *MP*, 33 (1935-6), 21-6. That article also mentions an independent Latin translation of the Song in the April Eclogue (British Library, Harley MS 532).

A further series of MS items which have not been given entries but which are of considerable interest is the annotations and comments made by early readers of Spenser's printed works. Notable is an exemplum of *The Faerie Queene*, Books I-III (London, 1590) containing copious notes, comments and glosses on the allegorical significance of the poem written probably in 1597 by John Dixon of Hilden, near Tonbridge, Kent. This volume is owned by the Earl of Bessborough (confirmed by letter 12 September 1975). The annotations are edited by Graham Hough in *The First Commentary on The Faerie Queene* (privately printed, 1964) and selections also published in *TLS* (9 April 1964), p. 294. Bent E. Juel-Jensen of Oxford reported possessing an exemplum of Books I-III (London, 1596) formerly owned by Charles Wesley and containing 'extensive contemporary manuscript notes, which must rival the claim made for the Weller-Poley-Bessborough *Faerie Queene* that it is the earliest to have contemporary notes' (*BC*, 15 (Summer 1966), p. 159). Other annotated exempla of this work include the following: Books I-III (1590) with notes by Sir Thomas Posthumous Hobby (1566-1641), now in the Bodleian (F. 2. 62 Linc.); Books IV-VI (1596) in Cambridge University Library (Sel. 5. 102); Books I-VI (1590-6) in the British Library (Department of Printed Books, C. 12. h. 17, 18, and G. 11535-6 (1)); and a 1617 folio with annotations in Latin in the Bodleian (K. 4. 23* Art.). These volumes, together with others containing later annotations, are discussed in the anonymous 'MS Notes to Spenser's "Faerie Queene"', *N & Q*, 202 (December 1957), 509-15, and in Alastair Fowler, 'Oxford and London Marginalia to "The Faerie Queene"', *N & Q*, 206 (November 1961), 416-18. For the 1617 folio annotated by members of Ralegh's family, see SIR WALTER RALEGH, INTRODUCTION.

Of Spenser's prose writings the only work extensively represented in the entries is *A View of the Present State of Ireland* (SpE 45-64), scribal copies of which proliferated since the work was of topical interest but was apparently denied a license for printing (see SpE 47). Very brief notes taken from the edition of 1633 can also be found in a miscellany compiled by Bishop Thomas Tanner (1674-1735), now in the British Library (Add. MS 6261, f. 87v). A pencil transcript of Spenser's other work on the same subject, *A Brief Note of Ireland*, is preserved at Trinity College, Dublin (MS 1789), but it was made by or for Caesar Litton Falkiner (1863-1908), probably from the MS in the Public Record Office (SpE 42).

The canon of Spenser's works accepted in the *Index* is based entirely on the Variorum edition. The MSS recorded have not been previously noted by editors unless otherwise stated.

PB.

ARRANGEMENT

Verse	SpE 1-41
Prose	SpE 42-64
Miscellaneous	SpE 65.

See also Addenda to Part 2, p. 634

FACSIMILE XXX — Edmund Spenser: Transcript of a letter in Latin from Erhardus Stibarus to Erasmus Neustetter about Petrus Lotichius, followed by two Latin poems on Lotichius (the leaf shaved at the top) (SpE 65). Folger, MS X.d.520, recto and verso. Reproduced by permission of the Folger Shakespeare Library.

[illegible] Servat. ac Erasmo
Neustetter Egnitj Erasmo S.
de P. Lotichio

Saepe soleo mihi ante oculos ponere crebrisque
usurpare sermonib. doctiss. Erasmi, suavitat.
ingenij tui morumque sanctimoniam atque venustate
quib. tantam tu laudem apud oes iamdiu retines,
ut sentio hoc petito et summa rerum omnium perturbatione
multj in spem amplam veniant excellente virtute
virtute tua et industria Reip. aliquando et bonis
saluti et ornamento futuram esse. Hac vero virtutisque
tuae recordatio singularis semper tuae mirabiles affe
rit, gloriaeque tuae admiratio ita animo meo haeret in
fixa, ut ea avelli nunquam possit. Mitto ergo ad te
Lotichij nostri Elegos, neque ita multos ut plerique fras,
idque eo facio libentius, quod tu nec minus optimarum
artium et literarum, quam et humanitatis et bonitatis laude
excellis, nec a Poetarum studijs abhorres, quib. animi
et ad virtutem erudiuntur et ad omnem alacritatem
redduntur aptiores. Extabat hic maxime otij nostri sin
[illegible] in hortis suburbanis, ubi crebro [illegible] pro
anima, quoties se calor fregisset aspirationis [illegible]
recumbebamus, Carminum eorum praecipue quae ad in
genij relaxationem erant accommodata pronuntiatio
exaque ego ibi cum Lotichio ad multam diem
et (ut Catullus inquit de Licinio)

Scribens versiculos uterque nostrum
Ludebat numero modo hoc, modo illo.

Hi nunc in manib. tuis sunt, quib. tu eo est [illegible]
bis amplius, quo magis hic studia reconditis atque
abditis e fontibus hauriuntur et ab imperitorum
intelligentia sensuque disiuncta sunt. Quod si uti
spero feceris, dabo operam, ut amor noster qui
librorum distantia interceptus hactenus fuit [illegible]
rib. testimonijs in posterum eluceat. Vale. In
monte [illegible] Id. Febru. Aº 1553.

Joannes de [illegible]
Lotichium.

Lotichi, si quid [illegible] sunt omnia nobis
Non opus in tenebris [illegible]
Atque aliquis spectans olim tua carmina dicet:
Venator vates Miles Amator erat.

Fr. Artifex Atheniensis

Lascivi, molles, teneri, simul atque salaces,
Thespiadum [illegible] iubet ire chorus
At quib. [illegible] Veneris [illegible]
Atque pharetrati spicula saeva Dei,
Hos legitote Elegos, mitj pietate refertos
Casta placent sanctis pectora numinibus.
Dulce poema fluens [illegible] petitur
Exhibet hic Vates suaviloquente stylo.

Edmund Spenser

VERSE

SpE 1 *Amoretti. Sonnet I* ('Happy ye leaues when as those lilly hands').

Copy, headed 'A sa mistresse', written in two scribal hands on a blank page in a printed exemplum of *The Faerie Queene*, Books I-III (London, 1590) possibly once owned by Spenser; c. 1590s?

First pub. in *Amoretti and Epithalamion* ([London], 1595); Variorum, *Minor Poems*, II, 191-232 (p. 195). This MS formerly but no longer thought to be autograph; printed, with A. Judson's discussion of its authenticity, in *Minor Poems*, II, 419-20; facsimile in Flower & Munby, *English Poetical Autographs*, p. 3.

Parke-Bernet, New York, 23-4 April 1946 (Frank Hogan sale), sold to Ray Hartz: see Edwin Wolf 2nd and J.F. Fleming, *Rosenbach* (London, 1960), pp. 433, 540.

SpE 2 ----- *Sonnet VIII* ('More then most faire, full of the liuing fire').

Copy, untitled and here ascribed to 'M[r] [Edward] Dier', in a miscellany compiled by a Cambridge student, possibly Sir John Finett (1571-1641) of Fordwich, Kent; c. 1586-91.

Variorum, *Minor Poems*, II, 198. Printed from this MS in L. Cummings, 'Spenser's *Amoretti VIII*: New Manuscript Versions', *SEL*, 4 (1964), 125-35 (p. 127).

Bodleian, MS Rawl. poet. 85, f. 7v.

SpE 3 ----- -----

Copy in a musical setting by Henry Lawes, in Lawes's autograph songbook; mid-17th century.

Facsimile of this MS in Willa McClung Evans, *Henry Lawes* (New York & London, 1941), p. 67.

British Library, Add. MS 53723, f. 17.

SpE 4 ----- -----

Copy of lines 1-4, untitled, in a verse miscellany compiled by the antiquary St Loe Kniveton of Gray's Inn; c. 1585-90s.

Printed from this MS in Cummings, p. 129.

British Library, Harley MS 7392, f. 28.

SpE 5 ----- -----

Copy in a verse miscellany probably compiled by Francis Baskerville of Malmesbury, Wiltshire, and owned in 1663 by William Wallrond; c. 1633.

Printed from this MS in Cummings, pp. 128-9.

British Library, Sloane MS 1446, f. 43.

SpE 6 ----- -----

Copy, untitled and here beginning 'More fayr then most fair full of the lyving fyre', in a verse miscellany compiled by Henry Stanford, household tutor in the Carey family; c. 1585-98.

Printed from this MS in Cummings, p. 128.

Cambridge University Library, MS Dd. 5. 75, f. 37v.

SpE 7 ----- -----

Copy inscribed in a printed exemplum of Fulke Greville, *Certaine Learned and Elegant Workes* (London, 1633), formerly in the library at Warwick Castle; late 17th century.

This MS noted by W. Hilton Kelliher in *BMQ*, 34 (1969-70), 120.

Christie's, 2 July 1969, Lot 58, sold to Hatchards.

SpE 7.5, 7.8 See Addenda, p. 634.

--- *Complaints*.

Poems from this work are recorded individually.

SpE 8 *The Faerie Queene*.

Copy of the Preface to Book I (beginning 'Lo I the man, whose Muse whilome did maske') and Canto I, stanzas 1-5 (beginning 'A Gentle Knight was pricking on the plaine'), in one hand, followed (on pp. 3-4) by Canto IV, stanzas 46-51 (beginning 'With gentle wordes he can her fairely greet') and Canto V, stanzas 1-32 (beginning 'The noble hart, that harbours vertuous thought'), in another hand; 17th century.

Books I-III first pub. London, 1590; Books IV-VI pub. London, 1596; Variorum, (I, pp. 3-6, 54-64).

Chetham's Library, Manchester, Halliwell-Phillipps No. 1373.

SpE 9 -----

Extracts, including Book III, Canto IX, stanza 20, in a composite volume of verse written by or relating to members of the Fairfax family; early 17th century.

British Library, Add. MS 11743, f. 25.

SpE 10 -----

Copy of Book IV, Canto IX, stanza 2, here beginning 'All naturall affection soone doth cesse', quoted in an undated letter from Francis Beaumont, later Master of the

Charterhouse (d. 1624), to Lady Anne Newdegate ('m^{r} Spensers opinion' in these 'honest verses' agrees with his own); c. 1611.

This letter printed in Lady Newdigate-Newdegate, *Gossip from a Muniment Room* (London, 1897), p. 132, and see T.W. Baldwin, 'The Three Francis Beaumonts', *MLN*, 39 (1924), 505-7.

Warwickshire Record Office, CR 136/ B25.

--- -----

See also INTRODUCTION and SpE 32.

SpE 11 *Iambicum Trimetrum* ('Vnhappie Verse, the witnesse of my vnhappie state').

Copy, untitled, in a verse miscellany compiled by John Harington of Stepney (1520?-82) and his son Sir John Harington of Kelston (1560-1612); late 16th century.

First pub. in *Two Other, very commendable Letters* [of Spenser and Gabriel Harvey] (London, 1580); Variorum, *Minor Poems*, II, 267. Printed from this MS in Hughey, *Arundel Harington MS*, I, No. 185, p. 234.

Owned by the Duke of Norfolk, Arundel Castle, MSS (Special Press), 'Harrington MS Temp. Eliz.', f. 142.

--- *Mother Hubberds Tale.*

See SpE 14-20.

SpE 12 *Muiopotmos: or The Fate of the Butterflie* ('I sing of deadly dolorous debate').

Copy, transcribed from *Complaints* (London, 1591), in a verse miscellany; c. 1596-1601.

First pub. (with a separate title page dated 1590) in *Complaints* (London, 1591); Variorum, *Minor Poems*, II, 157-73. This MS recorded in *Minor Poems*, II, 678, 687; described in *The Poetical Works of Spenser*, ed. E. de Sélincourt, III (Oxford, 1910), pp. xviii-xix.

British Library, Harley MS 6910, ff. 41v-8.

SpE 13 -----

Copy in a transcript of *Complaints* probably made from the edition of 1591; c. 1591.

Harvard, MS Eng 266, ff. 68-75v.

SpE 14 *Prosopopoia: or Mother Hubberds Tale* ('It was the month, in which the righteous Maide').

Copy in a miscellany compiled by John Ramsey (b. 1578) of Peterhouse, Cambridge; early 17th century.

First pub. in *Complaints* (London, 1591); Variorum, *Minor Poems*, II, 103-40.

Bodleian, MS Douce 280, ff. 22-34v.

SpE 15 -----

Extracts ranging from line 353 to line 659, beginning 'And now the Foxe had gotten him a gowne' and wrongly entitled 'The Ruines of Time', apparently transcribed from a MS source, in a verse miscellany owned in 1596 by one Anthony Babington of Warrington; c. 1600.

This MS recorded in Variorum, *Minor Poems* II, 687-8; first collated in P.M. Buck, Jr., 'Add. MS 34064 and Spenser's *Ruins of Time* and *Mother Hubberd's Tale*', *MLN*, 22 (1907), 41-6.

British Library, Add. MS 34064, ff. 33v-5.

SpE 15.5 -----

Copy in a miscellany; a slip with lines 1-6 also pasted on f. 1; c. 1591-early 17th century.

British Library, Harley MS 677, ff. 87-104.

SpE 16 -----

Copy, transcribed from *Complaints* (London, 1591), in a verse miscellany; c. 1596-1601.

This MS recorded in *Minor Poems*, II, 678, 687.

British Library, Harley MS 6910, ff. 2*-20.

SpE 17 -----

Copy in a transcript of *Complaints* probably made from the edition of 1591; c. 1591.

Harvard, MS Eng 266, ff. 38-58.

SpE 18 -----

Copy; 28 pages; 1607.

This MS formerly owned by Alexander B. Grosart and collated in his edition of *The Complete Works in Verse and Prose of Edmund Spenser*, 9 vols (privately printed, 1882-4), III, 148-52: see Variorum, *Minor Poems*, II, 688.

Owned by Arthur A. Houghton, Jr. (to be sold at Christie's, 1980).

Prosopopoia: or Mother Hubberds Tale

SpE 19 -----

Extracts in a composite volume of MSS collected by William Parkhurst (fl. 1604-67), among the papers of the Finch family of Burley-on-the-Hill, Rutland; 1600s-41.

Leicestershire Record Office, DG. 7/Lit. 2, f. 320v.

SpE 20 -----

Copy in a miscellany; incomplete; mid-17th century.

Yale, Osborn Collection, b 65, pp. 53-63.

SpE 21 *Ruines of Rome: by Bellay* ('Ye heauenly spirites, whose ashie cinders lie').

Copy, transcribed from *Complaints* (London, 1591), in a verse miscellany; c. 1596-1601.

First pub. in *Complaints* (London, 1591); Variorum, *Minor Poems*, II, 141-54. This MS recorded in *Minor Poems*, II, 678, 687.

British Library, Harley MS 6910, ff. 59v-66v.

SpE 22 -----

Copy in a transcript of *Complaints* probably made from the edition of 1591; c. 1591.

Harvard, MS Eng 266, ff. 59-67.

SpE 23 *The Ruines of Time* ('It chaunced me on day beside the shore').

Extracts ranging from line 183 to line 572, beginning 'It is not long, since these two eyes beheld', apparently transcribed from a MS source, in a verse miscellany owned in 1596 by one Anthony Babington of Warrington; c. 1600.

First pub. in *Complaints* (London, 1591); Variorum, *Minor Poems*, II, 35-56. This MS recorded in *Minor Poems*, II, 687-8; first collated in P.M. Buck, Jr., 'Add. MS 34064 and Spenser's *Ruins of Time* and *Mother Hubberd's Tale*', *MLN*, 22 (1907), 41-6.

British Library, Add. MS 34064, ff. 31-3.

SpE 24 -----

Copy, transcribed from *Complaints* (London, 1591), in a verse miscellany; c. 1596-1601.

This MS recorded in *Minor Poems*, II, 678, 687.

British Library, Harley MS 6910, ff. 48v-59.

SpE 25 -----

Copy in a transcript of *Complaints* probably made from the edition of 1591; c. 1591.

Harvard, MS Eng 266, ff. 2-15.

SpE 26 -----

Extracts in a composite volume of MSS collected by William Parkhurst (fl. 1604-67), among the papers of the Finch family of Burley-on-the-Hill, Rutland; 1600s-41.

Leicestershire Record Office, DG. 7/Lit. 2, ff. 317-20.

SpE 27 -----

Copy, beginning at stanza 24 ('But me no man bewaileth, but in game'), in a miscellany; imperfect, lacking the first part and a title; mid-17th century.

Yale, Osborn Collection, b 65, pp. 11-23.

--- -----

See also INTRODUCTION.

--- *The Shepheardes Calender.*

See INTRODUCTION.

SpE 28 *The Teares of the Muses* ('Rehearse to me ye sacred Sisters nine').

Copy in a miscellany compiled by John Ramsey (b. 1578) of Peterhouse, Cambridge; early 17th century.

First pub. in *Complaints* (London, 1591); Variorum, *Minor Poems*, II, 59-79.

Bodleian, MS Douce 280, ff. 36-43.

SpE 29 -----

Copy, transcribed from *Complaints* (London, 1591), in a verse miscellany; c. 1596-1601.

This MS recorded in *Minor Poems*, II, 678, 687.

British Library, Harley MS 6910, ff. 20v-30.

SpE 30 -----

Copy in a transcript of *Complaints* probably made from the edition of 1591; c. 1591.

Harvard, MS Eng 266, ff. 16-26.

The Teares of the Muses

SpE 31 -----

Copy, headed 'Musarum Lachrymae Dominae Strange dedicatae', in a miscellany; mid-17th century.

Yale, Osborn Collection, b 65, pp. 24-36.

SpE 32 *To the right honourable the Earle of Northumberland* ('The sacred Muses have made alwaies clame').

Copy of Spenser's dedicatory sonnet (in Book III of *The Faerie Queene*) written in a 19th-century hand in a miscellany compiled c. 1644 by one William Han.

First pub. in *The Faerie Queene*, Books I-III (London, 1590); Variorum, III, 191.

Yale, Osborn Collection, b 150, p. 277.

SpE 33 *Virgils Gnat* ('We now haue playde (Augustus) wantonly').

Copy (including the dedication beginning 'Wrong'd, yet not daring to expresse my paine'), transcribed from *Complaints* (London, 1591), in a verse miscellany; c. 1596-1601.

First pub. in *Complaints* (London, 1591); Variorum, *Minor Poems*, II, 678, 687.

British Library, Harley MS 6910, ff. 30v-41.

SpE 34 -----

Copy (including the dedication) in a transcript of *Complaints* probably made from the edition of 1591; c. 1591.

Harvard, MS Eng 266, ff. 26v-37v.

SpE 35 -----

Copy, headed 'Virgiliana Culex', in a miscellany; mid-17th century.

Yale, Osborn Collection, b 65, pp. 37-52.

SpE 36 *The Visions of Bellay* ('It was the time, when rest soft sliding downe').

Copy, transcribed from *Complaints* (London, 1591), in a verse miscellany; c. 1596-1601.

First pub. in *Complaints* (London, 1591); Variorum, *Minor Poems*, II, 179-85. This MS recorded in *Minor Poems*, II, 678, 687.

British Library, Harley MS 6910, ff. 69v-72v.

SpE 37 *The Visions of Petrarch* ('Being one day at my window all alone').

Copy in a miscellany compiled by John Ramsey (b. 1578) of Peterhouse, Cambridge; early 17th century.

First pub. in *Complaints* (London, 1591); Variorum, *Minor Poems*, II, 186-8.

Bodleian, MS Douce 280, ff. 44-5.

SpE 38 -----

Copy in a transcript of Sir John Davies's *Nosce Teipsum* (DaJ 73); late 17th century.

British Library, Add. MS 25304, f. 44v.

SpE 39 -----

Copy, transcribed from *Complaints* (London, 1591), in a verse miscellany; c. 1596-1601.

This MS recorded in *Minor Poems*, II, 678, 687.

British Library, Harley MS 6910, ff. 73-4v.

SpE 40 *Visions of the worlds vanitie* ('One day, whiles that my daylie cares did sleepe').

Copy, transcribed from *Complaints* (London, 1591), in a verse miscellany; c. 1596-1601.

First pub. in *Complaints* (London, 1591); Variorum, *Minor Poems*, II, 174-8. This MS recorded in *Minor Poems*, II, 678, 687.

British Library, Harley MS 6910, ff. 67-9v.

SpE 41 -----

Copy in a transcript of *Complaints* probably made from the edition of 1591; c. 1591.

Harvard, MS Eng 266, ff. 77-9.

PROSE

SpE 42 *A Brief Note of Ireland.*

Copy in the hand of Sir Dudley Carleton (1573-1632), inscribed in a later hand 'A briefe discourse of Ireland, by Spencer'; probably the MS delivered by Spenser to the Secretary of State in London; 1598.

First pub. (from this MS) in *The Complete Works of Spenser*, ed. Alexander B. Grosart (London, 1882-4), I, 537-55; printed from this MS in Variorum, *Prose Works* (ed. Rudolf Gottfried), pp. 233-45.

Public Record Office, SP.63/202 pt. 4/59.

A Brief Note of Ireland

SpE 43 -----

Copy of part of the third section, headed 'Certaine notes to be considered of in the recovering of the Realme of Irelande', in a volume of miscellaneous verse and prose transcribed from the papers of Sir Christopher Yelverton (1535?-1612); early 17th century.

All Souls College, Oxford, MS 155, ff. 58r-v.

SpE 44 -----

Copy of part of the third section, headed 'Spensers discours briefly of Irelande', in a composite volume of tracts and papers; early 17th century.

This MS collated in Variorum.

British Library, Harley MS 3787, f. 184.

--- -----

See also INTRODUCTION.

SpE 45 *A View of the Present State of Ireland.*

Copy, one in a collection of unbound tracts relating to Irish affairs probably collected by Sir William Trumbull (1639-1716) of Easthampstead Park; mid-17th century.

First pub. in Sir James Ware, *The Historie of Ireland* (Dublin, 1633); Variorum, *Prose Works* (ed. Rudolf Gottfried), pp. 39-231.

Berkshire Record Office, Trumbull Add. MS 11(b).

SpE 46 -----

Copy; 1596-early 17th century.

This MS collated in Variorum.

Bodleian, MS Gough Ireland 2.

SpE 47 -----

Copy, prepared for intended publication in 1598; with a note at the end from the Warden of the Stationer's Company to the Secretary, 'Mr. Collinges I pray enter this Copie for mathew Lownes to be prynted when he do bringe other authorytie. Thomas Man'; [1598].

Entered in the Stationers' Register under the date 14 April 1598; this MS collated in Variorum.

Bodleian, MS Rawl. B. 478.

SpE 48 -----

Copy, once owned by Sir Arthur Chichester (1563-1625), Lord-Deputy of Ireland in 1604-13; 1596-early 17th century.

This MS collated in Variorum.

British Library, Add. MS 22022.

SpE 49 -----

Copy in a volume of tracts relating to Ireland; 1596-early 17th century.

This MS collated in Variorum.

British Library, Harley MS 1932, ff. 1-90.

SpE 50 -----

Copy; 1596-early 17th century.

This MS collated in Variorum.

British Library, Harley MS 7388.

SpE 51 -----

Copy; 1596-early 17th century.

British Library, Sloane MS 1695.

SpE 52 -----

Copy; 1596-early 17th century.

This MS collated in Variorum.

Cambridge University Library, MS Dd. 10. 60.

SpE 53 -----

Copy; bound with a tract by Sir Robert Cotton; 1596-early 17th century.

This MS collated in Variorum.

Cambridge University Library, MS Dd. 14. 28 (1).

SpE 54 -----

Copy, apparently transcribed from SpE 63, in a volume of state tracts compiled by someone associated with Robert Devereux, second Earl of Essex (d. 1601) and owned in 1601 by one Richard Greene; imperfect; c. 1601.

Formerly MS 6185, this MS collated in Variorum.

Folger, MS V. b. 214, ff. 136v-93.

A View of the Present State of Ireland

SpE 55 -----

Copy; 1596-early 17th century.

This MS collated in Variorum.

Gonville and Caius College, Cambridge, MS 188/221.

SpE 56 -----

Copy; bound with a 15-leaf MS 'Breviate of ye gettinge of Irelande and of the Decaye of the same'; 1596-early 17th century.

This MS formerly owned by Richard Townley and W.H. Crawford; collated in Variorum; recorded in De Ricci, *Supplement*, p. 201. A negative photocopy is in the Folger, PR 1405 S7.

Owned by Arthur A. Houghton, Jr., MS, ff. 1-63v (to be sold at Christie's, 1980).

SpE 57 -----

Copy; 83 leaves; 1596-early 17th century.

Owned by Arthur A. Houghton, Jr. (and to be sold at Christie's, 1980).

SpE 58 -----

Copy, with an index in the hand of Sir Thomas Egerton (1540?-1617); c. 1596.

Printed from this MS in Variorum.

Huntington, EL 7041.

SpE 59 -----

Copy in several hands; 1596-early 17th century.

This MS collated in Variorum.

Lambeth Palace, MS 510.

SpE 60 -----

Copy; early 17th century.

Formerly owned by John Henry Gurney of Keswick Hall, Norfolk; this MS recorded in *HMC*, 12th Report, Appendix IX (1891), p. 123; collated in Variorum. Facsimile of last page in Sotheby's sale catalogue, 31 March 1936, Lot 200.

National Library of Ireland, MS 661.

SpE 61 -----

Copy; 1596-early 17th century.

This MS collated in Variorum.

Public Record Office, SP.63/202 pt. 4/58.

SpE 62 -----

Copy, once owned by Archbishop James Ussher (1581-1656) and used as the copy-text for Ware's edition of 1633; 141 leaves; 1596-early 17th century.

Formerly MS E.3.26, this MS collated in Variorum.

Trinity College, Dublin, MS 589.

SpE 63 -----

Copy in six hands; once owned by Sir Henry St George (1581-1644); 1597-early 17th century.

This MS formerly Phillipps MS 13761. A microfilm is in the British Library (RP 207).

Yale, Osborn Collection, fa 12.

SpE 64 -----

Précis of Spenser's arguments, headed 'Spensers discourse of Ireland termed Irelands good' and beginning '1. The cause of Tyrons and the rests Rebellion in Ulster was the new Counteyinge of Monahon...', in a legal miscellany owned in the late 17th-early 18th century by one Thomas Smethurst; 1st half 17th century.

Bodleian, MS Eng. misc. f. 473, pp. 51-66.

--- -----

See also INTRODUCTION.

MARGINALIA IN PRINTED BOOKS AND MANUSCRIPTS

See INTRODUCTION.

MISCELLANEOUS

*SpE 65 [*Miscellaneous*].

Transcript in Spenser's italic hand, on a single leaf, of a letter in Latin from Erhardus Stibarus to Erasmus Neustetter from Monte Pesentano, 1553, and of two Latin poems, 'Joannes de Sylva ad Lotichium' and 'Fr. Artifex Athensis'; later bound in a printed exemplum of Georgius Sabinus, *Poemata* (Leipzig, 1563) and now separate; the top edge slightly cropped.

See FACSIMILE XXX and INTRODUCTION.

Folger, MS X. d. 520.

Henry Howard Earl of Surrey

1517?-47

ABBREVIATIONS

Hughey, *Arundel* Ruth Hughey, *The Arundel Harington Manuscript of Tudor Poetry*, 2 vols (Columbus, Ohio, 1960).

Hughey, *Harington of Stepney* Ruth Hughey, *John Harington of Stepney: Tudor Gentleman* (Columbus, Ohio, 1971).

Hughey, *Library* (1935) Ruth Hughey, 'The Harington Manuscript at Arundel Castle and Related Documents', *The Library*, 4th Ser. 15 (1934-5), 388-444.

Mumford Ivy Lilian Mumford, 'Musical Settings to the Poems of Henry Howard, Earl of Surrey', *English Miscellany*, 8 (1957), 9-20.

Padelford *The Poems of Henry Howard, Earl of Surrey*, ed. Frederick Morgan Padelford, 2nd edition (Seattle, 1928; reprinted New York, 1966).

Rollins *Tottel's Miscellany (1557-1587)*, ed. Hyder Edward Rollins, 2 vols (Cambridge, Mass., 1928-9).

For abbreviations used throughout Volume I, see p.xi.

INTRODUCTION

No poetical MS survives in Surrey's autograph. The only examples of his hand are a few letters in the Public Record Office and in the British Library; certain of them are entirely in his hand but most are written by scribes and signed by him. These documents have been extensively quoted by Surrey's biographers: see particularly Edwin Casady, *Henry Howard, Earl of Surrey* (New York, 1938). A facsimile example of Surrey's hand from Cotton MS Titus B. II, ff. 39-40v, in the British Library, appears in *The Works of Henry Howard, Earl of Surrey, and of Sir Thomas Wyatt the Elder*, ed. George F. Nott, 2 vols (London, 1815-16), I, facing p. 167, and a facsimile example from Harley MS 283, f. 329, in the British Library, appears in Petti, *English Literary Hands*, No. 20.

Apart from an interesting scribal copy of his translation of Virgil's *Aeneid*, Book IV (SuH 70), there are two main MS texts of Surrey's poems. Both are miscellanies which were begun by John Harington of Stepney (1520?-82) and continued by his son, Sir John Harington of Kelston (1560-1612). One, a collection of verse and some prose, is in the British Library (Add. MS 36529); the other, an anthology of Tudor poems, is the Arundel Harington MS: for further particulars of the two MSS see SIR JOHN HARINGTON, HrJ 339, 337. The complete text of the second MS is printed in Hughey, *Arundel*; a MS transcript made c. 1810 for George F. Nott is in the British Library (Add. MS 28635) and was used by Padelford and Rollins in place of the Arundel MS itself (this transcript is not given entries). These MSS essentially supplement the main printed text of Surrey's poems, Richard Tottel's Miscellany *Songes and Sonettes* (London, 1557).

A few copies of particular poems are to be found in other 16th-century MS miscellanies and are recorded in the entries. A copy of one poem of Surrey's, '*When ragyng loue, with extreme payne*', can be found in a mid-17th-century miscellany in the Folger (MS V. a. 339, f. 127v), but it is a forgery by J. P. Collier: see Giles E. Dawson, 'John Payne Collier's Great Forgery', *SB*, 24 (1971), 1-26 (p. 9).

The canon accepted in the *Index* is based on Padelford, from which first lines (but not his supplied titles) are cited. Although, as with Wyatt, the canon is likely to remain a subject of debate, there have been no convincing attempts as yet to amend Padelford's version of it. In his article 'Surrey Poems in the Blage Manuscript', *N & Q*, 205 (October 1960), 368-70, Kenneth Muir attributed to Surrey a verse fragment beginning '... degrese of Lyghtnes lefte be hy[nd]e' and a poem beginning 'If right be rackt, and ouerronne', both of which appear in the Blage MS at Trinity College, Dublin (MS 160, ff. 176v, 179). The second poem also appears in the Arundel Harington MS (f. 22r-v) and is inscribed in part by Queen Elizabeth in a New Testament in the British Library (Department of Printed Books, C. 45. a. 13), but it appears in the Blage MS in the autograph of John Harington (d. 1582); both pieces are attributed to him on clear evidence in Hughey, *Harington of Stepney*, pp. 87, 257, and 85-6, 256 (with a facsimile of f. 179 facing p. 53). Ruth Hughey herself (*Arundel*, II, 84-5) tentatively attributed to Surrey a poem beginning 'Vnto thee lyving lord for pardon do I praye' which appears in the Arundel Harington MS (f. 37v) and elsewhere, but because of the lack of positive evidence to support this attribution this poem has been similarly excluded from the entries.

MS musical settings of Surrey's poems are included, even those cases where only the incipit is quoted. Most of the settings are discussed in Mumford. That work, and

Hughey, *Library* (1935), 394-5, mention also a printed exemplum of *Songes and Sonettes* (London, 1557) which was once owned by Sir W. W. Wynne and in which contemporary MS musical notation was written in the margins against three of Surrey's poems: '*In winters iust returne, when Boreas gan his raigne*', '*Marshall, the thinges for to attayne*', and '*When youthe had ledd me half the race*'. This volume was probably destroyed by fire with the bulk of the Wynnstay library on 5-6 March 1858. The tunes were printed in George F. Nott's edition of *Songs and Sonnets* (1814?), but that edition suffered the similar fate of being almost totally destroyed by fire; the only surviving exemplum to contain the music is owned by the Duke of Norfolk at Arundel Castle (ref. 13C).

In his edition of *The Works of Surrey and Wyatt* (1815-16), I, Appendix II, iii-vi, Nott prints the text of a MS household book of the Howard family which is cited in Casady's biography of Surrey (p. 23 seq.) as an important biographical source. The MS is now at the University of California at Berkeley: see Melvin J. Tucker, 'California MS. AC 523, formerly Phillipps MS. 3841', *N & Q*, 209 (October 1964), 374-6.

Some additional items of possible editorial interest are certain printed volumes annotated by George F. Nott. Nott's annotations on sources of Surrey's poems and his collations of MSS and printed texts can be found in the following: in two imperfect exempla of his edition of *Songs and Sonnets* (1814?) in the British Library (Department of Printed Books, C. 60. 0. 13, and 11623. ff. 1), the first of which is accompanied by an octavo volume of his MS notes; in an exemplum of *Poems of Henry Howard, Earl of Surrey*, printed for W. Meares and J. Brown (London, 1717), at Arundel Castle; and in an exemplum of *Songes and Sonettes*, reprinted by E. Curll (London, 1717), also at Arundel Castle. It should be noted that in his annotations Nott cites the Arundel Harington MS as 'Harington MS. No. II' and the Harington miscellany, Add. MS 36529, as the 'Hill MS' (it once belonged to Thomas Hill (1760-1840)). Those volumes, as well as other interesting volumes of Surrey's poems at Arundel Castle, are discussed in Hughey, *Library* (1935). Among other printed exempla of Surrey's poems which contain notable MS annotations are an exemplum of *Songes and Sonnets* (London, 1587) annotated by John Horne Tooke (1736-1812), now at Arundel Castle; two exempla of the Meares-Brown edition of Surrey's poems (1717), one annotated by Thomas Park (1759-1834), the other annotated by Park and by Joseph Haslewood (1769-1833), now in the British Library (Department of Printed Books, 1077. g. 17 and 1077. g. 13. (1)); and an exemplum of *The Poems of Henry Howard, Earl of Surrey*, ed. W. Pickering (London, 1831), annotated by F. T. Palgrave (1824-97), also in the British Library (Department of Printed Books, 11612. i. 3).

PB.

ARRANGEMENT

Verse: Poems and translations SuH 1-75.

See also Addenda to Part 2, p. 634

Henry Howard, Earl of Surrey

VERSE

POEMS AND TRANSLATIONS

SuH 1 *'As oft as I behold and see'.*

Copy of lines 1-24, 30-6, in a Harington miscellany; mid-late 16th century.

First pub. in *Songes and Sonettes* (London, 1557). Printed from this MS in Padelford, No. 14, pp. 64-5.

British Library, Add. MS 36529, f. 53v.

SuH 2 *'Brittle beautie, that nature made so fraile'.*

Copy, with a correction in another hand, in the Arundel Harington MS; mid-late 16th century.

First pub. in *Songes and Sonettes* (London, 1557); Padelford, No. 7, p. 59; doubtfully ascribed to Surrey and possibly written by Thomas, Lord Vaux: see Hughey, *Arundel*, II, 444-6, and Rollins, II, 137. Printed from this MS in Hughey, *Arundel*, I, No. 298, pp. 346-6; the Nott transcript of this MS recorded in Padelford, p. 209.

Owned by the Duke of Norfolk, Arundel Castle, MSS (Special Press), 'Harrington MS. Temp. Eliz', f. 212v.

--- *'...degrese of Lyghtnes lefte be hy[nd]e'.*

See INTRODUCTION.

SuH 3 *'Dyvers thy death doo dyverslye bemone'.*

Copy in a Harington miscellany; mid-late 16th century.

First pub. in *Songes and Sonettes* (London, 1557). Printed from this MS in Padelford, No. 45, p. 97.

British Library, Add. MS 36529, f. 57.

SuH 4 *'Eache beeste can chuse his feere according to his minde'.*

Copy in the Arundel Harington MS; mid-late 16th century.

First pub. in *Songes and Sonettes* (London, 1557); Padelford, No. 34, pp. 88-90. Printed from this MS in Hughey, *Arundel*, I, No. 78, pp. 123-5; printed from the Nott transcript of this MS in Padelford.

Owned by the Duke of Norfolk, Arundel Castle, MSS (Special Press), 'Harrington MS. Temp. Eliz.', ff. 51-2.

SuH 5 *Ecclesiastes 1* ('I, Salamon, Dauids sonne, King of Ierusalem').

Copy in the Arundel Harington MS; mid-late 16th century.

First pub. in *Nugae Antiquae* (London, 1804), II, 339-42; Padelford, No. 48, pp. 100-1. Printed from this MS in Hughey, *Arundel*, I, No. 86, pp. 133-4; the Nott transcript of this MS collated in Padelford.

Owned by the Duke of Norfolk, Arundel Castle, MSS (Special Press), 'Harrington MS. Temp. Eliz.', f. 55r-v.

SuH 6 -----

Copy, with corrections, in a Harington miscellany; mid-late 16th century.

Printed from this MS in Padelford; collated in Hughey, *Arundel*, II, 113-14.

British Library, Add. MS 36529, ff. 58v-9.

SuH 7 *Ecclesiastes 2* ('From pensif fanzies, then, I gan my hart reuoke').

Copy in the Arundel Harington MS; mid-late 16th century.

First pub. in *Nugae Antiquae* (London, 1804), II, 343-8; Padelford, No. 49, pp. 101-3. Printed from this MS in Hughey, *Arundel*, I, No. 87, pp. 134-6; the Nott transcript of this MS collated in Padelford.

Owned by the Duke of Norfolk, Arundel Castle, MSS (Special Press), 'Harrington MS. Temp. Eliz', ff. 55v-6v.

SuH 8 -----

Copy in a Harington miscellany; mid-late 16th century.

Printed from this MS in Padelford; collated in Hughey, *Arundel*, II, 114-15.

British Library, Add. MS 36529, ff. 59-60.

SuH 9 *Ecclesiastes 3* ('Like to the stereles boote that swerues with euery wynde').

Copy in the Arundel Harington MS; mid-late 16th century.

First pub. in *Nugae Antiquae* (London, 1804), II, 348-52; Padelford, No. 50, pp. 103-5. Printed from this MS in Hughey, *Arundel*, I, No. 88, pp. 136-8; the Nott transcript of this MS collated in Padelford.

Owned by the Duke of Norfolk, Arundel Castle, MSS (Special Press), 'Harrington MS. Temp. Eliz.', ff. 56v-7v.

Ecclesiastes 3

SuH 10 -----

Copy, with corrections in another hand, in a Harington miscellany; mid-late 16th century.

Printed from this MS in Padelford; collated in Hughey, *Arundel*, II, 116-17.

British Library, Add. MS 36529, ff. 60-1.

SuH 11 *Ecclesiastes 4* ('When I be thought me well, vnder the restles soon').

Copy in the Arundel Harington MS; mid-late 16th century.

First pub. in *Nugae Antiquae* (London, 1804), II, 352-6; Padelford, No. 51, pp. 105-6. Printed from this MS in Hughey, *Arundel*, I, No. 89, pp. 138-40; the Nott transcript of this MS collated in Padelford.

Owned by the Duke of Norfolk, Arundel Castle, MSS (Special Press), 'Harrington MS. Temp. Eliz.', ff. 57v-8.

SuH 12 -----

Copy, with corrections in another hand, in a Harington miscellany; mid-late 16th century.

Printed from this MS in Padelford; collated in Hughey, *Arundel*, II, 117-18.

British Library, Add. MS 36529, ff. 61-2.

SuH 13 *Ecclesiastes 5* ('When that repentant teares hathe clensyd clere from ill').

Copy in the Arundel Harington MS; mid-late 16th century.

First pub. in *Nugae Antiquae* (London, 1804), II, 356-60; Padelford, No. 52, pp. 107-8. Printed from this MS in Hughey, *Arundel*, I, No. 90, pp. 140-2; the Nott transcript of this MS collated in Padelford.

Owned by the Duke of Norfolk, Arundel Castle, MSS (Special Press), 'Harrington MS. Temp. Eliz.', ff. 58-9.

SuH 14 -----

Copy, with corrections in another hand, in a Harington miscellany; mid-late 16th century.

Printed from this MS in Padelford; collated in Hughey, *Arundel*, II, 118-20.

British Library, Add. MS 36529, f. 62r-v.

SuH 15 *'From Tuscan cam my ladies worthi race'*.

Copy, with a correction in another hand, in a Harington miscellany; mid-late 16th century.

First pub. in *Songes and Sonettes* (London, 1557). Printed from this MS in Padelford, No. 29, p. 83.

British Library, Add. MS 36529, f. 55.

SuH 16 *'Good ladies, you that have your pleasure in exyle'*.

Copy in the Arundel Harington MS; mid-late 16th century.

First pub. in *Songes and Sonettes* (London, 1557); Padelford, No. 33, pp. 87-8. Printed from this MS in Hughey, *Arundel*, I, No. 85, pp. 132-3; printed from the Nott transcript of this MS in Padelford.

Owned by the Duke of Norfolk, Arundel Castle, MSS (Special Press), 'Harrington MS. Temp. Eliz.', f. 54r-v.

SuH 17 *'Gyrtt in my glitlesse gowne, as I sytt heare and sowe'*.

Copy, with corrections in one or more other hands, in the Arundel Harington MS; mid-late 16th century.

First pub. in *Songes and Sonettes* (London, 1557); Padelford, No. 27, pp. 79-80. Printed from this MS in Hughey, *Arundel*, I, No. 72, pp. 117-18; printed from the Nott transcript of this MS in Padelford.

Owned by the Duke of Norfolk, Arundel Castle, MSS (Special Press), 'Harrington MS. Temp. Eliz.', f. 37.

SuH 18 *'I neuer saw youe, madam, laye aparte'*.

Copy in a Harington miscellany; mid-late 16th century.

First pub. in *Songes and Sonettes* (London, 1557). Printed from this MS in Padelford, No. 3, p. 57.

British Library, Add. MS 36529, f. 55v.

SuH 19 *'I that Vlysses yeres haue spent'*.

Copy, ascribed to Surrey, in a composite volume of MSS; mid-late 16th century.

First pub. in *Songes and Sonettes* (London, 1557); Padelford, No. 20, pp. 70-1. Edited from this MS in Padelford, where Surrey's authorship is doubted; see also Rollins, II, 322-3.

British Library, Harley MS 78, f. 30v.

SuH 20 *'If care do cause men cry, why do not I complaine?'*.

Copy in a composite volume of MSS, chiefly

astrological papers; late 16th-early 17th century.

First pub. in *Songes and Sonettes* (London, 1557); Padelford, No. 28, pp. 80-2. This MS recorded in Rollins, II, 313.

Bodleian, MS Ashmole 176, f. 97r-v.

SuH 21 -----

Copy in a musical setting in a MS songbook compiled by Robert Taitt, schoolmaster of Lauder, Berwickshire; [1676-89].

This MS recorded in Walter H. Rubsamen, 'Scottish and English Music in the Renaissance in a Newly-Discovered Manuscript', *Festschrift Heinrich Besseler* (Leipzig, 1961), 259-84.

Clark Library, Los Angeles, T 135Z. B724 1677-89 Bound, Cantus 7, ff. 37, 53'-54.

SuH 22 -----

Copy of a ten-stanza version in a musical setting in a Scottish MS book of roundels compiled by David Melvill; 1612.

Printed from this MS in *The Melvill Book of Roundels*, ed. Granville Bantock and H. Orsmond Anderton, Roxburghe Club (London, 1916), pp. 47-8, 199-200; recorded in Mumford, p. 12, and in Rollins, II, 313.

Library of Congress, Music Division, PR1105.R7 1916c.

SuH 22.5 See Addenda, p. 634.

SuH 23 -----

Copy in a musical setting in a MS transcript of the first edition (Aberdeen, 1662) of John Forbes, *Cantus, Songs and Fancies*; c. 1662.

Sandeman Library, Perth, N 16 (No. i).

SuH 24 -----

Copy in a musical setting in a MS book of verse and lute music; formerly among the papers of Lord Braye at Stanford Hall, Rugby; c. 1560.

Yale, Osborn Collection, Music MS 13, f. 22.

SuH 25 -----

Copy of the incipit in a musical setting, written in the counter-tenor MS part book of the 'St Andrews Psalter'; early 17th century.

This MS discussed, with a facsimile, in Mumford.

British Library, Add. MS 33933, f. 85.

SuH 26 -----

Copy of the incipit in a musical setting for the lute in a MS music book; early 17th century.

This MS discussed, with a facsimile, in Mumford.

British Library, Royal MS App. 58, f. 52.

SuH 27 -----

Copy of the incipit in a musical setting for the lute, transcribed by one Ralph Bowle on the end-papers of a 15th century MS volume of statutes of the reigns of Henry V and Henry VI; 18 May 1558.

This MS discussed, with a facsimile, in Mumford.

British Library, Stowe MS 389, f. 120.

SuH 28 -----

Copy of the incipit in a musical setting, written in one of the MS part books of the 'St Andrews Psalter'; early 17th century.

Trinity College, Dublin, MS 412, f. 55.

--- *'If he that erst the fourme so liuely drewe'*.

See SuH 75.

--- *'If right be rackt, and ouerronne'*.

See INTRODUCTION.

SuH 29 *'In Cipres springes — wheras dame Venus dwelt'*.

Copy in a Harington miscellany; mid-late 16th century.

First pub. in *Songes and Sonettes* (London, 1557). Printed from this MS in Padelford, No. 5, p. 58.

British Library, Add. MS 36529, f. 56.

SuH 30 *'In the rude age when scyence was not so rife'*.

Copy in a Harington miscellany; mid-late 16th century.

First pub. in *Songes and Sonettes* (London, 1557). Printed from this MS in Padelford, No. 44, p. 97.

British Library, Add. MS 36529, f. 56v.

SuH 31 *'In winters iust returne, when Boreas gan his raigne'*.

Copy of the incipit in a musical setting for the lute in a MS music book; early 16th century.

'In winters iust returne, when Boreas gan his raigne'

First pub. in *Songes and Sonettes* (London, 1557); Padelford, No. 24, pp. 75-7. This MS discussed, with a facsimile, in Mumford.

British Library, Royal MS App. 58, f. 52.

SuH 32 -----

Copy of the incipit in a musical setting for the lute in a miscellany; c. 1559-1610.

This MS discussed in Mumford.

Folger, MS V. a. 159, f. 13.

SuH 32.5 See Addenda, p. 634.

--- -----

See also INTRODUCTION.

SuH 33 *'Laid in my quyett bedd, in study as I weare'.*

Copy in the Arundel Harington MS; mid-late 16th century.

First pub. in *Songes and Sonettes* (London, 1557); Padelford, No. 43, pp. 95-6. Printed from this MS in Hughey, *Arundel*, I, No. 76, pp. 121-2; printed from the Nott transcript of this MS in Padelford.

Owned by the Duke of Norfolk, Arundel Castle, MSS (Special Press), 'Harrington MS. Temp. Eliz.', f. 50.

SuH 34 -----

Copy of lines 1-12 in a composite volume of MSS; mid-16th century.

Printed from this MS in Hughey, *Arundel*, II, 91-2; recorded in Rollins, II, 157.

British Library, Cotton MS Titus A. XXIV, f. 83.

SuH 35 *'London, hast thow accused me'.*

Copy in the Arundel Harington MS; mid-late 16th century.

First pub. in *Nugae Antiquae* (London, 1804), II, 336-8; Padelford, No. 32, pp. 85-7. Printed from this MS in Hughey, *Arundel*, I, No. 75, pp. 119-21; the Nott transcript of this MS collated in Padelford.

Owned by the Duke of Norfolk, Arundel Castle, MSS (Special Press), 'Harrington MS. Temp. Eliz.', f. 49r-v.

SuH 36 -----

Copy in a Harington miscellany; mid-late 16th century.

Printed from this MS in Padelford.

British Library, Add. MS 36529, f. 52r-v.

SuH 37 *'Love that doth raine and liue within my thought'.*

Copy in a Harington miscellany; mid-late 16th century.

First pub. in *Songes and Sonettes* (London, 1557). Printed from this MS in Padelford, No. 4, p. 57.

British Library, Add. MS 36529, f. 55v.

SuH 38 *'Marshall, the thinges for to attayne'.*

Copy, headed 'A translation of the Earl of Surreys out of Martiall directed by him to one Maister Warner' and here beginning 'Warner the things for to attayn', in a MS of the Epigrams of Sir John Harington (see HrJ 20); c. 1603.

First pub. at the end of Book III in William Baldwin, *A treatise of Morrall phylosophye* (London, 1547/8); *Songes and Sonettes* (London, 1557). Printed from this MS (together with Harington's own appended epigram to John Davies of Hereford) by 'EU. Hood' [i.e. Joseph Haslewood] in *The Gentleman's Magazine*, 97. ii (November 1827), 392.

British Library, Add. MS 12049, p. 150.

SuH 39 -----

Copy in a Harington miscellany; mid-late 16th century.

Printed from this MS in Padelford, No. 41, p. 94.

British Library, Add. MS 36529, f. 54v.

SuH 40 -----

Copy, here beginning 'My frende the thinges for to attayne', in a composite volume of MSS; mid-16th century.

This MS recorded in Rollins, II, 150.

British Library, Cotton MS Titus A. XXIV, f. 80.

SuH 41 -----

Copy in the hand of Sir John Harington, headed 'A translation of the Earle of Surreys out of Martiall, directed by him to one Maister Warner' and here beginning 'Warner the things for to attayne', in the autograph copy of Harington's Epigrams which he presented to Prince Henry (see HrJ 21); 1605.

Folger, MS V. a. 249, pp. 200-1.

SuH 42 -----

Copy written on the last leaf (Gg 4^v) of a printed exemplum of *Songes and Sonettes* (London, 1557); late 16th century.

'Marshall, the thinges for to attayne'

This item recorded in Rollins, II, 150.

Trinity College, Cambridge, Capell W. 1.

SuH 42.5 See Addenda, p. 635.

SuH 43 -----

Copy of the incipit, here 'My friends', in a musical setting for the keyboard in a MS music book compiled by Thomas Mulliner; mid-16th century.

This MS discussed, with a facsimile, in Mumford; edited in *The Mulliner Book*, ed. Denis Stevens, 2nd edition, Musica Britannica I (London, 1973), p. 50.

British Library, Add. MS 30513, f. 65v.

SuH 44 -----

Copy of the incipit, here 'My friends', in a musical setting by John Shepherd, in a MS music part book (bass); 16th century.

This MS recorded in Mumford, p. 15.

Public Record Office, SP.1/246, f. 25v.

--- -----

See also INTRODUCTION.

SuH 45 *'O happy dames, that may embrace'.*

Copy in a verse miscellany compiled principally by some ladies of the Royal Household, later owned by the Dukes of Devonshire; c. 1530s-40s.

First pub. in *Songes and Sonettes* (London, 1557); Padelford, No. 21, pp. 71-2; printed and tentatively attributed to John Harington (1520?-82) in Hughey, *Harington of Stepney*, pp. 131-2, 286-9. This MS collated in Padelford and in Hughey, *Harington of Stepney*.

British Library, Add. MS 17492, f. 55r-v.

SuH 46 -----

Copy in a musical setting by John Shepherd in a MS music part book (bass); 16th century.

This MS recorded in Mumford, p. 15.

Public Record Office, SP.1/246, ff. 31v-2v.

SuH 47 -----

Copy of the first stanza in a composite volume of MSS; mid-late 16th century.

This MS collated in Hughey, *Harington of Stepney*; recorded in Padelford, p. 197.

British Library, Harley MS 78, f. 30v.

SuH 48 -----

Copy of the incipit in a musical setting for the keyboard by John Shepherd, in a MS music book compiled by Thomas Mulliner; mid-16th century.

Edited from this MS in *The Mulliner Book*, ed. Denis Stevens, 2nd edition, Musica Britannica I (London, 1973), pp. 81-2; discussed, with a facsimile, in Mumford; recorded in Rollins, II, 143. Another setting of a song 'O ye happy dames', possibly the same poem, is on f. 3r-v (see Stevens, p. 1).

British Library, Add. MS 30513, ff. 107-8.

SuH 49 *'Of thy lyfe, Thomas, this compasse well mark'.*

Copy, with corrections, in a composite volume of MSS; mid-late 16th century.

First pub. in *Songes and Sonettes* (London, 1557); Padelford, No. 42, pp. 94-5. This MS collated in Padelford, p. 201.

British Library, Harley MS 78, f. 29.

SuH 50 *Psalm 8* ('Thie name, O Lord, howe greate is fownd before our sight!').

Copy, with corrections in another hand, in the Arundel Harington MS; mid-late 16th century.

First pub. (from this MS) in *The Works of Henry Howard, Earl of Surrey, and of Sir Thomas Wyatt the Elder*, ed. G.F. Nott, 2 vols (London, 1815-16), I, 85-6; Padelford, No. 53, pp. 108-10. Printed from this MS in Hughey, *Arundel*, I, No. 79, pp. 125-7; printed from the Nott MS transcript of this MS in Padelford.

Owned by the Duke of Norfolk, Arundel Castle, MSS (Special Press), 'Harrington MS. Temp. Eliz.', f. 52r-v.

SuH 51 *Psalm 55* ('Giue eare to my suit, Lord! fromward hide not thy face').

Copy, headed 'Exaudi Deus orationem meam. Ps:-55', in the Arundel Harington MS; mid-late 16th century.

First pub. in *Nugae Antiquae* (London, 1804), II, 368-71; Padelford, No. 54, pp. 110-11. Printed from this MS in Hughey, *Arundel*, I, No. 84, pp. 130-2; the Nott transcript of this MS collated in Padelford.

Owned by the Duke of Norfolk, Arundel Castle, MSS (Special Press), 'Harrington MS. Temp. Eliz.', ff. 53v-4.

SuH 52 -----

Copy, with corrections in another hand, headed 'Exaudi Deus orationem meam. Ps:-55', in a

Harington miscellany; mid-late 16th century.

Printed from this MS in Padelford; collated in Hughey, *Arundel*, II, 107-8.

British Library, Add. MS 36529, f. 65r-v.

SuH 53 *Psalm 73* ('Thoughe, Lorde, to Israell thy graces plentuous be').

Copy headed 'Qm̃ bonus Israel Deus. Ps. Lxxiij', in the Arundel Harington MS; mid-late 16th century.

First pub. in *Nugae Antiquae* (London, 1804), II, 364-8; Padelford, No. 56, pp. 112-14. Printed from this MS in Hughey, *Arundel*, I, No. 83, pp. 128-30; the Nott transcript of this MS collated in Padelford.

Owned by the Duke of Norfolk, Arundel Castle, MSS (Special Press), 'Harrington MS. Temp. Eliz.', ff. 53-3v (bis).

SuH 54 -----

Copy, with corrections in another hand, headed 'Qm̃ bonus Israel Deus. Ps. Lxxiij', in a Harington miscellany; mid-late 16th century.

Printed from this MS in Padelford; collated in Hughey, *Arundel*, II, 105.

British Library, Add. MS 36529, f. 64r-v.

SuH 55 *Psalm 88* ('Oh Lorde, vppon whose will dependeth my welfare').

Copy, headed 'Domine deus salutis. Psal: 98', in the Arundel Harington MS; mid-late 16th century.

First pub. in *Nugae Antiquae* (London, 1804), II, 361-3; Padelford, No. 55, pp. 111-12. Printed from this MS in Hughey, *Arundel*, I, No. 81, pp. 127-8; the Nott transcript of this MS collated in Padelford.

Owned by the Duke of Norfolk, Arundel Castle, MSS (Special Press), 'Harrington MS. Temp. Eliz.', ff. 52v-3.

SuH 56 -----

Copy, headed 'Domine deus salutis. Psal: 98', in a Harington miscellany; mid-late 16th century.

Printed from this MS in Padelford; collated in Hughey, *Arundel*, II, 102-4.

British Library, Add. MS 36529, f. 63r-v.

SuH 57 *'Set me wheras the sonne doth perche the grene'*.

Copy in a Harington miscellany; mid-late 16th century.

First pub. in *Songes and Sonettes* (London, 1557). Printed from this MS in Padelford, No. 6, p. 58.

British Library, Add. MS 36529, f. 57.

SuH 58 -----

Copy in a verse miscellany; c. 1630.

British Library, Egerton MS 2230, f. 62.

SuH 59 *'So crewell prison! howe could betyde, alas!'*.

Copy in a Harington miscellany; mid-late 16th century.

First pub. in *Songes and Sonettes* (London, 1557). Printed from this MS in Padelford, No. 31, pp. 84-5.

British Library, Add. MS 36529, f. 51r-v.

SuH 60 *'Suche waywarde wais hath love, that moste parte in discorde'*.

Copy in the Arundel Harington MS; mid-late 16th century.

First pub. in *Songes and Sonettes* (London, 1557); Padelford, No. 22, pp. 73-4. Printed from this MS in Hughey, *Arundel*, I, No. 77, pp. 122-3; the Nott transcript of this MS collated in Padelford.

Owned by the Duke of Norfolk, Arundel Castle, MSS (Special Press), 'Harrington MS. Temp. Eliz.', ff. 50-1.

SuH 61 -----

Copy of lines 1-30, 33-50, with corrections in a later hand, in a Harington miscellany; mid-late 16th century.

Printed from this MS in Padelford; collated in Hughey, *Arundel*, II, 93-5.

British Library, Add. MS 36529, f. 53.

SuH 62 -----

Copy in the hand of John Harington of Stepney (1520?-82), ascribed to 'H. S.', in a verse miscellany owned c. 1545-6 by Sir George Blage (1512-51); mid-16th century.

Printed from this MS in Kenneth Muir, 'Surrey Poems in the Blage Manuscript', *N & Q*, 205 (October 1960), 368-70.

Trinity College, Dublin, MS 160, f. 178r-v.

SuH 63 *'Th' Assyryans king — in peas, with fowle desyre'*.

Copy in a Harington miscellany; mid-late 16th century.

'Th' Assyryans king -- in peas, with fowle desyre'

First pub. in *Songes and Sonettes* (London, 1557). Printed from this MS in Padelford, No. 40, pp. 93-4.

British Library, Add. MS 36529, f. 56v.

SuH 64 *'The greate Macedon, that out of Persy chased'.*

Copy in a Harington miscellany; mid-late 16th century.

First pub. in *Songes and Sonettes* (London, 1557). Printed from this MS in Padelford, No. 38, p. 93.

British Library, Add. MS 36529, f. 56.

SuH 65 -----

Copy in the 'Egerton MS' of Sir Thomas Wyatt's poems; c. 1539-42?

This MS collated in Padelford.

British Library, Egerton MS 2711, f. 85v.

SuH 66 *'The sonne hath twyse brought forthe the tender grene'.*

Copy of lines 50-5, here beginning 'Vnto my self, vnlesse this carefull song', in the Arundel Harington MS; imperfect; mid-late 16th century.

First pub. in *Songes and Sonettes* (London, 1557); Padelford, No. 11, pp. 60-2. Printed from this MS in Hughey, *Arundel*, I, No. 74, p. 119; the Nott transcript of this MS collated in Padelford.

Owned by the Duke of Norfolk, Arundel Castle, MSS (Special Press), 'Harrington MS. Temp. Eliz.', f. 49.

SuH 67 -----

Copy of lines 1-18, 21-55, with corrections in a later hand, in a Harington miscellany; mid-late 16th century.

Printed from this MS in Padelford and in Hughey, *Arundel*, II, 86-8.

British Library, Add. MS 36529, f. 50r-v.

SuH 68 *'The soudden stormes that heaue me to and froo'.*

Copy in the Arundel Harington MS; mid-late 16th century.

First pub. in *Nugae Antiquae* (London, 1804), II, 364; Padelford, No. 36, p. 91. Printed from this MS in Hughey, *Arundel*, I, No. 82, p. 128; printed from the Nott transcript of this MS in Padelford.

Owned by the Duke of Norfolk, Arundel Castle, MSS (Special Press), 'Harrington MS. Temp. Eliz.', f. 53.

SuH 69 -----

Copy in a Harington miscellany; mid-late 16th century.

This MS collated in Padelford and in Hughey, *Arundel*, II, 104-5.

British Library, Add. MS 36529, f. 63v.

--- *'Vnto thee lyving lord for pardon do I praye'.*

See INTRODUCTION.

SuH 70 *'Virgil's Aeneid. Book IV* ('But now the wounded quene, with heavie care').

Copy, headed 'P. Virgilii Maronis Aeneidos Liber Quartus Britannica Sermoni Donatus per Comitem S.'; c. 1568.

First pub. London, [1554], ed. John Day; ed. Richard Tottel (London, 1557); ed. Florence H. Ridley (Berkeley & Los Angeles, 1963). Printed from this MS (with the text of the 1557 edition on facing pages) in Padelford, No. 58, pp. 122-65; collated in Ridley.

British Library, Hargrave MS 205, ff. 1-8.

--- *'When ragyng loue, with extreme payne'.*

See INTRODUCTION.

SuH 71 *'When Windesor walles sustained my wearied arme'.*

Copy in a Harington miscellany; mid-late 16th century.

First pub. in *Songes and Sonettes* (London, 1557). Printed from this MS in Padelford, No. 30, p. 83.

British Library, Add. MS 36529, f. 55.

SuH 72 *'When youthe had ledd me half the race'.*

Copy in a Harington miscellany; mid-late 16th century.

First pub. in *Songes and Sonettes* (London, 1557). Printed from this MS in Padelford, No. 15, pp. 65-6.

British Library, Add. MS 36529, f. 54.

'When youthe had ledd me half the race'

--- -----

See also INTRODUCTION.

SuH 63 *'Wher recheles youthe in a vnquiet brest'.*

Copy in the Arundel Harington MS; mid-late 16th century.

First pub. in *Nugae Antiquae* (London, 1804), II, 360; Padelford, No. 35, p. 91. Printed from this MS in Hughey, *Arundel*, I, No. 80, p. 127; the Nott transcript of this MS collated in Padelford.

Owned by the Duke of Norfolk, Arundel Castle, MSS (Special Press), 'Harrington MS. Temp. Eliz.', f. 52v.

SuH 74 -----

Copy in a Harington miscellany; mid-late 16th century.

Printed from this MS in Padelford; collated in Hughey, *Arundel*, II, 102-4.

British Library, Add. MS 36529, f. 63.

SuH 75 *'Yf he that erst the fourme so liuelye drewe'.*

Copy in a Harington miscellany; mid-late 16th century.

First pub. (from this MS) in *Nugae Antiquae* (London, 1804), II, 339. Printed from this MS in Padelford, No. 10, p. 60.

British Library, Add. MS 36529, f. 56v.

William Tindale

1494?-1536

For abbreviations used throughout Volume I, see p.xi.

INTRODUCTION

A single autograph of Tindale is known. It is a letter in Latin written from his cell to the Prison Governor at Vilvorde, the Marquis of Bergen, asking for warmer clothes for the winter, a lamp to relieve the tedium of dark evenings, and his Hebrew Bible, grammar and dictionary; it was written a few months before he was burned at the stake. The letter, which is preserved in the Archives générales du Royaume in Brussels (Office fiscal, liasse 1330), is printed in J. F. Mozley, *William Tyndale* (London, 1937), pp. 333-5; a reduced facsimile and English translation appear in G. E. Duffield, *The Work of William Tyndale* (Appleford, Berkshire, 1964), pp. 400-1. It is here reproduced full-size in FACSIMILE XXXI.

None of the works or translations attributed to Tindale by his biographers is known to exist in manuscript. The only item to receive an entry in the *Index* is an 18th-century transcript of a MS tract which appears to belong to Tindale's religious faction and has some stylistic affinities with his work.

PB.

ARRANGEMENT

Prose TiW 1.

FACSIMILE XXXI — William Tindale: Letter in Latin to the Marquis of Bergen (Prison Governor at Vilvorde), [1535-6]. Archives générales du royaume, Brussels, Office fiscal, liasse 1330. Reproduced by permission of the Archives generales du Royaume, Belguim.

Credo non latere te, vir prestantissime, qd de me statutu sit.
Quam ob rem, tuaz dnationem rogatam habeo, idqz per dnm Jesum,
vt si mihi per hyeme hic manendu sit, sollicites apud dnm
cōmissariu, si forte dignari velit, de rebz meis quas habet,
mittere calidiore biretu, frigg enim patior i capite nimiu,
oppssus perpetuo catarro, qui sub testudine nonnihil augetr.
Calidiore qz tunicam, na hec qua heo admodu tenuis e. Ite
pannu ad caligas reficiendas. Duplois detrita e. Camisee
detrite sut etiaz. Camiseaz laneaz hz, si mittere velit.
Habeo qz apud eu, ~~capro~~ caligas ex crassiori panno
ad superinduendu. Nocturna birreta calidiora habet etia
Vtqz vesperi lucerna habere liceat, Tediosu qde e per tenebras
solitariu sedere. Maxime aute omniu tuaz clementiaz
rogo atqz obsecro, vt ex aio agere velit apud dnm
cōmissariu, quatenus dignari velit mihi cōcedere
bibliaz hebraica, grammatica hebraica, et vocabulariu
hebraicu, vt eo studio tepus cōteraz. Sic tibi obtingat
qd maxime optas, modo cu aie tue salute fiat. Veru
si aliud cōsiliu de me ceptu est, ante hyeme pficiendu,
patiens ero, dei expectans voluntate, ad gloriaz gre dni
mei Jesu Christi, cuius Sps tuu semper regat pectus. Ame.

W. Tindalus.

William Tindale

PROSE

TiW 1 *A commyssion sent to the bloudy byshop of London, and to al conuents of Frers By the high and mighty prince and king, lord Sathanas the deuill of hell.*

Copy of a tract possibly by Tindale (?); inscribed 'Transcribed from a copy in the hands of Mr. George Ballard, September 20th: 1740'.

First pub. (from this MS) in John Fines, 'An Unnoticed Tract of the Tyndale-More Dispute?', *Bulletin of the Institute of Historical Research*, 42 (1969), 220-30.

British Library, Stowe MS 269.

Cyril Tourneur

1575?-1626

ABBREVIATIONS

Nicoll *The Works of Cyril Tourneur*, ed. Allardyce Nicoll (London, [1930]).

For abbreviations used throughout Volume I, see p.xi.

INTRODUCTION

Cyril Tourneur is known to have written a few plays and other works but his reputation is largely based on *The Revenger's Tragedy*, a play which, however, may well have been written by Thomas Middleton. There are no MSS of this drama (or of any part of it); nor is there any known specimen of Tourneur's autograph.

Five early copies have been located of the *Character of Salisbury* (ToC 2-6). This prose piece was attributed by Logan Pearsall Smith to Sir Henry Wotton because of its presence in the Burley MS (ToC 2) but was assigned to Tourneur by Nicoll. Tourneur's authorship is supported by ascription in three of the MSS, whereas it is nowhere assigned to Wotton, and only part of the Burley MS is transcribed from Wotton's papers (see SIR HENRY WOTTON, INTRODUCTION). One other item, a poem overlooked by Nicoll, may be added to the canon on the evidence of the attribution in a MS source (ToC 1).

Some music which has been thought to belong to Tourneur's lost play *The Nobleman* is preserved in the British Library (Add. MSS 10444, ff. 30v, 82, and 38539, f. 19): see Nicoll, pp. 25, 257-8, and Cutts, *Musique de la troupe de Shakespeare*, pp. 31-3, 138-9. However, it seems unlikely that this music has any connection with such a play but is rather for dances performed by a 'nobleman' in a masque: see *Four Hundred Songs and Dances from the Stuart Masque*, ed. Andrew J. Sabol (Providence, Rhode Island, 1978), No. 106.

PB.

ARRANGEMENT

Verse	ToC 1
Prose	ToC 2-6
Dramatic works	ToC 7

Cyril Tourneur

VERSE

ToC 1 *On the death of a child but one year old* ('How can Heaven's voyage, long or hard appear?').

Copy of a poem ascribed to 'Cecill Turner' in a verse miscellany appended to a MS volume of poems by John Donne; c. 1630s.

First pub. (from this MS) in A.B. Grosart, 'Literary-Finds in Trinity College, Dublin, and Elsewhere', *ES*, 26 (1899), 1-19 (pp. 16-17).

Trinity College, Dublin, MS 877, f. 257.

PROSE

ToC 2 *The Character of Robert Earl of Salisbury*.

Copy (unascribed) in the hand of William Parkhurst (fl. 1604-67), in a composite volume of MSS collected by him, among the papers of the Finch family of Burley-on-the-Hill, Rutland; [1612-41].

First pub. (from this MS) in Logan Pearsall Smith, *The Life and Letters of Sir Henry Wotton* (Oxford, 1907), II, 487-9; Nicoll, pp. 259-63. This MS recorded in Nicoll, pp. 330-6 (but not seen by him).

Leicestershire Record Office, DG. 7/Lit. 2, ff. 1-2v.

ToC 3 -----

Copy, here ascribed to 'William Turneur' but signed 'Cyrill Tourneur', in a volume of state papers; early 17th century.

Printed from this MS in Nicoll, pp. 259-63.

British Library, Harley MS 36, ff. 394-6v.

ToC 4 -----

Copy of an early version, ascribed to 'Jerill Turner', among the papers of the Clifton family of Clifton Hall, Nottinghamshire; early 17th century.

This MS recorded in *HMC*, 4th Report (1873), Appendix, p. 361, and *HMC* 55, *Various Collections*, Vol. VII (1914), p. 265; printed in Nicoll, pp. 297-8.

University of Nottingham, Clifton MS Cl LP 45.

ToC 5 -----

Copy (unascribed); early 17th century.

This MS collated in Nicoll, pp. 330-6.

Public Record Office, SP.14/69/59.

ToC 6 -----

Copy, here ascribed to 'Mr Serill Turneur', in a volume of historical tracts; 9 pages; c. 1625-40s.

Formerly Mostyn MS 262, this MS recorded in *HMC*, 4th Report (1874), Appendix, p. 361; recorded in Nicoll, pp. 330-6 (but not seen by him).

University College London, MS Ogden 36/1, item I.

DRAMATIC WORKS

ToC 7 *The Atheist's Tragedy*.

Extracts in a miscellany compiled by Edward Pudsey (1573-1613); 1600s.

First pub. London, 1611; Nicoll, pp. 173-255. This MS not recorded in Nicoll.

Bodleian, MS Eng. poet. d. 3, ff. 80v-1v.

Nicholas Udall

c.1505-56

For abbreviations used throughout Volume I, see p.xi.

INTRODUCTION

Only a few autographs of Nicholas Udall are known. One is an undated letter sent by him to a patron (? Sir Thomas Wriothesley), now in the British Library (Cotton MS Titus B. VIII, ff. 386-8); it is reproduced in part in Greg, *English Literary Autographs*, plate XXXII(a-b), and the full text is printed in *Nicholas Udall's Roister Doister*, ed. G. Scheurweghs, *Materials for the Study of the Old English Drama*, NS 16 (Louvain, 1939), pp. xxv-xxxii. This letter enables one to identify as autograph all the English verse ascribed to 'Vdallus' and some of the Latin verse in the presentation copy of the verses written by Udall and John Leland for the Coronation of Anne Boleyn (UdN 1). For a page of this MS see FACSIMILE XXXII. In addition, there is a series of autograph annotations in a printed grammar in the Folger (UdN 5), and the inscription 'Sum Nicolai Udalli, 1549' is found on the title page of a printed Zurich Latin Bible (1543) which was item 56 in catalogue No. 35 (1976) of Alan G. Thomas, and which is now in private hands.

Early MS copies of two other works which have been attributed to Udall are extant (UdN 2-3), but, except for an extract from a printed source (UdN 4), there is no MS of his most celebrated piece, *Roister Doister*. An early 19th-century transcript of a printed exemplum of *Thersites* (pub. 1562?), a play which has also been attributed to Udall, is in the Osborn Collection at Yale (d 68). Certain of the Loseley Papers (formerly at Loseley Park, Guildford) which relate to the Office of Revels and to performances arranged by Udall are now in the Folger (MSS L. b. 23; L. b. 26; L. b. 302). An indenture between John Ryther and Benjamin Gonson acknowledging that Ryther had handed over 66 bills, including one of Udall's of 5 February [1544/5], is in the Robert H. Taylor Collection at Princeton.

For the canon of works now attributed to Udall, see *NCBEL*, I, cols. 1414-15. A list of his works, including items no longer preserved or identified, is supplied in John Bale, *Scriptorum illustrium Maioris Brytanniae catalogus* (Basle, 1557), p. 717.

PB.

ARRANGEMENT

Verse	UdN 1
Prose	UdN 2
Dramatic works	UdN 3-4
Marginalia in printed books and manuscripts	UdN 5.

FACSIMILE XXXII — Nicholas Udall: One page of verses made for the coronation of Queen Anne, [1533] (UdN 1). British Library, Royal MS 18 A. LXIV, folio 11 verso. Reproduced by permission of the British Library.

Vdallus Queene Anne behold your seruaunts the three Graces,
Geuyng vnto your grace faithfull assistence,
With their moste goodly amiable faces.
Thei attend with their contynuall presence
Where your grace goeth, absent in your absence.
While your grace is here, thei also here dwell.
About the pleasaunte brinkes of this liue well.

Now here to bee thei thought it their duetie,
And presentely to salue you gracious queene,
Entring this daye in to this noble citie,
In suche triumphaunte wise, as hathe not been seene.
Whiche thing to your honour, and ioye, maye it beene.
These three sisters thought it their rebuke and shame,
This daye to bee slacke in honouring their Dame./.

Then ymmediatly folowed the
speches of the three graces in
this wise.

Aglaia. Hartie gladnes.

Vdallus. Queene Anne, whom to see this citie dooth reioyse,
Wee three Graces, ladies of all pleasaunce,
Clasped hand in hand, as of oon mynd and voice,
With our three giftes in all good assuraunce,
Shall now full your grace endue and enhaunce.
For I hartie gladnes by my name called,
Shall your harte replenishe with ioye vnfained.

Thaleia. Stable honour.

Vdallus And I stable honour ~~moste~~ gracious Queene Anne,
Ioynyng in your ioye, with this noble citie,
In honour and dignitee all that I can,
Shall you aduaunce, as yor grace is moste worthie.
You to assiste I am bound by my duetie,
For your vertues beinge incomparable,
You cannot but liue aye moste honourable.

Nicholas Udall

VERSE

*UdN 1 [*Verses made at the Coronation of Queen Anne*].

Autograph fair copy of Udall's English and Latin verses, together with John Leland's autograph Latin verses (see LeJ 8), for the coronation procession of Queen Anne Boleyn, 31 May 1533; presumably the copy presented to the Queen; [1533].

First pub. (from this MS) in John Nichols, *The Progresses and Public Processions of Queen Elizabeth*, I (London, 1788), i-xx; printed from this MS in F.J. Furnivall, 'Leland's and Udall's Verses before the Coronation of Anne Boleyn', *Ballads from Manuscripts*, Ballad Society (London, 1870), I, 364-401. Facsimile of one page (Udall's hand in the upper half) in Alfred Fairbank and Berthold Wolpe, *Renaissance Handwriting: An Anthology of Italic Scripts* (London, 1960), plate 23, and see also FACSIMILE XXXII. J.P. Collier's transcript of this MS (c. 1850) is in the Folger, MS N. b. 48.

British Library, Royal MS 18 A. LXIV.

PROSE

UdN 2 *An Answer to the articles of the commoners of Devonsheir and Cornewall.*

Copy, inscribed by a later hand 'Udall's ansuer to the Devon men'; c. 1549.

First pub. (from this MS) in *Troubles connected with the Prayer Book of 1549*, ed. Nicholas Pocock, Camden Society NS 37 (London, 1884), 141-93. G. Scheurweghs attributes this work to Philip Nichol in 'On An Answer to the Articles of the Rebels of Cornwall and Devonshire', *BMQ*, 8 (1933), 24-5; but see John Bale, *Scriptorum illustrium Maioris Brytanniae catalogus* (Basle, 1557), p. 717; William Peery, 'Udall as Timeserver, Part II', *N & Q*, 194 (2 April 1949), 138-41; William L. Edgerton, *Nicholas Udall* (New York, 1965), pp. 52, 118.

British Library, Royal MS 18 B. XI.

DRAMATIC WORKS

UdN 3 *Respublica.*

Copy of a play possibly by Udall, headed 'A merye enterlude entitled Respublica made in the year of oure Lord 1553...'; once owned by Sir Henry Spelman (1564?-1641) and by the Rev. Cox Macro (1683-1767); mid-16th century.

First pub. (from this MS) in John Payne Collier, *Illustrations of Old English Literature* (London, 1866), Vol. I; ed. W.W. Greg, EETS 226 (London, 1952); reproduced in facsimile in *The Macro Plays*, Tudor Facsimile Texts, Folio Series, No. 4 (1908). Collier's transcript of this MS is in the Folger, MS D. a. 40.

Pforzheimer Library, MS 40A.

UdN 4 *Roister Doister.*

Copy of Custance's letter (III, iv, 1074-1108, beginning 'Sweete mistresse where as I loue you nothing at all'), headed 'Their words make two contrary senses according as you distinguishe them', transcribed from the quotation in Thomas Wilson, *Rule of Reason*, 3rd edition (1553), in a composite volume of verse and prose owned c. 1669 by one John Cooke of Bury St Edmunds, Suffolk; c. 1620s-30s.

First pub. [London, 1566?]; ed. W.W. Greg, Malone Society (Oxford, 1935). This MS not recorded in Greg.

Bodleian, MS Rawl. poet. 26, f. 16v.

--- *Thersites.*

See INTRODUCTION.

MARGINALIA IN PRINTED BOOKS AND MANUSCRIPTS

*UdN 5 Linacre, Thomas. *De emendata structura Latini sermonis libri sex* (London, [1524]).

Extensive autograph annotations, with Udall's signature and the date '1525'.

This item recorded in William L. Edgerton, *Nicholas Udall* (New York, 1965), pp. 31-2, 114. Facsimile of title page in Maggs catalogue 493 (1927), item 591 (plate XLVI, facing p. 329).

Folger, STC 15634.

--- -----

See also INTRODUCTION.

John Webster

c.1578-c.1634

ABBREVIATIONS

Lucas *The Complete Works of John Webster*, ed. F. L. Lucas, 4 vols (London, 1927; reprinted 1966).

For abbreviations used throughout Volume I, see p.xi.

INTRODUCTION

There are no known specimens of Webster's handwriting nor any contemporary MSS of his plays other than a few songs and extracts in early miscellanies.

Each of Webster's plays has been edited several times, but the standard collected edition remains Lucas. None of the MSS recorded in the *Index* (except WeJ 13) was known to Lucas. For the Webster canon, see Bentley, V, 1239-56.

For recently discovered documents relating to Webster's life see Mary Edmond, 'In Search of John Webster', *TLS* (24 December 1976), pp. 1621-2; Mark Eccles's correspondence in *TLS* (21 January 1977), p. 71; and Mary Edmond's reply, *TLS* (11 March 1977), p. 272; also Charles R. Forker, 'Two Notes on John Webster and Anthony Munday: Unpublished Entries in the Records of the Merchant Taylors', *ELN*, 6 (September 1968), 26-34.

PB.

ARRANGEMENT

Verse	WeJ 1
Prose	WeJ 2
Dramatic works	WeJ 3-14.

John Webster

VERSE

WeJ 1 *'Some giue there wiues these tytles'.*

Copy of untitled verses possibly by Webster, inscribed at the end (sig. S3) of a printed exemplum of Sir Thomas Overbury, *A Wife*, 9th impression (London, 1616); c. 1616.

First pub. (from this MS, with a facsimile) in James E. Savage, 'An Unpublished Epigram, Possibly by John Webster', *University of Mississippi Studies in English*, 8 (1967), 13-18.

Huntington, RB 62806.

PROSE

WeJ 2 *A Purueiour of Tobacco.*

Copy of Webster's 'Character' inscribed at the end (sig. S3^{v}) of a printed exemplum of Sir Thomas Overbury, *A Wife*, 9th impression (London, 1616); c. 1616.

First pub. in Sir Thomas Overbury, *A Wife*, 6th impression (London, 1615); Lucas, IV, 44. Printed from this MS, with a facsimile, in James E. Savage, 'An Unpublished Epigram, Possibly by John Webster', *University of Mississippi Studies in English*, 8 (1967), 13-18.

Huntington, RB 62806.

DRAMATIC WORKS

WeJ 3 *The Devil's Law-Case.*

Excerpts, with comments on the play, in a miscellany compiled by Abraham Wright (1611-90); c. 1640.

First pub. London, 1623; Lucas, II, 229-372. Wright's comments printed in Arthur C. Kirsch, 'A Caroline Commentary on the Drama', *MP*, 66 (1968-9), 256-61 (p. 257), and in James G. McManaway, 'Excerpta quaedam per A.W. adolescentem', *Studies in Shakespeare, Bibliography and Theater* (New York, 1969), 279-91 (p. 287).

British Library, Add. MS 22608, ff. 74-5v.

WeJ 4 *The Duchess of Malfi.*

Excerpts, with comments on the play, in a miscellany compiled by Abraham Wright (1611-90); c. 1640.

First pub. London, 1623; Lucas, II, 1-210. Wright's comments printed in Arthur C. Kirsch, 'A Caroline Commentary on the Drama', *MP*, 66 (1968-9), 256-61 (p. 258).

British Library, Add. MS 22608, ff. 87-8v.

WeJ 5 -----

Copy of Bosola's couplet beginning 'Glories (like glowe-wormes) afarre off, shine bright' (IV, ii, 141-2), headed 'of Glories', transcribed by Katherine Butler at the back of Knightley Chetwode's MS copy of sermons by Donne which she used as a commonplace book; 1696.

Lucas, II, 97.

St Paul's Cathedral, MS 52. D. 14.

WeJ 6 ----- IV, ii, 65-76. Song: 'O let us howle, some heavy note'.

Copy of the Madman's song in a musical setting by Robert Johnson in a MS songbook once owned by one Richard Elliotts and possibly by the composer Adrian Batten (d. 1637); c. 1630.

Lucas, II, 95. Printed from this MS in John P. Cutts, 'Two Jacobean Theatre Songs', *M & L*, 33 (1952), 333-4; collated in Cutts, *Musique de la troupe de Shakespeare*, pp. 143-4.

British Library, Add. MS 29481, ff. 5v-6.

WeJ 7 ----- -----

Copy in a musical setting by Robert Johnson in a MS songbook ('Earl Ferrers' MS'); c. 1640.

This MS collated in Cutts, *Musique de la troupe de Shakespeare*, pp. 143-4.

New York Public Library, Music Division, Drexel MS 4041, No. 126, ff. 107v-8.

WeJ 8 ----- -----

Copy in a musical setting by Robert Johnson in a MS songbook once owned by a certain Anne Twice; c. 1620.

This MS collated in Cutts, *Musique de la troupe de Shakespeare*, pp. 143-4.

New York Public Library, Music Division, Drexel MS 4175, No. xlii.

WeJ 9 ----- -----

Copy, untitled and here beginning 'Come, lett vs howle some heavy Note', in a verse miscellany compiled by an Oxford man; c. 1630s.

Folger, MS V. a. 170, pp. 29-30.

The Duchess of Malfi. Song: 'O let us howle'

WeJ 10 ----- -----

Copy, headed 'Lovers deluded by their M[rss]', in a verse miscellany compiled by one Richard Archard; c. 1650-7.

Folger, MS V. a. 124, ff. 43v-4.

--- *Westward Ho*.

See THOMAS DEKKER, DkT 47.

WeJ 11 *The White Devil*.

Extracts in a miscellany compiled by Edward Pudsey (1573-1613); 1600s.

First pub. London, 1612; Lucas, I.

Bodleian, MS Eng. poet. d. 3, f. 81r-v.

WeJ 12 -----

Excerpts, with comments on the play, in a miscellany compiled by Abraham Wright (1611-90); c. 1640.

Wright's comments printed in Arthur C. Kirsch, 'A Caroline Commentary on the Drama', *MP*, 66 (1968-9), 256-61 (p. 258).

British Library, Add. MS 22608, ff. 88v-9.

WeJ 13 -----

Exemplum of the edition of 1612, formerly owned by David Garrick, with a few minor MS corrections; 17th century.

These corrections recorded in Lucas, I, 276 seq.

British Library, Department of Printed Books, C. 34. e. 18.

WeJ 14 -----

Exemplum of the edition of 1612 with numerous minor MS annotations consisting of alterations of directions, punctuation or spelling, the deletion or insertion of single words, underlinings, and the insertion of act or scene numbers; 17th century.

This item formerly in the Halliwell-Phillipps collection in the Penzance Library, Cornwall.

Edinburgh University Library, JA 297.

Thomas Wilson

1524?-81

For abbreviations used throughout Volume I, see p.xi.

INTRODUCTION

Dr Thomas Wilson (not to be confused with Sir Thomas Wilson (1560?-1629)) occupies a place among the distinguished literary men of his time as a notable humanist statesman and scholar. His achievements are summarised by Albert J. Schmidt in 'Thomas Wilson, Tudor Scholar-Statesman', *HLQ*, 20 (1956-7), 205-18, and in 'Thomas Wilson and the Tudor Commonwealth: An Essay in Civil Humanism', *HLQ*, 23 (1959-60), 49-60.

Apart from a mnemonic couplet copied from a printed source in John Lilliat's miscellany (Bodleian, MS Rawl. poet. 148, f. 5v), there is no MS of Wilson's most famous work, *The Arte of Rhetorique* (1553). Nor, apart from one extract from a printed source (see NICHOLAS UDALL, UdN 4), are there any known MSS of his *Rule of Reason* (1551), or *Discourse upon Usury* (1572), or any other work of his published during his lifetime (see *NCBEL*, I, col. 1824). An address to the Queen on New Year's Day, 1566/7, however, is preserved in his autograph presentation copy (WiT 2), and an autograph political tract of 1578 survives (WiT 1, and see FACSIMILE XXXIII).

There are also substantial and largely unedited collections of his official correspondence in the Public Record Office and the British Library (Additional, Cotton, Harley and Lansdowne MSS). Scribal copies of certain letters are in Cambridge University Library (MS Ee. 2. 34, ff. 87, 101, 105v) and in Bradford Central Library (Hopkinson MSS, Vol. 19, f. 19). Three autograph letters in the British Library (Lansdowne MS 12, f. 6; Harley MSS 6991, f. 52, and 6992, f. 116) are reproduced in part in Greg, *English Literary Autographs*, plate LXIV. A letter in Latin to Sir William Cecil (Lansdowne MS 12, f. 32) in which he mentions his translation of orations by Demosthenes (published London, 1570) is printed in *Original Letters of Eminent Literary Men*, ed. Sir Henry Ellis, Camden Society 23 (London, 1843), pp. 28-32.

A long Latin oration on English commercial grievances delivered by Wilson in 1567 on his embassy to the King of Portugal is preserved in the British Library (Cotton MS Nero B. I, f. 131). Two of his speeches in parliament against usury and vagabonds (1571) are in Cotton MS Titus F. I, ff. 152v, 163. His speech against Mary Queen of Scots in 1572 is copied in a parliamentary diary at Trinity College, Dublin (MS 1045). A MS 'Actio contra Mariam Scotorum reginam' ascribed to Wilson is preserved in the Pierpont Morgan Library (MA 41).

PB.

ARRANGEMENT

Prose WiT 1-2.

FACSIMILE XXXIII—Thomas Wilson: Part of last page of *A Discourse touching this Kingdom's Perils with their Remedies*, 2 April 1578 (WiT1). Public Record Office, SP 12/123/17, folio [2 verso]. Crown Copyright. Reproduced by permission of the Controller of H.M. Stationery Office.

The remedies of al the evil that may fawle upon this Realme, are to bee reduced to fowre principale heads. whereof the first is, that as I said at the first beginninge, Christ must bee our foundacion; and the corner stone of our buildinge, neyther must we suffer any to laboure in the Lords harvest, that do not seeke his glorie, sufficient teachers, and in most fault places would have them the rather that papists who are ... so that who be seduced, as in tymes past, might bee brought to lyve in dew obedience to God, and their Soveraigne.

The seconde poynte is, that theye abrode who are faythful and of the same religion that we professe, might bee united to us, and we to them, I do meane for France, the Kinge of Navarre, and the Prince of Condee with their allies. for the Low Countries, the States with the Prince of Orenge and the reformed churches there. for Germanye, the Princes of the religion, and specially Duke Casimire. for Scotland, the Kinge to bee made assured unto this Realme, and the nobilitie there beinge godlie affected, and not poore, to bee releeved from hence, with yearlie pensions in suche sorte as shal best seeme to her Ma[jes]tie to your sealle and to increase of those of the religion & more in the affected ... abrode. And great reason it is, that as others seeke to make themselves stronge both at home and abrode, so our most gracious Soveraigne, shoulde indevour to strengthen her selfe, with her frends, allyes and good subiects that are true and have foresight, the more respected here, & above al, ...

to the glorie of God, and preservation of her selfe, and her people committed to her charge.

Thomas Wilson

PROSE

*WiT 1 *A Discourse touching this Kingdom's Perils with their Remedies.*

Autograph; 2 leaves; 2 April 1578.

First pub. (from this MS) in Albert J. Schmidt, 'A Treatise on England's Perils, 1578', *Archiv für Reformationsgeschichte*, 46 (1955), 243-9. See FACSIMILE XXXIII.

Public Record Office, SP.12/123/17.

*WiT 2 *Oratio de Clementia.*

Autograph fair copy of a Latin address presented to Queen Elizabeth on 1 January 1566/7; 17 pages.

Unpublished.

British Library, Royal MS 12 A. L.

Sir Henry Wotton

1568-1639

ABBREVIATIONS

Dyce *Poems by Sir Henry Wotton*, ed. Alexander Dyce, Percy Society (London, 1843).

Hannah *Poems by Sir Henry Wotton, Sir Walter Raleigh, and others*, ed. John Hannah (London, 1845).

Pearsall Smith Logan Pearsall Smith, *The Life and Letters of Sir Henry Wotton*, 2 vols (Oxford, 1907).

For abbreviations used throughout Volume I, see p.xi.

INTRODUCTION

Sir Henry Wotton, diplomat and later provost of Eton College, is known as a writer chiefly on account of a small number of poems, some of which were extremely popular in their own time and remain standard anthology pieces. He also conducted a very extensive correspondence and wrote several prose tracts.

The *Reliquiae Wottonianae* (London, 1651), a posthumous collection of Wotton's verse and prose edited by Izaak Walton, includes various poems allegedly found among his papers, fourteen of which are specifically ascribed to him. These poems were reprinted in Dyce (1843) and in Hannah (1845). New editions of Hannah appeared under variant titles in 1870, 1875, and 1892; Hannah's own annotated exemplum of his 1845 edition is in the Bodleian (13. *θ*. 132). Two poems were added to the canon in Pearsall Smith (1907), II, 415-16. One, *To the rarely accomplished, and worthy of best employment, Master Howel, upon his Vocall Forrest* (beginning 'Believe it, Sir, you happily have hit'), is printed in Hannah (1845), pp. xii-xiii, but no MS copies are known. The other, *A Dialogue between Sir Henry Wotton and Mr. Donne* (beginning 'If her disdaine least change in you can move') was printed in Donne's *Poems*, 2nd edition (London, 1635), p. 195, and was included in H. J. C. Grierson edition of Donne (Oxford, 1912), I, 430-2; it appears in numerous MSS but is more generally assigned to William Herbert, Earl of Pembroke, or to Sir Benjamin Rudyard (see Grierson, II, cxxxix), so is not included in the entries below. In an article in *MLR*, 6 (1911), 154-5, Grierson added one more poem to the canon: the verses addressed to Donne '*'Tis not a coate of gray or Shepherds life*' (WoH 168-73).

The entries include two poems which both Hannah and Pearsall Smith classified as of doubtful authorship. One, *A Description of the Country's Recreations* (WoH 216-18), appeared anonymously in *Reliquiae Wottonianae*. The other, *A Farewell to the Vanities of the World* (WoH 219-57.5), was ascribed to Wotton in Izaak Walton's *Compleat Angler*, 3rd edition (London, 1661), p. 251, but is also ascribed in various sources to Donne, to Henry King, and to Sir Kenelm Digby; in most MS copies the poem is anonymous.

No poem is preserved in Wotton's autograph, but a remarkably large number of early MS copies of his poems have survived, sometimes representing widely different versions. Certain copies are of particular interest since they were wholly or partly written by his fellow poets, Ben Jonson (WoH 2) and Robert Herrick (WoH 4). A fairly close connection with the author can be argued for at least two items (WoH 63, 134), belonging to the Wyatt family with whom Wotton was acquainted. The possible authority of other MSS still requires investigation. Unless otherwise stated, the MSS recorded (both verse and prose) have not been previously noted by editors.

The only recorded MS texts of verse which may be thought to have a special connection with Wotton (WoH 1, 62) belong to what Pearsall Smith called the 'Burley MS'. In the hundred years since Alfred J. Horwood first recorded this MS, in *HMC*, 7th Report (1879), Appendix, p. 516, it has had a curious history, which can be briefly summarised. The MS belonged to the Finch family at Burley-on-the-Hill House, Rutland, where Pearsall Smith examined it some time before 1907. He described it (II, 489-90) as a 'commonplace book' which 'belonged to [Wotton], or to some one connected with him', a MS in which were copied various documents relating to Wotton, as well as miscellaneous state papers; none was in Wotton's own hand, but some appeared to be in the hand of William Parkhurst, one of his secretaries. The MS was again examined by H. J. C. Grierson, who noted in his edition of Donne's poems (1912), II, cxi, that since his visit 'the house at Burley-on-the-Hill has been burned down and the manuscript volume has perished'. In his account of the MS in *Unforgotten Years* (London, 1938), pp. 218-23 — an account which has now found a place in *The Oxford Book of Literary Anecdotes* — Pearsall Smith repeated that 'shortly after the volume was returned to the place where I had found it, the house was burnt down and the manuscript destroyed', a statement which serves neatly to point his anecdote about the MS. A partial transcript made for Pearsall Smith was, however, preserved by the Clarendon Press (who also own the copyright of the volume), and has been occasionally used by editors of Donne, though curiously this too has now gone astray. The statements of Grierson and Pearsall Smith seemed to be confirmed by the absence of the MS from the huge collection of Finch MSS transferred to the Leicestershire Record Office in the 1960s; yet a MS inventory of the Finch MSS made at some time in this century for the HMC still included the Burley MS. After various enquiries it emerged that the MS had been discovered, almost by accident, at the National Register of Archives in 1960 by I. A. Shapiro, now Fellow of the Shakespeare Institute, University of Birmingham, who had then been given temporary custody of it. Mr Shapiro believed that the MS was subsequently returned to the HMC, but it was only after further investigations that the Burley MS was finally rediscovered in January 1976, in a safe in the University Library at Birmingham where it had been lying for thirteen years. At present (1979) the MS remains in Mr Shapiro's custody (and is being used for his edition of Donne's letters) but it will shortly rejoin the main Finch Collection now in the Leicestershire Record Office (to be classified as 'DG. 7/Lit. 2').

The Burley MS proves upon examination to be a large folio of numerous independent documents bound together. By comparing it with relevant letters in the public records, Mr Shapiro has been able to establish that at least half the volume is indeed in the hand of William Parkhurst, who was in Wotton's employment as early as 1604 (see Pearsall Smith, II, 476-8) and who died in 1667. The volume was almost certainly Parkhurst's personal compilation; those documents not in his own hand may reasonably be assumed to have belonged to him, the very last item (f. 360) being a poem on the death of Strafford (1641), and perhaps indicating approximately when the volume was bound. A number of the earlier documents were evidently copied from Wotton's papers while Parkhurst was his secretary in Venice (1604-10). It is difficult to date particular pages with exactness, but the two poems by Wotton (WoH 1, 62) appear in the volume among later poems and could have been transcribed by Parkhurst in the 1620s or even 1630s, long after he had left Wotton's employment.

By contrast, various MS copies of Wotton's poems are to be found elsewhere which have not been given entries. Eighteenth-century copies of the doubtful poem *A Farewell to the Vanities of the World* can be found in the Bodleian (MSS Rawl. D. 260, f. 38; Rawl. poet. 90, f. 1; Rawl. poet. 153, ff. 45v-6) and in the British Library (Stowe MS 972, f. 5). The last MS also includes (f. 8) a copy of *The Character of a Happy Life*, as does a MS in the Huntington (HM 106, p. 89). An 18th-century copy of *A Hymn to my God in a night of my late sickness* is in the Brotherton Collection at the University of Leeds (MS Lt. 13, f. 44), and a copy of *On his Mistress, the Queen of Bohemia* was inscribed in the late 18th century by one James Bisset, Jr., of Montrose, in a printed exemplum of Tasso's *La Gerusalemme liberata* (Ferrara, 1581), now in the Folger (PQ 4638/A881b/Cage). Two 18th-century copies of the couplet *Upon the Death of Sir Albert Morton's Wife* are in the Bodleian (MSS Ballard 50, f. 196; Eng. poet. e. 40, f. 408). A MS copy of a poem which passed through the hands of A. S. W. Rosenbach has not been located or identified and is recorded in the first-line index of MS verse at the Rosenbach Foundation. A copy of *An Ode to the King, at his returning from Scotland* appeared in what Rosenbach called 'Ettington MS 19, p. 78' (? from the Shirley papers at Ettington Park, Stratford-upon-Avon).

Wotton's various prose works are listed in Pearsall Smith (II, 413-14). The items which Pearsall Smith calls *Table Talk* (WoH 303) and prints from the Burley MS in his Appendix IV (II, 489-500) require explanation. His Nos. 35-145 (MS, ff. 82-6) seem to be a series of remarks and anecdotes recorded by Parkhurst from Wotton's conversation in Venice in 1610. The list was clearly a constantly growing one, compiled over a period of time, and various marginal dashes, crosses, and pointers indicate those items which Parkhurst, or perhaps other readers, thought were particularly interesting. On the other hand, Nos. 1-34 (MS, ff. 255v-6), which are a completely separate list, are simply a selection of aphorisms copied out by Parkhurst from Sir Thomas Overbury's *Characters* (London, 1614), and have no connection with Wotton. Pearsall Smith rightly excludes from the canon (II, 414) the essay *Concerning Duellos in Spain*, which is ascribed to Wotton in Stowe MS 569, ff. 70-2v, in the British Library, but which was evidently written by a resident in Spain; another copy is in the British Library (Harley MS 4176, ff. 37-8). An essay which should be similarly excluded from the canon is *The Character of Robert, Late Earl of Salisbury*, which Pearsall Smith found in the Burley MS and thus identified with a 'character' of Salisbury which Wotton was reported to have intended writing in 1613 (see Pearsall Smith, II, 487-9). In other MS sources this essay is specifically ascribed to Cyril Tourneur (see ToC 2-6). Parkhurst's copy-text probably had no connection with Wotton, but if the essay had come to Wotton's attention this would help to explain why he never bothered to write a 'character' of his own.

As with his verse, none of the recorded MSS of Wotton's prose works is in his own hand, although it is possible that certain items — including, perhaps, six important and hitherto unrecorded scribal copies of *The State of Christendom* (WoH 296-301) (if indeed this work is by Wotton) — are transcripts of his autographs or of authorised texts. On the other hand, several printed exempla of *The Elements of Architecture* (London, 1624) bear his autograph presentation inscriptions. One, with an autograph dedicatory epistle to Prince Charles and, on page 88, an autograph 'Note omitted in the Presse', is now in the British Library (Department of Printed Books, C. 45. c. 6); the epistle is reproduced in Greg, *English Literary Autographs*, plate LXXXI(b), and is transcribed in Pearsall Smith, II, 284-5. Another exemplum, inscribed to Archbishop George Abbot, is at Lambeth Palace, and yet another, inscribed to William Boswell, is in the Berg Collection in the New York Public Library. Hannah (1845), pp. xv-xvi, prints the text of the dedicatory epistle to the Earl of Middlesex written in an exemplum owned by 'Mr. [William] Pickering', and he mentions volumes known to have been inscribed to 'M[r] Doctor Goslin, the most worthie Master of Caies Colledge', and to William Juxon (1582-1663) when he was Lord High Treasurer.

Wotton also formally inscribed and presented to the Bodleian in 1633 a hand-coloured exemplum of

Tycho Brahe, *Astronomiae instauratae mechanica* (Wandesburg, 1598), a volume once owned by Brahe himself (see Pearsall Smith, II, 347); it is now pressmark Arch. B. c. 3. The autograph album of Captain Francis Segar, now in the Huntington (HM 743), contains (f. 56) a full-page inscription by 'Henry Wotton', dated 'At Cassels 26. of January. 1602'; the hand is not immediately recognisable as Sir Henry Wotton's but he adopted several styles of writing and it can probably be accepted as an early version of the script represented in FACSIMILE XXXIV. Wotton wrote a much more famous inscription, at Augsburg in 1604, in the album of the merchant Christopher Flecamore or Fleckmore. Wotton's Latin joke to the effect that an ambassador is an honest man sent to lie abroad for the good of his country (see Pearsall Smith, I, 49) would cost him his post. The album with the original inscription is not known to have survived, but 17th-century copies of the inscription are to be found, including one in the Bodleian (MS Sancroft 98, p. 173) and one made by William Camden, now at Trinity College, Cambridge (in MS R. 5. 20).

A few other miscellaneous items are to be found. Brief extracts from *The Elements of Architecture* (1624) and *A Philosophical Survey of Education* (*Reliquiae Wottonianae* (1651), pp. 309-35) appear in a miscellany belonging to the Cartwright family of Aynho, Northamptonshire, now in the Bodleian (MS Don. e. 6, ff. 42-40v rev.). Brief extracts from the second work also appear in a miscellany owned by William Drake (1606-69) of Shardeloes, near Amersham, Buckinghamshire, preserved at University College London (MS Ogden 7/28). An 'Abstract' of 'Wotton on Education' made in 1706 and owned by the Massachusetts Historical Society is presumably a synopsis of the same work, or possibly of Wotton's *Aphorisms of Education* (*Reliquiae Wottonianae*, 2nd edition (1654), pp. 305-20). Wotton's system of cypher, which is mentioned in a letter of 1623 (Pearsall Smith, II, 265), can be found in copies in the British Library (Add. MS 4277, f. 200, and Add. MS 39853, f. 15). Copies of Wotton's Will appear among Archbishop Sancroft's collections in the Bodleian (MS Tanner 88, ff. 10v-11) and among the collections of John Hopkinson (1610-80) in Bradford Central Library (Hopkinson MSS, Vol. 34, pp. 178-81). The Latin epitaph on Wotton's tomb at Eton 'commanded by his will' was copied by Sir Francis Fane (c. 1612-80) in a miscellany now in the Shakespeare Birthplace Trust Record Office (ER 93/1, p. 141).

It remain's to note the most substantial body of Wotton MSS: his correspondence. Wotton's letters abound, particularly those written while he was Ambassador in Venice, letters which throw considerable light on the politics of early 17th-century Europe. Pearsall Smith, who with some justification considered Wotton 'the best letter-writer of his time', knew of 'nearly one thousand of Wotton's letters and dispatches' (I, v-vi); he printed the text of 511 of them. The main collections are in the Public Record Office, the British Library, at Eton College, and in the State Archives of Venice, Florence, and Lucca (see Pearsall Smith's inventory, I, xxi-xxii, and II, 417-54). A number of previously unedited letters in the State Archives of Florence were printed by Anna Maria Crinò in *Fatti e Figure del Seicento Anglo-Toscano*, Biblioteca dell 'Archivum Romanicum', Ser. I, 48 (Florence, 1957), 7-40. Letters which Pearsall Smith cites as being in the 'Hofbibliothek' are in what is today the Österreichische Nationalbibliothek, Vienna (Cod. 9737 z, 14-18; 6686, 4, fol. 56-7v, 59v); the 'Clifton Hall' letters are now at the University of Nottingham (Clifton MSS, Cl C 568-70); the Alfred Morrison letter, of 30 May 1617, is now at Eton College (added to MS 188); and the 'Knole MS' is among the Cranfield papers in the Kent Archives Office. No doubt there are many more letters of Wotton in existence: for instance, his correspondence with William Trumbull in 1614-25, now in the Berkshire Record Office (Trumbull MSS, Alphabetical Series Vol. XLIX); additional items in the British Library (Add. MS 34727); an item once owned by R. B. Adam and now in the Hyde Collection, Somerville (*Life*, II, 2, 170, of which there is a microfilm at Princeton); letters which were among the papers bound in an interleaved volume of Henry King's *Poems* (1842) sold at Sotheby's, 9 December 1929, Lot 152, to Dobell (though Wotton's letters are not mentioned in the sale catalogue); and a letter of 5 June 1604 sold at Parke-Bernet Galleries, 22 October 1963, Lot 408. Additional transcripts of letters by Wotton include items at All Souls College, Oxford (MS 218, f. 95), in the British Library (Add. MS 44848), in the National Library of Scotland (Adv. MS 34. 2.10, ff. 83-5), at The Queen's College, Oxford (MSS 36, 154), and at the Rosenbach Foundation (MS 239/18). It may also be noted that the State Archives of Venice contain hundreds of unpublished verbatim reports of Wotton's speeches (see the *Calendar of State Papers, Venetian*, Vols X and XI). A facsimile of an autograph letter of 17 April 1609 in the British Library (Add. MS 12504, f. 260) can be found in Greg, *English Literary Autographs*, plate LXXXI(a), and a letter of 19/29 January 1621/2 at Corpus Christi College, Oxford, is reproduced in Pearsall Smith, II, facing p. 224. For another example, see FACSIMILE XXXIV.

PB.

ARRANGEMENT

Verse:	(1) Poems by Wotton	WoH 1-215
	(2) Poems of uncertain authorship	WoH 216-57.5
Prose		WoH 258-304.

See also Addenda to Part 2, p. 635

FACSIMILE XXXIV — Sir Henry Wotton: Letter to Samuel Collins, Provost of King's College, Cambridge, 13 April 1620. King's College, Cambridge, Provost's Letter-Book, Volume III, No. 28. Reproduced by permission of the Provost and Fellows of King's College, Cambridge.

(28)

Sir

Without any familiar acquayntance with you heeretofore, or any abilitie of serving you heereafter I take boldenesse frō mine owne good meaning to beseeche you to graunt unto Mr Thomas Rowe a license for traveling abroade for some tyme in my companie without preiudice of his place at home in the meane while. For which fauour towardes him I shall be greatly obliged unto you: beeing a gentleman to whose name I am much beholden, and towardes whose person I haue much affection.

I was readdie aboute this purpose to procure unto you letters frō greater personages But in deede (Sir) besides the suite it self It shalbe a seconde obligation if it shall please you to spare me that labour and to value my poore lines aboue the merit of the writer: who will remayne desirouse to serve you.

Henry Wotton

From my Lodging in Westminster this 13th of Aprile 1620.

Sir Henry Wotton

VERSE

(1) POEMS BY WOTTON

WoH 1 *The Character of a Happy Life* ('How happy is he born and taught').

Copy in the hand of William Parkhurst (fl. 1604-67), a secretary of Wotton's, untitled, in a composite volume of MSS collected by Parkhurst; among the papers of the Finch family of Burley-on-the-Hill, Rutland (the 'Burley MS'); 1600s-41.

First pub. in Sir Thomas Overbury, *A Wife*, 5th impression (London, 1614); *Reliquiae Wottonianae* (London, 1651), pp. 522-3; Hannah (1845), pp. 28-31. Some texts of this poem discussed in C.F. Main, 'Wotton's "The Character of a Happy Life"', *The Library*, 5th Ser. 10 (1955), 270-4, and in Ted-Larry Pebworth, 'New Light on Sir Henry Wotton's "The Character of a Happy Life"', *The Library*, 5th Ser. 33 (1978), 223-6. This MS recorded in Pearsall Smith, II, 490.

Leicestershire Record Office, DG. 7/Lit. 2, f. 278.

WoH 2 -----

Copy in the hand of Ben Jonson; among the papers of the actor Edward Alleyn (1566-1626); early 17th century.

Printed (inaccurately) from this MS in John Payne Collier, *Memoirs of Edward Alleyn* (London, 1841), p. 53; printed from this MS, with a facsimile, in Pebworth; also collated in Hannah and recorded in Main, and another facsimile in *The Henslowe Papers*, ed. R.A. Foakes (London, 1977), II, 136.

Dulwich College, Alleyn Papers, Vol. I, No. 136, f. 259r-v.

WoH 3 -----

Copy of part of the first stanza, alleged by J.P. Collier to be in the hand of Edward Alleyn 'upon a scrap of paper on the back of which is a memorandum respecting some agricultural implements bought by him, bearing date in 1616'.

This MS allegedly found by Collier among the Alleyn Papers in Dulwich College: see Collier, *Memoirs of Alleyn* (1841), p. 54.

Unlocated.

WoH 4 -----

Copy, with corrections made by Robert Herrick, headed 'Sir He: Wotton, of happinesse', in a miscellany partly compiled by Herrick; c. 1614-23.

Facsimile and transcript of this MS in Norman K. Farmer, Jr., 'Poems from a Seventeenth-Century Manuscript with the Hand of Robert Herrick', *TQ*, 16, No. 4 (Supplement) (Winter, 1973), pp. 50-1; also printed from this MS, with a facsimile, in Pebworth.

University of Texas at Austin, Ms File/(Herrick, R)/Works B, pp. 78-9.

WoH 5 -----

Copy in a verse miscellany partly compiled by Elias Ashmole (1617-92); c. 1630s-40s.

Bodleian, MS Ashmole 47, f. 29v.

WoH 6 -----

Copy of two stanzas in a musical setting in a MS songbook; c. 1640s.

This MS collated in John P. Cutts, 'A Bodleian Song-Book: Don. C. 57', *M & L*, 34 (1953), 192-211 (p. 205).

Bodleian, MS Don. c. 57, f. 51v.

WoH 7 -----

Copy in a verse miscellany; mid-17th century.

This MS collated in Hannah; recorded in Main.

Bodleian, MS Malone 13, p. 11.

WoH 8 -----

Copy in a verse miscellany probably compiled by a member of New College, Oxford; c. 1620s-30s.

This MS collated in Hannah; recorded in Main.

Bodleian, MS Malone 19, p. 146.

WoH 9 -----

Copy in a miscellany; early 17th century.

Bodleian, MS Rawl. D. 1048, f. 58.

WoH 10 -----

Copy in a composite volume of verse and prose owned c. 1669 by one John Cooke of Bury St Edmunds, Suffolk; c. 1617-30s.

Bodleian, MS Rawl. poet. 26, f. 1v.

WoH 11 -----

Copy, untitled, in a verse miscellany; c. 1620-33.

Bodleian, MS Rawl. poet. 31, f. 5r-v.

The Character of a Happy Life

WoH 12 -----

Copy in a verse miscellany; c. 1650-75.

Bodleian, MS Rawl. poet. 66, f. 55.

WoH 13 -----

Copy in a verse miscellany compiled by one John Hooper of Devon; c. 1660s.

Bodleian, MS Rawl. poet. 208, f. 1.

WoH 14 -----

Copy in a miscellany compiled by an Oxford man; early 17th century.

Printed from this MS in Norman Ault, *Elizabethan Lyrics*, 4th edition (London, 1966), pp. 459-60; recorded in Main.

Bodleian, MS Rawl. poet. 212, f. 150 rev.

WoH 14.5 See Addenda, p. 635.

WoH 15 -----

Copy, headed 'S[r] Henry wootton on mr Roger Askam', in a verse miscellany compiled by the Yorkshire antiquary John Hopkinson (1610-80); late 17th century.

Bradford Central Library, Hopkinson MSS, Vol. 17, f. [124].

WoH 16 -----

Copy, headed 'Upon a private life', in a verse miscellany compiled by John Hopkinson; mid-17th century.

Bradford Central Library, Hopkinson MSS, Vol. 34, p. 44.

WoH 17 -----

Copy of a five-stanza version, untitled, transcribed from WoH 18, with a note in a later hand after line 6 saying '4 lines omitted here', in a verse miscellany possibly compiled by a member of an Inn of Court; c. 1630s.

This MS the Pickering MS collated in Hannah.

British Library, Add. MS 21433, ff. 115v-16.

WoH 18 -----

Copy of a five-stanza version, untitled, in a miscellany possibly compiled by a member of an Inn of Court; c. 1620s-30s.

British Library, Add. MS 25303, f. 121.

WoH 19 -----

Copy, untitled, in a composite volume of verse belonging to the Skipwith family of Cotes, Leicestershire; early-mid-17th century.

British Library, Add. MS 25707, f. 34v.

WoH 20 -----

Copy in a verse miscellany owned in 1688 by one H. Packwood; late 17th century.

British Library, Add. MS 29921, f. 42.

WoH 21 -----

Copy, headed 'Song', in a verse miscellany compiled by Daniel Leare (a distant cousin of William Strode) probably while at Christ Church, Oxford; c. 1631-3.

British Library, Add. MS 30982, f. 160.

WoH 22 -----

Copy, untitled, in a miscellany; c. 1630s.

British Library, Egerton MS 2026, f. 11v.

WoH 23 -----

Copy, untitled, in a verse miscellany; c. 1630.

British Library, Egerton MS 2230, f. 20v.

WoH 24 -----

Copy, untitled, in a composite volume of MSS; early-mid-17th century.

British Library, Harley MS 1576, f. 2.

WoH 25 -----

Copy, untitled, in a verse miscellany; c. 1620-33.

British Library, Harley MS 4064, f. 234v.

WoH 26 -----

Copy, untitled, in a verse miscellany compiled by one Thomas Crosse; c. 1630s.

British Library, Harley MS 6057, f. 18.

WoH 27 -----

Copy among poems at the end of a MS volume of poems by William Browne of Tavistock, possibly compiled by a member of an Inn of Court; bound in a composite volume of MSS; c. 1637-50.

British Library, Lansdowne MS 777, f. 65.

The Character of a Happy Life

WoH 28 -----

Copy in a verse miscellany; late 17th century.

British Library, Sloane MS 3769, f. 2.

WoH 29 -----

Copy in a verse miscellany; c. 1637.

British Library, Stowe MS 962, f. 176r-v.

WoH 30 -----

Copy, untitled, in a MS volume of poems chiefly by Donne; c. 1620-33.

Cambridge University Library, MS Ee. 4. 14, f. 76.

WoH 31 -----

Copy among some MS poems bound with a printed exemplum of Sir William Davenant, *Two Excellent Plays* (London, 1665); late 17th century.

Folger, D347, pp. 5-6 (at end of volume).

WoH 32 -----

Copy, headed 'A Contented Life', in a verse miscellany; c. 1630.

Folger, MS V. a. 103, Part I, f. 77.

WoH 33 -----

Copy, untitled, in a verse miscellany probably compiled by a member of an Inn of Court; mid-17th century.

Folger, MS V. a. 262, p. 89.

WoH 34 -----

Copy, headed 'S[r] Hen: wootton on a pvate life', in a miscellany; c. 1630.

Folger, MS V. a. 345, p. 63.

WoH 35 -----

Copy, untitled, in a memorandum book compiled by Richard Dering (d. 1612) of Surrenden, Kent, his son Anthony (1558-1635), and his grandson Sir Edward (1598-1644); c. 1614-44.

Folger, MS V. b. 296, f. 332.

WoH 36 -----

Copy, untitled, in a verse miscellany compiled by one or two Oxford men, possibly connected with New College and afterwards with the Inns of Court; 1630s.

This MS recorded in Main.

Harvard, MS Eng 686, ff. 15v-16.

WoH 37 -----

Copy, untitled, in a MS volume of poems chiefly by Donne; c. 1620s.

Formerly Norton 4620, this MS recorded in Main.

Harvard, MS Eng 966.7, f. 17v.

WoH 37.5 See Addenda, p. 635.

WoH 38 -----

Copy in a journal compiled by one Thomas Grocer; 1657.

Huntington, HM 93, p. 183.

WoH 39 -----

Copy, untitled, in a miscellany; imperfect; early 17th century.

University of Leeds, Brotherton Collection, MS Lt. 25, f. 7.

WoH 40 -----

Copy of a five-stanza version, headed 'A Caracter of a happy man', in a miscellany; c. 1700.

University of Leeds, Brotherton Collection, MS Lt. 48, f. [48].

WoH 41 -----

Copy, untitled, in a MS volume of poems chiefly by Donne, later used as a medical notebook by the Royal physician Sir John Wedderburn (1599-1679); c. 1620-33.

National Library of Scotland, MS 6504, f. 85v.

WoH 42 -----

Copy, headed 'A contented life', in a verse miscellany; c. 1630.

University of Nottingham, Portland MS Pw V 37, p. 169.

WoH 43 -----

Copy, untitled, in a verse miscellany used by members of the Holgate family of Saffron Walden, Essex; c. 1630s.

Pierpont Morgan Library, MA 1057, p. 137.

WoH 43.5 See Addenda, p. 635.

The Character of a Happy Life

WoH 44 -----

Copy in a verse miscellany entitled *Recueil Choisi De Pieces fugitives En Vers Anglois*; c. 1713.

Rosenbach Foundation, MS 239/16, p. 18.

WoH 45 -----

Copy, headed 'S[r] Henry Wotton on a private life', in a verse miscellany; c. 1638-45.

Rosenbach Foundation, MS 239/22, f. 25v.

WoH 46 -----

Copy, untitled, in a MS volume of poems chiefly by Donne, among the family papers of the Earl of Dalhousie; c. 1620-5.

Scottish Record Office, GD45/26/95/1, f. 11.

WoH 47 -----

Copy, untitled, in a verse miscellany appended to a MS volume of poems by Donne; c. 1630s.

Trinity College, Dublin, MS 877, ff. 165v-6.

WoH 47.5 See Addenda, p. 635.

WoH 48 -----

Copy, untitled, in a verse miscellany compiled by Tobias Alston (1620-c.1639) of Sayham Hall, near Sudbury, Suffolk; c. 1639.

Yale, Osborn Collection, b 197, p. 49.

--- -----

See also INTRODUCTION.

--- *A Dialogue between Sir Henry Wotton and Mr. Donne* ('If her disdaine least change in you can move').

See INTRODUCTION.

WoH 49 *A Hymn to my God, in a night of my late sickness* ('Oh Thou great power! in whom I move').

Copy, headed 'A shorte Hymne by S Hen: Wotton In a nyght of his present sicknes', in a verse miscellany compiled by Nicholas Burghe (d. 1670); c. 1638.

First pub. in *Reliquiae Wottonianae* (London, 1651), p. 515; Hannah (1845), pp. 49-51. This MS collated in Hannah.

Bodleian, MS Ashmole 38, p. 132.

WoH 50 -----

Copy in a verse miscellany compiled by one 'H.S.', a Cambridge man; c. 1640s-50s.

This MS collated in Hannah.

Bodleian, MS Rawl. poet. 147, p. 101.

WoH 51 -----

Copy in a verse miscellany compiled by Archbishop William Sancroft (1617-93); mid-late 17th century.

This MS collated in Hannah; facsimile in the appendix of the Scolar Press facsimile edition of Richard Crashaw, *Steps to the Temple* < 1646 > (Menston, 1970).

Bodleian, MS Tanner 465, f. 41.

WoH 52 -----

Copy in a verse miscellany compiled by Archbishop William Sancroft; mid-late 17th century.

Bodleian, MS Tanner 466, f. 4v.

WoH 53 -----

Copy, transcribed from a printed exemplum of *Reliquiae Wottonianae*, in a verse miscellany probably compiled by Marmaduke Rawdon (c.1610-68) of Hoddesdon, Hertfordshire; c. 1662.

British Library, Add. MS 18044, ff. 147v-54.

WoH 54 -----

Copy in a verse miscellany entitled *Recueil Choisi De Pieces fugitives En Vers Anglois*; c. 1713.

Rosenbach Foundation, MS 239/16, p. 11.

WoH 55 -----

Copy, untitled, in a verse miscellany; c. 1640.

Yale, Osborn Collection, b 62, p. 115.

--- -----

See also INTRODUCTION.

WoH 56 *An Ode to the King, at his returning from Scotland to the Queen after his coronation there* ('Rouse up thyself, my gentle Muse').

Copy of the first stanza in a musical setting in a MS songbook; c. 1640s.

First pub. in Ben Jonson's *Vnder-wood* in his

An Ode to the King, at his returning from Scotland

Workes (London, 1640); *Reliquiae Wottonianae* (London, 1651), p. 521; Hannah (1845), pp. 21-4; ed. C.H. Herford and Percy and Evelyn Simpson, *Ben Jonson*, VIII (Oxford, 1947), p. 267.

Bodleian, MS Don. c. 57, f. 29v.

WoH 57 -----

Copy in a verse miscellany compiled by one 'H.S.', a Cambridge man; c. 1640s-50s.

This MS recorded in Hannah.

Bodleian, MS Rawl. poet. 147, pp. 96-7.

WoH 58 -----

Copy in a verse miscellany compiled by Archbishop William Sancroft (1617-93); mid-late 17th century.

This MS recorded in Hannah.

Bodleian, MS Tanner 465, f. 61v.

--- -----

See also INTRODUCTION.

WoH 59 *On a Bank as I sat a-Fishing. A Description of the Spring* ('And now all nature seemed in love').

Copy, headed 'On the Spring', in a verse miscellany compiled by one 'H.S.', a Cambridge man; c. 1640s-50s.

First pub. in *Reliquiae Wottonianae* (London, 1651), p. 524; Hannah (1845), pp. 32-5. This MS collated in Hannah.

Bodleian, MS Rawl. poet. 147, p. 47.

WoH 60 -----

Copy, headed 'On the Spring', in a verse miscellany compiled by Archbishop William Sancroft (1617-93); mid-late 17th century.

This MS collated in Hannah.

Bodleian, MS Tanner 465, f. 61v.

WoH 60.5 See Addenda, p. 635.

WoH 61 -----

Copy, headed 'Of ye Springe: S: Hen: Wotton', subscribed in a much later hand 'Iz: W.', on a single leaf; c. 1620s.

A later note on this MS incorrectly claims that it is in the hand of Izaak Walton.

Harvard, MS Eng 886.

WoH 62 *On his Mistress, the Queen of Bohemia* ('You meaner beauties of the night').

Copy of a four-stanza version in the hand of William Parkhurst (fl. 1604-67), a secretary of Wotton's, headed 'The Lady Eliza: Queene of Bohemia', in a composite volume of MSS collected by Parkhurst; among the papers of the Finch family of Burley-on-the-Hill, Rutland 'Burley MS'); 1600s-41.

First pub. (in a musical setting) in Michael East, *Sixt Set of Bookes* (London, 1624); *Reliquiae Wottonianae* (London, 1651), p. 518; Hannah (1845), pp. 12-15. Some texts of this poem discussed in J.B. Leishman, '"You Meaner Beauties of the Night" A Study in Transmission and Transmogrification', *The Library*, 4th Ser. 26 (1945-6), 99-121. Some musical versions edited in *English Songs 1625-1660*, ed. Ian Spink, Musica Britannica XXXIII (London, 1971), Nos. 66, 122.

Leicestershire Record Office, DG. 7/Lit. 2, f. 336v.

WoH 63 -----

Copy of a five-stanza version, untitled, here beginning 'You glorious trifles of the East', and ascribed to 'Sr H.W.', in a verse miscellany compiled by Sir Francis Wyatt (1575-1644), bound in a composite volume of papers of the Wyatt family; c. 1630.

Printed from this MS in Agnes Conway, 'A New Stanza to "You Meaner Beauties of the Night"', *TLS* (4 September 1924), p. 540; also discussed by her in *TLS* (30 October 1924), p. 686; recorded in Leishman.

British Library, Loan MS 15 / Part 2 (Wyatt Commonplace Book), No. 29, ff. [25v-6].

WoH 64 -----

Copy of a five-stanza version in a verse miscellany compiled by Nicholas Burghe (d. 1670); c. 1638.

This MS recorded in Leishman.

Bodleian, MS Ashmole 38, p. 118.

WoH 65 -----

Copy of a six-stanza version in a miscellany compiled by one Philip Kynder (b. 1597); mid-17th century.

This MS recorded in Leishman. The text followed on f. 22 by a parodied version, beginning 'Ladies that guild the glittering moone', on the fall of Charles I.

Bodleian, MS Ashmole 788, f. 21v.

On his Mistress, the Queen of Bohemia

WoH 66 -----

Copy of a six-stanza version, headed 'To ye Lady Elizabeth', in a verse miscellany compiled by an Oxford man, possibly a member of Wadham College, and later used by William Fulman (1632-88); c. late 1630s.

Bodleian, MS CCC. 328, f. 79v.

WoH 67 -----

Copy of a six-stanza version in a musical setting in a MS songbook; c. 1640s.

This MS collated in John P. Cutts, 'A Bodleian Song-Book: Don. C. 57', *M & L*, 34 (1953), 192-211 (pp. 202-3).

Bodleian, MS Don. c. 57, f. 39.

WoH 68 -----

Copy of a five-stanza version in a verse miscellany compiled by the Yorkshire antiquary John Hopkinson (1610-80); c. 1647.

Bodleian, MS Don. d. 58, f. 21.

WoH 69 -----

Copy, here beginning 'Ye glorious trifles of the east', in a MS volume of political poems; mid-late 17th century.

The text accompanied by a Latin version by one 'T.L.'.

Bodleian, MS Douce 357, f. 19.

WoH 70 -----

Copy, untitled and here beginning 'You glorious trifles of the East', in a verse miscellany once owned by one Peter Daniell; c. 1630s-40s.

Bodleian, MS Eng. poet. c. 50, f. 77.

WoH 71 -----

Copy of a six-stanza version, headed 'Sr Henry Wotton vpon ye La: Elizab: Que: of Bohemia' (the last two stanzas headed 'Two other Staves added by Another') and here beginning 'Yee violetts wch first appear', in a verse miscellany compiled by an Oxford man and once owned by one Henry Lawson; c. 1630s.

Bodleian, MS Eng. poet. e. 14, f. 68v.

WoH 72 -----

Copy, headed 'On his Mrs, in a verse miscellany compiled by Robert Codrington (1602-65); c. 1638.

Bodleian, MS Eng. poet. f. 27, p. 198.

WoH 73 -----

Copy, headed 'To the Spanish Lady', in a verse miscellany probably compiled by a member of New College, Oxford; c. 1620s-30s.

This MS collated in Hannah; recorded in Leishman.

Bodleian, MS Malone 19, p. 37.

WoH 74 -----

Copy of a six-stanza version, untitled, in a verse miscellany compiled by an Oxford man and once owned by one William Bloys; c. 1630s.

Bodleian, MS Rawl. poet. 142, f. 46.

WoH 75 -----

Copy in a composite volume of MSS; late 17th century.

Bodleian, MS Rawl. poet. 159, f. 142.

WoH 76 -----

Copy, headed 'On my Princesse and Mrs. the Lady Elisabeth elected Queene of Bohemia' and here beginning 'Yow violets yt doe first appeare', in a verse miscellany; c. 1630s.

Bodleian, MS Rawl. poet. 160, f. 109r-v.

WoH 77 -----

Copy, here beginning 'Ye glorious trifles of the East' in a verse miscellany; c. 1630s.

Bodleian, MS Rawl. poet. 199, p. 2.

WoH 78 -----

Copy of a six-stanza version in a verse miscellany compiled by Archbishop William Sancroft (1617-93); mid-late 17th century.

This MS collated in Hannah; recorded in Leishman.

Bodleian, MS Tanner 465, f. 43.

WoH 79 -----

Copy of a five-stanza version, headed 'An Ode upon this mariage' (i.e. of the Prince Elector with the Princess Elizabeth), in a volume of transcripts of historical documents made by the Yorkshire antiquary John Hopkinson (1610-80) chiefly from papers belonging to John Savile, Baron of Pontefract, and Edward Taylor, of Furnivall's Inn, Holborn; 1674.

Bradford Central Library, Hopkinson MSS, Vol. 27, ff. 122v-3.

On his Mistress, the Queen of Bohemia

WoH 80 -----

Copy, here beginning 'Yee violetts, y^t first appeare', in a musical setting by John Hilton in a MS songbook chiefly compiled by one 'T.C.'; c. 1656-9.

British Library, Add. MS 11608, f. 52.

WoH 81 -----

Copy, here beginning 'Yee meaner beauties of the night', in an anonymous musical setting in a MS songbook chiefly compiled by one 'T.C.'; c. 1656-9.

British Library, Add. MS 11608, f. 52v.

WoH 82 -----

Copy, headed 'An ode upon ye Lady Elizab: Qu: of Bohemia', in a verse miscellany probably compiled by a Cambridge man; c. 1630s.

British Library, Add. MS 15227, f. 76.

WoH 83 -----

Copy of a six-stanza version, headed 'On ye Queene of Bohemia', in a verse miscellany; c. 1630s.

This MS recorded in Leishman.

British Library, Add. MS 22118, f. 37.

WoH 84 -----

Copy, headed 'Vpon the Queene of Bohemia', in a composite volume of verse among the 'Conway Papers' chiefly descended from Sir Edward Conway, Viscount Conway (d. 1631) of Conway Castle; early 17th century.

British Library, Add. MS 23229, f. 62v.

WoH 85 -----

Copy, headed 'On Sr Henery Wootton to Qu. Anne', in a verse miscellany compiled by Daniel Leare (a distant cousin of William Strode) probably while at Christ Church, Oxford; c. 1631-3.

British Library, Add. MS 30982, f. 145v rev.

WoH 86 -----

Copy, headed 'To ye Q of Bohemia', in a miscellany compiled by Anthony Scattergood (1611-87) of Trinity College, Cambridge; c. 1632-40.

British Library, Add. MS 44963, ff. 21v-2.

WoH 87 -----

Copy of a six-stanza version, headed 'Sr H. Wootton on the Lady crownd Q of Bohemia' and here beginning 'Yee glorious trifles of the East', in a miscellany compiled by Sir John Perceval, Bart. (1629-65), probably while at Magdalene College, Cambridge; c. 1646-9.

British Library, Add. MS 47111, f. 7r-v.

WoH 88 -----

Copy of a six-stanza version, untitled, in a verse miscellany compiled by Thomas Manne (1582?-1641) of Christ Church, Oxford; c. 1630s.

British Library, Add. MS 58215, pp. 192-3.

WoH 89 -----

Copy of a six-stanza version, headed 'On Ladie Eliz: Queene of Bohemia by S^r H: Wotton', in a verse miscellany probably compiled by Francis Baskerville of Malmesbury, Wiltshire, and owned in 1663 by William Wallrond; c. 1633.

This MS recorded by Agnes Conway in *TLS* (4 September 1924), p. 540.

British Library, Sloane MS 1446, ff. 43v-4.

WoH 90 -----

Copy of a six-stanza version, headed 'Sir H. Wotton. on the Lady Elizabeth when she was first crowned Que. of Bohemia' and here beginning 'Ye glorious trifles of the East', in a verse miscellany probably compiled by one 'I.A.' of Christ Church, Oxford, and later owned by Robert Killigrew; c. early 1630s.

This MS recorded by Agnes Conway in *TLS* (4 September 1924), p. 540.

British Library, Sloane MS 1792, f. 2r-v.

WoH 91 -----

Copy of a six-stanza version, untitled, in a verse miscellany compiled by a Cambridge man; c. 1653-60s.

Cambridge University Library, MS Add. 79, f. 11r-v.

WoH 92 -----

Copy, here beginning 'Yow minor beauties of the night', in a musical setting in a MS songbook compiled by Robert Taitt, schoolmaster of Lauder, Berwickshire; [1676-89].

This MS recorded in Walter H. Rubsamen,

'Scottish and English Music in the Renaissance in a Newly-Discovered Manuscript', *Festschrift Heinrich Besseler* (Leipzig, 1961), 259-84.

Clark Library, Los Angeles, T135Z.B724 1677-89 Bound, Cantus 3, ff. 35, 52.

WoH 93 -----

Copy, headed 'On ye Queen of Bohemia', in a miscellany among the papers of the Sheridan family of Frampton Court, Dorset; c. 1660s.

Dorset Record Office, D51/5, p. 211.

WoH 94 -----

Copy, untitled and here beginning 'Yow minor beautyes of the night', in a verse miscellany; c. 1630s-40s.

Edinburgh University Library, MS La. III. 436, pp. 24-5.

WoH 95 -----

Copies of the incipit, here 'You meaner beauties &c.', in a musical setting, written in three of the MS part books of the 'St Andrews Psalter'; early 17th century.

Edinburgh University Library, MS La. III. 483, Tenor, p. 185; Treble, pp. 192-3; Bassus, pp. 194, 202.

WoH 96 -----

Copy of a version in eight three-line stanzas, here beginning 'Yow minor beawties of the night', in a musical setting, in a MS music book compiled by one John Squyer; [1697-1701].

Edinburgh University Library, MS La. III. 490, pp. 63-4.

WoH 97 -----

Copy of a six-stanza version, headed 'On the Lady Elizabeth, when shee was first crowned Queene of Bohemia' and here beginning 'Yee glorious trifles of ye East', in a verse miscellany; c. 1630.

The text followed on ff. 53v-4 by a Latin version.

Folger, MS V. a. 103, Part I, f. 53r-v.

WoH 98 -----

Copy in a verse miscellany; c. 1660.

Folger, MS V. a. 148, Part I, f. 48.

WoH 99 -----

Copy, headed 'On the Spanish Lady wch the prince should marry', in a verse miscellany compiled by an Oxford man and once owned by one Stephen Welden; mid-17th century.

Folger, MS V. a. 162, f. 79r-v.

WoH 100 -----

Copy of lines 1-7, deleted, in a miscellany owned by James Bateman (b. 1633/4) of Christ's College, Cambridge, by Robert Pierrepont (either the son of Col. Francis Pierrepont, M.P. (d. 1659), or the third Earl of Kingston (1650/1-82)) of Holme-Pierrepoint, Nottinghamshire, and by the poet John Oldham (1653-83); c. 1650s-60s.

Folger, MS V. a. 169, Part II, f. 16.

WoH 101 -----

Copy of a four-stanza version in the miscellany of Robert Pierrepont et al.; c. 1650s-60s.

Folger, MS V. a. 169, Part II, f. 19v.

WoH 102 -----

Copy, headed 'On Q: Anne. By S^r^. H: W.', in a verse miscellany compiled by an Oxford man; c. 1630s.

Folger, MS V. a. 170, p. 43.

WoH 103 -----

Copy of a six-stanza version, headed 'Vpon the La: Elizabeth: By S^r^. H: Wootton' and here beginning 'You glorious trifles of the East', in a verse miscellany compiled by an Oxford man; c. 1630s.

Folger, MS V. a. 170, pp. 100-1.

WoH 104 -----

Copy, headed 'Sr Henr: Wotton on Queene Anne', in a verse miscellany; c. 1630s.

Folger, MS V. a. 245, f. 42v.

WoH 105 -----

Copy, headed 'Sir Henry Wotton on the Lady Elizabeth Queene of Bohemia', in a verse miscellany probably compiled by a member of an Inn of Court; mid-17th century.

Folger, MS V. a. 262, p. 88.

On his Mistress, the Queen of Bohemia

WoH 106 -----

Copy, headed 'Song', in a verse miscellany; c. 1640.

Folger, MS V. a. 319, f. 32.

WoH 107 -----

Copy, headed 'Song', in a verse miscellany; mid-17th century.

Folger, MS V. a. 322, p. 56.

WoH 108 -----

Copy, headed 'On ye Queen of Bohemia', in a miscellany; c. 1630.

Folger, MS V. a. 345, pp. 148-9.

WoH 109 -----

Copy of a five-stanza version, untitled and here beginning 'You glorious trifles of the East', in a verse miscellany owned in 1640 by Anthony St John (1618-73) and Ann St John, of Bletsoe, Bedfordshire; c. 1630s.

Harvard, fMS Eng 626, f. 8r-v.

WoH 110 -----

Copy of a five-stanza version, headed 'To the Spanish Lady', in a verse miscellany compiled by one or two Oxford men, possibly connected with New College and afterwards with the Inns of Court; 1630s.

Harvard, MS Eng 686, ff. 9v-10.

WoH 111 -----

Copy of a four-stanza version, headed 'In reginam Bohemiae', in a verse miscellany compiled by one or two Oxford men, possibly connected with New College and afterwards with the Inns of Court; 1630s.

Harvard, MS Eng 686, f. 84.

WoH 112 -----

Copy of a five-stanza version, untitled and here beginning 'You glorious trifles of the Easte', in a miscellany compiled by or for Sir Henry Cholmley, brother of Sir Hugh Cholmley (1600-57); c. 1624-41.

Harvard, MS Eng 703, ff. 32v-3.

WoH 113 -----

Copy, headed 'On the Q. of Bohemia', in a verse miscellany compiled by one Edward Hyde, perhaps the future first Earl of Clarendon (1609-74); c. 1630s.

Owned by Sir Geoffrey Keynes, *Bibliotheca Bibliographici* No. 1863, f. 2v.

WoH 114 -----

Copy, headed 'Upon the Queen of Bohemia, by Sir John Harrington' and afterwards inscribed 'By Sir H. Wotton', here beginning 'Ye twinckling starrs that in the night', transcribed from an early MS source, in a collection of transcripts of ballads made chiefly by Robert Jamieson (1780?-1844); c. 1800.

This MS recorded in G. Neilson, 'A Bundle of Ballads', *E & S*, 7 (1921), 108-42 (p. 112).

Mitchell Library, Glasgow, 308897, pp. 21-2.

WoH 115 -----

Copy, here beginning 'Youe twinkling stars that in the night', in a musical setting, in a MS songbook possibly compiled by one William Stirling with later additions by John Leyden (1775-1811); c. 1639.

Printed from this MS in Nelly Diem, *Beiträge zur Geschichte der Schottischen Musik im XVII Jahrhundert* (Zürich & Leipzig, 1919), pp. 83-4.

National Library of Scotland, Adv. MS 5. 2. 14, f. 10.

WoH 116 -----

Copy, headed 'Upon ye queen of Bohemia', in a composite volume of verse and dramatic works compiled by members of the Salusbury family of Llewenni, Denbighshire; early-mid-17th century.

National Library of Wales, NLW. MS 5390D, p. 152.

WoH 117 -----

Copy in a musical setting in a MS songbook once owned by a certain Anne Twice; c. 1620.

New York Public Library, Music Division, Drexel MS 4175, No. i.

WoH 118 -----

Copy of a five-stanza version in a musical setting in a MS music book owned (in 1659) and partly compiled by the composer John Gamble; c. 1630s-50s.

New York Public Library, Music Division, Drexel MS 4257, No. 98.

On his Mistress, the Queen of Bohemia

WoH 119 -----

Copy of a six-stanza version, headed 'On the Lady Elizabeth, when shee was first crowned Queene of Bohemia' and here beginning 'Yee glorious trifles of the East', in a verse miscellany; c. 1630.

The text followed on p. 111 by a Latin version.

University of Nottingham, Portland MS Pw V 37, p. 110.

WoH 120 -----

Copy, headed 'Uppon the Queene of Bohemia', in a verse miscellany used by members of the Holgate family of Saffron Walden, Essex; c. 1630s.

Pierpont Morgan Library, MA 1057, p. 72.

WoH 121 -----

Copy, headed 'On the Lady Elizabeth', in a verse miscellany; c. 1634.

Rosenbach Foundation, MS 239/27, p. 42.

WoH 122 -----

Copy of a five-stanza version, headed 'S^r^. H. Wotton on ye L. Elizabeth when she was first crown'd Q: of Bohemia' and here beginning 'Yee glorious trifles of ye East', in a verse miscellany; c. 1635.

The text followed on pp. 34-5 by a Latin version.

Rosenbach Foundation, MS 240/7, pp. 33-4.

WoH 123 -----

Copy, headed 'Vpon the Queene of Bohemya', here beginning 'Ye twinckling Starrs, that in the night' and ascribed to 'Sr John Harrington', in a miscellany compiled by or for Sir Thomas Finch, Viscount Maidstone and Earl of Winchelsea; c. 1634.

Rosenbach Foundation, MS 243/4, p. 48.

WoH 124 -----

Copy, headed 'An Ode upon ye Lady Elizabeth', in a verse miscellany owned in 1642 by one Horatio Carey; c. 1638-42.

Rosenbach Foundation, MS 1083/17, f. 136r-v.

WoH 125 -----

Copy, here beginning 'You minor beauties of the night', in a musical setting in a MS transcript of the first edition of John Forbes, *Cantus, Songs and Fancies* (Aberdeen, 1662); c. 1662.

Sandeman Library, Perth, N16 (No. liv).

WoH 126 -----

Copy in a musical setting written in one of the MS part books of the 'St Andrews Psalter'; early 17th century.

Trinity College, Dublin, MS 412, f. 46v.

WoH 127 -----

Copy written in a MS volume of poems by Donne; c. 1630.

Trinity College, Dublin, MS 877, f. 162v.

WoH 128 -----

Copy, untitled, in a verse miscellany appended to a MS volume of poems by Donne; c. 1630s.

Trinity College, Dublin, MS 877, f. 192.

WoH 129 -----

Copy, untitled, in a verse miscellany connected with Christ Church, Oxford, owned and perhaps partly compiled by George Morley, later Bishop of Winchester (1598-1684); c. 1625-30s.

Westminster Abbey, MS 41, f. 48.

WoH 129.5 See Addenda, p. 635.

WoH 130 -----

Copy in a verse miscellany compiled by Herbert Aston, son of Sir Walter Aston (1584-1639) of Tixall, Staffordshire; c. 1634.

Yale, Osborn Collection, b 4, f. 39r-v.

WoH 131 -----

Copy written in a 19th-century hand in a miscellany originally compiled c. 1644 by one William Han.

Yale, Osborn Collection, b 150, pp. 205-6.

WoH 132 -----

Copy, here beginning 'You violetts that doe first appeare', in a verse miscellany compiled by Tobias Alston (1620-c.1639) of Sayham Hall near Sudbury, Suffolk; c. 1639.

Yale, Osborn Collection, b 197, pp. 44-5.

On his Mistress, the Queen of Bohemia

WoH 133 -----

Copy in a miscellany; late 17th century.

Yale, Osborn Collection, b 213, pp. 28-9.

WoH 133.5 See Addenda, p. 635.

--- -----

See also INTRODUCTION.

WoH 134 *A Poem written by Sir Henry Wotton in his Youth* ('O faithless world, and thy most faithless part').

Copy, untitled and ascribed to 'S[r] H.W.', in a verse miscellany compiled by Sir Francis Wyatt (1575-1644), bound in a composite volume of papers of the Wyatt family; c. 1630.

First pub. in Francis Davison, *Poetical Rapsody* (London, 1602); *Reliquiae Wottonianae* (London, 1651), p. 516; Hannah (1845), pp. 3-5. This MS collated in Dyce (1843), pp. 1-2, and in Hannah.

British Library, Loan MS 15 / Part 2 (Wyatt Commonplace Book), No. 29, ff. [19v-20].

WoH 135 -----

Copy, possibly made by William Fulman (1632-88), in the second volume of the miscellaneous collections of Richard Davis of Sandford; late 17th century.

Bodleian, MS CCC. 318, f. 43.

WoH 136 -----

Copy, untitled, in a MS volume of poems chiefly by Donne compiled by Henry Champernowne (1600-56) of Dartington, Devon; c. 1623.

Bodleian, MS Eng. poet. f. 9, pp. 193-4.

WoH 137 -----

Copy, untitled, in a verse miscellany; c. 1620-33.

Bodleian, MS Rawl. poet. 31, ff. 5v-6.

WoH 138 -----

Copy in a verse miscellany compiled by one 'H.S.', a Cambridge man; c. 1640s-50s.

This MS collated in Hannah.

Bodleian, MS Rawl. poet. 147, p. 74.

WoH 139 -----

Copy, headed 'His M[rs] Constancie', in a composite volume of verse; mid-17th century.

British Library, Add. MS 11811, ff. 31v-2.

WoH 140 -----

Copy in the hand of a playhouse scribe, headed 'On his Mistris falshood', in a verse miscellany possibly compiled for the lawyer Chaloner Chute and belonging to his family in Hampshire; this MS in the same hand as *Dick of Devonshire* (HyT 5) and *Blurt Master Constable* (MiT 6); c. 1630s.

British Library, Add. MS 33998, f. 31v.

WoH 141 -----

Copy, in a verse miscellany once owned by one W. Allen; c. 1630s.

British Library, Egerton MS 923, f. 17.

WoH 142 -----

Copy, headed 'On his loues unconstancy', in a miscellany once owned by Sir Thomas Meres (1634-1715) of Kirton, Lincolnshire; c. 1640s.

British Library, Egerton MS 2725, f. 102r-v.

WoH 143 -----

Copy, untitled, in a verse miscellany; c. 1620-33.

British Library, Harley MS 4064, f. 235.

WoH 144 -----

Copy, untitled, in a verse miscellany; c. 1637.

British Library, Stowe MS 962, f. 170.

WoH 145 -----

Copy, headed 'On his loues Inconstancy', among poems at the end of a MS volume of poems by Donne later used by Dr William Balam (1651-1726) of Ely, Cambridgeshire; c. 1620s-30s.

Cambridge University Library, MS Add. 5778, f. 85.

WoH 146 -----

Copy, untitled, in a verse miscellany among the papers of the Gell family, formerly of Hopton Hall, possibly once owned by Sir John Gell (1593-1671); early-mid-17th century.

Derbyshire Record Office, D258/31/16, p. 12.

WoH 147 -----

Copy, headed 'On Women', in a miscellany among the papers of the Sheridan family of Frampton Court, Dorset; c. 1660s.

Dorset Record Office, D51/5, p. 211.

A Poem written by Sir Henry Wotton in his Youth

WoH 148 -----

Copy among some MS poems bound with a printed exemplum of Sir William Davenant, *Two Excellent Plays* (London, 1665); late 17th century.

Folger, D347, pp. 4-5 (at end of volume).

WoH 149 -----

Copy, headed 'of loues inconstance by: Sr: H: Wotton', in a verse miscellany compiled by William Jordan, schoolmaster of Denbigh or Caernarvon; c. 1674-84.

Folger, MS V. a. 276, Part II, ff. 15v-16.

WoH 150 -----

Copy, untitled, in a miscellany compiled by or for Sir Henry Cholmley, brother of Sir Hugh Cholmley (1600-57); c. 1624-41.

Harvard, MS Eng 703, f. 19v.

WoH 151 -----

Copy, untitled, in a MS volume of poems chiefly by Donne once owned by one Meriall Tracy; c. 1620-33.

Huntington, HM 198, Part II, f. 46r-v.

WoH 152 -----

Copy, untitled, in a MS volume of poems chiefly by Donne later used as a medical notebook by the Royal physician Sir John Wedderburn (1599-1679); c. 1620-33.

National Library of Scotland, MS 6504, f. 85.

WoH 153 -----

Copy of lines 7-26, headed 'Verses made by Sr Henry Wotton' and beginning 'Why was she born to please? or I to trust', in a verse miscellany; c. 1630.

National Library of Wales, Peniarth MS 500B, pp. 18-20.

WoH 154 -----

Copy, untitled, in a verse miscellany of Welsh origin bound with a miscellany owned by one Edward Lewis; c. 1630s.

National Library of Wales, NLW. MS 12443A, Part ii, pp. 52-3.

WoH 155 -----

Copy, headed 'On his Mistris Inconstancie', in a verse miscellany used by members of the Holgate family of Saffron Walden, Essex; c. 1630s.

Pierpont Morgan Library, MA 1057, p. 63.

WoH 156 -----

Copy, headed 'On his Mrs proouing false to his affections', in a verse miscellany appended to a MS volume of poems by Donne; c. 1630s.

Trinity College, Dublin, MS 877, f. 232r-v.

WoH 157 -----

Copy, untitled, in a MS volume of poems chiefly by Donne; c. 1622-33.

Yale, Osborn Collection, b 148, pp. 142-3.

WoH 158 *Tears at the Grave of Sir Albertus Morton who was buried at Southampton* ('Silence in truth would speak my sorrow best').

Copy, headed 'At the tombe of Sr Albertus Morton The teares of a friende', in a verse miscellany compiled by Robert Codrington (1602-65); c. 1638.

First pub. in *Reliquiae Wottonianae* (London, 1651), p. 528; Hannah (1845), pp. 40-3.

Bodleian, MS Eng. poet. f. 27, pp. 20-1.

WoH 159 -----

Copy, headed 'On the Death of Sr Albertus Morton', in a verse miscellany compiled by one 'H.S.', a Cambridge man; c. 1640s-50s.

This MS collated in Hannah.

Bodleian, MS Rawl. poet. 147, p. 107.

WoH 160 -----

Copy in a verse miscellany compiled by the Yorkshire antiquary John Hopkinson (1610-80); late 17th century.

Bradford Central Library, Hopkinson MSS, Vol. 17, f. [122r-v].

WoH 161 *This Hymn was made by Sir H. Wotton, when he was an Ambassador at Venice, in the time of a great sickness there* ('Eternal mover, whose diffused glory').

Copy in a verse miscellany once owned by one Peter Daniell; c. 1630s-40s.

First pub. in *Reliquiae Wottonianae* (London, 1651), p. 529; Hannah (1845), pp. 45-8.

Bodleian, MS Eng. poet. c. 50, f. 53r-v.

This Hymn was made by Sir H. Wotton, when he was an Ambassador at Venice

WoH 162 -----

Copy in a verse miscellany; c. 1630s.

Bodleian, MS Rawl. poet. 160, f. 85.

WoH 163 -----

Copy in a verse miscellany compiled by Archbishop William Sancroft (1617-93); mid-late 17th century.

Bodleian, MS Tanner 466, ff. 4v-5.

WoH 164 -----

Copy on a single leaf, imperfect, in a composite volume of MSS; 17th century.

British Library, Lansdowne MS 98, f. 189.

WoH 165 -----

Copy, headed 'Sr Walter Raleigh in the vnquiett rest of his last sicknes', in a verse miscellany probably compiled by Francis Baskerville of Malmesbury, Wiltshire, and owned in 1663 by William Wallrond; c. 1633.

British Library, Sloane MS 1446, f. 41r-v.

WoH 166 -----

Copy, headed 'An other Hymn made by him on the same occasion', in a verse miscellany entitled *Recueil Choisi De Pieces fugitives En Vers Anglois*; c. 1713.

Rosenbach Foundation, MS 239/16, pp. 11-13.

WoH 167 *To a Noble Friend in his Sickness* ('Untimely fever, rude insulting guest').

Copy, headed 'On the Duke of Buckingham sicke of a feaver', in a verse miscellany compiled by one 'H.S.', a Cambridge man; c. 1640s-50s.

First pub. in *Reliquiae Wottonianae* (London, 1651), p. 519; Hannah (1845), pp. 16-17. This MS collated in Hannah.

Bodleian, MS Rawl. poet. 147, p. 101.

WoH 168 *To J: D: from Mr H: W:* (''Tis not a coate of gray or Shepherds life').

Copy, untitled and here ascribed to 'J[ohn]. D[onne]:', in a MS volume of poems chiefly by Donne compiled by Henry Champernowne (1600-56) of Dartington, Devon; c. 1623.

First pub. in Herbert J.C. Grierson, 'Bacon's Poem, "The World": Its Date and Relation to Certain Other Poems', *MLR*, 6 (1911), 145-56 (p. 155). This MS probably one of the two unspecified MSS known to Grierson.

Bodleian, MS Eng. poet. f. 9, pp. 10-11.

WoH 169 -----

Copy, headed 'Agaynst Solitarines', in a miscellany compiled partly by the Oxford printer Christopher Wase (1627-90); mid-17th century.

Bodleian, MS Rawl. poet. 117, f. 29.

WoH 170 -----

Copy, headed 'A Letter Against Solitarines', in a verse miscellany; c. 1630.

Folger, MS V. a. 103, Part I, f. 69r-v.

WoH 171 -----

Copy, in a MS volume of poems by Donne once owned by John Egerton, first Earl of Bridgewater (1579-1649); c. 1622-33.

Printed probably from this MS in Grierson.

Huntington, EL 6893, f. 74r-v.

WoH 172 -----

Copy, headed 'To his freind on solitarines', in a miscellany compiled by or for Sir Thomas Finch, Viscount Maidstone and Earl of Winchelsea; c. 1634.

Rosenbach Foundation, MS 243/4, pp. 112-13.

WoH 173 -----

Copy, untitled, in a MS volume of poems chiefly by Donne; c. 1622-33.

Yale, Osborn Collection, b 148, p. 1.

WoH 174 *A Translation of the CIV. Psalm to the original sense* ('My soul exalt the Lord with hymns of praise').

Copy in a verse miscellany compiled by Archbishop William Sancroft (1617-93); mid-late 17th century.

First pub. in *Reliquiae Wottonianae* (London, 1651), p. 525; Hannah (1845), pp. 36-9.

Bodleian, MS Tanner 466, f. 16r-v.

WoH 175 *Upon the Death of Sir Albert Morton's Wife* ('He first deceased; she for a little tried').

Copy in a miscellany probably compiled by members of the Cartwright family of Aynho, Northamptonshire; mid-17th century.

First pub. in William Camden, *Remaines* (London, 1636); *Reliquiae Wottonianae* (London, 1651), p. 529; Hannah (1845), p. 44.

Bodleian, MS Don. e. 6, f. 16.

Upon the Death of Sir Albert Morton's Wife

WoH 176 -----

Second copy in a miscellany probably compiled by members of the Cartwright family; mid-17th century.

Bodleian, MS Don. e. 6, f. 17.

WoH 177 -----

Copy, headed 'On a Gent: dying soon after his wife' and here beginning 'His wife deceas'd hee after liu'd & try'de', in a verse miscellany compiled by a member of Christ Church, Oxford; c. 1630s-40s.

Bodleian, MS Eng. poet. e. 97, p. 153.

WoH 178 -----

Copy, here beginning 'She first deceased, he for a little tried', in a miscellany compiled by Edward Natley, fellow of Queens' College, Cambridge; c. 1635-44.

Bodleian, MS Eng. poet. f. 25, f. 10v.

WoH 179 -----

Copy, here beginning 'She first deceased, he for a little tried', in a verse miscellany; c. 1640.

Bodleian, MS Firth e. 4, p. 6.

WoH 180 -----

Copy, headed 'on Sir Henry Woottons Lady', in a miscellany compiled by John Gandye (b. 1604/5) of Oriel College, Oxford; c. 1620s.

Bodleian, MS Rawl. D. 947, f. 80 rev.

WoH 181 -----

Copy in a verse miscellany belonging to the Paulet family and owned in 1659 by one Egigius Frampton; mid-17th century.

Bodleian, MS Rawl. poet. 84, f. 46.

WoH 182 -----

Copy in a MS book of jests compiled by Archbishop William Sancroft (1617-93); mid-late 17th century.

Bodleian, MS Sancroft 53, p. 44.

WoH 183 -----

Copy, in a verse miscellany compiled by the Yorkshire antiquary John Hopkinson (1610-80); late 17th century.

Bradford Central Library, Hopkinson MSS, Vol. 17, f. [122v].

WoH 184 -----

Copy, headed 'An Epitaph', in a composite volume of verse; mid-17th century.

British Library, Add. MS 11811, f. 2.

WoH 185 -----

Copy, headed 'An epitaph of two Louers', in a composite volume of verse belonging to the Skipwith family of Cotes, Leicestershire; early-mid-17th century.

British Library, Add. MS 25707, f. 100v.

WoH 186 -----

Copy, headed 'On a gentleman dying presently after his wife' and here beginning 'She first deceased, he after liv'd, & tried', in a verse miscellany compiled by Daniel Leare (a distant cousin of William Strode) probably while at Christ Church, Oxford; c. 1631-3.

British Library, Add. MS 30982, f. 37.

WoH 187 -----

Copy, here beginning 'Shee first deceas'd hee after liv'd & tried', in a verse miscellany once owned by the physician Nathaniel Highmore (1613-85); c. 1630s.

British Library, Sloane MS 542, f. 56.

WoH 188 -----

Copy, untitled, in a miscellany; mid-17th century.

British Library, Sloane MS 1925, f. 30v.

WoH 189 -----

Copy in a miscellany compiled by Richard Boyle, Viscount Dungarvon, later Earl of Burlington (1612-98); c. 1630s.

Folger, MS V. a. 125, Part I, f. 9v.

WoH 190 -----

Copy, headed 'Epitaph 13. On a lady dying quickly after her husband', in a miscellany compiled by one Theophilus Alye; c. 1679-1718.

Folger, MS V. a. 147, f. 5.

WoH 191 -----

Copy, headed 'Of a gentlewoman y[t] dyed within a few dayes after her Husband', in a verse miscellany possibly once owned by Sir John Reresby (d. 1646); among the papers of the

Upon the Death of Sir Albert Morton's Wife

Savile family, formerly of Methley Hall, near Pontefract; c. 1630s.

Leeds Archives Department, MX 237, f. 30v.

WoH 192 -----

Copy, headed 'on one dyinge p[r]sently after her husband' and here beginning 'He first deceasts, she after liv'd & tryed', in a miscellany owned and probably compiled by Hugh Barrow (b. 1617/18) of Brasenose College, Oxford; c. 1638.

New York Public Library, Arents Collection, Cat. No. S288, p. 23.

WoH 193 -----

Copy in a verse miscellany used by members of the Holgate family of Saffron Walden, Essex; c. 1630s.

Pierpont Morgan Library, MA 1057, p. 169.

WoH 194 -----

Copy, headed 'Epitaph' and here beginning 'The man dy'd first, shee livd a while & try'd', in a verse miscellany; c. 1630.

Rosenbach Foundation, MS 239/23, p. 166.

WoH 195 -----

Copy, headed 'An Epitaph on a Gentlewoman who died for greife within a few daies after her husband', in a verse miscellany; c. 1635.

Rosenbach Foundation, MS 240/7, p. 36.

WoH 196 -----

Copy, headed 'On a Lady y[t] dyd soon after her husband' and here beginning 'He first deceased she liv'd, and try'd', in a verse miscellany; late 17th century.

Owned by John Sparrow, Oxford, MS, p. 135.

WoH 196.5 See Addenda, p. 635.

WoH 197 -----

Copy in a verse miscellany; c. 1635.

Edwin Wolf 2nd, Philadelphia, MS, p. 52.

WoH 197.5, 197.8 See Addenda, p. 635.

WoH 198 -----

Copy, here ascribed to 'W.S.' and beginning 'She first deceas'd, he after liv'd, and try'd', in a 12° miscellany compiled by Jeremie Baines (fl. 1639-51) of Hampshire; mid-17th century.

Formerly owned by Rev. Thomas William Webb, of Hardwick Vicarage, Herefordshire, this volume recorded and this text printed in *HMC*, 7th Report, Part I (1879), Appendix, p. 691.

Unlocated.

--- -----

See also INTRODUCTION.

WoH 199 *Upon the Sudden Restraint of the Earl of Somerset then falling from favour* ('Dazzled thus with the height of place').

Copy, originally headed 'S[r] H.W. (on y[e] Duke of Somer.)' and headed in a later hand 'On the suddaine restraint of a Favorite. Impressa', in a verse miscellany compiled by one 'H.S.', a Cambridge man; c. 1640s-50s.

First pub. in *Reliquiae Wottonianae* (London, 1651), p. 522; Hannah (1845), pp. 25-7. Some texts of this poem discussed in Ted-Larry Pebworth, 'Sir Henry Wotton's "Dazel'd Thus, with Height of Place" and the Appropriation of Political Poetry in the Earlier Seventeenth Century', *PBSA*, 71 (1977), 151-69. This MS collated in Hannah and in Pebworth, p. 161 seq.

Bodleian, MS Rawl. poet. 147, pp. 97-8.

WoH 200 -----

Copy, headed 'By y[e] moste Illustrious Prince George Duke of Buckingham &c.' and here beginning 'Dazeled wth y[e] height of place', in a MS volume of poems by and probably in the hand of one 'Alphonso Mervall' (i.e. James Cobbes?); c. 1629.

Printed from this MS in Pebworth, pp. 154-5. On p. 82 of the MS are three Latin versions added later by one James Harvey.

Bodleian, MS Rawl. poet. 166, p. 83.

WoH 201 -----

Copy, headed 'On the suddaine restraint of a Favourite' and here beginning 'Thus dazel'd wth y[e] height of place', in a verse miscellany compiled by Archbishop William Sancroft (1617-93); mid-late 17th century.

This MS collated in Hannah and in Pebworth, p. 161 seq.

Bodleian, MS Tanner 465, f. 61v.

WoH 201.5 See Addenda, p. 635.

WoH 202 -----

Copy, headed 'Upon Secretarye Da: fall' and here ascribed to 'F.B.', in a verse miscellany compiled by the Yorkshire antiquary John Hopkinson (1610-80); late 17th century.

Printed from this MS (or from the second copy:

WoH 203) in *HMC*, 3rd Report (1872), Appendix, p. 295.

Bradford Central Library, Hopkinson MSS, Vol. 17, f. [26v].

WoH 203 -----

Second copy, headed 'On Secretarye Dauison fall' and ascribed to 'F.B.', in a verse miscellany compiled by John Hopkinson; late 17th century.

See WoH 202.

Bradford Central Library, Hopkinson MSS, Vol. 17, f. [124v].

WoH 204 -----

Copy, headed 'Vpon the sudden restraint of a Fauorite', in a composite volume of verse belonging to the Skipwith family of Cotes, Leicestershire; early-mid-17th century.

This MS collated in Pebworth, p. 161 seq.

British Library, Add. MS 25707, f. 185v.

WoH 205 -----

Copy, untitled, in a composite volume of MSS; mid-17th century.

This MS collated in Pebworth, p. 161 seq. The text accompanied by two Latin versions.

British Library, Harley MS 1221, f. 110.

WoH 206 -----

Copy, untitled, in a verse miscellany; mid-17th century.

This MS collated in Pebworth, p. 161 seq. The text accompanied by two Latin versions.

British Library, Harley MS 6038, f. 44r-v.

WoH 207 -----

Copy, headed 'To a Favorite', among poems at the end of a MS volume of poems by William Browne of Tavistock possibly compiled by a member of an Inn of Court; c. 1637-50.

This MS collated in Pebworth, p. 161 seq.

British Library, Lansdowne MS 777, f. 64v.

WoH 208 -----

Copy, headed 'Of ffauorites', in a verse miscellany probably compiled by Francis Baskerville of Malmesbury, Wiltshire, and owned in 1663 by William Wallrond; c. 1633.

This MS collated in Pebworth, p. 161 seq.

British Library, Sloane MS 1446, f. 76.

WoH 209 -----

Copy, headed 'Vpon Somersets fall', in a miscellany; mid-17th century.

This MS collated in Pebworth, p. 160 seq.

British Library, Sloane MS 1925, ff. 30v, 29v.

WoH 210 -----

Copy, headed 'To the Lord Bacon then falling from favour', in a miscellany of Scottish provenance compiled by Gideon and Jean Rutherford; c. 1690-1725.

Folger, MS V. a. 255, f. 17v.

WoH 211 -----

Copy, untitled and here beginning 'Thus dazelled with height of place', in a verse miscellany; mid-17th century.

Folger, MS V. a. 322, p. 182.

WoH 212 -----

Copy, headed 'Of Fauorites' and here ascribed to 'Sr Water Ralegh', in a verse miscellany possibly once owned by Sir John Reresby (d. 1646); among the papers of the Savile family, formerly of Methley Hall, near Pontefract; c. 1630s.

Leeds Archives Department, MX 237, f. 56v.

WoH 213 -----

Copy, untitled and here beginning 'Dazled with the height of Place', with alternating Latin verses, written on the first page of a single bifolium, among the collections of the Duke of Portland, of Welbeck Abbey, Nottinghamshire; early-mid-17th century.

University of Nottingham, Portland MS Pw V 518.

WoH 214 -----

Copy, untitled and here beginning 'Thus dazelled with height of place', in a verse miscellany; c. 1630.

Rosenbach Foundation, MS 239/23, pp. 202-3.

WoH 215 -----

Copy in the hand of 'Johs. Rasbrick vic. de Kirkton', headed 'To the Lord Bacon when Falling from Favour', written on the flyleaf of what

Upon the Sudden Restraint of the Earl of Somerset

Rimbault calls 'an Old Music Book'; 17th century.

Printed from this MS (then in his possession) by Edward F. Rimbault in 'Ten Queries concerning Poets and Poetry', *N & Q*, 1 (9 March 1850), 302; this source recorded in Pebworth, p. 161.

Unlocated.

(2) POEMS OF UNCERTAIN AUTHORSHIP

WoH 216 *A Description of the Country's Recreations* ('Quivering fears, heart-tearing cares').

Copy among some MS poems bound with a printed exemplum of Sir William Davenant, *Two Excellent Plays* (London, 1665); late 17th century.

First pub. in *Reliquiae Wottonianae* (London, 1651), p. 531; Hannah (1845), pp. 55-9.

Folger, D347, pp. 6-8 (at end of volume).

WoH 217 -----

Copy, untitled, in a miscellany owned by Jamés Bateman (b. 1633/4) of Christ's College, Cambridge, by Robert Pierrepont (either the son of Col. Francis Pierrepont, M.P. (d. 1659), or the third Earl of Kingston (1650/1-82)) of Holme-Pierrepoint, Nottinghamshire, and by the poet John Oldham (1653-83); c. 1650s-60s.

Folger, MS V. a. 169, Part II, f. 4-5.

WoH 217.5 See Addenda, p. 635.

WoH 218 -----

Copy, headed 'Rusticatio Religiosi in Vacantiis', in a collection of unbound MS verse belonging to the Aston family of Tixall, Staffordshire; 17th century?

Printed from this MS in Arthur Clifford, *Tixall Poetry* (Edinburgh, 1813), pp. 297-300; collated from this publication in Hannah.

Unlocated.

WoH 219 *A Farewell to the Vanities of the World* ('Farewell, ye gilded follies, pleasing troubles!').

Copy, headed 'Doctor Donn's valadiction to the worlde', in a verse miscellany compiled by Nicholas Burghe (d. 1670); c. 1638.

First pub. in Izaak Walton, *The Compleat Angler* (London, 1653), pp. 243-5; Hannah (1845), pp. 109-13; *The Poems of John Donne*, ed. Herbert J.C. Grierson (Oxford, 1912), I, 465-7. This MS recorded in Hannah.

Bodleian, MS Ashmole 38, p. 1a.

WoH 220 -----

Copy, headed 'A Hermitts Meditation in the Grote', in a verse miscellany compiled by an Oxford man; mid-17th century.

Bodleian, MS CCC. 176, f. 30.

WoH 221 -----

Copy, headed 'Dr Donnes farewell to ye world', in a verse miscellany compiled by an Oxford man, possibly a member of Wadham College, and later used by William Fulman (1632-88); c. late 1630s.

This MS (erroneously cited as 'MS. 324') collated in Grierson.

Bodleian, MS CCC. 328, f. 20r-v.

WoH 222 -----

Copy, headed 'Sir Kellam Digbyes farewell to the World', in a miscellany probably compiled by members of the Cartwright family of Aynho, Northamptonshire; mid-17th century.

Bodleian, MS Don. e. 6, f. 7.

WoH 223 -----

Copy, headed 'An Invention for an Arbour', with a lengthy prose introduction describing a 'devise' with an emblem of a man with his foot on a globe &c., in a miscellany; early-mid-17th century.

Bodleian, MS Eng. poet. e. 57, ff. 15v-16v.

WoH 224 -----

Copy, headed 'Dr Dunne's farrewell to the world', in a verse miscellany compiled by Robert Codrington (1602-65); c. 1638.

Bodleian, MS Eng. poet. f. 27, pp. 79-80.

WoH 225 -----

Copy in a volume of genealogical collections of Sir William Dugdale (1605-86); early-mid-17th century.

Bodleian, MS Rawl. B. 144, f. 68.

WoH 226 -----

Copy, headed 'A Poeme made by D^r: Donne a Litle befor his death', in a verse miscellany; c. 1640.

Bodleian, MS Rawl. poet. 153, f. 16.

A Farewell to the Vanities of the World

WoH 227 -----

Copy in a composite volume of verse and prose; early-mid-17th century.

Bodleian, MS Rawl. poet. 172, f. 106.

WoH 228 -----

Copy, headed 'An Hermite in an Arbour, wth a prayer booke in his hand, his foote spurning a globe, thus speaketh', in a verse miscellany compiled by Archbishop William Sancroft (1617-93); mid-late 17th century.

This MS recorded in Hannah.

Bodleian, MS Tanner 465, f. 59r-v.

WoH 228.5 See Addenda, p. 636.

WoH 229 -----

Copy, headed 'Sr Kenelm Digbys Farewell to England', in a miscellany compiled by one John Watson; c. 1667-73.

This MS collated in Grierson.

British Library, Add. MS 18220, f. 69.

WoH 230 -----

Copy of lines 1-26, headed 'D^r^. Donne his farewell to the world', in a verse miscellany once owned by Francis Norreys (? Sir Francis Norris (1609-69)) and Henry Balle; mid-17th century.

British Library, Egerton MS 2421, f. 42v.

WoH 231 -----

Copy, headed 'A ffarewell to the world by S^r^. Kenelme Digby', in a composite volume of miscellaneous papers; 17th century.

This MS collated in Grierson.

British Library, Egerton MS 2603, f. 63.

WoH 232 -----

Copy, headed 'Doctor King his Farewell to the World', in a miscellany once owned by Sir Thomas Meres (1634-1715) of Kirton, Lincolnshire; c. 1640s.

British Library, Egerton MS 2725, f. 61r-v.

WoH 233 -----

Copy, headed 'A Good night to the world', in a verse miscellany compiled by one Thomas Crosse; c. 1630s.

This MS collated in Grierson.

British Library, Harley MS 6057, f. 14.

WoH 234 -----

Copy in a verse miscellany bound in a composite volume of MSS; late 17th century.

British Library, Lansdowne MS 223, f. 134v.

WoH 235 -----

Copy, headed 'A Farwell to ye world. May ye 16', transcribed by Francis Mortoft in his MS *Journal of a Voyage through France and Italy in 1658-59*; 16 May [1659].

This MS recorded in *Francis Mortoft: His Book*, ed. Malcolm Letts, Hakluyt Society, 2nd Ser. 57 (London, 1925), p. xiii.

British Library, Sloane MS 2142, f. 87.

WoH 236 -----

Copy, headed 'A farewell to ye world, per Sir Kell Digby. 1635', in a verse miscellany; c. 1637.

British Library, Stowe MS 962, ff. 33-4.

WoH 237 -----

Copy, headed 'Dr Donne's farewell to ye world', in a verse miscellany once owned by William Godolphin and Henry Savile; late 17th century.

Printed from this MS in *The Complete Poems of John Donne*, ed. A.B. Grosart, 2 vols, (privately printed, 1871-2), II, 248-9; recorded in Grierson.

Cambridge University Library, MS Dd. 6. 43, ff. 18v-19v.

WoH 238 -----

Copy, headed 'D: Dun's fairrweell', in a verse miscellany; c. 1630s-40s.

Edinburgh University Library, MS La. III. 436, pp. 115-16.

WoH 239 -----

Copy, headed 'Dr Dunn's farwell to ye world', in a verse miscellany compiled by an Oxford man, possibly a member of Christ Church; c. late 1630s.

Folger, MS V. a. 97, pp. 66-7.

WoH 240 -----

Copy, here ascribed to 'Dr Donn[e]', in a miscellany owned by James Bateman (b. 1633/4) of Christ's College, Cambridge, by Robert Pierrepont (either the son of Col. Francis Pierrepont, M.P. (d. 1659), or the third Earl of Kingston (1650/1-82)) of Holme-Pierrepoint, Nottinghamshire, and by the poet John Oldham

A Farewell to the Vanities of the World

(1653-83); c. 1650s-60s.

Folger, MS V. a. 169, Part II, ff. 6-7.

WoH 241 -----

Copy, headed 'Upon Solitud and the vanity of other things', in a miscellany of Scottish provenance compiled by Gideon and Jean Rutherford; c. 1690-1725.

Folger, MS V. a. 255, f. 6.

WoH 242 -----

Copy, headed 'A Hermitt in an Arbor wth a prayer booke in his hand spurning the Globe', in a verse miscellany compiled by William Jordan, schoolmaster of Denbigh or Caernarvon; c. 1674-84.

Folger, MS V. a. 276, Part II, f. 32r-v.

WoH 243 -----

Copy, headed 'A Farewell to Folly', in a verse miscellany; c. 1690-1730.

Folger, MS V. a. 308, f. 41v.

WoH 244 -----

Copy, untitled and here ascribed to Donne, in a verse miscellany; c. 1640.

Folger, MS V. a. 319, f. 34r-v.

WoH 245 -----

Copy, here ascribed to Donne, in a verse miscellany; mid-17th century.

Folger, MS V. a. 322, pp. 36-7.

WoH 246 -----

Copy, headed 'Dr Dunns good night to ye world', in a miscellany compiled by an Oxford man, possibly a member of Brasenose College; c. late 1630s.

Huntington, HM 116, p. 78.

WoH 247 -----

Copy, headed 'A contempt of ye world', in a miscellany possibly compiled by one William Leigh; c. 1650.

University of Illinois, Leigh, William (?) comp., Commonplace book (ca. 1650), pp. 20-1.

WoH 248 -----

Copy, untitled, in a MS volume of poems chiefly by Donne later used as a medical notebook by the Royal physician Sir John Wedderburn (1599-1679); c. 1620-33.

National Library of Scotland, MS 6504, f. 85.

WoH 249 -----

Copy, headed 'Sr Kenellam Digbies farwell to the Worlde', in a composite volume of verse and dramatic works compiled by members of the Salusbury family of Llewenni, Denbighshire; early-mid-17th century.

National Library of Wales, NLW. MS 5390D, pp. 318-19.

WoH 250 -----

Copy, headed 'Contempt of ye World' and here ascribed to 'Sr Kenelme Digby', in a verse miscellany entitled *Recueil Choisi De Pieces fugitives En Vers Anglois*; c. 1713.

Rosenbach Foundation, MS 239/16, pp. 41-2.

WoH 251 -----

Copy, headed 'His last goodnight. Dr Don', in a miscellany; c. 1660.

Rosenbach Foundation, MS 239/18, pp. 50-1.

WoH 252 -----

Copy, headed 'To the world D^r^: Dunne', in a miscellany partly compiled by one Robert Berkeley; c. 1640.

Rosenbach Foundation, MS 240/2, pp. 85, 87.

WoH 253 -----

Copy, headed 'Dr Dons last verses', in a verse miscellany owned and possibly compiled by John Pike of Cambridge; c. 1636-40s.

St John's College, Cambridge, MS S. 32 (James 423), f. 26r-v.

WoH 254 -----

Copy, headed 'Sr Kellam Digbie's Farewell to the World', in a miscellany; c. 1636-40.

St John's College, Cambridge, MS S. 44 (James 434), f. [6r-v rev.].

WoH 255 -----

Copy, headed 'A hermite in an arboure, wth a prayer booke in his hand, his foote spurninge

A Globe', in a verse miscellany compiled by John Cruso (1618-81) of Gonville and Caius College, Cambridge; c. 1630s.

St John's College, Cambridge, MS U. 26 (James 548), pp. 84-6.

WoH 256 -----

Copy, headed 'D[r] Duns Goodnight to the world', in a verse miscellany; c. 1640.

Yale, Osborn Collection, b 62, pp. 20-2.

WoH 257 -----

Copy, headed 'On an Hermite in a grove wth A prayer booke in his hand', in a miscellany; mid-17th century.

Yale, Osborn Collection, b 200, pp. 110-12.

WoH 257.5 See Addenda, p. 636.

--- -----

See also INTRODUCTION.

PROSE

--- *Aphorisms of Education.*

See INTRODUCTION.

WoH 258 *A Brief Discourse concerning the Emperor's Election, the Netherlands, and the Low Countries' Greatness, with some other affairs of State.*

Copy, in the same hand as SiP 211, in a composite volume of state tracts; mid-17th century.

Believed to be unpublished. This MS recorded in Pearsall Smith, II, 414.

Bodleian, MS Rawl. A. 141, ff. 65-70.

--- *Character of Robert, late Earl of Salisbury.*

See CYRIL TOURNEUR, ToC 2-6.

WoH 259 *A Concept of some Observations intended upon Things most Remarkable in the Civil History of this Kingdom.*

Copy of 'The preface to my sayd discourse' in a volume of letters and papers once owned by Archbishop William Sancroft (1617-93); mid-late 17th century.

First pub. in *Reliquiae Wottonianae* (London, 1651), pp. 163-74. This preface first pub. (from this MS) in John Gutch, *Collectanea Curiosa*, 2 vols (Oxford, 1781), I, 215-22.

Bodleian, MS Tanner 461, ff. 51-2v.

--- *Concerning Duellos in Spain.*

See INTRODUCTION.

--- *The Elements of Architecture.*

See INTRODUCTION.

WoH 260 *Italian Authors selected and censured by Sir Hen. Wotton.*

Copy of Wotton's list and comments in a volume of miscellaneous papers partly compiled by Archbishop William Sancroft (1617-93); mid-17th century.

First pub. (from this MS) in Pearsall Smith (1907), II, 484-6.

Bodleian, MS Tanner 88, ff. 142-3.

WoH 261 *A Meditation upon the XXIIth Chapter of Genesis. By H.W.*

Copy in the hand of Archbishop William Sancroft (1617-93) in a volume of miscellaneous papers; mid-late 17th century.

First pub. in *Reliquiae Wottonianae* (London, 1651), pp. 343-50.

Bodleian, MS Tanner 88, ff. 11v-12.

WoH 262 *A Parallel between Robert Earl of Essex and George Duke of Buckingham.*

Copy; c. 1634-41.

First pub. London, 1641; ed. Sir Robert Egerton Brydges (Lee Priory Press, Ickham, 1814).

Bodleian, MS Add. A. 104.

WoH 263 -----

Copy, endorsed 'for M[r] hide', in a miscellany compiled by Edward Hyde, first earl of Clarendon (1609-74); c. 1634-41.

Bodleian, MS Clarendon 127, ff. 5-10.

WoH 264 -----

Copy in a volume of miscellaneous collections of Roger Dodsworth (1585-1654); c. 1634-41.

Bodleian, MS Dodsw. 49, ff. 120-5.

WoH 265 -----

Copy in a volume of letters and tracts compiled by Archbishop William Sancroft (1617-93); mid-late 17th century.

Bodleian, MS Tanner 299, ff. 76-83v.

A Parallel between Essex and Buckingham

WoH 266 -----

Copy in a volume of state tracts owned by Browne Willis (1682-1760); c. 1634-41.

Bodleian, MS Willis 58, ff. 426-60v.

WoH 267 -----

Copy in a composite volume of papers relating to Queen Elizabeth and the Earl of Essex collected by Thomas Birch (1705-66); c. 1634-41.

British Library, Add. MS 4130, ff. 121-59v.

WoH 268 -----

Copy in a volume of antiquarian and state tracts; c. 1634-41.

British Library, Add. MS 22591, ff. 306-11.

WoH 269 -----

Copy in a volume of state tracts; late 17th century.

British Library, Hargrave MS 168, ff. 414-37.

WoH 270 -----

Copy in a composite volume of state tracts; c. 1634-41.

British Library, Harley MS 293, ff. 132-51v.

WoH 271 -----

Copy in a composite volume of tracts; c. 1634-41.

British Library, Harley MS 4685, ff. 31-49v.

WoH 272 -----

Copy in a composite volume of MSS; c. 1634-41.

British Library, Harley MS 5111, ff. 94-116v.

WoH 273 -----

Copy in a composite volume of state papers; c. 1634-41.

British Library, Harley MS 6854, ff. 130-41.

WoH 274 -----

Copy in a volume of state tracts; late 17th century.

British Library, Lansdowne MS 213, ff. 203-13v.

WoH 275 -----

Copy in two hands in a volume of state papers; c. 1640.

British Library, Lansdowne MS 489, ff. 111-18v.

WoH 276 -----

Copy; c. 1634-41.

British Library, Stowe MS 289.

WoH 277 -----

Copy, imperfect, consisting of only one leaf and fragments of two others, in a composite volume of tracts and state papers collected by the pamphleteer John Nalson (1638?-86); c. 1634-41.

Cambridge University Library, MS Add. 5872, f. 157.

WoH 278 -----

Copy in a volume of tracts; c. 1634-41.

Cambridge University Library, MS Dd. 6. 8, ff. 1-17v.

WoH 279 -----

Copy in a volume of state tracts and speeches; c. 1634-41.

Cambridge University Library, MS Ii. 5. 9, ff. 60-8v.

WoH 280 -----

Copy in a small volume of state tracts; c. 1634-41.

Eton College, MS 194, ff. 1-13v.

WoH 281 -----

Copy; c. 1634-41.

Formerly among the papers of the Shirley family at Ettington Park, Stratford-upon-Avon (MS 22); this MS sold at Sotheby's, 29 April 1947, Lot 346.

Eton College, MS 251.

WoH 282 -----

Copy; c. 1634-41.

This MS formerly Phillipps MS 19020.

Folger, MS V. b. 82.

A Parallel between Essex and Buckingham

WoH 283 -----

Copy, including a prefatory letter to the Earl of Portland; c. 1634-41.

Folger, MS X. d. 244.

WoH 284 -----

Copy in a volume of state and theological tracts; c. 1634-41.

Gonville and Caius College, Cambridge, MS 389/609, pp. 423-43.

WoH 285 -----

Copy; c. 1634-41.

This MS sold at Sotheby's, 5 July 1955 (André De Coppet sale), Lot 1019.

Harvard, MS Eng 979.

WoH 286 -----

Copy in a volume of state papers; c. 1634-41.

An 'Answer' to this tract is on ff. 188-208.

Inner Temple Library, Petyt MS 538, Vol. 43, ff. 60-81.

WoH 287 -----

Copy in a volume of state tracts; once owned by Sir Richard Betenson, Bart. (? the first baronet, d. 1679); c. 1634-41.

This MS formerly Phillipps MS 2519.

University of London Library, MS 309, ff. 179-83.

WoH 288 -----

Copy in a volume of state papers; c. 1640.

The Queen's College, Oxford, MS 121, pp. 173-82.

WoH 289 -----

Copy in a volume of state tracts; c. 1634-41.

Trinity College, Dublin, MS 545, ff. 173-87.

WoH 290 -----

Copy in a miscellany possibly compiled by an Oxford man; c. 1640.

This MS sold at Sotheby's, 5 July 1955 (André De Coppet sale), Lot 952.

Yale, Osborn Collection, fb 41, ff. 84-9.

WoH 291 -----

Copy, on 18 pages, inscribed 'Fragment of a Comparison between the Earle of Essex, and Duke of Buckingham, which I judge to be writ about the reign of king Charles the first', in a collection of state papers once owned by John Perceval, first Earl of Egmont (1683-1748); mid-17th century.

This collection formerly Phillipps MS 13964; sold at Sotheby's, 15 June 1971, Lot 1627.

Yale, Osborn Collection, Egmont Box, folder 7.

WoH 292 -----

Copy, unbound, among the papers of the Middletons, a Yorkshire recusant family; c. 1634-41.

Yorkshire Archaeological Society, Leeds, MD 59/22, [no item number].

WoH 293 -----

Copy, the last item in a miscellany once owned (in Paris) by Michael Heneage (? son or grandson of the antiquary Michael Heneage (1540-1600)); c. 1634-41.

Privately owned in England.

WoH 294 -----

Copy, in a 4to MS also containing *Leicester's Commonwealth*; 17th century.

Formerly among the papers of the Isham family at Lamport Hall, Northamptonshire, this MS recorded in *HMC*, 3rd Report (1872), Appendix p. 253.

Unlocated (not among the Isham MSS in the Northamptonshire Record Office).

WoH 295 -----

Copy; 4to; 17th century.

Formerly among the family papers of the Marquis of Westminster at Eaton Hall, Cheshire, this MS recorded in *HMC*, 3rd Report (1872), Appendix, p. 215.

Unlocated.

--- *Philosophical Survey of Education.*

See INTRODUCTION.

WoH 296 *The State of Christendom.*

Copy, lacking a title page; 387 leaves; 1st half 17th century.

The State of Christendom

First pub. London, 1657. Wotton's authorship is not certain.

British Library, Harley MS 3499.

WoH 297 -----

Copy, entitled 'A large and excellent discourse of the Estate of Christiandome Written by An vnknowne Author about the years of our Lord 1594...'; 554 leaves, with a table of contents in another hand; 1st half 17th century.

British Library, Stowe MS 274.

WoH 298 -----

Copy, lacking a title page; 427 leaves, with a table of contents; 1st half 17th century.

Clark Library, Los Angeles, W 937M3/5797.

WoH 299 -----

Copy in two hands; 340 leaves of text plus seven leaves of preliminaries, &c; a title page, inscribed 'A large and excellent discourse of the Estate of Christendome. Written by an vnknowne Author about the yeare of o^r Lord 1594...', added in another hand, that of the scribe who wrote SiP 206 and some tracts among the Acland-Hood MSS in the Somerset Record Office (DD/AH Box 51 Vols. III & V); 1st half 17th century.

This MS presented to Eton College in 1941 by Logan Pearsall Smith. A note on the title page claims incorrectly that marginal notes in the MS are in Wotton's hand.

Eton College, MS 247.

WoH 300 -----

Copy; 457 leaves of text, plus preliminaries and a table of contents; 1st half 17th century.

Huntington, EL 8378.

WoH 301 -----

Copy in two hands; small folio (12" x 7⅝"), 292 leaves; owned in the 18th century by the Marquess of Lothian; 17th century.

Facsimile page in Anderson Galleries sale catalogue, 27-8 January 1932.

Anderson Galleries, 27 January 1932, Lot 30.

WoH 302 -----

A brief synopsis of part of the work, headed 'Notes from a Discourse of the State of Christendom in the year 1589', inscribed in the margin 'Lent me by Mr Stansby August the 10th 1633', in a miscellany partly compiled by William Drake (1606-69) of Shardeloes, near Amersham, Buckinghamshire; c. 1633.

University College London, MS Ogden 7/21, ff. 5-11v.

WoH 303 *Table Talk.*

Copy of a series of anecdotes and sayings, evidently by Wotton, in the hand of his secretary William Parkhurst (fl. 1604-67), with pencil markings in the margin, untitled, in a composite volume of MSS collected by Parkhurst; among the papers of the Finch family of Burley-on-the-Hill, Rutland (the 'Burley MS'); c. 1610.

First pub. (from this MS) in Pearsall Smith (1907), II, 489-500 (his Nos. 35-145); Nos. 1-34, on ff. 255v-6, are not by Wotton: see INTRODUCTION.

Leicestershire Record Office, DG. 7/Lit. 2, ff. 82-6.

WoH 304 -----

A series of notes, anecdotes and sayings, similar in nature to WoH 303 (including references to Venice and to 'Sr H: W.'), also in the hand of William Parkhurst, in a composite volume of MSS; c. 1610.

This MS unrecorded and unpublished.

British Library, Harley MS 3998, ff. 63-7v.

Sir Thomas Wyatt

1503?-42

Foxwell *The Poems of Sir Thomas Wiat*, ed. A.K. Foxwell, 2 vols (London, 1913).

Harrier Richard Harrier, *The Canon of Sir Thomas Wyatt's Poetry* (Cambridge, Massachusetts, 1975).

Hughey Ruth Hughey, *The Arundel Harington Manuscript of Tudor Poetry*, 2 vols (Columbus, Ohio, 1960).

Muir & Thomson *Collected Poems of Sir Thomas Wyatt*, ed. Kenneth Muir and Patricia Thomson (Liverpool, 1969).

For abbreviations used throughout Volume I, see p.xi.

INTRODUCTION

There are four important MS collections of poems by Wyatt, one of which is of special significance since it was compiled by the poet himself:

(1) The EGERTON MS (British Library, Egerton MS 2711). A MS volume, now comprising 136 leaves (several original leaves missing) foliated from 2 to 120; ff. 3-101 occupied by copies of 107 of Wyatt's poems plus his *Penitential Psalms*, two of his letters, and three other poems, one of which is by Surrey (see SuH 65); written in several hands, with one scribal hand predominating on ff. 4-49, 50v-4, 55-62. Poems on ff. 50, 54v, 66, 67-9v, 86-98v, 100-1, and a couplet at the top of f. 70 are in Wyatt's own hand, and his autograph corrections and revisions occur intermittently in the scribal copies between ff. 29v and 66v. The collection was probably compiled in the 1530s, perhaps chiefly in 1537-9 (and certainly before Wyatt's death in 1542). Various other contemporary hands altered and annotated the poems; one of these hands can be identified as that of Nicholas Grimald (1519-62). The volume later passed into the possession of the Harington family, folios 104-7 being filled by Sir John Harington (see HrJ 2), and later members of his family using it as a rough notebook (see HrJ 342).

The Egerton MS has been taken as the main text by all Wyatt's modern editors. The text of ff. 3-101 is printed verbatim in Harrier. A transcript of the MS made c. 1810 for George F. Nott is in the British Library (Add. MS 28636) (this has not been given entries below).

(2) The DEVONSHIRE MS (British Library, Add. MS 17492). A verse miscellany, now comprising 96 numbered leaves (plus blanks), including 122 poems which have been attributed to Wyatt (four copied twice); written in between fifteen and twenty hands; probably compiled in the 1530s-40s by various noblemen and ladies in the Court circle, particularly members of the Howard family. The compilers included Margaret Howard (née Douglas), who transcribed some of the Wyatt poems, Mary Fitzroy (née Howard), Duchess of Richmond, and Mary Shelton. The volume later passed into the possession of the Cavendish family and successive Dukes of Devonshire.

The fragment of flyleaf (f.1) bearing the name of Mary Shelton and part of the signature of Mary Howard is reproduced in Foxwell, I, after p. 250.

(3) The ARUNDEL HARINGTON MS (owned by the Duke of Norfolk, Arundel Castle, MSS (Special Press), 'Harrington MS. Temp. Eliz.'). A verse miscellany, now comprising 145 leaves (of the original 228), including 55 poems which have been attributed to Wyatt (one copied twice) as well as his *Penitential Psalms*; written in several hands; begun by, or for, John Harington of Stepney (1520?-82) and continued by his son, Sir John Harington of Kelston, whose hand occurs frequently in the MS (see HrJ 335); mid-late 16th century.

A transcript of the MS made c. 1810 for George F. Nott is in the British Library (Add. MS 28635) (this has not been given entries below). The complete text of the Arundel Harington MS is printed in Hughey.

(4) The BLAGE MS (Trinity College, Dublin, MS 160). A verse miscellany, now bound in two volumes (volumes two and three (ff. 57-186) of a three-volume set), including 85 poems which have been attributed to Wyatt; written in various hands (including that of John Harington of Stepney), and owned c. 1545-6 by Sir George Blage (1512-51); c. 1530s-40s.

This MS was first described by Kenneth Muir ('An Unrecorded Wyatt Manuscript', *TLS* (20 May 1960), p. 328), and a selection of the poems was printed by him in *Sir Thomas Wyatt and his circle: Unpublished Poems* (Liverpool, 1961).

Copies of particular poems are to be found in various other miscellanies, one of which (British Library, Add. MS 36529), containing nine poems which have been attributed to Wyatt, is yet another volume compiled for John Harington of Stepney (see HrJ 339).

These MS collections, together with a few early printed texts — notably Richard Tottel's Miscellany, *Songes and Sonettes* (London, 1557) — are the materials with which Wyatt's modern editors have attempted to establish both canon and text. There is, however, considerable disagreement among scholars over editorial procedures and the interpretation of MS sources; neither can any account of the MSS offered by editors hitherto, especially with regard to the identification of hands, be accepted without qualification. For contributions to the scholarly debate, in addition to the works cited in the list of abbreviations above, see particularly *The Works of Henry Howard, Earl of Surrey, and of Sir Thomas Wyatt the Elder*, ed. George F. Nott, 2 vols (London, 1815-16); Ruth Hughey, 'The Harington Manuscript at Arundel Castle and Related Documents', *The Library*, 4th Ser. 15 (1934-5), 388-444; Raymond Southall, *The Nature and Significance of Rhythm in the Poetry of Sir Thomas Wyatt, with transcripts of two principal manuscripts (the Devonshire and Egerton MSS)* (unpub. Ph. D. diss., 3 vols, University of Birmingham, 1961); Raymond Southall, *The Courtly Maker* (Oxford, 1964); Raymond Southall, 'The Devonshire Manuscript Collection of Early Tudor Poetry, 1532-41', *RES*, NS 15 (1964), 142-50; Richard Harrier's review of the Muir-Thomson edition, *RQ*, 23 (1970), 471-4; H.A. Mason, *Editing Wyatt: An Examination of Collected Poems of Sir Thomas Wyatt together with suggestions for an improved edition* (Cambridge, 1972); Joost Daalder's review of Mason's book, *EC*, 23 (1973), 399-413; Sir Thomas Wyatt, *Collected Poems*, ed. Joost Daalder (London, 1975); H.A. Mason's review of Daalder's edition and Harrier's book (1975), *Sewanee Review*, 84.ii (1976), 675-83; and Sir Thomas Wyatt, *The Complete Poems*, ed. R.A. Rebholz (Penguin Books, 1978). It should be noted that H.A. Mason (1972), besides discussing certain texts in detail, offers a considerable number of corrections to the texts printed in Muir & Thomson (these corrections are not recorded for each individual poem in the entries below). A completely fresh study of the main MSS, and of the editorial problems associated with Wyatt, is now being made by Helen Baron and is to be published by Oxford University Press. This study is partly based on her unpublished doctoral thesis, *Sir Thomas Wyatt's Seven Penitential Psalms: A study of textual and source materials* (Cambridge, 1977). Some of the details incorporated in the entries below derive from Helen Baron's current work.

The Wyatt canon is an especially debatable subject. For instance, Muir & Thomson admit into the canon, on stylistic grounds, a considerable number of poems found only in the Blage MS, whereas Harrier and Daalder are reluctant to accept as Wyatt's any poem not found in the Egerton MS or clearly ascribed to him in other 16th-century texts. For present purposes the *Index* accepts the canon established in Muir & Thomson, and also cites titles and first lines from that edition. But it is recognised that the canon is very far from certain.

The other important MSS associated with Wyatt are his letters, which provide the evidence for the identification of Wyatt's autograph in the Egerton MS. Thirty-five letters of Wyatt are printed in Kenneth Muir, *Life and Letters of Sir Thomas Wyatt* (Liverpool, 1963). Most of the letters, preserved in the Public Record Office and the British Library (Harley MS 282; Cotton MSS Vespasian C. VII and F. XIII), are autograph. A facsimile of one of the Cotton letters appears in Foxwell (I, after p. 134), and one of the Harley letters is reproduced in Muir (facing p. 101). Contemporary transcripts of certain of Wyatt's letters are preserved in the British Library (Add. MS 5498). There are also a number of 16th and early 17th-century transcripts (some plainly 'edited' versions) of Wyatt's two letters to his son from Spain. Muir prints them (pp. 38-44) from the contemporary transcript found in the Egerton MS (ff. 71-3). Another transcript in the British Library (Add. MS 33271, ff. 25-6) is collated in Albert McHarg Hayes, 'Wyatt's Letters to his Son', *MLN*, 49 (1934), 446-9. Yet more transcripts are preserved in the British Library (Add. MS 32379, ff. 59-62v), in the Bodleian (MS Eng. hist. c. 272, pp. 1-6 (Gurney MS XXXV, recorded in *HMC*, 12th Report, Appendix IX (1891), p. 145)), in Bradford Central Library (Hopkinson MSS, Vol. 18, ff. 43-6), and in a MS volume of state letters in my possession ('Elizabethan MSS', pp. 1000-7).

Muir also prints (*op. cit.*, pp. 178-84, 187-209) Wyatt's formal declaration of innocence and his defence at his indictment in 1541, preserved in a scribal copy in Harley MS 78, ff. 1-15. Another text is in Yelverton MS 21 (recorded in *HMC*, 2nd Report (1871), Appendix, p. 40), now in the British Library (Add. MS 48020, ff. 132-44v), and was collated in Nott's 1815-16 edition of Wyatt.

A number of 16th and 17th-century papers belonging to the Wyatt family are now owned by the Earl of Romney. The only documents which appear to relate to Sir Thomas Wyatt himself, however, are two contemporary copies (one incomplete) of an anonymous 'answer unto 2 most lewde and false allegations, the one against Sr Tho: Wiat th' elder, the other against Sr Tho: ye yonger, his sonne, published in a certen slaunderous and seditious Booke, written against the state by [Nicholas] Saunders ye Papist'. The two copies of this work, which was written c. 1595-8, are bound in a volume of Wyatt family papers now on deposit in the British Library (Loan MS 15 / Part 2 (Wyatt Commonplace Book), Nos. 10 and 24), and the complete text is printed in *The Papers of George Wyatt Esquire of Boxley Abbey in the County of Kent, Son and Heir of Sir Thomas Wyatt the Younger*, ed. D.M. Loades, Camden Society, 4th Ser. 5 (1968), pp. 181-205.

An additional item of interest is a printed exemplum of *Songes and Sonettes* (London, 1557) (now lost) which contained musical notation written against certain of the poems in a contemporary hand. One of the poems annotated in this way was Wyatt's '*If euer man might him auaunt*' (Muir & Thomson, pp. 246-7). The volume was once owned by Sir W.W. Wynne, but was probably destroyed with the bulk of the Wynnstay Library in 1858. The musical notation was transcribed in George F. Nott's edition of *Songs and Sonnets* (1814?), but that edition too was almost totally destroyed by fire and the only extant exemplum known to contain the music is owned by the Duke of Norfolk, Arundel Castle (ref. 13C). For this edition, and other exempla of *Songes and Sonettes* with editors' annotations, see **EARL OF SURREY, INTRODUCTION.**

PB.

ARRANGEMENT

Verse: Poems attributed to Wyatt WyT 1-422.

Sir Thomas Wyatt

VERSE

POEMS ATTRIBUTED TO WYATT

WyT 1 *'A face that shuld content me wonders well'*.

Copy in the Blage MS; c. 1530s-40s.

First pub. in *Songes and Sonettes* (London, 1557). Printed from this MS in Muir & Thomson, pp. 132-3.

Trinity College, Dublin, MS 160, f. 72.

WyT 2 -----

Copy in a Harington miscellany; mid-late 16th century.

This MS collated in Muir & Thomson.

British Library, Add. MS 36529, f. 32v.

WyT 3 *'A Ladye gave me a gyfte she had not'*.

Copy in the Arundel Harington MS; mid-late 16th century.

First pub. in *Songes and Sonettes* (London, 1557). Printed from this MS in Muir & Thomson, pp. 238-9, and in Hughey, I, No. 97, p. 145.

Owned by the Duke of Norfolk, Arundel Castle, MSS (Special Press), 'Harrington MS. Temp. Eliz.', f. 60v.

WyT 4 -----

Copy in a composite volume of verse and prose; early 17th century.

This MS collated in Hughey, II, 126.

Bodleian, MS Rawl. poet. 172, f. 3v.

WyT 5 *'A! my harte, A! what aleth the!'*.

Copy in the Devonshire MS; c. 1530s-40s.

Not pub. in 16th century; Muir & Thomson, p. 129. This MS collated in Muir & Thomson.

British Library, Add. MS 17492, f. 78v.

WyT 6 -----

Copy in the Blage MS; c. 1530s-40s.

Printed from this MS in Muir & Thomson.

Trinity College, Dublin, MS 160, f. 66.

WyT 7 *'A Robyn'*.

Copy of lines 1-16, 21-8, including speech-prefixes, in the Egerton MS; c. 1537-9.

Not pub. (in this form) in 16th century. Printed from this MS in Muir & Thomson, pp. 41-2 (and see WyT 9), and in Harrier, pp. 147-8.

British Library, Egerton MS 2711, f. 37v.

WyT 8 -----

Copy of lines 1-8 in the Devonshire MS; c. 1530s-40s.

This MS collated in Muir & Thomson and in Harrier.

British Library, Add. MS 17492, f. 22v.

WyT 9 -----

Copy (not in the same hand as WyT 8) in the Devonshire MS; c. 1530s-40s.

This MS collated (and lines 17-20 printed) in Muir & Thomson and in Harrier.

British Library, Add. MS 17492, f. 24r-v.

WyT 10 -----

Copy of lines 1-12 in a musical setting by William Cornish (d. 1523) in a MS volume of musical pieces; c. 1515.

Printed from this MS in J.E. Stevens, *Music and Poetry in the Early Tudor Court* (London, 1961), p. 405, and in Muir & Thomson, p. 309; discussed, with a facsimile, in Ivy L. Mumford, 'Musical Settings to the Poems of Sir Thomas Wyatt', *M & L*, 37 (1956), 315-22; facsimile also in Foxwell, I, after p. 62. This text probably the popular song which was the basis for Wyatt's version.

British Library, Add. MS 31922, ff. 53v-4.

WyT 11 -----

Copy of the incipit (here 'Joly Robyn') in an anonymous musical setting in a MS music book; c. 1595.

This MS discussed in Mumford, *op. cit.*, p. 316, and in Mumford, 'Sir Thomas Wyatt's Songs: A Trio of Problems in Manuscript Sources', *M & L*, 39 (1958), 262-4. See WyT 10.

British Library, Add. MS 31392, f. 25.

WyT 12 *'A spending hand that alway powreth owte'*.

Copy in the Egerton MS; c. 1537-9.

First pub. in *Songes and Sonettes* (London, 1557). Printed from this MS in Muir & Thomson, pp. 95-7, and in Harrier, pp. 183-5.

British Library, Egerton MS 2711, ff. 56-7v.

WyT 13 -----

Copy in the Arundel Harington MS; mid-late 16th century.

Printed from this MS in Hughey, I, No. 141, pp. 170-2; collated in Muir & Thomson and in Harrier.

Owned by the Duke of Norfolk, Arundel Castle, MSS (Special Press), 'Harrington MS. Temp. Eliz.', ff. 99 (bis)-100.

WyT 14 *'Absence, alas'.*

Copy in the Blage MS; c. 1530s-40s.

Not pub. in 16th century. Printed from this MS in Muir & Thomson, pp. 127-8.

Trinity College, Dublin, MS 160, f. 64.

WyT 15 *'Absens absenting causithe me to complaine'.*

Copy in the Devonshire MS; c. 1530s-40s.

Not pub. in 16th century. Printed from this MS in Muir & Thomson, pp. 231-2.

British Library, Add. MS 17492, ff. 81v-2.

WyT 16 *'Accusyd thoo I be without desert'.*

Copy in the Blage MS; c. 1530s-40s.

First pub. in *Songes and Sonettes* (London, 1557). Printed from this MS in Muir & Thomson, p. 132.

Trinity College, Dublin, MS 160, f. 70.

WyT 17 *'After great stormes the cawme retornis'.*

Copy in the Egerton MS; c. 1537-9.

Not pub. in 16th century. Printed from this MS in Muir & Thomson, pp. 61-2, and in Harrier, pp. 182-3.

British Library, Egerton MS 2711, f. 55v.

WyT 18 -----

Copy in the Arundel Harington MS; mid-late 16th century.

Printed from this MS in Hughey, I, No. 138, pp. 164-5; collated in Muir & Thomson and in Harrier.

Owned by the Duke of Norfolk, Arundel Castle, MSS (Special Press), 'Harrington MS. Temp. Eliz.', f. 97r-v.

WyT 19 *'Agaynste the Rock I clyme both hy and hard'.*

Copy in the Blage MS; c. 1530s-40s.

Not pub. in 16th century. Printed from this MS in Muir & Thomson, p. 132.

Trinity College, Dublin, MS 160, f. 71.

WyT 20 *'Alas! dere herte, what happe had I'.*

Copy in the Blage MS; c. 1530s-40s.

Not pub. in 16th century. Printed from this MS in Muir & Thomson, p. 126.

Trinity College, Dublin, MS 160, f. 62.

WyT 21 -----

Copy, immediately following on from lines 1-8 of 'Mornyng my hart dothe sore opres' (see WyT 189), in a composite volume of verse and prose tracts; 16th century.

This MS collated in Muir & Thomson.

British Library, Add. MS 18752, f. 89.

WyT 22 *'Alas, fortune, what alith the'.*

Copy in the Blage MS; c. 1530s-40s.

Not pub. in 16th century. Printed from this MS in Muir & Thomson, pp. 128-9.

Trinity College, Dublin, MS 160, f. 65.

*WyT 23 *'Alas madame for stelyng of a kysse'.*

Copy, with autograph revisions and with alterations in another hand, in the Egerton MS; c. 1537-9.

First pub. in *Songes and Sonettes* (London, 1557). Printed from this MS in Muir & Thomson, pp. 33-4, and in Harrier, p. 138. Facsimile in Foxwell, I, after p. 44.

British Library, Egerton MS 2711, f. 31.

WyT 24 -----

Copy in the Arundel Harington MS; mid-late 16th century.

Printed from this MS in Hughey, I, No. 103, p. 147; collated in Muir & Thomson and in Harrier.

Owned by the Duke of Norfolk, Arundel Castle, MSS (Special Press), 'Harrington MS. Temp. Eliz.', f. 63v.

WyT 25 *'Alas! my Dere, the word thow spakest'.*

Copy in the Blage MS; c. 1530s-40s.

Not pub. in 16th century. Printed from this MS in Muir & Thomson, pp. 133-4.

Trinity College, Dublin, MS 160, f. 75.

WyT 26 *'Alas, poor man, what hap have I'.*

Copy in the Devonshire MS; c. 1530s-40s.

Not pub. in 16th century. Printed from this MS in Muir & Thomson, pp. 195-6.

British Library, Add. MS 17492, ff. 15v-16.

WyT 27 *'Alas the greiff, and dedly wofull smert'.*

Copy, with later alterations in the hand of Nicholas Grimald, in the Egerton MS; c. 1537-9.

Not pub. in 16th century. Printed from this MS in Muir & Thomson, pp. 3-4, and in Harrier, pp. 102-3.

British Library, Egerton MS 2711, ff. 5v-6v.

WyT 28 -----

Copy of lines 13-30, beginning 'O cruel causer of vndeserued chaunge', in the Devonshire MS; c. 1530s-40s.

This MS collated in Muir & Thomson and in Harrier.

British Library, Add. MS 17492, f. 2v.

WyT 29 -----

Copy in the Blage MS; c. 1530s-40s.

This MS collated in Muir & Thomson and in Harrier.

Trinity College, Dublin, MS 160, f. 74.

WyT 30 *'All hevy myndes'.*

Copy in the Egerton MS; c. 1537-9.

Not pub. in 16th century. Printed from this MS in Muir & Thomson, pp. 62-4, and in Harrier, pp. 185-8.

British Library, Egerton MS 2711, f. 58r-v.

WyT 31 *'All yn thi sight my lif doth hole depende'.*

Copy in the Devonshire MS; c. 1530s-40s.

First pub. in *Songes and Sonettes* (London, 1557). Printed from this MS in Muir & Thomson, p. 214.

British Library, Add. MS 17492, f. 69.

WyT 32 *'Alle ye that knowe of care and heuynes'.*

Copy in the Blage MS; c. 1530s-40s.

Not pub. in 16th century. Printed from this MS in Muir & Thomson, p. 131.

Trinity College, Dublin, MS 160, f. 69.

WyT 33 *'Alone musyng'.*

Copy in the Blage MS; c. 1530s-40s.

Not pub. in 16th century. Printed from this MS in Muir & Thomson, p. 127.

Trinity College, Dublin, MS 160, f. 63.

WyT 34 *'And if an Iye may save or sleye'.*

Copy of a 42-line version in the Egerton MS; c. 1537-9.

Not pub. in 16th century. Printed from this MS in Muir & Thomson, pp. 73-4, and in Harrier, pp. 199-200.

British Library, Egerton MS 2711, f. 65.

WyT 35 -----

Copy of a 28-line version (not in the same hand as WyT 34), deleted, in the Egerton MS; c. 1537-9.

Printed from this MS in Harrier, pp. 194-5; collated in Muir & Thomson.

British Library, Egerton MS 2711, f. 62v.

WyT 36 *'And wylt thow leve me thus?'.*

Copy in the Devonshire MS; c. 1530s-40s.

Not pub. in 16th century. Printed from this MS in Muir & Thomson, pp. 196-7. Facsimile in Foxwell, I, after p. 272.

British Library, Add. MS 17492, f. 17.

--- *Th' Argument* ('Somtyme the pryde of mye assured trothe').

See WyT 283.

WyT 37 *'As power and wytt wyll me Assyst'.*

Copy in the Devonshire MS; c. 1530s-40s.

Not pub. in 16th century. Printed from this MS in Muir & Thomson, pp. 198-9.

British Library, Add. MS 17492, f. 20.

'As power and wytt wyll me Assyst'

WyT 38 -----

Copy of lines 3-37, here beginning 'Evyn as you lyst my wyll ys bent', in a composite volume of verse and prose tracts; 16th century.

This MS collated in Muir & Thomson.

British Library, Add. MS 18752, f. 89v.

WyT 39 *'At last withdraw youre crueltye'.*

Copy in the Devonshire MS; c. 1530s-40s.

Not pub. in 16th century; Muir & Thomson, pp. 129-30. This MS collated in Muir & Thomson.

British Library, Add. MS 17492, f. 4r-v.

WyT 40 -----

Copy in the Blage MS; c. 1530s-40s.

Printed from this MS in Muir & Thomson.

Trinity College, Dublin, MS 160, f. 67.

*WyT 41 *'At moost myschief'.*

Copy of lines 1-41, with autograph corrections (line 30 inserted), in the Egerton MS; c. 1537-9.

Not pub. in 16th century. Printed from this MS in Muir & Thomson, pp. 36-7 (and see WyT 42-3), and in Harrier, pp. 142-3.

British Library, Egerton MS 2711, f. 34r-v.

WyT 42 -----

Copy in the Devonshire MS; c. 1530s-40s.

This MS collated (and lines 42-8 printed) in Muir & Thomson and in Harrier.

British Library, Add. MS 17492, f. 12.

WyT 43 -----

Copy in the Blage MS; c. 1530s-40s.

This MS collated (and lines 42-8 printed) in Muir & Thomson and in Harrier.

Trinity College, Dublin, MS 160, f. 68.

--- *The Aunswere* ('Your ffolyshe fayned hast').

See WyT 420.

WyT 44 *'Auysing the bright bemes of these fayer Iyes'.*

Copy in the Egerton MS; c. 1537-9.

First pub. in *Songes and Sonettes* (London, 1557). Printed from this MS in Muir & Thomson, p. 22, and in Harrier, p. 125.

British Library, Egerton MS 2711, f. 22.

WyT 45 -----

Copy in the Arundel Harington MS; mid-late 16th century.

Printed from this MS in Hughey, I, No. 113, p. 153; collated in Muir & Thomson and in Harrier.

Owned by the Duke of Norfolk, Arundel Castle, MSS (Special Press), 'Harrington MS. Temp. Eliz.', f. 67.

--- *'Because I have thee still kept from lies and blame'.*

See WyT 49-50.

WyT 46 *'Behold, love, thy power how she dispiseth!'.*

Copy, with later alterations in the hand of Nicholas Grimald, in the Egerton MS; c. 1537-9.

First pub. in *Songes and Sonettes* (London, 1557). Printed from this MS in Muir & Thomson, p. 1, and in Harrier, p. 97. Facsimile in Foxwell, I, after p. 2.

British Library, Egerton MS 2711, f. 4.

WyT 47 -----

Copy in the Devonshire MS; c. 1530s-40s.

This MS collated in Muir & Thomson and in Harrier.

British Library, Add. MS 17492, f. 69v.

WyT 48 *'Beyng as noone ys I doo complayne'.*

Copy in the Blage MS; c. 1530s-40s.

Not pub. in 16th century. Printed from this MS in Muir & Thomson, pp. 134-5.

Trinity College, Dublin, MS 160, f. 77.

WyT 49 *'Bicause I have the still kept fro lyes and blame'.*

Copy, with an alteration in another hand (that responsible for the 'Aunswer' to WyT 183), in the Egerton MS; c. 1537-9.

First pub. in *Songes and Sonettes* (London, 1557). Printed from this MS in Muir & Thomson, p. 20, and in Harrier, p. 123.

British Library, Egerton MS 2711, f. 20.

'Bicause I have the still kept fro lyes and blame'

WyT 50 -----

Copy in the Arundel Harington MS; mid-late 16th century.

Printed from this MS in Hughey, I, No. 110, p. 152; collated in Muir & Thomson and in Harrier.

Owned by the Duke of Norfolk, Arundel Castle, MSS (Special Press), 'Harrington MS. Temp. Eliz.', f. 66r-v.

WyT 51 *'Blame not my lute, for he must sound'.*

Copy in the Devonshire MS; c. 1530s-40s.

Not pub. in 16th century. Printed from this MS in Muir & Thomson, pp. 212-13.

British Library, Add. MS 17492, f. 64r-v.

WyT 52 -----

Copy of the incipit in a musical setting in a miscellany; c. 1559-1610.

Formerly MS 448.16, edited from this MS and discussed in Ivy L. Mumford, 'Musical Settings to the Poems of Sir Thomas Wyatt', *M & L*, 37 (1956), 315-22, and in John H. Long, 'Blame not Wyatt's Lute', *RN*, 7 (1954), 127-30 (and see also Vol. 8 (1955), 12-14).

Folger, MS V. a. 159, f. 4v.

WyT 53 -----

Copy of the incipit in a musical setting, in a MS book of cittern music (item 9) compiled by John Ridout (b. 1608); c. 1625-65.

This MS sold at Sotheby's, 15 June 1971, Lot 1602; not recorded by editors.

Owned by John M. Ward; deposited at Harvard.

WyT 54 *'But sethens you it asaye to kyll'.*

Copy, with later alterations in the hand of Nicholas Grimald, in the Egerton MS; imperfect, lacking the beginning; c. 1537-9.

Not pub. in 16th century. Printed from this MS in Muir & Thomson, p. 4, and in Harrier, pp. 103-4.

British Library, Egerton MS 2711, f. 7.

WyT 55 *'By belstred wordes I am borne in hand'.*

Copy in the Blage MS; c. 1530s-40s.

Not pub. in 16th century. Printed from this MS in Muir & Thomson, p. 134.

Trinity College, Dublin, MS 160, f. 76.

WyT 56 *'Caesar, when that the traytour of Egipt'.*

Copy in the Egerton MS; c. 1537-9.

First pub. in *Songes and Sonettes* (London, 1557). Printed from this MS in Muir & Thomson, p. 2, and in Harrier, pp. 99-100.

British Library, Egerton MS 2711, ff. 4v-5.

WyT 57 -----

Copy in the Devonshire MS; c. 1530s-40s.

This MS collated in Muir & Thomson and in Harrier.

British Library, Add. MS 17492, f. 70.

WyT 58 *'Comeforthe at hand, pluck vp thy harte!'.*

Copy in the Blage MS; c. 1530s-40s.

Not pub. in 16th century. Printed from this MS in Muir & Thomson, p. 136.

Trinity College, Dublin, MS 160, f. 81.

WyT 59 *'Comfort thy self my wofull hert'.*

Copy in the Egerton MS; c. 1537-9.

Not pub. in 16th century. Printed from this MS in Muir & Thomson, pp. 56-7, and in Harrier, p. 166.

British Library, Egerton MS 2711, f. 48v.

WyT 60 -----

Copy in the Devonshire MS; c. 1530s-40s.

This MS collated in Muir & Thomson and in Harrier.

British Library, Add. MS 17492, f. 74.

WyT 61 *'Complaynyng, alas, without redres'.*

Copy in the Blage MS; c. 1530s-40s.

Not pub. in 16th century. Printed from this MS in Muir & Thomson, pp. 135-6.

Trinity College, Dublin, MS 160, f. 80.

--- *'Deem as ye list upon good cause'.*

See WyT 63.

WyT 62 *'Defamed gyltynes by sylens vnkept'.*

Copy in the Blage MS; c. 1530s-40s.

Not pub. in 16th century. Printed from this

'Defamed gyltynes by sylens vnkept'

MS in Muir & Thomson, p. 139.

Trinity College, Dublin, MS 160, f. 86.

WyT 63 *'Deme as ye list vpon goode cause'.*

Copy in the Devonshire MS; c. 1530s-40s.

First pub. in *The Gorgeous Gallery of Gallant Inventions* (London, 1578). Printed from this MS in Muir & Thomson, pp. 235-6.

British Library, Add. MS 17492, f. 84v.

*WyT 64 *'Desire, alas, my master and my foo'.*

Autograph fair copy, with revisions, in the Egerton MS; c. 1537-9.

First pub. in *Songes and Sonettes* (London, 1557). Printed from this MS in Muir & Thomson, p. 57, and in Harrier, p. 173.

British Library, Egerton MS 2711, f. 50.

WyT 65 -----

Copy of an early version beginning 'Cruel desire my master and my foo', in the Devonshire MS; c. 1530s-40s.

This MS collated in Muir & Thomson and in Harrier.

British Library, Add. MS 17492, f. 73.

WyT 66 *'Desyre to Sorow doth me constrayne'.*

Copy in the Blage MS; c. 1530s-40s.

Not pub. in 16th century. Printed from this MS in Muir & Thomson, pp. 138-9.

Trinity College, Dublin, MS 160, f. 85.

--- *'Dido am I, the founder first of Carthage'.*

See WyT 73.

--- *'Disdain me not without desert'.*

See WyT 74.

--- *'Disdain not, madam, on him to look'.*

See WyT 75.

--- *'Divers doth use as I have heard and know'.*

See WyT 76.

WyT 67 *'Do way, do way, ye lytyll wyly prat!'.*

Copy in the Blage MS; c. 1530s-40s.

Not pub. in 16th century. Printed from this MS in Muir & Thomson, p. 138.

Trinity College, Dublin, MS 160, f. 84.

WyT 68 *'Dobell, dyuerse, soleyn and straunge'.*

Copy in the Blage MS; c. 1530s-40s.

Not pub. in 16th century. Printed from this MS in Muir & Thomson, p. 141.

Trinity College, Dublin, MS 160, f. 89.

WyT 69 *'Dryuyn to Desyre, a drad also to Dare'.*

Copy in the Blage MS; c. 1530s-40s.

Not pub. in 16th century. Printed from this MS in Muir & Thomson, pp. 140-1.

Trinity College, Dublin, MS 160, f. 88.

WyT 70 *'Dryven to Desire I Dyd this Dede'.*

Copy of lines 1-7 in the Devonshire MS; c. 1530s-40s.

Lines 1-7 first pub. in *Songes and Sonettes* (London, 1557); Muir & Thomson, pp. 139-40. This MS collated in Muir & Thomson.

British Library, Add. MS 17492, f. 81v.

WyT 71 -----

Copy (31 lines) in the Blage MS; c. 1530s-40s.

Printed from this MS in Muir & Thomson.

Trinity College Dublin, MS 160, f. 87.

WyT 72 *'Durese of paynes and grevus Smarte'.*

Copy in the Blage MS; c. 1530s-40s.

First pub. in *The Court of Venus*, [c. 1538]. Printed from this MS in Muir & Thomson, p. 137.

Trinity College, Dublin, MS 160, f. 83.

WyT 73 *'Dydo am I, the founder first of Cartage'.*

Copy in the Blage MS; c. 1530s-40s.

Not pub. in 16th century. Printed from this MS in Muir & Thomson, p. 141.

Trinity College, Dublin, MS 160, f. 90.

WyT 74 *'Dysdaine me not without desert'.*

Copy in a composite volume of verse and prose tracts; 16th century.

First pub. in *The Court of Venus*, [? c. 1538]

'Dysdaine me not without desert'

(no perfect exemplum known; it is in the later edition of c. 1563); *Songes and Sonettes* (London, 1557); Muir & Thomson, pp. 257-8. This MS collated in Muir & Thomson.

British Library, Add. MS 18752, f. 163v.

WyT 75 *'Dysdayne not, madam, on hym to louke'.*

Copy in the Blage MS; c. 1530s-40s.

Not pub. in 16th century. Printed from this MS in Muir & Thomson, p. 142.

Trinity College, Dublin, MS 160, f. 92.

WyT 76 *'Dyvers doth vse as I have hard and kno'.*

Copy in the Devonshire MS; c. 1530s-40s.

Not pub. in 16th century. Printed from this MS in Muir & Thomson, pp. 222-3.

British Library, Add. MS 17492, f. 77v.

WyT 77 *'Eche man me telleth I chaunge moost my devise'.*

Copy in the Egerton MS; c. 1537-9.

First pub. in *Songes and Sonettes* (London, 1557). Printed from this MS in Muir & Thomson, p. 11, and in Harrier, p. 112.

British Library, Egerton MS 2711, f. 11v.

WyT 78 -----

Copy in the Devonshire MS; c. 1530s-40s.

This MS collated in Muir & Thomson and in Harrier.

British Library, Add. MS 17492, f. 75v.

WyT 79 -----

Copy in the Arundel Harington MS; mid-late 16th century.

Printed from this MS in Hughey, I, No. 102, p. 147; collated in Muir & Thomson and in Harrier.

Owned by the Duke of Norfolk, Arundel Castle, MSS (Special Press), 'Harrington MS. Temp. Eliz.', f. 63v.

--- *'Even when you lust ye may refrain'.*

See WyT 82.

WyT 80 *'Ever myn happe is slack and slo in commyng'.*

Copy in the Egerton MS; c. 1537-9.

First pub. in *Songes and Sonettes* (London, 1557). Printed from this MS in Muir & Thomson, p. 23, and in Harrier, p. 126.

British Library, Egerton MS 2711, f. 22v.

WyT 81 -----

Copy in the Arundel Harington MS; mid-late 16th century.

Printed from this MS in Hughey, I, No. 114, pp. 153-4; collated in Muir & Thomson and in Harrier.

Owned by the Duke of Norfolk, Arundel Castle, MSS (Special Press), 'Harrington MS. Temp. Eliz.', f. 67.

WyT 82 *'Evyn when you lust ye may refrayne'.*

Copy, headed 'The answere', in the Blage MS; c. 1530s-40s.

Not pub. in 16th century. Printed from this MS in Muir & Thomson, pp. 146-7.

Trinity College, Dublin, MS 160, f. 105.

WyT 83 *'Farewell all my wellfare'.*

Copy in the Devonshire MS; c. 1530s-40s.

Not pub. in 16th century. Printed from this MS in Muir & Thomson, pp. 192-3.

British Library, Add. MS 17492, ff. 9v-10.

WyT 84 *'Ffarewell, Love, and all thy lawes for ever'.*

Copy in the Egerton MS; c. 1537-9.

First pub. in *Songes and Sonettes* (London, 1557). Printed from this MS in Muir & Thomson, pp. 12-13, and in Harrier, p. 114.

British Library, Egerton MS 2711, f. 13.

WyT 85 -----

Copy, here beginning 'Nowe farewell love and thye lawes forever', in the Devonshire MS; c. 1530s-40s.

This MS collated in Muir & Thomson and in Harrier.

British Library, Add. MS 17492, f. 75.

WyT 86 -----

Copy in the Arundel Harington MS; mid-late 16th century.

Printed from this MS in Hughey, I, No. 106,

p. 150; collated in Muir & Thomson and in Harrier.

Owned by the Duke of Norfolk, Arundel Castle, MSS (Special Press), 'Harrington MS. Temp. Eliz.', f. 65v.

WyT 87 *'Ffarewell, the rayn of crueltie!'*.

Copy in the Egerton MS; c. 1537-9.

First pub. in *Songes and Sonettes* (London, 1557). Printed from this MS in Muir & Thomson, pp. 11-12, and in Harrier, p. 113.

British Library, Egerton MS 2711, f. 12.

WyT 88 *'Ffor to love her for her lokes lovely'*.

Copy in the Egerton MS; c. 1537-9.

Not pub. in 16th century. Printed from this MS in Muir & Thomson, p. 14, and in Harrier, pp. 115-16.

British Library, Egerton MS 2711, f. 14.

WyT 89 -----

Copy in the Devonshire MS; c. 1530s-40s.

This MS collated in Muir & Thomson and in Harrier.

British Library, Add. MS 17492, f. 75.

WyT 90 *'Fforget not yet the tryde entent'*.

Copy in the Devonshire MS; c. 1530s-40s.

Not pub. in 16th century. Printed from this MS, with a facsimile, in Muir & Thomson, pp. 211-12.

British Library, Add. MS 17492, f. 54v.

WyT 91 *'Ffortune dothe frowne'*.

Copy in the Devonshire MS; c. 1530s-40s.

Not pub. in 16th century. Printed from this MS in Muir & Thomson, p. 225.

British Library, Add. MS 17492, f. 78v.

WyT 92 *'Ffortune what ayleth the'*.

Copy in the Blage MS; c. 1530s-40s.

First pub. in *The Court of Venus*, [c. 1538]. Printed from this MS in Muir & Thomson, pp. 173-4.

Trinity College, Dublin, MS 160, f. 151.

WyT 93 *'Fful well yt maye be sene'*.

Copy in the Devonshire MS; c. 1530s-40s.

Not pub. in 16th century. Printed from this MS in Muir & Thomson, pp. 207-8.

British Library, Add. MS 17492, f. 51.

*WyT 94 *'From thes hye hilles as when a spryng doth fall'*.

Autograph copy, with extensive revisions, in the Egerton MS; c. 1537-9.

First pub. in *Songes and Sonettes* (London, 1557). Printed from this MS in Muir & Thomson, p. 78, and in Harrier, pp. 203-4.

British Library, Egerton MS 2711, f. 66.

WyT 95 -----

Copy in the Blage MS; c. 1530s-40s.

This MS collated in Muir & Thomson and in Harrier.

Trinity College, Dublin, MS 160, f. 73.

*WyT 96 *'From thowght to thowght from hill to hill love doth me lede'*.

Autograph, in the Egerton MS; c. 1539.

Not pub. in 16th century. Printed from this MS in Muir & Thomson, p. 84, and in Harrier, p. 213.

British Library, Egerton MS 2711, f. 70.

--- *'Full well it may be seen'*.

See WyT 93.

--- *'Give place all ye that doth rejoyce'*.

See WyT 101.

WyT 97 *'Goo burnyng sighes Vnto the frosen hert!'*.

Copy, with an alteration in another hand (that responsible for the 'Aunswer' to WyT 183), in the Egerton MS; c. 1537-9.

First pub. in *Songes and Sonettes* (London, 1557). Printed from this MS in Muir & Thomson, pp. 16-17, and in Harrier, p. 119.

British Library, Egerton MS 2711, f. 16v.

WyT 98 -----

Copy in the Devonshire MS; c. 1530s-40s.

'Goo burnyng sighes Vnto the frosen hert!'

This MS collated in Muir & Thomson and in Harrier.

British Library, Add. MS 17492, f. 61v.

WyT 99 *'Greting to you bothe yn hertye wyse'.*

Copy in the Devonshire MS; c. 1530s-40s.

Not pub. in 16th century. Printed from this MS in Muir & Thomson, pp. 225-6.

British Library, Add. MS 17492, f. 79r-v.

WyT 100 *'Grudge on who list, this ys my lott'.*

Copy in the Devonshire MS; c. 1530s-40s.

Not pub. in 16th century; authorship discussed in Richard Leighton Greene, 'A Carol of Anne Boleyn by Wyatt', *RES*, NS 25 (1974), 437-9. Printed from this MS in Muir & Thomson, pp. 224-5.

British Library, Add. MS 17492, f. 78v.

WyT 101 *'Gyve place all ye that doth reioise'.*

Copy in the Devonshire MS; c. 1530s-40s.

Not pub. in 16th century. Printed from this MS in Muir & Thomson, pp. 221-2.

British Library, Add. MS 17492, f. 77v.

WyT 102 *'Had I wiste that now I wott'.*

Copy in the Blage MS; c. 1530s-40s.

Not pub. in 16th century. Printed from this MS in Muir & Thomson, p. 142.

Trinity College, Dublin, MS 160, f. 96.

WyT 103 *'Happe happith ofte vnloked for'.*

Copy in the Blage MS; c. 1530s-40s.

Not pub. in 16th century. Printed from this MS in Muir & Thomson, p. 144.

Trinity College, Dublin, MS 160, f. 99.

WyT 104 *'Hart oppressyd with desp'rat thought'.*

Copy in the Devonshire MS; c. 1530s-40s.

Not pub. in 16th century; Muir & Thomson, p. 237. This MS collated in Muir & Thomson.

British Library, Add. MS 17492, ff. 47v-8.

WyT 105 -----

Copy in the Arundel Harington MS; mid-late 16th century.

Printed from this MS in Muir & Thomson, and in Hughey, I, No. 312, p. 356.

Owned by the Duke of Norfolk, Arundel Castle, MSS (Special Press), 'Harrington MS. Temp. Eliz.', f. 217.

WyT 106 *'Hate whome ye lyste, I care not'.*

Copy in the Devonshire MS; c. 1530s-40s.

Not pub. in 16th century; Muir & Thomson, p. 145. This MS collated in Muir & Thomson.

British Library, Add. MS 17492, f. 78v.

WyT 107 -----

Copy in the Blage MS; c. 1530s-40s.

Printed from this MS in Muir & Thomson.

Trinity College, Dublin, MS 160, f. 100.

*WyT 108 *'He is not ded that somtyme hath a fall'.*

Copy, with autograph corrections, in the Egerton MS; c. 1537-9.

First pub. in *Songes and Sonettes* (London, 1557). Printed from this MS in Muir & Thomson, p. 45, and in Harrier, p. 152.

British Library, Egerton MS 2711, f. 40.

WyT 109 -----

Copy, here beginning 'Iam not ded altho I had a fall' (agreeing with the uncorrected state of the poem in WyT 108), in the Devonshire MS; c. 1530s-40s.

This MS collated in Muir & Thomson and in Harrier.

British Library, Add. MS 17492, f. 74.

WyT 110 -----

Copy in a Harington miscellany; mid-late 16th century.

This MS collated in Muir & Thomson and in Harrier.

British Library, Add. MS 37529, f. 32.

--- *'Heart oppressed with desperate thought'.*

See WyT 104-5.

--- *'Heaven and earth and all that hear me plain'.*

See WyT 112-14.

WyT 111 *'Helpe me to seke for I lost it there'.*

Copy in the Egerton MS; c. 1537-9.

Not pub. in 16th century. Printed from this MS in Muir & Thomson, p. 15, and in Harrier, p. 117.

British Library, Egerton MS 2711, f. 15.

WyT 112 *'Hevyn and erth and all that here me plain'.*

Copy in the Egerton MS; c. 1537-9.

Not pub. in 16th century. Printed from this MS in Muir & Thomson, pp. 55-6, and in Harrier, p. 165.

British Library, Egerton MS 2711, ff. 47v-8.

WyT 113 -----

Copy of lines 25-36, beginning 'Yf I had suffered this to you vnware', in the Devonshire MS; c. 1530s-40s.

This MS collated in Muir & Thomson and in Harrier.

British Library, Add. MS 17492, f. 11.

WyT 114 -----

Copy of lines 1-4 in a musical setting in a MS volume of madrigals and musical pieces; early 16th century.

This MS discussed, with a facsimile, in Ivy L. Mumford, 'Musical Settings to the Poems of Sir Thomas Wyatt', *M & L*, 37 (1956), 315-22.

British Library, Royal MS App. 58, ff. 52, 55v.

WyT 115 *'Horrybell of hew, hidyus to behold'.*

Copy in the Blage MS; c. 1530s-40s.

Not pub. in 16th century. Printed from this MS in Muir & Thomson, p. 143.

Trinity College, Dublin, MS 160, f. 97.

WyT 116 *'How oft have I, my dere and cruell foo'.*

Copy in the Egerton MS; c. 1537-9.

First pub. in *Songes and Sonettes* (London, 1557). Printed from this MS in Muir & Thomson, p. 24, and in Harrier, p. 127.

British Library, Egerton MS 2711, f. 23v.

WyT 117 -----

Copy in the Arundel Harington MS; mid-late 16th century.

Printed from this MS in Hughey, I, No. 116, p. 154; collated in Muir & Thomson and in Harrier.

Owned by the Duke of Norfolk, Arundel Castle, MSS (Special Press), 'Harrington MS. Temp. Eliz.', f. 67v.

WyT 118 *'Howe shulde I'.*

Copy of lines 1-34, 47-52, 59-62, in the hand of Margaret Douglas, in the Devonshire MS; c. 1530s-40s.

Not pub. in 16th century. Edited from this MS in Muir & Thomson, pp. 205-7 (and see WyT 119).

British Library, Add. MS 17492, f. 43.

WyT 119 -----

Copy of lines 1-22, 29-62, in the Devonshire MS; c. 1530s-40s.

Edited from this MS in Muir & Thomson (and see WyT 118).

British Library, Add. MS 17492, f. 77r-v.

WyT 120 *'I abide and abide and better abide'.*

Copy in the Devonshire MS; c. 1530s-40s.

Not pub. in 16th century. Printed from this MS in Muir & Thomson, p. 231.

British Library, Add. MS 17492, f. 81v.

WyT 121 *'I am as I am and so wil I be'.*

Copy in the Devonshire MS; c. 1530s-40s.

Not pub. in 16th century; Muir & Thomson, pp. 148-50. This MS collated and lines 1-18 printed in Muir & Thomson.

British Library, Add. MS 17492, f. 85.

WyT 122 -----

Copy of lines 9-40, beginning 'I doo not rejoise nor yet complayne', in the Blage MS; c. 1530s-40s.

Printed from this MS in Muir & Thomson (and see WyT 121).

Trinity College, Dublin, MS 160, f. 107.

WyT 123 -----

Copy of a shortened version in the form of a carol, written on a front flyleaf of a 15th century MS volume of sermons by John Felton, Vicar of St Mary Magdalene, Oxford; early 16th century.

'I am as I am and so wil I be'

Printed from this MS in Richard Leighton Greene, 'Wyatt's "I am as I am" in Carol-Form', *RES*, NS 15 (1964), 175-80; reprinted from this article in Muir & Thomson, pp. 399-400.

University of Pennsylvania, MS Latin 35, f. [iii].

WyT 124 -----

Copy of a version in a MS volume of Scottish poetry compiled by George Bannatyne; c. 1568.

Printed from this MS in *The Bannatyne Manuscript*, ed. J. Barclay Murdoch, Hunterian Club (Glasgow, 1896), III, 731-2; in *The Bannatyne Manuscript*, ed. W. Tod Ritchie, STS NS 26 (Edinburgh & London, 1930), pp. 2-3; and in H.A. Mason, '"I am as I am"', *RES*, NS 23 (1972), 304-8.

National Library of Scotland, Adv. MS 1. 1. 6, Vol. II, f. 250r-v (pp. 555-6).

WyT 125 *'I am redy and euer wyll be'.*

Copy in the Blage MS; c. 1530s-40s.

Not pub. in 16th century. Printed from this MS in Muir & Thomson, pp. 147-8.

Trinity College, Dublin, MS 160, f. 106.

WyT 126 *'I fynde no peace and all my warr is done'.*

Copy, headed 'Petrarke' in another hand (that responsible for the 'Aunswer' to WyT 183), in the Egerton MS; c. 1537-9.

First pub. in *Songes and Sonettes* (London, 1557). Printed from this MS in Muir & Thomson, pp. 20-1, and in Harrier, pp. 123-4.

British Library, Egerton MS 2711, f. 20v.

WyT 127 -----

Copy in the Devonshire MS; c. 1530s-40s.

This MS collated in Muir & Thomson and in Harrier.

British Library, Add. MS 17492, f. 82r-v.

WyT 128 -----

Copy, headed 'Pace non trouo', in a Harington miscellany; mid-late 16th century.

This MS collated in Muir & Thomson and in Harrier.

British Library, Add. MS 36529, f. 32.

WyT 129 -----

Copy of the incipit possibly of this poem (here 'No peace I find') in a musical setting in a MS music book; c. 1595.

This MS discussed in Ivy L. Mumford, 'Musical Settings to the Poems of Sir Thomas Wyatt', *M & L*, 37 (1956), 315-22 (p. 321), and in Mumford, 'Sir Thomas Wyatt's Songs: A Trio of Problems in Manuscript Sources', *M & L*, 39 (1958), 262-4 (where it is argued that this song may not be the same as Wyatt's poem); recorded in Muir & Thomson, p. 286.

British Library, Add. MS 31392, f. 52v.

WyT 130 *'I have benne a lover'.*

Copy in the Blage MS; c. 1530s-40s.

Not pub. in 16th century. Printed from this MS in Muir & Thomson, pp. 155-7.

Trinity College, Dublin, MS 160, f. 113.

WyT 131 *'I have sought long with stedfastnes'.*

Copy, with an alteration in an italic hand (that responsible for WyT 372), in the Egerton MS; c. 1537-9.

Not pub. in 16th century. Printed from this MS in Muir & Thomson, pp. 51-2, and in Harrier, pp. 160-1.

British Library, Egerton MS 2711, f. 45v.

WyT 132 -----

Copy in the Devonshire MS; c. 1530s-40s.

This MS collated in Muir & Thomson and in Harrier.

British Library, Add. MS 17492, f. 71v.

WyT 133 *'I knowe not where my heuy syghys to hyd'.*

Copy in the Blage MS; c. 1530s-40s.

Not pub. in 16th century. Printed from this MS in Muir & Thomson, pp. 154-5.

Trinity College, Dublin, MS 160, f. 112.

WyT 134 *'I lede a liff vnpleasant, nothing glad'.*

Copy in the Egerton MS; c. 1537-9.

Not pub. in 16th century. Printed from this MS in Muir & Thomson, p. 70, and in Harrier, p. 194.

British Library, Egerton MS 2711, f. 62.

WyT 135 *'I love lovyd and so doithe she'.*

Copy in the Devonshire MS; c. 1530s-40s.

Not pub. in 16th century. Printed from this MS

in Muir & Thomson, p. 191.

British Library, Add. MS 17492, f. 6.

WyT 136 *'I muste go walke the woodes so wyld'.*

Copy in the Blage MS; c. 1530s-40s.

Not pub. in 16th century. Printed from this MS in Muir & Thomson, pp. 150-2 (with a facsimile facing p. 196).

Trinity College, Dublin, MS 160, f. 108.

WyT 137 -----

Copy in a MS volume of legal works; early 16th century.

Printed from this MS in Rossell Hope Robbins, *Secular Lyrics of the XIVth and XVth Centuries* (Oxford, 1952), p. 14; recorded in Muir & Thomson, p. 400.

Huntington, EL 1160, f. 11v.

WyT 138 -----

Copy of a rough version in a MS volume of legal works; early 16th century.

This MS collated in Robbins, p. 14.

Huntington, EL 1160, ff. 108v, 107v, 109.

WyT 139 *'I se the change ffrom that that was'.*

Copy in the hand of Margaret Douglas in the Devonshire MS; c. 1530s-40s.

Not pub. in 16th century. Printed from this MS in Muir & Thomson, pp. 204-5.

British Library, Add. MS 17492, ff. 40v-1.

WyT 140 *'I see my plaint with open eares'.*

Copy in a Harington miscellany; mid-late 16th century.

Not pub. in 16th century. Printed from this MS in Muir & Thomson, p. 242.

British Library, Add. MS 36529, f. 33.

--- *'I see the change from that that was'.*

See WyT 139.

WyT 141 *'I wyll allthow I may not'.*

Copy of lines 1-8, 13-24, in the Blage MS; c. 1530s-40s.

Not pub. in 16th century. Printed from this MS in Muir & Thomson, pp. 153-4 (and see WyT 142).

Trinity College, Dublin, MS 160, f. 111.

WyT 142 -----

Copy, headed 'A balad of witt', in a composite volume of MSS; mid-late 16th century.

This MS collated (and lines 9-12 printed) in Muir & Thomson.

British Library, Harley MS 78, f. 28.

--- *'If armour's faith, an heart unfeigned'.*

See WyT 411-12.

WyT 143 *'If chaunce assynd'.*

Copy in the Egerton MS; c. 1537-9.

Not pub. in 16th century. Printed from this MS in Muir & Thomson, pp. 50-1, and in Harrier, pp. 158-9.

British Library, Egerton MS 2711, ff. 44v-5.

WyT 144 -----

Copy in the Devonshire MS; c. 1530s-40s.

This MS collated in Muir & Thomson and in Harrier.

British Library, Add. MS 17492, f. 70v.

WyT 145 -----

Copy of lines 1-4 in the Blage MS; c. 1530s-40s.

This MS recorded in Harrier.

Trinity College, Dublin, MS 160, f. 109.

--- *'If euer man might him auaunt'.*

See INTRODUCTION.

WyT 146 *'If fansy would favour'.*

Copy in the Egerton MS; c. 1537-9.

First pub. in *The Court of Venus*, [c. 1538]. Printed from this MS in Muir & Thomson, pp. 32-3, and in Harrier, pp. 136-7.

British Library, Egerton MS 2711, f. 30r-v.

WyT 147 -----

Copy of lines 1-12, 17-36, in the Devonshire MS; c. 1530s-40s.

'If fansy would favour'

This MS collated in Muir & Thomson and in Harrier.

British Library, Add. MS 17492, f. 34v.

WyT 148 -----

Copy of lines 9-36, here beginning 'ffansye dothe know how', in the Arundel Harington MS; imperfect, lacking the beginning; mid-late 16th century.

Printed from this MS in Hughey, I, No. 130, p. 159; collated in Muir & Thomson and in Harrier.

Owned by the Duke of Norfolk, Arundel Castle, MSS (Special Press), 'Harrington MS. Temp. Eliz.', f. 75.

--- *'If I might have at mine own will'.*

See WyT 413.

--- *'If in the world there be more woe'.*

See WyT 414-15.

--- *'If it be so that I forsake thee'.*

See WyT 416.

*WyT 149 *'If waker care if sodayne pale Coulour'.*

Copy, with autograph corrections, in the Egerton MS; c. 1537-9.

First pub. in *Songes and Sonettes* (London, 1557). Printed from this MS in Muir & Thomson, p. 78, and in Harrier, pp. 204-5.

British Library, Egerton MS 2711, f. 66v.

WyT 150 -----

Copy in the Arundel Harington MS; mid-late 16th century.

Printed from this MS in Hughey, I, No. 124, p. 157; collated in Muir & Thomson and in Harrier.

Owned by the Duke of Norfolk, Arundel Castle, MSS (Special Press), 'Harrington MS. Temp. Eliz.', f. 68.

--- *'If with complaint the pain might be expressed'.*

See WyT 417.

*WyT 151 *'In dowtfull brest, whilst moderly pitie'.*

Autograph fair copy, with revisions, in the Egerton MS; c. 1537-9.

First pub. in *Songes and Sonettes* (London, 1557). Printed from this MS in Muir & Thomson, p. 60, and in Harrier, pp. 180-1.

British Library, Egerton MS 2711, f. 54v.

WyT 152 *'In eternum I was ons determed'.*

Copy in the Egerton MS; imperfect; c. 1537-9.

Not pub. in 16th century. Printed from this MS in Muir & Thomson, pp. 53-4, and in Harrier, pp. 162-3.

British Library, Egerton MS 2711, f. 46v.

WyT 153 -----

Copy in the Devonshire MS; c. 1530s-40s.

This MS collated in Muir & Thomson and in Harrier.

British Library, Add. MS 17492, f. 72v.

WyT 154 *'In faith I wot not well what to say'.*

Copy in the Egerton MS; c. 1537-9.

First pub. in *Songes and Sonettes* (London, 1557). Printed from this MS in Muir & Thomson, p. 19, and in Harrier, pp. 121-2.

British Library, Egerton MS 2711, f. 19.

WyT 155 *'In mornyng wyse syns daylye I Increas'.*

Copy in the Blage MS; c. 1530s-40s.

Not pub. in 16th century. Printed from this MS in Muir & Thomson, pp. 157-9.

Trinity College, Dublin, MS 160, f. 114.

--- *In Spayne* ('So feble is the threde that doth the burden stay').

See WyT 273-5.

--- *'Is it possible'.*

See WyT 422.

WyT 156 *'It may be good, like it who list'.*

Copy in the Egerton MS; c. 1537-9.

First pub. in *Songes and Sonettes* (London, 1557). Printed from this MS in Muir & Thomson, pp. 17-18, and in Harrier, pp. 119-20.

British Library, Egerton MS 2711, f. 17.

WyT 157 -----

Copy in the Blage MS; c. 1530s-40s.

This MS collated in Muir & Thomson and in Harrier.

Trinity College, Dublin, MS 160, f. 98.

WyT 158 *'It was my choyse, it was no chaunce'.*

Copy in the Devonshire MS; c. 1530s-40s.

Not pub. in 16th century. Printed from this MS in Muir & Thomson, pp. 201-2.

British Library, Add. MS 17492, f. 30v.

WyT 159 -----

Copy of lines 1-13 (not in the same hand as WyT 158) in the Devonshire MS; c. 1530s-40s.

This MS recorded (but not collated) in Muir & Thomson (p. 202).

British Library, Add. MS 17492, ff. 24v-5.

*WyT 160 *Jopas' Song* ('When Dido festid first the wandryng Troian knyght').

Autograph, with extensive revisions, in the Egerton MS; c. 1539.

First pub. in *Songes and Sonettes* (London, 1557). Printed from this MS in Muir & Thomson, pp. 84-7, and in Harrier, pp. 250-2.

British Library, Egerton MS 2711, ff. 100-1.

WyT 161 -----

Copy in the Arundel Harington MS; mid-late 16th century.

Printed from this MS in Hughey, I, No. 140, pp. 168-70; collated in Muir & Thomson and in Harrier.

Owned by the Duke of Norfolk, Arundel Castle, MSS (Special Press), 'Harrington MS. Temp. Eliz.', f. 99r-v.

WyT 162 *'Lament my losse, my labor, and my payne'.*

Copy in the Devonshire MS; c. 1530s-40s.

Not pub. in 16th century. Printed from this MS in Muir & Thomson, pp. 219-20.

British Library, Add. MS 17492, f. 76v.

WyT 163 *'Lengre to muse'.*

Copy in the Devonshire MS; c. 1530s-40s.

Not pub. in 16th century. Printed from this MS in Muir & Thomson, pp. 228-9.

British Library, Add. MS 17492, f. 80.

--- *'Leve thus to slaunder love'.*

See WyT 168-9.

WyT 164 *'Like as the byrde in the cage enclosed'.*

Copy in a volume of miscellaneous documents relating to Richard Cox, Bishop of Ely (1500-81); 16th century.

First pub. in *Songes and Sonettes* (London, 1557). Printed from this MS in Muir & Thomson pp. 243-4.

Corpus Christi College, Cambridge, MS 168, No. 21.

--- *'Like as the swan towards her death'.*

See WyT 177-9.

--- *'Like as the wind with raging blast'.*

See WyT 180.

WyT 165 *'Like to these vnmesurable montayns'.*

Copy in the Egerton MS; c. 1537-9.

First pub. in *Songes and Sonettes* (London, 1557). Printed from this MS in Muir & Thomson, pp. 24-5, and in Harrier, p. 128.

British Library, Egerton MS 2711, f. 24.

WyT 166 -----

Copy in the Arundel Harington MS; mid-late 16th century.

Printed from this MS in Hughey, I, No. 117, pp. 154-5; collated in Muir & Thomson and in Harrier.

Owned by the Duke of Norfolk, Arundel Castle, MSS (Special Press), 'Harrington MS. Temp. Eliz.', ff. 67v-67(bis).

--- *'Live thou gladly, if so thou may'.*

See WyT 181.

WyT 167 *'Lo! how I seke and sew to haue'.*

Copy in the Devonshire MS; c. 1530s-40s.

Not pub. in 16th century. Printed from this MS in Muir & Thomson, pp. 209-10.

British Library, Add. MS 17492, f. 52v.

'Lo what it is to love!'

*WyT 168 *'Lo what it is to love!'.*

Copy of a sequence of three poems, with an autograph alteration, in the Egerton MS; c. 1537-9.

Not pub. in 16th century. Printed from this MS in Muir & Thomson, pp. 66-9, and in Harrier, pp. 190-4 (printed as separate poems).

British Library, Egerton MS 2711, ff. 60-2.

WyT 169 -----

Copy in the Blage MS; c. 1530s-40s.

This MS collated in Muir & Thomson and in Harrier.

Trinity College, Dublin, MS 160, ff. 117-18v.

--- *'Longer to muse'.*

See WyT 163.

WyT 170 *'Longer to troo ye'.*

Copy of stanzas 1-5 in the Blage MS; c. 1530s-40s.

Not pub. in 16th century. Printed from this MS in Muir & Thomson, pp. 159-60, (and see WyT 171).

Trinity College, Dublin, MS 160, f. 119r-v.

WyT 171 -----

Copy, here beginning 'Longer to prove ye, what may it availe me', in the Arundel Harington MS; mid-late 16th century.

Printed from this MS in Hughey, I, No. 244, p. 282; collated (and stanzas 6-7 printed) in Muir & Thomson.

Owned by the Duke of Norfolk, Arundel Castle, MSS (Special Press), 'Harrington MS. Temp. Eliz.', f. 168r-v.

WyT 172 *'Love and fortune and my mynde, remembre'.*

Copy, with an alteration in another hand (that responsible for the 'Aunswer' to WyT 183), in the Egerton MS; c. 1537-9.

First pub. in *Songes and Sonettes* (London, 1557). Printed from this MS in Muir & Thomson, pp. 23-4, and in Harrier, pp. 126-7.

British Library, Egerton MS 2711, f. 23.

WyT 173 -----

Copy in the Arundel Harington MS; mid-late 16th century.

Printed from this MS in Hughey, I, No. 115, p. 154; collated in Muir & Thomson and in Harrier.

Owned by the Duke of Norfolk, Arundel Castle, MSS (Special Press), 'Harrington MS. Temp. Eliz.', f. 67r-v.

WyT 174 *'Love hathe agayne'.*

Copy in the Devonshire MS; c. 1530s-40s.

Not pub. in 16th century; Muir & Thomson, pp. 161-2. This MS collated in Muir & Thomson.

British Library, Add. MS 17492, f. 80v.

WyT 175 -----

Copy in the Blage MS; c. 1530s-40s.

Printed from this MS in Muir & Thomson.

Trinity College, Dublin, MS 160, f. 120.

WyT 176 *'Luckes, my fair falcon, and your fellowes all'.*

Copy in a Harington miscellany; mid-late 16th century.

First pub. in *Songes and Sonettes* (London, 1557). Printed from this MS in Muir & Thomson, p. 241.

British Library, Add. MS 36529, f. 32v.

•WyT 177 *'Lyke as the Swanne towardis her dethe'.*

Copy in the Egerton MS; imperfect; c. 1537-9.

Not pub. in 16th century. Printed from this MS in Muir & Thomson, pp. 52-3, and in Harrier, pp. 161-2.

British Library, Egerton MS 2711, f. 46.

WyT 178 -----

Copy in the Devonshire MS; c. 1530s-40s.

This MS collated (and printed in part) in Muir & Thomson and in Harrier.

British Library, Add. MS 17492, f. 73.

WyT 179 -----

Copy in the Blage MS; c. 1530s-40s.

This MS collated in Muir & Thomson and in Harrier.

Trinity College, Dublin, MS 160, f. 122.

WyT 180 *'Lyke as the wynde with raginge blaste'.*

Copy, headed 'T. Wyat of Loue', in a composite volume of MSS; mid-late 16th century.

Not pub. in 16th century. Printed from this MS in Muir & Thomson, pp. 242-3.

British Library, Harley MS 78, f. 27v.

WyT 181 *'Lyue thowe gladly, yff so thowe may'.*

Copy in the Blage MS; c. 1530s-40s.

Not pub. in 16th century. Printed from this MS in Muir & Thomson, pp. 162-3.

Trinity College, Dublin, MS 160, f. 123.

WyT 182 *'Madame, I you requyere'.*

Copy in the Blage MS; c. 1530s-40s.

Not pub. in 16th century. Printed from this MS in Muir & Thomson, pp. 163-4.

Trinity College, Dublin, MS 160, f. 127.

WyT 183 *'Madame, withouten many wordes'.*

Copy in the Egerton MS; c. 1537-9.

First pub. in *Songes and Sonettes* (London, 1557). Printed from this MS in Muir & Thomson, p. 25, and in Harrier, pp. 128-9. The text followed by a 12-line 'Aunswer' in a later hand responsible for alterations to eleven other poems in the Egerton MS (this 'Aunswer' printed in Muir & Thomson, p. 298, and in Harrier, p. 129).

British Library, Egerton MS 2711, f. 24v.

WyT 184 -----

Copy, here beginning 'Mestres what nedis many wordis', in the Blage MS; c. 1530s-40s.

This MS collated in Muir & Thomson and in Harrier. The text followed by a 12-line 'Aunswer' in the same hand (see WyT 183).

Trinity College, Dublin, MS 160, f. 128.

WyT 185 *'Marvaill no more, all tho'.*

Copy, with an alteration in another hand (that responsible for the 'Aunswer' to WyT 183), in the Egerton MS; c. 1537-9.

First pub. in *The Court of Venus*, [c. 1538]; *Songes and Sonettes* (London, 1557). Printed from this MS in Muir & Thomson, pp. 38-9, and in Harrier, pp. 143-4.

British Library, Egerton MS 2711, f. 35r-v.

WyT 186 -----

Copy in the Devonshire MS; c. 1530s-40s.

This MS collated in Muir & Thomson and in Harrier.

British Library, Add. MS 17492, f. 16v.

WyT 187 *'Me list no more to sing'.*

Copy in the Devonshire MS; c. 1530s-40s.

Not pub. in 16th century. Printed from this MS in Muir & Thomson, pp. 215-17.

British Library, Add. MS 17492, f. 74v.

--- *'Might I as well within my song belay'.*

See WyT 211-12.

--- *'Mine old dear enemy, my froward master'.*

See WyT 213-14.

--- *'Mine own John Poins, since ye delight to know'.*

See WyT 215-20.

WyT 188 *'Mornyng my hart dothe sore opres'.*

Copy in the Blage MS; c. 1530s-40s.

Not pub. in 16th century. Printed from this MS in Muir & Thomson, p. 163.

Trinity College, Dublin, MS 160, f. 126.

WyT 189 -----

Copy of lines 1-8 in a composite volume of verse and prose tracts; 16th century.

This MS collated in Muir & Thomson. See also WyT 21.

British Library, Add. MS 18752, f. 89.

WyT 190 -----

Copy, here beginning 'Morenyng my hart doithe sore opress', in a musical setting, in a composite volume of papers of the Ramsden family; c. 1560-74.

This MS recorded (but not collated) in Muir & Thomson, p. 405.

Huddersfield Central Library, DD/R5/30, f. 2.

WyT 191 *'Most wretchid hart most myserable'.*

Copy in two hands, in the Egerton MS; c. 1537-9.

'Most wretchid hart most myserable'.

Not pub. in 16th century. Printed from this MS in Muir & Thomson, pp. 71-3, and in Harrier, pp. 197-8.

British Library, Egerton MS 2711, ff. 63v-4v.

--- *'Mourning my heart doth sore oppress'.*

See WyT 188-90.

WyT 192 *'My galy charged with forgetfulnes'.*

Copy in the Egerton MS; c. 1537-9.

First pub. in *Songes and Sonettes* (London, 1557). Printed from this MS in Muir & Thomson, pp. 21-2, and in Harrier, p. 125.

British Library, Egerton MS 2711, f. 21v.

WyT 193 -----

Copy, with alterations in another hand, in the Arundel Harington MS; mid-late 16th century.

Printed from this MS in Hughey, I, No. 112, pp. 152-3; collated in Muir & Thomson and in Harrier.

Owned by the Duke of Norfolk, Arundel Castle, MSS (Special Press), 'Harrington MS. Temp. Eliz.', f. 66v.

WyT 194 *'My hert I gave the not to do it payn'.*

Copy in the Egerton MS; c. 1537-9.

First pub. in *Songes and Sonettes* (London, 1557). Printed from this MS in Muir & Thomson, p. 13, and in Harrier, p. 115.

British Library, Egerton MS 2711, f. 13v.

WyT 195 -----

Copy, begun by an amanuensis and corrected and completed by Margaret Douglas (omitting lines 10-11), in the Devonshire MS; c. 1530s-40s.

This MS collated in Muir & Thomson and in Harrier.

British Library, Add. MS 17492, f. 3.

WyT 196 -----

Copy in the Devonshire MS; c. 1530s-40s.

This MS collated in Muir & Thomson and in Harrier.

British Library, Add. MS 17492, f. 75v.

WyT 197 -----

Copy in the Arundel Harington MS; mid-late 16th century.

Printed from this MS in Hughey, I, No. 107, pp. 150-1; collated in Muir & Thomson and in Harrier.

Owned by the Duke of Norfolk, Arundel Castle, MSS (Special Press), 'Harrington MS. Temp. Eliz.', f. 65v.

WyT 198 *'My hope, Alas, hath me abused'.*

Copy in the Egerton MS; c. 1537-9.

Not pub. in 16th century. Printed from this MS in Muir & Thomson, pp. 45-6, and in Harrier, pp. 153-4.

British Library, Egerton MS 2711, f. 41r-v.

WyT 199 -----

Copy in the Devonshire MS; c. 1530s-40s.

This MS collated in Muir & Thomson and in Harrier.

British Library, Add. MS 17492, f. 74v.

WyT 200 -----

Copy in the Arundel Harington MS; mid-late 16th century.

Printed from this MS in Hughey, I, No. 134, pp. 161-2; collated in Muir & Thomson and in Harrier.

Owned by the Duke of Norfolk, Arundel Castle, MSS (Special Press), 'Harrington MS. Temp. Eliz.', f. 77r-v.

--- *'My love took scorn my service to retain'.*

See WyT 210.

WyT 201 *'My loue ys lyke vnto th'eternall fyre'.*

Copy in the Devonshire MS; c. 1530s-40s.

Not pub. in 16th century. Printed from this MS in Muir & Thomson, p. 210.

British Library, Add. MS 17492, f. 53.

WyT 202 *'My lute, awake! perfourme the last'.*

Copy, with a correction in an italic hand (that responsible for WyT 372), in the Egerton MS; c. 1537-9.

'My lute, awake! perfourme the last'

First pub. in *The Court of Venus*, [c. 1538]; *Songes and Sonettes* (London, 1557). Printed from this MS in Muir & Thomson, pp. 48-50, and in Harrier, pp. 157-8.

British Library, Egerton MS 2711, ff. 43v-4.

WyT 203 -----

Copy in the Devonshire MS; c. 1530s-40s.

This MS collated in Muir & Thomson and in Harrier.

British Library, Add. MS 17492, f. 14v-15.

WyT 204 -----

Copy in the Blage MS; c. 1530s-40s.

This MS collated in Muir & Thomson and in Harrier.

Trinity College, Dublin, MS 160, f. 125.

WyT 205 *'My mothers maydes when they did sowe and spynne'.*

Copy in the Egerton MS; c. 1537-9.

First pub. in *Songes and Sonettes* (London, 1557). Printed from this MS in Muir & Thomson, pp. 91-5, and in Harrier, pp. 174-7.

British Library, Egerton MS 2711, ff. 50v-2v.

WyT 206 -----

Copy of lines 1-18 in the Devonshire MS; c. 1530s-40s.

This MS collated in Muir & Thomson and in Harrier.

British Library, Add. MS 17492, f. 87v.

WyT 207 -----

Copy in the Arundel Harington MS; mid-late 16th century.

Printed from this MS in Hughey, I, No. 142, pp. 172-5; collated in Muir & Thomson and in Harrier.

Owned by the Duke of Norfolk, Arundel Castle, MSS (Special Press), 'Harrington MS. Temp. Eliz.', ff. 100-1v.

WyT 208 *'My pen, take payn a lytyll space'.*

Copy in the Devonshire MS; c. 1530s-40s.

First pub. in *The Court of Venus*, [c. 1538]. Printed from this MS in Muir & Thomson, pp. 190-1.

British Library, Add. MS 17492, f. 3v.

WyT 209 *'My swet, alas, fforget me not'.*

Copy in the Blage MS; c. 1530s-40s.

Not pub. in 16th century. Printed from this MS in Muir & Thomson, pp. 165-6.

Trinity College, Dublin, MS 160, f. 130.

WyT 210 *'Mye love toke skorne my servise to retaine'.*

Copy in the Devonshire MS; c. 1530s-40s.

First pub. in *Songes and Sonettes* (London, 1557). Printed from this MS in Muir & Thomson, p. 227.

British Library, Add. MS 17492, f. 79v.

WyT 211 *'Myght I as well within my songe belaye'.*

Copy of lines 1-4 in the hand of Margaret Douglas in the Devonshire MS; (also a smudged copy of lines 1-2 in another hand on f. 66); c. 1530s-40s.

Not pub. in 16th century; Muir & Thomson, pp. 164-5. This MS collated in Muir & Thomson.

British Library, Add. MS 17492, f. 65v.

WyT 212 -----

Copy in the Blage MS; c. 1530s-40s.

Printed from this MS in Muir & Thomson.

Trinity College, Dublin, MS 160, f. 129.

WyT 213 *'Myne olde dere En'mye, my froward master'.*

Copy of lines 22-147, beginning 'O small hony, much aloes & gall', with later alterations in the hand of Nicholas Grimald, in the Egerton MS; imperfect; c. 1537-9.

First pub. in *Songes and Sonettes* (London, 1557). Printed from this MS in Muir & Thomson, pp. 5-10 (and see WyT 214) and in Harrier, pp. 105-8.

British Library, Egerton MS 2711, ff. 8-10v.

WyT 214 -----

Copy of lines 1-79 in the Arundel Harington MS; imperfect, lacking ending; mid-late 16th century.

Printed from this MS in Hughey, I, No. 144, pp. 176-8; collated and lines 1-21 printed in Muir & Thomson; lines 22-79 collated in Harrier.

Owned by the Duke of Norfolk, Arundel Castle, MSS (Special Press), 'Harrington MS. Temp. Eliz.', f. 102r-v.

'Myne owne John Poyntz, sins ye delight to know'

WyT 215 *'Myne owne John Poyntz, sins ye delight to know'.*

Copy of lines 52-103, beginning 'Praise him for counceill that is droncke of ale', in the Egerton MS; imperfect; c. 1537-9.

First pub. in *Songes and Sonettes* (London, 1557). Printed from this MS in Muir & Thomson, pp. 88-91 (and see WyT 216), and in Harrier, pp. 167-8.

British Library, Egerton MS 2711, f. 49r-v.

WyT 216 -----

Copy of lines 1-27, 31-103, in the Devonshire MS; c. 1530s-40s.

This MS collated and lines 1-27, 31-52 printed in Muir & Thomson; collated in Harrier.

British Library, Add. MS 17492, ff. 85v-7.

WyT 217 -----

Copy of lines 1-17, 20-8, 32-103, with corrections in another hand, in the Arundel Harington MS; mid-late 16th century.

Printed from this MS in Hughey, I, No. 104, pp. 147-9; collated in Muir & Thomson and in Harrier.

Owned by the Duke of Norfolk, Arundel Castle, MSS (Special Press), 'Harrington MS. Temp. Eliz.', ff. 64-5.

WyT 218 -----

Copy of lines 1-17, 20-8, 32-103, in a Harington miscellany; mid-late 16th century.

This MS collated in Muir & Thomson and in Harrier.

British Library, Add. MS 36529, ff. 30-1.

WyT 219 -----

Copy in a volume of miscellaneous papers relating to Richard Cox, Bishop of Ely (1500-81); 16th century.

This MS collated in Muir & Thomson and in Harrier.

Corpus Christi College, Cambridge, MS 168, No. 22.

WyT 220 -----

Copy, immediately following on from 'Venemus thornes that ar so sharp and kene' (see WyT 370), in a miscellany once owned by one W. Kytton; c. 1580.

This MS collated in F.D. Hoeniger, 'A Wyatt Manuscript', *N & Q*, 202 (March 1957), 103-4, and in Harrier; recorded in Muir & Thomson, p. 350.

Cambridge University Library, MS Ff. 5. 14, ff. 5v-7.

*WyT 221 *'Nature, that gave the bee so feet a grace'.*

Copy, with autograph corrections, in the Egerton MS; c. 1537-9.

First pub. in *Songes and Sonettes* (London, 1557). Printed from this MS in Muir & Thomson, p. 51, and in Harrier, p. 160.

British Library, Egerton MS 2711, f. 45.

WyT 222 -----

Copy in the Devonshire MS; c. 1530s-40s.

This MS collated in Muir & Thomson and in Harrier.

British Library, Add. MS 17492, f. 71v.

WyT 223 -----

Copy in the Blage MS; c. 1530s-40s.

This MS collated in Muir & Thomson and in Harrier.

Trinity College, Dublin, MS 160, f. 129v.

WyT 224 -----

Copy in a composite volume of MSS; mid-late 16th century.

This MS collated in Muir & Thomson and in Harrier.

British Library, Harley MS 78, f. 27.

WyT 225 *'Now all of chaunge'.*

Copy in the Devonshire MS; c. 1530s-40s.

Not pub. in 16th century. Printed from this MS in Muir & Thomson, pp. 230-1.

British Library, Add. MS 17492, f. 81r-v.

WyT 226 -----

Copy of lines 1-36, 43-8, subscribed 'To Smithe of Camden', in the Arundel Harington MS; mid-late 16th century.

Printed from this MS in Hughey, I, No. 6, p. 82; collated in Muir & Thomson.

Owned by the Duke of Norfolk, Arundel Castle, MSS (Special Press), 'Harrington MS. Temp. Eliz.', f. 17v.

WyT 227 *'Now must I lerne to lyue at rest'.*

Copy in the Devonshire MS; c. 1530s-40s.

Not pub. in 16th century. Printed from this MS in Muir & Thomson, p. 211.

British Library, Add. MS 17492, f. 54.

WyT 228 *'O crewell hart, wher ys thy ffaythe?'.*

Copy in the Blage MS; c. 1530s-40s.

Not pub. in 16th century. Printed from this MS in Muir & Thomson, pp. 168-9.

Trinity College, Dublin, MS 160, f. 139.

WyT 229 *'O goodely hand'.*

Copy in the Egerton MS; c. 1537-9.

Not pub. in 16th century. Printed from this MS in Muir & Thomson, pp. 65-6, and in Harrier, pp. 189-90.

British Library, Egerton MS 2711, f. 59v.

WyT 230 -----

Copy in a composite volume of MSS; mid-late 16th century.

This MS collated in Muir & Thomson and in Harrier.

British Library, Harley MS 78, f. 28.

WyT 231 *'O myserable sorow withowten cure!'.*

Copy in the Devonshire MS; c. 1530s-40s.

Not pub. in 16th century. Printed from this MS in Muir & Thomson, p. 212.

British Library, Add. MS 17492, f. 58v.

WyT 232 *'O what vndeseruyd creweltye'.*

Copy in the Blage MS; c. 1530-40s.

Not pub. in 16th century. Printed from this MS in Muir & Thomson, pp. 166-7.

Trinity College, Dublin, MS 160, f. 137.

*WyT 233 *'Off Cartage he that worthie warrier'.*

Autograph fair copy, with one revision, in the Egerton MS; c. 1537-9.

First pub. in *Songes and Sonettes* (London, 1557). Printed from this MS in Muir & Thomson, p. 61, and in Harrier, p. 181.

British Library, Egerton MS 2711, f. 54v.

*WyT 234 *'Off purpos Love chase first for to be blynd'.*

Autograph, with revisions, in the Egerton MS; c. 1539.

First pub. in *Songes and Sonettes* (London, 1557). Printed from this MS in Muir & Thomson, p. 83, and in Harrier, p. 211. Facsimile in Croft, *Autograph Poetry*, I, 9.

British Library, Egerton MS 2711, f. 69.

WyT 235 *'Ons as me thought fortune me kyst'.*

Copy in the Egerton MS; c. 1537-9.

First pub. in *Songes and Sonettes* (London, 1557). Printed from this MS in Muir & Thomson, pp. 47-8, and in Harrier, p. 156.

British Library, Egerton MS 2711, ff. 42v-3.

WyT 236 -----

Copy of lines 1-8 in the Devonshire MS; c. 1530s-40s.

This MS collated in Muir & Thomson and in Harrier.

British Library, Add. MS 17492, f. 71v.

WyT 237 -----

Copy in the Devonshire MS; c. 1530s-40s.

This MS collated in Muir & Thomson and in Harrier.

British Library, Add. MS 17492, ff. 73v-4.

WyT 238 *'Ons in your grace I knowe I was'.*

Copy in the Blage MS; c. 1530s-40s.

Not pub. in 16th century. Printed from this MS in Muir & Thomson, pp. 167-8.

Trinity College, Dublin, MS 160, f. 138.

WyT 239 *'Pacyence of all my smart'.*

Copy in the Devonshire MS; c. 1530s-40s.

Not pub. in 16th century. Printed from this MS in Muir & Thomson, pp. 200-1.

British Library, Add. MS 17492, f. 21.

--- *'Pain of all pain, the most grievous pain'.*

See WyT 250.

WyT 240 *'Pas fourthe, my wountyd cries'.*

Copy in the Blage MS; c. 1530s-40s.

First pub. in *Songes and Sonettes* (London, 1557). Printed from this MS in Muir & Thomson, pp. 171-2.

Trinity College, Dublin, MS 160, f. 148.

--- *'Patience, for I have wrong'.*

See WyT 245.

--- *'Patience for my device'.*

See WyT 246-9.

--- *'Patience of all my smart'.*

See WyT 239.

WyT 241 *'Patience, though I have not'.*

Copy, with an alteration in an italic hand (that responsible for WyT 372), in the Egerton MS; c. 1537-9.

Not pub. in 16th century. Printed from this MS in Muir & Thomson, p. 29, and in Harrier, pp. 133-4.

British Library, Egerton MS 2711, f. 28.

WyT 242 -----

Copy in the Devonshire MS; c. 1530s-40s.

This MS collated in Muir & Thomson and in Harrier.

British Library, Add. MS 17492, f. 13v.

WyT 243 -----

Copy in the Arundel Harington MS; mid-late 16th century.

Printed from this MS in Hughey, I, No. 131, pp. 159-60; collated in Muir & Thomson and in Harrier.

Owned by the Duke of Norfolk, Arundel Castle, MSS (Special Press), 'Harrington MS. Temp. 'Eliz.', f. 75v.

WyT 244 -----

Copy, with the third stanza placed first and here beginning 'Patiens off all my blame', in the Blage MS; c. 1530s-40s.

This MS collated in Muir & Thomson and in Harrier.

Trinity College, Dublin, MS 160, f. 146.

WyT 245 *'Patiens, for I have wrong'.*

Copy in the Devonshire MS; c. 1530s-40s.

Not pub. in 16th century. Printed from this MS in Muir & Thomson, p. 232.

British Library, Add. MS 17492, f. 82v.

WyT 246 *'Patiens for my devise'.*

Copy in the Egerton MS; c. 1537-9.

Not pub. in 16th century. Printed from this MS in Muir & Thomson, pp. 29-30, and in Harrier, pp. 134-5.

British Library, Egerton MS 2711, f. 28v.

WyT 247 -----

Copy in the Devonshire MS; c. 1530s-40s.

This MS collated in Muir & Thomson and in Harrier.

British Library, Add. MS 17492, f. 71.

WyT 248 -----

Copy of lines 1-8 in the Arundel Harington MS; imperfect; mid-late 16th century.

Printed from this MS in Hughey, I, No. 132, p. 160; collated in Muir & Thomson and in Harrier.

Owned by the Duke of Norfolk, Arundel Castle, MSS (Special Press), 'Harrington MS. Temp. Eliz.', f. 75v.

WyT 249 -----

Copy, immediately following on from 'Patiens off all my blame' (see WyT 244), in the Blage MS; c. 1530s-40s.

This MS collated in Muir & Thomson and in Harrier.

Trinity College, Dublin, MS 160, f. 147.

WyT 250 *'Payne of all payne, the most grevous paine'.*

Copy in the Devonshire MS; c. 1530s-40s.

Not pub. in 16th century; considered of doubtful authorship by H.A. Mason in *Sewanee Review*, 84. ii (1976), 679-80. Printed from this MS in Muir & Thomson, pp. 218-19.

British Library, Add. MS 17492, f. 75v.

*WyT 251 *Penitential Psalms* ('Love to gyve law vnto his subiect hertes').

Autograph of Wyatt's seven Penitential Psalms

and their prologues, with extensive revisions, in the Egerton MS; imperfect, lacking lines 100-51 (lines 28-80 in Psalm 6); [1534-42].

First pub. in *Certayne psalmes* (London, 1549). Printed from this MS (with a facsimile of one page) in Muir & Thomson, pp. 98-125, and in Harrier, pp. 214-49.

British Library, Egerton MS 2711, ff. 86-98v.

WyT 252 -----

Copy of the seven Penitential Psalms and their prologues, in the Arundel Harington MS; mid-late 16th century.

Printed from this MS in Hughey, I, Nos. 154-67, pp. 186-206; collated in Muir & Thomson and in Harrier.

Owned by the Duke of Norfolk, Arundel Castle, MSS (Special Press), 'Harrington MS. Temp. Eliz.', ff. 108-18.

WyT 253 -----

Copy of the seven Penitential Psalms and their prologues; mid-16th century.

This MS collated in Muir & Thomson (with a facsimile of two pages facing p. 116), and in Harrier.

British Library, Royal MS 17 A. XXII.

WyT 254 *'Perdy I sayd hytt nott'.*

Copy in the Devonshire MS; c. 1530s-40s.

First pub. in *Songes and Sonettes* (London, 1557); Muir & Thomson, pp. 170-1. This MS collated in Muir & Thomson.

British Library, Add. MS 17492, ff. 70v-1.

WyT 255 -----

Copy in the Blage MS; c. 1530s-40s.

Printed from this MS in Muir & Thomson.

Trinity College, Dublin, MS 160, f. 145.

WyT 256 *'Playn ye, myn eyes, accompany my hart'.*

Copy in a Harington miscellany; mid-late 16th century.

Not pub. in 16th century. Printed from this MS in Muir & Thomson, p. 241.

British Library, Add. MS 36529, f. 33.

WyT 257 *'Processe of tyme worketh such wounder'.*

Copy in the Egerton MS; c. 1537-9.

Not pub. in 16th century. Printed from this MS in Muir & Thomson, p. 61, and in Harrier, pp. 181-2.

British Library, Egerton MS 2711, f. 55.

WyT 258 -----

Copy in the Arundel Harington MS; mid-late 16th century.

Printed from this MS in Hughey, I, No. 137, p. 164; collated in Muir & Thomson and in Harrier.

Owned by the Duke of Norfolk, Arundel Castle, MSS (Special Press), 'Harrington MS. Temp. Eliz.', f. 97.

*WyT 259 *'Prove wythr I do chainge, my dere'.*

Autograph unfinished draft, in the Egerton MS; c. 1537-9.

Not pub. in 16th century. Printed from this MS in Muir & Thomson, p. 78, and in Harrier, p. 204.

British Library, Egerton MS 2711, f. 66.

*WyT 260 *Psalm 37. Noli emulare in maligna* ('Altho thow se th'owtragius clime aloft').

Copy of lines 1-36, with an autograph addition, in the Egerton MS; c. 1537-9.

Not pub. in 16th century. Printed from this MS in Muir & Thomson, pp. 75-7 (and see WyT 261) and in Harrier, pp. 201-2.

British Library, Egerton MS 2711, f. 65v.

WyT 261 -----

Copy of lines 1-69, 72-112, in the Arundel Harington MS; mid-late 16th century.

Printed from this MS in Hughey, I, No. 168, pp. 206-8; collated (and printed in part) in Muir & Thomson and in Harrier, pp. 202-3.

Owned by the Duke of Norfolk, Arundel Castle, MSS (Special Press), 'Harrington MS. Temp. Eliz.', ff. 118-19v.

WyT 262 *'Quondam was I in my Ladys gras'.*

Copy in the Blage MS; c. 1530s-40s.

Not pub. in 16th century. Printed from this MS in Muir & Thomson, pp. 172-3.

Trinity College, Dublin, MS 160, f. 150.

WyT 263 *'Resound my voyse, ye woodes that here me plain'.*

Copy in the Egerton MS; c. 1537-9.

'Resound my voyse, ye woodes that here me plain'

First pub. in *Songes and Sonettes* (London, 1557). Printed from this MS in Muir & Thomson, p. 18, and in Harrier, pp. 120-1.

British Library, Egerton MS 2711, f. 17v.

WyT 264 -----

Copy in the Devonshire MS; c. 1530s-40s.

This MS collated in Muir & Thomson and in Harrier.

British Library, Add. MS 17492, f. 72.

WyT 265 *'Ryght true it is, and said full yore agoo'.*

Copy in the Egerton MS; c. 1537-9.

First pub. in *Songes and Sonettes* (London, 1557). Printed from this MS in Muir & Thomson, pp. 35-6, and in Harrier, p. 141.

British Library, Egerton MS 2711, f. 33.

WyT 266 -----

Copy in the Arundel Harington MS; mid-late 16th century.

Printed from this MS in Hughey, I, No. 119, pp. 155-6; collated in Muir & Thomson and in Harrier. See also WyT 393.

Owned by the Duke of Norfolk, Arundel Castle, MSS (Special Press), 'Harrington MS. Temp. Eliz.', f. 67 (bis).

WyT 267 *'Sche that shuld most, percevythe lest'.*

Copy in the Blage MS; c. 1530s-40s.

Not pub. in 16th century. Printed from this MS in Muir & Thomson, p. 174.

Trinity College, Dublin, MS 160, f. 155.

WyT 268 *'Shall she neuer out of my mynde'.*

Copy in a composite volume of verse and prose tracts; 16th century.

First pub. (?) in *A Boke of Balettes*, [c. 1548]; *The Court of Venus*, later edition [c. 1563]. This MS collated in Muir & Thomson, pp. 255-6.

British Library, Add. MS 18752, f. 87v.

*WyT 269 *'She sat and sowde that hath done me the wrong'.*

Copy, with autograph corrections, in the Egerton MS; c. 1537-9.

First pub. in *Songes and Sonettes* (London, 1557). Printed from this MS in Muir & Thomson, p. 40, and in Harrier, pp. 146-7.

British Library, Egerton MS 2711, f. 37.

WyT 270 -----

Copy in the Devonshire MS; c. 1530s-40s.

This MS collated in Muir & Thomson and in Harrier.

British Library, Add. MS 17492, f. 73.

WyT 271 -----

Copy in the Arundel Harington MS; mid-late 16th century.

Printed from this MS in Hughey, I, No. 127, p. 158; collated in Muir & Thomson and in Harrier.

Owned by the Duke of Norfolk, Arundel Castle, MSS (Special Press), 'Harrington MS. Temp. Eliz.', f. 68v.

--- *'She that should most, perceiveth least'.*

See WyT 267.

--- *'Sighs are my food, drink are my tears'.*

See WyT 295.

--- *'Since love is such that, as ye wot'.*

See WyT 296.

--- *'Since so ye please to hear me plain'.*

See WyT 297.

--- *'Since ye delight to know'.*

See WyT 298-300.

WyT 272 *'Sins you will nedes that I shall sing'.*

Copy in the Devonshire MS; c. 1530s-40s.

Not pub. in 16th century. Printed from this MS in Muir & Thomson, p. 215.

British Library, Add. MS 17492, f. 73v.

--- *'Sith I myself displease thee'.*

See WyT 301.

--- *'Sith it is so that I am thus refused'.*

See WyT 294.

WyT 273 *'So feble is the threde that doth the burden stay'.*

Autograph copy, with extensive revisions, headed 'In Spayne' in an italic hand (that responsible for WyT 372), in the Egerton MS; c. 1537-9.

First pub. in *Songes and Sonettes* (London, 1557). Printed from this MS in Muir & Thomson, pp. 79-82, and in Harrier, pp. 205-9.

British Library, Egerton MS 2711, ff. 67-8v.

WyT 274 -----

Copy in the Devonshire MS; c. 1530s-40s.

This MS collated in Muir & Thomson and in Harrier.

British Library, Add. MS 17492, ff. 49-50v.

WyT 275 -----

Copy, with numerous alterations, in the Arundel Harington MS; mid-late 16th century.

Printed from this MS in Hughey, I, No. 139, pp. 165-8; collated in Muir & Thomson and in Harrier.

Owned by the Duke of Norfolk, Arundel Castle, MSS (Special Press), 'Harrington MS. Temp. Eliz.', ff. 97v-8v.

WyT 276 *'So vnwarely was never no man cawght'.*

Copy in the Devonshire MS; c. 1530s-40s.

First pub. in *Songes and Sonettes* (London, 1557). Printed from this MS in Muir & Thomson, pp. 202-3.

British Library, Add. MS 17492, f. 32.

WyT 277 *'Som fowles there be that have so perfaict sight'.*

Copy in the Egerton MS; c. 1537-9.

First pub. in *Songes and Sonettes* (London, 1557). Printed from this MS in Muir & Thomson, pp. 19-20, and in Harrier, p. 122.

British Library, Egerton MS 2711, f. 19v.

WyT 278 -----

Copy in the Arundel Harington MS; mid-late 16th century.

Printed from this MS in Hughey, I, No. 109, p. 151; collated in Muir & Thomson and in Harrier.

Owned by the Duke of Norfolk, Arundel Castle, MSS (Special Press), 'Harrington MS. Temp. Eliz.', f. 66.

*WyT 279 *'Some tyme I fled the fyre that me brent'.*

Copy, with autograph corrections, in the Egerton MS; c. 1537-9.

First pub. in *Songes and Sonettes* (London, 1557). Printed from this MS in Muir & Thomson, p. 44, and in Harrier, p. 151.

British Library, Egerton MS 2711, f. 40.

WyT 280 -----

Copy in the Devonshire MS; c. 1530s-40s.

This MS collated in Muir & Thomson and in Harrier.

British Library, Add. MS 17492, f. 38v.

WyT 281 -----

Copy in the Arundel Harington MS; mid-late 16th century.

Printed from this MS in Hughey, I, No. 128, p. 158; collated in Muir & Thomson and in Harrier.

Owned by the Duke of Norfolk, Arundel Castle, MSS (Special Press), 'Harrington MS. Temp. Eliz.', f. 68v.

WyT 282 -----

Copy of lines 1-4 in a composite volume of MSS; mid-late 16th century.

This MS collated in Muir & Thomson and in Harrier.

British Library, Harley MS 78, f. 27.

--- *'Some time I sigh, some time I sing'.*

See WyT 293.

WyT 283 *'Somtyme the pryde of mye assured trothe'.*

Copy, headed 'Th' Argument', in the Arundel Harington MS; mid-late 16th century.

Not pub. in 16th century. Printed from this MS in Muir & Thomson, p. 240, and in Hughey, I, No. 169, pp. 208-9.

Owned by the Duke of Norfolk, Arundel Castle, MSS (Special Press), 'Harrington MS. Temp. Eliz.', f. 119v.

WyT 284 *'Spight hath no powre to make me sadde'.*

Copy in the Devonshire MS; c. 1530s-40s.

'Spight hath no powre to make me sadde'.

Not pub. in 16th century. Printed from this MS in Muir & Thomson, pp. 223-4.

British Library, Add. MS 17492, f. 78.

WyT 285 *'Spytt off the spytt whiche they in vayne'.*

Copy in the Blage MS; c. 1530s-40s.

Not pub. in 16th century. Printed from this MS in Muir & Thomson, pp. 174-5.

Trinity College, Dublin, MS 160, f. 157.

WyT 286 *'Stone who so list vpon the Slipper toppe'.*

Copy in the Arundel Harington MS; mid-late 16th century.

First pub. in *Songes and Sonettes* (London, 1557). Printed from this MS in Muir & Thomson, p. 240, and in Hughey, I, No. 311, p. 356.

Owned by the Duke of Norfolk, Arundel Castle, MSS (Special Press), 'Harrington MS. Temp. Eliz.', f. 216v.

WyT 287 *'Such happe as I ame happed in'.*

Copy in the Egerton MS; c. 1537-9.

Not pub. in 16th century. Printed from this MS in Muir & Thomson, pp. 26-7, and in Harrier, pp. 130-1.

British Library, Egerton MS 2711, ff. 25v-6.

*WyT 288 *'Suche vayn thought as wonted to myslede me'.*

Copy, with an autograph alteration, in the Egerton MS; c. 1537-9.

First pub. in *Songes and Sonettes* (London, 1557). Printed from this MS in Muir & Thomson, p. 42, and in Harrier, pp. 148-9.

British Library, Egerton MS 2711, f. 38.

WyT 289 -----

Copy in the Devonshire MS; c. 1530s-40s.

This MS collated in Muir & Thomson and in Harrier.

British Library, Add. MS 17492, f. 31.

WyT 290 -----

Copy in the Arundel Harington MS; mid-late 16th century.

Printed from this MS in Hughey, I, No. 121, p. 156; collated in Muir & Thomson and in Harrier.

Owned by the Duke of Norfolk, Arundel Castle, MSS (Special Press), 'Harrington MS. Temp. Eliz.', f. 67 (bis)^{v}.

WyT 291 *'Suffryng in sorrowe in hope to Attayne'.*

Copy in the Devonshire MS; c. 1530s-40s.

Not pub. in 16th century. This MS collated in Muir & Thomson, pp. 176-7.

British Library, Add. MS 17492, f. 6v.

WyT 292 -----

Copy in the Blage MS; c. 1530s-40s.

Printed from this MS in Muir & Thomson.

Trinity College, Dublin, MS 160, f. 159.

WyT 293 *'Sum tyme I syghe, sumtyme I syng'.*

Copy in the Devonshire MS; c. 1530s-40s.

Not pub. in 16th century. Printed from this MS in Muir & Thomson, pp. 199-200.

British Library, Add. MS 17492, f. 20v.

WyT 294 *'Syethe yt ys so that I am thus refusyd'.*

Copy in the Blage MS; c. 1530s-40s.

Not pub. in 16th century. Printed from this MS in Muir & Thomson, pp. 175-6.

Trinity College, Dublin, MS 160, f. 158.

WyT 295 *'Syghes ar my foode, drynke are my teares'.*

Copy in a composite volume of MSS; mid-late 16th century.

First pub. in *Songes and Sonettes* (London, 1557). Printed from this MS in Muir & Thomson, p. 242.

British Library, Harley MS 78, f. 27.

WyT 296 *'Synes loue ys suche that, as ye wott'.*

Copy in the Devonshire MS; c. 1530s-40s.

Not pub. in 16th century. Printed from this MS in Muir & Thomson, pp. 208-9.

British Library, Add. MS 17492, ff. 51v-2.

WyT 297 *'Synes so ye please to here me playn'.*

Copy in the Devonshire MS; c. 1530s-40s.

Not pub. in 16th century. Printed from this MS in Muir & Thomson, p. 210.

British Library, Add. MS 17492, f. 53.

WyT 298 *'Syns ye delite to knowe'.*

Copy in the Egerton MS; c. 1537-9.

Not pub. in 16th century. Printed from this MS in Muir & Thomson, pp. 54-5, and in Harrier, pp. 163-4.

British Library, Egerton MS 2711, f. 47r-v.

WyT 299 -----

Copy in the Devonshire MS; c. 1530s-40s.

This MS collated in Muir & Thomson and in Harrier.

British Library, Add. MS 17492, f. 72v.

WyT 300 -----

Copy of lines 1-6, 15-35, in the Blage MS; c. 1530s-40s.

This MS collated in Muir & Thomson and in Harrier.

Trinity College, Dublin, MS 160, f. 156.

WyT 301 *'Sythe I my selffe dysplease the'.*

Copy in the Blage MS; c. 1530s-40s.

Not pub. in 16th century. Printed from this MS in Muir & Thomson, pp. 177-8.

Trinity College, Dublin, MS 160, f. 160.

*WyT 302 *'Tagus, fare well, that westward with thy stremes'.*

Autograph, with minor revisions, in the Egerton MS; c. 1539.

First pub. in *Songes and Sonettes* (London, 1557). Printed from this MS in Muir & Thomson, p. 82, and in Harrier, p. 211. Facsimiles in Croft, *Autograph Poetry*, I, 9; Petti, *English Literary Hands*, No. 19.

British Library, Egerton MS 2711, f. 69.

WyT 302.5 See Addenda, p. 636

WyT 303 *'Take hede be tyme leste ye be spyede'.*

Copy in the Devonshire MS; c. 1530s-40s.

Not pub. in 16th century. Printed from this MS in Muir & Thomson, p. 189.

British Library, Add. MS 17492, f. 2.

WyT 304 *'Tanglid I was yn loves snare'.*

Copy in the Devonshire MS; c. 1530s-40s.

Not pub. in 16th century. Printed from this MS in Muir & Thomson, pp. 227-8.

British Library, Add. MS 17492, ff. 79v-80.

WyT 305 *'That tyme that myrthe dyed stere my shypp'.*

Copy in the Devonshire MS; c. 1530s-40s.

Not pub. in 16th century; Muir & Thomson, pp. 184-5. This MS collated in Muir & Thomson.

British Library, Add. MS 17492, f. 17v.

WyT 306 -----

Copy in the Blage MS; c. 1530s-40s.

Printed from this MS in Muir & Thomson.

Trinity College, Dublin, MS 160, f. 175.

WyT 307 *'Th'answere that ye made to me, my dere'.*

Copy in the Egerton MS; c. 1537-9.

First pub. in *Songes and Sonettes* (London, 1557). Printed from this MS in Muir & Thomson, pp. 70-1, and in Harrier, p. 196.

British Library, Egerton MS 2711, f. 63r-v.

*WyT 308 *'Th'enmy of liff, decayer of all kynde'.*

Copy, with autograph corrections, in the Egerton MS; c. 1537-9.

First pub. in *Songes and Sonettes* (London, 1557). Printed from this MS in Muir & Thomson, p. 47, and in Harrier, p. 155.

British Library, Egerton MS 2711, f. 42v.

WyT 309 *'The flaming Sighes that boile within my brest'.*

Copy in the Arundel Harington MS; mid-late 16th century.

First pub. in *Songes and Sonettes* (London, 1557). Printed from this MS in Muir & Thomson, p. 239, and in Hughey, I, No. 310, p. 355.

Owned by the Duke of Norfolk, Arundel Castle, MSS (Special Press), 'Harrington MS. Temp. Eliz.', f. 216v.

WyT 310 *'The fructe of all the seruise that I serue'.*

Copy in the Devonshire MS; c. 1530s-40s.

Not pub. in 16th century. Printed from this MS in Muir & Thomson, p. 214.

British Library, Add. MS 17492, f. 72.

'The furyous gonne in his rajing yre'.

*WyT 311 *'The furyous gonne in his rajing yre'.*

Copy, with autograph revisions, in the Egerton MS; c. 1537-9.

First pub. in *Songes and Sonettes* (London, 1557). Printed from this MS in Muir & Thomson, p. 45, and in Harrier, pp. 152-3.

British Library, Egerton MS 2711, f. 40v.

WyT 312 -----

Copy in the Arundel Harington MS; mid-late 16th century.

Printed from this MS in Hughey, I, No. 129, p. 158; collated in Muir & Thomson and in Harrier.

Owned by the Duke of Norfolk, Arundel Castle, MSS (Special Press), 'Harrington MS. Temp. Eliz.', f. 68v.

WyT 313 *'The hart and servys to yow profferd'.*

Copy in the Devonshire MS; c. 1530s-40s.

Not pub. in 16th century. Printed from this MS in Muir & Thomson, p. 193.

British Library, Add. MS 17492, f. 11v.

WyT 314 *'The Joye so short, alas, the paine so nere'.*

Copy in the Devonshire MS; c. 1530s-40s.

Not pub. in 16th century. Printed from this MS in Muir & Thomson, pp. 217-18.

British Library, Add. MS 17492, f. 75v.

WyT 315 *'The knott that furst my hart dyd strayn'.*

Copy, preceded (f. 22v) by a version of lines 1-4 in the same hand, in the Devonshire MS; c. 1530s-40s.

Not pub. in 16th century; Muir & Thomson, pp. 183-4. This MS collated in Muir & Thomson.

British Library, Add. MS 17492, f. 23r-v.

WyT 316 -----

Copy in the Devonshire MS; c. 1530s-40s.

This MS collated in Muir & Thomson.

British Library, Add. MS 17492, f. 33r-v.

WyT 317 -----

Copy in the Blage MS; c. 1530s-40s.

Printed from this MS in Muir & Thomson.

Trinity College, Dublin, MS 160, f. 173.

--- *'The lively sparks that issue from those eyes'.*

See WyT 321-3.

WyT 318 *'The longe love, that in my thought doeth harbar'.*

Copy, with later alterations in the hand of Nicholas Grimald, in the Egerton MS; c. 1537-9.

First pub. in *Songes and Sonettes* (London, 1557). Printed from this MS in Muir & Thomson, p. 3, and in Harrier, p. 101.

British Library, Egerton MS 2711, f. 5r-v.

WyT 319 -----

Copy in the Arundel Harington MS; mid-late 16th century.

Printed from this MS in Hughey, I, No. 99, pp. 145-6; collated in Muir & Thomson and in Harrier.

Owned by the Duke of Norfolk, Arundel Castle, MSS (Special Press), 'Harrington MS. Temp. Eliz.', f. 63.

WyT 320 *'The losse is small to lese such one'.*

Copy in the Devonshire MS; c. 1530s-40s.

Not pub. in 16th century. Printed from this MS in Muir & Thomson, p. 223.

British Library, Add. MS 17492, f. 77v.

WyT 321 *'The lyvely sperkes that issue from those Iyes'.*

Copy in the Egerton MS; c. 1537-9.

First pub. in *Songes and Sonettes* (London, 1557). Printed from this MS in Muir & Thomson, p. 35, and in Harrier, p. 140.

British Library, Egerton MS 2711, f. 32v.

WyT 322 -----

Copy in the Devonshire MS; c. 1530s-40s.

This MS collated in Muir & Thomson and in Harrier.

British Library, Add. MS 17492, f. 36v.

WyT 323 -----

Copy in the Arundel Harington MS; mid-late 16th century.

Printed from this MS in Hughey, I, No. 118, p. 155; collated in Muir & Thomson and in Harrier.

Owned by the Duke of Norfolk, Arundel Castle, MSS (Special Press), 'Harrington MS. Temp. Eliz.', f. 67 (bis).

WyT 324 *'The piller pearisht in whearto I Lent'.*

Copy in the Arundel Harington MS; mid-late 16th century.

First pub. in *Songes and Sonettes* (London, 1557). Printed from this MS in Muir & Thomson, p. 238, and in Hughey, I, No. 96, pp. 144-5.

Owned by the Duke of Norfolk, Arundel Castle, MSS (Special Press), 'Harrington MS. Temp. Eliz.', f. 60v.

WyT 325 *'The restfull place, Revyver of my smarte'.*

Copy of lines 1-7 in a variant version, including an extra line between lines 5 and 6, in the hand of Nicholas Grimald, headed 'To hiz bedde' and here beginning 'O restfull place: reneewer of my smart', in the Egerton MS; c. 1540s-50s.

First pub. (in a three 7-line stanza version) in *Songes and Sonettes* (London, 1557); Muir & Thomson, pp. 197-8. Printed from this MS in Harrier, p. 105; collated in Muir & Thomson. Facsimile in Ruth Hughey, 'The Harington Manuscript at Arundel Castle and Related Documents', *The Library*, 4th Ser. 15 (1934-5), 388-444 (after p. 414).

British Library, Egerton MS 2711, f. 7v.

WyT 326 -----

Copy of the three 7-line stanza version in the Devonshire MS; c. 1530s-40s.

Printed from this MS in Muir & Thomson.

British Library, Add. MS 17492, f. 18.

*WyT 327 *'The wandering gadlyng in the sommer tyde'.*

Copy, with autograph corrections, in the Egerton MS; c. 1537-9.

First pub. in *Songes and Sonettes* (London, 1557). Printed from this MS in Muir & Thomson, p. 34, and in Harrier, p. 139.

British Library, Egerton MS 2711, f. 32.

WyT 328 -----

Copy in the Devonshire MS; c. 1530s-40s.

This MS collated in Muir & Thomson and in Harrier.

British Library, Add. MS 17492, f. 35v.

WyT 329 -----

Copy in a Harington miscellany; mid-late 16th century.

This MS collated in Muir & Thomson and in Harrier.

British Library, Add. MS 36529, f. 32v.

WyT 330 *'There was never ffile half so well filed'.*

Copy, with alterations in another hand (that responsible for the 'Aunswer' to WyT 183), in the Egerton MS; c. 1537-9.

First pub. in *Songes and Sonettes* (London, 1557). Printed from this MS in Muir & Thomson, p. 14, and in Harrier, p. 116.

British Library, Egerton MS 2711, f. 14v.

WyT 331 -----

Copy, headed 'To my [ ]', in the Devonshire MS; c. 1530s-40s.

This MS collated in Muir & Thomson and in Harrier.

British Library, Add. MS 17492, f. 19v.

WyT 332 -----

Copy in the Arundel Harington MS; mid-late 16th century.

Printed from this MS in Hughey, I, No. 98, p. 145; collated in Muir & Thomson and in Harrier.

Owned by the Duke of Norfolk, Arundel Castle, MSS (Special Press), 'Harrington MS. Temp. Eliz.', f. 60v.

WyT 333 -----

Second copy in the Arundel Harington MS; mid-late 16th century.

Printed from this MS in Hughey, I, No. 108, p. 151; collated in Muir & Thomson and in Harrier.

Owned by the Duke of Norfolk, Arundel Castle, MSS (Special Press), 'Harrington MS. Temp. Eliz.', ff. 65v-6.

WyT 334 -----

Copy in the Blage MS; c. 1530s-40s.

This MS collated in Muir & Thomson and in Harrier.

Trinity College, Dublin, MS 160, f. 174.

WyT 335 *'There was never nothing more me payned'.*

Copy in the Egerton MS; c. 1537-9.

'There was never nothing more me payned'

Not pub. in 16th century. Printed from this MS in Muir & Thomson, p. 28, and in Harrier, pp. 132-3.

British Library, Egerton MS 2711, f. 27r-v.

WyT 336 *'They fle from me that sometyme did me seke'.*

Copy in the Egerton MS; c. 1537-9.

First pub. in *Songes and Sonettes* (London, 1557). Printed from this MS in Muir & Thomson, p. 27 (with a facsimile facing p. 68), and in Harrier, pp. 131-2; facsimile also in Flower & Munby, *English Poetical Autographs*, plate 1.

British Library, Egerton MS 2711, f. 26v.

WyT 337 -----

Copy in the Devonshire MS; c. 1530s-40s.

This MS collated in Muir & Thomson and in Harrier.

British Library, Add. MS 17492, ff. 69v-70.

*WyT 338 *'Tho I cannot your crueltie constrain'.*

Copy, with autograph corrections, in the Egerton MS; c. 1537-9.

First pub. in *Songes and Sonettes* (London, 1557). Printed from this MS in Muir & Thomson, pp. 42-3, and in Harrier, p. 149.

British Library, Egerton MS 2711, f. 38v.

WyT 339 -----

Copy in the Devonshire MS; c. 1530s-40s.

This MS collated in Muir & Thomson and in Harrier.

British Library, Add. MS 17492, f. 37v.

WyT 340 -----

Copy of lines 1-17 in the Arundel Harington MS; imperfect, lacking ending; mid-late 16th century.

Printed from this MS in Hughey, I, No. 136, pp. 163-4; collated in Muir & Thomson and in Harrier.

Owned by the Duke of Norfolk, Arundel Castle, MSS (Special Press), 'Harrington MS. Temp. Eliz.', f. 78v.

WyT 341 *'Tho of the sort ther be that ffayne'.*

Copy in the Blage MS; c. 1530s-40s.

Not pub. in 16th century. Printed from this MS in Muir & Thomson, pp. 180-1.

Trinity College, Dublin, MS 160, f. 169.

WyT 342 *'Tho some do grodge to se me joye'.*

Copy in the Blage MS; c. 1530s-40s.

Not pub. in 16th century. Printed from this MS in Muir & Thomson, pp. 179-80.

Trinity College, Dublin, MS 160, f. 168.

WyT 343 *'Thou hast no faith of him that hath none'.*

Copy, with an alteration in another hand (that responsible for the 'Aunswer' to WyT 183), in the Egerton MS; c. 1537-9.

Not pub. in 16th century. Printed from this MS in Muir & Thomson, p. 16, and in Harrier, p. 118.

British Library, Egerton MS 2711, f. 16.

WyT 344 -----

Copy in the Devonshire MS; c. 1530s-40s.

This MS collated in Muir & Thomson and in Harrier.

British Library, Add. MS 17492, f. 69v.

WyT 345 *'Thou slepest ffast; and I with wofull hart'.*

Copy in the Blage MS; c. 1530s-40s.

Not pub. in 16th century; attributed to Wyatt in Annabel M. Endicott, 'A Note on Wyatt and Serafino D'Aquilano', *RN*, 17 (1964), 301-3. Printed from this MS in Muir & Thomson, p. 179.

Trinity College, Dublin, MS 160, f. 167.

--- *'Though I cannot your cruelty constrain'.*

See WyT 338-40.

WyT 346 *'Though I my self be bridilled of my mynde'.*

Copy in the Egerton MS; c. 1537-9.

Not pub. in 16th century. Printed from this MS in Muir & Thomson, p. 21, and in Harrier, p. 124.

British Library, Egerton MS 2711, f. 21.

WyT 347 -----

Copy in the Arundel Harington MS; mid-late 16th century.

Printed from this MS in Hughey, I, No. 111,

p. 152; collated in Muir & Thomson and in Harrier.

Owned by the Duke of Norfolk, Arundel Castle, MSS (Special Press), 'Harrington MS. Temp. Eliz.', f. 66v.

--- *'Though of the sort there be that feign'.*

See WyT 341.

--- *'Though some do grudge to see my joy'.*

See WyT 342.

WyT 348 *'Though this thy port and I thy seruaunt true'.*

Copy in the Egerton MS; c. 1537-9.

Not pub. in 16th century. Printed from this MS in Muir & Thomson, p. 59, and in Harrier, p. 179.

British Library, Egerton MS 2711, ff. 53v-4.

WyT 349 -----

Copy in the Blage MS; c. 1530s-40s.

This MS collated in Muir & Thomson and in Harrier.

Trinity College, Dublin, MS 160, f. 171.

WyT 350 *'Thy promese was to loue me best'.*

Copy in the hand of Margaret Douglas in the Devonshire MS; c. 1530s-40s.

Not pub. in 16th century. Printed from this MS in Muir & Thomson, pp. 203-4.

British Library, Add. MS 17492, f. 40.

WyT 351 *'To cause accord or to aggre'.*

Copy in the Egerton MS; c. 1537-9.

Not pub. in 16th century. Printed from this MS in Muir & Thomson, p. 58, and in Harrier, p. 178.

British Library, Egerton MS 2711, f. 53.

WyT 352 -----

Copy in the Devonshire MS; c. 1530s-40s.

This MS collated in Muir & Thomson and in Harrier.

British Library, Add. MS 17492, f. 69.

WyT 353 *'To make an ende of all this strif'.*

Copy in the Devonshire MS; c. 1530s-40s.

Not pub. in 16th century. Printed from this MS in Muir & Thomson, pp. 233-4.

British Library, Add. MS 17492, f. 83r-v.

WyT 354 *'To my myshap alas I fynd'.*

Copy in the hand of Margaret Douglas in the Devonshire MS; c. 1530s-40s.

First pub. in *Songes and Sonettes* (London, 1557); attributed to Sir Francis Bryan in A. Stuart Daley, 'The Uncertain Author of Poem 225, Tottel's *Miscellany*', *SP*, 47 (1950), 485-93; Muir & Thomson, pp. 181-3. This MS collated in Muir & Thomson.

British Library, Add. MS 17492, f. 42r-v.

WyT 355 -----

Copy in the Blage MS; c. 1530s-40s.

Printed from this MS in Muir & Thomson.

Trinity College, Dublin, MS 160, f. 172.

WyT 356 -----

Copy, with the second stanza placed first, headed 'Tempore quo fodiebat' and beginning 'Amydes my myrth and pleasantnes', in a MS volume of ballads owned in 1642 by one Gabriell Penne; mid-late 16th century.

This MS collated in Muir & Thomson.

Bodleian, MS Ashmole 48, f. 1r-v.

WyT 357 *'To Rayle or geste ye kno I vse it not'.*

Copy in the Devonshire MS; c. 1530s-40s.

Not pub. in 16th century. Printed from this MS in Muir & Thomson, p. 217.

British Library, Add. MS 17492, f. 75r-v.

WyT 358 *'To seke eche where, where man doth lyve'.*

Copy, with a revision in another hand, in the Egerton MS; c. 1538-9.

Not pub. in 16th century. Printed from this MS in Muir & Thomson, pp. 64-5, and in Harrier, pp. 188-9.

British Library, Egerton MS 2711, f. 59.

'To wette your yee withoutyn teare'

WyT 359 *'To wette your yee withoutyn teare'.*

Copy in the Devonshire MS; c. 1530s-40s.

Not pub. in 16th century; Muir & Thomson, p. 181. This MS collated in Muir & Thomson.

British Library, Add. MS 17492, f. 5.

WyT 360 -----

Copy in the Blage MS; c. 1530s-40s.

Printed from this MS in Muir & Thomson.

Trinity College, Dublin, MS 160, f. 170.

WyT 361 *'To wisshe and want and not obtain'.*

Copy, with two alterations in another hand (that responsible for the 'Aunswer' to WyT 183), in the Egerton MS; c. 1537-9.

Not pub. in 16th century. Printed from this MS in Muir & Thomson, pp. 43-4, and in Harrier, pp. 150-1.

British Library, Egerton MS 2711, f. 39.

WyT 362 -----

Copy in the Devonshire MS; c. 1530s-40s.

This MS collated in Muir & Thomson and in Harrier.

British Library, Add. MS 17492, f. 71v.

WyT 363 -----

Copy of lines 11-36, here beginning 'Yf then I burne to playne me so', in the Arundel Harington MS; imperfect, lacking the beginning; mid-late 16th century.

Printed from this MS in Hughey, I, No. 133, pp. 160-1; collated in Muir & Thomson and in Harrier.

Owned by the Duke of Norfolk, Arundel Castle, MSS (Special Press), 'Harrington MS. Temp. Eliz.', f. 77.

WyT 364 *'Vnstable dreme according to the place'.*

Copy in the Egerton MS; c. 1537-9.

First pub. in *Songes and Sonettes* (London, 1557). Printed from this MS in Muir & Thomson, pp. 59-60, and in Harrier, p. 180.

British Library, Egerton MS 2711, f. 54.

WyT 365 -----

Copy in the Arundel Harington MS; mid-late 16th century.

Printed from this MS in Hughey, I, No. 122, p. 156; collated in Muir & Thomson and in Harrier.

Owned by the Duke of Norfolk, Arundel Castle, MSS (Special Press), 'Harrington MS. Temp. Eliz.', f. 67 (bis)^{v}.

*WyT 366 *'Venemus thornes that ar so sharp and kene'.*

Autograph, in the Egerton MS; c. 1537-9.

First pub. in *Songes and Sonettes* (London, 1557). Printed from this MS in Muir & Thomson, pp. 57-8, and in Harrier, p. 173.

British Library, Egerton MS 2711, f. 50.

WyT 367 -----

Copy in the Devonshire MS; c. 1530s-40s.

This MS collated in Muir & Thomson and in Harrier.

British Library, Add. MS 17492, f. 72v.

WyT 368 -----

Copy in a Harington miscellany; mid-late 16th century.

This MS collated in Muir & Thomson and in Harrier.

British Library, Add. MS 36529, f. 32.

WyT 369 -----

Copy in a composite volume of MSS; mid-late 16th century.

This MS collated in Muir & Thomson and in Harrier.

British Library, Harley MS 78, f. 27.

WyT 370 -----

Copy, omitting line 4, in a miscellany once owned by one W. Kytton; c. 1580.

This MS collated in Muir & Thomson and in Harrier. See also WyT 220.

Cambridge University Library, MS Ff. 5. 14, f. 5v.

WyT 371 *'Venus, in sport, to please therwith her dere'.*

Copy in the Blage MS; c. 1530s-40s.

Not pub. in 16th century. Printed from this MS in Muir & Thomson, p. 188.

Trinity College, Dublin, MS 160, f. 184.

--- *'Vnstable dreme according to the place'*.

See WyT 364-5.

WyT 372 *'Vulcane bygat me; Mynerua me taught'*.

Copy in an italic hand, in the Egerton MS; c. 1539.

First pub. in *Songes and Sonettes* (London, 1557). Printed from this MS in Muir & Thomson, p. 84, and in Harrier, p. 213; discussed in Wayne H. Siek, 'A Note on Some Handwriting in Wyatt's Holograph Poetic Manuscript', *N & Q*, 222 (December 1977), 496-7.

British Library, Egerton MS 2711, f. 70.

WyT 373 -----

Copy, headed 'A Ridell. Tho. W.', in a composite volume of MSS; mid-late 16th century.

The text followed by the Latin poem from which Wyatt's poem was translated. This MS collated in Muir & Thomson and in Harrier.

British Library, Harley MS 78, f. 29v.

WyT 374 *'Was I never, yet, of your love greeved'*.

Copy, with later alterations in the hand of Nicholas Grimald, in the Egerton MS; c. 1537-9.

First pub. in *Songes and Sonettes* (London, 1557). Printed from this MS in Muir & Thomson, pp. 10-11, and in Harrier, p. 111.

British Library, Egerton MS 2711, f. 11.

WyT 375 -----

Copy in the Arundel Harington MS; mid-late 16th century.

Printed from this MS in Hughey, I, No. 101, p. 146; collated in Muir & Thomson and in Harrier.

Owned by the Duke of Norfolk, Arundel Castle, MSS (Special Press), 'Harrington MS. Temp. Eliz.', f. 63r-v.

WyT 376 *'Whan that I call vnto my mynde'*.

Copy in the Devonshire MS; c. 1530s-40s.

Not pub. in 16th century. Printed from this MS in Muir & Thomson, pp. 232-3.

British Library, Add. MS 17492, ff. 82v-3.

*WyT 377 *'What deth is worse then this'*.

Copy, with autograph revisions, in the Egerton MS; c. 1537-9.

Not pub. in 16th century. Printed from this MS in Muir & Thomson, pp. 46-7, and in Harrier, pp. 154-5.

British Library, Egerton MS 2711, f. 42.

WyT 378 -----

Copy in the Devonshire MS; c. 1530s-40s.

This MS collated in Muir & Thomson and in Harrier.

British Library, Add. MS 17492, f. 39v.

WyT 379 -----

Copy in the Devonshire MS; c. 1530s-40s.

This MS collated in Muir & Thomson and in Harrier.

British Library, Add. MS 17492, f. 74.

WyT 380 *'What menythe thys when I lye alone?'*.

Copy in the Devonshire MS; c. 1530s-40s.

Not pub. in 16th century. Printed from this MS in Muir & Thomson, pp. 193-4.

British Library, Add. MS 17492, ff. 12v-13.

WyT 381 *'What nedeth these thretning wordes and wasted wynde?'*.

Copy in the Egerton MS; c. 1537-9.

First pub. in *Songes and Sonettes* (London, 1557). Printed from this MS in Muir & Thomson, p. 35, and in Harrier, p. 141.

British Library, Egerton MS 2711, f. 33.

WyT 382 -----

Copy in the Arundel Harington MS; mid-late 16th century.

Printed from this MS in Hughey, I, No. 126, p. 158; collated in Muir & Thomson and in Harrier.

Owned by the Duke of Norfolk, Arundel Castle, MSS (Special Press), 'Harrington MS. Temp. Eliz.', f. 68r-v.

WyT 383 *'What no, perdy, ye may be sure!'*.

Copy, with a correction and line 15 written in an italic hand (that responsible for WyT 372), in the Egerton MS; c. 1537-9.

'What no, perdy, ye may be sure!'

Not pub. in 16th century. Printed from this MS in Muir & Thomson, p. 34, and in Harrier, pp. 138-9.

British Library, Egerton MS 2711, f. 31v.

WyT 384 -----

Copy in the Devonshire MS; c. 1530s-40s.

This MS collated in Muir & Thomson and in Harrier.

British Library, Add. MS 17492, f. 19.

*WyT 385 *'What rage is this? What furour of what kynd?'.*

Autograph draft, with revisions, in the Egerton MS; c. 1539.

First pub. in *Songes and Sonettes* (London, 1557). Printed from this MS (with a facsimile) in Muir & Thomson, pp. 83-4, and in Harrier, pp. 212-13; discussed (with a facsimile) in Helen V. Baron, 'Wyatt's "What rage"', *The Library*, 5th Ser. 31 (September 1976), 188-204.

British Library, Egerton MS 2711, f. 69v.

WyT 386 *'What shulde I saye'.*

Copy in the Devonshire MS; c. 1530s-40s.

Not pub. in 16th century. Printed from this MS in Muir & Thomson, pp. 220-1.

British Library, Add. MS 17492, f. 77.

WyT 387 *'What thing is that, that I both have and lack'.*

Copy in the Arundel Harington MS; mid-late 16th century.

First pub. in *Songes and Sonettes* (London, 1557). Printed from this MS in Muir & Thomson, pp. 237-8, and in Hughey, I, No. 313, pp. 356-7.

Owned by the Duke of Norfolk, Arundel Castle, MSS (Special Press), 'Harrington MS. Temp. Eliz.', f. 217.

WyT 388 -----

Copy of lines 1-7, headed 'A Ridle', in a composite volume of MSS; mid-late 16th century.

This MS collated in Muir & Thomson.

British Library, Harley MS 78, f. 29v.

WyT 389 *'What vaileth trouth? or, by it, to take payn?'.*

Copy, with later alterations in the hand of Nicholas Grimald, in the Egerton MS; c. 1537-9.

First pub. in *Songes and Sonettes* (London, 1557). Printed from this MS in Muir & Thomson, pp. 1-2, and in Harrier, p. 98.

British Library, Egerton MS 2711, f. 4.

WyT 390 -----

Copy of the incipit (here 'What vaileth') in a musical setting in a MS music book; c. 1595.

This MS discussed in Ivy L. Mumford, 'Musical Settings to the Poems of Sir Thomas Wyatt', *M & L*, 37 (1956), 315-22 (p. 321), and in Mumford, 'Sir Thomas Wyatt's Songs: A Trio of Problems in Manuscript Sources', *M & L*, 39 (1958), 262-4 (where it is argued that this song may not be the same as Wyatt's poem).

British Library, Add. MS 31392, f. 54v.

WyT 391 *'What wolde ye mor of me, your slav, Requyere'.*

Copy in the Blage MS; c. 1530s-40s.

Not pub. in 16th century. Printed from this MS in Muir & Thomson, pp. 186-7.

Trinity College, Dublin, MS 160, f. 182.

WyT 392 *'What wourde is that that chaungeth not'.*

Copy, headed in a later hand 'Anna', in the Egerton MS; c. 1537-9.

First pub. in *Songes and Sonettes* (London, 1557). Printed from this MS in Muir & Thomson, p. 36, and in Harrier, pp. 141-2.

British Library, Egerton MS 2711, f. 33v.

WyT 393 -----

Copy, immediately following on from 'Ryght true it is, and said full yore agoo' (see WyT 266), in the Arundel Harington MS; mid-late 16th century.

Printed from this MS in Hughey, I, No. 120, p. 155; collated in Muir & Thomson and in Harrier.

Owned by the Duke of Norfolk, Arundel Castle, MSS (Special Press), 'Harrington MS. Temp. Eliz.', f. 67 (bis).

--- *'When Dido festid first the wandryng Troian knyght'.*

See WyT 160-1.

--- *'When that I call unto my mind'.*

See WyT 376.

WyT 394 *'Where shall I have at myn owne will'.*

Copy, with alterations in another hand (that responsible for the 'Aunswer' to WyT 183), in the Egerton MS; c. 1537-9.

First pub. in *Songes and Sonettes* (London, 1557). Printed from this MS in Muir & Thomson, pp. 39-40, and in Harrier, pp. 145-6.

British Library, Egerton MS 2711, f. 36r-v.

WyT 395 -----

Copy in the Arundel Harington MS; mid-late 16th century.

Printed from this MS in Hughey, I, No. 135, pp. 162-3; collated in Muir & Thomson and in Harrier.

Owned by the Duke of Norfolk, Arundel Castle, MSS (Special Press), 'Harrington MS. Temp. Eliz.', f. 78r-v.

*WyT 396 *'Who hath herd of suche crueltye before?'.*

Copy, with autograph corrections, in the Egerton MS; c. 1537-9.

First pub. in *Songes and Sonettes* (London, 1557). Printed from this MS in Muir & Thomson, p. 32, and in Harrier, p. 136.

British Library, Egerton MS 2711, f. 29v.

WyT 397 -----

Copy in the Devonshire MS; c. 1530s-40s.

This MS collated in Muir & Thomson and in Harrier.

British Library, Add. MS 17492, f. 73.

WyT 398 -----

Copy in the Arundel Harington MS; mid-late 16th century.

Printed from this MS in Hughey, I, No. 125, p. 157; collated in Harrier.

Owned by the Duke of Norfolk, Arundel Castle, MSS (Special Press), 'Harrington MS. Temp. Eliz.', f. 68.

WyT 399 *'Who lyst his welthe and eas Retayne'.*

Copy in the Blage MS; c. 1530s-40s.

Not pub. in 16th century. Printed from this MS in Muir & Thomson, pp. 187-8.

Trinity College, Dublin, MS 160, f. 183.

--- *'Who most doeth slaunder love'.*

See WyT 168-9.

WyT 400 *'Who so list to hounte I know where is an hynde'.*

Copy, with later alterations in the hand of Nicholas Grimald, in the Egerton MS; c. 1537-9.

Not pub. in 16th century. Printed from this MS in Muir & Thomson, p. 5, and in Harrier, p. 104. Facsimile in Ruth Hughey, 'The Harington Manuscript at Arundel Castle and Related Documents', *The Library*, 4th Ser. 15 (1934-5), 388-444 (after p. 414).

British Library, Egerton MS 2711, f. 7v.

WyT 401 -----

Copy in the Arundel Harington MS; mid-late 16th century.

Printed from this MS in Hughey, I, No. 100, p. 146; collated in Muir & Thomson and in Harrier.

Owned by the Duke of Norfolk, Arundel Castle, MSS (Special Press), 'Harrington MS. Temp. Eliz.', f. 63.

WyT 402 -----

Copy in the Blage MS; c. 1530s-40s.

This MS collated in Muir & Thomson and in Harrier.

Trinity College, Dublin, MS 160, f. 185.

WyT 403 -----

Copy in a verse miscellany among the papers of the Gell family, formerly of Hopton Hall, possibly once owned by Sir John Gell (1593-1671); c. 1620s-30s.

This MS not recorded by editors.

Derbyshire Record Office, D258/60/26a, f. [37v].

WyT 404 *'Who would haue euer thowght'.*

Copy in the Devonshire MS; c. 1530s-40s.

Not pub. in 16th century. Printed from this MS in Muir & Thomson, p. 201.

British Library, Add. MS 17492, f. 21.

WyT 405 *'Wyll ye se what wonders love hathe wrought?'.*

Copy in the Devonshire MS; c. 1530s-40s.

Not pub. in 16th century. Printed from this MS in Muir & Thomson, pp. 234-5.

British Library, Add. MS 17492, f. 84.

'Wythe seruyng styll'

WyT 406 *'Wythe seruyng styll'*.

Copy in the Devonshire MS; c. 1530s-40s.

Not pub. in 16th century; Muir & Thomson, pp. 185-6. This MS collated in Muir & Thomson.

British Library, Add. MS 17492, f. 81.

WyT 407 -----

Copy in the Blage MS; c. 1530s-40s.

Printed from this MS in Muir & Thomson.

Trinity College, Dublin, MS 160, f. 181.

WyT 408 *'Ye know my herte, my ladye dere'*.

Copy of lines 24-39, beginning 'all to my harme', with an alteration in another hand (that responsible for the 'Aunswer' to WyT 183), in the Egerton MS; imperfect, lacking the beginning; c. 1537-9.

Not pub. in 16th century. Printed from this MS in Muir & Thomson, pp. 30-1 (and see WyT 409), and in Harrier, p. 135.

British Library, Egerton MS 2711, f. 29.

WyT 409 -----

Copy in the Devonshire MS; c. 1530s-40s.

This MS collated (and lines 1-23 printed) in Muir & Thomson; lines 24-39 collated in Harrier.

British Library, Add. MS 17492, f. 73v.

WyT 410 *'Ye old mule that thinck your self so fayre'*.

Copy in the Egerton MS; c. 1537-9.

Not pub. in 16th century. Printed from this MS in Muir & Thomson, pp. 25-6, and in Harrier, p. 130.

British Library, Egerton MS 2711, f. 25.

WyT 411 *'Yf amours faith, an hert vnfayned'*.

Copy in the Egerton MS; c. 1537-9.

First pub. in *Songes and Sonettes* (London, 1557). Printed from this MS in Muir & Thomson, p. 12, and in Harrier, pp. 113-14.

British Library, Egerton MS 2711, f. 12v.

WyT 412 -----

Copy in the Arundel Harington MS; mid-late 16th century.

Printed from this MS in Hughey, I, No. 105, p. 150; collated in Muir & Thomson and in Harrier.

Owned by the Duke of Norfolk, Arundel Castle, MSS (Special Press), 'Harrington MS. Temp. Eliz.', f. 65.

WyT 413 *'Yf I myght hau at myne owne wyll'*.

Copy in the Blage MS; c. 1530s-40s.

Not pub. in 16th century. Printed from this MS in Muir & Thomson, pp. 152-3.

Trinity College, Dublin, MS 160, f. 110.

WyT 414 *'Yf in the world ther be more woo'*.

Copy in the Egerton MS; c. 1537-9.

Not pub. in 16th century. Printed from this MS in Muir & Thomson, p. 70, and in Harrier, p. 195.

British Library, Egerton MS 2711, ff. 62v-3.

WyT 415 -----

Copy in the Devonshire MS; c. 1530s-40s.

This MS collated in Muir & Thomson and in Harrier.

British Library, Add. MS 17492, f. 53v.

WyT 416 *'Yf it be so that I forsake the'*.

Copy, with an alteration in another hand (that responsible for the 'Aunswer' to WyT 183), in the Egerton MS; c. 1537-9.

Not pub. in 16th century. Printed from this MS in Muir & Thomson, pp. 15-16, and in Harrier, pp. 117-18.

British Library, Egerton MS 2711, f. 15v.

WyT 417 *'Yf with complaint the paine might be exprest'*.

Copy in the Devonshire MS; c. 1530s-40s.

Not pub. in 16th century. Printed from this MS in Muir & Thomson, p. 214.

British Library, Add. MS 17492, f. 73.

WyT 418 *'You that in love finde lucke and habundance'*.

Copy in the Egerton MS; c. 1537-9.

First pub. in *Songes and Sonettes* (London, 1557). Printed from this MS in Muir & Thomson, p. 73, and in Harrier, p. 199.

British Library, Egerton MS 2711, f. 64v.

'You that in love finde lucke and habundance'

WyT 419 -----

Copy, omitting line 6, in the Arundel Harington MS; mid-late 16th century.

Printed from this MS in Hughey, I, No. 123, pp. 156-7; collated in Muir & Thomson and in Harrier.

Owned by the Duke of Norfolk, Arundel Castle, MSS (Special Press), 'Harrington MS. Temp. Eliz.', ff. 67 (bis)^{v}-68.

WyT 420 *'Your ffolyshe fayned hast'.*

Copy, headed 'The Aunswere', in the Blage MS; c. 1530s-40s.

Not pub. in 16th century. Printed from this MS in Muir & Thomson, p. 164.

Trinity College, Dublin, MS 160, f. 127.

WyT 421 *'Your lokes so often cast'.*

Copy in the Blage MS; c. 1530s-40s.

First pub. in *Songes and Sonettes* (London, 1557). Printed from this MS in Muir & Thomson, pp. 145-6.

Trinity College, Dublin, MS 160, f. 104.

WyT 422 *'Ys yt possyble'.*

Copy in the Devonshire MS; c. 1530s-40s.

Not pub. in 16th century. Printed from this MS in Muir & Thomson, pp. 194-5.

British Library, Add. MS 17492, f. 14.

ADDENDA TO PART 2

MICHAEL DRAYTON

(INTRODUCTION). What purports to be another autograph of Drayton is the inscription 'Mi Drayton 1613' on the verso of the title leaf of an exemplum of Spenser's *The Faerie Queene*, a volume now owned by Arthur A. Houghton, Jr. (and to be sold at Christie's in June 1980). The authenticity of this inscription is highly dubious and it may well be a forgery by John Payne Collier, who once owned the volume.

DrM 36.5 *The Cryer* ('Good Folke, for Gold or Hyre').

Copy in a verse miscellany (the 'Monckton Milnes MS'); c. 1624-33.

Privately owned in England, MS, p. 63.

JOHN FOXE

(INTRODUCTION). Another printed book once owned by Foxe is in the Pierpont Morgan Library. It is a Bible (1571) with his inscription on the title page 'Ex dono Reverendiss. in Chrō prīs Matthaeī Cantuariensis Archiepī 1571'.

FULKE GREVILLE

GrF 4.3 *Caelica. Sonnet lii* ('Away with these self-louing lads').

Copy of stanzas 1-2 in a musical setting by John Dowland in a MS songbook compiled by Thomas Hamond (d. 1662) of Suffolk; c. 1630.

This MS collated in Doughtie, *Lyrics from English Airs*, p. 469.

Bodleian, MS Mus. f. 7-10: f. 7, fol. 12v.

GrF 4.5 ----- -----

Copy in a four-part musical setting by John Dowland in a MS songbook once owned by one Thomas Myriell; early 17th century.

This MS collated in Doughtie, p. 469.

Bibliothèque Royale, Brussels, MS II. 4. 109 (Fétis 3095), pp. 8-9.

GrF 4.8 ----- -----

Copy of the incipit in a musical setting by John Dowland in a MS songbook compiled by Sir William Mure of Rowallan; c. 1600-20.

This MS recorded in Doughtie, p. 469.

Edinburgh University Library, MS La. III. 488, f. 26v.

GrF 16.5 *Letter to Grevill Varney on his Travels.*

Copy, headed 'S[r] Fulk Grevill to his kinsman in France', in a composite volume of MSS; mid-17th century.

British Library, Harley MS 6908, ff. 89-87 rev.

GrF 22.5 -----

Copy in a volume of transcripts of 15th-17th-century letters owned and probably compiled by the novelist Jane Porter (1776-1850); 1806.

This volume formerly Phillipps MS 16688.

University of Kansas, MS 153:10, pp. [23-31].

GrF 23.5 -----

Copy, headed 'A letter written by S[r] ffulke Grevill to a Cosen of his residinge in ffrance wherein he setts downe what obser-vacōns he thinks fitt for him to make vse of his travells', in a portion of a volume of state letters; early-mid-17th century.

This volume formerly Phillipps MS 29759.

Yale, Osborn Collection, fb 117, pp. 16-18.

JOSEPH HALL

(INTRODUCTION). Further poems are found ascribed to Hall in MS sources. In Yale, Osborn Collection (b 197, p. 59) is a two-line Latin epigram *On Queene Elizabeths Armes*, followed by an eight-line English version ('The lyon is the Forrest kinge') and a six-line 'explanation' of the poem ('The lyon awe, the flower her faire estate'), the whole subscribed 'Jos: Hall'. An anonymous version occurs in the Bodleian (MS Rawl. poet. 26, f. 82). In Yale, Osborn Collection (b 137, p. 198) a poem *On his Majestyes Death & his Incomparable Booke* ('Soe falls that stately Caedar, whyle it stood') is ascribed to 'J: Hall. Bp Norwitch:'. A copy ascribed to 'J.H.' occurs in the Bodleian (MS Rawl. D. 954, f. 23), and an anonymous copy is in Yale, Osborn Collection (fb 143, p. 37). The poem was first published (as 'An Epitaph upon King Charles 1st') in *Eikon Basilike* (1649), p. 312. -- Yet another autograph letter of Hall, to James Calthorp, 21 December 1649, is in the Pierpont Morgan Library (R-V Autogrs. Bishops English), and a document on vellum signed by Hall, 28 September 1637, is at Harvard (Autograph file).

HlJ 27.5 *Episcopal Admonition, Sent in a Letter to the House of Commons, April 28, 1628.*

Copy in a volume of speeches and proceedings in the House of Commons in 1627-8; mid-17th century.

University of Kansas, MS E103, f. 130.

JOSEPH HALL, *Episcopal Admonition*

HlJ 28.5 -----

Copy in a volume of state letters; mid-17th century.

Owned by Lord Egremont, Petworth House, HMC MS 61, pp. 521-3.

HlJ 29.5 -----

Copy in a volume of speeches and proceedings in the House of Commons in 1627-8; mid-17th century.

Yale, Osborn Collection, fb 164, ff. 199v-200.

HlJ 29.8 -----

Copy in a volume of speeches and proceedings in the House of Commons in 1627-8; mid-17th century.

This volume formerly Phillipps MS 10819.

Yale, Osborn Collection, fb 175, f. 33.

SIR JOHN HARINGTON

HrJ 60.5 *The Author to Queene Elizabeth, in praise of her reading* ('For euer deare, for euer dreaded Prince').

Copy, untitled, in a verse miscellany; c. 1638-45.

Rosenbach Foundation, MS 239/22, f. 8.

HrJ 70.5 *A good answere of a Gentlewoman to a Lawyer* ('A vertuous Dame, that saw a Lawyer rome').

Copy, headed 'On a lawyers absence', in a miscellany; mid-17th century.

Yale, Osborn Collection, b 205, f. 96.

HrJ 96.5 *Of a certaine Man* ('There was (not certain when) a certaine preacher').

Copy, headed 'Erat quidam homo' and here beginning 'Ther was no certayne when a Certyne teacher', in a verse miscellany compiled by John Cruso (1618-81) of Gonville and Caius College, Cambridge; c. 1630s.

The text followed (pp. 116-17) by an 'answear' (here beginning 'That noe man yet could in the Bible find').

St John's College, Cambridge, MS U. 26 (James 548), p. 116.

HrJ 98.5 -----

Copy, untitled and here beginning 'A tyme vncertayne when as a certayne preacher', in a verse miscellany; c. 1620.

The text followed (f. 72v) by an answer (here beginning 'That no man yet could in y[e] bible finde' and subscribed 'S[r]. J.H.').

Victoria and Albert Museum, Dyce Collection, Cat. No. 44 (Pressmark 25. F. 39), f. 72.

HrJ 98.8 -----

Copy, headed 'Quidam homo' and here beginning 'There was a time when that a certain teacher', in a miscellany; mid-17th century.

The text followed (f. 48r-v) by 'An answer by y[e] Lady checke' (here beginning 'That no man yet could in y[e] bible find').

Yale, Osborn Collection, b 205, f. 48.

HrJ 122.5 *Of a Lady that giues the cheek* ('Is't for a grace, or is't for some disleeke').

Copy, untitled, in a verse miscellany; c. 1620.

Victoria and Albert Museum, Dyce Collection, Cat. No. 44 (Pressmark 25. F. 39), f. 64v.

HrJ 159.5 *Of a Lady that left open her Cabbinett* ('A vertuose Lady sitting in a muse').

Copy, headed 'On A Lady sitting stradling' and here beginning 'A gallant Lady sitting in A muse', in a verse miscellany; mid-17th century.

Yale, Osborn Collection, b 200, p. 430.

HrJ 164.5 *Of a Precise Cobler, and an ignorant Curat* ('A Cobler, and a Curat, once disputed').

Copy, untitled and here beginning 'A curate & a Cobler longe disputed', in a verse miscellany compiled by an Oxford man and once owned by one Stephen Welden; mid-17th century.

Folger, MS V. a. 162, f. 65v.

HrJ 183.5 *Of a Precise Tayler* ('A Taylor, thought a man of vpright dealling').

Copy, untitled and here beginning 'A taylor ta'ne to be of vpright dealing', in a verse miscellany; c. 1620.

Victoria and Albert Museum, Dyce Collection, Cat. No. 44 (Pressmark 25. F. 39), f. 84.

HrJ 208.5 *Of a pregnant pure sister* ('I learned a tale more fitt to be forgotten').

Copy of a ten-line version, untitled and here beginning 'A godlie mayde wth one of her societie', in a verse miscellany; c. 1620.

Victoria and Albert Museum, Dyce Collection, Cat. No. 44 (Pressmark 25. F. 39), f. 64.

SIR JOHN HARINGTON, *Of a pregnant pure sister*

HrJ 209.5 -----

Copy of a ten-line version, headed 'parturiens puritana' and here beginning 'A godly sister by one of hir society', in a miscellany; mid-17th century.

Yale, Osborn Collection, b 205, f. 43v.

HrJ 209.8 -----

Copy of a ten-line version, headed 'Vpon a woman gotten with child by a Scholler and here beginning 'A puritane maide with her society', on f. [21] in a verse miscellany associated with Cambridge and owned in 1637 by Francis Rolfe (1618-78), later Town Clerk of [King's] Lynn; c. 1637.

Privately owned in England.

HrJ 237.5 *Of certain puritan wenches* ('Six of the weakest sex and purest sect').

Copy, headed 'Six holie Sisters' and here beginning 'Six holie sisters of the Purest sect', in the hand of George Faulcon, receiver or secretary to Roger Manners, fifth Earl of Rutland (1576-1612) and to Sir George Manners, seventh Earl of Rutland, in a composite volume of verse belonging to the Manners family; early 17th century.

This MS recorded (erroneously as part of 'Volume XXIV') in *HMC*, 12th Report, Appendix V, Rutland II (1889), p. 317.

Owned by the Duke of Rutland, Belvoir Castle, *Letters and Papers*, Verses, Vol. XXV, f. 18.

HrJ 268.5 *Of Treason* ('Treason doth neuer prosper, what's the reason?').

Copy, untitled, in a miscellany; c. 1630s.

John Rylands University Library of Manchester, Rylands English MS 410, f. 22v.

HrJ 289.5 *Of Women learned in the tongues* ('You wisht me to a wife, faire, rich and young').

Copy, headed 'In Amorosum Epig:' and here beginning 'A wife you wisht me s^r^ rich, faire, & young', in a miscellany; mid-17th century.

Yale, Osborn Collection, b 205, f. 40v.

HrJ 299.5 *To his Wife* ('Because I once in verse did hap to call').

Copy, headed 'S^r^ Jo: Harringtonn to his wife', in a verse miscellany compiled by John Cruso (1618-81) of Gonville and Caius College, Cambridge, c. 1630s.

First pub. in *1618*, Book II, No. 81; McClure No. 177, p. 218.

St John's College, Cambridge, MS U. 26 (James 548), p. 149.

HrJ 313.5 *A Tragicall Epigram* ('When doome of Peeres & Iudges fore-appointed').

Copy, headed 'Vpon ye death of ye Queen of Scots' and here beginning 'When doome of death by iudgm^t^. foreappointed', in a verse miscellany owned in 1642 by one Horatio Carey; c. 1638-42.

Rosenbach Foundation, MS 1083/17, p. 6.

HrJ 314.5 *A witty choice of a Country fellow* ('A rich Lord had a poore Lout to his ghest').

Copy, headed 'Vpon a lord and a Countryman', in a miscellany; mid-17th century.

First pub. in *1615*; *1618*, Book IV, No. 70; McClure No. 324, p. 276.

Yale, Osborn Collection, b 205, f. 47.

EDWARD, LORD HERBERT OF CHERBURY

HrE 78.5 *Inconstancy* ('Inconstancy's the greatest of synns').

Copy, the first stanza headed 'Of Inconstancy', the second headed 'The Aunswere, in praise of itt', in a verse miscellany; c. 1630.

University of Nottingham, Portland MS Pw V 37, p. 204.

HrE 95.5 *Autobiography.*

Extract made by Thomas Birch (1705-66) in 1755 from a transcript of Herbert's autograph (?) made in 1718 (? HrE 95), in a volume of Birch's transcripts of letters of John Chamberlain.

British Library, Add. MS 4173, ff. 5-20v.

GEORGE HERBERT

HrG 29.5 *Bitter-sweet* ('Ah my deare angrie Lord').

Copy in a miscellany compiled by Sir John Gibson (1606-65) of Welburn, near Kirkby Moorside, Yorkshire, a Royalist prisoner in Durham Castle; c. 1653-60; [1655-60].

This MS not recorded in Hutchinson.

British Library, Add. MS 37719, f. 272v.

GEORGE HERBERT

HrG 281.5 *Vertue* ('Sweet day, so cool, so calm, so bright').

Copy, untitled, in a miscellany entitled *Vade mecum or A Pocket-Booke* compiled by John Gibson (b. 1630) of Welburn, near Kirkby Moorside, Yorkshire; c. 1678.

This MS not recorded in Hutchinson.

Bodleian, Broxbourne R 359, f. [51].

HrG 302.5 *Ad Autorem Instaurationis Magnae* ('Per strages licet autorum veterũmque ruinam').

Copy in a verse miscellany compiled by Tobias Alston (1620-c.1639) of Sayham Hall, near Sudbury, Suffolk; c. 1639.

This MS not recorded in Hutchinson.

Yale, Osborn Collection, b 197, p. 26.

HrG 304.5 *Aethiopissa ambit Cestum Diuersi Coloris Virum* ('Qvid mihi si facies nigra est? hoc, Ceste, colore').

Copy in a verse miscellany compiled by Tobias Alston (1620-c.1639) of Sayham Hall, near Sudbury, Suffolk; c. 1639.

The text followed by an answer, 'Cestae ad Aethiopissam responsio' (beginning 'Vota precesq tuas negro signato lapillo') also ascribed to Herbert. This MS not recorded in Hutchinson.

Yale, Osborn Collection, b 197, pp. 167-8.

BEN JONSON

(INTRODUCTION). Some other printed books from Jonson's library can be located. Jonson's exemplum of Daniel's *Works* (1602) (McPherson, No. 47) is at Yale (see SAMUEL DANIEL, INTRODUCTION); his exemplum of *Lucretius* (Amsterdam, 1620) (McPherson, No. 108) is at Harvard (*EC.J7382.Zz6201); and his exemplum of John Selden, *Dis Syris* (1629) (McPherson, No. 173) is at the Rosenbach Foundation (401/21). His exemplum of Blasius Barnardius, *De laudibus vitae rusticae* (1613) is at Yale (Ih J738 Zz613).

JnB 4.5 *An Answer to Alexander Gill* ('Shall the prosperity of a Pardon still').

Copy, headed 'Ben: Johnsons reply' and here beginning 'Doeth ye prosperity of a pardon, still', in a verse miscellany; mid-17th century.

Yale, Osborn Collection, b 200, p. 15.

JnB 44.5 *A Celebration of Charis in ten Lyrick Peeces. 7. Begging another, on colour of mending the former* ('For Loves-sake, kisse me once againe').

Copy, headed 'Clayminge anothe^r kiss on coullo^r of mending ye former. by Ben: J.', in a miscellany owned and probably compiled by one John Hale; late 17th century.

Yale, Osborn Collection, b 104, p. 115.

JnB 136.5 *Epitaph on Elizabeth, L.H.* ('Would'st thou heare, what man can say').

Copy, headed 'On ye death of the Lady Eliz: Hobby' and here beginning 'Wilt thou heare w^t man can say?', in a verse miscellany; mid-17th century.

Yale, Osborn Collection, b 200, p. 100.

JnB 192.5 *Eupheme: or, The Faire Fame Left to Posteritie Of that truly noble Lady, the Lady Venetia Digby. 3. The Picture of the Body* ('Sitting, and ready to be drawne').

Copy in a verse miscellany (the 'Monckton Milnes MS'); c. 1624-33.

Privately owned in England, MS, p. 61.

JnB 379.5 *Ode to himselfe* ('Come leaue the lothed stage').

Copy, together with (stanza-for-stanza) a Latin version by William Strode and a Greek version by 'Mr Maisters of New=colledge', on three pages near the end of a miscellany compiled by Vincent Sparkes, Minister of Northwood, Isle of Wight; mid-17th century.

This MS recorded in Mary Damant, 'A Cromwellian Commonplace Book', *N & Q*, 7th Ser. 10 (13 September 1890), 204-5.

Isle of Wight Record Office, Cromwellian commonplace book, [no page numbers].

JnB 380.5 -----

Copy of the first stanza, untitled, followed by the first stanza of Randolph's answer and two Latin versions, all these verses then repeated, followed by the second stanza of Jonson's poem and the second stanza of Randolph's answer, in a verse miscellany appended to a MS volume of poems by Donne; c. 1630s.

Trinity College, Dublin, MS 877, ff. 279v-71v.

BEN JONSON

JnB 417.5 *On the Vnion* ('When was there contract better driuen by Fate?').

Copy, here beginning 'Never was Union better driven by fate', in a verse miscellany; c. 1630.

Folger, MS V. a. 103, Part I, f. 77.

JnB 417.8 -----

Copy, headed 'De vnione Brittaniae' and here beginning 'Was ever contract better driven by fate?', in a miscellany; c. 1630s.

John Rylands University Library of Manchester, Rylands English MS 410, f. 21.

JnB 422.5 -----

Copy, here beginning 'Was euer contract driuen by better fate?', in a verse miscellany compiled by Tobias Alston (1620-c.1639) of Sayham Hall, near Sudbury, Suffolk; c. 1639.

Yale, Osborn Collection, b 197, p. 36.

JnB 566.5 *Christmas his Masque*, lines 71-8, 93-101, 172-9, 182-245. Song: 'Now God preserve, as you well doe deserve'.

Copy, headed 'Ben: Johnsons Masque Before the Kinge', in a verse miscellany compiled by Tobias Alston (1620-c.1639) of Sayham Hall, near Sudbury, Suffolk; c. 1639.

Yale, Osborn Collection, b 197, pp. 132-4.

JnB 576.5 *An Entertainment of the King and Queen at Theobalds, 22 May 1607.*

Copy of a 115-line version (without the prose description) in the hand of Sir Henry Goodyer (1571-1627), on two unbound conjugate leaves in a small bundle of MS poems among the papers of Sir Joseph Williamson (1633-1701) [but probably derived from the 'Conway Papers': see JOHN DONNE, INTRODUCTION]; c. 1607.

Public Record Office, SP.9/51/40-39.

JnB 670.5 *The Gypsies Metamorphosed.* Song: 'ffrom a Gypsie in the morninge'.

Copy in a miscellany (pp. 27-8) probably compiled by one or two members of the Calverley family; c. 1623-30s.

Christie's, 13 June 1979 (Arthur A. Houghton, Jr. sale), Lot 135, sold to Maggs; thence to Huntington.

JnB 674.5 *The Haddington Masque*, lines 86 seq. Song: 'Beauties, haue yee seene this toy'.

Copy, headed 'A Cry for Cupide B: J:', in a verse miscellany (the 'Monckton Milnes MS'); c. 1624-33.

Privately owned in England, MS, p. 8.

JnB 714.5 *The Poetaster*, II, ii, 163 seq. Song: 'If I freely may discouer'.

Copy, headed 'Qualities for a Louer', in a verse miscellany (the 'Monckton Milnes MS'); c. 1624-33.

Privately owned in England, MS, p. 49.

JnB 731.5 *Sejanus his Fall.*

Copy of Sejanus's speech beginning 'Swell, swell my ioys and faint not to declare' (V, 1-3, 6-24), in a verse miscellany (the 'Monckton Milnes MS'); c. 1624-33.

Privately owned in England, MS, p. 6.

JOHN LYLY

(INTRODUCTION). Further copies of Lyly's two petitions to the Queen are found in the Pierpont Morgan Library (MA 1162, pp. 19-22) and in Yale, Osborn Collection (b 200, pp. 82-4).

CHRISTOPHER MARLOWE

MrC 9.5 *Ovid's Elegies. II, iv* ('I meane not to defend the scapes of any').

Copy, headed 'Ouid Amor: Lib: 2 Eleg. 4' and here beginning 'I will not seek to excuse the faults of any', in a verse miscellany compiled by the Yorkshire antiquary John Hopkinson (1610-80); c. 1647.

Bodleian, MS Don. d. 58, ff. 45v-6a.

MrC 9.8 ----- *III, xiii* ('Seeing thou art faire, I barre not thy false playing').

Copy, headed 'Ouid Amor: Lib: 3. Eleg: 13', in a verse miscellany compiled by John Hopkinson (1610-80); c. 1647.

Bowers, II, 390-2; Tucker Brooke, pp. 625-6.

Bodleian, MS Don. d. 58, f. 46a r-v.

PHILIP MASSINGER

MsP 21.5 *The Fatal Dowry*, IV, ii, 51-8. Song: 'Courtier, if thou needs wilt wiue'.

Copy in a verse miscellany entitled *The Theatre of Complements erected* owned in 1682 by Narcissus Luttrell (1657-1732); c. 1670s.

Yale, Osborn Collection, fb 107, p. 42.

THOMAS MIDDLETON

MiT 4.5 *Petition to King James* ('A harmless game raised merely for delight').

Copy of an eight-line version, headed 'to ye Kinge Middletons Verses who was comitted to ye Fleet for ye play called the "Game at chess:"', in a verse miscellany (the 'Monckton Milnes MS'); c. 1624-33.

Privately owned in England, MS, p. 62.

GEORGE PEELE

PlG 11.5 *A Sonet* ('His Golden lockes, Time hath to Silver turn'd').

Copy in a four-part musical setting by John Dowland in a MS songbook once owned by one Thomas Myriell; early 17th century.

Bibliothèque Royale, Brussels, MS II. 4. 109 (Fétis 3095), pp. 16-17.

SIR WALTER RALEGH

(INTRODUCTION). *Apocryphal tracts*: Another copy of *A Military Discourse* is in Yale, Osborn Collection (fb 39, pp. 27-63), and further copies of *The Present Stat of Thinges as they now Stand betweene the three great Kingdomes, France, England, and Spaine* are in the Pierpont Morgan Library (MA 664, pp. 5-23), Rosenbach Foundation (MS 239/4/5), and Yale, Osborn Collection (b 52/1, pp. 8-11). -- Transcripts of letters of Ralegh are also in the Pierpont Morgan Library (MA 1162, pp. 436-68).

RaW 124.5 *A Farewell to false Love* ('Farewell false Loue, the oracle of lies').

Copy in a five-part musical setting by William Byrd in a MS songbook once owned by one Thomas Myriell; early 17th century.

Bibliothèque Royale, Brussels, MS II. 4. 109 (Fétis 3095), pp. 110-11.

RaW 179.5 *Like to a Hermite poore* ('Like to a Hermite poore in place obscure').

Copy in a musical setting by Nicholas Lanier in a MS songbook compiled by Edward Lowe (c.1610-82); [1654-70s].

This MS recorded in *English Songs 1625-1660*, ed. Ian Spink, Musica Britannica XXXIII (London, 1971), No. 7.

British Library, Add. MS 29396, ff. 31v-2.

RaW 186.5 -----

Copy in a miscellany; late 17th century.

Yale, Osborn Collection, b 213, p. 65.

RaW 223.5 *On the Cardes, and Dice* ('Beefore the sixt day of the next new year').

Copy, headed 'Sr Walter Rawley his provesie', on ff. [21v-2] in a verse miscellany associated with Cambridge and owned in 1637 by Francis Rolfe (1618-78), later Town Clerk of [King's] Lynn; c. 1637.

Privately owned in England.

RaW 389.5 *'Here lyes the noble warryor that never bludyed sword'.*

Copy of an eight-line version, here beginning 'Heere lyeth y^t^ noble Counselloure | That never kept his worde', in a verse miscellany; c. 1620.

Victoria and Albert Museum, Dyce Collection, Cat. No. 44 (Pressmark 25. F. 39), f. 60.

RaW 410.5 *'ICUR, good Mounser Carr'.*

Copy, here beginning 'I.C.V.R. brave monser Car', in a composite volume of verse belonging to the Manners family, Dukes of Rutland; c. 1615.

This volume recorded (erroneously as 'Volume XXIV') in *HMC*, 12th Report, Appendix V, Rutland II (1889), pp. 316-31.

Owned by the Duke of Rutland, Belvoir Castle, *Letters and Papers*, Verses, Vol. XXV, f. 53.

RaW 411.5 -----

Copy in a verse miscellany; c. 1620.

Victoria and Albert Museum, Dyce Collection, Cat. No. 44 (Pressmark 25. F. 39), f. 97.

RaW 419.5 *'I cannot bend the bow'.*

Copy, untitled and here beginning 'There is a Bowe wherein to shoote I sue', in a MS volume of poems chiefly by Donne once owned by one Edward Smyth; c. 1620-33.

Cambridge University Library, MS Add. 29, f. 37v.

RaW 453.5 *'Say not you love, unless you do'.*

Copy written in a MS journal of proceedings in Parliament from January to March 1628/9, owned on 1 May 1629 by one Arthur Langford; among the papers of the Trumbull family of Easthampstead Park; c. 1630.

Berkshire Record Office, Trumbull Add. MS 51, f. [61].

SIR WALTER RALEGH, *'Say not you love, unless you do'*

RaW 462.5 -----

Copy, here ascribed to 'J.D.', in a volume of state papers once owned by Robert Drake and Stephen Foster; c. 1630s.

British Library, Egerton MS 2026, f. 65v.

RaW 476.3 -----

Copy, headed 'A gentlewoman to her loue', in a verse miscellany; c. 1634.

Rosenbach Foundation, MS 239/27, p. 163.

RaW 476.5 -----

Copy, headed 'An epigram. T: S:', in a miscellany partly compiled by one Robert Berkeley; c. 1640.

Rosenbach Foundation, MS 240/2, p. 39.

RaW 476.8 -----

Copy, here beginning 'Love or doe not say you doe', in a verse miscellany compiled by one Robert Bishop; c. 1630.

Rosenbach Foundation, MS 1083/16, p. 32.

RaW 488.5 *'The state of Fraunce as nowe it standes'.*

Copy of an eleven-stanza version, headed 'The frenche Prymero. 1585', in the miscellany of Robert Commaundre; late 16th-early 17th century.

British Library, Egerton MS 2642, ff. 324v-5.

RaW 496.5 -----

Copy in a volume of state papers; c. 1610.

Yale, Osborn Collection, fb 9, f. 38v.

RaW 556.5 *Apology for his Voyage to Guiana.*

Copy in two or three hands, on 20 unbound pages among papers of the North family; early-mid-17th century.

University of Kansas, MS P519.

RaW 732.3 *Ralegh's Second Testamentary Note.*

Copy, headed 'Accusations against S[r] W Rawleigh cleared by him at his death'; early-mid-17th century.

Public Record Office, SP.14/103/51.

RaW 732.5 -----

Copy, untitled; early-mid-17th century.

Public Record Office, SP.14/103/51.I.

RaW 732.8 -----

Copy, headed 'S[r] Walter Raleighs Protestacon at his Death', in a volume of state papers compiled by one John Browne; late 17th century.

Formerly among the MSS of Lord Braye at Stanford Hall, Rugby, this MS recorded in *HMC* 15, 10th Report, Appendix VI (1887), p. 122.

Yale, Osborn Collection, fb 155, pp. 381-2.

WILLIAM SHAKESPEARE

ShW 2.5 *The Rape of Lucrece* ('From the besieged Ardea all in post').

Copy of lines 386-95, headed 'An imperfect coppy of Wil: Shackespears', here beginning 'One of her hands one of her Cheeks lay vnder' and followed by three other lines, in a verse miscellany entitled *Recueil Choisi De Pieces fugitives En Vers Anglois*; c. 1713.

This version appears in Sir John Suckling, *Fragmenta Aurea* (London, 1646), pp. 29-30.

Rosenbach Foundation, MS 239/16, p. 146.

ShW 94.5 *The Tempest*, I, ii, 400-9. Song: 'Full fathom five thy father lies'.

Copies in a musical setting by Robert Johnson (as edited by John Wilson) in three MS music part books; mid-17th century.

Yale Music Library, Misc. MS 170, Filmer MS 4, (a) f. 20v; (b) f. 14v; (c) f. 20.

ShW 103.5 ----- V, i, 88-94. Song: 'Where the bee sucks, there suck I'.

Copies in a musical setting by Robert Johnson (as edited by John Wilson) in three MS music part books; mid-17th century.

Yale Music Library, Misc. MS 170, Filmer MS 4, (a) f. 21; (b) f. 15; (c) f. 20v.

SIR PHILIP SIDNEY

(INTRODUCTION). Another copy of Sidney's letter to his brother on travel is in Yale, Osborn Collection (fb 117, pp. 4-8). -- A MS 'addition' to *Arcadia* (in 255 pages), once belonging to the family of Sir Charles Holt of Warwickshire, is in Yale, Osborn Collection (b 107).

SIR PHILIP SIDNEY

SiP 108 *The New Arcadia.*

Verse and prose extracts, including lines from poems No. 2, 4, 6, 14, 19, and 51, transcribed for writing practice by Lady Katherine Manners (later wife of the first Duke of Buckingham), in a small booklet bound in a composite volume of verse belonging to the Manners family, Dukes of Rutland; c. 1612-20.

This volume recorded (erroneously as 'Volume XXIV') in *HMC*, 12th Report, Appendix V, Rutland II (1889), p. 319; discussed in Josephine Roberts, 'Extracts from *Arcadia* in the Manuscript Notebook of Lady Katherine Manners', *N & Q* (forthcoming).

Owned by the Duke of Rutland, Belvoir Castle, *Letters and Papers*, Verse, Vol. XXV, ff. 32-46v (passim).

SiP 126.5 *The Old Arcadia. Book II, No. 15* ('Let not old age disgrace my high desire').

Copy, headed 'An old man a suitor' and here beginning 'Why should old age disgrace my high desire', inscribed 'An old paper of my Coz. Burrows', in a miscellany; c. 1660.

Rosenbach Foundation, MS 239/18, p. 81.

JOHN SKELTON

SkJ 22.3 *Verses Presented to King Henry VII* ('O moste famous noble king! thy fame doth spring and spreade').

Copy, occurring in a herald's chronicle of ceremonial events in the reign of Henry VII, in a heraldic miscellany, once owned by Sir William Le Neve (1600?-61) and by Arthur, Earl of Anglesey; early 17th century.

Canon, D57, p. 18; first pub. (from this MS) in Elias Ashmole, *The Institutional Laws and Ceremonies of the Most Noble Order of the Garter* (London, 1672); Dyce, II, 387-8; discussed and Skelton's authorship rejected in Richard Firth Green, 'The *Verses Presented to King Henry VII*: A Poem in the Skelton Apocrypha', *ELN*, 16 (1978), 5-8. This MS discussed and collated in Green.

Bodleian, MS Rawl. B. 146, f. 169r-v.

SkJ 22.5 -----

Copy, with two introductory lines beginning 'Englande now Roioysse fore Ioyous may thou bee', occurring in a herald's chronicle of ceremonial events in the reign of Henry VII, in a volume of historical collections; 16th century.

Printed from this MS in Green.

British Library, Cotton MS Julius B. XII, ff. 50v-1.

SkJ 22.8 -----

Copy, with two introductory lines beginning 'Englande now reioyse, for ioyous may thow be', occurring in a herald's chronicle of ceremonial events in the reign of Henry VII, in a volume of accounts of state events; late 16th-early 17th century.

British Library, Egerton MS 985, f. 32v.

EDMUND SPENSER

(INTRODUCTION). Another printed book known to have been owned by Spenser in an exemplum of *The Traveiler of Ierome Turler* (London, 1575) at the Rosenbach Foundation (1003/28). This work is bound in the middle of a composite volume of printed pamphlets owned and annotated by Spenser's friend Gabriel Harvey and the title page bears Harvey's inscription, 'Ex dono Edmundi Spenserij, Episcopi Roffensis Secretarij. 1578'. -- A further copy of Digby's *Observations on...Spensers Faery queen* is in the Pierpont Morgan Library (MA 1162, pp. 657-71).

SpE 7.5 *Amoretti. Sonnet XXIII* ('Penelope for her Vlisses sake').

Copy in a composite miscellany; mid-17th century.

Variorum, *Minor Poems*, II, 204.

British Library, Harley MS 6908, f. 2.

SpE 7.8 ----- *Sonnet LXIIII* ('Comming to kisse her lyps, (such grace I found)').

Copy in a composite miscellany; mid-17th century.

Variorum, *Minor Poems*, II, 221-2.

British Library, Harley MS 6908, f. 1v.

HENRY HOWARD, EARL OF SURREY

SuH 22.5 *'If care do cause men cry, why do not I complaine?'.*

Copy, headed 'An Absent Louer hath noe comfort but in hope', in a miscellany partly compiled by one Robert Berkeley; c. 1640.

Rosenbach Foundation, MS 240/2, p. 45.

SuH 32.5 *'In winters iust returne, when Boreas gan his raigne'.*

Copy of the incipit in a musical setting in a MS book of verse and lute music; formerly among the papers of Lord Braye at Stanford Hall, Rugby; c. 1560.

Yale, Osborn Collection, Music MS 13, f. 41v.

HENRY HOWARD, EARL OF SURREY

SuH 42.5 *'Marshall, the thinges for to attayne'.*

Copy, here beginning 'Warner the things for to obtayne', written on the last blank leaf of a printed exemplum of Martial, *Epigrammata* (Venice, 1501) possibly once owned by Robert Pember (d. 1560); early-mid-16th century.

Facsimile of this MS in Sotheby's sale catalogue, 14 March 1979, p. 347.

Sotheby's, 14 March 1979, Lot 443, sold to A.G. Thomas.

SIR HENRY WOTTON

WoH 14.5 *The Character of a Happy Life* ('How happy is he born and taught').

Copy, transcribed from a printed source (p. 497), in a miscellany entitled *Vade mecum or A Pocket-Booke* compiled by John Gibson (b. 1630) of Welburn, near Kirkby Moorside, Yorkshire; c. 1678.

Bodleian, Broxbourne R 359, f. [40v].

WoH 37.5 -----

Copy in a verse miscellany; late 17th century.

Harvard, MS Eng 1035, f. 10.

WoH 43.5 -----

Copy, headed 'The Happy Man', in a miscellany compiled by Judge John Saffin (1632-1710) of New England; c. 1665-1708.

Printed from this MS in *John Saffin his Book (1665-1708)*, ed. Caroline Hazard (New York, 1928), pp. 123-4.

Rhode Island Historical Society, [no ref. number].

WoH 47.5 -----

Copy, headed 'The prayse of a priuate life', in a verse miscellany appended to a MS volume of poems by Donne; c. 1630s.

Trinity College, Dublin, MS 877, ff. 261v-2.

WoH 60.5 *On a Bank as I sat a-Fishing. A Description of the Spring* ('And now all nature seemed in love').

Copy, headed 'Sr Hen: Wotton's Description of ye Spring' and here beginning 'This day dame Nature seemd in Love', in a miscellany entitled *Vade Mecum or A Pocket-Booke* compiled by John Gibson (b. 1630) of Welburn, near Kirkby Moorside, Yorkshire; c. 1678.

Bodleian, Broxbourne R 359, f. [45].

WoH 129.5 *On his Mistress, the Queen of Bohemia* ('You meaner beauties of the night').

Copy in a miscellany; c. 1635.

The text followed (p. 4) by a Latin version.

Owned by Edwin Wolf 2nd, Philadelphia, MS, p. 3.

WoH 133.5 -----

Copy of a five-stanza version in a miscellany (p. 6) probably compiled by one or two members of the Calverley family; c. 1623-30s.

Christie's, 13 June 1979 (Arthur A. Houghton, Jr. sale), Lot 135, sold to Maggs; thence to Huntington.

WoH 196.5 *Upon the Death of Sir Albert Morton's Wife* ('He first deceased; she for a little tried').

Copy in a verse miscellany; c. 1700.

Victoria and Albert Museum, Dyce Collection, Cat. No. 43 (Pressmark 25. F. 37), p. 70.

WoH 197.5 -----

Copy, headed 'An Epitaph on two louers who beinge Espoused dyed before they were marryed' and here beginning 'She first deceased; he for a little tryde', in a verse miscellany compiled by Tobias Alston (1620-c.1639) of Sayham Hall, near Sudbury, Suffolk; c. 1639.

Yale, Osborn Collection, b 197, p. 57.

WoH 197.8 -----

Copy, headed 'On two Louers who did before they were married' and here beginning 'She ffirst deceas'd, he for a Little tryed', in a volume of epitaphs; c. 1694.

Yale, Osborn Collection, fb 143, p. 43.

WoH 201.5 *Upon the Sudden Restraint of the Earl of Somerset then falling from favour* ('Dazzled thus with the height of place').

Copy, headed 'On Somersets Fall. Sr H.W.', in a miscellany entitled *Vade mecum or A Pocket-Booke* compiled by John Gibson (b. 1630) of Welburn, near Kirkby Moorside, Yorkshire; c. 1678.

Bodleian, Broxbourne R 359, f. [41].

WoH 217.5 *A Description of the Country's Recreations* ('Quivering fears, heart-tearing cares').

Copy, untitled and transcribed from a printed source (p. 348), in a miscellany entitled

SIR HENRY WOTTON

Vade mecum or A Pocket-Booke compiled by John Gibson (b. 1630) of Welburn, near Kirkby Moorside, Yorkshire; c. 1678.

Bodleian, Broxbourne R 359, f. [41v-2].

WoH 228.5 *A Farewell to the Vanities of the World* ('Farewell, ye gilded follies, pleasing troubles!').

Copy, untitled and transcribed from a printed source (p. 351), in a miscellany entitled *Vade mecum or A Pocket-Booke* compiled by John Gibson (b. 1630) of Welburn, near Kirkby Moorside, Yorkshire; c. 1678.

Bodleian, Broxbourne R 359, ff. [42v-3].

WoH 257.5 -----

Copy, headed 'The Pilgrim', on ff. [27v-8] in a verse miscellany associated with Cambridge and owned in 1637 by Francis Rolfe (1618-78), later Town Clerk of [King's] Lynn; c. 1637.

Privately owned in England.

SIR THOMAS WYATT

WyT 302.5 *'Tagus, fare well, that westward with thy stremes'.*

Copy in a verse miscellany compiled by the Leicestershire antiquary William Burton (1575-1645); c. 1637.

Owned by the Marquess of Bath, Longleat House, MS 261, p. 36.